A History of Literary Criticism

For Yasmeen

A History of Literary Criticism

From Plato to the Present

M. A. R. Habib

Blackwell
Publishing

© 2005 by M. A. R. Habib

BLACKWELL PUBLISHING
350 Main Street, Malden, MA 02148-5020, USA
9600 Garsington Road, Oxford OX4 2DQ, UK
550 Swanston Street, Carlton, Victoria 3053, Australia

The right of M. A. R. Habib to be identified as the Author of this Work has been
asserted in accordance with the UK Copyright, Designs, and Patents Act 1988.

First published 2005 by Blackwell Publishing Ltd

3   2007

Library of Congress Cataloging-in-Publication Data

Habib, Rafey.
   A history of literary criticism: from Plato to the present / M. A. R. Habib.
      p.   cm.
   Includes bibliographical references and index.
   ISBN-13: 978-0-631-23200-1 (hard cover: alk. paper)
   ISBN-10: 0-631-23200-1 (hard cover: alk. paper)
   1. Criticism—History.   I. Title.

   PN86.H23 2005
   801′.95′09—dc22
                                                                    2005004898

ISBN-13: 978-0-631-23200-1 (hard cover: alk. paper)

A catalogue record for this title is available from the British Library.

Set in 10/12.5pt Minion
by Graphicraft Limited, Hong Kong
Printed and bound in the United Kingdom
by TJ International Ltd, Padstow, Cornwall

The publisher's policy is to use permanent paper from mills that operate a
sustainable forestry policy, and which has been manufactured from pulp
processed using acid-free and elementary chlorine-free practices. Furthermore,
the publisher ensures that the text paper and cover board used have met
acceptable environmental accreditation standards.

For further information on
Blackwell Publishing, visit our website:
www.blackwellpublishing.com

CONTENTS

ACKNOWLEDGMENTS

I would like to express my deepest gratitude to the following people for their advice, their suggestions, their encouragement, and inspiration: Michael Payne, Chris Fitter, Terry Eagleton, Frank Kermode, Andrew McNeillie, Kimberly Adams, Mughni Tabassum, William Lutz, Geoffrey Sill, Robert Ryan, Monica Dantonio, Sandra Sokowski, Mary Ellen Bray, Tommy Wright, Jenny Hunt, Emma Bennett, Mariam Patel, Julie Still, Karen Wilson, and Ernest Hilbert. I would like to thank Tim Laquintano for his invaluable assistance with the bibliography. I owe an inexpressible debt to my mother Siddiqua Shabnam; to my children Hishaam and Hasan, who live within this book; and to my wife Yasmeen, incomparable, to whom I dedicate it.

ABBREVIATIONS OF FREQUENTLY CITED WORKS

CCP   *The Cambridge Companion to Plato*, ed. Richard Kraut (Cambridge: Cambridge University Press, 1992).

CHLC   *The Cambridge History of Literary Criticism* (Cambridge: Cambridge University Press); V.I: *Volume I: Classical Criticism*, ed. George A. Kennedy (1997); V.III: *Volume III: The Renaissance*, ed. Glyn P. Norton (1999); V.IV: *Volume IV: The Eighteenth Century*, ed. H. B. Nisbet and Claude Rawson (1997); V.V: *Volume V: Romanticism*, ed. Marshall Brown (2000).

Curtius   Ernst Robert Curtius, *European Literature and the Latin Middle Ages*, trans. Willard R. Trask (London: Routledge and Kegan Paul, 1979).

GI   Karl Marx and Friedrich Engels, *The German Ideology: Part One*, ed. C. J. Arthur (1970; rpt. London: Lawrence and Wishart, 1982).

HWP   Bertrand Russell, *History of Western Philosophy* (London: George Allen and Unwin, 1974).

LWC   *Literature and Western Civilization: The Classical World*, ed. David Daiches and Anthony Thorlby (London: Aldus Books, 1972).

MLC   *Medieval Literary Criticism: Translations and Interpretations*, ed. O. B. Hardison, Jr. (New York: Frederick Ungar, 1974).

MLTC   *Medieval Literary Theory and Criticism, c.1100–c.1375: The Commentary Tradition*, ed. A. J. Minnis, A. B. Scott, and David Wallace (Oxford: Clarendon Press, 1988).

PF   Perry Anderson, *Passages From Antiquity to Feudalism* (London: Verso, 1985).

INTRODUCTION

I n our world it has become more important than ever that we learn to read critically. The events of September 11, 2001 and their aftermath have shown us – with
a new urgency – the dangers of misunderstanding and inadequate education. It
has become more important than ever that we understand the various voices crying
from afar in other languages; and it is just as urgent that we understand the bewilder-
ing multitude of voices in our own culture. In order to make sense of our own present,
we need to understand our own past. We need to look critically at the various
documents, cultural, political, and religious, which furnish our identity, which tell us
who we are, who we should be, and what we might become. As a black American
scholar has recently said, "the challenge of mutual understanding among the world's
multifarious cultures will be the single greatest task that we face, after the failure of the
world to feed itself."[1]

It has become indisputably clear that the study of the humanities in general is no
longer a luxury but a necessity, vital to our very survival as an enlightened civilization.
We cannot form an articulate vision of our own moral, educational, and political
values without some knowledge of where those values come from, the struggles in
which they were forged, and the historical contexts which generated those struggles. To
study the Bible, Plato, Greek tragedy, Shakespeare, or Roman Law, to study Jewish or
African-American history, to examine the Qur'an and the long history of the Western
world's fraught engagement with Islam, is to study the sources of the conflicts and
cultural tendencies which inform our present world. We cannot be good citizens –
either of a particular country or of the world – by succumbing to the endless forces
operating worldwide that encourage us to remain ignorant, to follow blindly, whether
in the form of blind nationalism, blind religiosity, or blind chauvinism in all its
manifold guises. One of the keys to counteracting those forces which would keep us in
darkness lies in education, and in particular in the process which forms the core of
education: the individual and institutional practice of *reading*, of close, careful, critical reading. Such reading entails a great deal more than merely close attention to the
words on the page, or the text as it immediately confronts us. We need to know
why a text was written, for whom it was written, what religious or moral or political

purposes motivated it, as well as its historical and cultural circumstances. Then, indeed, we can move on to the issues of its style, its language, its structure, and its deployment of rhetorical and literary techniques.

All disciplines in the humanities (and arguably those in the sciences) call for such close, critical, and comprehensive reading. There is one discipline which is *defined* by its insistence on such strategies: this is the discipline of literary criticism, as operating through both practice and theory. At the most basic level, we might say that the practice of literary criticism is applied to various given texts. The theory is devoted to examining the principles behind such practice. We might say that theory is a systematic explanation of practice or a situation of practice in broader framework; theory brings to light the motives behind our practice; it shows us the connection of practice to ideology, power structures, our own unconscious, our political and religious attitudes, our economic structures; above all, theory shows us that practice is not something natural but is a specific historical construct. Hence, to look over the history of literary criticism, a journey we are about to undertake in this book, is not only to revisit some of the profoundest sources of our identity but also to renew our connections with some of the deepest resources of our present and future sustenance.

Methodology of this Book

The methodology of this book rests on five basic principles. One of the central difficulties encountered by readers of modern literary criticism and theory derives from the fact that the latter often employs concepts and terminology that are rooted in philosophy and other disciplines. In addressing this difficulty, the first principle and purpose of this book is to provide not just an isolated history of literary criticism, but to locate this history within the context of the main currents of Western thought. This means, for example, not just examining what Plato and Kant say about poetry or aesthetics but situating their aesthetic views within the framework of their philosophical systems. Without those systems, we can have merely a haphazard understanding of their views on literature and art; moreover, those systems themselves are still with us in many guises, and they still inform the ways in which we think about the world.

The reaction of many literary scholars against modern literary and cultural theory is often underlain by a distrust of philosophy, of technical jargon, and a lack of familiarity with the great philosophical systems. I hope that this book goes some way toward making the works of great thinkers such as Plato, Aristotle, Kant, and Hegel a little less daunting. The truth is that without some grasp of their major ideas, we simply cannot begin to understand thinkers such as Derrida, Foucault, and Kristeva. A great deal of literary theory presupposes familiarity with a broad range of philosophical ideas. More importantly, the philosophical systems of these thinkers are crucial for any understanding of modern Western thought. For example, we cannot begin to understand the world that we have inherited without understanding liberalism as it was formulated by Locke, without understanding the main directions of Enlightenment thought such as rationalism, empiricism, and pragmatism, as well as the attempts of Kant and Hegel to situate such trends within larger, more comprehensive accounts of the world. Again, we cannot understand who we are without recognizing the diverse reactions against mainstream bourgeois thought, ranging from Romanticism through symbolism to Marxism, Freudianism, and existentialism. We need to recognize that today we are complex creatures who are the product of a long and complex historical development that embraces all of these movements and dispositions. We bear, in our own mentalities and our own broad outlooks toward the world, traces and vestiges of these often conflicting modes of thought. For example, we may live out our public lives on the basis of largely bourgeois values such as the use of reason, the reliance on experience and observation, and a commitment to competition, efficiency, practicality, and of course profit-making. Yet each of us, usually in our private lives, is also familiar with a set of values deriving sometimes from feudal Christianity or Judaism or Islam (loyalty, devotion, faith) or from Romantic attitudes (an emphasis on imagination, creativity, emotion, and a sense of the mystery of the world), as well as from Marxism (a belief in equality of opportunity, an openness to various modes of reconceiving history, and a redefinition of bourgeois values such as freedom in a comprehensive sense that applies to all people), not to mention certain radical ideas of the human psyche deriving from Freud and other pioneers in the fields of psychoanalysis. The history of literary criticism is profoundly imbricated in the history of thought in a broad range of spheres, philosophical, religious, social, economic, and psychological. Part of the purpose of this book, then, is to place modern literary theory within a historically broader context, to view it from a perspective that might evince its connections and lines of origin, descent, and reaction.

Secondly, given that this book proceeds by way of close textual analysis, it is necessarily selective, focusing on the most important and influential texts of some of the most important figures. There are certainly a number of major figures omitted: readers may object that there is no detailed treatment of Paul de Man and other deconstructionists, or of many feminist writers, or of Fredric Jameson or certain proponents of New Historicism. I must plead guilty to all of these omissions. My reason is simply that there is not enough room. The intent of this book is not to provide encyclopedic coverage, nor to offer a cursory treatment of all possible major figures. These valuable tasks have already been performed by several eminent authors. This book aims to redress a deficiency that students have repeatedly voiced to me: the need for a text that will guide them through the intricacies of many difficult literary-critical and theoretical works, by focusing on close readings of them. To illustrate the point: a one- or two-page summary of Plato or Kant will not help the student in her reading of the *Republic* or the *Critique of Judgment*. This book aims, rather, to undertake close readings of selected texts which represent or embody the principles of given literary-critical tendencies. What also appears to be needed is a clear but detailed account of the historical backgrounds of these texts. These two aims, then, have guided the present work which, I hope, might be used in conjunction with any of the excellent anthologies of literary criticism and theory now available.

Thirdly, while no section of this book is, strictly speaking, self-contained, I am hopeful that each section is independently intelligible inasmuch as it is situated within an intellectual and historical context. This strategy aims to answer a repeated practical concern that I have heard from students over the years: that their reading of one thinker always presupposes knowledge of other thinkers and the inevitable network of cross-references tends to confuse students who confront a difficult thinker for the first time. I have attempted to follow this strategy while minimizing the need for repetition: the section on Coleridge, for example, or on Wordsworth, should provide a fairly comprehensive overview of the basic principles and themes of Romanticism, such as the connection between reason and imagination, the high status accorded to poetry, and the problematic nature of the notion of subjectivity. In other words, these sections should be intelligible without first reading the chapters on Plato, Kant, Hume, and other thinkers. Of course, the connections between these thinkers *are* formulated; but a knowledge of them is not debilitatingly presupposed on the part of the student.

A fourth principle of the present volume is the need to correct an imbalanced perception, prevalent through many graduate schools, of the originality and status of modern literary theory, an imbalance reflected in certain anthologies of theory and criticism. Often, the critical output of previous historical eras is implicitly treated as an inadequate and benighted prolegomenon to the dazzling insights of modern theory. The history of philosophy is sometimes seen, through the alleged lens of deconstruction, as a series of deconstructed domains: in this distorted projection, Plato, Kant, and Hegel are treated as minor thinkers, whose mistakes and blindnesses were acutely brought to the surface by major thinkers such as Derrida, Lacan, and Foucault. Only an ignorance of the history of philosophy could sanction such an attitude. The truth is that, as all of these modern thinkers recognize, far deeper contributions to philosophy were made by Kant, by Hegel, and by Marx: without these thinkers, the work of modern theorists could not have arisen and in many ways it remains frozen within the problematics defined by the earlier figures. In general, modern theory – to its credit – is less original than is often imagined; I hope the following pages will show, among other things, that many of its insights were anticipated or made possible as controversions of positions and themes explored by earlier – sometimes far earlier – thinkers and literary scholars. It is natural that anthologies and modern accounts of criticism should exhibit a bias toward our own era; but this emphasis should not be allowed to obscure the true nature of our own contributions, which should be situated historically and assessed in the light of their far-reaching connections with the thought of previous ages.

The final principle informing this book is an aspiration toward clarity. Unfortunately, much of the theory that has enabled new modes of analysis and generated extraordinarily rich insights has isolated itself from public and political discourse by its difficult language and by its reliance on jargon. There is a difference between genuine complexity – which one finds in the great thinkers and in the major literary theorists – and confusion; between a command of language that can express truly difficult concepts and needlessly difficult language that offers a mere show or pretense of complexity, recycling worn ideas, and sacrificing in this process not only clarity but also subtlety and accuracy of expression.

Having said this, I am aware of some of the compelling reasons behind the refusal of some theorists to be dragged into an ideology of clarity. I am painfully aware that certain texts of poststructuralism and feminism are here expounded in a manner that somewhat betrays their aversion to theory and systematic thought based on the centuries-old categories of a male European (and Eurocentric) tradition. In the absence of the talent and creativity necessary to do justice to the stylistic import of these texts, I have resigned myself to the task of attempting to make them, and their contexts, accessible to a relatively wide range of readers.

Note

1 Henry Louis Gates, Jr., *Loose Canons: Notes on the Culture Wars* (New York and Oxford: Oxford University Press, 1992), p. xii.

PART I

ANCIENT GREEK CRITICISM

CLASSICAL LITERARY CRITICISM: INTELLECTUAL AND POLITICAL BACKGROUNDS

Our English word "criticism" derives from the ancient Greek term *krites*, meaning "judge." Perhaps the first type of criticism was that which occurred in the process of poetic creation itself: in composing his poetry, a poet would have made certain "judgments" about the themes and techniques to be used in his verse, about what his audience was likely to approve, and about his own relationship to his predecessors in the oral or literary tradition. Hence, the creative act itself was also a critical act, involving not just inspiration but some kind of self-assessment, reflection, and judgment. Moreover, in ancient Greece, the art of the "rhapsode" or professional singer involved an element of interpretation: a rhapsode would usually perform verse that he himself had not composed, and his art must have been a highly self-conscious and interpretative one, just as the performance of a Shakespeare play is effectively an interpretation of it.[1] In the written text of Shakespeare's *The Merchant of Venice*, the character of the Jewish moneylender Shylock has conventionally been seen as domineering, greedy, and vindictive. Yet our perception of his character and his situation can be transformed by a performance where we see him kneeling, surrounded by aggressively self-righteous Christian adversaries. In the same way, different performances of Homer's *Iliad* or *Odyssey* might have had very different effects. One can imagine Achilles presented as the archetypal Greek hero, valiant and (almost) invincible; but also as cruel, childish, and selfish. There are many incidents and situations in Homer – such as King Priam's entreaty to Achilles or Odysseus' confronting of the suitors – which must have yielded a rich range of interpretative and performative possibilities. Even performances of lyric poetry must have shared this potential for diverse interpretation, a potential which has remained alive through the centuries. An ode of Sappho, a sonnet by Shakespeare, Donne's "A Valediction: Forbidding Mourning," Shelley's "Ode to the West Wind," Eliot's "Prufrock," or the verse of a contemporary Israeli or Palestinian poet can each be "performed" or read aloud in a variety of ways and with vastly differing effects. In each case, the performance must be somewhat self-conscious and informed by critical judgment.

In this broad sense, literary criticism goes at least as far back as archaic Greece, which begins around 800 years before the birth of Christ. This is the era of the epic poets Homer and Hesiod, and of the lyric poets Archilochus, Ibycus, Alcaeus, and Sappho. What we call the "classical" period emerges around 500 BC, the period of the great dramatists Euripides, Aeschylus, and Sophocles, the philosophers Socrates, Plato, and Aristotle, the schools of rhetoric, and the rise of Athenian democracy and power. After this is the "Hellenistic" period, witnessing the diffusion of Greek culture through much of the Mediterranean and Middle East, a diffusion vastly accelerated by the conquests of Alexander the Great, and the various dynasties established by his generals after his death in 323 BC. Over the Hellenized domains there was a common ruling-class culture, using a common literary dialect and a common education system.[2] The city of Alexandria in Egypt, founded by Alexander in 331 BC, became a center of scholarship and letters, housing an enormous library and museum, and hosting such renowned poets and grammarians as Callimachus, Apollonius Rhodius, Aristarchus, and Zenodotus. We know of these figures partly through the work of Suetonius (ca. 69–140 AD), who wrote the first histories of literature and criticism.[3]

The Hellenistic period is usually said to end with the battle of Actium in 31 BC in which the last portion of Alexander's empire, Egypt, was annexed by the increasingly powerful and expanding Roman republic. After his victory at Actium, the entire Roman world fell under the sole rulership of Julius Caesar's nephew, Octavian, soon to become revered as the first Roman emperor, Augustus. During this span of almost a thousand years, poets, philosophers, rhetoricians, grammarians, and critics laid down many of the basic terms, concepts, and questions that were to shape the future of literary criticism as it evolved all the way through to our own century. These include the concept of "mimesis" or imitation; the concept of beauty and its connection with truth and goodness; the ideal of the organic unity of a literary work; the social, political, and moral functions of literature; the connection between literature, philosophy, and rhetoric; the nature and status of language; the impact of literary performance on an audience; the definition of figures of speech such as metaphor, metonymy, and symbol; the notion of a "canon" of the most important literary works; and the development of various genres such as epic, tragedy, comedy, lyric poetry, and song.

The first recorded instances of criticism go back to dramatic festivals in ancient Athens, which were organized as contests, requiring an official judgment as to which author had produced the best drama. A particularly striking literary-critical discussion occurs in Aristophanes' play *The Frogs*, first performed in 405 BC, just before the ending of the Peloponnesian War in 404 BC in the utter defeat of Athens at the hands of its rival, Sparta. It may seem odd, in our age of highly technical and specialized approaches to literature, that literary criticism should be used to entertain and amuse a large audience of several thousand people. This fact alone is testimony to the highly literate nature of the Athenian citizens, who were expected to recognize many allusions to previous literary works, and to understand the terms of a critical debate, as well as its broader political and social implications. In fact, the chorus in the play itself commends the erudition of the audience, claiming that the citizens are so "sharp" and "keen" that they will not miss "a single point."[4]

The plot of Aristophanes' comedy is built around the idea that there are no good poets left in the world; the current living dramatists are "jabberers ... degraders of their art" (*Frogs*, l. 93). The only way of obtaining the services of a good poet is to bring a dead one back from Hades. In order to determine which of the dead tragedians, Euripides or Aeschylus, is the more suitable for this task, a trial is conducted before the court of Pluto, the god of the underworld. The judge of course will be Dionysus, the patron god of drama. Aristophanes portrays the comic adventures of Dionysus and his slave Xanthias, as they make their way to the court and hear the arguments offered by each of the two tragic poets.

This is not merely a contest between two literary theories, representing older and younger generations; it is a contest in poetic art (*Frogs*, ll. 786, 796). Aeschylus represents the more traditional virtues of a bygone generation, such as martial prowess, heroism, and respect for social hierarchy – all embodied in a lofty, decorous, and sublime style of speech – while Euripides is the voice of a more recent, democratic, secular, and plain-speaking generation. In talking of the general functions of poetry, Aeschylus explains that poets such as Orpheus have taught humankind religious rites, moral codes, and medicine; Hesiod gave instruction concerning farming; and Homer sang of valor, honor, and the execution of war (*Frogs*, ll. 1030–1036). Aeschylus places himself in this tradition, reminding the audience how his own dramas inspired manly passions for war (*Frogs*, ll. 1021, 1040). He cautions that "we, the poets, are teachers of men" and that the "sacred poet" should avoid depicting any kind of evil, especially the harlotry and incest that we can find in Euripides (*Frogs*, l. 1055).

Euripides agrees that in general the poet is valued for his "ready wit" and wise counsels, and because he trains the citizens to be "better townsmen and worthier men" (*Frogs*, l. 1009). But he claims that, in contrast with Aeschylus, he himself employs a "democratic" manner, allowing characters from all classes to speak, showing "scenes of common life," and teaching the public to reason (*Frogs*, ll. 952, 959, 971–978). He insists that the poet should speak in "human fashion," and accuses Aeschylus of using language that is "bombastiloquent," obscure, and repetitious (*Frogs*, ll. 839, 1122, 1179). Aeschylus rejoins that a high style and lofty speech is appropriate for "mighty thoughts and heroic aims" (*Frogs*, ll. 1058–1060); and he upbraids Euripides for teaching the youth of the city to "prate, to harangue, to debate . . . to challenge, discuss, and refute," as well as bringing to the stage "debauchery" and "scandal" (*Frogs*, ll. 1070–1073).

Ultimately, to great comic effect, a pair of scales is brought in, showing Aeschylus' verse to be "weightier" (*Frogs*, ll. 1366, 1404–1410). Significantly, there are two factors involved in deciding the issue: Dionysus explains that not only does Athens need a true poet who will enable her to continue with her dramatic festivals and "choral games," but this poet will be called upon to give the city some much-needed advice on a political problem, namely, what should be done about Alcibiades (a brilliant but selfish and indulgent general currently in exile and who had been a threat to the state and the democracy) (*Frogs*, ll. 1419–1422). Aeschylus basically repeats the advice offered at the beginning of the war by the Athenian statesman Pericles: that Athens' true wealth lies in her fleet. Dionysus pronounces as victor Aeschylus in whom his "soul delights" (*Frogs*, ll. 1465–1467). Interestingly, the chorus sings the praises of Aeschylus as a "[k]een intelligent mind." This intelligence, however, is of a peculiar kind; it embodies the wisdom required for the art of tragedy; and it is pointedly contrasted with the "[i]dle talk" and "[f]ine-drawn quibbles" of the philosopher Socrates (*Frogs*, ll. 1489–1497). This quarrel between poetry and philosophy will surface again and again in the history of literary criticism.

It is clear that Aristophanes' play both embodies and enacts the civic duty of poetry and literary criticism. In fact, the play was uniquely honored by being acted a second time, since Aeschylus was deemed to have performed an important patriotic service to the city (*Frogs*, Introd., p. 293). Such an accolade may rest on his evident call for Athenians – about to suffer a humiliating military defeat – to return to the martial and "manly" values represented by Aeschylean drama. His play *The Frogs* stages the drama of Athens' political and cultural dilemma as a literary-critical dilemma. This first recorded instance of a sustained literary-critical debate reveals a number of salient features of both poetry and criticism in the ancient Greek world. Firstly, our some-times narrow focus on the "purely" aesthetic or literary dimension of a text would have been incomprehensible to the ancient Greeks; poetry for them was an important element in the educational process; its ramifications extended over morality, religion, and the entire sphere of civic responsibility; as such, poetry itself was a forum for the discussion of larger issues; it owed a large measure of its high esteem to its public and political nature, as well as to its technical or artistic dimension. In fact, these various dimensions of poetry and literature were not mutually separated as they sometimes appear to be for us. Hence, to understand the origins and nature of literary criticism in the Greek world – especially in the work of Plato and Aristotle, which we shall look at soon – we need to know something of the political, social, and intellectual forces that shaped their understanding of the world.

Political and Historical Contexts

"Classical" Athens in the fifth century BC – just prior to the time of Plato – was a thriving democratic city-state with a population estimated at about 300,000. However, this democracy differed considerably from our modern democracies: not only was it a direct rather than a representative democracy, it was also highly exclusive. Only the adult male citizens, numbering about 40–45,000, were eligible to participate in the decision-making process. The rest of the community, composed of women, resident aliens, and a vast number of slaves, formed a permanently excluded majority. Even most free men, whether working on the land or in the cities, were poor and had little hope of economic betterment (*LWC*, 32). This circumstance, widespread in the Greek world, was responsible in part not only for class conflict but also for a perennial struggle between different forms of government. The philosophies and literary the-ories of both Plato and Aristotle were integrally shaped by awareness of these political struggles.

By this stage of her history, Athens was not only a democracy but also an imperial power, head of the so-called Delian League of more than a hundred city-states, from whom she exacted tribute. Her rise to such predominance had been relatively recent and swift, though democracy itself had taken some centuries to evolve, displacing earlier systems such as oligarchy or tyranny and monarchy where power had resided in the hands of a small elite or one man. By 500 BC the tyrants had been overthrown in all the major Greek cities (*LWC*, 31). The ideals of social equality and democratic struc-ture were furthered in Athens by leaders and lawgivers such as Solon, who made the lawcourts democratic; Cleisthenes, who organized the political structure into ten tribes, each represented by 50 members in the Council of the Areopagus; and Pericles, who instituted pay for people to serve as state officials, so that such service might not be a privilege of the wealthy. In his funeral oration, Pericles defined democracy as a system in which power lies in the hands of "the whole people," "everyone is equal before the law," and public responsibility is determined not by class but by "actual ability."[5]

What propelled Athens into prominence was largely her leading role in repelling two invasions of Greece by Persia. In the first of these, the Athenians, without Spartan aid, defeated the Persian forces led by King Darius at Marathon in 490 BC. The second invasion was halted by Athens' powerful navy at Salamis in 480 BC and on land at Plataea in 479 BC. Despite the fact that the land battle was won with the help of Sparta, it was Athens who assumed the leadership of the Greek allies, organizing them into a confederation, the Delian League, with the aim of liberating the Greek cities of Asia Minor (now Turkey) from Persian rule. These postwar years were the years of Athens' power, prosperity, and cultural centrality: Pericles dominated Athenian politics; the Parthenon and Propylaea were built; the tragedies of Sophocles and Euripides were staged; the city was host to professional teachers of philosophy such as Protagoras, and to schools of rhetoric, which taught young men of the nobility the art of public speaking and debate (*PV*, 22–23). The city was alive with free political discussion and intellectual inquiry. Pericles called Athens the "school of Hellas" (*LWC*, 35).

In all of these historical circumstances, there were at least three developments that profoundly influenced the nature of literature and criticism, as well as of philosophy and rhetoric. The first was the evolution of the *polis* or city-state. The Greeks differentiated between themselves and the non-Greeks known as "barbarians" primarily by this political structure, the *polis*, which alone in their view could allow man to achieve his full potential as a human being. When Aristotle defined man as a "political animal," it was this structure that he had in mind. As the scholar M. I. Finley puts it, the *polis* was comprised of "people acting in concert, a community," where people could "assemble and deal with problems face to face" (*LWC*, 27–28). As later thinkers such as Hegel, Marx, and Durkheim reiterated, man's very being is social and public in its essential orientation, and his own fulfillment lies in advancing, not sacrificing, the public interest. These assumptions are common to the otherwise differing literary theories of Plato and Aristotle, who are both obliged to consider literature as a public or state concern. Finley states that "religion and culture were as much public concerns as economics or politics . . . the great occasions for religious ceremonial, for music, drama, poetry and athletics, were the public festivals, local or pan-Hellenic. With the state thus the universal patron, Greek tragedy and comedy . . . were as much part of the process of face-to-face discussion as a debate in a legislative assembly" (*LWC*, 28). Even the internal structure of drama was influenced by the ideal of the *polis*: the chorus (whether comprised of a group of dancers and singers, or a single speaking character) was the representative of the community or *polis*. As Gregory Nagy so eloquently puts it, the chorus was a "microcosm of social hierarchy," and embodied "an educational collectivisation of experience" (*CHLC*, V.I, 50). It is clear that literature and poetry had a public, even political, function, which was largely educational. T. H. Irwin states that "Athenian dramatic festivals took the place of some of the mass media familiar to us."[6] No one was more deeply aware than Plato of the cultural impact of literature. In fact,

13

Irwin points out that the "moral outlook of the Homeric poems permanently influenced Greek thought," in ways that conflicted with democratic attitudes. We might add that Plato – no democrat – also took great pains to counter the influence of Homer and the poets. Poetry had a primary role in education: children were taught letters for the purpose of memorizing poetry and ultimately of performing and interpreting it (*CHLC*, V.I, 74). In the ancient Greek world, poetry not only had a public nature but also served several functions which have been displaced in our world by news media, film, music, religious education, and the sciences. Ironically, as we shall see, the image of Plato himself looms behind some of these long-term displacements.

The second political development pertinent to literature and criticism lay in the fact that Athens' predominance in the Greek world did not go unchallenged. The other major power in the Greek world was Sparta, who counterbalanced Athens' leadership of the Delian League with her own system of defensive alliances known as the Peloponnesian League. The struggle between these two superpowers was not only military but also ideological: Athens everywhere attempted to foster her own style of democracy, whereas Sparta everywhere encouraged her own brand of oligarchy. This struggle convulsed the entire Greek world and eventually led to the Peloponnesian War, which lasted twenty-seven years, beginning in 431 BC and ending with the utter defeat of Athens in 404 BC. The first twenty-four years of Plato's life were lived during this war, and the issues raised by the conflict affected many areas of his thought, including his literary theory. Even before Athens' defeat, she had witnessed a brief coup at the hands of the oligarchical party in 411–410 BC (the regime of the "four hundred"). It was during this repressive period that Socrates was tried and executed in 399 BC on a charge of impiety. The Spartans imposed another oligarchy in 404 BC, the so-called regime of the "thirty," which included two of Plato's relatives, Critias and Charmides, who were also friends of Socrates. In 403, however, democracy was restored after a civil struggle. The struggle was effectively between two ways of life, between the "open-minded social and cultural atmosphere" of Athenian democracy, and the "rigidly controlled, militaristic" oligarchy of Sparta (*CCP*, 60–62). It was this struggle which underlay the opposition between Plato's anti-democratic and somewhat authoritarian philosophical vision and the more fluid, skeptical, and relativistic visions expressed by poetry, sophistic, and rhetoric. It is in this struggle, as we shall see, that Western philosophy as we know it was born.

A third factor that shaped the evolution of literature in archaic and classical Greece was pan-Hellenism, or the development of certain literary ideals and standards among the elites of the various city-states of Greece (*CHLC*, V.I, 22). Gregory Nagy points out that pan-Hellenism was crucial in the process of the continuous modification and diffusion of the Homeric poems and of poetry generally. It is well known that the *Iliad* and the *Odyssey* were products of an oral tradition, cumulatively composed over a long period of time; a given poet would take a story whose basic content was already familiar and modify it in the process of his own retelling; in turn, he would pass these poetic skills and this poetic lore down through his own successors. Nagy's point is that the process of "ongoing recomposition and diffusion" of the Homeric and other poems acquired a degree of stability in virtue of the development of pan-Hellenism. The standardization of literary ideals led to a process of decreasing novelty and "text-fixation" in "ever-widening circles of diffusion" (*CHLC*, V.I, 34). According to Nagy, then, pan-Hellenism had a number of important consequences. Firstly, it provided a context in which poetry was no longer merely an expression or ritual reenactment of local myths. The traveling poet was obliged to select those aspects of myth common to the various locales he visited. The word that came to express this "convergence of features" drawn from myth was *aletheia* or truth. Hence the concept of "poet" or singer evolved into the concept of "the master of truth." The poet becomes the purveyor of truth, which is general, as distinct from myth, which is local and particular. Interestingly, Nagy etymologically relates the word *mousa* or "muse" to *mne-*, which means "have the mind connected with." In this reading, the muse "is one who connects the mind with what *really* happens in the past, present, and future" (*CHLC*, V.I, 29–31). Nagy's perception is crucial for understanding subsequent Greek literary theory: the domain of truth becomes an arena of fierce contention between poetry and philosophy.

A second consequence of pan-Hellenism, furthering the process of standardization, was the evolution of a certain group or "canon" of texts into the status of classics (*CHLC*, V.I, 44). It was in the period of Alexandrian scholarship that the term "criticism" or "judgment" was used to differentiate between works that deserved to be included within a canon. Nagy points out that in this era, nine names comprised the "inherited canon of lyric poetry": Alcman, Stesichorus, Alcaeus, Sappho, Ibycus, Anacreon, Simonides, Bacchylides, and Pindar. Hence, "a pre-existing multitude of local traditions in oral song" had evolved into "a finite tradition of fixed lyric compositions suited for all Hellenes" (*CHLC*, V.I, 44). The third, related, consequence was the development of the concept of imitation or *mimesis* into a "concept of authority." Mimesis designates "the re-enactment, through ritual, of the events of myth" by the poet; it also designates "the present re-enacting of previous re-enactments," as in the performer's subsequent imitation of the poet. Mimesis becomes an authoritative concept inasmuch as the author speaks with the authority of myth which is accepted as not local but universal, timeless, and unchanging. It becomes an "implicit promise" that the performer will coin no changes to "accommodate the interests of any local audience," and will give rise to "the pleasure of exact performance" (*CHLC*, V.I, 47–49). Even after such oral performance traditions were obsolete, this authoritative or authoritarian ethic of exact mimesis was preserved in education where the text "becomes simply a sample piece of writing, potentially there to be imitated by other sample pieces of writing" (*CHLC*, V.I, 73). All of these developments outlined by Nagy might be seen as pointing in one general direction: over the centuries, from Homeric times onward, poetry had acquired an increasing authority, established in its function as a repository of *universal* myth and truth, its fixation into a canon of privileged texts which were no longer open to recomposition but merely to exact imitation or performance, and the predominating educational role of poetry in this exalted status. A final point that we can take from Nagy's splendid account of early Greek views of poetry is that by the time of Plato, the theater had become the primary medium of poetry, absorbing the repertoire of both epic and lyric. Tragedy had become the craft of poetry par excellence (*CHLC*, V.I, 66–67). The stage is almost set for our understanding of the literary theories of Plato and Aristotle; before considering these, we must say a few words about the intellectual currents through and against which these theories took form.

Intellectual Contexts

The single most important factor in understanding Plato's conception of poetry is precisely the authority and status it had achieved by his time. As we have seen, the evolution of this authority had been multifaceted: poetry claimed to present a vision of the world, of the gods, of ethics and morality that was *true*. Poetry was not only the repository of collective wisdom, as accumulated over the ages, but was also the expression of universalized myth. It had a public function that was most evident in its supreme embodiment, tragedy, which assumed for the ancient Greeks the roles of our theologies and religious institutions, our histories, our modern mass media, our education system, and our various modes of ascertaining truth.

There are a number of intellectual currents which formed the background of the philosophies of Plato and Aristotle. Interestingly, these currents merged in important ways with the main stream of culture that was comprised by poetry. The first of these was sophistic, which arose in fifth-century Athens, and whose major exponents such as Protagoras and Gorgias were contemporaries of Plato. The second was rhetoric, the art of public speaking, an art vital to the effective functioning of Athenian democracy. Both the Sophists and the rhetoricians offered training in public debate and speaking, often for very high fees; their curriculum aimed to prepare young men of the nobility for political life. While the two currents, sophistic and rhetoric, were so closely connected that the Sophists were indeed the first teachers of rhetoric, there was a distinction between them: rhetoric was, strictly speaking, restricted to the techniques of argument and persuasion; the more ambitious Sophists promised a more general education extending over the areas considered by philosophy: morality, politics, as well as the nature of reality and truth (*CCP*, 64, 66).

Plato was opposed to both sophistic and rhetoric. He objected to sophistic accounts of the world, which were essentially secular, humanistic, and relativistic. These accounts rejected the authority of religion and viewed truth as a human and pragmatic construct. In other words, there was no truth which ultimately stood above or beyond human perception. What Plato rejects in rhetoric is also based on its alleged exclusion of truth: rhetoric is concerned not with truth but merely with persuasion, often preying on the ignorance of an audience and merely pandering to its prejudices rather than seeking a moral and objective foundation. Clearly, the attitudes of sophistic and rhetoric arise in a democratic environment: just as in our modern-day democracies, the concept of truth as some kind of transcendent datum is extinguished; as in our lawcourts, we can argue only that one version of events is more probable and internally coherent than another. We do not claim that this superior version somehow expresses an infallible truth. Much of Plato's philosophy is generated by a desire to impose order on chaos, to enclose change and temporality within a scheme of permanence, and to ground our thinking about morality, politics, and religion on timeless and universal truths that are independent of human cognition. So profound was Plato's opposition to sophistical and rhetorical ways of thinking that his own philosophy is internally shaped and generated by negating their claims. His so-called dialectical method, which proceeds by systematic question and answer, arises largely in contradistinction to their methods. What is important for us is that Plato finds the same vision of the world in literature. In fact, he sees tragedy as a form of rhetoric. T. H. Irwin states that "[i]n attacking rhetoric, Plato also attacks a much older Athenian institution, tragic drama." Like rhetoric, tragedy "makes particular moral views appear attractive to the ignorant and irrational audience" (*CCP*, 67–68). Jennifer T. Roberts reminds us of "the important role played in the education of Athenian citizens by attendance at tragedies. It was tragic drama that afforded Athenians an opportunity to ponder and debate many of the same issues that arose in Plato's dialogues."[7] Hence, for Plato, sophistic and rhetoric effectively expressed a vision of the world that had long been advanced by the much older art of poetry. It is not only his dialectical method but also the content of his philosophy that arises in the sharpest opposition to that vision.

What was that poetic vision? It was a vision going all the way back to Homer: we may recall the squabbling between Zeus and his queen Hera, the laughable scene with Hephaestus, the disputes between various goddesses such as Athena and Aphrodite, and in general the often indecorous conduct of the gods. This is a vision of the world as ruled by chance, a world where "natural processes are basically irregular and unpredictable" where "gods can interfere with them or manipulate them as they please" (*CCP*, 52). Plato firmly rejects this undignified and unsystematic (and perhaps liberal) vision. As many scholars have pointed out, partly on Aristotle's authority, Plato's own ideas were indebted to a pre-Socratic tradition of naturalism, which attempts to offer an alternative account of the world, one that is not poetic or mythical or based on tradition but which appeals rather to natural processes in the service of a rational explanation. Irwin points out that in agreeing with the pre-Socratics, both Socrates and Plato were challenging "widespread and deep-seated religious assumptions of their contemporaries." In rejecting the Homeric irregular picture of the universe, they, like the naturalists, were rejecting the view that we incur divine punishment by failing to make the appropriate sacrifices or by fighting on an ill-omened day or by securing a god's favor by offering gifts. In Plato's view, the gods are "entirely just and good, with no anger, jealousy, spite or lust." Both of these views, says Irwin, existed in an unreconciled fashion in Greek tradition (*CCP*, 52–53). Moreover, like the naturalists, Socrates and Plato distinguished between mere evidence of the senses, which was "appearance," and an underlying reality accessible only through reason (*CCP*, 54). Hence, Greek philosophy begins with the application of rational thinking to all areas of human life: "In the lifetime of Socrates reflection on morality and human society ceased to be the monopoly of Homer and the poets; it became another area for critical thinking" (*CCP*, 58). In other words, Greek philosophy begins as a challenge to the monopoly of poetry and the extension of its vision in more recent trends such as sophistic and rhetoric. Plato's opposition of philosophy to poetry effectively sets the stage for more than two thousand years of literary theory and criticism.

Notes

1 In an excellent article, to which my account here is indebted, Gregory Nagy points out that even the word "rhapsode . . . is built on a concept of artistic self-reference." "Early Greek Views of Poets and Poetry," in *CHLC*, V.I, 7.
2 See M. I. Finley, "The World of Greece and Rome," in *LWC*, 38.

3   Gaius Suetonius Tranquillus, *De grammaticis et rhetoribus*, ed. Francesco della Corte (Turin, 1968); *De poetis*, ed. Augusto Rostagni (Turin, 1944). The latter contains accounts of the lives of various poets, including Vergil, Horace, Lucan, and Terence.
4   *Frogs*, ll. 1115–1117, in *Aristophanes, Volume II: The Peace, The Birds, The Frogs*, trans. Benjamin Bickley Rogers, Loeb Classical Library (Cambridge, MA and London: Harvard University Press/Heinemann, 1968). Hereafter cited as *Frogs*.
5   Irving M. Zeitlin, *Plato's Vision: The Classical Origins of Social and Political Thought* (Englewood Cliffs, NJ: Prentice-Hall, 1993), pp. 16–19. Hereafter cited as *PV*.
6   T. H. Irwin, "Plato: The Intellectual Background," in *CCP*, 68.
7   Jennifer Tolbert Roberts, *Athens on Trial: The Antidemocratic Tradition in Western Thought* (Princeton: Princeton University Press, 1994), p. 84.

CHAPTER 1

PLATO (428–CA. 347 BC)

It is widely acknowledged that the Greek philosopher Plato laid the foundations of Western philosophy. The mathematician and philosopher A. N. Whitehead emphasized this point when he stated that Western philosophy is a series of footnotes to Plato. While this claim may be exaggerated, it rightly suggests that Plato gave initial formulation to the most basic questions and problems of Western thought: How can we define goodness and virtue? How do we arrive at truth and knowledge? What is the connection between soul and body? What is the ideal political state? Of what use are literature and the arts? Plato's answers to these questions are still disputed; yet the questions themselves have endured, often in the forms and contexts posed by Plato.

Plato was born in 428 BC in Athens to a family of long aristocratic lineage, a fact which must eventually have shaped his philosophy at many levels. At the age of 20, Plato, like many other young men, fell under the spell of the controversial thinker and teacher Socrates. The impact on Plato was profound: he relinquished his political ambitions and devoted himself to philosophy. In a story later to be recounted in Plato's *Apology*, Socrates had been hailed by the Oracle at Delphi as "the wisest man alive." Incredulous as to the truth of this, Socrates was nonetheless inspired to devote his life to the pursuit of knowledge, wisdom, and virtue. Using a dialectical method of question and answer, he would often arouse hostility by deflating the pretensions of those who claimed to be wise and who professed to teach. A wide range of people, including rhetoricians, poets, politicians, and artisans, felt the razor edge of his intellect. Socrates' unpopularity in some circles was aggravated by his undermining of conventional views of goodness and truth as well as by his opposition to the principles of democracy. Eventually he was tried on a charge of impiety and condemned to death in 399 BC.

After the death of his revered master, Plato left Athens and traveled to Italy, Sicily, and Egypt. He later returned, to found an Academy (together with the mathematician Thaetetus) in Athens. As indicated by the inscription at the entrance – "Let none without geometry enter" – geometry was foremost in the curriculum, along with mathematics and philosophy. Astronomy, biology, and political theory were also taught.

Students at the Academy included Aristotle, much of whose philosophy was developed as a critique or extension of Plato's ideas.

Plato's thought was influenced by a number of pre-Socratic thinkers who rejected the physical world known through our senses as mere "appearance." They sought to describe a reality underlying physical appearances. Heraclitus' theory was that all things in the universe are in a state of flux; Parmenides viewed reality as unchanging and unitary. Plato was also influenced by mathematical concepts derived from Pythagoras. From Socrates, Plato learned the dialectical method of pursuing truth by a systematic questioning of received ideas and opinions ("dialectic" derives from the Greek *dialegomai*, "to converse"). As exhibited in his early dialogues, he also inherited Socrates' central concern with ethical issues and with the precise definition of moral concepts.

Most of Plato's philosophy is expounded in dialogue form, with Socrates usually cast as the main speaker. The canon attributed to Plato includes thirty-five dialogues and thirteen letters. The authenticity of some of the dialogues and of all the letters has been questioned. It has become conventional to divide Plato's dialogues according to early, middle, and later periods of composition. Most scholars seem to agree that the early dialogues expound the central philosophical concerns and method of Socrates. These dialogues, which include the *Apology, Charmides, Crito, Euthyphro, Gorgias, Ion, Laches, Protagoras, Lysis*, and the first book of the *Republic*, are devoted to exploring and defining concepts such as virtue, temperance, courage, piety, and justice. Such early works exhibit a naturalist tendency to seek by rational analysis a definition of the essence of such concepts, challenging and often rejecting their meanings as conferred by conventional authority and tradition. For example, in *Euthyphro* Socrates rejects the definition of piety as that which merely happens to please the gods; rather, an act pleases the gods *because* it is pious; hence the essence of piety must be sought elsewhere. In general, both Socrates and Plato reject the morally incoherent vision of the universe – found in Homer, Sophocles, and other poets – as disordered, irregular, unpredictable, and subject to the whims of the gods. One has only to think of the intolerable network of contradictions in which Achilles, Oedipus, and other legendary figures are trapped to appreciate the profound irrationality of that poetic vision, as instanced spectacularly in the arbitrary connections it posits between human and divine spheres. This irrationality will eventually inform Plato's indictment of the whole sphere of poetry.

The major dialogues of Plato's middle period – *Gorgias, Meno, Apology, Crito, Phaedo, Symposium, Republic* – move beyond the largely moral concerns of the historical Socrates into the realms of epistemology (theory of knowledge), metaphysics, political theory, and art. The style of the dialogues changes. Whereas the earlier dialogues presented Socrates in the role of a systematic questioner, he is now made to expound Plato's own doctrines in lengthy expositions that go largely unchallenged. At this stage of Plato's development, what unifies these various concerns is his renowned theory of Forms, underlain by his increasing reverence for mathematics as an archetype or model of human inquiry. It should be said that Plato was reacting not only against the disordered and mythical vision of the world offered by the poets but also against the skepticism of thinkers such as Democritus and Protagoras, who had both effectively rejected the notion of a truly objective world existing somehow outside the human mind and independent of human interpretation. The theory of Forms, expounded systematically in the *Phaedo* and the *Republic*, can be summarized as follows. The familiar world of objects which surrounds us, and which we apprehend by our senses, is not independent and self-sufficient. Indeed, it is not the *real* world (even though the objects in it *exist*) because it is dependent upon another world, the realm of pure Forms or ideas, which can be apprehended only by reason and not by our bodily sense-perceptions. What is the connection between the two realms? Plato says that the qualities of any object in the physical world are derived from the ideal Forms of those qualities. For example, an object in the physical world is beautiful because it partakes of the ideal Form of Beauty which exists in the higher realm. And so with Tallness, Equality, or Goodness, which Plato sees as the highest of the Forms. Plato even characterizes entire objects as having their essence in the ideal Forms; hence a bed in the physical world is an imperfect copy of the ideal bed in the world of Forms. The connection between the two realms can best be illustrated using examples from geometry: any triangle or square that we construct using physical instruments is bound to be imperfect. At most it can merely approximate the ideal triangle which is perfect and which is perceived not by the senses but by reason: the ideal triangle is not a physical object but a *concept*, an idea, a Form.

According to Plato, the world of Forms, being changeless and eternal, alone constitutes reality. It is the world of essences, unity, and universality, whereas the physical world is characterized by perpetual change and decay, mere existence (as opposed to essence), multiplicity and particularity. These contrasts become clearer if we consider that each Form is effectively a name or category under which many objects in the physical world can be classified. Returning to the example of the bed, we might say that there are numerous objects constructed for the purpose of sleeping on; what they have in common is a given kind of construction which facilitates this function, say, a flat surface with four legs; hence they fall under the general category of "bed." Similarly, "Goodness" – which Plato regards as the primal Form – can be used to classify a broad range of actions and attitudes, which would otherwise remain mutually disparate and unconnected. We can see, then, that a central function of the theory of Forms is to unify groups of objects or concepts in the world, referring them back to a common essence, and thereby to help make sense of our innumerably diverse experiences. Moreover, the theory attempts to give reality an objective foundation which transcends mere subjective opinion. Plato's theory may sound strange to modern-day readers brought up on empiricist assumptions: we tend to value what is particular and unique; much of our modern science rests on accurate observation of physical phenomena; and we are trained to view the world immediately before us as real. Such thinking was entirely foreign to Plato, whose insistence that reality lies in the universal rather than in the particular profoundly influenced philosophy and theology until at least the eighteenth century, when Enlightenment thinkers began to see knowledge not as innately present in the mind but as deriving from the particulars of sense-experience.

A renowned expression of Plato's theory occurs in the seventh book of the *Republic* where he recounts, through his main speaker Socrates, the so-called "myth of the cave." Socrates outlines the following scenario:

> Picture men dwelling in a sort of subterranean cavern with a long entrance open to the
> light on its entire width. Conceive them as having their legs and necks fettered from

childhood, so that they remain in the same spot, able to look forward only, and prevented by the fetters from turning their heads. Picture further the light from a fire burning higher up and at a distance behind them, and between the fire and the prisoners and above them a road along which a low wall has been built . . .

See also . . . men carrying past the wall implements of all kinds that rise above the wall, and human images and shapes of animals as well, wrought in stone and wood and every material, some of these bearers presumably speaking and others silent.[1]

Since the men are facing the wall of the cave with their backs to the opening, they can see only shadows, cast by the fire on that wall, of the people and objects which are passing behind them. When these people speak, they will hear the echo from the wall, imagining the passing shadows to be the speakers. Plato's point is that people who have known only these shadows will take them for realities: if they were forced to stand up and turn around, they would, at first dazzled by the light coming into the entrance of the cave, be unable to see the objects whose shadows they had previously seen. Indeed, they would insist that those shadows were more real. If they were now forced to ascend the road, which was "rough and steep," they would be yet more blinded. After habituating themselves to the new light, however, they would gradually discern the shadows and reflections of the real objects and eventually would be able "to look upon the sun," realizing that it "presides over all things in the visible region," and was in a sense their underlying "cause" (*Republic*, 515c–516c). These people, newly enlightened, would now pity those who still dwelt in the darkness of the cave mistaking shadows for reality. Plato makes it clear that the cave in which men are imprisoned represents the physical world, and that the journey toward the light is the "soul's ascension" to the world of Forms, the highest of which, like the sun, is the Form of the Good which is "the cause . . . of all that is right and beautiful" (*Republic*, 517b–c).

As beautiful as this myth is, there are many problems with Plato's theory of Forms. For one thing, he himself is never unequivocally clear as to what precisely is the connection between the realm of Forms and the physical world; the Greek words he uses can be translated as "imitation," "participation," and "commonness." Aristotle pointed out that Plato was mistaken in viewing the Forms themselves as actually existing in some abstract realm, on the grounds that such a model would make impossible the subject–predicate structure of language. If, for instance, we say "this table (subject) is beautiful (predicate)," we are stating that the table possesses a quality of beauty which is a universal. To posit that beauty *exists* in its own right is to argue that the quality can exist independently of any object to which it is attached. Notwithstanding such difficulties, this theory underlies all areas of Plato's thinking and is indispensable for understanding his views of art and poetry. The theory of Forms is an archetypal insistence that what we call reality cannot be confined to the here and now; that reality encompasses an organized and interconnected totality whose elements need to be understood as part of a comprehensive pattern. This idea has remained profoundly influential even into our own era.

In later dialogues such as the *Philebus*, *Sophist*, and the *Parmenides*, however, Plato subjects his own theory of Forms to a scrupulous questioning. The *Parmenides* suggests that the theory would require an infinite regression, whereby a further Form would have to be posited as lying behind the initial Form. In the *Sophist*, Plato offers a different view of reality: it is now defined as the power to affect or be affected. He argues, as against the theory of Forms, that such power must operate in the world of becoming and change. This world, then, must be part of reality. It is not clear from these later works, however, what Plato's final position is regarding the Forms. Other late dialogues include *Thaetetus*, concerned with knowledge, *Timaeus*, which expresses Plato's cosmology, and the *Laws*, which contains further analysis of political issues.

Plato on Poetry

Plato makes comments on poetry in many of his dialogues. In the *Apology*, Socrates affirms that poetry derives from inspiration rather than wisdom, and he also remarks on the pretensions of poets to knowledge that they do not possess (22c–d). In *Protagoras*, the role of poetry in education and the inculcation of virtue is discussed (325e–326d). The *Symposium* talks of the motives behind poetic composition, such as the desire to embody and preserve certain concepts of wisdom and virtue (209a). The *Phaedrus* distinguishes between productive and unproductive inspiration (245a), as well as between the relative virtues of speech and writing. And the *Cratylus* discusses, inconclusively, various aspects of the nature of language, such as the connection between words and things.

Plato's most systematic comments on poetry, however, occur in two texts, separated by several years. The first is *Ion*, where Socrates cross-examines a rhapsode or singer on the nature of his art. The second, more sustained, commentary occurs in the *Republic*, some of which is reiterated in a more practical context in the *Laws*. In the first of these dialogues, Socrates discourses with a rhapsode (a singer and interpreter) named Ion. In Socrates' understanding, there are basically two components of the rhapsodist's art: learning the lines of a given poet must be backed by understanding of his thought (*Ion*, 530b–c). Most of Socrates' argument concerning rhapsody addresses its interpretative, critical function rather than its musical and emotional power. Throughout the ostensible "dialogue," Ion acts as the willing and naive tool of Socrates' own perspective, unwittingly dragged through the implications of his own initial boast that he "of all men . . . [has] the finest things to say on Homer" (*Ion*, 530c). Characteristically, Socrates' strategy is not to contradict this statement directly but to unfold various contexts in whose light the connections between the constituent elements of Ion's claim very precisely emerge as absurd.

Ion's claim is strangely self-limited: he claims to recite and interpret only one poet, Homer, and to be ignorant of and indifferent to the work of other poets (*Ion*, 531a). Socrates demonstrates to Ion that genuine knowledge must have a comparative basis: if one can talk about how Homer excels in certain features, one must also be able to talk about how other poets are deficient in these respects (*Ion*, 532a–b). Moreover, Socrates points out that each separate art has its own area of expertise, its own apportioned sphere of knowledge (*Ion*, 537c). Hence, when Homer talks about charioteering, it is the charioteer, not the rhapsode, who can judge the truth of what Homer says; similarly, the physician, the diviner, and the fisherman will be better placed than the rhapsode to judge passages that relate to their professions (*Ion*, 538b–539e). Ion is unable to identify any area in which the rhapsode could interpret Homer's poetry better than the practitioners of other arts. And yet he stands by his claim that he can speak better on Homer than anyone else. How can this be so? Socrates explains that Ion's power as a rhapsode is based not on art or knowledge – if it were, he would be able to speak equally well of other poets – but rather on divine inspiration (*Ion*, 533d–534e).

According to Socrates, the rhapsode, like the poet himself, is in a state of "divine possession" and speaks not with his own voice, which is merely a medium through which a god speaks. The Muse inspires the poet, who in turn passes on this inspiration to the rhapsode, who produces an inspired emotional effect on the spectators (*Ion*, 534c–e). Socrates likens this process to a magnet, which transmits its attractive power to a series of iron rings, which in turn pass on the attraction to other rings, suspended from the first set. The Muse is the magnet or loadstone; the poet is the first ring, the rhapsode is the middle ring, and the audience the last one (*Ion*, 533a, 536a–b). In this way, the poet conveys and interprets the utterances of the gods, and the rhapsode interprets the poets. Hence, the rhapsodes are "interpreters of interpreters" (*Ion*, 535a).

The poet, insists Socrates, is "a light and winged thing, and holy, and never able to compose until he has become inspired, and is beside himself, and reason is no longer in him" (*Ion*, 534b). Not only poetry, according to Socrates, but even criticism is irrational and inspired. Hence, in this early dialogue, composed several years before the *Republic*, Plato has already sharply separated the provinces of poetry and philosophy; the former has its very basis in a divorce from reason, which is the realm of philosophy; poetry in its very nature is steeped in emotional transport and lack of self-possession. Having said this, Plato in this earlier dialogue accords poetry a certain reverence: he speaks of the poet as "holy," and as divinely inspired.

Plato's theory of poetry in the *Republic* is much less flattering. In fact, a modern-day reader is likely to be exasperated at the space devoted to poetry in what is, after all, a political tract concerned primarily with justice in both individual and state. Plato's text has inspired several defenses of poetry, notably by Sidney[2] and Shelley.[3] In general, political commentators have devoted their attention to the notion of justice while literary critics have tended to isolate the commentary on aesthetics from the overall discussion.[4] However, there is an intimate connection between Plato's aesthetics and his formulation of the ideal of justice. Plato's entire conception of justice arises explicitly in opposition to poetic lore, and the close connection between poetry and justice shapes the entire discussion, in political as well as aesthetic terms. It will be useful to consider three broad issues: (1) how Plato's commentary on poetry structures the form of his text; (2) the political motivations of Plato's aesthetics; and (3) the underlying philosophical premises of these aesthetics as well as the contradictions in Plato's argument.

Poetry and the Formal Structure of the *Republic*

It is only toward the end of the *Republic* that Socrates mentions "an ancient quarrel" between philosophy and poetry (*Republic*, 607b). Yet this conflict clearly emerges in the opening pages not only as Plato's starting point but also as a structural premise of his text. Before Socrates offers his own account of justice he is made to hear a number of other, more popular, definitions. In characteristic dialectical strain, the Socratic version is cumulatively articulated as a refutation of those popular assessments, finding its very premises within their negation. Hence what is at stake is not simply an impartial pursuit of the meaning of justice argued directly from first principles, but rather a power struggle, where the historical claims to authority of philosophy and poetry clash. Through this dialectic, the status of poetry as usurper of the throne of wisdom, and especially of popular wisdom, is cumulatively exposed.[5]

The claims of the individual speakers emerge as mouthpieces of poetic authority. Socrates is arguing with a man called Polemarchus over the definition of "justice." Polemarchus invokes the "wise and inspired man" Simonides in arguing that justice is the rendering to each his due. This provokes Socrates into saying that it "was a riddling definition of justice . . . that Simonides gave after the manner of the poets" (331d–332c). It is Socrates himself who makes the connection between his immediate antagonists and poetic lore, saying to Polemarchus: "A kind of thief then the just man it seems has turned out to be, and it is likely that you acquired this idea from Homer. For he regards with complacency Autolycus, the maternal uncle of Odysseus, and says, 'he was gifted beyond all men in thievery and perjury.' So justice, *according to you and Homer and Simonides*, seems to be a kind of stealing, with the qualification that it is for the benefit of friends and the harm of enemies" (334a–b, emphasis added). Hence Socrates explicitly attributes Polemarchus' erratic notion of "justice" to a poetic tradition.

Even this is only the prelude to a more comprehensive assault on the entire Hellenic store of poetic wisdom. At the beginning of book II Socrates affirms that justice must be loved not only for the results it engenders but also "for its own sake" (358a). We have here, perhaps, the first hint in the *Republic* of a distinction between reality and appearance, between the self-subsisting Forms as ultimate ends of knowledge and action, and the more immediate or proximate ends of worldly activity.

Socrates argues that poetry has failed to examine justice "in itself" because poetic knowledge is confined to the world of appearance. This fact is further evinced through the argument of another speaker Adeimantus, who reinforces Socrates' critique of poetry. Adeimantus says that what is popularly considered praiseworthy is not justice itself but the good reputation arising from it. Again, Adeimantus invokes Homer and Hesiod – whom he misreads – in support of his position (363a–d). Adeimantus proceeds to survey the overall shortcomings of poetry in expressing justice, thereby providing a context of received wisdom against which philosophy's "true" search for justice can emerge as a refutation. Against the "language about justice and injustice employed by both laymen and poets," he brings four charges: laymen and poets acknowledge sobriety and righteousness as honorable but unpleasant; they view licentiousness and injustice as not only pleasant but also as "only in opinion and by convention disgraceful"; they hold that injustice "pays better" than justice, and do not scruple to honor the wicked if they are rich and powerful; and, strangest of all, they portray the gods both as assigning misfortunes to good men and as easy to propitiate or manipulate by sacrifices, spells, and enchantments. "And for all these sayings," continues Adeimantus, "they cite the poets as witnesses" (364a–c). Once again, poetry is equated with popular wisdom; it is also associated with the sophistic view that beliefs, laws, and practices

25

claim only conventional rather than absolute validity (a charge to be repeated in book X); and its vision of the gods is deemed morally incoherent.

The ground has now been prepared for the emerging hegemony of philosophy. Poetry, concludes Adeimantus, teaches young men that appearance "masters" reality and that *seeming* just is more profitable than *being* just. It is this pursuit of a phantom, this honoring of dissemblance, which has led to social corruption whose symptoms include the organization of secret societies, political clubs, and the sophistic teaching of "cajolery" whereby the "arts of the popular assembly and the courtroom" are imparted (365a–e). Adeimantus now offers his crucial observation that no one, in either poetry or prose, has adequately inquired as to what justice is "in itself" (366e). Hence the starting point of Socrates' inquiry is finally arrived at through a complex strategy whereby (1) poetry is held to be the repository of received popular wisdom concerning justice; (2) as such, poetry is a codification of the rationale of individual self-interest and desire, a rationale which makes necessary the imposition of laws to constrain selfishness; (3) in consequence, such "wisdom" is morally incoherent, furnishing a divine and human apparatus for the greater prosperity of the *unjust* man; (4) most fundamentally, the poets' account is confined to the *appearance* of justice, not real justice or justice "in itself."

This "poetic" account, according to Socrates, confuses justice with its effects, its material results, the reputation it engenders, and its psychological motivation. The implicit charge is that poetry fails to abstract justice itself from its contingent surroundings and conditions, failing to apprehend its essential, universally applicable, unity. Poetry can perceive only an incoherent multiplicity, only particular appearances, and is intrinsically unable to see these as part of a larger totality. The aim of philosophy emerges cumulatively, then, from this series of negations: in pursuing the *real* nature of justice the philosopher will, on the one hand, isolate its essence by abstraction from particular circumstances and, on the other hand, will apprehend its coherent participation in a totalizing system of knowledge. Hence the assault on poetry, in all of its guises, is moved inexorably forward by Plato's most fundamental strategy, that of hypostatization, or the treatment of a concept as if it had a fixed essence: justice is viewed as a unity, having a single essence (479a). Moreover, the commentary on poetry furnishes the major elements which philosophy sets out to overcome: popular wisdom must be controverted by the higher knowledge of a specialized elite; the ethics of individualism and desire must be displaced by the predomination of state interest; justice must be shown to be more profitable than injustice; and the gods must be assumed to be just. In these crucial ways, the significance of poetry defines the very purpose and method of the *Republic*.

The Politics of Plato's Aesthetics

Poetry's deeper structural function in this text is not confined to the first two books. In books III and X that function extends to the program of education Plato advocates for the guardians or rulers of his ideal city. The initial elements prescribed for this training comprise the conventional Athenian combination of gymnastics and music. The Greek word *mousike*, as its form suggests, refers broadly to any art over which the Muses preside, including poetry, letters, and music. Plato shrewdly sees the importance of this entire sphere in the ideological conditioning of youth: "education in music is most sovereign, because more than anything else rhythm and harmony find their way to the inmost soul and take strongest hold upon it" (401d–e). Ideology operates, then, far more by its formal expression than by its explicit content, and poetry, as we have seen, is viewed by Plato as a powerful force in molding public opinion. Hence he does not underestimate the danger it presents to his ideal city, ordered as this is in a strict hierarchy whereby the guardians (philosophers) and their helpers (soldiers) comprise an elect minority which rules over a large majority of farmers, craftsmen, and "money-makers" (415a–b; 434c).

Just how seriously Plato takes this threat is signaled by the fact that it is music which primarily defines the function of guardianship: "It is here . . . in music . . . that our guardians must build their guardhouse and post of watch." Alert to the potential "insensible corruption" of the state, what they must guard against above all are "innovations in music and gymnastics counter to the established order . . . For a change to a new type of music is something to beware of as a hazard of all our fortunes. For the modes of music are never disturbed without unsettling of the most fundamental political and social conventions." Such innovations, fears Plato (who is speaking through Adeimantus), encourage a "lawlessness" which "by gradual infiltration . . . softly overflows the characters and pursuits of men and from these issues forth grown greater to attack their business dealings, and from these relations it proceeds against the laws and the constitution with wanton license . . . till finally it overthrows all things public and private" (IV, 424b–e). Plato here implicitly acknowledges what Marx and Engels were to theorize over two thousand years later: that the ruling ideas of a society are those of its ruling class. Moreover, he also anticipates Gramsci's theory that such hegemony is not an automatic process but must be achieved by means of a conscious and deliberate program. The molding of subjectivity itself toward unconscious complicity with the aims of the rulers preempts the need for excessive and dangerously provocative coercion by law and by force. That poetry, as the most articulate voice of ideology, must be subjected to constant vigilance lest it unleash forces which undermine the political, economic, and legal structure suggests that Plato accredited it with an inherent subversiveness, a mark of his hypostatization of the entire realm of poetry. Before examining this reductive account of poetic form, however, the precise nature of poetry's subversive potential as elaborated by Plato needs to be evinced.

Socrates suggests that justice would better be examined first in a city rather than as characterizing an individual, on the grounds that justice in the "larger" object will be more clearly discernible (II, 368e). Given that the desired city will be wise, brave, sober, and just (IV, 427e), the guardians themselves must possess a number of qualities: keen senses, strength, bravery, high-spiritedness, and love of wisdom (376e). Plato regards *both* music and gymnastics as directed to the improvement of the soul: gymnastics alone would foster a brutal and harsh disposition, while an exclusively musical training would render the soul too soft. Hence the guardians' nature must achieve a harmony between both dispositions, high-spiritedness on the one hand, and gentleness, together with a love of knowledge, on the other. Plato's terminology here is revealing: such a guardian would be "the most perfect and harmonious musician" (III, 410c–412a).

27

This terminology enables us better to understand just how Plato conceives of poetry as an ideologically destabilizing force. The harmony in the soul of the guardian is not innate; it is achieved only by long training and ideological inculcation. In describing such a guardian as a musician, in arrogating to this class of society the governance of music, in appropriating from poets themselves jurisdiction over their art, Plato is once again marking out music as the arena of ideological conflict between poetry and philosophy. Poetry's main threat resides in its ability to upset the finely attuned balance achieved as a model of subjectivity in rulers. In book X, Plato will allege that poetry establishes a "vicious constitution" in the soul, setting up emotions as rulers in place of reason (X, 605b–c, 606d). Hence in the earlier book Plato advocates an open and strict censorship of poetry, introducing certain charges hitherto unelaborated: (1) the falsity of its claims and representations regarding both gods and men; (2) its corruptive effect on character; and (3) its "disorderly" complexity and encouragement of individualism in the sphere of sensibility and feeling.

Music, observes Socrates, includes tales and stories. Those currently being told, he urges, especially those by Homer and Hesiod, should be suppressed on account of their degrading portrayal of the gods; or at most, they should be allowed circulation among "a very small audience." These include Hesiod's account of the struggles between Uranus and Cronus, and Homer's depiction of Hera's squabbles with Zeus. Even if allegorical, such tales are impermissible since "the young are not able to distinguish what is and what is not allegory" (II, 377c–378e). Such representations falsify the actual nature of God who is "good in reality" and cannot, further, be the cause of evil things as these poets and Aeschylus suggest (II, 379b–e). Nor should poets be allowed to present the gods as assuming manifold forms since, in actuality, "each of them, being the fairest and best possible, abides forever simply in his own form" (II, 381c–d). Finally, poets must not present the gods as deceitful since, affirms Socrates, "there is no lying poet in God" (II, 382d). Again, this phrase suggests that poetry by its very nature is a falsifying rhetorical activity. The underlying point is that such portrayals of gods and men will inculcate false and corruptive ideals into the guardians. What also emerges here as a crucial element in the conflict between philosophy and poetry is the right to name the divine, to authorize a particular vision of the divine world: for poetry, that world is presented as an anthropomorphic projection of human values centered on self-interest, a world of dark chance, irrational, in flux, and devoid of a unifying structure. The project of philosophy, in Plato's hands, is to stabilize that world, drawing all of its scattered elements into the form of order and unity under which alone they can be posited as absolute and transcendent. It might be more accurate to say that, whatever the world is like in actuality, the only version of it to which the guardians should be exposed is that which sees it as orderly and coherent. We can see that a pattern begins to emerge here: in each of the areas of its indictment, whether it be the expression of justice, truth, or depiction of the gods, poetry offers a vision of ungovernable and irreducible multiplicity where the transcendence of any ideal is only sporadically and therefore incompletely achieved.

In addition to its confused conception of the gods, poetry is also charged with speaking falsehood "about men in matters of the greatest moment," portraying unjust men as happy, just men as wretched, and concealed injustice as profitable. Such speech must be prohibited (III, 392b). In view of the qualities which need to be fostered in the guardians, this proscription must extend to certain specific features. Given that the guardians must be brave, tales of the underworld must be "supervised" and stripped of their "entire vocabulary" of terror and fear so as to avoid the risk of "softness" infecting the rulers. The portrayal of both lamentation and laughter in gods and men must be forbidden, since these are not conducive to sobriety and self-control. Poetry must also be prevented from presenting gods and men as greedy or bribable (III, 390e) and in fact from representing "the evil disposition, the licentious, the illiberal, the graceless" (III, 401b). This will help prevent the guardians from being "bred among symbols of evil" lest they "unawares accumulate and build up a huge mass of evil in their own souls." From earliest childhood, they must be "insensibly" guided "to likeness, to friendship, to harmony with beautiful reason" (III, 401c–d).

Given the desired psychical constitution of the guardians as brave, sober, and self-controlled, we might sympathize or at least understand Plato's proscriptions of such passages – until we come across his actual definitions of these qualities. Courage, for example, is defined as the "unfailing conservation of right and lawful belief about things to be and not to be feared." In qualification, Plato explains that the courage thus defined is "the courage of a citizen" (IV, 430b). He likens the implantation of such courage in the guardians to a dye which "might not be washed out by those lyes that have such dread power to scour our faiths away" (IV, 430a). Likewise, sobriety consists in the mastery over the "multitude" of one's appetites; by extension, sobriety in a city means that the rabble or multitude of people is dominated by a minority "of the better sort." Plato goes so far as to define sobriety as a condition of "unanimity" in which both rulers and ruled are of one mind, are harmonious in their agreement, as to who ought to rule (IV, 430e–432a). In similar vein, self-control, for both rulers and "multitude," means control over one's appetites; but for the multitude it also entails being "obedient to their rulers." Plato adds that authors should be forbidden from portraying "impertinences in prose or verse of private citizens to their rulers" (III, 389e–390a). These definitions reveal two glaring features of the connection Plato makes between aesthetics and politics. Firstly, despite his claims that each of these concepts should be examined "in itself," his definitions of them are politically motivated in that they arbitrarily import into these concepts a reference to the relation between classes in a hierarchically ordered state. In Plato's scheme, a man can be brave, self-controlled, or sober only by acknowledging inwardly, as well as outwardly, the validity of the political status quo. What this implies on a broader level is that not only knowledge but also language itself is structured by a political teleology whereby the meaning of concepts is given less in their mutual relations than in the subservient relation of each of them to the desired political end. In view of this, the struggle between philosophy and poetry emerges as a struggle for language, a struggle not merely to define the qualities of human nature or of the divine world, but to define these qualities "in themselves." The guardians must be protected from exposure to the ideological and linguistic matrix of poetry so that philosophy might work on the ideologically instituted *tabula rasa* or blank slate of the soul, enjoying a freely receptive domain not only for the inscription of its own ideological agenda but for its effective kenosis and remolding of language itself.

Secondly, what facilitates Plato's politically slanted definitions is his earlier parallelism between the individual and state. His aesthetics emerged as politically motivated in

29

the sense that they are determined by what the guardians should believe concerning men and gods, and the character as individuals toward which they must aspire. The definitions of the virtues of an individual as cited above comprise variously refracted facets of the same basic ethical model: the control and domination of the "multitude" by a unity. As applied to the individual, the "multitude" refers to the potentially endless variety of appetites and desires that need to be constrained by reason, which is a unity. In book X, it will emerge explicitly that poetry appeals to the "inferior" part of the soul, the appetitive portion (X, 603b–c). It is, in other words, an encouragement toward variety and multiplicity, toward valuing the particular for its own sake, thereby distracting from contemplation of the universal. In projecting this model onto the state as a whole, Plato aligns the mass of people with the unruly multitude of desires in the soul, and the guardians considered collectively with the unity of reason. The individuality of the guardians is to be all but erased, not merely through ideological conditioning but through their compulsory existence as a community: they are to possess no private property or wealth; they must live together, nourished on a simple diet, and receiving a stipend from the other citizens (III, 416d–417b). Collectively, then, the guardians' function in the city is a projection of the unifying function of reason in the individual soul. Hence, the political motivation of Plato's aesthetics lies not only in the desired character of the guardians, but also in the nature and origin of the ideal city as a whole.

It is here that Plato's overarching disposition toward unity asserts itself most pervasively and at every level, from the point of origin of a city to its formally articulated bureaucratic structure. Just as what is ultimately achieved in the guardians is a harmonious unity of soul, so the ultimate political aim of the city is to attain and preserve unity. What needs to be observed here is how unity – even more than the alleged goals of justice or the Good – is the ultimate teleological principle informing the interrelation of elements comprising the city's overall constitution.

According to Plato, the originating circumstance of a city is that individuals are not self-sufficient. No person can adequately provide the total of his or her own needs (II, 369b). The deeper premise beneath this is a strict specialization of function whereby "One man is naturally fitted for one task" (II, 370b). Plato is adamant on this point, insisting that "it is impossible for one man to do the work of many arts well" and that in the ideal city every man would work at "one occupation . . . all his days" (II, 374a–c). This rigid division of labor is the foundation of the entire analogy between the just individual and the just city. And this is perhaps where we approach the heart of Plato's overall argument concerning justice and poetry. The definition of justice in the state is reached in book IV: justice is a condition where "each one man must perform one social service in the state for which his nature was best adapted." It is also defined as the "principle of doing one's own business" and "not to be a busybody" (IV, 433a–b). Socrates recognizes here that this "principle" for which he had been seeking had in fact already been laid down as "a universal requirement" in the very origin of a city (as cited above). If the definitions of the other virtues of a city and an individual, such as wisdom, courage, sobriety, and self-control, appeared semantically to coerce these concepts into vehicles of social order, the same strategy emerges all the more blatantly in Plato's emptying of the concept of justice of all predicates even remotely recognizable as inhering in it by disinterested pursuit: fairness, impartiality, proportion, and all such predicates which might reasonably be invoked as necessary components of the definition of justice are effectively exiled from the concept, in what is perhaps one of the most high-handed attempts in the history of philosophy to overturn consensual language, and to reassign the semantic valency of words, in the name of a clarity accessible only to the epistemic elite. Justice "in itself" is a phantom exorcised by its very pursuit in the *Republic*: its function is reduced to pure circularity, acting at once as the origin and end of the state, with no intermediary logic connecting these extremes of its ostensibly structuring polarity. The circularity of argument is even more pronounced in Plato's remolding of his analogy between the state and the individual. Socrates argues that since "the city was thought to be just because three natural kinds existing in it performed each its own function, . . . we shall thus expect the individual also to have these same forms in his soul" (IV, 435b–c). And, predictably, justice in an individual is defined as a condition of the soul where "the several parts . . . perform each their own task," and where reason rules. He in whom this condition obtains "will be a just man and one who minds his own affair." Such a harmonious soul will, of course, be fostered by a correct blending of gymnastics and music (IV, 441e–442a). Injustice, then, comprises "a kind of civil war" of the three principles of the soul, upsetting the natural relation of dominance (IV, 444a–d).

This entire argument, based on strict division of function, is what underlies Plato's earlier disparagement of poetry. In political terms, poetry's greatest crime is its insubordination in respect of specialization of labor. Plato urges that the same man ought not to imitate "many things": any poetic imitation involving "manifold forms" will, says Socrates, "be ill suited to our polity, because there is no twofold or manifold man among us, since every man does one thing" (III, 397b–e). Plato then arrives at the renowned passage urging banishment of the "manifold" poet, a passage whose logic merits reconsideration:

> If a man . . . who was capable by his cunning of assuming every kind of shape and imitating all things should arrive in our city, bringing with himself the poems which he wished to exhibit, we should fall down and worship him as a holy and wondrous and delightful creature, but should say to him that there is no man of that kind among us in our city, nor is it lawful for such a man to arise among us, and we should send him away to another city, after pouring myrrh down over his head and crowning him with fillets of wool. (III, 398a)

These lines have sometimes been held to harbor an ambivalent attitude to poetry, but book X appears to confirm that the falling down and worshipping of the poet is suggested in an entirely mocking and sarcastic vein. The central argument of this passage is not that poetry corrupts, nor that it expresses falsehood; rather, it is in its very nature a contradiction of the possibility of a just framework of social and political existence: a city consists of several kinds of people each through some specific function contributing to the welfare of the whole. The poet, however, is engaged in an activity which per se resists such specialization; it is important to appreciate here that what is at issue for Plato is not the disposition of any individual poet but that of poetry itself.

This general charge against poetry is elucidated in book X. Once again, it is an index of how deeply poetry structures the entire discussion that this final book is devoted not

31

to justice or polity but to poetry. Socrates, perhaps shaky in his conviction of his own earlier arguments, returns to give second thoughts to the subject – with the biased intention of convincing himself more deeply. Using the dialogue between Socrates and Glaucon, Plato now presents the poet as a "most marvelous Sophist" and a "truly clever and wondrous man" who "makes all the things that all handicraftsmen severally produce" (X, 596c–d). The political implication of this claim that Plato attributes to poetry is that poetry can have no *definable* (and therefore limited) function in a state ordered according to a strict hierarchy of inexchangeable function. That poetry impinges indiscriminately on all areas of production and knowledge means that by definition it pervades all strata of the hierarchy, which it thereby undermines as a whole. It literally does not know its place and it can never be clear in relation to which activity or discipline it can be subordinated or superordinated. It spreads its influence limitlessly, dissolving social relations as it pleases and recreating them from its own store of inspired wisdom whose opacity to reason renders it resistant to classification and definition. In this sense, poetry is the incarnation of indefinability and the limits of reason. It is in its nature a rebel, a usurper, which desires to rule; and as such it is the most potent threat to the throne of philosophy, which is also the throne of polity in the state of the philosopher-king.

There is, moreover, a further political valency in poetry's indeterminacy of function. Plato sees poetry as pandering primarily to two types of constitution, the democratic and the tyrannical (VIII, 568a–d). Tyranny, moreover, is viewed by Plato as somehow not opposed to democracy but a logical extension of it. The precise significance of this association of poetry with democracy may be evinced from a broader political context. Plato suggests that there five basic forms of government. His own ideal constitution can be conceived as either royalty or aristocracy (IV, 445d). The other four forms represent a progressive degeneration away from this model: timocracy (where the pursuit of honor is paramount), oligarchy, democracy, and tyranny (such an evolution, it might be added, has no basis in Greek history). In line with his earlier parallelism of individual and state, Plato sees five basic kinds of individual characters or souls, corresponding to the forms of government (VIII, 544e–545c).

Even the ideal city, acknowledges Plato, will ultimately crumble. Its deterioration will be caused initially by flaws in the selective breeding of guardians, generating intermixture and dissension in the ruling class itself (VIII, 545d–547a). The timocracy eventually produced will retain some features of the aristocracy such as honoring of rulers and the abstention of the warrior class from money-making; but in admitting to office men of high spirit rather than reason it will hold itself perpetually in a posture of war, and "a fierce secret lust for gold and silver" and private gain will infect its rulers. Such will be a state guided by the coveting of honor (VIII, 547d–548c). This system naturally gives way to oligarchy where government office is attached to a property qualification (VIII, 550c) and where the city is no longer a unity but divided effectively into two cities, between rich and poor (VIII, 551d). Owing to this inequitable condition, such a city will be marked by crime and the pervasive presence of beggars (VIII, 552d). What is perhaps most interesting here is the way Plato characterizes the "soul" of the oligarchic man. Though he prizes wealth and property above everything, he is "thrifty and laborious, satisfying only his own necessary appetites and desires . . . but subduing his other appetites as vain and unprofitable." He is, in Socrates' words, "a squalid fellow, . . . looking for a surplus of profit in everything" (VIII, 554a–b). These words anticipate, almost verbatim, Weber's description of the mentality of early capitalists. Ironically, while Plato's "ideal" account of the evolution from monarchy and aristocracy to democracy and tyranny has little basis in the actual history of Greek society, it might be read as a valuable idealization of the historical transitions in Europe from petty kingdoms through the vast edifice of feudalism to the hegemony of capitalism, each of these emerging, as Marx would have it, from internal discord within the previous system. In virtue of the "internal dissension" of the oligarchic man, whose control over his ebbing appetites is motivated by fear for his possessions, Plato characterizes him as not a unity but a "double man" (VIII, 554d–e). Again, this might be paralleled with the ironic self-division of human beings in modern bourgeois society, as theorized by commentators from diverse traditions, including some of the Romantics, Hegel, Lukács, de Tocqueville, and Sartre.

When Plato describes the evolution of democracy from oligarchy, we can begin finally to discern the depth of political motivation on which his polemic against poetry rests. Democracy comes about as a popular revolution against the rich oligarchs, the people being granted an equal share in citizenship and political office (VIII, 556e–557b). What is worshipped here is individual liberty, leading to a number of undesirable consequences. Firstly, "every man has license to do as he likes" and "would arrange a plan for leading his own life in the way that pleases him." Secondly, this constitution would generate all "sorts and conditions of men," a greater variety than any other form of government. A democracy is thus "diversified with every type of character" and, shopping through the "bazaar of [individual] constitutions," each person could "establish his own." Thirdly, the government would be "anarchic and motley, assigning a kind of equality indiscriminately to equals and unequals alike" (VIII, 557b–558c). Moreover, the disorder of a democratic society extends into private life: the relation of authority is undermined between parents and children, teachers and pupils, freemen and slaves, men and women. The spirit of liberty waxes so strong that eventually even the laws are disregarded and a condition of lawlessness prevails (VIII, 562e–563e).

And what kind of citizen, what kind of soul, would such a democracy foster? To begin with, the distinction between "necessary" and "unnecessary" appetites which constrained the desires of the oligarchic man is now abrogated. The "brood of desires" now "seize the citadel of the young man's soul, finding it empty and unoccupied by studies and honorable pursuits" (VIII, 560b–561a). The democratic man fosters all parts of the soul equally and "avers that they are all alike and to be equally esteemed." His life will be run by "indulging the appetite of the day," and "he says and does whatever enters his head." In other words, "there is no order or compulsion in his existence" (VIII, 561d). Most tellingly, Plato affirms that the democratic man "is a manifold man stuffed with most excellent differences, . . . containing within himself the greatest number of patterns of constitutions and qualities" (VIII, 561e).

We can see here, quite apart from Plato's explicit association of poetry and democracy, that poetry is charged with the same fundamental traits as democracy. Like democracy, poetry fosters genuine individuals, "manifold" men who are "stuffed" with differences and resist the reduction of their social function, or indeed their natural potential, into one exclusive dimension. Also, like democracy, poetry nurtures all parts of the soul, refusing obeisance to the law of reason. By implication, then, poetry itself is spurred by the "greed" for liberty which is the hallmark of a democratic society. Poetry is, in the sphere of ideology, the archetype of social disorder, individuality, emphasis rather than suppression of difference, and insubordination to reason. Like that of democracy, its nature is rooted in self-will and physical pleasure, in a refusal to acknowledge the hierarchy either within the soul or between the soul and body.

From the disorder of the democratic state, maintains Plato, tyranny will arise, with one man claiming to represent the interests of both social order and the downtrodden majority. In terms of the evolution of one system of government from another, Plato's point is that tyranny, though ostensibly initiated as a reaction against the chaos of democracy, is in fact an extension of it. The tyrant, far from being king over his own soul, is in fact the most miserable of creatures, enslaved as he is to that "terrible brood" of lawless desires which have dethroned reason in his individual constitution. He gives full vent to the "mob" of his unconscious appetites and instincts which know no constraint. Accordingly, tyranny embodies the utmost depths of anarchy and lawlessness. Hence the degeneration from aristocracy through oligarchy to democracy and tyranny represents the collapse not only of the original unity of the state but also, equally importantly, of the unity of the individual into a lawless multiplicity. The unified, integrated person of the aristocracy who enjoyed a harmony between the various "classes" of his soul is fragmented first into the "double" man of oligarchy and then the "manifold" man produced by democracy; finally, even the vestiges of the soul's structure collapse, in tyranny, into an uncontrollable proliferation of desires, an abyss of irreducible particularity, multiplicity, and relativity.

Metaphysical Presuppositions and Impasses

It is crucial to see that Plato aligns the potential of poetry explicitly with such degradation of political and psychical unity. The notion of unity acts as the metaphysical premise of Plato's entire argument on a number of levels.[6] What has emerged cumulatively from the foregoing account of the connections between justice and poetry is Plato's presupposition that unity is the desired end of both individual and state constitution. He has repeatedly asserted that the democratic "mob," be it the mob of appetites in the soul or the mob of citizens, must be controlled by a rational element (IV, 431a–d). Moreover, it is the goal of unity which dictates a strict division of labor, based on Plato's view that individuals exercising a variety of functions would lead to the state's ruin (IV, 434b). Plato actually makes explicit his assumption that unity is intrinsically a positive value while multiplicity is associated with disorder, indulgence, and evil. He states, for example, that excellence is "one" while the varieties of evil are infinite (IV, 445c). The greatest evil for a state is that it should be "many" instead of "one."

In like manner, Plato sees reason itself as a unity while emotion is variable (X, 604e–605c). The structure of knowledge as Plato conceives it comprises a movement toward the apprehension of data as an interconnected whole or system: the science of dialectic both uncovers the first principles and essences of things and sees them as part of an ordered structure (VII, 533c–d, 534b, 537c). What enables this perception of order is that each of the Forms is itself a unity which has distilled into itself, as it were, the concentrated essence of various manifestations in the material world (V, 476a–b). It underlies, categorizes, and explains these. But the unity of the Forms is apprehended only by philosophers; the multitude, says Plato, are dreamers who "wander amid multiplicities," mistaking resemblance for identity and particular for universal (V, 476c; VI, 484b). Hence the guardians, after their initial study of music and gymnastics, must undertake the study of unity "as such" (VII, 524e), fostered by training in number or arithmetic, geometry, and astronomy. These sciences depend, according to Plato, on the use of reason rather than the senses. The most fundamental strategy toward the political implementation of unity is to unite the functions of ruler and philosopher. Plato sees the current separation of these roles as itself an expression of multiplicity; at present, a "motley horde" pursues either task independently (V, 473d).

Plato here unwittingly reveals that, if the movement toward knowledge and justice is essentially a movement toward unity whether in individual or state, it is also a movement of coercion. The ruling faculty in the soul and the ruling body in the state do not unify any real differences: the unity Plato has in mind is achieved by suppressing all difference and imperiously positing itself as the constant inner structure of a given type of variety in the physical world. For example, there is no compromise either between the multitude of competing appetites and desires in the soul or between these and reason: they must fall under the absolute sovereignty of reason. Similarly, the unity of the state is not achieved by any true harmony of the conflicting claims of various classes or groups; the guardians, the privileged political embodiment of reason, determine absolutely the interests of the state. Hence "unity" is anything but a confluence or coexistence of equal parts. Rather, it is effectively a euphemism for a system of dominance, a rigid hierarchy whereby the "lower" (referable to the body, the appetites, or the majority of people in a state) is not merely subsumed under the "higher" but is divested by such subsumption of any independent claim to reality, meaning, or value. The lower – which spans the various particulars of the material world – can have meaning or reality only in proportion with its potential to exemplify a pregiven Form. For example, a beautiful object as portrayed by a poet or painter must have its beauty already and completely contained within a pregiven Form or definition of the beautiful. The uniqueness of the poet's expression of a particular object in a particular setting must be reducible to an exemplary status. It is precisely the uniqueness or particularity which must be foregone or sacrificed in the interests of unifiability. Should the poet attempt to extend or alter the assessment of beauty, this becomes in Plato's eyes a falsification of the nature or essence of this Form. In this way, the imperious demand of unity further precludes any contemplation of a material object "in itself." For Plato, it is only the enabling ideal Form (such as beauty) of an object which can be studied "in itself." The object itself cannot be so studied and is thereby reduced to purely referential status, pointing beyond itself to the Form of which it is merely the superfluously unique material realization. This is not the interconnected system of references in terms of which many modern theorists, from Saussure to Derrida, have viewed language. In Plato, the referentiality is directed only one way: from the material object, which alone is reduced to a referential status, to the self-subsisting Form. Moreover, the reference operates along the lines of a stringent hierarchy. It can be seen shortly, then, that much of Plato's censure of poetry rests on the fact that the objects of its apprehension are merely references, not things in themselves.

A second, and deeply related, metaphysical presupposition underlying Plato's work generally is contained in his strategy of hypostatization, of reducing variety and multiplicity to a constant and definable essence. In terms of its bearing on the status of poetry, a number of inconsistencies inhering in this strategy need to be considered. Plato hypostatizes not only the Forms but also the mode of their apprehension, philosophy, as well as the entire realm of poetry. This means that philosophy and poetry have rigidly defined essences, the point here being that these essences are determined in explicit mutual contrast. Plato's argument simply does not comprehend the possibility that two genuine philosophers (as opposed to Sophists) could entertain sharply divergent visions of reality or that two poets could hold sharply opposed views. Despite his abundant use of examples from poetic tradition, his view of poetry is not constituted by inductive abstraction from the empirical practice of actual poets; rather, it is an a priori definition which coerces the potentially endless variety of that practice into a uniform assailability. Likewise, "philosophy" as a scientific discipline is viewed as an ideal pursuit standing above the actual practice of philosophers.

Yet, even if we approach Plato's hypostatized opposition of philosophy and poetry on its own terms, it is incoherent, entailing as it does an essentializing of the notions of truth, singularity of function, reason, emotion, and imitation. Plato's indictment of poetry has been based on (1) its *intrinsic* expression of falsehood, (2) its intrinsic operation in the realm of imitation, (3) its combination of a variety of functions, (4) its appeal to the lower aspects of the soul such as emotion and appetite, and (5) its expression of irreducible particularity and multiplicity rather than unity. The argument "from truth" breaks down very early in the *Republic*. Having urged that most of the current "stories" told by poets – such as Hesiod's account of the unseemly behavior between Uranus, Cronus, and Zeus – must be censored, Socrates adds: "Even if they were true . . . as few as possible should have heard these tales" (II, 377c–378a). It becomes immediately transparent here that it is not truth but political and educational expediency which is the criterion of censorship. Moreover, Plato repeatedly states that the guardians themselves (though no one else) must employ lies "for the benefit of the state" (III, 389b; V, 459c–d; VII, 535d–e). The entire point of the notorious "noble lie" is to persuade the citizens, and possibly the rulers themselves, that their social status and function are not products of circumstance and ideological conditioning but were endowed naturally by their "mother" earth (III, 414c–415c).

Plato, of course, is not unaware of this incoherence. He attempts to explain and overcome it by extending still further the strategy of hypostatization, urging that there is a distinction between "Essential falsehood" and "falsehood in words." The former, contends Plato, is abhorred by both gods and men while the latter can be "serviceable" (II, 382c–d). By this stroke of essentializing the notion of truth, Plato at once removes it from the realm of language and the possibility of poetic access. The point is that, no matter what a poet says, it cannot express "essential" truth because it is confined in terms of its objects to the realm of appearance and in terms of its mode of operation to imitation. In other words, it is not the content of poetry which renders it false; its falsehood is embodied in its very form.[7]

The notion of imitation, in fact, complements truth as the basis of Plato's reductive and incoherent opposition of philosophy and poetry. Plato's comments concerning poetic imitation are not restricted to book X. In book III he had expressed an ideological preference for poetry in which the proportion of narration to imitation was high: the more imitative poetry is, the more degraded it will be, involving mimicry of all kinds of "unworthy" objects; as such, it requires "manifold forms of variation" (III, 396c–397d). In book X the poet is held up as a Sophist, a "marvelous" handicraftsman who can "make" anything: "all implements, . . . all plants and animals, including himself, and thereto earth and heaven and the gods and all things in heaven and in Hades." Indeed, then, the poet "makes all the things that all handicraftsmen severally produce" (X, 596c–d). Hence poetic imitation in its very nature violates the political principle of singularity of function. And what the poet imitates is of course the appearance, not the reality, of things, since he merely imitates what others actually produce (X, 596e, 597e). Plato elaborates his famous triad: we find three beds, one existing in nature, which is made by God; another which is the work of the carpenter; and a third, the work of the painter or poet. Hence, the carpenter imitates the real bed and the painter or poet imitates the physical bed. The poet's work, then, like that of the rhapsode, is the "imitation of an imitation." It is worth recalling the precise order of Plato's argument here: he does not simply argue that poetic imitation is thrice removed from truth; he first states that the imitation in general is "three removes from nature" and then subsumes poetic practice under this limitation (X, 597e). He states later that the imitator (not merely the poet) knows nothing of reality but only appearance (X, b–c). What, then, does the poet "know"? Plato's answer is that the poet knows *only* how to imitate (X, 601a). Hence, just as Plato essentialized the pursuit of philosophy, assigning pregiven attributes to it, so he essentializes imitation itself, the mode to which poetry is confined. Moreover, he claims that poetry will deceive only those "who . . . judge only by forms and colors" (X, 601a), implying that a purely formal or aesthetic evaluation of poetry is necessarily indifferent to truth-value.

This procedure at once becomes problematic. To begin with, even if we grant what Plato says about imitation – that it is limited to appearance and that its potentially endless extension through indefinite fields is not based on knowledge – this is surely not enough to preclude imitation being an art or skill in its own right. Surely, by Plato's own logic, we could grant that the one thing the poet *does* know, how to imitate, is as specialized a field as carpentry or bed-making. Hence, if we follow Plato's own terms, we need not characterize the poet as someone who claims to know everything. He only claims to know the art of imitation and imitations will constitute precisely the field of his production. What apparently underlies Plato's refusal to grant this is his insistence that imitation must by its nature refer beyond itself to the thing it imitates. Plato will not concede that the imitation itself could have a reality or value independent of its presumed reference. Plato leaves no room for the possibility (subsequently taken up by the philosopher Plotinus) that the painter or poet imitates the Form of the bed itself, just as much as the carpenter does. He apparently refuses to acknowledge the image created by poetry or painting as a part of the sensible world on a par with other physical objects. This not only entraps poetry within a referential circle but also misses the point of reference to which poetry might aspire. For example, the painter portraying a carpenter needs to know not about carpenters but about painting. He does not mean to pretend that the image is the carpenter: the image has a function and a value that the real carpenter could not possess. Plato goes so far as to characterize imitation as "a form of play, not to be taken seriously" (X, 602b).

What, then, are we to make of Plato's *general* indictment of imitation when we recall that the guardians must undertake a considerable amount of "imitation" themselves?[8] Plato tells us that they must imitate "men . . . who are brave, sober, pious, free, and all things of that kind" (III, 395c). Plato does not distinguish between the two kinds of imitation – that used by the poets and that incumbent upon the guardians – and uses the same word in Greek. Moreover, he holds that the philosopher will "imitate" the eternal Forms (VI, 500b–c): would the philosopher not then be at least *twice* removed from truth? Finally, that Plato's hypostatization of the opposition of philosophy and poetry rests upon their definition by each other is shown in his general characterizations of each. A poet's work, maintains Plato, narrates "past, present, or future things" (III, 392d) and as such is concerned with bodily appetites, emotion, particulars, and multiplicities. In contrast, the philosopher, far from "wandering between the two poles of generation and decay," is concerned with eternal essences, with the soul, reason, and with knowledge as a whole (VI, 485a–c). Philosophy, the medium through which the form of justice "in itself" will be clearly perceived, is defined in explicit opposition to poetry, which it must displace in order to enable a truly and ideally just state. It is perhaps no accident that, despite Socrates' repeated and sarcastic disclaimers that he is not a poet (II, 379a; III, 393d), he describes the construction of the state as conducted by a "political artist" who fashions the city by imitating a "heavenly model." The constitution Socrates has in mind "will be realized when this philosophical Muse has taken control of the state" (VI, 499d; 500e–501c). The philosophical Muse invoked by the *Republic* must define itself against the poetic Muse whose abdication from the throne of state it must first compel.

The Influence and Legacy of Plato

The influence of Plato on many fundamental areas of Western thought, including literary theory, has been profound and pervasive, and continues to the present day. First and foremost has been the impact of the theory of Forms: discredited though this may have been since the time of Aristotle, it nonetheless exerted a powerful attraction through its implications that the world was a unity, that our experience of manifold qualities in the world could be brought under certain unifying concepts, that the physical world itself is only a small part, or manifestation, of a higher reality, and that there exists a higher, ideal pattern for earthly endeavors. The idea of the temporal world pointing beyond itself to an invisible eternal world has been an integral element in both Judeo-Christian and Islamic theology and philosophy. The distinctions between reason and sense, reason and emotion, soul and body, while not original to Plato, continued through his influence to provide some of the basic terminology of philosophical and religious thinking.

In historical terms, there have been a number of eras in which Platonism exerted a notable impact. The Academy founded by Plato in Athens continued beyond his death until AD 529 when it was closed on account of its paganism by the emperor Justinian. During this period, the philosophy known as Neo-Platonism was founded by Plotinus (AD 204/5–270) and his disciple and popularizer Porphyry (ca. AD 232–305), who combined Platonic notions with elements derived from Pythagoras, Aristotle, and the Stoics. Plotinus modified Plato's view of poetic imitation, and the Neo-Platonists in general used the theory of poetic inspiration, derived from Plato's *Ion* and *Phaedrus*, to argue that poetry transcends human reason. Neo-Platonism was the predominant philosophy in Europe for more than a thousand years; its major exponents included Iamblichus (ca. AD 250–ca. 325), Proclus, and the Alexandrian theologians Philo Judaeus, Clement, and Origen. Some of these thinkers, inspired partly by Plato, developed a system of allegorical readings of texts, especially of the Bible. Philo, for example, constructed an allegorical reading of Genesis. St. Augustine's theology as well as his figurative readings of certain parts of scripture were heavily influenced by Plato.

In the Middle Ages, only the *Timaeus* and a handful of other Platonic texts were available in Latin. Yet the influence of Platonism on St. Augustine ensured its survival in medieval Christian thought. It was further transmitted by the works of Chalcidius, Macrobius, and Boethius. Plotinus and Proclus influenced the mystical writings of Dionysius the pseudo-Areopagite (ca. AD 500), which were translated in the ninth century and inspired much mystical poetry, based on the premise that divine truth is ineffable in ordinary language. Dionysius also transmitted a Neo-Platonist view of creation as a hierarchy as expressed in the "Book of Nature." Such a view is broadly expressed in Dante's *Paradiso*. By the thirteenth century, however, Plato's influence was largely eclipsed by the recently translated works of Aristotle, used by Aquinas and the scholastics to undertake a rational account of Christian doctrine.

The Renaissance saw a reaction against scholastic thinking by humanists who returned to classical sources, preferring Plato over Aristotle. Notable humanists included leaders of the Platonic Academy in Florence such as Marsilio Ficino (1433–1499) and Pico della Mirandola (1463–1494), as well as John Colet, Erasmus, and Sir Thomas More in England. Renaissance Platonism stressed the didactic functions of poetry and Platonic concepts such as the "ladder of love," leading from the physical to the spiritual realm. Both defenders of poetry, such as Sir Philip Sidney, and detractors, such as Savonarola, appealed to their understanding of Plato's arguments concerning poetry. A century or so later, Platonic doctrines were again revived by a group of theologians and poets known as the Cambridge Platonists who included Ralph Cudworth, Benjamin Whichcote, and Henry More. At a time when religious ideas were increasingly under attack, these thinkers attempted to elaborate a rational basis for Christian theology, as did later Anglicans, also influenced by Platonic ideas, in the nineteenth century. Other figures indebted to Plato included the philosopher Leibniz and the astronomers Kepler and Galileo.

Some Platonic notions, such as the distinction between appearance and reality, emerge in highly refracted forms in the philosophies of Kant and Hegel, and some of Hegel's followers. Such notions also inform the work of English Romantic poets such as Blake, Wordsworth, and Shelley. In America, Emerson's transcendentalism bore the imprint of Plato's thought, as did the poetic theory and practice of Poe, Baudelaire, and the French symbolists. Literary figures such as Matthew Arnold have effectively turned Plato's own arguments against him, urging that poetry is a repository of humanistic values and nurtures sensibility. Plato's influence extends into the twentieth century, in the work of Yeats, Rilke, Wallace Stevens, and others. It is clear that Plato's literary and critical influence cannot be separated from the broader influence of his philosophical notions. Nonetheless, his impact on literary critics and theorists has embraced certain identifiable areas and issues: the doctrine of imitation; the educational and didactic functions of poetry; the place of poetry in the political state and the question of censorship; the treatment of poetry as a species of rhetoric; the nature of poetic inspiration; and the opposition of poetry to various other disciplines and dispositions, such as philosophy, science, reason, and mechanism. We are still grappling with the problems laid down by Plato.

Notes

1 *Republic*, in *Collected Dialogues of Plato*, ed. Edith Hamilton and Huntington Cairns (Princeton: Princeton University Press, 1969), 514a–c. Hereafter cited as *Republic*. All further citations of Plato's works refer to this edition, unless otherwise stated.
2 Sir Philip Sidney, *A Defence of Poetry*, ed. J. A. Van Dorsten (Oxford: Oxford University Press, 1966), pp. 60–61.
3 Unlike Sidney, Shelley does see Plato's views of poetry as part of the overall productive mechanism of a state; his direct "argument" against Plato, however, is restricted largely to asserting that Plato was himself a poet; *Shelley's Defence of Poetry; Browning's Essay on Shelley*, ed. L. Winstanley (Boston and London: D. C. Heath, 1911), pp. 13, 35.
4 Among the numerous political and philosophical commentaries on the *Republic* some notable works include: N. R. Murphy, *The Interpretation of Plato's Republic* (Oxford: Oxford University Press, 1951); R. C. Cross and A. D. Woozley, *Plato's Republic: A Philosophical Commentary* (London: Macmillan, 1964); Terence Irwin, *Plato's Moral Theory* (Oxford: Oxford University Press, 1977); Julia Annas, *An Introduction to Plato's Republic* (Oxford: Oxford University Press, 1981), and C. D. C. Reeve, *Philosopher Kings: The Argument of Plato's Republic* (Princeton: Princeton University Press, 1988). Interpretations of Plato's aesthetics include: R. G. Collingwood, "Plato's Philosophy of Art," *Mind* 34 (1925): 154–172; Iris Murdoch, *The Fire and the Sun: Why Plato Banished the Artists* (Oxford: Oxford University Press, 1977); Julius Moravcsik and Philip Temko, eds., *Plato on Beauty, Wisdom, and the Arts* (Totowa, NJ: Rowman and Littlefield, 1982); Elizabeth Belfiore, "A Theory of Imitation in Plato's *Republic*," *Transactions of the American Philological Association* 114 (1984): 121–146; G. R. F. Ferrari, "Plato and Poetry," in the *Cambridge History of Literary Criticism*, vol. 1 ed. George A. Kennedy (Cambridge: Cambridge University Press, 1989), pp. 92–148. Like most of the foregoing works, Irving M. Zeitlin's *Plato's Vision: The Classical Origins of Social and Political Thought* (Englewood Cliffs, NJ: Prentice-Hall, 1993) effectively treats Plato's views of justice and his aesthetics as two distinct classes of argument. Julius A. Elias' *Plato's Defence of Poetry* (Albany: State University of New York Press, 1984) does attempt to contextualize Plato's assessment of poetry within a background of eschatological, political, and methodological myth but his argument is quite different – if not opposed – to that advanced here.
5 Eric Havelock discusses the educational importance of poetry in Greek society of Plato's time in his classic study *Preface to Plato* (Cambridge, MA: Harvard University Press, 1963).
6 For a further but somewhat brief discussion of unity in the *Republic*, see Nicholas P. White, *A Companion to Plato's Republic* (Indianapolis, 1979), pp. 38–40.
7 See also Collingwood's argument that imitation by its very nature cannot adequately express its model; "Plato's Philosophy of Art," 157–159.
8 For a useful discussion of the various possible meanings of "imitation" see Elizabeth Asmis, "Plato on Poetic Creativity," in *CCP*, 350–355; Asmis does not, however, address the problem posed here.

CHAPTER 2

ARISTOTLE
(384–322 BC)

Life and Philosophy

The most brilliant student at Plato's Academy was Aristotle, who had come to Athens in 367 from his native Stageira in Macedonia to study with Plato. Aristotle's enormous contribution to the history of thought spans several areas: metaphysics, logic, ethics, politics, literary criticism, and various branches of natural science. Indeed, Aristotle's treatment of these subjects profoundly shaped the subsequent formulation of problems in these areas for two thousand years. Born in 384, Aristotle was the son of Nicomachus, court physician to Amyntas II, father of Philip of Macedon. Nicomachus died when Aristotle was young, but it is said that he taught his son some anatomy, an early training which may have contributed to Aristotle's eventual philosophical outlook. Indeed, Aristotle was more interested than Plato in empirical observation of natural phenomena, especially in biology, a difference which helps account for the fundamentally differing outlooks of the two thinkers.

In 343 King Philip of Macedon invited Aristotle to serve as tutor to his son Alexander at his court in Pella. Aristotle attended for four years to the education of the future king and conqueror, after which he was commissioned by Philip to oversee the restoration of Stageira, now devastated by war, and to establish a legal code for the city. Having completed this project successfully, Aristotle returned to Athens to open his own school of rhetoric and philosophy. The school was called the Lyceum (it was dedicated to Apollo Lyceus, god of shepherds) and housed a large library, a natural history museum, and a zoological garden. Unlike Plato's Academy, whose students came mostly from the aristocracy, the Lyceum drew largely from middle-class citizens, and a rivalry developed between the two schools. Indeed, this rivalry effectively continued, in the works of subsequent thinkers and schools, for many centuries. The Academy placed emphasis on mathematics, metaphysics, and politics, while at the Lyceum natural science predominated, its curriculum including botany, music, mathematics, medicine, the constitutions of the Greek cities, zoology, and the customs of the so-called barbarians.

It is recorded that Aristotle wrote twenty-seven dialogues; it was by these, not the works handed down to us, that he was known in the ancient world. Unfortunately, none of them has survived. What we now have of Aristotle's works, which represent only one-quarter of his actual output, are Aristotle's lecture notes, composed by himself and his students, largely in the last twelve years of his life. These were published by Andronicus of Rhodes in the first century BC. When Alexander of Macedon died in 323, Athens was the seat of much ill-feeling toward the Macedonians (who, under Philip, had conquered them) and it was expedient for Aristotle to leave. In fact, he was charged, like Socrates, with impiety; unlike Socrates, who freely faced his death sentence, Aristotle chose to avoid letting the Athenians "sin twice against philosophy" and moved to Chalcis in Macedonia.

Aristotle's Metaphysics

At the heart of Aristotle's metaphysics and logic is the concept of substance. In his *Metaphysics* Aristotle states that the subject matter of metaphysics is "being *qua* being."[1] In other words, metaphysics studies existence in general and what it means for things to exist. Aristotle tells us in *Posterior Analytics* that before we can know *what* a thing is, before we can know its true nature or essence, we must be aware *that* it exists. However, such awareness of existence is not distinct from, but part of, our knowledge of the thing's essence. To have true knowledge, we must know the thing's essence and the causes of it. For instance, we could be aware of the *existence* of something, such as "a noise in the clouds," but until we are *essentially* aware of it, until we know *what* the thing is (thunder/the causes of thunder), we do not even know that it exists.[2] Hence, the phrase "being *qua* being" does not refer to existence as an isolated, abstracted condition, but to existence as understood in its connections with essence. Given these considerations, Aristotle reformulates the question confronted by metaphysics ("what is being?") as "what is substance?" (*Met. I–IX*, pp. 312–313). The Greek word for "substance" (*ousia*) can also be translated as "essence." Hence the notion of substance comprehends the connection between existence and essence.

The notion of substance as formulated by Aristotle pervades the subsequent history of Western logic and metaphysics. It is indeed the underlying principle of Aristotle's work in these areas, central as it is to his *Categories* as well as his *Metaphysics*. In the former, Aristotle basically holds that there are ten categories through which we can view the world: whatness (substance), quantity, quality, relation, place, time, position, state, action, and affection.[3] A mere glance at these categories tells us that they still permeate our own thought about the world at the profoundest levels. When we think of any entity with a view to understanding it, we approach it in terms of its qualities, its relations to other entities, its position in space and time, and so on. But, according to Aristotle, there must be an underlying substrate or substance to which these qualities and relations belong. Hence substance, for Aristotle, has primacy of place in these categories: it both underlies the other categories, as their substratum, and bears to them a relation of subject to predicate (the Greek word for category means "predicate"). This primacy of substance can be explained by referring to Aristotle's definitions of it in the *Metaphysics*. In book V, it is defined as "the ultimate subject which cannot be predicated of something else" and as "whatever has an individual and separate existence" (*Met.*, V.viii.4). Aristotle maintains that the categories indicate the various modes of "being," and that all of these modes of being refer to substance. In book VII, Aristotle calls substance the primary sense of "being." Only substance, then, and none of the other categories, can exist separately since they are dependent upon substance (*Met. I–IX*, pp. 147–149, 310–313). Aristotle puts this in another way in the *Categories*, where he makes a distinction between primary substance and secondary substance: primary substance is "that which is neither asserted of nor can be found in a subject" (*Cat.*, p. 19). Examples of primary substance would include a particular man or a horse. The other categories, such as quantity and quality, would act as predicates or qualifications of these particular entities. Secondary substance, for Aristotle, designates the species or genera under which these individual entities are classified. So a particular man would belong to the species "man" and this species itself would fall under the genus of "animal." We can see, then, that all primary substance is individual, each denoting an indivisible unit. Secondary substance refers to many things, not one entity, as the genus "animal" would refer to all animals, and not to any particular animal. Aristotle tells us that the most outstanding characteristic of substance is that it can receive contrary qualifications or predicates while remaining numerically one and the same. For example, it could be predicated of the same man that he is both good and bad in various aspects. Substance seems to have the function, then, of an indivisible substrate to which various elements in the other categories can be attached, as predicates.

From a historical perspective, it is worth remarking that Aristotle's view of substance as the subject of predication represents a sharp break from the Platonic Forms, and was indeed to some extent worked out as part of Aristotle's critique of those Forms. Aristotle sometimes expresses great impatience with the Forms, referring to them as "empty phrases and poetical metaphors" (*Met.*, I.ix.12) and even dismissing them at one point as "mere prattle" (*PA*, I.xxii.83a, 33). However, he undertakes a serious critique of those Forms on several accounts. Plato had made a distinction between particular objects, such as a man or a bed, and "universals" or qualities such as goodness or tallness. Plato thought that these universals possessed an independent existence in the world of Forms which somehow transcends the world of physical, sensible, objects. Plato sees goodness in a particular man as deriving from, or participating in, the ideal Form of goodness. Aristotle, however, sees that this view of the connection between particulars and universals, between separate existing things and qualities, would make it impossible to explain the subject–predicate structure of language (*PA*, I.xxii.83a, 33). For example, if we want to say that a particular object has a certain quality, for instance, "This horse is tall" (where "This horse" is the subject and "is tall" is the predicate), it does not help us to think of "tallness" as a separate entity to which the first entity (horse) is somehow related. If tallness is truly a universal applying to many objects, we must view it as a *quality* which is possessed by a class of objects rather than as a *thing* which exists in its own right. Aristotle urges, the Forms introduce a great deal of confusion into our explanations of the sensible world and are simply not necessary (*Met.*, I.viii–ix).

However, Aristotle does develop certain implications of the Forms to arrive at his own theory of universals, namely, that universals refer to qualities which can be predicated of many subjects (or a class of subjects), and these qualities have no independent existence. Reversing the Platonic hierarchy, Aristotle urges that universals depend on particular things for their existence, not vice versa. A quality such as "blackness" can exist in a man but it has no independent life. Aristotle's rejection of the world of Forms and his location of universals as simply describing things in this world represents a major shift from Plato's vision and offers a metaphysics more centered on *this* world (rather than another, higher world). Though Aristotle would agree with Plato that reason has access to a higher knowledge than our senses, Aristotle insists that the senses are the starting point and the source of knowledge. He attempts to balance Plato's unilateral emphasis on reason with due attention to our actual experience and to close observation of the world. In a broad sense, the history of Western thought has often emerged as a conflict between these two visions: the idealistic Platonic vision which views reality as above and beyond our own world, and the more empirical Aristotelian view which seeks to find reality within our world.

Having said this, Aristotle's philosophy was a far cry from our own modern modes of realism and pragmatism. Modern realism, as dating from the nineteenth century, tends to view particular things as real and universals as abstractions from a group of particular entities. For example, we might observe that numerous particular animals have a given characteristic in common, the ability to live both on land and in water. From this we abstract the characteristic of "amphibiousness" and devise the category "amphibian" to group such animals together. In Aristotle's view (one followed by most philosophy through the Middle Ages and extending even into the work of Kant and Hegel) it is universals, not particular things, which are real. Even though, in terms of immediate perception, particulars precede the universal, it is the universal which can explain the particular. Also, as seen earlier, Aristotle's vision depends on the notion of substance. Without primary substance, says Aristotle, nothing else could even exist (*Cat.*, p. 22). In book XII of his *Metaphysics*, Aristotle says that, however we regard the universe as a whole, substance is its primary reality. So the notion of substance holds together the entire Aristotelian system, from the most meager level of existence to God who, as the ultimate or First Cause of the universe, is the ultimate guarantor of substance.

However, the notion of substance itself is problematic. On the one hand, Aristotle sees substance as underlying the other categories; on the other hand, he views substance as identical with any attributes in the other categories which can be essentially predicated of it (*PA*, p. 121). For example, if we say of the subject "horse" that it has "four legs," the latter predicate is part of the subject, since having four legs is essential to the definition of a horse. We may well ask, if we strip away all of the attributes in the other categories, what else is left? The very principle on which the categories are founded appears to be self-contradictory, and in one sense the subsequent history of Western philosophy (until Derrida and beyond) might be viewed as an attempt to grapple with this problem.

Aristotle's Logic

Aristotle's greatest contribution to philosophy lies in the realm of logic. Aristotle viewed logic as an instrument (or organon) which was a preliminary requirement for the study of every branch of knowledge. His own name for logic was "analytics" and his logical treatises include *Categories*, *Interpretation*, *Prior Analytics*, *Posterior Analytics*, and *Topics*. These works came to be referred to collectively by Aristotle's followers (known as Peripatetics) as the *Organon*. While Aristotle drew some elements of his logic from the pre-Socratics and Plato, he was the first philosopher to formalize the rules and methods of logic, and to treat it as a systematic prelude to scientific thinking. Aristotle attempted to clarify the structure of propositions which assert truth or false-hood, the nature of demonstration, the connection of universal and particular propositions, the isolation of the essential qualities of a subject by definition, and so on. The basis of Aristotelian logic, which acted as the foundation of logic for over two thousand years, was the syllogism. The Aristotelian syllogism typically consists of a major premise, a minor premise, and an inferred conclusion, as in the classic example of a syllogism: "All men are mortal; Socrates is a man; therefore, Socrates is mortal." Aristotle classified a number of different kinds of syllogism, ranging from this simple "if . . . then" structure to far more complex formats. Among Aristotle's contributions to logic are the provision of a mathematical foundation for logic, the use of the dialectical mode of argument as an instrument of proof, and the employment of empirical data. The influence of Aristotle's logic has been even greater than that of his metaphysics or politics. Even during periods such as late antiquity or the later Renaissance which saw Aristotle's general influence eclipsed by Plato's, Aristotle still remained the supreme authority in logic.

Nonetheless, Aristotle's logic has been severely criticized by thinkers such as Bertrand Russell, who regards the two-thousand-year influence of Aristotle as a period of "stagnation," and states that Aristotle's "present-day influence is . . . inimical to clear thinking" (*HWP*, 206). Among Russell's objections are that Aristotle puts too much stress on the syllogism, which is by no means the only kind of deductive argument; like the Greeks generally, Aristotle gave "undue prominence to deduction" over induction; the notion of "substance" or "essence," says Russell, may be applied to a word but not to a thing, hence Aristotle mistakenly applies the subject–predicate structure of language to the world itself. Russell goes so far as to say that "practically every advance in science, in logic, or in philosophy has had to be made in the teeth of opposition from Aristotle's disciples" (*HWP*, 207–212). Aristotle's logic has come under fire not only from modern mathematicians but also from physicists, philosophers such as Hegel and his followers, Marxist thinkers, and modern literary and cultural theorists such as Derrida.

Even more fundamental than the syllogism and deductive reasoning are the three so-called laws of logic (sometimes called the "laws of thought") as formulated by Aristotle and developed by numerous subsequent thinkers into our own day. The first of these is the law of identity, which states that A is A; the second is the law of non-contradiction, which dictates that something cannot be both A and not-A; and the third, the law of the excluded middle, holds that something must be *either* A *or* not-A.

These "laws," which can be regarded as the same law expressed from three different perspectives, have served for over two millennia as the (almost) unshakeable foundation of Western thought. As such, they bear examination in a little more detail. In general, the first of these laws, that of identity, is contained in Aristotle's notion of primary substance as "individual" and as denoting a "unit" (*Cat.* 3a10–13) and as not admitting degrees (*Cat.* 3b34), and, perhaps above all, as never being defined with "reference to something beyond or outside" (*Cat.* 8a19). But what does it mean to say that A is A? Is this not an obvious and empty tautology? We can see that it is no trite proposition the moment we substitute any important term for the letter A. Let us, for example, use the term "man." When we say that a man is a man, we are appealing to certain qualities which compose the essence of man; we are saying that this essence is fixed and unalterable; we are *also* saying that a man is somehow different from a woman, from an animal, from a plant, and so forth. We can quickly begin to see how our definition will have vast economic and political implications: if we define our "man" as rational, as political, as moral, and as free, it will seem natural to us that he should partake in the political process. The woman, whom we define as lacking these qualities, will by our definition be excluded. That this law of identity is highly coercive and hierarchical will become even clearer in the case of the terms "master" and "slave." The master might well be defined in terms of attributes that collectively signify "civilized," while the slave is constricted within designations of "savage" (Aristotle himself defines a slave as a "speaking instrument"). Such hierarchical oppositions have in history embraced the terms Greek and barbarian, Christian and Jew, white and black, noble and serf.

The second and third laws of logic will merely confirm our implicit degradation of the woman or slave. The law of contradiction, on which Aristotle insists (*Met. I–IX*, 1011b–13), tells us that something/someone cannot both be a man and not a man. Again, isn't this obvious? Surely it tells us nothing new? In fact, we are stating a further implication of the law of identity: that a certain set of qualities is attributed to "man" and a *different* set of qualities is accorded to woman, there being no overlap between these two sets of qualities. According to this logic, we cannot speak of a person who might come in between these two poles: a man who had womanly qualities or a woman with manly attributes. The law of the excluded middle explicitly forbids this middle ground (*Met. I–IX*, 1011b–23) in its urging that something must be *either* A *or* not-A. Either one must be a man or not a man; either American or not-American; either Muslim or Jew; either good or bad; either for or against. Hence, these "laws," which unfortunately still largely govern our thinking today, are not only coercive but also encourage a vision of the world as divided up sharply into categories, classes, nations, races, and religions, each with its own distinctive essence or character. The elimination of the middle ground has long been an ideological, political, and economic strategy, one that removes all possibility of definitional flexibility and change according to altered circumstances. So deeply rooted is this way of thinking that even attempted subversions of it, such as have issued from Marxism, feminism, deconstruction, and psychoanalysis, must operate within a broader network of complicity with what they challenge. It must be recalled that the notion of identity is firmly instituted within the concept of substance; hence, not only logic but metaphysics as well as political thought have fallen under the sway of these so-called laws.

Aristotle's Politics

Aristotle's views of poetry are underlain not only by his metaphysical principles but also by his vision of the political state. Unlike that of Plato, Aristotle's method is analytic and empirical, beginning with the notion of a composite whole and breaking it down into its smallest parts.[4] This analytic mentality underlies Aristotle's rejection of Plato's view that the state should comprise a unity. Unity, in fact, would destroy the state's self-sufficiency since the state harbors not only a plurality of numbers but also different kinds of men with diverse functions which support one another (*Pol.*, II.ii). The unity of a state arises out of its harmonization of various interests; it is also a function of education in the "spirit" of a given constitution, an education which entails training of both habits and the intellect (*Pol.*, II.v). We will see that poetry and the arts have an essential function in this kind of education.

A second premise deriving from Aristotle's metaphysics concerns the teleology of the state. Aristotle's view is that the state does not simply exist for the utilitarian functions of providing a living, protection, and the exchange of goods (*Pol.*, III.ix). The state is more than this. It is a political association which aims at the "highest good" (*Pol.*, I.i). According to Aristotle, the chief purpose or end of men, both communally and individually, is the "good life" (*Pol.*, III.vi). In defining this good life, Aristotle has recourse to his own earlier formulations in the *Ethics*: "the life which is best for men, both separately, as individuals, and in the mass, as states, is the life which has virtue sufficiently supported by material resources to facilitate participation in the actions that virtue calls for" (*Pol.*, VII.i). And, again repeating statements in his *Ethics*, he says that happiness is proportionate to the achievement of virtue and *phronesis* or practical wisdom (*Pol.*, VII.i). Hence the ultimate end of a state is primarily the achievement of virtue; the state exists, says Aristotle, for the sake of "noble actions" (*Pol.*, III.ix). Again, these political views underlie Aristotle's treatment of action in the *Poetics*.

The third metaphysical premise, also repeated from the *Ethics*, is the principle that virtue is a mean between excess and defect (*Pol.*, IV.xi). Aristotle, calling this the "principle of the middle way," extends its applicability to the formation of constitutions (*Pol.*, V.ix). Hence, in a political context, Aristotle defines the best life as "the middle life," which harbors a middle path or "mean" open to men of every kind (*Pol.*, IV.xi). This principle will become important in both Aristotle's assessment of democracy and his formulation of what he considers to be the most desirable constitution, which he calls "polity." It is also important in his definitions of poetry and the arts in general; each of these, Aristotle suggests, should aim at the mean. The political state advocated by Aristotle is itself a "mean." Like Plato, Aristotle sees many actual or potential evils in democracy. The two hallmarks of democracy he cites as the sovereignty of the majority and liberty (*Pol.*, V.ix). He also reiterates Plato's charges that democracy may be marked by a general disorder and disrespect for the law, and lack of control over slaves, women, and children. The constitution which Aristotle himself advocates, called polity, is offered as a mixture of oligarchy and democracy, a mixture which can lean in either direction (*Pol.*, IV.vi).

47

Aristotle's Poetics

The Metaphysical and Ethical Contexts of the Poetics

In the opening statement of his *Poetics*, Aristotle proposes to examine poetry "in itself." We should not be misled by this statement into thinking that Aristotle somehow embraced some of our nineteenth- and twentieth-century notions of poetic autonomy. For Aristotle poetry and rhetoric had the status of "productive" sciences; these disciplines had their place in a hierarchy of knowledge; and Aristotle viewed them as rational pursuits, as seeking a knowledge of universals (rather than of random particulars), and as serving a social and moral function. We have seen that the entire structure of the Aristotelian system was governed by the notion of substance, from the lowest level to God as the First Cause, or Unmoved Mover. Each element within this hierarchical order had its proper place, function, and purpose. Aristotle's universe is effectively a closed system where each entity is guided by an internalized purpose toward the fulfillment of its own nature, and ultimately toward realization of its harmony with the divine. Poetry, in this system, is analyzed and classified in the same way as the other branches of human knowledge and activity. The notion of poetic autonomy as developed in modern times, the notion of poetry as an end in itself, as an independent sphere with its own laws, would have been meaningless to Aristotle. In *Nicomachean Ethics*, he states quite clearly concerning productive activity that "the act of making is not an end in itself, it is only a means, and belongs to something else."[5] The purpose of art, like that of metaphysics, is to attain to a knowledge of universals. For Aristotle, the subject matter of art is the "cause" behind experiential fact. The *Poetics*, then, is a theoretical treatise on the nature and functions of poetry; it was part of a broader course of philosophical study offered by Aristotle at the Lyceum. And part of its motivation was to oppose Plato's powerful critique of poetry which condemned it on both moral and epistemological grounds.

Aristotle's *Poetics* has often been analyzed in terms of its prescriptions for tragedy, its distinctions of tragedy, epic, and other genres, as well as its comments on plot and character. So profound has been the influence of these notions that in academic institutions to this day works of literature are analyzed through such categories as theme, character, plot, and authorial presence in the text. However, in assessing the significance of Aristotle's *Poetics* within the various traditions of literary criticism, and in understanding the position of poetry and the arts in Aristotle's general scheme, we need to consider the political, ethical, and metaphysical frameworks of his text. Like Plato, Aristotle considers the question of whether "music" should form an integral part of state education, especially for children. "Music," we need to recall, had a broad significance, encompassing not only performances using instruments and songs but also dancing, and it referred to the arts in general. The question Aristotle raises, then, is effectively about the value of what we might call a liberal education. It was seen earlier that Aristotle criticized Plato's ideal republic as being confined within strictly utilitarian ends. Aristotle's own state, in contrast, was directed toward "the highest good" as its ultimate purpose, and enabling men to live "the good life." In his *Politics* he suggests that an integral aspect of this good life is the leisure to engage in civilized pursuits (*Pol.*, VIII.iii). He urges that "there is a form of education which we must provide for our sons, not as being useful or essential but as elevated and worthy of free men." He decries the constant demand for the usefulness of a given pursuit as "unbecoming to those of broad vision" (*Pol.*, VIII.iii). He even goes so far as to suggest that, at one level, the pleasure we derive from music might be an end in itself. However, he is quick to qualify this remark by adding that such pleasure is only an "incidental result," and that the true nature of music lies in its being a stimulus to virtue and is expressed in its "effect on the character and the soul" (*Pol.*, VIII.v). We can see here that, while Aristotle opposes a bland and mechanical utilitarianism, he yet insists that what gives music value is its potential use in education and in forming character. Typically, however, Aristotle suggests an organic connection between the pleasure derived from music and the virtue inspired by it. For virtue, says Aristotle, "has to do with enjoying oneself in the right way, with liking and hating the right things." He concludes that "clearly there is no more important lesson to be learned or habit to be formed than that of right judgment and of delighting in good characters and noble actions" (*Pol.*, VIII.v).

In the *Poetics* these statements emerge as being equally applicable to poetry. Aristotle's overall conclusion concerning music is that, since it has "the power to induce a certain character of the soul . . . , it must be applied to education, and the young must be educated in it."[6] Music is all the more valuable in educating the young, says Aristotle, because it is pleasant. This argument will be repeated by many subsequent critics, including Horace and Sidney. It is clear, then, that while the arts and poetry may have their own laws and offer pleasure, this pleasure is integral to a further, moral, aim which is institutionalized in education. In contrast with Plato's ideal state, where it is viewed as an obstacle to morality, rationality, and genuine knowledge, poetry would seem to have a positive function in Aristotle's state. However, in his own way, Aristotle is just as censorious as Plato regarding the propriety of material to which children should be exposed: they should be shielded from artistic representations of "unseemly actions," they must not be allowed to view comedies or scurrilous performances, and must in general be protected from any performance containing "wickedness or hostility" (*Pol.*, VII.xvii).

In addition to Aristotle's ethical and political dispositions, there are a number of epistemological and metaphysical principles which underlie his arguments and prescriptions in the *Poetics*. Some of these have already been mentioned: Aristotle's empirical method, his acceptance of plurality, the teleology of both individual and state, and the principle of moderation. To these we might add the notions of unity, probability, necessity, rationality, universality, and truth. All of these notions, together with Aristotle's ethical and political principles, underlie his views of the characteristics of good literature. The issues at stake here include the meaning and desirability of realism, the presentation of character, the use of detail, the use of language, and the way in which various components of a literary work are mutually integrated and harmonized.

Aristotle's General Views of Imitation and Action

At the core of Aristotle's *Poetics* are two complex notions, imitation and action, which are imbued with both Aristotle's metaphysical principles and his ethical/political dispositions. Like Plato, Aristotle holds that poetry is essentially a mode of imitation. But Aristotle propounds an entirely different view of imitation, one which leads him to regard poetry as having a positive function. For Plato, imitation itself embodied a step away from truth, since it produced an imperfect copy of the Form or essence of a given entity. In this sense, the entire world of physical phenomena for Plato was an imperfect imitation of the world of Forms. Poetry, for Plato, ranked even lower than the sensible world of appearances since it was obliged to imitate those appearances, which were already imitations of Forms. Aristotle, however, invests imitation with positive significance. Rather than viewing it as a necessarily denigrative activity, he sees it as a basic human instinct and allows it as an avenue toward truth and knowledge. In the *Poetics* he states that from childhood men have an "instinct" for imitation, and that what distinguishes man from other animals is that he is far more imitative (IV.2–3). Aristotle boldly adds that not just philosophers but all men in varying degrees find pleasure in learning. And human beings rely on imitation to learn; through this process they infer the nature of each object. Hence, for Aristotle, imitation is both a mode of learning and associated with pleasure. This view is reinforced in Aristotle's *Rhetoric* where he infers that, since learning and admiration are pleasant, the imitative arts such as drawing, sculpture, and poetry must also be pleasant. He holds that the pleasure lies not in the object which is imitated but in the process of imitation itself, which yields learning through a process of inference.[7] In his *Politics*, Aristotle also suggests that we delight in imitation inasmuch as it yields a likeness of reality (*Pol.*, VIII.v). The very distance between artistic representation and reality which Plato derided is offered up by Aristotle as a source of pleasure, based upon contrast. This delight in realism is something he will address again in the *Poetics*. It is clear, then, that for Aristotle, the notion of imitation is heavily charged with moral and epistemological functions.

The other crucial notion in the *Poetics*, that of action, is equally complex in Aristotle's scheme. In the *Politics* Aristotle attempts to evaluate the relative merits of contemplation and action. It is clear that he places a high priority on action. He states that "virtue in itself is not enough; there must also be the power to translate it into action" (*Pol.*, VII.iii). At one point he even proclaims that "happiness is action; and the actions of just and restrained men represent the consummation of many fine things." As such, the active life will be best both for the state and the individual (*Pol.*, VII.iii). However, Aristotle regards contemplation and intelligence, which are engaged in for their own sake, as even more active "because the aim in such thinking is to do well, and therefore also, in a sense, action" (*Pol.*, VII.iii). What these statements indicate is that action, for Aristotle, whether it be physical or mental, communal or individual, has a moral end or purpose. Art imitates human action; but human action must have as its ultimate purpose "the Supreme Good" (*PA*, p. 171).

In the *Ethics*, the moral nature of action is brought out in more depth and detail. The notion of action involves a number of elements: the (efficient) cause of action is choice, and the cause of choice is "desire and reasoning directed to some end." Hence, says, Aristotle, choice necessarily involves the exercise of intellect and a certain disposition of character (*NE*, VI.ii.4). Aristotle further explains that action which conforms to virtue requires certain conditions on the part of the agent: he must act with knowledge; he must deliberately choose the act; and the act must spring from "a fixed and permanent disposition of character." As such, virtue results from the *repeated* performance of just and temperate actions (*NE*, II.iv.3). Aristotle holds that the objects of virtue, what virtue is essentially concerned with, are feelings and actions (*NE*, II.vi.10–12). He defines virtue as "a settled disposition of the mind determining the choice of actions and emotions, consisting essentially in the observance of the mean relative to us . . . and it is a mean state between two vices, one of excess and one of defect" (*NE*, II.vi.15). These statements furnish a background against which we might understand the central notions of the *Poetics*: the nature of imitation; and the nature of action, and its relation to virtue, thought, emotion, and character.

In general terms, then, the connection between poetic imitation and action might be described as follows. Poetry, as a productive art, is not an end in itself. Its purpose is to represent action, which according to Aristotle is an end in itself inasmuch as it seeks to be virtuous. Hence, the initial relationship between imitation and action is that of means and end. However, the connection between them is also underlain by the concept of the mean or middle way. Just as virtuous action will aim at the mean, art itself in its imitative or representative endeavors must aim at the mean and apply this as the standard in its productions. We are now perhaps in a better position to understand the implications of these terms, imitation and action, in the *Poetics*.

The Concept of Imitation in the Poetics

Near the beginning of his text, Aristotle asserts that all the various modes of poetry and music are imitations. These imitations can differ in three ways: in the means used, in the kinds of objects represented, or in the manner of presentation. The means can include color, shape, sound, rhythm, speech, and harmony. The art that imitates by words, says Aristotle, is poetry. As against popular notions which equate poetry with the use of meter, Aristotle insists that the essential characteristic of the poet is imitation (*Poetics*, I). Given that Aristotle later suggests that the origins of the poetic art lie in natural causes, namely, our imitative nature and the pleasure we derive from learning through imitation, it would seem that the art of the poet is a formalization of impulses possessed in common by human beings. Again, this stands in sharp contrast with Plato's view of the poet as divinely possessed, composing in an irrational frenzy, and standing aloof from his fellow human creatures. For Aristotle, the poet is an integral part of human society, rationally developing and refining basic traits which he shares with other human beings.

The second way in which artistic imitations differ from one another is in the kinds of objects they address. What is common to all arts, however, is that they imitate men involved in action (*Poetics*, II). As suggested earlier, the actions Aristotle has in mind are those which have a significant moral valency. The actions imitated, says Aristotle, must either be noble or base since human character conforms to these distinctions. What lies at the basis of both human action and human character, then, is morality: it is this moral component of action and character which the artist must imitate or represent. It is within this general imperative of all art that distinctions can be made concerning the kinds of objects imitated: the latter can be better, worse, or like the norm (*Poetics*, II). In this one stroke Aristotle lays the foundations of two broad issues: distinctions of genre, on the one hand, and the nature of an artwork's connection to reality, on the other. Moreover, the two kinds of discussions remain indissolubly tied

51

to the moral basis from which they proceed. Tragedy, says Aristotle, represents men as better than the norm, comedy as worse than the norm. While this respective deviation from moral realism yields the genres of tragedy and comedy, there is no poetic genre generated by moral realism or "likeness" to the norm. As will emerge shortly, it seems that Aristotle relegates such mechanical moral realism to the discipline of history.

The final way in which imitations can be distinguished is in the manner of presentation. Aristotle allows only two basic types: narration, in which the poet speaks in his own person or through a character, and dramatic presentation, in which the story is performed and acted out (*Poetics*, III). Aristotle traces tragedy back to heroic and epic poetry, hymns, and encomia, while comedy, he suggests, has its roots in invective and iambic poetry.

The contrast between poetry and history is taken up later in the *Poetics* where Aristotle offers some further general comments on imitation. It is not the function of the poet, maintains Aristotle, to narrate events that have actually happened, but rather "events such as might occur . . . in accordance with the laws of probability or necessity" (*Poetics*, IX). What distinguishes the poet from the historian is not that one writes in verse and the other in prose, but precisely the fact that the poet, unlike the historian, is not constrained by the obligation to express actual events. The conclusion Aristotle draws from this is in many ways far removed from our modern conceptions of poetry, history, and realism. He infers that poetry is more "philosophical" and "serious" (*spoudaioteron*) than history because poetry expresses what is universal (*ta kathalou*), while history merely deals with individuals. Another way of putting this is to say that poetry yields general truths while history gives us particular facts. Today, we tend to think of the poet as expressing general truths only through the treatment of particular objects and detailed situations; we think of history as not merely recounting a series of events but as descrying broad patterns within these events, and as being advanced from a variety of perspectives. However, some of our notions of realism, as formulated through the nineteenth century, share with Aristotle the insistence on probability or necessity. That poetry does not depict the details of actual events does not, for Aristotle, detract from its realism. What poetry expresses is the universal, which, for Aristotle, is more real than particular events. The poet expresses the inner structure of probability or causality which shapes events, and as such is universalizable and transferable to other sets of events. Thus a poet will not express the contingent or accidental properties of a given person's actions, only those elements which might operate in the actions of others. The historian is actually bound by such contingency, such inextricable immersion in particularity as divested of universal application. We can see here how profoundly the notion of substance or essence underlies Aristotle's notions of literature.

Another important difference between poetry and history emerges in section XXIII of the *Poetics*. The poet's vision has a unity which the historian's work lacks. History is concerned not with one action but with one period of time, dealing with a sequence of events whose diversity is not necessarily united by a single purpose or goal. The poet, however, must imitate a single action that is "whole" and "complete"; his subject matter must be comprehended "in a single view." Implied here is a view of art which has been pervasive even to our own day: that art somehow orders and unifies the elements of the external world through appeal to what is universal in these elements, and through enlisting them in the service of an artistic end which itself subserves a moral and educational purpose. In this sense, it is the poet rather than the historian who attempts to make sense of experience by harmonizing its elements and situating it within broader intellectual contexts and moral imperatives.

Having said all of this, Aristotle does not rule out that the poet can imitate actions which have actually occurred. Certain actual events may harbor universal components, and the poet, unlike the historian, has the liberty to select which events shall be represented. It is for this reason that Aristotle says that the poet's primary attention must be directed not toward use of meter but toward the construction of plots. The worst kind of poet would be a kind of historian, using "episodic" plots whereby episodes merely followed one another without regard for probability or necessity. Indeed, it is the poet's use of plots which situates him within a tradition of literary imitation. As in all things, Aristotle desires a balance, between the poet's own inventiveness and the use of traditional elements. The poet should not cling exclusively to stories which have been handed down by tradition (*Poetics*, IX); on the other hand, says Aristotle, it is not possible for the poet to alter completely the traditional stories, which he is free only to adapt (*Poetics*, XIV). What emerges as a crucial component of Aristotle's poetics here is that imitation is not a process which can occur in a vacuum, or as a purely individual enterprise. The imitation of action is expressed essentially in the construction of a plot, and the poet is obliged to learn from the trials and errors of previous masters of imitation and plot construction (*Poetics*, XIV).

Toward the end of the *Poetics* Aristotle seems to have broadened his definition of poetic imitation, making it less exclusive. He now says that the poet must imitate in one of three possible ways. He must imitate things that were, things that are now or things that people say and think to be, or things which ought to be. A number of complex issues are raised here, including realism, convention, rationality, and probability. If we look closely at this later definition of poetic imitation, it reveals itself as entirely different from the earlier definitions in the *Poetics*. Those earlier definitions, we may recall, referred imitation not to morality or realism but to probability and universality. What distinguished the poet from the historian was the former's ability to express universal truths, as given in the representation of events connected by probability. The emphasis now, however, is upon realism: the poet represents events which happened in the past or occur in the present. Moreover, two important factors are introduced. The first is an appeal to the moral imperative of imitation, the second an appeal to the conventional opinions of people. Possibly in answer to Plato's indictment of poetry, Aristotle suggests that the criticism that a work of art is not a "truthful representation" can be met by the argument that it represents the situation not as it is but "as it should be." This argument, taken up later by Sidney and others, assigns to poetic imitation a moral function whereby it should present situations which are morally instructive or edifying. This moral function may have been implicit in Aristotle's earlier definition that poetry imitates human actions; however, the moral element was only obliquely implied inasmuch as it pertained to the object of imitation, the moral component of human actions. Now, it seems, Aristotle invests the act of imitation itself with a moral purpose as part of its very definition. Again, the situation here is somewhat complicated by the fact that the poet now seems to have a choice: to represent either what is actual or the morally idealized elements of actuality. It seems that for

Aristotle the moral purpose of imitation takes priority over any realist endeavor; he refers to a situation "as it should be" as "better than actuality" (*Poetics*, XXV). But the connection between the two functions is not clear: is realism in art at all related to its moral aims? Are the two functions separate? Are they, in fact, mutually exclusive, alternatives to each other? While Aristotle's text provides no clear answers to these questions, its value lies primarily in raising them.

The second new factor in the later definition of poetic imitation is an appeal to convention. Again responding to the possible criticism that poetry does not represent the truth, Aristotle urges that we can appeal to "men's opinions." For example, while a poet may not represent the gods truthfully, he is justified in presenting them in accordance with prevailing opinions and myths which are told about the gods. Again, by this stage of Aristotle's text we have come a long way from Plato's use of truth as a criterion by which to condemn poetry. The very basis of Plato's indictment – that poetry both appeals to and reinforces popular opinions, misconceptions, and falsehoods – is used by Aristotle to undermine any criterion of absolute and transcendent truth. Aristotle's acknowledgment that prevailing opinion cannot be simply dismissed takes a huge step toward suggesting that truth is not somehow transcendent and that it is realized within, not beyond, a human community. In his *Rhetoric*, Aristotle states that "truth is not beyond human nature and men do, for the most part, achieve it" (*Rhet.*, 1355a). Once again, Aristotle's application of the criterion of truth to poetry reflects a major philosophical difference from Plato. Reality, for Aristotle, lies within the purview of human endeavor; it falls within the compass of human society and human history. It is this reality which the poet must confront, not a Platonic reality abstracted into unattainable transcendence. The final point here is that at least two unreconciled definitions of poetic imitation occur in the *Poetics*, the one stressing probability and universality, while the other is far broader, appealing to realism, morality, and convention.

The Concept of Action in Aristotle's View of Tragedy

Aristotle's analysis of tragedy is by far the most well-known section of the *Poetics*. It remained influential for many centuries and was not seriously challenged until the eighteenth century. It is in this treatment of tragedy that the connections between the foregoing notions – imitation, action, character, morality, and plot – emerge most clearly. Here is Aristotle's famous definition of what he calls the "essence" (*ousia*) of tragedy:

> Tragedy is, then, an imitation of an action that is serious, complete and of a certain magnitude – by means of language enriched with all kinds of ornament, each used separately in the different parts of the play: it represents men in action and does not use narrative, and through pity and fear it effects relief to these and similar emotions. (*Poetics*, VI.2–3)[8]

The Greek word used for "action" is *praxis*, which here refers not to a particular isolated action but to an entire course of action and events that includes not only what the protagonist does but also what happens to him. In qualifying this action Aristotle again uses the word *spoudaios*, which means "serious" or "weighty." As Aristotle's later comments will reveal, this seriousness is essentially a *moral* seriousness. The word

Aristotle uses for "complete" is *telaios*, which refers to a situation which has reached its end or is finished. And the word *megethos* refers to greatness, stature, or magnitude. It seems, then, that the subject matter of tragedy is a course of action which is morally serious, presents a completed unity, and occupies a certain magnitude not only in terms of importance but also, as will be seen, in terms of certain prescribed constraints of time, place, and complexity. Moreover, since a tragedy is essentially dramatic rather than narrative, it represents men in action, and a properly constructed tragedy will provide relief or *katharsis* for various emotions, primarily pity and fear. Hence the *effect* of tragedy on the audience is part of its very definition.

The notion of action is central to Aristotle's view of tragedy because it underlies the other components and features, which include plot, character, diction, thought, spectacle, and song. These elements include the means of imitation (diction and song), the manner of imitation (spectacle), and the objects of imitation (actions as arranged in a plot, the character and thought of the actors). It will be remembered that Aristotle also prescribes other requirements such as completeness of action, artistic unity, and emotional impact. The element of tragedy which imitates human actions is not primarily the depiction of character but the plot, which Aristotle calls the "first principle" and "the soul of tragedy" (*Poetics*, VI.19–20). Aristotle's explanation of the connection between character and plot is complex and somewhat confusing. It was already seen that, in the *Nicomachean Ethics*, he viewed action as arising from "choice," which in turn was generated by thought or intellect and a certain disposition of character. He also saw virtue as concerning both emotions and actions and as arising from a "fixed disposition of character." These statements seem to imply that a given character, exercising thought in a certain way, will generate a given action. And in the *Poetics* he repeats this formula, saying that "thought and character are the natural causes of any action" (*Poetics*, VI.7–8). Yet, a little later in the *Poetics*, he accords priority to action in poetic representation. His reasoning seems to run as follows: tragedy is not a representation of men or of character; rather, it represents a sphere "of action, of life, of happiness and unhappiness, which come under the head of action" (*Poetics*, VI.12).

It would be a mistake here to think that Aristotle is somehow espousing an existentialist view whereby action precedes character and the latter is actually the cumulative effect or product of a series of actions. Aristotle has said quite clearly that a fixed disposition of character causes a given action, not vice versa. Why, then, does he insist that what must be represented is action rather than character? Aristotle's subsequent comments in the *Poetics* help us to answer this question. It is not that he separates action from its causal basis in character. Rather, as mentioned earlier, the action represented by tragedy is not the action of a single character; it is action in a much broader sense, a sphere "of life" in which the protagonist both acts and is acted upon. This wider sense of action is given in Aristotle's definition of the plot as "the arrangement of the incidents" (*Poetics*, VI.12). Because tragedy is essentially dramatic, its basis cannot be the depiction of character; as Aristotle points out, one cannot have a tragedy without action, but a tragedy without character study is quite feasible (*Poetics*, VI.14–15). A tragedy must be based on a certain structure of events or incidents to which the specific actions of given characters contribute. This overall dramatic structure, the plot, is "the end at which tragedy aims" (*Poetics*, VI.13).

This connection between action and character can be further clarified by Aristotle's subsequent comments on the kind of plot which is necessary for tragedy. For Aristotle, the most important feature of the plot is *unity*. This unity is not based on character: simply dealing with a single hero does not achieve such unity. Aristotle suggests that innumerable and diverse things can happen to a single individual, and this diversity cannot be unified with reference to that individual. Implied here is Aristotle's political disposition that individuals do not act in isolation but that their very nature is social, and that their actions occur within a complex network of human relationships and events which affect far more than a single individual. For Aristotle, then, unity is given by the representation not of an individual but of "a single object," a "single piece of action" (*Poetics*, VIII.1–4). In other words, the entire complex of events or incidents depicted must be subjected to an organic unity whereby each incident has an indispensable place in the whole. As Aristotle puts it, "the component incidents must be so arranged that if one of them be transposed or removed, the unity of the whole is dislocated and destroyed" (*Poetics*, VIII.4). Aristotle sees the entire complex as *one* unified action.

How is such organic unity achieved? Aristotle has already told us that the events must be connected by "probability or necessity." In section VII of the *Poetics*, he discusses in more detail the structure of the plot. Repeating his initial formulation that tragedy represents an action that is "whole and complete," Aristotle offers the following definition: "A whole is what has a beginning and middle and end" (*Poetics*, VII.2–3). A beginning, for Aristotle, is that which is not necessarily caused by anything else, but itself causes something else. A middle both follows from something else and results in something else. An end is what necessarily follows from something else but does not produce a further result. Clearly, the unity of the plot for Aristotle is based on a notion of causality. His point here seems to be that well-constructed plots do not "begin and end at random, but must embody the formulae we have stated" (*Poetics*, VII.7). It hardly needs stating here that Aristotle's formulae concerning beginning, middle, and end have been profoundly influential, extending far beyond the confines of tragedy or drama, and deeply infusing modes of thinking and writing even into our own times. Equally evident, however, is that the notion of causality underlying these formulae has been widely challenged, especially over the last two centuries. The notion of a "beginning" has been reformulated in much more complex ways, from Hegel to Derrida. In our own times, we are far more reluctant to acknowledge that any set of events can have the status of an absolute beginning or origin; or that an ending can be anything more than an arbitrarily imposed limit or closure upon the events we wish to fall under our consideration.

There are further dimensions, however, to Aristotle's view of the unity of the plot. One of these is an aesthetic dimension, regarding the beauty of representation; the other is an affective dimension, concerned with the emotions that tragedy will generate in an audience. Aristotle holds that for any entity to be beautiful, its parts not only must be arranged in an orderly fashion but also that the whole must have a certain magnitude (*Poetics*, VII.8–9). Aristotle defines this magnitude in terms of both space and time; and in both cases, the definition is referred not only to the beautiful object itself but also to the person who perceives its beauty. In terms of spatial representation, the beautiful object must have a magnitude which can be taken in by the eye "all at once" so as to produce "the effect of a single whole." If something is too small or too big for the eye to perceive, it cannot be beautiful. The same requirement of unity applies to time: whatever events are depicted must be accessible to our memory. As with beautiful objects, says Aristotle, "so too with plots: they must have length but must be easily taken in by the memory" (*Poetics*, VII.9–11). Aristotle holds that the longer the action is the better, provided it can "all be grasped at once." Aristotle now offers an important definition of the desirable magnitude of a plot, one which introduces another factor beyond causality and magnitude, namely, the qualitative progression or deterioration of events: "the magnitude which admits of a change from bad fortune to good or from good fortune to bad, in a sequence of events which follow one another either inevitably or according to probability, that is the proper limit" (*Poetics*, VII.12). This helps further to explain why a tragedy could not be based upon character: its essential purpose is the arrangement of events not only according to causality and necessity or probability but also according to their generation of a qualitative change in circumstances, a change which in the case of tragedy must be in the direction of good to bad fortune (*Poetics*, XIII.6–7). Though Aristotle does not explicitly state it, without this change in fortune all of the other elements combined could hardly result in a tragedy.

Aristotle's recognition of this fact is embodied in his further explanation of the unity of the plot in terms of both the plot's formal structure and the emotions produced in an audience. While Aristotle divides the formal structure of the plot into prologue, episode, exode, parode, and stasimon, it is clear that for him the real structure of the plot consists in the movement of the action. He divides plots into simple plots, which exhibit a continuous action, and complex plots – as exemplified in Sophocles' *Oedipus Rex* – whose action is marked by a movement through reversal, recognition, and suffering. Much later in his text, he divides the action into two parts, the "complication" which includes all of the events until the change in fortune, and the "dénouement" or unraveling which proceeds from the change in fortune until the end of the play. In this way, the change in fortune is indeed placed at the center of the play: the action as divided both leads to it and flows from it; and it is in relation to it that reversal, recognition, and suffering take their significance. Aristotle prefers complex plots because it is through the processes of reversal, recognition, and suffering that the emotions of pity and fear are evoked, which themselves contribute to the plot's unity.

The plot's unity, then, integrates not only causality, probability, and change of fortune but also the emotions of fear and pity which are generated in an audience. After repeating his formula that tragedy represents not only a complete action but also incidents that cause fear and pity, Aristotle adds an important qualification. Fear and pity are most effectively aroused when "the incidents are unexpected and yet one is a consequence of the other" (*Poetics*, IX.11–12). In other words, even the generation of these emotions must result from the sequence of cause and effect represented in the play. Though the effect of pity and fear may come as a surprise, it must nonetheless be perceived as resulting inevitably from previous events. The arousal of pity and fear, then, is an integral aspect of the unity of the plot. Aristotle does concede later that these emotions could be inspired by spectacular means (i.e., visual elements of the play on stage), but he still maintains that a better poet will produce them from the inner structure of the plot (*Poetics*, XIV.1–2).

Aristotle's explanations of the effects of fear and pity provide a further insight into the connection between character and action, as given in his renowned statement of what later came to be termed the "tragic flaw" of the protagonist. Pity, says Aristotle, is aroused by undeserved misfortune; fear is aroused when we realize that the man who suffers such misfortune is "like ourselves" (*Poetics*, XIII.4). Hence, these emotions cannot be inspired by a wicked man prospering; nor can they issue from seeing the misfortune suffered by either an entirely worthy man or a thoroughly bad man (*Poetics*, XIII.2–4). Rather, the character in question must occupy a mean between these extremes: he must be a man "who is not pre-eminently virtuous and just, and yet it is through no badness or villainy of his own that he falls into the misfortune, but rather through some flaw in him" (*Poetics*, XIII.5–6). These statements clarify considerably why a tragedy represents action rather than character. For the "flaw" which results in misfortune is not *necessarily* an outcome of a person's "fixed disposition of character." Rather, it is an oversight, an error, into which the protagonist falls, through lack of judgment or knowledge, and it flows from his character only in an *accidental* and contingent manner. Hence, it is the sequence of actions, and not character, on which tragedy must focus since a given action might be uncharacteristic and might occupy a position in the sequence of cause and effect beyond the knowledge or control of any given character and beyond the status of mere expression of character.

Aristotle's comments on the portrayal of character in tragedy raise some further problematic issues. He suggests four points. The first is that the character must be "good." What reveals character, above all, whether through dialogue or the actions, is "choice" (*Poetics*, XV.1). Earlier, in section VI, Aristotle had explained that this choice must occur "in circumstances where the choice is not obvious" (*Poetics*, VI.24). What Aristotle is referring to here is *moral* choice: the word he uses is *proairesis*, which can also be translated as "will," and refers to the deliberate choice of a given course of conduct. Again, this places the relation between action and character in a problematic light. Aristotle had said in his *Ethics*, we recall, that action arises from choice. Hence, it is in the choice of a given action that character is revealed. Yet the emphasis still seems to be on the particular, morally significant, action rather than on character. The revelation of character is not an end in itself; it merely coincides with the generation of morally significant action. Nor is it plausible to assume that the entire character is expressed in a given sequence of choice and action. It is rather character as concentrated into expression through that particular action.

Two other features of Aristotle's foregoing comments need to be considered. What does he mean by saying that the character portrayed must be "good"? The word Aristotle uses for "good" is *chrestos*, which can mean morally good, honest, or worthy; but it can also mean useful, valuable, or serviceable. We can infer from the immediate context that Aristotle is talking about the value or propriety of using certain personages in tragedy. He states that the goodness of character "is relative to each class of people." He concedes that women and slaves can be "good" even though "a woman is an inferior thing and a slave beneath consideration" (*Poetics*, XV.1–3). The implication is that the most appropriate personages for tragedy must not only be male and free citizens, but also that these citizens must come from the upper ranks of society. In section XIV he had claimed that the appropriate material for tragedy would be found by perpetual recourse to "a few families" which were beset by frightening calamities. Aristotle thus reserves the province of literature for the cultural expression of a male social elite; the dilemmas and experience of women and slaves are relegated to secondary importance. While there are of course exceptions to such exclusiveness in Greek tragedy and elsewhere, these tendencies have dominated most of Western literature. The other, more general, point which emerges from Aristotle's foregoing comments on character is that not just any action is suitable for imitation, but only action which entails a moral dilemma. There are many actions which are contingent in that they do not necessarily follow from or cause anything; and, more importantly, there are many actions which do not involve moral choice. Again, we see here an implicit distinction between the substantial or essential and the accidental, a distinction central to Aristotle's metaphysics.

Aristotle's second prescription is that the characters depicted should be "appropriate." A man, for example, should not act like a woman, or vice versa. This is related to the fourth prescription, that a character should be "consistent" (*Poetics*, XV.4, 6). Aristotle allows some flexibility here: a character may well be "consistently inconsistent"; hence, the connection between action and a "fixed disposition of character" is not always one of causal necessity or probability. Having said this, Aristotle does lay down that in the depiction of character the poet must seek what is inevitable or probable (*Poetics*, XV.10). Again, in contrast with Plato, Aristotle seems to make allowance for the actual complexity of action, which cannot always be predicted or accurately quantified in its effects. Even a character acting uncharacteristically could fall within the realm of the probable.

Aristotle's third prescription is more problematic. He urges that a character should be "like"; some translations interpret this as saying that the character should be "like reality." The word Aristotle uses is *homoios*, which can mean not only "like" or "resembling" but also "of the same rank or station." What did Aristotle have in mind here? It seems implausible, given the entire movement of Aristotle's aesthetic ideas away from Plato's, that Aristotle is advocating an ethical realism in the sense that the character portrayed should be somehow "true to life" except in a universal sense as described earlier. The notions of probability and necessity have been invoked often in Aristotle's text so as not to forego any connection between artistic representation and reality. Those notions, however, ensure that this connection is formalized and idealized: simply imitating the random course of actual events will produce neither unity nor true realism. The latter is achieved by the discernment and presentation of what is universal in the actual flux of particular events. Another translator of Aristotle suggests that by "like" Aristotle means "like the traditional person," inasmuch as Achilles should not be portrayed as soft or Odysseus as stupid (*Poetics*, p. 54 n. C). This seems a more fruitful approach toward understanding Aristotle's meaning: Aristotle explicitly says that this third requirement is distinct from the appropriateness or consistency of character, hence the "like" may well refer to the need for characters to be drawn in accordance with traditional portrayals and to be based on universal characteristics.

59

The Legacy of Aristotle's *Poetics*

The legacy of Aristotle's aesthetics, like that of his philosophy as a whole, is a distinctly classical one. Indeed, Aristotle's thought as a whole laid the foundation for the entire classical tradition of thought and literature in the Western world. It may be useful to furnish a concise statement of the elements of Aristotle's classicism.

The most fundamental premise is a political one, namely, that the individual achieves his or her nature and purpose only within a society and a state. Our own notions of individualism, often Romantic in origin, were quite foreign to Aristotle. Poetry, for Aristotle, does not express what is unique about individuals but rather their universal characteristics, what they share with other members of society. While Aristotle grants to poetry a certain autonomy, it yet occupies a definite place within the state as an instrument of education and moral edification. Poetry is not, as in Romantic thought, exalted to an eminence beyond other pursuits.

Poetry is also subject to the classical principles of Aristotle's philosophy in general. From the most minute level of diction to the highest level of plot construction, poetry is held to be a rational, deliberative activity which must always observe the mean and be guided by the principle of moderation. Like philosophy, it seeks to express universal truths, which are not constrained by reference to particular elements of reality. Its relation to reality is governed by the notions of probability and necessity. Also classical in outlook is Aristotle's insistence on distinguishing clearly between different genres in a hierarchical manner: comedy, which deals with "low" characters and trivial matter, ranks lowest; epic, which includes various plots and lengthy narration, falls below tragedy, which is more concentrated and produces a greater effect of unity. Again, the insistence on propriety and consistency of character is classical. Finally, Aristotle's view of the audience as an elite profoundly affects his prescriptions for the construction of tragedy. Aristotle's notions anticipate developments in several areas of literary criticism: the issue of poetic imitation, the connection between art and reality, the distinction between genres as well as between high and low art, the study of grammar and language, the psychological and moral effects of literature, the nature and function of the audience, the structure and rules of drama, as well as the notions of plot, narrative, and character. All of these notions are still profoundly pervasive in our thinking about literature and the world.

The *Poetics* is usually recognized as the most influential treatise in the history of literary criticism. For a long time, however, the *Poetics* was lost to the Western world and often misrepresented. It was available through the Middle Ages and the early part of the Renaissance only through a Latin translation of an Arabic version written by the philosopher Ibn Rushd, known to the Latin West as Averroës. While Aristotle by the later Middle Ages had supplanted Plato as the predominant influence on philosophy and theology, Horace remained the most powerful classical influence on literary criticism. It was not until the late fifteenth century that the *Poetics* was rediscovered and disseminated through numerous translations and commentaries, beginning with a Latin translation by Giorgio Valla in 1498. The most renowned commentaries were Minturno's *De poeta* (1559), Julius Caesar Scaliger's *Poetices libri septem* (1561), and Lodovico Castelvetro's *Poetica d'Aristotele vulgarizzata e sposta*, which eventually established the predominance of Aristotelian notions in literary criticism, especially as impinging on the theory and practice of drama. These notions exerted a sustained impact on seventeenth-century French dramatists such as Pierre Corneille and on the neoclassical writers of the eighteenth century. Aristotle's influence was somewhat eclipsed in the nineteenth century when the Romantics and Symbolists turned more to Plato and Longinus. Yet critics still continued to reexamine fundamental Aristotelian notions such as *katharsis* and *hamartia*. In the earlier twentieth century, the impact of Aristotle's attempt to treat poetry systemically as a distinctive sphere can be seen in Russian Formalists such as Boris Eichenbaum, in some of the New Critics, and in the systematic archetypal criticism of figures such as Northrop Frye. An interest in Aristotle was rekindled in the latter half of the twentieth century by the Chicago School of critics. His distinctive treatment of genre has been the foundation of genre theory, and his notions of plot and narrative structure continue to underlie narrative theories. Finally, his consideration of audience reaction as a crucial factor in the composition of tragedy presages much reader-response criticism. Above and beyond all of these influences, however, is his doctrine of substance, a notion that continues to underlie our thinking, and even our attempts to undermine conventional modes of thought.

Notes

1   Aristotle, *The Metaphysics I–IX*, trans. Hugh Tredennick, Loeb Classical Library (Cambridge, MA and London: Harvard University Press/Heinemann, 1947), p. 147. Hereafter cited as *Met. I–IX*.

2   Aristotle, *Posterior Analytics; Topica*, trans. Hugh Tredennick and E. S. Forster, Loeb Classical Library (Cambridge, MA and London: Harvard University Press/Heinemann, 1976), p. 202. Hereafter cited as *PA*.

3   Aristotle, *The Categories; On Interpretation; Prior Analytics*, trans. Harold P. Cooke and Hugh Tredennick, Loeb Classical Library (Cambridge, MA and London: Harvard University Press/Heinemann, 1973), pp. 16–19. Hereafter cited as *Cat.*

4   Aristotle, *Politics*, trans. T. A. Sinclair (Harmondsworth: Penguin, 1986), I.i. Hereafter cited as *Pol.*

5   Aristotle, *Nicomachean Ethics*, trans. H. Rackham, Loeb Classical Library (London and New York: Heinemann/Harvard University Press, 1934), VI.ii.5. Hereafter cited as *NE*.

6   *Aristotle: Poetics; Longinus: On the Sublime; Demetrius: On Style*, trans. W. Hamilton Fyfe (Cambridge, MA and London: Harvard University Press/Heinemann, 1965), VIII.v. Unless otherwise stated, I have used this translation of the *Poetics*. I have slightly amended some of the translations.

7   *The Art of Rhetoric*, trans. H. C. Lawson-Tancred (Harmondsworth: Penguin, 1991), 5.I.11. Hereafter cited as *Rhet.*

8   I have substituted the word "serious" for "heroic" as the translation of *spoudaios*.

PART II

THE TRADITIONS OF RHETORIC

CHAPTER 3

GREEK RHETORIC

T he word "rhetoric" derives from the Greek word *rhetor*, meaning "speaker," and originally referred to the art of public speaking. This art embraced a broad range of techniques whereby a speaker could compose and arrange the elements of a speech which would be persuasive through its intellectual, emotional, and dramatic appeal to an audience. Over the last two millennia, the scope and application of rhetoric have radically changed, and it has accumulated multifold significance through changing literary, intellectual, and social contexts. There are a number of spheres in relation to which the art and cultural practice of rhetoric has achieved articulation: the political sphere, which oversaw the birth of rhetoric; the institution and discipline of philosophy, whose spokesmen have often derogated rhetoric, placing it below logic and metaphysics; the institution of theology, which at most has placed rhetoric in subservience to the expression of divine revelation; the entire sphere of education, in which rhetoric has often assumed a central role, and continues to this day to exert a pervasive influence in the teaching of composition; and, of course, the sphere of literary criticism, which continues to draw from the wellsprings of rhetoric, especially in its focus on language, tropes, and the relation between speaker or writer and audience.

Rhetoric originated in ancient Greece in the fifth century BC. It owed its early development to the Sophists, Aristotle, and then, in the Roman world, to Cato, Cicero, and Quintilian. The Church Father St. Augustine enlisted rhetoric in the service of Christian doctrine. Classical rhetoric, as developed until the time of Cicero, had five parts or "offices": invention, arrangement, style, memory, and delivery. The first of these, "invention" (*heuresis/inventio*), referred to the content of a speech. This content would include a statement of the issue at stake, the means of persuasion, which embraced direct evidence, an account of the speaker's character, logical argument, and consideration of the emotions of the audience as well as of the ethical and political premises of the speech. The second office was the "arrangement" (*taxis/dispositio*) of the speech into a given order. The speech would begin with an "introduction" to arouse audience interest and sympathy; it would then engage in "narration" of a given background and context, as well as of relevant facts; it would proceed to a "proof," which would consist of logical arguments as well as refutation of objections or counter-arguments; it would end with a "conclusion," which might recapitulate the essential argument and appeal further to the emotions of the audience. The third office, "style," (*lexis/elocutio*) referred to the manner in which the ideas already arranged were expressed in language. Style conventionally had two elements, diction or word-choice, and composition, which referred to various elements of sentence construction, such as structure, rhythm, and the use of figures.

These three offices were common to both public speaking and written composition. There were two further offices, identified by Aristotle, peculiar to speaking: "memory," which signified the memorization of the speech for oral performance; and "delivery," which embraced control of voice and control of gesture. Style was conventionally evaluated on the basis of four virtues of style formulated by Aristotle's student Theophrastus: correctness (of grammar and language usage); clarity; ornamentation (using tropes and figures of speech); and propriety. Styles were classified as grand, middle, and plain.

According to one tradition, expressed in Aristotle, Cicero, and Quintilian, the art of rhetoric was formally founded in 476 BC by a native of Syracuse, Corax, whose student Tisias transmitted his master's teachings to the mainland. Very little is known about these figures and some scholars have argued that they were in fact the same person.[1] In its origins, rhetoric was an integral part of the political process in ancient Greece, especially in Athens and Syracuse of the fifth century BC. It has long been acknowledged that rhetoric has profound and perhaps intrinsic ties to the political system of democracy. The ability to express oneself independently and articulately, whether in speech or in writing, has always been held to be one of the foundation stones of democracy. It is usually the case that the ruling class in a given society controls not only political and economic power but also the instruments of culture and the prevailing ideas and concepts, especially language itself. It could be argued that it is ultimately through control of language, through control of the ideas and possible worldviews available to people, that a given class exerts control in the political and economic spheres.

It has sometimes been held that one of the failings of modern democracy is that language, and therefore the definitions of reality, self, truth, and morality, is indeed controlled by a given sector of the population which thereby determines not only what is seen as true, possible, and morally correct, but also to whom and in what degree access to the language can be given. In today's composition classrooms, for example, we witness this process operating inasmuch as we coerce the thought process and the writing of students into the categories and format of the Aristotelian rhetoric that underlies much of our pedagogy. The mastery, use, and control of language lie at the heart of the political process, and this centrality is most profoundly evident in a political democracy such as existed in ancient Athens. On the ability to speak persuasively could depend the entire future of a state or family or individual. On rhetoric often hung the balance of life or death, war or peace, prosperity or destruction, freedom or slavery.

Given that public speaking and public discourse were so vital in ancient Athens, there emerged a group of professional teachers of the art of rhetoric. These first teachers were called Sophists (from *sophos*, meaning "wise"), and their enterprise was to teach the art of rhetoric for use in the courts, the legislature, political forums, as well as for philosophical reflection and debate. The influence of the Sophists became so pervasive that rhetoric came to assume a central role in Greek education. It would be misleading to view the Sophists as having brought rhetoric to Athens; they were merely responding to the heightened importance of rhetoric in a Greek world where democracy was evolving in some city-states. It has been argued by numerous scholars that the rhetorical tradition evolved gradually,[2] and that the Greeks possessed a rhetorical consciousness in their epic and dramatic literature which relies to a large extent on the power of speeches to bring to life certain moral, religious, and political dilemmas; they also manifested this consciousness of rhetoric in their conceptions of the gods as anthropomorphic entities who might be moved by human speech, which often had a bartering and bargaining function. Ancient Greek texts rely heavily on the power of speech-making. A renowned example of this is Homer's *Odyssey*, which consists almost entirely of speeches: we have speeches made to Zeus by Athena, as well as by other gods such as Poseidon, Calypso, and Hermes; to the Ithacan assembly by Telemachus and the suitors; and the various narratives of Nestor, Menelaus, Alcinoos, Penelope, and Odysseus himself. The importance of speech-making is clear also in a drama such as Sophocles' *Oedipus the King*, where Oedipus' journey from ignorance to self-knowledge is mediated by oratorical clashes with Creon and Tiresias. Hence the contribution of the Sophists was to systematize and refine the rules of an art which had long flourished before their advent.

The most influential of the Sophists were Protagoras, Gorgias, Antiphon, Lysias, and Isocrates. Protagoras was born in the Greek colony of Abdera, and he traveled throughout Greece delivering speeches and teaching. He enjoyed great popularity and wealth but was eventually tried in Athens in 411 BC for his opposition to democracy. Protagoras' most famous belief was that "man is the measure of all things." This was essentially a secular humanistic and individualistic idea: each person constructs his own view of reality on the basis of sensations individually received. Protagoras also taught the very influential notion that every argument or position had two sides, which could be equally rational. He was therefore accused (by Socrates among others) of encouraging expediency in argument, of inducing people to make the worse cause appear better, and the better worse. It is clear that Protagoras' teachings, in promoting a humanistic rationalism which argued from the conditions of things themselves (rather than invoking external agencies such as divine forces), encouraged relativism, skepticism, and agnosticism. The conventional notion that truth somehow stood beyond human perception and language was thus profoundly challenged, and it is only in the nineteenth and twentieth centuries that this challenge was pervasively renewed.

Another powerful figure among the Sophists was Gorgias (ca. 485–380 BC), who was a native of the Greek colony of Sicily. He initially came to Athens to seek military aid on behalf of his home town Leontini against Syracuse. While the Athenians refused this request, he nonetheless quickly established a reputation as a stylish speaker and became a teacher of rhetoric in Athens. He studied with Empedocles, Corax, and Tisias. What marks his rhetorical practice and theory was a stress on the need for rhetoric to learn from the use of language by poets. He saw the world as containing fundamental contradictions, opposites, and polarities, which could only be reconciled by language. Like many of the Romantics, Coleridge in particular, he viewed the poet's language as the archetypal instrument of such reconciliation. Like Shelley, he saw the poet as rousing people to consciousness of their shared humanity; poetry was an agent of empathic identification with others.

Given that Gorgias saw rhetoric as the art of leading and persuading souls, he insisted on the need for rhetoric to borrow figures of speech from poetry and to use all kinds of stylistic devices, including the very sounds of words, in order to win over an audience. As with Protagoras, the notion of truth is subordinated to the presentation of a particular viewpoint or experience in language, and to the persuasion of a given audience.

The third major Sophist was Antiphon (ca. 480–411 BC), a native of Athens and a contemporary of Protagoras. Like Protagoras, he was opposed to the Athenian democracy and was eventually executed for treason. Nonetheless, he espoused the conventional Athenian belief in reconciling individual and communal, private and public interests. He both taught sophistry and was a professional speechwriter. His contribution to rhetoric was pioneering inasmuch as he elaborated systematic rules for it. He believed that the best speeches would appeal to actual experience of both the speaker and the audience. Many of his speeches were tailored for the Athenian courtrooms, and while they followed a conventional structure consisting of preface, introduction, a narrative of the facts, arguments, proofs, and an appeal to the jury, they were striking inasmuch as they were written in a lofty and formal style.

The most renowned rhetorician in the courts of Athens was Lysias (ca. 458–380 BC), who studied under both Tisias and Protagoras. Lysias was exiled to Athens along with his brother Polemarchus from the Athenian colony of Sicily when the democracy there was overthrown. He became famous as a rhetorician when he brought a suit against the man who had brought about his brother's execution. Many of the court cases in Athens were related to the struggle to retain democracy. Lysias was well known for his ability to write a speech in a plain style and which was adapted in tone and substance to the particular situation at hand. His speeches were simple in organization, consisting of an introduction, narrative, proof, and conclusion.

Like those of the other Sophists, the teachings of Isocrates (436–338 BC) were heavily influenced by political events, especially the Peloponnesian War (431–404 BC) between Athens and Sparta, as well as his insistence on the need for Greek unity in the face of possible threats from Asia. He opened a school of oratory in Athens and his students included some of the most powerful men in Greece. Isocrates' political views and his teachings on education, derived in part from his teachers including Tisias, Gorgias, and Socrates, were widely influential in his own time and in later periods. Also influential was his emphasis on rhetoric as the basis of education. He viewed the essential purpose of oratory as political: to train politicians in promoting the values and unity of Greek culture. Like Socrates, he believed that education should primarily foster moral virtue. Also like Socrates, he was skeptical of some of the techniques of other Sophists, and insisted that pursuit of truth and virtue were integral components of rhetoric, and that the rhetorician must have a broad education, which, like that suggested by Plato for the statesman, should include training of the mind and training of the body as complementary activities.

Given the conventional associations of rhetoric and democracy, it is something of an irony that the rhetoricians mentioned above were opponents of democracy. However, it is equally clear that their forging of the techniques of rhetoric emerged only in struggles over various kinds of political constitution and political, cultural, and educational causes.

Plato's Critique of Rhetoric

The Sophists' apparent monopoly on the art of speaking did not go unchallenged. Given the overwhelming importance of rhetoric in Athenian public life, it is hardly surprising that this art was subject to abuse. The actual speeches presented in Athenian lawcourts and political assemblies often diverged considerably from the rules laid down by the Sophists, relying excessively on passions, prejudices, the pity of the judges, and indeed any manner of persuading the audience. The Sophists nurtured in their students an ability to argue both or many sides of a case; they were consequently accused of training people in "making the worse cause appear the better" by a clever use of language and in thereby sacrificing truth, morality, and justice to unabated self-interest. Aristophanes satirized the Sophists in his comedy *The Clouds*. A more serious, and permanently damaging, challenge was issued by Socrates as represented in Plato's dialogues, especially in *Gorgias* and *Phaedrus*.

Plato's *Gorgias* is worth considering in some depth since it evokes several contexts which may help us to pursue the profound ramifications of classical rhetoric. The initial dialogue occurs between Plato's spokesman Socrates and the famed rhetorician Gorgias, whose disciple Polus eventually takes over on his behalf; finally, Socrates continues the debate with an aspiring and cynical young politician, Callicles. While Socrates employs his conventional dialectical strategy of question and answer in an ostensible attempt to investigate the nature of rhetoric, it is clear by the end of the text that his entire argument is premised on a sharp opposition and contrast between the spheres of philosophy and rhetoric.

Early in the dialogue, when Socrates hears of Gorgias' presence at his friend's house, he wishes to know who Gorgias "is"; in other words, what is his profession or area of expertise. Again and again, he insists on asking, what is the object of rhetoric? What is its province? What is it *about*?

When Gorgias responds that the province of rhetoric is speech, Socrates rejoins that *many* areas of inquiry are concerned with speech, and that speech is merely the *means* employed by rhetoric: his earlier question as to what is the object of rhetoric has still not been answered. Gorgias explains that rhetoric procures freedom for an individual and political power in a community. What *is* rhetoric? Gorgias offers a neat definition: it is "the ability to use the spoken word to persuade – to persuade the jurors in the courts, the members of the Council, the citizens attending the Assembly – in short, to win over any and every form of public meeting of the citizen body" (*Gorgias*, 452e).[3]

Socrates, however, is still not satisfied. He grants that rhetoric is an agent of persuasion of an audience; this, indeed, is its whole aim. But what is it persuasion *about*? What is its sphere of operation? He rejects Gorgias' lame assertion that this sphere is the distinction of right and wrong: there are two kinds of persuasion, maintains Socrates, one which confers conviction without understanding and one which confers knowledge. Rhetoric, he insists, leads to conviction without educating people as to right and wrong (*Gorgias*, 455a). Still on the theme of conviction, the argument takes another turn: Socrates suggests that when we require advice in a given field, we seek out a specialist in that field. On the contrary, rejoins Gorgias, in a public forum, it is the rhetoricians whose opinions prevail over the specialists or professionals. The rhetorician will be more persuasive in front of a crowd. Socrates cleverly turns this appeal to a mass audience against rhetoric: the rhetorician will indeed persuade a crowd if the crowd consists of non-experts. He will not be more persuasive before an audience of experts. Hence the rhetorician is a non-expert persuading other non-experts. He never need know the actual facts of a situation; he needs no expertise, merely a persuasive ploy (*Gorgias*, 459a–c).

It is at this juncture that Socrates either willfully or unwittingly misunderstands the nature of Gorgias' response: rhetoric, says Gorgias, is itself the area of expertise. Socrates' entire approach posits rhetoric as content, as a field of inquiry which must refer to a definite class of objects. He fails to understand Gorgias' implication that rhetoric is a *form*, that it has no intrinsic content, that its lack of content need not be viewed as emptiness but as a means of systematizing and controlling any type of content whatsoever. It is premised on a recognition that no content, whether political, philosophical, scientific, or literary, is inherently persuasive or even inherently meaningful until it is organized such as to maximize its reception by an audience. Meaning arises only as a result of this interaction or relation between speaker, audience, and context.

It is precisely this relational status of meaning and truth which Socrates attempts to suppress. His impugnment of rhetoric's intrinsic appeal to an audience is underlain by Plato's notion of truth as transcending human opinion. In the lawcourts, says Socrates, rhetoric relies on producing a large number of eminent witnesses; but such argument or refutation is worthless, he says, in the context of truth. Socrates accuses rhetoricians of changing what they say to suit the whims of their audiences, whereas the views of philosophy, he says, never change. In effect, suggests Socrates, the rhetorician and the politician are forced to pander to the existing power structure and the views of the majority; the overlapping function of rhetoric and politics is the assimilation of one's views to those which prevail in political practice (*Gorgias*, 481d–482c).

What is disturbing about Socrates' argument is its explicit rejection of the notion that rhetoric is a rational pursuit which might be based on knowledge. He insists that there is no expertise involved in rhetoric, and that it requires merely a mind good at guessing, some courage, and a natural talent for interacting with people. In general, he classifies rhetoric as a branch of flattery, along with imitative arts such as poetry, music, and tragedy; flattery is indifferent to encouraging good action; it simply promises to maximize immediate pleasure, and is based on knack not expertise because it lacks a rational understanding of its object (*Gorgias*, 502b–503b).

The sharp opposition between philosophy and rhetoric in this dialogue is highlighted by the harsh rejoinders of Socrates' political opponent Callicles: philosophers, he claims, do not understand the legal system or politics or human nature; they are hidden in private discussions instead of openly expressing important ideas; Callicles taunts that Socrates himself could not deliver a proper speech or defend himself in a court – "he'd end up dead!" (*Gorgias*, 484a–486c). Of course, Callicles' words are prophetic: Socrates does indeed eventually refuse to speak like a rhetorician at his own trial and, indifferent to the opinions of the many, he does end up dead. Callicles' other accusations about philosophers simply go unanswered by Socrates, who arrives at his own conclusions in an eminently non-dialectical fashion, notwithstanding his expressed intent.

Socrates' argument moves in a different register from that of Callicles. Callicles' concern is wholly pragmatic: how to persuade actual assemblies and courtrooms. Socrates' idealistic critique of rhetoric is precisely that it is based on nothing more than practical expediency. It is founded on no underlying principles of goodness or of the purpose and function of individual and communal life. The ultimate purpose of all activity is the good, and all else should be a means toward this end (*Gorgias*, 499e). Socrates equates goodness with order; the universe is an ordered whole and our ideal in the community should be justice, self-discipline, and happiness (*Gorgias*, 507d–508a). If rhetoric is to be used, its motivation must be moral; it should improve people, and alter the community's needs for the better rather than pandering to already existing needs (*Gorgias*, 517a–b). It must aim not at the *appearance* of truth and goodness but at their *reality* (*Gorgias*, 527a–c). What Socrates is effectively doing here is not redeeming rhetoric in a desirable form but transforming it beyond recognition into philosophy. The only justifiable way for rhetoric to survive is to take on the essential characteristics of philosophy.

This call for rhetoric to extinguish itself and to rekindle itself as philosophy receives further specification in Plato's *Phaedrus*. Here, Socrates defines what he takes to be the conventional understanding of rhetoric: "Must not the art of rhetoric, taken as a whole, be a kind of influencing of the mind by means of words, not only in courts of law and other public gatherings, but in private places also? And must it not be the same art that is concerned with great issues and small, its right employment commanding no more respect when dealing with important matters than with unimportant?" (*Phaedrus*, 261a–b).[4] Moreover, a professor of rhetoric "can make the same thing appear to the same people now just, now unjust, at will" (*Phaedrus*, 261c–d). Indeed, the whole art of rhetoric, insists Socrates, is contained in the claim of rhetoricians such as Tisias and Gorgias that truth is not important; what matters is conviction, which is based not on truth but probability. It is probability, therefore, which the orator should keep in view; and such rhetoricians define probability as "that which commends itself to the multitude" (*Phaedrus*, 273a–b).

Again, Socrates turns their own argument against the rhetoricians. If probability is engendered by the mere appearance of truth, it follows that the rhetorician, especially the rhetorician who wishes to deceive his audience, must have knowledge of the truth. The better his knowledge of the truth, the more easily he can present appearances of the truth (*Phaedrus*, 273d–274a). The speaker must therefore know his subject: he must know how to understand scattered particulars as expressions of one idea, or how to perceive the One in the Many; he must be able to divide and classify those particulars and know how to generalize; he must be able to discern the nature of the soul and the different modes of discourse which might affect different natures (*Phaedrus*, 277b–c). In short, for Socrates there is no real art of speaking divorced from truth (*Phaedrus*, 260e). Once again, rhetoric is permissible provided it dons the vesture of philosophy; provided that it impossibly reconfigures itself according to a conception of truth which is alien to its very nature.

Aristotle and the Further Development of Rhetoric

Aristotle's influential *Rhetoric* begins by stating that rhetoric is the "counterpart" of dialectic or logical argument. What has been neglected in previous treatments of rhetoric, says Aristotle, is the most important part of rhetoric, proof, which rests on the enthymeme. The enthymeme is a syllogism whose premises are not certain or necessary but probable.[5] Whereas dialectic uses logical syllogisms, rhetoric uses the enthymeme (*Rhet.*, 1355a). In contrast with Plato, who saw conventional rhetoric as divorced from the notion of truth, Aristotle urges that rhetoric is a useful skill precisely because it can promote the causes of truth and justice. In fact, the true position is naturally superior and more easily argued. Inasmuch as rhetoric is susceptible to abuse, it shares this liability with all good things (*Rhet.*, 1355b). Moreover, argues Aristotle, we need the capacity to argue contradictory positions not so that we can either argue indiscriminately or persuade men to evil but so that we have a fuller understanding of the case and can refute unjust counter-arguments (*Rhet.*, 1355a). This capacity is employed only in rhetoric and dialectic. In a later chapter, Aristotle states that "rhetoric is a compound of the science of dialectic and the deliberative study of morality and is akin both to dialectic and to sophistry" (*Rhet.*, 1359b).

Again in pointed contrast with Plato, Aristotle contends that rhetoric, like dialectic, is not concerned with any single field. The function of rhetoric is not persuasion; rather, it is the "detection of the persuasive aspects of each matter" and it is the same art which can detect what is truly persuasive and what is apparently persuasive, just as dialectic can distinguish the real from the apparent syllogism (*Rhet.*, 1355b). Aristotle later indicates that whereas each of the other arts is persuasive and instructive about a special province, rhetoric deals with the element of persuasiveness in any field. For example, physics might "persuade" and instruct people about certain features of matter and motion; political science might persuade and inform people as to certain features of government. Rhetoric would examine solely the elements of persuasion in both fields, independently of their actual content.

Aristotle classifies proof, the most important component of rhetoric, into three basic types, according as these relate to (1) the character of the speaker, (2) the disposition of the audience, and (3) the demonstrative nature of the speech itself. Proof from the speaker's character derives from the latter's credibility and reasonableness, a credibility which must not be pregiven but rather established in the course of the speech. Proofs from the disposition of the audience are produced when the audience is induced into a certain emotional state by the speech. Lastly, proof is achieved by the speech inasmuch as it demonstrates the persuasive aspects of a given issue (*Rhet.*, 1356a). To master these various proofs, one must master the syllogism, one must have a scientific understanding of character and virtue, and one must understand each emotion and how it is brought about. Given that rhetoric requires this broad mastery, Aristotle considers it to be an offshoot of dialectic and ethics. He in fact suggests that rhetoric "is quite properly categorized as political." Aristotle adds that both rhetoric and dialectic are "kinds of capacity to furnish arguments" (*Rhet.*, 1356a).

Dialectic and rhetoric are somewhat parallel in the procedures they use for proof. Where logic uses induction, rhetoric employs example; and where logic uses syllogism, rhetoric has its counterpart in enthymeme. But Aristotle makes an important distinction between rhetoric and dialectic. Dialectic is the province of specialists whereas rhetoric concerns matters of common interest which call for public discussion. The premises of rhetoric "are matters about which it is the established custom to deliberate" (*Rhet.*, 1356b–1357a). These are matters concerning which "we have no arts," matters which admit of various interpretations, and which are deliberated with audiences of limited intellectual scope who cannot follow lengthy reasoning.

Aristotle cites three genres of rhetoric, which are distinguished according to the kind of audience they address and their purpose. He tells us that a speech is composed of three elements, the speaker, the subject, and the listener; it is to the last of these that the purpose is related. The first genre is "deliberative" rhetoric, whose province is politics and which concerns what future actions should be taken by the state. The audience here is the assembly, and the objective is to use either exhortation to persuade the audience of some advantage or deterrence to demonstrate the harm that could arise from a given course of action. "Forensic" rhetoric is used in the lawcourts; it concerns actions already performed in the past, and it employs prosecution and defense in its objective of achieving justice. The final genre is "display" rhetoric, which focuses on the present and involves praise and denigration in its aim of displaying nobility. Aristotle acknowledges that these aims might overlap, but the primary aim of these genres is what distinguishes them (*Rhet.*, 1358b–1359a).

Aristotle devotes the next several chapters to these various branches of rhetoric. He explains that the most important topics of deliberative speeches are: revenue, war and peace, the defense of the realm, imports and exports, and legislation. These are the matters of which deliberative orators must possess detailed knowledge (*Rhet.*, 1359b–1360b). An assumption which underlies these chapters is that, in order to find the sources of persuasion in deliberative speeches, one must investigate what men most profoundly seek. The answer to this question, for Aristotle, is happiness: "all exhortations and dissuasions are concerned with happiness and things conducive to it and contrary to it" (*Rhet.*, 1360b).

According to Aristotle, the most important and decisive factor in rhetorical persuasiveness is an understanding of the various kinds of political constitution. His reasoning for this is that all men are persuaded by their interest and their interest is what preserves the constitution (*Rhet.*, 1365b). Aristotle states that the dominant group or class in any constitution will be decisive, implying that the rhetorician must shape his speech to accommodate this fact. Aristotle suggests that there are four constitutions: democracy, where offices are assigned by lot and whose fundamental purpose is freedom; oligarchy, directed toward wealth and governed by propertied men; aristocracy, where offices are assigned by men of noble birth and which aims at preserving customs and inculcating a certain kind of education; and monarchy or rule by one man, which can take the form of either kingship, where kingly power is subject to restraints, or tyranny, where there are no such limits.

Aristotle now devotes a brief chapter to display rhetoric, where the purpose is to display the virtue or vice, the nobility or baseness of a given issue. He cites the elements of virtue as justice, courage, restraint, splendor, magnanimity, liberality, prudence, and wisdom. The greatest virtues are those most useful to others and those pertaining to serious persons who engage in purposive actions (*Rhet.*, 1366b–1367b).

Proceeding to forensic oratory and litigation, Aristotle turns to the discussion of prosecution and defense and to the subject of litigation, injustice. In terms of deductions that need to be made in litigation, three areas must be understood: the motives for which men commit injustice, their disposition when doing so, and to what type of people (*Rhet.*, 1368b). The motives for which men seek to do harm are vice and lack of self-control as well as appetite. Actions spurred by appetite aim at pleasure (*Rhet.*, 1372a). Aristotle gives advice on how to oppose or enlist the service of written and unwritten laws, how to appeal to ancient authorities and modern notables as witnesses, and how to use or oppose evidence extracted under torture (*Rhet.*, 1375b–1377b). It is notable that, unlike previous writers on rhetoric, he accords arguments from probability a higher place than non-technical proofs. Probability, he affirms, cannot be deceived or corrupted (*Rhet.*, 1376a).

The next major divisions of the *Rhetoric* are devoted to emotion and character. Aristotle has already told us that the province of rhetoric is the study of demonstrations or proofs that are based on probability rather than logic, and that rhetoric rests on the enthymeme and the example, which are the counterparts of syllogism and induction in logic. However, Aristotle had also cited proofs based on emotion and character, which could not be viewed as demonstrative. He tells us now that we must regard not merely the demonstrative and persuasive aspects of a speech but also the speaker's establishing of his own credibility and bringing the audience into a certain emotional condition. The speaker's image is more important, he says, in political oratory while the disposition of the audience is more significant in the courts. A speaker himself can be persuasive on account of his common sense, virtue, and goodwill (*Rhet.*, 1378a). In order for the orator to manipulate his audience in respect of a given emotion such as anger, he must understand the psychological state men are in when they are angry, with whom they are disposed to be angry, and in what circumstances. The remainder of the section on emotion discusses ten basic emotions in the light of these three factors.

Aristotle's subsequent discussion of character focuses, somewhat unexpectedly, not on the speaker's attempt to establish a certain character for himself but rather on the attributes of the audience which the speaker should know. These attributes are affected by emotion and psychological state, which have already been discussed. They are also influenced by age and fortune, to which Aristotle now turns. He cites three "ages," youth, prime, and old age. In general he describes the character of youth as appetitive, subject to passion and change, craving excess, devoted to ideals and nobility rather than money, optimistic, overconfident, possessing courage, credulous and loving humor. Old age is marked generally by opposing qualities: lack of confidence, cynicism, sour temper, cowardice, self-interest, love of money, and pessimism. Middle age, or what Aristotle calls the prime of life, achieves a mean between the extremes of the other two ages; it is characterized by avoiding excess, balance, moderation, judging according to the truth, and living for both nobility and self-interest. Fortune, by which Aristotle means the accidents of birth, wealth, and power, also affects character. Wealth, for example, breeds arrogance and haughtiness, power breeds ambition, manliness, and seriousness of public interest. Again, these sections say little of rhetorical strategy in any particular situation. Rather, they offer a very general guide for the speaker who would know his audience in terms of its social class, aspirations, and its general interests (*Rhet.*, 1389a–1391b).

Having so far covered the material which is specific to the demonstrative proofs of the various genres, as well as the use of emotion and character to influence an audience, Aristotle now proceeds to discuss elements of oratory which are germane to any kind of speech. These elements are the "common topics," style and composition. The common topics are standard premises which can be used in the service of any content. He focuses on two types of common topic, which all speakers must use. The first of these is the possible and impossible, whereby a speaker will try to show that something will happen or has happened. The second is extent or degree, whereby a speaker will demonstrate the greatness or smallness of a given matter (*Rhet.*, 1392a).

Moving to a discussion of common proofs, Aristotle reminds us that there are two types, the enthymeme and the example; he here adduces a further subdivision of the enthymeme, the maxim. There are, he says, two species of example, the narration of past events and the invention of events, the latter being subdivided into comparison and fables. Example by narration would offer previous examples of a given sequence of actions; for example, both Xerxes and Darius invaded Greece only after conquering Egypt; therefore if the present king were to conquer Egypt, he would invade Greece. Comparison could be used to show how a given course of action in one field would be absurd (or wise) when applied in another field (*Rhet.*, 1393b). A fable would effectively use a parable to illustrate the wisdom or folly of a proposed action (*Rhet.*, 1394a).

Proceeding to the maxim, Aristotle defines this as a general declaration not about particulars nor about universal certainties but about things in connection with which actions are performed. A maxim is effectively the conclusion or premise of a syllogism or enthymeme where the reasoning has been removed. The use of maxims, suggests Aristotle, suits older age, and they should be used of things of which one has had experience. One should not frown on using even banal commonplaces, if these are useful, since all people agree with them. Maxims help speeches in several ways; firstly, they can accommodate the "stupidity" of listeners, if they are attuned to the prejudices and presuppositions of a given audience. They also give speeches character, by which Aristotle means the possession of a clear moral purpose; if the maxims are good, they make the speaker seem to be of a good character (*Rhet.*, 1395b).

Aristotle now gives a general account of the enthymeme as a syllogism whose premises and conclusions are related as probability rather than necessity (in contrast with logical syllogism). The most important prerequisite on the speaker's part is to have a sound grasp of the properties peculiar to a given subject. Aristotle divides enthymemes into two types, the demonstrative and the refutational. The former demonstrates, from uncontroversial premises, that something is or is not the case; the latter arrives at controversial conclusions (*Rhet.*, 1396b). Aristotle provides a long list of demonstrative and refutational common topics or premises. The former includes premises based on contraries, similarities, things in mutual relation, degree, definition, division, induction, listing parts, consequences, prediction by analogy, and cause (*Rhet.*, 1397b–1400b). These are the kinds of topics or premises which it is the speaker's function to invent. Refutational enthymemes, says Aristotle, are better known than demonstrative ones because they offer a single conclusion from opposing premises in a short space so that the opposition is apparent to the audience.

So far Aristotle has devoted his study to what he has claimed is the central function of rhetoric, the invention of proof. He now turns to the discussion of style which, though not part of rhetoric proper, warrants discussion on practical grounds: the presentation of a speech needs to be tailored to the nature of a given audience. In this regard, Aristotle observes that the entire enterprise of rhetoric has to do with opinion, and therefore consideration of style is needed because style has a great impact on the character of a speech and has a great effect because of the "baseness" of the audience (*Rhet.*, 1404a). He even goes so far as to say that written speeches have more effect through their style than their intellectual content. There are, he tells us, three basic components to consider in the construction of a speech (*Rhet.*, 1403b). The first of these, the grounds from which the proofs are drawn, have already been discussed (the sources of proof being the effect on the audience or judges, the speaker's character, and the demonstration given by the speech itself). The second is style, the subject of the present discussion, and the third is the actual mode of delivery of the speech, which Aristotle will take up later. Aristotle observes that the inquiries into style and delivery concern both rhetoric and poetics since stylistic devices were taken over into rhetoric from tragedy. It was the poets who first began these inquiries and their techniques were taken up into the "poetic prose" style of rhetoricians such as Gorgias. Aristotle objects to the common and uneducated view that such a poetic style is the finest discourse. He insists that argument and poetry have different styles, and goes on to consider the various elements of prose style.

Aristotle lays down that the virtue of style is to be clear and to be appropriate to the subject. It is the main verbs and nouns which make the style clear. However, an appropriate use of unusual words can endow the style with loftiness; such use must be sparing and concealed and must give the impression of speaking naturally rather than artificially, since the former is persuasive (1404b). Metaphor is a central element of style but, again, must be used proportionately and moderately, being drawn from familiar things in the same species (*Rhet.*, 1405a–1405b). Aristotle objects to the Sophists' "mischievous" device of using homonyms, as claiming that different words can mean the same thing. Aristotle insists that "one word or another does not indicate the same thing under different conditions" (*Rhet.*, 1405b).

Hence the overarching virtue of rhetorical speech is clarity, which accommodates unfamiliarity and metaphor. But in the quest for this virtue, the speaker may lapse into various kinds of frigidity: the immoderate or inappropriate use of compound names, exotic words, epithets, and metaphors. In all of these cases, an attempt to speak poetically can lead to absurd and ridiculous effects, obscurity, and therefore unpersuasiveness (*Rhet.*, 1406a–1406b). A further element of style, simile, Aristotle considers to be only slightly different from metaphor. He defines similes as "metaphors that invite explanation." A simile is essentially poetic but may be used in prose in small doses (*Rhet.*, 1406b–1407a).

Aristotle's next concern is with purity of language. He suggests that the prime principle of style is to speak Greek. For this five elements are required: the proper management of conjunctions, used such that they fall within the scope of the hearer's memory; the use of particular, rather than general, words; the avoidance of ambiguity; and proper agreement of words in respect of gender and number. In general, a speech should be easy to read and easy to speak, without a long series of connections and indicating places of punctuation clearly. The main clause should be uninterrupted by any long sequence of qualifying words or phrases (*Rhet.*, 1407b).

Aristotle has told us that, as well as clarity, propriety is the prime attribute of style. Propriety refers to the suitability of a given content to the way it is expressed. Grave matters should be addressed gravely; simple words should not be decorated. Also integral to propriety are the use of emotion and tailoring of the speech to the audience's character, as well as timeliness, the use of the appropriate expression at the appropriate time. In general, fitting style makes the matter persuasive. Aristotle observes that a man who speaks emotively with justification (such as a man angry over an outrage) always wins the empathy of an audience even if he is talking nonsense (*Rhet.*, 1408a–1408b). So with soft thoughts spoken in a hard manner and vice versa. Another feature of speeches which first developed in poetry is rhythm. A prose speech should not be wholly rhythmless; however, it should not have precise rhythm; nor should it have meter, otherwise it will be a poem (*Rhet.*, 1409a).

Aristotle produces some interesting observations in his discussion of wit and metaphor. As in so many other places in his writings, he suggests that learning is a pleasant activity, hence we will derive pleasure from words which produce knowledge. Of the various devices used in a speech, it is metaphor which has this effect (as opposed to exotic words which are unfamiliar or pertinent words which we already know). Metaphor produces understanding and recognition through its use of generic similarity, whereby the mind must think out the resemblance. For example, when a poet calls old age a reed, he generates such reflection and recognition through the fact that both have lost their flower. Another example offered by Aristotle of such intellectual illumination is, "a god set the intellect in the soul as its lamp." Interestingly, long anticipating the insights of Derrida, Aristotle aligns metaphor not only with poetry but also with philosophical reflection: "even in philosophy it requires a speculative capacity to observe the similarity even in very mutually remote things" (*Rhet.*, 1412a). Similes can also have a similar, though less powerful, effect. Aristotle identifies such metaphors and similes, as well as the general effect of vividness, with wit. Riddles and paradoxical or antithetical thought can also be witty insofar as they entail learning and greater clarity (*Rhet.*, 1412a). Understanding, says Aristotle, is made greater by contrast and swifter through happening in a short space (*Rhet.*, 1412b).

The final requirement of good style is its appropriateness to a given genre of rhetoric. The style of written composition differs from that of altercation, and the styles of political, forensic, and display oratory are different. Written composition, says Aristotle, needs to be the most precise and it needs to avoid frequent repetition and use of asyndeton (the omission of conjunctions), which are appropriate for a speech. In deliberative rhetoric precision is unnecessary since the audience will be a large crowd which will not be prone to engage in close inspection. But the forensic style, used in the lawcourts, needs to be more meticulous, all the more so if the audience is a single judge. In this latter case, the smallest amount of rhetoric will be involved, the facts are clearly evident, and debate is absent, so that the judgment is "pure" (*Rhet.*, 1414a).

The final section of the *Rhetoric* concerns composition, which, like the subject of style, Aristotle is including for practical purposes rather than for its comprising a constituent of rhetoric proper. A speech must have two basic components, since it is necessary both to state or present the subject matter or case and to demonstrate or prove it. Overall, the speech will have four parts: the introduction; the presentation or main narrative; the proof of the speaker's claims, which includes refutation of counter-arguments; and finally a summarizing epilogue (*Rhet.*, 1414b).

The nature of a speech's introduction will vary according to the genre. The introductions to display speeches will be drawn from praise or blame, exhortation, dissuasion, appeals to the audience, and in general will set the tone of the speech. In forensic oratory the introduction must give the purpose of the speech; it can also be used to dissolve prejudices against the speaker or to create prejudices against his adversary, to engender the audience's sympathy, and to manipulate the audience's emotional state and degree of attentiveness (*Rhet.*, 1415a–1416a). The narrative section of the speech is most important in forensic oratory. The narration should not be lengthy but strike a mean. It must have character, insofar as it exhibits a moral (rather than intellectual) purpose. It should establish the speaker as being of a certain character and credibility, giving clear reasons for unusual claims, and offering details when these are persuasive (*Rhet.*, 1417a–1417b). As far as proofs are concerned, Aristotle suggests that, in forensic oratory, they must demonstrate one of four things: that an action or event did or did not happen, that it did no harm, that it was not as important as claimed, or that it was done with justice.

Two speakers contesting each other's claims may end in altercation. Aristotle gives a number of devices to use, such as pointing out the incoherence or self-contradiction or sophistry or confusion of the opponent's claims. But only questions clearly designed to elicit these weaknesses should be used. Jokes and irony can also be weapons in altercation.

The final section of the speech is the epilogue, which has four elements: disposing the audience favorably toward oneself and negatively toward the adversary; amplifying or diminishing the facts demonstrated; bringing the audience into an emotional state; and recapitulation. The latter could summarize the points by which one's claims have been demonstrated, or engage in a systematic point-by-point contrast of one's own points with the opponent's claims, interrogation ("What, then, has he shown?"), or irony ("He said that, but I said this"). Finally, an asyndetic ending is appropriate for the speech so that it is a peroration rather than an oration.

Aristotle's *Rhetoric* has had a profound influence in certain areas on the subsequent treatment of rhetoric, especially his analysis of the basic forms of enthymemes, fallacious enthymemes, character, and common topics. However, his emphasis on the connection of the enthymeme with dialectic was not renewed until the Renaissance.

Notes

1 George A. Kennedy, *A New History of Classical Rhetoric* (Princeton: Princeton University Press, 1994), p. 34.
2 James J. Murphy and Richard A. Katula, *A Synoptic History of Classical Rhetoric* (Davis, CA: Hermagoras Press, 1994), p. 18. Hereafter cited as *SH*. Part of the exposition of Greek rhetoric in this chapter is indebted to the accounts offered by Murphy and Katula, as well as Kennedy.

3 The edition used here is Plato, *Gorgias*, trans. Robin Waterfield (New York and Oxford: Oxford University Press, 1994).

4 *Collected Dialogues of Plato*, ed. Edith Hamilton and Huntington Cairns (Princeton: Princeton University Press, 1969).

5 Aristotle, *The Art of Rhetoric*, trans. H. C. Lawson-Tancred (Harmondsworth: Penguin, 1991), 1354a. Hereafter cited as *Rhet*.

CHAPTER 4

THE HELLENISTIC PERIOD AND ROMAN RHETORIC

Historical Backgrounds

C lassical Greek culture based on the *polis* or city-state effectively ended with the defeat of Athens by Philip of Macedon at the battle of Chaeronea in 338 BC. Shortly after Aristotle's death in 332 BC his "student" Alexander the Great, son of Philip, conquered the vast Persian Empire in its entirety. The Hellenistic period is said to begin with Alexander's death in 323 BC, after which his empire was divided up among his generals, who initiated various dynasties: Ptolemy in Egypt (and later Phoenicia and Palestine), Seleucus in Syria, Persia, and Mesopotamia, and Cassander in Macedonia. Notwithstanding these divisions, Greek language and culture were spread all across the conquered territories. While some elements of classical Hellenic culture were retained, the age of the *polis* or city-state gave way before more despotic and monarchical forms of government; there was, moreover, a vast intermingling and fusion of diverse peoples and cultures. This new Hellenistic era was characterized by a merging of Greek and Oriental traditions. Nonetheless, there were continuities with the classical Greek period: the language of the new ruling classes was predominantly Greek, their education was uniform, and Greek science and logic continued to exert a fundamental impact on Hellenistic thought.

Economically, the Hellenistic world saw a vast expansion of trade, commercial investment, and large-scale production. A system of international finance grew up. Not only was much industry regulated by governments, but also large amounts of land were concentrated in the hands of rulers, hence small farmers were reduced to the status of serfs. As part of this economic revolution, a great many cities arose, with large populations. The most splendid of these was Alexandria, with a population of over half a million people, a museum, and a vast library, housing three quarters of a million volumes. One result of this centralization and regulation was that the gulf between rich and poor, between the rulers, the nobility, and traders, on the one hand, and peasants and workers, on the other, widened.

Given the hard and oppressive conditions for the vast majority of the population, it is perhaps not surprising that the main tendencies of Hellenistic philosophy were

Cynicism, Epicureanism, Stoicism, and Skepticism. Two of these, Stoicism and Epicureanism, were based in Athens alongside the older Academy founded by Plato and the Peripatetic School of Aristotle. What these newer modes of thought broadly shared was an indifference to politics and the harsh world of everyday existence. In general, they advocated some form of withdrawal from society. Cynic philosophy was founded by Diogenes of Sinope (ca. 400–325 BC); he was derisively called *kuon* or "dog" on account of his public exhibitionism, hence the name "cynic." He called for a return to nature, a satisfying of only the necessary physical requirements, and shunning everything that was conventional or artificial. In this way, he thought, a person could achieve self-sufficiency and freedom. This sect was active in the third century and experienced a revival in the first century AD.

Stoicism, named after the Stoa Poikile or hall in Athens where it was first taught, was founded around 300 BC by Zeno of Citium (335–263 BC) and developed by Chrysippus, Diogenes of Babylon, and others. Their central doctrines utilized Heraclitus' concept of the Logos or universal reason. They believed that this cosmic reason governed the universe as an ordered whole, and that any evil or misfortune was merely part of a larger pattern of ultimate good. Man asserts his own rational nature by accepting the order of the universe and his own part in it; he thereby achieves contentment and peace of mind. To this end, the Stoics stressed self-discipline, tolerance, and peacefulness, as well as the equality of human beings. While they held that one should indeed engage in social life, they believed that this engagement should be based on the recognition that the supreme good is to live in accordance with both reason and nature and thereby to achieve virtue. Later Roman Stoicism, as expressed by Cicero (106–43 BC), Seneca (4 BC–AD 65), Epictetus, a freed slave (ca. 55–AD 135), and the emperor Marcus Aurelius (AD 121–180), focused increasingly on nurturing an inward spirituality and detachment from the external world. The Stoics made contributions to literary criticism in the fields of grammatical theory and allegorical interpretation (*CHLC*, V.I, 210). Of particular interest is their notion of *phantasia* or imagination, which referred to the presentation of images to the mind, either by the impact of the outside world or the operation of a text. George Kennedy points out that while the Stoics generally held to a view of art as imitation, some of them saw *phantasia* as a higher creative process. Mere imitation, they held, can only represent what has been seen, whereas *phantasia* can create what has not been seen, according to an ideal standard (*CHLC*, V.I, 211). For example, a portrait might be based on an ideal of beauty rather than on any existing person. Kennedy states that the notion of *phantasia* became a part of the critical vocabulary of Greek and Roman writers; it would much later become an integral component of Romantic literary theory. While the Stoics accepted that a poem imitates life, their application of this principle in allegorical interpretation viewed such imitation as symbolic rather than literal. The Stoic influence in rhetoric was generally "prosaic," eschewing any strong appeal to emotion or excessive use of ornamentation and figures of speech (*CHLC*, V.I, 212).

Epicureanism, named after its founder Epicurus (342–270 BC), also began around 300 BC. It is well known that Epicurus taught that the highest good is pleasure. But he did not advocate uncontrolled debauchery and indulgence; while allowing that bodily appetites should be satisfied, he suggested that the highest pleasure was mental and contemplative; we achieve such mental peace both by freedom from pain and by recognizing that the universe operates according to its own laws without interference from the gods. The soul, which is material, dies with the body and cannot be subjected to punishment. While the Epicureans did not have much to say about literature, Epicurus and some of his followers did provide an account of language whereby words were seen as originating in the impressions of human beings and meanings created through consensus and convention (*CHLC*, V.I, 214). Such a view anticipates many modern theories.

The philosophy known as Skepticism, which experienced something of a revival in later thinkers such as David Hume and twentieth-century modes of thought such as deconstruction, goes back to the pre-Socratics such as Xenophanes and was developed by the Sophists Gorgias and Protagoras. Plato's Academy later professed adherence to this doctrine. Skepticism basically holds that we cannot have certain knowledge: our senses – which are ultimately the source of all our knowledge – are fallible and can mislead us. Skepticism became more systematic and formalized in the Hellenistic period, expressed through notable proponents such as Pyrrho, Carneades, and Aenesidemus, who identified ten reasons for withholding belief about things. The Hellenistic Skeptics, partly in opposition to the Stoics, argued that since we can have no certain or definite knowledge about the world, we can achieve happiness only through a noncommittal attitude whereby we suspend positive judgment about things. If it is necessary to act, we must do so on the basis of practical considerations and probabilities.

These philosophies were largely rational and materialist, believing that even the gods and the souls of human beings were composed of matter. A rather different dimension of Hellenistic philosophy was expressed in the endeavor to reconcile Hebrew with Hellenistic conceptions, as embodied in the work of the Jewish scholar Philo of Alexandria (also known as Philo Judaeus, ca. 20 BC–ca. AD 40), influenced by both Stoicism and Platonism. Translation of the Old Testament into Greek (called the Septuagint, since seventy-two translators were commissioned for the task) had begun during the middle of the third century BC (*LWC*, 39). Philo's synthesis of Hebrew and Greek notions was based on an allegorical interpretation of scripture. Philo believed the Old Testament to be "a divine allegory of the human soul and its relation to God," and his writings, says Kennedy, "are the earliest extended allegorical interpretations in Greek" (*CHLC*, V.I, 213). The Greek notion of Logos was central to Philo's system, as both the order of the universe and the intermediary through which God could be known. Philo distinguished between the spiritual and material aspects of the universe, urging that the soul can escape the matter in which it is imprisoned only through ascetic denial; the ultimate aim of our journey is a mystical union with God, who is otherwise not knowable. Philo's doctrines exerted a considerable influence on Christian thought.

Despite their sometimes fundamental differences, all of these Hellenistic philosophies were in their broad outlines defeatist, advocating either withdrawal from the world or simply resigning oneself to it. The attainment of happiness or a tranquil state of mind, for all of them, lay not in any action upon or transformation of the world but in a mental attitude of detachment. In one sense Philo's doctrines can be seen as a culmination of this attitude, and as paving the way for Christian theology: for Philo, the entire world of matter is evil and merely an obstacle to the development of the soul. In this period generally the approach to literature and criticism became much more technical, elucidating and classifying the style of classical texts and encouraging their imitation (*CHLC*, V.I, 219). These Hellenistic dispositions, alongside many mystical religious cults, were continued into the Roman world, partly in consequence of authoritarian political systems in which freedom was absent and where political debate, to the extent that it occurred, was constrained within rigid parameters. It was within an increasingly constrained political framework, as will emerge shortly, that Roman rhetoric, literature, and criticism developed, on the basis of Greek models. With the establishment of monarchies came patronage and an inevitable tendency toward sycophancy, hyperbole, and excess.

Hellenistic Rhetoric

The great library and museum of Alexandria was a center of scholarship in the fields of science, textual criticism, and poetic composition. Hellenistic scholars working in the library further systematized the content and rules of rhetoric. A major surviving text of this period is the *Rhetorica ad Alexandrum* (dedicated to Alexander the Great), written in Greek in the fourth century BC. Greek rhetoricians of this period include Theophrastus (ca. 370–285 BC), who may have initiated the study of figures of speech and figures of thought and who may have founded the notion of three levels of style, high, middle, and plain. The most important Greek rhetorician of this time was Hermagoras of Temnos, who lived in the second century BC. His work on rhetoric, which has been reconstructed by scholars, influenced the rhetorical ideas of major Roman figures such as Cicero and Quintilian. Especially influential was Hermagoras' doctrine of *stasis*, which identified the "position" or "stance" toward the issue at stake in an argument. He made a distinction between general cases and specific cases which could be argued according to four possible issues. This theory was designed to help students formulate issues and compose speeches (*CHLC*, V.I, 198). As George Kennedy observes, Hellenistic education focused on "acquiring practical arts of written and oral composition," and by the Roman imperial era, exercises for students included the retelling of a narrative in the student's own words, description, a speech in the persona of a mythological or historical character, the comparison of two things or persons, and the arguing of a thesis along with the practice of refutation and confirmation. Some of the compositional processes thereby learned were often taken over into literary composition (*CHLC*, V.I, 199). Many of these compositional exercises have been in use until very recently in our own classrooms and are still found in textbooks that cater for the teaching of modern rhetoric and composition.

Roman Rhetoric

Greek rhetoric made its entry into Rome in the second century BC. Hermagoras had a great influence on two of the major early Roman texts of rhetoric, the *Rhetorica ad Herennium* (*Rhetoric for Herennius*, ca. 90 BC) and Cicero's *De inventione* (87 BC). The

Rhetorica, whose author is anonymous (though sometimes known as "Pseudo-Cicero" since the work was attributed for 1,500 years to Cicero), is the first text to present a detailed discussion of the five-part system (invention, arrangement, style, memory, delivery) which was central to the Roman tradition of rhetoric. The author insists that this is a practical treatise and that the task of the speaker is to discuss competently those matters that law and custom have fixed for "the uses of citizenship."[1] Like Aristotle, he divides rhetoric into the three branches of epideictic, deliberative, and judicial (corresponding to "display," "deliberative," and "forensic" in Aristotle's account). He defines the five parts of rhetoric as follows: invention is the devising of matter which will make a given case convincing (invention being the most difficult and important of the speaker's tasks); arrangement is the ordering of the matter; style is the adaptation of words and sentences to the matter invented; memory is the firm retention in the mind of the matter; and delivery refers to the regulation of voice, countenance, and gesture (*RH*, I.ii.3).

The author cites the standard pattern of a discourse, as six parts: introduction, statement of facts, division, proof, refutation, and conclusion. There are, he states, two kinds of introductions, direct and subtle. The purpose of the introduction is to make hearers receptive, well disposed, and attentive, by means of four methods: talking about the speaker; talking about the adversary; talking about the audience; and discussing the facts themselves (*RH*, I.iii.4–I.iv.7). The most complete argument, he tells us, has five parts: proposition, reason, proof of the reason, embellishment, and résumé or conclusion. A conclusion is tripartite and includes summary, amplification, and appeal to pity.

As regards delivery and memory, the author explains that good delivery ensures that the speaker appears to be speaking in earnest. Memory is of two kinds, natural and artificial. The latter depends on the use of backgrounds and images (*RH*, III.xvi.28–29). The author suggests that there are three levels of style: the grand or high style, which uses ornate arrangements of impressive words; the middle style, which uses a lower class of words which, however, are not colloquial; and the simple or plain style, which uses the most current idiom of standard speech (*RH*, IV.viii.11). This concept of the three styles was adapted by critics in the Middle Ages, such as Geoffrey de Vinsauf and Matthew of Vendôme, who saw the three levels respectively as applying to narratives about the court, the town, and the peasantry.

Finally, the author provides a long list of figures of speech and figures of thought. The former are produced by an adornment of language, the latter by a distinction in the idea or conception itself (*RH*, IV.xii.18). The section on figures of speech goes through the standard figures such as antistrophe, apostrophe, reasoning by question and answer, and reasoning by contraries. An interesting distinction is made here between metonymy and synecdoche. Metonymy is defined as a figure which draws from an object closely akin to the intended object but substitutes a different name. It could substitute the name of the greater for that of the lesser, the thing invented for the inventor, the instrument for the possessor, the cause for the effect or vice versa, the container for the content or vice versa. Synecdoche occurs when the whole is understood from the part or vice versa, or when the singular is understood from the plural or vice versa (*RH*, IV.xxxii.43–xxxiii.45). Metaphor is said to occur when a word applying to one thing is transferred to another, on the basis of a given similarity; it is used to create vividness, brevity, to avoid obscenity, to magnify or diminish, or to embellish. Finally, allegory is defined as a manner of speech denoting one thing by the letter of the words but another by their meaning. It can assume three aspects: comparison, when a number of metaphors originating in a similarity are set together; argument, when a similitude is drawn from an object in order to magnify or minimize it; and contrast, when one mockingly refers to a thing by its contrary (*RH*, IV.xxxiv.45–46). The list of figures of thought includes frankness of speech, understatement, division (of the alternatives of a question), refining, dwelling on a point, comparison, exemplification, simile, character portrayal, dialogue, personification, emphasis, and conciseness.

Cicero's Rhetorical Theory

Marcus Tullius Cicero (106–43 BC) is the most renowned of the classical rhetoricians. Born into the equestrian order or upper middle class, he was a prominent practitioner of the art of public speaking in the Roman senate and the lawcourts. He drew upon Plato, Aristotle, Demosthenes, Isocrates, and Theophrastus in creating his own rhetorical synthesis which was also informed by his own rich experience. As a student in Rome, he entered an educational system which was centered on rhetoric and assigned exercises in writing, speaking, arguing a thesis, legislative and judicial declamations, as well as the learning of rhetorical rules, the exercise of memory, and the proper delivery of a speech. Cicero himself regarded delivery as of predominant importance in a speech. At an early age he published his rhetorical treatise *De inventione* in the early part of the first century BC. This was followed by other rhetorical texts, *De oratore* (55 BC), *Brutus* (46 BC), a history of Roman oratory, *Orator* (46 BC), *De optimo genere oratorum* [*On the Ideal Classification of Orators*] (46 BC), *Partitione oratoria* [*On the Divisions of Rhetoric*] (45 BC), a discussion of the components of a speech, the nature of audiences, and the resources on which a speaker can draw, and *Topica* (44 BC), an application of Aristotelian logic to Roman rhetoric.

Cicero lived at a turbulent time, when the Roman republic was convulsed with political, social, and military turmoil. Slave uprisings had broken out in Sicily in 139 BC and 103 BC. A third slave uprising, led by Spartacus, had arisen in 73 BC. Sulla had established a dictatorship in Rome in 82 BC. An agrarian revolution in Italy, as well as numerous civil wars, had shaken the Roman republic, which was riven by class warfare, itself driven by the huge discrepancy between the opulent luxury of the upper classes and the miserable poverty of the plebeians and peasants. Cicero was fearful of further revolution and the possibility of mob rule; he supported a "concord of the orders," a cooperation of the aristocracy and the business class. Cicero's major opponent was Lucius Sergius Catiline, who attempted to unite the various revolutionary factions. In 64 BC Cicero ran against Catiline for the consulate and defeated him, having the united support of the upper classes. Eventually, hostilities broke out and Catiline's forces were defeated in battle and a number of his followers were executed. After his crucial role in quelling this revolution, Cicero was hailed by the Romans as the father and savior of his country.[2] Plutarch describes Cicero at this time as being "the most powerful man in Rome" (*Fall*, 296).

Cicero's acerbic wit, however, made enemies. He eventually became caught up in the messy power struggles between Caesar and Pompey, and then between Antony and Octavian. His loyalties, generally to the preservation of the Roman republic as against rule by an emperor, wavered between these powerful figures. He took no part in the assassination of Caesar though he was a friend of Brutus; he argued before the senate that Brutus and Cassius should be granted an amnesty after Caesar's murder. Fearful that Antony would seek supreme power for himself, Cicero produced a series of speeches against Antony, called the *Philippics* (named after Demosthenes' speeches to the Athenians concerning Philip of Macedon). At first, Octavian provided protection for Cicero while the latter was useful in promoting his career. Eventually, however, Octavian acceded to Antony's demand that Cicero be placed on a list of names marked for death; Antony's soldiers eventually caught up with Cicero at one of his summer estates; they cut off his head and his hands, which were displayed on the public rostra in the forum in Rome.

In *De inventione* Cicero stresses the political importance of rhetoric. He also affirms that the function of rhetoric is to help promote a society based on justice and common welfare rather than physical strength. As such, the speaker must possess not only eloquence but also wisdom.[3] It is worth stating briefly Cicero's definitions of the six parts of a speech. (1) The *exordium* is intended to make the audience well disposed, attentive, and receptive. It is divided into the *introduction*, which accomplishes these three things directly, and the *insinuation*, which achieves them indirectly and through dissimulation. The latter is used to begin a speech when the audience is hostile (I.20). (2) The *narrative* is an account of the events which are alleged to have occurred (I.25). (3) The *partition* makes the whole speech lucid, and has two forms: one indicates the areas of agreement or disagreement with the opponent, and the other is a preview of the remainder of our own argument (I.30). (4) The *confirmation* is that part of a narrative which supports our case by enlisting arguments. Cicero here makes a number of general observations concerning argumentation. Arguments can lend support to propositions by reference to attributes of persons or of actions. All argumentation is either necessary or probable. Necessary arguments cannot be refuted; probability operates in people's ordinary beliefs. Moreover, all argumentation is conducted either by analogy (drawing a likeness between one's own case and facts which are undisputed) or by enthymeme, which draws a probable conclusion from the facts (I.35–65). (5) The *refutation* undermines the confirmation or proof in the opponent's speech, by denying its assumptions or conclusions or showing the opponent's form of argument to be fallacious (I.75). (6) The *peroration* which concludes the speech has three parts: a resume of the speech's substantial points, arousal of animosity against the opponent, and the arousing of sympathy for one's own case. A peroration might also include personification as well as appealing to the pity of the jury (I.80.100–105). In *De inventione* Cicero also tells us that every speech depends on one of the *stases* or issues for deliberation, and elaborates the specific rules for each kind of speech, forensic, deliberative, and epideictic.

De oratore is written as a conversation between four speakers. Cicero's own views are largely expressed through the character of Crassus, a renowned orator under whom Cicero had studied rhetoric. This treatise presents some further insights on style, notably that each proof in a speech should be related to an emotion since most decisions are made on the basis of emotion;[4] also, that each emotion naturally has a specific look and tone which the speaker must master in delivery (II.213). Other suggestions for speaking include knowing that the audience is most receptive at the beginning of the speech, which therefore should be used to make one's most probative statements; and using metaphor, since this – the discovery of new relationships among common terms – is what gives audiences most pleasure. Cicero considers delivery to be the supreme factor in successful oratory (III.213). The orator is defined in general as someone who can express ideas clearly to an "ordinary" audience (I.85).

What is most interesting about the *De oratore* is the way it addresses two important topics: the cultural value of rhetoric, and the connection between rhetoric, philosophy, and other forms of knowledge. Cicero, speaking through Crassus, maintains that the art of rhetoric has flourished especially in states which have enjoyed freedom, peace, and tranquility. Moreover, this art above all others distinguishes men from animals; it is this art which has brought unity and civilization to humanity (I, VIII). As such, the orator must combine in himself a multitude of virtues which are found but singly in other men (XXV–XXVI). Cicero also takes issue with Plato's criticism of rhetoric. Where Plato sees rhetoric as focused on style and divorced from philosophy, Cicero insists that the good rhetorician must speak on the basis of knowledge and under-standing of his subject, and that philosophy and rhetoric are complementary. A speaker must have knowledge of philosophy, law, and human psychology, and must be trained in the liberal arts (I, XI–XII). According to Cicero, Socrates "separated . . . the ability of thinking wisely and speaking gracefully, though they are naturally united." Interest-ingly, Cicero aligns this with an equally unnatural "divorce . . . of the tongue from the heart" (III, XVI). In short, Cicero insists, in contrast with Plato – a contrast so sharp that it verges on identity – that the rhetorician and the philosopher can be united in one person; whether he is called a rhetorician or a philosopher is a matter of indiffer-ence (III, XXXV). Plato, we may recall, effectively redefined the good rhetorician as a philosopher.

In *De optimo genere oratorum*, Cicero considers Demosthenes the greatest of all orators. In *Brutus* he argues that the ultimate test of a speaker's success is not acclaim by the critics but the approval of the people. He also adds a few other precepts such as avoiding bombast, and pursuing the path of moderation. In *Orator* Cicero argues that the functions of oratory – to teach, delight, and affect an audience – are related to the three levels of style, grand, middle, and plain. The ideal orator, says Cicero, will use the plain style for proving his case, the middle style for delighting his audience, and the grand style for evoking specific emotional responses. An orator using the grand style has the greatest power, but this should be mixed with other styles as appropriate. Commonplace subjects should be treated in a simple way, great subjects in the grand style, and subjects falling between these in the middle style. Cicero states that the orator should be familiar with logic as formulated by Aristotle, as well as history, civil law, religion, and morality. He considers figures of thought more important to elo-quence than figures of language, since embellishment and adornment are essential to oratory. In *De partitione oratoria* Cicero offers a more systematic account of the prin-ciples and divisions of rhetoric. His final rhetorical treatise, *Topica*, which purports to be an interpretation of Aristotle's *Topics*, actually attempts to show how philo-sophy and rhetoric draw on common themes or topics for invention. Where Plato had derided rhetoric as indifferent to truth and as based on emotional appeal rather than valid argumentation, Aristotle and his followers had developed the topics or "categories of reasoning," and had "established a complete system of argumentation" (*CHLC*, V.I, 229).

Indeed, Cicero's greatest achievement might be said to be a rhetorical synthesis between the principles of various schools, as well as an attempted fusion of philosophy and rhetoric. He undoubtedly increased the philosophical and literary-critical vocabulary of the Latin language, thereby paving the way for further rhetorical and philosophical refinements. Perhaps the best – and most flattering – tribute to Cicero was expressed by Plutarch in these words: "Cicero, more than anyone, made the Romans see how great is the charm which eloquence confers on what is good, how invincible justice is if it is well expressed in words, and how the good and efficient statesman should always in his actions prefer what is right to what will win popularity, and in his words should express the public interest in a manner that will please rather than prove offensive" (*Fall*, p. 287).

Quintilian

It is reputed that Cicero's last words were, "With me dies the republic!" The world inhabited by Cicero's rhetorical successors was very different. With the establishment and consolidation of imperial rule – whereby power lay in the hands of one man – came a considerable decrease in personal and political freedom, the ability to speak freely and to argue sincerely. A character in Tacitus' "Dialogue on Oratory" remarks that the period of peace inaugurated by Augustus effectively produced "tranquillity" in the senate as a result of the "restraints on eloquence as well as on all else."[5] The changes involved in the transformation from republic to empire have been succinctly expressed by Murphy and Katula:

> Conditions in the new Empire were inimical to creative oratory: the length of speeches, number of advocates, and duration of court trials were reduced; orators ran the risk of offending the Emperor in every speech they gave; the dynamic issues of the past were, for the most part, absent; the power of the monarchy steadily encroached on the self-governing bodies . . . In short, the social and political conditions productive of creative rhetoric no longer marked the Roman world.[6]

With some irony, Tacitus explains the dearth of great oratory in his day. One of his characters, Maternus, states, "the great and famous eloquence of old is the nursling of the licence which fools call freedom." In an ordered state, where "a sound morality and willing obedience to authority prevail," there is no need of eloquence or long speeches. What need is there of long speeches in the senate, he asks, "when political questions are decided not by an ignorant multitude, but by one man of pre-eminent wisdom?" (*Tacitus*, pp. 768–769). Perhaps not far beneath the surface of these comments is an underlying longing for the freedom in which other voices beyond the emperor's might be heard.

Though these circumstances oversaw a general decline of rhetoric in the first century AD in Rome, they nonetheless produced in Quintilian a figure whose enduring influence closely rivaled that of Cicero. Quintilian (Marcus Fabius Quintilianus) was born in northern Spain in AD 35 and died shortly after 96, the year of publication of his *Institutio orataria*. This text was a major contribution to rhetorical and educational theory as well as to literary criticism; its influence has been vast, second only to Cicero's in the Renaissance, and reaching into our own educational systems.

Quintilian studied oratory in Rome under the training of the leading orator of the time, Domitius Afer. He practiced as a lawyer and started a school of rhetoric which counted Tacitus, Pliny the Younger, Juvenal, and Suetonius among its students. He was appointed to a state professorship of rhetoric by the emperor Vespasian; his renown continued under the emperors Titus and Domitian, and he was eventually awarded the title of honorary consul.

In the *Institutio* Quintilian both describes in detail the Roman education system, which was centered on rhetoric, and offers a program for the education of an ideal orator from childhood. In a preface, Quintilian stresses what is perhaps the most original theme of his text, the dependence of true oratory on moral goodness: "the perfect orator . . . cannot exist unless he is above all a good man."[7] The orator thus requires "every excellence of mind." Like Cicero, Quintilian opposes Plato's separation of rhetoric and philosophy. Quintilian's integration of these activities is based on morality: the orator must be morally good – and cannot leave the principles of moral conduct to the philosophers – because he is actively involved as a citizen in the various enterprises of the state, civil, legal, judicial, private, and public. Like Cicero, then, Quintilian views wisdom and eloquence as naturally and necessarily accompanying each other. Hence the orator will require the broad training detailed in the *Institutio*, which consists of twelve books. The first book outlines the required education for a child prior to beginning his rhetorical studies, which are described in the second book. The third to ninth books deal with the five parts of rhetoric: invention, arrangement, style, memory, and delivery. The tenth book is a survey of Greek and Latin rhetoricians, the eleventh concerns the arts of memory and delivery, while the final book deals with the character of the ideal orator, his style, and the rules he must follow. The following discussion will focus on the first two books, which are renowned for their general insights into education, and the twelfth book, which crystallizes Quintilian's views of the orator.

In book I, concerning the education of children, Quintilian urges education in a public school over private tuition; the latter does not necessarily guard against possible bad habits and immorality at a school. Moreover, an eminent teacher will seek out a larger audience of students; one student alone will not provide an adequate forum for his speaking ability and teaching gifts. As Quintilian puts it, "There would be no eloquence in the world, if we were to speak only with one person at a time" (I.ii.31). However, by being a "kind friend" to his students, the teacher can establish a relationship of affection which will make every student feel individually treated rather than a member of a multitude. The caring teacher will also "let himself down to the capacity of the learner" (I.ii.15–16, 27–28). Quintilian goes on to say that the chief symptoms of ability in children are memory and imitation. He recommends some relaxation and play, which is both a sign of vivacity and expresses a child's moral disposition. He is against corporal punishment since it produces no change for the better in a child.

Once a child has learned how to read and write, he must next learn grammar. Quintilian defines the province of grammar as comprising two parts, the art of speaking correctly and the interpretation of literature. He warns against viewing grammar as trivial, since it lays a sure foundation for the future orator. The grammarian needs a knowledge of music in order to understand meter and rhythm; he must know some astronomy and philosophy, since poetry often draws upon these (I.iv.2–5). In general, Quintilian tells us that language is based on reason, antiquity, authority, and custom. While the judgment of eminent men of the past can sometimes be followed and while moderate use of archaic language is permissible, the surest guide to proper use of language in speaking is custom; it must have "the public stamp" (I.vi.2–3). However, Quintilian cautions that custom cannot be aligned with the practice of the majority; rather, it is "the agreement of the educated" (I.vi.45). This principle will reemerge in many writers, and is active in many reader-response theories of literature.

Regarding exercises in reading, Quintilian suggests that a student's mode of reading aloud should be "manly," uniting gravity with sweetness (I.viii.2). The passages chosen for reading should portray moral goodness; Quintilian recommends the reading of Homer and Vergil in order to sense the sublimity and magnitude of conception of heroic verse; the reading of tragedy and lyric poetry; and comedy, since it can contribute much to eloquence. Quintilian's appeal to Homer, Vergil, and Horace indicates the authority achieved by these poets as models for rhetorical composition. In analyzing poetry, the student must be taught to read closely, to specify the parts of speech, the feet and meter, to identify the correct usage of words, to know the various senses of a given word, to recognize all kinds of tropes, figures of speech, and figures of thought, to be acquainted with relevant historical facts, and above all, to understand the merit in the way the whole work is organized (I.viii.5–18). He defines a trope as "the conversion of a word or phrase from its proper signification to another, in order to increase its force" (VIII.vi.1). He defines a figure as "a form of speech artfully varied from common usage" (IX.i.14). In addition, boys should learn to relate orally Aesop's fables, and should practice paraphrasing poetry in their own words. They should practice writing aphorisms and character sketches. In general, the stories told by poets should be used to increase their knowledge rather than simply treated as models of eloquence (I.ix.2–6).

Having thus described the studies preliminary to rhetoric, Quintilian turns, in book II, to the teaching and learning which fall under the province of rhetoric proper. His foremost point here is that the teacher of rhetoric, receiving boys at an impressionable age, should be of exemplary morality. His description of the ideal teacher is still pertinent in our own time and is worth quoting in full:

> Let him [the teacher] adopt, then, above all things, the feelings of a parent toward his pupils, and consider that he succeeds to the place of those by whom the children were entrusted to him. Let him neither have vices in himself, nor tolerate them in others. Let his austerity not be stern, nor his affability too easy, lest dislike arise from the one, or contempt from the other. Let him discourse frequently on what is honourable and good, for the oftener he admonishes, the more seldom will he have to chastise. Let him not be of

an angry temper, and yet not a conniver at what ought to be corrected. Let him be plain in his mode of teaching, and patient of labor . . . Let him reply readily to those who put questions to him, and question of his own accord those who do not. In commending the exercises of his pupils, let him be neither niggardly nor lavish; for the one quality begets dislike of labor, and the other self-complacency. In amending what requires correction, let him not be harsh, and, least of all, not reproachful . . . Let him speak much every day himself, for the edification of his pupils. Although he may point out to them, in their course of reading, plenty of examples for their imitation, yet the living voice . . . feeds the mind more nutritiously – especially the voice of the teacher, whom his pupils, if they are but rightly instructed, both love and reverence. (II. ii.4–8)

This passage seems strangely modern in its precepts – especially those concerning responding to students' work – with the exception, perhaps, that we are not quite so insistent on stressing the instructor's moral character. So important is the moral element of teaching to Quintilian that, in its absence, he maintains, all other rules are useless (II.ii.10–11, 15).

Quintilian also suggests that, from the very beginning, the child should be given the best teachers; it is a mistake to think that his early education can be turned over to inferior teachers. Eminent teachers, who know their subject well and accurately, will not be above teaching elementary matters. Moreover, they will be people of good sense who know how to adapt their teaching to the standards of their pupils. Above all, their command of their learning will enable them to achieve in their teaching the virtue of clarity, which is "the chief virtue of eloquence." The less able a teacher is, the more obscure and pretentious he will be (II.iii.2–9).

It will be recalled that Cicero divided a speech into six parts, an essential one of which was the narration. Quintilian suggests that the teacher of rhetoric might begin with a subject such as narration, which has already been studied. He observes that there are three kinds of narration: the fable, which draws on imaginary material as exemplified in tragedies and poetry, the *argumentum*, which has an appearance of truth, as used in comedy, and the history, which is a statement of facts. It is this last and most substantial kind that the student must learn from the teacher of rhetoric. The student should be taught to compose a narrative which is neither dry or insipid nor adorned with far-fetched ornamentation (II.iv.2–4). Here also Quintilian offers valuable advice on pedagogy. A dry instructor should be avoided, and maturity should not be encouraged with overdue haste. A teacher should not be severe in correcting faults; he should be as agreeable as possible; he "ought to praise some parts of his pupils' performances, to tolerate some, and to alter others, giving his reasons why the alterations are made; and also to make some passages clearer by adding something of his own" (II.iv.8–12).

As well as practicing narrations, students must engage in the tasks of refuting and confirming them, praising illustrious characters and censuring immoral ones, and studying *commonplaces* (general claims on points of morality or law) and *theses* (arguments on a general topic, often comparing the virtues of two things) (II.iv.18–25). Students must also undergo exercises in the praise or denunciation of laws. It is within the province of the teacher of rhetoric, says Quintilian, to point out the beauties and faults of texts, helping them, if necessary, line by line through a text. He should point out to his students anything significant in thought or language. In particular, he should be on

91

the alert for the purpose of the entire passage, the clarity of the narration, the subtlety and urgency of the argumentation, and the speaker's ability to control his own and the audience's feelings. He should also remark stylistic elegances and defects, as, for example, in the appropriate use of metaphors and figures (II.v.7–9). In a subsequent chapter Quintilian stresses that the art of declamation is by far the most useful of exercises (II.x.2–3). Exercises in declamation are to be properly regarded as preparation for the pleading of actual cases and therefore should imitate them (II.x.12–13).

Quintilian has a number of interesting general observations on the nature and value of rhetoric. Rhetoric is foremost a practical art which is concerned with action, rather than a theoretical art concerned with understanding or a productive art such as painting or sculpture (II.xviii). As such, there are no rigid rules for rhetoric; the rules must be adapted to the specific nature and circumstances of each case (II.xiii). Quintilian refuses the classical definition of rhetoric as the art of persuasion since the latter can be achieved by many means. He prefers to name rhetoric the science of speaking well (II.xv). Rhetoric is by no means a morally indifferent art; it belongs to the province of a good person since one cannot give forensic and epideictic speeches without a knowledge of goodness and justice (II.xx). Finally, like Cicero, Quintilian turns Plato's critique of rhetoric against him: the material of rhetoric can indeed be anything, and this is why the orator must receive a comprehensive education (II.xxi). In books III and IV Quintilian goes over some of the history of rhetoric and informs us that his own position is eclectic rather than affiliated to any given school (III.i). He basically accepts the traditional division of rhetoric into forensic, deliberative, and epideictic branches, and states that questions pertain either to law or to fact (III.iv–v). His account of the various parts of a speech – exordium, narration, confirmation, proof, partition – is similar to Cicero's.

Having dealt with invention, Quintilian turns in book VII to arrangement. Among the general principles he advocates are that the prosecution should assemble its proofs while the defense should consider them separately, and that arguments should move from the general to the particular (VII.i). Book VIII deals with style, which Quintilian regards as the most difficult subject. He advocates a style which has clarity, elegance, and is adapted to its audience (VIII.i–ii). However, tropes, such as metaphor, synecdoche, and metonymy, can be used to enhance one's meaning or to decorate one's style (VIII.vi).

Simply to follow these stylistic precepts, however, is not enough in Quintilian's eyes to make a good orator. One must develop a certain facility and habitual competence, both through writing (which Cicero too had emphasized) and through reading and imitation of the best authors, ancient and modern, in poetry, history, philosophy, and oratory. However, mere passive imitation is not enough; the student must be inventive, adding something of his own. As regards writing, Quintilian insists that this should be careful rather than hasty and that self-correction through extensive revision is an integral part of the process of composition (X.i–iv). In achieving fluency and facility, other exercises, such as translation, paraphrase, theses, commonplaces, and writing out declamations, are also valuable (X.v). Moreover, young men should start to attend actual cases in court and learn to think out a plan for various kinds of cases. This will foster their ability in improvisation, which Quintilian calls the "highest achievement" of the orator (X.vi–vii).

Turning now to memory and delivery, Quintilian urges memorizing a speech. As to delivery, he concurs with Cicero that it has the most powerful effect; indeed, it is even more important than the content itself of the speech since it is what will move the audience. Delivery must follow the same principles as style: it must be clear, correct, duly ornamented, and appropriate to the given audience, occasion, and nature of the case (XI.iii).

In the final and most renowned book of the *Institutio*, Quintilian stakes a claim to originality inasmuch as he describes the character of the ideal orator. He repeats his initial affirmation that no man can be an orator unless he is a good man. His reasoning is that a truly intelligent man will not choose vice over virtue, and that only a good man can be sincere in his speeches. Moreover, the goal of oratory is to express what is good, just, and honorable (XII.i). Hence the orator must form himself into a noble character by acquiring an extensive knowledge of what is just and honorable from the philosophers, as well as real and fictitious examples of justice and honor through history and poetry. However, he must not become a philosopher, since the latter merely thinks without acting. The orator's duty is to utilize his learning and knowledge in practical affairs. He must also have a knowledge of civil law, religion, and the customs of his country, as well as a sound command of the three levels of style. Quintilian urges that the robust Attic style of oratory is superior to the more extravagant Asiatic style. Finally, he urges the orator to engage in constant practice, referring pointedly to the decadence and distractions of the current day – such as the theater and feasting – which surround him (XII.x–xi).

In general, it can be seen that Quintilian's major contribution to the fields of rhetorical and educational theory lies in his insistence that all aspects of these fields are underlain by morality. The purpose of his entire treatise is to indicate the type of training a person must undergo in order to be an orator and a statesman, one who can contribute in a virtuous and effective manner to the administration of the state. Not only must he be versed in the art of eloquence; he must also be trained in philosophy, law, and liberal studies. He must be practical, adaptable, kind, and moderate, and maintain a Stoic sense of duty to his country. His insistence on these moral and intellectual qualities of the orator is a reflection of, and proposed remedy for, the decay of rhetoric in his day caused in large part by political circumstances that did not encourage freedom of thought and speech. Sadly, in these circumstances, his educational program could not be realized. Nor was it realized in the Renaissance despite the reverence in which his treatise was held.

The Subsequent History of Rhetoric: An Overview

After the civil war in which Octavius defeated Antony at the battle of Actium, Octavius became emperor of the entire Roman world in 27 BC and ruled until AD 14. The republic had permanently collapsed and Rome was ruled by emperors until its fall in AD 410. In this period, the freedom to speak – and the art of rhetoric – was profoundly constrained: speakers focused on style and delivery and rhetorical ornamentation rather than substance. The period is generally referred to as the Second Sophistic

(27 BC–AD 410), named after a new generation of Sophists who advocated a return to the language and style of classical Athens. Deliberative speeches concerning state policy became less important and, as the empire expanded, rhetoric came to be dominated by narrowly defined legal and technical speeches. Rhetoric as taught in the schools was further and further removed from everyday life and the actual affairs of the state. It focused instead on imitation of earlier models, especially those of fourth-century Athens. Nonetheless, there was a proliferation of theories. In both respects – the withdrawal from *realpolitik* and the proliferation of theories – this state of affairs bears some resemblance to the late twentieth century where theories multiplied, nearly all of them estranged from the apparatus of political and economic power.

Marked by such circumstances, the Second Sophistic produced no major rhetorical treatises, with the exception of Longinus' *On the Sublime*. Given that rhetoric had effectively been denuded of its social and political functions, the art of rhetoric henceforth lost its public role, focusing increasingly on the formalization of rules for literary composition, which was seen through the Middle Ages as part of the province of rhetoric. In fact, the prevailing philosophy of this period, especially during the third and fourth centuries, was Neo-Platonism, deriving from Philo Judaeus and Plotinus; in stark contrast to the public, political, and rational nature of classical rhetoric, Neo-Platonism was mystical and ascetic in orientation, advocating absolute indifference to the political and economic world. Like the rhetoricians of the Second Sophistic, the Neo-Platonists shared in the "universal reverence" for the classical texts, viewing them as the fountains of wisdom. As such, the Neo-Platonists attempted to smooth away differences and conflicts between classical authors. They aimed to resolve the "ancient quarrel" between philosophy and poetry, by reconciling Plato and Homer. To do this, they were obliged, as Donald Russell says, to develop "techniques of allegorical and symbolic interpretation," paving the way for medieval conceptions of discourse which viewed the physical world as inherently symbolic of a higher world. Though this was a Greek development, it was the Latin writer Macrobius who ensured the legacy of such techniques in Western culture.[8] The Neo-Platonists were effectively continuing a Stoic tradition of allegorical interpretation aimed largely at defending Homer and other poets from charges initially brought by Plato (*CHLC*, V.I, 298–299).

Some rhetoricians of this period did exert an enduring influence. Under the dominant preoccupation with style, grammarians flourished. In the fourth century the grammarian Donatus produced two manuals, *Ars minor*, an exposition of the eight parts of speech, and *Ars maior*, which also dealt with figures of speech and tropes. Another influential grammarian was Priscian, who wrote his *Institutiones grammaticae* around the beginning of the sixth century, dealing with the parts of speech as well as problems of composition. During the Middle Ages Priscian's text was used in university education and Donatus' in elementary schools. Other rhetoricians of this period such as Victorinus influenced scriptural exegesis and rhetorical treatises in the Middle Ages. Donald Russell remarks that the Second Sophistic had an enduring social and educational impact on the way in which literature was approached: a technique of close reading was developed, which could be used to study the strategies both of great orators and of Homer and the great dramatists; this technique was later applied to the fundamental texts of Christianity (*CHLC*, V.I, 298).

By the end of the fourth century, Christianity had risen to a predominant status in the Roman Empire. This process had been initiated by a series of edicts issued by the emperor Constantine in 313 allowing Christianity to be tolerated; one of Constantine's successors, Theodosius I, had issued a decree in 380 demanding the practice of Christianity. As a result of this predominance, a reaction set in against the use of classical pagan methods and mythology in education. The Christian Council of Nicaea organized a structure of dioceses, each of which was to be presided over by a bishop responsible for preaching in his district. Augustine, who was trained in classical rhetoric, produced his *De doctrina christiana* in 426, in which he argued that language was a system of signs for conveying thoughts and emotions; but his fourth book argued for the importance of rhetoric, especially that of Cicero, as an instrument of explaining and conveying the Christian message through preaching and education. Eventually, the Church adopted Cicero's rhetoric as a guide for preachers. Augustine thus provides a link between classical and medieval rhetoric (*SH*, 205–211).

In the Middle Ages rhetoric was one part of the educational "trivium," the other two components being grammar and logic. Rhetoric was concerned primarily with the means of persuasion of an audience, whereas the focus of grammar was on the rules of linguistic correctness, and that of logic on valid argumentation. There was, according to some scholars, a "confusion" of rhetoric and poetic, indicating that the boundaries between these disciplines were not clearly established. If this is so, it is traceable partly to the "practical and didactic temper" of classical literary criticism, and partly to the fact that much classical criticism, as O. B. Hardison, Jr. states, was "really oratorical criticism which is applicable to poetry."[9] The primary source of medieval rhetorical criticism was in fact Horace's *Ars poetica*, which drew heavily on Alexandrian poetic theory (itself influenced by rhetorical theory) and Roman rhetoric, in particular that of Cicero. Horace's text effectively attributes to poetry some of the aims of rhetoric: to instruct, delight, and "move" an audience. Hardison points out that the concept of any sharp separation between poetic and rhetoric did not even arise until the sixteenth century rediscovered Aristotle's *Poetics*. Some Renaissance critics such as Julius Caesar Scaliger attempted to restrict the rules of rhetoric to the composition of prose.

The most influential rhetorical treatises during the Middle Ages were the *Rhetorica ad Herennium* and Cicero's *De inventione*. From these texts, medieval writers such as Conrad of Hirsau, Geoffrey de Vinsauf, John of Garland, and John of Salisbury took the notion of the three styles, as well as the classification of rhetorical figures. Other notable figures included Bede and Alcuin. Also influential were two works dating from the fourth century AD, the *Interpretationes Vergilianae* of Tiberius Claudius Donatus and Macrobius' *Saturnalia*. Both works discuss Vergil's *Aeneid* in terms of its mastery of the various provinces of rhetoric, and the second revives a standard theme, namely, whether Vergil was an orator or poet (*MLC*, 12). In the Carolingian period, purely rhetorical criticism after the fashion of Donatus and Macrobius disappeared, and was not revived until the fifteenth century (*MLC*, 13). Hardison suggests that there was a "lively debate during the twelfth and thirteenth centuries concerning the relative importance of the disciplines of the trivium," which shows that, far from being confused, the participants had an acute understanding of what was at stake. Poetry was henceforth treated under the province of grammar (*MLC*, 13). In general, rhetoric in the Middle Ages took second place to the development of logic, especially in the hands of the scholastic theologians such as Thomas Aquinas.

In the Renaissance, which returned to classical sources, rhetoric enjoyed a revived centrality in the educational curriculum. The Renaissance humanists drew profusely on the teachings of Cicero.[10] Whereas poetics and rhetoric in the Middle Ages had drawn on Cicero's earlier text *De inventione* to emphasize the two rhetorical offices concerning *form*, namely style and arrangement, the Renaissance writers used his mature work *De oratore*, as well as Quintilian's newly recovered treatise, in their emphasis on *content* and the strategies of invention ("RP," 1048–1049). As the Renaissance progressed, however, this emphasis on invention gave way to a preoccupation with style, which was seen as the central province of rhetoric, as indicated by influential texts such as *De inventione dialectica* of Rudolphus Agricola (d. 1485). What these developments effectively indicate is a subsumption of rhetoric – itself reduced to style – under poetics, and the loss of the rhetorical concern with audience, modes of argumentation, and persuasion. As Thomas Sloane so eloquently puts it, "this rhetoricizing of poetics did little to salvage the rapidly disappearing uniqueness of rhetorical thought" ("RP," 1049). Rhetoric as such was dead.

Indeed, the rediscovery of Aristotle's *Poetics*, along with a new edition of Longinus produced by Robortelli in 1554, inspired a new emphasis on poetic form and a view of poetry as not wholly analyzable as merely a branch of rhetoric. The new literary theories of humanists such as Robortelli and Castelvetro, inspired by the *Poetics*, were not grounded in a rhetorical approach. The three "unities" attributed to Aristotle – of time, place, and action – became widely prescribed for drama. There was also an Aristotelian insistence on the organic unity of a poem, whereas the various "offices" of rhetoric tended to distinguish sharply between the formal elements of a composition and its content. This formalism, as will emerge in a later chapter, was particularly intensified by the Romantic poets and reached a climax in the earlier part of the twentieth century in Russian Formalism, the New Criticism, and the Aristotelian critics of the so-called Chicago School ("RP," 1047). These modern formalisms were, in a sense, a revived reaction against the constraints of traditional rhetorical terms and classifications.

In subsequent eras, rhetoric survived only in a disintegrated form, as in the Ramist reformers who, following the French thinker Petrus Ramus, reduced it to style (by excluding the offices of invention and disposition, which they assigned to dialectics) and viewed the various offices of rhetoric as distinct spheres of study. The remaining component of rhetoric, *pronunciation*, became a subject of independent study – a study of gesture, elocution, and language as performance – in the seventeenth and eighteenth centuries in the hands of Francis Bacon, John Bulwer, and actors such as Thomas Sheridan. In seventeenth- and eighteenth-century poetics Ciceronian elements, such as the amplification of ideas to evoke and manipulate the "passions" of an audience, survived alongside terminology from Aristotle's *Poetics* such as plot, character, and thought. Poetic invention of course retained its importance but it was not, as in traditional rhetoric, oriented primarily toward an audience. Rather, it became a private, meditative act, the composition of a solitary mind in isolation. The figures of speech were less directed toward the passions of an audience; composition was viewed more as a form of self-expression, an indication of the author's psyche, and began to be examined by the new discipline of psychology ("RP," 1049). Such an approach was expressed by some of the important rhetorical treatises of this period which included George Campbell's *Philosophy of Rhetoric* (1776) and Richard Whately's *Elements of Rhetoric* (1828). This mode of thinking achieved a new intensity in Romanticism, which offered a new account of poetic creation on the basis of the faculty of imagination. The Romantics tended to draw upon Plato and Longinus, attacking the remnants of Aristotelian poetics and rhetoric that infused neoclassical poetics. They turned again to Plato's doctrine of poetry as a divine madness or possession, rather than Aristotle's view of poetry as a rational activity, subject to the processes of rhetorical invention. They also had recourse to Longinus' view of poetry as transporting its listeners to a higher state rather than persuading them.

Interestingly, this mutual separation of the elements of rhetoric into a study of the performative aspects of language on the one hand, and language as private meditation on the other, signifies a rift between speech and writing, a rift that broadened and intensified irreversibly with the development of printing. The profusion of written culture encouraged the theory and practice of invention and creativity as an isolated and solitary process. In general, after the Renaissance, rhetoric has experienced a disintegration whereby some of its functions have been preserved in other domains, such as law, politics, and poetics, some of its functions absorbed by literary and linguistic analysis, and its essentially public and social character dissolved in its modern reconfigurations. The original impulse of rhetoric (as Plato recognized, albeit in a negative way) was holistic. It aimed to subsume everything in its path, aspiring to a universal applicability to all domains of discourse. Whether one talked about politics, law, religion, or poetry, one could mold the *form* of discourse in each domain according to certain broad principles. Indeed, Plato failed to recognize that rhetoric was not composed of content but was essentially a form: in other words, it does not have a specific content and is a mode of imposing form on the content of *other* disciplines.

In the Middle Ages, this formal function of rhetoric was already being displaced by logic and theology. After the Renaissance, the gradual rise of bourgeois economy and modes of thought, reaching an explosive predominance in the late eighteenth and nineteenth centuries, contributed to the disintegration of rhetoric in several ways: through increasing specialization, whereby each area of inquiry aspired to a relative autonomy, possessing not only its own unique content but also its own methods; for example, it was argued that literature be treated *as* literature, rather than as a social or moral or political document. In this highly compartmentalized scheme of knowledge, rhetoric became treated as a specific content rather than as a form applicable to other disciplines. Moreover, the predominance of rationalist, empirical, and experimental outlooks fostered a distrust of predetermined categories of thought and expression, as well as promoting a more straightforward and literal use of language, divesting language of its allegorical potential as so richly realized in medieval texts. By the end of the nineteenth century and indeed into present times, "rhetoric" has become a derogatory term, signifying emptiness of content, bombast, superfluous ornamentation. Nonetheless, as indicated below, rhetoric has experienced some significant revivals during the twentieth century.

The Legacy of Rhetoric

The inheritance of the modern Western world from classical rhetoric is profound and pervasive. Rhetoric has played a central role in politics and law; for two millennia rhetoric has been at the center of the educational system in Europe, and its influence in education is still visible in its continued domination of the teaching of composition, influenced by theorists of argumentation such as Stephen Toulmin. In this field, however, rhetoric has had a somewhat narrow application, being transposed from the province of public speaking into the art of writing and even there often reduced to issues of thematic coherence and essay development; while there is some acknowledgment of a potential audience, this recognition is often abstract (the audience often blandly identified as a student's peers or instructor), with the act of invention remaining essentially private and meditative, an expression of the author's individual perspective. Having said this, approaches to teaching composition have begun to feel the reverberations of a rhetorical revival in literary studies. Rhetoric has recently exercised a renewed impact on the vast area of cultural and critical theory, spanning numerous disciplines, especially those such as speech act theory which are directly concerned with the nature of communication. The influence of rhetoric on literary criticism and theory extends much further than the stylistic analysis of figures of speech such as metaphor and metonymy. A rhetorical approach to a text must concern itself not only with the author's intentions but also with all the features implicated in the text as a persuasive or argumentative use of language: the structure of the text as a means of communication, the nature and response of the audience or reader, the text's relation to other discourses, and the social and political contexts of the interaction between author, text, and reader, as well as a historicist concern with the differences between a modern reception of the text and its original performative conditions. In short, a rhetorical approach views a literary text not as an isolated act (merely recording, for example, the private thoughts of an author) but as a *performance* in a social context.

In this broad sense, rhetoric has been an integral element in many approaches to literature and philosophy, ranging from Marxist and feminist perspectives through hermeneutic to reception theories. From the earlier parts of the twentieth century, philosophers such as Ludwig Wittgenstein and Gilbert Ryle have recognized the importance of studying the use of language in philosophical propositions. Later linguistic philosophers such as J. L. Austin have studied the performative aspects of language. A study of the nature of language as a system of signs, as comprehending both its communicative and "literary" functions, has been central to the project of much formalism, including the New Criticism. But as with earlier formalisms, this modern formalism – expressed partly in manifesto slogans such as "a poem should not mean, but be" – tended to undermine a rhetorical approach to literature as an effective form of communication, and to view the literary text either as an isolated verbal structure abstracted from all context or as enabled by an equally isolated structure of language in general viewed as a system of relations between signs. Most of these formalist approaches drew attention to the literary work not as a means of communication but as a material entity, existing for its own sake, possessing a certain pattern and structure.

One of the figures associated with New Critical tendencies, I. A. Richards, produced a book, *Philosophy of Rhetoric* (1936), in which he made a distinction, deriving partly from John Locke, between poetry, which draws on the entire semantic richness and multiple meanings of words, rhetoric, designed to persuade, and expository language, in which the meaning of each word should be clear and the language used neutral or impartial. However, as against Locke's call for a clear language free from figures and polysemy, Richards acknowledges that such purity is impossible, suggesting that it is the task of rhetoric to examine the semantic richness of language.

However, Richards' insights gave way before the predominance of New Critical and other formalisms. A more general revival of rhetoric was heralded by Kenneth Burke's reaction against these various modern formalisms and his call for the renewal of a rhetorical approach to literary form and interpretation. Writers such as T. S. Eliot and Wayne Booth tended to focus on the author's relation to the text, as in Eliot's essay "The Three Voices of Poetry"; Northrop Frye's *Anatomy of Criticism* (1957) also ultimately rejected any sharp distinction between a literary or rhetorical use of language that made use of figures and tropes, and a philosophical and expository use of language; the latter is also marked by ambivalence and connotation. Reception and reader-response theorists, including Iser, Holland, and Fish, have focused on the role and situation of the reader; other critics, such as Burke, Jakobson, Lacan, Derrida, and Paul de Man, resurrected the idea of certain foundational rhetorical tropes such as irony, metaphor, and metonymy, some arguing that these tropes are integral to language and the process of thought. Derrida sees all language, whether philosophical or literary, as intrinsically metaphorical (since the process of interpretation or exposition involves the endless displacement of one signifier for another, never being arrested at any signified), and in an important sense rhetorical. De Man aligns rhetoric with an indeterminacy and openness that cannot be coerced into a grammatical or logical system. Linguists and structuralists such as Todorov, Genette, and Barthes have often modified rhetorical classifications of tropes. A rhetorical perspective is explicitly acknowledged in the so-called Law and Literature movement: the narrative of a prosecution or defense in a courtroom will employ many literary and rhetorical strategies. But the influence is not one-sided: literary and other texts can themselves be viewed in the light of rhetorical strategies designed for the courtroom. The entire arsenal of "literary" figures, in fact, was devised by rhetoricians. In this broad sense, then, rhetoric might be viewed as an inevitable component of all kinds of discourse. A literary, philosophical, or historical text, for example, might be seen as arguing a case by an author in specific circumstances who has certain motives; the audience or reader is the judge, with its own motives and interests. Indeed, modern rhetoricians and theorists tend to view all of the figures of speech identified by classical rhetoric – such as metaphor, simile, metonymy, irony – as not merely external additions to language or ornaments but as conditioning the very process of thinking by means of language; as such, an analysis of these figures is integral to understanding the nature of language, the process of conceptualizing, and the reaction of an audience or reader.

It is clear, then, that the rhetorical heritage in Western literature and education has been countered by a long tradition of philosophy which has seen itself as devoted to the rational pursuit of truth, the definition of the good life and happiness; in short, the mainstream Western philosophical tradition has tended to reject rhetorical considerations of style, passion, and effect on audience, in favor of an emphasis on content. This tradition was effectively inaugurated by Plato; it runs through medieval logic and theology, as well as disputes in the Middle Ages concerning the status of logic, grammar, and rhetoric in the educational trivium; it continues through Renaissance attempts to stress the formal elements of poetry as well as through Ramist logic in the seventeenth century into the empiricist and rationalist philosophy of the Enlightenment, as expressed in Locke's insistence that philosophical language be free of figures and tropes; it survives into the twentieth century in the analytic philosophy of G. E. Moore and Bertrand Russell, as well as logical positivism, speech act theory, and various branches of semiology. Interestingly, whereas the philosophical disparagement of rhetoric has usually aligned the latter with poetry, sometimes the advocates of poetry have themselves opposed the alleged rigidity and prescriptiveness of rhetoric, as in Romanticism, late nineteenth-century symbolism, and modern formalism. Sometimes, influenced by Longinus, these advocates have argued that the primary function of poetry is not to communicate but to produce a certain state of mind in the reader, to produce verbal patterns that point to a transcendent world or to create a relatively autonomous verbal structure that highlights the material qualities of language.

The persistent struggle between philosophy and rhetoric has obliged thinkers in both fields to articulate and define not only various conceptions of truth but equally the connections between truth and style. While it is arguable that there is still today a conflict between rhetoric and more conventional analytic and empirical modes of philosophizing, it is equally clear that, as in the late Roman imperial period, there is also a mutual influence, for example in more recent philosophical views of language. Both this conflict and concurrence force us even today not to view truth somehow as subsisting in a vacuum, abstracted from all practical and political concerns, but to acknowledge that our definitions of truth are intrinsically tied to prevailing political structures. The notion of truth which rhetoric must inevitably harbor is truth as consensus. Even if its ostensible aim is persuasion or conviction, such persuasion can be achieved rationally on the basis of argument whose overall end is to give the appearance of approximating truth. To argue a case is never a matter of ostensive definition; it is never a matter of simply putting people in possession of the facts; not only do the facts need to be interpreted, but also what count as facts in the first place are the results of interpretations. Facts themselves are interpretations from various viewpoints. In fact, the very possibility of rhetoric is premised on the absence of truth as anything but an ideal limit. All that is possible is appearance of truth or approximation to truth; any actual truth which transcended the viewpoints of the interpreters would eliminate the need for rhetoric. Rhetoric originates and is workable only in a democracy, or at least only in a state which allows freedom of speech. In a democracy, truth is not merely relative, it is *necessarily* absent or non-existent as *content*; it can subsist only as a point of view which is forced to confront its limitations in collision with another point of view. There is no truth to measure it against, only perhaps degrees of comprehensiveness and coherence with solidified interpretations which have achieved conventionally the status of fact. But there must be an element of externality which brings into relief the limitation of a given viewpoint. The danger of this democratic situation is that the majority could affirm something to be true which is false.

Notes

1   [Cicero] *Ad C. Herennium: De ratione dicendi (Rhetorica ad Herennium)*, trans. Harry Caplan (Cambridge, MA and London: Harvard University Press/Heinemann, 1968), I, ii, 2. Hereafter cited as *RH*.

2   Plutarch, *Fall of the Roman Republic* (Harmondsworth: Penguin, 1968), p. 95. Hereafter cited as *Fall*.

3   Marcus Tullius Cicero, *De inventione; De optimo genere oratorum; Topica*, trans. H. M. Hubbell, Loeb Classical Library (Cambridge, MA and London: Harvard University Press/Heinemann, 1968), I.5.

4   Marcus Tullius Cicero, *De oratore* (Cambridge, MA: Harvard University Press, 1967–1968), II.165.

5   *The Complete Works of Tacitus*, ed. M. Hadas, trans. A. J. Church and W. J. Brodribb (New York: Random House, 1942), p. 767. Hereafter cited as *Tacitus*.

6   James J. Murphy and Richard A. Katula, *A Synoptic History of Classical Rhetoric* (Davis, CA: Hermagoras Press, 1994), p. 178. Hereafter cited as *SH*.

7   *Quintilian: On the Teaching of Speaking and Writing: Translations from Books One, Two, and Ten of the Institutio oratoria*, ed. James J. Murphy (Carbondale: Southern Illinois University Press, 1987), p. 6.

8   Donald Russell, "Greek Criticism of the Empire," in *CHLC*, V.I, 298–299.

9   "Introduction," in *MLC*, 10. My sketch of rhetoric in the Middle Ages is indebted to Hardison's insightful account.

10   Some of the insights in this section are indebted to the extremely learned article, "Rhetoric and Poetry," by Thomas O. Sloane in *The New Princeton Encyclopedia of Poetry and Poetics*, ed. Alex Preminger and T. V. F. Brogan (Princeton: Princeton University Press, 1993). Hereafter cited as "RP."

PART III

GREEK AND LATIN CRITICISM DURING THE ROMAN EMPIRE

CHAPTER 5

HORACE (65–8 BC)

The influence of Horace's *Ars poetica*, composed toward the end of his life, has been vast, exceeding the influence of Plato, and in many periods, even that of Aristotle. Horace (Quintus Horatius Flaccus) is known primarily as a poet, a composer of odes, satires, and epistles. In the realm of literary criticism, he has conventionally been associated with the notions that "a poem is like a painting," that poetry should "teach and delight," as well as the idea that poetry is a craft which requires labor. Horace's text was initially known as "Epistle to the Pisones" and the title *Ars poetica* is first found in Quintilian; the text actually takes the form of an informal letter from an established poet giving advice to the would-be poets of the wealthy Piso family in Rome. Though the *Ars poetica* is technically a work of literary-critical and rhetorical theory, it is itself written as a poem, a fact which dictates its structure and rhythm. The *Ars* is the first-known poem about poetics, and such a poetic expression of literary-critical principles was imitated by several men of letters, including the medieval writer Geoffrey de Vinsauf, the Renaissance writer Pierre de Ronsard, the neoclassical poets Nicolas Boileau-Despréaux and Alexander Pope, the Romantic poet Lord Byron, and twentieth-century poets such as Wallace Stevens. The influence of Horace's critical tenets, expressed primarily in *Ars poetica* but also in some of his letters such as the "Epistle to Florus" and the "Epistle to Augustus," has been even more extensive and continuous.

Horace's life intersected poignantly with the turbulent events of Roman history and politics in the first century BC. Born the son of a freedman (a freed slave), he was educated at Rome then Athens. It was during his lifetime that Rome was transformed from an oligarchic republic, ruled by the senate and elected consuls, to an empire ruled by one man, Octavian (later known as Augustus). Initially, Horace's sympathies were with the republicans Brutus and Cassius who had assassinated Julius Caesar, fearing that he had ambitions of becoming emperor. Horace fought with Brutus and Cassius against Caesar's nephew Octavian and Mark Antony at the battle of Philippi in 42 BC. The republicans were defeated, after which yet another civil war broke out, this time between Octavian and Mark Antony who allied himself with Queen Cleopatra of Egypt. Octavian's resounding victory at the battle of Actium left him the sole ruler of the

Roman world; he was given the title Augustus and revered as a god. Horace, however, was fortunate. Granted a pardon for his part in opposing Octavian, he was introduced by the poet Vergil to Gaius Maecenas, an extremely wealthy patron of the arts. Eventually, Horace enjoyed the patronage of the emperor himself. Nonetheless, it is arguable that Horace's loyalties remained somewhat mixed.

In assessing the temper of Horace's work and worldview, we need to know something about the prevailing intellectual and literary attitudes in the Roman world of his day. The most pervasive philosophical perspective was that of Stoicism, whose emphasis on duty, discipline, political and civic involvement, as well as an acceptance of one's place in the cosmic scheme, seemed peculiarly well adapted to the needs of the Romans, absorbed as they were in military conquest, political administration, and legal reform. Indeed, Roman Stoicism was imbued with a more practical orientation than its Hellenistic forebears, though it still preached that inner contentment based on acceptance of the universal order should be the primary goal of human beings. Stoic philosophy had some impact on Horace's worldview as expressed in his *Odes*, though the major Roman Stoic philosophers, such as Seneca (4 BC–AD 65), Epictetus (ca. AD 60–120), and the emperor Marcus Aurelius (121–180) all wrote after Horace's death. Other philosophical attitudes alive in Horace's day included Epicureanism and Skepticism; elements of both philosophies, especially the former, profoundly inform his poems and his literary criticism. While Horace's attitudes cannot be described as hedonistic, he acknowledges the fulfillment afforded by private pleasures and a quiet withdrawal from public cares; his work betrays an ironic skepticism concerning the ideals of empire and conventional religion.

Indeed, Horace's philosophical and poetic vision is thrown into sharper relief when placed alongside the work of his contemporaries. The greatest poet of his age was Vergil (70–19 BC), whose epic poem the *Aeneid* is founded on Stoic ideals such as *pietas*, duty, self-discipline, and sacrifice of individual interests for the sake of a larger cause. All of these qualities are expressed in its hero Aeneas, who must undergo severe hardships, who must forego his personal happiness and the love of Queen Dido, for the larger purpose of the founding of Rome. The *Aeneid* as a whole is intended to glorify and celebrate the Roman Empire, and in particular the reign of Augustus. Against this overtly political poetic enterprise, the political ambivalence of Horace's poetry and literary criticism emerges in a clearer light. Our view of Horace is sharpened even further when we consider the writings of the other major poet of this era, Ovid (ca. 43 BC–AD 17), whose works such as the *Ars amoris* led to his banishment by Augustus. Ovid, evidently influenced by the Cynics and Skeptics, expressed the decadent and seamy – even steamy – side of Roman life, grounded in individualism and self-interest rather than public duty or piety. His *Metamorphoses* – depicting, for example, Zeus as rapacious, deceitful, and embroiled in petty quarrels with his wife Hera – appears to be the very antithesis of Vergil's *Aeneid*, perhaps an anti-epic revealing the true motivation of empire as rapacious, ephemeral, and founded on subjective self-interest rather than noble ideals and historical destiny. Horace's work lies somewhere between these two poles of outright affiliation with, and undisguised cynicism toward, the entire political and religious register of imperial ideals.

Scholars such as Doreen C. Innes have remarked a pervasive general feature of both Greek and Latin literature: poets had a highly self-conscious attitude toward their place in the literary tradition. After the period of the great Alexandrian scholars and poets, the Greek canon of writers was rigidly established. As such, writers tended to imitate previous authors and to achieve originality within this traditional framework. Hence, poets such as Vergil, Ovid, and Horace accepted the Greek theory of imitation while striving for originality in a Roman context (*CHLC*, V.I, 246–247). For example, Vergil's *Aeneid* echoes many of the devices and strategies used in the Homeric epics while infusing new themes such as historical destiny and new ideals such as duty. The aesthetic framework of the Augustan poets was inherited from Alexandrian writers such as Callimachus who justified a movement away from the writing of epic and the magniloquent praising of famous deeds toward smaller genres and a focus on technical polish. This legacy also included a debate between genius (*ingenium*) and technique (*ars*) as the proper basis of poetry. The ideal of "art for art's sake" had been espoused by some Alexandrian writers such as Zenodotus, Eratosthenes, and Aristarchus (*CHLC*, V.I, 205, 248–252). This also was a question among the Augustans: should poetry primarily give pleasure or should this pleasure subserve a social, moral, and educational function?

Horace's apparently desultory treatment of these and other issues might be organized under certain broad headings: (1) the relation of a writer to his work, his knowledge of tradition, and his own ability; (2) characteristics of the *Ars poetica* as a verbal structure, such as unity, propriety, and arrangement; (3) the moral and social functions of poetry, such as establishing a repository of conventional wisdom, providing moral examples through characterization, and promoting civic virtue and sensibility, as well as affording pleasure; (4) the contribution of an audience to the composition of poetry, viewed both as an art and as a commodity; (5) an awareness of literary history and historical change in language and genre. These are the largely conventional themes that preoccupy Horace's text, to appreciate which we must consider his poetry as well as key elements of his political circumstances.

Although the letter was an acknowledged Roman literary genre, the highly personalized form of Horace's text disclaims any intention of writing a "technical" treatise in the sense of Aristotle. Some of Horace's richest insights take the form of asides and almost accidental digressions, and the entire piece is casual in tone. Horace's "principles" are drawn from experience, not theory.

Rome in Horace's day was a vast metropolis of three quarters of a million people; it was also a center of artistic patronage, crawling with poets. Horace closes his letter with an image of the mad poet as a leech that sucks the blood out of its audience: "if he once catches you, he holds tight and kills you with his recitation, a leech that will not release the skin till gorged with blood."[1] Horace's immediate point here is that the poet should rely on learning and art rather than on untutored inspiration, which is indistinguishable from madness. But this ending is also an index of Horace's skepticism toward would-be poets. Such an ending impels us to go back and read the text again, on another level.

These levels of interpretation effectively destabilize each other. In book X of the *Republic*, Plato had viewed poetry not as a self-subsistent entity but as an imitation of reality: indeed, it was to be judged by its distance from reality. Aristotle had considered poetry worthy to be studied as a sphere in its own right but had introduced subjective elements of the audience's response into his definition of tragedy, which was thereby partly "affective" (producing certain effects). But this was merely a pseudo-subjectivity: it assumed that members of an (hypothetical) audience would respond in a uniform way. With Horace, however, the definition of art contains a genuine subjective element, in terms of both author and audience. To begin with, the writer's materials are not pregiven but must be selected according to his capacity: "When you are writing, choose a subject that matches your powers, and test again and again what weight your shoulders will take and what they won't take" (*AP*, 38–40). In a striking image of reciprocity, Horace views the reader's response as part of the existence of the poem: "As you find the human face breaks into a smile when others smile, so it weeps when others weep: if you wish me to weep, you must first express suffering yourself" (*AP*, 102–103). Talking of drama, Horace reinforces his point: "Here is what the public and I are both looking for" (*AP*, 153). Not only, then, is the audience the ultimate criterion of genuine artistry, but also literature is intrinsically dialogic: the presumed response of a particular audience guides its "creation." The audience that Horace has in mind is no abstract entity. He is keenly aware of its changing moods and historical shifts of taste. Interestingly, Horace embeds this changeability firmly within the substratum of language. He considers it to be perfectly in order for a poet to "render a known word novel" and even to "mint" words: "when words advance in age, they pass away, and others born but lately, like the young, flourish and thrive" (*AP*, 48, 60–62). In talking of both changes in the composition of audiences and the need for growth in language, Horace displays historical self-consciousness and awareness of literary history as integral elements in literary criticism.

A prominent and influential principle expressed in Horace's text is the then standard rhetorical principle of "decorum," which calls for a "proper" relationship between form and content, expression and thought, style and subject matter, diction and character. Like many modern theorists, Horace's notion of "form" encompasses language itself, and he seems to think that there is an intrinsic or internal connection between form and content; in other words, the content cannot somehow be prior to or independent of the form as implied in Pope's view of language as the external "dress of thought." Neither can the content and thought be prior to language. This is why Horace can talk of the old order of words passing away, as well as of words acquiring a new meaning. When he speaks of "minting" words, this seems to entail language being extended through increasing recognition of its inadequacy.

This brings us to the other side of Horace's ambivalence as regards the "objective" status of literature. Having insisted on the *ontological* contribution of the reader or audience to what is termed "literature," he describes recent changes in the make-up of the audience itself. Once, he says, the audience for a play was "a public . . . easily counted, not too large, sparing in their ways, pure in their habits, modest in their attitude." But as Rome began to expand her territories and cities encompassed a greater variety of populace, "more and more freedoms were granted in meter and music" (*AP*, 205–207, 211). This enlargement and "corruption" of the audience dictate directly what is permissible and desirable on stage. But if the audience now lacks "taste," where does this leave Horace's characterizations of *good* literature? Horace frankly admits that often a "play that is . . . properly characterized, though lacking charm and without profundity or art, draws the public more strongly and holds its attention better than verses deficient in substance and tuneful trivialities" (*AP*, 319–322). Horace here effectively reverses Aristotle's priority of plot over characterization; for Horace, who rejects the Alexandrian attitude of "art for art's sake," and insists on the moral function of literature, the depiction of good character is indispensable. Indeed, this function should be effected in drama partly by the chorus which, says Horace, "should favor the good, give friendly advice, restrain the enraged, approve those who scruple to do wrong; it should praise the delights of a modest table, the bracing influence of justice and laws and the leisure afforded by peace; it should . . . offer supplication and prayer to the gods that fortune return to the unhappy and leave the proud" (*AP*, 196–201). Horace here states a comprehensive moral vision, embracing many aspects of life, from the formation of character by restraining negative emotions, through appreciation of social and political achievements to religious sentiment. And yet this vision is so commonplace that, coming from Horace's pen, it could be ironic.

If a poet is to convey character with propriety, he must learn "the duties owed to country and friends, the affection fit for parent, brother, and guest, the proper business of senator and judge, the part to be played by a general sent to war" (*AP*, 312–315). As against Plato, who had regarded the poet as necessarily distorting reality by offering a mere imitation of it, Horace insists that the "principal fountainhead of writing correctly is wisdom" (*AP*, 309) and he sees poetry as a repository of social and religious wisdom (*AP*, 396–407). In the depiction of character, the poet must be aware of the various characteristics of men from childhood, youth, manhood to old age (this repertoire of the ages of man is taken from rhetoric) (*AP*, 158–174). Hence, the poet's work must be based on knowledge; not bookish knowledge but a detailed empirical knowledge derived from acute observation of numerous situations in actual life. In other words, Horace demands a high degree of realism from the poet, as expressed in this statement: "My instruction would be to examine the model of human life and manners as an informed copyist and to elicit from it a speech that lives" (*AP*, 317–318). This appears to be a relatively modern sentiment, urging (as Wordsworth and T. S. Eliot were to do much later) that the poet use a language that "lives" as opposed to language derived from the stockpiles of rhetoric and previous poetic usage. Horace insists that poets invent on the basis of the "common resource" of "what is known" so that others can relate (*AP*, 240–243). Here again, the response of the listener or audience is integral to the very process of composition.

It is symptomatic of Horace's pragmatic approach to poetry that he repeatedly alludes to the "role" of wealth in the production of literature. On the one hand he can say that like "a crier gathering a crowd to buy goods, a poet, who is rich in property, rich in money put out at interest, is inviting people to come and flatter him for gain" (*AP*, 419–421). And, echoing Plato, he derides a situation where poetry alone of all the professions can be practiced without knowledge and with impunity: "a person who has no idea how to compose verses nevertheless dares to. Why shouldn't he? He is free and well-born" (*AP*, 382–383). Yet, this derision goes hand in hand with Horace's sincere advice on how to succeed in the midst of this sorry state of affairs:

> a poet has matched every demand if he mingles the useful with the pleasant [*miscuit utile dulci*], by charming and, not less, advising the reader; that is a book that earns money for the Sosii [publishers]; a book that crosses the sea and, making its writer known, forecasts a long life for him. (*AP*, 342–346)

109

This matching "every demand" carries the thrust of Horace's approach to literature, which views aesthetics as a practical combination. It's not just that literature is written well or badly and subsequently sells better or worse. The recipe for its financial success is already inscribed in its aesthetic function (in which is inscribed its moral function), literature being a commodity in both aesthetic and monetary respects. Horace's call for literature to be socially useful as well as pleasing was vastly influential; as was his insistence that a poem not only charm the reader but also offer moral advice.

In reminding the would-be poet of his obligations – such as self-knowledge or knowledge of his own abilities – Horace stresses the amount of labor required for composing good poetry. Part of this labor is seeking out valid criticism of his work from sincere and qualified people. Horace admonishes the poet to store his work away for nine years. He warns that, once a poem is published, the words used by the poet will forever become public property, part of a language inescapably social: "it will be permissible to destroy what you have not published: the voice once sent forth cannot return" [*nescit vox missa reverti*] (AP, 386–390). Horace's imagery here, using *vox* (voice) instead of, say, *liber* (book), could be read as implying that the act of publication effects a disembodiment of voice: once personalized, in the form of speech, it now leaves the author forever to become entwined in the huge network of presupposition and openness to alternative meaning known as "writing." Indeed, Horace's argument seems strikingly modern in rejecting an author's intention as the sole determinant or ultimate criterion of a poem's meaning. The poem's meaning is determined by its situation within larger structures of signification which lie beyond the poet's control.

But what has Horace, in this "classic," really told us about art and literature? Effectively, he has merely reiterated the then customary notion of literature as a compromise of pleasing and instructing. Even his deprecation of poetry as a "game" is conventional. And his emphasis on poetry as an act of labor, as effort (*ars*) rather than innate creativity (*ingenium*), was hardly original: a controversy had long been raging concerning these.[2] Even here, Horace traverses a safe *via media*: "I do not see of what value is application [*studium*] without abundant talent or of what value is genius [*ingenium*] when uncultivated" (AP, 409–410). It's true that Horace made an advance in terms of the persistence with which he insisted on poetry as an act of labor. Moreover, beyond these traditional concerns, Horace advocates a loose concept of poetic unity, whereby the various parts of a poem should be appropriately arranged. Horace, after all, had opened the *Ars poetica* with a grotesque image of what the artist should avoid: a human head attached to a horse's neck, covered with "a variety of feathers on limbs assembled from any and everywhere" (AP, 1–2). Horace also shared in a new concern with literary history, and downplayed the distinctions between genres such as tragedy and comedy (*CHLC*, V.I, 258, 261–262). It is arguable that what is original is Horace's blending of conventional and newer attitudes. It may, indeed, be his lack of originality, his ability to give striking poetic and epigrammatic expression to a body of accumulated wisdom or "common sense," the critic speaking with the authority of a poet, that ensured the classic status of his text.

Whatever the case, it is clear that so much recycling of traditional attitudes has a partial basis in Horace's political circumstances. Once a republican, having fought on the side of Brutus against Antony and Octavian, Horace gradually moved toward acceptance of the divine status of the new emperor Octavian, now Augustus. Though till late in life Augustus cherished a liberal stance toward men of letters, poets provided one platform for the propagation of his programs of religious, cultural, and agricultural reform. The complexity of Horace's shifting allegiance is recorded in his poems which, like most Roman literary texts, were highly self-conscious artifacts. We can perhaps read the *Ars poetica* as a distilled form of this poetic self-consciousness, as well as a rationalization of conventional poetic practice.

This rationalization is based partly in Horace's vision of poetic and political disharmony. The same ambiguities and hesitancies which plague the *Ars* pervade the poems to an even more striking extent. And it seems to be precisely this series of hesitancies, *aporiai* if you will, with its modern emphasis on individualized creation and its withdrawal from political or aesthetic commitment, which distinguishes Horace's work from anything written by Aristotle, Vergil, or later writers such as Longinus. It is the indelible writing of himself, his personal background, into his poetic significance which, ironically, is universalizable. Many of Horace's odes are concerned with death, a common enough theme; what is relatively peculiar to him is that his (conventional) endeavor to transcend death, his refusal to accept death as an absolute limitation on meaning and language, is indissolubly tied to his acute consciousness of his humble origin. The issue of "origins" lies at the heart of Horace's political ambivalence which, in turn, underpins his polyvalent aesthetic stance. Despite Juvenal's cynical remark that "When Horace cried '*Rejoice!*' / His stomach was comfortably full,"[3] Horace tends to see his art as something aligned with poverty rather than riches. He appears almost obsessed with his mediocre subsistence. (We might share Juvenal's cynicism on the ground that Horace's "modest" house was actually a twenty-four-room mansion with three bathing pools, though this was indeed modest compared with the vast possessions of many of the senatorial class.) In the *Ars*, Horace had erected a sharp opposition between a business mentality and the frame of mind conducive to writing poetry: "do you think that when once this . . . anxiety about property has stained the mind, we can hope for the composition of poems?" (*AP*, 330–331). The same opposition informs the poems, not merely in the form of passing disgruntlement but as part of the worldview controlling them. Horace's views of poetry are ostensibly entirely practical in their motives and devoid of metaphysical, political, or religious implications. He is more concerned with the immediate labor behind poetry as a craft. But those broader concerns, deflected into the status of formal phenomena in Horace's verse, lurk underneath the guise of philosophical, political, and financial indifference.

Horace's equivocation toward Augustus is well known. In some odes, such as II.12, he disclaims any ability to sing of Caesar's exploits. This, says Horace with typical irony, would require "plain prose."[4] By the fifth ode of book IV (i.e., after being commissioned by Augustus to compose the *Carmen saeculare*), he seems to accept Caesar's rule as secure and prosperous. But underlying this chronological movement from equivocation to allegiance is a more subtle emotional development; more subtle because less overtly political, but political nonetheless. Horace's apparent recalcitrance from politics is couched in a quasi-religious and aesthetic language, decked with the ornaments of Roman mythology and ethics. But his devotion to the Muses and the gods is half-hearted: even where he self-corrects his earlier "illusions" (perhaps "inspired" by Augustus' renovation of religious pieties), as in *Odes*, I.34:

> I, who have never been
> A generous or keen
> Friend of the gods, must now confess
> Myself professor in pure foolishness . . .

it seems that his "devotion" to these external powers is channeled largely through his manipulation of them: "I am the Muses' priest" (*Odes*, III.1). Certain insights of Hegel on the Roman Empire cast an interesting light on Horace's situation here. In *The Philosophy of History* Hegel characterizes Roman religion as "an instrument in the power of the devotee; it is taken possession of by the individual, who seeks his private objects and interests; whereas the truly Divine possesses on the contrary a concrete power in itself."[5] Yet when Horace speaks of his verse as an immortal monument, this is not mere self-aggrandizement, boasting that somehow he alone will survive death. It is equally an assertion that life's most important and durable gifts are those unconstrained by immediate political circumstances or contingencies of religious and ethical practice. Hence the monument is as much political as aesthetic, affirming as an ultimate value the withdrawal from temporal affairs, a withdrawal that is enshrined in and defines subjectivity. This cherishing of the private over the public is a symptom of Horace's refusal to see the meaning of subjectivity as dispersed through the objective forms of Roman law and duty. In his *Phenomenology*, Hegel drew a famous analogy between the later Roman Empire and the modern bourgeois state. In these societies, individuality is abstract; valued only in terms of property and possessions, it has no real content. Hegel says that in this period, any true ethical spirit perishes in the condition of "right" or "law"; the "Unhappy Consciousness" is the "tragic fate of the certainty of self that aims to be absolute."[6] Horace inhabits a world where this kenosis or emptying of subjectivity has already begun. He himself laments the passing of earlier generations with hardier morals and a less decadent approach to life (*Odes*, III.6).

Horace's inconsistency is almost systematic. He pays lip service to the gods, the Muses, and the administrative exploits of Augustus Caesar. But it's the vacuum in subjectivity, as later noted by Hegel, which he longs to fill. Even the themes of conquest and government are assessed in the deflected form of their implications for subjectivity:

> Govern your appetites: thereby you'll rule more
> Than if you merged Libya with distant Gades . . .
> (*Odes*, II.2)

In the same poem Horace warns against greed which, "when indulged, grows like the savage dropsy." Moreover, conquest has its limitations: "the swift years . . . Old age and death . . . no one conquers" (*Odes*, II.14). Horace insists that death's lake will be crossed by both "Rulers of kingdoms" and "needy peasants" alike. And even piety will not avert this end. These apprehensions eventually ripen into a blatant questioning of the very notion of conquest:

> Why do we aim so high, when time must foil our
> Brave archery? Why hanker after countries
> Heated by foreign suns? What exile ever
> Fled his own mind?
> (*Odes*, II.16)

It's worth recalling here a point argued effectively by Perry Anderson: since the economy of the entire Roman world depended on the slave mode of production, systematized on a massive scale and involving a rupture between labor and the intellectual-political activities of free citizens, the empire was stagnant in technological terms and only through geographical conquest could it maintain itself. Anderson's point derives of course from Marx, who had noted that in the Roman Empire all productive work was vilified as slave labor: "the labor of the free was under a moral ban."[7] What incentives could slaves have to increase their efficiency by technological or economic advances? The only route for expansion was a "lateral" one of military conquest, which in turn yielded more wealth and more slave labor. As Anderson has it, "Classical civilization was . . . inherently *colonial* in character" (*PF*, 26–28). From this point of view, Horace's text can be read as questioning the very foundation of Roman civilization. Given his inclination to the "inward" in the midst of a brutal Roman world where inwardness, where the content of human subjectivity, had little significance, could we read Horace's attitudes as subversive? They certainly invert conventional Roman values and the Roman emphasis on public duty; it is only poetry, in Horace's eyes, which can conquer death (*Odes*, IV.8). And poetry is of its essence private; Horace at one stage mockingly writes a poem about being asked to compose a poem. He asserts his own scheme of values: simple living, a mind free from envy, and devotion to his Muses.

Ironically, although Horace is generally against the idea of private property, looking back as he does to an age where there was "Small private wealth, large communal property" (*Odes*, II.15), he is all for this principle in the realm of poetry, as he states in the *Ars*: "A subject in the public domain you will have the right to make your own, if you do not keep slavishly to the beaten track" [*publica materies privati iuris erit, si / non circa vilem patulumque moraberis orbem*] (*AP*, 131–132). Once again, Horace is concerned to redefine the connection between *publicus* and *privatus*. His insight here may go deeper than at first appears. His opposition to the principle of "private property" is not simply a reaction against the social imbalance of wealth or even the financial rat-race (a favorite point of commentators on Horace). The notion of "private property" is closely tied to the *nature* of the individual. Talking of the Roman legal system, Perry Anderson affirms that the "great, decisive accomplishment of the new Roman law was . . . its invention of the concept of 'absolute property'" (*PF*, 66). This had also been affirmed by Hegel, whose treatment of its implications for subjectivity is illuminating. Hegel is altogether cynical of the concept of private right. He argues that in the figure of the emperor, whose will was absolute, "isolated subjectivity . . . gained a perfectly unlimited realization." And this one, capricious, monstrous will presided over a bland equality of subjects: "Individuals were perfectly equal . . . and without any political right . . . Private Right developed and perfected this equality . . . the principle of abstract Subjectivity . . . now realizes itself as Personality in the recognition of Private Right." The point here is that, as Hegel goes on to say, "Private Right is . . . *ipso facto*, a nullity, an ignoring of the personality."[8]

For Hegel, the principle of private right is a symptom of the *necessary* collapse of the Roman republic: there is no object (spiritual or political) beyond the objects dictated by individual greed and caprice. We needn't assert that Horace was thinking in Hegelian terms in order to believe that he too was aware of private right as an index of moral and spiritual disintegration, of the absence of a genuine subjectivity measurable in human, rather than merely abstract legal, terms. And, for all the emphasis he places on the need for literature to satisfy an audience, his withdrawal into a reconstituted subjectivity encompasses his aesthetics. He tends to regard himself as a recluse, preferring to satisfy the poetic standards of a chosen few. He assumes the posture of *recusatio*, refusing to attempt any epic praise of imperial and public deeds (*CHLC*, V.I, 251). The inky cloak of scholarly elitism fits him with a conventional smugness: "I bar the gross crowd. Give me reverent silence. / I am the Muses' priest" (*Odes*, III.1). Horace's religion, of course, is poetry. This securing of a heaven of invention, a haven of privacy in the midst of a callously public world, this refilling of the substantive emptiness of "privacy," amounts to a redefinition of values, as well as of the essentially "human." This redefinition does carry a subversive potential.

But, in common with much deconstructive criticism, this withholding of political complicity is an isolated gesture, with no contextualizing framework of practice to render it politically meaningful or effective. What exactly is the "human" into which Horace retreats? To begin with, it entails in the *Ars* an essentialism whereby human nature is fixed: "nature forms us within from the start to every set of fortune" (*AP*, 108). This goes hand in hand with an abstract view of the determinants of social changes: "The years as they come bring many advantages with them and take as many away as they withdraw" (*AP*, 175–176). This is almost on a par with Derrida's attribution of the historical growth of various philosophical oppositions to one indifferent cause: "the movement of différance." Moreover, Horace seems to view "truth" and "beauty" as unproblematic concepts.

Again, Horace's reaction against the present is too often couched in praise of the past. The virtues he commends are unequivocally classical: which isn't intrinsically culpable except that these virtues are unashamedly associated with peace of mind and avoidance of hazard:

> auream quisquis mediocritatem
> diligit tutus . . .

> All who love safety make their prize
> The golden mean and hate extremes . . .
> (*Odes*, II.10)

Although, unlike the translation given above, Horace's Latin does not include the word "extreme," his lines imply an Aristotelian hypostatization of the concept "extreme": as with Aristotle, the mean is defined in negative terms, by what it is not. The "extreme" is treated as an entity in itself, held up as something to be avoided. This could be read as a concerted peripheralization of what is viewed as unconventional or threatening to the established order. But we should also recall that for Aristotle the "mean" was a moral *end* in itself. Horace's reduction of it to the status of a mere *means* toward attaining the privileged end of "safety" is even more conservative than Aristotle's formulation. Aristotle had at least qualified his definition of moral virtue, which consists "essentially in the observance of the mean *relative to us*" (my emphasis).[9]

Moreover, it is not just safety which Horace cherishes. All his "riches," the things he craves, such as good health, peace of mind, and poetry (*Odes*, I.31), derive from his lack of commitment even to non-commitment. These lines have a self-betraying twist:

As wealth grows, worry grows, and thirst for more wealth.
Splendid Maecenas (splendid yet still a knight),
Have I not done right in ducking low to keep
    My headpiece out of sight?

(Odes, III.16)

By "ducking low," by refusing to raise his head, Horace is referring to his shrinking from material ambition and greed. But he has ducked low in another sense: politically his head was indeed out of sight. His work makes radical gestures but they remain just that, gestures. Horace is often held up as a bold spokesman for the Roman republican ideals he saw crumbling all around him. While there can be no doubt of Horace's powerful poetic gifts of satire, subtlety, and concision, that is a perspective which mirrors the history of Horace criticism, which has made the *Ars* a classic, more than it does the actual narratives of the Augustan state.

Two such narratives occur in the writings of Tacitus and Suetonius. These surely tell us that no assessment of Horace's views can be undertaken without some political perspective as to the nature of Augustus' rule. Suetonius portrays Augustus as evolving from an earlier, ruthless and fickle character into a clement and benevolent ruler "assiduous in his administration of justice."[10] Suetonius emphasizes that the senate even insisted on Augustus' absolute authority. Ironically, Tacitus, who has invoked the censure of left-wing historians for his "quietist" expression of the worldview of the Roman senatorial class, offers a more cynical account. There was no opposition to imperial rule, says Tacitus, because "the boldest spirits had fallen in battle . . . while the remaining nobles . . . preferred the safety of the present to the dangerous past."[11] Would this be an apt description of Horace's mentality? Horace, as the son of a freedman, was hardly "noble." Nor, having fled the field at the battle of Philippi, was he one of the "boldest spirits" even before Octavian's rule was consolidated. Tacitus seemingly laments the passing of republican ideals, urging that in the new order "there was not a vestige left of the old sound morality" (*Tacitus*, 5–11). And yet, despite certain comments suggesting that "liberty" and "sovereignty" are incompatible (*Tacitus*, 678), Tacitus begins his *History* by saying that after "the conflict at Actium, . . . it became essential to peace, that all power should be centered in one man" (*Tacitus*, 419). Nonetheless, in his history of Agricola, Tacitus makes a British chieftain describe to his troops the Roman imperial enterprise as follows: "To robbery, slaughter, plunder, they give the lying name of empire; they make a solitude [wilderness] and call it peace" (*Tacitus*, 695).

That the principate was necessary to peace is a common enough view. It is accepted by Hegel,[12] and even Perry Anderson writes that the "Roman monarchy of Augustus . . . punctually arrived when its hour struck" (*PF*, 70). But our problem remains: if this view was genuinely accepted by Horace, why his equivocation? And why was his criticism so tempered? One solution would be to say, with R. M. Ogilvie, that in contrast with other renowned poets of his day, Horace lacked the social standing (something he was ever conscious of) to make authoritative pronouncements, and had no real prospect of a political career.[13] In support of this, we might adduce Cicero's statement that certain political offices are "reserved to men of ancient family or to men of wealth."[14] But Cicero, like Ovid and Propertius, took risks. What better evidence is there for this than Plutarch's description of Antony's soldiers cutting off Cicero's head and hands for his writing of the *Philippics*?[15] Or Ovid's banishment to a dreary outpost, never revoked? Moreover, Suetonius states that some of Augustus' decrees, such as his marriage laws, aroused open opposition. His views were often impugned openly in the senate, without retribution.[16] In the sphere of literature, "Augustus gave all possible encouragement to intellectuals." He was, however, chiefly interested in moral precepts in literature and "expressed contempt for both innovators and archaizers . . . and would attack them with great violence: especially his dear friend Maecenas."[17] How vulnerable, then, was Horace, that other "dear friend" of Maecenas? It's a favorite line of Horace commentators to say that his poems "avoid the appearance of systematic argument." In doing this, does Horace avoid systematic argument itself? Perhaps the baby went out with the bathwater – in all three of his bathing pools.

But let us not be unduly harsh. Many historians agree that, all said and done, the republic in its final phase was already rotten: individual self-aggrandizement had already replaced loyalty to the state. Hence we have the individual (rather than state-sanctioned) military exploits of Caesar and Crassus. The republic had been, in any case, only a nominal democracy, actual power residing with unbroken continuity in the aristocratic class. The imperial administration, moreover, kept intact the basic legal framework of the republic, especially its economic laws. The primary change was that the will of a monarch replaced that of an oligarchy. Both during and after the republic, the will of the citizen in practice counted for little. This is reflected in the prevailing philosophies of the time: Stoicism, Skepticism, and Epicureanism. It was Epicureanism more than Stoicism which claimed Horace's lifelong allegiance, a school of thought which was cynical of the gods and which discouraged social and political involvement. No doubt a poet in Horace's equivocal position found here a platform for his own non-involvement.

But again, Hegel's views here are illuminating. He suggests that the purpose of *all* of these philosophies was the same: to render the soul indifferent to the real world. They were all a "counsel of despair to a world which no longer possessed anything stable."[18] Marx says much the same thing: "the Epicurean, [and the] Stoic philosophy was the boon of its time; thus, when the universal sun has gone down, the moth seeks the lamplight of the private individual."[19] A common saying of the Epicurean sect was that "tyrants for all their violence could not destroy the internal happiness of the wise man."[20] Hence, although we can sympathize with Horace's position, we should bear in mind that his potentially subversive withdrawals into subjectivity, like his prescriptions in the *Ars poetica*, were not original but merely commonplaces of his day. His originality was exclusively on the level of form, and it is here that he merits undoubted praise. It seems that Augustus has been universally praised for bringing "order" to the Roman state. Within this scheme of thinking, Horace's text is indeed marked by the merits and limitations of ambivalence. But it took a thinker of Marx's historical acuity to assert blandly that the "order" of Rome "was worse than the worst disorder." The emperors had simply regularized the republican exploitation of the provinces, resulting eventually in "universal impoverishment" throughout the empire.[21] Perhaps we should give the last word to Engels:

Old Horace reminds me in places of Heine, who learned so much from him and who was also *au fond* quite as much a scoundrel *politice*. Imagine this honest man, who challenges the *vultus instantis tyranni* [the threatening face of a tyrant] and grovels before Augustus. Apart from this, the foul-mouthed old so and so is still very lovable.[22]

What greater, and more honest, tribute could Horace ask for?

Notes

1   Horace, *The Art of Poetry*, trans. Burton Raffel (New York, 1974), p. 62. This volume contains a verse translation by Raffel and a prose translation by James Hynd. For the most part I have cited Hynd's translation except where Raffel's somewhat unorthodox (but effective) rendering emphatically registers points that the present chapter is attempting to evince. Hereafter cited as *AP*, using line numbers.

2   For a valuable account of these aspects of Horace, see Steele Commager, *The Odes of Horace: A Critical Study* (Bloomington and London: Indiana University Press, 1967), pp. 42–49.

3   Satire VII, in Juvenal, *The Sixteen Satires* (London: Penguin, 1974), p. 165.

4   *The Odes of Horace*, trans. James Michic (Harmondsworth: Penguin, 1976). Hereafter cited as *Odes*.

5   G. W. F. Hegel, *The Philosophy of History* (New York: Dover, 1956), p. 295.

6   G. W. F. Hegel, *Phenomenology of Spirit*, trans. A. V. Miller (Oxford: Oxford University Press, 1977), p. 455.

7   "Origin of Family, Private Property and State," in *Marx and Engels: Selected Works* (London: Lawrence and Wishart, 1968), p. 560.

8   Hegel, *Philosophy of History*, pp. 315–316, 320.

9   Aristotle, *NE*, II.vi.15.

10 Suetonius, *The Twelve Caesars*, trans. Robert Graves (Harmondsworth: Penguin, 1989), p. 73.

11 *The Complete Works of Tacitus*, ed. M. Hadas, trans. A. J. Church and W. J. Brodribb (New York: Random House, 1942), p. 4. Hereafter cited as *Tacitus*.

12 Hegel, *Philosophy of History*, p. 313.

13 R. M. Ogilvie, *Roman Literature and Society* (London: Penguin, 1980), pp. 142, 144.

14 Cicero, *On the Commonwealth*, trans. G. H. Sabine and S. B. Smith (New York: Bobbs-Merrill, 1929), p. 135.

15 Plutarch, *Fall of the Roman Republic* (Harmondsworth: Penguin, 1968), p. 319.

16 Suetonius, *The Twelve Caesars*, pp. 73, 85.

17 Ibid., pp. 101–102.

18 Hegel, *Philosophy of History*, p. 318.

19 Karl Marx and Friedrich Engels, *On Literature and Art* (Moscow: Progress Publishers, 1978), pp. 207–208.

20 Ogilvie, *Roman Literature*, p. 81.

21 *Marx and Engels: Selected Works*, p. 559.

22 Engels, letter to Marx, December 21, 1866, in Marx and Engels, *On Literature and Art*, p. 210.

CHAPTER 6

LONGINUS (FIRST CENTURY AD)

After the period of the early principate, there were two broad intellectual currents that emerged during the first four centuries. The first of these was known as the Second Sophistic (27 BC–AD 410), named after a new generation of Sophists and rhetoricians who took for their model the classical language and style of Attic Greece. The second was the philosophy of Neo-Platonism, whose prime exponent Plotinus will be considered in the next chapter. The major rhetorical treatise of this period was written in Greek: entitled *peri hupsous* or *On the Sublime*, it is conventionally attributed to "Longinus," and dates from the first or second century AD. It was the most influential rhetorical text through much of the period of the Second Sophistic, and has subsequently exerted a pronounced influence on literary criticism since the seventeenth century, somewhat against the grain of the classical heritage derived from Aristotle and Horace. It has fascinated critics of the modern period on account of its treatment of the sublime as a quality of the soul or spirit rather than as a matter of mere technique. In the later classical period and the Middle Ages, the treatise appeared to be little known. It was initially published during the Renaissance by Robortelli in 1554. It was subsequently translated into Latin in 1572 and then into English by John Hall in 1652. In modern times the concept of the sublime owed its resurgence to a translation in 1674 by Nicolas Boileau, the most important figure of French neoclassicism. The sublime became an important element in the broad Romantic reaction in Europe against neoclassicism as well as in the newly rising domain of aesthetics in the work of thinkers such as Immanuel Kant.

There is only one surviving manuscript of *On the Sublime*, with a third of the text missing, and it is not known for certain who the author was. The manuscript bears the name "Dionysius Longinus," which led ancient scholars to ascribe the work to either Dionysius of Halicarnassus or a third-century rhetorician, Cassius Longinus. Modern scholars have been more inclined to date the manuscript to the first or second century. The author must certainly have been a rhetorician and his essay is personal in tone, addressed to Postumius Terentianus, his friend and one of his Roman students.

At the beginning of his text, Longinus proposes to write a systematic treatise on the sublime, whereby he will both define his subject and relay the means of understanding it.[1] He offers an initial definition, stating that the sublime consists "in a consummate excellence and distinction of language, and . . . this alone gave to the greatest poets and historians their pre-eminence . . . For the effect of genius is not to persuade the audience but rather to transport them out of themselves." Longinus adds that "what inspires wonder casts a spell upon us and is always superior to what is merely convincing and pleasing" (I.3–4). The difference between such inspiration and conviction, as he explains, relates to power and control: we can control our reasoning but the sublime exerts a power which we cannot resist (I.4). Longinus distinguishes dramatically between other compositional skills and the sublime. Inventive skill and appropriate use of facts, for example, are expressed through an entire composition. But the sublime, he says, appears like a bolt of lightning, scattering everything before it and revealing the power of the speaker "at a single stroke." Longinus appeals to experience to confirm the truth of these claims (I.4).

Like Horace before him, Longinus now enters the long-raging debate as to whether art comes from innate genius or from conscious application of methodology and rules. His answer echoes the compromise offered by Horace. Longinus argues that nature is indeed the prime cause of all production but that the operations of genius cannot be wholly random and unsystematic, and need the "good judgment" supplied by the rules of art (II.2–3). At this point two pages of the manuscript are missing; when the text resumes, we find Longinus giving examples, taken from various poets, of the faults which an artist can fall into when reaching for grandeur. The first fault is "tumidity" when the artist or poet aims too high and, instead of achieving ecstasy, merely lapses into "folly," producing effects which are overblown or bombastic. Tumidity "comes of trying to outdo the sublime." Longinus identifies the opposite fault, "puerility," as the most ignoble of faults. He defines it as "the academic attitude, where over-elaboration ends in frigid failure" (III.3–4). When writers try too hard to please or to be exquisite, says Longinus, they fall into affectation. A third fault is what the first-century rhetorician Theodorus called "Parenthyrson."[2] Longinus explains that this term refers to "emotion misplaced and pointless where none is needed or unrestrained where restraint is required." Emotion which is not warranted by the subject is "purely subjective" and hence is not shared by the audience (III.5).

After proceeding to offer several examples of frigidity, Longinus reaches a generalization which sounds strangely familiar to us: "all these improprieties in literature," he urges, "are weeds sprung from the same seed, namely that passion for novel ideas which is the prevalent craze of the present day" (IV.5). His real point, however, is that virtues and vices spring from the same sources: it is the very pursuit of beauty, sublimity, agreeable phrasing, and exaggeration – in short, the very pursuit of an elevated style – which can result in the faults earlier described (IV.5).

How can the poet avoid these faults? The first thing he needs is a "clear knowledge and appreciation" of what is truly sublime. Yet such knowledge does not come easily; like all literary judgment, it must be the fruit of ripe experience (IV.6). Longinus' subsequent definition of the sublime indeed appeals to experience in a manner later echoed by Arnold, Leavis, and others. The true sublime, Longinus tells us, "elevates us" so that "uplifted with a sense of proud possession, we are filled with joyful pride, as if we had ourselves produced the very thing we heard." Such genuine sublimity is to be distinguished from a mere "outward show of grandeur" which turns out to be "empty bombast" (VII.1–3). The true sublime will produce a lasting and repeated effect on "a man of sense, well-versed in literature"; this effect will be irresistible and the memory of it will be "stubborn and indelible." As with Arnold and Leavis, Longinus' view of greatness in literature appears to be an *affective* one: we judge it by its emotional effects on the reader or listener (the Latin *affectus* as a noun means "disposition" or "state," and as a verb, "affected by"). Also anticipating these much later critics, he posits an ideal listener as a man of culture and sensibility. Longinus broadens his definition to say that the "truly beautiful and sublime . . . pleases all people at all times" (VII.4). By this, he appears to mean all "qualified" people of various periods and tastes: when there is enduring consensus among a community of cultured listeners, this is evidence of the truly sublime nature of a literary work. In a broad sense, Longinus also anticipates various consensual theories ranging from those of Edmund Burke to reader-response critics.

In an important passage, Longinus cites five "genuine sources" of the sublime: (1) the command of "full-blooded" or robust ideas (sometimes expressed by translators as "grandeur of thought"); (2) the inspiration of "vehement emotion"; (3) the proper construction of figures – both figures of thought and figures of speech; (4) nobility of phrase, which includes diction and the use of metaphor; and (5) the general effect of dignity and elevation. This general effect, Longinus tells us, embraces the previous four elements. Longinus intends, so he claims, to consider these elements systematically but he sometimes digresses. To begin with, he argues, as against a previous writer on the sublime, Cecilius, that sublimity is not identical with emotion or always dependent upon it. Certain emotions can be mean or base and many sublime passages exhibit no emotion (VIII.1–2). Returning now to the first source of the sublime, the command of solid or weighty ideas, Longinus refers to this faculty as "natural genius," affirming that it is a gift of nature rather than something acquired; this facility, he says, plays a greater part in sublimity than the other sources. His examples of sublimity here are intended to express what might be viewed as his fundamental position: citing Homer,[3] he reflects that "a great style is the natural outcome of weighty thoughts, and sublime sayings naturally fall to men of spirit" (IX.1–3). At this point, six further pages of the manuscript are missing; when the text resumes, Longinus cites two passages from the *Iliad*. One of these attains sublimity, he says, because it "magnifies the powers of heaven [the gods]" and the other falls short because it is "irreligious" and shows "no sense of what is fitting" (IX.5–7). Those passages in Homer are sublime "which represent the divine nature in its true attributes, pure, majestic, and unique" (IX.8). Interestingly, Longinus also cites early passages from the Old Testament ("Let there be light") as expressing "a worthy conception of divine power" (IX.9). In these passages Longinus seems to find sublimity in the expression of profound and appropriate religious sentiment which displays a sense of decorum and which justly marks the relation of divine and human. Great writers, then, achieve sublimity through their grandeur of thought, by expressing a vision of the universe that is morally and theologically elevated. It is not clear, however, how these qualities of sublimity could fall under the five "sources" initially listed by Longinus; one might conjecture that they could answer to either the demand for "weighty" ideas or "the general effect of dignity."

In a famous passage on Homer, Longinus draws some further inferences: Homer shows us, he claims, that "as genius ebbs, it is the love of romance that characterizes old age." The *Iliad*, composed in the heyday of Homer's genius, is alive with dramatic action; it is marked by "consistent sublimity" that resides in the "sustained energy" of the poem which is "brimful of images drawn from real life." In contrast, as is characteristic of old age, narrative predominates in the *Odyssey*, which is a mere "epilogue" to the *Iliad*. In the later poem, the "grandeur remains without the intensity." In the ebbing tide of his genius, Homer "wanders in the incredible regions of romance," and indeed "reality is worsted by romance" in the *Odyssey* (IX.12–14). Longinus here appears to add two further dimensions to his conception of the sublime: firstly, it is associated with dramatic action rather than narrative; and secondly, it is firmly rooted in reality as opposed to romance. Another inference made by Longinus is that "with the decline of their emotional power great writers and poets give way to character-study." Homer's character sketches in the *Odyssey*, says Longinus, follow the style of the "comedy of character" (IX.15). Again, we might ask whether these attributes of sublimity are related to the five "sources" of the sublime. It may be that dramatic action is associated by Longinus with "vehement emotion" and that realism is the medium for the expression of "solid" or "robust" ideas: clearly, for Longinus, the fanciful nature of romance represents a departure from such solidity.

Longinus adds a further factor to his notion of sublimity: the power of combining certain elements appropriately into an organic whole (X.1). Citing examples from Sappho and Homer, he suggests that these writers have organized "all the main points by order of merit . . . , allowing nothing affected or undignified or pedantic to intervene" so as to produce the effect of sublimity by means of an "ordered and . . . coherent structure" (X.7). Closely connected with, but distinct from, this power of combination, says Longinus, is the device of "amplification": whenever the subject matter admits of fresh starts and halting places, phrases can be multiplied with increasing force, using exaggeration, emphasis on arguments or events, or by careful assemblage of facts or feelings (XI.1–2). However, Longinus departs from previous definitions which equate amplification with sublimity. Sublimity, he suggests, "lies in elevation" and is found "in a single idea," whereas amplification lies in quantity and redundance. Amplification consists "in accumulating all the aspects and topics inherent in the subject and thus strengthening the argument by dwelling upon it. Therein it differs from proof, which demonstrates the required point" (XII.1–3).[4] In illustration of this difference between sublimity and amplification, Longinus cites the rhetorical styles of Demosthenes and Cicero: the former has a sublime power of rhetoric which "scatters everything before him" like a flash of lightning while the latter, using amplification, is like "a widespread conflagration" devouring all around it (XII.4). What also emerges from Longinus' comments here is that, while sublimity and amplification are mutually distinct, they both differ from formal argument in that they employ alternative means of persuasion: sublimity strikes the hearer and possesses him whereas amplification ponders over an argument, bringing it out in various guises.

There is another road which leads to sublimity, remarks Longinus, and it is Plato who lights up this path for us: the path of imitation of great historians and poets of the past. Just as the priestess of Apollo is inspired by the divine power of this god, so too a writer can be inspired by the "natural genius of those old writers" (XIII.2–3). Plato himself borrowed profusely from Homer. And such borrowing, Longinus reassures, is not theft but "rather like taking an impression from fine characters . . . moulded figures"

(XIII.4). Moreover, Longinus sees the process of influence not as passive and static but as an active endeavor of the contemporary writer to vie with the ancient poets. Such was Plato's relationship with Homer: one of striving "to contest the prize." Longinus adds that "even to be worsted by our forerunners is not without glory" (XIII.4). He (and the Hellenistic tradition behind his insights here) also anticipates Arnold's "touchstone" theory of tradition whereby we measure contemporary works against a set of acknowledged classics: when we are attempting to achieve sublimity, urges Longinus, we should ask ourselves how Homer or Plato or Demosthenes would have pursued this task. We must also ask ourselves how such great writers would have responded to our own work: "Great indeed is the ordeal, if we propose such a jury and audience as this to listen to our own utterances." Longinus adds that we should also bear in mind the judgment of posterity; if we refuse to say anything which "exceeds the comprehension" of our own time, our conceptions will be "blind" and "half-formed" (XIV.1–3). In these important passages, Longinus articulates a conservative concept of tradition which proved to have lasting influence: not only Arnold, but also Eliot, Leavis, and earlier writers such as Pope (and, before Longinus, the Alexandrian scholars) formulated similar prescriptions whereby a contemporary writer's greatness could be measured only in relation to standards set by an acknowledged canon of great writers. Nonetheless, Longinus' own formulation allows for creative strife between past and present writers, acknowledging that present authors can in principle achieve sublimity. In this, he anticipates more liberal attitudes toward tradition such as that enshrined in Harold Bloom's notion of the "anxiety of influence" whereby an author "misreads" previous writers so as to stake out for himself an area of originality.

If imitation is one path to the sublime, another path is through the highway of imagination. In delineating this path, Longinus anticipates many discussions of this topic by the Romantics. He observes that "Weight, grandeur, and energy" (i.e., the basic components of the sublime) are largely produced by the use of images. He states the prevailing use of the term "Imagination": it is applied to "passages where, inspired by strong emotion, you seem to see what you describe and bring it vividly before the eyes of your audience" (XV.1–2). However, whereas the Romantics tended to see imagination primarily or exclusively as a characteristic of poetry, Longinus distinguishes between the use of imagination in poetry and in prose or oratory. In both of these, the aim is to excite the audience's emotions and to present things vividly. What distinguishes them is that the deployment of imagination in poetry "shows a romantic exaggeration, far exceeding the limits of credibility, whereas the most perfect effect of imagination in oratory is always one of reality and truth" (XV.2, 8). In contrast with many modern critical theories which see no sharp division between poetry and prose, Longinus is skeptical of the attempts of "modern" orators in his day to transgress these boundaries: certain orators, he observes, make their speech poetical, deviating "into all sorts of impossibilities." The appropriate use of imagination in rhetoric, says Longinus, "is to introduce a great deal of vigour and emotion into one's speeches, but when combined with argumentative treatment it not only convinces the audience, it positively masters them" (XV.8–9). In such cases, he explains, the imaginative conceptions of the speaker far surpass "mere persuasion": "our attention is drawn from the reasoning to the enthralling effect of the imagination, and the technique is concealed in a halo of brilliance" (XV.11–12). Hence, while reason is by no means dispensable in argument, it is clear that imagination is seen as a higher power.

So far, Longinus has analyzed three sources of sublimity: natural genius, imitation, and imagination. He now moves to a further source, the use of figures. The first example he offers here is the use of an oath or what Longinus terms an "apostrophe" in a speech by Demosthenes. This renowned speaker advocated a policy of war for the Athenians to resist domination by Philip of Macedon, father of Alexander the Great: "You were not wrong, men of Athens, in undertaking that struggle for the freedom of Greece . . . no, by those who bore the brunt at Marathon." In using this oath, asserts Longinus, Demosthenes transforms his argument "into a passage of transcendent sublimity and emotion." The use of this figure allows the speaker "to carry the audience away with him" and to convince the defeated Athenians that they should no longer view the defeat at Chaeronea as a disaster (XVI.2–3).

While once again, in the example given above, Longinus shows how an argument can be rendered more powerful and persuasive by figurative rather than purely rational means, he cautions his reader that there is a general suspicion toward the "unconscionable use" of figures. A judge, for example, or a king, might feel offended or manipulated by the figurative strategies of a skilled speaker, in which case he will become hostile to the actual reasoning of the speech. Hence Longinus recommends that a figure is most effective when it is unnoticed: it can be appropriately obscured by sublimity and a powerful effect on the emotions. Demosthenes' use of the oath is cited as an example of this covert procedure: the figure is concealed "by its very brilliance." What is sublime and emotionally moving, urges Longinus, is closer to our hearts and always strikes us before we even realize that figures are being used. Longinus cites a number of other important figures. One of these is the figure of rhetorical "question and answer, which involves the audience emotionally" (XVIII.1–2). Another figure which conveys apparently genuine and vehement emotion is inversion of the order of words, phrases, or sentences. Such inversion mimics the actual use of language by people in situations of fear, worry, or anger. The best prose writers, says Longinus, use inversions to "imitate nature and achieve the same effect. For art is only perfect when it looks like nature and Nature succeeds only by concealing art about her person" (XXII.1). Such inversion, which alters the natural sequence of words and phrases, gives the effect of improvisation, allowing the audience to share the excitement of the situation (XXII.3–4).

Other figures cited by Longinus are accumulation, variation, and climax: these figures range over changes of case, tense, person, number, and gender. Such changes can produce a "sublime and emotional effect." What all of these figures help us to see, according to Longinus, is that emotion is an important element in the sublime. What is emphasized in Longinus' treatment of them is the ability of language to take control suddenly – and irrationally – over the emotions, the power of language when used in unusual combinations, when it is forced to deviate from a conventionally anticipated structure. It is small wonder that Longinus falls outside of the classical tradition and provided so much inspiration for Romantic views of art. Indeed, his view that a powerful passage cannot be paraphrased without loss has become part of the thinking of the whole modern era about poetry, from the Romantics through the New Criticism. Moreover, in appealing to numerous examples, Longinus illustrates the rhetorical practice of close textual reading; such close attention to the text as a verbal structure was not the monopoly of modern formalists and New Critics but had been part of the repertoire of rhetoric for centuries.

Longinus now moves to other aspects of what he had earlier cited as the fourth source of the sublime, nobility of diction, thought, and metaphor. He is in no doubt that all orators and historians aim at the use of appropriate diction as "their supreme object." It is fine diction which gives the style "grandeur, beauty, a classical flavour . . . and endues the facts as it were with a living voice." Again, he warns that majestic diction is to be reserved for stately and important situations (XXX.1–2).[5] Metaphors are especially useful in treating commonplace subjects and descriptions: figurative writing has a natural grandeur and metaphors contribute to sublimity (XXXII.5–6).

Longinus raises a long-debated question: "Which is better in poetry and in prose, grandeur with a few flaws or correct composition of mediocre quality, yet entirely sound and impeccable?" A related question, he remarks, is whether literary value should be accorded to the largest number of merits or to the merits that are intrinsically great (XXXIII.1–2). Predictably, Longinus' own position is that great excellence , even if it is not uniformly sustained, should always be valued more highly: perfect precision risks being trivial; mediocre natures take no risks; genius and divine inspiration will not easily fall under any rule (XXXIII.2–5). Hypereides, explains Longinus, has more merits than Demosthenes; nonetheless his speeches "lack grandeur; they are dispassionate, born of sober sense, and do not trouble the peace of the audience." Demosthenes, in contrast, "seems to dumbfound the world's orators with his thunder and lightning. You could sooner open your eyes to the descent of a thunderbolt than face unwinking his repeated outbursts of emotion" (XXXIV.4). Perhaps here it becomes clearer than anywhere else in Longinus' text how, faced with an audience immediately embroiled in a given political situation, a speaker could not attain maximum persuasive power merely by deploying reason and an abstractly convincing argument or even by producing a speech which was technically perfect. All of this could be mobilized into persuasive power only if the audience could be "disturbed," only if its emotions were first kindled as if by a bolt of lightning and then fanned by the technical virtues of the speech.

Longinus' next passage effectively presents the metaphysical assumptions underlying his entire text. It is a passage which clearly anticipates the aesthetics of Kant and many of the Romantics. "Nature," he says, has distinguished us over other creatures, and has

> from the first breathed into our hearts an unconquerable passion for whatever is great and more divine than ourselves. Thus within the scope of human enterprise there lie such powers of contemplation and thought that even the whole universe cannot satisfy them, but our ideas often pass beyond the limits that enring us. Look at life from all sides and see how in all things the extraordinary, the great, the beautiful stand supreme, and you will soon realize the object of our creation . . . The little fire we kindle for ourselves keeps clear and steady, yet we do not therefore regard it with more amazement than the fires of Heaven, which are often darkened, or think it more wonderful than the craters of Etna in eruption, hurling up rocks and whole hills from their depths and sometimes shooting forth rivers of that pure Titanic fire . . . what is useful and indeed necessary is cheap enough; it is always the unusual which wins our wonder. (XXXV.2–5)

Hence Longinus' stress on emotion as a vital element of the sublime does not rest on a simple appeal to the heart over abstract reasoning but is an intrinsic expression of his view of the purpose of humankind. This purpose, far from according with a classical recognition of our finitude and proper place in the cosmic scheme, is to strive beyond our own human nature toward the divine; and this striving is accomplished on the wings of "unconquerable passion." Longinus subsequently says that sublimity lifts men "near the mighty mind of God" (XXXVI.1). All of these dispositions anticipate the Romantics; also like the Romantics, Longinus superordinates the "wonderful" and sublime over that which is merely "useful" and "necessary." This seemingly simple opposition and prioritization is an index of a broad shift away from a classical world-view: whereas Aristotle actually prescribed necessity and probability, universality and typicality, as the bases for poetry's engagement with the world, Longinus advocates precisely what deviates from such universality. It is an aesthetic premised not on what is central to human experience but precisely on what escapes such centrality, on what stands as rare at the pinnacle of experience and is expressible only by genius. When we appeal to emotion through the achievement of sublimity in writing, we appeal to that which relates us primally to our highest purpose in life, the recognition through nature of the limitless potential of our own being.

Indeed, Longinus refers to Homer, Demosthenes, and Plato as "demi-gods" who, redeeming their other faults through "a single touch of sublimity," are justly revered by posterity. The more compromising conclusion at which Longinus arrives is that since technical correctness is due to art and the height of excellence is achieved by genius, "it is proper that art should always assist Nature. Their co-operation may thus result in perfection" (XXXVI.3–6).

Longinus now turns to the final source of sublimity, "the arrangement of the words themselves in a certain order" (XXXIX.1). Melody, he says, is a natural instrument of persuasion and pleasure; it is also a means of achieving grandeur and emotion. Composition, he proceeds, is "a kind of melody in words – words which are part of man's nature and reach not his ears only but his very soul" such that the speaker's actual emotion is brought into the hearts of his hearers (XXXIX.1–3). Citing as an example two lines of a speech by Demosthenes, Longinus explains in detail how the effect of sublimity is produced as much by the melody – resting on dactyls, the "noblest of rhythms" – as by the thought (XXXIX.4).

More fundamental than anything else in the production of sublimity is the composition or arrangement of the various elements of a passage into a unified, single system. Longinus advocates an artistic organicism, using an analogy which has subsequently served countless writers: just as with the members of the human body, so it is with the elements of sublimity: "None of the members has any value by itself apart from the others, yet one with another they all constitute a perfect organism" (XL.1). Some phrases may actually be vulgar or commonplace; but in their appropriate place they may contribute to the overall sublimity of a passage (XL.3). Longinus makes a distinction here between "extreme conciseness" which "cripples the sense" and "true brevity" which "goes straight to the point." On the other hand, prolix passages are "lifeless" (XLII.1–2). Trivial or commonplace words and phrases can also debase a passage, says Longinus (XLIII.1–2): "the proper course is to suit the words to the dignity of the subject and thus imitate Nature, the artist that created man" (XLIII.5). These prescriptions for art were not undermined until the advent of realism in the latter nineteenth century.

The final surviving part of the manuscript is perhaps the most revealing of Longinus' world view and how his notions of literature grew out of his clearly negative assessment of his own era. Many scholars have cautioned that the purpose of Longinus' entire manuscript is simply to produce a practical treatise on style, and that his use of the word "sublime" refers to no more than an elevated or lofty style. While it is true that Longinus' treatment of sublimity is far more general than that of modern critics who viewed it as a distinct aesthetic category, that treatment is nonetheless grounded in circumstances exhibiting certain important parallels with those behind many Romantic aesthetics.

As with many of the preceding sections, Longinus addresses this last section to Terentianus, relating to him a "problem" which characterizes their era: "in this age of ours we find natures that are supremely persuasive and suited for public life, shrewd and versatile and especially rich in literary charm, yet really sublime and transcendent natures are no longer, or only very rarely, now produced. Such a world-wide dearth of literature besets our times" (XLIV.1–2). The problem seems to be that while there are some writers who possess technical competence, truly great or sublime literature is no longer being produced. Longinus purports to offer two explanations of this phenomenon, the first by an acquaintance of his, a philosopher; the second, his own. The philosopher challenges what he calls the "hackneyed" explanation that true genius flourishes only in a democracy. Rather, he seems to suggest, democracy in his time has degenerated into an "equitable slavery" in which "we seem to be schooled from childhood." We never drink, says the philosopher, from "the fairest and most fertile source of literature, which is freedom." Consequently, he argues, we are prone to servile ways and flattery. Just as prison confines and stunts the body, so all slavery, however equitable, "might well be described as a cage for the human soul, a common prison." The philosopher remarks that, while in such circumstances slaves can be granted some faculties, "no slave ever becomes an orator" (XLIV.3–6) for he does not have the habit of speaking freely.

Longinus appears to dispute such an explanation. The real source of mediocrity in literary composition he locates in the "love of money, that insatiable sickness from which we all now suffer, and the love of pleasure," both of which "enslave us." After wealth is thus made a "god," there follow in its wake other vices: extravagance, swagger, conceit, luxury, insolence, disorder, and shamelessness. The result of this process is that "men no longer then look upwards . . . their greatness of soul wastes away from inanition and is no longer their ideal, since they value that part of them which is mortal and consumes away, and neglect the development of their immortal souls." Given that "we have sold our souls for profit at any price," Longinus asks, can we expect that "there is left a single free and unbribed judge of the things that are great and last to all eternity?" Finally, in a passage whose import extends readily to our own world of mass consumerism, he states: "what spends the spirit of the present generation is the apathy in which all but a few of us pass our lives, only exerting ourselves . . . for the sake of getting praise or pleasure out of it, never from the honourable and admirable motive of doing good to the world" (XLIV.6–11). Some scholars, such as G. E. M. de Ste. Croix, have found Longinus' reply "bitterly disappointing" on the grounds that it almost ignores the philosopher's substantial comments and that it merely rehearses commonplaces of Stoic thought, attributing the prevailing frivolity and general ethical malaise to greed and the pursuit of pleasure. Ste. Croix also disputes the conventional scholarly assumption that, in talking of a degeneration from democracy to slavery, the philosopher is referring to the transformation of the Roman republic into an empire ruled by one man. He points out that, typically of Greek works of this period, Longinus' text is almost exclusively concerned with Greek literature, and reveals almost no interest in Roman letters. As such, it makes no sense to claim that the institution of the principate somehow debilitated Greek literature, which was hardly affected by changes in the Roman form of government. A far better case can be made, argues Ste. Croix, "for saying that Greek literature, apart from Homer and the early poets, did indeed rise and fall with *demokratia* – in the original and proper sense!" In other words, the sentiment about literary decline originated with the Greeks, who realized that Greek literature had flourished most under democracy.[6]

However we view it, the worldview expressed in Longinus' account is quite clear in its system of values: the soul over the body, the immortal, permanent, and selfless over the perishable, transient, and self-interested. The world view is Stoic and Platonic – even Neo-Platonic – but also somewhat Christian in its emphasis. In an argument which is now perhaps controverted by many scholars, O. B. Hardison fascinatingly suggested that Longinus' text, if its author was indeed a pupil of Plotinus as some scholars have claimed, "illustrates the late classical Neo-platonic aesthetic which also appears to have encouraged late classical Asianism." What is interesting about this speculation is Hardison's correlative insight that this Asianism was the closest approximation to a theory of art for art's sake during this period, and that it took not only literary form but also a "flowering of epideictic oratory."[7] This tendency toward artistic autonomy was stimulated by rhetorical rather than poetic theory.

Whether we accept or dispute Hardison's insight, the parallels between Longinus' worldview and those of the Romantics are clear. Moreover, if we view Longinus' influence as moving in a broadly "aesthetic" direction toward notions of relative artistic autonomy, we can see that the debate between classicism and Romanticism was played out not only from the eighteenth through the twentieth centuries but also in the Hellenistic world itself and in the early Roman Empire (as in the Stoic, moral, and educational tenor of Vergil's epic as opposed to the more aesthetic and individualistic flavor of Ovid's poems). Indeed, Longinus' explanation of the dearth of sublimity in his world is remarkably close to Shelley's condemnation of the modern capitalist world where the principle of utility and profit is opposed to the selfless principles of poetry. We find here, inasmuch as we can judge from an incomplete manuscript, the true motives for Longinus' need to explain the sublime, and his stress on emotion as the avenue to the fulfillment of our higher nature whereas mere reason, as in Shelley's view, is constrained within the realm of pragmatic interests.

In the light of the context sketched above, Longinus' preoccupation with the sublime might be seen as a call for spiritual reorientation, a movement away from rationality and merely technical competence, itself a reflex of materialist and pragmatic thinking, toward acknowledgment of a profounder and more authentic strain in human nature that, through its exercise of emotion and imagination, sees itself not in isolation but as part of a vaster and divine scheme. This call has been repeated endlessly in numerous guises in various literary periods. The themes raised by Longinus, and much of his mode of treating them, persist into our own day, in the realms of literature, politics, law, and the media: the idea that poetry or indeed prose can emotionally transport, rather than merely persuade, a listener; the idea of organic unity and totality; the nature of imitation; the connection between reason and imagination, reason and emotion, beauty and utility, art and genius, art and nature; and, most importantly, a recognition of the power of language – founded on grandeur of thought and the skillful use of figures – to attain sublimity, thereby transforming our perception of the world.

Notes

1 *Aristotle: Poetics; Longinus: On the Sublime; Demetrius: On Style*, trans. Stephen Halliwell, W. Hamilton Fyfe, Doreen C. Innes, and W. Rhys Roberts (Cambridge, MA and London: Harvard University Press/Heinemann, 1996), I.1. Hereafter citations are given in the text.
2 This refers to the inappropriate use of the "thyrsus." The thyrsus was a staff carried by the Greek god Dionysus and his devotees, made of a reed often bearing a spear point topped by a pine cone. "Parenthyrson" thus refers metaphorically to an affectation of Dionysiac frenzy.
3 The example is taken from book XI of the *Odyssey* where Ajax in Hades appears to Odysseus and refuses to speak, still bitter over the awarding of the dead Achilles' arms to Odysseus, an action which prompted Ajax's suicide. Longinus suggests that this silence is "more sublime than any speech."
4 Two further pages of the manuscript are missing here.
5 Four pages of the manuscript are missing here; when the text resumes, Longinus is talking of metaphor.
6 G. E. M. de Ste. Croix, *The Class Struggle in the Ancient Greek World* (Ithaca and New York: Cornell University Press, 1981), pp. 324–325.
7 "Introduction," in *MLC*, 10.

CHAPTER 7

NEO-PLATONISM

The philosophy of Neo-Platonism was predominant during the third and fourth centuries of the Christian era. It derived some inspiration from the doctrines of Philo Judaeus and was developed systematically by Plotinus, the Syrian philosopher Porphyry, and Proclus. Like the rhetoricians of the Second Sophistic, the Neo-Platonists held the classical authors in the highest esteem; so high, in fact, that they attempted to reconcile discrepancies between various classical authors such as Plato and Aristotle, as well as between philosophy and poetry; they attempted in particular to reconcile Plato's theories of poetry with the poetic practice of Homer and other poets. Their fundamental method of achieving this was through allegorical and symbolic modes of interpretation, opening the way for Christian medieval conceptions of allegory and discourse which viewed the physical world as inherently symbolic of a higher world. It was a Latin writer, Macrobius, who transmitted these essentially Greek developments in the art of interpretation to the Middle Ages (*CHLC*, V.I, 298). From a literary-critical perspective, the great achievement of the Neo-Platonists was to provide a metaphysical framework for the previous Stoic attempts to defend Homer and other poets from the charges initially leveled by Plato and his followers. In this sense, the Neo-Platonists reformulated Plato's metaphysical framework so as to rehabilitate and accommodate the arts. The three major exponents to be examined here are Plotinus, Macrobius, and Boethius.

Plotinus (AD 204/5–270)

The third-century philosopher Plotinus has been variously referred to by scholars as the greatest metaphysician of antiquity, the founder of Neo-Platonism, and the most profound single influence on Christian thought. The philosophy of Neo-Platonism takes from Plato the idea that ultimate reality subsists in another world, a transcendent and spiritual realm, from which the physical world takes its existence and meaning. Nonetheless, Plato's system was considerably modified, if not thoroughly transformed, in its Neo-Platonic guises. Plotinus' philosophy exerted an enormous influence, in terms of its theological and mystical components, extending from Augustine, Macrobius, Boethius, and medieval Christian Platonism through Italian Renaissance humanism, the seventeenth-century Cambridge Platonists and the Romantic poets to modern thinkers and critics such as William James, Henri Bergson, A. N. Whitehead, and Harold Bloom.

Plotinus' life was recorded primarily by his disciple, the Greek philosopher Porphyry, who also edited his works. Plotinus was born (according to the Greek Sophist Eunapius) in Lycopolis in upper Egypt. Despite his Roman name, his cultural background appears to have been Greek and he wrote in Greek. He studied philosophy in Alexandria under the Platonist Ammonius Saccas; he was also acquainted with the works of the Jewish philosopher Philo and was influenced not only by Plato and Aristotle but also by Stoicism, Gnosticism, and the Neo-Pythagoreans, as well as by Eastern mystery cults. His interest in Persian and Indian philosophy prompted him to join the emperor Gordian's expedition against the Persians, an endeavor that was aborted when the emperor was murdered. In 244 Plotinus established a school of philosophy in Rome where he unsuccessfully attempted to persuade the emperor Gallienus to found a city in Campania based on the principles of Plato's *Republic*. After Plotinus' death, his teaching was continued by his disciples Porphyry and Iamblichus; its last great expression as an independent philosophy was in the work of Proclus (411–485), after which it was integrated into Christianity, in the works of the Church Fathers and in Christian mysticism.[1]

Plotinus' philosophical essays or treatises grew directly out of his teaching. At his death, he left fifty-four such treatises, which were compiled under the title *Enneads* by Porphyry. The Greek word *ennea* means "nine," and Porphyry arranged the texts as six *Enneads,* i.e., six sets each containing nine treatises. Plotinus thought of his work as essentially a commentary and exposition of Plato's ideas, and it was thus unwittingly that he gave rise to a new school or movement of Neo-Platonism. While he basically accepts Plato's bifurcation of the world into a higher intelligible realm of eternal Forms and a lower sensible world of time and change, what distinguishes his scheme from Plato's is his elaboration of a more refined hierarchy of levels of reality, as well as his explanation of the connection between these various levels. His scheme can be represented as follows:

The One
Embodies: Unity/Truth/Origin/Good
Is Source of Essence and Existence

Eternal	*Act/Utterance*	
	Divine Mind: Presides Over	
	Intellectual Realm	
"There"	*Act/Utterance*	
	Inner	Soul
	All-Soul/World-Soul/Great Soul	Humans
	Outer (Nature-Principle)	Body
"Here"	World of Matter, Sense, Time	

According to Plotinus, all the various phases of existence emanate from the divinity; the goal of all things is ultimately to return to the divine. Reality is basically bifurcated into an eternal spiritual and intellectual realm (which comprehends the One, the Intellectual Realm, and the All-Soul), and a physical realm of matter, sense, space, and time. Human beings belong to both of these worlds: their souls belong to the higher realm of All-Soul, while their bodies occupy the spatial and temporal world of matter, sense, and extension. The task of philosophy is to facilitate the soul's transcendence of the physical realm, to rise to intellectual intuition and ultimately to attain an ecstatic and mystical union with the One.

In Plotinus' system, the divinity itself is a hierarchical triad expressed in three principles or "hypostases": the One, the Divine Mind or Intellect, and the All-Soul. The One can also be termed the Absolute, the Good, or the Father. From this One emanates the Divine Mind, which presides over the realm of Divine Thought or Intellection (this intellectual realm is equivalent to Plato's eternal Ideas or Forms). This Divine Intelligence contains all particular intelligences, and the intellectual forms in this realm are the archetypes of all that exists in the lower, sensible sphere. Moreover, the Divine Intelligence is an expression of the One which is unknowable by mere intellect or reason. From the Divine Mind emanates the All-Soul, or Soul of all things. The All-Soul has three phases: the intellective soul, which contemplates the Divine Thought of the intellectual realm; the Reasoning Soul, which generates the sensible universe on the model of the archetypes in the intellectual realm; and the Unreasoning Soul, which is the principle of animal life. Hence the All-Soul forms and orders the physical world.

It can be seen that each of these phases or levels subsists in two relations, oriented both to that which is higher than itself and to what lies lower. Only the first phase, that of the One, is unrelated to any preceding phase, since it is the absolute cause of the others. Unlike Plato, Plotinus does not view these relationships as imitation; rather, each phase is an "emanation" from the preceding phase, retaining the latter's archetypal imprint as a goal to which it must return or conform on its path toward its ultimate reunion with the One.

The Soul, then, has an intermediary function, on the one hand gazing back at its own source in the Divine Mind and, on the other, generating all life below it. Plotinus describes the Soul as "the author of all living things, . . . whatever is nourished by earth and sea, all the creatures of the air, the divine stars in heaven; it is the maker of the sun; itself formed and ordered this vast heaven and conducts all its rhythmic motion." As such, the Soul is "far more honorable than anything bodily" (*Enneads*, V.i.2). He explains the connection between this Great Soul or All-Soul and the Divine Mind as follows: "Soul is but an image and an utterance of Divine Mind, the stream of life sent forth by It to the production of further being . . . Sprung from Divine Mind, Soul is intellective too; for its perfecting it must look to that Divine Mind which may be thought of as a father watching over his child." On its "upper level," says Plotinus, Soul is united with Divine Mind and "participant in Its nature, but on the lower level in contact with the realm beneath" (*Enneads*, V.i.3). Hence, Soul is created by an "utterance" of Divine Mind and the two levels are characterized as in the relation of father and child.

Plotinus explains this intermediary function of Soul in another way, in terms of intellect and sense. If we look at the world of sense, he says, at its "vastness and beauty and . . . order," we can ascend to the Archetype of this world, the more authentic sphere of the intellectual realm, where thoughts are invested with "perfect knowledge." Presiding over this sphere is the Divine Mind containing "unapproachable wisdom" (*Enneads*, V.i.4). The Soul, says Plotinus, has an "inner phase, intent upon Divine Mind, and an outer, facing to the external." By its gazing on the Divine Mind (its inner phase), it retains a likeness to its source; by its external phase, it engages in "action and reproduction . . . so that all its creations bear traces of the Divine Intellection." In other words, all the creations of the soul are molded – as emanations and images – upon archetypes in the Intellectual sphere (*Enneads*, V.iii.5).

The realm of Divine Mind, like that of Soul, is eternal. Plotinus describes it as "pure being in eternal actuality; nowhere is there any future, for every then is a now; nor is there any past, for nothing There has ever ceased to be" (*Enneads*, V.i.4). This intellectual realm is the equivalent of Plato's eternal Forms. Yet Plotinus argues that, since this realm is one of multiplicity, since it contains multiple archetypes and thought-essences, it must have its origin in something which is One, something which is an absolute Unity (*Enneads*, V.i.5). Hence Divine Mind, the intellectual realm, is itself a radiation of the Supreme One: just as Soul is "an act and utterance of Divine Mind," so the Divine Mind "is act and utterance of the One" (*Enneads*, V.i.6).

What, then, is this One to which Plotinus accords absolute sovereignty? Its attributes might be categorized under the headings of unity and presence, truth and goodness. Its most immediate attribute is absolute unity: it is the "All-Transcendent, utterly void of multiplicity," and independent of all else; other entities acquire unity in proportion to their nearness to it. It is the absolute beginning (*Enneads*, V.iii.15–16). It is the "power from which Life and Intelligence proceed," and it is "the source of essence and existence" (*Enneads*, V.v.10–11). It cannot be divided, nor is it bound to space and time (*Enneads*, V.i.11). It is infinite, having no definition and no limit; it transcends all being (*Enneads*, V.v.6). It does not change, and it has no constituent parts, no pattern, and no shape (*Enneads*, V.v.10–11). What Plotinus says about the "presence" of the One illustrates perhaps more than any other philosophy the significance that Derrida will later attach to this term. The One is "omnipresent; at the same time, It is not present, not being circumscribed by anything; yet, as utterly unattached, not inhibited from presence at any point." Indeed, the presence of the One is "an instantaneous presence everywhere, nothing containing, nothing left void, everything therefore fully held by Him" (*Enneads*, V.v.9). Effectively, then, the One is an absolute and immediate presence which contains and comprehends all other presences; He is the archetypal presence in relation to which all other presence (of other entities) is defined.

In terms of knowing and truth, Plotinus states that the "entire Intellectual Order may be figured as a kind of light with the One in repose at its summit as its King . . . But the One, as transcending intellect, transcends knowing. The One is, in truth, beyond all statement" (*Enneads*, V.iii.12–13). Hence the One stands above all discursive knowledge, beyond the horizons of reason; it can only be grasped partially by those who are "divinely possessed" (*Enneads*, V.iii.14). Moreover, the object contemplated by the One is not external: "It sees Itself," and in its self-knowing it comprehends all things (*Enneads*, V.iii.8), being the "King of Truth" (*Enneads*, V.v.3).

As well as embodying absolute unity, presence, and truth, the One equally embodies absolute goodness. It is the primary goodness toward which the being of all things in the universe is oriented; things rise above other things in proportion as they possess greater goodness, and in the same proportion they possess more authentic being (*Enneads*, V.v.9). The One embodies a "Good absolute and unique, the Good . . . unalloyed, all-transcending, Cause of all" (*Enneads*, V.v.13).

How do human beings apprehend the One? We must, says Plotinus, "put aside the system of sense with desires and impulses" (*Enneads*, V.iii.9), in order to adjust ourselves for a vision of the One, in a posture of "perfect surrender," enabling us to gleam "in the light of that Presence" (*Enneads*, V.v.8). Hence Plotinus' system is expressed in terms that might lend themselves in a very direct way to later deconstructive strategies: the One is explicitly a "transcendental signified" which authorizes the entire system: it is the absolute origin and goal of human life; it embodies absolute truth and goodness; its presence is not only ubiquitous but all-containing, preemptively defining all human endeavor and history within the closure of its absolute epistemological and moral authority. This closure is effected by sharp oppositions between infinite and finite, eternal and temporal, intellect and sense, soul and body. Moreover, each phase in the hierarchy of reality is created by speech, by an utterance. In a real sense, Plotinus' thought might well be viewed as evincing and elaborating characteristics of Plato's vision, unwittingly preparing that vision for its later crucial integration into much Christian theology.

Plotinus' views of art and beauty must be understood in the context of his philosophical and theological system as outlined above. Plotinus treats the concept of beauty in two of the *Enneads*, the sixth treatise of the first *Ennead* and the eighth section of the fifth *Ennead*, entitled "On the Intellectual Beauty." The more comprehensive latter essay might be considered first here; it locates the nature and function of art, beauty, imitation, and knowledge within a profoundly elaborated philosophical and theological vision. This influential treatise effectively sets the stage for centuries of Christian medieval thinking about beauty and its connections with God and the entire realm of being; it does so, in part, by overturning Plato's views on art and imitation; or, rather, by pursuing the logic of Plato's own theory of Forms toward a more self-consistent account of the connection between various levels of reality, an account comprehensive enough to legitimately accommodate, rather than exclude, the value of art.

The first point that Plotinus establishes in this essay is that beauty is ideal: in other words, it belongs essentially to the realm of ideas rather than to the realm of sensible, physical objects. He gives the example of two stones, one which has been wrought by the artist's hands into a statue, and the other untouched by art. The former, says Plotinus, is beautiful not as stone (i.e., not as matter) but "in virtue of the Form or Idea introduced by the art." And this form exists in the artist's mind before it enters the stone. In the designer's mind, in fact, the beauty exists in a far higher form, since it is "concentrated in unity," than it does when it is diffused by entering into matter. Art creates things by an idea it already has of the beautiful object. Plotinus calls this idea the "Reason-Principle" (*Enneads*, V.viii.1). And this idea is more beautiful in its pure form than when it is mingled with matter. Indeed, it is only as an idea that beauty can enter the mind. Hence, beauty is not in the concrete object but in "soul or mind" (*Enneads*, V.viii.2).

Plotinus now explains the origin of beauty, with reference to his cosmological hierarchy. The Nature, he says, which creates beautiful things must itself be produced by a "far earlier beauty." The "Nature-Principle" (which lies below the level of the All-Soul) contains "an Ideal archetype of the beauty that is found in material forms." But this archetype itself has its source in a still more beautiful archetype in Soul. And this archetype, in turn, has its source in the Intellectual-Principle, in the realm of pure intellectual Forms. Plotinus' term for this intellectual realm is "There." He designates the sensible world as "Here" (*Enneads*, V.viii.3). Plotinus sees the realm of "There" as inhabited by "gods," a term he uses somewhat metaphorically to designate the divine order, or certain exalted beings who minister to the supreme God.[2] These "gods" or inhabitants of the intellectual realm are beautiful not on account of their corporeal forms but in virtue of their intellect. In that realm, which is a realm of authentic, eternal being and not of process and becoming, everything is clear and transparent: "every being is lucid to every other . . . And each of them contains all within itself, and at the same time sees all in every other, so that everywhere there is all . . . While some one manner of being is dominant in each, all are mirrored in every other." And all the beings of that world are engaged in "contemplation of an infinite self" (*Enneads*, V.viii.4). Plotinus sees the many gods of the divine realm as being "distinct in powers but all one god in virtue of that one divine power of many facets . . . this is the one God who is all the gods" (*Enneads*, V.viii.9). The wisdom of that realm is "not a wisdom built up by reasonings but complete from the beginning, . . . a wisdom primal, unborrowed, not something added to the Being, but its very essence" (*Enneads*, V.viii.4). Hence, the world of "There" or the intellectual realm is a world of complete unity, where all the beings merge into an infinite divine identity. Moreover, the system of wisdom is also a unity, complete, self-enclosed, and acting as the measure of all subsequent wisdom. Anticipating Aquinas, Plotinus suggests that knowledge or wisdom is not something extraneous to existence; it is part of the very essence of being. He goes so far as to define reality as wisdom: "Being is Real in virtue of its origin in wisdom." Knowledge in that realm, then, is not discursive; it is not expressed in language; it exists "There not as inscription but as authentic existence." Like Plato, he regards the Ideas or Forms as actual existents or beings (*Enneads*, V.viii.5). Like the ancient Egyptian hieroglyphs, each manifestation of knowledge and wisdom in the intellectual realm "is a distinct image, an object in itself, an immediate unity, not an aggregate of discursive reasoning." Plotinus calls this "wisdom in unity" (*Enneads*, V.viii.6).

In the world of "Here," the sensible world, things are very different. Everything is "partial," including our knowledge, which exists as "a mass of theorems and an accumulation of propositions" (*Enneads*, V.viii.4). The kind of wisdom we possess is only an image of the original "wisdom in unity," an image that reproduces the original in discursive form, in language, using reasoning (*Enneads*, V.viii.6). The one exception to this limitation lies in art: the artist goes back to "that wisdom in Nature which is embodied in himself; and this is not a wisdom built up of theorems but one totality, not a wisdom consisting of manifold detail co-ordinated into a unity but rather a unity working out into detail" (*Enneads*, V.viii.5). Hence the artist, according to Plotinus, seems to have a more direct intuitive access into that earlier wisdom than does the philosopher or the scientist. His vision begins as an immediate unity that extends to comprehend greater and greater detail whereas the philosopher's knowledge is cumulative, starting with details or parts and then arriving at a totality.

Indeed, according to Plotinus, the entire universe was created in this "artistic" fashion: it could not have been thought out in detail and built up step by step. Rather, its existence and nature "come to it from beyond itself . . . all things must exist in something else." In other words, the entire universe is a copy or image of a preexisting world: "the entire aggregate of existence springs from the divine world, in greater beauty" (*Enneads*, V.viii.7). The beauty of the divine world is greater because it exists in a pure form, unmingled with matter. According to this account of creation, everything that could possibly exist in our sensible world already existed as an archetype in the realm of Forms: "From the beginning to end," says Plotinus, "all is gripped by the Forms of the Intellectual Realm" (*Enneads*, V.viii.7). Even matter is an Idea, though it is the lowest of the ideas. Hence, the universe in its entirety is essentially ideal: its reality consists not in its material aspects but in the archetypal ideas underlying all its material forms, and the crucial elements in its creation were "Being and Idea" (*Enneads*, V.viii.7).

Earthly beauty, then, derives from the perfect beauty of the divine world. This conception of beauty, which we will find again in Aquinas and medieval thinkers, is at first difficult for us to grasp since in our world we are accustomed to perceiving beauty through our senses. In Plotinus' system, beauty is perceived not at all by the senses but by the intellect and this is one of the bases of his divergence from Plato's views of art and poetry. He actually cites an observation from Plato's *Timaeus* that the Creator approves his work, once he has created the universe. For Plotinus, beauty plays an important role in drawing human souls toward the truth of the higher realm. The Creator's intention, he says, was "to make us feel the lovable beauty of the archetype and of the Divine Idea" (*Enneads*, V.viii.8). Hence, whereas Plato sees poetry as appealing to man's lower nature, his desires and passions, Plotinus sees in art a means of access to the divine world, based on art's reproduction of the beauty of that world, a beauty discernible not to the senses and passions but to the intellect.

A further crucial way in which Plotinus diverges from Plato is his insistence on a logic of continuity between the two realms, intellectual and sensible: Plato's denigration of the sensible world does not make sense, according to Plotinus, since this world derives from and is modeled after the archetypes of the higher realm. Where Plato equates "imitation" with ontological and epistemological inferiority, Plotinus stresses the continuity with an original that imitation embodies: "to admire a representation," he urges, "is to admire the original upon which it was made." Moreover, there is no intrinsic defect in the sensible world, which is itself beautiful: "if the divine did not exist, the transcendently beautiful, in a beauty beyond all thought, what could be lovelier than the things we see? Certainly no reproach can rightly be brought against this world save only that it is not That" (*Enneads*, V.viii.8). Hence, the sensible world appears defective only in comparison with the intellectual; but, by the same token, it perpetuates and expresses the beauty of that higher world according to its own capacity and appropriate position in that hierarchy. Plotinus says that this "second Cosmos [i.e., our human world] at every point copies the archetype: it has life and being in copy . . . In its character of image it holds, too, that divine perpetuity" (*Enneads*, V.viii.12). These statements are crucial: "life and being in copy": Plotinus ascribes an independent function and value to imitation, to copy, to image. Where Plato treated the images offered by art as merely adjectival upon their originals, Plotinus sees the image itself as valuable, as a further level of reality that perpetuates the divine ideas or originals whose trace it bears. Plato would see a painting of a horse merely as a relation, a relation to an actual horse. Plotinus sees a value and function in the painting itself, in the image, which may in some respects be superior to the natural object. As Plotinus states, Plato "fails to see that as long as the Supreme is radiant there can be no failing of its sequel" (*Enneads*, V.viii.12). Hence, image and copy are modes of exalting and continuing the divine ideas, rather than imperfect betrayals and distortions of them. Here we see the roots of a medieval Christian notion of beauty that ascribes beauty to the entirety of God's creation. Moreover, in opposition to Plato's notion of art as an imitation of nature, which is itself an imitation of the eternal Forms, Plotinus holds that art does not engage in a bare reproduction of things in nature but goes "back to the Reason-Principles from which Nature itself derives . . . they are holders of beauty and add where nature is lacking" (*Enneads*, V.viii.1). Hence, where Plato thought of art as imitating what was already an imitation (of eternal Forms), Plotinus sees art as directly imitating the Forms themselves, and with a directness inaccessible to the discursive reasoning of philosophy.

Plotinus accords priority to the notion of beauty in yet another way. Just as he defines wisdom as part of the essence of being, so he includes beauty within that essence: "Beauty without Being could not be, nor Being voided of Beauty: abandoned of Beauty, Being loses something of its essence. Being is desirable because it is identical with Beauty" (*Enneads*, V.viii.9). Hence beauty, like wisdom, is not an attribute that is externally added to existence: things have being *only* to the extent that they possess beauty and wisdom. This perception of the core or essence of being as intrinsically laden with predicates such as beauty and wisdom will dominate medieval thinking: the creation, being the handiwork of God, is intrinsically beautiful and is an intrinsic expression of His wisdom. Indeed, for Plotinus, "the final object of all seeing," or the ultimate purpose of our contemplation, is "the entire beauty upon all things" (*Enneads*, V.viii.10). Again, "beauty" here is a far richer term than it is in our world: discerned by the intellect, it comprehends the order, proportion, and perfection of the world on a number of levels, including those of knowledge and goodness, which might be said to harbor aesthetic dimensions.

Plotinus ends his treatise with what is perhaps one of the most beautiful and insightful passages ever composed by a philosopher. The perception of beauty is not a passive act, of gazing upon a beautiful object that is external to the spectator. If our vision of beauty is merely partial and sensual, says Plotinus, "the immediate impression is alone taken into account" and we remain passive observers. However, if our souls are "penetrated by this beauty," we cannot remain mere gazers, mere spectators: "one must bring the vision within and see no longer in that mode of separation but as we know ourselves" (*Enneads*, V.viii.10). For example, if we seek a vision of God, we must find that vision within ourselves. Plotinus offers an account of mystical union with God, an account that shares much with, and indeed influenced, subsequent Christian and Islamic mysticism. If we submit ourselves to the vision of God, we will lose our own self, and be unable to see our own image; possessed by God, we will see our own image "lifted to a better beauty"; progressing further, we will "sink into a perfect self-identity," forming "a multiple unity with the God silently present" (*Enneads*, V.viii.11). Hence the first stage of this ascent to union with God is separation, a state in which we are aware of self; but if we turn away from sense and desire, we become "one in the Divine": instead of remaining in the mode of separation, of mere spectator or seer, we ourselves become "the seen," the object of our own vision or self-knowledge. Hence, truly to know beauty is to *become* it: we must put behind us reliance on sense or sight, which "deals with the external." There can be no vision of beauty, says Plotinus, "unless in the sense of identification with the object . . . And this identification amounts to a self-knowing, a self-consciousness." We are "most completely aware of ourselves when we are most completely identified with the object of our knowledge" (*Enneads*, V.viii.11). In these passages, Plotinus anticipates not only numerous forms of mysticism, both Eastern and Western, but also the philosophies of such thinkers as Kant and Hegel who regard all consciousness as self-consciousness. For Plotinus, knowledge – of beauty or anything else – is a form of interaction, a mode of unity rather than separation, a manner of internalizing the object and being transformed by it, a process of mutual adaptation of self and object, losing the one in the other, in a merged identity.

Plotinus equates the Greek gods Uranus, Cronus, and Zeus respectively with the One, the Intellectual-Principle, and the All-Soul. Cronus, in this mythological explanation, holds a mid-position, standing between "a greater Father" (Uranus) and "an inferior son" (Zeus). Interesting here is Plotinus' observation that the "father" or the One "is too lofty to be thought of under the name of Beauty," hence it is the "second God" or Cronus who "remains the primally beautiful" (*Enneads*, V.viii.13). In other words, the primordial beauty belongs in Plotinus' system not to the One but to the intellectual realm. Plotinus says that we "ourselves possess beauty when we are true to our own being . . . our self-knowledge . . . is our beauty" (*Enneads*, V.viii.13). Truth to our own being would reside in acknowledging our purpose to return to the divine, to unity with the absolute Unity, and in laying aside the multifold temptations of the world of sense. This helps further explain Plotinus' view of knowledge as identification with our object: we know ourselves through the object, the latter being the form of our self-knowledge, and in such self-knowing we do not merely perceive beauty externally but become it, making it our very being. Where Plato distanced art and poetry from knowledge, Plotinus sees an internal connection between knowledge and beauty as predicates of being, whereby each of these shapes the other; hence beauty acquires a heightened importance which in turn underlies the significance of art.

In the essay called "Beauty" in the first *Ennead*, which exerted considerable influence on artists during the Renaissance, Plotinus approaches the concept of beauty in similar terms but from a slightly different perspective, that of the soul which seeks to apprehend true beauty. He acknowledges that, in our ordinary lives, beauty addresses itself chiefly to the senses, to sight and hearing; there is also a beauty, he says, in the noble conduct of life and the pursuits of the intellect, and in "all that derives from the Soul" (*Enneads*, I.vi.1). He affirms that there is a single principle underlying these various forms of beauty, a principle remembered by the soul from its previous, unbodily, existence. "The soul," he says, "includes a faculty peculiarly addressed to Beauty," a faculty that enables it to recognize beauty with certainty in the light of the soul's own earlier affiliation with the highest being (*Enneads*, I.vi.2). As in the other treatise, Plotinus maintains that all earthly beauty derives from the ideal Forms. What is interesting is his additional explanation of beauty as the formation of unity from multiplicity, a view that was profoundly influential in the medieval era. All shapelessness of

137

matter, he suggests, that has not been patterned and structured by the ideal Forms on the basis of reason is ugly in virtue of its "isolation from the Divine Thought." But where the ideal Form has operated, it has grouped and coordinated "a diversity of parts" into a unity: "it has rallied confusion into co-operation; it has made the sum one harmonious coherence; for the Idea is a unity and what it moulds must come to unity as far as multiplicity may." And it is on this unity that "Beauty enthrones itself" (*Enneads*, I.vi.2). Hence, not only is beauty intrinsically affiliated to order and unity, but also unity itself is a characteristic of the divine, of the highest realm of the hierarchy; the lower one descends in that hierarchy, the more existence or being spans out into multiplicity. Hence for Plotinus, as for many medieval thinkers who followed in his path, the ascent to God, to goodness, truth, and beauty, was effectively an escape from the bondage of worldly multiplicity and a return to the unity whence one came. Hence the "principle" underlying all beauty is a principle "whose labor is to dominate matter and bring pattern into being" (*Enneads*, I.vi.3). It is a principle of both order and unity.

The rest of Plotinus' essay is devoted to the means whereby the soul can rise to the perception of true beauty. He reminds us that there are "earlier and loftier beauties" than those perceived in the world of sense, but only the "soul sees and proclaims them." Indeed, only the soul can apprehend the beauty of noble conduct, virtue, and learning (*Enneads*, I.vi.4). But for the soul to attain a vision of the highest beauty, it must renounce the body, all material pursuits and desires, and live within its "veritable self." To attain to its authentic self, it must remove all "internal discord" and dissolve its "alien nature" as formed by commerce with the material world (*Enneads*, I.vi.5). The soul on this upward path is obliged to "renounce kingdoms and command over earth and ocean and sky" (*Enneads*, I.vi.7). When the soul is thus cleansed, it is comprised of "all Idea and Reason . . . Intellection and all that proceeds from Intellection are the soul's beauty." Indeed, in becoming a good and beautiful thing, the soul becomes like God, "for from the Divine comes all its beauty and the rest of its share in Existence. We may even say that Beauty *is* the Authentic Existence" (*Enneads*, I.vi.6). As in the other essay, Plotinus equates beauty with real being and explains that soul derives its beauty from the Divine Mind; in turn, the soul is "the author of the beauty found in the world of sense" (*Enneads*, I.vi.6).

To ascend to the beauty whence it came, the soul must withdraw inward, into itself, foregoing the mode of earthly sensual vision, and recognizing that earthly beauties are "copies, vestiges, shadows." The soul's journey, says Plotinus, is to the fatherland: "The Fatherland is There whence we have come, and There is the Father" (*Enneads*, I.vi.8). To undertake this journey, the soul must waken in itself its own power of vision, perfecting itself until it achieves an "inner unity," true to its "essential nature." At this point, says Plotinus, "you are now become very vision." In other words, the entire soul has become nothing but vision, losing itself in what it seeks, and acquiring its authentic self in God. Just as in the other treatise Plotinus urged that subject and object, knower and known, should become one, so here he suggests that the soul must itself become of the same nature as the object of its vision: "never did eye see the sun unless it had first become sunlike, and never can the soul have vision of the First Beauty unless itself be beautiful" (*Enneads*, I.vi.9). And the final object of vision, which may equally be called beauty, goodness, or truth, is of course God, the journey to whom must be conducted in isolation from all else: "each in the solitude of himself shall behold that solitary-dwelling Existence, the Apart, the Unmingled, the Pure, That from which all things depend, towards Which all look, the Source of Life, of Intellection and of Being" (*Enneads*, I.vi.7). Hence, in Plotinus' system, God circumscribes the entire journey of human life at every level: as beginning and end, as identity of truth, goodness, and beauty, and as the very constitution of being or existence by these three predicates. This conception of beauty, far removed from ours, was an integral part of the order and unity of the universe, and of the relation of finite creatures to the Divine.

It is clear that Plotinus' rehabilitation of poetry and the arts is enabled by his intricate reformulation of both Plato's metaphysics and his aesthetics. His followers continued this metaphysical and critical enterprise. Porphyry reinterpreted the *Odyssey*'s description of the cave of the nymphs on the island of Ithaca in an allegorical manner that defied any symbolic one-to-one interpretation. Donald Russell remarks that this "tolerance of polysemy" was "unusual" among classical critics, and was typical of the Neo-Platonic worldview which is dominated by the notion that "everything stands for something else, or indeed for several different things, in the various stages and levels of the hierarchy of the universe" (*CHLC*, V.I, 325). We might qualify Russell's valuable insight by noting that the notion of polysemy was to some extent inherent in the doctrines of the Sophists and the Skeptics, against the relativistic tendencies of which some of Plato's views achieved definition. What is also interesting is that allegory appears to arise, both in the Stoic and Neo-Platonic traditions, essentially as an effort to loosen the bonds between a word and its meaning, to formulate a larger framework of interpretation within which the word can mean other things; this effort is emphatically an effort to make a word mean something else; in this sense, polysemy might be seen as intrinsic to allegory. The reconciliation of poetry with philosophy, the explanation of internal inconsistencies within a text and between various classical texts, appeared to demand such a semantic loosening of conventional verbal affiliations and patterns. Hence, the fifth-century Neo-Platonist Proclus effectively reinterprets Plato's own account of poetry using Plato's own texts, arguing that poetry can serve the highest function, such as facilitating the soul's union with the divine, through enabling knowledge, to the function of imitation (where Plato had reduced it to this lowest function).

Macrobius (b. ca. 360)

Another influential Neo-Platonic metaphysical vision and perspective toward literature is contained in the work of Macrobius. Born around 360, he was the author of two texts that proved to be widely influential in the Middle Ages, the *Saturnalia* (ca. 395) and *Commentary on the Dream of Scipio* (ca. 400). Unlike his Christian contemporary St. Augustine, he belongs to a secular tradition devoted to the exposition of pagan texts. The *Saturnalia*, written in the form of a dialogue, discusses various aspects of liberal education appropriate for youth. Vergil is treated not merely as a poet but as the fundamental educational resource, an authority in all aspects of learning. This view of Vergil both characterized the Roman world in Macrobius' time and underlay medieval conceptions of Vergil's "omniscience." The text reaffirms certain classical literary-critical positions: that art imitates nature, that poets should be versed in the traditions of literature in relation to which they seek originality, that literature should both please and instruct.

The *Commentary on the Dream of Scipio* came to be regarded for many centuries as an authoritative account of the significance of dreams. Much later, Freud was rightly to remark that ancient cultures attached various kinds of serious significance to dreams whereas modern science had relegated them to the realm of superstition. Macrobius' *Commentary* takes as its starting point Cicero's work *De re publica* (the *Republic*), which, like Plato's text of the same title, was devoted to the art of government. The last book of this political and philosophical treatise narrates a dream of Scipio Africanus the Younger, a Roman general, in which he is visited by his grandfather Scipio Africanus the Elder, the famous general who saved Rome from defeat at the hands of the Carthaginian leader Hannibal in the Second Punic War. There are several interesting features of Macrobius' text. While ostensibly analyzing Scipio's dream, it engages far broader issues and implications. Its explanation of Neo-Platonic doctrines was influential through the Middle Ages, in particular the doctrine that reality is above and beyond the physical realm; it examines the nature of truth in such a scheme; and it considers the connections between literary and philosophical language, between figurative or allegorical uses of language and their role in providing an avenue to the truths of the higher realm; finally, it provides a systematic account of the meaning of dreams.

The central motivation of Macrobius' text is a question which is still controversial in the twenty-first century: is philosophy justified in employing fiction and figurative language? Noting that Plato's *Republic* and Cicero's *Republic* had been criticized for using such language, Macrobius wishes to investigate the "reason for including such a fiction and dream in books dealing with governmental problems."[3] He attempts to distinguish between justified and unjustified uses of fiction in philosophy. Fables, he suggests, can serve two purposes: "either to gratify the ear or to encourage the reader to good works." The former kind, which merely amuse, must be avoided in philosophy (*CDS*, I.ii.6–8). The second kind, which draws the reader's attention to certain virtues, can be divided into two types. In the first of these, as in *Aesop's Fables*, both the setting and the plot of the story are fictitious; the second type, however, which Macrobius calls a "fabulous narrative," "rests on a solid foundation of truth, which is treated in a fictitious style." As examples of this kind of story, Macrobius cites accounts of sacred rites, of the ancestry and deeds of the gods, and mystical conceptions. Even this second type, however, which is based on truth, admits of two divisions, since "there is more than one way of telling the truth." If the plot of the story involves matters which are "base and unworthy of divinities," this is a type of story that philosophers should reject. The only type of story acceptable for use in philosophy is one which presents "a decent and dignified conception of holy truths, with respectable events and characters, . . . presented beneath a modest veil of allegory" (*CDS*, I.ii.9–11).

A further reason for using fictions is that "a frank, open exposition of herself is distasteful to Nature" whose "sacred rites are veiled in mysterious representations so that . . . [o]nly eminent men of superior intelligence gain a revelation of her truths" (*CDS*, I.ii.17–18). Yet even the "fabulous narratives," warns Macrobius, are not always serviceable for philosophy. For example, when philosophers speak about "the Supreme God and Mind, they shun the use of fabulous narratives . . . It is a sacrilege for fables to approach this sphere." Macrobius explains that while fables may legitimately be used by philosophers to talk about the soul or about gods in general, they cannot be used to explain the highest notions such as primal Mind or Intellect or the original Forms of things. In fact, when philosophers do address these notions, they "resort to similes and analogies," since it is impossible for the human mind to grasp such notions (CDS, I.ii.13–16).

Before analyzing the text of Scipio's dream, Macrobius provides some general comments on dreams. Like the second-century Greek writer Artemidorus, Macrobius divides dreams into five types: enigmatic, prophetic, oracular, nightmare, and apparition. The last two of these, he notes, have no prophetic significance. The other three furnish us with the power of divination (CDS, I.iii.2–3). In an oracular dream, a parent, pious or revered man, or priest clearly reveals what will or will not transpire, and what action to take or to avoid. We call a dream a prophetic vision if it actually comes true. An enigmatic dream is one that conceals the true meaning and requires interpretation for its understanding. There are five varieties of the enigmatic dream: personal, alien, social, public, and universal.

Scipio's dream, says Macrobius, is oracular since the two men who appeared to him revealed his future. It is prophetic since Scipio saw the regions of his abode after death and his future condition. It is enigmatic because the truths were revealed to him in words whose profound meaning was hidden, and in fact it contains all five varieties of the enigmatic dream. Scipio's dream in Cicero's text is a remarkable document and is worth looking at in some detail, not only to appreciate Macrobius' analysis of it but also for the light it sheds on medieval views of the universe. It is certainly not a scientific analysis and its explanation of cosmology is not original; it is derived, in its various parts, from Pythagoras, Plato, Aristotle, and the Stoic philosophers. Yet it offers a neat summary of a cosmology that was influential for many centuries. The passage in Cicero's text, which occurs in the format of a dialogue with Scipio as the main speaker, begins with the elder Scipio Africanus (who had defeated Hannibal) appearing to his grandson Scipio, who is taken to heaven and looks down on earth and the other planets. Africanus points out to Scipio the city of Carthage which he (the younger Scipio) is destined to destroy. But he also predicts that the government of Rome will be in a state of anarchy and that the entire country will turn to Scipio on account of his integrity, talent, and wisdom. It will be Scipio's duty to "restore order in the commonwealth."[4] Africanus explains that people who preserve or defend their country are reserved a "special place" in heaven where they enjoy "an eternal life of happiness" (DRP, VI.xiii).

Scipio's father, Paulus, now comes to him and explains that he cannot yet leave his body and remain in paradise. Human beings, he states, have been given souls made out of the "eternal fires which you call stars and planets," each in its own orbit and animated by divine intelligence. It is destined that men's souls must remain imprisoned within their bodies. Only God, says Paulus, can free human souls from their bodies (DRP, VI.xv). He goes on to tell Scipio that while he is on earth, he must fulfill his duty. He must love justice and devotion, which are owed to his parents, kinsmen, and above all his country. Such a life, he urges, will lead to heaven (DRP, VI.xvi).

Something remarkable now happens. Scipio looks around at the universe and the spheres, remarking that the entire view "appeared wonderfully beautiful . . . indeed the earth seemed to me so small that I was scornful of our empire, which covers only a single point, as it were, upon its surface" (*DRP*, VI.xvi). Africanus' subsequent account of the structure of the universe is worth quoting in full since it succinctly expresses a pervasive and enduring medieval worldview:

> These are the nine circles, or rather spheres, by which the whole is joined. One of them, the outermost, is that of heaven; it contains all the rest, and is itself the supreme God, holding and embracing within itself all the other spheres; in it are fixed the eternal revolving courses of the stars. Beneath it are seven other spheres which revolve in the opposite direction to that of heaven. One of these globes is that light which on earth is called Saturn's. Next comes the star called Jupiter's, which brings fortune and health to mankind. Beneath it is that star, red and terrible to the dwellings of man, which you assign to Mars. Below it and almost midway of the distance is the Sun, the lord, chief, and ruler of the other lights, the mind and guiding principle of the universe, of such magnitude that he reveals and fills all things with his light. He is accompanied by his companions, as it were – Venus and Mercury in their orbits, and in the lowest sphere revolves the Moon, set on fire by the rays of the Sun. But below the Moon there is nothing except what is mortal and doomed to decay, save only the souls given to the human race by the bounty of the gods, while above the Moon all things are eternal. For the ninth and central sphere, which is the earth, is immovable and the lowest of all, and toward it all ponderable bodies are drawn by their own natural tendency downward. (*DRP*, VI.xvii)

Africanus also explains the "music of the spheres," which is created by the motion of the spheres. What is remarkable about the passage above is that, by giving Scipio a comprehensive view of the entire universe, Africanus enables him to see how petty the concerns of earth are, concerns which focus on the body and on earthly glory. Africanus himself chides Scipio when the latter keeps looking back to earth: "If it seems small to you, as it actually is, keep your gaze fixed upon these heavenly things, and scorn the earthly ... you will see what a small portion of it belongs to you Romans. For that whole territory which you hold ... is really only a small island ... Now you see how small it is in spite of its proud name!" (*DRP*, VI.xix- xx). He also tells Scipio that earthly glory is trivial: "it is not you that is mortal, but only your body. For that man whom your outward form reveals is not yourself; the spirit is the true self ... And just as the eternal God moves the universe, which is partly mortal, so an immortal spirit moves the frail body" (*DRP*, VI.xxiv).

Africanus explains that things which are always in motion are eternal and, as something eternal, the human soul is self-moving. This everlasting force, he says, should be used to undertake the "best pursuits" and the best tasks "are those undertaken in defence of your native land." The soul's flight will be quicker, he adds, if it contrives ways to detach itself "as much as may be from the body." Those who fail to do this and indulge in worldly pleasures and passions will not return to paradise but will "fly about close to the earth," returning to their proper place in the heavens only after "many ages of torture" (*DRP*, VI.xxvi).

In analyzing this dream, Macrobius affirms that "the purpose of the dream is to teach us that the souls of those who serve the state well are returned to the heavens after death and there enjoy everlasting blessedness" (*CDS*, I.iv.1). Much of Macrobius' "analysis" turns out to be an exposition of various elements of Neo-Platonic doctrine (such as the "One," Mind, and World-Soul) and the connection of these elements with Pythagorean theories of number and various cosmological theories deriving from Plato's *Timaeus* and other sources. He discusses the properties of bodies (as having three dimensions) and as always consisting of four elements, earth, water, air, and fire (*CDS*, I.vi.36). Using the dream of Scipio as his starting point, he explains his Neo-Platonic vision of the cosmos: "There is the Supreme God; then Mind sprung from him, in which the patterns of things are contained; there is the World-Soul, which is the fount of all souls; there are the celestial realms extending down to us; and last, the terrestrial realm" (*CDS*, I.vi.20). Macrobius also discusses the ambiguous nature of prophecy (*CDS*, I.vii.1–9).

Taking his cue from what Scipio's dream says about virtue, Macrobius lists the four virtues named in Plato's *Republic*. These virtues were later adapted to Christian theology by figures such as St. Ambrose, and they came to be known as the four "cardinal" or "natural" virtues of prudence, temperance, courage, and justice, which the Roman Catholic Church distinguished from the "theological" virtues of faith, hope, and charity (*CDS*, 120 n. 2). What is interesting here is Macrobius' influential definition of these four virtues, following Cicero, Plotinus, and Porphyry. Prudence consists in despising the world and attending only to divine things; temperance requires abstinence from bodily gratifications; courage refers to the soul's lack of fear as it escapes the body and ascends the celestial realms; and justice calls for "obedience to each virtue" (*CDS*, I.viii.3–4). Macrobius also cites (drawing on Plotinus and Porphyry) the secular implications of these virtues; for example, prudence is a "political" virtue, comprehending reason, understanding, and foresight (*CDS*, I.viii.5–9). Yet what is striking about these virtues is that, whatever worldly imperatives they sustain, they ultimately all call for a turning away from the things of this world toward divine things. Macrobius praises Cicero for stating that "*nothing that occurs on earth is more gratifying*" to the Supreme God than the associations of men under commonwealths (*CDS*, I.viii.12–13). In other words, Cicero acknowledges that while commonwealths are good, they are, like all earthly matters, insignificant in the context of the eternal.

Macrobius also commends the view of the soul presented in Scipio's dream, namely, that the soul originates in heaven and that while it occupies a body on earth, it is endowed with virtue by its ability to remember where it came from and to where it should return (*CDS*, I.ix.1–4). He praises Scipio's sense of justice (and of the other three virtues), which enables him "not to regard his own judgments as the criterion of truth" (*CDS*, I.x.3), as well as his perception of the soul's immortality (*CDS*, I.x.5–7). Among other issues which Macrobius considers to have been correctly presented in Scipio's dream are: God's omnipotence, the structure of the universe (*CDS*, I.xvii.5), the movement of the planets, the music of the spheres, the transient nature of earthly glory, and the nature of motion. Macrobius ends his *Commentary* by noting that there are three branches of philosophy: moral, physical, and rational. All three of these, he urges, are included in Scipio's dream, and he concludes that "we must declare that there is nothing more complete than this work, which embraces the entire body of philosophy" (*CDS*, II.xvii.15–17).

It would be tempting to see Macrobius as somehow anticipating much later views, of thinkers such as Nietzsche and Derrida, on the connection between the "literal" or direct language of philosophy and the figurative and fictional language of literature.

While Macrobius can be regarded as modern in the fact that he investigated this connection, we need also to bear in mind that his view of this connection expresses his Neo-Platonic disposition: that philosophy must use literary language as a means of access to higher, hidden truths reflects his belief that the physical world is an imperfect manifestation of a higher reality, a realm of pure Forms. Moreover, as seen above, he severely restricts the use of fiction in philosophy, primarily on moral grounds. His account of dreams is less modern than that of Artemidorus who, in proposing a system of symbolic and allegorical interpretation of dreams, anticipated Freudian ideas such as condensation and displacement. In summary, the reasons given by Macrobius for using fictions in philosophy are that: they may strengthen a philosophical argument through the use of vivid imaginative portrayals; they may convey profound truths in a dignified, allegorical form; that such allegorical or figurative presentation is appropriate when dealing with truths that cannot be otherwise conveyed; and that fictional presentation of higher truths serves to preserve their sanctity by restricting access to them. While some of these reasons overlap with those given by Christian writers such as Augustine and Aquinas for the figurative reading of the scriptures, Macrobius' work occupies a seminal position in the medieval commentary tradition on secular texts. His analysis of Scipio's dream serves not only to justify certain philosophical uses of fiction but also to bring out his own and Cicero's view, influenced by Plato, the Stoics, Plotinus, and Porphyry, that the concerns and events of the world must be situated in a far vaster cosmological scheme. This view was highly influential in the Middle Ages, underlying the widespread notion that occurrences in the world have not only a literal significance in earthly terms, but also an even greater significance that reverberates through the higher realms.

Boethius (ca. 480–524)

The Roman philosopher Boethius had a vast impact on medieval thinking, an impact that was foundational in the field of logic. He translated the four logical treatises comprising Aristotle's *Organon*, and also translated and commented on Porphyry's *Introduction to the Categories of Aristotle*. He wrote on Cicero and composed five essays on logic. Also of vast influence is the text that will be examined here, *The Consolation of Philosophy* (524), written in prison. This text effectively summarizes the most important components of many medieval world views, and was a foundation of later medieval humanism. Though in this work Boethius effectively justifies the ways of divine providence, he never explicitly identifies himself as a Christian, and his text shows the massive influence of Plato and Neo-Platonism. Nonetheless, the *Consolation* remained an authoritative text in discussions of Christian ethics for many centuries.

Born around 480 into a distinguished Roman aristocratic family, Boethius became consul in 510 and aligned himself with the interests of the senate. His downfall came in 523 when he incurred the disfavor of King Theodoric who, having conquered Italy, became Roman governor. The charges brought against him – underlined by the charge of treason – were politically motivated, leading to his exile, imprisonment, and his execution. It was in prison that he reflected upon the life he had led and was forced by his own philosophical principles to place it within the larger context of questions about God's providence, the injustice of the world, human free will, and the order and purpose of the world.

As Boethius is languishing in prison, he takes comfort in composing poetry, with the Muses presiding over his efforts. But there appears to him Lady Philosophy, a "woman of majestic countenance," who drives away the Muses of poetry, saying that they "kill the fruitful harvest of reason with the sterile thorns of the passions."[5] This overt displacement of poetry by philosophy provided fuel for later medieval enemies of poetry, though some writers such as Boccaccio qualified Boethius' attitude, saying that he only disapproved of obscene theatrical poetry (*CP*, 2 n. 2). Moreover, Lady Philosophy points out that her robe, which signifies the unity of philosophy – in turn symbolized by Plato, regarded by Boethius and most medieval thinkers until the thirteenth century as the greatest philosopher – has been torn by the factionalism of subsequent philosophies such as Epicureanism and Stoicism, as well as by the wicked worldly men whom it is the "main duty" of philosophy to oppose (*CP*, 5–6).

Philosophy attempts to place Boethius' misfortunes and his questions concerning the prosperity of wicked men within the broad perspective of God's nature and providence. Most fundamentally, she reminds Boethius that the world is governed not by accident or chance but by divine reason (*CP*, 16). She proceeds to show Boethius that the goddess Fortune is two-faced, bringing both prosperity and despair, that her very nature is to change (*CP*, 19–20). She reminds Boethius both of his own former fortune in being raised by a noble father-in-law, possessing a chaste wife, and having two sons who were made consuls – all of which he has now lost. The basic lesson is that this world "cannot stay the same," that it suffers violent changes, and that it is folly to trust man's inconstant fortunes (*CP*, 22). Philosophy asks: "Why . . . do men look outside themselves for happiness which is within?" (*CP*, 24). Philosophy remarks on the irony whereby man, who "is divine by his gift of reason thinks his excellence depends on the possession of lifeless bric-à-brac . . . God wished the human race to be superior to all earthly things" (*CP*, 27). She urges that "worldly power is not true power, and public honor is not true honor" (*CP*, 30). Even the repute won by virtuous men such as Boethius is of small value, and death "equalizes the high and low" (*CP*, 31–33).

Philosophy now begins the process of explaining and defining the highest good, which will "relieve man of all further desires." In pursuing material gain in terms of riches, honor, power, and fame, man is distracted from his true nature and purpose. Man is part of the unalterable order of the universe, whereby "Nature . . . providently governs the immense world by her laws . . . she controls all things, binding them with unbreakable bonds." Within this mighty scheme, "all things seek again their proper courses, and rejoice when they return to them. The only stable order in things is that which connects the beginning to the end." Even man, though blinded and distracted by worldly cares, has some vague recollection of his origin and his true goal (*CP*, 40–41). The honor and respect gained through "untrustworthy public opinion" is worthless and inconstant (*CP*, 44). The wise man, on the contrary, "measures his virtue by the truth of his conscience, not by popular esteem" (*CP*, 47).

Significantly, Philosophy explains that the various worldly ambitions which mislead men – power, fame, reverence, joy – are "in substance . . . one and the same thing." What "nature has made simple and indivisible, human error has divided." All of these

145

pursuits are interrelated and are equally defective (*CP*, 50–51). Philosophy now sings a poem which summarizes a portion of Plato's *Timaeus* and embodies important components of the medieval worldview. This song or poem was widely influential during the Middle Ages and is worth quoting at length:

> Oh God, Maker of heaven and earth, Who govern the world with eternal reason, at your command time passes from the beginning. You place all things in motion, though You are yourself without change. No external causes impelled You to make this work from chaotic matter. Rather it was the form of the highest good, existing within You without envy, which caused You to fashion all things according to the eternal exemplar. You who are most beautiful produce the beautiful world from your divine mind and, forming it in your image, You order the perfect parts in a perfect whole.
>
> You bind the elements in harmony so that cold and heat, dry and wet are joined, and the purer fire does not fly up through the air, nor the earth sink beneath the weight of water.
>
> You release the world-soul throughout the harmonious parts of the universe as your surrogate, threefold in its operations, to give motion to all things . . .
>
> In like manner You create souls and lesser living forms and, adapting them to their high flight in swift chariots, You scatter them through the earth and sky. And when they have turned again toward You, by your gracious law, You call them back like leaping flames.
>
> . . . The sight of Thee is beginning and end; one guide, leader, path, and goal. (*CP*, 53–54)

The characteristic medieval notions expressed here include: divine reason ruling the world; God as the "unmoved Mover"; the intrinsic beauty of the created world; the relation of the four elements; the Neo-Platonic notion of the World-Soul as intermediary between God and material things; and the circle of beginning and end, whereby God is not only the source but the end and goal of all created things.

Philosophy argues, on the assumption that there must be a source of goodness and perfection, that "the most high God is full of the highest and most perfect good." And, since the perfect good is true happiness, "it follows that true happiness has its dwelling in the most high God" (*CP*, 55). It further follows that "men become happy by acquiring divinity . . . although it is true that God is one by nature, still there may be many gods by participation" (*CP*, 56). Hence, if happiness is the highest good, and all other goods are aspects of this highest good, the "good and happiness are one and the same thing." Moreover, the essence of God "is to be found in the good, and nowhere else" (*CP*, 57).

Again, in characteristically Platonic and medieval fashion, Philosophy argues that if "every good is good by participating in the perfect good . . . the good and the one are the same" (*CP*, 59). All things, in seeking to survive, seek unity, for "without unity existence itself cannot be sustained." And, since unity is the same as goodness, "all things desire the good" (*CP*, 61). Hence the good is "that which is desired by all." The good is the "one thing to which all other things are related," without which they would "wander without direction or goal" (*CP*, 61).

To fulfill his true nature, man must "teach his spirit that it possesses hidden among its own treasures whatever it seeks outside itself." She adds, in an exquisite statement,

146

that the "seed of truth grows deep within and is roused to life by the breath of learning" (*CP*, 61–62). Understandably, however, Boethius wonders how there can in fact be evil in the world and how it can go unpunished given the existence of "an all-knowing and all-powerful God who desires only good" (*CP*, 67). Philosophy explains that the power to do evil is not a power at all; only the wise can do what they want; the wicked merely follow their irrational desires: "Lust rules their hearts . . . rage whips them," and they are slaves to both sorrow and delusive hope. Enslaved "by these evil powers, he cannot do what he wishes" (*CP*, 72–73). Moreover, the good are always rewarded and the wicked always punished because the aim or goal of an action is the reward of that action (*CP*, 73). Likewise, wickedness itself is the punishment of the wicked; more profoundly, since existence itself is identified with unity, and unity with goodness, it follows that whatever loses its goodness ceases to be; hence, to be wicked is to "lose one's human nature," to lose one's participation in the divine nature and to become a beast (*CP*, 74).

Philosophy further explains that what to mortal eyes may seem like unjust accident is actually directed by Providence toward ends which are good. She makes an interesting distinction between Providence and Fate. Providence is "the divine reason itself," which governs and connects all things; Fate, on the other hand, belongs to all mutable things. Thus, "Providence is the unfolding of temporal events as this is present to the vision of the divine mind; but this same unfolding of events as it is worked out in time is called Fate . . . Providence is the immovable and simple form of all things which come into being, while Fate is the moving connection and temporal order of all things" (*CP*, 82–83). Hence Fate itself is subject to Providence: "the changing course of Fate is to the simple stability of Providence as reasoning is to intellect . . . as time is to eternity, as a circle to its center" (*CP*, 83). Philosophy's answer to Boethius' question has itself remained unchanged through the centuries: the workings of Providence and divine wisdom are beyond human understanding, and even the actions of wicked men can be used to generate good (*CP*, 84, 86). We can see that, just as God relates to the world as One to the Many, unity to diversity, so Providence is the unity of Fate; and the distinction between them is one of viewpoint, divine and human. So profoundly ingrained within this worldview are the ideals of unity and order that they are characterized as "mutual love" between the elements of the universe themselves. It is this love which governs the eternal movements of the stars, and "the war of discord is excluded from the bounds of heaven." But love also governs the connections of the four elements: "Concord rules the elements with fair restraint . . . Only thus can things endure: drawn by love they turn again to the Cause which gave them being" (*CP*, 87–88). Hence, God is conceived of ultimately as a circle, a self-generating circle of causes which externalizes itself, which descends into multiplicity from unity, and then gathers all to itself in a renewed unity. All fortune has as its purpose the trial and reward of good men, and the correction of evil men. In such an ordered and just world, of course, there can be no such thing as chance (*CP*, 88, 91).

Philosophy explains that this scheme does not preclude human free will. Events do not happen *because* they are foreseen. Whatever is known is known not by the force and nature of the things that are known but by the power of the knower (*CP*, 100). And, just as human reason transcends but includes human sense-perception, so divine intelligence transcends human reason. This intelligence is intuitive and comprehends in a single perspective what human reason apprehends in a piecemeal and partial way. God's knowledge is effectively not a foreknowledge of future events but "knowledge of a never changing present" (*CP*, 106). So the same event is "necessary with respect to God's knowledge of it, but free and undetermined if considered in its own nature" (*CP*, 107–108). The lesson of this, says Philosophy, is that human free will remains inviolate, that God's laws are just, rewarding and punishing good and evil in human action, and that therefore men should "stand firm against vice and cultivate virtue" (*CP*, 108). This vision remained deeply ingrained within the medieval psyche for many centuries.

Notes

1   "Introduction," in *The Essence of Plotinus: Extracts from the Six Enneads and Porphyry's Life of Plotinus*, trans. Stephen Mackenna, ed. Grace H. Turnbull (New York and Oxford: Oxford University Press, 1948), pp. xvi–xix. Hereafter cited as *Enneads*.
2   This terminology is admirably explained by Grace Turnbull in *Enneads*, pp. 15–16.
3   Macrobius, *Commentary on the Dream of Scipio*, trans. William Harris Stahl (New York: Columbia University Press, 1990), I.i.1–3. Hereafter cited as *CDS*.
4   Cicero, *De re publica; De legibus*, trans. Clinton Walker Keyes (Cambridge, MA and London: Harvard University Press/Heinemann, 1966), VI.xii. Hereafter cited as *DRP*.
5   Boethius, *The Consolation of Philosophy*, trans. Richard H. Green (New York: Dover, 2002), 1–2. Hereafter cited as *CP*.

PART IV

THE MEDIEVAL ERA

CHAPTER 8

THE EARLY MIDDLE AGES

Historical Background

Over the last half-century or so, scholars have challenged the prior perception of the Middle Ages as an era of darkness, ignorance, and superstition. The term, and indeed the very idea of, the "Middle Age" (*medium aevum*) was devised by Italian humanist thinkers who wished to demarcate their own period – of renaissance, rebirth, and rediscovery of classical thinkers – from the preceding era. While it is true that the early Middle Ages, from the fall of Rome at the hands of Germanic tribes in the fifth century until around 1000, saw a reversion to various forms of economic and intellectual primitivism, there occurred not only the Carolingian Renaissance (named after the emperor Charlemagne or Carolus Magnus) in the ninth century, but a great deal of intellectual and cultural progress from the eleventh through the thirteenth centuries (known as the later Middle Ages). The Renaissance humanists extolled the classical Greek and Roman authors, viewing themselves as their first legitimate successors, and condemning medieval scholasticism which intervened between them and the classical period as benighted. This rejection of medieval philosophy and literature was reinforced by the Protestant Reformation, which associated it with Roman Catholicism.[1] However, more recent scholarship in a variety of fields, including literary criticism, has shown this picture to be erroneous. Much Renaissance thought and culture was in fact a development from the medieval period, which was by no means ignorant of the classical Greek and Roman traditions.

A number of factors contributed to the making of the Middle Ages: the evolving traditions of Christianity; the social and political patterns of the Germanic tribes who overran the Roman Empire; vestiges of the Roman administrative and legal system; the legacy of the classical world; and contact with Islamic civilization (which lies beyond the scope of this study). The most powerful force in the development of medieval civilization was Christianity. Even before the fall of Rome in 410, Christianity had been increasingly tolerated, as stipulated in a series of edicts, initiated by the emperor Constantine, from 313 onward; by 381 it was recognized as the official religion of the

Roman Empire. The beginnings of Christian thought in the letters of St. Paul, Clement of Rome, and the Gospel of St. John related the tenets of Christianity to Greek philosophical concepts. Subsequent Christian writers in the second century were concerned to justify their faith, their most articulate exponent being Justin Martyr, a teacher executed in Rome around 165.

Early Christianity had been heterogeneous, containing a large number of sects with disparate beliefs and practices, often embroiled in disputes. The Arians and Nestorians, for example, rejected the notion of the Trinity which was advocated by the Athanasians. The Docetae and Basilidans rejected the factuality of Christ's crucifixion. The Pelagians denied the notion of original sin and espoused human free will. Eventually, in order to settle these doctrinal disputes, a number of worldwide Church councils were convened, beginning with the Council of Nicaea in 325, which condemned the views of most of these sects as heretical and established the Athanasian view of the Trinity as orthodox Christian doctrine. The doctrine of the Incarnation was not formally adopted until the Council of Chalcedon in 451. The course of these debates was shaped by such figures as Athanasius of Alexandria (293–373), Gregory of Nyssa, St. Basil (ca. 330–379), Gregory of Nazianzus (ca. 330–ca. 389), John Chrysostom (ca. 347–407), Ambrose (ca. 339–397) and Augustine of Hippo (354–430). One of the greatest Christian thinkers of this period was Jerome (ca. 347–420), who translated the Bible from its original languages into Latin (known as the Vulgate edition). Other steps were also taken to promote unity of belief and practice: these included the promulgation of standard sermons, the training of bishops, and the growth of the papacy in power and prestige into a focus of allegiance and obedience. Having said this, Christian doctrine was never fully formalized in the early Middle Ages, and many of the Eastern churches adhered to unorthodox beliefs. It took further ecumenical councils until 681 for major schisms between the churches at Rome and Constantinople to be healed.

Notwithstanding these difficulties, after the collapse of the empire it was left to the Church to preserve unity, order, and guidance in many spheres. The Church's unity survived that of the empire. It was the Church, becoming increasingly sophisticated in its organization and increasingly dominated by the leadership of the papacy in Rome, which promoted moral values, fostered appropriate social conduct, and transmitted classical learning. The Church has been described as the "single institution" which enjoyed continuity in the "whole transition from Antiquity to the Middle Ages" (*PF*, 131). It not only preserved classical culture but facilitated its "assimilation and adaptation to a wider population," effectively Latinizing their speech and enabling the emergence of the Romance languages (*PF*, 135–136). Latin remained the language of scholarship and law during the Middle Ages. The Germanic tribes invading the empire retained Latin as the means of communication wherever they settled; as E. R. Curtius points out, however, the growth of vernacular languages and literatures from the twelfth and thirteenth centuries onward did not entail a dissolution of Latin but rather a bifurcation into two languages, used respectively by the learned and the common people. For centuries yet, Latin "remained alive as the language of education, of science, of government, of law, of diplomacy." Writers such as Boccaccio and Petrarch were "still affected by the heritage of the Latin Middle Ages," and the influence of medieval Latin literature persisted through the great movements of the modern period such as humanism, the Renaissance, and the Reformation (Curtius, 26–27). One particularly important aspect of Christianity was monasticism, with its roots in early Christian asceticism. Founded in the East by St. Basil and in the West by St. Benedict, monasticism entailed a strict regimen of poverty, obedience, humility, labor, and devotion. It was largely monks who were responsible for writing most books, transmitting early manuscripts, and maintaining schools, libraries, and hospitals. The monks would later develop into the regular clergy (following a strict rule or *regula*), as opposed to the secular clergy, the various ranks of priests and bishops who operated in the worldly sphere (*saeculum* meaning "world" or "time"). The slave mode of production in the ancient world had fostered a contempt for manual labor and a consequent stagnation in technology. The monastic orders united "intellectual and manual labour . . . in the service of God," and agrarian labor "acquired the dignity of divine worship" (*PF*, 135). Christianity thus promoted a "liberation" of technology, of labor, and of culture from "the limits of a world built on slavery" (*PF*, 132). In these crucial respects, Christianity was the "indispensable bridge between two epochs," between the ancient slave mode of production and the feudal mode of production (*PF*, 137).

Another force which overwhelmed the Western Roman Empire was the Germanic peoples, who included Scandinavians, Goths, Vandals, Franks, and Anglo-Saxons. Many of these peoples had already settled in various parts of the empire long before the fall of Rome. Eventually revolting against Roman rule, the Visigoths led by Alaric sacked Rome in 410. The city was taken again by the Vandals in 455. The lifestyle, as well as the legal, economic, and political structure, of the Germanic peoples was primitive in many respects. This structure, amalgamating with the administrative legacy of the Roman Empire, eventually developed into the system of feudalism, which involved contractual obligations between rulers and subjects, lords and vassals, obligations based on values such as courage, honor, loyalty, protection, and obedience. We see these values repeatedly expressed in poems such as *Beowulf*, often in uneasy coexistence with Christian values such as humility and trust in divine providence.

In the early Middle Ages commerce and industry declined, and land became increasingly concentrated in the hands of a few, with famine and disease often widespread. The economic system was limited largely to local trade. Ancient Roman culture gave way before a life centered on villages, feudal estates, and monasteries. This hierarchical and largely static way of life was sanctioned by the Church; the social order, where each person had his place, was seen as part of the larger, divinely established, cosmic order. One of the most significant figures of this period was Carolus Magnus or Charlemagne (742–814), who established an empire that extended over western and central Europe and much of Italy, and to some extent centralized law and government. He was crowned emperor by Pope Leo III in 800, an event which signified the formation of the Holy Roman Empire, a powerful and influential "alliance" between the Frankish dynasty and the papacy. The empire thus achieved both political unity under Charlemagne and religious unity under papal leadership. Perry Anderson remarks that the Carolingian monarchy, with the Church as its "official mentor," brought about a "real administrative and cultural revival" throughout the empire, sponsoring "a renovation of literature, philosophy, art and education." Even more importantly, it was in this era that the groundwork of feudalism was laid (*PF*, 137, 139). E. R. Curtius remarks that when

Christianity became the state religion of the Roman Empire in 381, Rome's universalism "acquired a twofold aspect. To the universal claim of the state was added that of the church." The medieval empire of Charlemagne took over from Rome, by the doctrine of "transference," the "idea of a world empire; thus it had a universal, not a national, character" (Curtius, 28–29). These ideas, as will emerge later, were taken up in contrasting ways by Augustine, who distinguished sharply between the earthly Rome and the heavenly city, and Dante, who saw a connection between the Rome of Vergil and the Rome of St. Peter. Curtius stresses the continuity between the two epochs: the language of Rome was also the language of the Bible, the Church, and of medieval learning (Curtius, 30). After Charlemagne's death, the empire was divided up but was revived in 962 when Otto the Great of Germany was crowned emperor by Pope John XII. The Holy Roman Empire lasted (though having lost much of its power) until 1806.

Intellectual and Theological Currents: Christianity and Classicism

The thought and literature of this entire period was formulated within the larger religious and evolving feudal context described above. The intellectual currents of the early Middle Ages were driven by two broad factors: the heritage of classical thought, and the varying relation of developing Christian theology to this heritage. The secular criticism of the late Roman period included some influential figures: Macrobius and Servius, who contributed to the prestige of Vergil and the knowledge of Neo-Platonism in the Middle Ages, Servius also being the author of the standard grammar of this period; the grammarian Aelius Donatus, who wrote a commentary on Terence, as well as handbooks entitled *Ars minor* and *Ars maior*, used throughout the Middle Ages; Priscian, whose *Institutio grammatica* was used in the Middle Ages; and Diomedes, who produced an exhaustive account of grammatical tropes and "the most systematic surviving account of poetic genres" (*CHLC*, V.I, 341, 344). Vergil was the basic text in schools of grammar, while Cicero held a privileged place in the teaching of rhetoric. One of the rhetoricians of late antiquity, Martianus Capella, who wrote in the early fifth century, was known in the Middle Ages primarily by his authoritative encyclopedia of the seven liberal arts. Later influential encyclopedias were produced by Cassiodorus, who produced the first Christian handbook of ecclesiastical learning and the secular arts (Curtius, 41), and Isidore of Seville (*CHLC*, V.I, 341, 344). Isidore transmitted "the sum of late antique knowledge to posterity" (Curtius, 23). These compendia anticipated the eventual formalization of the liberal arts curriculum at medieval universities into the "trivium," comprising logic, rhetoric, and grammar, and the "quadrivium," composed of astronomy, music, arithmetic, and geometry. A major thinker of this period was the Neo-Platonist Boethius (ca. 480–524), whose translations of Aristotle's logical treatises proved of paramount importance for the thinking of the later Middle Ages, especially scholasticism. Of the foregoing developments, two were especially germane to the early Middle Ages: Neo-Platonism (which, beginning prior to the Middle Ages, is considered in the previous chapter) and the closely related Christian tradition of allegorical interpretation, as embodied in the work of St. Augustine, which will be treated in the present chapter.

In the early Middle Ages, the Church's "other-worldly" disposition tended to subordinate the position of literature and the arts to the more pressing issues of salvation and preparation for the next life. In general, the widespread instability, insecurity, and illiteracy intensified religious feeling and promoted ideals of withdrawal from the world, condemning earthly life as worthless and merely a means of passage to the next life, to eternal salvation and bliss. As the theological content of Christianity developed, two broad approaches to classical literature emerged. The first of these sought to distance Christianity from paganism and accordingly frowned on the pagan origins of the arts in the cultures of Greece and Rome, while the second sought to continue the Christian appropriation of classical rhetoric and philosophy. The former stream of Christian thought, deriving from the third-century theologian Tertullian (ca. 160–ca. 225) and enduring until the last patristic author Pope Gregory the Great (540–604), laid stress on the authority of faith and revelation over reason. Both Tertullian and Gregory renounced all secular knowledge and viewed literature as a foolish pursuit. Tertullian saw drama as patronized by Bacchus and Venus, whom he called "devils" of passion and lust. Having said this, recent scholarship has recognized a synthesis in Tertullian's writings of Christian doctrines with Platonic and Stoic philosophical traditions, as well as with rhetoric (*CHLC*, V.I, 337). The ascetic dispositions of monasticism intensified Christian anxiety concerning worldly beauty and art: St. Jerome, St. Basil, St. Bernard, and St. Francis all turned away from the beauty of nature as a distraction from the contemplation of things divine. Generally, the early Christian philosophers echoed Plato's objections to art, namely that art, as relying on counterfeiting or image-making, is removed from the truth, and that it appeals to the lower, sensuous part of our nature and the passions. Tertullian condemned the practice of feigning and false imitation in drama. As for Plato's second objection, Christians saw pagan arts as expressing emotions such as pride, hypocrisy, ambition, violence, and greed which were blatantly opposed to the Christian virtues of humility, meekness, and love. Christian thinkers such as Boethius also echoed Plato's concern that the arts were seductive, and could distract men from the righteous path. There was also in the eighth and ninth centuries an "iconoclastic controversy" in Christianity, concerning the acceptability of portraying images. Christians held that it debased their spiritual doctrines to represent them to the senses. It was not until the Council of Nicaea in 787 that devotional images were deemed a legitimate resource for religious instruction.

The second stream of Christian thought, represented by the third-century Christian theologians Clement and Origen, both from Alexandria, displayed a rationalist emphasis and attempted to reconcile ancient Greek thought with the tenets of Christianity. Origen (ca. 185–ca. 254) was the Greek author of *On First Principles*, the first systematic account of Christian theology. The most renowned biblical scholar of the early Church, Origen formulated an allegorical method of scriptural exegesis whose influence endured for many centuries. The attempt of Christian philosophy to come to terms with its classical Greek and Roman heritage continued through Gregory of Nazianzus, Gregory of Nissa, John Chrysostom, and Ambrose, reaching unprecedented heights in the work of St. Augustine, St. Bonaventura, and St. Thomas Aquinas. These thinkers had a more accommodating view of classical learning and literature. While poetry and history gained some acceptance (the first major Christian poet was Prudentius and the first Christian historian Orosius), the Church remained for a long time opposed to drama, as well as to visual art, which was associated with idolatry. Augustine referred to stage-plays as "spectacles of uncleanness"[2] whose speeches were "smoke and wind."[3] In general, it is clear that Christian writers displayed a wide range of attitudes toward classical culture and that their writings cannot be categorized neatly in terms of straight-forward assent or dissent. George Kennedy usefully suggests that the Christian Fathers writing prior to the Council of Nicaea in 325 exhibit a broad agreement on certain general principles: that a Christian must acquire literacy, which must entail some reading of classical texts; that examples can be taken from classical works, and read allegorically so as to accord with Christian teaching; that classical philosophy and literature do contain certain truths; and that the Bible, being divinely inspired, is true at a literal level, but also harbors moral and theological levels of meaning (*CHLC*, V.I, 339–340).

In fact, it might be argued that Christian allegory had its origins in the need to confront classical thought, as well as in the imperative to reconcile the Old and New Testaments. There was a tradition of skeptical thought in the time of the Roman Empire, expressed in the writings of figures such as Cicero and the late second-century thinker Sextus Empiricus. Augustine himself was influenced by such skepticism prior to his eventual conversion, after which he came to believe that absolute truth came from divine revelation. More generally, Christian thought was obliged to confront skeptical attitudes toward the scriptures, based on textual inconsistencies as well as incompatibility with reason. Just as the Neo-Platonists were driven by an urge to reconcile Homer and Plato, poetry and philosophy, as well as to harmonize the doctrines of Plato and Aristotle, so Christian thinkers needed to reconcile the Old Testament with the New Testament, and scripture generally with the teachings of the Greek philosophers. In response to these needs, both Christian writers and Neo-Platonists developed the tradition of allegorical interpretation already formulated by the Stoics. The tradition of Christian allegorical interpretation effectively begins with St. Paul, and continues through Clement of Alexandria and his student Origen. Clement believed that reason was necessary for the understanding of scripture, and that the Greek philosophers had anticipated the Christian conception of God. He asserted that truth was veiled in symbols. Origen, who viewed the Bible as divinely inspired, formulated a vastly influential system of allegorical interpretation, according to three levels, literal, moral, and theological, corresponding to the composition of man as body, soul, and spirit (*CHLC*, V.I, 330–334). We can now see how these Christian attempts to accommodate and develop classical learning achieved a classic formulation in the views of St. Augustine.

St. Augustine (354–430)

Many of the foregoing tendencies can be found in, and indeed arose from, Augustine's views of art and literature. It is in his work (along with that of later writers such as Aquinas and Dante) that the profoundest synthesis of classical and Christian notions can be discerned. More than any other early Christian thinker, Augustine profoundly influenced the traditions of both Roman Catholic and Protestant thought. Chief of the Latin Church Fathers, he was born in North Africa. After studying in Carthage, Rome, and Milan, he was made bishop of Hippo in 395. In his *Confessions* (400), Augustine described the long and arduous process of his conversion to Christianity, a path which had included belief in Manicheism and Skepticism. He expounded his theology in *City of God* (412–427), where he viewed human history as the unfolding of a divine plan. In laying out a Christian scheme of history he was essentially defending Christianity against those who attributed the sack of Rome by the Goths in 410 to the abandonment of the pagan deities. While Augustine acknowledged that philosophy had a place in the pursuit of wisdom, he subordinated it to divine revelation, the task of reason being to promote a clearer understanding of things already accepted on faith. Augustine affirmed the supreme importance of original sin as responsible for man's departure from God and the depraved state of human nature. The cause of original sin, he affirmed, was pride, which Augustine equated with man's self-love and desire for self-sufficiency, whereby man regards himself as his own light. Augustine divided spiritual life into the "earthly city," characterized by "self-love reaching the point of contempt for God," and the "heavenly city," which rests on "the love of God carried as far as contempt of self" (*CG*, XIV.10–14). Though Augustine does not deny human free will (since it was man's depraved will which led to the original sin), he is often characterized as believing in determinism since only those who belong to the heavenly city, the elect, will attain salvation. The elect are chosen not on account of their goodness but for unknown reasons. This deterministic doctrine, originating in St. Paul, was later revived by Calvin. Augustine asserts that only God can restore the natural state of goodness in which man was created. The vehicle for man's redemption from sin is the Incarnation; only through Christ, who is the "mediator between God and men," can man have access to grace. Augustine's concept of the two cities had a pervasive influence during the Middle Ages, sanctioning the struggles of Church against the state. Augustine affirms the truth of the scriptures but his views often accommodate, or are influenced by, those of Plato, whom he regarded as the greatest philosopher.

In his *Confessions* Augustine had retrospectively regretted his own "foolish" immersion in classical literature (*Confessions*, I.xiii; III.ii). He condemned liberal studies, suggesting that only the scriptures were truly liberating. He somewhat modified his views in *De Doctrina Christiana* [*On Christian Doctrine*] and other works. While he sympathized with Plato's arguments for banishing poets and dramatists on moral grounds, his views of poetry's connection with truth were somewhat different. He suggests that paintings, sculptures, and plays were necessarily false, not from any intention to be such but merely from an inability to be that which they represent. Paradoxically, the artist cannot be true to his artistic intent unless he enacts falsehood. One of the problems of medieval aesthetics was to reconcile earthly beauty with spiritual preoccupations. For Augustine and other medieval philosophers such as Albertus Magnus and Bonaventura, beauty was not specifically concerned with physical objects; rather, it implied a relationship of harmony between certain terms, whether these were material, intellectual, or spiritual. Influenced by Cicero, Augustine viewed the essential elements of beauty as, firstly, harmonious wholeness and, secondly, unity of parts which are ordered in due proportion (*Confessions*, IV.xiii).

Augustine's aesthetics rely on a modified Platonic framework appealing to a higher spiritual realm to which the physical world is subordinated. As such, art, composed of sensuous elements, was assigned a lower degree of reality than spiritual life, far removed from God, the ultimate source of being, and the standard by which the reality accorded to anything was measured. The early Church, then, harbored a metaphysical idealism descended in part from Plato, insisting that reality is spiritual and that sense-perception and observation of the world were not reliable avenues to truth. However, owing to various theological controversies in which the Church became embroiled, the world of matter was not rejected as unreal but was admitted into the divine scheme of creation, occupying nonetheless a humble position. The beauty of earthly things was viewed as an expression of their divine origin, and rested on their unity – a unity in diversity – which imitated the Oneness of God. This relation expressed the medieval Christian vision of the One and the Many: it is ultimately God's unity which confers unity and harmony on the vast diversity of the world. The world is God's poem which proclaims its beauty through harmony and correct proportion (*CG*, XI.18).

Augustine's strategy of adapting classical thought and literature to Christian purposes proved to be profoundly influential in the disposition of medieval philosophy and theology. This strategy also marks Augustine's important work *De Doctrina Christiana*, which deserves consideration here since it not only concerns possible Christian uses of classical rhetoric and learning, but also details Augustine's theories of the sign and of figurative language. The first three books of *De Doctrina*, devoted to the understanding and interpretation of the scriptures, were written in 397. A fourth book, concerning the use of rhetoric in the teaching of the scriptures, was added in 426. To discover the meaning of the scriptures, suggests Augustine, we must consider both things and signs, in other words, the things which should be taught to Christians, and the signs or modes of expressions of these things. He distinguishes things from signs by saying that the former are never employed to signify anything else. He adds that "every sign is also a thing . . . but not every thing is also a sign."[4]

Book I is concerned with the nature of things. Augustine asserts that some things are for use while others are for enjoyment. He states that "to enjoy a thing is to rest with satisfaction in it for its own sake. To use, on the other hand, is to employ whatever means are at one's disposal to obtain what one desires" (I.4). To enjoy something, then, is to treat it as an end in itself and to find one's happiness in it (I.33). The only object, therefore, which should be enjoyed as such is the Triune God or Trinity, "who is our highest good and our true happiness." Augustine defines the characteristics of the Trinity as follows: "In the Father is unity, in the Son equality, in the Holy Spirit the harmony of unity and equality" (I.5). Hence the only "true objects of enjoyment" are those which are "eternal and unchangeable." All other objects are for use, being merely the means whereby we arrive at enjoyment of God (I.22). The distinction between use and enjoyment, then, embraces the distinctions of means and end, adjective and substantive, temporal and eternal, physical and spiritual, journey and goal. Essentially, these distinctions are based on a broad distinction of this-worldliness and other-worldliness that was central to Christian theology for centuries: the world itself can never rise above the status of a means; even the beauty of the world can never be an end in itself. Objects in the world are for such use, such instrumentality; even if they are loved, our love is not to rest in them, says Augustine, but to have reference to God.

The world is thus divested of any *literal* significance: its meaning resides not in its isolated parts or even in the system of relations connecting all of its parts, but in its potential to point beyond itself to what it signifies in another realm, such referral being governed by a transcendent goal. The mechanism of such self-transcendence is the presumed correspondence of the physical and spiritual: elements of the material world are not there for their own sake, but only to point beyond themselves to a spiritual realm. The world, then, is intrinsically symbolic, always referring beyond itself to achieve meaning, and our modes of expression must necessarily be allegorical since a purely literal level of significance is disabled. This level is enabled only by its own transcendence in symbolic levels of meaning: the system of meaning extends not laterally over relations with other terms on a literal level, as in Saussure's characterization of language, but upward through these various allegorical levels. No object in the world can have any significance, importance, or meaning except in reference to God. Augustine states that "no part of our life is to be unoccupied, and to afford room, as it were, for the wish to enjoy some other object . . . the love of God . . . suffers no stream to be drawn off from itself by whose diversion its own volume would be diminished" (I.22). Only God is to be loved for his own sake, and all other things are to be loved in reference to God (I.27). It is clear that the entire system of human knowledge and perception is sanctioned only by an end, externally imposed by divine agency, which is not itself epistemological. In other words, knowledge can progress only to what is already sanctioned and can follow only a path already prescribed. All "knowledge and prophecy are subservient," says Augustine, to faith, hope, and love (I.37).

Although Augustine ostensibly views the world as comprised of "things," his insistence that these things are to be used rather than enjoyed effectively accords to them the status of *signs*, since they carry meaning not in themselves but only in so far as they signify or enable spiritual elements. Indeed, the world itself, inasmuch as its elements are experienced in their potential to serve as a pathway towards God, is an expression of the Word of God. In other words, the world as experienced by a Christian is not essentially a thing or a series of things since it is transformed into a sign or a series of signs. Augustine states:

> the word which we have in our hearts becomes an outward sound and is called speech; and yet our thought does not lose itself in the sound, but remains complete in itself, and takes the form of speech without being modified in its own nature by the change: so the Divine Word, though suffering no change of nature, yet became flesh, that He might dwell among us. (I.13)

The analogy here is between the inward human word or thought which externalizes itself in speech, and the Divine Word which incarnates itself in human form as Christ. Through his material and spiritual existence, Christ provides access of human language into the Divine Word, a point of archetypal contact at which the Divine Word can give the world – and the human language which expresses this world – its idealized shape, direction, and purpose. Talking of divine wisdom, Augustine states that "though Wisdom was Himself our home, He made himself also the way by which we should reach our home" (I.11). As Father, God is both origin and goal; as Christ, he is the way. As Christ, as intermingling divine and human components, he imbues the relations of the world with a potential to overcome the materiality of their nature, to cast their signifying claims into the realm of spirit, and to achieve the status of a spiritual path leading ultimately to God. Thus the Word of God which is materialized as Christ in the world raises to a higher power of signification the externalization of human thought into speech which can thereby exalt the status of the world's contents above and beyond mere thinghood.

In book II Augustine turns to the study of signs. He defines a sign as "a thing which, over and above the impression it makes on the senses, causes something else to come to mind as a consequence of itself" (II.1). It is interesting that Augustine does not define a sign, as later thinkers did, by a duality between particular existence and universal meaning (for example, a rose exists as a particular object but may have a universal symbolism, signifying love). Instead, Augustine seems to view the sign in terms of a duality between isolated, sensuous existence on the one hand, and its causal agency in inducing further mental representations on the other. Many centuries before Saussure, Augustine distinguished between natural and conventional signs. A natural sign, he says, embodies no human intention yet still leads to the knowledge of something else, as when smoke signals fire. Such connections are revealed simply through experience (II.1). Conventional signs, in contrast, "are those which living beings mutually exchange for the purpose of showing . . . the feelings of their minds, or their perceptions, or their thoughts" (II.2). The most numerous and important conventional signs are, of course, words.

Even the signs given by God in the scriptures, says Augustine, were made known through men, and need to be studied. The difficulties of scripture, he thinks, spring largely from two sources, unknown and ambiguous signs. Signs are either proper or figurative; they are proper when they refer to their intended objects, and figurative when these intended objects are used to signify something else (II.10). The main remedy for unknown proper signs is knowledge of the languages of scripture (Latin, Hebrew, Greek); Augustine even admits that a diversity of interpretations is useful inasmuch as these will often throw light on obscure passages (II.11, 12). In the case of figurative signs, their meaning is to be traced partly by the knowledge of languages and partly by the knowledge of things. For example, researches into the meanings of "Adam," "Eve," and other names have helped clarify many figurative expressions in scripture; and sometimes these figures presuppose a knowledge of things, whether animals, minerals, or plants, which are used by way of comparison (II.16). In general, while Augustine acknowledges that some of the meanings of scripture are shrouded in the "thickest darkness," he explains that "all this was divinely arranged for the purpose of subduing pride by toil," as well as of increasing pleasure in the communication of knowledge through figures (II.6). Moreover, we must "believe that whatever is there written, even though it be hidden, is better and truer than anything we could devise by our own wisdom" (II.7). Once again, the system of knowledge is viewed as closed, bounded as it is by God's omniscience and foreknowledge. Human knowledge is forever a partial emulation of, and aspiration after, what is already known to God.

Augustine's advice to the Christian regarding pagan knowledge is that where the latter is immersed in superstition, it should be rejected; but whatever is useful in heathen science and philosophy should be appropriated for Christian use. For example, dialectics or the science of reasoning is of great service in helping us to understand scripture, provided that this science is not used for mere vanity and entrapping adversaries through clever uses of words. Moreover, only such verbal ornamentation should be used as is consistent with "seriousness of purpose" (II.31), and we should remember that the laws which govern logical inference do not guarantee truth, which is an entirely separate issue (II.34). Having acknowledged that dialectics and logic have been developed by pagan thinkers, Augustine does not view these sciences as devised by men, for logical sequence "exists eternally in the reason of things, and has its origin with God" (II.32). Similarly, the science of definition, of division and partition, is not invented by man but "is evolved from the reason of things" (II.35).

Augustine's prescriptions for the use of rhetoric are similar. Like dialectic, rhetoric can provide training for the intellect, but we should beware of the temptation to incline the intellect toward mischief and vanity. Moreover, both dialectic and rhetoric are instrumental, merely means to a higher end; of themselves, they cannot yield the secrets of a happy life (II.37). Once again, while insisting that the rules for eloquence are true, Augustine states that these rules were not devised by men; rather, the facts that certain affectionate expressions conciliate the audience or that a clear and concise narrative affects an audience or that variety maintains interest represent rules or circumstances that were merely discovered by men (II.36).

Augustine warns young Christian men "not to venture heedlessly" on the pursuit of all the branches of pagan learning, but to discriminate carefully among them (II.39). He accepts that pagan philosophers, especially the Platonists, have expressed not only "false and superstitious fancies" but also "liberal instruction which is better adapted to the use of truth, and some excellent precepts of morality." These should be taken by the Christian, who can devote them to their "proper" use in preaching the gospel (II.40). Finally, Augustine attempts to place the value of heathen knowledge in perspective by saying that such knowledge is poor "compared with the knowledge of Holy Scripture. For whatever man may have learnt from other sources, if it is hurtful, it is there condemned; if it is useful, it is therein contained" (II.42). It appears, then, that the relation between secular knowledge and scriptural knowledge is that between means and end. Scriptural knowledge is a kind of center or focus toward which all other knowledge converges, and by which all knowledge is ordered and valued.

In book III Augustine deals with ambiguous signs. Since these may be either direct or figurative, he is concerned to furnish rules which will guide the reader in knowing whether to interpret given passages of scripture literally or figuratively. Augustine states that a knowledge of figures of speech is necessary because tropes are used extensively in the scriptures and when passages taken literally give an absurd meaning, the possibility of their using figurative language must be considered (III.29). He defines a figure as an expression where "one thing is said with the intention that another should be understood" (III.37).

The general rule is that whatever passage taken literally is inconsistent with either "purity of life" or "soundness of doctrine" must be taken as figurative (III.10). Quoting St. Paul's statement that "The letter killeth, but the spirit giveth life," Augustine warns against taking a figurative expression literally. In doing this, we are understanding what is said in a "carnal" manner, thereby enacting the "death of the soul" and subjecting the intelligence to the flesh by such a "blind adherence to the letter." It is "a miserable slavery of the soul," he says, "to take signs for things, and to be unable to lift the eye of the mind above what is corporeal and created, that it may drink in eternal light" (III.5). These comments throw an interesting light on the foundations of Christian allegory. Literal meaning, whereby "things are to be understood just as they are expressed" (III.37), corresponds with the realm of materiality and bodily sensation. Figurative expressions, "in which one thing is expressed and another is to be understood," attempts to raise perception toward a spiritual and intellectual realm. Literal meaning is arrested at the opacity of "things" whereby figurative meaning looks *through* things, treating them as only signs of more exalted levels of truth, abolishing the thinghood of the world and imbuing it with a symbolic significance which refers all of its elements to the life hereafter. Thus is laid the foundation of various levels of meaning in allegory, each level sublating (both transcending and preserving in a higher synthesis) the previous levels. Augustine sees this process of ascension as a freedom from bondage: whoever pays homage to an object without knowing what it signifies is effectively in bondage to a sign; we escape such bondage to signs when we understand, firstly, that they *are* signs (and not things in themselves), and, secondly, the significance of the sign (III.9). We have already seen that Augustine's distinction of use and enjoyment effectively transformed, for the Christian, the world of things to a world of signs: to view the world as thinghood means viewing it as an end in itself; to view it as symbolic is to view it as a means to higher purposes. Figurative language, then, is a way of lifting our vision away from the temporal world as an object or end in itself toward God; it is not difficult to see how allegory would comprise a systematic use and control of such language.

One of the reasons we need to be aware of figurative expressions is that the same word does not always signify the same thing. In a comment which sounds surprisingly modern, Augustine states that "objects are not single in their signification, but each one of them denotes not two only but sometimes even several different things, according to the connection in which it is found" (III.25). This seems to suggest a relational view of meaning such as has been emphasized by many thinkers since Saussure. Augustine even encourages various interpretations of scripture provided that they are "in harmony with the truth . . . For what more liberal and more fruitful provision could God have made in regard to the Sacred Scriptures than that the same words might be understood in several senses, all of which are sanctioned by the concurring testimony of other passages equally divine?" (III.27). Hence the variety of interpretations of a given passage of scripture is subject to strict control inasmuch as it is restricted by the need to conform with other divinely sanctioned truths as expressed in other scriptural passages. Indeed, Augustine says that in explaining a doubtful passage, we may, in the absence of evidence from scripture, use the evidence of reason. "But," he warns, "this is a dangerous practice. For it is far safer to walk by the light of Holy Scripture" (III.28). Students of the scriptures should, above all, *pray* that they may understand them, for the "Lord giveth wisdom: out of His mouth comes knowledge and understanding" (III.37). Augustine also makes clear his belief that it was the Holy Spirit speaking through the human authors of the scriptures (III.27). The model of knowledge and wisdom presented here is that of a finished system over which God has control. All significant knowledge and wisdom is contained in the scriptures, which were inspired by the Holy Spirit; men can use their human faculty of reason and various branches of secular knowledge to a certain degree in understanding the Word of God. But ultimately, this Word stands above human language and reason, and men must ascend allegorically from a literal understanding of their world to a symbolic view of their world as a small part in a vast scheme which both subsumes and gives meaning to it. The *world* must be understood as the *Word* of God.

In the first three books of *De Doctrina* Augustine has dealt with the issue of discovering the meaning of sacred scripture. The fourth book is devoted to the expression and communication of that meaning, as in the activities of teaching and preaching. It is here that Augustine treats extensively of the need for the Christian preacher to draw upon rhetoric. Augustine quickly establishes that it is lawful for a Christian teacher to use the art of rhetoric; for, if "bad men use it to obtain the triumph of wicked and worthless causes . . . why do not good men study to engage it on the side of truth?" (IV.2). It is a duty, he says, of the Christian teacher to teach what is right and to refute what is wrong, using, as necessary, narrative for exposition, reasoning and proofs to dispel doubts, vigor of speech to move men to action, and various devices such as entreaties, exhortations, and reproaches to arouse emotions (IV.4).

However, while eloquence is useful to the Christian preacher, it is less important than wisdom, especially since the wisdom being dispensed is not human wisdom but a "heavenly wisdom which comes down from the Father." The Christian preacher, then, is but a minister of this higher wisdom (IV.5). As such, even if his powers of eloquence are weak, he can gain help by memorizing and drawing on the riches of scripture. Thereby, his own words will "gain strength and power" (IV.5). If the preacher can speak with eloquence as well as wisdom, however, he will be of greater service. Interesting again is the connection implied between human and divine wisdom; in the absence of the former (i.e., in the absence of rhetorical skills), the latter will still suffice if allowed to speak for itself; given the difficulties of scripture, however, it will be communicated more effectively by a speaker who understands its meaning and knows how to engage his audience. Augustine recommends that eloquence be learned by imitating men who combine eloquence with wisdom rather than from teachers of rhetoric (IV.5).

Such a combination of eloquence and wisdom is found foremost in the scriptures, which were "not composed by man's art and care, but . . . flowed forth in wisdom and eloquence from the divine mind" (IV.6). Augustine here throws further light on the conception of knowledge as descending from God to man. In the divine mind, all knowledge exists in a state of absolute clarity. To men, however, this knowledge is a mystery which cannot be penetrated without the aid of the scriptures. The scriptures themselves need to be interpreted and clarified by those who possess not only the necessary intellectual qualities but also the requisite spiritual purity and illumination. Augustine states that obscurity was a necessary element in the eloquence of scripture. Such obscurity, he maintains, is "useful and wholesome," for a number of reasons. Firstly, it was "designed to profit our understandings, not only by the discovery of truth, but also by the exercise of their powers" (IV.6). A second reason is that obscurity will "break in upon the satiety and stimulate the zeal of those who are willing to learn." Finally, obscurity will "throw a veil over the minds of the godless either that they may be converted to piety or shut out from a knowledge of the mysteries" (IV.8). While Augustine commends scriptural obscurity for these reasons, he insists that it is precisely such obscurity which must not be imitated by the Christian preacher, who cannot claim the authority of the divinely inspired sacred writers. On the contrary, his first and chief aim is to be understood by using clear speech, and to make "clear what was obscure" (IV.8, 11). Hence he should be anxious not so much about his eloquence as about the clarity of his teaching (IV.9). Having said this, if he is merely clear without stylistic grace, he will never appeal to more than a few eager students. He must use eloquence such that his message is "flavoured to meet the tastes of the majority" (IV.11). Augustine's own enormous resistance as a Christian notwithstanding, he is finally beginning to sound like a classical rhetorician, one of whose first concerns is how to adapt his speech to the composition and nature of the audience.

As if aware of this last point, Augustine quotes Cicero, perhaps both to confirm the latter's soundness and to distinguish his own formulations. Augustine commends Cicero's view that "an eloquent man must speak so as to teach, to delight, and to persuade." While Augustine agrees with Cicero that the speaker must not merely teach the hearer but also delight him in order to secure his attention and persuade him so as to move him to action, Augustine wishes to stress even more than Cicero the latter's emphasis on teaching as the most essential of the three functions. Augustine states that the true function of teaching is to point out the truth clearly; if the speaker is not understood he has not said what he intended to say. Though the style of the speech might add to its pleasing effects, Augustine insists that "the truth itself, when exhibited in its naked simplicity, gives pleasure, because it is the truth" (IV.12). This emphasis on truth over style seems to distinguish Augustine's Christian rhetoric from even those rhetoricians such as Cicero who themselves had stressed the importance of the substance of a speech.

Augustine traverses a precarious balance between a Christian emphasis on truth and a classical rhetorical consideration of style. Precarious, because the one tends to undermine the other: the balance is asymmetrical inasmuch as the expression of truth is viewed as necessary while the stylistic features are desirable but not essential. The situation is further complicated by Augustine's advice that the Christian orator "will succeed more by piety in prayer than by gifts of oratory." Though he must acquire knowledge as well as a facility for speech, when the hour of speech comes he should rely on God. "For," quotes Augustine, "it is not ye that speak, but the Spirit of your Father which speaketh in you" (IV.15). Here we have an important dimension of Christian oratory which is entirely absent in classical rhetoric. The Christian speaker's individual effort as a man is almost undermined by the fact that he himself is merely a vehicle for the speech of the Holy Spirit speaking through him. His own human knowledge and oratorical skill, then, are but a preparation for this displacement of his speaking persona by divine speech. One implication of this seems to be that even if the speaker is weak in his ability, his pure and truthful intentions may invoke the aid of the Holy Spirit, thereby raising his skill beyond anything normally accessible to him.

This important Christian qualification notwithstanding, Augustine reaffirms that the speaker who aims at enforcing what is good should not despise any of the three aims of teaching, giving pleasure, or moving the hearer. Augustine takes Cicero's three divisions of style as corresponding to these three respective aims. Modifying Cicero's formulation, Augustine writes: "He, then, shall be eloquent, who can say little things in a subdued style, in order to give instruction, moderate things in a temperate style, in order to give pleasure, and great things in a majestic style, in order to sway the mind" (IV.17). The Christian orator, however, since he is addressing the salvation of men's souls, is always dealing with great matters (IV.18). Nonetheless, he must use the stylistic level appropriate to his occasion (IV.19). While effective speeches, mixing these styles as occasion and subject matter demand, may teach and move, they may ultimately inspire a "change of life" (IV.24). The aims of giving pleasure and achieving beauty of expression must subserve the ends of the majestic style, which is to "persuade men to cultivate good habits and give up evil ones" (IV.25). In general, all speeches should aim at the three merits of perspicuity, beauty of style, and persuasive power (IV.26). Augustine's view of truth itself as the basis of good style underlies his new, Christianized, definition of rhetoric: "To speak eloquently, then, and wisely as well, is just to express truths which it is expedient to teach in fit and proper words" (IV.28). Hence, eloquence is wrested from its grounding in form, in style, and regrounded or refounded as a function of content.

Notes

1   *Cambridge Companion to Aquinas*, ed. Norman Kretzmann and Eleonore Stump (Cambridge: Cambridge University Press, 1993), pp. 4–5.
2   St. Augustine, *City of God*, trans. Henry Bettenson (Harmondsworth: Penguin, 1984), I.31. Hereafter cited as *CG*.
3   *The Confessions of St. Augustine*, trans. Rex Warner (New York: Mentor, 1963), I.xvii. Hereafter cited as *Confessions*.
4   St. Augustine, *De Doctrina Christiana* (Calvin College: Christian Classics Ethereal Library, 2003), I.2. This translation, which I find to be particularly effective, is in the public domain and can be found in electronic format at: www.ccel.org/ccel/augustine/doctrine.iii.html.

CHAPTER 9

THE LATER MIDDLE AGES

Historical Background

C ertain thinkers of the early medieval period continued to exercise a shaping
influence for many centuries. The influence of Augustine – in particular his
view of human will and the need for divine grace – persisted through the later
Middle Ages, though only as one strand of thought competing with the doctrines of
other theologians. Another thinker of the early medieval period, Boethius, also continued
to exert a profound impact, primarily through his translations of Aristotle's logical
treatises into Latin, and his commentaries both on these treatises and on their interpretation by the Neo-Platonist Porphyry. Likewise, some streams of literary criticism
of the early medieval period either continued into, or were resurrected in, the later
Middle Ages. The tradition of grammatical criticism and textual exegesis had been fairly
continuous from the late classical era onward. Allegorical criticism and exegesis of
both pagan and Christian texts enjoyed a similar continuity. One of the most prominent
streams of thought of the early Middle Ages, Neo-Platonism, saw a revival in the twelfth
century. Beyond these continuities, the later Middle Ages witnessed the growth of new
intellectual movements, chiefly various forms of humanism and scholasticism, which
arose from within the structures and divisions of knowledge that had grown in the later
medieval institutions of learning, namely, the cathedral schools and the universities.

In order to understand these new modes of thinking about literature – which were
inevitably tied to broader movements of thought – we must consider the larger social
and economic developments that marked the later medieval era. As mentioned in the
previous chapter, the early Middle Ages saw the collapse of the Roman Empire and the
centralized system of Roman administration and government, with a decline in commerce, trade, and agriculture, and in many areas a reversion to tribal customs and local
law. It had largely been left to the Church (and certain rulers such as Charlemagne) to
attempt some kind of social and moral cohesion and to preserve and transmit the
various intellectual and literary traditions. The later Middle Ages, beginning around
1050, witnessed considerable progress on many levels. Most fundamentally, there was

an economic revival. It was in this period that the system of feudalism achieved a relatively stable formation. The term "feudalism" derives from the word "fief" (the medieval term being *feudum* or "feud"), which means a piece of land held in "fee": in other words, the land was not owned, but a person had the right to cultivate it in return for rent or certain services performed for the landlord. Perry Anderson succinctly defines "fief" as "a delegated grant of land, vested with juridical and political powers, in exchange for military service" (*PF*, 140).

The basic contractual relation in feudal society was between a lord and a vassal: the lord, owning the land, would provide protection, in return for which the vassal was bound to obey his lord, to pay taxes or rent, and to provide military or other service. Often, small farmers would give up their independent ownership of land for the protection of powerful lords. Usually, fiefs (tracts of land or certain offices) were hereditary, and the feudal system was in general a static hierarchy, ranging from the highest lord, the monarch, through the various ranks of nobility such as castellans, barons, counts, and principals to the knights. Hence, each member of this hierarchy was both a lord and a vassal, involved in an intricate nexus of relationships with those above and below him. In a broader sense, however, society was increasingly divided into two classes, the one a landed aristocracy and clergy, the other composed of the mass of peasants, with a small middle class of merchants, traders, and craftsmen. The peasantry itself existed as a hierarchy, from villeins or tenant farmers through serfs (who were bound to a particular tract of land) to the poorest people who hired out their labor on an occasional basis. Clearly, this was not a system based on individual enterprise or merit or ability. The legal and political structure, as Hegel would observe later, was not rational but an outgrowth of hereditary status, existing practices, traditions, and customs. Having said that, the lord was obliged, in theory at least, to the terms of his contractual relationship with the peasant, affording him both military and economic protection. The basic unit of production in the feudal system was the manor or manorial estate: this comprised the lord's manor house and demesne (that part of his land not held by tenants), the parish church, one or more villages, and the land divided into strips between a multitude of peasants. The size of the estate varied between two to four thousand acres. The manor was largely self-contained, self-governed, existing in relative economic isolation, with minimal foreign trade (*PF*, 137).

Another constitutive element in feudalism was the city. By the later Middle Ages, significant urban communities had been formed. Major European cities included Palermo, Venice, Florence, Milan, Ghent, Bruges, and Paris. Many of these enjoyed a considerable degree of freedom from feudal restrictions concerning property and service. Economically, the cities were dominated by two types of organizations, merchant guilds and artisan guilds, whose purpose was to ensure a monopoly of local trade for their own members. The merchant guilds restricted foreign trade and established uniform prices. The members of the artisan guilds formed a hierarchy composed of master craftsmen, who owned their own businesses, and the "journeymen" who worked for them, as well as the apprentices, for whose training and upbringing the masters were responsible. The artisan guilds also regulated the means of production, attempting to preserve a stability and freedom from competition, with standard wages and prices, and even frowning on new technology or more efficient strategies. The guilds had a paternalistic attitude toward their members, sustaining them in times of hardship, providing for their widows and orphans, as well as exercising broader religious and social functions. The guild system rested partly on Christian doctrines, stemming from the Church Fathers and Aquinas, which frowned on excessive wealth or private property, condemned usury or the taking of interest, advocated fair prices, and encouraged an orientation toward the welfare of the community as a whole rather than that of the individual. At least, such were the ideals in theory.

Drawing on insights of Marx, Perry Anderson remarks certain structural features of feudalism. Most fundamentally, since feudal authority was transmitted through a complex chain of lordship and vassalage, "political sovereignty was never focused in a single centre." There were three structural consequences of this "parcellization of sovereignty." Firstly, there was no straightforward concentration of the two basic classes, lords and serfs, within a homogeneous form of property relation. The peasant class, from which the lord extracted an agrarian surplus or profit, "inhabited a world of overlapping claims and powers," a plurality which enabled, through the survival of a number of communal and peasant-owned lands, some degree of "peasant autonomy and resistance" (*PF*, 148–149). A more important result of this stratification of power was effectively the creation of the medieval town. The feudal system was the first to enable an autonomous development of the city within an agrarian economy. Even though the cities of the ancient world had been larger, they were governed by nobles who were primarily landowners. The medieval towns of Europe, in contrast, were "self-governing communes, enjoying corporate political and military autonomy from the nobility and the Church" (*PF*, 150). Marx had observed in feudalism a *dynamic* opposition of town and country. Anderson summarizes this conflict as one between "an urban economy of increasing commodity exchange, controlled by merchants and organized in guilds and corporations, and a rural economy of natural exchange, controlled by nobles and organized in manors and strips, with communal and individual peasant enclaves" (*PF*, 150–151). It was this opposition between the merchant class in the cities and the nobility in the countryside which eventually fueled the growth of the bourgeois class and of a capitalist economy.

The third result of the feudal power structure was yet another structural contradiction within feudalism. The monarch did not have supreme power over his subjects; rather, he was a "feudal suzerain [lord] of his vassals, to whom he was bound by reciprocal ties of fealty." The monarchy was not a true "integrating mechanism," a fact which "posed a permanent threat" to the stability and survival of the feudal system. At the same time, "actual royal power always had to be asserted and extended against the spontaneous grain of the feudal polity as a whole, in a constant struggle to establish a 'public' authority outside the compact web of private jurisdictions" (*PF*, 151–152).

Another contradiction in the structure of feudal power was that the Church, which in late antiquity had been integrated within the mechanisms of imperial power, was an autonomous institution within feudalism, and the sole source of religious authority. A number of factors had led to this circumstance. By the time of the Fourth Lateran Council in 1215, the theory of the priesthood (whereby the priest was vested with some of the pope's authority as inherited from Peter) and the fixing of theory of the seven sacraments increased the power and status of the clergy. The Church's role as spiritual guardian was reinforced and disseminated by the requirements of confession and the threat of excommunication. Furthermore, a number of religious reform movements had wrested the monasteries, clergy, and the appointment of church officials from the power of the feudal nobility, insisting on the authority of the pope and the Church in ecclesiastical matters. Bertrand Russell remarks that the Church's emancipation from the feudal aristocracy was "one of the causes of the emergence of Europe from the dark ages" (*HWP*, 305). Prior to this emancipation, conflict between Church and state power was "endemic in the medieval epoch," especially in the period from 1050 until around 1350, with considerable consequences for later intellectual development (*PF*, 152). The thought of Dante and Aquinas, for example, was marked by this struggle between temporal and spiritual power, just as Augustine had given archetypal expression to it. Augustine had effectively divided human experience into the categories of *civitas dei* or the City of God and *civitas terrena* or the Earthly City. These categories – and the conflict they embodied – persisted through many guises, spiritual against temporal, papacy against empire, the demands of the soul against those of the body.

These inherent structural contradictions all contributed to the decline of feudalism. One large-scale effect of the growth of feudalism was to increase the power of the landed aristocracy or nobles relative to that of the monarchy. In turn, one factor in the decline of feudalism was the growth and establishment of strong or even absolute monarchies in several countries, notably France, England, and Germany. Other factors contributed to the undermining of the feudal structure: the growing internationalization of trade; the expansion of cities and the increased opportunities for urban employment, which tempted peasants to move to the towns; the Crusades, beginning in 1096, which encouraged peasants to break their bonds to the soil of absentee landlords; the Hundred Years' War (1337–1453), which consolidated the monarchy in France; the plague known as the Black Death which spread over Europe, causing a shortage of labor; and, after 1517, the rise of various sects of Protestantism which intensified latent trends toward the sanctioning of worldly activity. All of these factors contributed to the explosion of economic practice, as well as its legitimation by religious and political ideologies, beyond the constraining boundaries of feudalism.

Intellectual Currents of the Later Middle Ages

The Medieval Curriculum

These were the broad historical developments that lay behind the intellectual currents of the later Middle Ages. The major currents comprised various forms of humanism deriving from the classical grammatical tradition, the heritage of Neo-Platonism and allegorical criticism, and the movement known as scholasticism, which was largely based on a revived Aristotelianism mediated through Islamic thinkers such as Ibn Rushd (Averroës). These later intellectual streams effectively began with Boethian logic, and were enabled by educational developments, primarily the rise of the cathedral schools and the universities. The universities were initially institutions or corporations for training teachers and were usually composed of faculties of liberal arts as well as faculties of medicine, law, and theology. The notion of the liberal arts can be traced as far back as the Sophist Hippias of Elis, a contemporary of Socrates, as well as to the rhetorician Isocrates who opposed Plato's insistence on a purely philosophical training with a broader system of education. The *locus classicus* for the system of *artes liberales* is a letter by the Roman thinker Seneca, who called these arts "liberal" because they are worthy of a free man, their purpose not being to make money.

By the end of antiquity the number of the liberal arts had been fixed at seven and arranged in the sequence that they were to retain through the medieval period. The first three, grammar, rhetoric, and dialectic (or logic), were known from the ninth century onwards as the "trivium" ("three roads"); the remaining four mathematical arts, arithmetic, geometry, music, and astronomy, had been designated by Boethius as the "quadruvium" ("four roads"), later known as the "quadrivium." It was Martianus Capella's description of the liberal arts, in the form of a romance entitled *De nuptiis Philologiae et Mercurii* (*The Wedding of Philology and Mercury*), which remained authoritative throughout the Middle Ages (Curtius, 36–38). Of the seven liberal arts, those of the trivium were most thoroughly cultivated, and the most exhaustively studied of these was grammar, which comprised the study of both language or correct speech and the interpretation of literature. The word *litteratura* was a translation of the Greek term *grammatike* and the *litteratus* referred to a person who knew grammar and poetry (Curtius, 42–43). The authors studied included Vergil, Ovid, Donatus, Martianus Capella, Horace, Juvenal, Boethius, Statius, Terence, Lucan, and Cicero, as well as Christian writers such as Juvencus, Arator, and Prudentius. This list continued to expand into the thirteenth century, with the pagan authors subjected to allegorical interpretation and viewed as sages. The teaching of grammar and rhetoric had already given them authoritative status, as *auctores* (whose etymology includes "authority" as well as "author" or "originator") in a normative and imposing curriculum (Curtius, 48–52).

It was the authority of this curriculum – along with the presuppositions sustaining it – which was dislodged by the dialectical or logical methods of the scholastic thinkers. As mentioned earlier, these rational methods had been fostered by the growth, from the beginning of the twelfth century, of the cathedral schools and the universities. The cathedral schools effectively displaced the surviving monasteries as centers of education. They were located in towns, the most renowned being at Paris, Chartres, and Canterbury. Each of these schools was directed by a canon, the *scholasticus*, who enjoyed a relative flexibility in arranging the curriculum. The French logician Peter Abelard (1079–1142) taught at the school of Mont Ste.-Geneviève, and the Italian theologian Peter Lombard (ca. 1100–1160) was educated at such a school. Perhaps the single greatest force animating these schools was the revival of philosophy, which, at the end of antiquity, had given way to the liberal arts and had "ceased to be a systematic discipline and an educational force" (Curtius, 37). In the new schools, however, philosophy was an important part of the curriculum.

This revival was spearheaded in the late eleventh and early twelfth centuries by Anselm of Canterbury (1033–1109) and the other theologians mentioned above. These thinkers effectively pioneered the broad school or movement of medieval thought known as scholasticism. They drew on Boethius' logic to attempt a rational and coherent interpretation of Christian doctrine as derived from scripture, the Church Fathers, and the decrees of the Church. One of the strategies for which St. Anselm is noted is the ontological argument, which attempts to prove God's existence by logical means. The most important of the early scholastic philosophers were Roscelin and his pupil

Peter Abelard. The latter exerted a considerable influence on later scholasticism through his volume entitled *Sic et Non* (*For and Against* or literally, *Yes and No*), which advanced a series of antitheses designed to reveal the incoherence of arguments based on authority. While Abelard upheld the foremost authority of the scriptures, he encouraged a fearless use of dialectic as an avenue to truth, viewing logic as the predominant Christian science. Peter Lombard, known as "Master of the Sentences," authored the *Libri quatuor sententiarum*, a collection of authoritative "judgments" (*sententiae*) on the Incarnation, Trinity, and sacraments, which eventually became a standard text of Catholic theology.

Even more important in this twelfth-century "renaissance" of thought was the widespread growth of universities. Ancient universities had been largely devoted to the teaching of grammar and rhetoric. It was in the Middle Ages that our modern notion of the university was created, with various faculties, a regular curriculum, and a hierarchy of degrees. The oldest universities were in Italy, France, and England, and included Bologna (1158), Oxford (ca. 1200), Paris (1208–1209), and Naples (1224). Through these universities swept the philosophy of the "new" Aristotle, the recently recovered works of Aristotle on natural history, metaphysics, ethics, and politics, made available to the West through translations from Arabic and Greek. The foremost of the Arab Aristotelian thinkers was Ibn Rushd, whose doctrines were irreconcilable with Church doctrine. At the instigation of the pope, the study of the "new" Aristotle was forbidden in 1215, but the stricture had little force. It was the Dominican scholars who attempted to reconcile the Christian faith with Greek philosophy (Curtius, 54–55). Thus came into being the great impetus of scholasticism, reaching its height in Albertus Magnus and then his student Thomas Aquinas. By the efforts of the Dominicans at the University of Paris, "the dangerous Aristotle was purified, rehabilitated, and authorized. Even more: his teaching was incorporated into Christian philosophy and theology, and in this form has remained authoritative" (Curtius, 56).

Because of these changes, the curricula of learning no longer gave primacy to the lists of authors, the *auctores*, who had been regarded for centuries as sources of technical knowledge and worldly wisdom in terms of both breadth of experience and moral precepts. The universities, in particular the University of Paris, which was one of the educational centers of Europe, had become instruments of the Church. Philosophy and theology acquired a new prominence, while the study of grammar, rhetoric, and literature was pushed somewhat into the background. There were a few enclaves of humanistic learning, such as the school of Chartres, under the directorship of Bishop John of Salisbury, and at the University of Oxford, where thinkers such as Roger Bacon prefigured a scientific approach to knowledge that would outlive scholasticism (Curtius, 56–57).

Medieval Criticism: A Historical Overview

In broadly historical terms, what falls under the rubric of "medieval criticism" has been classified by scholars such as O. B. Hardison, Jr. into a number of periods. It will be seen later that more recent scholarship has challenged this kind of classification, based as it was on a clear distinction between humanism and scholasticism. Nonetheless, Hardison's schema, as outlined below, is extremely useful as a starting point. The first period of the Middle Ages overlaps with the late classical period, which runs from around the first century BC to the seventh century. The dominant traditions of criticism in this era, discussed in the previous chapter, were grammatical, Neo-Platonic, and allegorical. Neo-Platonism arose and was developed in the works of Plotinus, Porphyry, and Proclus. The tradition of allegorical exegesis had been established, running from Philo through Clement and Origen, being absorbed by Ambrose and Augustine. The most important texts of this era for medieval criticism were the various commentaries and collections that were integrated into the grammar curriculum. These included the commentaries of Servius on Vergil, Donatus on Terence, Diomedes' *Ars grammatica*, and Isidore's *Encyclopaedia*. Christian writers including Tertullian, Lactantius, and Augustine grappled with the problem of assimilating pagan texts; eventually, Christian thinkers and teachers radically enlarged the curriculum of studies to include Old Testament authors and a body of Christian literature, thereby transforming both the chronology of world literature and the content of the classical "canon" of texts. As Hardison states, grammatical criticism was conservative, focusing on practical aids to understanding and imitation, and secondarily on the moral function of literature. Neo-Platonism promoted a view of poetry as a repository of esoteric wisdom.

The next period, the Carolingian, from the eighth through the tenth centuries, produced numerous commentaries, including works by Rabanus Maurus, Remigius of Auxerre, and Scotus Eriugena. The most comprehensive rhetorical treatise of the period was Alcuin's *Rhetoric*, which is Ciceronian in scope and emphasis. The only purely critical document from this period is the *Scholia Vindobonensia*, a commentary on Horace's *Ars poetica*, intended as an aid for reading Horace in the grammar curriculum. This text defines poetry as the "art of making [fictions]" and composing; it espouses the values of moderation, restraint, and verisimilitude, warning against the creation of impossible or incredible episodes. The author explains that poetry is fed by grammar, rhetoric, and logic; its content is ethics and the disciplines of the quadrivium. Poetry delights, offers moral instruction, and arouses patriotism (*MLC*, 23–28).

The ensuing period, from the eleventh through the thirteenth centuries (known as the High Middle Ages), saw a renewal of interest in Neo-Platonism which generated intellectual ferment in a number of directions. This ferment was initiated at the end of the tenth century by John Scotus Eriugena's translation of the works of Dionysius the pseudo-Areopagite (so called because, during the Middle Ages, he was confused with Dionysius of Athens who had conversed with St. Paul on the Areopagus). The supposed apostolic authority of Dionysius' writings – which were actually produced around the end of the fifth century – procured for them a profound impact on medieval theology. These writings attempt a synthesis of Christian doctrine and Neo-Platonism, and, along with the works of Calcidius, Macrobius, and Boethius, they laid the foundation for subsequent treatises on mysticism. Dionysius' works articulate a spiritual progress from the material world toward God, laying a renewed emphasis on inspiration, on a supra-rational intellect, and visionary experiences communicable only through symbols. Dionysius' symbolism generated a new interest in the transcendent, and, as Hardison states, his God "is an architect or a geometer making a world from numbers, or, alternately, a musician creating harmonies out of the discord of matter" (*MLC*, 29).

Dionysius' work was a seminal element in a broader pattern of medieval Platonism which included Bernard Silvestris' commentary on Vergil's *Aeneid*, and which was also expressed in a revival of grammatical humanism in the twelfth century. This human-istic revival was reflected in a series of treatises on the art of poetry (*artes poeticae*) influenced by Bernard, beginning with Matthew of Vendôme's *Ars versificatoria* in 1175 and extending to Gervase of Melcheley's *Ars poetica* of around 1215. One of these treatises, Geoffrey de Vinsauf's *Poetria Nova* (to be considered in more detail below), bears traces of this broad Neo-Platonic influence in its emphasis upon the inward and intellectual elements of poetry. The primary purpose of these treatises on poetry was educational; they were manuals and their emphasis was on imitative exercises and knowledge of grammatical and rhetorical figures.

Another main stream of criticism during this period, falling under grammatical exegesis, was the *accessus* tradition. The *accessus* was a formal introduction to a cur-riculum author, which followed a formula that became standard through the works of writers such as Bernard of Utrecht and Conrad of Hirsau, whose *Didascalon* is the fullest example. The formula for an *accessus* consisted of: name of author, title, genre, intention of the writer, number of books in the text, stylistic and didactic mode of pro-cedure, the order in which contents were arranged, the pedagogic and moral usefulness of the book, explanation or interpretation of the text, and the branch of knowledge to which it belonged. Such formulae have been traced back through Servius to Hellenistic times; and much of the material used by Bernard and Conrad draws upon late classical compendia such as Diomedes' *Ars grammatica* and Isidore's *Encyclopaedia*. Conrad offers a "list of authors" which indicates the curriculum used at the cathedral schools: pagan authors such as Homer, Vergil, Horace, Terence, and Statius are complemented by Christian authors. Conrad stresses the importance of imitation, practiced by all the great writers; he also emphasizes that the rationale for reading the poets is preparation for reading scripture, which effectively crowns the list of authors (*MLC*, 32–33).

The twelfth century also produced a number of surveys of knowledge in the tradition of Quintilian, Cassiodorus, and Rabanus Maurus. One of the most noted examples of this kind of treatise, Hugh of St. Victor's *Didascalicon*, will soon be examined. Also important is John of Salisbury's *Metalogicon*, which describes the grammar curriculum and its use of the *auctores*, and also sheds light on the controversy that raged between the so-called humanist advocates of literary studies, associated with the cathedral schools, and the promoters of logic, affiliated with the University of Paris. Gervase of Melcheley's *Ars poetica* (ca. 1215–1216), as Hardison usefully suggests, might be seen as a compro-mise between the older humanist and newer scholastic positions: in content it belongs with the *artes poeticae* of the cathedral schools, but it is scholastic in that it abandons rhetorical divisions of poetic figures and classifies them instead in terms of logical divisions of identity, similitude, and contrariety (*MLC*, 34).

The scholastic phase of medieval criticism, profoundly influenced by Islamic philo-sophers such as al-Farabi (ca. 870–950) and Ibn Rushd, was marked by a tendency to view poetry as a branch of logic rather than of grammar or rhetoric. Poetry was here conceived of as a faculty, a technique for manipulating language rather than as a subject with its own specific content. This view anticipates many modern formalist conceptions of poetry. Hence, whereas the grammar curriculum exalted poetry as both a source of delight and a means of offering moral instruction through examples of virtue, the scholastics tended to view poetry as a mere recreation or even as a diversion from the essential theological tasks of understanding scripture and clarifying Christian

doctrine. A link between poetry and logic had been made by late classical commentators on Aristotle, but during the early Middle Ages this connection was allowed to
lapse in favor of rhetorical and grammatical treatments of poetry. Bernard of Utrecht
and Conrad of Hirsau initiated a link between poetry and logic by relating the *accessus*
formula to Aristotle's four causes; and, as we have seen, Gervase of Melcheley used a
logical system of classifying figures. The issue of whether poetry belonged to logic or
grammar was part of a broader debate over the liberal arts: the cathedral schools
insisted on the primacy of grammar, in which a central place was given to the interpretation of literature using the traditional canon of *auctores*; in contrast, the newly
emergent universities held that logic should command pride of place in the trivium.

The scholastic phase is followed by another set of humanistic currents effectively
beginning with Dante's *De Vulgari Eloquentia*, which argues that the vernacular is an
appropriate medium for great poetry. Dante's successors, such as Petrarch, Mussato,
and Boccaccio, can be seen as transitional figures, aligned with either the declining
Middle Ages or the nascent Renaissance. In any case, they are humanistic advocates of
liberal studies and defenders of poetry against its late scholastic detractors, though they
often deploy scholastic arguments toward their own ends. Humanism saw a revival not
only in Italy but also in France, where the tradition of *artes poeticae* is renewed in the
works of Deschamps; the tradition of allegorical interpretation continues in the works
of Petrus Bercorius, John de Ridevall, and Christine de Pisan (who will be considered
in more detail in the next chapter). Allegorical poetry also found expression in such
enduring works as *Sir Gawain and the Green Knight*, the *Roman de la Rose*, Chaucer's
Canterbury Tales and other works, Gower's *Confessio Amantis*, and Sir Thomas Malory's
Morte Darthur and *Everyman*. In theoretical terms, the major issue was still the place of
poetry in the overall scheme of the sciences. Mussato and Boccaccio (to be considered
in the next chapter) saw poetry as a kind of inspired theology, and Petrarch saw it as
both a means of instruction and a vehicle of patriotism. All three were pitted against
conservative views that poetry was a means of manipulating language to express fictions
and falsehoods, and was devoid of any intrinsic moral content. Boccaccio anticipates
developments in Renaissance Platonism, and Petrarch anticipates the educational and
rhetorical strains of Renaissance humanism.

Overall, then, in literary-critical terms, the later Middle Ages was characterized by
an ongoing and widespread tradition of grammatical humanism which was continuous
from the late classical era. This tradition was complemented by developments in Neo-
Platonism and allegorical interpretation, and was somewhat eclipsed by movements in
scholasticism which in turn gave way before fourteenth-century revivals of humanism.
The foregoing picture of the various tendencies of medieval literary criticism is necessarily brief. It has also been challenged in its assumption that there was a clear distinction between scholasticism and the various currents of humanism. Scholars such as
A. J. Minnis and A. B. Scott have suggested that the conventional distinction between
scholasticism and humanism is "misleading," whether regarded chronologically or in
terms of the alleged characteristics of each movement.[1] For one thing, they claim,
thirteenth-century scholasticism actually grew out of twelfth-century humanism; moreover, the scholastics did not merely dismiss or bypass the classics that were so central
to the humanistic grammar curriculum; rather, they redeployed these works for their
own ends, and actually channeled earlier literary-critical methods into the study of

scripture. Again, they point out that much of the so-called humanist literary theory of the fourteenth and fifteenth centuries takes its point of departure and many basic ideas from scholasticism. These ideas include: the use of poetry, the place of poetry within the hierarchy of the sciences, the spiritual and moral senses of poetry, and the question of styles. The relation between humanism and scholasticism, according to these and other scholars, is best seen as dialectical, each school actually articulating its own positions against those of the other (*MLTC*, 7–10). More recently, Martin Irvine has ascribed conventional misconceptions about medieval literary criticism and history to two conventional "modern prejudices": firstly, a "humanist paradigm" of cultural history, and secondly, a fundamentalist reduction of medieval literary interests to a "strictly religious pragmatism."[2] Hence, the connections between humanism and scholasticism are best seen as fluid and mutually defining. The same might be said of the connections between the various elements of the trivium, grammar, rhetoric, and logic (dialectic). It was in relation to these disciplines that the significance of poetry was articulated in the later Middle Ages. These various placements of poetry can now be examined.

The Status of Literature

As indicated above, the various kinds of medieval criticism can be classified in terms of the broad divisions of knowledge that were embodied in the institutions of learning. All three elements of the medieval trivium – *grammatica*, *rhetorica*, *dialectica* – were sciences of language and discourse, concerned with interpretation and signification; their boundaries often overlapped and were indeed sometimes the subject of fierce dispute. Accordingly, the status and placement of literature varied. Since the late classical era, poetry had been positioned as a branch of rhetoric; in the later Middle Ages the study of poetry was increasingly absorbed by the grammatical tradition, but in the hands of scholastic thinkers it became part of the province of logic.

These various streams of medieval criticism can now be examined through a detailed consideration of one or two of the major writers representing each tendency. We can begin by considering the medieval disposition to situate literature within the entire scheme of knowledge, as will emerge in our analysis of Hugh of St. Victor. We can then consider the fundamental ideological importance of grammar in medieval thought generally, and the nature and value of the grammar curriculum (of which literature was an important part), in the work of John of Salisbury and Dante. We can then proceed to the placement of poetry, first within rhetoric (in the texts of Geoffrey de Vinsauf), and then within logic (as expressed in the scholastic thinkers Ibn Rushd and Aquinas, as well as in Dante). Finally, in the next chapter, we can see the placement of poetry as a part of philosophy or theology in the writings of Boccaccio and Christine de Pisan (in what is effectively a humanistic revival of allegorical traditions).

The Traditions of Medieval Criticism: Literature and Grammar

Most of the intellectual currents of the Middle Ages are founded on the tradition of textual exegesis deriving from the classical grammatical tradition, and extended by

Christian scholars to scriptural exegesis. Indeed, the most enduring placement of poetry was in the grammar curriculum, and the association of grammar with the reading of poetry can be traced back from medieval authors such as John of Salisbury and Rabanus Maurus through late classical figures such as Cassiodorus and Victorinus all the way to Quintilian who had defined grammar as comprising exposition of poets and the rules for the correct use of language.

The association of grammar with poetry spawned three characteristic types of treatise. The first was the *commentary* or *gloss*. The major commentaries, such as those of Servius and Donatus, date from the late classical period. Notable medieval examples include those of John Scotus Eriugena on Dionysius the pseudo-Areopagite, and Nicholas of Lyra's *Glossa Ordinaria*, which was the standard commentary on the Bible in the Middle Ages (*MLC*, 6–7). To understand the importance of the gloss and commentary in the teaching and transmission of texts, we need to bear in mind the physical characteristics of medieval books and manuscripts. To begin with, there was a great deal of textual variation: a text was not somehow fixed and closed. More significantly, the pages were designed to include gloss and substantial commentary within the very wide margins; this meant effectively that the division between the text and commentary was not as clear as it often seems with modern texts; the text was carefully and elaborately encoded – and even contained – within a broader system of meaning handed down by traditional interpretation (*GLT*, 17). Hence, even the material form of the text was enlisted in the ideological function of grammar which, as will be seen shortly, authorized certain conceptions of the world. In general, medieval literary theory gave priority to inherited forms of literature and stressed the virtue of treating traditional matter in novel ways rather than the invention of radically new viewpoints.

A second type of grammatical treatise was the *ars metrica*, since the grammar curriculum included prosody and a study of the standard poetic forms. A late classical example of this type of work is Bede's *De Arte Metrica*, which contains one of the earliest analyses of accentual prosody; notable among medieval Latin treatises was Dante's *De Vulgari Eloquentia* (ca. 1304–1307), which will be examined below. Medieval vernacular treatises included Eustace Deschamps' *L'art de dictier* (1392), which anticipates Renaissance texts such as Du Bellay's *Deffence et illustration de la langue francoyse* and George Gascoigne's *Certain Notes of Instruction*. The third type of grammatical treatise was the *accessus* or prologue to an author, which has already been discussed. This prologue or introduction to an author had its roots in Quintilian's *Institutio*, which offers a list of curriculum authors; the medieval practice of formulating a list or canon of *auctores* or standard authors was formalized in the early eleventh century in these treatises known as *accessus*. As will emerge below, Dante's *Epistle*, which is scholastic in its approach, is also influenced by the *accessus* tradition.

All three types of grammatical treatise – the commentary, the *ars metrica*, and the *accessus* – were vehicles of medieval humanism (*MLC*, 10). It should be said that medieval grammar or *grammatica* was much broader than our modern notion of "grammar," and its importance in the entire scheme of medieval thought and ideology cannot be overestimated. As Martin Irvine has recently argued, although grammar was the first of the arts of discourse (the others being rhetoric and logic), it was not merely one discipline among many. From late classical times until the early Renaissance, grammar had a foundational role, furnishing a model of learning, interpretation, and knowledge. It was a social practice that provided exclusive access to literacy, the understanding of scripture, knowledge of the literary canon, and membership of an international Latin textual community. *Grammatica* was sustained by the dominant social and political institutions of medieval Europe; in turn, *grammatica* functioned in support of those institutions: the courts, cathedrals, and all the major centers of power. As such, the authority of *grammatica* was a textual reflex of religious and political authority (*GLT*, 2, 13, 20). It was *grammatica* that elaborated the rules and interpretative strategies for constructing certain texts as repositories of authority and value; it effectively constructed language and texts as objects of knowledge and as such was presupposed by *all* of the arts of discourse, including biblical and literary interpretation, philosophy, theology, and law (*GLT*, 2). In the late classical era, both grammar and rhetoric had an important role in perpetuating the myth of Roman *imperium*. The texts of Vergil were promoted as a kind of national scripture, and he was regarded as the prime authority on grammar. Literary education in schools of grammar had an ideological function: to preserve the deeds and characters of illustrious ancestors and to provide cultural examples of heroism and virtue. Equally importantly, grammar was a vehicle for promulgating a certain view of history. History was an independent discipline but was taught through the standard *auctores* and the myths of empire, to foster an image of history and empire as continuous and unified, to foster the myth of a continuous tradition, as well as the myth of the unity of past and present. This imperial myth and the scriptural status of Vergil is revealed in the commentaries on Vergil by writers such as Donatus, Servius, and Macrobius. As the Christian textual community began to shape its own canon through thinkers such as Ambrose and Augustine, grammar continued to be fundamental (*GLT*, 78–86). The enlarged Christian canon did not displace the pagan classical texts but redeployed them, subjecting them to allegorical interpretation consistent with Christian doctrine and enlisting grammatical methods for the reading and interpretation of scripture.

The medieval model of grammar, based on that formulated by the Roman writer Varro (116–27 BC), consisted of two broad elements: the interpretation of literary texts and training in reading and writing. A later text influential in medieval times, the *Ars Victorini*, divided the interpretative dimension of grammar into four parts: *lectio*, the principles of prosody and reading aloud; *enarratio*, the exposition of content and the principles of interpretation; *emendatio*, the rules of linguistic correctness and textual authenticity; and *iudicium*, the criticism or evaluation of the text. Hence, grammar involved the study of both language and literature; it constituted both a special field of knowledge – a canon of traditional texts – and the rules of language as embodied in a standard written Latin (*latinitas*) (*GLT*, 3–4). Clearly, then, grammar was the foundation of the entire system of written knowledge as well as of systems of interpretation.

The language studied by grammar was of course not ordinary speech or vernacular idioms but the language of classical literary texts. The very nature of grammar and its fundamental role in late classical and medieval culture entailed a privileging of writing over speech. Hence, notwithstanding Derrida's comments about the priority of speech over writing in the Western tradition since Plato's *Phaedrus*, the fourth to the eleventh centuries saw, as Irvine says, a victory of *grammatica* and writing in official culture (*GLT*, 12). Medieval culture was based on the authority of a canon of classical texts, both pagan and Christian, ultimately crowned by scripture; it was grammar that articulated and enabled this authority and in turn received its authority from this function. Given that medieval culture was ultimately based on scripture, on *the* Book, *grammatica* was an essential precondition of this culture. The three sacred languages of scripture – Hebrew, Greek, and Latin – were regarded as divinely sanctioned; hence scripture and writing mutually sanctioned each other's authority. According to Rabanus Maurus, the letters of God's law contain and disclose all that is in the world, past, present, and future. Rabanus sees writing as a means of repelling temporality, change, and death (*GLT*, 14).

As Irvine states, modern forms of textuality and critical discourse are part of a much longer grammatical history that is often forgotten or overlooked. In fact, as he argues, *grammatica* continues to shape our understanding of texts, writing, and the literary canon. We might extend his insight to suggest that our modern theories of reading, writing, and textuality are perhaps not so radical when placed in this longer perspective. For one thing, our modern notions of intertextuality are anticipated and already formulated; as Irvine points out, *grammatica* produced a culture that was *intertextual*: a written work was constituted as a text by being accorded a position in a larger library of texts; it was interpreted as part of a larger textual system (*GLT*, 15). Further, it is clear that medieval scholars adhered to a system of reading and interpretation which was more intricate than the modes conventionally employed in our own day. Membership of a textual community required the highest degrees of literacy in the classical languages, especially Latin. Finally, much modern literary and cultural theory is premised on the primacy accorded to language in the construction of the world and of our ourselves. It is clear, however, that many centuries ago *grammatica* had already and very elaborately replaced the world of things by the world of signs; it had already reduced thinghood to language, in a vast and hierarchical system of signification that spanned many levels. This system was just as relational as any view of language to be found in Saussure. In other words, no element in that system was presumed to have any isolated or independent significance. In all these ways, medieval literary theory was far more sophisticated – and more foundational in our own ways of thinking – than was previously thought. The fully fledged encounter of modern theory with medieval *grammatica* has yet to occur, though it has begun in the work of scholars such as Rita Copeland and A. J. Minnis. It is an encounter that promises to transform our understanding of both.

Literature in the Scheme of Human Learning: The Sacred Hermeneutics of Hugh of St. Victor (ca. 1097–1141)

The work of Hugh of St. Victor illustrates the medieval tendency to situate literature as one component in an ordered and hierarchical scheme of learning, a scheme which is founded on the traditions of grammar. Moreover, many of the questions raised by Macrobius and other Neo-Platonists, concerning the connection between body and soul, man's ultimate destination, the use of literal and figurative language, and allegorical interpretation, were addressed in a widely influential treatise composed in the late 1120s called the *Didascalicon* (a Greek word meaning "instructive" or "fit for teaching").

Its author, Hugh of St. Victor, was born in the last decade of the eleventh century, and derives his name from the circumstance that he was a teacher and prior at the Abbey of St. Victor in Paris, from 1118 until his death. The abbey had been founded in 1108 by William of Champeaux.

The *Didascalicon*, as Hugh states in his preface, is essentially concerned with *reading*: it attempts to lay out guidelines for what people should read, as well as the order and manner of their reading, as applied to both the arts and sacred scripture.[3] Hence this text is an educational treatise, addressed primarily to teachers and students in the medieval curriculum. As Jerome Taylor remarks, in contrast with the specialized curricula of various medieval institutions, the *Didascalicon* "set forth a program insisting on the indispensability of a whole complex of the traditional arts and on the need for their scientific pursuit in a particular order by all men as a means both of relieving the physical weaknesses of earthly life and of restoring that union with the divine Wisdom for which man was made" (*DHV*, 4).

As a treatise on educational methods, the *Didascalicon* belongs to a tradition that goes all the way back, through Boethius, Augustine, Quintilian, and Cicero, to Plato, Aristotle, and the Sophists. In some ways it effects a synthesis of previous works, yet this synthesis was original. As Taylor notes, it appeared at a time when "learning itself was making secularist adaptations" (*DHV*, 4). This was broadly the period of the twelfth-century renaissance, a period in which the traditional medieval curriculum was challenged by secular and rationalist approaches toward learning, inspired in part by a rediscovery of Greek texts. Moreover, the methods of learning outlined in the *Didascalicon* were widely influential on curricula across Europe from the twelfth century onward; not only did it exert an impact on the ideas of thinkers such as John of Salisbury, Thomas Aquinas, and St. Bonaventure, but also the questions it raises about reading and interpretation are still pertinent in literary criticism and other disciplines today in our own educational institutions.

Hugh begins his treatise by stressing that the first thing we should seek is wisdom, for it is wisdom which "illuminates man so that he may recognize himself . . . if man had not forgotten his origin, he would recognize that everything subject to change is nothing" (I.i). The first precept that will advance us toward this wisdom is "know thyself": following Plato, Pythagoras, and others, Hugh asserts that our soul is analogous in its composition to the nature of things outside of us; it "represents within itself their imaged likeness." Hence in knowing ourselves, we know the nature of all things. Hugh explains that, in our earthly life, our mind is "stupefied by bodily sensations" and has thus "forgotten what it was." However, we can restore ourselves "through instruction, so that we may recognize our nature" (I.i). Hugh accepts Pythagoras' definition of philosophy as the pursuit of wisdom but he insists that this is not the practical wisdom needed for craftsmanship of various kinds; rather, it is "that Wisdom which is the sole primordial Idea or Pattern of things" (I.iv). And wisdom, says Hugh, should govern all human actions and pursuits; it is only by knowledge and virtue that we can restore the integrity of our fallen nature, since it is the contemplation of truth and the practice of virtue which restore our likeness to God. Since man is composed of an immortal soul and a perishable body, he is obliged in his pursuit of wisdom to give priority to his spiritual nature (I.v). Hugh divides wisdom into two parts: "understanding," which pertains to "human" actions, i.e., those actions we perform for our survival in the world of nature; and "knowledge," which applies to "divine" actions, the actions we undertake to restore our divine nature. Understanding itself is divided into two kinds, theoretical, which is concerned with the investigation of truth, and practical, which applies to our moral activity (I.viii).

Adapting the views of Platonic commentators (*DHV*, 55 n. 59), Hugh says, in a statement reminiscent of Plato's views in the tenth book of the *Republic*, that there are three types of works: the work of God, the work of nature, and the work of the artificer. God's work is to create out of nothing; nature brings forth that which was hidden; and the artificer imitates nature, and his art is a "mechanical" art (I.ix).

So far, Hugh has discussed the origins of the theoretical, practical, and mechanical arts. He now turns his attention to the origin of logic, which he regards as the fourth and last branch of knowledge. Logic was invented, he says, because we need to know "the nature of correct and true discourse" when we search the "nature of things." Interestingly, Hugh anticipates Kant somewhat in his view that without a knowledge of correct argumentation, we will fall easily into error since "real things do not precisely conform to the conclusions of our reasoning as they do to a mathematical count." Again, like Kant, he suggests that without a knowledge of our own discursive tools, we will arrive at conclusions that are "false and contrary to each other." Hugh says that rational or argumentative logic can be divided into dialectic and rhetoric; but rational logic itself is a subdivision of linguistic logic, which is divided into grammar, dialectic, and rhetoric (I.xi). He later defines grammar as the "knowledge of how to speak without error," dialectic as "clear-sighted argument" which separates truth from falsehood, and rhetoric as "the discipline of persuading" (II.xxx).

In general, all of the arts, says Hugh (using "arts" here in a broad sense to cover all disciplines of knowledge), are directed toward philosophy, which is a love of the divine wisdom which "in a single and simultaneous vision beholds all things past, present and future." Hence, the ultimate purpose of all arts is to "restore within us the divine likeness" (II.i). As stated earlier, Hugh divides philosophy into four branches, theoretical, practical, mechanical, and logical. The theoretical itself is divided into theology, mathematics, and physics (II.i); and it is the divisions of mathematics which comprise the "quadrivium": arithmetic, music, geometry, and astronomy (II.vi). Interestingly, Hugh sees the quadrivium as concerned with concepts, which "are internally conceived," whereas the trivium (grammar, dialectic, and rhetoric) is concerned with words, "which are external things" (II.xx). These seven "sciences," says Hugh, were "especially selected by the ancients for education since they excel all the rest in usefulness" as a foundation for subsequent independent inquiry, and since they best prepare the mind for "complete knowledge of philosophic truth" (III.iii). Indeed, Hugh reaffirms that these "seven liberal arts," which are parts of philosophy, provide "the foundation of all learning"; hence the student should devote himself to the mastery of these. These genuine arts, he warns, should be distinguished from mere "appendages of the arts," which include "all the songs of the poets – tragedies, comedies, satires, heroic verse and lyric, iambics, certain didactic poems, fables and histories," as well as pseudo-philosophical works which obscure "a simple meaning in confused discourses." These "appendages" may be read for entertainment, but should not be substituted for the arts. Moreover, he insists that the seven liberal arts "depend upon" and cohere with one another, so that not one of them can be omitted in the quest of becoming a philosopher (III.iv). And each art, he cautions, has its own peculiar domain, in terms of content and approach, a domain which should not be transgressed (III.v).

The foregoing represents the intellectual and pedagogical framework within which Hugh sets out his guidance for the reading process. When we need to expound a given text, he says, our exposition includes three elements: "the letter, the sense, and the inner meaning." By "letter" he refers to the suitable arrangement of words; the "sense" is "a certain ready and obvious meaning which the letter presents on the surface"; while the "inner meaning" is the "deeper understanding which can be found only through interpretation and commentary" (III.viii). The method of expounding is analysis, which "begins from things which are finite, or defined, and proceeds in the direction of things which are infinite, or undefined." Moreover, in our investigation, we "descend from universals to particulars" (III.ix).

Hugh provides a similar scheme of guidance for reading and expounding the sacred scriptures. In contrast with the writings of philosophers, where truth is mixed with falsehood, the sacred texts are defined, he says, by their absolute truth and by their freedom from falsehood. These scriptures were produced by men who "cultivated the catholic faith," and they are sanctioned by "the authority of the universal church" (IV.i). Another important way in which scripture differs from philosophical texts is that in scripture "not only words but even things have a meaning." The philosopher knows only the signification of words, which is established by convention and expresses the "voice of men"; but the significance of things, being dictated by nature, and expressing the "voice of God," is "far more excellent." Hugh defines a "word" as the "sign of man's perceptions," whereas a thing is a "resemblance of the divine Idea." The human voice, or the "external word," fades even as it is spoken whereas the "internal word," the idea in the mind, is eternal. Hence the understanding to be found in the scriptures is profound, because there we "come through the word to a concept, through the concept to a thing, through the thing to its idea, and through its idea arrive at Truth" (V.iii). And the fruit of sacred reading is that it "either instructs the mind with knowledge or it equips it with morals. It teaches us what it delights us to know and what it behooves us to imitate" (V.vi).

Unlike many authors in the tradition of allegorical exegesis (such as Augustine, Bede, Aquinas, and Dante), Hugh proposes a threefold (rather than fourfold) understanding of scripture, influenced by Gregory the Great and analogous to the allegorical levels proposed by Jerome and Origen (*DHV*, 120 n. 1). Sacred scripture, says Hugh, has "three ways of conveying meaning – namely, history, allegory and tropology." History represents the literal level of meaning; allegory refers to the spiritual or mystical sense; and tropology refers to the moral level of interpretation. Hugh warns that we should not attempt to find all of these levels of significance everywhere in the sacred texts, but should rather "assign individual things fittingly in their own places, as reason demands" (V.ii).

As for the order to be followed when reading scripture, Hugh insists that a literal or historical reading be mastered before proceeding to the other levels of allegorical interpretation. He defines "history" as "not only the recounting of actual deeds but also the first meaning of any narrative which uses words according to their proper nature." The "foundation and principle of sacred learning," he stresses, "is history, from which . . . the truth of allegory is extracted." Summarizing the threefold layers of interpretation, he suggests that history provides "the means through which to admire God's deeds"; allegory, the means through which "to believe his mysteries"; and morality, the means to "imitate his perfection" (VI.iii).

On the subject of allegory, Hugh likens divine scripture to a building: its foundation of stones laid in the earth is the literal meaning; the next layer of stones, a superstructure which acts as a "second foundation" for everything else, is the spiritual meaning. Scripture "in its literal sense, contains many things which seem both to be opposed to each other and, sometimes, to impart something which smacks of the absurd or the impossible. But the spiritual meaning admits no opposition; in it, many things can be different from one another, but none can be opposed" (VI.iv). The allegorical superstructure contains such mysteries as the Trinity, grace, original sin, and resurrection. Hugh cautions the student to establish a sound structure of accepted doctrine and "unshaken truth" so that he can safely build onto this structure "whatever he afterwards finds." He will subsequently "know how to bend all Scriptural passages whatever into fitting interpretations," being able to judge what is consonant with "sound faith" (VI.iv). While Hugh has earlier insisted on not overlooking a literal reading of scripture, he cautions here that "The letter killeth, but the spirit quickeneth." Simply following the letter alone, he warns, will cause one to fall soon into error. Hence, we must both "follow the letter in such a way as not to prefer our own sense to the divine authors," while ensuring that "we do not follow it in such a way as to deny that the entire pronouncement of truth is rendered in it" (VI.iv).

Hugh stresses that the order of reading in allegorical and historical study is different, for history "follows the order of time," whereas allegory follows "the order of knowledge" whereby we should proceed from clear things to obscure matters. Hence, he advises, the New Testament, in which the "evident truth is preached," should be studied before the Old Testament, in which "the same truth is announced in a hidden manner, shrouded in figures." For example, many prophecies were made in the Old Testament which came to light only through the life and works of Christ (VI.vi).

As with the exposition of secular texts, scriptural exegesis, says Hugh, includes "the letter, the sense, and the deeper meaning." As in his analysis of secular writings, the letter, referring to the arrangement of words and construction of sentences, is found in every discourse (VI.ix). The sense is the most apparent meaning of a certain arrangement of words; sometimes, however, the words themselves may have a clear meaning but their overall sense is obscure. Indeed some sense, says Hugh, can be incredible, impossible, absurd, or false (VI.x). In contrast, the "divine deeper meaning can never be absurd, never false." It "admits no contradiction, is always harmonious, always true." This level of meaning always requires interpretation and effort; if we are uncertain as to this meaning, we should hold fast to the author's intention (if this can be ascertained with certainty); where this is not possible, we should at least elicit a "deeper meaning consonant with sound faith." Once again, Hugh cautions against imposing our own opinion on the text: we should attempt to make our own thought identical with that of the scriptures, rather than coercing scripture into identity with our own thought (VI.xi). In all of these assumptions Hugh is effectively adhering to mainstream medieval literary-critical practice: novelty and individuality are discouraged, and the meanings of words must be constrained ultimately by the semantic field circumscribed by scripture.

Defending and Defining the Grammar Curriculum: John of Salisbury (ca. 1115–1180)

The work of John of Salisbury was equally symptomatic of the twelfth-century renais sance in medieval learning and education. This was a time in which the grammar curriculum was broadened, and the science of logic, thanks to a wider accessibility of Aristotle's logical treatises, assumed a central status in many disciplines, including not only the natural sciences but also literature, philosophy, and theology. John's *Metalogicon* (1159) both reflects and somewhat underlies these changes. Essentially, it is an educational treatise which vehemently defends the elements of the trivium against a group of detractors who denounced the value of grammar, logic, and rhetoric. John is known primarily for two works. The first of these is the *Policraticus*, a statesman's manual, which is considered to be a classical work of medieval political theory. The second, the *Metalogicon*, is to be examined here. On the completion of the *Metalogicon* in 1159, both texts were sent to the chancellor of England Thomas Becket, to whom they were addressed; such a distinguished audience assured the publication and circulation of the manuscript. John was also the author of poems in Latin and various biographies, including one of Becket.

Born near Salisbury in England, John went to Paris in 1136 where he studied logic under distinguished teachers such as Peter Abelard, Alberic of Reims, and Robert of Melun. From 1138 he studied grammar at the famous cathedral school of Chartres under the successor of Bernard of Chartres, Gilbert de la Porrée, and William of Conches; he learned rhetoric from Richard l'Évêque and the arts from Bernard's younger brother Theodoric. He returned to Paris in 1141 to study theology under Robert Pullus and Simon of Poissy. He spent a few years at the papal court of Rome and eventually became private secretary to Theobald, archbishop of Canterbury, and then to his successor Thomas Becket. He was involved in various missions to the Holy See and made the acquaintance of Pope Adrian IV. Like Becket, John incurred the displeasure of King Henry II for defending the rights of the Church against royal power and both men were obliged to go into exile, returning in 1170 when relations between Church and king somewhat improved. Nonetheless, further quarrels ensued, resulting in King Henry's ordering the murder of Becket in the same year, which was probably witnessed by John. In 1176 he was appointed bishop of Chartres, a position he occupied until his death. Significantly, the *Metalogicon* ends with an account of John's anguish over the schism in the Church following the death of Pope Adrian and the impending death of Archbishop Theobald. The only resource, suggests John, is to pray to God for a worthwhile successor to the papacy and for the kings appointed to care for their flocks.[4]

The *Metalogicon* was long renowned for its elegant Latinity, and it was the first medieval work that displayed a familiarity with, and promoted the authority of, the entire range of Aristotle's *Organon* or logical treatises. The explicit aim of the *Metalogicon* is to defend logic (which John uses in a broad sense to mean the entire trivium of grammar, rhetoric, and logic) against attacks from a group of skeptics. This group is led by a figure whom John mockingly dubs "Cornificius" (named after a notorious detractor of Vergil cited in a text by Donatus). The real name of John's despised adversary is unknown; and while it is clear that John is defending the traditional curriculum of grammar and logic, it would be simplistic to view him as somehow one-sidedly embroiled in the debate between the "humanistic" cathedral schools, with their stress on grammar, and the universities, with their increasing emphasis on logic (more narrowly defined).

In fact, John pleads for the merits of *both* the grammar curriculum and an intelligent devotion to logical and philosophical studies which does not somehow bypass the liberal arts but is grounded upon them. So what is the target of his polemic? He characterizes his opponents, the "Cornificians," as "pseudo-philosophers" whose byword is "reason," and who engage endlessly and pointlessly in "undisciplined disputation." These "overloquacious logicians," he says, despise everything but logic (as defined in a narrow sense) and are ignorant of grammar (*ML*, 14, 16, 86).

In fact, the members of this impoverished sect, he says, have effectively abandoned liberal and philosophical studies, and have migrated into four professions, which he mockingly calls their new "quasi-quadrivium": they have become monks and clerics; or doctors of medicine; or entered the service of the court; or are immersed in the pursuit of money-making (*ML*, 16–20). Hence the object of his scorn appears to be an incipient bourgeois mentality with a distinctly pragmatic orientation, jettisoning the entire sphere of liberal studies as useless, and salvaging only what was serviceable in its practical and worldly ambitions. John's endeavor, then, is complex: he seeks to defend logic in its *broader* sense as including grammar; to urge that the study of logic must not be pursued in isolation (which merely leads to excessive subtlety), but must be seen as integrated within a more comprehensive scheme of learning; and to stress that logic, even in a narrow sense, should be pursued in a disciplined manner informed by an understanding of Aristotle's newly recovered logical treatises.

This broad endeavor motivating the *Metalogicon* entails not only a defense of grammar, logic, and rhetoric, but also an attempt to define these disciplines and their interconnection. John also describes this curriculum as taught by some of his own masters. He situates these discussions within his broader insights into the nature of language, his views on art and poetry, his account of the human faculties, and the general framework of his religious world view.

John begins with the assertion that nature elevates man over other creatures in virtue of two faculties, reason and speech. These activities presuppose each other: reason and wisdom, if not expressed in appropriate and eloquent speech, are enfeebled and barren. John goes so far as to say that the art of eloquence is the foundation not only of all liberal and philosophical studies but also of all civilization, including politics, faith, and morality (*ML*, 9–12). As against the Cornificians who claim that eloquence is a natural gift, John asserts, following Horace, that study and exercise are needed to cultivate and realize this gift (*ML*, 30). This study is embodied in logic, which refers to the disciplines which promote eloquence. John defines logic broadly as "the science of verbal expression and [argumentative] reasoning."[5] He refers this definition back to the meaning of *logos* as both "word" and "reason." Hence, logic "includes all instruction relative to words" (*ML*, 32).

In this broad sense, logic refers to the liberal arts, which, John insists, are the foundation of all understanding. The first three of these arts, the trivium, disclose "the significance of all words." The arts of the quadrivium – arithmetic, geometry, music, and astronomy – unveil "the secrets of all nature" (*ML*, 36). The first among the liberal arts is logic, which, in its broad sense, includes grammar, which John (quoting Isidore) defines as "the science of speaking and writing correctly – the starting point of all liberal studies." John's subsequent comment gives us an idea of the overwhelming importance of the grammar curriculum: "Grammar is the cradle of all philosophy, and . . . the first nurse of the whole study of letters . . . It nurses us in our infancy, and guides our every forward step in philosophy. With motherly care, it fosters and protects the philosopher from the start to the finish [of his pursuits]." John goes so far as to say that one who is ignorant of grammar cannot philosophize (*ML*, 37–38). Interestingly, John's comments here reveal not only the humanistic medieval insight that philosophy and wisdom require expression in appropriate and eloquent language, but also the modern insight that philosophy is intrinsically a linguistic enterprise, that the very possibility of philosophy lies in a mastery of language, and that philosophy is shaped internally (rather than merely outwardly expressed) by the nature and scope of language as subjected to the rules of grammar.

Like many late classical and medieval thinkers, John sees grammar as furnishing a foundation for, and avenue toward, all other disciplines. He states that the "art [of grammar] is, as it were, a public highway, on which all have the right to journey" (*ML*, 54). He explains the broad function of grammar, which is "not narrowly confined to one subject. Rather, grammar prepares the mind to understand everything that can be taught in words . . . all other studies depend on grammar." Indeed, grammar is "the key to everything written, as well as the mother and arbiter of all speech" (*ML*, 60–61). Grammar is the gateway to eloquence and other philosophical pursuits (*ML*, 73). Grammar is even ultimately responsible for man's highest end, which is the practice of virtue in preparation for reunion with God. Virtue must be founded on knowledge; and since grammar is the root of scientific knowledge, it is grammar which initially implants the seed of virtue; hence the function of grammar extends beyond learning into the spheres of morality and theology (*ML*, 65). As mentioned earlier, the medieval conception of grammar was far more inclusive than ours. According to John, the study of grammar includes not only the nature and meanings of letters, syllables and words, but also prosody, the laws of poetry, the definition and uses of figures of speech, and the methods used in historical and fictional narratives (*ML*, 56–60).

Clearly, much that we might today classify under literary interpretation falls under the medieval notion of grammar. Indeed, John indicates that there was something of a dispute in his day concerning the appropriate placement of poetry. Poetry had long been regarded as a branch of rhetoric, and rhetoricians had conventionally enumerated and explained the various figures of speech. By the twelfth century, however, much of rhetoric had been absorbed into the study of grammar. And John insists that the study of poetry belongs to grammar. He argues that although grammar is a human invention, it closely imitates nature. One example of this is that the rules of poetry reflect nature, and that the poet must "follow nature as his guide" (*ML*, 51). What John has in mind here is Horace's statement that the poet expresses the range of human emotions furnished by nature. Following nature, for John, also entails considering factors such as age, place, time, and other circumstances in the poet's description of character or in endowing those characters with speech. However, according to John, some critics have used this close connection of poetry with nature to argue that poetry is a distinct art: "several have denied that poetry is a subdivision of grammar, and would have it to be a separate art. They maintain that poetry no more belongs to grammar than it does to rhetoric." John's own opinion is that "poetry belongs to grammar, which is its mother and the nurse of its study" (*ML*, 51–52).

Today, we are accustomed to the idea, deriving from thinkers and writers of the nineteenth and early twentieth centuries, that poetry is an autonomous realm that is not subject to rules imposed by other fields such as morality, politics, and education. If we think through the implications of poetry being subsumed under grammar rather than comprising an area of study in its own right, we can see that poetry essentially comes to subserve the same ideological functions as grammar. The principles of "correctness" which rule in grammar will also extend over the domain of poetry; in its very conception, poetry must harbor the fundamental rules which govern the creation of meaning and the relations of words. It is not that novelty in poetry is not allowed or possible; it is, rather, that novelty must be generated as a rational and predictable extrapolation of what already exists, that novelty can itself only travel along certain authorized channels. In short, poetry is a *governed* activity, a rule-governed enterprise, internally tied to the prevailing ideological structures sustained by, and sustaining, grammar.

This effective subservience of poetry to grammar can be further illuminated by considering John's views of language and his account of literary interpretation. His placing of poetry under grammar is ultimately based on the fact that poetry is just one instance of grammar's general conformity to nature. John suggests that "Letters, that is written symbols, in the first place represent sounds. And secondly they stand for things, which they conduct into the mind through the windows of the eyes." Grammar not only imparts the fundamental elements of language but also "trains our faculties of sight and hearing" (*ML*, 38). Hence grammar comprehends all aspects of the signifying process. Whereas our modern notions of the sign, deriving from Saussure and others, tend to relate a *sound* or signifier to a *concept*, and then this entire complex of sound–concept to a "thing" or object, the starting point of the sign, for John, is effectively the *written* inscription; in other words, the sound does not possess the status of a signifier until it has achieved written form, in virtue of which it is already a component and creation of grammar, subject in its very birth to the entire system of grammatical rules. The very manner in which our senses respond to these signifiers is regulated by grammar. Also, for John, there is no concept which mediates between sound and thing: the sound directly names the thing, language therefore having a transparent character, directly reflecting the world through a simple correspondence. The meaning of a word consists precisely in its unproblematic reference to a thing. The rules of grammar are thus imposed upon the operations of the world itself.

Hence, while John acknowledges that grammar is "an invention of man," that it is "arbitrary and subject to man's discretion," he qualifies this by asserting that grammar "imitates nature" and "tends, as far as possible, to conform to nature in all respects" (*ML*, 38–39). For example, claims John, nature has limited the number of vowel sounds to five "among all peoples." Moreover, man first named the things present to his senses, so that names are "stamped on all substances" (*ML*, 39). The parts of speech also imitate nature, verbs denoting changes in things, adverbs expressing differences in motion, and adjectives denoting the qualities present in things (*ML*, 39–41). John goes so far as to suggest that the "properties of things overflow into words," as when we call certain words "sweet" or "bitter," and that there is in general a "reciprocity between things and words" (*ML*, 47, 50). Hence, for John, poetry is merely a specialized and highly formalized instance of grammar's conformity to nature. This claim of conformity is of course itself ideologically motivated: the system of grammar, and the world views it encourages, are ultimately shaped by divine providence (*ML*, 39). Moreover, it is precisely the system of grammar that is the index of civilization and its distinctness from barbarianism; a barbarism, says John, is the "corruption of a civilized word, that is, of a Greek or Latin word" (*ML*, 52). Hence civilization excludes not only what is outside of Europe but also even contemporary Europe as taken in isolation; civilization is defined exclusively as founded on the classical past. John adds that the supreme arbiter of correct speech is custom: not, we might add, common custom, but "the practice of those who speak correctly" (*ML*, 49). Again, long anticipating this kind of conclusion by reader-response theorists, John suggests that the rules of grammar – of the entire field of reading, writing, and literary interpretation – are defined by a learned and scholarly elite, a privileged interpretative textual community whose minimal qualification was literacy in the "civilized" languages.

Belonging to such a community not only requires a high degree of literacy; it also entails the following of certain strict rules in the activity of literary interpretation. We have already seen that the *accessus* or introduction to an author followed a fairly fixed formula. In the course of his defense of grammar and logic, John offers an interesting account of the rationale behind medieval methods of teaching, exposition, and interpretation. He suggests that the most desirable quality in the use of language is "lucid clarity and easy comprehensibility." The use of figures of speech often impedes understanding, hence such use should be sparing and discriminating and should be "the exclusive privilege of the very learned" (*ML*, 56). The idea here is that only the learned will be aware of the rules of grammar, and a trope, according to Isidore, is "an excusable departure from the rule." Hence, the rules governing the use of tropes and figures are very strict, and even the deviations from rules are regulated (*ML*, 54). The requirement of clarity means that the "meaning of words should be carefully analyzed" so that we can determine "the precise force of each and every term . . . so that one may dispel the haze of sophistries that would otherwise obscure the truth" (*ML*, 57–58). Again, there is an implicit recognition here that the very process of thought is determined by language, and that confusion of thought arises out of an obscure use of language. There is also a presupposition, of course, that absolute clarity is possible in language.

A second principle of analysis is that a text should be analyzed in such a way that "the author's meaning is always preserved." The text should be "studied with sympathetic mildness, and not tortured on the rack" (*ML*, 146, 148). In order to understand a text, we need to consider its underlying purpose (*ML*, 57). Hence, typically of medieval exposition, there is a great deal of emphasis on authorial intention; this emphasis is again premised on the idea of linguistic clarity inasmuch as the author's intention is expressed in the text's literal meaning: we must "respect as inviolable the evident literal meaning of what is written" until we obtain a fuller grasp by "further reading or by divine revelation" (*ML*, 148).

A third principle, as exemplified by one of John's own teachers Bernard of Chartres, is the imitation of distinguished authors, in an endeavor to educate students not only in technical skills but also in fostering faith and morality. The question here, and one still pertinent in our own day, is that of the canon. Bernard did not believe in wasting time reading what was worthless, and prescribed as models for his students only the canon of distinguished authors. He urged his students to rise to "real imitation" rather than mere plagiarism, sometimes exhorting them and sometimes flogging them (*ML*, 68–69). The picture of Bernard flogging the value of "imitation" into his students is somewhat harshly symptomatic of an enduring trait in medieval literary criticism: "imitation" in this context did nor refer to imitation of the world of objects but of the writings of previous authors. Also characteristic of medieval educational methods, Bernard would oblige his students to memorize passages from the eminent authors. Such emphasis on imitation of past masters means effectively that the authorized modes of viewing the world are already determined and classified; all the student can hope to do is to emulate precisely and repeat these world views, not only installed within his memory but also codified by grammar and rhetoric so as to determine from the depths of the classical past the fundamental features of any future composition. In fact, long before Harold Bloom began speaking of the "anxiety of influence," whereby a contemporary author might deliberately "misread" his predecessors for creative purposes in order to stake out an area of originality for himself, John offers this very insight. Men always, he suggests, alter the opinions of their predecessors: "Each, to make a name for himself, coins his own special error. Wherewith, while promising to correct his master, he sets himself up as a target for correction and condemnation by his own disciples as well as by posterity. I recognize that the same rule threatens to apply in my own case" (*ML*, 117). That John includes himself in this chain of misreading suggests that, in his eyes, this manner of generating a literary tradition is inevitable. On the other hand, he is condemning a situation where (quoting Terence) he says that there "are as many opinions as there are heads" (*ML*, 116). Finally, it is central to the value of this humanistic curriculum that poetry was seen throughout the Middle Ages as having the dual function assigned by Horace: to instruct and please (*ML*, 92).

There are a number of general principles underlying the specific approach to literary interpretation outlined above. We have already seen that language was regarded as enjoying an intimate correspondence with reality or the world of objects; this correspondence was authorized ultimately by God, by the "thoughts of the Most High, whose depths no man can probe: the words said once and for all, and realized in the course of time, in accordance with the decrees of divine providence." The Word of God, as Augustine says, is "eternally begotten" (*ML*, 262–263). A further general premise is that "the principles of all branches of learning are interwoven, and each requires the aid of the others in order to attain its own perfection" (*ML*, 204).

Human learning and the human faculties of perception are gradated within this divine plan. Our knowledge of the material world, says John, begins with our senses; the imagination operates upon and orders the data received by sensation; our faculty of reason transcends sense-perception and contemplates heavenly things; our highest faculty is a kind of intuitive understanding which leads to a spiritual wisdom (*ML*, 227–230). These stages of knowledge, which will be recast in far more secular terms by thinkers such as Kant, are here made coterminous with and constrained by our relation with God, as mediated by obedience and grace. John states that these "successive steps are the result of grace" and we attain wisdom through the practice of piety and obedience (*ML*, 231–232). Our reason itself is divinely endowed: we possess reason because we participate in the "original reason," which is the "wisdom of God" (*ML*,

225). John goes as far as to urge that, since sensation and reason often err, faith is the "primary and fundamental requisite for understanding of the truth" (*ML*, 273). Hence all human learning – which must be directed by our striving toward goodness and wisdom – is circumscribed, from the outset, by religious categories. This scheme of course is dependent on a view of the universe as an ordered whole whose parts presuppose one another; all things are deficient when isolated and are perfected only when united with this totality (*ML*, 10). And it is the original reason of God which "embraces the nature, development, and ultimate end of all things" (*ML*, 250). Another important contribution of John's treatise is that it extensively surveys, for the first time in medieval writing, the entire corpus of Aristotle's logical works, explaining their value and import. All in all, the *Metalogicon* provides us with a revealing picture not only of the medieval curriculum but also of the religious world view and the conceptions of human nature underlying this curriculum.

Promoting the Vernacular: Dante's *De Vulgari Eloquentia*

While the works of Dante will be considered in more detail in the next section, his treatise *De Vulgari Eloquentia* (*Eloquence in the Vernacular Tongue*, ca. 1304–1308) impinges interestingly on the connection of literature and grammar, and can more appropriately be considered here, even though its influence was not active until the Renaissance. *De Vulgari Eloquentia*, though itself composed in Latin, is primarily an argument for the use of the vernacular in poetic composition. Like John of Salisbury, Dante sees man as distinguished from animals by his faculties of speech and reason.[6] Given this constitution, it is necessary that "the human race should have some sign, at once rational and sensible, for the inter-communication of its thoughts." According to Dante, the linguistic sign conveys thoughts from one person's reason to another's reason, using the medium of sense. The sign must have two components: sound, which is sensible, and meaning, which appeals to reason (*DVE*, 10–11). Hence Dante views language as the external instrument of thought (rather than as somehow determining the process of thought).

Dante defines the vernacular as "natural" speech, acquired when we are children through the practice of imitation without following any rules. Dante defines grammar as a "secondary speech," which arises from the first. Unlike the first, natural, speech, grammar is acquired only by a few persons through assiduous study and much expenditure of time. What is interesting are the reasons that Dante gives for the invention of grammar. He observes that no human language can be lasting and continuous (*DVE*, 17–20, 27). Grammar was invented as a kind of ideal stabilization of speech, as "a kind of unchangeable identity of speech in different times and places." Grammar posits an ideal, unchanging essence of language as underlying the fluctuations and malleability of actual speech. The main purposes behind the creation of grammar, says Dante, were twofold: the first was this requirement of stabilization, so that speech might not fluctuate at the mercy of individuals; the second, integrally related, motive was that we might "at least attain but a partial knowledge of the opinions and exploits of the ancients, or of those whom difference of place causes to differ from us" (*DVE*,

29). Hence, the idea of positing through grammar a "correct" and stable language is implicitly connected with a literary heritage which embodies, exemplifies, and indeed defines that grammar. Dante makes this connection explicit when he suggests that our practice should be modeled on imitation of the classics: "the more closely we copy the great poets, the more correct is the poetry we write . . . it behoves us . . . to emulate their poetic teaching" (DVE, 78). Hence, not only does grammar embody the ideals of unity, order, and permanence, as well as being emblematic of civilization itself, but also the poetic tradition is what lays the foundations of grammar.

As for the vernacular, which he wishes to show is suitable for poetic composition, Dante seeks a vernacular language that will be valid and suitable for all of Italy (DVE, 35). He defines the general vernacular as an illustrious, cardinal, and courtly language, and rejects the claims of various Italian dialects to possess these qualities and this general suitability. He defines this illustrious vernacular language as "that which belongs to all the towns in Italy but does not appear to belong to any one of them." Dante suggests that the illustrious language has been "chosen out" from the various dialects by the illustrious poets, including himself, who amalgamated these into a generally usable language (DVE, 56–57). This language is "cardinal" inasmuch as all the other dialects hinge upon it, and fluctuate in accordance with it. The vernacular language will also be "courtly" inasmuch as a "court is a common home of all the realm . . . hence it is that those who frequent all royal palaces always speak the illustrious vernacular" (DVE, 61). Dante pointedly notes, however, that Italy lacks an imperial court (implying, as an advocate of Italian unification and the resurrection of Roman *imperium*, that there should be one in Rome); hence, the illustrious vernacular in Italy "wanders about like a wayfarer" and is united only by the practice of the illustrious writers scattered through Italy, who are themselves "united by the gracious light of Reason" (DVE, 61–62). The Italian vernacular language, then, is that which "has been used by the illustrious writers who have written poetry in the vernacular throughout Italy" (DVE, 63).

Hence, just as correct Latinity was defined by grammar through reference to the practice of the classical writers, so the correct use of the vernacular is embodied in the practice of the great poets. In fact, Dante insists that the vernacular should *only* be used by men of genius and knowledge, and should be restricted to only the worthiest subjects such as war, love, and virtue, and should be expressed in the form of the canzone (DVE, 67–71). It is somewhat ironic that Dante's endeavor to extricate the writing of poetry from its expression in Latin, and from the correct Latinity embodied in *grammatica*, is itself written in Latin. Even more ironic is the fact that Dante's retreat from the sovereignty of grammar (which he sees as artificial and inferior to the natural speech of the vernacular) appears to replicate within the realm of the vernacular the same stringency and strict regulation of language and poetic forms that characterized grammar itself. On the other hand, in historical terms, Dante might help us to see the history of literature and literary criticism since the Middle Ages as a gradual extrication from *grammatica*, from this rule-governed body of knowledge, ideology, and method. Dante's text was not brought into prominence until Giangiorgio Trissino (1478–1550) used it to argue that the highest form of the language should be called Italian, not Tuscan. As we shall see, other Renaissance writers developed Dante's defense and promotion of the vernacular. Interestingly, Dante's own *Divine Comedy* violates the rules he himself lays down in *De Vulgari Eloquentia*. It treats of those worthy subjects of arms, love, and war but not in canzoni nor in the tragic style (*DVE*, 20). It is Dante's own poetic output, then, rather than his theorizing about the vernacular, which sets poetry on a different path, one whose future is not constrained by a centuries-old grammatical past.

The Traditions of Medieval Criticism: Literature and Rhetoric

As seen in the previous chapter, much literary criticism of the classical period – including the works of Dionysius of Halicarnassus, Horace, and "Longinus" – was actually rhetorical criticism applied to poetry. The heritage of rhetoric since late classical times included the system of the three styles (high, middle, low), the division of figures into schemes and tropes, the division of figures of thought from figures of speech, the relative importance of genius and art in poetic composition, the doctrine of imitation of the masterpieces, the distinction between content and language, as well as the concept of decorum (*MLC*, 5). Indeed, as Hardison observes, the concept of a sharp distinction between poetic and rhetoric was not even available until the renewed circulation of Aristotle's *Poetics* in the sixteenth century. Hence, throughout the Middle Ages, rhetoric continued to influence literary criticism through the widespread circulation of treatises such as the *Rhetorica ad Herennium* and Cicero's *De inventione*. The most important document in this regard was Horace's *Ars poetica*, which was viewed by medieval authors as part of grammar rather than rhetoric. Horace was one of the standard authors used in the grammar curriculum. In contrast, Longinus' *On the Sublime* had no traceable influence during the Middle Ages, and was not translated into Latin until the sixteenth century. The late classical rhetorical texts that were available in the Middle Ages were Tiberius Claudius Donatus' discussion of Vergil and Macrobius' *Saturnalia*. The former held up Vergil as a master of all areas of rhetoric; the latter raises what had become a standard question, namely, whether Vergil was an orator or poet, illustrating both Vergil's command of rhetorical rules and his adeptness as an imitator (*MLC*, 5).

As Hardison notes, after the Carolingian period, purely rhetorical criticism disappeared and was absorbed into grammatical treatises which drew much of their content from rhetoric. The *artes poeticae* of the twelfth and thirteenth centuries draw heavily on the *Rhetorica ad Herennium*. These centuries witnessed a debate on the relative importance of the disciplines of the trivium, as well as on the status of literature. As already seen, John of Salisbury placed poetry within the province of grammar. The *artes poeticae* were designed for the curriculum of the cathedral schools and hence were part of the grammar curriculum, even though they had been heavily influenced by rhetoric. One of the best examples of such a text is Geoffrey de Vinsauf's *Poetria Nova*, which will now be examined.

Geoffrey de Vinsauf (ca. 1200)

Geoffrey de Vinsauf derives his name (*de Vino Salvo* in Latin) from a treatise on the preservation of wine which was attributed to him. However, it was not wine but poetics which earned him renown, though almost nothing is known about his life except that he lived in the late twelfth and early thirteenth centuries, wrote poetry, studied in Paris, visited Rome, and taught rhetoric in England.[7] His treatise *Poetria Nova* (*New Poetics*) was widely influential; designed to provide guidance in the rules and practice of poetry, along with the study and imitation of great poets, it became one of the standard training manuals of poets in Europe from the thirteenth century until well into the Renaissance. Characteristically of medieval writers, Geoffrey viewed poetry as a branch of rhetoric, and consequently divided his treatise according to the five rhetorical "offices" of invention, arrangement, style, memory, and delivery. Indeed, his text is rooted, and intervenes, in the conventional medieval curriculum of rhetoric and poetics based on classical sources. The main source of Geoffrey's treatise was the *Rhetorica ad Herennium* (*Rhetoric to Herennius*), also called the *Rhetorica Nova* or *New Rhetoric* because it was newly placed in the medieval curriculum alongside the standard rhetorical treatise already in use since the later twelfth century, Cicero's *De inventione* (*On Invention*). Geoffrey's treatise *Poetria Nova* echoes the title *Rhetorica Nova*, indicating that he wishes to propound a new poetics. It also echoes the title of the second source on which it is based, Horace's *Ars poetica*, which was known in the Middle Ages as the *Poetria*. Like Horace's text, Geoffrey's treatise is written in Latin verse and, as Margaret Nims points out, it belongs to a "long tradition of versified manuals in the liberal arts which extended back beyond Horace and continued long after the twelfth century." The most renowned later work in this tradition was Alexander Pope's *Essay on Criticism*.

Significantly, Geoffrey's treatise is dedicated to Pope Innocent, who is addressed as "the world's sun" (*Poetria Nova*, 16). In his "General Remarks" on poetry, Geoffrey likens the creation of a poem's substance or subject matter to the building of a house: "The mind's hand shapes the entire house before the body's hand builds it. Its mode of being is archetypal before it is actual" (I.47–49). Geoffrey insists that before putting pen to paper, the poet must "construct the whole fabric" of the poem "within the mind's citadel; let it exist in the mind before it is on the lips" (I.57–59). This rational view of poetry, whereby the act of composition occurs entirely in the mind prior to writing, contrasts sharply with the Romantic notions of poetry that we have inherited. Shelley, for example, was later to view the actual poetic product as but a remote and faded version of the mind's original conception. Once the poem's substance has been created, says Geoffrey, we must create or invent the verbal expression: "let poetic art come forward to clothe the matter with words" (I.61–62). Later, he states that words "are instruments to unlock the closed mind; they are keys, as it were, of the mind" (IV.1065–1066). Again, in our age, we have become habituated to the idea that language is not merely the outer expression of thought but the very instrument that enables thought. Geoffrey's view that the entire domain of thought precedes language was an integral part of medieval thinking; this view continues through Pope and many other figures until we reach the nineteenth century.

Geoffrey remarks that there are two broad ways of ordering the poetic material or subject matter. The first is to follow the order of nature, the natural sequence of events, so that "the order of discourse does not depart from the order of occurrence" (II.88–91). If we follow the order of art, however, we will alter the order of nature, sometimes placing last things first, so as to dispose "the material to better effect" (II.120–126).

Indeed, the order of art, says Geoffrey, is "more elegant than natural order" (II.98–99). Given its insistence on the transformative power of art, it is clear that Geoffrey's text is taking a considerable stride away from the notion of art as mere imitation and the idea that it is somehow a step removed from the truth of nature.

The bulk of Geoffrey's treatise is devoted to style and the various "ornaments" that create given styles in poetry. His general advice is to "examine the mind of a word, and only then its face" (IV.739–740). In other words, we should use words not just for their superficial qualities of sound and appearance, but with due consideration of their meaning in a given context. We must "examine the words in relation to the meaning proposed . . . let rich meaning be honoured by rich diction" (IV.750–755). Geoffrey expounds ten basic tropes or figures of ornament, which include: metaphor, onomatopoeia, allegory, metonymy, hyperbole, and synecdoche (IV.959). Metaphor provides pleasure, he says, because "it comes from what is your own . . . a metaphor serves you as a mirror, for you see yourself in it and recognize your own sheep in another's field" (IV.796–799). The figurative use of language must be kept "in check" by reason (IV.1013–1014). In general, any kind of excess must be avoided in ornament (IV.1934–1935). Nonetheless, he encourages the poet to experiment, since altered "meaning . . . gives new vitality to a word" (IV.949–951). Indeed, all of the tropes, he explains, are "distinguished by the figurative status of the words and the uncommon meaning assigned them" (IV.963–964). In contrast with the long tradition of aesthetics which saw poetry as mere imitation of nature, Geoffrey places considerable emphasis on the transformation of nature by poetry, and the need for the poet to attain novelty. The resources of art provide "a means of avoiding worn-out paths and of travelling a more distinguished route" (IV.982–983).

Geoffrey has some wise remarks to make on the poet's relation to the audience, remarks which might apply equally to the teacher and the orator, even today. He cautions: "Be of average, not lofty, eloquence. The precept of the ancients is clear: speak as the many, think as the few . . . Regard not your own capacities, therefore, but rather his with whom you are speaking. Give to your words weight suited to his shoulders, and adapt your speech to the subject. When you are teaching the arts, let your speech be native to each art; each delights in its own idiom. But see that its idiom is kept within its own borders" (IV.1080–1089). Many of these statements are reminiscent of Horace's precepts, notably those which call for not only the adapting of words to their subject matter but also the use of the prospective audience as a guide in the process of composition itself.

In general, three elements "perfect a work: artistic theory by whose law you may be guided; experience, which you may foster by practice; and superior writers, whom you may imitate" (IV.1704–1707). Geoffrey stresses that in some respects verse and prose follow different paths. Inelegant things are permissible in prose but not in verse; the rustic form of a word will "embarrass" verse "by its ungainliness, and bring shame to the line . . . A line of prose is a coarser thing; it favours all words" (IV.1855–1863). In all other matters, he says, the artistic principles of verse and prose are the same (IV.1873–1880). Ordinary speech and colloquial language, he points out, are allowed only in comedy, which "demands plain words only" (IV.1885–1886). The final judgment in the usage of words must be a "triple judgment of mind and ear and usage" (IV.1947–1948).

193

While much of Geoffrey's text clearly points to a more modern poetics, he nonetheless sustains the classical precepts of moderation, decorum, propriety, and the appeal to reason, as well as to the important classical distinction between prose and verse and a hierarchy of genres whereby comedy occupies a lowly rank. Moreover, the examples of good writing that Geoffrey offers are replete with eulogies of the pope, with narratives of Christ's mission and of original sin – examples which are grounded in medieval theology. Having said this, it is striking that Geoffrey does not lay down explicit didactic or moral functions for poetry; its primary purpose, in his text, is to provide pleasure, though a refined and controlled pleasure. In terms of language, the central assumption that runs through his poetics and rhetoric is that there is a core of stable, literal meaning, a meaning which is preserved even through figurative transformation. Together with his retention of the classical dispositions cited above, this feature of Geoffrey's text indicates its somewhat contradictory and incoherent nature, marking it as a product of its time: classical values coexist uneasily with an impetus toward modernism. The modernism is of form, comprising a stress on artistic pleasure and delight; whereas the reason and moderation that must constrain modernistic innovation derive from a world view that is profoundly conservative.

The Traditions of Medieval Criticism: Literature and Logic

Scholasticism began in the twelfth century though, as noted above, its foundations were laid considerably earlier. In general, this mode of thinking, fostered in the medieval universities, was characterized by a number of tendencies. Firstly, scholastic philosophers worked with a commonly accepted background of Christian orthodoxy usually defined by ecumenical councils such as the various Councils of Nicaea. Secondly, the scholastic thinkers worked initially under the influence of the patristic philosophers enumerated above, especially Augustine. However, during the twelfth and thirteenth centuries the works of Aristotle became increasingly well known. Islamic scholars had translated into Arabic nearly the entire corpus of Aristotle and texts of Galen, Hippocrates, Euclid, and Porphyry. The Aristotelian corpus, transmitted largely by the Islamic philosophers Ibn Rushd and Ibn Sina (Avicenna), was translated into Latin from the mid-twelfth century. Eventually, Aristotle was taken as the fundamental philosophical foundation of the scholastics, and he replaced Plato as the primary philosophical basis of Christian theology. Thirdly, the tenor of the scholastic philosophers was argumentative and they relied primarily on dialectic and syllogistic reasoning. The pervasive methods of teaching were the *lectio* and the *disputatio*, which rested on presentation and argumentation via syllogisms. Finally, the issues which typically concerned these thinkers were: proving the existence of God, the connection between faith and reason, the relation of will and intellect, and the problem of universals on which the opposing factions were divided into realists (those thinkers such as Boethius and William of Champeaux who followed Plato in believing in the actual existence of universals) and nominalists (thinkers such as Roscelin and Peter Abelard who, like Aristotle, saw universals as merely names designating classes of objects). Above all, the scholastics attempted to establish a systematic and hierarchical synthesis of the various branches of learning, at the apex of which stood theology. The various schools of scholastic theology included those inspired by the Franciscan Duns Scotus (1266–1308) and the Dominican theologians Albertus Magnus (1193–ca. 1280) and Thomas Aquinas.

Aquinas' theology represented a break with Augustine's pessimistic view of fallen human nature. The early Middle Ages is better embodied in Augustine's other-worldly vision, expressing contempt for earthly life and a longing for the heavenly city. Aquinas' vision is more rational, intellectual, and grants a greater value to life in this world and to the political state. Nonetheless, the Augustinian impulse, viewing religious life as based on will rather than intellect, continued in thinkers such as St. Bonaventure (1221–1274), Duns Scotus, and William of Ockham (ca. 1285–1349). Eventually, scholasticism was eclipsed by nominalism (sometimes included within the repertoire of scholasticism), which flourished in the fourteenth century and which, along with the work of thinkers such as Roger Bacon (ca. 1214–1294), paved the way for the more scientific tenor of Renaissance thought, and an increasing separation of philosophy and theology.

It is clear that scholasticism was generated and sustained fundamentally by an emphasis on logic or dialectic. This emphasis extended to its treatment of literature, which was seen as a branch of logic, an instrument for the manipulation of language. Literature was seen as a form rather than as having any specific content. This conception was heavily influenced by Islamic philosophers such as al-Farabi and Ibn Rushd. Aristotle's logical texts had been translated into Arabic in the eighth and ninth centuries, after which Arab thinkers produced commentaries and encyclopedias systematizing and analyzing the Aristotelian corpus. In his *Catalogue of the Sciences* (translated into Latin by Gerard of Cremona), al-Farabi categorized Aristotle's logical treatises and included with them Aristotle's *Rhetoric* and *Poetics*. An even more important medium for the transmission of Aristotle's *Poetics* was Ibn Rushd's *Commentary on the Poetics of Aristotle*, translated into Latin in 1256 by Hermannus Alemannus. Significantly, Ibn Rushd's commentary – in its Latin rendering – was far more widely read in the Middle Ages than Aristotle's *Poetics* itself (which was translated by William of Moerbeke in 1278). As such, it was the most important theoretical literary-critical statement of the scholastic period (*MLC*, 14–15). These texts inspired such treatises as Dominicus Gundissalinus' *On the Division of the Sciences*. Gundissalinus denied the didactic function of poetry, and held that its distinctive feature lay in its being a technique for creating illusions, whereas the function of rhetoric was persuasion and that of logic was demonstration. He saw the distinctive instrument of poetry as the "imaginative syllogism" (*MLC*, 35).

It would be unfair, however, to think that the scholastics in general simply dismissed poetry and literature: in viewing it as a branch of logic, they accorded it a definite place in a hierarchy of sciences crowned by theology. The later scholastics such as Roger Bacon and Thomas Aquinas viewed poetry as having a dual status: it was both a faculty and a branch of moral philosophy with a specific ethical content (*MLC*, 34–35). Moreover, in reconceiving the *accessus* tradition in Aristotelian terms, they opened up important new pathways of literary investigation. The conventional formula for an *accessus* or introduction to an author was reformulated as the Aristotelian prologue, based on Aristotle's account of the four fundamental causes: the "efficient cause" of the text was the author himself as agent; the "material cause" was the materials he used; the "formal cause" was his literary style and structure; while the "final cause" was his ultimate purpose in writing. As A. J. Minnis and A. B. Scott explain, it was the terms of Aristotle's *Physics* and *Metaphysics*, rather than those of his *Poetics*, which underlay the parameters of much scholastic literary theory (*MLTC*, 3). This Aristotelian interpretative system allowed commentators to focus more on the human qualities of authors, as opposed to agency of divine inspiration (in the case of scripture) or the notion of *auctores* merely as impersonalized sources of authority to be imitated. Such a focus on the human author enabled an increasing sophistication in analyzing authorial roles (distinguishing between author, commentator, scribe, encyclopedist, etc.) and literary forms. Hence a new and more liberal critical vocabulary was eventually encouraged, allowing for a more comprehensive treatment of author, material, style, structure, and effect. In this section we will consider the most important scholastic treatise on poetry, Ibn Rushd's *Commentary* on Aristotle's *Poetics*, as well as the aesthetics of Aquinas in the context of his vastly influential world view, and finally Dante's *Epistle to Can Grande della Scala*, which is one of the foremost practical applications of scholastic criticism.

Ibn Rushd (Averroës) (1126–1198)

The Islamic philosopher and jurist Ibn Rushd is known primarily for his great commentaries on Aristotle, which had a profound impact on the medieval West, where he gained wide recognition among both Christian and Jewish scholars. Nearly all of his commentaries on Aristotle's major works were translated into Latin, and some into Hebrew. He also wrote extensive commentaries on Plato's *Republic* and Porphyry's *Isagoge*. In his interpretations of Aristotle he attempted to remove the elements of Neo-Platonism that had hitherto distorted previous Arabic readings of the Greek philosopher. It was through Ibn Rushd that the main corpus of Aristotle's texts was transmitted to Europe. The central endeavor of Ibn Rushd's own major philosophical treatises, such as the *Incoherence of the Incoherence* (which attempted to refute al-Ghazali's attack on philosophy, *The Incoherence of the Philosophers*), is to reconcile philosophy and religion, reason and revelation. While in general Ibn Rushd believed that philosophy yields truths which are certain, he argues not for a religion of pure reason but rather for a philosophical and rational understanding of the truths of revealed religion. Ironically, it was misinterpretations of Ibn Rushd's teachings by the Latin "Averroists" – who viewed him as believing that faith and reason were irreconcilable – that provoked the response of Aquinas' philosophy, which labored to harmonize these domains. Ironically, and sadly for the subsequent history of Islamic thought, Ibn Rushd's influence in the Islamic world was far smaller than his impact on Christian Europe; he failed to convince Islamic scholars and theologians of the propriety of philosophy within their religious visions.[8]

Born into a family of jurists, Ibn Rushd was trained in law and became a judge in Seville and Cordova. Around 1153 he was introduced by his friend, the philosopher Ibn Tufayl, to a prince of the Almohad court. There is a story that the prince asked him whether philosophers considered the world to be created in time or eternal, a conversation that instigated Ibn Rushd's commentaries on the Greek philosophers.

The text of Ibn Rushd to be considered here is his *Commentary on the Poetics of Aristotle*, translated into Latin in 1256 by Hermannus Alemannus, a monk living in Toledo. It was printed in 1481, the first version of Aristotle's text published during the Renaissance. Not long after the death of Aristotle, the text of his *Poetics* effectively vanished; for most of the late classical and early medieval periods, it was not known except through intermediaries such as Aristotle's pupil Theophrastus. The oldest surviving manuscript in the West dates from the eleventh century. But this was not the version that influenced the medieval West; the version that had such an impact on the Middle Ages was Arabic, a tenth-century translation of a Greek manuscript dating before the year 700. This version departed considerably from the Western manuscript, and is partly responsible for the altered form of Aristotle's ideas transmitted through Ibn Rushd's *Commentary* (*MLC*, 81–82).

As mentioned earlier, Arab philosophers such as al-Farabi (whose *Catalogue of the Sciences* was twice translated into Latin in the twelfth century) followed late Greek commentators in viewing Aristotle's *Rhetoric* and *Poetics* as part of his *Organon* or series of logical treatises. Poetry was thus viewed as a faculty or method of treating language without any specific content. As O. B. Hardison, Jr. states, this "interpretation ignores imitation, plot, characterization, catharsis and most of the other subjects stressed by Aristotle in favor of . . . the imaginative syllogism," which was considered to be the distinctive feature of poetry (*MLC*, 82). Inasmuch as this view is attributable to Ibn Rushd, however, it was somewhat modified, as we shall now see.

Since the form of Ibn Rushd's text is a commentary, purportedly following the contours of Aristotle's text, it contains a great deal of repetition and elaboration. We can distinguish three broad themes that are somewhat circuitously developed in the *Commentary*, themes that intersect at times only tangentially with the Greek text of Aristotle as we now have it. We might bear in mind that Ibn Rushd's text is written in Arabic and its immediate audience would have been not Western but Arab scholars and writers. He purports to bring to an Arab readership the insights of Aristotle as these might impinge on Arabic literary traditions. In this light, we might discern the following three theses: (1) poetry is defined broadly as the art of praise or blame, based on representations of moral choice; (2) the purpose of poetry is to produce a salutary effect upon its audience, through both excellence of imitative technique and performative elements such as melody, gesture, and intonation; and (3) poetry is viewed as a branch of logic, or logical discourse, which is compared and contrasted with rhetorical discourse.

While Aristotle is cited as the authority for all of these views, Ibn Rushd is effectively developing insights that are often only incidentally related to Aristotle's main arguments. For example, Ibn Rushd's central thesis that "Every poem and all poetry are either blame or praise" is developed from Aristotle's comment in chapter IV of the *Poetics* that the first forms of poetry were praises of famous men and satire. Ibn Rushd states that the subjects proper to poetry are those that "deal with matters of choice, both good and bad."[9] These subjects, then, are concerned directly with virtue and vice since the aim of poetic representation is "to impel people toward certain choices and discourage them from others." Like Aristotle, Ibn Rushd holds that all action and character are concerned with either virtue or vice (91). He further defines one species of poem as a song "praising and reciting beautiful and excellent deeds," while the other species is a song "blaming and denigrating base and immoral deeds." As an excellent example of a poem of praise, Ibn Rushd gives the epic, citing Aristotle's praise of Homer (93–94). Ibn Rushd holds that a poem of praise should represent "a virtuous act of choice which has universal application to virtuous activities and not a particular application to an individual instance of virtue." Only such a universally applicable representation can arouse the passions of pity or fear in the soul, through stimulating the imagination (94). A tragedy, for example, should not imitate men "as they are perceived individually," but should represent their "character" which "includes actions and moral attitudes" (95). Ibn Rushd insists that poetry should not evoke the pleasure of mere admiration, but should seek "the level of pleasure which moves to virtue through imagination. This is the pleasure proper to tragedy" (103). As with Aristotle, then, poetry should express what is universal, what is common to all men, not what is unique to them or their circumstances.

Another aspect of Ibn Rushd's claim is that a virtuous act must be based on moral choice, not mere habit; as he says later, the actions portrayed by the poet must be "based on free choice and knowledge" (104). Aristotle had urged that the action portrayed in tragedy must be "serious," meaning that the action must have a significant moral import. Ibn Rushd also urges that the emotions of "suffering and fear" can be aroused not by the presentation of "small and unimportant" actions but by portraying the "difficult and harsh experiences . . . which tend to befall mankind" (103).

Regarding poetic imitation, Ibn Rushd places great emphasis on realism. Whereas Aristotle talks of the poet representing what is probable, Ibn Rushd insists that the poet only engage in true representations, speaking "only of things that exist or may exist" (98). The poet in fact "only gives names to things that exist," and his representations are based on things that are in nature, not things that are "made up or imaginary." Like Aristotle, he suggests that the poet is close to the philosopher inasmuch as he speaks "in universal terms" (99). But Ibn Rushd insists that, just as "the skilled artist depicts an object as it is in reality . . . the poet should depict and form the object as it is in itself . . . so that he imitates and expresses the character and habits of the soul" (105). Aristotle's advocacy of poetic realism is couched in terms of "probability" and "necessity"; it is a realism that pertains not to the portrayal of objects but to the presentation of actions, events, and the connection of events in a "plot." In contrast, Ibn Rushd urges that a "good and skilled poet" should "describe and delineate things according to their proper qualities and their true natures" (111). Aristotle's own realism is largely restricted to expressing the events comprising the causal content of moral behavior. It seems that Ibn Rushd prescribes a broader pursuit of poetic objectivity which was strangely modern in its demand for objects in the world to be accurately represented; he goes so far as to say that poetry is most truthful when it is based on direct experience: like everyone else, the poet "does best in reporting those things that he has understood for himself and almost seen first-hand with all their accidents and circumstances" (110). This emphasis on direct experience (as opposed to scripture, authority, law, convention, or tradition) as the basis of understanding and poetic representation does not become a generally accepted maxim of philosophy in the West until the rise of empiricism and rationalism; it does not assume an important status in literature until the Romantics. To the extent that these insights influenced succeeding generations, their impact was restricted to the West, and did not extend to the majority of Islamic thinkers and poets.

It is clear that Ibn Rushd places at least as much emphasis as Aristotle on the moral purpose and function of poetry; he places greater emphasis on the realistic nature of poetic imitation; these emphases correspond with the greater weight that he accords to the affective elements of poetry, the elements that will produce an effect on the audience. In other words, unlike Aristotle, Ibn Rushd sees such realism or naturalism as directly increasing the affective and imaginative power, and therefore the moral impact, of poetry. Like Aristotle, Ibn Rushd attributes the pleasure we receive from poetry to the fact that representation is natural to human beings, and that we derive pleasure from images of things; he adds that we also derive pleasure from meter and melody (92). Aristotle had distinguished between elements intrinsic to poetry, such as mode of representation, plot, and character, and those elements which were "extrinsic" or belonged to the performance of the play or poem. Ibn Rushd rehearses Aristotle's distinction between "intrinsic" and "extrinsic" elements of poetry, using these two factors – imitation or representation and melody – as the basis of the distinction. In general, he acknowledges that the poet's skill in both of these domains will affect an audience. The various features of performance "make the language more representational" (94). Having said this, he tends to agree with Aristotle that the skilled poet does not rely on "extrinsic" performative aids (100). Indeed, poetic speeches that express truth vividly do not need external enhancements (112). A tragedy, says Ibn Rushd, should achieve its effect through representation.

In general, Ibn Rushd holds that excellence in poetic composition derives from two factors, arrangement and magnitude. Regarding the former, poetry should imitate nature and harbor a single subject and a single end; as for the latter, it should also have, as Aristotle had suggested, a "definite magnitude," being neither too large nor too small for the audience's perception and understanding. In this way, the representation as a whole will have a unity, comprising a beginning, middle, and end (98). Such a unified and ordered organization will produce the desired impact or effect upon the audience. In a formula strangely prefiguring T. S. Eliot's notion of the "objective correlative," Ibn Rushd stipulates that when the poet describes things as they truly are, the "imaginative stimulation is not in excess of the qualities of the things and their true natures" (111). Eliot had suggested that a poet's description of a series of objects and events would arouse a precisely determined emotion; Ibn Rushd also seems to recognize an internal connection between poetic representation and human emotion, based implicitly on a correspondence between the "external" world of objects and the "internal" world of human perception.

The third insight that structures Ibn Rushd's text is his treatment of poetry as a branch of logic. In general, he appears to divide speech into "logical" and "non-logical" speech (103). He often refers to poetry as "poetic speech," implying that this is one of the sub-genres of speech, varying from but fundamentally related to other types of speech. He characterizes rhetoric as "persuasive speech" and poetry as "representational speech" (96). Indeed, he goes so far as to define poetic speech as a "variation" of "truthful or standard speech" (117). He takes as his starting point for this claim Aristotle's view that poetry should engage in a moderate use of metaphorical and figurative language such that it will neither be wholly obscure nor degenerate into commonplace speech (115). The "variation" that occurs in poetry is through alteration of the meanings of words, the use of ornament, rhyme, and unfamiliar diction (117). Nonetheless,

Ibn Rushd sees this variation as strictly and rationally controlled: it seems that he measures poetry by the standards of prose, and indeed sees poetry, like rhetoric, as a special type of prose. In fact, Ibn Rushd might have fueled, or at least reinforced, the medieval tendency to situate poetry as a branch of either grammar or rhetoric. He suggests that "a syllogism is one statement and a rhetorical oration is one, and a poetical composition is one" (114). He suggests also that the epilogues or conclusions of poems should summarize the subject commemorated, "just as happens in rhetorical conclusions" (105). At one point, deviating entirely from Aristotle's explanation of the quantitative components of tragedy (which he uses only as a starting point), he states that Arab poems are divided into a "rhetorical exordium," the body of the praise itself, and a "rhetorical conclusion" (101). He is describing here the form of the Arabic *qasidah* or ode; interestingly, his description invokes some of the divisions of a rhetorical speech, and treats poetry as a logical statement.

Given that Ibn Rushd urges the poet to express truths, and sees this as having a morally persuasive impact on an audience, it is clear that for him poetry takes on some of the functions of philosophy, logic, and rhetoric. He defines the "decorous style" as one where "the speech offers open truth and is clear" (120). Interestingly, when poetic "variation" of language is emphatic, using excellent imagery, the purpose of this is "a more complete understanding of the thing represented" (118). Hence poetry is accredited with the goals of convincing and promoting understanding through the use of speech which is clear and departs minimally – and rationally – from "standard" speech. Not only are the modes of departure from ordinary speech strictly regulated toward the general end of precluding outlandish metaphors and figures, but also there are six basic errors that the poet should avoid: representing the impossible, distorted representation, representing rational beings by irrational ones, comparing a thing to its contrary, using words with ambiguous meanings, and resorting to rhetorical persuasion rather than poetic representation (120–121).

The tendency of all of these prohibitions is to direct the poet toward realism and clarity in the expression of truth: poetic speech, though contrasted with rhetorical speech, shares the same basis, and is part of the entire family of discourses. Ibn Rushd's emphasis on truth may derive partly from the fact that, like many Islamic thinkers, he appears to treat the Qur'an as the archetypal text. He sees the Qur'an as exceptional in Arabic literature inasmuch as it praises "worthy actions of the will and blame of unworthy ones." The Qur'an, he states, prohibits "poetic fictions" except those which rebuke vices and commend virtues (109). Even where the Qur'an uses emphatic variations from standard speech, this is not to produce an ornamental effect but a "more complete understanding" (118). In a striking commensurability with much medieval poetics, then, Ibn Rushd's views might be said to have a scriptural foundation: just as Vergil and the Bible were revered as authoritative texts (stylistically and grammatically, as well as in their content), so the Qur'an is invoked as a literary exemplar.

Hence, Ibn Rushd's treatise is archetypal of scholastic views of poetry, situating it as one form of discourse among a hierarchy of discourses, at whose pinnacle stood theology. Unlike many minor scholastic thinkers who saw poetry as one of the lowest branches of logical discourse, Ibn Rushd at least grants to poetry an important moral function (as does Aquinas somewhat); unlike Aquinas, he also accords it an epistemological function; in fact, for Ibn Rushd, the two functions are integrally related.

What would later medieval and Renaissance thinkers and writers have gleaned about Aristotle from Ibn Rushd's text? Certainly an emphasis on the moral function and the truth-value of poetry; in formal terms, a stress on unified poetic organization, and the need for poetry to produce a powerful impact on its audience. Also, they would have encountered the notion of poetry as one discourse intimately related to other discourses, and overlapping considerably with rhetoric and logic. In all of these aspects, it could be – a question scholars are still debating – that Ibn Rushd was reinforcing or confirming trends that were already present or congenial to medieval thinking. For example, Ibn Rushd fails to distinguish between drama and narrative, between tragedy and epic, a conflation also found in writers such as Dante and Chaucer (*MLC*, 85). Moreover, readers would have found in Ibn Rushd's text a highly un-Aristotelian description of the components of tragedy. Whereas Aristotle had insisted that the plot was the most important element and that action took priority over character, Ibn Rushd, characterizing tragedy along with epic as a "song of praise," sees its most important component as "character and belief." He describes the plot as composed of "representational speeches in the form of fables" (95). The reader would also seek in vain for Aristotle's characterizations of "reversal" and "recognition," though he would find the notion that pity and fear are inspired by the spectacle of undeserved misfortune (102).

Notwithstanding these sometimes drastic alterations of Aristotle's views, Ibn Rushd's text was widely influential and met with the approval of figures such as Roger Bacon. It was used extensively by critics such as Benvenuto da Imola, the fourteenth-century commentator on Dante, who saw Dante's *Commedia* as essentially a work of praise and blame. It also influenced Petrarch's humanist disciple Coluccio Salutati, who made use of the principle of praise and blame as well as of Ibn Rushd's definition of imitation. The influence is traceable in sixteenth-century writers such as Savonarola, Robortelli, and Mazzoni, who all believed that poetry was to some degree a branch of logic and who all cited Ibn Rushd in support of their own positions. As Hardison observes, throughout the sixteenth century the didactic theory of poetry coexisted uneasily with Aristotelian doctrines. Ibn Rushd's version of Aristotle was congenial to the moralistic attitudes of the humanists. The tension between the two modes of criticism reached explicit opposition in the work of Lodovico Castelvetro, whose interpretation of Aristotle's *Poetics*, though highly distorted, is free of Ibn Rushd's influence. Castelvetro was sharply opposed by his humanistic contemporary Torquato Tasso, who aligns his own views of heroic poetry as praise of virtue with the views of St. Basil, Ibn Rushd, Plutarch, and Aristotle (*MLC*, 88). Ironically, then, owing to a complex combination of historical circumstances, Ibn Rushd's version of Aristotle was for a long time given more credit than the views of Aristotle himself.

St. Thomas Aquinas (1224/5–1274)

Aristotle also assumes a prominent position in the thought of Thomas Aquinas, the greatest of the scholastic philosophers as well as the greatest philosopher of the Roman Catholic Church. Aquinas' philosophy took primarily Aristotle as its basis but was also influenced by the Stoics, the Neo-Platonists, Augustine, Boethius, Cicero, Ibn Sina, Ibn

Rushd, Ibn Gabirol, and Maimonides. Eventually, Aquinas was proclaimed to be the official "doctor" of the Church and his works were considered to be the expression of orthodox doctrine. His system is still widely taught in Catholic educational institutions.

Aquinas was born into a noble family in 1224 or 1225 in Italy near the city of Naples. He studied first at a Benedictine abbey until 1239 when he went to the University of Naples to study the liberal arts. In Naples he fell under the influence of Dominican friars who, like the Franciscans, were devoted to the ideals of poverty and simplicity. The Dominicans, however, were unique in their promotion of study and established houses for this purpose in many cities. Their central scholarly endeavor was to reconcile the teachings of Aristotle and Christ. Aquinas joined the order and under its auspices studied theology at the University in Paris, the intellectual center of Christendom. He also studied with the renowned Albertus Magnus, also a Dominican. Both figures effected the reconciliation just mentioned, and it was through their efforts that the Church established Aristotle, rather than Plato (who had been promoted by the Church Fathers for many centuries), at the center of Christian thought. For three years (1256–1259) Aquinas was a master in theology at the University of Paris, and for the next ten years taught in various Italian cities, after which he returned to teach in Paris. Aquinas died in 1274, at the age of 49, bequeathing to the Western world a legacy of theological and philosophical work greater than that of Plato and Aristotle combined.[10]

Aquinas is known primarily for two major works. The first, *Summa contra Gentiles*, was written between 1259 and 1264. Its essential purpose was to defend – or argue – the truth of Christianity against gentiles who did not accept the authority of the scriptures. In the first four books of the *Summa*, Aquinas relies, therefore, not on scripture but on "natural reason," which can be used to prove God's existence and the soul's immortality. The truths of the Incarnation, the Trinity, and the Last Judgment, however, are beyond the grasp of natural reason. Indeed, the provinces of reason and revelation need, according to Aquinas, to be clearly distinguished. He holds that these two provinces, while distinct, cannot contradict and must accord with each other. Religious truths capable of demonstration (for the learned) can also be known by faith, as in the case of simple people or children.

This insistence on a certain commensurability of reason and revelation reflects the intersection of Aquinas' life with certain important historical circumstances. In some respects his biography closely mirrors the abrogation of the feudal constraints into which he was born: the Dominican friars were institutionally poor and they moved away from the traditional monastic emphasis on prayer and manual labor to a life centered on scholarship and preaching. Secondly, the feudal world itself was changing, moving increasingly away from an agrarian to an urban economy organized on the basis of paternalistic trade guilds; hence a more rationalistic outlook toward the affairs of the world began to replace the other-worldliness and contempt for the world which had characterized the earlier Middle Ages. Finally, these developments coincided with the influx into Europe of a naturalistic and rationalistic Aristotelianism, as filtered through Islamic philosophers.

Indeed, it was in response to a controversy initiated by the influx of Arab philosophy that Aquinas maintained the harmony of reason and revelation. The Spanish Islamic philosopher Ibn Rushd had held that religious knowledge and rational knowledge were two distinct domains, which some disciples thought could conflict. This was unacceptable to Christian (as well as Islamic) orthodoxy, and Aquinas found himself engaged in a polemic against certain features of Averroism and the Averroist interpretation of Aristotle. Aquinas sees theology as a divine science, in relation to which all of the other elements of human knowledge are hierarchically ordered. While his scheme places theology at the apex of the human sciences, it also accommodates these sciences and views them as preparatory for man's last end as an intellectual creature, which is to know God. While Aquinas makes a distinction between intellection and reasoning, he sees them both as limited: they cannot discursively fathom the gift of God's grace yet they are complementary to the truths of revealed religion. Natural philosophy, he says, proceeds via reason whereas divine science observes intellection. Reason looks at many things in order to arrive at one truth, whereas the intellect grasps many things in one simple truth, "just as God in knowing His essence is cognizant of all things."[11] Aquinas terms divine science "first philosophy," given that it is this science "which confers principles on all the other sciences" (*MTA*, 111). Aquinas states that "God is the end of each thing, and hence each thing, to the greatest extent possible to it, intends to be united to God as its last end." And "the human intellect desires, loves and enjoys the knowledge of divine things, though it can grasp but little about them . . . the last end of all human knowledge and activity is the knowledge of God." Indeed, Aquinas avers that for man's happiness, which he equates with his last end, "no intellectual knowledge whatever suffices except the knowledge of God" (*MTA*, 113–117).

Correlative with the belief that the natural sciences were preparatory to divine science was the view that the physical world was not to be dismissed but had its place in God's creation. Rational investigation of the world of nature through the various sciences would prepare for the study of spiritual matters. Again, the main recourse for medieval scholars was Aristotle, and they turned to his *Physics*. In many areas – political theory, government, literature, law – the Augustinian view of nature as fallen and enveloped by God's providence began to give way before more rational and worldly accounts which emphasized the operations of causality and determined laws in nature. In Aquinas, the two seemingly disparate views are merged: God's providence does indeed rule the universe, but this providence accommodates the scientific laws to which nature is subject and wills all things to operate according to their specific nature. Aquinas also followed Aristotle in his conception of man's constitution, of which the body is matter and the soul the form.

It is important to remember that some of these views at the time were highly unorthodox and were opposed by many people, including Bonaventure, who saw Aquinas' views as threatening the transcendence of the soul, its freedom from the body and the natural world. A number of his doctrines were condemned by the universities of Paris and Oxford. In his own day, his theology was both controversial and radical. Aquinas' thought continued to receive much criticism during the later Middle Ages, and until the Enlightenment it was rivaled by the schools of thought derived from Duns Scotus and William of Ockham. Aquinas was not canonized until 1323, nor made a doctor of the Church until 1567. It was only from the Renaissance onward that most of the popes praised his system. The modern revival of Thomism began in 1879 with the publication of Pope Leo XIII's encyclical *Aeterni Patris*. From 1918 the ecclesiastical laws of the Catholic Church directed professors and students in seminaries to follow the "method, teaching and principles of the Angelic Doctor."

In his second major work, *Summa Theologiae*, Aquinas offers five proofs of the existence of God. The first is the argument of the unmoved Mover: in order to avoid an infinite regress, there must be something which moves other things without being moved itself. Second is the argument from First Cause, which follows a similar logic: there must be a cause which itself is not caused. Thirdly, there must be a primal source of all necessity. Fourthly, the various types and degrees of perfection which actually exist in the world must have their source in something absolutely perfect. Finally, even lifeless things serve a purpose, which must be directed toward some being beyond them. Some of the major characteristics of God, according to Aquinas, are as follows. God is eternal, unchanging, and he has no parts or composition since he is not material. In God, essence and existence are identical, and there are no accidents or contingencies in God. He does not belong to any genus and cannot be defined. God's intellection is his essence; he understands himself perfectly and in so doing understands the various elements of the world, which are like him in certain ways. As Aquinas puts it, "God himself, in knowing Himself, knows all other things" (*MTA*, 114). God's knowledge is comprehensive, holistic, and instantaneous; it is not discursive, piecemeal, and rational. Aquinas believes that God created the world *ex nihilo* or out of nothing; and that God is the end of all things, which tend toward likeness of God. The human intellect, which aspires after God, is a part of each man's soul, the soul being the form of the body. Aquinas agrees with Aristotle on the question of universals: these do not have an independent, substantial existence but are merely names or categories. On the questions of sin and predestination, Aquinas basically agrees with Augustine that only God's grace can redeem man from sin and that the election of some men for salvation is a mystery.

The picture of the world which emerges here is one which is rigidly coherent and closed off from all possible intrusion of accidence. It is also one which is balanced precariously on the narrow ground of coterminousness of revelation and reason, God's providence and natural law, essence and existence. Russell states that Aquinas' "appeal to reason is, in a sense, insincere, since the conclusion to be reached is fixed in advance" (*HWP*, 453). Moreover, since there is nothing entirely trivial in the world, all things except God have their true being outside of themselves, in their end, which is God. And God effectively acts as the boundaries of the universe since all things are replicated – in their true significance – in the sphere of God, his self-knowledge encompassing knowledge of them. In other words, things achieve their true identity only in God, and then only in God's act of self-knowledge, in the coerced relation of dependence to him in which they are obliged to subsist. They achieve identity, then, not as objects of knowledge in their own right but as projections or rather introjections of God's subjectivity. Furthermore, as noted above, man's ultimate happiness consists in contemplation of God. Hence man's own knowledge is internally directed toward the divine, and toward things in the world only insofar as they relate to the divine. God's essence delimits the world in several ways: as origin and purpose, as beginning and end, as subject and object, as knower and known, as center and circumference.

The foregoing represents the general world view which formed the background of Aquinas' aesthetics. Indeed, that world view is of great significance since its central elements furnish the context of much medieval thought and practice in general as well as of aesthetics. In his study of Aquinas, Umberto Eco describes Aquinas as "the person who gave most complete expression to the philosophical and theological thinking of the age."[12] Eco notes that medieval aesthetic sensibility was concerned not only with beauty as an abstraction (for example, as an attribute of God) but also with beauty in its concrete physical aspect (Eco, 12–13). He also remarks the medieval disposition, as evidenced in St. Bernard and others, to use the rejection of outward sensible beauty to elevate aesthetic sensibility to a higher level, one which could all the more appreciate inner, spiritual beauty (Eco, 10). Hence "the emphasis on an interior beauty which does not die was more than a simple opposition to an aesthetic of the sensible. It was, rather, a kind of reinstatement of such an aesthetic" because the permanent inner essence of beauty was the source of the beauty of sensible appearances. Inner beauty was seen as expressed in outer beauty (Eco, 10–11).

Such is the tenor of medieval aesthetic sensibility which Eco sees as forming the background of Aquinas' own aesthetics. In order to understand the aesthetics of Aquinas, we need to grasp some further basic features of his metaphysics, which were fundamental to the worldview of many medieval thinkers. In agreement with Aristotle, Aquinas states that the subject of metaphysics is being *as* being, or the essential attributes of being. Other sciences treat of being under particular aspects; for example, arithmetic treats being as number. Hence metaphysics is a fundamental science because it alone deals with universal being, and "on the knowledge of common or universal things hinges the knowledge of proper or individual things" (*MTA*, 20).

Again like Aristotle, he distinguishes the *essence* of a thing from its *existence* (*MTA*, 24–26). Essence and existence are identical only in God. In all created things they are distinct. Aquinas explains as follows: "The act of existing belongs to the first agent, God, through His own nature; for God's act of existing is His substance . . . But that which belongs to something according to its own nature, appertains to other things only by participation . . . Thus the act of existing is possessed by other things, from the First Agent, through a certain participation" (*MTA*, 33). Hence *it is the very essence of God to exist*, or, to put it a different way, *existence is His essence*. As Aquinas has it, "God alone *is* His act of existing" (*MTA*, 32, emphasis added). It is not in the nature or essence of created beings to exist and they possess existence only as a kind of refraction of God's existence; significantly, Aquinas uses the term "participation" to describe the connection between the two modes of existence. Plato had used the same word (*koinonia*) to express the connection between the world of Forms and the physical world. Hence the connection between God and man, at its profoundest level, is contained in the very notion of existence: God's *nature* is nothing other than to exist (though, as will emerge shortly, existence itself is not empty but replete with certain attributes); everything else has *another* nature, which is not existence, and which determines its individual being.

All of the characteristics of the connection between human and divine flow from this primary relation of uncreated and created, which represents the downward movement from the identity of existence and essence to their mutual separation. Seen in this light, the act of creation is the act of existence falling away from its coextensiveness with essence. The identity of existence and essence is a means of retaining within the controlling categories of essence the potentially infinite diversity of existence. In other words, all that could actually happen in the world is already assigned a place and a predetermined significance within a universal scheme. For anything to move beyond that scheme, for the content of existence to slide beyond the boundaries of essence, would be to enter a realm of contingency and accident. In a sense, this is precisely what the human *creature* does: as a *created* being who is also fallen, he falls away from the absolute universality and necessity inherent in the identity of essence and existence, into the contingency and particularity of externality to divine grace. The distance by which man's existence outspaces his essence expresses the area of this externality. Lost in the consequent contingent temptations of this world, he must find his way back to the divine, back to the retraction of existence into coterminousness with essence, back to the union of essence and existence which alone can give his life order, harmony, and significance by pursuing the configuration of the universal and essential beneath the chaotic variety and particularity of existence. As an intellectual creature, man seeks above all the knowledge of God, a path which proceeds by way of knowledge of essence and universals.

Since, however, all human existence is "participated" or achieved through participation in God's existence, human beings are never severed from relationship with God. Aquinas states that "every created substance attains likeness to God through the very act of existing" (*MTA*, 31). Aquinas proceeds to say that "the distance of nature between the creature and God cannot stand in the way of a community of analogy between them" (*MTA*, 36). Hence, the relation between God and created beings subsists not through nature but through analogy.

The Transcendentals

Following Aristotle and the scholastic tradition, Aquinas suggests that certain predicates, as expressed by the categories, apply to particular aspects of being. Other predicates, however, which he called "transcendentals," are qualities of all being. These include the predicates "one," "true," and "good." Further predicates added by Arab philosophers included "thing" and "something"; some commentators added a further transcendental predicate, "beautiful." These transcendental attributes are general features of all being and add nothing to the nature of being; each one of them is coextensive with the whole of being, and this is why Aquinas regards them as mutually convertible. In other words, it is possible to view being under any of these aspects, each aspect comprising a different perspective toward being.

It may well be asked why Aquinas, and scholastic thought generally, insisted that being possessed certain inherent properties. The answer lies partly in the medieval metaphysics which saw God's being and essence as identical: as the most perfect being, God inherently possessed certain attributes. Also, however, there was the need to combat certain heresies such as Manicheism, which saw the universe as a battleground of the forces of good and evil. The insistence on the intrinsic unity, truth, and goodness of being was a way of combating such views of the world and creation. When beauty is added to the list of transcendentals, this argument can be extended further: God's creation is intrinsically beautiful and, as Eco points out, beauty consequently "acquires a metaphysical worth, an unchanging objectivity, and an extension which is universal" (Eco, 22). This vision of the world as intrinsically beautiful derived from many sources. The most obvious influence was the Bible, which had extolled the beauty of God's creation. Also, Plato's *Timaeus* had envisioned the universe as governed by order and beauty. Then there were the influences deriving from Pythagoras, which had led figures such as St. Augustine to see the beauty of the world in terms of musical and numerical harmony. Finally, and perhaps most importantly, there was the influence of the Neo-Platonists Proclus, Porphyry, and especially Dionysius the pseudo-Areopagite (sometimes called pseudo-Dionysius), whose book *The Divine Names* had presented the universe as a dazzling hierarchy of beauty emanating from the First Principle. One of the important figures influenced by Dionysius was John Scotus Eriugena, who saw the universe as a vast structure of symbols, all of which pointed toward God (Eco, 23–24). Eco suggests that "Eriugena's aesthetic perspective was the most far-reaching . . . in the whole of the Middle Ages" (Eco, 24–25).

Aquinas adduces a number of arguments to prove that God is one. It was seen in an earlier chapter how important the notion of unity was for Plato, in two fundamental ways: the unity of the world of Forms effectively controlled and ordered the diversity of the physical world. Poetry was condemned precisely because of its unruly violation of such unity. In Aquinas we see the notion of unity exerting its controlling force at an even more fundamental level: it is one of the primary attributes not only of God but also of universal being; it is only by negation of this that division and multiplicity can arise. Moreover, the very notion of multiplicity is defined such that it is subsumable under unity; in other words, it arises only in neat symmetrical opposition with unity which remains as its underlying substratum of possibility and measurement. In the absence of such controlled polarity, multiplicity would lead to infinite regress and the lack of a secure foundation of knowledge or reality. Finally, the oneness of God is intrinsically bound with the order of the world: contingency and accidence are allowed to slide away to the periphery of this medieval vision, and lapse into the status of unreality. Another way of understanding this would be to say that only those elements of the divine as well as of the human world are allowed access into the status of reality which can fall under the coercive control of unity. What stands at the center of this vision, ensuring the stability of the entire framework, is the identity of existence and essence which comprises the profoundest perspective of God's unity.

In respect of the transcendental "true," Aquinas affirms that "Truth is a disposition of being . . . as something universally found in being" (*MTA*, 62–63). Hence being cannot be understood independently of the true "because being cannot be grasped without that which corresponds or is adequated to the intellect" (*MTA*, 62). In other words, being is already somehow oriented toward conformity with our intellectual faculties. Aquinas states that "even if the human intellect did not exist, things would still be said to be true in their relation to the divine intellect" (*MTA*, 68). Hence, the notion of truth as conceived of by Aquinas is not a humanistic one dependent on human structures of perception. Rather, truth precedes human perception and cognition: things are already in their appointed place and their truth-value already inscribed in their being; the human intellect merely supervenes passively on this preordered arrangement, merely registering truths of that arrangement in its own limited fashion. It is the preordered correspondence of being with the divine intellect that preserves the paradigm of unity of knowledge which the human intellect strives to emulate. The multiplicity infecting human knowledge and the world of things as sundered from their participation in correspondence with the divine intellect is something to be overcome as the human intellect points beyond itself to its completion in a higher mode.

In discussing the transcendental "beauty," Aquinas states: "Nothing exists which does not participate in beauty and goodness, since each thing is beautiful and good according to its proper form . . . created beauty is nothing other than a likeness of the divine beauty participated in things" (*MTA*, 88). This sounds somewhat like a Platonic formulation, and Aquinas adds that beauty and goodness are based upon the same reality but differ in reason. The good relates to the appetite, as an end, since it is what all desire; beauty, however, relates to the cognitive power, "because those things are said to be beautiful which please when seen," as a formal cause, since the pleasure yielded depends on due proportion of form. Three things are required for beauty: integrity or perfection, right proportion or consonance (*consonantia*), and splendor of form (*claritas*).

Again following Dionysius, Aquinas maintains that God's beauty is not subject to the limitations of the beauty of created beings: it is not subject to variability and corruption, nor is it confined within any given aspect since God is absolutely and in every way beautiful. Moreover, in God "the simple and supernatural Essence of . . . every beauty and every beautiful being pre-exists, not indeed dividedly, but uniformly [unitedly and simply], in the manner in which multiple effects pre-exist in their cause" (*MTA*, 90–92). Again the formulation seems Platonic inasmuch as a unified cause gives rise to multiple effects, and especially inasmuch as causality is not merely viewed as a formal relation but is imbued with content; thus "goodness" preexists the multiplicity of good things which are good through participation in that preexisting essence. Inasmuch as parts relate to a whole, the relations between these appertains to harmony or *consonantia* which is the essence of beauty (*MTA*, 94–95). The form upon which the proper nature of a thing depends pertains to *claritas*, and order to the end (finality) pertains to *consonantia* (*MTA*, 98).

Medieval Allegory and Aquinas

Numerous writers have observed a widespread tendency throughout the medieval period to view all things in the world and the universe as essentially symbolic, as signs in a vast lexicon through which God speaks to humanity. Everything points beyond itself, beyond its immediate worldly significance, toward a higher level of significance in a more comprehensive pattern of events and divine purpose. Among the influential propounders of such a view were pseudo-Dionysius, the Roman writer Macrobius, and John Scotus Eriugena who wrote that "there is nothing among visible and corporeal things which does not signify something incorporeal and intelligible" (Eco, 139). Such all-embracing symbolism provided a vision of a world constrained by unity, order, and purpose. In such a vision, human beings are obliged to read and decipher the book of the world or the book of the universe.

Christian allegory arose initially from the attempts by writers such as Origen to reconcile the Old and New Testaments, to show that they were mutually coherent and that they were both, in different ways, speaking the same truths. Allegory also had its basis in the endeavor to restrict the potentially infinite meanings of the scriptures, by subjecting them to a code of interpretation. The scriptures were regarded as an infinitely rich store of wisdom; St. Jerome saw them as "an infinite forest of meanings," and Origen spoke of "a most enormous forest of Scripture." Yet this view had to be reconciled with the assignment of specific and limited meanings to the sacred texts. Hence the Church Fathers devised an allegorical theory of interpretation of the Bible, according to three levels of meaning: the literal, the moral, and the mystical. Later, this system was expanded to include four levels: the literal, the allegorical, the moral, and the anagogical. Nicholas of Lyra summarized these four levels of significance as follows: "The literal sense tells us of events; the allegorical teaches our faith; the moral tells us what to do; the anagogical shows us where we are going" (Eco, 145). A related problem was that of deciding whether a given passage in scripture should be taken literally or figuratively; as we have seen, St. Augustine was the first to furnish rules for determining this.

In his *Summa Theologica*, Aquinas explained allegory in a formulation which comprehends the foregoing tendencies:

> that first signification whereby words signify things belongs to the first sense, the historical or literal. That signification whereby things signified by words have themselves also a signification is called the spiritual sense, which is based on the literal, and presupposes it. Now this spiritual sense has a threefold division. For as the Apostle says the Old Law is a figure of the New Law, and Dionysius says *the New Law itself is a figure of future glory* . . . Therefore, so far as the things of the Old Law signify the things of the New Law, there is the allegorical sense; so far as the things done in Christ, or so far as the things which signify Christ, are types of what we ought to do, there is the moral sense. But so far as they signify what relates to eternal glory, there is the anagogical sense. (*Summa Theologica*, Q.I, Tenth Article)[13]

What is notable about Aquinas' definition of allegory is the movement from the signification of *things* to that of *words*. The literal or historical sense denotes the connection between language and the world. The remaining levels of significance are contained within the realm of language and literary/biblical tradition. The most general name for this symbolism (itself, for Aquinas, denoting the connection between word and concept) is the "spiritual sense." The three divisions of this comprehend Christianity's attempt to appropriate the pre-Christian past into its own historical and theological framework (the allegorical sense); they also affirm the moral authority of Christ's own example (the moral sense); finally, they stress the Christian view of the transient, partial, and finite nature of this world, which has significance only in relation to the totality of God's eternal scheme which is accessible only by revelation and not by human reason (the anagogical or mystical sense).

Eco presents Aquinas' views of allegory as an integral part of a broad change which tended to demote the secular human world to the status of literal meaning, and which restricted spiritual and symbolic significance to the province of biblical history. In the first place, Aquinas held that poetry was *infima doctrina* or an inferior kind of teaching to that of scripture. It was inferior because of its deficiency in truth, which in turn rested on the fact that it dealt with objects which were imagined or invented rather than real. While, as Eco observes, such a view does not imply contempt for poetry on Aquinas' part, it expresses in part his sense of the hierarchy of various modes of knowledge (Eco, 148–149). It is because poetry talks of things unknown or previously unimagined that it cannot communicate via reason and must employ metaphors (Eco,

149 n. 53). However, unlike scripture, poetry can never achieve a true distinction between literal meaning and symbolic or spiritual meaning. Whereas poetry is *deficient* in knowledge, the mysteries of scripture *exceed* our capacities of understanding and therefore need to be expressed through metaphor and allegory (Eco, 150 n. 54). The literal historical events recounted in scripture have a spiritual sense which was known only to God and not necessarily known to its authors who, however, were writing under divine inspiration. The secular language of poetry, on the other hand, while it employs allegory and metaphor, deals with objects and events which possess no intrinsic spiritual significance. Aquinas views poetry as having only a literal sense; any further level of meaning (which Aquinas terms the "parabolic") is merely a sub-species of this literal sense; and he understands the literal meaning to express a given author's intention (Eco, 153 n. 66).

After Aquinas, according to Eco, certain thinkers such as John Duns Scotus, William of Ockham, and Nicholas of Autrecour questioned his concept of natural organic form, thereby providing the impetus for a new conception of art and beauty. These thinkers stressed the particularity and uniqueness rather than the universal qualities of beauty, furnishing novel possibilities for aesthetics, possibilities which were realized in many modern conceptions of art that emphasized art as creation rather than merely imitation, and stressed the particularity and uniqueness of beautiful things. Eco also sees the three figures as symptomatic of a crisis of scholasticism in the late medieval period. The disorder caused by the collapse of the Roman Empire and the invasion of the barbarians had led to desperate attempts at seeking order, as witnessed in the Pythagorean aesthetics of number, important in Augustine and other writers of this period. The relatively stable political order after the Carolingian renaissance had in-spired the systematic theological ordering of the universe in which scholasticism played so central a role. A number of factors, however, began to undermine this conception of world order and the theology which expressed it: the Crusades, the rise of the middle class, which was unable to see itself "in that image of universal order" expressed in Aquinas' aesthetics, nationalism, the use of vernacular languages, and mysticism (Eco, 212–213). In short, scholasticism "no longer reflected the economic and social rela-tions of the time . . . modern aesthetics conforms with a cognitive model brought to completion by the bourgeois society which was emerging at the time that medieval aesthetics was in crisis" (Eco, 214). These new views stressed the artist as a creator and inventor in contrast with Aquinas' view of the artist as applying the rules laid down by God. Nonetheless, Eco sees an enduring value in scholasticism and medieval aesthetics. For one thing, we can still learn from scholasticism's attempts to explain art in terms of intellect, its treatment of the connection between aesthetic autonomy and functional requirements, and its acknowledgment that what we call aesthetic emotion depends in fact upon systems of values, ideologies, and cultural codes (Eco, 215–216).

Dante Alighieri (1265–1321) and the Allegorical Mode

Allegory is integral to the work of Dante Alighieri, arguably the greatest poet the Western world has produced. He is best known for his epic poem *Divina Commedia*

(1307–1321) and his earlier cycle of love poems published as *La Vita Nuova* (*The New Life*, ca. 1295), written in honor of Beatrice Portinari. Dante also wrote literary criticism, which was in part indebted to Aristotle, Boethius, Cicero, and Aquinas. In *De Vulgari Eloquentia* he defended the use of the vernacular Italian as appropriate for the writing of poetry. In *Il Convivio* (*The Banquet*, 1306–1309) he produced a collection of fourteen odes with prose commentaries, designed to clear him of the charge of "unrestrained passion" in these odes and to explain the principles of allegory. And in 1319 he wrote a now famous letter, also treating of allegory, to his patron in Verona, Can Grande della Scala, though the authenticity of the letter has been questioned. In *Il Convivio* Dante states that allegory has four senses, which he enumerates and explains as follows:

> The first is called the literal, and this is the sense that does not go beyond the surface of the letter, as in the fables of the poets. The next is called the allegorical, and this is the one that is hidden beneath the cloak of these fables, and is a truth hidden beneath a beautiful fiction . . .
> The third sense is called moral, and this is the sense that teachers should intently seek to discover throughout the scriptures, for their own profit and that of their pupils . . .
> The fourth sense is called anagogical, that is to say, beyond the senses; and this occurs when a scripture is expounded in a spiritual sense which, although it is true also in the literal sense, signifies by means of the things signified a part of the supernal things of eternal glory.[14]

As an example of the allegorical sense, Dante offers Ovid's account of Orpheus taming wild beasts. The allegorical meaning of this, says Dante, is that the wise man makes cruel hearts grow tender and humble. The moral sense is illustrated, he says, by the gospel account of Christ ascending the mountain to be transfigured; that he took only three apostles with him means that "in matters of great secrecy we should have few companions." To exemplify the anagogical sense, Dante recalls Psalm 114 which states that when the people of Israel left Egypt, "Judea was made whole and free": this, remarks Dante, means that "when the soul departs from sin it is made whole and free in its power." Dante is insistent that in allegorical explication, "the literal sense should always come first, as being the sense in whose meaning the others are enclosed." Literal meaning is also the "subject and material" of the other senses, as well as their foundation. He pictures the literal meaning as being on the "outside," enclosing the other senses which are within (II.i.65–80). Many centuries later, Derrida will attempt to deconstruct such metaphors of outside and inside. In insisting on including literal meaning in any interpretation, Dante (like others before him) is partly reacting against the definitions of allegory and metaphor by classical rhetoricians as the mere substitution of one set of terms for another. He is also following many theologians who affirmed the truth of all four levels of meaning, as against rhetorical and poetic views of allegory which might view even the literal meaning as fictional. It becomes clear through *Il Convivio* that one of the functions of allegory is to express "darkly" and in a hidden manner what is otherwise ineffable concerning the mysteries of God and eternity which even philosophy, the noblest human pursuit, cannot fathom (III.xv.58–69). Having said this, the authority of Aristotle stands at the literal foundation of Dante's allegory; he sees Aristotle as the "master" and "leader" of human reason, and as worthy of "faith" and "obedience" (IV.vi.50–73).

In the "Letter to Can Grande" Dante dedicates his *Divine Comedy* to his patron and explains the allegorical structure of this poem. Dante begins by reiterating Aristotle's position that some things are self-sufficient, having being in themselves, while the being of other things is relational, lying beyond themselves in their connections with other things.[15] Dante uses this position to explain the need to outline the entire conception of his *Commedia*. However, it might well be used as an introduction to his explanation of allegory: the word in itself is incomplete. Dante explains that his text is "polysemous, that is, having several senses." The literal sense necessarily signifies beyond itself to higher senses which complete it. Dante's definition pursues the broad lines of Aquinas' formulation, but names the three spiritual senses as interchangeably "allegorical." The non-literal senses, although they are called by various names (allegorical, moral, anagogical) "may all be called allegorical, since they are all different from the literal or historical" ("LCG," par. 7). Hence he sees the structure of allegory as broadly dualistic, the literal sense being a narrative of this world and the allegorical sense referring to the spiritual domain.

In accordance with this duality, Dante sees the subject of the poem as twofold, corresponding to literal and allegorical senses. The subject of the work, taken literally, "is the state of souls after death." Allegorically, "the subject is man, in the exercise of his free will, earning or becoming liable to the rewards or punishments of justice" ("LCG," par. 8). This division of the subject implies a somewhat sharp separation and exact correlation between the two levels of significance, both of which could operate only in a context of a universe theologically viewed as closed, purposeful, and coherent. In other words, despite Dante's claim that his work is polysemous, and has "several senses," further possibilities of interpretation must be foreclosed for such separation and correlation to be functional. Again pursuing this dualism, Dante views the end or ultimate aim of the work as dual, as immediate and ultimate. This aim is viewed as a spiritual aim, namely, to lead souls from a state of sin and misery to a state of blessedness ("LCG," par. 15). Hence, the twofold structure of allegory as given in Dante's text informs every aspect of the reading process, from the author's intentions and use of language to the reader's response. All of these elements are figured into a highly structured framework.

What also underlies allegory, in the texts of both Aquinas and Dante, is a belief in the reality of universals rather than of particulars. The structure of allegory presupposes ease of conceptual movement between various levels of significance. This is only possible if each incident is prevented from being immersed in particularity and uniqueness and is compelled to bear the weight of its own self-transcendence, its own lack of self-sufficiency, its own partial participation in a broader spectrum of signification. Such self-transcendence can achieve coherence and precise allegorical expression in a closed system of meaning whereby a particular object or event on the literal plane can be invested with clear significance on an allegorical level. Indeed, like Cicero and Macrobius, Dante points out the virtues of pursuing knowledge as opposed to the worldly pursuits of wealth and power (*Il Convivio*, IV.xii–xiii). More fundamentally, in a number of his works, Dante gives expression to a characteristic medieval cosmology in terms of the positions of the planets, the concepts of motion and of first cause. In the "Letter to Can Grande," for example, he uses Aristotle's metaphysics, as did Aquinas, as a basis to argue that "all things which exist, except this one thing, have their being from another . . . , which is God. Thus everything which has its being, gets its being, either directly or indirectly, from Him" ("LCG," par. 20). And again like Aquinas, he states that God's self-sufficiency, as both being and essence, can be attested to by reason but even more by divine authority or scripture ("LCG," par. 20–22). Hence, it can be seen that allegory, wherein the meanings of words are intrinsically referred beyond the words themselves into a higher nexus of spiritual relationships and meanings whose terminus is God, expresses at its profoundest level a vision of the world in which the existence of things is not self-sufficient but always depends ultimately, through a series of mediating relationships, on God as the prime and absolutely self-sufficient existent. All worldly goals are subordinated to the ultimate goal of human life, which is to achieve blessedness by beholding God, the "Origin of Truth" ("LCG," par. 33).

Indeed, Dante's insights concerning poetry generally exhibit traits characteristic of many of the medieval writers already discussed. In *Il Convivio*, for example, he states that the "goodness" of a poem, like that of any other discourse, resides in its meaning, while its beauty resides in its adornment (II.xi.4–5). He suggests that poetry, being a form of persuasion, enlists the rules of rhetoric (II.vi.6; II.viii.2); Dante refers both to Aristotle's *Rhetoric* and the *Rhetorica Nova*, which he, like medieval writers generally, wrongly attributed to Cicero ("LCG," par. 18–19). And, like other discourses, poetry is a rational activity which is structured and uses various rhetorical figures (*Il Convivio*, III.ix.1–3). Yet Dante is somewhat modern, even beyond figures such as Geoffrey de Vinsauf, in his realization that language is limited: not only does it fail to express divine mysteries, but also it is an inadequate instrument even for the expression of human thought, which far outruns it and exceeds its capacity (III.iv.4, 12). In the "Letter to Can Grande," he says that "we see many things with the intellect for which there are no verbal signs." Plato, he notes, was aware of this fact, and of the consequent need to make use of metaphor ("LCG," par. 29). However, this inadequacy of language is for Dante ultimately an index of human limitation in relation to the divine; allegory is a form of verbal expression which, pointing metaphorically to mysteries beyond human comprehension, accommodates human limitation in a structured manner.

Notes

1 "Introduction," in *MLTC*, 5.
2 Martin Irvine, *The Making of Textual Culture: "Grammatica" and Literary Theory, 350–1100* (Cambridge and New York: Cambridge University Press, 1994), pp. 18–19. Hereafter cited as *GLT*.
3 *The Didascalicon of Hugh of St. Victor*, trans. Jerome Taylor (New York: Columbia University Press, 1991), p. 44. Hereafter cited as *DHV*.
4 *The Metalogicon of John of Salisbury: A Twelfth-Century Defense of the Verbal and Logical Arts of the Trivium*, trans. Daniel D. McGarry (Gloucester, MA: Peter Smith, 1971), pp. 275–276. Hereafter cited as *ML*.
5 The square brackets in all of the quotations from John are the editor's.
6 Dante, *De Vulgari Eloquentia*, in *The Latin Works of Dante: De Vulgari Eloquentia, De Monarchica, Epistles, Eclogues, and Quaestio de Aqua et Terra*, trans. A. G. Ferrers Howell (New York: Greenwood Press, 1904), pp. 4–6. Hereafter cited as *DVE*.

7 "Introduction," in Geoffrey of Vinsauf, *Poetria Nova*, trans. Margaret F. Nims (Toronto and Wetteren, Belgium: Pontifical Institute of Medieval Studies/Universa Press, 1967), pp. 10–11. Some of the other details presented here of Geoffrey's life and work are also taken from Nims' brief but useful introduction.

8 Much of this information is taken from W. Montgomery Watt's splendid account in *Islamic Philosophy and Theology* (Edinburgh: Edinburgh University Press, 1985), pp. 117–119.

9 Averroës, "The Middle Commentary of Averroës of Cordova on the *Poetics* of Aristotle," in *MLC*, 89. Hereafter citations are given in the text with references to the appropriate pages.

10 Norman Kretzmann and Eleonore Stump, eds., *Cambridge Companion to Aquinas* (Cambridge: Cambridge University Press, 1993), pp. 3, 12–13.

11 *An Introduction to the Metaphysics of St. Thomas Aquinas: Texts Selected and Translated*, preface by James F. Anderson (Indiana: Regnery/Gateway, 1953), p. 109. Hereafter cited as *MTA*.

12 Umberto Eco, *The Aesthetics of Thomas Aquinas*, trans. Hugh Bredin (Cambridge, MA: Harvard University Press, 1988), p. 140. Hereafter cited as Eco.

13 *Summa Theologica*, trans. Fathers of the English Dominican Province, 1920–1931.

14 Dante, *Il Convivio: The Banquet*, trans. Richard H. Lansing (New York and London: Garland, 1990), II.i.1, 20–60.

15 "The Letter to Can Grande," in *Literary Criticism of Dante Alighieri*, trans. Robert S. Haller (Nebraska: University of Nebraska Press, 1973), par. 5. Hereafter cited as "LCG," with numbers referring to paragraphs.

CHAPTER 10

TRANSITIONS: MEDIEVAL HUMANISM

Two medieval figures, Giovanni Boccaccio and Christine de Pisan, were important forerunners of the Renaissance humanism that eclipsed (but also grew out of) scholasticism. As will be seen in the accounts below, Boccaccio saw an urgent need to defend poetry and a humanistic curriculum against the onslaughts not so much of scholastics as of the rising mercantile classes who saw no practical value in literature and the arts. The basis of his defense was broadly humanistic, advocating a return to classical literature and the need for a knowledge of rhetoric and logic. Yet Boccaccio's defense of poetry effectively redefined this art, as independent of rhetoric, and also in terms of its effect on the reader, a notion that we can still relate to today. Christine's was a powerful humanistic voice in the medieval era which dared to enter into a literary debate with male authorities and which not only challenged male historiography and the portrayals and treatment of women by men, but also associated the very notion of reason with femininity.

The Defense of Poetry: Giovanni Boccaccio (1313–1375)

Though Boccaccio wished to be known as a scholar, he is most widely known for his *Decameron* (1358), a collection of a hundred, sometimes bawdy, stories told by ten characters against the background of the bubonic plague that overtook Italy in 1348. Boccaccio also wrote allegorical poetry and romances which influenced Chaucer and Shakespeare. Like Dante, he pressed the cause of Italian vernacular literature. Yet through his scholarly works, written in Latin, he was an influential forerunner of Renaissance humanism. His *De Mulieribus Claris* (*Concerning Famous Women*) (1361) was a source of Christine de Pisan's *City of Ladies* (1405). In terms of literary criticism, his most important work was *Genealogia Deorum Gentilium* (*Genealogy of the Gentile Gods*) (1350–1362), a huge encyclopedia of classical mythology in fifteen books. In the first thirteen books he attempts to compile, arrange, and offer allegorical interpretations of classical mythology. The last two books are devoted to a comprehensive defense of poetry, citing arguments for and against the art since the time of Plato. Hence, the book is not only an endeavor to expound the virtues of classical literature but also an attempt by a practicing poet to defend his art, in a tradition that stretches from Horace through Ronsard, Du Bellay, Sidney, Boileau, and Pope to Wordsworth, Coleridge, Shelley, and Arnold. As an encyclopedia of both literature and literary criticism, its influence on poets as well as critics was broad, and endured for more than two centuries. As Charles Osgood notes, along with Aristotle's *Poetics*, which was rediscovered in the fifteenth century, Boccaccio's text effectively furnished "the substance of literary theory for the Renaissance"; and traces of it appear in Chaucer, Spenser, Jonson, Milton, and Shelley.[1] Though he was born into a merchant family, he eventually shied away from commercial life and moved in aristocratic and courtly circles.

Boccaccio's preface to the *Genealogy* is addressed to Hugo IV, king of Cyprus and Jerusalem, who commissioned the work. This preface gives some indication of the magnitude of Boccaccio's task, and his own conception of his purpose. Concerning the ancient gods and myths, he says, "there is no one book that I know of which contains all this matter . . . The names and tribes of gods and their progenitors are scattered hither and yon all over the world" (*GDG*, 9). Hence, his work was to be a vast assemblage of myths and tales which were hitherto uncollected.

Boccaccio states two other intentions in his preface. The first is to expound the deeper, truthful meaning of ancient texts, a meaning often hidden by superficial absurdity or impossibility or adherence to a false theology. Secondly, in bringing to light the wisdom of the ancient poets, he proposes to defend the art of poetry against its detractors (*GDG*, 12). This defense is vehemently taken up in book XIV where, passing contemptuously over the cavils against poetry by the ignorant and the tasteless, Boccaccio confronts the criticisms of the jurists and the lawyers. These people, he says, are conspicuous, influential, and persuasive in speech. Their indictment of poetry rests on the ground that it does not bring wealth and power, and it is of no practical use, hence poets in general must be foolish to spend their lives in such unprofitable activity (XIV.iv). Such charges incite Boccaccio to launch into not only a defense of poetry but also an extolment of poverty. Whereas lawyers are tainted by the love of money, prestige, and worldly things – which are perishable – poetry, like theology and philosophy, rejects such pursuits: "Poetry devotes herself to something greater; for while she dwells in heaven, and mingles with the divine counsels, she moves the minds of a few men from on high to a yearning for the eternal" (XIV.iv). Moreover, poetry is "a stable and fixed science" which is the same "in all times and places," whereas the law is subject to change according to culture and circumstance (XIV.iv). Boccaccio effectively redefines true poverty as "a mental disease that often afflicts even the rich" (XIV.iv). This is a poverty of the imagination, whereby people pursue fleeting treasures with a hunger that is never satisfied (XIV.iv). Noticeable here in Boccaccio's spirited defense is an affiliation of poetry with philosophical and theological other-worldliness; it calls people to virtue in this life only by making them realize its trivial and transient nature, urging them to focus on the life of the spirit.

Boccaccio now constructs an allegory of a house devoted to sacred study: on a lofty throne "sits Philosophy, messenger from the very bosom of God, mistress of all knowledge" (XIV.v). Around her are men of learning and humility, seated in high places; beyond these is a noisy crowd of pretenders to knowledge, pseudo-philosophers who are interested not in truth or wisdom but in procuring a favorable reputation (XIV.v). It is these people that Boccaccio depicts as denouncing poetry in the most vociferous terms: poetry, they charge, is a "useless and absurd craft"; poets are "tale-mongers, or, in lower terms, liars"; the work of poets is not only false but also often obscure and lewd; moreover, poets are "seducers of the mind, prompters of crime." Such cavilers, notes Boccaccio, use Plato's authority to uphold their "mad denunciation of poets" (XIV.v). Boccaccio's initial response is to point out that "poetry, like other studies, is derived from God, Author of all wisdom." And if certain poets have pandered to a licentious taste, poetry itself cannot be universally condemned since it offers "so many inducements to virtue" and employs "exquisite style and diction" to direct "men's thoughts on things of heaven" (XIV.vi).

Boccaccio proceeds to define poetry, its origin and functions. He calls poetry a "fervid and exquisite invention," in speech or writing, that "proceeds from the bosom of God." Boccaccio cites the authority of Cicero to support his claim that poetry is an inspired art, for which there can be no rigid rules and formulae (XIV.vii). And the fervor of poetry is "sublime in its effects: it impels the soul to a longing for utterance; it brings forth strange and unheard-of creations of the mind; it arranges these meditations in a fixed order, adorns the whole composition with unusual interweaving of words and thoughts; and thus it veils truth in a fair and fitting garment of fiction" (XIV.vii). Interestingly, his definition is modern in that the product of poetry cannot be planned in advance since these productions are both inspired and new; it is less modern in its implication that poetry is intrinsically allegorical, always clothing truth with fiction. The functions of poetry are also practical; it can prepare kings for war, portray the various phases of human character, stimulate virtue, and subdue vice. Also modern is Boccaccio's insistence that poetry be defined primarily according to its effect. Indeed, he sees the derivation of the word "poetry" as based on its effect: it comes from the Greek word *poetes*, which he takes to mean "exquisite discourse" (XIV.vii). He sees poetry as derived from the Greeks, where it arose as a heightened form of language used for prayer and the praise of God, as well as for expressing "the high mysteries of things divine" (XIV.viii).

Boccaccio anticipates many of the Romantics in stating that poets prefer lonely haunts that are favorable to contemplation, especially contemplation of God. Here, the poet is free of the distractions of the city, such as "the greedy and mercenary markets," as well as the courts and noisy crowds. The pleasures of nature "soothe the soul; then they collect the scattered energies of the mind, and renew the power of the poet's genius," prompting it "to long for the contemplation of high themes" (XIV.xi).

For a poet to be effective, he must know not only the precepts of grammar and rhetoric but also "the principles of the other Liberal Arts, both moral and natural." He must have a comprehensive knowledge, encompassing the works not only of ancient writers but of the world, the history of nations and even their geography (XIV.vii). Having said this, he does not regard poetry as merely a branch of rhetoric, for, "among the disguises of fiction rhetoric has no part" (XIV.vii). Hence, Boccaccio sees poetry as a somewhat unique art, distinct from rhetoric and from other branches of learning in general.

Turning to the charge that poets are tale-mongers or liars, Boccaccio retorts that poets who compose fictions incur no more disgrace than philosophers who use syllogisms. Moreover, the word "fable" (*fabula*) has its origin in the Latin verb *for, fari*, and means "conversation" (*confabulatio*). He cites a definition framed by previous writers: "fiction is a form of discourse, which, under guise of invention, illustrates or proves an idea; and, as its superficial aspect is removed, the meaning of the author is clear" (XIV.ix). Hence fiction is always a way of presenting hidden truths. In fact, Boccaccio distinguishes four types of fiction: the first, such as Aesop's fables, on the surface lacks all appearance of truth; the second, appearing to mingle truth with fiction, has been used "to clothe in fiction divine and human matters alike"; the third appears more to be history than fiction but, as in Vergil's *Aeneid*, the hidden meaning is far different from the surface meaning (XIV.ix). The fourth kind of fiction contains no truth at all, either superficial or hidden, and Boccaccio dissociates this kind completely from poetry. Those who object to the first three forms of fiction, he says, might as well object to the scriptures since they are replete with figures and parables. In general, the positive capacity of fiction is such that "it pleases the unlearned by its external appearance, and exercises the minds of the learned with its hidden truth; and thus both are edified and delighted with one and the same perusal" (XIV.ix). Hence, fiction – by which Boccaccio means poetic invention – is imbued with the classical functions of teaching and delighting by presenting truth. It is also imbued with a theological function, that of cloaking divine mysteries. Indeed, opposing those who aver that truth and eloquence cannot go together, Boccaccio cites Quintilian's view that great "eloquence is inconsistent with falsehood," and affirms that Vergil was a philosopher, while "Dante was a great theologian as well as philosopher." It is because poetry is "brought up in the very home of philosophy, and disciplined in sacred studies" that it expresses "the very deepest meaning" (XIV.x). In book XV, Boccaccio seeks to show that while the use of poetry is not immediately apparent, it possesses a deeper usefulness of enduring value, partly on account of its ornamental qualities and partly because of the wisdom through which it brings "profit and pleasure" to the reader (XV.i).

As for the charge of obscurity, Boccaccio admits that much poetry is obscure; but in this it is no different from philosophy; the texts of Plato and Aristotle "abound in difficulties." Moreover, the sacred scriptures are "overflowing with obscurities and ambiguities." Boccaccio's defense of obscurity is partly theological: just as holy scripture is obscure so as to avoid casting pearls before swine and protect the sacred mysteries, so it is the office of the poet to protect such solemn matters "from the gaze of the irreverent." And, as Augustine said of sacred scripture, obscurity both obliges serious intellectual effort and generates a rich variety of interpretations (XIV.xii). The other part of Boccaccio's commendation of obscurity has more to do with the craft of poetry: "You must read, you must persevere, you must sit up nights, you must inquire, and exert the utmost power of your mind" (XIV.xii). Finally, Boccaccio acknowledges that the charge of obscurity rests on the ancient rhetorical precept that "a speech must be simple and clear." But, citing Petrarch to support his claim, Boccaccio insists that "oratory is quite different, in arrangement of words, from fiction, and that fiction has been consigned to the discretion of the inventor as being the legitimate work of another art than oratory" (XIV.xii). Hence, while Boccaccio sees poetry as concurrent in some of its aims with philosophy and theology, he is nonetheless concerned to mark out its domain as an autonomous province, finally extricated from rhetoric.

Boccaccio answers the charge that poets are liars by retorting that poetic fiction has nothing in common with falsehood. For, a poet's purpose is not to deceive; and poetic fiction differs from a lie in that it usually bears no resemblance at all to "the literal truth," the one exception being historical fiction. It is the very function of the poets to express hidden truths; they are not constrained "to employ literal truth on the surface of their inventions" (XIV.xiii). Hence if they must "sacrifice the literal truth in invention," they cannot be charged with lying (XIV.xiii). Again, Boccaccio points to the figurative language of the Bible where many passages, though at first glance they appear contrary to truth, possess a "majesty of inner sense" (XIV.xiii). In this chapter and in his text as a whole, Boccaccio diverges from notions of allegory which insist on the truth of the literal meaning; he in fact espouses a notion of poetry as intrinsically sacrificing literal truth in order to express more profound levels of meaning.

Having asserted, contrary to its critics, that the best poetry induces men to virtuous thoughts and deeds (XIV.xv), Boccaccio denies the charge that poets are merely "apes of the philosophers." He draws some interesting distinctions between philosophy and poetry. In a broad sense, poets are to be considered philosophers, since "they never veil with their inventions anything which is not wholly consonant with philosophy as judged by the opinions of the Ancients" (XIV.xvii). Yet, though the "destination" of poets is the same as that of the philosophers, the philosopher proceeds by syllogizing, and employs an "unadorned prose style, with something of scorn for literary embellishment." The poet, on the other hand, contemplates without the use of syllogism, and veils his thought "under the outward semblance of his invention," writing in meter with a scrupulous attention to style (XIV.xvii). Once again, we find the perennial distinction between philosophy and poetry articulated in terms of style rather than content: philosophy is credited with using a literal language whereas poetry always hides its truths, speaking through figure and metaphor. If the poet imitates anything, says Boccaccio, it is nature in "her eternal and unalterable operation" (XIV.xvii).

A large part of Boccaccio's endeavor is to show that poetry is not somehow contrary to the principles of Christianity. Critics, having charged poetry with blasphemy, obscenity, and falsehood, claim that it is a sin to read poetry. Boccaccio states that the theological errors and polytheism of the classical pagan poets are excusable since knowledge of the true God was not given to them. Moreover, the gospels and the Christian Church did not forbid the reading of poetry. While Boccaccio acknowledges that some poets, such as Ovid and Catullus, and various comic writers depicted licentious material, he cites the authority of St. Paul, his disciple Dionysius the Areopagite, Augustine, and Jerome himself (often cited as opposing poetry) to uphold his claim that poetry is an integral part of the gospels and the theological tradition (XIV.xviii). Moreover, if critics charge poetry with paganism, why, asks Boccaccio, do these same critics praise the pagan philosophies of Plato and Aristotle? Poetry, he remarks, has in this respect sinned no more than philosophy: "For while Philosophy is without question the keenest investigator of truth, Poetry is, obviously, its most faithful guardian, protecting it as she does beneath the veil of her art . . . She is Philosophy's maidservant" (XIV.xvii). It emerges clearly here that, for all his defense of poetry, Boccaccio situates this art in a hierarchy wherein it is subservient to both philosophy and theology. He acknowledges that "it would be far better to study the sacred books" than even the best works of poetry (XIV.xvii).

Boccaccio now treats in a sustained manner a theme that has recurred through his text: the relation of pagan writers to their Christian successors. He calls the pagan poets theologians, since they dealt with "mythical" theology (a term he derives from Augustine). The works of such poets contained many moral and physical truths, and despite their system of theology they often exhibited what was "right and honorable" (XV.viii). Hence, it is not improper or impious for Christians to study the pagan authors of antiquity. Boccaccio launches into a detailed affirmation of his faith and his belief in Christian doctrine, a faith which makes him immune to any adverse influence (XV.ix). He says that he was called, since childhood, to the profession of poetry "by God's will" (XV.x). And his defense of poetry, he remarks, was "a most urgent duty" (XV.xiv).

Feminism: Christine de Pisan (ca. 1365–1429)

Christine de Pisan was perhaps the most articulate and prolific female voice of the European Middle Ages. Being widowed at the age of 25 without an inheritance and with three children, she was obliged to earn her living as a writer. She was commissioned as biographer of Charles V. Her patrons included King Charles VI of France, King Charles of Navarre, and two dukes of Burgundy. Her publications, which were translated into English, Italian, and other languages, included *Epistle of the God of Love* (1399), where she impugned the misogynistic portrayals of women and the dearth of morality in the popular French work *Roman de la Rose*, an allegorical love poem written by Guillaume de Lorris and expanded by Jean de Meung. The controversial quarrel surrounding these texts was known as the *Querelle de la Rose*, with Christine and Jean Gerson, chancellor of the University of Paris, allied against the esteemed humanist royal secretaries Jean de Montreuil and Pierre Col. In a further work, *Christine's Vision* (1405), she complained against her fortune as a female writer and scholar burdened by the conventional obligations of womanhood. Another work produced in the same year, *Livre des Trois Vertus* (*Book of Three Virtues*), concerns the status and role of women in society. Her most renowned work was *The Book of the City of Ladies* (1405), which was influenced by Boccaccio's *Concerning Famous Women* (1361), as well as by the linguistic and allegorical theories of Quintilian, Augustine (to whose book *City of God* Christine's title alludes), Hugh of St. Victor, and Dante. Almost uniquely among women of her time, Christine was enabled to obtain a fine education through her family's connections to the royal court; her father, Tommaso di Benvenuto da Pizzano, was appointed court astrologer by Charles V, and her reading may well have included Ovid, Boethius, and John of Salisbury, as well as the figures mentioned above.[2] Christine also published a poem on Joan of Arc, *Ditie de la pucelle* (1429).

The Book of the City of Ladies attempts effectively to rewrite the history of women, its scope extending through past and future, as well as over pagan and Christian eras. Such rewriting entails an explosion of age-long male myths about women, such as their inability to govern, their unfitness for learning, and their moral deficiencies. It also entails both adapting and refashioning Boccaccio's text *Concerning Famous Women*, which had restricted its scope to pagan women, omitting treatment of both the renowned female figures of sacred history and contemporary women. Moreover, Boccaccio's "praise" of women had been deeply ironic, portraying them as mentally tardy and including numerous examples of unrighteous women. Christine's scope is far more comprehensive, including women from the Judeo-Christian tradition as well as illustrious women from her own time. Above all, all of her examples subserve her general argument which refutes the slanderous charges brought by men against women. As Earl Jeffrey Richards points out, the historical perspective of Christine's text is further deepened by its continuation in the vernacular, following Dante, of the poetic achievement of Vergil (*BCL*, xlii–xliv). Richards states that one of the purposes of Christine's text is to exhibit women's affinity for learning; and an effective means of doing this was to display her own erudition, in a "learned and cultivated prose," using Latinate syntax, such that her "defence and illustration" of the vernacular was also a "defence and illustration" of femininity (*BCL*, xxvii, xli).

Indeed, the nature of Christine's feminism has been a disputed issue, with some scholars pointing to her conservatism, her espousal of the medieval class structure, her appeals to tradition and above all to Christianity. Again, Richards provides a clear insight here, explaining that Christine's invocation of Christianity sees it as "a means of overcoming oppression," and that her defense of Christian marriage "was a call for the highest form of moral commitment between a man and a woman and not an endorsement of institutionalized domination." Not only this, but Christine hardly longed for a return to some idealized past; rather, she was calling for a "*realization* of the ideals transmitted by the tradition which she had inherited." Hence, her portrayal of women's suffering throughout history was "an appeal for change" (*BCL*, xxix–xxx).

The Book of the City of Ladies is written as a conversation between Christine and three allegorical virtues, Reason, Rectitude, and Justice. Just as Virginia Woolf, some six hundred years later, began *A Room of One's Own* by reflecting on the enormous number of books written about women by men, so Christine opens her text by wondering why so many treatises by men contain "so many wicked insults about women and their behavior" (*BCL*, I.1.1). All the philosophers and poets appear, she notes, to "concur in one conclusion: that the behavior of women is inclined to and full of every vice" (*BCL*, I.1.1). What puzzles Christine is the disparity between these male theories about women and her own practical experience of women of all social ranks, "princesses, great ladies, women of the middle and lower classes" (I.1.1). Initially, says Christine, she did not trust her own intellect and felt inclined to rely "more on the judgment of others than on what I myself felt and knew" (I.1.1). She describes herself as detesting both herself and "the entire feminine sex," and as wondering how God, who "could not go wrong in anything," could have made a creature so "abominable" (I.1.1–I.1.2). Christine's strategy here is both ingenious and disingenuous: she places herself initially in the customarily inferior position of woman, lacking confidence, distrustful of even her first-hand experience, and allowing herself to be intimidated by the traditions of male authority. Yet, as the book proceeds, the tentative testimony of her own experience is broadened to include the experience of women from a wide range of historical periods, until its comprehensiveness can be ranged theoretically against the male presumptions that were initially so overbearing.

As Christine ponders, debilitated, by these thoughts, there appears to her a vision of "three crowned ladies" (I.2.1). The first of these both consoles her and gently chides her for shunning the evidence of her senses and relying on the testimony of "many strange opinions." She points out to Christine that the "greatest philosophers" who hold these negative opinions about women "contradict and criticize one another." Hence, the claims of the philosophers are fallible and cannot be taken as "articles of faith" (I.2.2). As for the poets, the lady points out that they often speak in a fictional and ironic manner, often meaning the contrary of what their literal language appears to assert. The various attacks by men against the institution of marriage – which is a "holy state . . . ordained by God" – are refuted by experience: no husband can actually be found who will allow his wife to abuse and insult him as these male detractors claim (I.2.1).

The lady explains that she and her two companions are "celestial beings," whose function is to circulate among the world's people so as "to bring order and maintain in balance those institutions we created according to the will of God" (I.3.1–2). The first lady herself carries a mirror: whoever looks into this will achieve self-knowledge, as well as a knowledge of "the essences, qualities, proportions, and measures of all things" (I.3.2). The three ladies, however, are also embarked on a further mission: to provide a refuge for "ladies and all valiant women" against the numerous assailants of the female sex. In this mission, she tells Christine that she must, with the help of the three ladies, build a city, "which has been predestined," and where only ladies of fame and virtue will reside (I.3.3). The three ladies do not appear to everyone: Christine was chosen for her "great love of investigating the truth" (I.3.2). And the first lady, identifying herself as "Lady Reason," charges Christine with the foundation and building of this "City of Ladies," which will be both extremely beautiful and of "perpetual duration" in the world, notwithstanding the assaults of "jealous enemies" (I.4.1–3).

The second lady introduces herself as Rectitude: she is the messenger of God's goodness, exhorting and defending righteousness and resisting the power of evil-doers. She carries a straight ruler "which separates right from wrong and shows the difference between good and evil." Since all things are measured by this ruler, Christine must use it to measure the edifice of the City of Ladies (I.5.1). The third lady identifies herself as Justice: her duty is to judge fairly, to "dispense according to each man's just deserts." She teaches men and women of sound mind to correct themselves, "to speak the truth" and "to reject all viciousness." She carries in her hand a vessel of gold which serves "to measure out to each his rightful portion." She also explains that the other virtues are based on her, and that each of the three ladies could not exist without the others. Justice will construct the high roofs and towers of the city, and populate it with "worthy ladies and the mighty Queen," after which she will turn over the keys of the city to Christine (I.6.1).

Christine is given instructions to build the city on the "Field of Letters," which is a "flat and fertile plain." She must excavate the earth and lay the foundations there (I.8.1–2). In response to Christine's inquiry as to the motives behind men's attacks on women, Lady Reason explains that such behavior is "contrary to Nature, for no connection in the world is as great or as strong as the great love which, through the will of God, Nature places between a man and a woman" (I.8.3). As for the motives of men, she states that some men have been inspired by good intentions, to draw men away from the company of "vicious and dissolute women." Lady Reason states that such attacks, when indiscriminately extended to all women, are based on ignorance rather than Reason (I.8.3). Other motives have included men's own defects and vices, as well as jealousy of women's greater understanding and nobility of conduct; still others have merely imitated, in poetry or prose, received opinions whose repetition might bring them repute (I.8.5–10). These attacks are metaphorically viewed as part of the rubbish which Christine must clear away in order to lay the city's foundations. Indeed, the city itself will be a city of words, as Lady Reason's subsequent exhortations – "Take the trowel of your pen and ready yourself to lay down bricks" – make clear (I.14.4).

Christine now asks Lady Reason how the eminence of various eminent poets and thinkers, such as Ovid, Cecco d'Ascoli, Cicero, and Cato, is to be reconciled with their severe attacks on women. Lady Reason responds by discussing the complex theological issues of the creation of woman and original sin. That woman was created from a rib of Adam, she says, signified that "she should stand at his side as a companion and never lie at his feet like a slave, and also that he should love her as his own flesh." Moreover, if God, the "Supreme Craftsman," was not ashamed of creating woman, why should Nature be ashamed? Indeed, woman "was created in the image of God." Lady Reason corrects those who refer this statement to the material body: this was not the case because "God had not yet taken a human body." The statement is meant to refer to the soul: "God created the soul and placed wholly similar souls, equally good and noble in the feminine and in the masculine bodies" (I.9.2). Contradicting Cicero's statement that woman is lower than man, she states that loftiness or lowliness resides not in the gendered body but in "the perfection of conduct and virtues" (I.9.3). As for Cato's statement that men would be able to converse with the gods if there were no women, she retorts that more was gained through the Virgin Mary than was lost through Eve: "humanity was conjoined to the Godhead, which would never have taken place if Eve's misdeed had not occurred . . . as low as human nature fell through this creature woman, was human nature lifted higher by this same creature." Lady Reason observes, regarding Cato: "You can now see the foolishness of the man who is considered wise" (I.8.3).

It may be worth remarking at this point on some of the strategies used by Christine in defense of women. On the surface, she appears to be invoking, in conventional medieval fashion, a theological sanction for her position, resting ultimately on the absolute authority of God. Yet the three virtues she cites as divinely descended – Reason, Rectitude, and Justice – could equally be seen as idealized projections of human – and humanistic – virtues. And the first of these, Reason, could be correlated with independent thinking rather than basing one's beliefs on the authority of others. Indeed, their initial purpose was to furnish Christine with the confidence to rely on her own experience rather than on the testimony of male writers. Ironically, then, what the divine authorizes here is the validity of female experience. Moreover, the personification of "Reason" as a woman also extricates the faculty of reason from its history of male appropriation and abuse. So Christine's appeal to Christianity might be viewed as broadly humanistic. A further strategy is to destabilize male interpretations of scripture and to show that male reputations, such as those of Cicero and Cato, are often based on misconceptions. In this manner, Christine's rewriting of history is conducted on several concurrent levels: theological exegesis, the literary tradition as defined by males, and the psychological constitution of human beings.

Lady Reason contradicts those men who say that women have no natural sense for politics and government, by citing several examples of "great women rulers" of the past, as well as of contemporary women who managed their affairs well after the deaths of their husbands (I.11–13). She also relates narratives of women who possessed a physical strength and courage matching those of men, such as Queen Semiramis (I.15), the Amazons and Queen Thamiris (I.16–17), Queen Penthesilea, and many others (I.19–26). Concerning the intellectual capacity of women, Lady Reason states that if women were not kept at home and had access to learning, they would do even better than men since, just as they have weaker bodies, so "they have minds that are freer and sharper whenever they apply themselves" (I.27.1). And "there is nothing which so instructs a reasonable creature as the exercise and experience of many different things" (I.27.1). Again, what is remarkable about this passage is that, despite its ostensibly theological framework, it anticipates the major strands of Enlightenment thought, combining a proposed rationalism with actual experience of the variety of the world.

Though Christine's reaction against male traditions of theology and literature might be viewed as effected by an appeal to collective personal experience of women to shatter the claims of abstract reason and authority, her appeal to experience is sanctioned by broadening the compass of reason beyond its theological confines. Lady Reason assures Christine that, as before, she will offer "proof through examples," examples which range from Cornificia, the Roman lady Proba, the Greek poetess Sappho to Queen Circe (I.28–32). She also cites women who furthered the path of knowledge by discovering new arts and sciences: Carmentis invented laws for the region where Rome was subsequently founded; she "established the Latin alphabet and syntax, spelling, . . . as well as a complete introduction to the science of grammar." For her contributions she was honored and even considered a goddess (I.33.2). Other examples given include Minerva, Ceres, and Isis, who respectively invented the arts of making armor, cultivating the earth, and planting. Citing the authority of Boccaccio for her observations, Lady Reason infers from such examples that "God . . . wished to show men that He does not despise the feminine sex" (I.37.1). Christine herself concludes that the contribution of these women was greater even than that of Aristotle, and she admonishes: "Henceforth, let all writers be silent who speak badly of women . . . in their books and poems, and all their accomplices and supporters too – let them lower their eyes, ashamed for having dared to speak so badly, in view of the truth which runs counter to their poems" (I.38.4). As for the knights and nobles, who are indebted to Minerva, her message is unambiguous: "From now on let them keep their mouths shut" (I.38.5). Significantly, Christine's stance has developed from an initial tentativeness to categorical assertion.

Having established that women can possess strength, understanding, and inventiveness, Lady Reason proceeds to argue that women are capable of prudence, which she equates with practical and moral intelligence, learning from the past, reflecting on the future, and wise management of present affairs (I.43.1). She points out that prudence can be both a natural gift or acquired. It is the latter, acquired learning, which is the more valuable because it endures. Again, Lady Reason provides several examples of prudent women, including Queen Gaia Cirilla, Queen Dido, Queen Ops of Crete, and Lavinia, daughter of King Latinus, who married Aeneas (I.44–48).

In the second book Christine describes how the city inside the walls was constructed and by whom it was peopled. Rectitude tells her that foremost among the ladies of dignity are the ten sibyls, upon whom God bestowed "greater honor in revelation" than upon any other prophet (II.1.3). Rectitude speaks in detail of some of the sibyls and also points out that there were many female prophets in the Jewish religion, such as Deborah, Elizabeth, who was cousin of the Virgin Mary, and Anna, who recognized Christ in the temple (II.4.1).

Eventually, Rectitude announces that she has finished building the houses and palaces of the city, and that it is time to people the city: "Now a New Kingdom of Femininity is begun" (II.12.1). She explains that after it has been populated with noble citizens – women of "integrity, of great beauty and authority" – Lady Justice will lead in the queen and high princesses to reside in the loftiest apartments (II.12.2). Christine broaches the topic of marriage; she cites authorities such as Valerius and Theophrastus who claim that the institution of marriage is unhappy and intolerable on account of women's faults of rancor, impetuousness, and indifference. Rectitude replies that it is women who have been abused, beaten, and subjected to cruelty. Importantly, however, she states that not all marriages are full of spite and ill-feeling; some husbands are "very good" and some couples live together in "great peacefulness, love and loyalty" (II.13.1).

Christine raises a variety of other charges brought against women by men, all of which are refuted by Rectitude's appeal to experience and numerous examples. These include women's inability to keep secrets (II.25.1–27.1), and the paucity of women's advice (II.28.1–29.3). Rectitude gives examples of women who saved their people, or made peace among hostile factions, or converted their kin to Christianity (II.31.1–35.3), as well as examples of women who were both beautiful and chaste (II.37.1–43.3). Numerous other allegations are confronted: women's inconstancy (II.47.1–52.2), infidelity (II.54.1), coquettishness (II.62.1–63.11), and greed (II.66.1–67.2). Interestingly, Rectitude defines inconstancy as "nothing but acting against the commands of Reason, for it exhorts every reasonable creature to act well. When a man or woman allows regard for Reason to be conquered by sensuality, this is frailty or inconstancy, and the deeper one falls into error or sin, the greater the weakness is, the more one is removed from regard for reason" (II.49.5). By this standard, says Rectitude, not only does history show men to have been more inconstant than women but also the Church itself has long declined from the standards of Reason (II.49.4–5). Also significant here is the absolute equation Christine makes between reason and righteousness; her formulation is secular insofar as it exalts reason far beyond the function assigned to it in the theologies of Aquinas and other major formulators of orthodox Christian doctrine. Here Christine appears to extricate reason not only from its male history but also from the theological contexts by which it was constrained. Her strategy differs sharply from those twentieth-century feminists who reject reason altogether as too deeply tainted, and as perhaps constituted, by male values.

Concerning many men's belief that education is harmful to a woman's mores, Rectitude states that "not all opinions of men are based on reason" (II.36.1). She cites the most famous example of an accomplished woman in Christine's text: Novella, the daughter of a law professor Giovanni Andrea, was so well educated in law that sometimes he "would send Novella . . . in his place to lecture to the students from his chair.

And to prevent her beauty from distracting the concentration of her audience, she had a little curtain drawn in front of her" (II.36.3). Few images could match this portrayal of female power! Rectitude also refers to Christine's own father who took pleasure from seeing his daughter learn (II.36.4). Indeed, Rectitude affirms that, in God's plan, "everything comes to a head at the right time," and that the task of defending women has been reserved for Christine.

At the end of book II, Rectitude announces that her task – of erecting beautiful palaces and populating the city with noble ladies – is complete. In turn, Christine remarks that she must now turn to Lady Justice to execute the remaining work in the city (II.68.11–69.1). In the third book, Lady Justice explains to Christine that the queen must be brought into the city so that she may govern it. She must be received with honor by all the inhabitants of the city for she is "not only their Queen but also has ministry and dominion over all created powers after the only Son whom she conceived of the Holy Spirit and carried and who is the Son of God the Father" (III.1.1). After all the women beseech her presence, the "Queen of Heaven" enters and announces: "I am and will always be the head of the feminine sex. This arrangement was present in the mind of God the Father from the start, revealed and ordained previously in the council of the Trinity" (III.1.3). Other ladies, including Mary Magdalene, and a host of saints and virgins are then invited to reside with the queen.

Christine ends the book in a manner that must disappoint modern feminists. While she reminds the city's inhabitants that the city is a refuge against their enemies and assailants, she advises the women not to "scorn being subject to your husbands" (III.19.1–2). If their husbands are good or moderate, they should praise God; if their husbands are "cruel, mean, and savage," they should display forbearance and attempt to lead them back to a life of reason and virtue (III.19.2). Addressing all classes of women, she admonishes: "all women – whether noble, bourgeois, or lower-class – be well-informed in all things and cautious in defending your honor" (III.19.6). Modern feminists might also raise the possibility that the city embodies a form of ghettoization, whereby women are protected from the evils of male institutions at the cost of foregoing any active and transformative participation. The reverse side of this situation is that the conversation between Christine and the three ladies invites participation by females only and that men are excluded, able only to overhear the proceedings in projected silence. In this manner, women are allowed the space they need, the room, to extricate themselves from the male writing of their history and to rearticulate that history without interference.

Notes

1   Charles G. Osgood, "Introduction," in *Boccaccio on Poetry: Being the Preface and the Fourteenth and Fifteenth Books of Boccaccio's Genealogia Deorum Gentilium* (Indianapolis and New York: Bobbs-Merrill, 1956), p. xxx. Hereafter cited as *GDG*.
2   "Introduction," in Christine de Pisan, *The Book of the City of Ladies*, trans. Earl Jeffrey Richards (New York: Persea, 1982), pp. xix, xxvii. Many of the details of this account of Christine's life, as well as of the significance of her work, are taken from Richards' excellent introduction to his translation. Hereafter cited as *BCL*.

PART V

THE EARLY MODERN PERIOD TO THE ENLIGHTENMENT

CHAPTER 11

THE EARLY MODERN PERIOD

Historical Background

The period beginning around the fourteenth century and extending midway into the seventeenth has conventionally been designated as the Renaissance, referring to a "rebirth" or rediscovery of the values, ethics, and styles of classical Greece and Rome. The term was devised by Italian humanists who sought to mark their own period as reaffirming its continuity with the classical humanist heritage after an interlude of over a thousand years, a period of alleged superstition and stagnation known as the Dark Ages and Middle Ages. In this view, the Renaissance overturned the medieval theological worldview, replacing it with a more secular and humanist vision, promoting a newly awakened interest in the temporal world both in economic and in scientific terms, and according a new importance to the individual – all inspired by a rediscovery of the classics. This view has been somewhat shaken, with even the term "Renaissance" itself becoming suspect and often replaced by the broader and more neutral term "early modern," which tends to distance itself from the self-images of Renaissance writers.

Historians and scholars in several fields now tend to recognize that many developments in the Renaissance were in fact continuations or modifications of medieval dispositions. For example, much medieval thinking was characterized by a reverence for – and indeed, a knowledge of – the classics; and certain periods, such as the ninth-century Carolingian renaissance and the renaissance of the twelfth century, were marked by humanistic tendencies. In fact, as was seen in chapter 9, the very distinction between scholastic and humanistic modes of thought has been challenged, and scholastic thought continued to exert an influence well beyond the medieval period. Moreover, the early modern period's undoubtedly dazzling achievements in literature, art, science, and religion were often unrelated, or only remotely related, to the classical past. Nonetheless, as scholars such as David Norbrook have argued, there may be a case for retaining the label "Renaissance." The early modern usage of the word, Norbrook points out, was largely restricted to the spheres of literature and painting. It was in the nineteenth century that historians saw culture as "a unified system in which economic, social and political factors all had their influence on the arts." While such unity was artificial and retrospectively imposed, the idea of the Renaissance may "offer a way of understanding how modernity changed the world." Images of the Renaissance have of course been forged in conflict with one another: Jacob Burckhardt's "highly courtly notion" of the Renaissance, as expressed in his *The Civilization of the Renaissance in Italy* (1860), has been challenged by the more populist notions of scholars such as F. J. Furnivall (1825–1910). And New Critical notions of Renaissance poetry which stress its isolatable formal qualities have been contested by New Historicists, notably Stephen Greenblatt, who have insisted on locating poetry within contexts of social power, and explaining the formation of literary canons with reference to the interests of a social elite.[1]

Indeed, if the early modern period was not a renaissance as such, it certainly bore certain distinctive traits marking it as an era of profound transformation and even revolution. The most dominant trait of this new period has conventionally been identified as "humanism," a term ultimately deriving from Cicero and used by Italian thinkers and writers to distinguish themselves from the medieval scholastics. The term "humanism" has been very broadly used and cuts across boundaries of political affiliation and class. In general, it implies a world view and a set of values centered around the human rather than the divine, using a self-subsistent definition of human nature (rather than referring this to God), and focusing on human achievements and potential rather than on theological doctrines and dilemmas; the term also retained its Ciceronian connection with the liberal arts (one of the original definitions of a humanist was a teacher of the humanities) and in general with secular and independent inquiry in all fields, as opposed to viewing these areas of study as hierarchically bound within a theological framework.

In this broad sense, humanism was indeed characteristic of much Renaissance thought. However, humanism itself was only one manifestation of a more profound shift in sensibility which encompassed other areas. This shift might be aptly characterized as moving from a broadly "other-worldly" disposition – viewing this earthly life as a merely transitory phase, as a preparation for the life hereafter – to a "this-worldly" attitude, which saw actions and events in this world as significant in their own right without referring them to any ultimate divine meaning and purpose. This shift from "other-worldliness" to "this-worldliness" both underlies and reflects the major transformations of the early modern period. The most fundamental of these changes were economic and political: the fundamental institutions of the later Middle Ages – the feudal system, the universal authority of the pope, the Holy Roman Empire, and the system of trade regulated by medieval guilds – were all undermined. As a result of large-scale investment of capital, booming manufacture, and expanding trade and commerce, the focus of economic life increasingly shifted away from the manorial estates of the feudal nobility to the newly emerging cities such as Florence, Milan, Venice, and Rome, whose affluence enabled their prominence as centers of cultural efflorescence. This "renaissance" extended to several other European cities such as Paris, London, Antwerp, and Augsburg, which also contributed to humanist culture. Many factors contributed to the decline of feudalism: the rise of monarchies and centralized governments, and the ability of serfs and villeins (helped by the absence of their warrior overlords during the Crusades) to free themselves from the land and to find work in the expanding cities, which were increasingly emancipated from the control of feudal lords. All of these developments went hand in hand with the weakening of the feudal nobility and the rise of an increasingly powerful and rich middle class. The decline of the Holy Roman Empire and the power and prestige of the papacy resulted in the increasing independence of states in Italy and elsewhere. Indeed, our modern conception of the state – fundamental to the social, religious, and literary currents of the Renaissance – derives from this period: the rulers of the most powerful Italian states such as Florence, Milan, and Venice rejected any religious conception of the state and stressed its independent and secular nature, promoting a new "civic consciousness" as to the responsibility of the citizen, patriotism, and the pursuit of the economic and political interests of the state as an end in itself. Like so many other innovative notions in the Renaissance, this political modernity was born of a return to classical political ideals of civic humanism and devotion to the common welfare.

It was these broad economic and political transformations that enabled the development of other features of the early modern period such as a more this-worldly orientation, the growth of humanism, the development of a secular political philosophy, and the beginnings of a systematic examination of the world of nature as well as of the human body and mind. Other characteristics include the increasing importance of vernacular languages (and literatures) as opposed to, and alongside, Latin, and a more pronounced focus on style and aesthetics, as opposed to theology or logic. Indeed, most of the literary and artistic accomplishments of this period were achieved by laymen rather than clergy, and the patrons of art, such as the Medici rulers of Florence, were increasingly secular rather than ecclesiastical.

Elsewhere, in northern and western Europe, feudalism underwent a similar decline, giving way before the centralized authority of monarchs and absolute rulers who, with the help of the upwardly moving middle classes, eroded the power of the nobles and of the feudal guilds. The Tudor dynasty was established in England by Henry VII in 1485. The Hundred Years' War between France and England (1337–1453) enabled the French monarchs to establish their rule; Louis XI's kingdom extended over nearly all of France; and Spain was united in 1469 by the marriage of Ferdinand of Aragon and Isabella of Castile. All of these states experienced a rapid upsurge of national consciousness; only Italy, still torn by factional strife, and Germany, still part of the Holy Roman Empire, did not become national states during this period. The empire itself, however, was virtually a relic by this time, with real power in the hands not of the emperor but of the princes of the various states.

These struggles were decisive both in fostering the growth of humanism and in shaping the literature and criticism of the period. With the consolidation of a centralized monarchy, the composition of the aristocracy changed from the landed nobility as a warrior class to a newly rising and expanding court aristocracy. Status and social advancement were no longer determined solely by military power and service or by inheritance of birth and rank; increasingly important were the humanist values of rhetorical skill, literary accomplishment, and various kinds of administrative and ideological service to the court. The circle of court patronage was expanded and the fortunes of major literary figures were indissolubly tied to court politics. The rise of vernacular languages was molded by poetic, rhetorical, and ideological theories which stood in reciprocal relation to the growth of national consciousness. Nearly all of the poets of this era were actively involved in the political process, and formed an important constituent of the "public sphere," the arena of public debate and discourse which began to emerge during the later Renaissance. English poets, for example, wrote vehemently in favor of both royalist and parliamentary sides during the English Civil War; John Milton (1608–1674) was the leading literary advocate of the Puritan revolution, and his epic *Paradise Lost* celebrated the Protestant notion of the individual's moral responsibility, while his *Areopagitica* (1644) was a passionate defense of free speech and a critique of dogmatic traditionalism in the interests of civic humanism.

Intellectual Background

Humanism and the Classics

While classical writers had been influential through much of the Middle Ages, the revival of the classics in the early modern period took an entirely different character and scope. To begin with, in the Middle Ages scholarship was undertaken largely by the clergy, usually monks, and later by scholars in the cathedral schools. One of the major persisting endeavors throughout the Middle Ages was to reconcile classical philosophy and literature with the teachings of Christian scripture. The early modern period witnessed the growth of a new secular class of educated people and a more secular employment of the classics in fields such as rhetoric and law. The most distinguished humanists and classicists of this period fostered the revival of classical literary forms in poetry and rhetoric. These figures included Albertino Mussato, who is credited with writing the first tragedy of this period, and, even more important, Francesco Petrarca (1304–1374), who outlined a curriculum of classical studies, focusing on the study of classical languages and the traditional grammatical requirement of imitating the classical authors. Eloquence, based on a study of classical models, was important for Petrarch, since it inspired people to virtue. Petrarch's program, based on a combination of moral philosophy and rhetoric, inspired others such as Leonardo Bruni to formulate curricula for the study of the humanities, deriving in part from the liberal arts curriculum recommended by Cicero and Quintilian.

These new curricula overlapped to some extent with the medieval trivium (rhetoric, grammar, logic) and quadrivium (music, astronomy, algebra, geometry) but laid a renewed emphasis on rhetoric, poetry, history, and moral philosophy. Another major difference between medieval and humanist attitudes to the classics was that the latter insisted upon a thorough knowledge of the classical languages, not only Latin but also Greek, which began to be studied at the end of the fourteenth century. In the Middle Ages the classics had been studied largely through Latin translations. Moreover, the humanists attempted to return to the pure Latin of the ancient authors as opposed to the medieval Latin of the Church. The humanists also insisted on the direct study of ancient texts, unencumbered by the constraining framework of medieval glosses and commentaries. Another difference was that in the early modern period the classical texts were far more widely disseminated, partly for the pedagogical reasons just outlined and partly because of the development of printing. Finally, the monopoly of

Latin as the language of learned discourse and literature was undermined, and in the works of Dante, Petrarch, Boccaccio, and many humanists the rules of grammar and composition were adapted to theorize about vernacular tongues. Hence the humanists created a set of techniques and a framework of interpretation for both classical and vernacular texts. In general, the humanists supplanted the scholastic aversion to poetry and rhetoric with an emphasis upon the moral value of these disciplines and upon worldly achievement in general. David Norbrook has stated that humanism originated in a defense of rhetoric against scholastic philosophy, effectively reviving the "ancient quarrel" between philosophy and rhetoric (*PBRV*, 8, 53). In this process the humanists reaffirmed both the classical emphasis on style and the logical or rational and rhetorical or persuasive components of literature, thereby combining the disciplines of rhetoric, logic, and poetics which the Middle Ages had kept somewhat separate.

These poets not only theorized about the vernacular but also wrote in it and cultivated its elegant expression. Petrarch's friend Giovanni Boccaccio adapted classical forms to the vernacular, developing literary forms such as the pastoral, idyll, and romance. Through his best-known works such as the *Decameron*, Boccaccio provided models of Italian prose which influenced both Italian writers such as Tasso and writers in other countries such as Chaucer. The cultivation of prose – in narratives, epistles, and dialogues – was an important achievement of the humanists. A renowned example is Baldassare Castiglione's treatise entitled *The Courtier*, a discussion of attitudes toward love, and of the courtly behavior and education appropriate for a gentleman. This text is often seen as an embodiment of Renaissance ideals and had a far-reaching influence throughout Europe. Later Italian writers developed other literary forms: the epic reached its height in the *Orlando Furioso* of Ludovico Ariosto (1474–1533), which departs from the idealistic and moralistic nature of medieval epics. Historiography and political writing also achieved a new level of realism: Machiavelli wrote a history of Florence that was free of theological explanations and based upon "natural" laws. Machiavelli's political writings entirely undermined medieval notions of government: in his treatise *The Prince* (1513), he treated politics as an autonomous domain, free of the incursions of morality or religious doctrine. He saw the state as an independent entity, whose prime goal was the promotion of civic rather than religious virtue, and self-preservation at any cost. An even more important figure in historiography was Francesco Guicciardini (1483–1540), whose *History of Italy* is characterized by realistic, detailed analysis of character, motive, and events. Lorenzo Valla (1406–1457) applied critical methods of scholarship and analysis to biblical texts, and he challenged the authenticity of certain authoritative documents, opening the way for later attacks upon Christian doctrine.

Humanism flourished also in other parts of Europe. The Dutch thinker Desiderius Erasmus (1466–1536) was the most renowned humanist of his time and his works were widely read. His strong humanistic convictions in reason, naturalism, tolerance, and the inherent goodness of man led him to oppose dogmatic theology and scholasticism, and to propound instead a rational religion of simple piety based on the example of Christ. His *Colloquia* (1519), criticizing the abuses of the Catholic Church, has often been viewed as paving the way for the Lutheran Reformation; but Erasmus himself was also opposed to the dogmatism and violence of some of the Lutherans. His most famous work, *Encomium moriae* (*The Praise of Folly*, 1509), satirized theological dogmatism and the gullibility of the masses. France also produced notable figures such as François Rabelais (ca. 1494–1553), whose *Gargantua and Pantagruel* expounded a naturalistic and secular philosophy glorifying humanity and ridiculing scholastic theology, Church abuses, and all forms of bigotry. In England, the most renowned humanist was Sir Thomas More (1478–1535), whose *Utopia* (1516) was a thinly veiled condemnation of the social and economic defects of his time: religious intolerance, financial greed, the glaring discrepancy between rich and poor, the notions of conquest, imperialism, and war. The creation of such fictive worlds, as theorized by writers such as Sidney, allowed a measure of critical and moral distance from political reality. According to Norbrook, such utopian realms created by the literary imagination were ironically an integral part of the public sphere, facilitating a measure of intellectual independence from the "everyday discourses of public life" (*PBRV*, 13).

The humanist tradition was richly expressed in the rise of English vernacular literature of this period. Even Chaucer, often treated as a medieval writer, expressed a somewhat secular humanistic vision in his *Canterbury Tales*, which tends to bypass simple moralism in the interest of broader stylistic ends such as verisimilitude and realistic portrayal of character, situation, and motive. English drama achieved unprecedented heights in the work of Christopher Marlowe (1564–1593), Ben Jonson (1573?–1637), and William Shakespeare (1564–1616). Marlowe's *Doctor Faustus* expresses an overwhelming craving for experience and a humanistic desire to subjugate the world to human intellection and ingenuity. Shakespeare's plays not only expressed a profound analysis of human character and emotion but also embodied the vast struggle between the values of a declining feudal system and an emerging bourgeois structure of values. As Chris Fitter has shown, the Shakespearian stage illustrates precisely the truth of Norbrook's claim that Renaissance theater provided a forum for varied ideological perspectives contradicting the self-images of monarchical and official theory.[2] The rise of national consciousness in many countries during this period was reflected in the growth of vernacular literatures in Italy, England, France, Germany, and Spain.

Philosophy and Science

In general, the humanists tended to turn away from scholastic philosophy with its emphasis upon logic and theology and its Aristotelian basis. Poets such as Sidney and Milton argued, as against Plato (though adducing his own style in support of their claims), for the elevation of poetry above the languages of prose such as philosophy and history. The humanists, concerned more with the material aspects of language, the achievement of eloquence, and with the ennobling, moral impact of discourse, turned to classical rhetoricians such as Cicero, and promoted the revival of other ancient philosophies such as Platonism. In fact, the major philosophers of this period, such as Marsilio Ficino (1433–1499) and Pico della Mirandola (1463–1494), were Neo-Platonists, affiliated with the Platonic Academy in Florence founded by Cosimo de' Medici. Other thinkers revived the ancient movements of Stoicism, Epicureanism, and Skepticism. They included Lorenzo Valla who, in addition to his historical writing, wrote a *Dialogue of Free Will* and a sympathetic examination of Epicurean ethics; and of course the political philosopher Machiavelli who, also informed by the philosophy of Epicurus, condemned asceticism and other-worldliness. In France, Michel de

Montaigne (1533–1592) expounded a philosophy of skepticism which held that the deliverances of the senses are often deceptive and that even reason can misguide us. We should recognize, he held, that there is no absolute truth, and it is the humble acknowledgment of uncertainty alone that can free us from superstition and bigotry. Like the later skeptical thinker David Hume, Montaigne saw religious, philosophical, and moral systems as ultimately the product of custom. The most renowned English philosopher of this period was Sir Francis Bacon (1561–1626), whose most significant contributions were contained in his *Novum Organon* and *The Advancement of Learning*. Bacon was the forerunner of the empiricist tradition in Britain, urging the use of the inductive method and direct observation as against scholastic reliance upon authority, faith, and deductive reasoning.

There can be no doubt that a major distinction between the medieval and early modern periods lies in a momentous transformation in scientific outlook. Medieval cosmology and scholastic theology were premised on a Ptolemaic geocentric view of the earth as being at the center of the universe, surrounded by a series of seven concentric spheres (the orbits of the planets), beyond which was the Empyrean and the throne of God, who was the "unmoved Mover" and the "First Cause" of all things. The universe was thought to be composed of four elements, earth, air, fire, and water, combined in varying proportions; and human beings were constituted by four "humors." The earth, as in Dante's *Divine Comedy*, was thought to be populated only in its northern hemisphere, which was composed of Asia, Africa, and Europe. This world view, based largely on the physics and metaphysics of Aristotle, was shattered in the early modern era by the heliocentric theory of Nicholas Copernicus (1473–1543), whose truth was demonstrated by Galileo Galilei (1564–1642) and thus paved the way for modern mechanistic (rather than spiritual) conceptions of the universe. Even much of this humanistic scientific revolution returned to neglected ancient sources in Greek science and astronomy, such as the third-century BC Hellenistic astronomer Aristarchus, who had first propounded a heliocentric theory. Great advances were made also in mathematical theory and in medicine; Andreas Vesalius (1514–1564) produced a description of the human body based on careful observation. A particularly significant invention of this time was that of printing, developed in Germany by Johannes Gutenberg and spreading quickly through Europe. Needless to say, the transformations engendered in every area of communication were profound and far-reaching, enabling vast and rapid dissemination not only of information but also of all forms of ideology.

Religion

One of the most profound and large-scale transformations in the early modern period was the Protestant Reformation, erupting in 1517 and resulting in a major schism in the Christian world. Most of northern Europe broke away from Roman Catholicism and the authority of the pope. There also occurred the Catholic Reformation (sometimes known as the Counter-Reformation), which reached its most fervent intensity in the mid-sixteenth century, changing the shape of Catholicism considerably from its medieval character. Indeed, these reformations embodied a sharper break from medieval thinking and institutions than many of the changes wrought by the other currents of humanism. National consciousness played an even more integral role in the Reformation, since the Protestant cause was affiliated with reaction against a system of ecclesiastical control at whose apex sat the pope.

While it may have been immediately incited by abuses within the Catholic Church – such as the amassing of wealth for private self-interest, the sale of indulgences, and the veneration of material objects as holy relics – the Protestant Reformation was directed in essence against some of the cardinal tenets of medieval theology, such as its theory of the sacraments, its elaborate ecclesiastical hierarchy of intermediation between God and human beings, and its insistence that religious faith must be complemented by good deeds. As seen earlier, medieval theology had been broadly propagated through two systems: the theology of the early Middle Ages had been based on the teachings of St. Augustine that man is fallen (through original sin), his will is depraved, and that only those whom God has so predestined can attain eternal salvation. This largely fatalistic system, whereby humans were entirely and mysteriously dependent on God, was largely supplanted in the twelfth and thirteenth centuries by the theologies of Peter Lombard and Thomas Aquinas, which acknowledged man's free will, but urged that he needed divine grace to attain salvation. Such grace was furnished to man through the sacraments, such as baptism, penance, and the eucharist or mass. It was the ecclesiastical hierarchy, tracing its authority all the way through the pope to the apostle Peter, which had the power to administer these sacraments and hence to gain access to divine grace.

The Protestant reformers such as Martin Luther reacted against this complex system of intermediation between God and man, advocating a return to the actual doctrines of the scriptures and the writings of the Church Fathers such as Augustine. They rejected the theory of the priesthood as well as worship of the Virgin, the intermediation of the saints, and the reverence for sacred relics. In general, they returned to the Augustinian visions of original sin, the depraved state of man's will, and, in the case of Calvinism, a strong belief in predestination. The causes of the Protestant Reformation were multifold and complex. The papacy's decline in power and prestige reached a nadir in the "Great Schism," a division into two conflicting claims to the papacy, contested by popes in Rome and Avignon. Many movements had helped prepare the way for the Reformation, including mystics and the fourteenth-century English reformer John Wyclif, who attacked the abuses of the Catholic Church. Many of the humanist thinkers mentioned earlier, such as Erasmus and Sir Thomas More, had contributed to a renaissance in religion, associated with the "Brethren of Common Life," a group of laymen who established schools in Germany and the Low Countries. They professed a religion of simple piety based on the model of Christ, as expressed in Thomas à Kempis' *The Imitation of Christ*. This book enjoyed a wide readership and inspired Ignatius of Loyola to found the Society of Jesus. In the writings of these thinkers, known as Christian humanists, Christianity was freed from its superstitious and ritualistic elements, the absolute authority of the pope was rejected, and the need for a rational and reasonable faith was urged. The growth of national consciousness, affiliated with the increasing power of absolute rulers, was another factor. Perhaps the most fundamental causes were economic: not merely the desire of rulers to appropriate Church wealth but, more significantly, the growth and increasing power and wealth of the middle class, whose commercial interests clashed with both feudalism and the ideals of Catholic Christianity, which, as in the writings of Aquinas, condemned profit-making and usury.

Martin Luther effectively initiated the Reformation in 1517 by drawing up ninety-five theses against indulgences and nailing them to the door of the church in Wittenberg. In his published writings, he called upon the German princes to reform the Church themselves, independently of the pope. He rejected the Roman Catholic interpretation of the eucharist as well as the notion that the Church held supremacy over the state. His central doctrine was "justification by faith": man's sins are remitted and his salvation achieved through faith alone, not through good works. In effect, Luther emphasized the primacy of individual conscience, and the directness of man's relation with God, unmediated by priests, saints, relics, or pilgrimages to shrines. Luther's views were denounced as heretical and in 1521 he was excommunicated. Germany was swept by a series of uprisings culminating in the Peasants' Revolt of 1524–1525. A Protestant revolution in Switzerland was incited by Ulrich Zwingli (1484–1531) and the Frenchman John Calvin (1509–1564); the latter strongly reaffirmed the Augustinian doctrine of predestination, whereby God has already predestined his elect for salvation, and the remainder to damnation. However, rather than this doctrine fostering an indifference to life on earth, it taught that, while none can know whether he or she is of the elect or damned, a "sign" of election is a life of piety, good works, and abstinence. Ironically, as Max Weber was to argue, the influence of Calvin's world view and the "Protestant ethic" – which could be used to sanction the worldly activities of disciplined trading and commerce – played an integral role in the rise of capitalism. Indeed, Calvinism spread in communities and countries where the new capitalist ethic was growing, taking root among the English Puritans, the Scottish Presbyterians, the French Huguenots, and the Church in Holland.

The Catholic Reformation, which was to some degree independent of the Protestant revolution, resulted eventually in a redefinition of Catholic doctrines at the Council of Trent (1545–1563), convened by Pope Paul III. The doctrines challenged by the Protestants were reaffirmed: the necessity for good works to attain salvation; the theory of the sacraments as the only means of attaining divine grace; papal supremacy over the entire ecclesiastical system; and equal authority accorded to the Bible and the teachings of the apostles. A large part of the work of the Catholic Reformation was accomplished by the Jesuits, members of the Society of Jesus founded by Ignatius of Loyola in 1534, and operating through missionary activities, colleges, and seminaries.

These momentous religious transformations induced a vast schism in the Christian world: northern Germany and Scandinavia became Lutheran; England adopted a compromise, integrating Catholic doctrine with allegiance to the English crown; Calvinism held sway in Scotland, Holland, and French Switzerland. The countries still expressing allegiance to the pope now numbered only Italy, France, Spain, Portugal, Austria, Poland, Ireland, and southern Germany. The Protestant Reformation promoted not only individualism but also nationalism (as coextensive with independence from the Church at Rome), increased sanction for bourgeois thought and practice, as well as a broader education accessible to more of the masses. Many of the values of Protestantism and humanism overlapped or reinforced each other: these included self-discipline, industry, and intellectual achievement.

Literary Criticism

Just as many of our own institutions are descended from the early modern period, much of our own literary criticism, and indeed the very notion of criticism as a relatively autonomous domain, derives from this era. In particular, the rise of the independent state and of a liberal bourgeoisie enabled the pervasive growth of humanist culture and of national sentiment; the literature and criticism of the period tend to reflect civic values, a sense of national identity, and a sense of place in history, especially as gauged in relation to the classics. The technology of the period, such as the development and dissemination of printing, transformed the conditions of reading, facilitating the process of editing (of especially classical texts), and vastly extending the sphere of the reading public. Some of the innovative characteristics of Renaissance literary criticism, as Glyn P. Norton has noted, include reappraisals of the nature and function of language, moving away from the scholastic fourfold allegorical structure – grounded on a literal, referential, view of meaning – to a view of language as dialogic and as subject to historical evolution. Such a shift entailed new approaches to reading, interpretation, and an increasing recognition that all literary criticism is intrinsically tied to specific social contexts (*CHLC*, V.III, 3–4).

It is clear also that the general transformation in Europe from feudal power to the absolutist state engendered profound changes in the conditions of production of literature and criticism. Scholars such as Robert Matz have argued that, whereas a number of different forms of power – economic, social, and judicial – were merged in the authority of the feudal lord, the sixteenth and seventeenth centuries witnessed an increasing separation of these spheres. An important literary and literary-critical consequence was that the artist exercised a greater autonomy, in a number of ways: his support came less from "personal patronage" and more from the "anonymous market"; there was an increasing "separation of art from the church and the sacred"; and, perhaps above all, the emergence of the absolutist state as "a locus of authority to some degree distinct from and opposed to that of the feudal lord . . . created the opportunity for the social assertion of secular-bourgeois intellectuals who gained power within the expanding bureaucratic state and whose identity lay in their humanist language skills and disciplined conduct rather than warrior function or traditional landed status." These cultural transformations, which wore the countenance of humanism, were associated not only with the emerging bourgeoisie but also with the transformation of the aristocracy itself from a "warrior elite into a civil elite."[3] Matz argues that this transformation generated different views of appropriate aristocratic conduct, and a struggle within factions of the aristocracy itself, which were both reflected in, and shaped, some of the major defenses and definitions of poetry during this period.

In our own day, and especially in Western culture, where poetry and good literature have been marginalized, it is easy to forget how deeply poetry and literary criticism were embroiled in the political process during the Renaissance. In a number of groundbreaking studies, David Norbrook has extrapolated Jürgen Habermas' notion of the "bourgeois public sphere, a realm of debate in which citizens could participate as equals, independently of pressure from monopolies of power." Habermas saw this public sphere as emerging fully around 1695. Norbrook traces its emergence somewhat earlier on the English scene, attributing its growth to a number of factors such as an educational revolution, the reformers' campaign for widely available public education, relaxed censorship of Protestant writings, the rise of a literary market which allowed greater independence from court patronage, increased circulation of newspapers and the size of the electorate in public life, and of course the growth of a wider reading public (*PBRV*, 18, 24, 28, 32). The important point made by Norbrook is the poet's involvement in this sphere: the poet was a public figure, and all of the English Renaissance poets "tried to influence public affairs through their writings."[4] After the rise of monarchies and the decline of the feudal nobility, many poets could entertain career prospects only in serving the crown. While this of course entailed compromise with courtly discourse, the expansion of the public sphere and the other factors mentioned above enabled the poet to create fictive and utopian worlds, to mold the image of public events (as in Marvell's Horatian Ode), and to assert some degree of individualism. Moreover, textual criticism was charged with a potent political potential to demystify the power and language of corrupt institutions: the exposure by humanist scholarship of the "Donation of Constantine" as a forgery helped undermine the power of the papacy, and the translation of the Bible into vernacular languages shifted the privilege of interpretative authority away from the clergy to the individual reader. In such a climate, poets and critics inevitably placed emphasis on the practical and social functions of poetry and its dependence on rhetorical strategies (*PBRV*, 9, 11, 13–15).

Indeed, much Renaissance criticism was forged in the struggle to defend poetry and literature from charges – brought within both clerical and secular circles – of immorality, triviality, and irrelevance to practical and political life. The types of criticism proliferating in the early modern period also included a large body of humanist commentary and scholarship on classical texts. The most influential classical treatises during the sixteenth and seventeenth centuries were Aristotle's *Poetics* and Horace's *Ars poetica*. A third important body of criticism in this period is comprised of commentaries on Aristotle's *Poetics* and debates between the relative virtues of the Aristotelian and Horatian texts as well as attempts to harmonize their insights. Alongside Aristotle and Horace, the influential rhetorical voices of Cicero and Quintilian were recovered in the early fifteenth century: Renaissance critics tended to adapt, and even distort, these voices to their own needs.

Almost all of these defenses, commentaries, and debates concern a number of fundamental notions: imitation (of both the external world and the tradition of classical authors), which Glyn Norton characterizes as "arguably the predominant poetic issue of the entire period" (*CHLC*, V.III, 4); the truth-value and didactic role of literature; the classical "unities"; the notion of verisimilitude; the use of the vernacular; the definition of poetic genres such as narrative and drama; the invention of new, mixed genres such as the romantic epic and the tragicomedy; the use of rhyme in poetry; the relative values of quantitative and qualitative verse; and the place of literature and poetry in relation to other disciplines such as moral philosophy and history. In the sections below, we shall look at the treatment of these issues by some of the influential writers of the period, as well as the major defenders of poetry and the main contenders in the various debates. It will be useful to divide them into three broad categories, while remembering that the concerns and motives of each set of writers overlap considerably. The first set of writers, all Italian (Giraldi, Castelvetro, Mazzoni, and Tasso), are concerned to formulate or reformulate their connections with the classical tradition; the second group, comprising both French and English writers (Du Bellay, Ronsard, and Sidney), endeavors to defend poetry and the use of the vernacular; the third, represented here by Gascoigne and Puttenham, aims to define the art of poetry, drawing on the traditions of rhetoric. In many of these writers, the promotion of the vernacular and the very definition of the poetic is intrinsically tied to their political and often nationalistic affiliations.

Confronting the Classical Heritage: Giraldi, Castelvetro, Mazzoni, Tasso

As Renaissance writers returned to the classical past, they did so critically and inevitably with their own agendas in mind. In using classical texts for their own ends, they were obliged to formulate their own stances toward the classical heritage – especially the poetic and rhetorical heritage of Aristotle, Horace, and Cicero – and to articulate their own positions on issues raised by the ancient writers. These issues included the meaning of "imitation," the definition and expansion of genres, the formulation of the classical unities, and the connection of poetics and rhetoric. As mentioned in chapter 9, during the Middle Ages Aristotle's *Poetics* had been known primarily through a commentary by the Islamic philosopher Ibn Rushd, which had seen the central thesis of Aristotle's text as the notion that the function of poetry is either praise of virtuous action or blame of base deeds.

A new and powerful stimulus to literary criticism arose when the Greek text of the *Poetics* was made available in 1508 and translated into Latin in 1536. A number of editions of Horace's *Ars poetica* were circulated, one of the most influential of which was produced in Paris in 1500. While poetics had overlapped increasingly with rhetoric, as evident in the work of Renaissance writers such as Minturno, Scaliger, Du Bellay, and Puttenham, the recovery of Aristotle's text fostered a new examination of literary form and organic unity that was not wholly grounded in rhetoric. Many commentaries on Aristotle appeared during the sixteenth century. The earlier ones, such as those by Robortelli (1548), blended Aristotelian insights with precepts from Horace and the Ciceronian rhetorical tradition. The later ones, notably that by Castelvetro (1570, 1576), were virtually free of rhetorical influences. Somewhat ironically (given the availability of the actual text of Aristotle's *Poetics*), many writers saw literature as Ibn Rushd had, as exercising a moral function through the depiction of virtue and vice; they combined this with Horace's precept that literature should also please; hence the formula that literature should "teach and delight" (used by Sidney) pervaded the thinking of this era.

Aristotle's influence was profoundest on the Italian writers and critics who, however, used his work as a starting point for their own conceptions of the poetic art. The salient issues raised by these writers include the "unities," discussed by Giraldi and Castelvetro; the theory of genres, which informs the work of Giraldi and Tasso; the doctrine of poetic imitation, treated by all of these writers, and most innovatively examined in the work of Mazzoni. In practice, many of these notions were intertwined. Renaissance writers added the doctrine of the unities of time and place to Aristotle's original demand for the unity of action; debates over these unities encompassed the discussion of classical genres, notably the lyric, epic, tragedy, and comedy, as well as mixed genres such as the romantic epic and the tragicomedy. The newer, characteristically humanist, genres also included the essay and the dialogue form, as well as increasing focus on the epigram as an instrument of wit. Boccaccio's work stimulated inquiry into the nature of prose fiction, and into its constituent elements such as verisimilitude or realism. These inquiries paved the way for subsequent analyses of the novel as a genre distinct from the *nouvelle* and the romance (*CHLC*, V.III, 10–11). Imitation was used by most writers of this period to refer to poetic representation of the real world in terms of what is typical or probable, the license of the poet to mix fantasy with fact, and imitation of classical authors as models. As will be seen in the writers now to be examined, the treatment of these issues varied along a broad range of perspectives, displaying emphatically how each writer's adaptation of classical norms was fueled by specific contemporary agendas.

Giambattista Giraldi (1504–1573)

The Italian dramatist, poet, and literary critic Giraldi was embroiled in a number of controversies. Like Dante, he spoke in favor of the use of vernacular languages and, as against the influential classical notions of literature deriving from Aristotle and Horace, he advocated a new genre, the romance, a lengthy narrative poem which combined elements of the classical epic with those of medieval romances. The most noteworthy contemporary example of such a romance was Ariosto's *Orlando Furioso* (1516). Hence Giraldi was effectively involved in a quarrel between "ancients" and "moderns" which was to last for many centuries. Giraldi's leaning toward the modern is shown in a number of ways. To begin with, he tends to view literature in a historical context, which means that classical values are not necessarily applicable to all ages. He also reacted, both in his dramas and in his theory, against many of Aristotle's prescriptions for tragedy, such as unity of action and unity of time. His drama and poetry influenced many subsequent writers, including Pierre Corneille and Shakespeare. His literary criticism, of which his *Discorso intorno al comporre dei romanzi* (1554; *Discourse on the Composition of Romances*) was the most controversial and influential, anticipates and parallels some of the views of Mazzoni, Du Bellay, and Coleridge.

In his *Discourse* Giraldi states unapologetically that romances directly contravene Aristotle's precept that an epic should imitate a single action. Romances deal not only with many actions but with many characters, building "the whole fabric of their work upon eight or ten persons."[5] Giraldi pointedly remarks that the romance came neither from the Greeks nor from the Romans but "came laudably from our own language." The great writers of this language, he adds, gave to this genre "the same authority" that Homer and Vergil gave to their epics. Giraldi also promotes an ideal of organic unity, suggesting that the parts of a poem must "fit together as do the parts of the body" (*DCR*, 24). However, this is not exactly the kind of organicism advocated by the Romantics and later poets. Indeed, it has more in common with classical and neoclassical views of organic unity. Giraldi, like Pope two centuries later, holds that the "prudent poet . . . can with varied ornaments embellish the body of his work," giving each part "a just measure and decorous ornament" so that each part "may be set with beautiful order in its place" (*DCR*, 24). This ideal of organic unity depends upon the classical notions of appropriate proportion, harmony, and moderation; it also views form as having an ornamental connection with content, whereas later writers viewed appropriate form as growing out of a particular content.

However, Giraldi strikes a more Romantic and modern tone when he insists that authors should not limit their freedom by restricting themselves within the bounds of their predecessors' rules. Such restraint would be a "bad use of the gifts that mother nature gave them" (*DCR*, 39). Even Vergil and Homer, he notes, showed how poets can turn away from the habits of the ancients. Giraldi's arguments here have a nationalistic strain: the Tuscan poets, he maintains, need not be bound by the poetic forms or literary confines of the Greeks and Romans. After all, he remarks, Aristotle and Horace did not even know the Italian tongue or the manners of composing fitting to it (*DCR*, 40). And Ovid, who ignored Aristotle's poetics, emerged "as a beautifully artistic poet" because he was writing about things for which there were no rules or examples. However, Giraldi's modernism is constrained in its call to innovation: he recommends that Italian poets follow the example laid down by the better poets in this language who have already written excellent romances (*DCR*, 41).

In other respects, Giraldi's views of poetry echo those of Horace and other classical writers. As regards the civil function of the poet, Giraldi insists that poetry must "praise virtuous actions and censure the vicious." He claims that Italian poets, such as Dante, Petrarch, and Ariosto, are actually more decisive in this regard than the Greeks and Romans "who only hinted at such censures and praises" (*DCR*, 52). Moreover, the poet should always observe "decorum, which is none other than what is fitting to places, times, and persons" (*DCR*, 56). Giraldi also urges the use of moderation when employing principles of allegorical explanation, being sure not to veer into "chimeras and fantasies completely foreign to the meaning of the things on which they comment" (*DCR*, 67). Hence, Giraldi attempts a balance or compromise between classical virtues and contemporary artistic needs.

Lodovico Castelvetro (1505–1571)

Castelvetro is best known for his stringent reformulation of Aristotle's unities of time and place in drama, his rigid approach being subsequently endorsed by neoclassical writers. Also important in his writings, however, are his treatment of imitation, plot, the distinction between poetry and history, and his views of the purpose and audience of poetry. Indeed, many of his views went against the grain of contemporary critical orthodoxy. As against a long critical tradition, deriving in part from Horace, that the function of poetry was to be "useful" as well as to entertain, Castelvetro insisted, in a strikingly modern pose, that the sole end of poetry was to yield pleasure. He also dismissed the long-held notion, arising most influentially with Plato, of poetry as somehow divinely inspired and the poet as possessed by a divine furor or madness. The poet, he insisted, is made, not born: his creations are the product of study, training, and art.[6] Unlike most of his predecessors and contemporaries who had written commentaries on Aristotle's *Poetics*, Castelvetro saw Aristotle's text as merely the unfinished draft of an uncompleted work (*PA*, 19). His own commentary, *Poetica d'Aristotele vulgarizzata e sposta* (*The Poetics of Aristotle*

Translated and Explained, 1570, 1576), purports not only to elucidate and often refine or even controvert Aristotle's views, but also to provide a comprehensive guide for the aspiring poet.

Among Castelvetro's major heterodoxies is his insistence that pleasure, not instruction or usefulness, is the sole end of poetry, and further, that the appropriate audience for poetry is the common people (*PA*, 19). Critical orthodoxy until the Renaissance and beyond had accepted Horace's formulation of the dual function of the poet as he who combines usefulness with pleasure (*qui miscuit utile dulci*). This formulation had been repeated by classical rhetorical theorists such as Cicero, as well as Renaissance theorists such as Julius Caesar Scaliger. In various parts of his text, Castelvetro does concede that poetry may have a salutary effect on its audience, but such an effect is not essential to the nature of poetry (*PA*, 150, 171).

Castelvetro denies the title of poet to those who have written history or science or art in verse form; the true poet, according to him, is "essentially an inventor" (*PA*, 105). True invention is the product of great labor, a point often repeated by Castelvetro. Poetry must be verisimilar in two respects: it must imitate objects that are real, not fantastic; and its manner of imitation must appear probable or at least possible to the audience (*PA*, 48, 92); however, Castelvetro qualifies this by urging that the poet's portrayal of events must be marvelous, since "the marvelous is especially capable of giving pleasure" (*PA*, 254). Nonetheless, the marvelous cannot include the impossible (*PA*, 290).

Castelvetro's views of tragedy usually agree with Aristotle's, though often for different reasons: like Aristotle, he considers plot the most important element, on the grounds that it requires more labor than the other elements (*PA*, 66). He ranks tragedy above epic on the grounds that the former requires a greater exertion of the poet's genius (*PA*, 321). The unities of time and place were first formulated by Castelvetro and it was his authority that underlay their popular dissemination. His formulation of these unities, mistakenly thought to be based on Aristotle, endowed the doctrine with high authority for over two hundred years. Both this specific doctrine and Aristotle's authority in general were eventually undermined by the Romantics. Castelvetro's conception reached the height of its influence in the seventeenth century, on French classical drama. Yet in the spirit of his theories, he was a precursor of the realism and naturalism that flourished in the nineteenth century.

Taking Aristotle as his starting point, Castelvetro asserts that history and the arts and sciences are not fit subjects for poetry, for a number of reasons. The subject matter of history is not furnished by the author's genius but by "the course of earthly events or by the manifest or hidden will of God." In contrast, the matter of poetry "is invented and imagined by the poet's genius" (*PA*, 18). The true office of the poet is to exert his "intellectual faculties to imitate human actions . . . and through his imitations to provide pleasure for his audiences." The final reason given by Castelvetro for the poet's avoiding treatment of the arts and sciences is perhaps the most integral to his own conception of poetry: "poetry was invented for the sole purpose of providing pleasure and recreation . . . to the souls of the common people and the rude multitude." And, in Castelvetro's eyes, the common people are "incapable" of understanding, and therefore impatient of, the subtle arguments and rational proofs employed in the arts and sciences. The subjects of poetry should be suited to the common understanding, consisting of "the everyday happenings that are talked about among the people"

(*PA*, 20). Aristotle, in stark contrast, had held that appropriate subjects of poetry were the fortunes of noble families.

Equally divergent from Aristotle is Castelvetro's view that the species of poetry is determined not by the moral qualities of men but rather by their social rank. Aristotle had said that the persons imitated by poetry must be good or bad and that they must be better or worse than ourselves or like us. Tragedy, according to Aristotle, imitates better men and comedy, worse. Castelvetro, taking Aristotle's statement to be incomplete and inconsistent with his later comments, cites these factors as proof that the text of Aristotle's *Poetics* "is no more than an accumulation of notes" intended to serve as the basis of a more complete and consistent text (*PA*, 22). Given that poetry imitates men in action, its species, says Castelvetro, are determined not by the moral nature of men but by "whether they are royal personages, burghers, or peasants." And the purpose of poetry is not to increase knowledge of good and bad in human character but "to offer the common people the greatest possible pleasure in their representations of actions never before seen" (i.e., actions which are invented rather than taken from history) (*PA*, 23).

Where Aristotle had distinguished three types of imitation, the first being narrative, the second dramatic, and the third a combination of these two, Castelvetro suggests an alternative catalogue of types: narrative, dramatic, and similitudinary. The narrative mode, he suggests, uses words only to represent both words and things: it recounts both what people say and the entire range of their interaction with the physical world. The dramatic mode uses both words and things (i.e., material objects, people, scenic backgrounds) to represent words and things. The dramatic mode differs from the narrative in that it is more restricted in space and time, it can only represent things that are audible and visible, and its actions must take place in real time (i.e., the actual duration in which the events portrayed would occur) (*PA*, 31–33). The similitudinary mode, which is Castelvetro's own invention, either uses direct quotation or substitutes words that are similar to those originally used. This third mode, however, is not usually found alone but embedded within a narrative (*PA*, 33–35).

On the subject of pleasure, Castelvetro has some interesting insights. Aristotle had asserted that men obtain pleasure from the learning that is entailed in imitation: imitation involves an intellectual process of observing similarities and differences among objects. Again, Castelvetro does not deny this; he merely adds that there are other reasons, ignored by Aristotle, why man finds imitations pleasurable. He derives pleasure from imitating other human beings, from imitating animals, from imitating nature or fortune; in all of these cases, his pleasure lies in the fact that "his imitations seem to him to constitute a new order of nature or of fortune or a new course of earthly affairs and to partake somehow of creations transcending human capabilities" (*PA*, 45–46).

We now come to what Castelvetro was renowned for: the unities. In general, he agrees with Aristotle's doctrine of the unities, and even extends their application, but offers a different rationale for them. Concerning the magnitude or duration of the plot, he agrees that a tragic plot – that is apprehended by both sight and hearing – must not exceed "one revolution of the sun," which Castelvetro takes to be twelve hours. However, he argues that the plot in epic (narrative) poetry, which appeals to the hearing only, can last longer than twelve hours, provided that no one of its sections exceeds twelve hours (for this would tire an audience at one sitting) (*PA*, 82–83).

However, Castelvetro rejects Aristotle's reason for this time constraint, namely, "the limited capacity and retentiveness of the audience's memory." The real cause, suggests Castelvetro, is that "since the imaginary action from which the plot is formed represents words directly with words and things with things, it must of necessity fill as many hours on the stage as the imaginary action it represents would have filled . . . if it had actually occurred" (PA, 82, 87). Castelvetro accepts Aristotle's definition of the unity of a plot as consisting of a "single action of a single person" or, at most, two actions which are closely interrelated (PA, 87, 89). Castelvetro finds no justification for this position in Aristotle's text beyond an appeal to the authority of Homer and the tragic poets (PA, 89). The reasons offered by Castelvetro himself are, firstly, that the temporal limitation of twelve hours on tragedy will not allow the representation of many actions; and, secondly, that the epic poet who restricts his representations to one action will all the more exhibit his "judgment and skill" (PA, 89–90). Moreover, Castelvetro argues that Aristotle's criterion of unity – that actions should have a probable or necessary relationship among themselves – is too narrow; actions can also be related, he suggests, by pertaining to one person or one place or one nation (PA, 91). Indeed, he appears to extrapolate the Aristotelian unity of time to extend to space: the action "must be set in a place no larger than the stage on which the actors perform and in a period of time no longer than that which is filled by their performance" (PA, 243). As this last sentence indicates, Castelvetro reformulates Aristotle's notion of the unities into a prescription for detailed realism. However, his general discussion of the probable accords with Aristotle's requirement that the poet represent the probable and the necessary, allowing for certain improbable events provided that these are excluded from the plot as such.

Giacopo Mazzoni (1548–1598)

Born in Cesena, Italy, the Italian scholar Giacopo Mazzoni's major work was a philosophical treatise called *De Triplici Hominum Vita, Activa Nempe, Contemplativa, e Religiosa Methodi Tres*, 1576 (*On the Three Ways of Man's Life: The Active, the Contemplative, and the Religious*). In this text Mazzoni attempted to reconcile the philosophies of Plato and Aristotle. What concerns us here is Mazzoni's aesthetics, which were formulated in connection with his enduring interest in Dante's work. Just as Giraldi laid down a defense of the romantic epic, so Mazzoni found it necessary to defend Dante's allegory against critics who condemned its subject matter as being fantastic and unreal. In his essay *Della difesa della Commedia di Dante* (1587; *On the Defense of the Comedy of Dante*), the central issue at stake is the nature of poetic imitation. In defending Dante's poem, Mazzoni formulated a comprehensive and systematic aesthetics of poetic imitation.

In his introduction, Mazzoni opposes the view, which he finds common among philosophers, that metaphysics is a comprehensive science, of which all the other arts and sciences are a part. Instead, following Aristotle, Mazzoni insists that the real distinction between the various arts and sciences lies in their differing ways of knowing and constructing the same object.[7] A particular art or science, then, is distinguished by its mode of knowing and constructing a given object (DCD, 39–40). In explaining this basis of distinction, Mazzoni claims to be following Plato. There are three types of objects, says Mazzoni, and three ways in which they can be approached. These objects are "idea," "work," and "idol." These are, respectively, the objects of the "ruling" arts, the "fabricating" arts, and the "imitating" arts. The objects are therefore approached as observable, fabricable, or imitable. Mazzoni offers an example also given by Plato. Let us suppose that the object is a bridle. The "ruling" art here will be the art of horsemanship, which is concerned only with the *idea* of how the bridle must work; the art of the bridle-maker will have "work" or fabrication as its object, since this is the art that will actually make the bridle; the imitating arts will be concerned with the bridle only inasmuch as it is imitable, by means of an "idol" or image (*DCD*, 40). Unlike Plato, however, Mazzoni wishes to establish a firm distinction between the imitating arts and the fabricating arts; after all, Plato had seen the fabricating arts (for example, bridle-making) as imitating the idea of the object; Mazzoni retorts that while the art of bridle-making does indeed represent or copy the idea supplied by the ruling art, it also serves other purposes, such as managing horses. So, while all the arts may involve some kind of imitation, states Mazzoni, what distinguishes the imitative from other arts is that they have no other end or purpose beyond that of representation (*DCD*, 41).

Mazzoni further explains that the idol or image which is the object of the imitative arts arises from human artifice or fantasy. In other words, arts such as painting and sculpture do not properly imitate actually existing objects but objects devised by their own imagination. Mazzoni draws upon a distinction made by Plato in his dialogue, the *Sophist*, between two kinds of imitation. The first kind, which imitates actual things, is "icastic"; the second type, which imitates things of the artist's invention, is "phantastic" (*DCD*, 46).

Acknowledging that poetry is an imitative art, Mazzoni seeks to define it according to its medium, its subject matter, its efficient cause, and its final cause. The proper medium or instrument of poetry, he urges, is harmony, number, and meter, all taken from music since they produce pleasure in an orderly fashion (*DCD*, 57–58). While Mazzoni has insisted that the imitative arts such as poetry deal with objects of fantasy, he nonetheless rejects "the opinion of many" that the subject matter of poetry is merely "the fabulous and false." He appeals to the authority of Aristotle and even of Plato (for whom certain types of poetry which gave a truthful presentation of the gods were acceptable) to affirm that the poet may indeed depict the truth as well as portraying fantasies; to put it another way, the poet may use "icastic" imitation. Again following Aristotle (who had urged that poetry should imitate what is probable), Mazzoni states that the appropriate subject of poetry is the "credible": this category would include both truth and falsity (since what is false can sometimes be presented in a credible fashion) (*DCD*, 72–73).

What does it mean, in practice, for the poet to treat his subject in a "credible" fashion? Mazzoni urges that the poet must always use particular and concrete means that will appeal to the senses; he can by all means talk of things which are speculative and abstract, but his manner of speaking will differ from that of the scientist or the philosopher; the poet must present even complex ideas by means of images and idols; he must instruct by using comparisons and similitudes taken from physical things. Why? Because the poet must address "the people, among whom are many rude and uneducated." By way of example, Mazzoni cites a passage from the end of Dante's *Paradiso*, presenting an image of the Trinity as three circles. Had Plato witnessed Dante's inventiveness, Mazzoni suggests, he would have recognized the poet's superiority in this regard, and consequently the superior potential of poetry (*DCD*, 78).

Regarding credibility, says Mazzoni, a second conclusion is incumbent upon the poet: if the poet has a choice between two circumstances, one credible but false, and the other true but incredible, he must always follow the path of the credible. Finally, since poetry should give more importance to what is credible than what is true, poetry should be placed under the category of ancient "sophistic." Although the term "sophist" had long acquired negative connotations, Mazzoni cites Philostratus' *Lives of the Sophists* to argue that the Sophists had certain virtues. They treated everything rhetorically – which Mazzoni understands as "credibly" – and confidently represented their claims by means of idols and images, just as the poet should (*DCD*, 80). Philostratus, observes Mazzoni, did not, like Plato and Boethius, consider the sophistic art as "low and scandalous" but as a worthy and noble pursuit which in some ways participated in the "rectitude of true philosophy" (*DCD*, 82). True philosophy, says Mazzoni, directs the intellect by truth and the will by goodness. But not all sophistry is opposed in these regards to philosophy. Plato, he claims, was opposed only to the species of sophistry which misdirected the intellect and the will (*DCD*, 83). Mazzoni considers that another, second species of sophistic – which Philostratus called the old sophistic – does set feigned things before the intellect but does not mislead the will; this kind, he notes, was not condemned by the ancients. It is under this ancient sophistic that Mazzoni classifies phantastic poetry, which often contains under the cover of fiction "the truth of many noble concepts" (*DCD*, 83).

The last species of sophistic – called the second sophistic by Philostratus – employs true names and real actions as the basis for discussions "appropriate to the rules of justice." Under this species Mazzoni places icastic poetry, which "represents true actions and persons but always in a credible way" (*DCD*, 84). Mazzoni concludes that poetry is a "rational faculty" and must be classified with those rational faculties which are concerned not with truth but with "the apparent credible." He cites the authority of Plato, who had called the poet a "marvelous sophist" who never represents the true but always the apparent. Plutarch, also, had "shown that poetry willingly accepts the lie in order better to please." Hence, Mazzoni sees poetry as a "sophistic art" whose proper genus is imitation, whose subject is the credible, and whose end or purpose is delight; given these qualities, poetry is often obliged to accommodate falsehood (*DCD*, 85). But if the subject of poetry – the credible – is the same as that of rhetoric, how does it differ? Mazzoni's answer is that rhetoric deals with the credible insofar as it is credible, whereas poetry treats of the credible inasmuch as it is marvelous. This definition, he insists, does not exclude truth since truth, in both nature and human history, can be marvelous (*DCD*, 86). Mazzoni also argues that Plato did not view all poetry as falsifying (*DCD*, 87–88).

As for the "efficient cause" of poetry (i.e., the agency which makes it possible), Mazzoni locates this in what he calls the "civil faculty." By this term, which he himself defines as "moral philosophy" (*DCD*, 98), he refers to the general social discourse which lays down the rules for ethical behavior. He divides the civil faculty into two parts. The first is concerned with the laws behind the justness of human actions, and this part is called politics or civil law. The second part has to do with the laws of "recreational activities" (or what Mazzoni calls the laws of cessation of serious and difficult activities), and this part is called poetics. In other words, the civil faculty comprehends both the serious work performed in the state as well as the recreational activities or games which provide relief from that work (*DCD*, 90–91). Among all "games," says Mazzoni, none is "more worthy, more noble, and more central" than poetry.

Mazzoni now takes up the question of the "final cause" or purpose of poetry. The same object, he says, can have different aims when considered from differing perspectives. For example, the principal purpose of the tongue is to provide the sensation of taste; yet, in animals, it can also be used for defense; and in humans, it is an instrument of speech, an instrument of reason (*DCD*, 94). In the same way, poetry can be viewed, in three different modes, as having three different ends or purposes: in its mode of imitation, its end is to provide a correct imitation or representation; considered as amusement, poetry's purpose is simply to produce delight; thirdly, it can be considered as "amusement directed, ruled, and defined by the civil faculty" (*DCD*, 95). In this mode, poetry has usefulness or moral betterment as its purpose: it "orders the appetite and submits it to the reason" (*DCD*, 98). What is interesting here is that Mazzoni uses this threefold definition of poetry to answer Plato's charges against poetry. The sort of poetry banished by Plato, says Mazzoni, was that which, unregulated by the civil faculty, produced a "free" delight which was independent of any law and which "disordered the appetite . . . producing complete rebellion against reason and bringing damage and loss to a virtuous life" (*DCD*, 97). Mazzoni even cites Plato as conceding that poetry can bring useful things to our minds by means of the delight it can offer. Not only this, but in the second, third, and tenth books of the *Republic* and in the second book of the *Laws*, observes Mazzoni, Plato suggests that the poetic faculty is the civil faculty and provides instruction in a sweetened way to those who are otherwise not amenable to learning (*DCD*, 99). Mazzoni's strategy here employs considerable irony: rather than refuting Plato's arguments against poetry, he searches Plato's texts for support of his own more comprehensive and stratified view of poetic imitation, thereby evincing the actually complex nature of Plato's scattered views of poetry, foregrounding these over the conventionally reductive view usually assigned to the Greek philosopher.

What Mazzoni does next is even more surprising. He takes the very framework of Plato's banishment of poetry and brings out its potential to accommodate poetry as defined in a more comprehensive manner. Plato's ideal republic, he observes, consists of three classes of people: the artisans (including lower- and middle-class citizens), the soldiers, and the magistrates (including the powerful citizens who rule the state). Mazzoni argues that, in accordance with this constitution of the state, there are three main kinds of poetry created by the civil faculty: the heroic, the tragic, and the comic. Heroic poetry is aimed primarily at the soldiers, spurring them to imitate the glorious deeds narrated in such verse. Tragedy, which characteristically depicts the "dreadful and terrible downfall of great persons," is aimed at the ruling classes, its function being to moderate "the pride characteristic of their state," so as to discourage them from becoming "insolent in their rule," and to "keep them always under the justice of the laws." And comedy is aimed at the lower classes, to "console them for their modest fortune," to "implant in the minds of humble citizens obedience to their superiors, so that . . . they should not be moved to disobedience or rebellion, and so that they should always remain content with their condition" (DCD, 105). These three types of poetry, then, because they are "ruled by the civil faculty," bring not only delight but also "utility and benefit to the republic, instructing in an almost concealed way" the three social classes (DCD, 106).

Mazzoni's next strategy is little short of remarkable, given the era in which he wrote. He offers, consecutively, three definitions of poetry. In the first of these, he designates poetry as an "art" that is "made with verse, number and harmony, . . . imitative of the credible marvelous, and invented by the human intellect to represent the images of things suitably." The second definition calls poetry a "game" which is also invented by the human intellect "in order to delight." The final definition, also denominating poetry as a "game," sees it as "invented by the civil faculty to delight the people in a useful way" (DCD, 108). These definitions stress, respectively, the imitative function of poetry, its status as a game, and its higher status as a "game modified by the civil faculty." Only poetry of the third kind, insists Mazzoni, is governed by the civil faculty, and it is this mode of poetry which should stand as the ideal of the "good poet," the foremost exemplar in this regard being Dante (DCD, 109).

The underlying significance of Mazzoni's text goes far beyond a mere defense of poetry or of allegory. His text is to a great extent structured by his progressive and increasingly comprehensive definitions of poetry. In repeatedly defining poetry according to increasingly comprehensive criteria, he is effectively laying bare the process of his own thought, a transparency which rescues from its reductive closure in Plato (and to some extent Aristotle) the definition of poetry, and which reopens the possibilities of a broader conception of the nature of poetry. Moreover, Mazzoni engages not merely in a rebuttal of Plato but rather in a *rereading* of Plato and Aristotle. By citing some of the less well-known passages from their works, he effectively rescues their texts from the conventionally reductive readings based on the commonly cited sources of their views (such as the tenth book of the *Republic*). Mazzoni evinces what he considers to be the actual but hitherto unpursued implications of their own arguments to redefine the nature of poetic imitation. By stratifying and refining the definitions of Plato and Aristotle, he shows how, within Plato's own constitutional framework, poetry has an important ideological function with respect to all the social classes in a political constitution. It is only poetry whose sole end is to produce delight, poetry produced by the human intellect without the guidance of the civil faculty, which can incite social disorder. The best poetry is indeed socially responsible, since it derives from the very same source – the civil faculty – as the ideal of political justice and order. A final strategy of Mazzoni's text is its attempt to rescue rhetoric from its scandalous reputation and to name poetry as a species of such a redeemed rhetoric. The redemption of both rhetoric and poetry rests upon Mazzoni's redefinition of their connection with truth, and of his reassessment of the value of truth itself: he deploys Aristotle's text to show that, as far as these disciplines are concerned, it is credibility rather than truth which stands as an appropriate ideal. In this insistence also, Mazzoni is modern, rescuing sophism, relativism, and author–audience interaction from the tyranny of absolute truth imposed by Plato and his successors.

Torquato Tasso (1544–1595)

Tasso has long enjoyed a reputation as both one of the finest poets of the Renaissance and an influential critic. He is best known for his epic poem *Jerusalem Delivered* (1581), whose topic was the First Crusade. This poem, initially completed in 1575, was revised into a longer version, *Jerusalem Conquered*. During the process of revision, Tasso undertook the writing of a long critical treatise, *Discorsi del Poema Eroica* (1594; *Discourses on the Heroic Poem*), which both defended the epic poem he had already written and anticipated some of the principles underlying its revision. The text of the *Discourses* itself represents a considerable amplification and revision of an earlier critical text, *Discourses on the Poetic Art*, which had appeared somewhat earlier, in 1587.

Tasso was born in Sorrento and spent some years at the court of Ferrara where his conduct obliged the duke, Alphonso II, to have him incarcerated on grounds of insanity. After his release in 1586 he wandered from court to court and died in Rome. "Paranoia" might be too strong a word; but certainly a great deal of insecurity and anxiety about adverse criticism of his epic informs Tasso's *Discourses*, which – characteristic, to some extent, of Renaissance scholarship – parades its learning and takes great pains to assert its points of originality, especially as against recent influential writers such as Lodovico Castelvetro. Tasso's own revised *Discourses on the Heroic Poem* had a considerable impact not only on Renaissance but also on subsequent literary theory in Italy, England, and France. Its influence stemmed no doubt partly from the fact that this theory of epic poetry was advanced by the first great epic poet in a European vernacular: it was effectively the theory behind his own epic composition, the theory that justified and explained his own epic.

Tasso well understood the important critical issues of his own day – such as the relative values of Homer and Vergil, ancients and moderns, as well as the issue of the usefulness of poetry as against its function of affording pleasure – and his text reflects his accommodation of the various demands on poetry and criticism. As the translators of Tasso's text point out, apropos of these demands, "Tasso took them all into account, reconciling society's demand that poetry should entertain, the Church's demand that poetry should encourage the faith, the humanist's veneration for Antiquity, the modernist's self-applause – and managed not to degrade poetry into entertainment, confuse it with propaganda . . . disparage ancients, medievals, or moderns; he even managed not to be anti-Aristotelian or anti-Platonic."[8] Indeed, Aristotle is one of the main sources of Tasso's text, the others being Horace and the canons of classical rhetoric. In a broad sense, Tasso might be said to adapt and extend Aristotle's insights into the basis of his own theory of the heroic poem, with a view to justifying the content, style, and diction of his own epic.

In book I of his treatise, prior to his task of defining a heroic poem, Tasso offers a series of attempts to define poetry in general. He suggests that all of the species of poetry, including epic, tragedy, comedy, and song, are forms of "imitation in verse" (*DHP*, 7). What do they imitate? Tasso takes up the Stoic view that poetry imitates human and divine actions. He rejects the idea that any divine action can be imitated as such, and concludes that poetry "is an imitation of human actions, fashioned to teach us how to live. And since every action is performed with some reflection and choice, poetry will deal with moral habit and with thought" (*DHP*, 10).

In arriving at this definition, Tasso began by acknowledging Aristotle's dictum that "in all things one must consider the end" or purpose; and in defining poetry, we must keep before our eyes its "excellent purpose" (*DHP*, 6, 10). However, he rejects the idea, derived from Horace's *Ars poetica*, that the purpose of poetry is twofold, encompassing both pleasure and utility. A single art, says Tasso, cannot have two purposes which are somehow unrelated. Hence, either poetry should set aside any "useful" purpose such as instructing and content itself wholly with delighting, or "if it wishes to be useful, it should direct its pleasure to this end. It may be that pleasure directed to usefulness is the end of poetry" (*DHP*, 10). The intrinsic connection between pleasure and usefulness demanded by Tasso proves effectively to be a subordination of pleasure to usefulness, in the relation of means and end: the poet, he says, "is to set as his purpose not delight . . . but usefulness, because poetry . . . is a first philosophy which instructs us from our early years in moral habits and the principles of life." At any rate, the pleasure produced by poetry should be circumscribed by its moral purpose: "We should at least grant that the end of poetry is not just any enjoyment but only that which is coupled with virtue" (*DHP*, 11). While this may seem a far cry from Romantic and postmodernist demands that pleasure should be unshackled and unrestricted, and allowed to indulge in free play, Tasso does point out that "to aim at pleasure is nobler than to aim at profit, since enjoyment is sought for itself, and other things for its sake . . . the useful is not sought for itself but for something else; this is why it is a less noble purpose than pleasure and has less resemblance to the final purpose" (*DHP*, 11). Tasso now expands his definition to the following: "poetry is an imitation of human actions with the purpose of being useful by pleasing, and the poet is an imitator who could, as many have, use his art to delight without profiting . . . the poet is both a good man and a good imitator of human actions and moral habits, whose purpose is profit with delight" (*DHP*, 12–13).

While Tasso does not entirely dismiss the opinion of Maximus of Tyre that "philosophy and poetry are two in name but of a single substance," he suggests that what differentiates the two disciplines is their manner of considering things: "poetry considers them in as much as they are beautiful, and philosophy in as much as they are good" (*DHP*, 13). Poetry strives to reveal beauty in two ways, by narration and by representation, both of which fall under the heading of "imitation." Tasso follows Aristotle in stating that narration is the mode proper to the epic or heroic poem. He suggests a further, un-Aristotelian, difference between epic poetry and tragedy, which is a difference in "the means or instruments employed to imitate; for tragedy, in order to purge the soul, uses rhythm and harmony in addition to verse." Hence, in Tasso's formulation, epic and tragedy agree in one element, the things imitated, since both represent the "actions of heroes." They differ in the means they use to imitate, as well as in their mode of imitating (*DHP*, 14). Tasso also, however, suggests a further important difference, a difference in effect upon the audience or listener. He initially defines the heroic poem as "an imitation of an action noble, great, and perfect, narrated in the loftiest verse, with the aim of giving profit through delight." But as he acknowledges, this definition does not differentiate between various kinds of poetry, since "the end of each ought to be peculiar to it" (*DHP*, 14–15). The effect of tragedy, he says (following Aristotle), is "to purge the soul by terror and compassion." That of comedy is "to move laughter at base things." Similarly, the epic poem ought to "afford its own delight with its own effect – which is perhaps to move wonder" (*DHP*, 15). While he acknowledges that tragedy and comedy may also produce a degree of wonder, this effect is peculiarly appropriate to epic poetry, since we will gladly accept in an epic "many wonders that might be unsuitable on stage . . . because the reader allows many liberties which the spectator forbids" (*DHP*, 16). The epic poet's primary purpose, moreover, is to produce wonder, whereas this is merely an ancillary effect of other forms of poetry (*DHP*, 17). A further feature of an epic poem, according to Tasso, is that it is a "whole," with four components: the fable, or imitation of the action; the moral habit of the persons in the fable; thought; and diction (*DHP*, 18–19).

This connection of poetry with truth is taken up in detail in book II, where Tasso says that the poet can either invent the matter or content of his poem or take it from history; the latter is more creditable in Tasso's eyes, on the general ground that "truth [as opposed to fiction] provides a more suitable basis for the heroic poet," who must "pursue the verisimilar" (*DHP*, 26). The poet delights the reader with the "semblance of truth," and "seeks to persuade us that what he treats deserves belief and credit." Citing the authority of Aristotle, Tasso urges that if poets are imitators, "it is fitting that they imitate truth" (*DHP*, 27). In contrast with Mazzoni, Tasso insists that poetry "belongs under dialectic along with rhetoric . . . its function being to consider not the false but the probable. It therefore deals with the false, not in so far as it is false, but in so far as it is probable. The probable in so far as it is verisimilar belongs to the poet" (*DHP*, 29). Following Aristotle, the principal subject of the poet, says Tasso, "is what is, or may be, or is believed, or is told; or all these together" (*DHP*, 30). Tasso thus attempts to rescue poetry from the province of sophistry and to bring it back under the realm of dialectic. The poet is a maker of idols or images not in the same sense as the sophist; rather, the poet "is a maker of images in the fashion of a speaking painter, and in that is like the divine theologian who forms images and commands them to be" (*DHP*, 31). Tasso associates poetry, however, not with the scholastic theologian but with the mystical theologian: "to lead to the contemplation of divine things and thus awaken the mind with images, as the mystical theologian and the poet do, is a far nobler work than to instruct by demonstration, the function of the scholastic theologian. The mystical theologian and the poet, then, are noble beyond all others" (*DHP*, 32). In summary, the poet, although a maker of images, "resembles the dialectician and the theologian rather than the sophist" (*DHP*, 33).

Moving to the other qualities of the epic, Tasso reminds us that he has hitherto cited two essential obligations of the epic poem: to be verisimilar and to express the marvelous. Tasso gives examples of how the same actions can be viewed from one perspective as verisimilar and from another as marvelous: the actions of God and of supernatural forces are marvelous when considered from a human and natural standpoint; they will be verisimilar, however, when regarded "in terms of their agent's efficacy and power," when viewed apart from human and natural limitations (*DHP*, 38).

In book VI Tasso takes up the question of the relative merits of epic and tragedy, and of course, for him, it is the epic poem that must be accorded the higher honor. He calls the epic poem "the most beautiful of all kinds," as well as "the most magnificent"; as such, it provides its own distinctive delight, a delight produced through metaphor and the other figures of speech (*DHP*, 172, 177). Tasso sharply contrasts the ornate diction and figurativeness of the epic with the plain or low style of speech. His views are especially interesting if seen as an unwitting but prescient commentary on our own preference for plain speech and clarity, a preference embodied in our theories of composition and attributed by many thinkers to the predominating philosophies and requirements of the bourgeois world. Tasso names the "lowly form of speech" the "thin or spare" style: "This style suits slight matters; and the words should be common and ordinary, since whatever departs from common usage is magnificent. Words that are metaphorical, invented, foreign . . . are unsuitable . . . What the lowly style requires above all else is likelihood and what the Latins called *evidentia*, the Greeks energy, which we might no less properly call clarity or expressiveness. This is the power that makes us almost behold the things narrated; it comes from a minutely attentive narration that omits nothing" (*DHP*, 188–189). What these comments help us to see is that the linguistic dispositions that have sometimes been called bourgeois clarity and bourgeois realism – and even naturalism – did not arise in recent history. These modes have always been available, but only as elements of a "low" or "common" style which took its place as one level of approach to language, within a hierarchy of levels. Ascent on this hierarchy was measured precisely by departure from the "ordinary" and the mundanely likely or probable and expressiveness of detail. The approach to language, and hence the world view embodied in or enabled by language, that was integral to the later bourgeois revolutions was a reductive approach inasmuch as language was stripped of its figurative capacity, a capacity which enshrined the ability to express the present world as one element in a larger, providential, and ultimately mysterious order. The reduction to so-called "literal" language implied a world infinitely intelligible, intelligible to its very foundations on the basis of reason and experience and observation. What to Renaissance writers was the lowest common denominator in terms not just of style but of the world views implied in style became in recent history the predominant mode of expression and thought, as in the pervasiveness of realism, naturalism, and the expression of "ordinary" life.

In arguing the superiority of epic, Tasso is of course challenging the authority of Aristotle, who urged the superiority of tragedy given that it has all of the elements of epic but in greater concentration and unity. In fact, Tasso himself has recourse to the authority of Plato whom he cites as preferring epic because it relies less on extrinsic aids (such as actors). Tasso adds that inasmuch as tragedy has epic elements, it borrows these from the epic (*DHP*, 204). While Tasso concedes that tragedy is more concentrated because smaller, he urges that the epic, being larger, has greater power and gives greater pleasure, which is "true pleasure" as opposed to that offered by tragedy, which is "mingled with weeping and tears." Tasso denies that tragedy achieves its end better; it achieves this by "an oblique and tortuous road, while epic takes the direct way. For if there are two ways of improving us through example, one inciting us to good works by showing the reward of excellence and an almost divine worth, the other frightening us from evil with penalties, the first is the way of epic, the second that of tragedy, which for this reason is less useful and gives less delight" (*DHP*, 205). What is interesting here is Tasso's recognition that he is vying with the revered authority of Aristotle: he suggests that he is parting company with Aristotle in a few matters so that he "may not abandon him in things of greater moment, that is, in the desire to discover truth and in the love of philosophy" (*DHP*, 205). It is perhaps characteristic of his status as an important Renaissance theorist that Tasso builds his own theory of epic on the foundation of Aristotle's poetics by refashioning that very foundation to serve his own purpose. Where later thinkers will reject Aristotle outright, Tasso's relation to the ancient master is such that he must invoke the very authority he is called upon to subvert by his own actual poetic practice.

Defending the Vernacular: Du Bellay, Ronsard

Notwithstanding the humanist reverence for the classics, many of the most illustrious minds of the Renaissance, including such writers as Dante, Petrarch, Boccaccio, William Langland, John Gower, and Geoffrey Chaucer, wrote in the vernacular; some of these, such as Petrarch and Dante, felt called upon to theorize and defend their practice. Ironically, humanism itself had done much to undermine the authority of *grammatica* by dismantling the edifice of late medieval scholasticism and the peculiar legacy of Aristotle informing it. Much of the impetus for this self-extrication from the imperial language of Latin lay in nationalist sentiment, and the sixteenth century witnessed the growth of national literatures in several countries, notably Italy, England, France, and Germany. The Protestant Reformation not only fueled such nationalist sympathy but also fostered vernacular translations of the Bible as well as of liturgies and hymns, which in some cases laid broad foundations for the development of national languages. "National" epics were written by many of the major poets of the period, including Ariosto, Tasso, Ronsard, Spenser, and Milton.

In the case of Italy, which lacked a national language, Dante had been obliged to defend the "universal" dialect that had been used by major Italian poets. His arguments were subsequently reinforced by later writers such as Giangiorgio Trissino, Leone Battista Alberti, Pietro Bembo, who claimed that the Florentine dialect equaled Latin, and Baldassare Castiglione, who advocated the language of the court. Lorenzo Valla promoted a view of language as historically changing. Arguments in favor of the vernacular assumed a strongly nationalistic and patriotic posture in the work of the French writer Joachim Du Bellay and the English writer Roger Ascham. The cumulative effect of these endeavors was not so much to dislodge the authority of *grammatica* and Latinity as to assert an equal authority for vernacular literary culture. These writers were obliged to address issues of meter, rhyming, and versification in vernacular tongues. For a while, a number of vernacular poets attempted to imitate the quantitative meter of classical verse, whereby accent was measured by the length of syllables (rather than by stress as in the qualitative meters of vernacular poetry). Controversies also surrounded the use of rhyme. Many of these controversies can be seen in the work of Du Bellay and Ronsard.

Joachim Du Bellay (ca. 1522–1560)

Like Dante, who undertook to defend the virtues of his Italian vernacular language as against Latin, Joachim Du Bellay engaged in a sustained defense of his French vernacular. His motivation for this came when, having initially studied law at Poitiers, he was influenced by his friend Pierre de Ronsard to study at the Collège de Coqueret in Paris. This college was molded by its master, Jean Dorat, into a center of humanist learning and radical poetics. The students there formed themselves into a group known as the Pléiade, named after the constellation of seven stars: the seven poets were Dorat himself, Du Bellay, Ronsard, Etienne Jodelle, Jean-Antoine de Baïf, Pontus de Tyard, and Rémi Belleau. At that time Latin was the official language of the court, of scholarship, and of poetry, whereas the French vernacular was the idiom of the masses and of popular forms of entertainment.

Du Bellay's *Defence and Illustration of the French Language* (1549) was written as a response to a pamphlet published in 1548 that had urged the equality of French popular poetry with Latin verse. Du Bellay and his colleagues adopted a somewhat different stance: they wished indeed to defend and justify the use of the French vernacular, but by lifting it above its popular forms and basing it upon a new poetics such that it could match the gravity and decorum of the classical Greek and Latin languages.

Du Bellay begins his *Defence* by pointing out that languages are not somehow spontaneous products of nature but rather of the "desire and will of mortals" (281).[9] He acknowledges that some languages have indeed become richer than others; however, the reason for this is not the intrinsic virtue of those languages but the "artifice and industry of men." His basic purpose in this treatise is to show that the French vernacular is not "incapable of good letters and erudition" (282). In response to the charge that the French language is "barbarous," Du Bellay enlists two arguments, both of which highlight the nationalistic nature of his enterprise. To begin with, the appellation "barbarous" rests on no legitimate authority or privilege but is entirely relative: the Greeks in their arrogance called all other nations barbarous; yet "this Greek arrogance, admiring only its own inventions, had neither law nor privilege to legitimize its own nation and bastardize all the others" (282). The Greeks may have thought of the Scythians as barbarous, but they themselves were considered barbarians among the Scythians. And modern French culture, he affirms, is now in every respect the equal of Greek culture. In their turn the Romans did the same thing: Roman imperialism "sought not only to subjugate but to render other nations vile and abject" (282). In this context, Du Bellay raises the issue of historiography: the deeds of the Roman people are remembered and celebrated because of the distorted writing of history by numerous Roman writers who also conspired to neglect the "warlike glory" of the Gauls (283). Hence, the degradation of the French language is deeply rooted in a history of imperialism, not only in the military subjugation of other nations but also in their cultural and linguistic subjugation in fields such as historiography and literature. Du Bellay points out that the term "barbarous" is applied to a people's language and culture by its "enemies and by those who had no right to give us this name" (283).

If the French language is currently in an impoverished state, argues Du Bellay, this is not because of any intrinsic defects but rather due "to the ignorance of our ancestors" who chose to cultivate noble actions rather than words (283). The Greeks and Romans were "more diligent in the cultivation of their languages" (284). Du Bellay observes that the French tongue has at last begun to flower but has not yet "borne all the fruit that it might well produce" (283). He expresses the hope – no less political than cultural – that "when this noble and puissant kingdom will in its turn obtain the reins of sovereignty," the French language may "rise to such height and greatness, that it can equal the Greeks themselves and the Romans" (284). Again, Du Bellay's text clearly connects cultural greatness with political and economic power.

Having said all this, Du Bellay is adamant that the French language is not in such a poor state as admirers of foreign languages (Greek and Latin) allege. Commenting on the numerous translations into French in the 1530s and 1540s of ancient Greek and Roman texts, he observes that the French language is at least "a faithful interpreter of all others." The numerous French translations of foreign texts from many disciplines prove that "all sciences can faithfully and copiously be treated" in French. In another political gesture, Du Bellay praises Francis I, the late king of France, who has "restored all the good arts and sciences in their ancient dignity" and has promoted the elegance of the French language (285). However, while translation is a "praiseworthy labour," it will not suffice to elevate the French tongue to the height of its potential. Du Bellay lists the five parts or "offices" of rhetoric as established by ancient writers: invention, elocution, arrangement, memory, and pronunciation. The last three of these, he says, will depend on the speaker and his particular circumstances. Of the first two offices, invention can indeed be aided by translation. If invention is the ability to speak copiously of all things, this facility can be acquired "only by the perfect understanding of the sciences, which were first treated by the Greeks, and next by the Romans, imitators of them." Hence Greek and Latin must "be understood by him who would acquire this copiousness and richness of invention" (285). To this end, and up to this point, translation is useful. However, in the most important aspect of a speech – elocution or style – translation cannot help. Style depends on figures of speech, such as allegory, comparison, and similes, which depend on the "common usage of speech." And since "each language has a something proper to itself alone," in other words, a character and expressions that cannot be translated into other tongues, the virtues of elocution must be developed from within a given language; they cannot be imported from other languages (286). Hence, French writers must engage not only in translation but also in imitation of classical poets and forms. While the Romans indeed enriched their language by imitating Greek authors, they imitated the best writers and managed to enrich their own language by grafting their borrowings and applying them to their own tongue (287).

In like manner, Du Bellay calls upon French writers to imitate the good Greek and Roman authors, urging upon them the Horatian precepts of the need to labor over art, to exercise great discretion in the choice of which writers to imitate, and to know their own capacities (288–289). In a lengthy apostrophe to the future French poet, Du Bellay calls upon him to leave behind all popular verse forms and songs; to "turn the leaves of your Greek and Latin exemplars"; and, following Horace, to "mingle the profitable with the agreeable." He entreats and advises this future poet: "Sing me those odes, unknown as yet of the French muse, on a lute well-accorded to the sound of the Greek and Roman lyre, and let there be no line wherein appeareth not some vestige of rare and ancient erudition." For his subject matter, the poet should take praises of the gods and virtuous men, and the "immutable order of earthly things." Above all, he admonishes the poet to make his creations "far removed from the vulgar, enriched and made illustrious with proper words and epithets by no means idle, adorned with grave sentences, and varied with all manner of poetical colours and ornaments" (289). He encourages the poet to revive some of the verse forms of the ancients, such as heroic verse, eleven-syllable lines or hendecasyllables, and eclogues, and to restore both comedy and tragedy – currently usurped by farces and morality plays – to their ancient dignity. All the "archetypes" for the adorning of the French language will be found in the ancient authors (290).

In some ways, Du Bellay's message is deeply conservative and traditional. While he calls for a renovation and enrichment of French language and literature, his vision of such elevation is focused entirely on a return to the classics, not to be used for slavish imitation but rather as a perpetual resource for replenishment. His call is essentially a call for classical seriousness, gravity, command of form, and a deployment of poetic devices as catalogued by the ancient rhetoricians. The only novel feature of his vision is the insistence that, by returning to the resources and archetypes of the classical languages, the French language might fulfill its potential to displace them and dislodge them from their positions of cultural sovereignty. Together with Ronsard and other members of the Pléiade, Du Bellay helped inaugurate a new era of French poetry.

Pierre de Ronsard (1524–1585)

Like his friend and distant cousin Joachim Du Bellay, Pierre de Ronsard eventually studied under the supervision of the Hellenist Jean Dorat at the Collège de Coqueret in Paris, an institution that housed a nucleus of seven poets known as the Pléiade. This group, engaged in intense study of Greek and Latin poetry, was dedicated to a renewal of French poetry and language based on imitation and adaptation of classical models.

Ronsard came from a Catholic and noble family which had close connections with the royal court in France. His father worked for King Francis I, and he himself served as page to the royal prince Charles. While his family promoted the ideals of Renaissance scholarship and poetry, Ronsard, himself a member of the clergy, was a staunch defender of Catholicism, in an era of violent religious strife in France. He was opposed especially to the more puritanical forms of Protestantism which decried imitation of the pagan classics. Indeed, Ronsard is best known for his sonnets which, in the tradition of Plotinus and subsequent Neo-Platonism, bring into coexistence elements from both Christian theology and classical pagan philosophy. In accordance with the literary ideals of the Pléiade, he wrote in French but imitated classical and Italian verse forms. His poetic output included four books of *Odes* (1550), a collection of sonnets, *Les Amours de Cassandre* (1552), and an unfinished epic based on Vergil's *Aeneid* entitled the *Franciade* (1572), as well as his renowned *Sonnets to Helene* (1578).

Ronsard's "A Brief on the Art of French Poetry" was published in 1565. Like Horace's *Ars poetica*, this brief takes the form of a letter offering advice to a young poet, in this case a young nobleman, Alphonse Delbene. In this brief essay, Ronsard begins with a somewhat radical claim: the art of poetry "can be neither learned nor taught by precept, it being a thing more experiential than traditional."[10] In other words, the very nerve of poetry derives from the author's experience of life. Ronsard encourages the young poet to "frequent the practitioners of all trades, seamanship, hunting, falconry, . . . goldsmiths, foundrymen, blacksmiths, metallurgists." From such broad experience, the poet will be able to "store up many good and lively semblances" in order to "enrich and beautify" his work. This experience of life will provide him with the material needed for "excellent inventions, descriptions and comparisons," which will give charm and perfection to poetry, enabling it to be universal and "victorious over time" (182).

This apparently radical strain, in Ronsard's emphasis on experience as opposed to tradition, is somewhat counterbalanced by his vision of the theological origin and infrastructure of poetry, and its consequently intrinsic spiritual and moral function. This theological foundation appears to derive from Plotinus. It was through the classical Muses, says Ronsard, that God, "in his sacred grace . . . made known to ignorant peoples the excellence of his majesty. For poetry was in the earliest time only an allegorical theology, to carry into men's coarse brains, by charming and prettily colored fables, the secret truths which they could not comprehend if openly declared" (179). Like the medieval rhetoricians and poetic theorists, Ronsard sees poetry in its origins as intrinsically allegorical and as overlapping heavily with the offices of theology. At this early stage, says Ronsard in terms reminiscent of Plotinus, poets were called divine on account of their "god-like soul": they were in communion with "oracles, prophets, diviners, sibyls, interpreters of dreams," amplifying with color and commentary their prophetic utterances. What the prophets and sibyls were to the poets, the poets were to ordinary people. Hence the function of poetry was effectively to expound and translate into an accessible idiom the cryptic sayings of the divines. However, unlike most of his medieval predecessors, Ronsard sees later poetry as emerging from this intrinsic allegorical and theological function into a more humanistic mode: a "second school" of poets emerged during the days of Roman predominance, who were "human, as being more filled with artifice and labor, than with divine inspiration" (180).

This secular development is one that Ronsard, true to the belief of the Pléiade poets in the divine inspiration of poetry, does not welcome. His advice to the poet effectively calls for a return to the earlier theological foundation. The Muses, he says, are "not willing to reside in a soul unless it be kindly, saintly, virtuous . . . let nothing enter your soul which is not superhuman, divine. You are to bear in highest regard conceptions which are elevated, grand, beautiful – not those that lie around the earth. For the principal thing is invention, which comes as much from goodness of nature as from the lessons of the good ancient authors" (180). Again, we seem to hear the voice of Plotinus behind these words. What in Plotinus was general advice to all human beings is here transmuted into the special privilege and obligation of the poet. Plotinus admonished that only by casting aside the interests of the material earthly realm could the soul hope to sustain its journey toward the vision of the One or supreme God; for Ronsard, such elevation of oneself above earthly concerns is the paramount duty of the poet, a duty difficult to reconcile with Ronsard's earlier advice that the poet experience a broad spectrum of worldly affairs. Ronsard's strategy might be seen as effectively aestheticizing Plotinus' view of the ascent to God: Plotinus indeed saw the attractions of divine beauty as integral in this ascent, but Ronsard views the poet as the indispensable guide.

After urging this cleansing and upward orientation of the soul, Ronsard offers more worldly, Horatian, advice to the poet: he must study the works of the "good poets"; he must "correct and file" his verses; he must offer his work up to the scrutiny of fellow poets and friends; and obey the particular laws of French prosody. In a further respect, Ronsard's advice is radical: the language of poetry should not be restricted, as it often is by reliance on patronage, to the idiom of the court, but it should be enriched by selective appropriation from the numerous dialects of the provinces (182).

The remainder of Ronsard's "Brief" deals with three of the conventional offices of rhetoric, namely, invention, disposition, and arrangement, as well as French phonetics and various aspects of French grammar and verse. The aim of the poet, he says, is to "imitate, invent, and represent – things which are, or which may be – in a resemblance to truth" (183). This is a somewhat elliptical formulation of the poet's task: the poet may imitate or represent things which already exist, which already stand in "resemblance to truth"; but beyond simply imitating, he can also *invent* things that *may* hold such resemblance; what seems to be invoked elliptically here is the Aristotelian requirement of probability, whereby the poet is obliged to present not necessarily any actual truth about the world but something which, being probable, exhibits a resemblance to truth. Hence the poet can invent as well as imitate: he need not be tied to the real world. Indeed, Ronsard was later held up by the Romantics as a pioneer of freer verse forms. Yet the classical constraint of probability effectively limits what Ronsard's view of invention can encompass: in contrast with some of the Romantics, he insists that inventions should be "well-ordered and appointed"; they should not be "fantastic and melancholy," since such creations are like the "broken dreams of one in a frenzy," and are the products of "an imagination bruised or injured" (183).

Indeed, Ronsard is even more insistent on this point when he turns to the office of "disposition" or arrangement of one's material. Disposition, depending upon sound invention, consists in "an elegant and consummate placing and ordering of the things invented; it does not permit what appertains to one place to be put in another, but, operating by artifice, study, and application, it disposes and sets each matter to its proper point" (183). Again, the terms – "order," "proper," "application" – are profoundly classical and conservative. Notwithstanding his belief in the divine inspiration of poetry, Ronsard, like Aristotle and Horace, clearly views the poetic process as a rational and studied procedure (184).

Ronsard defines the third rhetorical office, elocution or style, as comprising "a propriety and splendor of words, properly chosen and adorned." A poem will shine "in proportion as the words be significant, and chosen with judgment" (184). But again, Ronsard's view of style is constrained by a need to return to the classics: the poet must guide himself in these elements of style "by imitation of Homer" (184). Again, there is an uneasy balance here: on the one hand, the poet must submit to ancient precedent; on the other, he must draw on life itself, on experience. With the Romantics, this classical equilibrium, precarious in Ronsard's text, was tilted heavily in favor of experience and sanctioned by a far more radical conception of imagination.

Poetics and the Defense of Poetry: Sidney

The defense of poetry, as seen in the previous chapter, had been undertaken aggressively by Boccaccio in his *Genealogy of the Gentile Gods*. Following Boccaccio's endeavor, notable manifestoes or defenses of poetry were undertaken by writers such as Joachim Du Bellay and Sir Philip Sidney. Such apologiae and defenses have been obliged to continue through the nineteenth century into our own day, highlighting the fact that the category of the "aesthetic," as a domain struggling to free itself from the constraints of theology, morality, politics, philosophy, and history, was in part a result of Renaissance poetics. The revival of Neo-Platonism, mentioned above, being in part a reaction against Aristotelian formalism, was instrumental in many of the early modern defenses, which argued that literature and specifically poetry was divinely inspired and created a world superior to the realm of nature.

Also integral to many of these defenses of poetry was a formula deriving from Horace: the function of poetry, according to the Roman poet, was "aut prodesse volunt aut delectare poetae / aut simul et iucunda et idonea dicere vitae" (*Ars poetica*, ll. 333–334; "Poets wish either to benefit or to delight or to say things that are both pleasing and apply to life"). Matz has deftly argued that the two aims of poetry prescribed here by Horace, first as alternatives and in the subsequent clause as a combination, were designed to satisfy two constituencies in the ancient Roman world, the cultured Greek-speaking elite and the more utilitarian-minded middle classes. This powerful Horatian formula, appealing to both pleasure and profit, both leisure and labor, was redeployed by Sidney and other Renaissance writers as an ideological instrument in advancing conflicting notions of the role of the aristocracy and of aristocratic conduct. These notions of aristocracy reciprocally influenced the definitions of poetry. A claim for the pleasure and profit of humanist study underlay Thomas Elyot's attempt to reform the conception of the aristocracy, from "a warrior and courtly elite into an intellectual and administrative" one, representing the upwardly mobile and industrious "new man." George Puttenham, as will be seen, urged that rhetorical skills were necessary for court, and courtiers saw humanist rhetoric as a means of access toward their objectives of privilege and power. In Sidney's case, the Horatian formula – couched as "delightful teaching" – was enlisted in his literary-critical and ideological response to his own ambiguous social status as both courtly and Protestant aristocrat. On the one hand Sidney defended the courtly pleasure of poetry as promoting warrior service. But, aware that the newly emerging intellectual and bureaucrat class had somewhat displaced the warrior class in importance in the absolutist state, Sidney (like many aristocrats bent on preserving their status as against the rising class of "new men" in the absolutist state) adopted humanist and Protestant conceptions of aristocratic function, urging these as sources of political and cultural authority (Matz, 17–19, 21–22). But, while adopting the humanist ideals of self-discipline, industry, and intellectual profit, the aristocracy demonstrated their status and their difference from the subordinate class through their access to pleasure.

Both of these emphases are reflected in Sidney's defense of poetry which, like aristocratic ideology, advanced alternative forms of social authority without relinquishing the previous ones. Matz argues that this dual function of poetry is also utilized by Edmund Spenser, who claimed that "the pleasure of poetry . . . inculcates forms of profitable pleasure." In doing this, Spenser helped "to organize the distinction between poetic and courtly pleasures," paving the way for "the appearance of the category of the aesthetic in a newly organized distinction between elevated poetic pleasures and stigmatized material ones." The crucial point here is that Horatian poetics were integrally involved in "a clash of cultural values" and in the attempt "to create poetry as a distinct and distinctive aesthetic pleasure" (Matz, 22). Another way of approaching this phenomenon – the incipient emergence of the aesthetic as a relatively autonomous realm – would be to recognize poetry's increasing extrication from surrounding spheres, such as rhetorical theory (much of which had been absorbed by poetics), logic, and theology. Some of these tendencies can now be analyzed in Sidney's work.

Sir Philip Sidney (1554–1586)

Sir Philip Sidney is often cited as an archetype of the well-rounded "Renaissance man": his talents were multifold, encompassing not only poetry and cultivated learning but also the virtues of statesmanship and military service. He was born into an aristocratic family, was eventually knighted, and held government appointments which included the governorship of Flushing in the Netherlands. He was involved in war waged by Queen Elizabeth I against Spain and died from a wound at the age of 32. His friends included the poet Edmund Spenser; he wrote a pastoral romance, *The Countess of Pembroke's Arcadia* (1581), and he was original in producing a sonnet cycle in the English language, influenced by the Italian poet Petrarch, entitled *Astrophil and Stella* (1581–1582).

Sidney's *Apologie for Poetrie* (1580–1581) is in many ways a seminal text of literary criticism. It is not only a defense but also one of the most acclaimed treatises on poetics of its time. While its ideas are not original, it represents the first synthesis in the English language of the various strands and concerns of Renaissance literary criticism, drawing on Aristotle, Horace, and more recent writers such as Boccaccio and Julius Caesar Scaliger. It raises issues – such as the value and function of poetry, the nature of imitation, and the concept of nature – which were to concern literary critics in numerous languages until the late eighteenth century. Sidney's writing of the *Apologie* as a defense of poetry was occasioned by an attack on poetry entitled *The School of Abuse* published in 1579 by a Puritan minister, Stephen Gosson. As mentioned earlier, Sidney rejects Gosson's Protestant attack on courtly pleasure, effectively defending poetry as a virtuous activity for the aristocracy (Matz, 22).

Toward the beginning of the *Apologie*, Sidney observes that poetry has fallen from its status as "the highest estimation of learning . . . to be the laughingstock of children."[11] He produces a wide range of arguments in defense of "poor Poetry," based on chronology, the authority of ancient tradition, the relation of poetry to nature, the function of poetry as imitation, the status of poetry among the various disciplines of learning, and the relationship of poetry to truth and morality. Sidney's initial argument is that poetry was the first form in which knowledge was expressed, the "first light-giver to ignorance," as bodied forth by figures such as Musaeus, Homer, and Hesiod, Livius, Ennius, Dante, Boccaccio, and Petrarch (216–217). And the first Greek philosophers Thales, Empedocles, Parmenides, and Pythagoras, he points out, expressed their vision in verse. Even Plato used poetic devices such as dialogue and description of setting and circumstance to adorn his philosophy (217). Again, historians such as Herodotus have borrowed the "fashion" and the "weight" of poetry. Sidney concludes here that "neither philosopher nor historiographer, could at the first have entered into the gates of popular judgments, if they had not taken a great passport of poetry" (218). His point is that an essential prerequisite of knowledge is pleasure in learning; and it is poetry that has made each of these varieties of knowledge – scientific, moral, philosophical, political – accessible by expressing them in pleasurable forms (218).

Sidney's second argument might be called the "argument from tradition" since it appeals to the ancient Roman and Greek conceptions of poetry and "stands upon their authorities" (219). The Roman term for the poet was *vates*, meaning "diviner, fore-seer, or prophet, . . . so heavenly a title did that excellent people bestow upon this heart-ravishing knowledge" (219). Sidney argues that this definition of the poet was quite "reasonable," as shown by the fact that the Psalms of David are a "divine poem," whereby prophecy is expressed in a poetic manner. Hence poetry does not deserve the "ridiculous . . . estimation" into which it has lapsed, and "deserveth not to be scourged out of the Church of God" (220).

The ancient Greek definition of poetry is even more important for Sidney, providing access into his own view of the connection between poetry and nature. Sidney reminds the reader that the Greek origin of the English word "poet" was the word *poiein*, meaning "to make" (220). Every art, says Sidney, has "the works of Nature" for its "principal object": the astronomer, for example, observes the stars as ordered in nature, and the geometrician and arithmetician examine quantities as ordered in nature; the natural philosopher examines physical nature, and the moral philosopher considers the natural virtues and vices; the grammarian, rhetorician, and logician expound respectively the rules of speech, persuasion, and reasoning as based on nature. Sidney names here all of the elements of the medieval trivium, quadrivium, and more. His point is that each of these disciplines *depends* on some aspect of nature, which furnishes the ground of its exploration. The poet, however, is free of any such subjection or dependence on nature: "only the poet, disdaining to be tied to any such subjection, lifted up with the vigor of his own invention, doth grow in effect into another Nature, in making things either better than Nature bringeth forth, or, quite anew forms such as never were in Nature, as the Heros, Demigods, Cyclops." Rather than being constrained within the "narrow" compass of nature, the poet ranges freely "only within the zodiac of his own wit" (221). As such, the poet's "making" or production is superior to nature: "Nature never set forth the earth in so rich tapestry, as divers poets have done . . . Her world is brazen, the poets only deliver a golden" (221).

Sidney is careful to situate this human creativity in a theological context. Though man is a "maker" or poet, his ability derives from his "heavenly Maker . . . who having made man to his own likeness, set him beyond and over all the works of that second nature, which in nothing he showeth so much as in poetry: when with the force of a divine breath, he bringeth things forth far surpassing her doings" (222). Sidney goes on to refer to original sin, as a result of which "our erected wit, maketh us know what perfection is, and yet our infected will, keepeth us from reaching unto it" (222). Significant here is the intrinsic connection Sidney attempts to establish between man's ability to "make" poetry and his status in relation to God. That man is made in the image of God is most profoundly expressed in man's replication, on a lower level, of God's function as a creator. It also implies that man is elevated above the world of physical nature (which Sidney calls "second nature"). This God-like activity in man which exalts him above the rest of nature is expressed above all in poetry; it is poetry, too, in its exercise of "wit," that allows us to glimpse perfection, even as our will, "infected" by original sin, prevents us from achieving it. This ultimately theological aim of poetry is elaborated later in Sidney's text.

It is clear that if, for Sidney, poetry is higher than nature, his conception of poetry as imitation does not imply a slavish copying of nature. He states that poetry "is an art of imitation, for so Aristotle termeth it in his word *mimesis*, that is to say, a representing, counterfeiting, or figuring forth: to speak metaphorically, a speaking picture: with this end, to teach and delight" (223). In this definition, Sidney adapts elements from

Aristotle and Horace to offer his own somewhat broader view of imitation. He suggests that there have been three kinds of poetic imitation. The first consists of poetry that "did imitate the inconceivable excellencies of God," as in the various poetical portions of the Old Testament. The second kind of imitation is effected by poetry that deals with subjects whose scope is philosophical, historical, or scientific, such as the works of Cato, Lucretius, Manilius, or Lucan (223). This kind, Sidney observes, is determined by its field of study, being "wrapped within the fold of the proposed subject," rather than relying on the poet's "own invention" (224). It is the final kind of imitation proposed by Sidney that lifts it free of the constraints imposed by Aristotle. This third kind, urges Sidney, is produced by "right poets . . . who having no law but wit, bestow that in colors upon you which is fittest for the eye to see." These are the poets who "most properly do imitate to teach and delight, and to imitate, borrow nothing of what is, hath been, or shall be: but range only . . . into the divine consideration of what may be, and should be" (224). Hence the poet is free of dependence on nature in at least two ways: firstly, he is not restricted to any given subject matter, any given sphere of nature. Secondly, his "imitation" does not actually reproduce anything in nature, since his concern is not with actuality but with portrayals of probability and of idealized situations.

The ultimate aim of this kind of poetry is moral: the poet imitates, says Sidney, in order "both to delight and teach." The object of both teaching and delighting is goodness: by delighting, the poet moves people to welcome goodness; and by teaching, he enables them to "know that goodness whereunto they are moved." And this, says Sidney, is "the noblest scope to which ever any learning was directed" (224). Given these aims of poetry, it is not surprising that Sidney relegates "rhyming and versing" to the status of ornaments: it is not these which produce a poet but, rather, the "feigning notable images of virtues, vices, . . . with . . . delightful teaching" (225). However, Sidney sees all learning, and not just poetry, as directed to this final end or purpose: "to lead and draw us to as high a perfection, as our degenerate souls made worse by their clayey lodgings, can be capable of" (225). All the spheres of learning, he states, endeavor "by knowledge to lift up the mind from the dungeon of the body, to the enjoying of his own divine essence" (226). While each of the sciences have "a private end in themselves," they are nonetheless all directed "to the highest end." And the "ending end of all earthly learning" is "virtuous action" (226). Many of these statements could have been made by Hugh of St. Victor, Geoffrey de Vinsauf, and many other medieval writers. What is interesting here is that Sidney's invocation of a theological framework of learning is characteristically medieval; what is distinctly more modern and characteristic of the Renaissance is his alteration of the medieval hierarchy of disciplines, to place poetry at the apex.

Indeed, Sidney's invocation of the ultimate aim of learning itself has an ulterior purpose: to establish poetry as the discipline most suited to this purpose. The poet's chief competitors in this regard, thinks Sidney, will be the moral philosopher and the historian. The former will claim that his path to virtue is the most direct since he will teach what virtue and vice are, how passion must be mastered, and how the domain of virtue extends into family and society (227). The historian, on the other hand, will claim that moral philosophers merely teach virtue "by certain abstract considerations," whereas his own discipline, history, will offer concrete examples of virtue based on the "experience of many ages" (227). Sidney cites a third possible contender for this office of teaching virtue, the lawyer. But he rapidly dismisses the lawyer's claim, since the lawyer "doth not endeavor to make men good, but that their evil hurt not others." The lawyer merely imposes upon people to follow the outward form of virtue without changing their inward disposition (228). Sidney summarizes the dispute between the moral philosopher and the historian by saying respectively that "the one giveth the precept, and the other the example" (228). Since both disciplines are thus one-sided, they are both deficient: the philosopher sets down the "bare rule" in difficult terms that are "abstract and general"; the historian, conversely, lacks the force of generalization and is "tied, not to what should be, but to what is, to the particular truth of things" (229). Indeed, since the historian is "captived to the truth of a foolish world," the lessons he is bound to impart will often be negative, showing in some cases how the wicked thrive and prosper (234).

It is the "peerless poet," according to Sidney, who performs both functions: "he coupleth the general notion with the particular example." The poet paints a "perfect picture" of the philosopher's abstract insight, providing an image of what in philosophy is merely a "wordish description" (229). It is poetry which can strike the soul and the inward sentiments by means of "a true lively knowledge." The philosopher's declarations remain dark "if they be not illuminated or figured forth by the speaking picture of poesy" (230). It is poetry which brings to life all the virtues, vices, and passions, and hence the "feigned images" of poetry have "more force in teaching" than the "regular instruction" of philosophy (231). And, whereas the philosopher teaches "obscurely" such that only learned people can understand him, the "poet is the food for the tenderest stomachs, the poet is indeed the right popular philosopher," as shown by Aesop's fables, which use accessible allegories (231). The power of poetry to move or influence people, says Sidney, "is of a higher degree than teaching . . . it is well nigh the cause and the effect of teaching" (236). For people to be taught, they must first be filled with desire to learn: citing Aristotle's dictum that the fruit of learning must not be merely *gnosis* (knowing) but *praxis* (doing), Sidney holds that poetry inspires people to *perform* what philosophy merely teaches in the abstract (236). Both Plato and Boethius, claims Sidney, were well aware of the power of poetry, and "therefore made mistress philosophy, very often borrow the masking raiment of poesy" (238).

As for the poet's superiority over the historian, Sidney appeals to Aristotle's statement that "poetry is *philosophoteron* and *spoudaioteron*, that is to say, it is more philosophical, and more studiously serious, than history" (232). Sidney cites Aristotle's view that poetry deals with the *kathalou* or universal, whereas history concerns the *kathekaston*, the particular; the particular is constrained by what actually happened, whereas the universal comprehends actions or words which are appropriate in terms of probability or necessity (232). Sidney even argues that a fictional presentation of a character as he "should be" is preferable to a portrayal of the actual historical character in his imperfection. A "feigned example," he says, has "as much force to teach, as a true example" (233). Since the historian is tied to reality, he is not at liberty to present the ideal pattern of people or events, whereas the poet can "frame his example to that which is most reasonable" (233). Moreover, whatever the historian can relate in terms of true events, the poet can make by his own imitation, "beautifying it both for further teaching, and more delighting, . . . having all . . . under the authority of his pen" (234).

The emphasis here is on the poet's freedom, which allows him to choose his material, to frame it in an ideal pattern, so that he can present virtue "in her best colors," setting out his words "in delightful proportion" (234, 237). For all of these reasons, proclaims Sidney, we must set "the laurel crown upon the poet as victorious, not only of the historian, but over the philosopher" (235). Sidney's tone is repeatedly triumphalistic and persistent in attempting to overturn the conventional hierarchy of knowledge: "of all sciences . . . is our poet the monarch" (236). The irony here is that Sidney uses a theological justification for poetry to dethrone theology and philosophy from their preeminent status. Another reading of his procedure might be to say that, by imbuing poetry itself with a theological function, he furnishes the terms whereby theology might be displaced by poetry. It is poetry which most effectively disposes man to overcome his own lower nature, thereby offering access into the divine: "as virtue is the most excellent resting place for all worldly learning . . . so poetry, being the most familiar to teach it, and most princely to move towards it . . . is the most excellent workman" (239). And yet, for poetry to assume the "monarchy" of learning undermines the very theological framework to which this claim appeals: it is unmistakably a step in the direction of secular humanism.

Sidney now undertakes a defense of the various genres of poetry that shows clearly the moral and theological functions he assigns to this art. Sidney considers heroic poetry to be the "best, and most accomplished kind of poetry" since it both "instructeth the mind" and "most inflameth the mind with desire to be worthy" (244). The function of poetry for Sidney, as manifested in these comments, is three-fold: to teach people the substance of virtue; to move people to virtuous action; and, underlying these two functions, to impress upon people the transitory and worthless nature of worldly affairs. The poet is historian and moral philosopher, but above all, preacher and theologian.

Sidney now addresses the specific charges brought against poetry. The first is that there are other kinds of knowledge more fruitful than poetry. Sidney states that the greatest gifts bestowed upon human beings are *oratio* and *ratio*, speech and reason. It is poetry which most polishes the gift of speech, and it "far exceedeth prose" on two accounts: it engenders delight because of its meticulous ordering of words, and therefore it is memorable. Since knowledge depends on memory, poetry has an affinity with knowledge (246–247). Moreover, since poetry "teacheth and moveth to virtue," there can be no "more fruitful knowledge" than this (248). The second charge is that poetry "is the mother of lies" (247). Sidney's famous retort is that "the poet . . . nothing affirms, and therefore never lieth" (248). Unlike the historian, the poet does not claim to be telling the truth; he is not relating "what is, or is not, but what should or should not be." He is writing "not affirmatively, but allegorically, and figuratively" (249). The next objection to poetry is that it "abuseth men's wit, training it to wanton sinfulness, and lustful love" (250). The fault here, says Sidney, is with particular poets who have abused their art, not with the art itself. It is not that "poetry abuseth man's wit, but that, man's wit abuseth poetry" (250). Even the word of God, says Sidney, when abused, can breed heresy and blasphemy (251).

The final, and perhaps most serious, charge that Sidney confronts is that Plato banished poets from his ideal republic, some claiming that, as a philosopher, Plato was "a natural enemy of poets" (253). Sidney suggests that Plato opposed the abuse of poetry rather than the art itself: he charged the poets of his day with promulgating false opinions of the gods which might corrupt the youth (255). The dangers of such false belief have now been removed by Christianity. Sidney also cites Plato's dialogue *Ion* as giving a "divine commendation to poetry," viewing poetry as inspired by "a divine force, far above man's wit" (255–256). He also cites the authority of many great figures who admired poetry, including Aristotle, Alexander, Plutarch, and Caesar (256).

Sidney ends his text with a lamentation, rather than an inquiry, over the impoverished state to which poetry has declined in England. Poetry has become the province of "base men, with servile wits" (258). While he acknowledges that poetry is a "divine gift" and dependent on genius, Sidney bemoans the fact that these would-be poets ignore the need to labor at their craft, a craft whose principles must be "art, imitation, and exercise" (i.e., genius, imitation of the models of earlier writers, and practice) (259). He concludes by admonishing the reader no more to scorn this sacred art, reminding him of his earlier arguments and the various authorities he has invoked. He entreats the reader to believe that "there are many mysteries contained in poetry, which of purpose were written darkly, least by profane wits, it should be abused" (269). And he curses those who are possessed of "so earth-creeping a mind, that it cannot lift itself up, to look to the sky of poetry" (270). The metaphor here truly encapsulates the entire thrust of Sidney's text. Formerly, sacred scripture was spoken of in this fashion, as written "darkly," so as to lie beyond the reach of unworthy eyes; in Sidney's text, poetry is elevated to that sacred status: in its very nature it is opposed to worldliness and "earth-creeping" concerns; it is the newly appointed heaven of human invention and endeavor.

Poetic Form and Rhetoric: Gascoigne, Puttenham

During the Renaissance, rhetoric – or at least rhetorical theory – enjoyed a renewed centrality in educational institutions. Drawing on Quintilian and on Cicero's mature work, Renaissance writers first focused on strategies of invention, and then on style. This new emphasis was partly fueled by the increasing displacement of Latin by vernacular languages which were in their turn subjected to stylistic analysis. The domains of poetics and rhetoric increasingly overlapped, as did the procedures for analyzing poetry and prose, and the conceptions of poet and orator. Poetry and prose were both seen to share the aims of persuasion, and, sometimes, of praising and blaming. The rhetorical curriculum entailed practice in various kinds of speeches in imagined and real circumstances, urging the speaker to assume a persona and to consider ways in which certain responses could be induced in an audience. Theorists and apologists of poetry such as Vida, Minturno, Scaliger, and Sidney effectively treated poetry as a higher form of rhetoric, drawing on Cicero and Quintilian, as well as incorporating insights from Aristotle concerning imitation and arguing along Horatian lines that the function of poetry was to teach and delight. An important dimension of poetry for these writers, taken over from rhetorical theory, was persuasiveness and the power to move an audience or reader.

George Puttenham's *The Arte of English Poesie* (1589) was based on rhetorical analysis of style; writers such as Du Bellay and Ronsard also offered a rhetorical treatment of poetry. While poetics had overlapped increasingly with rhetoric, the recovery of Aristotle's *Poetics* fostered a new examination of literary form and organic unity that was not wholly grounded in rhetoric, which had distinguished between the form and content of a poem. Indeed, one of the legacies of the Renaissance that has endured until today lay in the fact that the scope of poetics was broadened well beyond the constraining boundaries of rhetoric to encompass moral philosophy, metaphysics, science, and political thought. The central figures in this process of broadening and integration included Marco Giralamo Vida, whose *De arte poetica* (*The Art of Poetry*, 1527) integrated insights from the Horatian tradition and rhetorical treatment of invention and style with humanist notions of the genres and moral function of poetry, and Julius Caesar Scaliger, whose *Poetices libri septem* (*Seven Books of Poetics*, 1561) elaborated a highly influential account of literary criticism as an independent sphere with its own methods.

As seen earlier, vernacular poetic theory had been developed by writers such as Trissino in Italy and Du Bellay in France. The growth of the vernacular, along with the foregoing developments, fueled a number of problems of poetic form, concerning issues such as meter and rhyme. In returning to classical precedents, Renaissance poets rejected the regular stress-based alliterative meter of medieval poets. Some experimented with the idea of introducing classical quantitative meters, based on length of syllables rather than stress, into vernacular languages. In general, the humanists rejected rhyme as an unclassical barbarism; the controversy over rhyme was salient in the debate between Samuel Daniel, who wrote a *Defence of Rhyme* (1603), and Thomas Campion, who rejected rhyme in favor of classical forms. The aversion to rhyme on the part of figures such as William Webbe and George Puttenham, who went so far as to affiliate the use of rhyme with a Roman Catholic mentality, led to the search for a new metrical basis for English poetry and eventually stimulated the growth of blank verse. These tendencies can now be explored as they occurred on the English literary scene in the work of Gascoigne and Puttenham.

George Gascoigne (1542–1577)

The poet and dramatist George Gascoigne is credited with having written the first literary-critical essay in the English language, entitled "Certayne Notes of Instruction concerning the making of verse or ryme in English." This essay appeared in a collection of Gascoigne's works entitled *The Posies of George Gascoigne, Esquire, corrected, perfected, and augmented by the author* (1575). This collection contained *Jocasta*, the second-earliest English tragedy written in blank verse. Educated at Trinity College, Cambridge, and at Gray's Inn, Gascoigne was a poet and soldier, as well as a Member of Parliament for Bedfordshire. He fought as a mercenary in Holland (1572–1575) and was captured by the Spaniards. He produced numerous other dramatic and poetic works.

Gascoigne's essay "Certayne Notes" follows in the tradition of Horace's *Ars poetica* as a treatise or manual offering advice to the aspiring poet on the entire range of rhetorical issues, including invention, prosody, verse form, and style. The feature of poetic composition that Gascoigne most insists upon is "fine invention," or the finding of appropriate theme and material. It is not enough, he says, "to roll in pleasant words," or to indulge in alliterative "thunder" (alliterative verse being common in parts of England such as the north and the midlands).[12] Gascoigne insists that the poet must employ "some depth of device in the invention, and some figures also in the handling thereof," or else his work will "appear to the skilful reader but a tale of a tub" [i.e., some trite or ordinary matter] (163). Indeed, like many Renaissance literary theorists, Gascoigne advises the poet to "avoid the uncomely customs of common writers" (163). Gascoigne cautions against the use of "rhyme without reason" (164). In other words, a poet should not be distracted by rhyme for its own sake, nor should he allow the search for rhyme to guide the matter of the poem.

Gascoigne also advises the poet to be consistent in his use of meter throughout a poem. He admonishes the poet to situate every word such that it will receive its "natural *emphasis* or sound . . . as it is commonly pronounced or used." He indicates the three types of accent: *gravis* (\) or the long accent, *levis* (/) or the short accent, and *circumflexa* (~), which is "indifferent," capable of being either long or short (164). He notes that the most common foot in English is the foot of two syllables, the first short and the second long (the iambic foot), and he encourages the use of the iambic pentameter (in which, as many other writers have noted, the English language seems naturally to fall). Also furthering the cause of a distinctive English verse is Gascoigne's advice that the poet avoid words of many syllables, since "the most ancient English words are of one syllable, so that the more monosyllables that you use the truer Englishman you shall seem, and the less you shall smell of the inkhorn" (166).[13] A further reason is that long words "cloy a verse and make it unpleasant." Indeed, while Gascoigne follows Cicero in urging the poet to use the same figures or tropes that are used in prose, he generally opposes the use of strange and obscure words and asks the poet to find a middle ground between "haughty obscure verse" and "verse that is too easy" (167). Much of the advice offered by Gascoigne moves in the direction of both standardizing certain English poetic and metrical practices and differentiating these from "foreign" practices.

George Puttenham (d. 1590)

A long and influential treatise entitled *The Arte of English Poesie*, published anonymously in 1589, is attributed to George Puttenham, though the evidence for this is not conclusive and continues to be argued by scholars. Puttenham was educated at Oxford and presented Queen Elizabeth I with his poem *Partheniades* in 1579. The *Arte* is a text that belongs in a tradition of poetical and rhetorical treatises stretching from the *Rhetorica ad Herennium* and Quintilian's *Oratorio institutio* through Geoffrey de Vinsauf's *Poetria Nova* and Matthew of Vendôme's *The Art of Versification* to Dante's *Il Convivio*. The central purpose of Puttenham's treatise is similar to that of writers such as Dante and Joachim Du Bellay: to justify the use of the vernacular language for poetry, and specifically to establish English vernacular poetry as an *art*, requiring serious study and labor.

The *Arte* is divided into three books, the first justifying poetry as expressing the needs of individual and society; the second, "Of Proportion," devoted to the craft of poetry; and the third, "Of Ornament," offering a renaming of the figures and tropes of classical rhetoric. Puttenham's text was influential on his contemporaries, as well as on seventeenth-century writers; more recently, some of its terms and insights have figured in New Historicist studies. There is no doubt that Puttenham was writing at the advent of a great period of English letters, and his text amply exhibits how early English criticism was tied to certain controversies over language (such as the desirability of importing terms from Greek, Latin, and other languages), as well as to the emerging perception of certain features of English verse, such as the emphasis on stress of syllables. It might be said that his treatise not only contributed to the idea of a "standard" English, but also founded and enabled some of the terminology of early modern literary criticism in English. Terms such as "ode," "lyric," and "epigrammatist" were brought into standard currency partly through the agency and influence of Puttenham's text.[14] In short, his text helped establish the terms and methods of modern English criticism.

At the outset of his treatise, Puttenham defines the poet as both a "maker" and an imitator: he is able to create from his own mind the substance and form of his poetry, an ability that, as in Sidney's defense, raises poetry above all other arts and sciences. But unlike Sidney, for whom poetry presented things in their ideal, rather than actual, condition, Puttenham states that the poet may also express in a "true and lively" manner "every thing that is set before him" (3). Puttenham argues that English poetry, no less than Greek and Latin poetry, can be formulated as an art: "If . . . Art be but a certaine order of rules prescribed by reason, and gathered by experience," he asks, then English poetry is subject to just as many rules and subtle distinctions as classical verse. Moreover, English is just as rich in signification, in conceits, and in the possibilities of wit and invention. Though classical metrics are based on quantitative feet which are lacking in English verse, this is compensated by the richness of rhyme and melody (5–6).

Like Sidney, Puttenham notes the disrepute into which poetry has fallen, both in general and with royal patrons, attributing this to "barbarous ignoraunce" and the poet's externality to "the busie life and vayne ridiculous actions" of the people (16–18). In a passage that might well be thought to anticipate Matthew Arnold's lamentation over the state of modern mechanical civilization – to which he saw poetry and literature as the remedy – Puttenham bemoans his own "iron & malitious age," in which the energies of princes and rulers, and even gentlemen, are exhausted by "the affaires of Empire & ambition"; they have no leisure "to bestow upon any other civill or delectable Art of naturall or morall doctrine . . . whereby their troubled mindes might be moderated and brought to tranquillitie" (21).

The second book undertakes a survey and analysis of stanza (staffe), meter (measure), rhyme, and rhyme pattern, offering advice on all of these matters to those who would write English verse. Puttenham sees the English line of verse as based on meter and rhyme. It is the latter that creates much of the musical effect of English verse. Importantly, Puttenham moves toward a perception of the function of stress in English verse (78–80). Perhaps what is most significant about this section is that it formalizes and classifies the various meters actually employed in English at this time: in this sense, it is effectively the first English prosody.

The final book of the *Arte*, "Of Ornament," primarily addresses language as it can be analyzed for the poet's task. This section, which is a manual of rhetoric, reflects a broader background of humanistic concern with language and rhetoric. Puttenham describes this section as concerned with "the fashioning of our makers language and stile, to such purpose as it may delight and allure as well the mynde as the eare of the hearers with a certaine noveltie and strange maner of conveyance, disguising it no litle from the ordinary and accustomed" (137). Interestingly, the emphasis here is not on the classical balance of teaching and delighting, but on the latter: the poet delights both the mind and the ear, the sensible effects of poetry being viewed as important; moreover, this delight proceeds from a *new* mode of expression. These obligations of poetry will be repeated by many Romantics and modernists. In fact, according to Puttenham, a poet's chief merit lies in the skillful employment of figures (138).

Puttenham's chapter "Of Language" is a *locus classicus* of the issue of standard English. At the time there was a controversy, begun in the 1540s, known as the "Inkhorn term" controversy, concerning the extent to which Latin and Greek words could be imported into English. Puttenham's views appear to call for some compromise. Puttenham sees a point at which a language achieves a general consensus and standardization, a point beyond which only minor changes are admissible. However, as we progress through Puttenham's text, we see that this "consensus" is not truly the consensus of an entire country. The poet, he says, must use language which is "naturall, pure, and the most usuall of all his country." He identifies this "most usuall" language, however, with "that which is spoken in the kings Court, or in the good townes and Cities," and in general by "men civill and graciously behavoured and bred," rather than with the language spoken "in the marches and frontiers" or by "poore rusticall or uncivill people" or in universities where scholars suffer from "affectation" of words. Puttenham identifies "standard" English not only with the courtly class but also with geographical region: the language spoken north of the River Trent is not admissible since "it is not so Courtly nor so currant as our Southerne English is" (144–145). Puttenham goes so far as to suggest an inviolate linguistic perimeter, admonishing the poet: "ye shall therfore take the usuall speach of the Court, and that of London and the shires lying about London within lx. myles, and not much above" (145). He accepts the standardizing authority of the extant English dictionaries, and warns against using "ill affected . . . inkhorn termes" imported by secretaries and merchants and travelers (145). However, he acknowledges that many terms such as "significative," "figurative," and "penetrate" are indispensable in English. In partial support of his view, he quotes from Horace's *Ars poetica* lines which suggest that a language changes over time (146–148).

Puttenham defines style not as contained in particular words or phrases but as "a constant & continuall phrase or tenour of speaking and writing," a total impression that reveals the "disposition of the writers minde" (148). He reiterates the classical dictum that a man's style should conform to his subject matter and that the three principal styles are high, mean (middle), and low; the high style embraces hymns, tragedies, and histories, portraying the affairs of the gods and noble families; the mean style (as in comedy) deals with the business of ordinary men; the low style (as in the eclogue and pastoral) deals with commoners and craftsmen. Puttenham reaffirms the classical principle of decorum whereby a high style should express a lofty subject matter, and a low style a meaner subject, acknowledging that this principle can sometimes be violated for specific ends (149–150).

In his chapter "Of Figures," Puttenham points out that figures of speech have an intrinsic doubleness or duality, since they go beyond the limits of common utterance and plain speech. Metaphor, for example, is "an inversion of sense by transport"; allegory contains "a duplicitie of meaning or dissimulation under covert and dark intendments" (154). As such, all of these figures are subject to abuse; in the hands of the poet, however, whose only purpose is to please his hearers, such dissimulations are not vices but virtues, provided he observes decorum and measure in the use of his figures (155). Puttenham proceeds to explain that, just as the Greeks and Romans devised names for the various figures, so he will devise English terms for them. Puttenham reminds his reader that his text is intended "for the learning of Ladies and young Gentlewomen, or idle Courtiers, desirous to become skilful in their owne mother tongue." He wishes to instruct them for their "private recreation," for the purposes of "Courting" as well as of "poesie" (158). In chapter XV Puttenham begins by renewing his address to Queen Elizabeth, and reaffirming his own status as a court poet, providing "entertainment to Princes, Ladies of honour, Gentlewomen and Gentlemen," entertainment which includes offering solace and giving serious advice "in matters . . . profitable as pleasant and honest" (298–299).

Puttenham sees the arts of grammar, rhetoric, and logic as simply a formalization – acquired by "studious observation" and practice – of his natural abilities. And the poet's relation to nature comprehends all of the foregoing possibilities, integrating imitation, supplementation, and invention (306). But, like Sidney, Puttenham urges that poetry is unique among the arts inasmuch as it is enabled by "a cleare and bright phantasie and imagination." The poet, in fact, works in the same way that nature does: "even as nature her selfe working by her owne peculiar vertue and proper instinct and not by example or meditation or exercise as all other artificers do, [the poet] is then most admired when he is most naturall and least artificiall" (307). Puttenham's text represents in many ways an important stage in the development of modern English criticism, long anticipating what will become Romantic reactions against neoclassicism, and even moving toward a notion of art as primarily offering pleasure. The overt emphasis on pleasure, as opposed to moral instruction, is an implicit – though not at this stage a consciously or precisely formulated – gesture toward poetic autonomy.

Notes

1   David Norbrook, "Introduction," in *The Penguin Book of Renaissance Verse 1509–1659*, ed. H. R. Woudhuysen (Harmondsworth: Penguin, 1993), pp. xxii–xxv. Hereafter cited as *PBRV*.

2   Chris Fitter, "A Tale of Two Branaghs: Henry V, Ideology, and the Mekong Agincourt," in *Shakespeare Right and Left*, ed. Ivo Kamps (New York and London: Routledge, 1991), pp. 261–264.

3   Robert Matz, *Defending Literature in Early Modern England: Renaissance Literary Theory in Social Context* (Cambridge: Cambridge University Press, 2000). Hereafter cited as Matz.

4   David Norbrook, *Poetry and Politics in the English Renaissance*, revised edition (Oxford: Oxford University Press, 2002), p. 1. Hereafter cited as *PER*. See also Norbrook's seminal work, *Writing the English Republic: Poetry, Rhetoric and Politics 1627–1660* (Cambridge: Cambridge University Press, 2000).

5   *Giraldi Cinthio on Romances: Being a Translation of the Discorso intorno al comporre dei romanzi*, trans. Henry L. Snuggs (Lexington: University of Kentucky Press, 1968), p. 11. Hereafter cited as *DCR*.

6   Castelvetro, *On the Art of Poetry: An Abridged Translation of Lodovico Castelvetro's Poetica d'Aristotele vulgarizzata e sposta*, trans. Andrew Bongiorno (Binghamton, NY: Medieval and Renaissance Texts and Studies, 1984), pp. 42–43. Hereafter cited as *PA*.

7   Giacopo Mazzoni, *On the Defense of the Comedy of Dante: Introduction and Summary*, trans. Robert L. Montgomery (Tallahassee: University Presses of Florida, 1983), pp. 37–38. Hereafter cited as *DCD*.

8   "Introduction," in Torquato Tasso, *Discourses on the Heroic Poem*, trans. Mariella Cavalchini and Irene Samuel (Oxford: Clarendon Press, 1973), pp. xxii–xxiii. I am indebted for parts of my account to the translators' scholarly exposition of the background of Tasso's text. The translated text is hereafter cited as *DHP*.

9   Joachim Du Bellay, *La Deffence et Illustration de la Langue Francoyse* (Paris: Société des Textes Français Modernes, 1997). Since the English translation of this text, *The Defence and Illustration of the French Language* by Gladys M. Turquet, is not easily available, I have referred the reader to the excellent selections from this translation reprinted in *The Norton Anthology of Theory and Criticism*, ed. Vincent B. Leitch (New York and London: W. W. Norton, 2001), with the relevant page numbers given in parentheses.

10   Pierre de Ronsard, "A Brief on the Art of French Poetry," trans. J. H. Smith, in *The Great Critics*, ed. James Harry Smith and Edd Winfield Parks (New York: W. W. Norton, 1951), p. 179. All subsequent page citations of Ronsard's "Brief" refer to this translation.

11   *An Apology for Poetry*, in *The Selected Poetry and Prose of Sir Philip Sidney*, ed. David Kalstone (New York and Toronto: New American Library, 1970), p. 216. All subsequent page citations refer to this edition.

12   George Gascoigne, "Certayne Notes of Instruction," reprinted in *English Renaissance Literary Criticism*, ed. Brian Vickers (Oxford: Clarendon Press, 1999), p. 162. All subsequent page citations refer to this edition.

13   Around this time there was raging the "Inkhorn term" controversy concerning whether foreign words were desirable for use in English. The inkhorn was an inkwell and came to signify figuratively a certain pedantry associated with foreign, often polysyllabic, words.

14   George Puttenham, *The Arte of English Poesie*, ed. Gladys Doidge Willcock and Alice Walker (1936; rpt. Cambridge: Cambridge University Press, 1970), p. xcii. Some of my comments are indebted to the editors' introduction. All subsequent page citations refer to this edition.

CHAPTER 12

NEOCLASSICAL
LITERARY CRITICISM

Neoclassicism refers to a broad tendency in literature and art enduring from the early seventeenth century until around 1750. While the nature of this tendency inevitably varied across different cultures, it was usually marked by a number of common concerns and characteristics. Most fundamentally, neoclassicism comprised a return to the classical models, literary styles, and values of ancient Greek and Roman authors. In this, the neoclassicists were to some extent heirs of the Renaissance humanists. But many of them reacted sharply against what they perceived to be the stylistic excess, superfluous ornamentation, and linguistic oversophistication of some Renaissance writers; they also rejected the lavishness of the Gothic and Baroque styles.

Many major medieval and Renaissance writers, including Dante, Ariosto, More, Spenser, and Milton, had peopled their writings with fantastic and mythical beings. Authors such as Giraldi had attempted to justify the genre of the romance and the use of the "marvelous" and unreal elements. Sidney and others had even proposed, in an idealizing Neo-Platonist strain, that the poet's task was to create an ideal world, superior to the world of nature. The neoclassicists, reacting against this idealistic tendency in Renaissance poetics, might be thought of as heirs to the other major tendency in Renaissance poetics, which was Aristotelian. This latter impetus had been expressed in the work of Minturno, Scaliger, and Castelvetro, who all wrote commentaries on Aristotle's *Poetics* and stressed the Aristotelian notion of probability, as well as the "unities" of action, time, and place.

However, whereas many Renaissance poets had labored toward an individualism of outlook, even as they appropriated elements of the classical canon, the neoclassicists in general were less ambiguous in their emphasis upon the classical values of objectivity, impersonality, rationality, decorum, balance, harmony, proportion, and moderation. Whereas many Renaissance poets were beginning to understand profoundly the importance of invention and creativity, the neoclassical writers reaffirmed literary composition as a rational and rule-bound process, requiring a great deal of craft, labor, and study. Where Renaissance theorists and poets were advocating new and mixed genres, the neoclassicists tended to insist on the separation of poetry and prose, the purity of each genre, and the hierarchy of genres (though, unlike Aristotle, they generally placed the epic above tragedy). The typical verse forms of the neoclassical poets were the alexandrine in France and the heroic couplet in England. Much neoclassical thought was marked by a recognition of human finitude, in contrast with the humanists' (and, later, the Romantics') assertion of almost limitless human potential.

Two of the concepts central to neoclassical literary theory and practice were imitation and nature, which were intimately related. In one sense, the notion of imitation – of the external world, and primarily, of human action – was a reaffirmation of the ideals of objectivity and impersonality, as opposed to the increasingly sophisticated individualism and exploration of subjectivity found in Renaissance writers. But also integral to this notion was imitation of classical models, especially Homer and Vergil. In fact, these two aspects of imitation were often identified, as by Pope. The identification was based largely on the concept of nature. This complex concept had a number of senses. It referred to the harmonious and hierarchical order of the universe, including the various social and political hierarchies within the world. In this vast scheme of nature, everything had its proper and appointed place. The concept also referred to human nature: to what was central, timeless, and universal in human experience. Hence, "nature" had a deep moral significance, comprehending the modes of action that were permissible and excluding certain actions as "unnatural" (a term often used by Shakespeare to describe the murderous and cunning behavior of characters such as Lady Macbeth). Clearly, the neoclassical vision of nature was very different from the meanings later given to it by the Romantics; this vision inherited something of the medieval view of nature as a providential scheme but, as will emerge shortly, it was informed by more recent scientific views of nature rather than by Aristotelian physics. The neoclassical writers generally saw the ancients such as Homer and Vergil as having already discovered and expressed the fundamental laws of nature. Hence, the external world, including the world of human action, could best be expressed by modern writers if they followed the path of imitation already paved by the ancients. Invention was of course allowed, but only as a modification of past models, not in the form of a rupture.

Having said all of this, the neoclassicists were by no means devoted to slavish imitation of the classics. La Bruyère indeed thought that the ancients had already expressed everything that was worth saying; and Pope, in one of his more insistent moments, equated following the rules of nature with the imitation of Homer. But Ben Jonson, Corneille, Dryden, and many others were more flexible in their assimilation of classical values. Nearly all of them acknowledged the genius of Shakespeare, some the genius of Milton; Boileau recognized the contribution of an inexplicable element, the *je ne sais quoi*, in great art, and Pope acknowledged that geniuses could attain "a grace beyond the reach of art." Moreover, the neoclassicists attempted to develop and refine Aristotle's account of the emotions evoked by tragedy in an audience, and an important part of their endeavor to imitate nature consisted in portraying the human passions. There raged at the beginning of the eighteenth century various debates over the relative merits of "ancients" and "moderns." The ancients were held to be the repository of good sense, natural laws, and the classical values of order, balance, and moderation. Such arguments were found in Jonathan Swift's *The Battle of the Books* (1704) and in the writings of Boileau and Pope. Proponents of the "modern" laid stress on originality of form and content, flexibility of genre, and the license to engage in new modes of thought.

The connection of neoclassicism to recent science and what would eventually emerge as some of the core values of the Enlightenment was highly ambivalent and even paradoxical. On the one hand, the neoclassical concept of nature was informed by Newtonian physics, and the universe was acknowledged to be a vast machine, subject to fixed analyzable laws. On the other hand, the tenor of most neoclassical thought was retrospective and conservative. On the surface, it might seem that the neoclassical writers shared with Enlightenment thinkers a belief in the power of reason. The neoclassicists certainly saw literature as subject to a system of rules, and literary composition as a rational process, subject to the faculty of judgment (Pope uses the word "critic" in its original Greek sense of "judge"). But, while it is true that some neoclassical writers, especially in Germany, were influenced by Descartes and other rationalists, the "reason" to which the neoclassical writers appeal is in general not the individualistic and progressive reason of the Enlightenment (though, as will be seen in a later chapter, Enlightenment reason could from other perspectives be seen as a coercive and oppressive force); rather, it is the "reason" of the classical philosophers, a universal human faculty that provides access to general truths and which is aware of its own limitations. Alexander Pope and others emphasized the finitude of human reason, cautioning against its arrogant and unrestricted employment. Reason announced itself in neoclassical thought largely in Aristotelian and sometimes Horatian terms: an adherence to the requirements of probability and verisimilitude, as well as to the three unities, and the principle of decorum. But the verisimilitude or likeness to reality here sought after was different from nineteenth-century realism that sought to depict the typical elements and the universal truths about any given situation; it did not operate via an accumulation of empirical detail or a random recording of so-called reality. It was reason in this Aristotelian sense that lay behind the insistence on qualities such as order, restraint, moderation, and balance.

Interestingly, Michael Moriarty has argued that the neoclassical insistence on adherence to a body of rules embodies an ideological investment which must be understood in terms of broader developments in the literary market. A specifically literary criticism, he urges, began to emerge as a specialized and professional discipline in the seventeenth century, with literature being identified as an autonomous field of study and expertise. Seventeenth-century criticism addressed an expanded readership which it helped to create: this broader public ranged from the aristocracy of the court and the salons to the middle strata of the bourgeoisie. The critical ideology of this public was oriented toward pleasure and to evaluation based on polite "taste." The rise of periodical presses during the second half of the seventeenth century "provided a new channel for discourse about literature addressed to a non-scholarly social elite." But there was a reciprocal interaction: the habits of literary consumption modified critical discourse; for example, despite the epic's high theoretical status, the demands and tastes of an increasing theater-going public generated far more criticism about drama. Along with these developments, a class of literary men newly emerged from bourgeois backgrounds, the *nouveaux doctes*, specialized in a specifically literary training, and focused on language, rhetoric, and poetics. This mastery enabled them to establish a new, more respectable identity for themselves as men of letters, whereby they could offer polite society the kind of pleasure befitting its dignity. They defined this pleasure in Horatian terms, as necessarily conjoined with instruction; it was a refined pleasure,

275

issuing from a conformity to rules. It was these rules, impersonally and sacredly embodied in ancient authorities such as Aristotle and Horace, and in modern authorities such as the Académie Française, which consecrated the work as a product of art and which legitimated "the poet's status as a purveyor of pleasure" to the dominant groups.[1]

This general tendency of neoclassicism toward order, clarity, and standardization was manifested also in attempts during the seventeenth and eighteenth centuries to regulate the use of language and the meanings of words. In France, the Académie Française was established for this purpose in 1635, and writers such as François de Malherbe argued that meanings should be stabilized in the interests of linguistic clarity and communication. Samuel Johnson's *Dictionary* was published in 1755. The impetus behind these endeavors was reflected in John Locke's theory of language, and his insistence, following Descartes, that philosophy should proceed by defining its terms precisely, using "clear and distinct" ideas and avoiding figurative language. This ideal of clarity, of language as the outward sign of the operations of reason, permeated neoclassical poetry, which was often discursive, argumentative, and aimed to avoid obscurity. This movement toward clarity has been variously theorized as coinciding with the beginnings of bourgeois hegemony, as reacting against a proliferation of vocabulary and meanings during the Renaissance, and as marking a step further away from a medieval allegorical way of thinking toward an attempted literalization of language.

Ironically, neoclassicism helped prepare the way for its own demise. One avenue toward this self-transcendence of neoclassicism was through the concept of the sublime. The first-century treatise called *On the Sublime*, attributed to "Longinus," had viewed the sublime as a form of emotional transport beyond the rational faculty. Boileau's translation of this text in 1674 was followed by flourishing discussions of the topic in England and Germany, which were often accompanied, as we shall see in chapter 14 on Kant, by an extensive examination of the concept of beauty. In fact, in England, the contrast "between sublimity and correctness had socio-political resonance, since the former was associated with the English subject's liberty, the latter with both the English and the absolutist French court" (*CHLC*, V.III, 552–553). Another legacy of the neoclassicists was an examination of the notion of "taste" in terms of consensus of qualified people. This notion of consensus prepared the way for an aesthetic oriented toward reader response rather than mere adherence to an abstract body of rules. The following sections will consider some of the major figures of neoclassical literary criticism in the countries where it was most pronounced: France and England.

French Neoclassicism: Corneille, Boileau-Despréaux

Neoclassical literary criticism first took root in France from where its influence spread to other parts of Europe, notably England. It was Jean Chapelain who introduced into France the ideas of the Italian Aristotelian commentators Castelvetro and Scaliger. The French court during the reign of Louis XIV was a center of patronage for numerous poets and dramatists. The political conditions of relative peace, prosperity, and national unity after the religious wars of the sixteenth century, together with the growth of educated elites in the clergy and court aristocracy, proved ripe for the founding of the French Academy in 1635. The mission of the Academy, headed by Cardinal Richelieu, was partly to standardize language through the creation of a dictionary and grammar, as well as work on rhetoric and poetics, in pursuit of what Hugh M. Davidson has called the "rhetorical ideal," an eloquence perceived as vital to the development of civil society (*CHLC*, V.III, 500). One of the results of this was the emergence of a rhetorical context for the speculations of the various French theorists. Another result was the relatively uniform and systematic nature of French neoclassical theory. As Michael Moriarty has pointed out, the intimately related notions of *vraisemblance* (probability) and *bienséance* (decorum) as defined by the Académie Française could exercise a function of "ideological censorship," requiring the presentation of characters in conformity with public opinion or stereotypes of gender and class (*CHLC*, V.III, 523). The major figures of French neoclassicism were Corneille, Racine, Molière, and La Fontaine. Corneille's theories grew out of the need to defend his dramatic practice against strict classicists such as Scudéry and Jean Chapelain. The most prominent theorists were Dominique Bouhours, René Rapin, and Nicolas Boileau. Characteristically of the neoclassical tendency as a whole, Bouhours argued against excessive ornamentation and insisted on the principle of decorum. Boileau, perhaps the most influential French neoclassical critic, argued for retaining the strict divisions between classical verse forms.

Pierre Corneille (1606–1684)

Pierre Corneille, born in the French town of Rouen in Normandy, was primarily a playwright. Born into a middle-class family, and having failed in his initial endeavor as a lawyer, he launched into a stormy and controversial career in the theater. The most important text of his literary criticism, *Trois Discours sur le poème dramatique* (*Three Discourses on Dramatic Poetry*, 1660), was produced in response to the controversies he had ignited, to explain and justify his own dramatic practice. Those controversies had their origin in the varied reception of Corneille's most renowned play, *Le Cid*, which appeared in 1637. While the play enjoyed great popularity with audiences, it was attacked not only by critics but also by the French literary and political establishment. This attack was based on the play's alleged failure to observe the rules of classical theater as laid down by Aristotle and Horace. Critics claimed that the play violated the classical unities – of action, time, and place – as well as the Aristotelian precepts of probability and necessity; and in doing so, they argued, it undermined the morally didactic function of drama. Corneille responded to these charges both by writing further plays displaying his mastery of classical conventions and by producing his *Three Discourses*. While he is conventionally regarded as a champion of neoclassical virtues in the tradition of François de Malherbe and Racine, the actual texts of his *Discourses* suggest that he is concerned to adapt classical precepts to modern requirements of the stage and to provide a broader and more liberal interpretation of those precepts.

In his third *Discourse*, entitled "Of the Three Unities of Action, Time, and Place," Corneille attempts to explain the rationale behind his plays. Regarding the unity of action, Corneille resists any interpretation of this to mean that "tragedy should only show one action on the stage." He takes Aristotle's statement that a complete action should have a beginning, middle, and end to mean that these three parts are "separate actions which find their conclusion in the principal one." And, just as these three parts are subordinated to the main action, so, Corneille urges, each of these three parts can contain subordinate actions. In other words, while he agrees that "there must be only one complete action," he insists that "action can become complete only through several others . . . which, by serving as preparation, keep the spectator in a pleasant suspense." He suggests that the end of each act "leave us in the expectation of something which is to take place in the following one."[2] So what Corneille is disputing is not that the action in a play should be complete, but the definition of a complete action; interestingly, his own definition attempts to develop the implication of Aristotle's for the connections between the acts of a play; it also makes the audience's response an integral component. In addition he develops Aristotle's view, that one event must not simply follow another but be caused by it according to necessity or probability, into a rule which is "new and contrary to the usage of the ancients." This rule is that, not only should all parts of the action be closely and causally connected, but also they should "all have their source in the protasis" (the *protasis* being the introduction of events in the first act) (102–103).

Aristotle had divided a play into two parts: the "complication" leading up to the "change of fortune" of the protagonist; and the "resolution," the remaining part of the play. While Corneille accepts this division, he states that the "complication depends entirely upon the choice and industrious imagination of the poet and no rule can be given for it" beyond the requirements of probability and necessity (105). Corneille adds that the poet should not engage in lengthy narrations providing background to the play's actual action; this will annoy and burden the spectator. Narrations should be used only to explain or comment on actions that have occurred within the play. Corneille reaffirms Aristotle's view that the *deus ex machina* should be avoided, since this provides a "faulty resolution" of a plot. On the other hand, he finds Aristotle's criticism of the flying chariot in Euripides' *Medea* harsh since, Corneille argues, the audience has been adequately prepared for this otherwise improbable scene (106).

As for the number and unity of acts and scenes, there is no rule, Corneille asserts, for linking the various scenes which comprise each act; such linking indeed provides for continuity of action, but "it is only a beauty and not a rule." Linking of scenes was not always practiced by the ancients, he observes, and it has become a rule for modern audiences merely through habituation, so that "they cannot now witness a detached scene without considering it a defect" (103). The kind of linking that should be effected, according to Corneille, is that which depends on the presence and speech of a character. For example, a character's presence on stage must not simply fulfill the function of hearing what other characters say; his presence must be "dictated by the plot of the play," with the character performing an indispensable function in a given scene, to link it with other scenes (104). Likewise, the number of acts was not prescribed by Aristotle; and though Horace limits a play to five acts, we do not know for sure, says Corneille, how many acts ancient Greek plays contained since they made no distinction between acts and scenes, and since they would separate episodes by the chanting of the chorus. The modern theater, he reminds us, is not encumbered with such long choral songs, which impose a substantial burden on the spectator, who is obliged to recall the action of the play after hearing the chant (107–108). In general, Corneille advises that while each act should express a portion of the overall action, the latter should be weighted more toward the later acts since the first act merely depicts the "moral natures" and relevance of the characters to the plot (106).

As for the unity of time, Corneille notes Aristotle's precept that the action of a tragedy must be encompassed within one revolution of the sun. On the issue, argued by critics and dramatists, of whether this means twelve or twenty-four hours, Corneille is content to say that Aristotle's view must be interpreted liberally, allowing even up to thirty hours' duration of the action, since some subjects do not lend themselves to such brief treatment (109). Strict observance of this rule, Corneille points out, "forced some of the ancients to the very edge of the impossible," since their action included journeys of armies and battles. In general, however, Corneille believes that it is not merely Aristotle's authority but "common sense" that commends such a rule. The "dramatic poem," he reminds us, "is an imitation, or rather a portrait of human actions, and . . . portraits gain in excellence in proportion as they resemble the original more closely." On this basis, he recommends compressing the action "into the shortest possible period, so that the performance may more closely resemble reality and thus be more nearly perfect" (109–110). What Corneille appeals to here is realism as an aesthetic criterion. The realism that Aristotle espoused, as an option for tragic action, was one that "imitated" or portrayed the universal, the generalizable truths of a situation. The realism Corneille upholds is verisimilitude, the presentation of reality in "its proportionate dimensions" (110). Though constrained by time for these reasons, the poet can, points out Corneille, make known by devices such as narration what the background and circumstances of the hero are (111). As with the unity of action, Corneille gives the audience or spectator an integral role in determining what comprises the unity of time. The "matter of duration," he suggests, should be left to "the imagination of the spectators." It would be an "obtrusive affectation" to spell out in definite terms the portrayed duration of an action. He also appeals to audience response in proposing that the fifth act of a play has a "special privilege" to accelerate time: since it is the final act, it may recount offstage incidents which would take more time than allowed by the action of the stage itself. The reason behind this is, once again, the requirements of the audience, which by this stage of the play is impatient to know the conclusion (110).

For the unity of place, there is no rule, notes Corneille, prescribed by either Aristotle or Horace. Rather, this rule was established "as a consequence of the unity of one day," covering "the points to which a man may go and return in twenty-four hours." Corneille finds this opinion "a little too free": it would allow for two sides of the stage to represent two cities. While he concedes that precise unity of time and place may be desirable, these unities would impose constraints on a playwright's endeavor to depict probable actions. For example, many realistic situations would not admit of being portrayed in a single room or hall. Sophocles and many other successful dramatists, he points out, did not observe a rigorous unity of place. We should, thinks Corneille, adopt a compromise; for example, we could "concede that a whole city has unity of place," provided that scenes are changed only between, not within, the acts, and that different places do not require different stage settings. This would help, he suggests, "to deceive the spectator, who . . . would not notice the change" (113–114). Corneille proposes an interesting compromise: just as jurists speak of "legal fictions," so we might introduce "theatrical fictions," whereby, for example, if the action of a play were to take place in a number of apartments belonging to different characters, we might establish a room contiguous to all these other apartments, a room where it was understood that each of the characters could speak with secrecy (114–115).

In concluding his *Discourse*, Corneille effectively points out the underlying basis of his adaptation of the classical unities as propounded by Aristotle and Horace. It is easy, he remarks, for critics to be strict in their censure; but if they themselves had to produce plays, if they themselves "recognized through experience what constraint their precision brings about and how many beautiful things it banishes from our stage," they might reconsider their own severity. The test, Corneille insists, is experience, actual practice. Corneille's overall aim, as he suggests, is to "make ancient rules agree with modern pleasures" (115). In this endeavor, he is not so much making those rules more liberal – indeed, at times, he wishes them to be stricter – as reformulating them in the light of the needs and requirements of the audience, especially the modern audience. In this attempt to redefine their significance, he appeals not only to a broader vision of Aristotelian probability and necessity which enlists these in the service of a more modern verisimilitude, but also to other aesthetic criteria such as beauty, comprehensiveness, and unity. His text is an interesting example of ancient authority tempered not only by examples of the subversion of that authority by ancient writers themselves, but also above all by an appeal to experience and theatrical practice. Corneille effectively rescues the importance of performance from the peripheral status it meekly occupies in Aristotle's text.

Nicolas Boileau-Despréaux (1636–1711)

The French poet, satirist, and critic Boileau had a pervasive influence not only on French letters (of the old-fashioned kind) but also on English and German poets and critics. His *L'Art Poétique* (*The Art of Poetry*), first published in 1674, was translated into English by John Dryden. Boileau's text represents a formal statement of the principles of French classicism, and perhaps the most direct expression of neoclassical ideals anywhere. It drew heavily on Aristotle and Horace, and in its turn was a powerful influence on English neoclassical writers such as Pope; in fact, some of it is echoed very directly in Pope's *Essay on Criticism*. Boileau's text and authority enjoyed such prestige that he was known as the *législateur du Parnasse*, credited with the formation of French literary taste, fixing this taste through consistent criteria and extricating it from "unclassical" Spanish and Italian influences. Boileau helped the French public to appreciate the works of his friends Racine and Molière. Above all, Boileau became the embodiment of classical rationality, "good sense," and proportion.

Like Pope's *Essay on Criticism*, Boileau's *Art of Poetry* embodies some of the vast intellectual and political changes that were already beginning to sweep over Europe. In some ways, it embodies a rejection of the entire feudal system; characteristically of neoclassical thinking, it virtually ignores the Middle Ages and seeks to restore the classical principles of reason and nature, together with the classical view of the human being as essentially social. Just as Molière's plays effect a balance between religious belief and rationalism, arguing for an enlightened rather than authoritarian religion, so Boileau's text is marked by a central affirmation of the importance of reason, as well as observation. To this extent, Boileau's neoclassicism, like Molière's and Pope's, exhibits surface similarities with emerging bourgeois philosophy and relatively modern ways of thinking. It reacts against Christian puritanism, submitting the claims of the latter to the judgment of reason. But, as in the case of these other authors, the "reason" espoused by Boileau is a classical view of reason as a common human faculty which perceives what is universally true. It is not the individualistic reason of bourgeois philosophy that rejects all authority and relies ultimately on the findings of individual sense-perception. Moreover, Boileau appeals directly in his text, as does Molière in *Tartuffe*, to the authority of the king (Louis XIV) as an enlightened and near-omniscient monarch who has extinguished "rebellion" and has brought order to all of Europe.

Like Pope's *Essay*, Boileau's text is written as a poem, in the tradition of Horace's *Ars poetica*, and offers advice to the poet in various genres such as tragedy, comedy, epic, and ode, as well as summaries of various aspects of literary history. The parallels with Horace's text are clearly discernible in canto I, which offers general prescriptions to the poet. Boileau asks the poet to consider the extent of his own ability, his "own force and weight" (I, l. 12).[3] He insists, perhaps even more than Horace, on the craft, the labor, involved in writing poetry: "A hundred times consider what you've said; / Polish, repolish, every color lay," (I, ll. 172–173). Like Horace, he admonishes the poet to avoid showing his work to flatterers: "Embrace true counsel, but suspect false praise" (I, l. 192). He cautions the poet to avoid excessive detail, "barren superfluity," and to vary his discourse in the interests of "pleasing" the reader (I, ll. 60, 70–72, 105). The most significant parallel is perhaps afforded by Boileau's reiteration of the Horatian formula:

> In prudent lessons everywhere abound,
> With pleasant join the useful and the sound;
> A sober reader a vain tale will slight,
> He seeks as well instruction as delight.
> (IV, ll. 86–89)

That Boileau almost repeats Horace's most general statement of the function of poetry, with the added requirement that the content be "sound" (*Partout joigne au plaisant le solide et l'utile*), indicates that his text is not original in its fundamental claims. However, where it moves beyond Horace, where it embodies the long historical development of rhetoric and thought between its own time and Horace's era, is in its insistence on the centrality of reason to the poetic enterprise.

The principle of reason is at the heart of Boileau's text, receiving an emphasis well beyond that in Horace's text and greater even than that in Pope's text. Boileau's most general imperative that the poet employ reason is contained in the lines: "Love reason then; and let whate'er you write / Borrow from her its beauty, force, and light" (I, ll. 37–38). Boileau is skillful in drawing out the widely varied ramifications of the reliance on reason. To begin with, it underlies a poem's unity of form and content. Boileau says: "Whate'er you write of pleasant or sublime, / Always let sense accompany your rime" (I, ll. 27–28). Indeed, rhyming in poetry should not be allowed to dictate the poem's course; it must be subjected to the power of "master reason" (I, l. 36). It is reason which protects against the "excess" of "false glittering poetry," and the use of

"Extravagant and senseless objects" (I, ll. 40–45). The sounds in a poem should be informed by the light of reason; perfection of style will follow perfection of content:

> Learn then to think ere you pretend to write.
> As your idea's clear, or else obscure,
> The expression follows, perfect or impure;
> (I, ll. 150–152)

This view of thought as somehow preceding language and expression runs counter to our modern ideas of language itself as not only a vehicle but also a shaper of thought. Nonetheless, like Pope, Boileau demands a unity between the various parts of a poem, "One perfect whole of all the pieces joined" (I, l. 180). Later in his text, Boileau reiterates this counsel of classical moderation: "above all avoid the fond [foolish] excess" (II, l. 132). To steer a path between extremes, Boileau advises the writer to emulate the revered poets of antiquity such as Vergil and Theocritus: of Homer he says: "Let his example your endeavors raise; / To love his writings is a kind of praise" (III, ll. 306–307). Boileau even associates the classical dramatic unities with reason (III, ll. 43–46). In his second and third book, Boileau describes the characteristic of various poetic forms and genres such as the eclogue, elegy, ode, tragedy, comedy, and epic. On the issue of the relative merits of tragedy and epic, he appears to side with Tasso as against Aristotle's view of the superiority of tragedy. The heroic poem, says Boileau, "claims a loftier strain" (III. ll. 159–161).

Hence, poetic control, moderation, the unities of time and place, and the imitation of classical examples are all associated by Boileau with the exercise of reason; later, in Pope's *Essay*, all of these virtues will be associated with following nature. For Boileau, reason also urges against the subjection of poetry to religious puritanism. He states: "Our pious fathers, in their priest-rid age, / As impious and profane abhorred the stage." But "At last right reason did his laws reveal, / And showed the folly of their ill-placed zeal" (III, ll. 79–80, 85–86). Boileau's point is that religious zeal is misplaced in substituting angels, virgins, and saints for classical heroes. He also sees as misplaced the puritanical aversion to the use of poetic ornament. Ornament, he says, is indispensable to the poet's art: "Without these ornaments before our eyes / The unsinewed poem languishes and dies" (III, ll. 173–174, 188–191). Boileau denies that he is asking for Christian poems to be filled with "the fictions of idolatry," but that rejecting the heathen deities and poetic ornaments outright is to trouble oneself with "vain scruples" and to seek an impossible perfection (III, ll. 216–225). Boileau's point here is complex and perhaps incompletely coherent: in his desire to return to classical models, he countenances even those aspects of classical paganism that directly contradict Christian teaching, on the grounds that the gospels are not a fitting subject for verse and that removal of classical ornament will impoverish a poem. As many critics have pointed out, Boileau betrays here some of his own limitations: he entirely bypasses the contributions of medieval aesthetic theory and Christian notions of beauty. He is unable to envision a Christian mythology at all replacing classical mythology or even complementing it, as it does in Dante and Milton, whose work he does not seem to appreciate. He accords grudging praise to Tasso (III, ll. 208–215). His argument that the God of the gospels should not be mixed with accounts of the pagan gods effectively forestalls the very idea of a poem with Christian content. Against such religious and puritanical poets he invokes reason, which for him is not only classical but also pagan: "Leave them their pious follies to pursue, / But let our reason such vain fears subdue, / And let us not, amongst our vanities, / Of the true God create a god of lies" (III, ll. 232–235). Hence, for the Christian God to remain pure and true, his domain of portrayal must be restricted to the gospels and theology; he must not be allowed access to the province of poetry.

Like Pope after him, Boileau appeals to nature: "To study nature be your only care." The poet, he says, must know human nature and the "secrets of the heart." He must observe and be able to paint all kinds of people, at all stages in life. But even here, the following of nature is seen as obeying the rules of reason: "Your actors must by reason be controlled; / Let young men speak like young, old men like old" (III, ll. 390–391). Indeed, the poet must observe "exact decorum," which itself rests on a knowledge of human nature and on the exercise of reason: each person must be portrayed in his "proper character," which must be both self-consistent and consistent with the character's country, rank, and native customs (III, ll. 110–112, 121). Hence the poet must not only know human nature; he must also be an observer of various customs and ages; he must "Observe the town and study well the court" (III, l. 392). All of this emphasis on decorum is seen by Boileau as resting on the use of reason: "I like an author that reforms the age, / And keeps the right decorum of the stage, / That always pleases by just reason's rule" (III, ll. 422–424).

Reason has one final aspect in Boileau's text: a relation of harmony with feeling and emotion. Notwithstanding his emphasis on reason, Boileau expresses despite for "lukewarm authors" who describe "hot desire" in a "cold style," who "sigh by rule" (II, ll. 45–49), and in "all their raptures" keep "exactest time," guided only "by strictest rules of art" (II, ll. 73–78). Boileau's own advice is:

> In all you write observe with care and art
> To move the passions and incline the heart.
> ... The secret is, attention first to gain,
> To move our minds and then to entertain ...
> (III, ll. 15–21, 25–26)

Boileau is here repeating an old formula, used earlier by many Renaissance writers such as Sidney: inasmuch as poetry instructs, it must first delight. In Boileau's text, pervaded as this is by recourse to reason, the formula acquires a slightly new semantic texture: it effectively broadens the scope of reason. In other words, reason is equated by Boileau not with the observance of artistic rules but, rather, with a knowledge of *when* to observe rules. Reason itself prescribes that a poem should create an emotional impact.

While, like Horace, Boileau places a great deal of emphasis on pleasing the reader, he reminds the poet that he is not writing for present glory but for "immortal fame" (IV, ll. 124–125). In particular, he derides those who have reduced poetry to a "mercenary trade," flawed by flattery of patrons (IV, ll. 168–171). In a highly dubious argument, Boileau claims that there is no need to be concerned about earning a living under the rule of a "sharp-sighted prince" who "Rewards your merits, and prevents your wants" (IV, ll. 188–192). Boileau sings the praises of the monarch in question, Louis XIV, who has "Europe's balance in his steady hand," and who has driven out "rebellion, discord, vice, and rage, / That have in patriots' forms debauched our age" (IV, ll. 207, 214–215). Louis XIV (1643–1715) was the first of the Bourbon kings in France who exercised absolute monarchy; he believed that he was appointed by God to reign, and it is to him that the words *l'état, c'est moi* (I am the state) are attributed. His policy in religion was reactionary; in 1685, for example, he revoked the Edict of Nantes, which had granted freedom of belief to the Huguenots. His successors Louis XV and Louis XVI were also authoritarian in their rule, a disposition that contributed to the onset of the French Revolution of 1789. Under the reign of Louis XIV, France underwent a sustained policy of mercantilism aimed at enriching the business opportunities of the middle classes; people were discouraged from becoming monks or nuns.

Neoclassicism in England: Dryden, Pope, Behn, Johnson

A precursor of neoclassicism in England was Ben Jonson, who drew upon ancient Roman and Renaissance Italian sources and whose recourse to the laws of dramatic form was part of a combative mentality "in the battle to distinguish true poet from false rhymester."[4] The main streams of English neoclassical criticism were inspired by (and reacted against) the French example. French influence in England was intensified by the Restoration of 1660, whereby Charles II, exiled in France after the English Civil War, returned with his court to England. Boileau's *Art Poétique* was imported into England through a translation by Dryden. Boileau's influence, however, was most pronounced upon Pope; Dryden himself defended English drama against some of the French critics.

As noted earlier, the France of Louis XIV had embarked upon a neoclassical program of national proportions. While neoclassical criticism in England was not so systematic, many saw the adoption of neoclassical ideals as necessary to produce a stable and ordered political state (*CHLC*, V.III, 549). But Dryden and others decried the servility and enslavement of French critics to the royal court. England had its fair share of stern preceptors: Thomas Rymer was so insistent on adherence to the unities and the principle of probability that he indicted Shakespeare. But others, such as John Dennis, acknowledged that literature must change with varying religion and culture, and even extolled Milton above the ancients. As Joshua Scodel has pointed out, English neoclassicism was in general flexible enough to accommodate within the tradition authors such as Chaucer, Shakespeare, Donne, and Milton, who "did not fit a rigid classical paradigm." Moreover, classical norms being adapted to developments in England underwent certain shifts in meaning (*CHLC*, V.III, 543). While Addison too took a dim view of English drama, he anticipated discussions of the imagination, taste, beauty, and the sublime on the part of later writers such as Shaftesbury, whose *Characteristics* (1711) was the first large-scale treatment of aesthetics, Hutcheson, Burke, and Hume. Many of these writers drew upon the philosophical foundations of empiricism and associationism as established by Hobbes and Locke. The classical tendency in England embraced a number of major prose writers who laid the foundations of the modern English novel, such as Daniel Defoe (1660?–1731), Jonathan

Swift (1667–1745), and Henry Fielding (1707–1754). As will be seen below, Dryden and Johnson were perhaps the most flexible exponents of neoclassicism in England, attempting to mediate between the merits of ancients and moderns. In general, the critics ranging from Jonson to Dryden effectively advanced the notion of a viable English literary tradition.

John Dryden (1631–1700)

John Dryden occupies a seminal place in English critical history. Samuel Johnson called him "the father of English criticism," and affirmed of his *Essay of Dramatic Poesy* (1668) that "modern English prose begins here." Dryden's critical work was extensive, treating of various genres such as epic, tragedy, comedy and dramatic theory, satire, the relative virtues of ancient and modern writers, as well as the nature of poetry and translation. In addition to the *Essay*, he wrote numerous prefaces, reviews, and prologues, which together set the stage for later poetic and critical developments embodied in writers such as Pope, Johnson, Matthew Arnold, and T. S. Eliot.

Dryden was also a consummate poet, dramatist, and translator. His poetic output reflects his shifting religious and political allegiances. Born into a middle-class family just prior to the outbreak of the English Civil War between King Charles I and Parliament, he initially supported the latter, whose leaders, headed by Oliver Cromwell, were Puritans. Indeed, his poem *Heroic Stanzas* (1659) celebrated the achievements of Cromwell who, after the execution of Charles I by the victorious parliamentarians, ruled England as Lord Protector (1653–1658). However, with the restoration of the dead king's son, Charles II, to the throne in 1660, Dryden switched sides, celebrating the new monarchy in his poem *Astrea Redux* (*Justice Restored*). Dryden was appointed poet-laureate in 1668 and thereafter produced several major poems, including the mock-heroic "Mac Flecknoe" (1682), and a political satire *Absalom and Achitophel* (1681). In addition, he produced two poems that mirror his move from Anglicanism to Catholicism: "Religio Laici" (1682) defends the Anglican Church while *The Hind and the Panther*, just five years later, opposes Anglicanism. Dryden's renowned dramas include the comedy *Marriage a la Mode* (1671) and the tragedies *Aureng-Zebe* (1675) and *All for Love, or the World Well Lost* (1677). His translations include *Fables, Ancient and Modern* (1700), which includes renderings of Ovid, Boccaccio, and Chaucer.

Dryden's *Essay of Dramatic Poesy* is written as a debate on drama conducted by four speakers, Eugenius, Crites, Lisideius, and Neander. These personae have conventionally been identified with four of Dryden's contemporaries. Eugenius (meaning "well-born") may be Charles Sackville, who was Lord Buckhurst, a patron of Dryden and a poet himself. Crites (Greek for "judge" or "critic") perhaps represents Sir Robert Howard, Dryden's brother-in-law. Lisideius refers to Sir Charles Sedley, and Neander ("new man") is Dryden himself. The *Essay*, as Dryden himself was to point out in a later defense of it, was occasioned by a public dispute with Sir Robert Howard (Crites) over the use of rhyme in drama.[5] In a note to the reader prefacing the *Essay*, he suggests that the chief purpose of his text is "to vindicate the honour of our English writers, from the censure of those who unjustly prefer the French" (27). Yet the scope of the *Essay* extends far beyond these two topics, effectively ranging over a number of crucial debates concerning the nature and composition of drama.

The first of these debates is that between ancients and moderns, a debate that had intermittently surfaced for centuries in literature and criticism, and which acquired a new and topical intensity in European letters after the Renaissance, in the late seventeenth century. Traditionalists such as Jonathan Swift, in his controversial *Battle of the Books* (1704), bemoaned the modern "corruption" of religion and learning, and saw in the ancients the archetypal standards of literature. The moderns, inspired by various forms of progress through the Renaissance, sought to adapt or even abandon classical ideals in favor of the requirements of a changed world and a modern audience. Dryden's *Essay* is an important intervention in this debate, perhaps marking a distinction between Renaissance and neoclassical values. Like Tasso and Corneille, he attempted to strike a compromise between the claims of ancient authority and the exigencies of the modern writer.

In Dryden's text, this compromise subsumes a number of debates: one of these concerns the classical "unities" of time, place, and action; another focuses on the rigid classical distinction between various genres, such as tragedy and comedy; there was also the issue of classical decorum and propriety, as well as the use of rhyme in drama. All of these elements underlie the nature of drama. In addition, Dryden undertakes an influential assessment of the English dramatic tradition, comparing writers within this tradition itself as well as with their counterparts in French drama.

Dryden's *Essay* is skillfully wrought in terms of its own dramatic structure, its setting up of certain expectations (the authority of classical precepts), its climaxing in the reversal of these, and its denouement in the comparative assessment of French and English drama. What starts out, through the voice of Crites, as promising to lull the reader into complacent subordination to classical values ends up by deploying those very values against the ancients themselves and by undermining or redefining those values.

Lisideius offers the following definition of a play: "*A just and lively image of human nature, representing its passions and humours, and the changes of fortune to which it is subject, for the delight and instruction of mankind*" (36). Even a casual glance at the definition shows it to be very different from Aristotle's: the latter had defined tragedy not as the representation of "human nature" but as the imitation of a serious and complete action; moreover, while Aristotle had indeed cited a reversal in fortune as a component of tragedy, he had said nothing about "passions and humours"; and, while he accorded to literature in general a moral and intellectual function, he had said nothing about "delighting" the audience. The definition of drama used in Dryden's *Essay* embodies a history of progressive divergence from classical models; indeed, it is a definition already weighted in favor of modern drama, and it is a little surprising that Crites agrees to abide by it at all. Crites, described in Dryden's text as "a person of sharp judgment, and somewhat too delicate a taste in wit" (29), is, after all, the voice of classical conservatism.

Crites notes that poetry is now held in lower esteem, in an atmosphere of "few good poets, and so many severe judges" (37–38). His essential argument is that the ancients were "faithful imitators and wise observers of that Nature which is so torn and ill represented in our plays; they have handed down to us a perfect resemblance of her; which we, like ill copiers, neglecting to look on, have rendered monstrous, and disfigured." He reminds his companions that all the rules for drama – concerning the plot, the ornaments, descriptions, and narrations – were formulated by Aristotle, Horace, or their predecessors. As for us modern writers, he remarks, "we have added nothing of our own, except we have the confidence to say our wit is better" (38).

The most fundamental of these classical rules are the three unities, of time, place, and action. Crites claims that the ancients observed these rules in most of their plays (38–39). The unity of action, Crites urges, stipulates that the "poet is to aim at one great and complete action," to which all other things in the play "are to be subservient." The reason behind this, he explains, is that if there were two major actions, this would destroy the unity of the play (41). Crites cites a further reason from Corneille: the unity of action "leaves the mind of the audience in a full repose"; but such a unity must be engineered by the subordinate actions which will "hold the audience in a delightful suspense of what will be" (41). Most modern plays, says Crites, fail to endure the test imposed by these unities, and we must therefore acknowledge the superiority of the ancient authors (43).

This, then, is the presentation of classical authority in Dryden's text. It is Eugenius who first defends the moderns, saying that they have not restricted themselves to "dull imitation" of the ancients; they did not "draw after their lines, but those of Nature; and having the life before us, besides the experience of all they knew, it is no wonder if we hit some airs and features which they have missed" (44). This is an interesting and important argument which seems to have been subsequently overlooked by Alexander Pope, who in other respects followed Dryden's prescriptions for following the rules of "nature." In his *Essay on Criticism*, Pope had urged that to copy nature is to copy the ancient writers. Dryden, through the mouth of his persona Eugenius, completely topples this complacent equation: Eugenius effectively turns against Crites the latter's own observation that the arts and sciences have made huge advances since the time of Aristotle. Not only do we have the collective experience and wisdom of the ancients to draw upon, but also we have our own experience of the world, a world understood far better in scientific terms than in ages past: "if natural causes be more known now than in the time of Aristotle . . . it follows that poesy and other arts may, with the same pains, arrive still nearer to perfection" (44).

Turning to the unities, Eugenius points out (after Corneille) that by the time of Horace, the division of a play into five acts was firmly established, but this distinction was unknown to the Greeks. Indeed, the Greeks did not even confine themselves to a regular number of acts (44–46). Again, their plots were usually based on "some tale derived from Thebes or Troy," a plot "worn so threadbare . . . that before it came upon the stage, it was already known to all the audience." Since the pleasure in novelty was thereby dissolved, asserts Eugenius, "one main end of Dramatic Poesy in its definition, which was to cause delight, was of consequence destroyed" (47). These are strong words, threatening to undermine a long tradition of reverence for the classics. But Eugenius has hardly finished: not only do the ancients fail to fulfill one of the essential obligations of drama, that of delighting; they also fall short in the other requirement, that of instructing. Eugenius berates the narrow characterization by Greek and Roman dramatists, as well as their imperfect linking of scenes. He cites instances of their own violation of the unities. Even more acerbic is his observation, following Corneille, that when the classical authors such as Euripides and Terence do observe the unities, they are forced into absurdities (48–49). As for the unity of place, he points out, this is nowhere to be found in Aristotle or Horace; it was made a precept of the stage in our own age by the French dramatists (48). Moreover, instead of "punishing vice and rewarding virtue," the ancients "have often shown a prosperous wickedness, and an unhappy piety" (50).

Eugenius also berates the ancients for not dealing sufficiently with love, but rather with "lust, cruelty, revenge, ambition . . . which were more capable of raising horror than compassion in an audience" (54). Hence, in Dryden's text, not only is Aristotle's definition of tragedy violently displaced by a formulation that will accommodate modern poets, but also the ancient philosopher's definition itself is made to appear starkly unrealistic and problematic for ancient dramatists, who persistently violated its essential features.

The next point of debate is the relative quality of French and English writers; it is Lisideius who extols the virtues of the French while Neander (Dryden himself) undertakes to defend his compatriots. Lisideius argues that the current French theater surpasses all Europe, observing the unities of time, place, and action, and is not strewn with the cumbrous underplots that litter the English stage. Moreover, the French provide variety of emotion without sinking to the absurd genre of tragicomedy, which is a uniquely English invention (56–57). Lisideius also points out that the French are proficient at proportioning the time devoted to dialogue and action on the one hand, and narration on the other. There are certain actions, such as duels, battles, and death-scenes, that "can never be imitated to a just height"; they cannot be represented with decorum or with credibility and thus must be narrated rather than acted out on stage (62–63).

Neander's response takes us by surprise. He does not at all refute the claims made by Lisideius. He concedes that "the French contrive their plots more regularly, and observe the laws of comedy, and decorum of the stage . . . with more exactness than the English" (67). Neander effectively argues that the very "faults" of the English are actually virtues, virtues that take English drama far beyond the pale of its classical heritage. What Neander or Dryden takes as a valid presupposition is that a play should present a "lively imitation of Nature" (68). The beauties of French drama, he points out, are "the beauties of a statue, but not of a man, because not animated with the soul of Poesy, which is imitation of humour and passions" (68).

Indeed, in justifying the genre of tragicomedy, Neander states that the contrast between mirth and compassion will throw the important scenes into sharper relief (69). He urges that it is "to the honour of our nation, that we have invented, increased, and perfected a more pleasant way of writing for the stage, than was ever known to the ancients or moderns of any nation, which is tragi-comedy" (70). This exaltation of tragicomedy effectively overturns nearly all of the ancient prescriptions concerning purity of genre, decorum, and unity of plot. Neander poignantly repeats Corneille's observation that anyone with actual experience of the stage will see how constraining the classical rules are (76).

Neander now undertakes a brief assessment of the recent English dramatic tradition. Of all modern and perhaps ancient poets, he says, Shakespeare "had the largest and most comprehensive soul." He was "naturally learn'd," not through books but by the reading of nature and all her images: "he looked inwards, and found her there" (79–80). Again, the implication is that, in order to express nature, Shakespeare did not need to look outwards, toward the classics, but rather into his own humanity. Beaumont and Fletcher had both the precedent of Shakespeare's wit and natural gifts which they improved by study; what they excelled at was expressing "the conversation of gentlemen," and the representation of the passions, especially of love (80–81). Ben Jonson he regards as the "most learned and judicious writer which any theatre ever had," and his peculiar gift was the representation of humors (81–82). Neander defines "humour" as "some extravagant habit, passion, or affection" which defines the individuality of a person (84–85). In an important statement he affirms that "Shakespeare was the Homer, or father of our dramatic poets; Johnson was the Vergil, the pattern of elaborate writing" (82). What Neander – or Dryden – effectively does here is to stake out an independent tradition for English drama, with new archetypes displacing those of the classical tradition.

The final debate concerns the use of rhyme in drama. Crites argues that "rhyme is unnatural in a play" (91). Following Aristotle, Crites insists that the most natural verse form for the stage is blank verse, since ordinary speech follows an iambic pattern (91). Neander's reply is ambivalent (Dryden himself was later to change his mind on this issue): he does not deny that blank verse may be used; but he asserts that "in serious plays, where the subject and characters are great . . . rhyme is there as natural and more effectual than blank verse" (94). Moreover, in everyday life, people do not speak in blank verse, any more than they do in rhyme. He also observes that rhyme and accent are a modern substitute for the use of quantity as syllabic measure in classical verse (96–97).

Underlying Neander's argument in favor of rhyme is an observation fundamental to the very nature of drama. He insists that, while all drama represents nature, a distinction should be made between comedy, "which is the imitation of common persons and ordinary speaking," and tragedy, which "is indeed the representation of Nature, but 'tis Nature wrought up to an higher pitch. The plot, the characters, the wit, the passions, the descriptions, are all exalted above the level of common converse, as high as the imagination of the poet can carry them, with proportion to verisimility" (100–101). And while the use of verse and rhyme helps the poet control an otherwise "lawless imagination," it is nonetheless a great help to his "luxuriant fancy" (107). This concluding argument, which suggests that the poet use "imagination" to transcend nature, underlines Neander's (and Dryden's) departure from classical convention. If Dryden is neoclassical, it is in the sense that he acknowledges the classics as having furnished archetypes for drama; but modern writers are at liberty to create their own archetypes and their own literary traditions. Again, he might be called classical in view of the unquestioned persistence of certain presuppositions that are shared by all four speakers in this text: that the unity of a play, however conceived, is a paramount requirement; that a play present, through its use of plot and characterization, events and actions which are probable and express truth or at least a resemblance to truth; that the laws of "nature" be followed, if not through imitation of the ancients, then through looking inward at our own profoundest constitution; and finally, that every aspect of a play be contrived with the projected response of the audience in mind. But given Dryden's equal emphasis on the poet's wit, invention, and imagination, his text might be viewed as expressing a status of transition between neoclassicism and Romanticism.

Dryden's other essays and prefaces would seem to confirm the foregoing comments, and reveal important insights into his vision of the poet's craft. In his 1666 preface to *Annus Mirabilis*, he states that the "composition of all poems is, or ought to be, of wit; and wit . . . is no other than the faculty of imagination in the writer" (14). He subsequently offers a more comprehensive definition: "the first happiness of the poet's imagination is properly invention, or finding of the thought; the second is fancy, or the variation, deriving, or moulding, of that thought, as the judgment represents it proper to the subject; the third is elocution, or the art of clothing or adorning that thought, so found and varied, in apt, significant, and sounding words: the quickness of the imagination is seen in the invention, the fertility in the fancy, and the accuracy in the expression" (15). Again, the emphasis here is on wit, imagination, and invention rather than exclusively on the classical precept of imitation.

In fact, Dryden was later to write "Defence of *An Essay on Dramatic Poesy*," defending his earlier text against Sir Robert Howard's attack on Dryden's advocacy of rhyme in drama. Here, Dryden's defense of rhyme undergoes a shift of emphasis, revealing further his modification of classical prescriptions. He now argues that what most commends rhyme is the delight it produces: "for delight is the chief, if not the only, end of poesy: instruction can be admitted but in the second place, for poesy only instructs as it delights" (113). And Dryden states: "I confess my chief endeavours are to delight the age in which I live" (116). We have come a long way from Aristotle, and even from Sidney, who both regarded poetry as having primarily a moral or ethical purpose. To suggest that poetry's chief or only aim is to delight is to take a large step toward the later modern notion of literary autonomy. Dryden goes on to suggest that while a poet's task is to "imitate well," he must also "affect the soul, and excite the passions" as well as cause "admiration" or wonder. To this end, "bare imitation will not serve." Imitation must be "heightened with all the arts and ornaments of poesy" (113).

If, in such statements, Dryden appears to anticipate certain Romantic predispositions, these comments are counterbalanced by other positions which are deeply entrenched in a classical heritage. Later in the "Defence" he insists that "they cannot be good poets, who are not accustomed to argue well . . . for moral truth is the mistress of the poet as much as of the philosopher; Poesy must resemble natural truth, but it must *be* ethical. Indeed, the poet dresses truth, and adorns nature, but does not alter them" (121). Hence, notwithstanding the importance that he attaches to wit and imagination, Dryden still regards poetry as essentially a rational activity, with an ethical and epistemological responsibility. If the poet rises above nature and truth, this is merely by way of ornamentation; it does not displace or remold the truths of nature, but merely heightens them. Dryden states that imagination "is supposed to participate of Reason," and that when imagination creates fictions, reason allows itself to be temporarily deceived but will never be persuaded "of those things which are most remote from probability . . . Fancy and Reason go hand in hand; the first cannot leave the last behind" (127–128). These formulations differ from subsequent Romantic views of the primacy of imagination over reason. Imagination can indeed outrun reason, but only within the limits of classical probability. Dryden's entire poetic and critical enterprise might be summed up in his own words: he views all poetry, both ancient and modern, as based on "the imitation of Nature." Where he differs from the classics is the means with which he undertakes this poetic project (123). Following intimations in

Plato's *Timaeus* and Aristotle's *Poetics*, he suggests in his "Parallel of Poetry and Painting" (1695) that what the poet (and painter) should imitate are not individual instances of nature but the archetypal *ideas* behind natural forms.[6] While adhering to this classical position, he also suggests that, in imitating nature, modern writers should "vary the customs, according to the time and the country where the scene of the action lies; for this is still to imitate Nature, which is always the same, though in a different dress" (*Essays*, II, 139). This stance effectively embodies both Dryden's classicism and the nature of his departure from its strict boundaries.

Alexander Pope (1688–1744)

An Essay on Criticism, published anonymously by Alexander Pope in 1711, is perhaps the clearest statement of neoclassical principles in any language. In its broad outlines, it expresses a worldview which synthesizes elements of a Roman Catholic outlook with classical aesthetic principles and with deism. That Pope was born a Roman Catholic affected not only his verse and critical principles but also his life. In the year of his birth occurred the so-called "Glorious Revolution": England's Catholic monarch James II was displaced by the Protestant King William III of Orange, and the prevailing anti-Catholic laws constrained many areas of Pope's life; he could not obtain a university education, hold public or political office, or even reside in London. Pope's family, in fact, moved to a small farm in Windsor Forest, a neighborhood occupied by other Catholic families of the gentry, and he later moved with his mother to Twickenham. However, Pope was privately taught and moved in an elite circle of London writers which included the dramatists Wycherley and Congreve, the poet Granville, the critic William Walsh, as well as the writers Addison and Steele, and the deistic politician Bolingbroke. Pope's personal life was also afflicted by disease: he was a hunchback, only four and a half feet tall, and suffered from tuberculosis. He was in constant need of his maid to dress and care for him. Notwithstanding such social and personal obstacles, Pope produced some of the finest verse ever written. His most renowned publications include several mock-heroic poems such as *The Rape of the Lock* (1712; 1714), and *The Dunciad* (1728). His philosophical poem *An Essay on Man* (1733–1734) was a scathing attack on human arrogance or pride in failing to observe the due limits of human reason, in questioning divine authority and seeking to be self-reliant on the basis of rationality and science. Even *An Essay on Criticism* is written in verse, following the tradition of Horace's *Ars poetica*, and interestingly, much of the philosophical substance of *An Essay on Man* is already formulated in this earlier poem, in its application to literature and criticism. While *An Essay on Man* identifies the chief fault of humankind as the original sin of "pride" and espouses an ethic based on an ordered and hierarchical universe, it nonetheless depicts this order in terms of Newtonian mechanism and expresses a broadly deistic vision.

The same contradictions permeate the *Essay on Criticism*, which effects an eclectic mixture of a Roman Catholic vision premised on the (negative) significance of pride, a humanistic secularism perhaps influenced by Erasmus, a stylistic neoclassicism with roots in the rhetorical tradition from Aristotle, Horace, Longinus, and modern disciples such as Boileau, and a modernity in the wake of figures such as Bacon, Hobbes, and

Locke. Some critics have argued that the resulting conglomeration is inharmonious; in fairness to Pope, we might cite one of his portraits of the satirist:

> Verse-man or Prose-man, term me which you will,
> Papist or Protestant, or both between,
> Like good Erasmus in an honest Mean,
> In moderation placing all my glory,
> While Tories call me Whig, and Whigs a Tory.
>
> (*Satire* II.i)

Clearly, labels can oversimplify: yet it is beyond doubt that, on balance, Pope's overall vision was conservative and retrospective. He is essentially calling for a return to the past, a return to classical values, and the various secularizing movements that he bemoans are already overwhelming the view of nature, man, and God that he is attempting to redeem.

Indeed, Pope's poem has been variously called a study and defense of "nature" and of "wit." The word "nature" is used twenty-one times in the poem; the word "wit" forty-six times. Given the numerous meanings accumulated in the word "nature" as it has passed through various traditions, Pope's call for a "return to nature" is complex, and he exploits the multiple significance of the term to generate within his poem a comprehensive redefinition of it. Among other things, nature can refer, on a cosmic level, to the providential order of the world and the universe, an order which is hierarchical, in which each entity has its proper assigned place. In *An Essay on Man* Pope expounds the "Great Chain of Being," ranging from God and the angels through humans and the lower animals to plants and inanimate objects. Nature can also refer to what is normal, central, and universal in human experience, encompassing the spheres of morality and knowledge, the rules of proper moral conduct as well as the archetypal patterns of human reason.

The word "wit" in Pope's time also had a variety of meanings: it could refer in general to intelligence and intellectual acuity; it also meant "wit" in the modern sense of cleverness, as expressed for example in the ability to produce a concise and poignant figure of speech or pun; more specifically, it might designate a capacity to discern similarities between different entities and to perceive the hidden relationships underlying the appearances of things. In fact, during the late seventeenth and early eighteenth centuries, "wit" was the subject of a broad and heated debate. Various parties contested the right to define it and to invest it with moral significance. A number of writers such as Nicolas Malebranche and Joseph Addison, and philosophers such as John Locke, argued that wit was a negative quality, associated with a corrupting imagination, distortion of truth, profanity, and skepticism, a quality opposed to "judgment," which was a faculty of clear and truthful insight. Literature generally had come to be associated with wit and had been under attack from the Puritans also, who saw it as morally defective and corrupting. On the other side, writers such as John Dryden and William Wycherley, as well as moralists such as the third earl of Shaftesbury, defended the use and freedom of wit. Pope's notions of wit were worked out in the context of this debate, and his redefinition of "true" wit in *Essay on Criticism* was a means not only of upholding the proper uses of wit but also of defending literature itself, wit being a mode of knowing or apprehension unique to literature.[7]

It would be facile to dismiss Pope's *Essay on Criticism* as an unoriginal work, as a hotchpotch of adages drawn from the likes of Aristotle, Horace, Quintilian, Longinus, and Boileau. While the isolated insights offered by Pope may not be original, the poem as a whole undertakes a number of endeavors that, in their poetic unification, might well be viewed as novel. To begin with, Pope is not merely delineating the scope and nature of good literary criticism; in doing this, he redefines classical virtues in terms of an exploration of nature and wit, as necessary to both poetry and criticism; and this restatement of classicism is itself situated within a broader reformulation of literary history, tradition, and religion. Above all, these three endeavors are pursued in the form of a *poem*: the form of the work exemplifies and enacts much of its overt "meaning." And its power far exceeds its paraphrasable meaning: this power rests on the poetic effects generated by its own enactment of classical literary dispositions and its own organic unity.

While much of Pope's essay bemoans the abyss into which current literary criticism has fallen, he does not by any means denounce the practice of criticism itself. While he cautions that the best poets make the best critics ("Let such teach others who themselves excell," l. 15), and while he recognizes that some critics are failed poets (l. 105), he points out that both the best poetry and the best criticism are divinely inspired:

> Both must alike from Heav'n derive their Light,
> These *born* to Judge, as well as those to Write.
> (ll. 13–14)

By the word "judge," Pope refers to the critic, drawing on the meaning of the ancient Greek word *krites*. Pope sees the endeavor of criticism as a noble one, provided it abides by Horace's advice for the poet:

> But *you* who seek to *give* and *merit* Fame,
> And justly bear a Critick's noble Name,
> Be sure *your self* and your own *Reach* to know,
> How far your *Genius*, *Taste*, and *Learning* go;
> Launch not beyond your Depth . . .
> (ll. 46–50)

Indeed, Pope suggests in many portions of the *Essay* that criticism itself is an art and must be governed by the same rules that apply to literature itself. However, there are a number of precepts he advances as specific to criticism. Apart from knowing his own capacities, the critic must be conversant with every aspect of the author whom he is examining, including the author's

> . . . *Fable, Subject, Scope* in ev'ry Page,
> *Religion, Country, Genius* of his Age:
> Without all these at once before your Eyes,
> *Cavil* you may, but never *Criticize*.
> (ll. 120–123)

Perhaps ironically, Pope's advice here seems modern insofar as he calls for a knowledge of all aspects of the author's work, including not only its subject matter and artistic lineage but also its religious, national, and intellectual contexts. He is less modern in insisting that the critic base his interpretation on the author's intention: "In ev'ry Work regard the Writer's *End*, / Since none can compass more than they *Intend*" (ll. 233–234, 255–256).

Pope specifies two further guidelines for the critic. The first is to recognize the overall unity of a work, and thereby to avoid falling into partial assessments based on the author's use of poetic conceits, ornamented language, and meters, as well as those which are biased toward either archaic or modern styles or based on the reputations of given writers. Finally, a critic needs to possess a moral sensibility, as well as a sense of balance and proportion, as indicated in these lines: "Nor in the *Critick* let the *Man* be lost! / *Good-Nature* and *Good-Sense* must ever join" (ll. 523–525). In the interests of good nature and good sense, Pope urges the critic to adopt not only habits of self-criticism and integrity ("with pleasure own your Errors past, / And make each Day a *Critick* on the last," ll. 570–571), but also modesty and caution. To be truthful is not enough, he warns; truth must be accompanied by "Good Breeding" or else it will lose its effect (ll. 572–576). And mere bookish knowledge will often express itself in showiness, disdain, and an overactive tongue: "*Fools* rush in where *Angels* fear to tread. / Distrustful *Sense* with modest Caution speaks" (ll. 625–626). Pope ends his advice with this summary of the ideal critic:

> But where's the Man, who Counsel *can* bestow,
> Still *pleas'd* to *teach*, and yet not *proud to know*?
> Unbiass'd, or by *Favour* or by *Spite*;
> Not *dully prepossest*, nor *blindly right*;
> Tho learn'd, well-bred; and tho' well-bred, sincere;
> . . . Blest with a *Taste* exact, yet unconfin'd;
> A *Knowledge* both of *Books* and *Humankind*;
> *Gen'rous Converse*; a *Soul* exempt from *Pride*;
> And *Love* to *Praise*, with *Reason* on his Side?
> (ll. 631–642)

As we read through this synthesis of the qualities of a good critic, it becomes clear that they are primarily attributes of humanity or moral sensibility rather than aesthetic qualities. Indeed, the only specifically aesthetic quality mentioned here is "taste." The remaining virtues might be said to have a theological ground, resting on the ability to overcome pride. Pope effectively transposes the language of theology ("soul," "pride") to aesthetics. It is the disposition of humility – an aesthetic humility, if you will – which enables the critic to avoid the arrogant parading of his learning, to avoid falling into bias, and to open himself up to a knowledge of humanity. The "reason" to which Pope appeals is not the individualistic and secular "reason" of the Enlightenment philosophers; it is "reason" as understood by Aquinas and many medieval thinkers, reason as a universal archetype in human nature, constrained by a theological framework. Reason in this sense is a corollary of humility: it is humility which allows the critic to rise above egotistical dogmatism and thereby to be rational and impartial, and aware of his own limitations, in his striving after truth. Knowledge itself, then, has a moral basis in good breeding; and underlying good breeding is the still profounder quality of sincerity, which we might understand here as a disposition commensurate with humility: a genuine desire to pursue truth or true judgment, unclouded by personal ambitions and subjective prejudices. Interestingly, the entire summary takes the form not of an assertion but of an extended question, implying that what is proposed here is an ideal type, to which no contemporary critic can answer.

Pope's specific advice to the critic is grounded on virtues whose application extends far beyond literary criticism, into the realms of morality, theology, and art itself. It is something of an irony that the main part of his *Essay on Criticism* is devoted not specifically to criticism but to art itself, of which poetry and criticism are regarded as branches. In other words, Pope sees criticism itself as an art. Hence most of the guidance he offers, couched in the language of nature and wit, applies equally to poetry and criticism. Not only this, but there are several passages which suggest that criticism must be a part of the creative process, that poets themselves must possess critical faculties in order to execute their craft in a self-conscious and controlled manner. Hence there is a large overlap between these domains, between the artistic elements within criticism and the critical elements necessary to art. While Pope's central piece of advice to both poet and critic is to "follow Nature," his elaboration of this concept enlists the semantic service of both wit and judgment, establishing a close connection – sometimes indeed an identity – between all three terms; wit might be correlated with literature or poetry; and judgment with criticism. Because of the overlapping natures of poetry and criticism, however, both wit and judgment will be required in each of these pursuits.

Before inviting the poet and critic to follow nature, Pope is careful to explain one of the central functions of nature:

> Nature to all things fix'd the Limits fit,
> And wisely curb'd proud Man's pretending Wit;
> . . . One Science only will one Genius fit;
> So vast is Art, so narrow Human Wit . . .
> (ll. 52–53, 60–61)

Hence, even before he launches into any discussion of aesthetics, Pope designates human wit generally as an instrument of pride, as intrinsically liable to abuse. In the scheme of nature, however, man's wit is puny and occupies an apportioned place. It is in this context that Pope proclaims his famous maxim:

> First follow NATURE, and your Judgment frame
> By her just Standard, which is still the same:
> *Unerring Nature*, still divinely bright,
> Once *clear*, *unchang'd*, and *Universal* Light,
> Life, Force, and Beauty, must to all impart,
> At once the *Source*, and *End*, and *Test* of Art.
> (ll. 68–73)

The features attributed to nature include permanence or timelessness and universality. Ultimately, nature is a force which expresses the power of the divine, not in the later Romantic sense of a divine spirit pervading the physical appearances of nature but in the medieval sense of expressing the order, harmony, and beauty of God's creation. As such, nature provides the eternal and archetypal standard against which art must be measured: the implication in the lines above is not that art imitates nature but that it derives its inspiration, purpose, and aesthetic criteria from nature.

Pope's view of nature as furnishing the universal archetypes for art leads him to condemn excessive individualism, which he sees as an abuse of wit. Wit is abused when it contravenes sound judgment: "For *Wit* and *Judgment* often are at strife, Tho' meant each other's Aid, like *Man* and *Wife*" (ll. 80–83). However, Pope does not believe, like many medieval rhetoricians, that poetry is an entirely rational process that can be methodically worked out in advance. In poetry, as in music, he points out, are "*nameless* Graces which no Methods teach" (l. 144). Indeed, geniuses can sometimes transgress the boundaries of judgment and their very transgression or license becomes a rule for art:

> Great Wits sometimes may *gloriously offend*,
> And *rise* to *Faults* true Criticks *dare not mend*;
> From *vulgar Bounds* with *brave Disorder* part,
> And *snatch a Grace* beyond the Reach of Art,
> Which, without passing thro' the *Judgment*, gains
> The *Heart*, and all its End *at once* attains.
>
> (ll. 152–157)

If Kant had been a poet, he might have expressed his central aesthetic ideas in this very way. Kant also believed that a genius lays down the rules for art, that those rules cannot be prescribed in advance, and that aesthetic judgment bypasses the conventional concepts of our understanding. Indeed, Kant laid the groundwork for many Romantic aesthetics, and if Pope's passage above were taken in isolation, it might well be read as a formulation of Romantic aesthetic doctrine. It seems to assert the primacy of wit over judgment, of art over criticism, viewing art as inspired and as transcending the norms of conventional thinking in its direct appeal to the "heart." The critic's task here is to recognize the superiority of great wit. While Pope's passage does indeed in these respects stride beyond many medieval and Renaissance aesthetics, it must of course be read in its own poetic context: he immediately warns contemporary writers not to abuse such a license of wit: "*Moderns*, beware! Or if you must offend / Against the *Precept*, ne'er transgress its *End*" (ll. 163–164). In fact, the passage cited above is more than counterbalanced by Pope's subsequent insistence that modern writers not rely on their own insights. Modern writers should draw on the common store of poetic wisdom, established by the ancients, and acknowledged by "*Universal* Praise" (l. 190).

Pope's exploration of wit aligns it with the central classical virtues, which are themselves equated with nature. His initial definition of true wit identifies it as an expression of nature: "*True Wit* is *Nature* to Advantage drest, / What oft was *Thought*, but ne'er so well *Exprest*" (ll. 297–298). Pope subsequently says that expression is the "*Dress of Thought*," and that "true expression" throws light on objects without altering them (ll. 315–318). The lines above are a concentrated expression of Pope's classicism. If wit is the "dress" of nature, it will express nature without altering it. The poet's task here is twofold: not only to find the expression that will most truly convey nature, but also first to ensure that the substance that he is expressing is indeed a "natural" insight or thought. What the poet must express is a universal truth which we will instantly recognize as such. This classical commitment to the expression of objective and universal truth is echoed a number of times through Pope's text. For example, he admonishes both poet and critic: "Regard not then if Wit be *Old* or *New*, / But blame the *False*, and value still the *True*" (ll. 406–407).

A second classical ideal urged in the passage above is that of organic unity and wholeness. The expression or style, Pope insists, must be suited to the subject matter and meaning: "The *Sound* must seem an *Eccho* to the *Sense*" (l. 365). Elsewhere in the *Essay*, Pope stresses the importance, for both poet and critic, of considering a work of art in its totality, with all the parts given their due proportion and place (ll. 173–174). Once again, wit and nature become almost interchangeable in Pope's text. An essential component underlying such unity and proportion is the classical virtue of moderation. Pope advises both poet and critic to follow the Aristotelian ethical maxim: "Avoid *Extreams.*" Those who go to excess in any direction display "*Great Pride, or Little Sense*" (ll. 384–387). And once again, the ability to overcome pride – humility – is implicitly associated with what Pope calls "right Reason" (l. 211).

Indeed, the central passage in the *Essay on Criticism*, as in the later *Essay on Man*, views all of the major faults as stemming from pride:

> Of all the Causes which conspire to blind
> Man's erring Judgment, and misguide the Mind,
> . . . Is *Pride*, the *never-failing Vice of Fools.*
> (ll. 201–204)

It is pride which leads critics and poets alike to overlook universal truths in favor of subjective whims; pride which causes them to value particular parts instead of the whole; pride which disables them from achieving a harmony of wit and judgment; and pride which underlies their excesses and biases. And, as in the *Essay on Man*, Pope associates pride with individualism, with excessive reliance on one's own judgment and failure to observe the laws laid down by nature and by the classical tradition.

Pope's final strategy in the *Essay* is to equate the classical literary and critical traditions with nature, and to sketch a redefined outline of literary history from classical times to his own era. Pope insists that the rules of nature were merely discovered, not invented, by the ancients: "Those Rules of old *discover'd*, not *devis'd*, / Are *Nature* still, but *Nature Methodiz'd*" (ll. 88–89). He looks back to a time in ancient Greece when criticism admirably performed its function as "the Muse's Handmaid," and facilitated a rational admiration of poetry. But criticism later declined from this high status, and those who "cou'd not win the Mistress, woo'd the Maid" (ll. 100–105). Instead of aiding the appreciation of poetry, critics, perhaps in consequence of their own failure to master the poetic art, allowed the art of criticism to degenerate into irrational attacks on poets. Pope's advice, for both critic and poet, is clear: "Learn hence for Ancient *Rules* a just Esteem; / To copy *Nature* is to copy *Them*" (ll. 139–140).

Before offering his sketch of literary-critical history, Pope laments the passing of the "Golden Age" of letters (l. 478), and portrays the depths to which literature and criticism have sunk in the degenerate times of recent history:

> In the fat Age of Pleasure, Wealth, and Ease,
> Sprung the rank Weed, and thriv'd with large Increase;
> When *Love* was all an easie Monarch's Care;
> Seldom at *Council*, never in a *War* . . .
>
> . . . The following Licence of a Foreign Reign
> Did all the Dregs of bold *Socinus* drain;
> Then Unbelieving Priests reform'd the Nation,
> And taught more *Pleasant* Methods of Salvation;
> Where Heav'ns Free Subjects might their *Rights* dispute,
> Lest God himself shou'd seem too *Absolute*.
> . . . Encourag'd thus, Wit's *Titans* brav'd the Skies . . .
>
> (ll. 534–537, 544–552)

Pope cites two historical circumstances here. By "easie Monarch" he refers to the reign of Charles II (1660–1685), whose father King Charles I had engaged in a war with the English Parliament, provoked by his excessive authoritarianism. Having lost the war, Charles I was beheaded in 1649, and England was ruled by Parliament, under the leadership of the Puritan Oliver Cromwell. Shortly after Cromwell's death, a newly elected Parliament, reflecting the nation's unease with the era of puritanical rule, invited Prince Charles to take the throne of England as Charles II. The new king, as Pope indicates, had a reputation for easy living, lax morality, and laziness. The reigns of Charles II and his brother James II (1685–1688) are known as the period of the Restoration (of the monarchy). Both kings were strongly pro-Catholic and aroused considerable opposition, giving rise to the second historical event to which Pope refers above, the Glorious Revolution of 1688–1689. In 1688 the Protestants Prince William of Orange and his wife Mary (daughter of James II) were secretly invited to occupy the throne of England. Under their rule, which Pope refers to as the "Licence of a Foreign Reign," a Toleration Act was passed which granted religious freedom to all Christians except Catholics and Unitarians. Also enacted into law was a Bill of Rights which granted English citizens the right to trial by jury and various other rights.

Hence, as far as understanding Pope's passage is concerned, there were two broad consequences of the Glorious Revolution. First, various impulses of the earlier Protestant Reformation, such as religious individualism and amendment of the doctrines of the Church of England, were reconfirmed. Pope refers to Faustus Socinus (1539– 1604), who produced unorthodox doctrines denying Christ's divinity, as being of the same theological tenor as the "Unbelieving Priests," the Protestants, who reformed the nation. The second, even more significant, consequence of the revolution was the complete triumph of Parliament over the king, the monarchy's powers being permanently restricted. Protestantism in general had been associated with attempts to oppose absolute government; clearly, Pope's sympathies did not lie with these movements toward democracy. Significantly, his passage above wittily intertwines these two implications of the Glorious Revolution: he speaks sarcastically of "Heav'ns Free Subjects" disputing their rights not only with temporal power but also with God himself. Such is the social background, in Pope's estimation, of the modern decline of poetry and criticism: religious and political individualism, the craving for freedom, and the concomitant rejection of authority and tradition, underlie these same vices in the sphere of letters, vices which amount to pride and the contravention of nature.

Pope now furnishes an even broader historical context for these modern ills. He traces the genealogy of "nature," as embodied in classical authors, to Aristotle. Poets who accepted Aristotle's rules of poetic composition, he suggests, learned that "Who conquer'd *Nature*, shou'd preside oe'r *Wit*" (l. 652). In other words, the true and false uses of wit must be judged by those who have learned the rules of nature. Likewise, Horace, the next critic in the tradition Pope cites, was "Supream in Judgment, as in Wit" and "his *Precepts* teach but what his *Works* inspire" (ll. 657, 660). Other classical critics praised by Pope are Dionysius of Halicarnassus (ca. 30–7 BC) and the Roman authors of the first century Petronius and Quintilian, as well as Longinus, the first-century Greek author of *On the Sublime*. After these writers, who represent the classical tradition, Pope says, a dark age ensued with the collapse of the western Roman Empire at the hands of the Vandals and Goths, an age governed by "tyranny" and "superstition," an age where "Much was *Believ'd*, but little *understood*" (ll. 686–689). What is interesting here is that Pope sees the medieval era as a continuation of the so-called Dark Ages. He refers to the onset of medieval theology as a "*second Deluge*" whereby "the *Monks* finish'd what the *Goths* begun" (ll. 691–692). Hence, even though he was himself a Catholic and placed great stress on the original sin of pride, Pope seems to reject the traditions of Catholic theology as belonging to an age of superstition and irrational belief. He is writing here as a descendent of Renaissance thinkers who saw themselves as the true heirs of the classical authors and the medieval period as an aberration. What is even more striking is Pope's subsequent praise of the Renaissance humanist thinker Desiderius Erasmus, who "drove those *Holy Vandals* off the Stage" (ll. 693–694). Erasmus, like Pope, had a love for the classics grounded on rationality and tolerance. He rejected ecclesiastical Christianity, theological dogmatism, and superstition in favor of a religion of simple and reasonable piety. His writings helped pave the way for the Protestant Reformation, though he himself was skeptical of the bigotry he saw on both Protestant and Catholic sides.

Pope's implicit allegiance to Erasmus (and in part to contemporary figures such as Bolingbroke) points in the direction of a broad deism which, on the one hand, accommodates the significance of pride in secular rather than theological contexts, and, on the other hand, accommodates reason within its appropriate limits. His historical survey continues with praises of the "Golden Days" of Renaissance artistic accomplishments, and suggests that the arts and criticism thereafter flourished chiefly in Europe, especially in France, which produced the critic and poet Nicolas Boileau. Boileau was a classicist influenced greatly by Horace. Given Boileau's own impact on Pope's critical thought, we can see that Pope now begins to set the stage for his own entry into the history of criticism. While he notes that the English, "Fierce for the *Liberties of Wit*," were generally impervious to foreign literary influences, he observes that a handful of English writers were more sound: they sided with "the *juster Ancient Cause*, / And here restor'd Wit's *Fundamental Laws*" (ll. 721–722). The writers Pope now cites were either known to him or his tutors. He names the earl of Roscommon, who was acquainted with classical wit; William Walsh, his mentor; and finally himself, as offering "humble" tribute to his dead tutor (ll. 725–733). All in all, Pope's strategy here is remarkable: in retracing the lineage of good criticism, as based on nature and the true use of wit, he traces his own lineage as both poet and critic, thereby both redefining or reaffirming the true critical tradition and marking his own entry into it. Pope presents himself as abiding by and exemplifying the critical virtues he has hitherto commended.

Aphra Behn (1640–1689)

Aphra Behn was a pioneer in many respects. Because of her family circumstances and her husband's early death, she was obliged to support herself as a writer – the first woman to do so. She is one of the founders of the English novel; her extended stay in Surinam inspired her to write *Oroonoko* (1688), the first novel to oppose slavery. And her experience as a female playwright exposed her to the enormous obstacles faced by a woman in this profession, resulting in her highly unorthodox and controversial views about drama. These views are expressed largely in the prefaces to her plays, such as *The Dutch Lover* (1673), *The Rover* (1677), and *The Lucky Chance* (1687). If figures such as Pierre Corneille took a step away from the authority of classical rules of drama by appealing to experience, Aphra Behn's appeal to experience – to specifically female experience – was far more radical. Moreover, she (perhaps unwittingly) elevates to a newly important status the performative dimensions of drama, such as the ability and integrity of the actors.

In the "Epistle to the Reader" which prefaces *The Dutch Lover*, Behn strikes a tone of utter defiance. She defends the value of drama by contrasting it favorably with traditional learning as taught in the universities. This learning, she says, amounts to "more absolutely nothing than the errantest Play that e'er was writ."[8] Having said that, she equally denies that poets, especially dramatic poets, "can be justly charged with too great reformation of mens minds or manners." It is unrealistic, and lacks any foundation in experience, to expect drama to perform a moral function. On the contrary, such expectations are little short of absurd given that "the most assiduous Disciples of the Stage" are the most foolish and lewd group of people in the city (*Behn*, I, 222). Experience also encompasses the effects of the actual plays that have recently been written: these dramas, asserts Behn, have "not done much more towards the amending of mens Morals, or their Wit, than hath the frequent Preaching, which this last age hath been pester'd with" (*Behn*, I, 222). By "frequent preaching," Behn is referring to the moral condemnation of the theater which accompanied the rise of Puritanism in England. As far as moral intention goes, Behn is adamant that "no Play was ever writ with that design." Even the best characters in tragedy, she says, present "unlikely patterns for a wise man to pursue . . . And as for Comedie, the finest folks you meet with there, are still unfitter for your imitation." Behn's own, carefully unstudied, opinion is that drama represents the best entertainment that "wise men have"; to discourse formally about its rules, as if it were "the grand affair" of human life, is valueless. Behn's own purpose, in writing her play *The Dutch Lover*, was "only to make this as entertaining as I could," and the judges of her success will be the audience (*Behn*, I, 223).

Behn now takes up the murky issues surrounding female authorship. She heaps a barrage of insulting criticism ("ill-favour'd, wretched Fop" and more) upon a man who told the audience for her play to expect "a woful Play . . . for it was a womans." Replying to his presumption, she asserts that women, if given the same education as men, are just as capable of acquiring knowledge and in as many capacities as men. Moreover, successful plays, she points out, do not rest on the learning which is men's point of advantage over women, citing Shakespeare and Jonson as examples. Further, given that "affectation hath always had a greater share both in the actions and discourse of men than truth and judgment have," women might well reach the heights attained by men (*Behn*, I, 224). The classical rules of drama she dismisses in a breath: these "musty rules of Unity, . . . if they meant anything, they are enough intelligible, and as practicable by a woman" (*Behn*, I, 224). With no apology, she ends with: "Now, Reader, I have eas'd my mind of all I had to say" (*Behn*, I, 225).

In her preface to *The Lucky Chance*, written some fifteen years later, Behn states that she will defend her comedy against "those Censures that Malice, and ill Nature have thrown upon it, tho' in vain."[9] It is the very success of her play, she exclaims, that caused critics to "load it with all manner of Infamy." And they heap upon it, she says, "the old never failing Scandal – That 'tis not fit for the Ladys" (*Behn*, III, 185). She hastens to point out that many works of poetry have long treated the subject of women in an indecent fashion, but the offense is overlooked "because a Man writ them." She taunts the hypocritical critics: "I make a Challenge to any Person of common Sense and Reason . . . to read any of my Comedys and compare 'em with others of this Age, and if they can find one Word that can offend the chastest Ear, I will submit to all their peevish Cavills." She admonishes these critics not simply to condemn her work because it is a woman's, but to "examine whether it be guilty or not, with reading, comparing, or thinking" (*Behn*, III, 185). Her play has been read, she points out, not only by Sir Roger L'Estrange, licenser of published works, and by the owners of the theatrical company that produced *The Lucky Chance*, but by "several ladys of very great Quality"; none of these readers found any obscenity in her work. Moreover, she contests not only the charge of indecency but also the content of what counts as indecency. She points out several great plays with scenes that might be alleged to be offensive in this respect; yet these scenes are not indecent, she states, because they are artistically justified, containing what is "proper for the Characters" and falling "naturally . . . into the places they are design'd for" (*Behn*, III, 186).

What Behn effectively does here is to place the virtues of good judgment, critical reading, and thinking beyond the pale of traditional masculine learning and the conventional male literary establishment, which have both, on account of their transparent bias and maliciousness, forfeited their right to speak with authority. Behn presents another voice, a woman's voice, speaking not from a position below that establishment but rather from above; she takes no great pains to dislodge male assumptions about women writers; rather, she appropriates for women's use the categories of common sense and reason, extricating them from the tradition of male prejudice in which they have been misused and abused. However, the status of her "feminism" is unclear. For one thing, she was politically conservative, a consistent supporter of the royalists as against the English Parliament. Furthermore, she does not see herself as outside the male literary tradition, and indeed, pleads to be included in it. Or does she? These are her words: "All I ask, is the Priviledge for my Masculine Part the Poet in me . . . to tread in those successful Paths my Predecessors have so long thriv'd in, to take those Measures that both the Ancient and Modern Writers have set me" (*Behn*, III, 187). If she can so boldly attempt to redeem the notions of "common sense" and "reason" from their sullied masculine traditions, why can she not redeem "poetry" as a legitimately female activity? Why must she appeal to the poet in her as the "masculine" part? And why does she seem to be knocking on the doors of a literary tradition stretching all the way back to ancient writers?

These statements may serve a rhetorical purpose: perhaps to reassure male writers that she is not dismissing the tradition and that her disdain will dissolve once she gains entry. It would be unrealistic to expect her, writing in 1687, to be talking of a female tradition; but these final statements need to be read in the context of her having scorned both male learning and classical rules of literary composition. And her originality, surely, lies as much in the way she speaks as in what she speaks: her texts adopt a tone and a style unprecedented in the history of literary criticism. Defiant, unapologetic, and placing herself entirely outside of the traditional canons of male learning and literature (an externality achieved as much by her tone as by what she says), her writing does not follow a logical pattern; it seems to be punctuated, rather, by the movement of her righteous anger, her deliberate outpourings of emotion, the nodal points of her rebuttals of insubstantial criticism, and the flow of particularity or detail – of names, and particular circumstances – which itself infuses her general statements with substance in a newly immediate and transparent manner, the general being treated as being on the same level as the particulars which it comprehends, rather than loftily coercing particulars (in what she would regard as a conventionally male fashion) into the exemplificatory service of its own predetermined and prescriptive nature.

Samuel Johnson (1709–1784)

Of his numerous achievements, Samuel Johnson is perhaps best remembered for his two-volume *Dictionary of the English Language*, first published in 1755. Of almost equal renown are his *Lives of the English Poets* (1783) and his eight-volume edition of Shakespeare (1765). His most famous poem is *The Vanity of Human Wishes* (1749), a speculation on the emptiness of worldly pursuits. He also wrote drama and a fictional work, *The History of Rasselas* (1759), as well as numerous essays in periodicals such as the *Rambler*, the *Adventurer*, and the *Idler*. In 1737 Johnson moved from his native town of Lichfield to London, which became the center of his literary life; he moved in an intellectual circle that included the conservative thinker Edmund Burke, the painter Joshua Reynolds, and the economist Adam Smith. Johnson's own biography was recorded by his friend James Boswell, who published his celebrated *Life of Samuel Johnson* in 1791.

An integral dimension of Johnson's literary output and personality was his literary criticism, which was to have a huge impact on English letters. His famous "Preface" to, and edition of, Shakespeare's plays played a large part in establishing Shakespeare's reputation; his account of the lives of numerous English poets contributed to the forming of the English literary canon and the defining of qualities such as metaphysical wit; his remarks on criticism itself were also to have an enduring impact. His critical insights were witty, acerbic, provocative, sometimes radical, and always grounded on his enormous range of reading.

In his fictional work, *The History of Rasselas*, written during the evenings of a single week to pay for the funeral of his mother, Johnson expresses through one of his characters called Imlac certain central insights into the nature of poetry. In chapter X, Imlac undertakes a disquisition on poetry which has often been regarded as a summary of neoclassical principles; to what extent he represents Johnson's own opinions is debatable, especially since his requirements for the poet are shown in the text to be impossibly comprehensive. Yet much of what he says is reiterated by Johnson elsewhere and therefore deserves to be considered – even if tentatively – as part of Johnson's literary-critical outlook.

Imlac, who is a poet in ambition rather than in fact, states that wherever he went, he found "that Poetry was considered as the highest learning," and that, "in almost all countries, the most ancient poets are considered the best."[10] He suggests, anticipating later comments of Johnson's, that "the early writers are in possession of nature, and their followers of art: that the first excel in strength and invention, and the latter in elegance and refinement." This seems to suggest the conventional neoclassical view that modern writers can only proceed by broadly imitating and refining the work of classical writers. Yet Imlac quickly remarks that "no man was ever great by imitation" and that poetic excellence can be achieved only by attending "to nature and to life." Moreover, there is an emphasis in Johnson's text on the direct experience of life, as well as the writer's knowledge of his audience. Imlac also stresses that the poet must be conversant with all kinds of knowledge; he must store up "images and resemblances" such that his mind is furnished with "inexhaustible variety." The ultimate purpose of such varied knowledge is moral: "every idea is useful for the enforcement or decoration of moral or religious truth." In general, the business of the poet, says Imlac, is "to examine, not the individual, but the species; to remark general properties and large appearances . . . He is to exhibit in his portraits of nature such prominent and striking features, as recall the original to every mind." The poet must "divest himself of the prejudices of his age or country; he must consider right and wrong in their abstract and invariable state . . . and rise to general and transcendental truths, which will always be the same."

Imlac also points out that "knowledge of nature is only half the task of a poet; he must be acquainted likewise with all the modes of life." The poet must be able to estimate various conditions of happiness and misery, and to observe "all of the passions in all their combinations, and trace the changes of the human mind as they are modified by various institutions and accidental influences of climate or custom." These two sets of precepts appear to contradict: on the one hand, the poet is to express timeless, universal truths; on the other, he will show the changes that passions, cultures, and human mentality undergo. It could be that Johnson is attempting to voice through his character the need for the poet to be aware, through experience, both of the changes undergone by the human mind in different periods and of the universal truths underlying these shifting manifestations.

In a later chapter of *Rasselas*, Imlac makes certain comments on the faculty of imagination that again exhibit a neoclassical disposition toward the expression of truth.

Imlac's views are inspired by his encounter with a man of great learning, an astronomer, whose solitary immersion in profound thought has driven him mad, and who genuinely believes that he controls the weather. But Imlac also acknowledges that, while this "power of fancy over reason is a degree of insanity," we are all under this power to some extent: "There is no man whose imagination does not sometimes predominate over his reason," no man who does not "hope or fear beyond the limits of sober probability" (ch. XLIV). While Johnson follows the classical path of Plato, Aristotle, and numerous others in viewing reason as the avenue to truth, it is significant that what is opposed to reason here is not passion or emotion but imagination elevated to the status of a mental faculty or disposition. The very power and prevalence that Johnson accords to imagination here, as something dangerously distortive of truth and nature, will be held up by the Romantics as a transformative power, more comprehensive than reason, and as an avenue to truths of a higher and more spiritual nature.

However, Johnson's classical commitment to reason, probability, and truth was complemented by his equally classical insistence on the moral function of literature. In a brief essay written for the *Rambler* No. 4 (1750), he applauded contemporary romance fiction for moving beyond the stock, unrealistic themes of earlier romance, which had been filled with giants, knights, ladies in distress, and imaginary castles. Modern romances, he states, "exhibit life in its true state."[11] Hence, modern writers require not only the learning that is to be gained from books but also "that experience which can never be attained by solitary diligence, but must arise from general converse, and accurate observation of the living world" (*Rambler*, 10). However, given the audience for these modern romances, says Johnson, the prime concern of the author should not be verisimilitude but moral instruction. These books are chiefly addressed to "the young, the ignorant, and the idle, to whom they serve as lectures of conduct, and introductions into life" (*Rambler*, 11). Johnson acknowledges that "the greatest excellency of art" is to "imitate nature; but it is necessary to distinguish those parts of nature, which are most proper for imitation" (*Rambler*, 12–13). Hence the "realism" that Johnson advocates is highly selective, constrained by moral imperatives: while the author must indeed adhere to probability, he must not represent everything; he must not "confound the colors of right and wrong," and must indeed help to "settle their boundaries." Vice must always produce disgust, not admiration; and virtue must be shown in the most perfect form that probability will allow (*Rambler*, 14–15). Johnson's position appears to be solidly entrenched within the tradition of classical realism: like Aristotle, he desires literature, even the newly emerging genre of the novel, to express truth in general and universal terms, rather than being tied down by the need to represent a multitude of "accidental" events and circumstances; in this way, the author's choice of material and manner can be circumscribed by moral imperatives.

However, there are many instances in Johnson's work where he shows himself to be flexible in his adherence to classical formulations. Many of the rules and principles that have been long honored, he says, are nothing but the "arbitrary edicts" of self-appointed legislators who have "prohibited new experiments of wit, restrained fancy from the indulgence of her innate inclination to hazard and adventure, and condemned all future flights of genius to pursue the path of the Meonian eagle [Homer]." Johnson stresses that rules should be drawn from reason rather than from mere precedent (*Rambler*, 197–199). In No. 156 he had also urged that "many rules have been advanced without consulting nature or reason." Among these, he cites some long-held precepts about drama: the rule that only three persons should appear at one time on stage; the limitation of a play to five acts; and the unity of time, whereby a play should be performed in the compass of one day. Johnson retorts that these precepts, aimed at realism, fail to accommodate our general willingness to be "deceived" that the events on the stage are real: "some delusion must be admitted, I know not where the limits of imagination can be fixed" (*Rambler*, 193–194). He applauds the "mixed" genre of tragicomedy, suggesting that this does not violate either reason or the essential function of drama, which "pretends only to be the mirrour of life." Johnson does, however, commend the absolute need to observe the rules of unity of action and unity of character. In judging which rules to follow, he states that it "ought to be the first endeavor of a writer to distinguish nature from custom" (*Rambler*, 194–196). There seems to be an admission here, not that the foundations of classical precepts – adherence to nature, reason, and truth – were wrong, but that some rules have not been truly derived from these foundations.

Many of these issues are taken up in more detail in Johnson's renowned "Preface" to his edition of Shakespeare's plays. Three basic concerns inform this preface: how a poet's reputation is established; the poet's relation to nature; and the relative virtues of nature and experience of life as against a reliance on principles established by criticism and convention. Johnson begins his preface by intervening in the debate on the relative virtues of ancient and modern writers. He affirms that the excellence of the ancient authors is based on a "gradual and comparative" estimate, as tested by "observation and experience."[12] If we judge Shakespeare by these criteria – "length of duration and continuance of esteem" – we are justified, thinks Johnson, in allowing Shakespeare "to assume the dignity of an ancient," since his reputation has survived the customs, opinions, and circumstances of his time (60–61).

Inquiring into the reasons behind Shakespeare's enduring success, Johnson makes an important general statement: "Nothing can please many, and please long, but just representations of general nature" (61). Once again, by "general nature," Johnson refers to the avoidance of particular manners and passing customs and the foundation of one's work on the "stability of truth," i.e., truths that are permanent and universal. And it is Shakespeare above all writers, claims Johnson, who is "the poet of nature: the poet that holds up to his readers a faithful mirrour of manners and of life." His characters are not molded by the accidents of time, place, and local custom; rather, they are "the genuine progeny of common humanity," and they "act and speak by the influence of those general passions and principles by which all minds are agitated." Other poets, says Johnson, present a character as an individual; in Shakespeare, character "is commonly a species." It is by virtue of these facts that Shakespeare's plays are filled with "practical axioms and domestick wisdom . . . from his works may be collected a system of civil and oeconomical prudence" (62).

In contrast with the "hyperbolical or aggravated characters" of most playwrights, Shakespeare's personages are not heroes but men; he expresses "human sentiments in human language," using common occurrences. Indeed, in virtue of his use of durable speech derived from "the common intercourse of life," Johnson views Shakespeare as "one of the original masters of our language" (70). Though Shakespeare "approximates the remote, and familiarizes the wonderful," the events he portrays accord with probability. In view of these qualities, Shakespeare's drama "is the mirrour of life" (64–65).

Johnson now defends Shakespeare against charges brought by critics and writers such as John Dennis, Thomas Rymer, and Voltaire. These critics argue that Shakespeare's characters insufficiently reflect their time period and status, that his Romans, for example, are not sufficiently Roman, and his kings not sufficiently royal. Johnson retorts that Shakespeare "always makes nature predominate over accident; and . . . he preserves the essential character," extricated from accidental conventions and the "casual distinction of country and condition" (65–66). A more serious form of censure concerns Shakespeare's mixing of comic and tragic scenes, thereby violating the classical distinction between tragedy and comedy. Johnson acknowledges that Shakespeare's plays "are not in the rigorous and critical sense either tragedies or comedies, but compositions of a distinct kind; exhibiting the real state of sublunary nature, which partakes of good and evil, joy and sorrow, mingled with endless variety of proportion and innumerable modes of combination." The ancient poets selected certain aspects of this variety which they restricted to tragedy and comedy respectively; whereas Shakespeare "has united the powers of exciting laughter and sorrow not only in one mind but in one composition" (66–67). It is here, in his defense of tragicomedy, that Johnson appeals to nature as a higher authority than precedent. He allows that Shakespeare's practice is "contrary to the rules of criticism . . . but there is always an appeal open from criticism to nature. The end of writing is to instruct; the end of poetry is to instruct by pleasing. That the mingled drama may convey all the instruction of tragedy or comedy cannot be denied, . . . and approaches nearer than either to the appearance of life." Moreover, says Johnson, the mixed genre makes for greater variety, and "all pleasure consists in variety" (67). Johnson also points out that when Shakespeare's plays were first "edited" in 1623 by members of his acting company, these editors, though they divided the plays into comedies, histories, and tragedies, did not distinguish clearly between these three types. And through all of the three forms, Shakespeare's "mode of composition is the same; an interchange of seriousness and merriment," and he "never fails to attain his purpose" (68).

Johnson does concede, however, that Shakespeare had many faults. His first defect is that he is "more careful to please than to instruct, that he seems to write without any moral purpose." Johnson acknowledges that from Shakespeare's plays, a "system of social duty" may be culled. The problem is that Shakespeare's "precepts and axioms drop casually from him; he makes no just distribution of good or evil," leaving his examples of good and bad actions "to operate by chance." And it is always a writer's duty, Johnson insists, "to make the world better" (71). Among other faults of Shakespeare cited by Johnson are: the looseness of his plots, whereby he "omits opportunities of instructing or delighting"; the lack of regard for distinction of time or place, such that persons from one age or place are indiscriminately given attributes pertaining to other eras and locations; the grossness and licentiousness of his humor; the coldness and pomp of his narrations and set speeches; the failure to follow through with scenes that evoke terror and pity; and a perverse and digressive fascination with quibbles and wordplay (71–74).

There is one type of defect, however, from which Johnson exonerates Shakespeare: neglect of the classical unities of drama. Johnson takes this opportunity to elaborate on his earlier cynicism regarding these ancient rules. To begin with, he exempts Shakespeare's histories from any requirement of unity: since these are neither tragedies nor comedies, they are not subject to the laws governing these genres. All that is required in these histories is that "the changes of action be so prepared as to be understood, that the incidents be various and affecting, and the characters consistent, natural and distinct. No other unity is intended" (75). Johnson argues that Shakespeare does observe unity of action: his plots are not structured by a complication and denouement "for this is seldom the order of real events, and Shakespeare is the poet of nature." But he does observe Aristotle's requirement that a plot have a beginning, middle, and end.

For the unities of time and place, however, Shakespeare had no regard, a point on which Johnson defends Shakespeare by questioning these unities themselves. Like Corneille, he views these unities as having "given more trouble to the poet, than pleasure to the auditor" (75–76). Johnson sees these unities as arising from "the supposed necessity of making the drama credible." And such a requirement is premised on the view that the mind of a spectator or reader "revolts from evident falsehood, and fiction loses its force when it departs from the resemblance of reality." The unity of place is merely an inference from the unity of time, since in a short period of time, spectators cannot believe that given actors have traversed impossible distances to remote locations. Such are the grounds on which critics have objected to the irregularity of Shakespeare's drama. In Johnson's eyes, such premises are themselves spurious: in a striking counter-argument, he appeals to Shakespeare himself as a counter-authority, asserting: "It is false, that any representation is mistaken for reality; that any dramatick fable in its materiality was ever credible" (76). Spectators, Johnson observes, are always aware, in their very trip to the theater, that they are subjecting themselves to a fiction, to a form of temporary self-delusion. And we must acknowledge that, "if delusion be admitted," it has "no certain limitation." If we can believe that the battle being enacted on stage is real, why would we be counting the clock or dismissing the changing of places as unreal? We know, from first to last, that "the stage is only a stage, and that the players are only players" (77).

Imitations give us pleasure, says Johnson, "not because they are mistaken for realities, but because they bring realities to mind" (78). Johnson concludes that "nothing is essential to the fable, but unity of action," and that the unities of time and place both arise from "false assumptions" and diminish the variety of drama (79). Hence these unities are "to be sacrificed to the nobler beauties of variety and instruction," the greatest virtues of a play being "to copy nature and instruct life." Johnson is well aware of the forces arrayed against him on these points, and that he is effectively recalling "the principles of drama to a new examination" (80). Yet his strategy is both to argue logically against the incoherence of the unities of time and place and to set up Shakespeare as an alternative source of authority as against the classical tradition. Ironically, his own views are thus sanctioned by a playwright to whom he himself has painstakingly accorded the dignity of a classic.

Johnson broadly agrees with the tradition that Shakespeare lacked formal learning; the greater part of his excellence "was the product of his own genius." In contrast with most writers, who imitate their predecessors, Shakespeare directly obtained "an exact knowledge of many modes of life" as well as of the inanimate world, gathered "by contemplating things as they really exist" (89). He demonstrates clearly that "he has seen with his own eyes; he gives the image which he receives, not weakened or distorted by the intervention of any other mind." In summary, the "form, the characters, the language, and the shows of the English drama are his" (90). Johnson also shrewdly points out that Shakespeare's reputation owes something to his audience, to its willingness to praise his graces and overlook his defects (90–91). In this text, Johnson's appeal to nature and direct experience and observation over classical precedents and rules, as well as his assessment of Shakespeare as inaugurating a new tradition, effectively sets the stage for various broader perspectives of the role of the poet, the poet's relation to tradition and classical authority, and the virtues of individualistic poetic genius. His assessment of Shakespeare is backed by a laborious editing of his plays.

Another area in which Johnson exerted great influence on his successors was that of biography and comparative estimation of the poets in the English canon. His accounts of the lives and works of numerous English poets were first produced as a series of prefaces to a large edition of the works of the English poets. These prefaces, fifty-two in all, were published separately as *Lives of the English Poets* in 1781. In general, Johnson raises biography to an art: far from being slavishly adherent to facts, Johnson's text is replete with all the apparatus of imaginative texts: figures of speech, imaginative insights, hypothetical argumentation, vivid descriptions, and speculative judgments; he appeals not only to the intellects of his readers but also to their emotions, backgrounds, and moral sensibilities. His most fundamental appeal, throughout these prefaces, is to the notion of "nature," as encompassing reason, truth, and moral propriety. He considers various genres and styles of poetry, the nature of imitation, the problems of translation, the classical rules of art, and the duties of literary criticism.

The typical structure and composition of each preface contributes important elements to both the art of biography and the theory and practice of literary criticism. Johnson characteristically places the work of a given poet within a detailed account of his political context, his personal circumstances, his learning, his character, and his relationship with his literary contemporaries and with the public. He usually cites the ways in which a given poet was praised and blamed; he engages in a close analysis of some of the poet's verses; and he attempts a general, comparative estimate of the poet's greatness and significance, and his place in the English literary tradition. All of these accounts are to some extent informed by Johnson's own critical maxim that to "judge rightly of an author, we must transport ourselves to his time."[13] Johnson's assessments have proved influential in the establishing of an English canon or literary tradition. It was he, for example, who most comprehensively defended Shakespeare and other poets against the charge of violating the classical unities; it was he who named Dryden both "the father of English criticism" and the poet who transformed English poetry: "He found it brick, and he left it marble" (*Lives*, 157, 194). Likewise, it was Johnson who, after considering Pope's merits and defects, took it as a given that Pope's reputation as a poet had been secured: "If Pope be not a poet, where is poetry to be found?" (*Lives*, 402). Again, it was Johnson who saw Addison's prose as "the model of the middle style," and his essential literary-historical function as the presenting of "knowledge in the most alluring form, not lofty and austere, but accessible and familiar" (*Lives*, 236–237).

Considered as a whole, Johnson's assessments of the English poets have survived as what Arnold called "natural centres," points of reference to which criticism can repeatedly return. Though Johnson's criticism rested on the classical foundation of adherence to nature, reason, and truth, as well as moral instruction, what Johnson added was the need for historical contextualization (exemplified in his work on Shakespeare, in his *Lives*, and in his *Dictionary*) of authors and their works, as well as the obligation to place nature – in its most comprehensive sense – above the authority of mere precedent or classical authors, an obligation that might empower new or revised visions of the literary tradition. Johnson stresses that "truth . . . is . . . superior to rule" (*Lives*, 94). It is worth remembering also that by "nature," Johnson does not mean primarily the world of external, physical nature, but rather human nature in its universal and historical embodiment of reason and moral sensibility. In his essay on Milton he states that "the knowledge of external nature, and the sciences which that knowledge requires or includes, are not the great or the frequent business of the human mind . . . the first requisite is the religious and moral knowledge of right and wrong; the next is an acquaintance with the history of mankind, and with those examples which may be said to embody truth . . . Prudence and justice are virtues and excellences of all times and of all places; we are perpetually moralists, but we are geometricians only by chance" (*Lives*, 23). In both of these respects – the need for historical contextualization and comparison, and the appeal to nature and truth over convention – he anticipates, and sets the stage for, much Romantic and modern criticism.

Notes

1. Michael Moriarty, "French Literary Criticism in the Seventeenth Century," in *CHLC*, V.III, 556–558, 561–562.
2. Pierre Corneille, "Of the Three Unities of Action, Time, and Place," trans. Donald Schier, in *The Continental Model: Selected French Critical Essays of the Seventeenth Century, in English Translation*, ed. Scott Elledge and Donald Schier (Ithaca and London: Cornell University Press, 1970), pp. 101–102. Hereafter page citations are given in the text.
3. The text used here is the translation by William Soame and John Dryden. It is reprinted in *The Art of Poetry: The Poetical Treatises of Horace, Vida, and Boileau*, trans. Francis Howes, Christopher Pitt, and Sir William Soames, ed. Albert S. Cook (Boston: Ginn, 1892).
4. See Colin Burrow, "Combative Classicism: Classical Literary Criticism in Renaissance England," *CHLC*, V.III, 488.
5. John Dryden, "Defence of *An Essay of Dramatic Poesy*," in *Essays of John Dryden: Volume I*, ed. W. P. Ker (New York: Russell and Russell, 1961), p. 133. All subsequent citations of Dryden's essays are from this edition.
6. *Essays of John Dryden: Volume II*, ed. W. P. Ker (New York: Russell and Russell, 1961), pp. 119–125. Hereafter cited as *Essays*, II.
7. Some of my remarks on wit are indebted to the excellent exposition provided by Edward Niles Hooker's "Pope on Wit: *The Essay on Criticism*," in *The Seventeenth Century: Studies in the History of English Thought and Literature from Bacon to Pope*, R. F. Jones et al. (Stanford: Stanford University Press, 1951), pp. 225–246.
8. *The Works of Aphra Behn: Volume I*, ed. Montague Summers (New York: Benjamin Blom, 1967), p. 221. Hereafter cited as *Behn*, I.

 9 *The Works of Aphra Behn: Volume III*, ed. Montague Summers (New York: Benjamin Blom, 1967), p. 185. Hereafter cited as *Behn*, III.
10 Samuel Johnson, *The History of Rasselas, Prince of Abyssinia* (Harmondsworth: Penguin, 1986), ch. X. All citations are from this text.
11 Samuel Johnson, *Essays from the Rambler, Adventurer, and Idler*, ed. W. J. Bate (New Haven and London: Yale University Press, 1968), p. 9. Hereafter cited as *Rambler*.
12 *The Yale Edition of the Works of Samuel Johnson. Volume VII: Johnson on Shakespeare*, ed. Arthur Sherbo, introd. Bertrand H. Bronson (New Haven and London: Yale University Press, 1968), p. 59. All further page citations from Johnson's preface refer to this edition.
13 Samuel Johnson, *Lives of the English Poets*, introd. John Wain (London and New York: Dent/Dutton, 1975), p. 158. Hereafter cited as *Lives*.

CHAPTER 13

THE ENLIGHTENMENT

Historical and Intellectual Background

The Enlightenment was a broad intellectual tendency, spanning philosophy, literature, language, art, religion, and political theory, which lasted from around 1680 until the end of the eighteenth century. Conventionally, the Enlightenment has been called the "age of reason," though this designation is now regarded as somewhat reductive since it fails to comprehend the various intellectual trends of the period. The Enlightenment thinkers were by no means uniform in their outlooks, but in general they saw themselves as initiating an era of humanitarian, intellectual, and social progress, underlain by the increasing ability of human reason to subjugate analytically both the external world of nature and the human self. They viewed it as their mission to rid human thought and institutions of irrational prejudice and superstition, as well as to foster a society free of feudal caprice, political absolutism, and religious intolerance, and where human beings could realize their potential through making moral and political choices on the foundations of rationality and freedom. In political and economic terms, Enlightenment thought was integral to the rise of liberalism and the ascendancy to power of the bourgeois class through the French Revolution of 1789 and subsequent revolutions throughout Europe. Indeed, it should be remembered that reason was not merely a neutral knowledge-seeking human faculty given prominence by philosophy; the reverberations of reason as a way of life, as a fundamental disposition toward the world, had their foundations in the economic sphere, underlying newer, rational attitudes toward banking, investment, trade, and manufacture, and harboring profound implications for the status of science and technology.

These images of the Enlightenment, and in particular the power and objectivity of reason, have been challenged from many directions: initially, by certain figures usually included within the orbit of Enlightenment thought, such as Jean-Jacques Rousseau, who stressed the importance of emotion and instinct, and David Hume, whose skepticism embraced even the abilities of reason; by Theodor Adorno, Max Horkheimer, and many others such as Roland Barthes, who have developed the critique, originally advanced by Marx and Engels, of the "empire of reason" as a foundation of bourgeois ideology; by an alternative, heterological tradition of philosophy running from Schopenhauer, Nietzsche, and Bergson to Derrida which has emphasized the intrinsic connection of reason with ideological and pragmatic interests and physical survival; by the psychoanalytic traditions generated from Freud and Jung, which have stressed how small a component of human behavior is accounted for by reason; by feminisms which have viewed reason as a predominant factor in male constructions of the world and as internally constrained by the complex claims of the body; and by various forms of poststructuralist and postcolonial theory, which have situated reason as a peculiarly European phenomenon intrinsically tied to class interests and the projects of imperial hegemony. At its very heart, reason was from the beginning ideologically oriented, on many levels. Hence, all of these movements and tendencies have challenged the claims of reason to neutrality, impartiality, objectivity, and universality.

Notwithstanding these critiques, which have variously exerted force since the early twentieth century, the main streams of the Enlightenment continue to have a profound effect on our world. Much Enlightenment thought was underlain by a new scientific vision of the universe inspired by the work of the English mathematician Sir Isaac Newton (1642–1727): this conception of a mechanical universe ordered by laws which were scientifically ascertainable eventually displaced the view of the universe as ordered and historically directed by a benevolent divine providence. The very concept of reason issued a profound challenge to centuries-old traditions of thought and institutional practice. Reliance on reason was in itself nothing new; the classical philosophers such as Plato and Aristotle had urged reason as the faculty through which we could gain access to truths that were universal and certain. Medieval Christian philosophy acknowledged that reason was a necessary component of a proper spiritual disposition, but it was only one element and needed to be balanced by faith and revelation. In other words, reason was constrained within a broader pattern of human faculties and its limitations were stressed: reason alone could not gain access to God or salvation, nor could it probe the ultimate mysteries of the universe. What was novel to the Enlightenment was its insistence on reason as the primary faculty through which we could acquire knowledge, and on its potentially limitless application. The findings of reason need no longer be constrained by the requirements of faith or the dictates of divine revelation. More than this, the exaltation of reason, of man's individual capacity for reasoning, effectively undermined reliance on any form of authority, whether it be the authority of the Church, the state, of tradition, convention, or of any powerful individual. This way of thinking is particularly marked in modern democracies even today: as Alexis de Tocqueville noted about America, people in general prefer to rely on their own insight (however uninformed) rather than submit to the authority or testimony of others, even of experts.

Three seminal precursors of Enlightenment thought were the English thinker Francis Bacon (1561–1626), the French rationalist philosopher René Descartes (1596–1650), and the Dutch rationalist thinker Benedict (or Baruch) Spinoza (1632–1677). Bacon's major philosophical works were *The Advancement of Learning* (1605) and *The New Organon* (1620), in which he formulated the method of induction whereby we generalize on the basis of actual observation of a number of particular occurrences. He proposed that induction, as the method of modern science, was a more effective path to knowledge than the medieval reliance on deduction and a priori reasoning, whose premises were handed down by the authority of tradition. In *The New Organon* Bacon insisted that knowledge can arise only from actual observation of nature; the elements of logic, such as the syllogism, which underlie much medieval philosophy, he says, may form a coherent structure within itself but is not necessarily tied to actual fact. A syllogism, for example, could be valid inasmuch as its propositions flow logically, but these propositions could nonetheless be untrue. The only secure way to arrive at knowledge, then, is by a "true induction," whereby reason is applied to observed facts; only in this way can ideas and axioms be generated.

Even though certain systems of thought have commanded assent for centuries, Bacon asserts that we must begin anew from this alternative foundation. Up until now, he warns, the human mind has been misled by what he calls "idols" or false notions. He divides these idols into four classes. The first type are "Idols of the Tribe," which refer to the distorted impressions of nature caused by the deficiencies of sense and understanding common to all human beings. The next are "Idols of the Cave": each man, he says, has a private cave or den, through which or from which he sees the world. The cave is a metaphor for the peculiarity of an individual's nature and upbringing: his view of the world will be refracted and distorted by his subjective experiences. The third kind of idols are those of the "marketplace," again a metaphor for "the commerce and consort of men": when men enter into social bonds, a social discourse is created which panders to the "vulgar" in its vagueness and intellectual insufficiency. Finally, there are "Idols of the Theatre": these are the systems of philosophers and learned men which are "merely stage plays" because they represent "worlds of their own creation" rather than the actual world.[1] The upholders of these previous systems urge us to view the world through those fictions rather than experiencing it directly for ourselves.

René Descartes is often called the "father" of modern philosophy. Like Bacon, Descartes challenged the basic principles of medieval philosophy. In his *Discourse on Method* he began his thinking in a skeptical mode, doubting all things, including his own senses, understanding, and the reality of the external world, until he could find a secure and certain foundation on which to build his own system of thought. Descartes resolved to "reject as absolutely false everything as to which I could imagine the least ground of doubt" in order to see if any kind of certain knowledge remained. He first doubted the deliverances of our sense, since they often deceive us; he then doubted the process of reasoning; he imagined that the entire world might be a delusion. But, in assuming everything to be false, Descartes concluded: "it was absolutely essential that the 'I' who thought this should be somewhat [something], and remarking that this truth '*I think, therefore I am*' was so certain and so assured . . . I came to the conclusion that I could receive it . . . as the first principle of the Philosophy for which I was seeking." Descartes proceeded to identify his essential nature or self with the process of thinking, calling himself a "thinking being," independent of any place or any material circumstances. In this way, he made his famous dualism or distinction between the mind and the body. The mind is a thinking substance, whereas the body belongs to the world of space, time, and material extension. In this way, Descartes perpetuated a mechanistic view of the world. Descartes inferred from his earlier process of doubt that

313

he could take it as a general rule that the things which we conceive very "clearly and very distinctly" are all true.[2] Descartes took mathematics as his model of knowledge given that its ideas were clear and distinct and that its truths were certain.

The third seminal figure, Spinoza, was a Jew born in Amsterdam, who had studied Descartes' works closely. His own rationalist and unorthodox views led to his expulsion from the Jewish community in 1656 for heresy. He also offended Christian theologians by his unorthodox views of the Bible. Like Descartes, he believed in the primacy of deduction and in a mechanistic view of the universe; however, he did not adopt Cartesian dualism, arguing instead that the universe is composed of a single substance, which he viewed as God, and which is refracted differently in the attributes of mind and matter. In his major work, the *Ethics* (1677), he urged that the highest good consists in the rational mastery over one's passions and ultimately in the acceptance of the order and harmony in nature, which is an expression of the divine nature. Subsequent Enlightenment thinkers such as John Locke and David Hume in Britain, Voltaire, Diderot, and d'Alembert in France, as well as Gotthold Lessing in Germany, encouraged more skeptical, rational, and tolerant approaches to religion. The most common approach was "deism," which saw divine laws as natural and rational, and dismissed all superstition, miracles, and sacraments.

Bacon and Descartes represent what were to become two important strands of Enlightenment thought, empiricism and rationalism respectively. Bacon's empiricism placed emphasis on our experience and observation of the world; Descartes stressed the use of our reason to arrive at clear and distinct notions of the world. Another stream of Enlightenment thought was materialism, which marks the thought of the thinkers just discussed but is most fully represented by Thomas Hobbes (1588–1679). Hobbes expounded a materialistic view of even the mind, regarding sensation as caused by the impact and interaction of small particles.

In political terms, the Enlightenment produced several blueprints of what might be an ideal state. Several Enlightenment philosophers drew up a theory of the "social contract," or the contract that might be agreed upon by citizens of a state so that social life would be governed by laws and that the ruler's power and his relation to his subjects in terms of rights and duties would be defined. Many of these thinkers postulate what men would be like in a state of nature, prior to the formation of a social contract. Hobbes' view of this state, as expressed in his *Leviathan* (1651), is bleak: he suggests that, without any binding laws or contract, men would be in a perpetual state of war. His reasoning is that nature has basically made men equal; from this equality proceeds "diffidence" (by which Hobbes means hostility or aggressiveness), since men, whose principal purpose is self-conservation, would be competing for the same things. Eventually, war would result, since in order to secure themselves as fully as possible, men would attempt to master as many other people as they could. A third cause of quarrel would be the desire for glory and reputation. In this condition of war, says Hobbes, there would be no trade or industry, no culture, no arts, letters, or science. There would be merely "continual fear, and danger of violent death; and the life of man, solitary, poor, nasty, brutish, and short." In this state of nature, there would be no rules, no morality, no justice, and no law: these institutions, says Hobbes, belong to man as he lives in society, not in solitude. Even after a social contract is established between persons of a given state, says Hobbes, one state will nonetheless be in a posture of war against other states; this condition, however, unlike that of a war of individuals, may actually promote industry and happiness.

One of the major empiricist thinkers of the Enlightenment, and the most important philosopher in the formulation of political liberalism, was John Locke, whose most influential works were *An Essay Concerning Human Understanding* and *Two Treatises on Civil Government*, both published in 1690. In the *Essay* Locke denied Descartes' view that the mind has "innate ideas," or ideas that it is simply born with. Rather, the mind is initially a *tabula rasa* or blank slate upon which our experience of the world is written.[3] Locke argues that all our ideas come from experience, either through sensation or through reflection. We receive distinct ideas of the objects in the external world through our senses, such as the ideas of yellow, white, hard, cold, or soft; we also receive ideas through reflection on the internal operation of our own minds; these ideas include perception, thinking, doubting, reasoning, and believing. These two operations, he says, are "the fountains of knowledge" and there is no other source of knowledge or ideas (*Essay*, 89–90, 348). Where Locke does agree with Descartes is in his insistence on clear and distinct ideas; as we shall see, like some modern philosophers of language, Locke blamed the misuse or abuse of language for many of our misconceptions about the world, and proposed that language should be made more precise.

The Scottish philosopher David Hume developed some of Locke's empiricist notions toward more radical, skeptical, conclusions. Where Locke had urged that our minds know the external world through ideas, Hume argued that we know *only* ideas, not the external world itself. We can know external objects only by the "perceptions they occasion," and we can infer their existence only from "the coherence of our perceptions," whether they indeed are real or merely "illusions of the senses."[4] In fact, Locke himself acknowledged that even simple ideas, which were the very core of experience, cannot be proved to correspond with reality, and he admitted that the real essence of things is unknowable (*Essay*, 271–273, 287, 303). Both Locke and Hume rejected the Aristotelian concept of "substance" as the underlying substratum of reality. Hume develops the skepticism implicit in Locke's rejection of substance: there are no essences actually in the world, whether we are talking of external objects such as a table, or human identity, or moral concepts such as goodness. All of these are ultimately constructions of our minds, informed largely by custom and habit. Indeed, in Hume's view, even the human self was not a fixed datum but a construction through a "succession of perceptions" (*THN*, 135). Hence the very notion of human identity is called into question by Hume. Moreover, in Hume's eyes, the law of causality, on which the entire thrust of modern science was based and which was hailed as the "ultimate principle" of the universe, has merely a conventional validity, based on nothing more than the authority of custom (*THN*, 316). What we perceive in the world is not the operation of causality but mere "constant conjunction," in other words, our own long habit of associating two phenomena.

In France, the main figures of the Enlightenment were Voltaire (1694–1778), Denis Diderot (1713–1784), and Jean d'Alembert. Perhaps more than anyone else, Voltaire popularized the ideas of Newton and Locke. As a young man, he was imprisoned in the Bastille for his satiric verses on the aristocracy, and later exiled in England. His numerous works included the *Philosophical Dictionary* (1764) and a fictional philosophical tale, *Candide* (1759), in which he promulgated the necessity of reason and experience and the notion that the world is governed by natural laws. In *Candide* he mocked the optimism, determinism, and rationalism of the German philosopher Gottfried Leibniz, who believed in a preestablished harmony in the world, lampooning the latter's position in the phrase "Everything is for the best in this best of all possible worlds." The implication is that abstract reason of itself does not comprehend the infinite variety of human situations and human deficiencies. In this sense, reason is held up as a kind of comforting fiction, pandering to the human need for order. Voltaire satirizes the "rational" justifications for war, the intolerance of religions, the institutions of inequality, the search for a utopia, the greed which undermines human contentment, the gull-ibility of the masses, and the strength of human self-deception. One of the two stark lessons to emerge is the need to experience the world directly: "to know the world one must travel," concludes Candide. The only lesson is the need to work, in order to stave off the "three great evils, boredom, vice and poverty." In general, Voltaire championed liberty and freedom of speech, though his sympathies did not extend to the common man. The other French Enlightenment thinkers included the rationalists Diderot and d'Alembert, who were the leading members of the group which produced the *Encyclopaedia*, a compendium of the latest scientific and philosophical knowledge. In Germany, the tendencies of the Enlightenment were expressed by Gotthold Lessing (1729–1781) and Moses Mendelssohn (1729–1786), who both propounded philosophies of religious tolerance.

Certain Enlightenment philosophies had a formative influence on the ideals behind the French Revolution. These included Locke's *Second Treatise of Civil Government* (1690), which justified the new political system in England that prevailed after the 1688 revolution. Locke condemned despotic monarchy and the absolute sovereignty of parliaments, affirming that the people had a right to resist tyranny. Voltaire advocated an enlightened monarchy or republic governed by the bourgeois classes. Baron de Montesquieu (1689–1755) also influenced the first stage of the French Revolution, advancing a liberal theory based on a separation of executive, legislative, and judicial powers. Jean-Jacques Rousseau (1712–1778) exerted a powerful impact on the second stage of the Revolution through his theories of democracy, egalitarianism, and the evils of private property, as advocated in his *Social Contract* and *Discourse on the Origin of Inequality*. However, in some ways, Rousseau hardly belongs to the main trends of rationalist Enlightenment thought. Significantly, he is often hailed as the father of Romanticism on account of his exaltation of the state of nature over civilization, and of the emotions and instincts over reason and conventional learning.

In general, however, the major tendencies of Enlightenment philosophy were toward rationalism, empiricism, pragmatism, and utilitarianism; these tendencies formed the core of liberal-bourgeois thought. The main philosophical assumptions behind this tradition of thought were: that the world is composed of particular things which are distinct and separate from one another (philosophical pluralism); that consciousness (the human self) and the world are mutually distinct, and there is an external reality independent of our minds; and that general ideas are formed from the association and abstraction of particular ones (in other words, general ideas are constructions of our minds and are not found in the world). It is these assumptions that underlay the other trends of Enlightenment thinking: that the world is a machine, subject to laws; that human society is an aggregate of atomistic or separate individuals; that the individual is an autonomous and free rational agent; that reliance on reason and experience or observation will enable us to understand the world, the human self, and enable historical progress in humanitarian, moral, religious, and political terms.

These assumptions not only permeate Enlightenment discussions of literature, but also have continued to inform many literary-critical perspectives, ranging from the experiential theories of literature advanced by figures such as Matthew Arnold and Henry James to the New Criticism and other movements of the twentieth century such as neo-Aristotelianism. The rationalist disposition of the Enlightenment has in various modifications informed the aesthetics of Kant, Hegel, Marx, and Croce. Equally, much criticism flowing from the Romantics and French Symbolists, as well as from thinkers such as Schopenhauer, Nietzsche, Bergson, Heidegger, and Sartre, has urged the problematic nature of Enlightenment assumptions. The psychoanalytic criticism inspired by Freud and Jung, and more recent movements such as structuralism, deconstruction, and postcolonial criticism, have subjected Enlightenment rationalism and empiricism to searching intellectual and ideological scrutiny. They have questioned the idea that entities exist independently, the epistemological validity of subject–object dualism, the idea of an independent external world, and the notion that language somehow reflects or corresponds with reality. It should be remembered, however, that many of these critiques were initiated by the Enlightenment philosophers themselves and were most articulately expressed by Hegel long before the advent of the more modern developments.

Enlightenment Literary Criticism: Language, Taste, and Imagination

The historical and intellectual developments associated with the Enlightenment had far-reaching effects on literary criticism in terms of discussions of the language of poetry, notions of taste, and faculties such as wit, judgment, and imagination. These historical developments included: the increasing power of the bourgeoisie and corresponding decline of the nobility and clergy; constraint of the absolute power of monarchs and developments of constitutional forms of government; the promulgation of ideals of political equality; the increasing prestige and power of newer scientific perspectives; the continued expansion of the public sphere and of the reading public; and the development of rationalism and empiricism as the main streams of Western thought.

A very direct connection between Enlightenment philosophy and literary criticism occurs through the various philosophies of language that mark the eighteenth century. The most important of these theories of language was formulated by John Locke, and the specific influence on literary criticism of his views of language reinforced the general impact of his empiricism on this and other fields. Many scholars have argued that the scientific and observational dimension of Locke's empiricism affected the writing of poetry, stimulating a relatively novel preoccupation with sensory detail, scientific description, and what was known as the "doctrine of particularity," advocated by writers such as Joseph Warton and Hugh Blair. In this sense, Locke's influence undermined the neoclassical conception, argued by Samuel Johnson and others (and

317

stretching all the way back through Renaissance and medieval writers to Aristotle), that poetry speaks a universal language and expresses general truths. But, as William Keach and others have argued, other dimensions of Locke's empiricism were equally influential. The subjective and mentalistic aspects of empiricism, presenting the mind not merely as receiving ideas passively from the external world but as *active* in constructing experience through its associating the ideas received in various combinations, led to a preoccupation in eighteenth-century literature and criticism with the representation of mental experiences. Poetry attempted to express human psychology and to register the mind's association of ideas. In fact, the doctrine of "associationism," running through thinkers such as Locke, Hume, Hartley, and Condillac, became a force in literary-critical discussions of poetic language. In turn, this doctrine sparked a new interest in synaesthetic language, the representation of one of the five senses through appealing to another. Such language was held to be the privileged potential of poetry. Locke's discussions also impinged on the development of an important feature of eighteenth-century poetic style, personification, which variously raised the connection between universal and particular.[5]

From a broader perspective, it has been observed that the reform of literature and criticism in the eighteenth century reflected the empirical thrust of broader scientific and philosophical developments. Interestingly, Susan Manning has argued that language in the eighteenth century had not yet been specialized into a number of distinct discourses, each with its characteristic jargon. Rather, scientists, philosophers, theologians, and literary critics all attempted to describe human experience and used essentially the same language, which she designates as a *literary* language. In this view, the concerns of the literary critic, the philosopher, and the scientist were broadly united. The empirical method was common to them all.[6] Locke effectively extended Newton's empirical methods to the analysis of the human mind, and in England, France, and Germany his empiricism, describing the mind's reception of ideas in sensation, "largely commanded the aims and methods of literary criticism" throughout the eighteenth century (*CHLC*, V.IV, 590). Manning's account enumerates other ways in which Locke's influence can be discerned: in Johnson who applies the "test of experience" to literary standards, and in Burke's definition of the sublime in terms of experience, of its impact upon the senses of the reader or hearer. Johnson rehearses Locke's strictures on the abuse of words; and his *Dictionary* of 1755 epitomizes the denotative and definitional aspects of the empirical attitude toward language (*CHLC*, V.IV, 600–601). And, in the broader sense suggested above, Locke's empiricism furnished a starting point for eighteenth-century thinking regarding human nature.

A further important influence was exerted in the direction of relativism: Locke's philosophy harbored an implicit skepticism, recognizing that the mind knows not the real world but only ideas, and that the connection between words and ideas is not natural but conventional. This skeptical position encouraged eighteenth-century literary criticism and philosophy to "abandon absolutes," and to search for foundations in "relation and relativity" (*CHLC*, V.IV, 590, 596). The aesthetics of reader response, as will be seen in the section on Hume, was relativized, and this relativism was restrained by appealing to the shared nature of experience. More importantly, literary criticism "becomes historically based rather than rule-based for the first time, recognizing its dependence on human perception and its confinement to time and place" (*CHLC*,

V.IV, 596). Clearly, the tendencies set in motion by Enlightenment philosophy and science have reached not just through the eighteenth century but through the nineteenth and twentieth centuries into our own day, embracing the growth of aesthetics as a distinct field, discussions of taste, the sublime, historicism, and the aesthetics of reader response.

Locke's influence also extends to subversions of his own views. While he himself, as will be seen shortly, championed a literal, denotative, and clear language free of all figurative infection, many eighteenth-century theorists of language saw his views as reductive and as disempowering the creative and expressive potential of language and its ability to express human emotion and passion rather than merely reeling before the tyranny of reason. Many of these theorists offered historical accounts of the origins of language, and espoused primitivist positions. Rousseau and Diderot saw language as a system of signs which had developed from a natural to a conventional state, being corrupted and made artificial with the increasing advance of so-called civilization. As Keach observes, both Diderot and Burke celebrated the indefinite as poetic and sublime respectively, instead of condemning it. Blackwell saw language as originally full of metaphor and increasingly becoming stale through refinement; Vico, as we shall see, saw primitive language as not rational but sensuous and imaginative, harboring poetic wisdom; Herder, also, identified primitive language with poetry (*CHLC*, V.IV, 135–138). Condillac and Rousseau saw modern language as less melodious and musical, and more exact, lucid, and harsh. Sheridan criticized Locke for ignoring the passions, and like Herder and many others in the eighteenth century, he expressed a distrust of written language (*CHLC*, V.IV, 343–344). In these reactions, we witness both the predominance of the ideals of clarity and "literalness" and an incipient reaction to such strict regimentation of language, a reaction that would eventually blossom into various branches of Romanticism.

A specific area in which Locke's influence was broadly felt was his distinction between wit and judgment, which will be discussed below. For the metaphysical poets such as John Donne, wit had embodied a kind of conceptual and linguistic cleverness and quickness, being celebrated the more as it increased in ingenuity. As we have seen in Dryden and Pope, the neoclassical writers urged that wit be tempered by judgment. Locke, aligning wit with poetry and pleasure, and judgment with philosophical clarity and knowledge, effectively recasts in stringent form an opposition formulated by Thomas Hobbes. As James Sambrook notes, Locke's philosophy was popularized by Addison, who urged that knowledge of Locke was necessary for the literary critic. Addison's own investigations into imagination and the psychology of aesthetic response were influenced by Locke. What is interesting in Addison's aesthetics is his attempt to integrate Lockean principles into his analysis of literature while retaining certain neoclassical presuppositions concerning poetic imitation, and even anticipating Romantic views of the imagination and of art as having the capacity to excel nature (*CHLC*, V.IV, 618–621).

The philosophical assumptions of the Enlightenment can now be examined in the literary and cultural criticism of certain major thinkers, as they inform various critical trends. We shall consider the views of language formulated by Locke and Vico; the popularization of Locke's ideas and their integration with neoclassical and even precursive Romantic notions in the work of Addison; the theories of taste and judgment offered by Hume and Burke (whose thinking, specifically opposed to many Enlightenment values, can fruitfully be considered here); and the analysis of women's social and educational status undertaken by Mary Wollstonecraft, who effectively extends Enlightenment ideals to the notion of gender.

John Locke (1632–1704)

Locke's philosophy has been enduring and widespread in its influence. He laid the foundations of classical British empiricism, and his thought is often characterized as marked by tolerance, moderation, and common sense. In general, Locke's affiliations were with the Puritans; his father had supported the parliamentarians against the king, and he attended Oxford, which was Puritan in sympathy. While at Oxford, he fell under the influence of the leading British scientist Sir Robert Boyle, who advocated an experimental and empirical method. He also read closely the work of Descartes, and was a friend of Isaac Newton. In 1668 he was elected Fellow of the Royal Society. After the death of his patron, the earl of Shaftesbury, Locke sought refuge in Holland until the Glorious Revolution of 1688, which restored to the throne a Protestant monarch, William of Orange. Locke's most important work, his *Essay Concerning Human Understanding* (1690), immediately won for him a high reputation amid some opposition.

The implications of Locke's empiricism are still with us: many ideological forces still encourage us to look at the world as an assemblage of particular facts, yielding sensations which our minds then process in arriving at abstract ideas and general truths. In our context, Locke's views of language are particularly interesting since they not only provided the starting point for subsequent theories of language in the eighteenth century (both for and against Locke's views) but also anticipate a great deal of modern literary-critical thinking about language.

Locke's fundamental endeavor is to show how closely language is connected with the process of thought and therefore to urge the need to use language in the most precise way so as to avoid unnecessary confusion in our concepts. Before turning to his views of language in general, it is worth remarking on two influential passages that impinge profoundly on literature and poetry. In the first of these passages, Locke makes his famous distinction between two faculties, wit and judgment:

> men who have a great deal of wit, and prompt memories, have not always the clearest judgment or deepest reason. For wit lying most in the assemblage of ideas, and putting those together with quickness and variety, wherein can be found any resemblance or congruity, thereby to make up pleasant pictures and agreeable visions in the fancy; judgment, on the contrary, lies quite on the other side, in separating carefully, one from another, ideas wherein can be found the least difference, thereby to avoid being misled by similitude, and by affinity to take one thing for another. This is a way of proceeding quite contrary to metaphor and allusion; wherein for the most part lies that entertainment and pleasantry of wit, which strikes so lively on the fancy, and therefore is so acceptable to all people, because its beauty appears at first sight, and there is required no labor of thought to examine what truth or reason there is in it. (*Essay*, II, xi, 2)

In this passage, Locke effectively revives the age-old antagonism between philosophy, on the one side, and poetry and rhetoric, on the other. Where much classical and Renaissance thought had endeavored to combine the functions of poetry, as producing both pleasure and (moral) profit, Locke reawakens the ghost of a hard Platonism, separating (and even opposing) the spheres not only of profit and pleasure, but also of the faculties respectively enlisted by poetry and philosophy. The domain of poetry is governed by wit, which sees identities and affinities between disparate things, an imaginative and fictive operation designed to please the fancy. The realm of philosophy, on the other hand, is presided over by judgment, by the clear, cool ability to *separate* what does not belong together, to distinguish clearly between things, in the interests of furthering knowledge. The impulse of one lies toward confusion and conflation, while the impetus of the other is toward clarity. The poetic realm is the realm of fancy, of figurative language, of metaphor and allusion; the language of philosophy shuns adornment, and engages with the real world. Locke attempts to dismantle the effort of many centuries to fuse the claims of delight and instruction, viewing these as opposed rather than allied.

Hence, at the end of book III of the *Essay*, entitled "Of Words," Locke urges that figurative speech comprises one of the "abuses" of language. He acknowledges that "in discourses where we seek rather pleasure and delight than information and improvement," the ornaments of figurative speech and rhetoric may not be considered faults. "But," he warns, "if we would speak of things as they are, we must allow that all the art of rhetoric, besides order and clearness; all the artificial and figurative application of words eloquence hath invented, are for nothing else but to insinuate wrong ideas, move the passions, and thereby mislead the judgment; and so are perfect cheats: and therefore . . . they are certainly, in all discourses that pretend to inform or instruct, wholly to be avoided." Locke goes so far as to call rhetoric a "powerful instrument of error and deceit." In this passage, Locke opposes pleasure and delight to both the pursuit of knowledge and moral improvement. He acknowledges, however, that the attraction of eloquence, "like the fair sex," has hitherto prevailed: rhetoric is "publicly taught," and the "arts of fallacy are endowed and preferred" (*Essay*, III, x, 34). Whereas the Renaissance humanists aspired toward an integration of human pursuits and faculties, Locke demands a clear separation. Locke is here calling for a literalization of language, an extrication of words from their metaphorical and allegorical potential, a potential accumulated over many centuries. When language is thus reduced to denotation, stripped of all connotative potential, the word effectively becomes a transparent window onto meaning, and its material dimension is suppressed. Locke's voice is perhaps the most pronounced sign of the bourgeois refashioning of language into a utilitarian instrument, a scientist tendency that still infects some of our composition classrooms to this day.

Locke's seemingly harsh views of figurative speech need to be appraised in the context of his views of language in general. These views unwittingly highlight some of the skeptical implications of Locke's empiricism, which were also evinced in various ways by George Berkeley and David Hume. Locke defines words as the "signs of ideas" or "internal conceptions" (*Essay*, III, i, 2). Anticipating Saussure and many modern theorists of language, he emphasizes that the connection between signs (words) and ideas is not natural but is made by "a perfectly arbitrary imposition" which is regulated by "common use, by a tacit consent" (*Essay*, III, ii, 8). He also points out that whereas all things in existence are particular, the vast majority of words (apart from proper names) are general and do not designate specific objects, since to have a word for every object would not only be impractical and cumbersome but would also disable the very process of thought, which depends heavily on our ability to abstract from given circumstances and to generalize. Hence one word will usually cover an entire class of objects (*Essay*, III, iii, 1–6). Again Locke emphasizes that "general" and "universal" do not belong to "real existence" or to "things themselves": they are inventions of the human mind, designed to facilitate our understanding of the world. In fact, the essences of genera and species are nothing more than abstract ideas: for example, "to be a man, or of the *species* man, and to have the right to the name 'man' is the same thing" (*Essay*, III, iii, 11–12). In other words, the essence of any general idea such as "man" is not found in the world; it is a purely verbal essence, though Locke hints that in forming abstract or general ideas, we are attempting to follow the similitude we appear to find among things in nature. He denies, however, that there are in the world any "real essences" that we can know (*Essay*, III, iii, 13).

In other parts of the *Essay*, Locke effectively acknowledges a skeptical position that what our minds know is not the world itself but the ideas we have of it. His discussion of language reinforces this implicit skepticism, especially in relation to the notion of essence which had dominated philosophy and theology for more than two thousand years. He suggests that there are two meanings of the term "essence": it can be taken to refer to the "real internal . . . constitution of things," which, however, is unknown; or it refers to the constituting characteristics of each genus, which is represented by an abstract or general idea, to which a given word is attached (*Essay*, III, iii, 15). Locke uses these two definitions to make his famous distinction between "real" and "nominal" essence: he urges that real essence and nominal essence are the same when we are talking about simple ideas and "modes" but that they are different in substances. The names of simple ideas – which cannot be broken down into smaller components – are the least doubtful because each of them represents a single perception (*Essay*, III, iv, 12–13). Simple ideas are not manufactured by the mind but are "presented to it by the real existence of things operating upon it" (*Essay*, III, v, 2). The names of modes (complex ideas which cannot subsist by themselves but depend on substances, such as "triangle," "goodness," "patricide") are purely inventions of the mind and have no direct connection to real existence, hence their real and nominal essences coincide. But in the case of substances (which Locke defines as "distinct particular things subsisting by themselves") such as "gold," the real and nominal essences will be different: the nominal essence cannot be embodied in any particular real thing. Essentiality refers only to types and species, not to individuals (*Essay*, II, xii, 4–6; III, vi, 3–4). If there is a real essence of substances, we can only conjecture what this might be (*Essay*, III, vi, 6). Locke dismisses as fruitless any search after "substantial forms," which are "wholly unintelligible" (*Essay*, III, vi, 10). Our knowledge of species and genera is constructed by the "complex ideas in *us*, and not according to precise, distinct, real essences in *them*." Locke insists that we do not know real essences (*Essay*, III, vi, 8–9). He is here moving away from a conception of nature as harboring "certain regulated established essences." He does acknowledge, however, that while the nominal essences of substances are made by the mind and not by nature, they are not entirely arbitrary, but attempt to follow the pattern of nature: we see certain qualities conjoined in nature, and we attempt to imitate these combinations in our complex ideas (*Essay*, III, vi, 15, 28).

In his chapter "Of the Imperfection of Words," Locke suggests that language is used primarily for two purposes: for recording our own thoughts and for communicating these thoughts to others (*Essay*, III, ix, 1). He also defines language as "the instrument of knowledge" (*Essay*, III, ix, 21). The imperfection of words lies in the uncertainty of what they signify. He appears to define clarity as a situation where a word or group of words will "excite in the hearer the same idea which it stands for in the mind of the speaker" (*Essay*, III, ix, 4). Locke attributes inaccuracy to a number of causes: since there is no natural connection between words and their meanings, and no natural standards, different people will attach different ideas to the same words; the rules governing meaning are not always clear or understood; and words are often learned without awareness of their full range of meaning (as by children). These imperfections tend not to disable everyday or "civil" discourse but are of serious consequence in philosophy, which seeks general truths (*Essay*, III, ix, 4–15).

In an even more strongly entitled chapter, "The Abuse of Words," Locke lists a number of willful faults which contribute to the failure of communication. These include: the use of words without "clear and distinct ideas," or the use of "signs without anything signified"; using words inconstantly and without distinct meanings; affecting obscurity, by using words in new and unusual ways; using obscurity to cover up conceptual difficulties and inadequacies; taking words for things (i.e., assuming that one's own views describe reality itself); and assuming that the meanings of certain words are known and need not be explained (*Essay*, III, x, 2–22). Locke's remedies for these situations are to annex clear and distinct ideas to words, respecting their common usage, elaborating their meanings where necessary, ensuring that words agree as far as possible "with the truth of things" or what actually exists, and using the meanings of words with constancy. Locke even airs the idea, which he thinks to be unrealistic, of a dictionary, which might standardize and clarify all language usage. If this advice were followed, he believes, many of the current controversies would end, and "many of the philosophers' . . . as well as poets' works might be contained in a nutshell" rather than in long-winded tomes (*Essay*, III, xi, 9–26).

In his philosophy of language, as in his general advocacy of empiricism, Locke wavers uneasily between a view of the human mind constructing the world with which it engages, and the mind "receiving" this world from without. The general thrust of his commentary suggests that we construct the world through language: we ourselves impose general ideas, categories, and classifications upon the world. We can no longer talk of Platonic Forms or Aristotelian essence or substance: the essences that we "find" are our own constructions, constructions of language. Nature itself contains only particulars, and its apparent regularity and order are projections of our own thought processes whose medium is language. All of this points to a "coherence" theory of language, whereby language is not referential (referring to some external reality), but acquires meaning only through the systematic nature and coherence of its expression of our perceptions. On the other hand, Locke seems to intimate that the connection between language and reality is not entirely arbitrary: at some level – that of simple ideas – our perceptions do somehow correspond to external reality. Locke is at a loss to explain this correspondence, but he will not relinquish this last vestige of purported objectivity. Indeed, his urgent desire for linguistic clarity is perhaps a reaction to the failing system of referentiality: the entire edifice, the entire equation and harmony of language and reality, promulgated through centuries of theological building on the notion of the Logos (embracing the idea of God as both Word and the order of creation expressed by this), is about to crumble.

Joseph Addison (1672–1719)

Though he was also a poet and dramatist, Joseph Addison is best known as an essayist, and indeed he contributed much to the development of the essay form, which, like the literary form of the letter, flourished in the eighteenth century. Together with his friend and colleague Richard Steele whom he had known since his schooldays, he authored a series of articles in the periodicals the *Tatler* (1709–1711) and the *Spectator* (1711–1714). It was his ambition to bring philosophical, political, and literary discussion within the reach of the middle classes. He was a politician as well as a writer, holding positions of undersecretary of state, lord lieutenant, and then chief secretary for Ireland, as well as being a member of the Whig or Liberal Party from 1708 until his death. Steele too was a political liberal, and the two men used their periodicals for literary, moral, and educational purposes. To these ends, they offered character sketches of fictional personages which commented on contemporary issues and manners, and offered satiric portraits from a broadly humanitarian and largely middle-class framework of values. The "essay" as developed by these two writers – who wrote anonymously for their periodicals – was both a personal document as well as an attempt to probe the truth of things, in a dramatic and witty manner but ultimately for the moral enlightenment of their readers. The essays were journalistic inasmuch as they addressed a cross-section of topical events and concerns, ranging from codes of conduct, fashions in dress, marriage conventions, to political propaganda. Catering as it did for an increasingly literate middle-class readership, the *Tatler* was immediately popular and its undoing was its involvement in political partisanship; committed to Whig or Liberal causes, it saw the downfall of the Whig Party and was increasingly attacked by the Tory press, as the Conservative Party rose to power. Only two months after its demise in January 1711, the two writers launched the *Spectator*, which they managed to keep free of political partisanship. This latter periodical became famous for its characterizations of fictitious personae, such as Sir Roger, Sir Andrew, and Will Honeycomb, which were conducted with a vitality and coherence that affected subsequent novelistic writing.

After the closing of the *Spectator* in 1712, Addison and Steele launched the *Guardian*. This, however, never achieved the popularity of its predecessors, and it was the *Tatler* and the *Spectator* in their reprinted forms which continued to command a significant reading public through the nineteenth century. Most of the valuable literary criticism is contained in the pages of the *Spectator*, which had included extended series of essays on more serious issues, including philosophy and literature, in an attempt to mold and refine the critical tastes of its readership. These tastes were partly confined within a neoclassical scheme of values, drawing on Aristotle and Longinus, as evident in the essays on wit, tragedy, and Milton's *Paradise Lost*. Yet they also made use of more recent observations, such as those on psychology by John Locke.

Indeed, although these periodicals were addressed to the middle classes, their function was to reform the values of this class rather than merely to propagate or expound them. In the *Spectator* No. 6, Steele referred to his age as "a corrupt Age," devoted to luxury, wealth, and ambition rather than to the virtues of "good-will, of Friendship, of Innocence."[7] Steele urges that people's actions should be directed toward the public good rather than merely private interests, and that these actions should be governed by the dictates of reason, religion, and nature (*Spectator*, 68–70). In the *Spectator* there are several essays or articles dealing with specifically literary-critical issues, such as the nature of tragedy, wit, genius, the sublime, and the imagination. As far as tragedy goes, Addison and Steele advise following the precepts of Aristotle and Horace. Their general prescription is to follow nature, reason, and the practice of the ancients (*Spectator*, 87).

In 1711, the year in which Pope's *Essay on Criticism* attempted to distinguish between true and false wit, Addison attempted the same task in Nos. 61 and 62 of the *Spectator*. In the first of these, he argues that puns and quibbles are species of "false" wit; with the exception of Quintilian and Longinus, none of the ancient writers, he says, made a distinction between puns and true wit. In his second piece on wit, Addison finds Dryden's definition of wit as "a Propriety of Words and Thoughts adapted to the Subject" to be too broad: it could apply to all good writing, not merely to wit (*Spectator*, 108). He prefers John Locke's distinction, in his *Essay Concerning Human Understanding*, between wit and judgment, cited above. Locke had argued that those endowed with wit and those capable of judgment are not usually the same persons, since these involve diverse procedures. Wit consists in bringing together ideas which resemble one another, with "quickness" and "variety." Under this general procedure fall the various rhetorical tropes such as metaphor and allusion. Judgment, on the other hand, lies in separating ideas carefully, such that one idea is not mistaken for another (*Essay*, II, xi, 2). Addison himself adds that not every resemblance of ideas can be termed wit: the resemblance must give delight and surprise to the reader (*Spectator*, 105). He includes under Locke's definition of wit not only metaphor but also similes, allegories, parables, fables, dreams, and dramatic writing. He further adds that resemblance of ideas is not the only source of wit: the opposition of ideas can also produce wit (*Spectator*, 110).

On the basis of Locke's definition of wit, Addison produces a definition of false wit: whereas true wit consists in the resemblance and congruity of ideas, false wit is produced by the resemblance and congruity of single letters, as in anagrams; of syllables, as in doggerel rhymes; of words, as in puns and quibbles; and of entire sentences. Addison suggests that, in addition to true and false wit, there is a hybrid species, which he calls "mixed wit," which consists partly in the resemblance of words and partly in the resemblance of ideas. Such mixed wit, which he finds in writers such as Cowley and Ovid (but not in Dryden, Milton, the Greeks, and most Roman authors), is a "Composition of Punn and true Wit . . . Its Foundations are laid partly in Falsehood and partly in Truth" (*Spectator*, 107–108). Addison cites with approval the French critic Bouhours' view that "it is impossible for any Thought to be beautiful which is not just, and has not its Foundation in the Nature of Things: That the Basis of all Wit is Truth; and that no thought can be valuable, of which good Sense is not the Ground-work" (*Spectator*, 108–109). These remarks come strikingly close to Pope's definition of true wit as

"Nature to advantage dress'd": both formulations ground wit in truth, the similarity here revealing the profoundly neoclassical disposition adopted by Addison. In No. 65 of the *Spectator*, Steele similarly states: "I shall always make Reason, Truth, and Nature the Measures of Praise and Dispraise," urging the use of these standards rather than the "generality of Opinion" (*Spectator*, 111).

However, while Addison and Steele assume a neoclassical stance in invoking absolute standards rather than public opinion, they do in later essays somewhat anticipate the more modern tendency to appeal to the collective taste of a community of readers. In No. 409 of the *Spectator*, Addison defines taste as "*that faculty of the Soul, which discerns the Beauties of an Author with Pleasure, and the Imperfections with Dislike.*" The test of whether someone possesses this faculty, he says, is to read the "celebrated Works of Antiquity" which have withstood the test of time, as well as those modern works which "have the Sanction of the Politer Part of our Contemporaries" (*Spectator*, 202). The person of taste will appreciate the beauties of these texts. Like Dryden, and later writers such as Arnold and Eliot, Addison appeals here to the authority of a cultured community of readers, as well as to the "timeless" principles embodied in the classics. His position appears to straddle both a classical disposition centered on the authority of the text and a modern attitude that accords the readership an integral role in the assigning of literary value. With similar ambivalence, he views the faculty of taste as "in some degree born with us," but as capable of cultivation through exposure to refined writings, to conversation with cultured people so as to rectify the partiality of our assessment, and to the best critics of both ancient and modern times (*Spectator*, 203– 204). Deepening this ambivalence still further, Addison states that although in poetry the unities of time, place, and action, as well as other classical precepts, are "absolutely necessary," he also insists that "there is still something more essential to the Art, something that elevates and astonishes the Fancy, and gives a Greatness of Mind to the Reader, which few of the Cricks besides *Longinus* have considered" (*Spectator*, 204). The insistence of the appeal to fancy as *more* essential than merely observing the classical rules, as well as the appeal to Longinus, suggests a dissatisfaction with the view of art as a purely rational, wholly explicable process. This kind of dissatisfaction, some-what amorphous at this transitional stage of literary-critical history, will later blossom into certain Romantic formulations of art.

Such blossoming has one of its germs in Addison's essay in No. 411 of the *Spectator* on the pleasures of the imagination. Addison suggests here that our sight is the most perfect and delightful sense: "It fills the Mind with the largest Variety of Ideas, converses with its Objects at the greatest Distance, . . . spreads itself over an infinite Multitude of Bodies, comprehends the largest Figures, and brings into our reach some of the most remote Parts of the Universe" (*Spectator*, 205–206). It is the sense of sight that furnishes the imagination with its ideas. Addison defines the pleasures of imagination (a term he uses interchangeably with "fancy") as arising "from visible Objects, either when we have them actually in our View, or when we call up their Ideas into our Minds" by various forms of art. While Addison acknowledges that there can be no image in the imagination which we do not first receive through our sight, he also points out that "we have the Power of retaining, altering and compounding those Images, which we have once received, into all the varieties of Picture and Vision that are most agreeable to the Imagination." And through this faculty we can create scenes "more beautiful than any that can be found in the whole Compass of Nature" (*Spectator*, 206). These comments anticipate the formulations of many Romantic writers, suggesting as they do that we have a powerful faculty in imagination for transcending and transforming nature.

Addison obliquely anticipates Coleridge in distinguishing between the "primary pleasures" of imagination, which proceed from objects that lie before us, and "secondary pleasures" which flow from the *ideas* of visible objects, called up in our memories, in the absence of the objects themselves (*Spectator*, 206–207). Like Kant, Addison situates imagination somewhere between sense and understanding; it is higher than sense but lower than understanding. The pleasures of understanding are more "preferable" because they are based on new knowledge; yet the pleasures of imagination, Addison adds, are just "as great and as transporting"; they are also more accessible, inciting our immediate assent to beauty (*Spectator*, 207). Moreover, someone possessed of refined imagination "looks upon the World, as it were, in another Light, and discovers in it a multitude of Charms, that conceal themselves from the generality of Mankind" (*Spectator*, 207). He also points out that the pleasures of the fancy or imagination, derived from scenes of nature or art, have a healthful and restorative influence on our bodies and minds (*Spectator*, 208). Here we seem to reach a precarious balance between classical or neoclassical insistence on the superiority of reason and intellect and a Romantic insight into the transformative powers of imagination, a power that is potentially infinite, that can raise our insight above conventional perceptions of the world, and that can even exert a morally beneficent influence on our sensibilities.

In a second essay on imagination, in No. 412 of the *Spectator*, Addison deals briefly with both beauty and sublimity. The primary pleasures of imagination, he says, arise from the sight of objects that are great, uncommon, or beautiful. The first of these attributes, greatness, he defines as the "Largeness of a whole View, considered as one entire Piece," as exemplified by vast uncultivated stretches of desert or mountain. Again, somewhat anticipating Kant, he suggests that our imagination "loves to be filled with an Object, or to grasp at anything that is too big for its Capacity." At such unbounded views, we experience a stillness and amazement of the soul, in virtue of our hatred of confinement and our profound desire for freedom. Kant's view will be somewhat different, but nonetheless grounded on our desire for freedom: while the immensity of nature exceeds the power of imagination, that immensity is itself comprehended by a higher power, the faculty of reason. For Addison, the pleasure in such unlimited views derives from the fact that the eye can expatiate on the immensity of its vision and "lose it self amidst the Variety of Objects" (*Spectator*, 209). While Kant thus restrains the boundaries of imagination, subordinating this faculty to reason, Addison postulates a more Romantic attitude, almost Keatsian, whereby the perceiving subject merges with the objects of its vision.

Also Romantic is Addison's view that we derive imaginative pleasure from whatever is new or uncommon; such novelty offers "agreeable Surprise" and gratifies our curiosity because we are "tired out with so many repeated Shows of the same Things," and welcome "Strangeness of . . . Appearance" (*Spectator*, 210). We enjoy scenes that are perpetually shifting and dynamic rather than static. This insistence on novelty, strangeness, and the dynamism of nature was to be an integral element of many Romantic visions of the world. The third kind of primary pleasure of imagination is caused by beauty. Again, like Kant, and anticipating modern Romantic conceptions, Addison views the perception of beauty not in the objective terms inherited from medieval aesthetics – harmony, proportion, order – but as a process bypassing reason entirely and as governed by imagination. The effect of beauty is immediate and definite: beauty "diffuses a secret Satisfaction . . . through the Imagination . . . there are several Modifications of Matter which the Mind, without any previous Consideration, pronounces at first sight Beautiful or Deformed" (*Spectator*, 211). However, Addison acknowledges that there is a second kind of beauty that consists in "the Gaiety or Variety of Colours, in the Symmetry and Proportion of Parts, in the Arrangement and Disposition of Bodies, or in a just Mixture and Concurrence of all together" (*Spectator*, 212). What is interesting about this definition is that it preserves some of the elements of classical notions of beauty (symmetry, order, proportion) but locates these not exclusively in objects but in our subjective response, which he characterizes as a "secret Delight," a pleasure beyond the explanatory range of reason. Finally, he points out that, while objects that are great, uncommon, or beautiful all produce pleasure, this pleasure is multiplied and intensified when these qualities merge, and when the senses on which they are based, such as sight and sound, enter the mind together.

All in all, the views of Addison and Steele express an interesting combination of neoclassical values with dispositions that, in their more sustained treatment by later writers, will be articulated into elements of a Romantic vision of the world and the human self. Addressing themselves to a broad middle-class public immersed in the materialist and pragmatist ideologies of bourgeois thought, their insistence on classical values might be seen as part of their endeavor to cultivate the moral, religious, and literary sensibilities of this class; they were nonetheless obliged, however, to accommodate the more recent attitudes toward beauty and the imagination, attitudes gesturing in the direction of Romanticism, which equally undermined the conventional values of this political class.

Giambattista Vico (1668–1744)

The Italian philosopher Vico expressed in his writings a historical view of the progress of human thought, language, and culture that anticipates the evolutionary perspectives of Hegel, Marx, and others. His major work was his *Scienza Nuova* (*New Science*), first published in 1725, with subsequent editions in 1730 and 1744. Like his more famous successors, he views human nature not as timeless and unchanging but as produced by specific social, religious, and economic circumstances.

Born in Naples, Vico was educated in rhetoric and medieval philosophy, and had a wide range of interests, extending from philology and poetry to sociology, theology, and law. In his early life he was affiliated with a group of radical intellectuals who reacted against the central tenets of medieval philosophy and whose vision expressed the rationalist and empiricist values of the Enlightenment, being based on the works of such people as Galileo Galilei (1564–1642), Francis Bacon, and Descartes. After he became professor of rhetoric at the University of Naples, Vico joined another group of thinkers, the Palatine Academy, which was also committed to Enlightenment and the liberation of philosophy and science from theology. Vico made a number of speeches on humanistic education. His historical poetics have influenced such thinkers as Edward Said and Harold Bloom.

Vico explains that the purpose of his *New Science* is to study "the common nature of nations in the light of divine providence."[8] He points out that the "world of civil society" – which encompasses human social, political, and legal institutions – "has certainly been made by men, and that its principles are therefore to be found within the modifications of our own human mind" (*NS*, para. 331, p. 96). His point is that philosophers have devoted their energies to studying nature which, having been made by God, is knowable only by him. In doing this, they have neglected to study the civil world, which we can know about since we created it. However, like Hegel, he rejects the notion, advanced for example by Stoics and Epicureans, that human history is a random or blind series of events. Rather, it has been ordered by divine providence. Hence the "new science" must be "a rational civil theology of divine providence," demonstrating in its analysis of human institutions "what providence has wrought in history." Indeed, true "wisdom . . . should teach the knowledge of divine institutions in order to conduct human institutions to the highest good" (*NS*, para. 364, p. 110). This science, therefore, describes "an ideal eternal history traversed in time by the history of every nation" (*NS*, para. 349, p. 104). Equally, however, Vico's "science" will be "a history of the ideas, the customs, and the deeds of mankind," from which he will attempt to derive "the principles of the history of human nature" (*NS*, para. 368, p. 112). Like Hegel's historical scheme, then, and perhaps equally reflective of the Enlightenment ideals imbibed by both writers, Vico's vision of historical progress allows for a mutual accommodation or equivalence of divine and human agency. Those Enlightenment ideals – pertaining to the primacy of reason, science, and human free will – had begun to undermine notions of history as simply the unilateral unfolding of divine providence. Vico's thought reflects his affiliation with the early stages of Enlightenment thinking: providence and human agency are brought into an uneasy equivalence; human agency is now admitted into the scheme, making for a precarious balance between human and divine operations. After Hegel, this balance will become permanently upset in favor of human directiveness and natural causality (as divested of its divine expressiveness).

In a strikingly new fashion, Vico's insights into poetry form an integral part of his attempt to explain the origins and development of human society. He takes his three-fold division of history from the Egyptians: the age of gods, of heroes, and of men. Each of these periods, he says, had its own language, civil society, and form of government. The age of gods represents a time when people lived directly under "divine governments," and followed the commandments given by prophecies and oracles. The language spoken by this community was "a mute language of signs and physical objects" which had a "natural" connection to the ideas they expressed. Vico calls this a "hieroglyphic" or "sacred" language. The age of heroes refers to "aristocratic common-wealths" in which the "heroes," or those of superior nature, rule over the common people. The "heroic language" used here was a "symbolic" language comprised of "similitudes, comparisons, images, metaphors, and natural descriptions." This system in turn gave way to the age of men, in "which all men recognized themselves as equal in human nature," and established two forms of "human government," first popular commonwealths and then monarchies. The language used here was "epistolary" or "vulgar," serving the everyday requirements of life. It was agreed upon by convention, a language of which the common people were "absolute lords"; hence the common people had wrested control of the language and the laws from the nobles (*NS*, para. 31–32, p. 20).

One of the foundations of Vico's views of poetic language is his assertion, as against previous philologists, that letters and language were born together and developed together through the three historical periods. Indeed, in the first period, the first gentile peoples (by which Vico means pre-Christian peoples) "were poets who spoke in poetic characters." Contrary to our notions of poetry as requiring a heightened command of language, Vico sees the origin of poetry in a "poverty of language" and in the need to "to explain and be understood." The first people, he says, had "vigorous imaginations" and "great passions" but "the feeblest reasoning powers." Hence they used "poetic characters" such as images of animate substances, gods, and heroes. Vico calls these poetic characters "imaginative genera," which were effectively fables or myths used to explain the world (*NS*, para. 34, p. 21). Hence the first science to be learned, says Vico, should be mythology or the interpretation of fables (*NS*, para. 51, p. 33). The next, heroic, period used "heroic" speech, which was symbolic. In the third period, there was a progression from heroic verses to iambics, after which the language "finally settled into prose" (*NS*, para. 34, p. 22). These languages, says Vico, provide a "mental dictionary" which we need in order to understand all other languages: "Such a lexicon is necessary for learning the language spoken by the ideal eternal history traversed in time by the histories of all nations" (*NS*, para. 35, p. 23).

Wisdom itself changed its shape, says Vico, as history progressed. Among the first peoples, wisdom "began with the Muse" and the first sages were "theological poets" who practiced the "science of divining" (*NS*, para. 361–364, pp. 109–110). Such was the "vulgar wisdom of all nations" which consisted in "contemplating God under the attribute of his providence" (*NS*, para. 365, p. 111). Human institutions were regulated by "sensible signs believed to be divine counsels." Wisdom was then expanded to include "useful counsels given to mankind" and the effective ordering of common-wealths. Hence this poetic theology was also a "civil theology" (*NS*, para. 366, p. 111). After this period of "poetic theology" came the era of metaphysics or "natural theology." In this second period, wisdom consisted of a "knowledge of man's mind in God" and the recognition of God as "the source of all truth" and as "the regulator of all good" (*NS*, para. 365, p. 111). The metaphysics of this period moved beyond the senses and demonstrated providence by the use of reason (*NS*, para. 366, pp. 111–112). The final period was that of Christian theology, which comprehended the wisdom of the earlier periods and added "the science of eternal things revealed by God," a science which furnished knowledge "of the true good and true evil" (*NS*, para. 365, p. 111). Hence Christian theology was "a mixture of civil and natural with the loftiest revealed theology; all three united in the contemplation of divine providence" (*NS*, para. 366, p. 111). Vico also sees this progression of wisdom or knowledge as moving from the senses (the province of poetry) through reason (the sphere of philosophy) to revelation. Vico here is effectively historicizing Aristotle's dictum that what is in the human intellect is first received through the senses (*NS*, para. 363, p. 110; *De Anima*, 432a7f). As with Hegel, each stage of Vico's historical scheme does not simply leave earlier stages behind but incorporates their crucial elements even as it transcends them. Hence the Christian era incorporates both sense and reason even as it moves on to the higher plane of revelation. What is obviously different about Hegel's scheme, perhaps reflecting the historical points at which these two thinkers intersect with Enlightenment thought (Vico situated in the earlier stages and Hegel positioned subsequent to Enlightenment), is that human thought progresses through religion to its ultimate goal in philosophy.

What is interesting in Vico's system is that poetry, a mode of knowing the world through the senses, was the first form of metaphysics, and that the forms of this poetic metaphysics are retained somewhat in the later, rational and revealed metaphysics. The metaphysics of the first period, says Vico, was "not rational and abstract like that of learned men now, but felt and imagined . . . This metaphysics was their poetry" (NS, para. 375, p. 116). The poets of this period created things "according to their own ideas . . . by virtue of a wholly corporeal imagination," in other words, an imagination wholly grounded on sense rather than reason and therefore, according to Vico, possessing sublimity. At this time, the work of poetry was threefold: "to invent sublime fables suited to the popular understanding"; to possess the poet; and "to teach the vulgar to act virtuously" (NS, para. 376, p. 117). In this way, says Vico, the first theological poets "created the first divine fable, . . . that of Jove, king and father of men and gods" (NS, para. 379, p. 118). They believed that Jove commanded by sensible signs, that "such signs were real words, and that nature was the language of Jove." The science of this language was divination, the science of the language of the gods (NS, para. 379, p. 119). It was fear or terror of the present, says Vico, which made people create gods and the science of divination (NS, para. 382, p. 120). It was in this very fear that poetry had its origins, the fear that gave rise to both religion and the divinatory language of religion. The "proper material" of poetry is "the credible impossibility," which expresses the impossibility of attributing animation and agency to inanimate objects such as the sun and sky. Hence it was the poets, according to Vico, who founded religions among the earliest people (NS, para. 383, p. 120). Vico stresses that, in attributing the origins of poetry to a deficiency of reasoning power, he is upsetting all previous theories of the genesis of poetry given by Plato, Aristotle, and Italian Renaissance thinkers.

Indeed, the first poets, says Vico, spoke a language which, far from according with the actual nature of things, "was a fantastic speech making use of physical substances endowed with life and most of them imagined to be divine" (NS, para. 401, pp. 127–128). By means of divinities they explained everything connected with "the sky, the earth, and the sea." Our own modern era, Vico suggests, uses personifications to understand spiritual entities: we make human images of them. But the first poets, not having our power of abstraction, attributed senses and passions to inanimate objects (NS, para. 402, p. 128). All the tropes, says Vico, are reducible to four basic tropes: metaphor, metonymy, synecdoche, and irony (NS, para. 409, p. 131). These basic tropes are the forms taken by the "poetic logic" of the first peoples and they still underlie our basic apprehension of the world. The most "necessary and frequent" trope is metaphor, which "gives sense and passion to insensate things." Hence metaphor was a means of attributing human capacities to inanimate entities, of commensurating elements of the outside world with our own human capacities, and thereby making narratives or fables of those elements. Hence "every metaphor . . . is a fable in brief." Significantly, and anticipating some modern theories, Vico attributes to metaphor a seminal function in the creation of philosophy. The metaphors expressing analogies between the external world and the operation of our minds "must date from times when philosophies were taking shape." Hence these tropes lie at the foundation of human thinking in both arts and sciences (*NS*, para. 404–405, p. 129). Vico notes the numerous expressions in all languages that attempt to humanize elements of the outside world: we speak of the "brow or shoulder of a hill," of "a beard of wheat"; we say that the "sea smiles" or that the "wind whistles." Vico takes such endeavors, embodied in all languages, as an index of the ignorance of the first peoples: "man in his ignorance makes himself the rule of the universe . . . he has made of himself an entire world." Vico suggests that as our reasoning powers progress, we venture beyond our human constitution into the nature of things themselves, rather than imposing our own human image on the world around us. Vico raises some extremely complex issues here: the role of subjectivity in creating the external world; the nature of human understanding and the temptation to reduce everything outside of us to the mold of our own mental operations; and the poetic, metaphorical basis of our engagement with the world. His scheme here is very different from that of Hegel who, influenced by Kant, saw human knowledge progressing in the degree to which it recognized its own operations in the construction of the external world. Vico seems to suggest that intellectual progress is made as we remove subjective elements from our account of the world.

Because they did not have the capacity to abstract qualities from a given entity, the first poets, says Vico, also used metonymy and synecdoche, both of which helped them to name things on the basis of the "most particular and the most sensible ideas" (*NS*, para. 406, p. 130). However, irony – which is "fashioned of falsehood . . . which wears the mask of truth" – could not have begun until the "period of reflection." The first poets had the "simplicity of children" and were "truthful by nature"; hence the first fables must have been "true narrations" (*NS*, para. 408, p. 131). Implicit in Vico's remarks is the idea that irony can arise only in a more refined civilization where people can distance themselves from their own thought and language. These four tropes, says Vico, were "necessary modes of expression of all the first poetic nations." With further development of the human mind, these tropes became "figurative," since words were invented which could signify "abstract forms or genera" (*NS*, para. 409, p. 131). What Vico appears to mean here is that, in their initial use among primitive peoples, the four basic tropes represented the *only* engagement with the world: this engagement had no underlying literal basis. As the human mind developed, a more rational, scientific, and literal expression of our relationship with the world was established and the tropes were reduced to a figurative status, articulated in relation to this literal level. They remained, however, as integrally related to the literal and endured as its foundation. Thus, Vico attributes two important historical functions to poetry, or what he calls "poetic wisdom": on it was founded the religious and civil institutions of the first peoples; and it provided the embryonic basis for all further learning.

David Hume (1711–1776)

The Scottish philosopher David Hume was one of the major figures of the Enlightenment. Like John Locke and George Berkeley, he was an empiricist, believing that our knowledge derives from experience, and he pushed the empiricism of his predecessors toward a controversial skepticism as regards our knowledge of the external world, our subjective identities, and our religious beliefs. His major philosophical works were *A Treatise of Human Nature* (1739–1740), reproduced in a more accessible version in *An Enquiry Concerning Human Understanding* (1748), and *An Enquiry Concerning the Principles of Morals* (1751). He also produced *Political Discourses* (1752), and a number of treatises on religion, including *The Natural History of Religion* (1755) and *Three Dialogues Concerning Natural Religion*, which was not published until 1779, after his death. In addition to these striking accomplishments, he managed to write a six-volume *History of England* (1754–1762).

Hume's essay "Of the Standard of Taste" was published in his volume entitled *Four Dissertations* in 1757. The other three essays were on history of religion, the passions, and tragedy. The essay on taste raises questions about the standards of aesthetic judgment that are still pertinent today: how do we reconcile people's conflicting judgments about taste? Can we arrive at an objective standard? When we make judgments about beauty, are we expressing something about the object or ourselves? What role does the reader or audience have in determining the elements of taste?

Hume begins his essay by noting the inevitable fact that taste differs widely, even among people nurtured under the same circumstances, people who have imbibed the same general dispositions and prejudices. When we shift our consideration to a broader, intercultural context, this divergence is even more striking: we may call "barbarous" the tastes and conventions of other nations and cultures; but they are liable to throw such condemnation back at us.[9]

Hume sees such a divergence of opinion as marking the realm of taste far more than that of science where, often, an explanation of the disputed terms will resolve disagreements. In matters of taste, on the other hand, we might agree on the qualities we applaud, such as elegance, propriety, and simplicity; however, different people will affix different meanings to these terms ("OST," 2). Likewise, in the sphere of morality, the very nature of language generates a harmony between people's opinions. The terms of the language of morality are already inscribed with praise or blame: no one will contest that virtue is praiseworthy or that vice is to be frowned upon. Such terms are "the least liable to be perverted or mistaken" ("OST," 5). However, when we move from this general level to more particular instances, disagreements arise since the qualities people attribute to "virtue" will vary according to particular dispositions, historical and cultural circumstances.

Hume draws attention to a skeptical view of aesthetic standards advanced by certain previous thinkers who make a distinction between judgment and sentiment or feeling. According to this skeptical position, judgments of the understanding refer to something beyond themselves, namely to "real matter of fact," and hence there is only one correct judgment, which we have the capacity to determine. Sentiment, however, does not express anything about the real object, only about a relation between the object and our mental faculties. Hence all sentiments are correct: the same object could give rise to a thousand different sentiments and none of these can rightfully claim more validity than the others. In this view, beauty "is no quality in things themselves: It exists merely in the mind which contemplates them; and each mind perceives a different beauty" ("OST," 7).

Hume suggests that this skeptical position is undermined by appeal to our actual experience: in practice we do make certain judgments which are sanctioned by consensus: for example, Milton is regarded as a superior writer to Ogilby, and Addison to Bunyan. If some person were to deny this, we would not value that person's taste, and here the "principle of the natural equality of tastes is then totally forgot." Hume stresses that the rules of art are not fixed by a priori reasonings but by experience, by "general observations, concerning what has been universally found to please in all countries and all ages." This appeal to experience, to the experience of the reader or audience, accords the reader an integral role in determining the elements of art. Hume states that whatever elements of art are found to please people cannot be faults ("OST," 8–9).

However, Hume concedes that, though the general rules of art are founded on experience and the "common sentiments of human nature," the actual feelings and experience of people will not always conform to these rules. Aesthetic judgment involves the "finer emotions of the mind," which are of "a very tender and delicate nature." And the least hindrance will confound or cloud our judgment, distracting us from the "perfect serenity of mind" and the "due attention to the object." Such hindrances could be of an external or internal nature: an external hindrance might be our cultural remoteness from the aesthetic object; an internal obstacle might be our own prejudices or our undeveloped sense of taste. We can be affected by particular incidents which "throw a false light on the objects." Our "internal organs" of perception need to be in a healthy state. Hume here anticipates what Kant calls a "disinterested" or impartial assessment of the object. Even when we can distance ourselves from our personal circumstances and prejudices, says Hume, our appreciation of the artistic qualities of a given work must be part of a more "durable admiration," given by others of various times and cultures to this same work. For example, the "same Homer, who pleased at Athens and Rome two thousand years ago, is still admired at Paris and at London. All the changes of climate, government, religion, and language, have not been able to obscure his glory." The "general rules of beauty," then, are drawn from our appeal to "those models and principles, which have been established by the uniform consent and experience of nations and ages" ("OST," 11–12).

On the basis of this appeal to broad and consensual experience, Hume infers that there are "certain general principles" whereby we can approve or criticize a work of art. He even goes so far as to hint that there are particular forms and qualities of art which, correlating with "the original structure" of our mental apparatus, are liable to please us. Hume does not deny that beauty and other aesthetic qualities are subjective; but though they are "not qualities in objects . . . there are certain qualities in objects, which are fitted by nature to produce those particular feelings" of pleasure or displeasure ("OST," 16).

The only way in which we can convince a "bad critic" who disagrees with our judgment is to show him a principle of art and to offer examples, which he can submit to his own experience; if his experience does not conform, we at least persuade him that his taste is lacking. Indeed, a sense of aesthetic taste is developed not by following abstract rules but by "*practice* in a particular art." It is repeated experience of, repeated exposure to, artistic objects which refines our feeling or sentiment ("OST," 18). A further requirement for refining taste is to make comparisons of various art objects and various kinds of beauty, and various cultural perspectives. In order to examine carefully the object itself, we must not only remove personal prejudices but must, via an imaginative leap, place ourselves in the position of its original audience; we must make our own situation "conformable to that which is required by the performance." As a reader or spectator or listener, I must "forget, if possible, my individual being and my peculiar circumstances." The hearer, in Hume's language, must impose "a proper violence on his imagination" ("OST," 20–21).

True taste, according to Hume, is a rational process; we rely on good sense to check our prejudices, and reason is requisite to the formation of good taste in a number of ways. We must also be aware of the structure of the work, of the way the various parts relate to the whole, of the "consistence and uniformity of the whole," as well as the end or purpose of the work of art. Even poetry, says Hume, "is nothing but a chain of propositions and reasonings . . . however disguised by the colouring of the imagination." Hence the poet himself needs not only taste and invention but judgment; likewise, the "same excellence of faculties" is required by the critic who would achieve good taste ("OST," 22).

Needless to say, then, this combination of qualities required for sound critical judgment is rare. Hume says that though the principles of taste are universal, only a few are qualified to give judgment on a work of art, since most people cannot overcome the various obstacles in the way of achieving true taste. Here is Hume's summary of the qualities and function of the true critic: "Strong sense, united to delicate sentiment, improved by practice, perfected by comparison, and cleared of all prejudice, can alone entitle critics to this valuable character; and the joint verdict of such, wherever they are to be found, is the true standard of taste and beauty" ("OST," 23). The standard of taste, then, is not objective; rather, it is based on subjective consensus – but only the consensus of "qualified" people. Hume here anticipates both the "communities of interpretation" as formulated by modern reader-response theories and, more immediately, Kant's grounding of taste on a "subjective universality."

Hume now confronts the potentially embarrassing question, where are such critics to be found? His answer, as always, is based on an appeal to our actual experience. Unlike science and philosophy, where one theory is often exploded in favor of a newer explanation, the realm of art is stabilized by critical judgments that hold their validity more or less permanently. Great artists and literary figures "maintain an universal, undisputed empire over the minds of men." Prejudices may cloud people's judgment for a time, Hume acknowledges, but true genius will survive. Where disagreements do occur, "men can do no more than in other disputable questions, which are submitted to the understanding: They must produce the best arguments" and they must grant indulgence to those whose judgments differ. Hume cites two further possible sources of disagreement. One is the differing dispositions of particular men, and the other is the peculiar manners and beliefs of differing countries and times. While he admits that sometimes disagreements will be unresolvable, he insists that the "general principles of taste are uniform in human nature" and that a man of learning can make allowance for the differences of custom, nation, and age ("OST," 26–28).

Hume ends his essay by contrasting the aesthetic sphere with the realm of morality. Moral principles, he says, are "in continual flux and revolution." It requires a particularly violent effort of imagination for us to accept, even in art, the portrayal of moral ideals which contrast sharply from those with which we have been nurtured. Nonetheless, such an effort is to be made in our attempt to arrive at an aesthetic judgment; Hume

335

once again anticipates Kant, who will insist more emphatically on the separation of artistic and moral domains. Hume especially warns that critics must overlook differences of religion, since religious "errors" are "the most excusable in compositions of genius" ("OST," 33–34). For example, when we read Homer or Vergil, we must overlook "all the absurdities of the pagan system of theology." On the other hand, Hume suggests that religious bigotry can disfigure works of art, citing the influence of Roman Catholicism on the plays of Racine and Corneille. Hume seems to be implying that the poet himself must observe a certain decorum and propriety in avoiding an undue expression of religious principles, which exceeds the requirements of his artistic purpose ("OST," 35–36).

In attempting to rescue artistic taste from mere subjectivism, Hume appeals to a number of factors, all of which are based on experience. First, there is a canon of literature and art that has survived the judgment of various times and cultures, a canon established by consensus. Next, this consensus points to a common human nature which responds universally to certain features of art, such as elegance and organic unity. Finally, the consensus which matters is not democratically established; rather, it is the consensus of a qualified elite of critics who, through their ability to reach a disinterested aesthetic perspective, are authorized to act as the arbiters of true taste, as the voice of that common human nature in its intact, cultivated, and unbiased state. Essentially, Hume's answer to the question of how subjective aesthetic judgments may be based on a standard is to say that in practice, we already apply standards, as shown by our existing consensus regarding great artists. The question then becomes one of articulating the standards we already employ. Much of this strategy will underlie Kant's aesthetics; and, like Kant's, Hume's invites certain reproaches. For one thing, despite Hume's claim that the judgments of various ages should be taken into account, his approach is ahistorical in its appeal to a universal human nature, and in its failure to explain how a community of interpretation is actually formed in terms of its relation to the existing power structure; in other words, he talks of a community of qualified critics as an abstract entity rather than as situated and generated within a given historical location.

Edmund Burke (1729–1797)

Edmund Burke is best known for his political writings and his activities as a statesman. In 1765 he became secretary to the marquess of Rockingham, a leader of the Whig or Liberal political party in England. He also served as a member of the English Parliament; in this capacity he was involved in the struggle, on behalf of the Whigs, to limit the power of the king, George III. He expressed his views on this issue, as well as on the problems arising in the American colonies, in a pamphlet entitled *Thoughts on the Causes of the Present Discontents* (1770). By far his most famous work, however, was his *Reflections on the Revolution in France* (1790), a scathing attack on numerous aspects of the French Revolution of 1789.

In the *Reflections*, Burke expresses a desire to conserve the essential economic and political fabric of feudalism. He appeals to the authority of the past and opposes the collective wisdom and experience of the past to what he sees as the abstract rationalism of the French revolutionists. Like all conservatives, he maintains that, in reforming society, we must adopt a policy of gradual change, and our starting point must be the actual status quo rather than an idealistic and abstractly rational set of principles which may not be related at all to actual social and economic conditions. He insists on the validity and legitimacy of the feudal hierarchy, a hereditary monarchy, with a hereditary nobility and clergy occupying dominant positions. And finally, like many conservatives before and after him, he insists that the only practicable conception of liberty is one which ties it indissolubly to the notions of social responsibility and duty. In this text, Burke suggests that appeal to reason alone fails to accommodate a people's sensibility, feeling, as well as considerations of taste and elegance.

These political dispositions are somewhat anticipated in Burke's much earlier text, *A Philosophical Enquiry into the Origins of Our Ideas of the Sublime and Beautiful* (1757). Burke is here writing in a tradition that goes back to Longinus' treatise *On the Sublime* (which Burke had read), and which was revived in the eighteenth and nineteenth centuries largely under the auspices of Kant and Romantic writers. Burke's essay draws on the insights of Addison and Hume, and like these thinkers, he adopts a broadly empiricist perspective.

Burke begins by noting that we usually have fixed criteria for truth and falsehood and for the operations of reason. But where taste is concerned, a "superficial" view suggests that people differ widely. Yet, Like Hume and Kant, Burke suggests that, unless we had a standard of taste, just as we share a standard of reason, we would not be able to "maintain the ordinary correspondence of life."[10] While he acknowledges that taste, "like all other figurative terms," is not accurate in its signification, he uses the term to refer to those faculties of mind which are affected by, or form judgments about, works of imagination (*PE*, 12). Burke's attempt to show that certain standards of taste are common to all human beings shares some features with Kant's, although his procedure is empirical like Hume's.

His essential strategy is to divide the faculties whereby we know the external world into three: the senses, imagination, and judgment. Since the organs of all men are the same, he argues, the "manner of perceiving external objects is in all men the same." In other words, our sense-perceptions operate in the same way (*PE*, 13). Given that objects in the world present the same images to all of us, the "pleasures and pains which every object excites in one man, it must raise in all mankind" (*PE*, 13). For example, regarding the sense of taste, we all concur not only in finding certain foods sweet and others sour but also in finding sweetness pleasant and sourness or bitterness unpleasant. Where certain people diverge from this standard, says Burke, it is because an "acquired" taste has supervened upon natural taste. A man might find tobacco pleasant, but this taste for bitterness is acquired by habit and on account of certain effects of the drug (*PE*, 14). Such a man would still find other bitter tastes, with which he is unfamiliar, displeasing. Burke concludes that "the pleasures of all the senses" are "the same in all, high and low, learned and unlearned" (*PE*, 16).

Having established this uniformity at the level of sense-perception, Burke's strategy is to show, in characteristic empiricist fashion, that the other faculties, imagination and judgment, are also ultimately grounded on sense-perception. The imagination, says Burke, is a creative power; it can represent the images of things in the order in which

337

they were received by our senses or it can rearrange them in a new way. Imagination is the main province of the creative arts. However, in contrast with later, Romantic views of imagination, Burke denies that the imagination can produce anything absolutely new: it "can only vary the disposition of those ideas which it has received from the senses" (*PE*, 17). The imagination is the "most extensive province of pleasure and pain," and, since the imagination is merely the "representative" of the senses, the pleasure or displeasure it derives from images must rest on the same principle as the pleasure experienced by our senses. Burke concludes that "there must be just as close an agreement in the imaginations as in the senses of men" (*PE*, 17).

There are two ways in which we can receive pleasure from the operations of the imagination. We can derive pleasure from the properties of the object itself, or from the resemblance which the imitation produced by the imagination has to the original object. Burke sees both of these causes of pleasure as working uniformly in all people, since "they operate by principles in nature" and not by any peculiar habits that people have (*PE*, 17). Burke here invokes Locke's distinction between wit and judgment. Wit, according to Locke, is characterized by tracing resemblances among things, whereas judgment typically discerns differences. Following Locke, Burke insists that wit and judgment are entirely different in their nature. He urges that we derive far greater satisfaction from wit than from judgment; the latter is used in the distinctions we make in our everyday engagement with the world. But when we utilize wit, when we find resemblances among things, "we produce *new images*, we unite, we create, we enlarge our stock" (*PE*, 17–18). Burke anticipates here many Romantic views of the power of poetry to challenge conventional ways of representing the world.

Burke attempts to show how the pleasure deriving from resemblance between imitation and the actual object is generally the same in all people. Such pleasure varies not according to varying capacities of taste but according to people's knowledge of the real object, a knowledge which is accidentally acquired and circumstantial, a knowledge which depends upon "experience and observation" (*PE*, 18). Hence the taste underlying our pleasure in resemblance is uniform. However, like Hume, Burke concedes that this pleasure may be modified by comparison with other objects. A refined or superior taste depends not on one man having a greater faculty of taste but on his possessing greater knowledge and experience of the mode of art in question. "So far as taste is natural," says Burke, "it is nearly common to all" (*PE*, 19–20). In other words, taste unrefined by knowledge and experience is the same in all people.

Insofar as taste belongs to the imagination, then, "its principle is the same in all men" (*PE*, 20). However, people can differ in the *degree* to which they are affected by an object. This difference can arise from two causes: either from a greater degree of "natural sensibility" or from "a closer and longer attention to the object" (*PE*, 21). This type of difference brings us to the province of judgment. The imagination is engaged when we are dealing with the artistic representation of sensible objects or the passions, since we can represent these "without any recourse to reasoning" (*PE*, 22). But when works of imagination extend to the characters and actions of men, their relations, vices and virtues, says Burke, they fall under the province of judgment, which "is improved by attention and by the habit of reasoning" (*PE*, 22). Taste here becomes a "refined judgment." Burke concludes that taste "is not a simple idea, but is partly made up of a perception of the primary pleasures of sense, of the secondary pleasures of the imagination, and of the conclusions of the reasoning faculty, concerning the various relations of these, and concerning the human passions, manners and actions. All this is requisite to form Taste." Since the senses underlie the activities of imagination and judgment, says Burke, they are "the great originals of all our ideas, and consequently of all our pleasures." Hence the "whole ground-work of Taste is common to all" (*PE*, 22).

While Burke acknowledges that the principles of taste, though uniform, are present in different people in varying degrees, he attributes such variation to certain defects. Taste requires both sensibility and judgment; if sensibility is defective, this will result in a lack of taste, as for example in people whose feelings might be considered to be blunt. If judgment is weak, this will produce a "wrong" or "bad" taste. Factors contributing to weak judgment include "ignorance, inattention, prejudice, rashness, levity, obstinacy" (*PE*, 23). Having said this, Burke does not view taste as a separate faculty of the mind, as distinct from judgment and imagination. He insists that good taste is distinguished from bad taste only by the exercise of our understanding. Taste, he urges, "is improved exactly as we improve our judgment, by extending our knowledge, by a steady attention to our object, and by frequent exercise" (*PE*, 25).

Burke's comments on the sublime and beautiful anticipate in some respects the account later offered by Kant, which is otherwise very different. He says that whatever excites ideas of pain, danger, and terror is a source of the sublime; and the sublime is the "strongest emotion which the mind is capable of feeling," far more powerful than emotions of pleasure (*PE*, 36). Ultimately, pain is so potent a force because it is "an emissary" of death, the "king of terrors." It is when we are able to distance ourselves from such pain and terror that we can find them delightful; and it is this feeling which is sublime (*PE*, 36). The sublime differs from the beautiful in fundamental ways: sublime objects are vast, rugged, obscure, dark; beautiful objects are small, smooth, light, and delicate. Sublime objects are founded on pain while beautiful objects give pleasure (*PE*, 113).

Mary Wollstonecraft (1759–1797)

Acknowledged as one of the first feminist writers of modern times, Mary Wollstonecraft was a radical thinker whose central notions were framed by the debates and issues that arose directly out of the French Revolution of 1789. Her *Vindication of the Rights of Men* (1790), like Thomas Paine's *The Rights of Man*, was a defense of the Revolution against the scornful attacks expressed in Burke's *Reflections on the Revolution in France*. Wollstonecraft has rightly been characterized as an Enlightenment thinker, propounding arguments in favor of reason, against hereditary privilege and the entire inequitable apparatus of feudalism. Yet Wollstonecraft added to these conventional Enlightenment elements an important dimension: a concern for the economic and educational rights of women, as expressed in the work for which she is best known, *A Vindication of the Rights of Woman* (1792).

Wollstonecraft's troubled life reflects and underlies her ideological dispositions. One of six children, she suffered, with the rest of her family, at the hands of a somewhat despotic father. She experienced first hand the economic disadvantages to which women were subject, attempting to earn a living in the conventional female occupations of governess and lady's maid; she was a victim of unfortunate romantic encounters, first with the painter Henry Fuseli, and then with an American businessman, Gilbert Imlay, with whom she conceived a child and whose infidelity led her to two suicide attempts; she eventually married the political philosopher William Godwin (whose *Political Justice* appeared in 1793); a few days after giving birth to a daughter (who would marry the poet Shelley and write the novel *Frankenstein*), she died. Notwithstanding her turbulent life, she mixed with some of the prominent radical figures of her day: her publisher Joseph Johnson, the dissenter Dr. Richard Price (who initially provoked Burke's anti-revolutionary sentiments), Thomas Paine, and of course William Godwin himself.

Among Wollstonecraft's publications were *Thoughts on the Education of Daughters* (1786) and a novel, *Mary, A Fiction* (1788). While she did not directly write on literature, she did explore issues such as the nature of women, their innate abilities and their characteristics as arising from social and economic circumstances, and their capacity for education, issues which have remained central to many feminist theories and which underlie much feminist literary criticism.

The central purpose of *A Vindication of the Rights of Woman* is stated as follows: "Contending for the rights of woman, my main argument is built on this simple principle, that if she be not prepared by education to become the companion of man, she will stop the progress of knowledge and virtue; for truth must be common to all, or it will be inefficacious with respect to its influence on general practice."[11] She points out that woman can cooperate in this enterprise only if she understands why she ought to be virtuous, and only if "freedom strengthens her reason till she comprehends her duty," part of which is to be a "patriot" (86). If the rights of man merit consideration, claims Wollstonecraft, then by a "parity of reasoning," women's rights also claim attention. These claims, as Wollstonecraft implies, are founded on two fundamental principles: firstly, that not only men but also women have "the gift of reason"; and secondly, that no authority can simply coerce women into fulfilling a given set of duties (87–88). Wollstonecraft ends this section on a powerful note: "the rights of Woman may be respected, if it be fully proved that reason calls for this respect, and loudly demands JUSTICE for one-half of the human race" (89). What she is essentially appealing to in this dedication are the Enlightenment principles of reason, duty, freedom, self-determination, and even patriotism; her feminism consists in the demand that these same principles extend to women; she is not, like later feminists, devaluing these principles themselves as outgrowths of a patriarchal establishment and history. Many modern feminists, for example, have challenged the primacy of reason itself, as well as the various categories – such as substance and accident, identity, space, time, causality – according to which male thinkers, since Plato and Aristotle, have divided up the world.

However, Wollstonecraft is far from ignoring the defects of male categories or male employments of reason, and indeed she anticipates many of the objections of modern feminists. As with Christine de Pisan many centuries earlier, an essential part of Wollstonecraft's endeavor is to redeem the notion of reason from its history of male abuse and to appropriate it toward more equitable ends respecting gender. Her first chapter, concerning the rights and duties of mankind, provides an important historical and political context for her later specific arguments concerning the character and education of women. She asserts that the time has come "to go back to first principles in search of the most simple truths," truths that have become clouded by "prevailing prejudice" and custom. Man's preeminence over the brute creation, she affirms, consists in his power of reason; what exalts one being over another is virtue; and experience shows that, by struggling with our passions, we attain to a degree of knowledge denied to animals. These principles are brought together in the most fundamental premise of Wollstonecraft's entire argument: "the perfection of our nature and capability of happiness must be estimated by the degree of reason, virtue, and knowledge, that distinguish the individual, and direct the laws which bind society." We need to return to first principles in the search for truth, says Wollstonecraft, because for many centuries "deeply rooted prejudices have clouded reason, and . . . spurious qualities have assumed the name of virtues" (91). We must engage in independent thinking that has not been blurred by these prejudices and by expediency, both based on "shallow" reasoning.

Wollstonecraft sees the entire history and structure of feudalism as based on irrational expediency and prejudice, rather than on reason: "Such, indeed has been the wretchedness that has flowed from hereditary honours, riches, and monarchy, that men of lively sensibility have almost uttered blasphemy in order to justify the dispensations of Providence" (93). She sharply criticizes the institution of monarchy, which places the fate of nations in the hands of a few people whose position by its very nature incites them toward irrational caprice; she also impugns, as "injurious to morality," every profession based on subordination of rank, a hierarchical power structure, or blind submission to authority (96). While she sympathizes with some features of Rousseau's critique of civilized society, she rejects his view that a state of nature and solitude is superior to one of civilization: man is endowed with a gift, that of reason, which allows him to rise above mere brute existence; had Rousseau seen more clearly, he would have contemplated "the perfection of man in the establishment of true civilization, instead of taking his ferocious flight back to the night of sensual ignorance" (99).

In an important second chapter, Wollstonecraft attempts to undermine prevailing views of the character of women, views resting on political and economic circumstances as well as on a history of male writing about women. Women are taught, she explains, to nurture qualities such as cunning, an appearance of weakness, and a duplicitous "outward" obedience (100); they are encouraged to develop the "cardinal virtues" of gentleness, docility, and a "spaniel-like affection" (118); they are essentially "stripped of the virtues that should clothe humanity," and are pressured into the cultivation of "artificial graces" whereby "their sole ambition is to be fair, to raise emotion instead of inspiring respect" (121). Such attributes, they are advised, will earn them the "protection of man" (100).

A long tradition of male writers, says Wollstonecraft, has contributed to this degradation of women into "artificial, weak characters" (103). The "whole purport of those books," she exclaims, tends to "degrade one-half of the human species, and render women pleasing at the expense of every solid virtue" (104). She offers the examples of Milton, Rousseau, and the eighteenth-century writer John Gregory. In Milton she finds a contradiction: on the one hand, in *Paradise Lost* (IV.637–638) he portrays Eve as saying to Adam: "God is *thy law, thou mine*: to know no more / Is woman's *happiest* knowledge and her *praise*" (101). In a later book of his long poem, however (VIII.381–391), he presents Adam as complaining to God that he requires the fellowship of an *equal* being so that he can experience "rational delight" (102). Taking her cue from

341

this, Wollstonecraft suggests that we explore the principles on which women can cooperate with the "Supreme Being," such that they can have a productive role in the world.

Most male writers, however, effectively render women "useless members of society" (103). Even Rousseau, whom Wollstonecraft otherwise admires, suggests that woman should exercise cunning and coquetry to make herself "a more alluring object of desire"; her cultivation of "truth and fortitude" must be sharply restricted since "obedience is the grand lesson which ought to be impressed" on women. The fearlessness of Wollstonecraft's retort is an integral element in her feminist strategy: "What nonsense!" (108). Not only Rousseau but also most of the male writers who have followed in his footsteps have argued that the whole tendency of female education should be directed toward one purpose: to make women pleasing to men (110). A more recent example of such "nonsense" is to be found in John Gregory's handbook on proper female behavior, entitled *A Father's Legacy to his Daughters* (1774). Gregory advises women to cultivate such "virtues" as a "fondness for dress," a capacity for dissimulation, and the avoidance of "delicacy of sentiment" (111, 116). Wollstonecraft also attacks female writers such as Hester Lynch Thrale Piozzi, Mme. de Staël, and the celebrated French writer Mme. Felicité Genlis as effectively reiterating "masculine sentiments" (202–205).

Underlying all of these prescriptions for female behavior, Wollstonecraft sees one fundamental principle, rooted in educational strategy: an endeavor to "enslave women by cramping their understandings and sharpening their senses" (104). In the education of women, the "cultivation of the understanding is always subordinate to the acquirement of some corporeal accomplishment" (105). Whereas men are from their infancy regaled with "method" and the need for systematic and exact thought, women "receive only a disorderly kind of education," being taught to rely on "a sort of instinctive common sense never brought to the test of reason." This prevents women from generalizing on the basis of "matters of fact" (104). This desultory knowledge that women acquire is based more on "sheer observations on real life than from comparing what has been individually observed with the results of experience generalized by speculation" (105). Wollstonecraft's voice here reverberates with Enlightenment ideals; whereas many feminists, including Christine de Pisan, have appealed to direct experience to counter the theoretical reflections of men, Wollstonecraft recognizes that a mere appeal to direct experience can have little force: it is imprisoned within the domain of particular phenomena and events, divesting itself of the power to offer an alternative interpretation. In her view, women are effectively constrained within particularity, forced to look at the world as a series of discrete and unrelated phenomena, whose connections might as well be random. In being deprived of the ability to generalize, women are, in effect, deprived of the ability to think. Indeed, this entrapment within particularity is also a docile entrapment within the present: men are encouraged to exercise their thought in relation to the past and future, as well as the present. Women are told that they need focus only on the present, a narrowness of perspective that effectively increases and solidifies their dependence on men (116, 118).

There are a number of degrading and injurious consequences of women being given such a haphazard education. The most important is that women are unable to act as genuine moral agents: without the power of reason, they cannot make moral choices and are disposed to blind obedience of whatever power structure can claim authority over them. Another prerequisite of moral action is freedom; Wollstonecraft wisely states that liberty "is the mother of virtue" (121). Hence, for women to be able to contribute to society as moral agents, they must be able to understand the bases of their actions as well as have the freedom to make moral decisions. Wollstonecraft insists that "the conduct of an accountable being must be regulated by the operations of its own reason" (121); she equates with a "system of slavery" any attempt to "educate moral beings by any other rules than those deduced from pure reason." And these rules must "apply to the whole species" (117): the conduct of both sexes, she insists, "should be founded on the same principles, and have the same aim" (108).

Other consequences of conventional female education include women's inability to engage in "serious scientific study" in any given field, since their attention is diverted to "life and manners" (105). Further, women are prevented from becoming friends and partners to their husbands, for the effective management of their households or the education of their children (119). Having said all of this, Wollstonecraft is deeply aware that mere private education of particular women will not solve the overall problem. The educational system itself plays a fundamental role in the tyranny that men exercise over women, breeding all the womanly follies such as sentimentality, incoherent thinking, fondness of dress, and the cultivation of physical beauty (318–319). This problem, this inequality, has a structural basis, grounded in the very fabric of feudalism. Education itself needs to be reformulated on the basis of a more rational political structure; education will not be effective until "kings and nobles, enlightened by reason, and, preferring the real dignity of man to childish state, throw off their gaudy hereditary trappings" (103). "Brutal force," she says, "has hitherto governed the world": only when the hierarchies based on force yield to a society based on freedom will "mankind, including woman . . . become more wise and virtuous" (122). Wollstonecraft acknowledges that much of what she has said about the stunting of women's capacities applies equally to large numbers of men who themselves "have submitted to superior strength to enjoy with impunity the pleasure of the moment" (122). Her call is essentially for a society that will free not only women but also men from the servitude of blind obedience, of immersion in the present, and of losing sight of the rational foundations of morality.

As such, the national education of women is of the "utmost consequence" (297). Wollstonecraft argues that private and public education should be combined, a strategy that will bypass the one-sided defects of an exclusively public or private education. Public education, she says, "should be directed to form citizens." But the virtues of a good citizen must first be nurtured in the home, through exercise of affection and respect for family members and domestic duties: public affections, as well as public virtues, "must ever grow out of the private character" (279). To this end, of combining private and public teaching, Wollstonecraft recommends national day schools which will be free to all classes of society, and where both sexes will be educated together. In all respects, including dress, equality should be promoted, especially the principle that the virtue of both sexes rests upon reason, and not on outward obedience (283, 286). Such a system will cultivate friendship and love between the sexes, rather than domineering tyranny on one side and a duplicitous submissiveness on the other (288). It will also promote early marriage, an institution that she regards as the "cement of society" (283, 287). The subjects of study will include not only the conventional academic disciplines such as botany, astronomy, reading, writing, arithmetic, and natural history but also gymnastics (287). Besides, women should be taught the basic elements of anatomy and medicine, so as to make them "rational nurses of their infants"; they should also be taught "the anatomy of the mind," as well as the science of morality and, in general, the progress of the human understanding (298). The establishment of such day schools will enable children to sleep at home "that they may learn to love home," as well as encouraging them at school to "mix with a number of equals, for only by the jostlings of equality can we form a just opinion of ourselves" (293).

This last point is important in the educational method prescribed by Wollstonecraft: instead of rote-learning of what they do not comprehend, children must be encouraged to think for themselves, by exchanging and testing their ideas against those of their peers. Indeed, Wollstonecraft urges that religion, history, and politics "might also be taught by conversations in the Socratic form" (287). Her own educational principles might be said to have an aesthetic leaning: the kind of independence of thought she advocates in the classroom bears similarities with her view of the artist's independence. Both a taste for the fine arts and a taste for the emotions associated with virtue, she says, require great cultivation and an "enlargement of mind" (284). The true artist does not simply make a "servile copy" of nature but uses an "exalted imagination, . . . fine senses and enlarged understanding" to form an ideal picture or harmonious whole (290–291). And, like certain neoclassical writers, she holds that judgment or understanding is the "foundation of all taste" (284). She observes that true "taste is ever the work of the understanding employed in observing natural effects; and till women have more understanding, it is vain to expect them to possess domestic taste" (285). As with the artist, a woman cannot simply rely on others (such as her husband) for judgment, for no being can "act wisely from imitation, because in every circumstance of life there is a kind of individuality, which requires an exertion of judgment to modify general rules" (298). As a result of the education she prescribes, woman will have a fuller understanding of beauty in both its physical and moral dimensions. Woman will acquire a "dignified beauty . . . To render the person perfect, physical and moral beauty ought to be attained at the same time . . . Judgment must reside on the brow, affection and fancy beam in the eye, and humanity curve the cheek, or vain is the sparkling of the finest eye or the elegantly turned finish of the fairest features" (291). Wollstonecraft here effectively *redefines* female beauty as an integral product of a rational, affectionate, and independent disposition, a quality behind which lies not merely the accident of appearance but a revolutionizing of gender relations, based in turn on a revised educational and political program.

Indeed, it is ultimately on political and economic premises that Wollstonecraft sees the possibility of a more effective education resting. Social equality would be the basis of educational equality (287–288). She urges men to allow women "to share the advantages of education and government" (286). Only if they are enabled to undertake study of political and moral subjects can they be "properly attentive to their domestic duties. An active mind embraces the whole circle of its duties" (288). Women cannot fulfill their family duties until "their minds take a wider range," and until they are allowed to "found their virtue on knowledge, which is scarcely possible unless they be educated by the same pursuits as men" (294). She urges: "Make women rational creatures and free citizens, and they will quickly become good wives and mothers" (299).

Hence, Wollstonecraft seeks to extend to women the Enlightenment principles of basing both knowledge and morality upon reason, which itself presupposes access to the right kinds of information, to a nurturing of coherent thinking, and, above all, freedom in the sense of being allowed to judge and think for themselves. Without this independence, women cannot even be good, clear-thinking wives and mothers; Wollstonecraft implicitly rejects any sharp distinction between the private, "domestic" sphere of women and the public sphere of men. She also anticipates Hegel's master–slave dialectic and the arguments advanced in many African-American slave narratives, in insisting that a virtuous, prosperous, and happy society cannot be built on foundations of inequality with respect to gender or to opportunity in general. Later feminists have often diverged from Wollstonecraft, in viewing marriage as an institution irremediably pervaded by a history of patriarchal principles; they have rejected her view that morality and virtue should be founded on eternal and immutable principles; and they have left behind her own grounding of these views on a supreme being, as well as her appeal to reason. What is enduring about her vision, however, is its insistence that female equality in any sphere depends ultimately on a radical restructuring of the social and political order; her arguments for education remain pertinent today; and her view that genuine morality cannot be based on ignorance and blind obedience retain their inspiring force.

Notes

1 Francis Bacon, *The New Organon*, ed. Fulton H. Anderson (Indianapolis: Bobbs-Merrill, 1960), pp. 47–50.

2 *The Philosophical Works of Descartes: Volume I*, trans. E. S. Haldane and G. R. T. Ross (NP: Dover, 1955), p. 101.

3 John Locke, *An Essay Concerning Human Understanding*, ed. A. D. Woozley (Glasgow: Fontana/Collins, 1975), p. 89. Hereafter cited as *Essay*.

4 David Hume, *A Treatise of Human Nature: Book One*, ed. D. G. C. Macnabb (Glasgow: Fontana/Collins, 1978), pp. 113, 130–131. Hereafter cited as *THN*.

5 William Keach, "Poetry, after 1740," in *CHLC*, V.IV, 129–133.

6 Susan Manning, "Literature and Philosophy," in *CHLC*, V.IV, 587–588.

7 Addison and Steele, *Selections from the Tatler and the Spectator*, ed. Robert J. Allen (New York: Holt, Rinehart, and Winston, 1961), pp. 67–68. Hereafter cited as *Spectator*.

8 *The New Science of Giambattista Vico*, revised translation of third edition, Thomas Goddard Bergin and Max Harold Fisch (Ithaca and New York: Cornell University Press, 1968), para. 31, p. 20. Hereafter cited as *NS*.

9 David Hume, "Of the Standard of Taste," para 1. This essay was originally published in David Hume, *Four Dissertations* (New York: Garland, 1970); I have cited a more easily accessible online edition which is particularly convenient since its paragraphs are numbered: www.csulb.edu/~jvancamp/361r15.html. Hereafter cited as "OST"; numbers refer to paragraphs.

10 Edmund Burke, *A Philosophical Enquiry into the Origins of Our Ideas of the Sublime and Beautiful* (New York and Oxford: Oxford University Press, 1990), p. 11. Hereafter cited as *PE*.

11 Mary Wollstonecraft, *Vindication of the Rights of Woman*, ed. Miriam Brody Kramnick (Harmondsworth: Penguin, 1985), pp. 85–86. All subsequent page references are to this edition.

PART VI

THE EARLIER NINETEENTH CENTURY AND ROMANTICISM

INTRODUCTION TO
THE MODERN PERIOD

The period of European history from 1760 to 1860 was dominated by two broad
series of events, the French Revolution and the Industrial Revolution, which
oversaw the emergence and growth of Romanticism. Both of these phenomena
contributed decisively to the most profound structural change of this era, the transformation of Europe from a feudal to a bourgeois society. This introduction will briefly
examine that transformation in terms of the political, social, and economic causes and
effects of the French and Industrial Revolutions, the growth of nationalism, the kinds
of ideological and intellectual struggles emerging from these phenomena, and the
response of writers and critics, much of which was forged in the heat of those struggles.
The present account is based in part on analyses of this era by Eric Hobsbawm, Herbert
Marcuse, Georges Lefebvre, and others, while much of the historical material presented here derives from some of the general histories cited in the bibliography at the
end of the book.

The French Revolution: Background and Consequences

It would not be an exaggeration to say that the effects of the French Revolution of 1789
are still with us. The historian Eric Hobsbawm has suggested that most political struggles through the nineteenth century into the twentieth century have been for or against
the principles which were at stake in that Revolution.[1] The effect of the Revolution was
to bring about the destruction of the vast edifice of feudalism which had lasted for
centuries. Feudalism had been characterized by a static and localized economy, hereditary privilege, and concentration of power in the hands of monarchy and nobility,
together with vast Church wealth and influence. Each person was believed to have a
fixed place in the allegedly natural and divinely sanctioned order of things.

Essentially, the French Revolution, along with the numerous other revolutions that
succeeded it, initiated the displacement of the power of the king and nobility by the
power of the bourgeoisie or middle classes which comprised recently appointed nobles,

financiers, businessmen, traders, and members of the liberal professions.[2] In addition to the political and economic changes incited by the French Revolution, there was a fundamental change in the thinking of people. The feudal world had been characterized by values of static hierarchy, loyalty, authority, religious faith, and monarchical or oligarchical exercise of power; these values were increasingly displaced by bourgeois ideology, much of which stemmed from Enlightenment thought. Such ideology was predominantly secular, stressing reason, individual experience, efficiency, usefulness, and, above all, political liberalism based on a free rational economy aided by technology and science. Much Romanticism took its initial impetus as a response to the new world created by these vast structural transformations in the realms of politics, economy, philosophy, and aesthetics.

The broad background of the French Revolution was colored by a number of overarching circumstances. The first of these was the rise of absolute monarchies everywhere in Europe during the fourteenth and fifteenth centuries. In England, absolute government was instituted by the Tudor monarchs and continued by the Stuarts, James VI and Charles I. Their inflated conceptions of monarchy and their attempts to undermine Parliament eventually resulted in the Civil War (1642–1649) between the supporters of the king and those of Parliament. The latter, led by Oliver Cromwell, were victorious. Charles I was beheaded in 1649 and England was ruled for a short spell by Parliament. However, the so-called Restoration of 1660 placed Charles II upon the throne. In the Glorious Revolution of 1688, William and Mary of Orange were invited to rule England. This series of events put an end to absolute monarchy in England in favor of parliamentary government.

Central Europe and Spain were also under the rule of despots, some enlightened such as Frederick II the Great of Prussia (1740–1786) and Joseph II of Austria (1780–1790), and others more repressive such as Catherine the Great of Russia (1762–1796), who crushed a serf rebellion in 1773–1774. In France, however, the situation was dire. Henry IV, founder of the Bourbon dynasty, had promoted industry and manufacture and effectively minimized the sovereignty of the feudal nobility. The next three Bourbon kings, Louis XIV (1643–1715), Louis XV (1715–1774), and Louis XVI (1774–1792), took to new extremes the arrogation of power and the instruments of justice. Louis XIV had declared "*l'état, c'est moi,*" and both of his successors professed the divine right of kings. Absolutism as a political theory had been expressed by Jean Bodin (1530–1596), who had claimed that the monarch derives his authority from God, as well as by the philosopher Thomas Hobbes and the Dutch writer Hugo Grotius (1583–1645).

Hence, the French Revolution was in part a reaction against the excesses of absolute government which had grown both in theory and practice since the fourteenth century. Another factor was the economic transformation of society. The fourteenth through the seventeenth centuries had witnessed tendencies which would later foster the growth of capitalism: the accumulation of wealth which was invested for profit, the growth of banking and credit facilities, regulated associations of companies and joint-stock companies, the decline of the feudal manufacturing guilds, and the growth of new industries such as mining and wool, and the revolutionizing of agricultural methods. These trends were accompanied by economic nationalism, an ethic of competition, and imperialism. By the seventeenth century, England, France, Italy, Spain, Portugal, and Holland had become imperial powers; trade became a worldwide rather than a national or local phenomenon. By the end of the seventeenth century the bourgeoisie had achieved economic hegemony.

Against this background, it can be seen that the more proximate causes of the French Revolution were economic, political, and intellectual. The economic causes were perhaps the most important: though the middle classes had risen to a dominant economic position, they were without correlative political privileges; these classes were opposed to the age-old policies of mercantilism, which established monopolies and control of purchase, wages, and prices. Another economic cause was the survival of a feudal system of privileges, whereby the higher clergy and certain classes of nobles monopolized government. Peasants resented the fees and land taxes they were obliged to pay to their lords; and the urban masses suffered greatly from high prices. The political causes included a despotic monarchy, an unsystematic mode of government, finance, taxation, and law. Perhaps the most direct causes were the costly Seven Years' War (1756–1763) fought against England and Prussia, and the French involvement in the American War of Independence (1778), which both contributed to the economic bankruptcy of the government.

The intellectual influences stemmed largely from the Enlightenment, whose major tendencies, as seen in the previous chapter, were toward rationalism, empiricism, pragmatism, and utilitarianism; these tendencies, inspired by thinkers such as John Locke and David Hume in Britain, Voltaire, Diderot, and d'Alembert in France, as well as Gotthold Lessing in Germany, formed the core of liberal-bourgeois thought. The more specific influences on the French Revolution included Locke's *Second Treatise of Civil Government* (1690), which justified the new political system in England that prevailed after the English revolution of 1688. Locke condemned despotic monarchy and the absolute sovereignty of parliaments and suggested that the people had a right to resist tyranny. Voltaire advocated an enlightened monarchy or republic governed by the bourgeois classes. Baron de Montesquieu also influenced the first stage of the French Revolution, advancing a liberal theory based on a separation of executive, legislative, and judicial powers. Jean-Jacques Rousseau exerted a powerful impact on the second stage of the Revolution through his theories of democracy, egalitarianism, and the evils of private property, as advocated in his *Social Contract* and *Discourse on the Origin of Inequality*. A final intellectual factor in the background of the Revolution was the growth of bourgeois economics, which undermined mercantilism and advocated (with varying qualifications) the doctrine of economic laissez-faire, and labor theories of value.

The French Revolution began with aristocratic unrest with the monarchy and the nobility demanding increase of their privileges; but events were soon controlled by bourgeois interests which shaped the essentially bourgeois nature of the Revolution. In the first stage (1789–1792) Louis XVI called a meeting in 1789 of the Estates General, a parliamentary body which had been convened only irregularly in the past. The three estates represented there were the clergy, the nobility, and the common people. The Third Estate, of which the richest and most capable section was the bourgeoisie (*FR*, 43), formed itself into the National Assembly which, led by advocates of bourgeois reform, drafted a new constitution by 1791. It was in this first stage, in which the Bastille was stormed, the Church secularized, and the "Declaration of the Rights of

Man" enacted, which proclaimed liberty, security, and property as natural rights. The Declaration opposed feudal privilege but was not egalitarian in character. The structure of government was not democratic but a constitutional monarchy in which a propertied oligarchy would govern through a representative assembly. The document was also nationalist in character, viewing the source of authority as residing in the nation.

The second phase of the Revolution began in August of 1792. It was a more radical phase, involving the masses, whose leaders, such as Maximilien de Robespierre (1758–1794), Georges Jacques Danton (1759–1794), and Jean-Paul Marat (1743–1793), were devoted to the egalitarian doctrines of Rousseau. A National Convention was elected, its purpose being to draft a new democratic constitution which would include rights and provisions for the poor. France became a republic. In January 1793 Louis XVI was charged with treason and beheaded. France entered into war with, and was defeated by, Austria and Prussia whose rulers feared the spread of revolutionary ideals. The so-called "Reign of Terror" (1793–1794) was instigated by the executive arm of the National Convention, known as the Committee of Public Safety. This period is usually remembered for its violence and thousands of executions but, as Hobsbawm has pointed out, it was also a period of remarkable achievements. These included the drafting of the first genuinely democratic constitution produced by a modern state (though this was not put into effect), the abolition of all remaining feudal rights, the fixing of maximum prices on grain, the division of large estates to be sold to poorer citizens, the separation of Church and state, the abolition of slavery in the French colonies, the expulsion of the invading armies of Prussia and Britain from France, and the relative stabilizing of the French economy (*AR*, 90–91). Robespierre's execution in 1794 effectively marks the end of the second, radical stage of the Revolution. The Convention was now dominated by more moderate leaders who acted in bourgeois interests. In 1795 the Convention drafted a new constitution which was founded on the security of property and which restricted voting to wealthy proprietors. Power was vested in a five-man Directory. This stage was characterized by profiteering and a great deal of corruption, and the ensuing inflation and economic chaos paved the way for the coup d'état of Napoleon Bonaparte on November 9 (the eighteenth Brumaire), 1799, the date which marks the end of the French Revolution.

The Era of Napoleon

Napoleon had been exalted to the status of a national hero through his success in a French campaign against Austria. Eventually, his popularity and military power enabled him to overthrow the French government in 1799 and to become consul; he became Emperor Napoleon I of France in 1804 and his autocratic rule effectively put an end to the liberal ideals of the French Revolution. However, he confirmed and developed certain accomplishments of that Revolution, centralizing the government, continuing tax reforms, maintaining the redistribution of vast estates and the abolition of serfdom, and continuing reforms begun by the Revolution in the spheres of education and criminal and civil law (known in their revised form as the Code Napoléon). Some of the revolutionary fervor spread to Prussia, and these legal developments were transported into the legal structures of other countries such as Italy, Prussia, and Switzerland. However, Napoleon undermined the Revolution's separation of Church and state, establishing a Concordat with Pope Pius VII in 1801.

Napoleon inherited from revolutionary times a war against Britain, Austria, and Russia, defeating the latter two powers and extending the frontiers of France to encompass most of continental Europe, as well as placing his brothers on the thrones of Westphalia, Naples, and Holland. Eventually, Napoleon was defeated in turn by Britain, Austria, Prussia, and Russia. He was exiled until his death in 1821.

The Congress of Vienna and the Metternich System

In the aftermath of the French Revolution, ideological and political struggles between liberals and conservatives swept through the rest of Europe. The heads or representatives of many powers – including Prussia, Austria, Russia, and Britain – assembled at the Congress of Vienna (1814–1815) to decide the future of Europe. The Congress was dominated by Klemens von Metternich (1773–1859), the Austrian minister of foreign affairs who had helped forge the alliance which had defeated Napoleon. Metternich was a staunch conservative who was determined to return to the status quo before the Revolution of 1789. He engineered an agreement whereby the dynasties which had held power in 1789 should be restored and whereby each country should possess again the territories it had held at that time. Liberal movements challenged the conservatives in England, where the Reform Bill of 1832 implemented electoral reforms, enfranchising and establishing the hegemony of the middle class. Bourgeois entrepreneurs also agitated against the Corn Laws, protective tariffs benefiting the landowners; these laws were eventually repealed in 1846. There were uprisings against the restored Bourbon monarch Louis XVIII of France, who was succeeded in 1824 by his even more reactionary brother Charles X.

Intense ideological struggles shook Prussia and Russia also. In response, Metternich enforced in the former a repressive program known as the Carlsbad Decrees (1819), which, in response to student unrest, brought the entire university system and the press under strict control and censorship. However, the Metternich system of alliances began to crumble. Britain, primarily for economic motives, withdrew; and several revolutions erupted in Europe in 1830. The first was the July Revolution in France where bourgeois leaders ousted Charles X and replaced him with Louis-Philippe as head of a constitutional monarchy. The Belgian Netherlands revolted successfully against Dutch rule; and in 1831 Poland's rebellion against Russian rule was quelled severely by Tsar Nicholas I.

The Revolutions of 1848 and the Growth of Nationalism

The French Revolution, whose catchwords were "liberty, equality, fraternity," had fostered not only the idea of individual rights but also the obligations of the individual toward society or the nation as a whole, which was seen as having a specific history, culture, and direction. The revolutions of 1848 were partly inspired by discontent among liberals with reactionary regimes, and were generally fueled by nationalistic sentiment which had everywhere taken root since the French Revolution. In 1848 widespread dissatisfaction with the increasing despotism of Louis-Philippe led to his deposition. France was made a republic and Louis Napoleon Bonaparte (1808–1873), nephew of Napoleon I, was elected president by an overwhelming majority.

Inspired by the 1848 events in France, revolutions also occurred in Austria and Hungary. In the former, Metternich was forced to resign and the emperor obliged to accept a liberal constitution. Nationalism was an especially potent force for change in Germany and Italy, which eventually achieved unification. Another large empire that collapsed was the Ottoman Empire, which began to crumble as a result of nationalist uprisings, aided by Russia, in Greece and Serbia (1829), as well as in subject territories such as Bosnia, Herzegovina, and Bulgaria (1875–1876).

The Industrial Revolution

The Industrial Revolution, which was given its name by English and French socialists of the 1820s, is cited by Hobsbawm as "probably the most important event in world history" (AR, 44). It is usually divided into two phases, the first stretching from the mid-eighteenth to the mid-nineteenth centuries, and the second phase continuing effectively until the present day. Large-scale industrialization began first in Britain on account of her wealth, her encouragement of private profit, and her economic system backed by liberal policies which had ousted the feudal guild system, as well as her colonies and effective monopoly of the world market. Industrialism spread rapidly, however; by the mid-nineteenth century France and Belgium were engaged in mechanized production; by the end of the nineteenth century Germany had been transformed from an agricultural economy to the greatest industrial power; and industrialization reached Japan and Italy toward the end of the century. The economic transformation of Europe since the fourteenth century had witnessed several technological innovations in many industries such as cotton and iron, culminating in the invention of the steam engine and the large-scale use of coal, along with the development of a factory system using conveyor belts, assembly lines, and other techniques of mass production. Cotton manufacture became mechanized through the invention of the spinning jenny in 1767, the power loom in 1785, and the cotton gin in 1792.

The second phase of industrialization was marked by the use of electricity and oil, the development of the iron and steel industries, increased automation, division of labor, and an increasing harnessing of science by industry. The nineteenth century also saw vast improvements in travel with the establishment of better roads, the railway system, steamships, telecommunications, and cars. Agriculture also became rationally organized and mechanized. More importantly, the massively increased wealth of the bourgeois class sought more outlets for investment in markets that were expanding both in the countries of Europe themselves as a result of increased population and in the colonies of the European powers. Capital was increasingly dominated by investment, finance, and the formation of vast monopolies, while economic liberalism was increasingly displaced by government control, subsidy, and protectionism. By this period, the bourgeois classes had established hegemony and, as Hobsbawm states, the "gods and Kings of the past were powerless before the businessmen and steam-engines of the present" (AR, 69).

Notwithstanding its promotion of prosperity and economic expansion, industrialism was not without its social and economic problems and political crises. While wages increased, there was large-scale unemployment, partly on account of the use of women and children as cheap labor in factories. Extremely poor working conditions, long hours, and disease increased the misery of the working classes. These flaws in the capitalist economy helped precipitate the European revolutions of 1848 and the Chartist uprising in Britain (1838–1848), which struggled for the implementation of a People's Charter demanding universal suffrage, a secret ballot, and salaries as opposed to property qualifications for members of the House of Commons. By the end of the nineteenth century most of the population of Europe was occupied in industrial rather than agricultural labor, embroiled in a crowded urban way of life. These and other factors gave rise to a new political force, the industrial proletariat, which became the main opponent of the recently established hegemony of the new bourgeoisie, the bankers, the industrial magnates, the proprietors of factories, railroads, steelworks, and mines.

The Struggle between Liberal and Conservative Ideologies

The foregoing political struggles and economic transformations were naturally accompanied by a struggle between liberal and conservative ideologies, between those who wished to advance further the principles behind the French Revolution such as rationalism, individualism, and limited government, and those who wished to return to a pre-revolutionary emphasis on tradition, faith, and authority. During the Revolution itself, this struggle had expressed itself prominently in the debate between the liberal statesman Edmund Burke and Thomas Paine (1737–1809), one of the moderate members of the National Convention. In his *Reflections on the Revolution in France* (1790), Burke's attack on the Revolution was characterized by the usual elements of conservatism: an appeal to the authority of the past and the collective wisdom of tradition as opposed to what he sees as the abstract rationalism of the French revolutionists. Thomas Paine's radicalism, as expressed in his widely influential *Rights of Man* (1791), embraced the central thrust of the new bourgeois ideologies: freedom from the past, from tradition, from convention, and a marked emphasis on the present; the exaltation of rationalism so that people might work out for themselves what is the best way to live; insistence upon a somewhat democratic view that political authority is neither hereditary nor divinely bestowed, but derives from the people.

This ideological struggle was played out in many spheres, including religion, philosophy, literature, and art. Perhaps the most profound general ideological change was the secularization of thinking, consonant with the rationalist and materialist worldview of the bourgeoisie. For much of the nineteenth century, religion was engulfed in debates – with philosophy, science, and an entirely transformed way of life – which often threatened its very foundations. There developed in the 1830s in Germany a school of "Higher Criticism," devoted to a study of the sources and methods used by the authors of the Bible, often questioning the coherence and historical accuracy of biblical texts. One of the prominent studies in this field was David Strauss' *Life of Jesus* (1835). Later in the century, the Church would face further threats from discoveries in science, particularly those of Darwin. These developments, together with the onslaught of many governments against the wealth, property, legal rights, and temporal power of the Church, made secularization an institutional as well as an ideological phenomenon.

The formation of an organized proletariat in the nineteenth century was accompanied and promoted by some important political and economic theories. The liberal-bourgeois economic theories of Adam Smith, David Ricardo, and James Mill had dominated much nineteenth-century thought and practice with their notions of economic individualism, laissez-faire, and free competition; these were opposed by thinkers disposed toward representing the interests of the laboring classes, such as the utopian socialists Claude Henri de Saint-Simon (1760–1825), Charles Fourier (1772–1837), who advocated collective ownership of the means of production, and Robert Owen (1771–1858), who impugned the profit system as exploiting the labor of the worker. The most important of the socialist thinkers were Karl Marx (1818–1883) and Friedrich Engels (1820–1895). Marx and Engels developed a materialistic conception of history which saw capitalism as having evolved from a long history of various modes of production, from the ancient slave mode of production through the feudal system, this progression being driven essentially by class conflict. They argued that once technologically assisted capitalist accumulation and world expansion has led to a world of sharply contrasting wealth and poverty, and working classes become conscious of their historical role, capitalism itself will yield to a communism which will do away with private property and base itself on human need rather than the greed of a minority for increasing profit.

The foregoing historical developments, together with the ideological debates they spawned, comprised the crucial background to the emergence of the philosophies of Kant and Hegel, as well of as the broad movements of Romanticism.

Notes

1 E. J. Hobsbawm, *The Age of Revolution: Europe, 1789–1848* (London: Abacus, 1977), pp. 73–75. Hereafter cited as *AR*.
2 Georges Lefebvre, *The French Revolution: From its Origins to 1793*, trans. Elizabeth Moss Evanson (London and New York: Routledge and Kegan Paul/Columbia University Press, 1965), pp. 43–46. Hereafter cited as *FR*.

CHAPTER 14

THE KANTIAN SYSTEM AND KANT'S AESTHETICS

There is no science of the beautiful, but only critique.
Critique of Judgment, p. 172

Much modern literary and cultural theory has encouraged us to view literature and art within their historical and ideological contexts. However, in both academia and popular culture, we are still today very familiar with terms such as "art for art's sake" and we still hear poetry or music or art spoken of as "ends in themselves," to be enjoyed for their own sake. The idea behind such expressions is that literature must be free from any specific moral obligations or political purposes: its primary purpose is not to furnish moral lessons or to promote social causes but to give pleasure; we value it for its own sake, whatever other significance it may have. Most thinkers from Plato to the eighteenth century would have been puzzled or exasperated at such an idea: while they might admit that one function of literature is to "delight" us, they would insist that literature has an important moral, religious, or social dimension.

Strange as it may seem, the idea of literature as autonomous, as having no purpose beyond itself, received its first most articulate expression not by a poet or a literary critic but by a philosopher: Immanuel Kant (1724–1804). It was Kant's *Critique of Judgment,* first published in 1790, which synthesized previous haphazard attempts toward expressing literary autonomy or the idea that literature is ruled only by its own laws rather than by rules from other realms such as morality and education. This book proved to have a vast influence on subsequent aesthetics and poetry, an influence still alive today in our own reverence for the literary artifact as something which stands above and beyond the demands of morality, education, and politics. There are many people today, for example, who would frown on a movie which had an obvious purpose of political propaganda, or a poem whose sole purpose was to inculcate a moral lesson or espouse a given religious viewpoint. We tend to look for purposes which are *internal* to the literature or art itself; we do this by focusing on the *form* of literature as much as on what it seems to "say," and it is this form (for example, the way the various parts of a movie are synthesized) which gives us pleasure. All of these tendencies can be traced back to the aesthetics of Kant.

Immanuel Kant is usually considered, along with G. W. F. Hegel, as one of the two greatest philosophers of modern times. His writings exerted a profound influence upon the thought of Hegel and on several branches of modern philosophy; they furnished a touchstone for much subsequent German political and legal theory; and they had an enormous impact on the development of Romantic thought and many modern aesthetic theories.

Kant was born in 1724 in the town of Königsberg in East Prussia, to a family of modest means. His father was a harness-maker and his mother was uneducated. A formative influence on Kant's early life was his family's immersion in the tradition of pietism, a Protestant sect which emphasized inward and emotional spirituality. Kant's personal life was relatively uneventful, though he lived through the Seven Years' War (during part of which East Prussia was occupied by Russia), as well as the French Revolution. These events may have played a part in leading Kant away from pietism toward political and theological liberalism. He was a believer in democracy and sympathized with the French Revolution until the Reign of Terror in 1793–1794. Kant is often portrayed as a recluse of extremely regular habits; it has been noted that people were able to set their watches by the punctuality of his afternoon stroll. However, although Kant hardly ever left Königsberg and although he never married, he did enjoy social life among a group of articulate friends among whom he was known as vivacious and witty.

Kant studied at the University of Königsberg from 1740 to 1746. In 1755 he became an instructor at the same university, lecturing on a wide range of subjects, including the natural sciences, metaphysics, logic, ethics, theory of law, anthropology, and geography. In 1770 he was appointed professor of logic and metaphysics, a position he retained for most of his life. Unlike Hegel, Kant was a gifted lecturer, and his increasing fame was acknowledged in his appointment as rector of the university. Significantly, Kant's first publications were on scientific subjects. He was inspired by the earthquake of Lisbon to write a theory of earthquakes. His most important scientific treatise was his *General Natural History and Theory of the Heavens* (1755), in which he advanced an original account – similar to that later proposed by Laplace – of the origin of the universe. Part of Kant's endeavor in this work was to offer a philosophical justification of Newtonian physics. Kant's awareness of scientific developments was to prove crucial to his subsequent formulation of a "critical" philosophy, by which Kant meant a philosophy examining not just the objects which we know but our mode of knowing itself, its potential and its limits.

This "critical" philosophy received elaborate expression in Kant's most important work, the *Critique of Pure Reason* (1781; second edition, 1787). Kant himself saw this work as initiating a "Copernican Revolution" in philosophy, in virtue of its attempt to prove that, although our knowledge cannot transcend experience, some of it is a priori (not dependent on experience) and possesses deductive certainty. This was in part, as will be seen, a response to the skepticism of the Scottish philosopher David Hume. Kant's next important work, the *Critique of Practical Reason*, was published in 1788. Kant's third major work, the *Critique of Judgment*, came out in 1790. His only other treatise on aesthetics had been the *Observations on the Feeling of the Beautiful and Sublime*, published in 1764.

In his political writings, which grew organically out of his critical philosophy, Kant expressed a liberal outlook. Influenced by thinkers such as Locke and Rousseau, he attempted philosophically to justify man's right to political freedom and espoused a representative constitutional government. In this, he shared something of the ideals of the American and French Revolutions, with which he largely sympathized. Kant broadly inherited from the Enlightenment a belief in the power of reason not only to examine the external world of nature through a systematic application of scientific method, but also to investigate the nature of human beings, their mental apparatus, their morality and the political and social systems in which they coexist. Yet Kant's relationship to Enlightenment thought is ambivalent. Central to his investigation of morality and politics is a belief in human freedom; as a moral and political agent exercising free will, man is not simply a machine, completely subject to the laws of the physical world, which is the world of *phenomena* or things as they appear to us. Man's exercise of moral choice is grounded upon certain assumptions, one of which is his freedom to rise above the phenomenal world governed by sequences of cause and effect and to base his actions on reason, regardless of their material or physical consequences. Kant's belief in this inner moral sense may stem partly from the pietism which was pronounced in his family during his early years. Pietism was one of the trends in eighteenth-century Germany which was antithetical to Enlightenment thought, fostering as it did an emotionalistic outlook toward religion.

The assertion of political and religious freedom is indeed the central theme of Kant's essay "What is Enlightenment?" (1784). He says there that the motto of enlightenment is: "*Sapere aude!* Have courage to use your *own* understanding!"[1] The intelligentsia of a society, says Kant, should "disseminate the spirit of rational respect for personal value and for the duty of all men to think for themselves." Kant proceeds: "For enlightenment of this kind, all that is needed is *freedom* . . . freedom to make *public* use of one's reason in all matters . . . The *public* use of man's reason must always be free, and it alone can bring about enlightenment among men" (*KPW*, 55). Kant acknowledges that a *private* use of reason may be restricted without harm. By a "private" use of reason, he means the exercise of reason in a particular post or office, which requires obedience to one's superiors and certain institutional norms. For example, a preacher is obliged to teach certain doctrines to his congregation. However, in a "public" use of reason, the preacher will assume the role of a scholar addressing the "real public" or the world at large (rather than a specific audience); and in this capacity he should enjoy unlimited freedom, freedom even to criticize or undermine the very doctrines he preaches in his "private" capacity. Kant is utterly opposed to any rigid systematization of doctrines which are held to be unalterable and which are imposed on future generations. This "would be a crime against human nature, whose original destiny lies in . . . progress." Each age should be allowed to "extend and correct its knowledge." Even a monarch, says Kant, cannot impose views upon his people, for this would be "trampling underfoot the sacred rights of mankind." A monarch's "legislative authority depends precisely upon his uniting the collective will of the people in his own" (*KPW*, 56–58). We can hear the voice of Rousseau behind these words. Kant's views eventually brought him into conflict with the authorities. His treatise *Religion within the Limits of Reason*

Alone (1793; second edition, 1794) offended the king of Prussia, Frederick William II, on account of its rationalistic and unorthodox outlook. The king compelled the reluctant philosopher to promise that he would not write again on religious matters. Kant reneged on his promise after the king's death. The foregoing remarks illustrate how the notion of freedom was not only a touchstone of Kant's political thinking but also integral to his entire system as offered in the three *Critiques*. Hence these major works need to be situated within their historical context, a context which includes not only Enlightenment philosophy with its emphasis on rational inquiry but also the political thinking behind the American and French Revolutions, stressing human freedom and individual rights.

In order to understand Kant's aesthetic views as expressed in the *Critique of Judgment*, we need to see this work as part of a broader project which includes the first two *Critiques*. The *Critique of Pure Reason* is by far the most important and groundbreaking of Kant's works. The essential project of this first *Critique* is threefold: firstly, Kant wishes to define the boundaries of human reason: what kinds of things can reason tell us about and what kinds of things are beyond its grasp. Secondly, he wishes to establish a secure foundation for metaphysics. The empiricist philosophers Locke and Hume had argued that, since all of our knowledge comes from experience, this knowledge cannot be grounded on any necessary laws. For example, Hume argued that the concept of causality was not based on any necessary relation between a cause and an effect but rested rather on our habit of "constant conjunction," whereby we habitually associate two events, viewing one as cause and the other as effect. Locke and Hume had also undermined a concept which had been central to much ancient and medieval philosophy and theology: the Aristotelian–Thomist idea of "substance" as the primary reality on which all else was based. They had asserted that there is no primal substance or essence which underlies objects in the external world, and that our only connection with these objects is by means of our senses. In the wake of Hume's skepticism – a skepticism which, as Kant recalls, aroused him from his "dogmatic slumbers" – Kant was concerned to ground metaphysics on principles which were a priori (independent of experience) and necessary. In other words, such knowledge as we do have must be shown to possess absolute certainty. Such an endeavor represents in part Kant's desire to accommodate the findings of recent science, especially the fundamental laws of nature as formulated by Newton. Finally, Kant made a distinction between phenomena and noumena. Phenomena refer to the world of objects which we experience, objects as they appear to us; noumena, or objects as they might be in themselves, are objects which are merely thinkable and outside of our possible experience. This distinction served not only to secure the world of phenomena on a sure foundation (the project of the first *Critique*), but also to provide a feasible basis for the world of morality, which for Kant is the noumenal realm (the project of the second *Critique*).

In the *Critique of Pure Reason*, Kant acknowledges that all our knowledge begins with experience but does not accept the empiricist claim that all our knowledge is somehow derived from experience.[2] Knowledge not only consists of the impressions we receive from the world but also has a component which we ourselves supply in constructing the world as it appears to us. For example, Kant says that the concept of causality is not something that is found in the world; rather, it expresses one of the ways in which we *look* at the world. Similarly, the concept of "substance" (the essential properties of an object, on which its other qualities are based) is not found anywhere in the world: if we look at an object and remove all its qualities as given by experience (its shape, color, size, etc.) we are still left with the concept of substance, which, again, expresses our way of looking at objects. Kant uses these examples to show that the concepts of causality and substance are not somehow in the world but are rooted in our own faculty of a priori knowledge (*CPR*, 45); we *bring* these concepts to our experience of the world, and they structure that experience. The same applies to all of the twelve basic categories that Kant assigns to the understanding. These are divided into four types, according to the four basic ways in which we view the world: the categories of *quantity* are unity, plurality, and totality; under *quality* are included reality, negation, and limitation; under *relation* are substance, causality, community; finally, under the heading of *modality*, Kant lists possibility, existence, and necessity (*CPR*, 113). It is not necessary here to examine these categories in detail; the important point to realize is that collectively they represent what our own mental apparatus brings to our experience of the world. It is through these categories or basic concepts that we divide up and order our knowledge of the world.

In order to understand Kant's account of how our mind contributes to the formation of the world around it, we need to grasp two distinctions which are central to his thought: that between a priori and a posteriori, and that between *analytic* and *synthetic* judgments. Knowledge which is a priori is independent of all experience; it possesses necessity and universality. Empirical knowledge, on the other hand, is possible only a posteriori, i.e., through experience. This kind of knowledge is inductive and can never achieve necessity or universality. Kant explains the distinction between analytic and synthetic judgments as follows. In an analytic judgment, the predicate adds nothing to the concept already contained in the subject. To take the example offered by Kant, in the statement:

All bodies are extended

the subject is "All bodies" and the predicate is "are extended." Since the concept of extension (occupying a certain amount of space) is already included in the concept of "body," it is clear that the predicate here adds nothing to the concept of the subject. This is an analytic judgment, which must be *necessarily* true and which must apply *universally* to all bodies. It is also an a priori judgment since we do not need the testimony of experience to verify it; we need not go beyond the concept itself (*CPR*, 49). Indeed, we *apply* this concept to our experience. In a synthetic judgment, on the other hand, the predicate does add something to the subject. For example, if we say:

Everything which happens has its cause

the concept of cause (the predicate) is not contained in the concept of "everything which happens" (the subject). Hence this is a synthetic judgment. It also happens to be an a priori judgment since the concept of causality cannot (as Hume showed) be derived from experience, and since it has both necessity and universality (*CPR*, 50–51).

Kant insists that only synthetic judgments are "ampliative" or able to furnish genuine additions to our previous knowledge. Metaphysics, says Kant, ought to contain knowledge which is both a priori and synthetic, since its business is not only to analyze concepts but also to extend our a priori knowledge (*CPR*, 54). Hence the general problem of pure reason, says Kant, is: how are a priori synthetic judgments possible? Kant views this problem as so fundamental that on its solution rests the success or failure of metaphysics (*CPR*, 55). Kant here rejects Hume's skepticism, by appealing to existing bodies of knowledge. Kant sees pure mathematics and natural science as already containing bodies of a priori synthetic knowledge (*CPR*, 53–54). Kant wishes to establish metaphysics as a special science, a science of pure reason. He defines reason as the faculty which supplies the principles of a priori knowledge. He also entitles his philosophy "transcendental," by which he means a philosophy which is "occupied not so much with objects as with the mode of our knowledge of objects in so far as this mode of knowledge is to be possible *a priori*" (*CPR*, 58–59). In other words, Kant is concerned to make metaphysics scientific inasmuch as it will make reason a self-conscious realm: conscious of its limitations and of the precise manner in which it relates to the outside world. He is concerned to oppose not only skeptical empiricism but equally any "dogmatic" use of reason whereby reason transgresses its own boundaries and ends in mere speculations which can always be contradicted by other speculations (Kant refers to the possible self-contradictions produced by such unrestricted use of reason as "antinomies") (*CPR*, 57).

In raising the question of how a priori synthetic judgments are possible, Kant is effectively confronting the chasm between mind and reality as skeptically posited by Locke and Hume. If reality is outside of the mind, how can we know it truly? How can our knowledge of it be based on principles which are necessary and universal, and which can actually extend this knowledge? Kant suggests that there are two stems of human knowledge: sensibility and understanding. It is through sensibility that objects arc "given" or presented to us; and through the understanding, objects are subjected to the process of thought, by being placed under certain categories or concepts. Our experience of any object demands both of these procedures working in harmony. Objects are given to us by means of sensibility; it alone can furnish us with intuitions through which we relate immediately to objects; the process of thought acts upon the data provided by sensibility. Kant distinguishes between the *matter* of appearance, which is given by sensation (the object's effect on our senses), and the *form* of appearance, which is determined by our subjective apparatus (both sensibility and understanding) (*CPR*, 62–66). Hence, Kant's overall project is to show how both sensibility and understanding are not merely passive in their registering of objects from the external world but that they both contain a priori components which structure the form or the way in which we receive these objects. His attempt to show this in the case of sensibility is called the "transcendental aesthetic" (the word "aesthetic" derives from the Greek word *aisthesis*, meaning perception); and his endeavor to show how the concepts of the understanding structure the way we think about any object is called the "transcendental deduction." The word "transcendental" here reminds us that he is concerned to show, in the cases of both sensibility and understanding, not the connections between objects as they might be in themselves but the connection between the perceiving subject and the object perceived (or the object as it appears to us).

In the transcendental aesthetic, then, Kant argues that neither space nor time is a feature of the external world. Rather, they are both pure forms of sensible intuition, serving as principles of a priori knowledge. In other words, space and time are properties of our minds; they comprise the most fundamental feature of the way in which we look at the world; we *bring* space and time to our experience of the world (*CPR*, 67–68). Kant refers to space as "outer sense," since it is by means of our intuition of space that we represent all objects as outside of us and in space. He calls time the "inner sense" since this gives a determinate form to our intuition of our inner states. Hence space and time are the subjective conditions of sensibility; that is, they are the universal subjective conditions of the possibility of all appearances (i.e., all representations of objects). They are the pure forms of all sensible intuition and as such they make possible a priori and synthetic judgments (*CPR*, 75–80). This, in Kant's view, is what enables the various truths of geometry, mathematics, and natural science.

Just as space and time determine the form of objects as they are given to our senses, so, Kant argues in the transcendental deduction, the concepts or categories of the understanding determine in an a priori fashion the way in which we can think about these objects. In other words, the categories are a priori necessary conditions of thought (*CPR*, 138). And, like space and time, they are the a priori necessary conditions of the possibility of experience (*CPR*, 126). Kant argues that there are twelve basic categories of the understanding. In the transcendental deduction he states that there are three subjective sources of knowledge which make possible both the understanding and all experience as its empirical product (*CPR*, 130–131). The first of these is the *apprehension* of representations in intuition. The various impressions we receive from sensible experience must be ordered according to time (our inner sense) and held together as a single representation. Secondly, in order for us to make sense of our experience (or for us to have a unitary, rather than chaotic, experience), we must be able to reproduce these unified representations and unite them with other representations, in a way that they are not combined as directly presented to our senses (*CPR*, 131, 144). Such *reproduction* of representations, whereby they can be associated with one another, says Kant, is the function of the imagination, so called because it transforms the manifold of sensation in intuition into an image (*CPR*, 132–133). The senses supply impressions, says Kant, but cannot themselves combine these to give images of objects; in order to achieve this, a synthesis of imagination is needed (*CPR*, 144). It is, in fact, imagination which unites sensibility and understanding in a necessary connection (*CPR*, 146). Finally, the associated representations achieve conscious *recognition* in a concept (*CPR*, 134–135). That is, the sensuous content of intuition as ordered and reproduced by imagination is now subjected to the rules of thought by being brought under a given concept or category. Kant refers to understanding as the "faculty of judgement"; it is this which unites various concepts as well as various sensible representations of an object in intuition. By this threefold synthesis, then, consisting of *apprehension, reproduction*, and *recognition*, the initial indefinite mass of sensation which is presented by the world to our experience is unified into a definite, knowable content. Through this process, our experience of the objects in the world becomes ordered, rather than chaotic. But such ordered experience must belong to a unified self or ego, an ego which underlies all of the elements of the experience. For example, if I were to wake up tomorrow without the consciousness of myself as the same self that existed today or yesterday, then my experience would be chaotic. Such experience would be the moment-to-moment experience of my empirical self or ego, the ego which is the subject of each particular experience. For this experience to be ordered, and to be brought to recognition in a concept, there must be a unity underlying all of the functions and concepts of the understanding. Kant gives to this unity the name of the transcendental unity of apperception. This refers to a transcendental self or ego which we must presuppose or posit as standing behind and overlooking the experiences of our empirical ego. It is the transcendental ego (standing above experience) which unites and enables an ordering of the various experiences of the empirical ego.

However, the full import of these arguments cannot be appreciated without showing how they effectively bifurcate our conception not only of the human self but also of reality. In other words, they divide reality into two realms: the realm of phenomena, or things as they appear to us; and the realm of noumena, or things as they might be in themselves. Kant basically argues that each of the three stages of synthesis determines any representation of an object within the mind in an a priori fashion. Each stage demands the ironic bifurcation of our understanding of "object" into noumenon and phenomenon: we *must* postulate the thing in itself as unknowable for a necessary and a priori connection to obtain between the categories and the phenomena they determine. Kant effects, then, a dual strategy: on the one hand, whatever lies beyond human understanding is uniformly coerced and hypostatized into the category of the noumenal; by sharply distinguishing this sphere from that of knowable phenomena, the latter can obtain a necessary connection with the human self. The phenomena–noumena distinction, then, enables an ordering of knowledge through an a priori constraint toward certainty. On the other hand, this ordering could not be achieved without a duality in the self, whereby the detached transcendental ego overlooks the empirical ego's experiences. This bifurcation of the self and the world enables a unity both within the self (because another, detached self stands behind it) and between the self and the world (the world is a unity because, in its phenomenal aspect, its forms are determined by subjective sensibility and understanding).

Kant's phenomena–noumena distinction is often mistakenly taken as a distinction between two classes of objects, one real and one unreal. Kant uses the term noumenon not to mean "reality" or "real object" but in its Greek sense, meaning "something thought or conceived" (*CPR*, 266–267). Thus, phenomena are "sensible entities" because they are objects given in sensible intuition. Noumena are "intelligible entities" because they refer to what *would be* objects of pure understanding if it were possible for the concepts of the understanding to operate independently of sensibility. Kant is not saying that noumena *exist*. For Kant the noumenon is not "a special (kind of) object," and phenomena and noumena are not two classes of objects. The entire distinction between them is made from the standpoint of phenomena: the noumenon is merely a "*limiting concept*, the function of which is to . . . limit the objective validity of sensible knowledge" (*CPR*, 272). Kant urges that the noumenon "must be understood as being such only in a *negative* sense" (*CPR*, 270). So Kant is neither asserting that the noumenon is real nor even that it exists: it is a concept whose meaning subsists entirely in its negative reference to the phenomenon. It is simply the *indeterminate* concept of an object (not the object itself) that *would* be given to the understanding alone, were such separation from sense possible (*CPR*, 274). The reverse side of this crucial point is that Kant doesn't view phenomena as somehow unreal or illusory: "I do not mean to say that these objects [phenomena] are a mere illusion" (*CPR*, 88).

In his next major work, the *Critique of Practical Reason*, Kant's concerns shifted from theoretical knowledge of the world (the sphere of speculative reason) to the grounds of our moral behavior (the sphere of practical reason). Kant had argued that speculative reason is concerned exclusively with objects of the understanding, which are given in sensible intuition and are therefore empirically conditioned. Practical reason, says Kant, "has to do with a subject . . . with the grounds of determination of the will" and is therefore not bound by empirical conditions of objectivity, these "grounds" being purely rational.[3] Kant was concerned to show that practical reason, the moral faculty, makes its decisions on the basis of reason, not contingent empirical circumstances or the effects of these decisions in the physical world. The fundamental law of practical reason is a "categorical imperative" which, unlike a hypothetical imperative, determines the will irrespective of empirical effects: the categorical imperative effectively isolates moral action from all possible effects in the physical world (in their criticism of Kant's position, both Hegel and Marx were to point out later that what Kant does here is to render morality completely abstract). Categorical imperatives are laws which are universally applicable to experience (i.e., not bound by the contingencies of a particular situation); action under the obligation of such moral laws is "duty" (*CP*, 32). In other words, our consciousness that we are obliged to act according to such a priori moral laws requires us to fulfill our duty regardless of how difficult this is or whether it is in our own pragmatic interests. Our actions, then, according to Kant, must be based on duty rather than their outcomes. The ultimate object of the will, says Kant, is the highest good, which is a synthesis of virtue and happiness. To attempt to achieve this, practical reason must postulate three things: immortality, the freedom of a being qua noumenon (since our will must be free of the causality which pertains to phenomena, and indeed is itself a cause of new objects or situations), and God. These must be assumed if the will is to obey the moral law (*CP*, 117, 123, 137ff.). Kant is profoundly aware of the possible problem here: in the first *Critique* he had argued that the noumenon was merely a "limiting concept," empty of any positive content. And now, in the second *Critique*, he seems to be affirming the existence of noumenal entities, viz. God, freedom (of a noumenal human self), and immortality. Kant's strategy here is to assert that these entities must be *postulated* so that morality can have a firm basis; he admits that we cannot claim to have any speculative or theoretical knowledge of them. Of the reality of these entities, he says: "But this reality is still given only with reference to the practice of the moral law and not for any speculative use" (*CP*, 143).

Hence, the phenomena–noumena distinction, as articulated in the first and second *Critiques*, effectively preserves a domain for God and morality (by elevating these to the unknowable, noumenal world), securing this domain against the rationalist and empiricist onslaught of the Enlightenment thinkers. Kant held that only the phenomenal world, grounded in sense-experience, could be apprehended by the intellectual faculty of pure reason. The noumenal entities, viz. God, freedom, and immortality, were a function of the "practical" moral faculty, the will. This metaphysical gesture might be viewed as an attempt to reinstate Aquinas' separation of the domains of intellect and will, of reason and revelation, in a modern context which was obliged to accommodate the findings of science. Causality indeed reigns in Kant's phenomenal realm, which is effectively the world bequeathed by modern science; but its grasp cannot extend into the noumenal world, which is essentially the domain of faith. Hence Kant's bifurcation of reality into phenomenon and noumenon effectively forces into coexistence the fundamental principles of bourgeois thought with revamped feudal attitudes. In the process of arriving at this bifurcation, he ironizes the human self, separating it into an empirical ego which undergoes a variety of experiences and a transcendental ego which stands apart and detached from experience: this second ego both takes the first ego for its object and unifies it. Hence Kant's irony, as applied to both reality and the self, represents historically the first major attempt to reconcile the emerging contradictions of bourgeois thought within a larger, unifying perspective. Kant stood, then, in a highly ambivalent relation to the preceding tradition of bourgeois Enlightenment thought.

Kant's *Critique of Judgment*, which deals with the nature and extent of our aesthetic judgments, also attempts to reconcile various Enlightenment strands of thinking about aesthetics. One strand of Enlightenment thought, as we have seen, was rationalist, as expressed by such figures as Gottfried Wilhelm Leibniz (1646–1716) and his disciple Christian Wolff (1679–1754). The views of these two thinkers were further developed by Wolff's disciple Alexander Gottlieb Baumgarten (1714–1762) and his student Georg Friedrich Meier (1718–1777). On the empiricist side were the aesthetic theories of Francis Hutcheson (1694–1747), David Hume, and Edmund Burke.

The central problem that Kant raises in this third *Critique* is expressed in the same question that had provided the theme of the first two *Critiques*, a question which is now raised in a different context: how are synthetic a priori judgments possible in the realm of aesthetics? When we perceive beauty, we are making a subjective judgment yet we speak of beauty as if it were a characteristic of objects in the world or of works of art or literature. Essentially, Kant wishes to ground such judgments on necessary and universal principles while acknowledging their subjective and specifically aesthetic character. The rationalists Leibniz and Wolff had argued that sense-perception is a lower (and more confused) stage of thought; they believed that beauty and art could be cognized through sense-perception. The empiricists, on the other hand, did not view beauty as a quality of things themselves but rather as a sense possessed by our subjective apparatus. In other words, they thought that we possessed a sense of beauty, which was essentially the same in all human beings.

Kant wishes to retain the rationalist attribution of universality and necessity to aesthetic judgments while at the same time acknowledging the empiricist insistence on the subjective character of such judgments. As against the rationalists, he denied that beauty could be a quality of things themselves; as against the empiricists, he denied that universal assent in aesthetic judgments could be obtained inductively from the experiences of "qualified" people. This could only yield a "contingent uniformity." Hence, according to Kant, we need an analysis of aesthetic judgments which will show how they can be both subjective and possess universality and necessity.

The Divisions of Philosophy: Theoretical, Practical, Aesthetic

Central to Kant's account of aesthetic judgment is the concept of purposiveness. To grasp this concept, we need to refer to Kant's introduction to the *Critique of Judgment* which attempts to explain the role of this *Critique* in his system as a whole. Kant reminds us here that his first two *Critiques* had divided our cognitive power into two realms: the theoretical realm of the understanding, whose concepts prescribe a priori laws for nature; this was the sensible world of phenomena. There was also the practical realm of reason, a faculty which prescribes the laws for freedom, in the exercise of our will. This was the world of moral action, which engaged our free, noumenal, selves.[4] Kant now raises the question: how are these two realms, those of understanding and reason, of phenomena/nature and morality, harmonized? It was clear to Kant that decisions made in the moral realm could have an effect in the world of phenomena or nature; therefore, nature's laws must somehow harmonize with the possibility that we can achieve certain purposes in nature when we act in accordance with the laws of our moral freedom (*CJ*, 15).

But what, asks Kant, could be the basis which unites the two worlds, physical and moral? He finds the answer in the faculty of judgment, which he describes as a "mediating link" between understanding and reason. Kant sees our human powers as divided into three kinds: our cognitive power is legislated by the understanding; our power of desire (and will) is legislated by reason; it is our capacity to feel pleasure or displeasure which is legislated by judgment (*CJ*, 16–17). How exactly does judgment occupy a mediating role between the spheres of understanding and reason? Kant defines judgment as a twofold capacity. On the one hand, judgment is the ability to subsume a particular thing under a general law; for example, we might look at a rose and place it under the general category of "flower." This kind of judgment is a "determinative" judgment and in order to use it we must already have at our disposal the concepts provided by the understanding. It is these concepts which "determine" our judgment. However, Kant concedes that although the understanding provides the general a priori concepts through which we think of nature as subject to universal laws, these are nonetheless *general* concepts and do not necessarily apply to nature in all of its vast detail and diversity. The objects of nature, taken in their particularity and individuality, may be subject to all kinds of additional rules which are not encompassed by the concepts of the understanding. It is here that judgment must assume a different function: instead of subsuming something particular under a general law according to a pregiven concept, it must now *find* a universal or general law for the particular entity it confronts (*CJ*, 18–22). This kind of judgment is called a "reflective" judgment. And it is precisely here that the concept of purposiveness comes into play. Even though judgment must now proceed without the help of the concepts of the understanding, it must assume that all the varieties of nature in its details have a certain unity which is governed by laws and which exhibits some kind of order. In other words, it must proceed as if this unity had been prescribed by the understanding. It must assume such a coherence and connection among the appearances of nature so that we can reflect coherently upon nature, so that our exploration or investigation of nature will prove to be a coherent, rather than chaotic, experience. In presupposing this unity and order of nature's various manifestations, we are presupposing a harmony between nature and our cognitive powers: they are suited or adapted to each other. It is this harmony which Kant calls "purposiveness." Kant refers to this assumption as the "transcendental concept of the purposiveness of nature," which he regards as a subjective principle or maxim of judgment. It is subjective because it does not really tell us anything about nature in itself but about our own subjectivity; about the way in which we must proceed if we are to understand nature in an orderly manner (*CJ*, 22–25). It is through the concept of purposiveness that judgment mediates between the concepts of nature provided by the understanding and the concept of freedom as legislated by reason. Kant calls the concept of the purposiveness of nature provided by judgment a *regulative* principle of our cognitive power: in other words, the harmony which judgment assumes between nature and our cognitive powers is the basis which unites the phenomenal world of nature with the moral world ruled by reason. It is because of this harmony that our actions based on moral purposes can have an effect in the phenomenal world.

The Nature of Aesthetic Judgment

As mentioned earlier, this notion of purposiveness underlies Kant's account of aesthetic judgment. It is precisely this purposiveness – the harmony of nature's heterogeneous laws with our cognitive powers – which gives rise to pleasure. We experience pleasure when we discover that the empirical laws of nature can be unified under one principle, in other words, when we discover an order or pattern in nature (*CJ*, 26–27). Such pleasure is integral to our aesthetic experience. According to Kant, when we make an aesthetic judgment, we make a judgment about the *form* of an object (not its content as given through our senses); this judgment is reflective because we are not assessing the object from the perspective of any pregiven concept; the object's form gives rise to pleasure because it exhibits a harmony with our cognitive powers, namely, our understanding and imagination. We then call the object "beautiful" and our ability to judge the object by such a pleasure is "taste" (*CJ*, 30).

To understand Kant's account of aesthetic judgment, we need to recall his model, in the first *Critique*, of how we obtain knowledge. Kant had said that, when we encounter a formless object in the world, we first *apprehend* it through our sensible intuition; in other words, we create a mental representation of the object, a representation which is given a certain *form* by being ordered in space and time. After this, the imagination takes over and *reproduces* the representation into an image. The resulting representation is now referred to the understanding, which *recognizes* it by placing it under a given concept or category. In an aesthetic judgment, however, we go through only the first two of these processes: when the imagination has reproduced the representation as a mental image, this image is referred not to the understanding, which would give us conceptual knowledge of it, but instead to the subject, to our self and its feeling of pleasure or displeasure. Hence an aesthetic judgment is not a judgment of cognition; we do not objectively *know* an object through this kind of judgment, since its ground is subjective. An aesthetic judgment does not tell us anything about the object; it tells us only about how we, as subjects, are affected by our mental representation of the object.

There are, according to Kant, certain distinctive features of aesthetic judgment as we use it in describing an object as beautiful. Nearly all of these features are related to the concept of "purposiveness" as outlined above, whereby the underlying patterns we discover in objects of the world or in nature give rise to a harmonious interplay between our cognitive faculties of imagination and understanding, a harmony which affords us pleasure. To begin with, a judgment of taste is "disinterested." In other words, when we judge an object to be beautiful, we have no *interest*, no ulterior motive, in the object's actual existence. We do not care if the object produces certain effects in the world, or if it has some kind of utility or even if it has a positive moral value. To state this in Kantian terms, we might say that we have no interest in the object's *purpose*, or at least, in any external purposes which might be assigned to the object. We are content simply to contemplate the object and to take pleasure in it. As Kant says, beautiful things have no meaning, and he defines beauty as the object of a disinterested judgment of taste.

In contrast to such a pure and disinterested judgment of taste, our judgments concerning sensory pleasure and the morally good do have an "interest" in the existence of an object. These judgments both have reference to the faculty of desire: for example, if we experience pleasure from a certain food, our pleasure is based on the desire for that food and of course its actual existence. In a moral judgment, we must bring an object under the principles of reason, using the concept of a purpose. For example, a food could be pleasant or agreeable to our senses but judged by reason to be harmful; in this case, we give an objective value, not merely a subjective value, to the object. In both cases, the judgment is "interested" or constrained by a purpose; in both cases the judgment is no longer free and so cannot be an aesthetic judgment.

Do Aesthetic Judgments Have Universal Validity?

However, if we go along with what Kant has so far said, we confront a possible dilemma: if aesthetic judgment is subjective, if my perception of beauty says nothing about the object but reflects merely my feeling of pleasure, how can we ever hope to make others agree with our judgment? Kant's answer to this dilemma reverberates through much of modern literary theory, especially those branches which are based on reader-response theory. If our judgment of an object's beauty is *disinterested*, says Kant, this means that our judgment doesn't rest on any subjective inclination or private conditions, a feature which implies a ground of pleasure for all people. For example, if I like a particular portrait, I cannot base this liking on the fact that the portrait reminds me of my father, or that it is painted in particular colors which I happen to like, or that I see a certain moral significance in it: these would be private motives which obviously cannot apply to everyone. My judgment of the portrait as beautiful must be free of all such private reasons and conditions. According to Kant, we *can* claim that our judgment is universal – i.e., that others must agree with our judgment – provided we separate from our pleasure in beauty everything which has to do with mere sensory pleasure (which is based on private feeling) or with our ideas of the morally good (*CJ*, 379). Kant also states that taste is a kind of *sensus communis*, a sense shared by all of us. The principles of this common sense are to think for oneself, in an unbiased way; to think from the perspective of everyone else; and to think consistently. Our power of judgment takes account a priori of this common sense, of everyone else's way of presenting a given object. If we abstract from the limitations that happen to attach to our own judgment, we can focus on the formal features of our presentational state; we can thereby override the private conditions of our judgment and reflect on our own judgment from a universal point of view (*CJ*, 160–161). However, unlike judgments about the good which are based on a concept and therefore have an objectively universal validity, aesthetic judgments have merely a *subjective* universality. In other words, even though we speak of beauty as though it were a characteristic of the object (*CJ*, 378), what we are really claiming is that the connection between the object and the subject's feeling of pleasure will be the same in everyone. Kant offers a related insight here which is still highly pervasive today: no rule or rational argument, he says, can enforce our recognition of beauty. In aesthetic judgments we are unwilling to rely on the taste of other people; we always want to submit the object to our own eyes, to see whether or not *we* find it beautiful (*CJ*, 59). Later, Kant summarizes these principles as two peculiar characteristics of a judgment of taste. The first peculiarity is that a judgment of taste must be autonomous and a priori: a person should judge for himself, not rely on the judgments of others. Even when we follow classical models, says Kant, this is not imitation but simply drawing on the same resources as our predecessors did (*CJ*, 145). The second peculiarity is that there is no empirical basis of proof that could make anyone concur with a given judgment of taste; nor can a judgment of taste be determined by an a priori proof (for example, by appealing to what previous critics have cited as qualities of beauty) (*CJ*, 147–148). And when we make an aesthetic judgment, we expect confirmation not from rules as given by concepts but rather from the agreement of other people with our judgment (*CJ*, 379). We can see here not only the overwhelming importance Kant attaches to direct experience in aesthetic judgments, but also the grounds he establishes for arriving at a notion of beauty based on consensus.

It may well be objected: if this is the case, why do people's aesthetic judgments differ? Why does an object strike one person as beautiful and another person as plain? Though we claim our aesthetic judgment to be universally valid, it is often rejected by others. Kant's answer is that what people dispute is not whether such a claim is possible; they are merely unable to agree, in particular cases, on how to apply that claim (*CJ*, 58–59). For example, one person's judgment may be clouded by his failure to disengage his feeling from private circumstances, in which case his judgment will no longer be purely aesthetic: it may be partly a judgment of sensory pleasure or even a moral judgment. Indeed, although Kant sees aesthetic judgments as subjective (with the provision that this subjectivity can be presupposed as universally the same among people), such a judgment *can* become the basis of a logical or conceptual judgment. For example, in an aesthetic judgment we might say: "This rose is beautiful." This statement says nothing in itself about the rose (the object) but says something about the connection between the rose and my (the subject's) feeling of pleasure. But if we compare several such judgments about roses, we might proceed to make a broader statement such as: "Roses in general are beautiful." This new judgment is no longer aesthetic; it is a logical or conceptual judgment based on an aesthetic one (*CJ*, 379).

Kant provides an additional reason for our presupposing the same ground of pleasure in everyone, namely, that an object we consider beautiful will give rise to a harmonious interplay of the cognitive powers, imagination and understanding, in everyone. Such harmony between these two faculties, he says, is required not only for aesthetic judgments but also for cognition in general, hence we can assume that this harmony is a universal feature of our subjective apparatus (*CJ*, 62, 159). Moreover, this harmony in aesthetic judgments is a *felt* harmony; we do not know it intellectually but experience it through our senses (*CJ*, 62). Indeed, for this harmony to be universally communicable, explains Kant, we must presuppose a certain "common sense" in everyone. He defines this common sense as "the effect arising from the free play of our cognitive powers," which refers to a mutual attunement of imagination and understanding (*CJ*, 87–88). Such common sense, he says, cannot be based on experience, for it does not say that someone else *will* agree with my aesthetic judgment but that he *ought* to. Hence, this common sense, in Kant's eyes, is an ideal standard. If we presuppose this common sense, this standard, in everyone, we can make our aesthetic judgment into a rule for everyone (*CJ*, 89). What we are effectively saying is that if I, by means of a genuinely disinterested judgment (which is not based on my private feelings or circumstances), say that a certain natural scene is beautiful, I believe that everyone who makes a disinterested judgment in the same way will do so on the basis of a "sense" which is common to us all, and will thereby arrive at the same feeling of pleasure and the same assessment of beauty. This sense is the feeling of harmony in each person between the faculties of imagination and understanding.

Kant has used the term "purposiveness" to refer to the way in which nature *appears* to be adapted to our cognitive powers. To grasp this, we need to reflect on the distinction he makes between *purpose* and *purposiveness*. If, by means of reason, we have a concept of a certain object or outcome, and we exercise our will to achieve this object or outcome, that object is called a *purpose* (*CJ*, 64–65). However, when we confront the external world (or nature, as Kant calls it), we cannot say that nature is designed for a given purpose by a will. But if we are to proceed in an orderly and coherent manner in our investigations of nature, we must *assume* that nature is driven by a causality and a will such that it exhibits design and purpose. In other words, we regard nature as having "purposiveness without purpose"; we regard it as suited or adapted to the cognitive powers with which we confront it. A later analogy given by Kant may help us to understand this. We look at the endlessly varied phenomena of nature not as elements of a purposeless mechanism but rather as *art*, as something *assumed* to have a certain design and order amenable to our cognitive powers (*CJ*, 387). However, because this is a mere assumption, we cannot ascribe to nature any objective purpose: its purposiveness is something that belongs to our mental representation of it. And this mental representation is created by the harmonious interplay of our imagination and understanding. When we judge an object to be beautiful, we do so on the basis that this harmony yields a pleasure which we can communicate to, and presuppose in, everyone. Another way of saying this is that it is the mere *form* of purposiveness in our representation of an object which gives us this universally communicable pleasure (*CJ*, 380). And since our aesthetic judgment of

371

beauty is concerned only with the form of an object (or, rather, of our representation of an object), our judgment of beauty cannot include elements such as charm or emotion, which both belong to private sensation (*CJ*, 380–382). Nor can it include considerations of the object's utility or even its perfection (its fulfillment of what it is supposed to be according to some pregiven concept) (*CJ*, 382).

The Role of Imagination in Aesthetic Judgment

Hence aesthetic pleasure is really our consciousness of a "formal purposiveness" in the harmonious play of our cognitive powers (*CJ*, 67–68). It is the pleasure we might feel when we discover unexpected patterns or appearances of order in the phenomena of nature. In what exactly does this harmony consist? Kant's answer to this question laid the foundation for a great deal of Romantic theory and literary practice. This vast influence stemmed largely from Kant's account of the role of imagination in an aesthetic judgment. He defines an aesthetic judgment as an ability to judge an object in reference to the free lawfulness of imagination (*CJ*, 91). In an aesthetic judgment, the function of imagination is not reproductive as it is in our ordinary cognition of the world. In our everyday knowledge of objects, imagination reproduces the information given to us by our senses into images; and this reproduction is subject to certain laws of association, and to the rules of the understanding. In our day-to-day engagement with the world, our imagination is necessarily constrained by the actual objects with which we are confronted as well as the forms imposed upon them by our subjective apparatus (our sensibility and understanding). However, when we approach the world from an aesthetic perspective, our imagination is not required to undergo the same constraints. In this case, as Kant says, understanding serves imagination rather than vice versa (*CJ*, 91–92). The imagination can now be *productive* and spontaneous; it can originate its own choice of the forms of possible intuitions; it can combine images differently from their sequence in our ordinary experience, to yield new and surprising combinations. The understanding demands order and regularity everywhere and customarily imposes constraints on the imagination. What gives us pleasure is a subversion of these priorities: we can through imagination indulge in a free play of our representational powers, we can afford to be unstudied and experimental. In a statement which gave wings to much Romantic thought, Kant suggests that the demands of understanding can prove irksome, whereas "nature, extravagant in all its diversity, can nourish permanently" (*CJ*, 91–92). However, even in this creative role, imagination is not entirely free: its creations must still not violate the basic laws of understanding. This is why Kant refers to the "free lawfulness" of the imagination: it is a lawfulness (an adherence to the basic laws of understanding) which is not imposed on the imagination but self-exercised, even in its free play. This seems to be what Kant means when he talks of a subjective harmony of imagination and understanding, which he equates with a purposiveness without purpose. It is this *felt* harmony between our cognitive powers which gives us aesthetic pleasure. Because it is felt, each person must experience it for himself or herself and there can be no objective rule as to what constitutes beauty

(*CJ*, 384). We see here an important departure on Kant's part from Enlightenment thought, indeed, a point of transition to Romantic thought. Not only is an aesthetic judgment freed from the bondage of morality, not only is art transformed into an autonomous province, but it is also made the province of subjective experience, at the heart of which stands imagination in its supremely creative role, triumphing to some extent over our conceptual faculty.

The Characteristics of Beauty

Kant's comments on beauty may help clarify his views on the subjective universality of aesthetic judgments. His most famous definition of beauty reads as follows: "*Beauty is the form of the purposiveness of an object, so far as this is perceived without any representation of a purpose*" (*CJ*, 386). For example, we could find a certain purposiveness in a flower which, in our judgment, is referred to no purpose at all. In fact, Kant makes a distinction between two kinds of beauty. The first is *free* beauty (*pulchritudo vaga*), which does not presuppose any concept of what the object is meant to be. Again, an example of a free natural beauty might be a flower: when we judge it aesthetically, it represents nothing, and we like it for itself. Here, our imagination is in a state of play, contemplating merely the form of the flower. A botanist might judge it differently, since he knows its functions and what it is meant to be; in this case, he would be making a cognitive and rational judgment, not a pure judgment of taste. The second kind of beauty is *accessory* beauty (*pulchritudo adhaerens*), which does presuppose a concept of what the object is meant to be. Examples of accessory or adherent beauty would be the beauty of a human being, a church, palace, or summer-house. In each of these cases, beauty is merely accessory to a given purpose, as defined by a determinate concept of what the thing is meant to be. Hence, if we judged a church as beautiful, this would not be a pure judgment of taste since our assessment of its beauty is connected with our assessment of its goodness or perfection *as* a church. So our judgment is partly rational, based on a concept, and partly aesthetic, based on our feeling of pleasure (*CJ*, 76–77). Kant acknowledges that our taste is enriched by such a connection of aesthetic with intellectual liking: such a connection allows taste to become fixed and amenable to rules. However, these will not be rules of taste, but rules for uniting taste with reason, the beautiful with the good. And such a union will enable us to use the beautiful as an instrument for promoting a given kind of goodness (*CJ*, 78). Kant suggests that many disputes concerning beauty might be resolved by this distinction between free and adherent beauty. One person, judging an object as a free beauty, might earn the censure of another person who was looking primarily to the object's purpose and viewing its beauty as merely accessory. Yet each of these, in his own way, is judging correctly, the one aesthetically, by his feeling of pleasure, and the other intellectually, by concepts (*CJ*, 78). What begins to emerge in Kant's discussion here is that he is not somehow averse to using art and literature for moral purposes; he is simply concerned to establish that these spheres have a certain autonomy and that when they are connected with other spheres such as morality and practical usefulness, the nature of the connection be clearly understood. Another way of saying this would be to acknowledge that art and literature do not have external purposes inscribed in their very definition; once their status as beautiful works is acknowledged on independent grounds, they may serve all kinds of social, moral, and educational purposes.

So, while he is concerned to establish the freedom of aesthetic judgments from morality, mere sensory pleasure, utility, and concepts of perfection, Kant does acknowledge the need to situate aesthetic judgment in the broader contexts implied by these other realms. He even talks of an ideal of beauty which might be derived from "the broadest possible agreement among all ages and peoples" regarding the feeling of pleasure in beautiful objects. The fact that we can derive an ideal of beauty in such an empirical and inductive manner from the consensus of many people suggests, says Kant, that there must be a deeply hidden basis, common to all human beings, underlying this consensus (CJ, 79). This ideal or archetype of taste is of course a mere idea. And again Kant insists that we cannot acquire such ideal or exemplary taste simply by imitating someone else's. It is an ideal which everyone must generate within himself. It is not an ideal based on concepts which can then be taught to someone else; rather, it is an ideal of the imagination, which is based on the harmonious state of our representational powers and the consequent pleasure we feel (CJ, 80).

However, this ideal can be sought only for the kind of beauty which is "fixed" rather than free. In other words, the beauty must be fixed or determined by a concept of what the object is meant to be. The object of such "fixed" beauty will belong partly to an aesthetic judgment and partly to an intellectual one. It is meaningless, says Kant, to talk of an ideal of beautiful flowers or a beautiful view or even of a beautiful mansion or garden, since none of these objects has a sufficiently determined purpose (CJ, 80–81). Hence the only entity in relation to which an ideal of beauty can be sought is man, since only man has the purpose of his existence within himself. Man can determine his own purposes by reason. Kant says that this ideal of beauty has two components, the "aesthetic standard idea" and the "rational idea" (CJ, 81). The first of these is a standard arrived at by the imagination, a standard for judging each of the species aesthetically. This standard will point to a kind of average in terms of physical proportions and, as a standard, it will not be realized by any particular individual. Kant admits that the standard idea of a beautiful man or woman will vary according to culture and nation. It is in accordance with this standard that rules for judging become possible in the first place. This provides a further answer as to the question of how people's aesthetic judgments can reach a consensus: though we each make such judgments individually, on the basis of our own feelings, we do not do this in a cultural vacuum; our very judgment is made possible by the various archetypes of beauty that predominate in our culture (CJ, 82–83). The second component in the ideal of beauty is the "rational idea," according to which we judge a human being's appearance as the expression of his purpose and moral status (CJ, 81, 83). Unless we saw a human being's appearance as significant in these ways, we would not, according to Kant, be disposed to feel pleasure in it (CJ, 83). But again, this is not to say that in human beings, the aesthetic dimension intrinsically carries moral significance. Kant is careful to state that when we make a judgment according to such an ideal of beauty, our judgment is not a purely aesthetic judgment (CJ, 84).

The Sublime

In the second book of the *Critique of Judgment*, Kant turns his attention from the beautiful to the sublime. To grasp his vastly influential views on the sublime, we need to consider some important statements he makes in the first *Critique* on the faculty of reason and its connection with the understanding. Just as the concepts of the understanding give unity to the data of sense-experience, so the concepts of reason (which Kant calls *ideas*) give unity to the concepts of the understanding (*CPR*, 305). The concepts of reason are "transcendental" ideas because they are not derived from experience and indeed they transcend experience. For example, the idea of "virtue" or the idea of "humanity" is an idea of reason, not derived from experience, but held up by reason as an ideal to be aimed at (*CPR*, 311–312). We have already seen this application of reason in our moral life where, according to Kant, our actions should be determined by reason and not by empirical circumstances. Hence, in the moral sphere, our experience itself is made possible by ideas of reason (*CPR*, 313). We don't derive the idea of virtue from experience; what we do is formulate this idea via reason and then use it as a kind of paradigm or standard whereby we judge our experience. In the phenomenal realm, ideas of reason, says Kant, are formed from *pure* concepts of the understanding (i.e., without any corresponding intuitions of sense), and their function is to organize the concepts of the understanding such that they form a self-consistent unity and a totality (*CPR*, 314–318). Kant calls this a "regulative employment" of reason, by which he means that reason itself does not yield knowledge of experience or of objects but rather sets forth, by means of its ideas, an ideal of unity and totality toward which the understanding can aspire (*CPR*, 533). It is reason which gives us the idea of a *whole* of knowledge, which we must assume if we are to gain knowledge of the various parts or particular objects. These ideas, then, do not come from nature; rather, we use them to make assumptions of coherence in our investigations of nature. We presuppose a systematic unity of nature, as well as a systematic unity of our own understanding (*CPR*, 534–538). It will be recalled that Kant's definition of "purposiveness" was precisely the assumption that nature is adapted to our cognitive powers.

In fact, it is this issue of mutual adaptation between our powers of knowing and the world of nature which decisively separates the beautiful from the sublime. In some respects, Kant points out, the beautiful and the sublime are similar: they are both concerned with pleasure and not with cognition of an object; they are both based not on a logical or cognitive judgment but on a judgment of reflection (which seeks to *find* the general rule for a particular case); the pleasure we experience from them both concerns the way in which the object is presented (rather than the object itself) and with the faculty of presentation, the imagination. However, there are striking differences between the beautiful and the sublime. To begin with, beauty concerns the form of an object, which consists of definite boundaries; the sublime concerns *formless* objects, which represent boundlessness. Beauty is accompanied by a feeling of charm, of the furtherance of life, as well as by the play of our imagination; the sublime gives rise to a different response: we feel a momentary checking of our vital powers and then a stronger outflow of them; here our imagination is not engaged in play but is exercised in earnest; we feel repulsion from, as well as attraction to, the object. When we judge an object as beautiful, our mind reposes in a state of restful contemplation; but the feeling of the sublime involves a movement and agitation of the mind (*CJ*, 387). Kant characterizes our feeling about the sublime as a "negative pleasure": we feel not charm or love but admiration or respect (*CJ*, 386).

These differences between the beautiful and the sublime rest on the decisive difference mentioned above, a difference which involves the connection between understanding and reason: when we judge natural beauty as beautiful, we attribute to it a formal "purposiveness" whereby the object in nature seems to be preadapted to our cognitive powers, producing a harmonious interplay between our imagination and understanding that, in turn, gives rise to our feeling of pleasure. But an object which yields a feeling of sublimity seems to do the opposite: it seems formally to violate any concept of purpose or, in Kant's terms, it seems "contrapurposive" for our cognitive powers. For example, when we view nature as beautiful, we see it not as a purposeless mechanism but as harboring a design or pattern, as if it were art and as if it were somehow adapted to our powers of knowing. With the sublime, just the opposite happens: nature excites feelings of the sublime "in its chaos, its wildest disorder," provided that it is seen as possessing might and magnitude (*CJ*, 387). For this reason, we cannot experience a feeling of sublimity when confronted with products of art, since these are determined by human purposes. Nor can we experience the sublime in those objects of nature whose purpose can be clearly seen. Rather, we are talking about crude nature, nature which has come under no determinate concept (*CJ*, 109). Hence, the sublime presents a challenge to our cognitive faculties: when nature is viewed in this aspect, it is not purposive but contrapurposive: in its might and magnitude, it seems beyond the reach and control of our mental apparatus. What happens as a result of this challenge is that the very inadequacy of our imagination to represent such a magnitude of disordered nature forces us to realize that we have a faculty, namely reason, which transcends the entire world of nature and whose ideas are supersensible. As Kant puts it, we realize that we have a faculty of mind which surpasses every standard of sense (*CJ*, 388). It is this realization or ability to which Kant gives the name "sublime." So the sublime is not in fact a quality of nature but a quality of our own minds; nature, in certain of its manifestations which possess magnitude, might, and disorder, simply acts as the occasion for exciting this feeling of the sublime. When nature appears to us as infinite, this intuition excites in us the realization of an infinite power in ourselves, namely, the power of reason. The ideas of reason strive toward infinity and totality, and in comparison with this endeavor, all strivings of sense in the world of nature are small. Another way of saying this would be that we discover in ourselves a faculty of resistance to the apparent almightiness and immensity of nature. We find in our reason a faculty which can transcend even the infinity of nature (*CJ*, 390). So, just as an aesthetic judgment of beauty refers imagination in its free play to the understanding, to harmonize with its concepts in general, so in a judgment of the sublime the imagination is referred to reason, to harmonize with its ideas (*CJ*, 389). The difference is that in a judgment of beauty the harmony of imagination and understanding represents a subjective purposiveness (i.e., a state of adaptation to nature); in a judgment of the sublime, the "harmony" of imagination and reason is actually a conflict: whereas imagination (the greatest faculty of sense) cannot comprehend nature regarded as sublime, reason shows itself to be superior to both imagination and nature (*CJ*, 390).

Kant equates this feeling of the sublime, this recognition of the superiority of reason, with moral feeling and with respect for our own supersensible destination (*CJ*, 389). In judging nature sublime, says Kant, it may initially excite our fear, since we recognize our physical impotence as natural beings; but in consequence our imagination is elevated by referring itself to reason; hence we call forth our strength, "to regard as small the objects of our natural concerns, such as property, health and life" (*CJ*, 391).

The Beautiful, the Sublime, and the Moral

Kant says that the feeling for the sublime in nature is a mental attunement similar to that which we experience in moral feeling: reason exerts its dominance over sensibility, as it does in the moral sphere (*CJ*, 128). The feeling of sublimity in nature corresponds with a capacity of the mind to rise above obstacles of sense via moral principles (*CJ*, 131). In fact, Kant suggests that a judgment about the sublime requires more aesthetic cultivation and moral disposition than a judgment of beauty. Unlike Edmund's Burke's empirical exposition of the beautiful and sublime, which can demand only contingent assent from other people, Kant urges that such a demand must be based on an a priori principle, not merely in an empirical fashion "by gathering votes," if it is to have necessity and universal validity (*CJ*, 138–139, 143–144). In judging something sublime (or as occasioning a feeling of sublimity), our demand that other people agree with us is based on the fact that we presuppose moral feeling or a moral capacity in them (*CJ*, 124–125).

It is clear that the feeling of sublimity has an intrinsic connection with moral feeling. As Kant says, the pleasure we experience in the sublime is a pleasure involved in reasoning contemplation and has a moral foundation, hence this pleasure lays claim to universal participation (*CJ*, 158). What of beauty? Is there any intrinsic affinity, asks Kant, between a feeling for beauty and moral feeling? Kant insists that only *after* a pure aesthetic judgment of taste has been made can any kind of *interest* – moral, empirical, intellectual – be attached to it. It is in the social world that we connect these various interests with beauty. The urge to society is natural, says Kant, and sociability is a mark of our humanity. He even talks of an "original contract" whereby our humanity dictates a need for universal communication. When civilization reaches its peak, he says, such communication becomes our most refined activity and even sensations are valued only insofar as we can make them universally communicable. It is here, according to Kant, that our capacity for aesthetic judgment provides a transition from sense enjoyment to moral feeling, showing that judgment is "a mediating link in the chain of man's a priori powers" (*CJ*, 163–164).

Again, these insights of Kant were to prove vastly influential, leaving their trace not only in the views of Romantic writers but also, however indirectly, in the work of many literary figures of the late nineteenth century. To take a direct interest in the beauty of nature, asserts Kant, is always the "mark of a good soul." If this interest is habitual, it indicates a mental attunement favorable to moral feeling. Reason has an interest that nature should display some harmony with our pleasure; hence we cannot meditate on the beauty of nature without finding our moral interest aroused. Nature in its beauty exhibits itself as art, as if it were intentionally designed according to a lawful arrangement, as purposiveness without a purpose (*CJ*, 165–168). Kant even suggests that when we reflect on the form of sensations we receive from nature, these forms "contain, as it were, a language in which nature speaks to us and which seems to have a higher meaning" (*CJ*, 169). Such statements anticipate many comments made by Wordsworth, Coleridge, and other Romantics concerning the profound significance of nature, a significance inexpressible by rational thought.

Art, Imagination, and Genius

Kant's views on art and genius also laid the foundation for much Romantic thought. And, for all his endeavor to secure the realm of aesthetic judgment as an autonomous domain, his views on the connections between art and society were to reverberate through many subsequent theories about the social, educational, and moral functions of art. Kant initially defines art as "a production through freedom, i.e., through a power of choice that bases its acts on reason" (*CJ*, 170). Like Aristotle, Kant sees art as a productive or practical ability, as distinguished from the theoretical ability of science. He also makes an important distinction between art and mere craft. Genuine art is free art, "it is play . . . that is agreeable on its own account," whereas craft is "mercenary" art or labor which attracts us only through its product (*CJ*, 171). Mechanical or mercenary art merely makes a possible object actual, whereas aesthetic or free art intends directly to arouse a feeling of pleasure. If aesthetic art is merely agreeable, it produces pleasure through the presentation of mere sensations; if it is fine art, it yields pleasure by means of presentations that are ways of knowing. Kant defines fine art as "a way of presenting that is purposive on its own and that furthers, even though without a purpose, the culture of our mental powers to [facilitate] social communication" (*CJ*, 173, editor's parenthetical insert). It was seen above that Kant espouses a social function for art; even though our judgment of what counts as art must be based on formal aesthetic grounds, our judgment of art differs from our judgment of nature. To judge fine art as beautiful, we must have a concept of purpose, of what the artistic product is meant to be; and we must assess the artwork's perfection, or the degree to which it fulfills its purpose (*CJ*, 179). Kant says that the pleasure we take in the purposive form of fine art is also "culture." In other words, unlike the pleasure in mere sensory enjoyment, the pleasure in fine art somehow attunes us to moral ideas. Unless we connect the arts, either "closely or remotely," with moral ideas, they will ultimately serve only as diversion and will not satisfy the mind (*CJ*, 195–196). Beauty, says Kant, like sublimity, arouses in us a state of mind analogous to that produced by moral judgments; our capacity of aesthetic taste enables us to make a transition from mere sensory charm to a "habitual moral interest," since taste teaches us to like objects of sense "freely," i.e., for their form rather than their sensory content (*CJ*, 230). Kant also defines taste as an "ability to judge the way in which moral ideas are made sensible" (*CJ*, 232). Hence, Kant says, to study fine art, we cannot follow precepts or rules;

rather, we must cultivate our mental powers and expose ourselves to the humanities; this will promote a "universal feeling of sympathy" and an ability to engage in intimate communication. We can nurture our taste by developing our moral ideas and cultivating moral feeling (*CJ*, 232). What Kant anticipates here is later nineteenth-century and twentieth-century views of literary sensibility and the moral and educational function of literature. For example, in the late nineteenth century, Matthew Arnold was to urge that great literature cannot be defined; it must be experienced, and our literary sensibility is developed by increasing exposure to great works. Like F. R. Leavis in the twentieth century, Arnold saw in literature a redemptive and moral function: they both saw literary education as a means of fostering moral sensibility.

Kant's treatment of "genius" also influenced many Romantic and post-Romantic theories. He defines genius as the "innate mental disposition through which nature gives the rule to art" (*CJ*, 174). What he means by this is that, although every art has certain rules, there is no definite rule or set of rules for producing a work of art. Rather, it is "natural" genius, resting on a subjective attunement of the faculties of imagination and understanding, which produces something original and thereby provides an exemplary model or standard (*CJ*, 175). In contrast with much classical aesthetic theory, Kant considers genius to be the very opposite of the spirit of imitation. Learning, he says, is nothing but imitation. And the rules for art cannot be communicated directly as precepts; rather, they must be abstracted from the actual products of art which are created by genius. Hence the only way rules about art can be transmitted to posterity is by models of fine art (*CJ*, 176–178).

Not surprisingly, for Kant, imagination plays a crucial role in the operation of genius. He says that true works of art must be informed by "spirit" or an "animating principle" of the mind. And this principle is the "faculty of presenting aesthetic ideas." He defines an aesthetic idea as "a presentation of the imagination which prompts much thought, but to which . . . no [determinate] *concept*, can be adequate, so that no language can express it completely" (*CJ*, 182, translator's parenthetical insert). Kant goes on to say that an aesthetic idea is the "counterpart" of a rational idea. Just as an idea of reason transcends actual experience, so aesthetic ideas are representations of the imagination which strive beyond experience, seeking to offer a presentation of concepts of reason, i.e., ideas for which there are no intuitions in our sense-experience. As Kant says, imagination is powerful in creating "another nature" out of the material that actual nature gives it. When experience becomes too commonplace, we remold it in accordance with the "higher" principles of reason. In this way, says Kant, we feel our freedom, the freedom of our imagination from the laws of association which constrain it in ordinary cognition (*CJ*, 391). A presentation of the imagination (which Kant calls "aesthetic attributes," rather than conceptual attributes, of an object) occasions complex thought which exceeds any definite concept; the imagination thus "aesthetically enlarges" the concept, showing the concept's implications and its kinship with other concepts, opening the mind to an endless array of further associations, which cannot be expressed by existing concepts (*CJ*, 183). Hence genius consists in a peculiar combination of imagination and understanding. When the imagination is used for cognition, it falls under the rule of the understanding, and it is an ability to "exhibit," or give concrete form to, an aesthetic idea (*CJ*, 217). But when our purpose is an aesthetic one, the imagination is relatively free (*CJ*, 185). Kant here introduces a concept of symbolism, which again lay at the heart of much Romantic thought about poetry. Since both rational and aesthetic ideas exceed experience, they cannot be adequately "exhibited" or represented by a correlative sensible intuition. Such ideas or transcendent concepts can be exhibited sensibly only in a symbolic manner, which uses analogy. For example, there can be given to our senses no object which corresponds to the idea of God. So if we want to give sensible expression to this idea, we must do so in a symbolic way via analogy: we transfer our concepts of some other object which we *can* experience (e.g., Man) onto the concept of God, and all of the causal relations which exist within the concept of Man, we transfer to the concept of God. So the set of relations is the same in both cases, but the intrinsic character of the object (God) remains unknown. Hence our "knowledge" of God is not cognitive (or, in Kant's terms, "schematic") but symbolic (*CJ*, 225–228).

By way of example, Kant cites the poet who gives concrete, sensible expression to "rational ideas" of invisible entities and notions such as hell, eternity, death, envy, and love. The poet uses imagination, making it emulate the play of reason in its quest toward an ideal totality, to present these ideas to our sense with a completeness which is not actually found in nature (*CJ*, 391). Hence poetry can produce emotions which cannot be expressed by our ordinary, definite concepts, and it is poetry above all, according to Kant, which can manifest the power of aesthetic ideas (*CJ*, 183). Of all the fine arts, Kant accords the first rank to poetry since it is this art, more than any other, which sets the imagination free, whereby it presents a wealth of thought which we cannot express in language; poetry, says Kant, raises the mind above the phenomenal sphere of natural determination (*CJ*, 392–393). However, Kant is careful to repeat that the freedom of imagination is not absolute; if this faculty is left in a state of "lawless freedom," its ideas, however rich, will produce "nonsense." This is why Kant assigns to imagination in its aesthetic use a "lawful freedom" (*CJ*, 188–189).

Kant divides the fine arts into three types: the arts of speech, which consist of oratory and poetry; the visual arts, which can be plastic arts like sculpture, or arts of "sensible illusion" such as painting; and the arts of the "beautiful play of sensations," such as music (*CJ*, 190–192). Of all these, poetry is the highest, for the reasons given above by Kant. Poetry is the art of "conducting a free play of the imagination"; though poetry plays with illusion, it does not deceive since it openly declares itself as mere play of the imagination, a play which proceeds in harmony with the laws of the understanding (*CJ*, 393). Kant frowns on the art of rhetoric, which cannot be recommended, he says, either for legal or religious purposes since in such important matters there should be no trace of luxuriant wit or imagination or a subjective viewpoint (*CJ*, 393). The visual arts come next in the hierarchy since they also engage imagination in a free play which is nonetheless commensurate with the understanding (*CJ*, 200). For Kant, music occupies the lowest rank since it speaks merely "a language of sensations" (*CJ*, 199).

Kant's philosophy and aesthetics have had vast influence, especially on Romantic thought and Romantic conceptions of the literary imagination. His notions of aesthetic freedom, artistic form, genius, and the non-utilitarian, non-moral character of art exerted, for example, a profound impact on his contemporaries Goethe and Schiller, as well as on Coleridge, the American transcendentalists, and Poe. Both Romantic and non-Romantic thought attempted to overcome Kant's absolute distinction between phenomena and noumena: the noumenal world was brought back within the grasp of imagination and intellect. Indeed, in Kant's work lay the very possibility of Hegel's system whose vast influence encompassed philosophy and aesthetics. The philosophical problems raised by Kant heavily influenced Anglo-American idealists such as Josiah Royce, and inspired the growth of the Marburg School, whose prominent members included Ernst Cassirer (1874–1945) and Rudolph Stammler (1856–1938). Kant's ideal of aesthetic "disinterestedness" was applied by subsequent writers such as Matthew Arnold and T. S. Eliot to the sphere of literary criticism, which they saw as an activity ideally unencumbered by immediate political and social exigencies. The influence of Kant's aesthetics extended to Russia, where they were reflected in the views of art propounded by Leo Tolstoy and others. In their emphasis upon form and artistic autonomy, these aesthetics also held considerable attraction for some of the late nineteenth-century proponents of aestheticism, certain modernist writers, and the American New Critics. Kant's treatment of the sublime is an important component in critiques of this notion in the work of more recent writers such as Paul de Man and Jean-François Lyotard. In more general terms, Kant's philosophy has been profoundly influential in its distinction of phenomena and noumena, its insistence that the world is in fundamental ways our construction, and its grounding of morality on rationality and freedom. Finally, in Kant's thought, the notion of substance – the metaphysical foundation of Christian theology – is subjectivized and reduced to one of twelve basic categories of human understanding, thereby reduced to one of the viewpoints through which the world can be apprehended.

Notes

1 Immanuel Kant, *Political Writings*, trans. H. B. Nisbet, ed. Hans Reiss (Cambridge: Cambridge University Press, 1991), p. 54. Hereafter cited as *KPW*.
2 Immanuel Kant, *Critique of Pure Reason*, trans. Norman Kemp Smith (London: Macmillan, 1978), pp. 41–42. Hereafter cited as *CPR*.
3 Immanuel Kant, *Critique of Practical Reason*, trans. L. W. Beck (Indianapolis: Bobbs-Merrill, 1978), pp. 15–18. Hereafter cited as *CP*.
4 Immanuel Kant, *Critique of Judgment*, trans. Werner S. Pluhar (Indianapolis and Cambridge: Hackett, 1987), pp. 9–11. Hereafter cited as *CJ*.

CHAPTER 15

G. W. F. HEGEL (1770–1831)

Historical Context of Hegel's Thought

The Hegelian philosophical system occupies a central place in the history and genesis of modern Western thought. Its scope and influence cannot be overestimated. Along with Kant, George Wilhelm Friedrich Hegel is usually considered to be the greatest of modern Western philosophers. Hegel's system was initially inspired by the French Revolution of 1789, which for him embodied the revolutionary struggle of the bourgeois class throughout Europe to gain supremacy over the feudal aristocracies and the clergy, and to replace the decaying and irrational hierarchy of feudalism with a society based on reason, where both social institutions and the human community embodied a rational outlook. Revolutionary bourgeois philosophy and ideals received their most articulate expression in Hegel's work. In this sense, Hegel is a product of the Enlightenment, stressing as he does the supreme value of reason, which he brings into confluence with the other main impulse of Enlightenment philosophy, empiricism, or the doctrine that knowledge derives from experience. However, Hegel's system, while not itself Romantic, is also deeply informed by certain attributes derived from Romanticism: a commitment to the idea of unification or totality and a concomitant belief that subject and object, the human self and the world, are created and determined in their nature by each other. Hence Hegel's thought effects a vast synthesis of two major currents in European intellectual and social history, the Enlightenment and Romanticism, which are conventionally seen to be opposed in many respects (as in the respective primacy they attach to reason and imagination). In its inheritance of both of these trends, Hegel's philosophy was profoundly influenced by the work of Kant.

The historical and philosophical consequences of Hegel's thought were even more momentous. His system influenced a wide range of philosophies whose effects are still with us today: Marxism, the Anglo-American idealism of the late nineteenth and early twentieth centuries, various branches of existentialism, as well as the thought of many twentieth-century theorists ranging from feminists such as Simone de Beauvoir and Julia Kristeva to so-called "poststructuralist" thinkers such as Jacques Lacan and

Jacques Derrida. Hegel's doctrines have informed much Protestant theology, and his philosophy of history has profoundly affected numerous disciplines, including political and cultural theory. Equally, the Hegelian system has provoked much opposition to itself, in the form of the nineteenth-century positivism of Auguste Comte and Émile Durkheim, the early twentieth-century realism of Bertrand Russell, G. E. Moore, and others, as well as the logical positivism, the analytic philosophies, and the various brands of empiricism which have survived through the twentieth century.

What is it in Hegel's thought that has inspired both such broad and enduring acclaim and, on the other side, such fierce antagonism and contempt? To seek the answer in Hegel's personal life would be vain. It is true that, while living in Jena, Hegel impregnated his landlord's wife; one might be tempted to wonder if the three-phase dialectic did not have its origins partly in this dynamic triad of landlord, landlady, and tenant Hegel, with the wedlock-transcending child engendering the externalization or estrangement of the second phase of the dialectic. Beyond this seminal act, Hegel's biography was unremarkable: he was born in Stuttgart in Prussia to a father who was a minor civil servant; he studied theology and philosophy at a famous seminary in Tübingen, worked as a private tutor, and then began teaching at the University of Jena in 1801; in 1811 he married a far younger woman who bore him two children; in 1816 he became Professor of Philosophy at the University of Heidelberg; and in 1818 he was invited to assume the Chair of Philosophy at the University of Berlin, where he taught until his death. At Berlin he achieved the height of his reputation and scholars from all over Europe came to hear his lectures. Hegel's first major publication was *The Phenomenology of Spirit* (1807), perhaps the most difficult philosophical text ever written; this was followed by his three-volume *Science of Logic*, published between 1812 and 1816. His subsequent *Encyclopaedia of the Philosophical Sciences* was essentially a restatement of his philosophy as a whole; and the final work published in his lifetime was his *Philosophy of Right* (1821). After his death, his students and disciples edited and published his lectures on various subjects, including *Lectures on the Philosophy of History*, *Lectures on Aesthetics*, *Lectures on the Philosophy of Religion*, and *Lectures on the History of Philosophy*. Some of his earlier works were also posthumously published, and in some instances cast considerable light on his later ideas. These include his *Early Theological Writings* and *The Difference between Fichte's and Schelling's System of Philosophy*.

In a broader sense, however, Hegel's life was anything but uneventful. His life intersected, sometimes in startling immediacy, with vast historical transformations which have left an enduring imprint on the politics and culture of the modern Western world. When the French Revolution began in 1789, Hegel, like Wordsworth, Coleridge, and many others, welcomed it as the glorious dawn of a new era; together with his friend, the poet Hölderlin, he danced around a "liberty tree" that they had planted. Two years later, the French revolutionary armies invaded Germany, which was then a loose confederation of states known as the Holy Roman Empire, ruled by Francis I of Austria, and which included the German state of Prussia. In 1806 the French, led by Napoleon who had already vanquished the Austrians, defeated Prussia at the battle of Jena; this was during the very time that Hegel lived there and was attempting to complete his monumental work, *The Phenomenology of Spirit*, published the following year. Hegel saw with his own eyes the emperor Napoleon, as he records: "The

Emperor – this world soul – I saw riding through the city to review his troops; it is indeed a wonderful feeling to see such an individual who, here concentrated into a single point, sitting on a horse, reaches out over the world and dominates it." This statement has been held up for ridicule by later philosophers such as Bertrand Russell, who have untimely ripped it from its contexts. Hegel's point was that Napoleon, like Alexander the Great and Julius Caesar, was a "world-historical" figure whose actions and career crystallized and concentrated certain broad transformative historical tendencies. Hegel saw in the French Revolution and the expansion of its ideals to other countries an opportunity for Prussia to advance beyond feudalism into a more enlightened society. Indeed, until Napoleon's defeat in 1814, Prussia took steps in this direction, abolishing serfdom and moving toward a representative government. These movements were repressed after 1814 by the Prussian king, Frederick William III, and a series of statutes called the Carlsbad Decrees of 1819 implemented a broad system of censorship, extending to the press, the universities, and of course the arts.

It can be seen, then, that from the very beginning, Hegel's philosophy was forged in the heat of colossal, and sometimes violent, political struggles. The whole of Europe felt the shock not only of the French Revolution but also of subsequent revolutions in 1830 and 1848; the struggle for bourgeois supremacy against aristocracy and absolute power continued through the nineteenth century. The ideals of the French Revolution had largely been articulated by the thinkers associated with the Enlightenment: as Hegel was to note in his *Lectures on the History of Philosophy*, Descartes had effectively separated or extricated philosophy from theology, placing emphasis on reason (rather than revelation or external authority) as the primary avenue toward knowledge. Empiricist philosophers such as John Locke and David Hume had challenged the classical and medieval idea of "substance" as the primary reality on which all else was based; they emphasized the importance of experience in acquiring knowledge. In political terms, these thinkers had advocated some form of representative government (as did Locke) or even a democracy based on the "general will" of the people (as in Rousseau's *Social Contract*). While Hegel recognized the important contributions of the Enlightenment philosophers, he viewed their philosophies as one-sided, stressing reason at the expense of experience or vice versa. He saw the history of philosophy as a unity, which could progressively integrate the various elements that had been stressed separately by previous thinkers. And, to some extent, he saw this history as culminating in his own totalizing system.

The Enlightenment tradition was also one-sided in positing a gulf between thought and reality, subject and object, self and world. Thus Hegel integrates the insights of the Enlightenment with the insistence of Romantic thinkers on the unity of self and world. Kant's philosophy had taken a step in this direction. Hence, Hegel's own relationship with Enlightenment philosophy is largely mediated by the system of Kant, and adaptations of that system by Hegel's broadly Romantic German contemporaries and friends such as Fichte, Schiller, and Schelling. In his *Critique of Pure Reason* (1781), Kant had attempted to define the scope and limits of human reason, arguing that its operations can extend only to the world as it is already constituted by our subjective capacities, namely, sensibility and understanding. This world, to the making of which our minds contribute, he called the world of phenomena or the world of things as they appear to us; objects which we can only think of but do not present themselves to our senses he called noumena, or purely intelligible (and hypothetical) objects. Most of Kant's successors, including Fichte, Schiller, Schelling, and Hegel himself, took this distinction as one between things as they appear and things as they might be in themselves. They took it, in other words, as a distinction between appearance (the world as subjectively constructed by us) and external reality (the world as it might be in itself). They variously attempted to overcome this distinction: Hegel rejected the attempts of both Fichte and Schelling, saying that Fichte's identification of ego and nature consisted in a mere formal imposition of the categories of the former on the latter; and Schelling's because his identification of mind and nature was merely intuited (rather than rationally apprehended), which effectively denuded his absolute of difference and differentiation. For Hegel, this unity of subject and object, mind and nature, must be rationally comprehended.[1]

The Hegelian Dialectic

All aspects of Hegel's philosophy, logical, metaphysical, political, and aesthetic, are intimately tied to his philosophy of history. Hegel was the most articulate and influential advocate of what was later called "historicism," the belief that we can understand phenomena – people, nations, events, and objects – only within their specific historical contexts, and that these contexts form an integral element in the constitution of these phenomena. Nothing, in other words, can be examined in abstraction from its particular history, its causes, its effects, and its specific position in a broader historical scheme, a scheme often said to be driven toward specific goals through the operation of inexorable laws. In general, Hegel sees human history as a progress of absolute mind or consciousness toward self-conscious freedom. The movement toward freedom is equated by Hegel with a movement toward greater rationality, in both the operations of the human mind and the social and political arrangements which express these. Essentially, when our own minds have become rational and the laws and institutions that we live under are also rational, we shall freely consent to live by those laws. Hegel also characterizes this general movement as the progressive attainment of *self-consciousness* on the part of consciousness; in other words, as consciousness moves to higher levels, it perceives increasingly that what it previously took as the external world, as something alien and foreign to it, is in fact essentially constituted, at its deepest rational core, by its own operations. What was previously confronted as *substance* is now recognized as *subjectivity*. Hence Hegel also describes this entire movement as a progression from substance to subject. It is a process that works both in the logical workings of consciousness and in the progression of consciousness through history.

The most comprehensive avenue into understanding Hegel's philosophy as a whole is the notion of the dialectic, a notion which operates on three broad levels, logical, phenomenological (the forms taken by consciousness), and historical. And, as will emerge shortly, the dialectic also has certain political implications. To outline the logical operation of the dialectic, we might begin with an important passage in the *Phenomenology*:

everything turns on grasping and expressing the True, not only as *Substance*, but equally as *Subject* . . . This Substance is, as Subject, pure, *simple negativity*, and is for this very reason the bifurcation of the simple; it is the doubling which sets up opposition, and then again the negation of this indifferent diversity and of its antithesis (the immediate simplicity). Only this self-*restoring* sameness, or this reflection in otherness within itself – not an *original* or *immediate* unity as such – is the True. It is the process of its own becoming, the circle that presupposes its end as its goal, having its end also as its beginning; and only by being worked out to its end, is it actual. (*PS*, 17)

Here, the three "moments" or phases of the dialectic are given in terms of the concepts of identity and diversity; and the entire movement is defined as subjectivity (which is treated as a process rather than a static datum). The first phase is that of immediacy and simple self-identity. In this, which represents our first view of an object, we view it as an immediate datum, as mere existence, as independent, isolated from its context and having its identity within itself. In the second stage, that of *mediation* and *externalization*, we view the object's identity as externalized or mediated or dispersed through its relations with other objects. In other words, we locate the object's essence and identity not in itself but in *something else*, in its *relations*. In this second stage, we are concerned not with the fact of the object's immediate existence but with its content, its nature, its essence, the qualities that underlie its existence, the general or universal qualities that *exceed* its particular existence. The third stage is that of *mediated unity* or mediated identity: to arrive at this stage, we must formulate a principle of totality that can unite our first two perspectives of the object, i.e., the object as a particular existent and the object as embodying certain universal and essential qualities.

We can illustrate this process using an example given by Hegel himself. We might see the growth of a plant as having three stages, bud, blossom, and fruit. If we take the bud on its own (our first perspective), it appears to be self-identical, having its essence within itself. But soon the bud disappears when the blossom shows forth, and the blossom in its turn gives way to the fruit. So, in actuality, the essence of the bud was not contained in its own immediate existence: it referred beyond itself to the blossom. And the essence of the blossom extends back to its bud and forward to its fruit. So each of these stages actually has its essence outside of itself, and its very identity seems to be constituted by a diversity that is external to it. But they all achieve their true identity as essential elements of the overall process which is "plant" – the principle of totality which unites them in a necessary connection (*PS*, 2). Considered in isolation, merely as given, each aspect had the character of "substance." But considered as aspects in a process that is formulated by thought, they become "subject," or conscious elements of the movement of thought itself. Hence Hegel characterizes the entire process as a movement from substance to subject, from a perspective that initially views an entity as alien or "other," through an increasingly broadening perspective that recognizes that entity as constituted in its *essence* and universal significance by a subjective process. In other words, subjectivity for Hegel is a *process*, which apprehends what is rational, essential, and universal in the object as the product of the subject's own operations, as revealing the very form of subjectivity – not the personal and contingent subjectivity of any given individual but of universal subjectivity. Hence the dialectic is a mode of thinking that recognizes that the self and world stand in necessary connection, that thought is not a static system of classification but a self-criticizing process, and that the world as simply given to our senses is not worthy of the name "reality." Things in the world are to a large extent defined by their relations; they cannot be understood in isolation, abstracted from their connections with other things, but must be understood within their historical contexts. As Hegel states in his *Philosophy of Right*, "What is real is rational, and what is rational is real." Reality is not simply a vast and possibly incoherent assemblage of unrelated and unalterable facts (as crude empiricism would have it); rather, in its core, it is rational, historically progressive, and potentially unified, answering to the deepest demands of our own rational selves. Hence the dialectic is a mode of thought that is not only rational but also relational and historical.

As it is expounded in Hegel's *Logic*, it is clear that dialectical thinking constitutes an attack upon traditional logic which is based upon the notion of identity. Without understanding this, much of the import of modern literary and cultural theory – which reenacts this onslaught in altered contexts – will be lost. Hegel's own logic, enlisting the notion of "identity in diversity" or "identity in difference," is in part an attempt to overcome the separations between thought and reality, subject and object, which were implied in the empiricist philosophies of Locke and Hume and made explicit in Kant's distinction of phenomena and noumena.

Hegel's *Logic* undertakes a dialectical reexamination of the categories which have been fundamental to Western thought since Aristotle. Where Aristotle had begun his metaphysical inquiries with the question "What is being?" which he identified with the question "What is substance?," Hegel sees the category of "being" as a contentless abstraction: being in itself has no determinate qualities. Pure being, says Hegel, is "the absolute abstraction" because its purity consists in "an absolute absence of attributes." Hence being *is* nothing; there is no ground on which these two terms can be distinguished since both are without content.[2] Since being both implies its opposite (nothing) and is also indistinguishable from it, the ground of their simultaneous opposition and identity must lie outside of them. They are perpetually passing into each other, and this indefinite transition between them needs to be expressed by a third term, namely, "becoming." We began with "being" posited as simple self-identity; but when this was reflected upon by thought, its identity appeared to subsist outside of itself, in "nothing" (its "other"); on further broadening our perspective, we can see that they are both aspects of "becoming," which is the unity in which they can be distinguished (*SL*, 82–83, 92–93). Becoming, then, is the "truth" of being and nothing, the higher unity in which they are both "sublated" (transcended and yet preserved).

In this dialectical manner, Hegel examines the categories of what he designates as "objective logic" and "subjective logic," moving from the sphere of "being" through the sphere of "essence" to the sphere of the "notion" (notional thought being the highest mode of understanding, that which comprehends what is universal in an object). What is central to this entire enterprise is Hegel's insistence that becoming, not being, is the fundamental feature of all existence; and that the notion of identity cannot be thought apart from difference. This latter is the principle behind Hegel's departure from traditional logic (which attempts to comprehend a static world by means of fixed categories and laws), and indeed from any system of thought (such as one-sided empiricism or rationalism) which views the world as static, plural (made up of independent objects), and external (beyond the parameters of human subjectivity). Hegel points out that if we actually adhered to the first law of traditional logic, that A = A, we would be reduced to such empty tautological utterances as "A planet is a planet . . . Mind is mind." And even in making these statements we have presupposed a difference (between the named entities) as the very ground of their identity. Thus, identity has its nature beyond itself, in difference: the self-identity of a planet subsists entirely in its connections with what is different from it (an insight that many critics have seen as originating much later, with figures such as Saussure). Hence, identity and difference are inseparable.[3]

In his lesser *Logic*, Hegel distinguishes three basic modes of thought: *understanding*, which views the world as static and as composed of distinct particulars; *dialectic*, which ascertains the contradictory and dynamic nature of things, but is unable to resolve these contradictions (the term "dialectic" is here used in a specialized sense, distinct from that which characterizes Hegel's thought as a whole); and *speculation* or "positive reason," which "apprehends the unity of terms . . . in their opposition" (*Logic*, 118– 119). And for Hegel, subjectivity is the principle of the entire process: consciousness in the speculative stage is self-consciousness, because it has only itself, i.e., the whole process, for its object. One of the features Hegel brings out in this vast dialectic is that any given "thing" harbors a contradiction between its "matter" or content, which is dependent upon other things, and the immediate "form" of its existence (which appears to be self-contained) (*Logic*, 185, 187). In virtue of this dependence on what is beyond it, the thing is "appearance": for Hegel the only complete truth is the absolute, the whole. In other words, things do not exist in isolation; they are composed integrally by the relations into which they enter; hence Hegel's view of the world is relational: the relations between entities stretch out not only laterally in space but also through time and history, evolving to achieve a purposive totality and unity. As Hegel states in the *Phenomenology*, "The True is the whole . . . Of the Absolute it must be said that it is essentially a *result*, that only in the *end* is it what it truly is" (*PS*, 11).

In fact, the dialectic as formulated by Hegel is a historically cumulative process, harmonizing a number of broad tendencies and dispositions in modern philosophy: first, the principle of certainty in self-consciousness, as expressed in Descartes' cogito. According to Hegel, Descartes' thought marked the divorce (and liberation) of philosophy from theology. Descartes' cogito or self-consciousness signals the first real advance from the principle of substance toward the principle of self-conscious subjectivity.[4] But Descartes took self-consciousness merely as an immediate datum, whereas for Hegel it is a process that reveals God or the absolute through historical evolution. Again, Locke was right to see that "experience" was a necessary element in a totality (*Lectures*, 295), and empiricism in general is right to insist that what is true must pertain to the actual world (*Logic*, 61). For Hegel, Hume's importance is twofold. Firstly, he shows that Locke's empiricism leads to "no fixed standpoint" and culminates in "custom" which "is just a subjective universality" (*Lectures*, 363, 374). This denial of objectivity by Hume extends to God. Secondly, it was from Hume that Kant derived the starting point of his philosophy: the recognition that universality and necessity are not indeed in perception (*Lectures*, 369, 427). But Kant is right, according to Hegel, in locating these within subjectivity as necessary determinations of objectivity (*Lectures*, 427–428). This necessity is achieved by Kant, however, at the expense of positing an abstract noumenal world which can safeguard the concept of God from the onslaught of pure reason effected by the mainstream Enlightenment. Hence, Hegel's dialectic bears the trace of the Enlightenment influences noted above; but he holds that all of these Enlightenment philosophies effectively dirempt thought from being, subject from object. So Hegel integrates the truths of these philosophies with whatever truth is contained in the Romanticism of thinkers such as Goethe, Fichte, and Schelling. As noted above, however, he views the subject–object unity affirmed by Fichte and Schelling to be abstract; this identity must be achieved historically and it must be rationally, not intuitively, comprehended (*PS*, 11). Hence, Hegel attempts to unite the truths of both rationalist and empiricist strands of the Enlightenment with the insights of Romanticism, each of which alone is merely a potential phase or moment of the overall dialectic.

Writers such as Lukács and Marcuse have argued that the ideals of the French Revolution inform the very structure of the Hegelian dialectic. These bourgeois ideals included: the abolition of feudal absolutism and its replacement by an economic system (marked by free competition) and a political system (liberal-democratic, with equality before the law) attuned to the interests of the bourgeoisie, the emancipation of the individual from blind obedience to external authority, and the establishment of the individual's reliance on his free rational activity. It is clear that Hegel's dialectic, as described above, implies that the world as it *is*, as it is *given*, is not equated with reality. Empiricist philosophies, resting ultimately upon notions of "common sense" and custom, imply a somewhat conservative acceptance of the given order of things. In contrast, Hegel's thought expresses a more radical position, a philosophy of the negative, a philosophy that aims to negate or transcend the world as merely given. Such negation, then, is at the heart of the dialectical process: the dialectic contends that only when social and political structures are constructed in accordance with our rational demands can they be viewed as real. For Hegel, rational thought is correlative with freedom, a freedom to abolish the given-ness of the world; the world thus becomes a medium for the self-realization of the subject, the apex of which is self-consciousness, or the consciousness that, in apprehending what is real in the world, the subject sees only its own rational operations. Hegel sees this movement toward freedom operating historically, from the Oriental world, where only one person – the emperor – is free, to the Greek and Roman world, where some people are free, to the modern world, where all are free.

The Phenomenology of Spirit

The word "phenomenology" means something like "the science or study of appearance." Hegel attempts in this work to describe the various forms (manifestations or appearances) taken by absolute spirit or consciousness on its path toward freedom and self-consciousness, a movement that is correlative with the journey from substance to subject. The ultimate goal of this movement is self-consciousness, the point at which spirit or consciousness confronts the world no longer as "object" but as itself; in other words, it attains to the recognition that it has *itself* for object and that its consciousness of objectivity is ultimately consciousness of *self*, of its own profoundest nature. On this path, then, earlier formulations of truth are displaced, or rather sublated, by increasingly more comprehensive notions of truth, progressing toward absolute truth.

In the famous "Preface" to this work, Hegel explains the principles underlying the dialectic: that the nature of knowledge is not piecemeal but a coherent unity and totality; that knowledge expresses not a static system but an evolution, both logically and historically; that particular philosophies contribute to the development of a totalizing philosophy that includes all earlier stages (*PS*, 2); that knowledge consists in overcoming an initial opposition of subject and object, in overcoming the otherness (substantivality) of the object and perceiving it under the universal form of self or subjectivity (*PS*, 21); that truth is not a fixed result but a fluid, developing, process (*PS*, 23); that knowledge progresses from an initial perception of elements as mutually independent and externally connected, to seeing these elements as occupying a position in the development of a single, unified, content (*PS*, 36–38).

Hegel's starting point is the philosophical position that relies on sense-certainty, or the immediate data given by our senses, as a means of knowing the world. At first glance, sense-certainty, says Hegel, "appears to be the *truest* knowledge . . . But . . . this very *certainty* proves itself to be the most abstract and poorest *truth*" (*PS*, 58). All that sense-certainty can tell us about the object is that it *is*; and it similarly reduces consciousness itself to a pure "I," an abstract agent of perception. The relation here is between two particulars, between two entities in immediate relation. Immediacy is thought to be characterized by the terms "this," "here," and "now" (*PS*, 60). But Hegel points out that these terms – the very terms that are used to sanction immediate sense-experience – are in fact universals, because they can be applied indifferently to various objects. "This," for example, could refer to a house or a tree; "here" could refer to various points in space; and "now" to various points in time. "So it is in fact the universal that is the true [content] of sense-certainty" (*PS*, 60). Hegel also points out that we can never express individuality as such; language, which is intrinsically universal (in the sense that it is always bringing particular things under general categories), will allow us only to express individuality in general (*PS*, 60–62). Language can express not this particular "I" that designates me but an "I" that could refer to anyone; similarly with the terms "this," "here," and "now" (*PS*, 66). Sense-certainty also comes to realize that its essence lies not in the subject or object but in their unity, in the entire structured relation of subject and object (*PS*, 62).

Hegel's central argument here is that sense-data alone cannot give us knowledge; implicit in this argument is that (1) purely immediate experience is impossible, for we could not understand it, express it in language, or communicate it; (2) the elements of sense-experience can only be understood with reference to universals, and indeed many of those elements themselves are universals; what is true in sense-experience are precisely these universal elements; (3) nothing can be understood or even experienced in isolation from all else. We understand and experience within certain broader contexts. The supposedly "immediate" object of knowledge is already mediated – by language, by other objects, by its relation to me and by my relations to other selves.

Consciousness then moves to the next stage, that of "perception." Perception advances beyond sense-certainty in acknowledging the universal as its object, the universality that perception confronts is riven (as in Locke's account, and even Aristotle's account, of substance) by contradictions: between the universality of properties and the individuality of a thing, between the unity and diversity of properties themselves, and between the essence of the thing as intrinsic to it and as external to it (*PS*, 77). These contradictions persist, says Hegel, inasmuch as consciousness imagines that it is dealing with real substances and properties. Once it realizes that it is dealing with thoughts and concepts, it progresses to the stage of "understanding" (*PS*, 77, 79). In Hegel's terminology, consciousness has progressed to a *notional* understanding of the object; in other words, it recognizes that what is true about the object are its universal and essential features. But it still regards the notional object as alien to itself, not realizing that it is dealing with *its own* thoughts and conceptual constructs.

The foregoing description is intended to give some idea of how the dialectical process operates in the progressive forms taken by consciousness. But we cannot leave Hegel's *Phenomenology* without briefly considering one of its most important and influential sections, the master–slave dialectic. The section on "consciousness" (which consists of sense-certainty, perception, and understanding) is succeeded by the stages of "self-consciousness." Where Kant and nearly all of the Enlightenment philosophers formulated their notions of the human self as an isolated being, Hegel insists that human identity and consciousness are in their very nature social and historical. It is this fact which emerges most clearly – albeit somewhat metaphorically – in the master–slave dialectic.

Hegel begins the section on self-certainty by stating that the three forms of consciousness already examined, sense-certainty, perception, and understanding, can now be seen not as self-subsistent views of the world but as moments or phases of self-consciousness. For Hegel, the most fundamental form of self-consciousness is desire. As Hegel puts it: "self-consciousness is *Desire* in general" (*PS*, 105). Desire is the medium through which we abolish the foreignness of the object and make it ours. It is through such possession and transformation of the world that self-consciousness asserts and recognizes itself. It is by destroying the independence of the object that it achieves "certainty of itself" (*PS*, 109). But self-consciousness can achieve satisfaction only through recognition, which an object in the world is unable to give explicitly. This recognition can only be given by another self-consciousness. We may recognize ourselves in an object that we transform and possess so that it is stamped with our character; but in such an object we merely recognize ourselves implicitly. For true self-recognition, we need the mirror of another self-consciousness, in which we can see ourselves objectively affirmed – as subjects. As Hegel puts it, self-consciousness can achieve satisfaction and recognition "*only in another self-consciousness*" (*PS*, 110).

And this, as he states at the beginning of the master–slave section, is Hegel's major contention: "Self-consciousness exists . . . only in being acknowledged" (*PS*, 111). When one individual self-consciousness is confronted by another, each is certain of itself but not of the other, and therefore its certainty is not genuine; this certainty has truth only when "each is for the other what the other is for it" (*PS*, 113). In other words, to be certain of my humanity, my self-consciousness, I must obtain recognition not from an object, nor from a person whom I treat as an object, but from a person whose humanity I recognize: we each acknowledge the other not as objects but as free, autonomous *subjects*. How do we attain this recognition? Hegel suggests that there is a struggle for recognition between these two individuals. This struggle must be a life and death struggle because each individual must prove that he "is not attached to any specific *existence*, . . . not attached to life." This involves attempting to take the other's life and also risking one's own. It is "only through staking one's life that freedom is won," that the individual proves that his essential being is not imprisoned in the "immediate form" of individual existence; in seeking the other's death, the individual shows that he values the other person no more than himself, that his essential being – like his own – is present in the form of an other, external to him (*PS*, 114).

Needless to say, the death of either or both of these individuals would preclude any recognition of either consciousness. Hence the life and death struggle results not in death but in the victory and independence of one consciousness, which exists for itself, and the utter dependence or bondage of the other consciousness, which exists only for the other. Hegel calls the former the master and the latter the slave. The master is he who has risked his life, and has shown that he can transcend his material existence; the slave is he who has feared to risk his life, and holds on to his material being. It becomes evident at this point in Hegel's account that these two types of consciousness – independent and dependent, master and slave – might be seen as opposing and as yet unreconciled moments or aspects of one consciousness. In other words, as consciousness progresses, it reaches a state where it is divided between these two forms and is unable to reconcile them. The independent moment of consciousness is "immediate self-consciousness," or an "I" that has not yet been mediated by interaction with the world; the dependent moment is "consciousness in the form of *thinghood*. Both moments are essential. Since to begin with they are equal and opposed, and their reflection into a unity has not yet been achieved, they exist as two opposed shapes of consciousness . . . The former is lord, the other is bondsman" (*PS*, 114). So consciousness is opposed to itself: as consciousness of self, as subject, it is not yet reconciled with itself as constituting thinghood, as object. Hence, this model of master and slave, lord and bondsman, can be taken as a metaphor for the development of self-consciousness. It has also been interpreted in historical terms, as will emerge shortly.

The master's victory, however, is short-lived: it is true that, in reducing the other to slavery, to thinghood, he uses him to master the external world. The slave works on the world for the sake of the master. But precisely because the master has reduced the other consciousness to thinghood, he himself cannot obtain the reciprocal recognition that his own consciousness demands, since such recognition can be given only by another free and autonomous consciousness. In fact, it is the slave, rather than the master, who approaches the truth of independent self-consciousness. The slave has experienced the "fear of death, the absolute Lord," an experience in which his entire being has been "shaken to its foundations." And this "absolute melting away of everything stable," says Hegel, is the "essential nature of self-consciousness," which is "absolute negativity" (*PS*, 117). In other words, as Hegel maintains from the beginning to the end of his philosophy, the very nature of thinking and consciousness is to *negate* the given, to raise what is immediately given to the status of something mediated by thought. What the fear of death has given the slave is the implicit awareness that the entire range and depth of his world can be negated; in working on the world and transforming it (even for the sake of the master), he makes explicit this awareness by acting upon it. He overcomes his attachment to natural existence through his servitude, obedience, and discipline, all of which inform his formative activity of work.

Hence, he rids himself of his dependence on the material world by working on it and transforming it (*PS*, 117).

Hegel has already told us that we basically relate to objects in the form of desire: but the satisfaction arising from the fulfillment of desire, from the possession of the object, is merely a fleeting one, because it lacks such "objectivity and permanence" (*PS*, 118). "Work, on the other hand, is desire held in check . . . work forms and shapes the thing." Work, then, transforms the thing permanently and objectively; and the slave or worker recognizes his own essential and independent being in the object he creates: the slave "realizes that it is precisely in his work wherein he seemed to have only an alienated existence that he acquires a mind of his own" (*PS*, 119). Hence the slave advances beyond the master in acquiring an independence and an affirmation of his existence through the formative activity of his labor. We learn also that consciousness does not merely recognize itself in the world, but that it *creates* the world. Consciousness is not simply a theoretical stance but a formative practical *activity*. Hegel insists, however, that for work to have this significance – of providing an objective and independent form for the slave's existence – the moments of fear (of death) and service and obedience are necessary. If consciousness attempted to work on the world *without* experiencing the fear of death, its fashioning of the world would be merely an "empty self-centred attitude," and would not give it "a consciousness of itself as essential being." Such work would merely express "self-will" which was still "enmeshed in servitude" and would display merely localized skills. In contrast, the slave's work, informed as it is by this primordial existential fear, embodies the essential and universal nature of consciousness that realizes itself through negation of the world (*PS*, 119).

To be sure, there have been numerous interpretations of the master–slave dialectic, the most renowned ones offered by Marx and Sartre. In his *Economic and Philosophic Manuscripts of 1844*, Marx stated that the "outstanding achievement of Hegel's *Phanomenologie* and of its final outcome, the dialectic of negativity as the moving and generating principle, is . . . that Hegel conceives the self-creation of man as a process, conceives objectification as loss of the object, as alienation and as transcendence of this alienation; that he thus grasps the essence of *labor* and comprehends objective man – true, because real man – as the outcome of man's *own labor*."[5] Marx also states that Hegel's standpoint, in grasping labor as the essence of man, is that of the bourgeois political economists (such as Adam Smith, J. B. Say, and David Ricardo), and the limitation of this viewpoint is theirs: he "sees only the positive, not the negative side of labor" (*EPM*, 132). In other words, Hegel sees only that aspect of labor which serves the function of objectifying man's essence; he overlooks the possibility that labor could be *alienated*, that its products, far from embodying the essence of the laborer, could be estranged from the worker such that he is unable to see himself in them. Despite these criticisms, Hegel's fundamental insight concerning work as self-realization is the starting point of Marx's reflections on the subject. Moreover, Marx shares the fundamental premises of Hegel's view of consciousness. In *The German Ideology*, he states that the world is a construction of social activity, and that consciousness is a social product. He insists that "truth . . . is not a question of theory but is a *practical* question" (*GI*, 42, 51). He also states that "the human essence" is not somehow pregiven but is "the ensemble of social relations" (sixth thesis on Feuerbach).

In general, Hegel's account of master and slave might be regarded as embodying a necessary phase in the development of self-consciousness toward the recognition that it is a social product. It might also be viewed as a historical process expressing a state of oppression in a given society or in a pre-civil natural state where individuals vie with one another for recognition. In other words, in a civil society, where the rights of individuals are guaranteed, the phases of the master–slave dialectic have already been traversed. In Hegel's own account, the consciousness of both master and slave – unable to be reconciled into a unity – yields to other forms of consciousness. The first of these is Stoicism, which effects a retreat from a harsh world of "universal fear and bondage," the world of the later Roman Empire, into a realm of pure thought. Such Stoicism adopts an attitude of indifference to the hardships of the world, but its "freedom" from the world is abstract and without any determinate content (*PS*, 121). It gives way to another form of consciousness, skepticism, also a characteristic philosophy of the ancient Roman world. Whereas Stoicism is passively indifferent to the world, skepticism actively negates any determinate content of the world, and denies that we can have any certain knowledge of the world; but it, too, is abstract, and is also involved in the contradiction that it must *act* as if the world that it denies is real. At this stage, consciousness is reduced to a "confused medley, the dizziness of a perpetually self-engendered disorder" (*PS*, 124–125). Such is Hegel's anticipatory critique of the modern-day type of deconstruction which refuses any determinate vantage point. This contradictory and dual nature of skepticism, which effectively brings into unreconciled coexistence the moments of master and slave, then gives way before the "Unhappy consciousness," which is essentially a Christian consciousness divided between awareness of itself as an unchanging essence and as immersed in the world of change, multiplicity, and decay. This Unhappy consciousness ascetically denies its own individual and material self in order to project its true identity into a transcendent spiritual world. But its attempt at self-annihilation merely confirms its individuality, and its self-realization through work and action (*PS*, 136–138).

From this point onward, the development of consciousness as described in the *Phenomenology* assumes a social and historical status, progressing from the religious consciousness all the way through the Enlightenment and the French Revolution until the phase of absolute knowledge is reached. This development is considered in far more historical detail in Hegel's later work, published posthumously as *The Philosophy of History*. It is worth remarking briefly on Hegel's comments on the French Revolution and the goal of absolute knowledge in the *Phenomenology*. His assessment of the Enlightenment and the Revolution occurs in the section on "Spirit," where Hegel describes the disintegration of the Greek world. The unity between individual and society in that world is shattered and gives way before the Roman world, a world of atomistic individuals who have worth only insofar as they possess certain legal rights such as property rights. This "empty individuality" is incarnated in the person of the emperor, whose absolute power is experienced as something alien and oppressive (*PS*, 291–292). This condition of alienation between the individual and the social structure persists for centuries through European feudal society until the French Revolution. During these centuries of feudalism, individuals rise above their purely natural condition through the creation of state power and economic wealth. Self-consciousness sees itself embodied in these two forms of activity (*PS*, 301–302). In other words, these are the activities through which men create themselves. Hegel now details a dialectic between two attitudes toward state power and wealth: the "noble consciousness" is at first aligned with state power (which is personified in the form of absolute monarchy), but then its allegiance becomes merely linguistic, mere flattery, after which power passes from the monarch into its own hands (*PS*, 308 316). The "base consciousness" harbors a rebellious disposition toward state power (*PS*, 307). Though this contrast of noble and base consciousness seems to refer to the division between nobility and the bourgeoisie/peasantry in feudal society, it is clear that, ultimately, the noble consciousness assumes the stance of the base consciousness. However, it is the latter – the bourgeoisie and peasantry, not the nobility – that produces wealth. Hence, as in the master–slave dialectic, the noble consciousness relies on the activity of an other and thus fails to create the social and economic world in its own image. This, in brief, is Hegel's account of how power passes from the feudal nobility to the wealthy and enterprising bourgeoisie. The agent of this transition was the French Revolution.

In terms of historical development, then, the *Phenomenology* reaches a climax with the French Revolution, which ushers in a state of consciousness of absolute freedom to transform the world according to the dictates of reason. From this stage, Hegel moves to a description of absolute knowledge, or knowledge of the world as it truly is. Such knowledge is reached when mind or spirit reaches the awareness that the essential nature of the world is the result of its own rational operations of both thought and action. All objectivity is seen in the form of concepts, and the external, the substantial, is transmuted into the notional and the subjective (*PS*, 486–487). In this sense, absolute knowledge embodies a state of true self-consciousness, and part of its truth is its own historical journey. Knowledge and history, "the two together, comprehended History, form alike the inwardizing and the Calvary of absolute Spirit, the actuality, truth, and certainty of his throne, without which he would be lifeless and alone" (*PS*, 493). The absolute idea or God achieves self-realization only through a human community whose consciousness is raised through historical development to awareness of itself as expressing the divine. At the stage of absolute knowledge, the separation between subject and object is overcome since self-consciousness has itself for object; it sees itself, its own operations, through the natural, social, and political worlds. Another way of saying this is that the various forms of alienation between the subject and the world are finally overcome.

Hegel's Aesthetics

Hegel's aesthetics are very closely tied to his philosophy of history. As we have seen, Hegel sees human history as a progress of absolute mind or consciousness toward self-conscious rationality and freedom. Hegel sees art as one of the stages traversed by the absolute idea or spirit on this journey. Art, like religion and philosophy, is one of the modes through which spirit is expressed. Hegel begins his *Introduction to Aesthetics* by asserting boldly that art is higher than nature. Underlying this view is Hegel's more general observation that what is true, what is essential, in the world is spirit (or the absolute idea). In somewhat Platonic fashion, he suggests that whatever is beautiful in the world is so only because it partakes of this higher essence. Hence, "the beauty of nature appears only as a reflection of the beauty that belongs to spirit, as an imperfect incomplete mode [of beauty]."[6]

Like Kant, Hegel sees art and beauty as a realm that belongs to "*sense,* feeling, intuition, imagination." Its sphere is essentially different from that of thought, and it is "precisely the *freedom* of production and configurations that we enjoy in the beauty of art . . . it seems as if we escape from every fetter of rule and regularity . . . the source of works of art is the free activity of fancy which in its imaginations is itself more free than nature is" (*IA,* 5). Hegel is here using the words fancy and imagination interchangeably, rather than refining the distinction between them as Coleridge was to do. His main point is that the creative imagination can use the formations of nature but can also go beyond them in its free activity (*IA,* 6).

True art, Hegel says, must be free. Indeed, the art which Hegel wishes to consider here scientifically is "art which is *free* alike in its ends and its means" (*IA,* 7). Rather than subserving the ends of religion or morality, it must, like religion and philosophy, be a valid mode of expression of the universal truths of the spirit: "in this its freedom alone is fine art truly art, and it only fulfils its supreme task when it has placed itself in the same sphere as religion and philosophy, and when it is simply one way of bringing to our minds and expressing the *Divine,* the deepest interests of mankind, and the most comprehensive truths of the spirit" (*IA,* 7). In other words, it must fulfill the same functions and ends as these other disciplines in its own way, and stand with relative independence, rather than its end falling within those other disciplines. What distinguishes art from other modes of expression is its ability to present even the most abstruse ideas in sensuous form, such that our feelings and senses will be affected. Hence art reconciles the worlds of sense and intellect, nature and thought, the external and the internal. The unifying power accorded by Kant, Coleridge, and others to the imagination is assigned by Hegel to art in general. As for the objection that art deceives by presenting only appearances, Hegel rejoins that appearance is essential to reality, since the former embodies itself or "shines through" the latter (*IA,* 8). Moreover, the entire empirical world – both the inner world and the outer world – as immediately presented does not comprise genuine reality: "Only beyond the immediacy of feeling and external objects is genuine actuality to be found. For the truly actual is only that which has being in and for itself, the substance of nature and spirit . . . It is precisely the dominion of these universal powers which art emphasizes and reveals" (*IA,* 8). In other words, art actually helps us to perceive reality by organizing the chaos and contingency of the world such that we can see the "true meaning" of appearances (*IA,* 9). Hence the reality embodied in art is higher than "ordinary reality," infected as the latter is with contingency and chance.

Like Aristotle and Sidney, Hegel points out that history is burdened with the "contingency of ordinary life and its events," whereas art evinces the universal and "eternal powers that govern history" (*IA,* 9). Hegel is careful to point out, however, that art is not the highest mode of expressing the truths of the spirit; in this function, it is superseded by both religion and philosophy (*IA,* 9–10). The limitation of art lies in its being restricted to a specific content; only "one sphere and stage of truth" can be represented in art, that which is able to be embodied in sensuous, material forms (*IA,* 9). In the present era, says Hegel, there is a deeper comprehension of truth than that which art can provide: thought and reflection "have spread their wings above fine art" (*IA*, 10). Art no longer affords the satisfaction of spiritual needs that earlier ages had sought in it: in our world, thought has developed into a necessity, whereby we employ "general considerations and . . . regulate the particular by them" (*IA*, 10). Hegel here appears to suggest that art no longer serves the "real" functions of being the primary form through which we can apprehend truth, morality, cultural history, and ambition. And we no longer rely on art to shape our view of the world, to shape our very modes of feeling and perception. Rather, art has become reduced to an object of intellectual inquiry, an object of a somewhat distanced and detached apprehension: even when we are deeply moved, we raise our engagement with art to intellectual self-consciousness.

Nonetheless, Hegel rejects any view that spurns artistic activity as unserious and frivolous. On the contrary, he stresses that thinking is the "inmost essential nature of spirit," and art springs from the spirit and is in its nature spiritual even if its presentation assumes a sensuous form (*IA*, 12). And art, at least the highest art (which Hegel calls fine art), is not simply an expression of "wild unfettered fancy": rather, since it expresses the highest truths of spirit, this content will itself demand artistic control and quality (*IA*, 13).

Hegel briefly surveys a number of previous attempts to treat the arts systematically. The first approach he considers is an empirical approach, as exemplified in Aristotle's *Poetics*, Horace's *Ars poetica*, and Longinus' *On the Sublime* as well as practiced by more recent theorists such as the eighteenth-century writers Henry Home and Charles Batteux. Hegel regards the theorizing of the classical authors as unreliable and drawn empirically from a restricted range of art works; the modern theorists, as he objects, drew their empirical observations from an inadequate psychology (*IA*, 14–16). Hegel briefly considers the account of beauty offered by his contemporary and friend A. L. Hirt, as well as his friend Goethe's concept of the beautiful as underlying the external appearance of art, which has no immediate value (*IA*, 19–20). The second approach that Hegel considers is a theoretical examination of the *idea* of beauty. Here he cites Plato's general view that "objects should be understood not in their particularity, but in their universality, in their genus, in their essential reality" (*IA*, 21). But Hegel views Plato's (intellectual) treatment of the beautiful as abstract. Hence, Hegel rejects both purely empirical and purely theoretical accounts of art. The concept of the beautiful, he says, "must contain, reconciled within itself, both the extremes which have been mentioned, because it unites metaphysical universality with the precision of real particularity" (*IA*, 22).

Hegel stresses that the treatment of the beautiful is a part of philosophy generally. In other words, it cannot be an isolated science or study, but must form part of our total understanding of ourselves and the world. He offers here one of his clearest descriptions of the totalizing nature of philosophy, a description that will subsequently be brought under question by Derrida and other recent thinkers:

> it is only the *whole* of philosophy which is knowledge of the universe as in itself that *one* organic totality which develops itself out of its own Concept and which, in its self-relating necessity, withdrawing into itself to form a whole, closes with itself to form *one* world of truth. In the circle of this scientific necessity each single part is on the one hand a circle returning to itself, while on the other hand it has at the same time a necessary connection with other parts. (*IA*, 24)

In this important statement, Hegel stresses that philosophy is a system of concepts in organic and necessary connection; that *the* Concept or Idea goes out into the world and permeates everything with its own orderly, structured, and hierarchical nature, and returns to itself bringing the full wealth of the world under its own conceptual control, rejecting as unreal all that might be accidental and chaotic, and defining the true and the real as subsisting within a closed circle, itself composed of a number of other closed circles (its parts) whose mutual relations are determinate: these relations are controlled ultimately by the rational nature of the Idea. Both the larger circle and its constitutive circles carefully exclude what is not assimilable and capable of integration into this scheme of understanding. Presumably, the realm of art comprises one or a series of the smaller circles: it cannot exercise an unrestrained freedom. To put it another way, even its freedom – a freedom, independence, and relative autonomy on which Hegel insists – must conform to the larger pattern of the Idea's development in logic and history.

Hegel proceeds to examine certain common ideas of art: that it is brought about by human activity, that its domain is the field of our senses, and that it has an end in itself. On the first of these, Hegel cites classical conceptions of art as labor, as a craft pursued according to certain rules, and Romantic conceptions which attribute it to genius. Hegel's own view, like Horace's, is that both genius and reflection and workmanship are required (*IA*, 25–27). Like Sidney, Hegel views the creations of art as standing above those of nature; God is more honored by the conscious productions of the spirit (as in art) than by the unconscious and unreflective workings of nature, and he is equally operative in both (*IA*, 30).

But from where comes man's *need* to produce art? This "absolute need," says Hegel, originates in the fact that man is a thinking consciousness, that "man draws out of himself and puts *before himself* what he is and whatever else is. Things in nature are only *immediate* and *single*, while man as spirit *duplicates* himself" (*IA*, 30–31). In other words, man objectifies himself, both theoretically and practically: theoretically, because he represents himself (his own essence) to himself; and practically, because he has the impulse, in "whatever is directly given to him, in what is present to him externally, to produce himself and therein equally to recognize himself. This aim he achieves by altering external things whereon he impresses the seal of his inner being" (*IA*, 31). In this way, man strips the external world of its foreignness and sees in it an "external realization of himself." And art is one of these modes of "self-production" in external things (*IA*, 31). In this self-duplicating activity, says Hegel, we witness "the free rationality of man in which all acting and knowing, as well as art too, have their basis and necessary origin" (*IA*, 32). Hence art springs from the same source as thought and action, and in fact is itself a mode of action: this source is man's self-creation through intellectual, physical, and artistic labor. In such statements (similar to earlier statements in Hegel's *Phenomenology*) lie the germs of many philosophies. Marx developed Hegel's idea of man's self-creation through labor, his objectification, and, in certain circumstances, his alienation or estrangement from his own activity. Existentialists such as Sartre also laid emphasis on man's creation of himself through a series of acts; Hegel's insights here have also influenced phenomenology, feminism (as in the work of de Beauvoir, Kristeva, and others), as well as psychoanalysis (as in Lacan's theories).

One modern disposition that Hegel would not have sanctioned, however, is that of affective theories, such as reader-response and reception theory. Hegel rejects the argument that, since art is meant to arouse feelings in us, the investigation of art should be effectively an investigation of the feelings. Such an inquiry, he warns, does not advance beyond vagueness, and it confines us to "observing subjective emotional reaction in its particular character, instead of immersing itself in . . . the work of art" (*IA*, 32–33). Hence Hegel rejects theories such as those of Edmund Burke which rely on a specific sense or feeling of the beautiful, a feeling often labeled as "taste," and viewed as capable of refinement and education. Such theories, inordinately tied to the sensuous elements of art, are doomed to be vague and abstract (*IA*, 34).

Hegel's own account of how we should approach art is initially somewhat Kantian. He distinguishes the realm of art from, on the one hand, the realm of practical desire and utility, and, on the other hand, from the purely theoretical realm of science. Hegel explains here, as he does in the *Phenomenology*, that our basic mode of relating to the world is *desire* (thinkers such as Lacan were to reaffirm this fundamental relation between self and world). Sensuous apprehension, Hegel reminds us, is the most impoverished way of looking at the world: we are merely seeing, hearing, and feeling. Spirit goes beyond such sensuous apprehension of the external world; it "makes it [the world] into an object for its inner being which then is itself driven, once again in the form of sensuousness, to realize itself in things, and relates itself to them as *desire*. In this appetitive relation to the external world, man, as a sensuous individual, confronts things as being individuals" (*IA*, 36). In other words, once spirit or consciousness has worked on the world, refashioning it in its own deepest image, we nonetheless can relate to the objects in this world in a practical way, through our desire: we are not indifferent to the object; we do not let the object persist as something in its own right, something free, outside of us. Rather, we impose our own image on objects, and we relate to them as entities to be destroyed and consumed. When we are caught up in such personal interests of desire, neither the objects nor we are free, since our engagement with the object is based on restricted interests rather than on universal considerations and a rational will (*IA*, 36).

We do not, however, relate to art in this way: we leave it "free as an object to exist on its own account." In other words, our engagement with it is purely contemplative and we do not *use* its sensuous features. For example, we do not usually use a poem to convey a practical message; we regard the poem as an object in its own right; in this way, our relationship to it is not one of desire (*IA*, 37). Nor, on the other hand, do we adopt a scientific view toward art, a view that will evince only what is universal in it, for in engaging with a work of art, we cherish its individual and sensuous aspect (*IA*, 38). A work of art, says Hegel, "stands in the *middle* between immediate sensuousness and ideal thought." The sensuous aspect of art is itself ideal, since it is elevated above purely material nature: the sensuous aspect of art is not present for its own sake, it does not presume to independence, but is an embodiment of spiritual or ideal interests. Hence "the sensuous aspect of art is *spiritualized*, since the spirit appears in art as made *sensuous*" (*IA*, 39). Hegel speaks of the "essential figurativeness and sensuousness" of art, whose function is to exhibit the "profoundest and most universal human interests in pictorial and completely definite sensuous form" (*IA*, 40).

399

What is the aim of art? This is the question to which Hegel now proceeds. He rejects the centuries-old notion that the aim of art is imitation, that art awakens or purifies one's feelings and passions (*IA*, 47–49). He cites the views of Horace (and Sidney, whom he does not name) that art's instructive power is closely related to its capacity to afford pleasure or delight (*IA*, 50–51). But these views, says Hegel, suggest that "art does not carry its vocation, end, and aim in itself, but that its essence lies in something else to which it serves as a means." Art is reduced either to "an entertaining game" or a means of instruction (*IA*, 51). However, Hegel acknowledges that the view of art as providing moral betterment points to a "higher standpoint," which of course is his own. Art's vocation, he says, "is to unveil the *truth* in the form of sensuous artistic configuration, to set forth the reconciled opposition [between the worlds of thought and sense] . . . and so to have its end and aim in itself. For other ends, like instruction, purification, bettering, financial gain, struggling for fame and honor, have nothing to do with the work of art as such, and do not determine its nature" (*IA*, 55). What is interesting here is that, within the context of Hegel's overall thesis that art must express the truths of spirit, he nonetheless insists on the autonomy of art: its expression of spiritual truth is not in the interests of pleasure, morality, or instruction; rather, this expression of truth is an end in itself, the end and purpose of art.

Hegel considers Kant's aesthetics to signal the "reawakening of the science of art." It was Kant, he says, who brought to light the notion of art as effecting a union between the worlds of spirit and nature (*IA*, 56). The deficiency of Kant's philosophy lies in the fact that his union of subjective and objective elements occurs (in both his general philosophy and his aesthetics) as a union *within* subjectivity. In his general philosophy, this union occurs within the world of phenomena, leaving open an enduring gulf between this world and the world of noumena. Kant sees aesthetic judgment as bypassing the conceptual understanding and as based on the "free play of Understanding and imagination." Hegel's objection is that the actual nature of the work of art is not thereby known (*IA*, 58). Hegel appears to applaud Kant's attempt to define aesthetic judgment as disinterested and unrelated to desire and practical motives, as well as his views of the universally valid nature of such a judgment and his notion of beauty as "purposive," revealing a harmony of means and ends (*IA*, 58–59). Hegel views Kant's *Critique of Judgment* as the starting point for the "true comprehension of the beauty of art," though his deficiency – in locating the unity between universal and particular, etc. within subjectivity – needs to be overcome (*IA*, 60). According to Hegel, Schiller made some advances over Kant in attempting to grasp intellectually the essence of art as the unity of "universal and particular, freedom and necessity, spirit and nature" (*IA*, 62). Hegel also notes the notion of irony as developed by A. W. and Friedrich von Schlegel. He sees this irony as rooted in the philosophy of Fichte, which established the ego as the principle of all knowing and viewed all aspects of the world as modifications of itself (*IA*, 64–65). The *artistic* ego that does this undertakes a procedure of irony, viewing itself as detached from the conventions, laws, and morals that it expresses, and whose validity it questions (*IA*, 66–67). Hegel credits K. W. F. Solger with developing the notion that the infinite idea negates itself in the form of particularity and finitude (*IA*, 68–69). The stage is now set for Hegel's own intervention into aesthetics.

Prior to his analysis of the various stages of art in history, Hegel cites three requirements that are essential to art. Art, he says, synthesizes two elements into a "free reconciled totality": the content of art is the Idea, while its form is a "configuration of sensuous material." Given that the content of art is spiritual and the form is sensuous, the first requirement is that the content itself must be worthy of artistic representation. It should not be "prosaic" material, which is "ill-adapted to figurativeness" (IA, 70). Secondly, this content must not be abstract but concrete. Hegel observes here an integral element of his general philosophy, the notion of the concrete universal; what is true must be not only universal but also concrete: it must have "subjectivity and particularity in itself" (IA, 70). The example that Hegel gives to clarify this is the Christian trinitarian notion of God who, unlike the God of other religions, is not an abstract universal who remains completely transcendent and unknowable but rather is incarnated in Christ and achieves spiritual expression and realization in a community. As such a "person," God possesses subjectivity and concreteness: he expresses "essentiality or universality, and particularization, together with their reconciled unity" (IA, 70). Clearly, for Hegel, God himself is not an entity but a process, a dialectical process. Such a conception of God, originating in Hegel's early theological writings, might in fact be said to be an important source of the dialectic: the dialectic (at least in its origins) was partly an attempt to rationalize the Christian concept of the Trinity.

The third requirement for art is that not only the content but also the form must be individual, concrete, and possess unity. An example of this is the human form, which is a concrete sensuous object which embodies the spirit concretely. Hegel cautions that because such an object addresses itself to the "inner" apprehension, to our hearts and minds, not any object randomly chosen from nature will serve this purpose. Art does not seize upon its object randomly, for any given spiritual content already carries with it the appropriate elements of externality. The beauties of nature, for example, may go unseen or unheard. But the work of art is specifically addressed to human thought and emotion. The work of art "is essentially a question, an address to the responsive breast, a call to the mind and the spirit" (IA, 71).

Hegel is also careful to circumscribe with qualifications the high function of art. Although art has an important task in giving sensuous form to a concrete spiritual content, thought represents a higher mode of representing spirit. Hence in his overall scheme of the development of consciousness, Hegel assigns both religion and philosophy a higher place than art. These latter disciplines can express what art, limited by its sensuous form, cannot. For example, the Greek gods are closely related to the natural, human form and can be represented as such; but the Christian God, who is also indeed a "concrete personality," is "*pure* spirituality . . . His medium of existence is therefore essentially inner knowledge and not the external natural form through which he can be represented only imperfectly and not in the whole profundity of his nature" (IA, 72). In other words, mere art cannot adequately express the profundity of the Christian conception of God; this can only be expressed by thought. Within the framework of this limitation, the value of art lies in the correspondence and unity it can effect between spiritual content and sensuous embodiment. The criterion of art's excellence will be "the degree of inwardness and unity in which Idea and shape appear fused into one" (IA, 72). This general criterion, viz., the appropriateness of unity between spiritual content and sensuous form, is used by Hegel to classify the various historical stages through which art progresses. Spirit must pass through these stages on its journey toward self-understanding. This evolution is one of content, passing through various increasingly refined conceptions of the universe, nature, man, and god; it is also an evolution through various forms of sensuous artistic representation (i.e., the particular arts) (*IA*, 72–73). As will emerge shortly, Hegel sees these correlative developments as undergoing three broad stages.

Corresponding to this evolution of the Idea, as well as of the development of its particular configurations in art, Hegel divides the "science" of beauty into three parts: the first deals with the "universal Idea of artistic beauty as the ideal"; the second deals with the various artistic forms in which the Idea has been presented; and the final part considers the various arts as divided into their genera and species. Under the first heading, that dealing with the ideal of beauty, Hegel makes it clear that art is intrinsically related to truth: the highest art presents not just any content in a form suitable to it; rather, it embodies and presents the truth of the Idea. In turn, the Idea itself generates from within itself the appropriate artistic configurations for its own expression. In other words, artistic form is not just an external appendage to the content of the Idea but must derive from the very nature of the Idea (*IA*, 74–75). Hence, when we attempt to evaluate art, we cannot merely refer to the skill or defects of the artist. Some content, Hegel argues, is already defective and the artist must work within this inherent limitation. Thus, the spiritual content of certain religions was vague and obscure and could only be expressed in vague and inarticulate forms. Hegel cites the Chinese, Indians, and Egyptians, who "could not master true beauty because their mythological ideas . . . were still indeterminate." In general, as works of art "are all the more excellent in expressing true beauty, the deeper is the inner truth of their content and thought" (*IA*, 74).

Under the second heading, Hegel considers how the Idea has been expressed historically in particular forms of art. He cites three progressive configurations or stages of art: symbolic, classical, and romantic. At the first stage, that of *symbolic* art, the spiritual content or idea is still indefinite, obscure, and not well understood. Because it is indefinite it has not yet achieved individuality. The sensuous artistic form which attempts to embody such vagueness is itself defective and is characterized by Hegel as a searching after form rather than an actual "capacity for true representation." The spiritual idea assumes a form in matter which is not appropriate to it, which is still foreign and arbitrary. Spiritual meaning is attached randomly to objects in nature, and a true correspondence between content and form does not occur. For example, a lion might be held to represent strength. A block of stone might symbolize the divine but it does not truly represent it. Because the spiritual idea struggles in vain to find appropriate form, it exaggerates natural phenomena, distorting them into grotesqueness, hugeness, and diversity in attempting to raise these natural phenomena to a spiritual level. The spirit, says Hegel, "persists sublime above all this multiplicity of shapes which do not correspond with it" (*IA*, 76–77). Hegel characterizes this stage as the "artistic pantheism" of the Orient, which attempts to coerce any object, however trivial, into bearing a significance by which it can express the world view of the culture in question. This, then, is the first, symbolic, form of art, "with its quest, its fermentation, its mysteriousness, and its sublimity" (*IA*, 77).

The second form is *classical* art, which, says Hegel, annuls the twofold defect of symbolic art: the indeterminate nature of the Idea embodied in it and the inadequate nature of this embodiment itself, the inadequate "correspondence of meaning and shape" (*IA*, 77). In contrast, classical art "is the free and adequate embodiment of the Idea in the shape peculiarly appropriate to the Idea itself in its essential nature" (*IA*, 77). This adequate embodiment, however, is not merely a formal propriety between a given content and its external form; if this were the case, every copy or portrayal of nature would be classical, on the strength of its congruity between content and form. Rather, in classical art the content is the "concrete Idea, . . . the concretely spiritual" (*IA*, 78). In order to express this Idea or "free individual spirituality," we must find what form or shape in nature is peculiarly appropriate to its expression, to its embodiment. Hegel sees this shape as the human form, his reasoning being that God, or the "original Concept," created the human form as an expression of spirit. Hence art advances to anthropomorphism and personification, since the human form is the only sensuous expression appropriate to spirit (*IA*, 78). Such personification, however, constitutes precisely the limitation of classical art: "here the spirit is at once determined as particular and human, not as purely absolute and eternal" (*IA*, 79). In other words, while the human form is the most appropriate to expressing spirit, it nonetheless expresses it in a limited manner, weighed down by its particular and material nature.

This defect demands a transition to a higher stage, the *romantic* form of art. The unity which had been achieved between the Idea and its reality is here canceled or annulled once again; and the opposition or difference of these is reinstated, though at a higher plane than that of symbolic art. Hegel acknowledges that the classical mode is the "pinnacle" of artistic form, and its limitation is inherent in art itself, which must use sensuous forms to express a spiritual content. The defect (of art itself and even of its highest form as classical art) is that the Idea or spirit is not "represented in its *true nature*." For spirit, Hegel reminds us, is "absolute inwardness" or "infinite subjectivity" of the Idea; in other words, spirit is pure thought or ideality whose infinite and organic expansiveness cannot be restrained or expressed by outward, sensuous means (*IA*, 79).

Hence romantic art cancels the "undivided unity" of classical art because it expresses a higher content, it expresses spirit or idea at a higher stage of self-development. This content coincides with Christianity's view of God as spirit, in contrast with the Greek conception of the gods. In classical Greek art, the Idea is presented as an *implicit* unity of human and divine natures: the Greek god is known by "naive intuition and sensuous imagination, and therefore his shape is the bodily shape of man. The range of his power and his being is individual and particular" (*IA*, 79). In a higher stage of spirit's development, this unity, which was previously implicit and sensuously immediate, is elevated into "self-conscious knowledge," just as man is distinguished from animals by his knowledge (rather than intuitive awareness) of himself as an animal, a knowledge that enables him to rise above his animal nature and to know himself as spirit (*IA*, 80).

If, then, we are confronted with spirit at this higher stage, what could be the appropriate form for its embodiment or expression? The medium which will express such spiritual content can no longer be sensuous and material; rather, this medium must be the "*inwardness of self-consciousness.*" Christianity presents God not as an individual spirit but as absolute spirit, and therefore takes spiritual inwardness, not the human body, as its medium of expression. In other words, the unity of human and divine must be realized only by spiritual knowing, freed from immediate sensuous existence. In this way, Hegel suggests, "romantic art is the self-transcendence of art." Romantic "art" effectively transcends the sphere of art since the latter is defined as a presentation of spirit in sensuous form. In this third stage, then, "the subject-matter of art is *free concrete spirituality*, which is to be manifested as *spirituality* to the spiritually inward" (*IA*, 80). By this Hegel means that the object or subject matter of art is subjectivity itself, the inner world of emotion, spirituality, and thought. The artist no longer expresses what is in the world but what is at the depth of the human self. In this way, "Inwardness celebrates its triumph over the external . . . whereby what is apparent to the senses alone sinks into worthlessness" (*IA*, 81).

And yet, even if the romantic artist is concerned to express the depths of human subjectivity, how can he do this without an external, material medium of expression? Hegel's answer is that an external medium is indeed utilized but is recognized as "inessential and transient," a merely contingent circumstance employing expedient devices such as plot, character, action, incident, as devised by the imagination. This external medium, and the external world generally, however, is no longer viewed as harboring its own essence; its essence lies in the spirit that simultaneously embraces it and spurns it as the medium for its own manifestation (*IA*, 81). What Hegel appears to be saying here is that though elements of the external world are indeed used by the romantic artist, these elements are no longer used for their own meaning. For example, the phenomena of nature, such as the wind or a nightingale, are used symbolically and metaphorically to express human thoughts and emotions; they are recognized as merely contingent occasions for expressing the inner world of subjectivity. Hence, in romantic art the separation of Idea and form, their mutual indifference and inadequacy, emerge once again; the difference is that, in romantic art, the Idea is perfected in its development, and in this perfection it can suffer no adequate union with what is external; its true reality and manifestation lie within itself. In general, Hegel characterizes the symbolic, classical, and romantic forms of art as consisting, respectively, in the "striving for, the attainment, and the transcendence of the Ideal as the true Idea of beauty" (*IA*, 81). In general, the center of the entire world of art, for Hegel, is the "region of divine truth, artistically represented for contemplation and feeling." In passing from the symbolic through the classical to the romantic mode, we have effectively moved from a "spiritless objectivity" (where the configurations of the external world have their meaning not in themselves but beyond themselves, in spirit) to the presentation of the divine as something inward, as given a particularized subjective existence in human "knowledge, emotion, perception, and feeling" (*IA*, 83). Indeed, art at its highest stage is "immediately connected" with religion, and Hegel likens this threefold development of art with the triadic movement of the divine itself in human consciousness: first, we confront the natural world in its finitude, as subjects confronting objects; then, our consciousness makes God its object, abrogating the distinction between subjective and objective (we see our own subjectivity or consciousness as part of the divine subjectivity or self-consciousness); and thirdly, our consciousness of God as such (God per se, or God in himself) advances to a notion of God as present in the community, to God as "present in subjective consciousness" (*IA*, 83).

Hegel now passes on to the third part of his subject, which concerns the realization of the three general forms of art in specific arts, namely, architecture, sculpture, painting, music, and poetry. Each of the specific arts, says Hegel, primarily embodies one of the general art forms: for example, classical art is primarily suited to sculpture, and romantic art to poetry. There can, of course, be some overlap: epic poetry, for example, manifests classical objectivity, and poetry in fact runs as an undercurrent through all of the other varieties of art (*IA*, 82).

The first (and lowest) of the specific arts is architecture, which manipulates external organic nature as "an external world conformable to art," thereby making this world cognate with spirit. The material of architecture is matter confronted as "immediate externality as a mechanical heavy mass," i.e., matter subject to mechanical laws. Hence architecture is the fundamentally symbolic art because spirit cannot be realized in such material. However, architecture opens a path for spirit by working on nature to free it from "the jungle of finitude and the monstrosity of chance." It levels a space for the god and builds his temple, an enclosure for spiritual congregation (*IA*, 84). The next phase of art is contained in sculpture: into this temple, the "god enters himself as the lightning-flash of individuality striking and permeating the inert mass" (*IA*, 84). In sculpture, "the spiritual inner life, at which architecture can only hint, makes itself at home in the sensuous shape and its external material." Hence, sculpture, embodying the spirit, fundamentally expresses the classical form of art: through sculpture, the spirit stands in bodily form, in immediate unity with it. What this means is that the sensuous matter processed by sculpture is no longer manipulated according to its mechanical qualities alone, but rather according to the ideal forms of the human figure in all three spatial dimensions. But sculpture uses an "abstract spatiality" inasmuch as it deals with an ideal human form raised above the "play of accidents" and contingency of the external world (*IA*, 85).

So far, then, architecture has built the temple, and sculpture has set up therein the image of the god. Thirdly, this sensuously present god is confronted by the *community*: the "compact unity in itself which the god has in sculpture disperses into the plurality of the inner lives of individuals whose unity is not sensuous but purely ideal. And so only here is God himself truly spirit, spirit in his community" (*IA*, 85–86). God is released from his immediate immersion in a bodily medium and "is raised to spirituality and knowledge . . . which essentially appears as inward and as subjectivity" (*IA*, 86). Hence, in this third stage, the spirit moves to a higher level: instead of being embodied in material form, God – as spiritual knowledge – passes into the subjectivity of the community, into the beliefs, thoughts, and feelings of the community; it is these beliefs, not the act of physically congregating, that unites the community in an "ideal" way. God is seen as alternating between his own "inherent unity" and his realization in the knowledge of the individuals within a community. This third phase of God's development coincides with romantic art, for the object of artistic representation is now the inner world of human thought and feeling; it is "the most manifold subjectivity in its living movement and activity as human passion, action . . . and . . . the wide range of human feeling" (*IA*, 86).

The sensuous material used in romantic art must be appropriate to such "subjective inwardness." What is this material? It is of three broad types: color, musical sound, and "sound as the mere indication of inner intuitions and ideas." The modes of art corresponding to these materials are, respectively, painting, music, and poetry. These arts express a deeper intimacy between spirit and matter than was exhibited in architecture and sculpture: in painting, music, and poetry, the sensuous medium is posited as spiritual and ideal, hence these arts conform in general to the romantic mode (*IA*, 86–87). In each of these arts, the world of matter is raised to an ideal and spiritual status:

it is significant not in itself but in terms of the subjective human thoughts and emotions it embodies or expresses. The material of painting is "visibility as such," which is particularized as color. Unlike architecture, painting does not consider mechanical qualities; and unlike sculpture, it does not engage with "sensuous spatiality." Rather, the quality of visibility is "subjectivized and posited as ideal." Painting frees art from the spatiality of material things by restricting visibility to the dimensions of a plane surface (*IA*, 87). On the other hand, the content of painting can attain the "widest particularization," extending over the entire world of particular existence, including the full range of human emotion (*IA*, 87).

The second art which realizes romantic form is music, whose material delves still deeper into subjectivity and particularization. Music further negates and idealizes space by concentrating it into the isolated unity of a single point, a movement or tremor of the material body in relation to itself. In other words, in music, the ideality of matter appears no longer under the form of space but as a temporal ideality, in sound or tone. Succession in time is more ideal than coexistence in space, since the former is more exclusively registered in consciousness. The abstract visibility of matter, as presented in painting, is altered into audibility: "sound releases the Ideal, as it were, from its entanglement in matter" (*IA*, 88). Interestingly, Hegel sees music as standing at the center of the romantic arts, marking the "point of transition between the abstract spatial sensuousness of painting and the abstract spirituality of poetry" (*IA*, 88).

Indeed, the third and highest realization of romantic art is poetry, which completes the liberation of spirit from sensuousness that was begun by painting and music. Hegel's explanation is worth citing in full:

> For sound, the last external material which poetry keeps, is in poetry no longer the feeling of sonority itself, but a *sign*, by itself void of significance, a sign of the idea which has become concrete in itself, and not merely of indefinite feeling and its nuances and gradations. Sound in this way becomes a *word* as a voice inherently articulated, the meaning of which is to indicate ideas and thoughts. (*IA*, 88)

In this stage, the self-conscious individual – the poet – out of his own resources "unites the infinite *space* of his ideas with the *time* of sound." Poetry does indeed use sound, but only to express ideas, "only as a sign in itself without value or content." The audible, like the visible, has sunk into being "a mere indication of spirit" (*IA*, 89). Hegel sees the proper element of poetic representation as the imagination; and poetry itself "is the universal art of the spirit," which is not bound by sensuous material; instead, "it launches out exclusively in the inner space and the inner time of ideas and feelings" (*IA*, 89). And it is precisely at this stage that "art now transcends itself . . . and passes over from the poetry of the imagination to the prose of thought" (*IA*, 89). As a whole, Hegel characterizes architecture as an "external" art, sculpture as "objective," and painting, music, and poetry as "subjective" (*IA*, 89). Hegel stresses that poetry underlies all forms of the beautiful "because its proper element is beautiful imagination," necessary for every beautiful production in any form of art (*IA*, 90).

The influence of Hegel's philosophy on subsequent major developments in thought has already been mentioned at the beginning of this chapter. His aesthetics have also had a pervasive influence, on both literature (as, for example, on the dramas of

Friedrich Hebbel) and criticism. The late nineteenth-century thinker Wilhelm Dilthey was profoundly influenced by Hegel in his historicism; the major modern aestheticians Benedetto Croce and Giovanni Gentile developed many of Hegel's insights. Hegel anticipated some of the insights of Freud concerning the development of identity, and the insights of Saussure concerning the nature of language. The work of the Hungarian philosopher and aesthetician Georg Lukács is informed by an intimate knowledge of the entire corpus of Hegel's work. The leading members of the Frankfurt School, such as Max Horkheimer, Walter Benjamin, Theodor Adorno, Herbert Marcuse, and Jürgen Habermas, have stressed the debt of Marxism to certain features of Hegel's thought, such as the role of consciousness in creating the world, and have developed Marxist critiques in aesthetic, cultural, and linguistic dimensions. Hegel's thought was fundamental to the articulation of existentialism, as in the work of Jean-Paul Sartre, and feminism, as expounded by Simone de Beauvoir. Jacques Lacan, Jacques Derrida, and Jean-François Lyotard continued to develop or react against the insights originally offered by Hegel. Much of this recent criticism has reacted against what it sees as the totalizing nature of Hegel's vision, stressing instead the local, the particular, and the notion of "difference." But it was Hegel who first articulated the notion of relatedness, of human identity as a reciprocal and social phenomenon, of the world as a social and historical human construction, of identity as intrinsically constituted by diversity, of language as a system of human perception, and of the very idea of otherness or alterity as it informs much modern thought.

Notes

1 G. W. F. Hegel, *Phenomenology of Spirit*, trans. A. V. Miller (Oxford: Oxford University Press, 1977), pp. 11, 29–32. Hereafter cited as *PS*.
2 *Hegel's Science of Logic*, trans. A. V. Miller (London and New York: George Allen and Unwin/Humanities Press, 1976), pp. 128–132, 479. Hereafter cited as *SL*.
3 *Hegel's Logic: Being Part One of the Encyclopaedia of the Philosophical Sciences (1830)*, trans. William Wallace (Oxford: Oxford University Press, 1982), pp. 167–171. Hereafter cited as *Logic*.
4 *Hegel's Lectures on the History of Philosophy, III*, trans. E. S. Haldane and Frances H. Simson (London and New York: Routledge and Kegan Paul/Humanities Press, 1963), pp. 217–218. Hereafter cited as *Lectures*.
5 Karl Marx, *Economic and Philosophic Manuscripts of 1844*, English translation (Moscow and London: Progress Publishers/Lawrence and Wishart, 1981), p. 132. Hereafter cited as *EPM*.
6 *Hegel's Introduction to Aesthetics: Being the Introduction to the Berlin Aesthetic Lectures of the 1820s*, trans. T. M. Knox (Oxford: Oxford University Press, 1979), p. 2. Hereafter cited as *IA*.

CHAPTER 16

ROMANTICISM (I): GERMANY AND FRANCE

What gods will rescue us from all these ironies?
Friedrich von Schlegel,
"On Incomprehensibility," 1800

O riginally, the term "Romantic" had referred to medieval romance and tales of adventure; its connotations extended to what was fictitious and fantastic, to folklore and legend, as well as to the dazzling and rugged sights of nature. Romanticism, as we understand it, was a broad intellectual and artistic disposition that arose toward the end of the eighteenth century and reached its zenith during the early decades of the nineteenth century. The ideals of Romanticism included an intense focus on human subjectivity and its expression, an exaltation of nature, which was seen as a vast repository of symbols, of childhood and spontaneity, of primitive forms of society, of human passion and emotion, of the poet, of the sublime, and of imagination as a more comprehensive and inclusive faculty than reason. The most fundamental literary and philosophical disposition of Romanticism has often been seen as irony, an ability to accommodate conflicting perspectives of the world. Developing certain insights of Kant, the Romantics often insisted on artistic autonomy and attempted to free art from moralistic and utilitarian constraints, as expressed in the centuries-old formula, deriving from the ancient Roman poet Horace, that literature should both please and instruct.

It was in the fields of philosophy and literature that Romanticism – as a broad response to Enlightenment, neoclassical, and French revolutionary ideals – initially took root. In general, this period can best be seen as one in which the major upheavals such as the French Revolution, the Industrial Revolution, and the revolutions of 1830 and 1848, along with the growth of nationalism, impelled the bourgeois classes toward political, economic, cultural, and ideological hegemony. It was their world view – broadly, rationalist, empiricist, individualist, utilitarian, and economically liberal – which dominated the thought and practice of this period, and which spawned various oppositional movements such as socialism, anarchism, cults of irrationalism, and revivals of tradition and religion. Romanticism cannot be placed within any set of these movements since it effectively spanned them all.

A question that might fruitfully be addressed here is the complex connection of Romanticism to the predominating bourgeois world views. As writers such as Plekhanov, Marcuse, and Hobsbawm have pointed out, it is too simplistic to view Romanticism in any of its expressions as a straightforward reaction against the prevalent bourgeois way of life. Some of the Romantics, such as Blake, Wordsworth, and Hölderlin, initially saw the French Revolution as heralding the dawn of a new era of individual and social liberation. Schiller and Goethe in their own ways exalted the struggle for human freedom and mastery of knowledge. Shelley, Byron, Heine, George Sand, and Victor Hugo were passionate in their appeals for justice and liberation from oppressive social conventions and political regimes. Underlying nearly all Romantic views of literature was an intense individualism based on the authority of experience and, often, a broadly democratic orientation, as well as an optimistic and sometimes utopian belief in progress. Moreover, the Romantics shared Enlightenment notions of the infinite possibility of human achievement, and of a more optimistic conception of human nature as intrinsically good rather than as fallen and theologically depraved. In all these aspects, there was some continuity between Enlightenment and Romantic thought.

However, many of the Romantics, including some of the figures cited above such as Blake, Wordsworth, Shelley, and Byron, reacted against certain central features of the new bourgeois social and economic order. Appalled by the squalor and the mechanized, competitive routine of the cities, as well as by the moral mediocrity of a bourgeois world given over to what Shelley called the principles of "utility" and "calculation," they turned for spiritual relief to mysticism, to nature, to Rousseauistic dreams of a simple, primitive, and uncorrupted lifestyle, which they sometimes located in an idealized period of history such as the Middle Ages. Wordsworth held that the poet should emulate the "language of real life"; he, along with Blake and Coleridge, exalted the state of childhood and innocence of perception, untainted by conventional education; and many Romantic writers – in tune with growing nationalistic sentiments – revived primitive forms such as the folktale and the ballad. Nature, for the Romantics, departed from the conception of nature held by neoclassical writers such as Pope, for whom the term signified an eternal, unchangeable, and hierarchical order of the cosmos as well as certain criteria for human thought and behavior. Pope's view had been influenced by notions deriving from Newton of the universe as a vast machine, as well as by Christian providential notions of nature surviving from the Middle Ages. For the Romantics, nature was transfigured into a living force and held together as a unity by the breath of the divine spirit. It was infused with a comprehensive symbolism resting on its profound moral and emotional connection with human subjectivity. Coleridge referred to nature as the "language of God."

Perhaps the most fundamental trait of all Romanticism was its shift of emphasis away from classical objectivity toward subjectivity: in the wake of the philosophical systems of Fichte, Schelling, and above all, of Hegel, the worlds of subject and object, self and world, were viewed as mutually constructive processes, human perception playing an active role rather than merely receiving impressions passively from the outside world. Such an emphasis placed a high value on uniqueness, originality, novelty, and exploration of ever expanding horizons of experience, rather than the filtering of experience through historically accumulated layers of tradition and convention. The emphasis on uniqueness is amply exemplified in Rousseau's *Confessions*, which both in its very form asserts the value of the confessional mode, of private experience, and in its content places great value on uniqueness and particularity rather than typicality and conformity. Moreover, the self which is exalted in Romanticism was a far cry from the self as an atomistic (and economic) unit as premised in the political and economic philosophies of bourgeois individualism. The Romantic self was a profounder, more authentic ego lying beneath the layers of social convention, a self which attempted through principles such as irony to integrate the increasingly fragmented elements of the bourgeois world into a vision of unity. And it was primarily the poet who could achieve such a vision. In general, the Romantics exalted the status of the poet, as a genius whose originality was based on his ability to discern connections among apparently discrepant phenomena and to elevate human perception toward a comprehensive, unifying vision.

The most crucial human faculty for such integration was the imagination, which most Romantics saw as a unifying power, one which could harmonize the other strata of human perception such as sensation and reason. It should be noted that Romanticism is often wrongly characterized as displacing Enlightenment "reason" with emotion, instinct, spontaneity, and imagination. To understand what is at issue here, it is necessary to recall that much Romantic thought took Kant's philosophy (which itself was not at all Romantic) as its starting point, notably his distinction between phenomena and noumena, his treatment of imagination, and his establishing of a relative autonomy for the category of the aesthetic. Kant's relation to Enlightenment thought was indeed ambivalent inasmuch as he attempted to establish the limitations of reason. However, Kant declared that the categories of the understanding applied throughout the phenomenal world; his notion of the noumenon is merely a limiting concept and its actual existence is nothing more than a presupposition of morality and free will. He had, moreover, viewed imagination as a mediating principle which reconciled the deliverances of sensation with the categories of the understanding. The Romantics, like Hegel (who himself was certainly not a Romantic), placed the noumenal realm within the reach of human apprehension, and often exalted the function of imagination, viewing it as a vehicle for the attainment of truths beyond the phenomenal world and beyond the reach of reason alone. But they did not attempt to dismiss or discard the findings of logic and reason, merely to place these within a more embracing scheme of perception. Hence Coleridge saw the secondary imagination, peculiar to the poet, as a unifying power which could reconcile general and concrete, universal and particular. Shelley even saw imagination as having a moral function, as a power enabling the self to situate itself within a larger empathetic scheme, as opposed to reason, which expressed the selfish constraints of the liberal atomistic self. Hence the relation between Romanticism and the mainstreams of bourgeois thought, which had risen to hegemony on the waves of the Enlightenment, the French Revolution, and the Industrial Revolution, was deeply ambivalent. Our own era is profoundly pervaded by this ambivalent heritage.

This ambivalent connection of Romanticism to bourgeois thought operated through both the notion of imagination and the equally archetypal notion of Romantic irony. The ancient Roman authors Cicero and Quintilian had followed the Greeks in defining irony as a form of dissemblance whereby a speaker's intention differed from his statements. This broad definition of irony remained in currency through late antiquity, the Middle Ages, the Renaissance, and the neoclassical era. Both the French *Encyclopédie* of

1765 and Johnson's *Dictionary* reiterated the definition of irony as a figure of speech in which the meaning undermines or opposes the actual words used to express it.

It was only at the end of the eighteenth century that irony rose in status from a mere rhetorical device to an entire way of looking at the world, becoming, in the guise of Romantic irony, an index of a broad philosophic vision. The emergence of this change is usually dated to Schlegel's *Fragments* of 1797, which accords irony an epistemological and ontological function, seeing it as a mode of confronting and transcending the contradictions of the finite world. The theorizing of irony in this direction was furthered by numerous writers including Heine, Kierkegaard, and Nietzsche. At the core of irony as formulated by most nineteenth-century thinkers was a Romantic propensity to confront, rather than overlook, the obstinate disorder, contingency, flux, and mystery of the world. In this sense, an ironic vision accepts that the world can be viewed from numerous irreconcilable perspectives, and rejects any providential, rational, or logical foreclosure of the world's absurdity and contradictions into a spurious unity. Yet such Romantic irony is not entirely negative: while it rejects the "objective" order imposed upon experience or the world by religious or rational means, it seeks a higher transcendent unity and purpose, grounded ultimately in subjectivity. Modernist irony is seen by most theorists as a development of Romantic irony and as entailing a dual posture: a negation of prevailing values and institutions, and a helpless complicity with them. However, it diverges from Romantic irony in being more nihilistic, despairing over the possibility of transcending or changing the current state of affairs. Irony effectively entails a failed search for meaning and unity.

The "Romantic" metamorphosis of irony in the eighteenth century from a classical and medieval rhetorical device to an index of a metaphysical perspective was integrally tied to the broader social and political changes earlier invoked. The emergence and rapid theorizing of irony as a metaphysical perspective coincided with the era in which the hegemony of bourgeois interests and values was establishing itself not only in political life and economic practice but also in philosophy, literature, and science. Irony was essentially an idealistic reaction against the mainstream tendencies of bourgeois thought which attempted to define the world in terms of its own clear-cut categories, founded on rationalism, pragmatic efficiency, and an atomistic and utilitarian commodification of all the elements of the world, including the human subject. Underlying these tendencies lay the conviction that, in principle, knowledge, reason, and science could extend their control over all aspects of human life.

The Romantic thinkers who embraced an ironic vision reacted against the reductively mechanistic, utilitarian, and commercial impetus of bourgeois thought. Irony was a means of reinvesting the world with mystery, of limiting the arrogant claims of reason, of denying the ideals of absolute clarity and definition, of reaffirming the profound interconnection of things, and of seeking for the human spirit higher and more spiritual forms of fulfillment than those available through material and commercial efficiency. Yet irony as a very mode of reaction bore the imprint of defeat: it could merely voice subjective protests against colossal historical movements which were already in process of realization, protests which often floated free of any viable basis of institutional change. The Romantics were struggling against a world whose materialistic, pragmatic, utilitarian, and scientific foundations had already been laid since the Enlightenment and the French Revolution. Like the French symbolists after them, their

411

only recourse was to an ironic vision which insisted that reality is not confined to the here and now but embraces the past or is located in a Platonic ideal realm. The connections between Romanticism and subsequent eras have been influentially examined by M. H. Abrams, Frank Kermode, and others; as Marshall Brown notes, crucial elements of both elitist modernism and populist postmodernism can be traced back to Romantic criticism;[1] the rhetorical, textual, and skeptical dimensions of Romanticism have been explored extensively by critics such as Paul de Man, J. Hillis Miller, Harold Bloom, and Stanley Cavell. Feminist approaches to Romanticism – advanced by scholars such as Margaret Homans, Susan Levin, Anne Mellor, and Mary Jacobus – have attempted to rescue neglected female authors, examined the ways in which some of the Romantics exploited women, questioned the Romantic masculine obsession with self, and challenged what they have seen as the essentialist doctrines of Romanticism.

Romanticism in Germany

During the 1760s and 1770s, Germany witnessed the rise of the *Sturm und Drang* ("Storm and Stress") movement in which writers and critics such as Johann Gottfried von Herder (1744–1803), Goethe, and Schiller experimented with new subjective modes of expression and of the linguistic bases and cultural functions of art. This movement was followed by various expressions of classicism, after which Romantic writers renewed the impetus of experimentation and exploration. The major figures of Romanticism included Schiller and Heinrich Heine (1797–1856), who were both critics of conservatism and staunch advocates of freedom. The greatest poet of this period was Friedrich Hölderlin (1770–1843), whose view of history was mythical. The poetry and prose of Friedrich Novalis (1772–1801) explored the preconscious depths of human nature and looked back to the Middle Ages as an ideal. Another towering figure, Johann Wolfgang von Goethe (1749–1832) was in some respects an advocate of classicism; yet some of his major works, such as *Faust* and *The Sorrows of Young Werther*, express human subjectivity, creativity, passion, and the thirst for boundless experience with a Romantic intensity. The drama of Ludwig Tieck (1773–1853) expressed a Romantic ironic vision. Many poets looked back to primitive and fantastic forms of literature such as folktale and romance.

It was in Germany that Romantic philosophy and literary criticism achieved their foundation, in the work of Kant and Friedrich von Schlegel. Kant (as seen in chapter 14) had urged that aesthetic judgments belong to a category independent of moral judgments and judgments that express knowledge or information. This vision of aesthetic autonomy was enduringly influential through Romantic writers and beyond. What was even more profoundly influential was Kant's metaphysics, where he had argued that the mind actively and necessarily contributes to the construction of the world. This emphasis on the vital role of subjectivity in constructing the world of objects profoundly influenced the subsequent history of nearly all Western thought, not merely that of the Romantics. Kant held that the world that we know, as formed by our subjective apparatus – our senses and the various categories of our faculty of understanding – is the world of phenomena, the world as it appears to us. What the world might be *in itself* we do not know. The Romantics, like Hegel and many commentators on Kant, took this unknowable world to be the world of noumena (against the grain of Kant's own definition). Perhaps the first poet deeply influenced by Kant was Schiller, who develops Kant's view of the mediating role of the aesthetic, as reconciling sensation and reason, and who in fact views the aesthetic per se as a mode of freedom. The philosopher Johann Gottlieb Fichte (1762–1814) saw Kant's distinction of phenomena and noumena as harboring an irreconcilable chasm between appearance and reality, as well as between self and world; to overcome this, Fichte posited the ego or self as the primary reality, the thing in itself, and held that the external world was posited by this: in other words, the world is ultimately absorbed into the ego, of which it is an appearance or projection. This notion profoundly influenced the Romantics. The main philosopher of Romanticism, however, was Friedrich Schelling (1775–1854), who argued in his *System of Transcendental Idealism* (1800) that consciousness essentially knows only itself, and its knowledge of the external world is a mediated form of self-consciousness. The systems of both Fichte and Schelling effectively merge the realms of subject and object, self and nature. Unlike Hegel, who was in the most profound sense a rationalist and saw human history as the progressive unfurling of the operations of reason in both the world and the human mind, Schelling held that the mind achieves its highest self-consciousness in art, in a process of intuition. Schelling's influence extended to Coleridge and the other English Romantics. Hegel's philosophy offered a historicized account of the construction of the world by human categories, as well as a historical account of the progress of art through various forms, symbolic, classical, and romantic. Hegel was engaged in the constant interaction between philosophers, writers, and critics; though he was influenced to some extent by Goethe, Schelling, and Solger, in general he responded negatively to the ideas of the Romantics. Nonetheless, his own philosophical system shares some fundamental affinities with Romanticism, such as the view that subjectivity and objectivity are mutually dependent processes. Hegel's account of these processes took non-Romantic directions. But his impact extended to many literary figures, beginning with the literary history written by Gervinus. Hegel's friend Hölderlin also emphasized the historical dimensions of aesthetic experience.

It is clear, then, that one lineage of Romantic thought went back to Kant, pursuing the nature of subjectivity, examining aesthetics and the notion of the imagination. Another, overlapping, strand, can be traced to Friedrich von Schlegel, who first articulated the concept of Romantic irony. Though Schlegel was originally classicist in orientation, his disposition to Romanticism was transformed through his exposure to the ideas of Schiller and Fichte. Schlegel saw irony as the distinctive disposition of poetry. Schlegel's insights were collected into a series of "philosophical fragments." In one of these, his most influential definition of irony occurs as a recasting of Socratic irony: "In this sort of irony, everything should be playful and serious, guilelessly open and deeply hidden. It originates in the union of *savoir vivre* and scientific spirit, in the conjunction of a perfectly instinctive and a perfectly conscious philosophy. It contains and arouses a feeling of indissoluble antagonism between the absolute and the relative, between the impossibility and the necessity of complete communication."[2] Hence, irony harbors a movement between shifting perspectives of the world, relative and absolute, instinctive and rational, held together not by some higher order of harmony but by an acknowledgment of contradiction and paradox. Elsewhere, Schlegel in fact states that "Irony is the form of paradox. Paradox is everything simultaneously good and great" (Critical Fragment 48, in Schlegel, 6). In his essay of 1800 entitled "On Incomprehensibility," after citing several kinds of irony Schlegel speaks of the "irony of irony," which pervades discourse at such a profound level that "one can't disentangle oneself from irony anymore." Schlegel's general point is that the communication of ideas can never occur unequivocally and completely, there being no sharp line between comprehension and incomprehension. Anticipating much modern literary and cultural theory, he points out that "all incomprehension is relative" and that "words often understand themselves better than do those who use them." The greatest truths, he avers, are "completely trivial and hence nothing is more important than to express them forever in a new way and, where possible, forever more paradoxically, so that we won't forget they still exist and that they can never be expressed in their entirety." Far from regarding incomprehensibility as an "evil" in the manner of Enlightenment rationalist philosophers, Schlegel points out that the incomprehensible is an integral element of understanding, of acknowledging that the world cannot be entirely subjected to the rule of "blasphemous rationality," and that our systems of knowledge are based on principles that we cannot fully fathom.[3] In this sense, acknowledgment of incomprehensibility is itself integral to the notion of irony.

This notion of depth not entirely accessible to discursive reason forms the core of Schlegel's definition of Romantic poetry:

> Romantic poetry is a progressive, universal poetry . . . It tries to mix and fuse poetry and prose, inspiration and criticism . . . Other kinds of poetry are finished and are now capable of being fully analyzed. The romantic kind of poetry is still in the state of becoming; that, in fact, is its real essence . . . It can be exhausted by no theory . . . It alone is infinite, just as it alone is free; and it recognizes as its first commandment that the will of the poet can tolerate no law above itself. The romantic kind of poetry is . . . poetry itself. (*Athenaeum* Fragment 116, in Schlegel, 31–32)

Here is the archetypal statement of many of the principles of Romanticism: a reaction against the classical distinction of genres, and of poetry and prose. More importantly, poetry is viewed as supra-rational, involving a creative power that will not bow to the restrictive faculty of reason. At the heart of this Romantic creativity is an assertion that poetry subserves no other discipline, that it is free and autonomous. Schlegel's ideas were disseminated by his brother August Wilhelm von Schlegel (1767–1845), who helped found the *Athenaeum* journal. Schlegel influenced the notions of irony formulated by other writers and thinkers such as Karl Solger (1780–1819), Søren Kierkegaard (1813–1855), and Ludwig Tieck.

Schlegel's notion of irony as informing even philosophy and literary criticism is reenacted in the hermeneutic theory of Friedrich Schleiermacher. Like Schlegel, Schleiermacher sees the process of interpretation as an endless and infinite task that must always be partial, and always in need of increasing refinement. As Marshall Brown succinctly puts it, an important new strand of Romantic criticism "turns its attention to hermeneutics and interpretation: how do readers grasp what authors are saying?" (*CHLC*, V.V, 1). The work of Schiller and Schleiermacher can now be discussed in more detail.

Friedrich von Schiller (1759–1805)

Schiller was a poet, dramatist, and literary theorist whose development of Kant's aesthetic ideas had a great influence on other German Romantic writers and on Coleridge. He was a Romantic in many senses: writing in the aftermath of the most violent phase of the French Revolution (known as the Reign of Terror, 1793–1794), he saw art and letters as the solution to the malaise of a world corrupted by the principles of mechanism and utility; he was an advocate for freedom, staunchly opposed to authoritarianism of any kind; and he propounded a view of history as essentially divided between an ideal, harmonious past and a disintegrated present. His two most well-known pieces in the realm of literary theory are *On the Aesthetic Education of Man* (1795) and *On Naive and Sentimental Poetry* (1795–1796). *On the Aesthetic Education of Man* consists of a series of letters addressed by Schiller to his patron, the duke of Augustenburg. In the second letter, he answers a possible objection to his focusing on aesthetic matters at a time, in the wake of the French Revolution, when Europe is faced with a challenge to create the "most perfect" of all the arts of man, political freedom.[4] This question, Schiller suggests, has hitherto been decided by the "blind right of might" but is now being brought before "the tribunal of Pure Reason" (225).

In response to such an objection, Schiller urges that his own epoch is not conducive to art: it is mired beneath the "tyrannical yoke" of material needs: "*Utility* is the great idol of the time, for which all powers slave and all talents should pay homage" (225). In these circumstances, the kind of art Schiller advocates is an art that "must leave reality and elevate itself . . . above want." It is an art which "vanishes from the noisy mart of the century." What is needed, says Schiller, is to place "Beauty before Freedom": the political problem must be approached "through the aesthetical, because it is beauty, through which one proceeds to freedom" (226).

It is in the sixth letter that Schiller draws an idealistic, but nonetheless astute, contrast between the ancient Greek world and modern civilization. The Greeks, he says, combined both imagination and reason "in a glorious humanity." In their world, the powers of the mind, sense and intellect, worked in harmony, and they had not yet engaged in hostile partition and mutual separation of their frontiers (232). In the modern world, however, these aspects remain fragmented, with not only individuals but also entire classes developing only one part of their potential while the rest remains stunted. Greek society, says Schiller, received its form from "all-uniting Nature," whereas modern culture is based on "all-dividing understanding" (232). Schiller blames this divisiveness and fragmentation on the process of civilization itself. As knowledge increased, and modes of thought became more precise, sharp divisions between the various sciences ensued; moreover, anticipating Marx's comments on the division of labor, Schiller explains that the increasingly complex machinery of state necessitated a sharper separation of ranks and occupations. All of these developments shattered the "inner bond of human nature" and a "destructive struggle divided her harmonious powers" (233). In the Greek world there was a harmony between individual and state, an organic wholeness; the modern state, in contrast, is a mechanical assemblage of "lifeless parts." Schiller portrays poignantly the various dualisms which underlie modern social configurations: "the state and church, the laws and the customs, were

415

now torn asunder; enjoyment was separated from work, the means from the end, the effort from the reward. Eternally chained to only a single fragment of the Whole, man only develops himself as a fragment." And even this fragmentary participation in the state is dictated in a manner that inhibits freedom of thought. In this manner the "concrete life" of the individual is destroyed so that "the abstract of the Whole may devour his scanty existence, and eternally the state remains foreign to its citizens" (234). Anticipating the ideas of both Hegel and Marx on alienation, Schiller suggests here that human individuality is reduced to an abstract notion which takes no account of its actual range and potential.

Schiller admits that civilization could have taken no other course. The spirit of abstract speculation was bound to become a stranger to sensual world; the intellect was compelled to free itself from feeling and intuition in an attempt to arrive at exact understanding (235). And the practical spirit inevitably became imprisoned within the dull sphere of material objects, judging all experience on the basis of its own narrow experience. The former stood too high to view the particular, the latter too low to see the whole (235). The damage thereby done extended beyond knowledge and production into the realm of feeling and imagination, whose range and richness were impoverished (236). Schiller concedes that this hostility of faculties and functions is the instrument of civilization: both thought and sense were obliged to usurp each other's domains in order to develop to their fullest potential. Hence, while this one-sidedness might lead the individual astray, it leads the species as a whole to truth. Given the damage done to the unity and potential of the individual, such a movement of civilization cannot go unanswered. It must be open to us, Schiller asserts, to restore "this totality in our nature, which art hath destroyed, through a higher art" (237).

The logic behind Schiller's argument is elaborated in the ninth letter, where he claims that all improvement in the political sphere must come from the ennobling of character, and the instrument for such ennobling is fine art, which lies beyond the jurisdiction of state activities. But how can the artist rise above the "barbarous" nature and constitution of his age? Schiller answers that the "artist is indeed the son of his time." But he should not be its ward or minion (241). Schiller regards both art and science as free from the constraints imposed by human conventions; the sphere of art is beyond the reach and damage of political constitutions or legislation. The artist must retreat from his own times and allow his sensibility to mature under the light of a "Grecian sky." He can then return to his own age "in order to purify it." He will necessarily take his theme from the degraded present; but he will borrow his form from a "nobler time," or rather, "from beyond all time, from the absolute immutable unity of his essence" (241). By way of example, Schiller says that Romans of the first century were obliged to kneel before their emperor; but statues still portrayed people erect, recalling the time of the republic when such ingratiation and obedience to absolute rule was not enjoined. In this way, where humanity has lost its dignity, "art hath saved it and preserved it in meaningful stone; the truth lives on in illusion, and from the copy the original will be restored" (241). In this way, art prepares what lies ahead.

So Schiller admonishes the artist to disdain the opinion of his age, by directing his gaze upward, away from the needs of ordinary life to his true calling and the "universal Law." He must "abandon to the understanding . . . the sphere of the actual; let him strive however, to produce the ideal from the bond of the possible with the necessary.

Let him stamp this on illusion and truth" (241). Such a recourse, for Schiller, is far more effective than yielding to the temptation of addressing the ills of the current age by immediate action. The pure moral instinct, he says, "is directed at the unconditioned" (242). The artist must impart to the world a direction toward the "necessary and eternal." However, the changes which the artist seeks to bring about are not merely in the external world but "in man's inner being." He must project the form of beauty out of himself in a manner that appeals not only to thought but also to the senses, for this will be more attractive to the world. It is the leisure hours of people, not their overt principles or practice, that the artist must take as his province. For if he can banish caprice and frivolity and coarseness from their pleasures, he will imperceptibly banish these from their actions and inclinations. He must surround them with "Noble, with great, with ingenious forms, enclose them all around with symbols of excellence, until appearance overcomes reality and art, nature" (243).

Schiller's text is a seminal point of many important Romantic doctrines. Foremost in significance is his urging of the artist to turn away from reality, to seek inspiration from an ideal world or from a bygone golden age, and to recreate the world in the artistic image of such ideality. Such a process lies at the core of Romantic irony, which will be expressed by Schlegel and numerous other Romantics. The withdrawal from the world into subjectivity and the creation of ideal forms was one of the functions attributed by many Romantics to the imagination, and this avenue of thought was continued by the French symbolist poets of the later nineteenth century. Also characteristic of much Romantic thought is Schiller's retreat from political solutions and his effective substitution of art for religion, his delineation of the realm of art as possessing moral and spiritual functions. Notwithstanding these functions, he sees art as an autonomous domain, free from the incursions and constraints of politics and morality. The recourse to literature and art as a source of moral sensibility will be continued in writers such as Matthew Arnold and F. R. Leavis.

Friedrich Schleiermacher (1768–1834)

The German philosopher and Protestant theologian Friedrich Schleiermacher is generally credited with having laid the foundations of modern hermeneutics, or the art of systematic textual interpretation. His most important text in this regard was his *Hermeneutics and Criticism*, published posthumously in 1838, in which he formulates principles for the textual interpretation of the New Testament. These principles, though they were often contested and modified, had a profound effect on the work of both contemporaries such as Ralph Waldo Emerson and later thinkers such as Wilhelm Dilthey, Martin Heidegger, and Hans Georg Gadamer. Some of Schleiermacher's positions have been expressed by thinkers such as Lyotard, Rorty, Lacan, Derrida, and Donald Davidson. Indeed, hermeneutics is currently a controversial issue in contemporary philosophy.

Schleiermacher's work straddled both philosophy and theology, and hermeneutics plays a central role for him in both fields. Born in Prussia to a family steeped in Moravian pietism, he studied at Moravian Brethren schools; he translated many of

Plato's works into German; he contributed to the journal *Athenaeum*, founded by his friend and early Romantic Friedrich von Schlegel; he taught philosophy and theology first at the University of Halle and then at Berlin. He advocated many views which are now seen as Romantic: the freedom of the Church; the importance of the intuitive and emotional, rather than the moral, dimensions of religion, as in his books *On Religion: Speeches to Its Cultured Despisers* (1799), addressed to his Romantic colleagues, and *The Christian Faith* (1821–1822); he also supported the causes of various rights for workers and women.

Schleiermacher's *Hermeneutics and Criticism* is the first text to establish hermeneutics as a modern, systematic discipline, and many of his principles are so fundamental that they are still in use today in a wide range of fields: these principles include the central role of language in human understanding, the reciprocal relationship between individual speech acts and the structure of language as a whole, the intimate interdependence of the various elements in language, and the historicist principle of understanding the differences between our own culture and that of the text we are interpreting. Schleiermacher initially defines hermeneutics as "the art of understanding particularly the written discourse of another person correctly," and criticism as "the art of judging correctly and establishing the authenticity of texts." Both of these activities, he stresses, presuppose each other.[5] Moreover, both of them must be categorized, along with grammar, as philological disciplines (4). Schleiermacher points out that as yet, there exists no general art of hermeneutics: it has been treated as an appendix to logic or as a branch of philology (5, 21).

In attempting to define the nature of hermeneutics, Schleiermacher elaborates the connection between speech and thought. For him, language is integral to the thought process. The notes of Schleiermacher's lecture of 1832 state that "language is the manner in which thought is real. For there are no thoughts without speech . . . no one can think without words" (8). What hermeneutics attempts is to clarify the connection between these two elements, speech and understanding. Since speech is "the mediation of the communal nature of thought," the art of hermeneutics belongs together with the art of rhetoric: if rhetoric comprehends acts of speech, every act of understanding is the "inversion" of those speech acts, attempting to grasp the thought which is at the basis of speech. Moreover, both rhetoric and hermeneutics have a common connection with dialectic, the art of logical thinking, since the development of all knowledge depends on both speech and understanding (7).

In general, speech stands in a twofold relation: on the one hand, it is related to "the totality of language"; on the other hand, it bears a relation to the "whole thought" of its author or creator. All understanding, therefore, must accommodate these two components: the utterance as derived both from the language as a whole and from the mind of the thinker (8). These two components react reciprocally on each other: we can say that every speech or utterance arises from a given language; but we must also acknowledge that language comes into being only through speech. Hence Schleiermacher sees every person as both a locus "in which a given language forms itself in an individual manner" and a speaker whose discourse or speech needs to be understood as situated in the totality of the language system (8). The notes of Schleiermacher's 1832 lecture explain that the "individual is determined in his thought by the (common) language and can think only the thoughts which already have their designation in his language." Schleiermacher characterizes thinking as an "inner speaking," and concludes that "language determines the progress of the individual in thought. For language is not just a complex of single representations, but also a system of relatedness of representations . . . Every complex word is a relation." And it is because language is a system of relations that "every utterance can only be recognized as a moment of the life of the language-user in the determinedness of all the moments of their life, and this only from the totality of their environments . . . their nationality and their era" (9). In other words, to understand a given act of speech, we must take into account not only the structure of the language and how this determines individual speech, but also the unique psychological and social circumstances of a given speaker.

Hermeneutics or the understanding of speech, then, consists in just this interaction of these two elements: the "grammatical" interpretation, which attends to the place of an individual's speech within language as a whole, and the "psychological" (or what Schleiermacher calls the "technical") interpretation, which focuses on the psychological and cultural conditions of the speaker. These two aspects of interpretation are intrinsically related and complementary: an utterance must be understood both as a modification of the language in general, since "the innateness of language modifies the mind," and as "an act of the mind" of the individual speaker (11). Schleiermacher acknowledges that not all texts are equally open to a given type of exposition. For example, when a work lends itself primarily to a grammatical interpretation, this propensity is called *classical*. When a work disposes itself to a psychological interpretation, such a disposition is named *original* (13). Hence it is not necessary to use both sides of the hermeneutic procedure for all cases (14).

Laying down some general rules on the art of hermeneutics, Schleiermacher stresses that our aim is to attain an *exact* understanding of texts (20). We begin with "misunderstanding," which can be "qualitative," where we mistake the meanings of certain expressions, or take irony as meant seriously or vice versa; in "quantitative" misunderstanding, we take parts of the text out of context or err in our view of the speaker's own elaboration of the text, or fail to grasp the main thought or indeed the whole itself (22, 28). From this misunderstanding we progress to a "precise understanding" (22). In order to achieve this, we must first place ourselves "in the place of the author," by means of what Schleiermacher calls objective and subjective reconstruction of the speaker's utterance (24). In the case of a text far removed from us in time and culture, we must first employ a knowledge of language and history to understand the differences between the author's culture and our own: we must attempt to identify the text's original meaning (20).

Schleiermacher offers a "formula" for interpretation, whereby we can identify with the author's overall situation, a formula which includes: *objective historical* reconstruction, which considers how a given utterance relates to language as a whole, and how the knowledge in a text is the product of language; *objective divinatory* reconstruction, which conjectures how the utterance or discourse itself will contribute to the language's development; *subjective historical* reconstruction, which examines a discourse as a product of an individual writer's mind; and, finally, *subjective divinatory* reconstruction, which assesses how the process of composition affects the speaker. Strikingly modern in this apparently anti-intentionalist insight, Schleiermacher asserts that the task of hermeneutics is to understand the text or utterance "just as well and then better than its author." All our knowledge of him is not immediate (like his own) but mediated; and we can therefore attempt to make conscious elements of which he may have been unconscious (23). By attaining such knowledge of the language as he himself had, we will possess a more exact understanding of it than even his original readers had (24).

This emphasis on two poles of interpretation, individual elements and their broader contexts, leads Schleiermacher to expound the famous "hermeneutic circle" of interpretation or understanding: "Complete knowledge is always in this apparent circle, that each particular can only be understood via the general, of which it is part, and vice versa" (24). The point is that, since the particular is integrally part of a totality, knowledge of the general and knowledge of the particular presuppose each other. We must begin, therefore, with "provisional understanding," based on the knowledge we obtain about particulars from a general knowledge of the language. Hence, though we must contextualize any given idea, and find in a text the "leading ideas according to which the other ideas must be assessed," we must begin with the interpretation that has larger scope, the grammatical interpretation (27).

It must be remembered, however, that Schleiermacher's own purpose was to formulate a systematic method for the interpretation and criticism of the New Testament. A number of his insights are worth mentioning. Addressing the question of whether there are special and unique modes of interpretation that apply only to the New Testament, he agrees with advocates of the historical interpretation that the New Testament writers are essentially products of their time. However, this insistence should be balanced by recognizing the power of Christianity to give rise to new concepts. Moreover, we should be wary of viewing these ancient texts through modern eyes; the task of interpretation is to reconstruct "the relationship between the speaker and the original listener" (15). Schleiermacher also offers some observations on the allegorical interpretation of scripture and the exposition of myths. He affirms, like Dante and some other medieval thinkers, that allegorical interpretation should be based on truth. However, the test of the propriety of an alleged figurative meaning is whether or not this is "woven into the main sequence of thoughts." With myths, says Schleiermacher, no psychological interpretation is possible, since there is no single text and no given author (15–16).

Schleiermacher cautions against certain errors in expounding the New Testament. Firstly, its connection with the Old Testament often encouraged scholars to use the same methods of exegesis as for the former. Secondly, there was a tendency to view the Holy Spirit as the author of the New Testament. But such an author, observes Schleiermacher, "cannot be thought of as a temporally changing individual consciousness," and this view generated a disposition "to find everything" in the sacred text (16). He rejects claims that the scriptures should be treated differently than other texts: for one thing, the "whole of Christianity" is not contained in the writings of the apostles: they were directed at specific communities, each of which stressed certain characteristics of the gospel stories. These texts, therefore, must be explicated using the same methods that are applied to secular works, and assume that even if the Holy Spirit did speak through the New Testament authors, it "could only have spoken through them in the way they themselves would have spoken" (17). Hence Schleiermacher's work was modern not only in its formulating of the general principles of textual exposition but also, as part of the same program, in its effective constrainment of sacred texts within these hermeneutic boundaries.

420

In part I of his *Hermeneutics*, which is devoted to expounding the process of grammatical interpretation, Schleiermacher advances certain general principles: a given utterance must be clarified by referring to the uses of language that are common to the author and his original audience (30); the sense of particular words and passages must be determined by their linguistic context, the words and passages that surround it (44); the main thought of a text can be established by reference to other texts in the same vein by a given author (51). In applying these rules to New Testament explication, Schleiermacher states that if we cannot definitively determine the elements of a sentence from its contexts, we must proceed via an alternative route: we must obtain an overview of the whole text, attempting to distinguish between the main thought and secondary thoughts; if the meaning of a word or sentence is unclear, we can refer to a parallel passage where these expressions are used in a similar manner; we can use oppositions and analogies as hermeneutic aids (61–63). He rejects the ancient maxim that scripture should never be interpreted figuratively if it can be read on a literal level, suggesting instead that, as with every other text, the level of reading should be determined by the context (81–82).

Schleiermacher offers some interesting observations on the interpretation of poetry which, along with prose, he takes as the two "end- and limit-points" of hermeneutics. The aforementioned procedure of obtaining an overview of a text and distinguishing leading ideas and secondary thoughts is not strictly applicable to poetry. Lyric poetry presents a particular challenge to hermeneutics since it "eludes logical analysis" and proceeds via "a free movement of thoughts" linked primarily by the self-consciousness of the subject. It is difficult to distinguish here what is the main thought, the secondary thought, and what is merely means of presentation (64). Normal hermeneutical principles are based on the assumption of a "bound" train of thought, i.e., thought that is subject to rules. But in lyric poetry, "unboundedness prevails." However, though such a poem may appear as the negation of a bound train of thought, there are certain points in the poem which are bound, since "even the most free movement of thought cannot free itself" (64–65). In a lyric poem, says Schleiermacher, the linguistic elements are the same but they exist in different relationships than in prose. Because "logical opposition and subordination are lacking it is best to go straight into the detail after getting an impression of the whole" (65). In this type of explication, "the hermeneutic operation encroaches on the psychological side." In other words, if we are attempting to follow the "free" train of thought in a lyric poem, our knowledge of the individuality of the author, his psychology and circumstances, may help us to determine the linguistic value of a given expression (67).

With scientific writing, the obverse is the case, since here "everything stands in the relationship of subordination or co-ordination of the individual parts of the whole." But difficulties can arise even in the explication of scientific texts if scientific revolutions have prevailed; in such cases, one must first compare entire systems with one another before attempting to grasp differences of detail. Schleiermacher states that "the general hermeneutic difference between poetry and prose is that in the former the particular wishes to have its specific value as such, in the latter the particular has it only in the whole, in relation to the main thought" (65–66). This is an important affirmation, which anticipates various kinds of Romanticism and formalism. It stresses that in poetry, words can have a value independent of their mere semantic relation to their context and the leading ideas contained by this context. For example, a word can have value for its material qualities, its sound, its shape, and its ability to excite certain associations and emotions.

The second part of *Hermeneutics* is devoted to what Schleiermacher calls the "psychological" or "technical" aspect of interpretation.[6] He states that the task of psychological interpretation in general is to understand "every given structure of thoughts as a moment of the life of a particular person" (101). Offering certain basic principles for this task, he affirms that, as with the grammatical interpretation, the starting point of psychological interpretation is "the general overview which grasps the unity of the work and the main characteristics of the composition." The work's basic qualities are seen as flowing from his "individual nature" (90). In grammatical explication, the work's unity is seen as the manner in which the grammatical constructions of the language are composed and connected; this unity is "objective." But the author orders this object in his own individual manner, and adopts secondary ideas which also reveal his individuality. Hence Schleiermacher characterizes the author's function within the language as twofold: on the one hand, he produces something new in his use of language; on the other, he "preserves what he repeats and reproduces." Both methods, the grammatical and the psychological, are "the same, only looked at from a different side" (91). Hence there must be continuity between both perspectives, those which view the whole and parts respectively; and the grammatical perspective must not overlook the genesis of the work (91). Schleiermacher points out that there can never be a perfect interpretation; no individual explication can be exhaustive, and can always be rectified or improved (91).

Before beginning the psychological interpretation, there are a number of things we need to know: how the subject occurred to the author, how he acquired the language, earlier developments in the genre in which he wrote, the uses made of that genre, as well as "the contemporary related literature" on which the author may have drawn (92). On the whole, we need to adopt two methods. The first is the divinatory, whereby we "transform" ourselves, as it were, into the author; our ability to do this depends on our power of empathy or "receptivity for all other people," which in turn rests on our possession of certain universal human characteristics. The second is the comparative method, which places the work under a general category alongside similar works. Both of these methods refer back to each other because "divination is . . . excited by comparison with oneself" (93). It is through the main idea of the work that the author's purpose reveals itself; this purpose must be gleaned through the way the material is developed and by ascertaining the entire "sphere of its effect," which would include such factors as its audience and its intended effect on that audience (93). Schleiermacher points out elsewhere that we cannot simply rely on the author's own statement of his purpose, since many "texts indicate something which is far below the real theme in importance as their object" (101). Overall, then, the psychological task involves two aspects: "understanding of the whole basic thought of the work," and "comprehension of the individual parts of the work via the life of the author" (107). Whereas grammatical interpretation situates an author within the language, effectively viewing him as a linguistic site, the psychological perspective will view language as "the living deed of the individual, his will has produced what is individual in it" (132).

Schleiermacher distinguishes three stages of the hermeneutical task in general. The first stage is an interest in history, so as to establish the relevant facts in a case of interpretation. The second stage is "artistic interest or the interest of taste." This is more specialized and depends on knowledge of both language and the arts. The third stage is the speculative, under which Schleiermacher includes both scientific and religious interests, which "both emerge from the highest aspect of the human spirit." The former comprehends the development of humanity and its consciousness through language; this, too, is a specialized interest, but it is counterbalanced by the universal nature of the religious interest; again it is through language that humankind becomes "clear and certain" about its religious ideas (156–157).

The principles of hermeneutics as formulated by Schleiermacher include important insights into language and the construction of meaning: that language is historically determined; that any element of a text must be situated not only within the text as a totality but also in the context of the writer's work and historical situation as a whole; that the cultural and psychological constitution of the subject has an active role in the creation of meaning; that an author's work is to a large extent determined by his location within the history of language and literature, while he himself may exert a reciprocal influence on the development of both; and that our knowledge itself moves in endless circles such that we must often acknowledge its provisional and progressive nature.

Romanticism in France

One of the founders of Romanticism, its so-called father, was the French thinker Jean-Jacques Rousseau, who espoused a return to nature and equated the increasing growth and refinement of civilization with corruption, artificiality, and mechanization. Rousseau's *Social Contract* espouses democratic principles and begins with the famous sentence "Man is born free, and everywhere he is in chains." This statement was as important for Romanticism as it was for the French Revolution, and Rousseau's influence on subsequent Romantic writers was profound. Post-revolutionary France witnessed an attempt on the part of one group of writers, led by Louis de Fontanes (1757–1821), to return to the classical values of the seventeenth century. This group saw the rules of art, founded on nature, as immutable. An opposing group, basing itself more on Enlightenment ideals, included Georges Cabanis (1757–1808) and Claude Fauriel (1772–1844): this faction located beauty and artistic values generally not in the observance of universal rules but rather in the reader's response: the effect of literature on the impressions, emotions, and imagination. They also rejected strict neoclassical definitions of genres. The more modern and Romantic currents eventually triumphed, as in the work of Germaine de Staël and François de Chateaubriand (1768–1848). As will be seen below, de Staël, influenced by Schlegel, essentially rejected classical ideals as outdated and identified Romantic notions as progressive, working toward cultural relativism and historical specificity in her literary criticism. Influenced by de Staël and an important critic in his own right, Charles Augustin Sainte-Beuve (1804–1869) developed biographical criticism which attempted "scientifically" to contextualize the creative work of given individuals. His criticism embodies an amalgam of Romantic notions such as a belief in genius with neoclassical principles of order and decorum. Chateaubriand, effectively opposed to Enlightenment principles, promoted a Catholic revival, but exalted the life of the lowly strata of society; George Sand (1804–1876) also made heroes and heroines of peasants and rustics in her novels; and Victor Hugo (1802–1885) demonstrated his relentless opposition to social injustice and oppression in his *Les Misérables*. Hugo insisted as against the conservatives such as Désiré Nisard (1806–1883) and Gustave Planche (1808–1857) that art and poetry must be autonomous and free, not restricted by classical constraints.

However, the ideals of classicism and Romanticism often coexisted uneasily in the work of many of these writers, where the form and content might collide. A case in point is Théophile Gautier's carefully sculptured poems: though ostensibly returning to a hard-edged classicism, they effectively participate in and perpetuate a Romantic ethic, and also prefigure French symbolism. This "hard" stanzaic poetry recoiled just as much from contemporary experience as any of the forms which preceded or followed from it: its idealizations merely assumed a more formal expression. In Gautier's work lay the founding rationale of the Parnassians, who continued fundamental Romantic aspirations while excluding personal feelings and freer verse forms. Their aesthetics were underlain by a Romantic insistence on artistic autonomy: in the preface to his *Mademoiselle de Maupin* (1835), Gautier offered his theory of "art for art's sake," deriding any utilitarian conception of art.[7] His attack on the bourgeois concept of utility is even more derisive than that in Shelley's *Defence of Poetry* (1821).[8]

George Plekhanov's *Art and Social Life* (1912) argues that artists tend to proclaim artistic autonomy when they find themselves in *hopeless* disaccord with their social environment. He observes that the scorn which Gautier poured on bourgeois life was directed against its "boredom and vulgarity," not its economic and social order.[9] Once the bourgeoisie had gained hegemony, no longer fired by revolutionary struggle, the new Parnassian art, says Plekhanov, could merely indulge in "the idealization of the opposition to the bourgeois manner of life. Romanticism became such an idealization."[10] Equally, Gautier's impersonality and formal stringency subserve – as with T. S. Eliot's early so-called classical poetic endeavors – not a classical realism but an extreme subjectivism and insularity from the vulgar everyday manifestations of bourgeois reality, as recorded in Gautier's own notorious preface.

Germaine de Staël (1766–1817)

Mme. de Staël's life and writings intersect profoundly with a number of political, intellectual, and literary movements. To begin with, she was one of the heirs of Enlightenment thought; her friends and acquaintances included the Encyclopedists Denis Diderot and Jean d'Alembert. From her mother, influenced by Rousseau's views of education, she inherited an independence and a passion for freedom. Her family was also intimately connected with the incipient events of the French Revolution: her father was finance minister to King Louis XVI of France and extremely popular with the people; his dismissal was part of the series of events that triggered the onset of the

Revolution. Yet she also had affiliations with Romanticism, moving in a circle that included writers such as Goethe and Lord Byron.

Given her extraordinary abilities and lifestyle, it is not surprising that Mme. de Staël was embroiled in various controversies, political, personal, and literary. She had numerous lovers, gave birth to four children outside of wedlock, and hosted a salon frequented by many of the leading literary figures of her day. Her writings offended Napoleon, who exiled her from Paris. Politically, she espoused a constitutional monarchy; in letters she advanced the cause of Romanticism while anticipating later developments in realism; she was a staunch believer in freedom and the notion of historical progress. She published two novels, *Delphine* (1802) and *Corinne, or Italy* (1807); her important contributions to literary criticism are contained in her "Essay on Fiction" (1795) and her longer work, *On Literature Considered in its Relationship to Social Institutions* (1800).

In the introduction to her "Essay on Fiction," de Staël states that man has only two distinct faculties, reason and imagination. And it is the imagination which is the most valuable of the two. The province of reason is limited and cannot alone satisfy the human mind or heart because metaphysical precision cannot be applied to man's emotions. Human beings need distraction and pleasure. Yet fictions, whose province is the imagination, have a more important function than providing merely pleasure; they can influence greatly our moral ideas and they may be the "most powerful means of guidance or enlightenment."[11]

De Staël divides fictions into three types: marvelous or allegorical; historical; and fictions, consisting of "events at once entirely invented and imitated, in which nothing is true but everything is believable" ("EF," 203). She is concerned to show that it is this last type, the realistic fiction, that takes "life as it is," which is the most useful. These realist or "natural fictions," as de Staël calls them, must present their material such that everything looks true to life. She does not include tragedies among these since they usually present an extraordinary situation, and their morality applies to few people. Nor does she include comedy because theatrical conventions allow only for broadly defined situations, with little room for commentary. And life itself, she says, is not concentrated in such a way. Only the modern novel, she says, can achieve the persistent and accurate usefulness we can get from the portrayal of our ordinary, habitual feelings. A novel need not be focused on one principal idea, since the author is bound to follow the rules of probability, which may not allow such focus. Of all creations of the human mind, the novel is one of the most influential on individual morality, which ultimately determines public morality ("EF," 204–205).

The novel has a bad reputation, according to de Staël, because it is considered to be devoted exclusively to portraying love. And yet love is something we experience largely during our youth. The novel needs to broaden its scope, then, to include the various passions and interests which preoccupy the later stages of life ("EF," 205). She also answers the objection here that one might simply go to history for an accurate record of men's various passions. History, she says, does not usually touch the lives of private people; the lessons of history are public; they apply to nations, not individuals. Hence the "moral" offered by history is often unclear, and history leaves lacunae as far as private happiness and misery are concerned. Moreover, reality itself often fails to make an impact whereas novels can depict characters and feelings with such force and

425

vivacity that they will make a moral impression. And the morality expressed in novels relates not so much to the events they relate as to the development of the "inner emotions of the heart" ("EF," 206).

Another objection against novels is that they falsify reality. De Staël retorts that, while this may be true of poor novels, good novels provide an "intimate understanding of the human heart," employing great detail rather than generalities ("EF," 206–207). She offers a somewhat refined notion of verisimilitude. Even if people could give an accurate and truthful account of their lives, it "would be necessary to add to the truth a kind of dramatic effect." Nature sometimes presents things all on the same level; and if we were to imitate her in a slavish manner, we would actually be distorting nature. A scrupulously detailed account of an ordinary event "diminishes its credibility rather than adding to it." Our representation itself must possess harmony, and the only truth fiction has is "the impression it produces" ("EF," 207).

Nor can moral philosophy somehow replace this function of novels. A simple statement of moral duty will not make an impression. Virtue must be "animated." Novels make moral truths tangible by "putting them into action." And the more power the novel has for moving people, the more important it becomes to "extend its influence to the emotions of people of all ages and to the obligations of all classes" ("EF," 208). Indeed, the novel would thereby aid in avoiding negative passions because it would allow those passions to be recognized and analyzed. While the impression the novel makes might resemble the impression we derive from real facts we have witnessed, the fictional impression has more unity and is less distracting, because it is always "directed toward the same end." Reality, in contrast, is often a "disconnected picture of events," from which we could draw no clear moral lesson. The novel might foster the ability to be moved by examples of vice and virtue ("EF," 208–209).

In *On Literature Considered in its Relationship to Social Institutions* de Staël examines the various social obstacles to the success of women writers. She points out that the existence of women is still "uncertain" in many ways; they belong "neither to the natural nor to the social order."[12] Women are likely to be forgiven for negligence in their domestic virtues or for mental mediocrity; they will be forgiven even for sacrificing their household occupations for the sake of society and its pleasures (*GS*, 202); they will not be forgiven by the public for displaying unusual talent. De Staël places her analysis of women's literary possibilities in historical context, discussing both monarchies and republics. In a monarchy, she explains, "the sense of right and proper is so acute that any unusual act or impulse to change one's situation looks ridiculous right away" (*GS*, 201–202). Moreover, in the French monarchy there still lingered a "spirit of chivalry" which frowned upon the excessive cultivation of letters even among men; it disdained such pursuits all the more among women, since such interests distracted them from "their primary concern, the sentiments of the heart" (*GS*, 202). One would not expect to find such disadvantages in republics, especially in republics that allegedly encouraged the process of enlightenment. However, she notes that since the Revolution, "men have deemed it politically and morally useful to reduce women to a state of the most absurd mediocrity" (*GS*, 203).

De Staël urges that women must be enlightened and taught together with men; this is necessary, she warns, in order to establish any "permanent social or political relationships." The development of reason in women will promote "both enlightenment and the happiness of society in general" (*GS*, 205). Without such education, women would not be able to direct their children's education, they would not be able to allay men's "furious passions," they would not be able to contribute to society life and, above all, they "would no longer have any useful influence over opinion" (*GS*, 204). She makes the important point that women "are the only human beings outside the realm of political interest and the career of ambition, able to pour scorn on base actions, point out ingratitude, and honor even disgrace if that disgrace is caused by noble sentiments" (*GS*, 204). She here sees women as occupying not only a position of externality to the public sphere, but also one of disinterestedness, whereby they can act as a voice of conscience in this sphere since they have no direct interests vested in it. The public's prejudice against female talent and genius, she explains, is based on the safeguards of routine and mediocrity. A woman provides the most vulnerable target because she is unable to defend herself and no one comes to her aid, not even other women (*GS*, 206–207).

Notes

1 "Introduction," in *CHLC*, V.V, 3.
2 "Critical Fragments," 108, in Friedrich von Schlegel, *Philosophical Fragments*, trans. Peter Firchow (Minneapolis and Oxford: University of Minnesota Press, 1991), p. 13. Hereafter cited as Schlegel.
3 Friedrich von Schlegel, "On Incomprehensibility," in *German Aesthetic and Literary Criticism: The Romantic Ironists and Goethe*, ed. Kathleen M. Wheeler (Cambridge and New York: Cambridge University Press, 1984), pp. 33–38.
4 "On the Aesthetic Education of Man," in *Friedrich Schiller: Poet of Freedom*, trans. William F. Wertz, Jr. (New York: New Benjamin Franklin House, 1985), p. 224. Hereafter page citations are given in the text.
5 Friedrich Schleiermacher, *Hermeneutics and Criticism and Other Writings*, trans. and ed. Andrew Bowie (Cambridge: Cambridge University Press, 1998), p. 3. Notes from various lectures of Schleiermacher are integrated into this text. Hereafter page citations are given in the text.
6 As the editors of the text used here point out, Schleiermacher actually divides the "psychological" aspect into the *purely psychological* and the *technical* (*Hermeneutics and Criticism*, p. 90n.).
7 Théophile Gautier, "Preface," in *Mademoiselle de Maupin* (1835; rpt. Paris: Garnier, 1955), pp. 2–3, 11, 22–24.
8 "A Defence of Poetry," in *The Complete Works of Percy Bysshe Shelley, Volume VII*, ed. Roger Ingpen and Walter E. Peck (London and New York: Ernest Benn/Gordian Press, 1965), pp. 132–133.
9 George V. Plekhanov, *Art and Social Life* (New York: Oriole Editions, 1974), p. 17.
10 Ibid., p. 18.
11 Germaine de Staël, "Essay on Fiction," in *Madame de Staël on Politics, Literature and National Character*, trans. Morroe Berger (London: Sidgwick and Jackson, 1964), p. 203. Hereafter cited as "EF."
12 Germaine de Staël, *On Literature Considered in its Relationship to Social Institutions*, in *An Extraordinary Woman: Selected Writings of Germaine de Staël*, trans. Vivian Folkenflik (New York: Columbia University Press, 1987), p. 201. Hereafter cited as GS.

CHAPTER 17

ROMANTICISM (II): ENGLAND AND AMERICA

Romanticism in England

In England, the ground for Romanticism was prepared in the latter half of the eighteenth century through the economic, political, and cultural transformations mentioned in the preceding chapters. The system of absolute government crumbled even earlier in Britain than elsewhere; nationalistic sentiment sharpened, imperialistic endeavors widened, and the century saw an increasing growth of periodical literature which catered to the middle classes. The ideals of neoclassicism, such as decorum, order, normality of experience, and moderation, were increasingly displaced by an emphasis on individual experience. The moral function of literature was increasingly counterbalanced by an emphasis on aesthetic pleasure and the psychology of the reader's response to beauty and sublimity. An emphasis on originality and genius supplanted the primacy of imitation of classical authors or nature. Thinkers such as Locke, Hume, and Burke had been instrumental in these shifts of taste and philosophical orientation. Critics such as Edward Young, William Duff, and Joseph Warton produced influential treatises: Young's *Conjectures on Original Composition* (1759) and Duff's *An Essay on Original Genius* (1767) stressed the claims of originality, genius, and the creative imagination. Poets and critics of this period, such as Richard Hurd, idealized the Middle Ages and expressed an admiration for primitive societies and a native literary tradition, in which the figures of Chaucer, Spenser, and Shakespeare were accorded prominence. The artist Sir Joshua Reynolds praised the genius and sublimity of the Renaissance painter Michelangelo.

The early British practitioners of Romanticism included Thomas Gray, Oliver Goldsmith, and Robert Burns. The English movement reached its most mature expression in the work of William Wordsworth, who saw nature as embodying a universal spirit, and Samuel Taylor Coleridge who, drawing on the work of Kant, Fichte, and Schelling, gave archetypal formulation to the powers of the poetic imagination. Like their European counterparts, the English Romantics reacted at first favorably to the French Revolution and saw their own cultural and literary program as revolutionary. As many critics, ranging from Lukács to Abrams and Raymond Williams, have noted, the Romantics saw themselves as inheriting a world disfigured by the squalor of bourgeois economic and political practice, a world fragmented by dualisms such as individual and society, past and present, sensation and intellect, reason and emotion; their task was to seek once again a unifying vision, usually through the aesthetic and cultural realms.

The first major figure of English Romanticism, William Blake (1757–1827), had recourse to mysticism and a mythical vision of history; he saw the world as inherently harboring opposites and contradictions, which it was the poet's task to harmonize. His own idiosyncratic religious views were presented in poems such as *The Marriage of Heaven and Hell* (1793). In other poems, he expressed powerfully a vision of the new urban world as plagued by social injustice, and he railed against what he saw as the oppressive rationality embodied by figures such as Voltaire and Rousseau. In his *Pursuits of Literature* (1794–1798) the writer T. J. Mathias accorded to literature an explicitly ideological function. Other writers such as the liberal William Hazlitt attempted to separate the political and aesthetic realms, though he saw the literature of the new era as no longer subservient to the forces of absolutism. The literary-critical insights of Wordsworth and Coleridge, concerning the nature of poetry, language, and the imagination, in the context of their ideological orientations, will be discussed below. The other English Romantics included Dorothy Wordsworth (1771–1855), who authored letters, poems, and a series of journals, and who had a considerable influence on her brother and Coleridge; John Keats (1795–1821), Percy Bysshe Shelley (1792–1822), Mary Shelley (1797–1851), author of *Frankenstein* (1818), and George Gordon Lord Byron (1788–1824).

Shelley's *Defence of Poetry* is a powerful and beautifully expressed manifesto of fundamental Romantic principles, detailing the supremacy of imagination over reason, and the exalted status of poetry. Keats' brief literary-critical insights are centered around the notion of "negative capability." In a letter to Benjamin Bailey, Keats suggests that, in poetic creation, the poet acts as a catalyst for the reaction of other elements, stating that "Men of Genius are great as certain ethereal Chemicals operating on the Mass of neutral intellect . . . they have not any individuality, any determined Character."[1] Writing to Richard Woodhouse, Keats distances himself from "the wordsworthian or egotistical sublime": "the poetical Character . . . has no self – it is every thing and nothing – It has no character . . . A Poet . . . has no Identity – he is continually in for – and filling some other Body" (*Letters*, 386–387). The idea behind this "annihilation" of character is that the poet's mentality infuses, and is infused by, everything. Deploying what Keats calls the "negative capability" of abstaining from particular positions or dogmas, it loses itself wholly among the objects and events of the external world which are its poetic material (*Letters*, 184, 386–387). The ego, then, should not interpose itself between the poet and his "direct" sensations. Keats' apparent identification of beauty with truth in his "Ode on a Grecian Urn" has received much critical attention. Though the Romantics are often viewed as writing confessional poetry and expressing personality, it is significant that both Keats and Shelley rejected this notion. Like Shelley, Byron rebelled against conventional beliefs, and in his poems such as *Don Juan* engaged in pungent satire of the hypocrisy and corruption of those in power. His stormy and eccentric life ended in the struggle for Greek independence. Many of these issues can now be examined in detail in the literary theories of Wordsworth and Coleridge.

William Wordsworth (1770–1850)

It was Wordsworth who wrote the following famous lines about the French Revolution as it first appeared to many of its sympathizers:

> Bliss was it in that dawn to be alive,
> But to be young was very Heaven! O times,
> In which the meagre, stale, forbidding ways
> Of custom, law, and statute, took at once
> The attraction of a country in romance!
> When Reason seemed the most to assert her rights . . .
> *Prelude*, XI, 108–113

These lines, first published in 1809, embodied the initial promise of the Revolution, and the hopes of reform it inspired in many hearts: the old world, resting on the tottering foundations of feudalism, a world based on authority, caprice, hierarchy, and inheritance, was about to give way before a gleaming new era based on reason, equality, and freedom. It is no accident that many Romantic theories of literature were forged in the heat of such revolutionary enthusiasm. But, as Wordsworth's own modified reactions reveal, Romantic literary theory has an oblique and complex, often contradictory, connection with the ideals behind – and the reality of – the Revolution. The foregoing lines were eventually incorporated into Wordsworth's long autobiographical poem, the *Prelude*, completed in 1805 but not published until just after his death. Three books of this poem are concerned with revolutionary events in France; and these books effectively contextualize the somewhat idealistic impulse of his own early revolutionary fervor and republican sympathies.

Wordsworth describes in the *Prelude* how he forsook the "crowded solitude" of London society, resolving to go to France. There, he saw "the Revolutionary Power / Toss like a ship at anchor, rocked by storms," and witnessed how the "silent zephyrs sported with the dust / Of the Bastille" (IX, 50–51, 66–67). He describes the time as "an hour / Of universal ferment," and himself as a "patriot" whose heart was given over to the French people (IX, 123–124, 161–162). What is interesting here is that, on account of his upbringing, whereby he learned to disdain the feudal values of "wealth and titles," in favor of republican ideals such as "talents, worth, and prosperous industry," Wordsworth hailed the first part of the Revolution as simply an expression of "nature's certain course" (IX, 215–247). Wordsworth's devotion to nature was life-long; from first to last, he viewed himself as a follower of nature. What is striking, at this point of his autobiographical masterpiece, is the *equation* of nature – a concept fundamental to the work of nearly all Romantic poets – with certain political events, events directed, at least in theory, toward a "government of equal rights" and a republic where, as Wordsworth states, "all stood thus far / Upon equal ground," and where "we were brothers all / In honour, as in one community" (IX, 226–228). Nature is regarded by Wordsworth as a fundamental unity, and here a human community resting on equality is held to be an integral part of that unity. At this stage, Wordsworth regarded the entire feudal fabric, resting on the power of royal courts and "voluptuous life," as removed from "the natural inlets of just sentiment, / From lowly sympathy and chastening truth" (IX, 350–351). He expressed a desire to see:

> ... the earth
> Unthwarted in her wish to recompense
> The meek, the lowly, the patient child of toil, ...
> And finally, as sum and crown of all,
> Should see the people having a strong hand
> In framing their own laws; whence better days
> To all mankind.
>
> (IX, 522–532)

Wordsworth even names the violent outbursts against prevailing power as "Nature's rebellion against monstrous law" (IX, 571). He states also that "nothing hath a natural right to last / But equity and reason" (IX, 205–206). In book X, however, Wordsworth begins to describe the conflict he felt, as an Englishman who thought of himself as a "patriot of the world," when England declared war against France on February 11, 1793; he actually rejoiced to hear of English setbacks in the war (X, 285–290). His inner conflicts intensified as he learned of the "domestic carnage" in France, and were palliated briefly when the death of Robespierre seemed to presage the end of the "reign of terror" (September 1793–July 1794) and to renew the promise of future "golden times" (X, 573–578). In book XI, Wordsworth once again equates this seemingly positive turn of events with nature: "To Nature, then, / Power had reverted" (XI, 31–32). It is in this section that he recalls his youthful confidence in the outcome of the Revolution: "Bliss was it in that dawn to be alive" (XI, 108).

Wordsworth described himself at this stage as an "active partisan" (XI, 153). Retrospecting, however, he believes he had lent too careless an ear to "wild theories" that were not borne out by actual events. The French became "oppressors in their turn," changing "a war of self-defence / For one of conquest, losing sight of all / Which they had struggled for" (XI, 206–209). Wordsworth is referring to the French aggression against Spain, Italy, Holland, and Germany in 1794–1795. This was a time, he recalls, fed on "speculative schemes" based on the worship of abstract reason, or as Wordsworth puts it, "Reason's naked self" (XI, 224, 234). Wordsworth's own disposition was already becoming distanced from these events. He pursued:

> ... what seemed
> A more exalted nature; wished that Man
> Should start out of his earthy, worm-like state,
> And spread abroad the wings of Liberty,
> Lord of himself ...
>
> (XI, 250–254)

While Wordsworth insists that he will always retain this aspiration toward human liberty, he notes also that he fell into errors, betrayed by false reasonings that had turned him aside "From Nature's way by outward accidents" (XI, 288–291). Despairing of moral questions, and losing his faith in the authority of abstract reason alone, he describes himself as turning to the realm of "abstract science" where reason might operate undisturbed by the world of space and time, matter, and "human will and power" (XI, 328–332). Guided by nature, he returns to his "true self," his fundamental identity as a poet, open "To those sweet counsels between head and heart / Whence grew that genuine knowledge, fraught with peace." External events, of course, aided this redirection of Wordsworth's energies, the last straw for him being the coronation of Napoleon as emperor in 1804, attended by Pope Pius VII. In a passage reminiscent of Burke, Wordsworth comes to the conclusion that:

> There is
> One great society alone on earth:
> The noble living and the noble Dead.
> (XI, 393–395)

And he addresses his friend Coleridge, commending their common turning toward nature for solace and restoration, after the tumultuous events which have proved to be a "sorrowful reverse for all mankind" (XI, 404). Hence, for Wordsworth, the equation of nature with republican ideals has dissolved: his continued pursuit of nature retains these ideals – liberty, equality, reason – at most in a form abstracted from immediate political applicability. His return to nature is marked by a balancing of reason (the "head") with the counsels of the heart; by a vision of human life as extending beyond merely present concerns to encompass past and future; by an assertion of certain ideals, such as liberty, as timelessly valid.

The most elemental factor in Wordsworth's return to nature was imagination. Earlier in the *Prelude*, he had referred to imagination as an "awful Power" that reveals with a flash the "invisible world" (VI, 594–602). In the conclusion of the poem, he says that imagination is "but another name for absolute power / And clearest insight, amplitude of mind, / And Reason in her most exalted mood" (XIV, 188–193). This faculty has been his "feeding source," and it is a power which enables one to engage in "spiritual Love," whereby one can transcend the dictates of custom, the pressures of conventional opinion, and the narrowness of concerns that are confined to the present. It is also a faculty which allows communion with nature and in fact with all things (XIV, 160–188). In book XIII, he called imagination "a Power / That is the visible quality and shape / And image of right reason," a power which teaches us humility by presenting us with "a temperate show / Of objects that endure," the permanent forms of goodness in man and nature (XIII, 30–37). Interestingly, Wordsworth does not merely associate imagination with reason as two concurrent powers; rather, he identifies the two powers, imagination being the sensible image of reason. The idea here seems to be that imagination is an intermediary power that stands above both reason and sense even as it connects them. Imagination, in its capacity as "right reason," orients our sensibility to the things that are truly universal and permanent; by implication, a "wrong" use of reason, abstracted entirely from things of the sense, would either impel us to impose false schemes upon the world of sense, or to be at the mercy of the world of sense, taking this alone as reality, and understanding its own function as ordering this reality which is already given, already presented to our senses.

In contrast, imagination frees us from what Wordsworth calls this "tyranny" of sense, bringing us to the realization that we are *creative* in our interaction with nature and the world, and that the "mind is lord and master" over outward sense (XII, 127–136, 203–206, 222–223). In this passage Wordsworth makes his celebrated declaration that there are in our existence "spots of time," or moments of imaginative insight, whereby our minds are "nourished" and renovated above the "deadly weight" of trivial and present occupations. In "Lines Composed a Few Miles above Tintern Abbey," Wordsworth also recalls his progress from a merely sensual to an imaginative apprehension of nature, which allows him to see the unity of nature in itself as well as the unity of humankind with nature: he perceives in "the round ocean and the living air, / And the blue sky, and in the mind of man: / A motion and a spirit, that impels / All thinking things, all objects of all thought, / And rolls through all things" (*Tintern Abbey*, 95–102). The human mind here is no longer regarded as a passive receiver of external impressions but as active in the construction of its world.

In the *Prelude* Wordsworth opposes such insight as furnished by the imagination to conventional education, the conventional misleading "wisdom" of books, and the stunting of the passions by overcrowded life in the cities where "the human heart is sick." Such wisdom, he states, is fostered by the wealthy few in the service of their own interests (XIII, 169–212). The poet above all, having the gift of imagination, apprehends a "mighty scheme of truth," and, exercising his mind upon "the vulgar form of present things" and the appearances of the everyday world, discerns "a new world" that is founded on permanent and universal principles (XIII, 300–312, 355–370). Hence, imagination is a power that does not simply, like abstract reason, leave behind the world of sense altogether and impose its abstract ideals; rather, it has its foundation in the world of sense but transcends that world in its ability to discern what is truly enduring and universal in it; imagination is a comprehensive and unifying power, allowing the poet to connect sympathetically with all of nature and human nature; it lifts us beyond the world we see through our eyes to an invisible world that acts as an ideal. Imagination has not only an important perceptual function, showing that human perception is creative, but also a vital moral function, guiding us to the realization of truths that are beyond mere sensation and that are not located in the world as it is given. Wordsworth has effectively relocated the idealism of political revolutionary movements to a transcendent realm.

Some of Wordsworth's early republican sentiments, however, appear to inform his most important contribution to literary criticism, the celebrated and controversial *Preface* to *Lyrical Ballads*. This collection of poems was published jointly by Wordsworth and Coleridge in 1798; Wordsworth added his preface to the 1800 edition, and revised it for subsequent editions.[2] In the "Advertisement" which accompanied the first publication of the *Lyrical Ballads* in 1798, Wordsworth's primary concern is with the language of poetry. He states that the poems in this volume are "experiments," written chiefly to discover "how far the language of conversation in the middle and lower classes of society is adapted to the purposes of poetic pleasure" (*PLB*, 116). This apparently democratic sentiment underlies his central argument in this text, that the poet is a "man speaking to men"; such sentiment, however, is associated, as in Wordsworth's modified political reaction, not with reason but with a balance between emotion and thought.

Wordsworth's *Preface* is intended to justify the style, subject matter, and language of the poems included in *Lyrical Ballads*. But the underlying intention is to make some more general statements which effectively redefine what properly constitutes poetic language, as well as the nature and scope of the poet. Some of these comments have become classic statements of Romantic aesthetic doctrine, sometimes through isolation from their contexts. Wordsworth's initial claim is that his poems attempt to present "the real language of men in a state of vivid sensation" (*PLB*, 119). What Wordsworth is reacting against here, as he explains in an Appendix to the *Preface*, is the stylized and artificial modes of expression that poetry has accumulated over the centuries. The earliest poets, writes Wordsworth in this Appendix, used a language that was "daring, and figurative," inspired by powerful feelings and passions. Later poets, however, desiring to reproduce the effects of such language, adopted these figures of speech in a mechanical and automatic manner, applying them to feelings and thoughts with which they had no natural connection. Over time, the language of poetry was largely separated from that of "common life," the use of meter in poetry further deepening this chasm (*PLB*, 160–162). What Wordsworth is calling for, then, is a return to a kind of realism, a descent of poetic language from its stylized status, from its self-created world of metaphorical expression and artificial diction, to the language actually used by human beings in "common life." These expressions – "real language," "common life" – are of course highly problematic, as Coleridge will later point out.

In what is perhaps the most striking and important passage of the *Preface*, Wordsworth states that the central aim of the poems in *Lyrical Ballads* was:

> to choose incidents and situations from common life, and to relate or describe them, throughout, as far as was possible in a selection of language really used by men, and, at the same time, to throw over them a certain colouring of imagination, whereby ordinary things should be presented to the mind in an unusual aspect . . . to make these incidents and situations interesting by tracing in them . . . the primary laws of our nature: chiefly, as far as regards the manner in which we associate ideas in a state of excitement. Humble and rustic life was generally chosen, because, in that condition, the essential passions of the heart . . . are under less restraint, and speak a plainer and more emphatic language; because in that condition of life our elementary feelings co-exist in a state of greater simplicity, and, . . . in that condition the passions of men are incorporated with the beautiful and permanent forms of nature . . . Accordingly, such a language, arising out of repeated experience and regular feelings, is a more permanent, and a far more philosophical language, than that which is frequently substituted for it by Poets, who think that they are conferring honour upon themselves and their art, in proportion as they separate themselves from the sympathies of men . . . in order to furnish food for fickle tastes, and fickle appetites, of their own creation. (*PLB*, 123–125)

In many ways, this statement embodies the aesthetic impulse of Wordsworth's entire text. If it is a pivotal statement of Romantic doctrine, it is nonetheless a complex statement, fraught with difficulty and irony. Even in the central thrust of its import, the passage appears to harbor conflicting dispositions: the passage reacts fundamentally against urban, industrialized society. By implication, city life promotes vanity, artifice and confusion, and even vulgarity in our feelings. But this is the very society produced by ostensibly democratic ideals. The ideal held up in opposition to such "urbanity" is the artless simplicity of rural life: people living close to nature experience emotions in their fundamental, unadulterated state, emotions that are capable of clear expression. Such an ideal is of course not original to Wordsworth; the primitivistic theories of such eighteenth-century writers as Rousseau, William Duff, and James Beattie had already extolled the simple manners and passions of earlier peoples living in a state of nature. Hence, the "common life" that Wordsworth claims to portray is hardly the common life of modern industrial society; rather, it is the life of those on the periphery of such a social order, those whose lifestyles are the vestiges of a pre-industrial, agricultural era. So, what first appears to be a democratic sentiment on Wordsworth's part is effectively a desire to return to nature, which is now equated not with republican political ideals but with an externality to the very world in which those ideals might operate, the squalid world of political and economic conflict, the world of reason and calculation, the world of industrialism, factories, and crowded cities, the world bequeathed by Enlightenment thought and bourgeois revolution. Instead of seeking nature within that world, Wordsworth now sees the two realms not as standing outside of each other but as sharply opposed. Nature is viewed as eternal, the repository and projection of what is permanent in human nature; the city is an ephemeral product of ephemeral philosophies and ephemeral political movements.

As for the democratic impulse of Wordsworth's comments on poetic language, these are somewhat tempered by his view of imagination as well as his conception of a poet. Wordsworth's suggestion that rural people speak a more "philosophical" language may have been influenced by the theories of Hartley and Joseph Priestley, who anticipated the formation of a philosophical language among humankind, a language that would be universal and accurate in its expression of human conceptions and emotions. Wordsworth's underlying aim is that the poet return to the expression of permanent and fundamental human emotions, which are fostered by perpetual communion with nature. He regards both the human mind and nature as possessed of "inherent and indestructible qualities" which have been clouded over and corrupted by recent historical transformations:

> a multitude of causes, unknown to former times, are now acting with a combined force to blunt the discriminating powers of the mind, and, unfitting it for all voluntary exertion, to reduce it to a state of almost savage torpor. The most effective of these causes are the great national events which are daily taking place, and the increasing accumulation of men in cities, where the uniformity of their occupations produces a craving for extraordinary incident, which the rapid communication of intelligence hourly gratifies. To this tendency of life and manners the literature and theatrical exhibitions of the country have conformed themselves. (*PLB*, 129, 131)

Such a statement has perhaps even more pertinence in our world where the tendencies Wordsworth bemoans have reached an intensity beyond what he might have imagined: the mail coach and the telegraph, recent inventions in Wordsworth's memory, have been ousted by almost instantaneous means of communication and by far more powerful channels of blunting the human senses and imagination. Wordsworth is indeed lamenting the woes caused by an earlier phase of industrial capitalism, a phase brought into being by "national events" such as the French Revolution and the ensuing wars between France and other nations, as well as the struggles of the bourgeoisie to gain political hegemony. While Wordsworth has acknowledged in the past that the ideals behind these historical tendencies may have been noble, he is now addressing their actual effects: the chief of these is the artificial stimulation of people's passions, the blunting of their imaginations, and the degradation of their moral sensibilities. Wordsworth sees "nature" as harboring the remedy for all of these effects, and he sees part of the poet's task as using nature to enlarge people's original, undistorted sensibilities. Hence he calls on the poet to return to an uncorrupted idiom, an idiom that does not pander to the vulgarity of modern taste.

Yet this imperative for the poet to return to a purer language, a language that can express not only purer human emotions but also the often forgotten and blurred connection between humanity and nature, is fraught with complexity and contradiction. While Wordsworth insists that the poet is "a man speaking to men," that he should weep "natural and human tears," and that there is no essential difference between the language of poetry and that of prose (*PLB*, 135, 138), he acknowledges that the poet's composition must be informed by "true taste and feeling" such as will separate it entirely "from the vulgarity and meanness of ordinary life" (*PLB*, 137). Even in the passage cited above where he claims to take incidents from "common life," he is careful to state that the poet must "throw over them a certain colouring of imagination, whereby ordinary things should be presented to the mind in an unusual aspect." So the poet does not, after all, present ordinary things in an ordinary way: he selects ordinary things but makes them appear extraordinary, through the transforming power of imagination.

What, then, is the difference between the poet and other men? According to Wordsworth, the poet is endowed with a "more lively sensibility, . . . greater knowledge of human nature, and a more comprehensive soul." In addition to these qualities, he has a "disposition to be affected more than other men by absent things as if they were present; an ability of conjuring up in himself passions," passions that are closer to those produced by real events than those that most men can otherwise reproduce (*PLB*, 138). The power to which Wordsworth alludes here, without naming it, is the power of imagination, or the "image-making" power. It is this which allows the poet both to recreate in his mind the images of absent things and also to respond to these images with appropriate emotions, thereby acquiring a "greater readiness and power in expressing what he thinks and feels" than that possessed by other men (*PLB*, 138). In a sense, then, the very faculty which characterizes the poet – imagination – is not a faculty oriented toward realism; rather, in its very nature, it is a transformative faculty which uses the "real" world as its raw material. And yet, the imaginary world created by the poet must "resemble" that real world: Wordsworth encourages the poet to slip into "entire delusion," so as to identify completely with the person whose feelings he is describing. Indeed, he suggests that no words which the poet's *own* "fancy or imagination can suggest" can be "compared with those which are the emanations of reality and truth" (*PLB*, 139). Hence even the poetic imagination here is enlisted in the service of a broad realism, rather than the ideal world associated with many Romantic aesthetic theories.

In support of such realism, Wordsworth cites a classical authority: "Aristotle, I have been told, has said, that Poetry is the most philosophic of all writing: it is so: its object is truth, not individual and local, but general, and operative; not standing upon external testimony, but carried alive into the heart by passion; truth which is its own testimony" (*PLB*, 139). The reaffirmation of Aristotle's definition has a quite different valency in Wordsworth's era than in its original context: Wordsworth is not espousing the realism of the Enlightenment, or the realism that will dominate much nineteenth-century literature, a realism based on close and "scientific" observation of particulars. Rather, he is reaffirming a realism of the universal: poetry expresses timeless and universal truths. Once again, Wordsworth sees in poetry a means of transcending what he considers to be ephemeral political and literary fashions.

Notwithstanding the fact that Wordsworth's *Preface* is often held up as one of the seminal manifestos of Romanticism, it is clear that the poetic ideal he is espousing here is a classical one: poetry does not so much express private emotions and the particulars of a given situation as the universal truths underlying these. Wordsworth insists that the poet "converses with general nature," and directs his attention to the knowledge and sympathies shared by all human beings (*PLB*, 140). The passions and feelings that are produced in the poet "are the general passions and thoughts and feelings of men" (*PLB*, 142). All of the qualities possessed by the poet, according to Wordsworth, imply that he does not differ "in kind from other men, but only in degree" (*PLB*, 142). In a long and famous statement which anticipates Shelley, Wordsworth urges the claims of poetry: in contrast with the other arts and sciences which work within the constraints of a particular field, the poet writes "as a Man"; he sings "a song in which all human beings join with him . . . '. . . he looks before and after.' He is the rock of defence of human nature; . . . carrying everywhere with him relationship and love . . . the Poet binds together by passion and knowledge the vast empire of human society, as it is spread over the whole earth, and over all time" (*PLB*, 139, 141). If the poet is the same in kind as other men, his language, infers Wordsworth, cannot "differ in any material degree from that of all other men who feel vividly and see clearly . . . Poets do not write for Poets alone, but for men . . . the Poet must descend from this supposed height; and, in order to excite rational sympathy, he must express himself as other men express themselves" (*PLB*, 142–143). And the object of his writing will be "the great and universal passions of men, the most general and interesting of their occupations, and the entire world of nature" (*PLB*, 145). Wordsworth insists that such poetry will "interest mankind permanently" (*PLB*, 159). Again, the impulse behind these sentiments is classical: Wordsworth sees poetry as concerned with what is central and universal in human experience, rather than with accidental attributes produced by particular times, customs, or circumstances. In transcending his time, the poet reestablishes the unity of humankind, reaffirming the relationship and unity of all things.

Also classical is Wordsworth's insistence on poetry as a "rational" art: in the lines above, he talks of the poet as exciting "rational sympathy." And at the very beginning of the *Preface* he speaks of the pleasure that "a Poet may rationally endeavour to impart" (*PLB*, 119). Wordsworth's comments on the nature of poetic composition reinforce this view of poetry as a conscious and controlled activity. His statement that "all good poetry is the spontaneous overflow of powerful feelings" has often been torn from its context to illustrate an allegedly Romantic view of poetic creation as an expression of immediate feelings. Yet Wordsworth's statement continues:

> and though this be true, Poems to which any value can be attached were never produced on any variety of subjects but by a man who . . . had also thought long and deeply. For

437

our continued influxes of feeling are modified and directed by our thoughts, which are indeed the representatives of all our past feelings. (*PLB*, 127)

Wordsworth adds that when we contemplate the connections between these thoughts or "general representatives," we discover "what is really important to men" and, by continued experience we can make this process automatic: we shall describe objects, sentiments, and their connection in a way that the "understanding of the Reader must necessarily be in some degree enlightened, and his affections strengthened and purified" (*PLB*, 127). This view is far removed from any notion of poetry as an outpouring of emotion. Wordsworth sees such a close connection between thought and feeling that these can actually pass into each other: not only is feeling directed and governed by thought, but the content of past feelings *becomes* thought. The process merely *appears* automatic when it is subjected to continued practice. Moreover, it is not merely the emotions of the reader, but also his understanding, to which poetry appeals. What the poet expresses, then, is neither thought nor feeling alone but a complex of both; and what appears as spontaneity is the result of long reflection and practice.

This view of poetry as a meditated craft is elaborated in Wordsworth's other renowned comment in the *Preface* concerning poetic composition. After repeating his original statement that "poetry is the spontaneous overflow of powerful feelings," he adds that poetry

> takes its origin from emotion recollected in tranquillity: the emotion is contemplated till, by a species of re-action, the tranquillity gradually disappears, and an emotion, kindred to that which was before the subject of contemplation, is gradually produced, and does itself actually exist in the mind. In this mood successful composition generally begins. (*PLB*, 149)

So the poetic process begins with emotion that is *remembered* and subjected to thought; in this initial state, the emotion *is* thought. The word "tranquillity" implies a certain distance from, and perhaps a certain contextualization of, the original emotion: the disappearing of this tranquillity is the process whereby the thought reverts to emotion; the original emotion which is represented by the current thought is once again *felt*, is brought to life again as a feeling, extricated from its current context, a context which allowed it to be contemplated dispassionately. To put it another way, we leave behind the current emotion as mediated by thought and retrospection, returning to it in its immediate state. In this sense, poetic composition *begins* in feeling, but this feeling will be subsequently modified again by thought.

While Wordsworth accepts Aristotle's definition of poetry, then, as expressing universal truths, and while he sees poetry as an activity controlled by thought, he enlists these classical views in the service of a more Romantic aesthetic purpose. The poet's essential focus is not on the external world, or supposedly "objective" events and actions, but on the *connection* between the inner world of human nature and the world of external nature. Archetypally Romantic is his view that these two worlds are created by mutual interaction. He also diverges from Aristotle and other classical thinkers in his views of the purpose of poetry. This purpose, he says, is to give "immediate pleasure" (*PLB*, 139). He does not consider such an aim to be a degradation of the poet's art because this "grand elementary principle of pleasure" is "an acknowledgment of the beauty of the universe." We have no sympathy or knowledge, Wordsworth says, except that which is founded on pleasure. The poet "considers man and the objects that surround him as acting and re-acting upon each other, so as to produce an infinite complexity of pain and pleasure" (*PLB*, 140). In a later passage, Wordsworth reaffirms that the "end of Poetry is to produce excitement in co-existence with an overbalance of pleasure; but by the supposition, excitement is an unusual and irregular state of the mind; ideas and feelings do not, in that state, succeed each other in accustomed order" (*PLB*, 147).

While Wordsworth does not believe that the use of meter is an integral component of poetry, he concedes that we receive pleasure from metrical language; the source of this is "the pleasure which the mind derives from the perception of similitude in dissimilitude. This principle is the great spring of the activity of our minds . . . From this principle the direction of the sexual appetite, and all the passions connected with it, take their origin: it is the life of our ordinary conversation; and upon the accuracy with which similitude in dissimilitude, and dissimilitude in similitude are perceived, depend our taste and our moral feelings" (*PLB*, 149). Hence the principle of pleasure is more profound than at first appears: it is founded on our ability to perceive similarity in difference and vice versa. This ability, in turn, is a capacity for viewing objects, for seeing the world, in a new light: we discern patterns in nature, as well as in thought, emotion, and experience, that were hitherto overlooked. The order of ideas and emotions in ordinary perception is changed. We also effectively return to a more authentic view of things that penetrates through their character as accumulated by convention. Wordsworth sees the whole of life as governed by this principle, from our sexuality to our moral sensibility. So the poet's task, in giving "pleasure," is a difficult one, that of searching for the universal "truths" which have been clouded by convention, authority, and prejudice. But where classical thinkers regarded such truths as objective and accessible to reason, Wordsworth sees such truths as discernible only by poetic insight.

Samuel Taylor Coleridge (1772–1834)

The genius of Samuel Taylor Coleridge extended over many domains. In poetry he is best known for compositions such as "The Rime of the Ancient Mariner," "Frost at Midnight," "Christabel," and "Kubla Khan," as well as *Lyrical Ballads* (1798), which he co-authored with Wordsworth. He also wrote on educational, social, political, and religious matters in his *Lectures on Politics and Religion* (1795), *Lay Sermons* (1816), and *On the Constitution of the Church and State* (1829). Much of his thinking on philosophical issues is contained in his *Logic*. His literary criticism includes detailed studies of Shakespeare and Milton, and a highly influential text, *Biographia Literaria* (1817). The *Biographia* is an eclectic work, combining intellectual autobiography, philosophy, and literary theory; some critics have praised the insight and originality of this work, viewing Coleridge as the first English critic to build literary criticism on a philosophical foundation, which he derived from German idealist thinkers such as Immanuel Kant, and German Romantics such as Schiller, the Schlegels, and Schelling. Other critics have viewed Coleridge's efforts as a philosopher as haphazard and irrelevant to his essential literary-critical insights.

Indeed, Coleridge's genius was somewhat thwarted by his eccentric character and his tendency to undertake ambitious projects that proved abortive. In 1794 he left Cambridge University without completing his degree. In the same year he devised a plan with the poet Robert Southey to establish a society of equals ruled by all, a "pantisocracy," in Pennsylvania, a plan that rapidly dissolved. Coleridge's marriage to Sara Fricker in 1815 eventually went awry, and he fell in love with Sara Hutchinson. He became dependent on laudanum, a form of opium. Nonetheless, his achievement was vast: not only did he lecture on a broad range of topics, but also, in addition to his other writings, published two journals, first the *Watchman* in 1796, and then the *Friend* from 1809 to 1810. Two experiences were central to his future development as a poet and thinker: the first was his meeting with the poet Wordsworth in 1795, resulting in a friendship that lasted until 1810. Coleridge and his wife Sara lived close to Wordsworth and his sister Dorothy from 1796; in 1800 they all moved to the Lake District, which proved to be a rich source of poetic inspiration. The other experience was travel (with the Wordsworths) to Germany in 1798 where Coleridge studied the work of Kant and the German Romantic thinkers.

Coleridge's *Biographia Literaria* is his most significant literary-critical work, and will be the focus of the following discussion. The insights achieved in that text, however, need to be contextualized within some broader developments in Coleridge's life and work. Like Wordsworth, Coleridge was at first of radical mind, inspired by the promise of the French Revolution. In an early poem, *Ode on the Destruction of the Bastille* in 1789, he had written:

> I see, I see! glad Liberty succeed
> With every patriot virtue in her train!
> And mark yon peasant's raptured eyes;
> Secure he views his harvests rise;
> No fetter vile the mind shall know,
> And Eloquence shall fearless glow.
> Yes! Liberty the soul of Life shall reign,
> Shall throb in every pulse, shall flow thro' every vein![3]

In the same poem Coleridge expressed the hope that the influence of France might spread "Till every land from pole to pole / Shall boast one independent soul."

By 1792, while at Cambridge, Coleridge had befriended the radical leader William Frend, an active sympathizer of the Revolution. Frend's political opinions brought him into conflict with the university authorities after the beginning of war between France and England in 1793. A few years earlier, Frend's religious views had also roused antagonism: he had been dismissed from his post as tutor in the university on account of his Unitarian beliefs. It was under the influence of Frend that Coleridge himself became a Unitarian by 1794 and, in 1796, decided to become a Unitarian minister (a decision, for various reasons, not realized). Other radical acquaintances of Coleridge's at this time included John Thelwall, often in trouble for his Jacobin sympathies. Coleridge himself gave numerous radical lectures at Bristol and a number of cities in the midlands, with the Unitarians. Thelwall described Coleridge's talks as replete with "*levelling* sedition and constructive treason."

However, like Wordsworth – near whom he was living at the time – Coleridge became disillusioned with the revolutionary movement. France's invasion of Switzerland in 1798 provoked him to write and publish a poem which he first entitled "Recantation," and then simply "France: An Ode." Here, Coleridge neatly recounts the history of his own attitudes toward the Revolution. The poem is interestingly structured: it begins by addressing the clouds, the ocean waves, and the woods, elements of nature which pay homage only to "eternal laws" and which have inspired the poet to adore the "spirit of divinest Liberty" (*CPW*, 244). The second stanza describes how Coleridge "hoped and feared" with the Revolution's promise of freedom; and, like Wordsworth, he describes himself as torn between love of liberty and loyalty to his native country when Britain warred against France. At this stage, however, liberty won the day: Coleridge recalls how he "blessed the paeans of delivered France, / And hung my head and wept at Britain's name" (*CPW*, 245).

The poet's doubts begin to creep to the surface of the third stanza: though shocked by the "blasphemies" and horrors of the Reign of Terror, he took these as an understandable reaction to the despotism of former times; and he still embraced the hope that "conquering by her happiness alone, / Shall France compel the nations to be free." By the beginning of the fourth stanza, however, the poet has nothing but remorse for his early revolutionary fervor. He hears freedom's "loud lament," and addresses France now in less flattering terms: "O France, that mockest Heaven, adulterous, blind, / And patriot only in pernicious toils! . . . To insult the shrine of Liberty with spoils / From freemen torn" (*CPW*, 246). In *Biographia* Coleridge described himself, after the invasion of Switzerland, as "a more vehement anti-gallican, and still more intensely an anti-jacobin."[4] The final stanza is a direct address to Liberty, which the poet dissociates from any possibility of realization in human government; rather, he finds the spirit of liberty in the mind's contemplation of its own individuality and the surrounding sublime objects of nature, as pervaded by the love of God.

> O Liberty! . . .
> The guide of homeless winds, and playmate of the waves!
> And there I felt thee! – on that sea-cliff's verge,
> . . . Possessing all things with intensest love,
> O Liberty! my spirit felt thee there.
>
> (*CPW*, 247)

This reads very much like Wordsworth's retraction of the ideal of liberty from political affairs into the connection between humanity and nature; whatever the direction of nce (several commentators have suggested that it was Coleridge who impressed s on Wordsworth), it is clear that for both men the notion of liberty is m its status as a political ideal commensurate with certain forms of onomic structures to an eternal ideal, raised above the sphere of subsisting, in somewhat Kantian fashion, within the self-dual. For Coleridge, such an ideal of liberty implied an e world, one that went hand in hand with political conservatism. Shortly after his explicit disillusionment with French revolutionary principles and practice, he also questioned his own unorthodox Unitarian views, and by 1805 he had made positive overtures toward trinitarianism. On several occasions in both his prose and poetry Coleridge expressed admiration for Edmund Burke (*BL*, I, 191). Likewise, though Coleridge was accused of being a renegade, he claimed that he had adhered to principles rather than loyalty to nation or political party. Coleridge eventually took his place in the tradition of English conservatism, on which he exerted considerable influence.

At the heart of Coleridge's conservatism was his insistence, similar to Burke's, that truth cannot be reached by focusing on the present alone. Rather, both men appealed to what they called universal principles that would comprehend past, present, and future. Both men reacted against the prevailing philosophies of the Enlightenment, and especially against what they saw as the principle of "abstract reason" governing French and other revolutionary attempts to reform society according to "abstract" principles rather than on the basis of actual history and culture. Many of Coleridge's views on these issues are contained in *The Statesman's Manual* (1816), the first essay in what was planned as a series of three "lay sermons" intended to address the ills of contemporary society. In these sermons, Coleridge bemoaned the modern spirit of commerce and speculation that had thwarted the diverse potential of human beings;[5] like Wordsworth, he lamented the contemporary "frivolous craving for novelty," and what he called the "general contagion" of the "mechanical" philosophies of the Enlightenment derived from thinkers such as Locke, Hume, and David Hartley (*LS*, 25, 28). He saw this commercial spirit as underlying the principles of the French Revolution, principles which erected "immediate utility" and the gratification of the senses into the ultimate criteria of value, and which reduced all relations into essentially economic relations (*LS*, 74–76). He saw the Revolution as deifying *human* reason and as arrogantly misapplying this reason in the presumption that "states and governments might be and ought to be constructed as machines," rather than evolving naturally on universal principles (*LS*, 34, 62–63).

Coleridge sought the antidote to these evils in "the collation of the present with the past, in the habit of thoughtfully assimilating the events of our own age to those of the time before us" (*LS*, 9). He saw the universal principles of truth and morality as contained in the Bible, which he advocated as the "end and center of our reading" (*LS*, 17, 70). He insisted that the Bible was the true moral and intellectual foundation of Europe, and that it expressed "a Science of *Realities* . . . freed from the phenomena of time and space" (*LS*, 31, 49–50).

In a formulation which proved to have great impact on later writers such as Poe and Baudelaire, Coleridge returned to the medieval idea of the Book of Nature, whereby the world of nature itself contained the "correspondences and symbols of the spiritual world" (*LS*, 70). He made a distinction between symbol and allegory, defining the latter as merely a "translation of abstract notions into a picture-language which is itself nothing but an abstraction from objects of the senses." A symbol, on the other hand, "is characterized by a translucence of the Special in the Individual or of the General the Especial or of the Universal in the General. Above all by the translucence Eternal through and in the Temporal. It always partakes of the Reality which is intelligible; and while it enunciates the whole, abides itself as a living part in of which it is the representative." The poverty of the modern age, argued Coleridge, rests partly on its inability to recognize any "medium between *Literal* and *Metaphorical*": modern thinking either buries faith in the "dead letter" or replaces it with products of a mechanical understanding. Coleridge was to be followed by many others, both radical and conservative, in his reaction against the reduction of thought and language to a literal, aggregative character. What is perhaps most interesting about Coleridge's perspective is the way he presents "eternal" and vital scripture as opposed to modern "mechanical" or "dead" philosophies in terms of the faculties of the human mind. His elaboration of this is integral to his aesthetics.

In the first place, Coleridge attempted to redeem the notion of reason from its reductive and abstract status as bequeathed by the Enlightenment. He accused modern thinkers of seducing understanding from its "natural allegiance," whereby it stood in the courts of faith and reason, allowing it to operate instead in a misguided independence. Coleridge effectively charged modern bourgeois thought with reducing reason to understanding. His thinking here appears to have been influenced by Kant: he sees reason as a higher and more comprehensive faculty than understanding. The understanding, according to Coleridge, "concerns itself exclusively with the quantities, qualities, and relations of *particulars* in time and space" (*LS*, 59). The understanding, then, gives us a piecemeal knowledge of what Kant called the "phenomenal" world, the world of our sense-experience in space and time. Mere understanding, as elaborated by empiricist philosophers such as David Hume, is fragmentary; moreover, it cannot comprehend the realm of morality (*LS*, 20–22). Reason, says Coleridge, "is the knowledge of the laws of the Whole considered as One." It is "the science of the *universal*" (*LS*, 59). So, as with Kant, reason is a faculty which stands above the understanding, organizing the knowledge derived from the latter into a more comprehensive unity. If the understanding is employed in isolation from reason, says Coleridge, it can be directed only to the material world and our worldly interests; he insists that the understanding is merely "the means not the end of knowledge" (*LS*, 68–69).

This contrast and connection between reason and understanding furnishes the broader context for Coleridge's view of the imagination. Like Kant, he sees understanding as a limited power, which, used in independence, "entangles itself in contradictions." Unlike Kant, he sees the corrective and contextualizing relation of reason to understanding as mediated by the imagination: "The completing power which unites clearness with depth, the plenitude of the sense with the comprehensibility of the understanding, is the IMAGINATION, impregnated with which the understanding itself becomes intuitive, and a living power" (*LS*, 69). So Coleridge seems to follow Kant (and much eighteenth-century thought) in viewing the imagination as a faculty which unites what we receive through our senses with the concepts of our understanding; but he goes further than Kant in viewing imagination as a power which "completes" and enlivens the understanding so that the understanding itself becomes a more comprehensive and intuitive (rather than merely discursive) faculty. The Romantics, including Coleridge, are often characterized as extolling imagination as the supreme human faculty. Nonetheless, Coleridge appears to view reason as the supreme faculty, one which contains all the others: "The REASON, (not the abstract reason, not the reason as the mere *organ* of science . . .) . . . the REASON without being either the SENSE, the UNDERSTAND-ING or the IMAGINATION contains all three within itself, even as the mind contains

443

its thoughts, and is present in and through them all" (*LS*, 69–70). Hence, just as imagination combines sense with understanding, so reason, placed at a higher vantage point, unites the knowledge derived from all three of these. And while Coleridge insists that each individual must bear witness to the light of reason in his own mind, this reason is not strictly a faculty or personal property of any individual; rather, the individual partakes of the light of a reason which is universal and divine. Coleridge is now very far from Kant, who had indeed viewed reason as a higher, regulative faculty but one which was human, not divine.

What, in fact, Coleridge does in attempting to rescue reason from its modern reduction to mere fragmentary understanding is to redefine it. What the Enlightenment philosophers called "reason" was essentially an individualistic reason based on direct but piecemeal observation and experience. This is not the same conception of reason as was espoused by the classical philosophers, or by Christian theologians, who viewed it as a faculty through which we could acquire a universalizing knowledge that might contextualize in both moral and intellectual terms the information we received through our senses. In a sense, then, Coleridge is returning to an earlier and broader notion of reason, one that he elaborates, however, in post-Kantian terms. What he does, in a bold and drastic gesture, is to *equate* reason with religion. He suggests that "Reason and Religion differ only as a two-fold application of the same power . . . Reason as the science of All as the Whole, must be interpenetrated by a Power, that represents the concentration of All in Each – a Power that acts by a contraction of universal truths into individual duties, as the only form in which those truths can attain life and reality. Now this is RELIGION, which is the EXECUTIVE of our nature, and on this account the name of highest dignity, and the symbol of sovereignty" (*LS*, 59, 64). Hence Coleridge sees the precepts and duties inscribed in religion as an expression of reason itself. And this "reason," for Coleridge, is divine reason: he argues that human understanding merely "snatches at truth"; it is partial, fragmentary, and uncertain; whereas God's knowledge is absolute and certain (*LS*, 20). If God alone is the ground and cause of all things, if God alone contains "in himself the ground of his own nature, and therein of *all* natures," then "Reason hath faith in itself, in its own revelations" (*LS*, 32). The primal act of faith, says Coleridge, "is enunciated in the word, GOD: a faith not derived from experience, but its ground and source, and without which the fleeting *chaos of facts* would no more form experience, than the dust of the grave can of itself make a living man. The imperative and oracular form of the inspired Scripture is the form of reason itself in all things purely rational and moral" (*LS*, 18). Whereas, for Kant, the ultimate ground and enabling principle of experience was the transcendental ego that stood aloof from and organized particular experiences, Coleridge sees this transcendental ground not in ourselves but in the Word of God; for him, reason itself is equated with divine scripture, and thereby made transcendental; in other words, reason is not, as for the Enlightenment thinkers, a faculty that operates directly on the data derived from experience; rather, it precedes, enables, and defines the very possibility of experience. According to Coleridge, it is the distinguishing principle of Christianity "that in it alone . . . the Understanding in its utmost power and opulence . . . *culminates* in Faith, as in its crown of Glory" (*LS*, 46). These assertions bear broad similarities to the arguments of Aquinas on the commensurability and mutual complementarity of faith and reason.

Coleridge sees reason defined in this broader sense as a means of counteracting the tendency of Enlightenment philosophy to reduce reason to a merely human faculty and one which operates independently of faith: "To this tendency . . . RELIGION, as the consideration of the Particular and Individual (in which respect it takes up and identifies with itself the excellence of the *Understanding*) but of the Individual, as it exists and has its being in the Universal (in which respect it is one with the pure *Reason*,) – to this tendency, I say, RELIGION assigns the due limits" (*LS*, 62). As Coleridge later states, the "elements . . . of Religion are Reason and Understanding" (*LS*, 89). Hence, if modern thought has reduced all knowledge to the piecemeal knowledge of the understanding, religion does not dismiss such knowledge but situates this within a unifying context, one which delves beneath the particularity of things to their true reality as contained in their universal characteristics and the pattern of their connections with other entities. Coleridge states that, because religion comprehends both faculties, of reason and understanding, throughout civilized history, religion has been the fosterer of poetry and the fine arts (*LS*, 62).

Coleridge's views of the connection of the various faculties and their intersection with religion have interesting implications for his aesthetics. Reason is the supreme faculty or power which embraces the senses, the understanding, and the imagination. Coleridge equates this supreme faculty with religious revelation, i.e., revelation that precedes and enables human experience, furnishing it with a transcendent foundation and meaning. He aligns scripture with a mode of writing that he calls symbolic, and for Coleridge, the symbolic is the realm of the imagination. In *The Statesman's Manual* he calls imagination a "reconciling and mediatory power, which incorporating the Reason in Images of the Sense, and organizing (as it were) the flux of the Senses by the permanence and self-circling energies of the Reason, gives birth to a system of symbols, harmonious in themselves, and consubstantial with the truths, of which they are the *conductors*" (*LS*, 62). Hence Coleridge sees the notion of a symbol as intrinsically religious; or, to put it conversely, he sees religious writing as intrinsically symbolic, whereby events on the worldly temporal level are understood as meaningful ultimately in their symbolic capacity, their capacity to refer to a higher, spiritual system of significance.

Coleridge's views of imagination, and specifically of poetic imagination, are elaborated in his *Biographia Literaria* (1817), published shortly after his *Lay Sermons*. The *Biographia* is a highly eclectic mixture of literary autobiography, literary theory, philosophical speculation, and polemic. It is here that Coleridge offers his best-known definitions of imagination, definitions which, however, need to be understood in the context outlined above. In the fourth chapter of the *Biographia*, Coleridge makes his famous suggestion that fancy and imagination, contrary to widespread belief, are "two distinct and widely different faculties": they are not "two names with one meaning, or . . . the lower and higher degree of one and the same power." Coleridge sees his distinction between these faculties, inspired in part by Wordsworth's writings, as part of a broader historical tendency, concomitant with cultural and linguistic refinement, to "desynonymize" words that originally shared the same meaning (*BL*, I, 82–83). It is not, however, until the thirteenth chapter, "On the Imagination," that Coleridge explains his distinction. And even here, his elaboration is drastically compacted: Coleridge interrupts his own meditations by quoting a letter (allegedly from a friend, but actually written by Coleridge himself) urging him to reserve the treatment of imagination for a later work where it can be more fully contextualized. The "later" work was never written and Coleridge's analysis of imagination and fancy is restricted to the following definitions, which are worth quoting in full:

> The IMAGINATION then I consider either as primary, or secondary. The primary IMAGINATION I hold to be the living Power and prime Agent of all human Perception, and as a repetition in the finite mind of the eternal act of creation in the infinite I AM. The secondary I consider as an echo of the former, co-existing with the conscious will, yet still as identical with the primary in the *kind* of its agency, and differing only in *degree*, and in the *mode* of its operation. It dissolves, diffuses, dissipates, in order to re-create; or where this process is rendered impossible, yet still at all events it struggles to idealize and to unify. It is essentially *vital*, even as all objects (*as* objects) are essentially fixed and dead.
>
> FANCY, on the contrary, has no other counters to play with, but fixities and definites. The Fancy is indeed no other than a mode of Memory emancipated from the order of time and space; and blended with, and modified by that empirical phenomenon of the will, which we express by the word CHOICE. But equally with the ordinary memory it must receive all its materials ready made from the laws of association. (*BL*, I, 304–305)

What Coleridge designates as the primary imagination is roughly equivalent to what Kant views as the reproductive imagination: it operates in our normal perception, combining the various data received through the senses into a unifying image, which can then be conceptualized by the understanding. In this role, imagination is an intermediary faculty, uniting the data of the senses with the concepts of the understanding. Even in this primary role, however, imagination as formulated by Coleridge evokes a wider, cosmic context: the very act of perception "repeats" on a finite level the divine act of creation. In other words, human perception actively recreates or copies elements in the world of nature, reproducing these into images that can be processed further by the understanding. The imagination in this primary capacity helps us to form an intelligible perspective of the world; this understanding, however, is fragmentary: we do indeed perceive God's creation but in a piecemeal, cumulative fashion. Moreover, there is no originality in the primary imagination: like Kant's reproductive imagination, it is bound by what we actually experience through the senses as well as the laws for associating these data.

It is the secondary imagination which is poetic: like Kant's productive or spontaneous imagination, this is creative and forms new syntheses, new and more complex unities out of the raw furnishings of sense-data. As Coleridge indicates in the passage above, it breaks down the customary order and pattern in which our senses present the world to us, recreating these into new combinations that follow its own rules, rather than the usual laws of association. Coleridge also stresses in this passage the voluntary and controlled nature of the secondary or poetic imagination; whereas the primary imagination operates in an involuntary manner in all people, the secondary imagination belongs to the poet and is put into action by the "conscious will." Nonetheless, this poetic imagination is still dependent for its raw material on the primary imagination: Coleridge is careful to state that the two types of imagination differ not in kind but only in degree. The secondary imagination must exert its creative powers on the very perceptions supplied by the primary imagination; it cannot operate independently of them. Another way of putting this might be to say that even the creative poetic imagination is ultimately rooted in our actual perceptions of the world: it cannot simply create from nothing, or from the insubstantiality of its own dreams. For, ultimately, the secondary imagination is perceiving the world at a higher level of truth, one that sees beneath the surface appearances of things into their deeper reality, their deeper connections, and their significance within a more comprehensive scheme that relates objects and events in their human, finite significance to their symbolic place in the divine, infinite order of things.

We might simply regard Coleridge's passage as an index of a reaction against the primacy of Enlightenment reason, and its displacement by imagination as the higher and more creative power. Such an explanation, however, tends to be based on the isolated passage above and tends to oversimplify the Romanticism of both Coleridge and many of the thinkers on whom he drew. It needs to be recalled that, even for Coleridge, it is not imagination but reason which is the highest faculty. As seen earlier, reason for Coleridge is a comprehensive faculty, whose unifying disposition far exceeds the fragmentary and cumulative operations of the mere understanding. Coleridge does talk in the *Biographia* of a "philosophic imagination," which he also calls "the sacred power of self-intuition" (*BL*, I, 241). But this use of the term "imagination" seems to be generic: Coleridge uses it synonymously with what he calls "philosophic consciousness" or the use of the higher and intuitive power of reason which alone can view the concepts of the understanding as an essentially symbolic expression of a higher unity (*BL*, I, 241–242). Hence the secondary, poetic imagination occupies an intermediary role between the primary imagination, which unifies the data of sense so that these can be brought under the concepts of the understanding, and reason, whose ideas unite those concepts into a still higher unity.[6]

Coleridge's view of imagination may be somewhat indebted to Kant, to Schelling, who identified three levels of imagination (perceptual, philosophical, and artistic), and to the psychologist Johann Nicolaus Tetens.[7] The important point here is that Coleridge's work was part of a growing tendency to ascribe to the imagination a role beyond the merely perceptual function assigned to it by Hobbes, Berkeley, and Enlightenment empiricists such as Locke and Hume. An important element in this elevation of imagination's role was the distinction between this higher faculty and mere fancy. In the passage above, Coleridge reproduces with his own modifications a distinction between fancy and imagination made by several German thinkers such as Tetens, Kant, Ernst Platner, and Schelling. A long tradition of classical and medieval thought, prevailing into the eighteenth century, had viewed fancy (the Greek *phantasia*) as a more creative power than imagination (from the Latin *imaginatio*): fancy was associated with the free play of thought whereas imagination had been restricted to the role of recalling images. The German thinkers cited above overturned this hierarchy, lifting imagination above its merely perceptual role and viewing it as a creative and unifying force, and assigning to fancy the more mundane role of selecting and connecting images.[8] In Coleridge's formulation, fancy is a more mechanical mode of creativity: it receives its materials "ready made from the law of association," and Coleridge calls it merely "a mode of Memory." In other words, it is a mode of recalling and recombining images that have actually been experienced.

It may well be asked: what is the difference between fancy and the primary imagination, which, after all, is also constrained by the experience of our senses? Two factors might distinguish these faculties. Firstly, though fancy is a mode of recalling, it is nonetheless "emancipated from the order of time and space." Secondly, it is "modified by that empirical phenomenon of the will, which we express by the word choice." So fancy has a degree of freedom in the way it recalls images; it is not restricted to the original order of images in time and space; and it can exercise some choice in the way it combines images. Unlike the primary imagination, then, fancy is not merely a perceptual agent; rather, it is a creative power but operates at a lower level of creativity than the secondary or poetic imagination, which has the power to dissolve perceptions entirely and create new combinations. Elsewhere, Coleridge calls imagination a "shaping and modifying power," and fancy "the aggregative and associative power" (*BL*, I, 293 and n. 4). Indeed, Coleridge refers to imagination as the "esemplastic" power, a term he derives from the Greek *eis hen plattein* meaning "to shape into one" (*BL*, I, 168). Collectively, these statements suggest that imagination unifies material in an internal organic matter, changing the very elements themselves that are united, whereas the combinations produced by fancy are aggregative, comprising merely external addition, as in the placing of images side by side.

Coleridge's passage on imagination and fancy is an index of some broader and more profound changes of world view between eighteenth-century thought, especially Enlightenment thought, and Romanticism. He saw much modern philosophy as beset by a dualism between the self and the world, a dualism introduced into modern philosophy by Descartes in the form of a distinction between mind and body: "To the best of my knowledge Des Cartes was the first philosopher, who introduced the absolute and essential heterogeneity of the soul as intelligence, and the body as matter" (*BL*, 129). Descartes had characterized the mind (or what Coleridge calls "soul") as a thinking substance, a substance that he identified as the essential human self, whereas matter for him was of a completely different nature, characterized primarily by extension in space and time. Coleridge sees this distinction as further refined in modern thought by philosophies such as materialism, hylozoism, and empiricism. The empiricists Locke and Hume were unable to reconcile the self and the external world, saying that we could only know our own ideas or impressions of the world rather than the world itself. Coleridge rejects the various theories of associationism expounded by Hume and psychologists such as David Hartley as offering any feasible means of explaining the connection between mind and body or between self and world, though he accepts Aristotle's explanation of the ways in which ideas are associated (*BL*, I, 102–103).

Coleridge saw most of these philosophies as reducing nature to a dead and lifeless entity, subject merely to mechanical laws (*BL*, I, 129 n. 1). He viewed Kant's metaphysics as having taken an important step in overcoming this fundamental dualism between self and world, or self and nature. He acknowledged that Kant's writings, "more than any work, at once invigorated and disciplined my understanding" (*BL*, I, 153). Kant had attempted to display a necessary connection between our mental faculties and the world of phenomena or the world as it appears to us: our minds have an active and necessary role in constructing this world. However, Kant achieved this necessity at the expense of positing a noumenal world (the world of things in themselves) which we could never know through our intellectual apparatus. Like Fichte and Schelling (and Hegel), Coleridge saw Kant's phenomena–noumena distinction as reintroducing a distinction or dualism between reality as we know it and ultimate reality which is unknowable. And, like these other thinkers, he rejected what he took to be Kant's explanation of the noumenon (*BL*, I, 155).

The German philosophers Fichte and Schelling had attempted to overcome Kant's distinction. Fichte placed emphasis on the ego, which he identified as the primary reality: the ego posits itself in a primal act of affirmation, and subsequently posits nature or the non-ego as a limitation of itself. But Coleridge saw this stress on the ego as inordinate, and sees Fichte's theory as degenerating into a crude egoism, opposed to nature which is "lifeless, godless, and altogether unholy" (*BL*, I, 158–159). It is primarily to Schelling that Coleridge turns for the resolution of the dualism between self and nature. However, Coleridge qualifies his debt to Schelling, tracing the similarities between their ideas to their common reading of Jacob Bohme (*BL*, I, 160–161). Though Coleridge claims to have arrived at his fundamental ideas independently, he calls Schelling the "founder" of the "dynamic" philosophy of nature (as opposed to the empiricist and materialist traditions which rendered nature lifeless) (*BL*, I, 162–163).

As Coleridge sees it, "philosophy is neither a science of the reason or understanding only, nor merely a science of morals, but the science of BEING altogether": it must combine the realms of the speculative and the practical (or moral). Moreover, all knowledge "rests on the coincidence of an object with a subject" (*BL*, I, 252). For knowledge to arise, then, the dualism of subjective and objective, inherent in modern philosophy since Descartes, must be overcome. Coleridge thinks that we can arrive at this reconciliation whether we start from the subjective or objective pole. If we begin with the objective, or nature, our initial perspective is that of the natural philosopher: the more we examine the world of nature, the more we realize that its essence subsists not in material objects but in the laws that govern those objects and their connections, the very laws that subsist in man as intelligence and self-consciousness. We realize, in other words, the essential identity of nature as object and ourselves as subjects (*BL*, I, 255–256). If, on the other hand, we start out from the subjective side, our initial position will be that of a transcendental philosopher: like Kant, Coleridge sees transcendental philosophy as assuming that there is a reality beyond our senses, but it is nonetheless ultimately grounded in our senses: it cannot simply construct schemes of its own that bear no relation to our actual experience (the latter kind of philosophy would be "transcendent") (*BL*, I, 237). Transcendental philosophy, then, would start out from the fundamental fact of subjectivity, the "I AM" or immediate self-consciousness, which Coleridge sees as "the ground of all other certainty." In proceeding to examine nature, we would find that this is identical with our self-consciousness (*BL*, I, 260). In other words, all the "external" objects that we view are in fact modifications of this self-consciousness or "I AM" which is the fundamental principle of all philosophy: "Only in the self-consciousness of a spirit is there the required identity of object and representation . . . the spirit in all the objects which it views, views only itself" (*BL*, I, 272, 278). Hence, though Coleridge begins with the ostensibly Cartesian principle of self-consciousness, he adopts this principle toward a very different conclusion: instead of arriving at the dualism of Descartes or other modern philosophers, he is concerned to abrogate that antithesis, by means of viewing the external world as a development of self-consciousness. But Coleridge of course situates this identity of subject and object within an "absolute identity of subject and object" that expresses the eternal and divine "I AM" (*BL*, I, 285). Hence all nature is an expression of the self-conscious will or intelligence of God: "We begin with the I KNOW MYSELF, in order to end with the absolute I AM. We proceed from the SELF, in order to lose and find all self in GOD." What Coleridge desires is a "total and undivided philosophy" where "philosophy would pass into religion, and religion become inclusive of philosophy" (*BL*, I, 282–283).

Though many of these ideas may have come directly from Schelling, it is worth noting that they bear similarities with those of Hegel, whose system also attempts to overcome the fundamental dualisms and contradictions of bourgeois thought. What is interesting here is Coleridge's historical position as an English Romantic who introduced or imported into his native tradition some of the principal tenets of German speculative philosophy, tenets that have become identified with the broad spectrum of Romantic movements. These tenets, aimed in part against the mechanistic, fragmentary, and secular spirit of much Enlightenment thought, include the primacy of subjectivity and self-consciousness, the elevation of nature beyond mere lifeless mechanism to a spiritual status, and the perception of a fundamental unity between the human self and the world of nature.

Coleridge's views on the nature of poetry and poetic language are intrinsically tied to his broader vision as outlined above and, in particular, to his views of poetic imagination. While he shares some components of this broader vision with Wordsworth, he takes some pains, in *Biographia*, to distinguish his positions precisely from those of his friend. The most basic point on which he differs from Wordsworth is in his insistence that the language of poetry is *essentially* different from that of prose (*BL*, II, 73). Whereas Wordsworth saw the poet as a "man speaking to men," using the language of "real" life (albeit in a more refined form), Coleridge, like the New Critics of the early twentieth century, saw poetry as essentially untranslatable into prose. Indeed, Coleridge criticized the poetic practice of neoclassical writers such as Pope for precisely this, that their poetry took the form of logical argument and that it seemed to be "characterized not so much by poetic thoughts, as by thoughts *translated* into the language of poetry" (*BL*, I, 18–19).

Coleridge acknowledges that poetry is formed from the same elements as prose; the difference lies in the different combination of these elements and the difference of purpose (*BL*, II, 11). Whereas science, history, and other disciplines have the communication of truth as their immediate purpose, this conveyance of truth is for poetry an *ultimate* purpose. Poetry is distinguished from these other realms "by proposing for its *immediate* object pleasure, not truth; it is also distinguished by its insistence on organic unity, such that the pleasure yielded by any component part of the poem is consonant with the pleasure afforded by any other part and by the poem as a whole" (*BL*, II, 12–13). Coleridge later gives something like a definition of organic unity: "*all* the parts of an organized whole must be assimilated to the more *important* and *essential* parts" (*BL*, II, 72). Hence, unlike Pope, who viewed language as the external "dress" of thought, Coleridge sees the unity of a poem as shaped from within, through internal connections of its elements. Wordsworth, too, had seen the immediate purpose of poetry as producing pleasure. Coleridge's explanation of this, however, is different: the ultimate aim of poetry is indeed the expression of truth, but pleasure is derived not merely from our view of this final goal but "by the attractions of the journey itself" (*BL*, II, 14). This view anticipates many modern conceptions of poetry and poetic autonomy: the primary purpose of poetry is not referential, but rather to draw attention to itself as a linguistic and material construct, to the journey or *means* whereby truth is achieved. Coleridge's renowned definition of "poetic faith" as a "willing suspension of disbelief" helps explain this poetic autonomy: the images in poetry have a force and logic of their own that urge the reader to enter the world of poetic illusion and to suspend judgment as to whether the images of that poetic world have a real existence. In other words, the question of poetry's reference to reality is suspended, and the reader's gaze is focused on the "autonomous" poetic world which is temporarily isolated from all contexts.

Coleridge's most comprehensive definition of the activity of the poet adumbrates the essential features of the foregoing discussion:

> The poet, described in *ideal* perfection, brings the whole soul of man into activity, with the subordination of its faculties to each other, according to their relative worth and dignity. He diffuses a tone, and spirit of unity, that blends, and (as it were) *fuses*, each into each, by that synthetic and magical power, to which we have exclusively appropriated the name of imagination. This power, first put in action by the will and understanding, and retained under their irremissive, though gentle and unnoticed, controul . . . reveals itself in the balance or reconciliation of opposite or discordant qualities: of sameness, with difference; of the general, with the concrete; the idea, with the image; the individual, with the representative; the sense of novelty and freshness, with old and familiar objects; a more than usual state of emotion, with more than usual order; judgment ever awake and steady self-possession, with enthusiasm and feeling profound or vehement; and while it blends and harmonizes the natural and the artificial, still subordinates art to nature; the manner to the matter; and our admiration of the poet to our sympathy with the poetry. (*BL*, II, 16–17)

Once again, the composing of poetry is seen as distinct, relying primarily on the unifying power of imagination, which is put into effect in a voluntary and controlled manner. What the mere understanding can perceive only in terms of opposites – general, concrete, individual, representative, etc. – imagination has the power to reconcile in a higher vision of unity. This use of the imaginative power lies at the core of poetry's distinction from prose or from any discursive activity that brings us conventional perceptions of the world: the poet, through imagination, can not only reassemble whatever elements the world presents to our senses but also see the profounder connection of those elements. Nonetheless, while the poet for Coleridge is a kind of genius, set apart from other men, he insists that the reader's engagement should be with the poetry itself, not with the poet. Such an insistence contributes to a conception of poetry as autonomous, and will be repeated by the twentieth-century formalists and New Critics.

Given Coleridge's views of the unique status of the poet, it is hardly surprising that he takes issue with Wordsworth's views of poetic language. In his *Preface* to the *Lyrical Ballads*, Wordsworth had urged the poet to abandon the artificial language of poetic tradition and instead to adopt what he called the "real" language of men. He claimed that language in its purest and most philosophical form was exhibited in rustic life, which had been uncontaminated by the vulgar idioms and emotions of the city.

451

Coleridge's many objections to these statements can be distilled into two central arguments: firstly, the term "real" is equivocal. Every man's language, says Coleridge, has its individualities, as well as properties common to his social class and certain words or phrases that are universally used. Moreover, language varies in every country and every village; given such variety, what would "real" language mean? Hence, for "real," thinks Coleridge, we should substitute the term "ordinary" or *lingua communis* (*BL*, II, 55–56). And this, he says, is no more to be found in the language of rustics than in that of any other class.

The second, more fundamental, objection to Wordsworth is that, far from being the most philosophical language, the rustic's discourse is marked by scanty vocabulary and the communication of isolated facts, rather than the connections or general laws which constitute the "true being" of things (*BL*, II, 55–56). The best part of language, according to Coleridge, "is derived from reflection on the acts of the mind itself. It is formed by a voluntary appropriation of fixed symbols to internal acts, to processes and results of imagination, the greater part of which have no place in the consciousness of uneducated man" (*BL*, II, 54). Hence, it is imagination which underlies not only the poet's distinctive role, as set above the sphere of conventional perception, but also his refined use of language: it is this power through which the poet has the ability to see the connections and underlying patterns behind the facts that are received discretely or in a fragmentary and isolated way by the ordinary consciousness.

Interestingly, and somewhat ironically, though Coleridge and Wordsworth differ on the issue of how poetic language relates to ordinary language, they both claim to abide by Aristotle's view that poetry expresses truths which are general and universal rather than individual. Coleridge states: "I adopt with full faith the principle of Aristotle, that poetry is essentially *ideal*, that it avoids and excludes all *accident*; that its apparent individualities of rank, character, or occupation must be *representative* of a class; and that the *persons* of poetry must be clothed with *generic* attributes, with the *common* attributes of the class; not with such as one gifted individual might *possibly* possess, but such as from his situation . . . that he *would* possess" (*BL*, II, 45–46). Hence for Coleridge too, poetry focuses on the essential and universal features of a particular situation, and though it might employ individualization to create an emotional impact, such use always carries a broader, generalizing significance (*BL*, II, 72).

Hence, as with Wordsworth, Coleridge uses classical Aristotelian precepts – in this case, the poetic expression of universal truths, and poetry as an imitation of nature or human nature – toward Romantic ends. What allows the poet to communicate general and essential truths is the unifying power of imagination, which sees the connections between particular and general, concrete and abstract, individual and representative. It is through this very power that the poet's "imitation" is itself creative, reaffirming and replicating on a lower level the original creative act of the divine "I AM."

Romanticism in America

As stated in an earlier chapter, the French Revolution of 1789 marked a watershed for the future of Europe, a fact keenly discerned by writers on both sides of the Atlantic, such as Irving Babbitt and Matthew Arnold. Not only did that Revolution initiate the political ascendancy of the bourgeoisie, a struggle continued through the violent European revolutions of 1830 and 1848; but also its dimensions were so momentous, overturning the centuries-old economic edifice of feudalism and absolutism, as well as their sanction in classical Christian thought, that its imprint was indelibly impressed on all areas of life, economic, religious, philosophical, scientific, and literary.

The major characteristics of capitalist development in America during the nineteenth century were consonant with those in Europe. Henry Adams observed an "instinctive kinship" between the later nineteenth-century bourgeoisie of Paris and London and that of New England; for the latter, "England's middle-class government was the ideal of human progress."[9] In both Europe and America, industrial capitalism, where business interests had been predominantly organized as individual enterprises or partnerships, began to be superseded in mid-century by the much more impersonal organization of finance capitalism, so called because of the monopolization of industry by huge investment banking empires. The new ruling class now comprised industrialists and investment bankers. Adams effectively captured the ruthless spirit of this transition: "The Trusts and Corporations stood for the larger part of the new power that had been created since 1840, and were obnoxious because of their vigorous and unscrupulous energy. They were revolutionary, troubling all the old conventions and values . . . They tore society to pieces and trampled it under foot."[10] In the 1880s John D. Rockefeller and Andrew Carnegie became symbols of such monopoly through their respective enterprises in petroleum and steel. By the 1860s it was the railroads which represented the most powerful economic interest in America; the rapid expansion and incorporation of the railroad network in the following years paved the way for large corporations and centralized management in other industries such as steel. It is no accident that in Adams' autobiography the railroad becomes a subtle metaphor for the restructuring of society by industrial interests.

These developments were accompanied by a massive increase in population from about five million in 1800 to around a hundred million in 1914, as well as by a huge influx of immigration and, as in Europe, a large-scale movement of people from the countryside to the towns. By the late nineteenth century there had arisen a vast urban industrial landscape linked by railroad and telegraph, a metallic and concrete world in which the rhythms of rural life, the seasonal work cycles, the links between successive generations, the sense of identity between individual and community, and the strength of family ties were all severely shaken. The greater part of individual identity, as Ferdinand Tonnies suggests, was endowed by a person's social role. Equally consequent upon this increasing division of labor was the disintegration of the individual's psychic unity into a one-dimensional orientation toward utilitarian and rational practice at the expense of what many writers called sensibility. All of these features – finance capitalism, the railroad, centralization of management and authority, a mechanical concept of time (as money), and the displacement of Gemeinschaft by Gesellschaft – formed the conditions to which American Romantics responded.

Like Europe, America had its fair share of economic liberals such as Nassau Senior, as well as its propagators of the myth of the "self-made man," a myth through whose core ran the Puritan Protestant ethic of hard work and thrift. As stated above, the notion of self-creation through work or labor lies at the center of a nexus of bourgeois ideals which, as Engels, Max Weber, and others have argued, are underpinned by a devotion to the rational organization of society and in particular the rational accumulation of capital. In America, economic liberalism (which, however, was constrained by America's protectionist policy since 1816 and the emergence of corporations and monopolies) was somewhat tempered by the "gospel of wealth," which was but one of numerous attempts to argue the commensurability of capitalism and Christianity. This doctrine, elaborated for example in Carnegie's *The Gospel of Wealth* (1901), decreed that possession of wealth brought along with it a Christian responsibility to donate to the good of the community. Many churches in fact formulated their doctrines so as to harmonize with contemporary economic practice and material conditions. One of these was the Unitarian Church, whose liberalism facilitated the influx into America of European Romantic ideas.

Romanticism in America flowered somewhat later than in Europe, embroiled as the new nation was in the struggle for self-definition in political, economic, and religious terms. It was American independence from British rule, achieved in 1776, that opened the path to examining national identity, the development of a distinctly American literary tradition in the light of Romantically reconceived visions of the self and nature. The major American Romantics included Ralph Waldo Emerson, Walt Whitman, Nathaniel Hawthorne, Margaret Fuller, Henry David Thoreau, and Herman Melville. While some of these writers were influenced by European Romantics and philosophers, nearly all of them were inspired by a nationalistic concern to develop an indigenous cultural tradition and a distinctly American literature. Indeed, they helped to define – at a far deeper and more intelligent level than the crude definitions offered by politicians since then until the present day – the very concept of American national identity. Like the European Romantics, these American writers reacted against what they perceived to be the mechanistic and utilitarian tenor of Enlightenment thinking and the industrial, urbanized world governed by the ethics and ideals of bourgeois commercialism. They sought to redeem the ideas of spirit, nature, and the richness of the human self within a specifically American context.

It was Emerson who laid the foundations of American Romanticism. Utilizing the ideas of Wordsworth, Coleridge, and Thomas Carlyle, he developed organicist ideas of nature, language, and imagination, and called for American writers to depart from the strict genres and formal hierarchies of European literary tradition and to forge their own modes of expression. Both Emerson and Whitman referred to America as a "poem" which needed to be written. In the preface to his *Leaves of Grass* (1855), Whitman saw himself as writing "the great psalm of the republic," and in a subsequent preface identified the expression of individual identity with national identity. Like Emerson, he reacted against the strictures of genre and form and wrote in a freer form using colloquial speech, or what Whitman called "the dialect of common sense," intended to convey the vastness of the American spirit. He saw the "genius" of the United States as residing in the common people, and thought that the redemption of America from its rotten commercialism lay in the realization of its authentic self.[11] Whitman's *Song of Myself* begins with the line "I celebrate myself." But the narrative "I" that controls the movement of this poem is symbolic ("In all people I see myself," l. 401). Emphasizing a common humanity, Whitman locates this human nature in both soul and body, spurning didactic aims and boldly celebrating the divine in all dimensions of his humanity, and assuming indifference to conventional morality, as in his questioning "What blurt is it about virtue and about vice?" (l. 468). Whitman moves toward a total acceptance of humanity, free from the artifice of conventional perception, and the false imposition of coherence: "Do I contradict myself? / Very well then ... I contradict myself; / I am large ... I contain multitudes" (ll. 1314–1316). Whitman saw the human personality as integrating and accommodating all kinds of development, scientific, artistic, religious, and economic.

Another major figure influenced by Emerson, as well as by Thomas Carlyle, was Henry David Thoreau (1817–1862). In his most famous work, *Walden* (1854), based on his sojourn at Emerson's property at Walden pond, he advocated a life free of social artifice, routine, and consumerism, simplified in its needs, devoted to nature and art, imaginatively exploring the depths of the self, and developing an authentic language. Thoreau's highly Romantic and eccentric vision was also expressed in his views of the rights of the individual and of the need to resist oppression; he was a fervent abolitionist, and his essay "Resistance to Civil Government" (1849; later entitled "Civil Disobedience") influenced Mohandas K. Gandhi's struggle for Indian independence from British rule as well as the American civil rights movement led by Martin Luther King, Jr.

Margaret Fuller (1810–1850) also voiced fervent opposition to what she saw as a society soiled by material greed, crime, and the perpetuation of slavery. Influenced at various times by Goethe, Carlyle, Mary Wollstonecraft, and George Sand, and a friend of Emerson's, she edited the transcendentalists' journal the *Dial* from 1840 to 1842, and published a notable feminist work, *Woman in the Nineteenth Century* (1844), in which she argued that the development of men and women cannot occur in mutual independence, there being no wholly masculine man, or purely feminine woman. She was distinctive in making gender an issue, and this text can be read as an effort to make Emersonian self-reliance an option for women.

Nathaniel Hawthorne (1804–1864) drew upon Emerson's theories, Enlightenment philosophy, and Coleridge's views on imagination to define the genre of romance fiction as a locus where the real and the imaginary intersect and influence each other, in a unified vision. For Hawthorne, recognition of textual history and the history of American institutions is just an integral element of such a vision as is nature. Both Hawthorne and his friend and admirer Herman Melville reacted, like the other American Romantics, against the mechanism and commercialism at the core of American life. Striving to attain the passion and originality to develop a national literature, they yet recognized that the modern fragmented world defied the attempts of romance and imagination to achieve a harmonious and comprehensive vision of life.

Ralph Waldo Emerson (1803–1882)

Emerson, the most articulate exponent of American Romanticism, was a poet; but he was distinguished primarily by his contributions to literary and cultural criticism. He was the leading advocate of American "transcendentalism" with its insistence on the value of intuition, individuality of perception, the goodness of human nature, and the unity of the entire creation. His views of nature and self-reliance not only influenced American literary figures of his own day, such as Thoreau, Whitman, and Dickinson, but also left their mark on European writers such as George Eliot and Nietzsche, as well as the American pragmatist philosophers William James and John Dewey.

Though he graduated from Harvard Divinity School and became a minister at a Unitarian church in Boston, his personal circumstances (his first wife dying of tuberculosis) and intellectual development led him to harbor doubts about conventional Christian doctrine. He traveled to Europe in 1832, meeting with Wordsworth and Coleridge, as well as Thomas Carlyle, with whom he maintained a long correspondence. Beyond the influences of these European literary figures, Emerson's work bears traces of the ideas of Kant, Hegel, and Schleiermacher. His most renowned volumes and essays include "Nature" (1836), "The American Scholar" (1837), the "Address Delivered before the Senior Class in Divinity College" (1838) (where he criticized institutional religion for thwarting individual self-discovery), "History," "Self-Reliance," and "The Poet."

Emerson's essay "Nature" is one of the most powerful and succinct expressions of a Romantic world view. Emerson sees the universe as composed of "Nature" and the "Soul," taking up a distinction of Carlyle and some German philosophers such as Fichte between the "self" and the "not-self."[12] Everything that falls under the "not-self" or the "not-me" is considered by Emerson to fall under the term "Nature." Characteristically of Romanticism, Emerson believes that nature is apprehensible not to most adults but to the "eye and the heart of the child," of someone who "has retained the spirit of infancy" (25). He stresses that nature is part of God and through it circulate the "currents of the Universal Being" (26). Whatever is furnished to our senses by nature Emerson calls "commodities." A higher gift of nature is the love of beauty. Emerson sees beauty as having three aspects: at the lowest level, we derive pleasure from the "simple perception of natural forms." But this beauty is merely "seen and felt," and its elements are the mere physical appearances of nature which in themselves have no reality (29–30). Such nature reflects a higher and divine beauty which inspires man to virtue. The highest form under which beauty may be viewed is when it becomes "an object of the intellect," which "searches out the absolute order of things as they stand in the mind of God" (32). Hence the beauty in nature "is not ultimate. It is the herald of inward and eternal beauty" (33).

A third use provided by nature to man is language. Nature, says Emerson, is "the vehicle of thought," in a threefold manner. Firstly, words are "signs of natural facts": the root of every word is ultimately "borrowed from some material appearance." For example, "right" originally meant "straight" and "wrong" meant "twisted" (33). Secondly, "it is not words only that are emblematic; it is things which are emblematic. Every natural fact is a symbol of some spiritual facts. Every appearance in nature corresponds to some state of the mind" (34). For example, light and darkness are familiarly associated with knowledge and ignorance; a river expresses the flux of all things. Nature makes man conscious of "a universal soul within or behind his individual life, wherein, as in a firmament, the natures of Justice, Truth, Love, Freedom, arise and shine. This universal soul he calls Reason . . . That which intellectually considered we call Reason, considered in relation to nature, we call Spirit. Spirit is the Creator" (34). What Emerson is indicating here is that nature taken in itself is a mere catalogue of facts. But once it is married to human history, it becomes alive, expressing a "radical correspondence between visible things and human thoughts." In this sense, nature is an "interpreter." It remains for wise men and poet to redeem language from its corruption and to "fasten words again to visible things" (35–36). In other words, language is reconnected with material images, and good writing and discourse are "perpetual allegories." Like Wordsworth, Emerson advocates the life of the country, a withdrawal from "the roar of cities or the broil of politics," in order to facilitate such a rejuvenation of language. Emerson goes on to explain that the "world is emblematic. Parts of speech are metaphors, because the whole of nature is a metaphor of the human mind" (36). In a Hegelian sentiment, Emerson notes that "there seems to be a necessity in spirit to manifest itself in material forms." Material phenomena "preexist in necessary Ideas in the mind of God . . . A Fact is the end or last issue of spirit" (37). Hence language is rooted in the divinely overseen and progressive connection between the human spirit and nature; things in the world are themselves signs, are themselves allegorical enactments of higher truths; nature or the world does not exist in and for itself but as a vehicle of man's spiritual expression.

Nature, according to Emerson, also provides a "discipline" to our understanding, offering an immense variety of material which can educate our understanding and reason (38–39). Moreover, nature disposes us toward "idealism," toward overcoming our immersion in material things and recognizing that the material world is merely an expression of something higher, namely, a system of truth, morality, and beauty. Nature "is made to conspire with spirit to emancipate us" (45). The poet communicates this detached pleasure, arising from his ability to lift things from their immediate context and to situate them in larger, spiritual and intellectual realms: "The sensual man conforms thoughts to things; the poet conforms things to his thoughts" (45). The poet has a freedom whereby he can rearrange elements of the given world into a more profound, symbolic reality, effectively asserting the "predominance of the soul" over nature (47).

The poet, says Emerson, "proposes Beauty as his main end," whereas the philosopher proposes Truth. Nonetheless, they both seek to ground the world of phenomena in stable and permanent laws in an *idea* whose beauty is infinite. Hence, the "true philosopher and the true poet are one, and a beauty, which is truth, and a truth, which is beauty, is the aim of both" (47). Whereas later writers such as Poe will subordinate the considerations of truth and morality to the overarching aim of beauty, Emerson holds these together in a precarious balance flown into the modern world direct from Plato's Athens.

Like many Romantics, Emerson laments that the current age is reduced to a mechanical understanding of the world. Man at present, says Emerson, "works on the world with his understanding alone. He lives in it and masters it by a penny-wisdom" (55). Understanding, we recall, is regarded by most Romantics as a categorizing faculty, able to divide up the world in a mechanical way but unable to reach the unifying vision of reason or imagination. In such a view of the world, says Emerson, the "axis of vision is not coincident with the axis of things . . . The reason why the world lacks unity, and lies broken and in heaps, is because man is disunited with himself." The problem of "restoring to the world original and eternal beauty is solved by the redemption of the soul" (56). By altering ourselves, by transforming the spirit that moves within us, we will transform the world of nature, since the latter is moved and molded by spirit (57).

It is Emerson's essay "The American Scholar" that perhaps best articulates some of the distinctive concerns of American Romanticism. Emerson here attempts to give voice to the composition and duties of the American scholar in the context not only of contemporary American culture but also of the broader implications of Emerson's transcendental beliefs in the unity of the world, and of the human soul, as well as the nature of their connection. At the beginning of the essay, Emerson declares that America's "day of dependence" on foreign learning is drawing to a close (58). At one level, the essay might be read as a justification of, or as arguing the need for, such cultural and intellectual independence, and a relative freedom from the past. But Emerson's text skillfully integrates the parameters of this freedom, this independence, this cultural nationalism, within a vision of the overall unity of humankind. His most fundamental premise is that "there is One Man," who is present to a partial degree in all men: "Man is not a farmer, or a professor, or an engineer, but he is all. Man is priest, and scholar, and statesman, and producer, and soldier. In the *divided* or social state, these functions are parcelled out to individuals," and the "original unit, this fountain of power . . . has been so minutely subdivided and peddled out, that it is spilled into drops, and cannot be gathered . . . Man is thus metamorphosed into a thing, into many things" (59). Hence, instead of envisioning these subdivisions as "Man farming" or "Man trading" or "Man thinking," we have effectively *reduced* man to the specific functions of "farmer," "trader," or "scholar" (59). None of these is equipped to look beyond his narrow function; the trader, for example, loses sight of the "ideal worth" of his work and, being entrenched within the "routine of his craft," his "soul is subject to dollars" (59).

Like Marx, what Emerson is bemoaning here is the fragmentation of the human by division of labor into various isolated and ossified aspects, a fragmentation that has reached a new intensity with the extreme specialization of function in bourgeois society. This specialization has effectively caused the various human faculties to be separated out according to function, losing sight of their original coexistence and unity. Emerson's proposed remedy for this fragmentation of the human being is, of course, markedly different from the revolutionary strategies of Marx. But it is worth noting the overlap between their perceptions of the circumstance of alienation in the emerging capitalist world. For Emerson, as for many of the Romantic and Victorian thinkers, it is the man of letters, rather than any economic or political agency, who holds the keys to salvation.

In the foregoing statements Emerson expresses a characteristically Romantic vision in his own exquisite mode. Like other Romantics, he rejects the world of mainstream bourgeois philosophy, the world of separate, atomistically conceived entities; a world where the human faculties have fallen from their original unity, and grope in presumed independence; a world of dualism, where nature is viewed as external to the human self, where object and subject, no longer coterminous and enjoying mutual harmony, glide beyond each other's limits in the mode of alienation and incommensurability. Emerson is not returning to some pre-bourgeois vision of preestablished harmony between the self and world; he seems to be articulating a more Hegelian position, one that sees subjectivity and objectivity arising as part of the same movement and in necessary mutual relation. The atomism and fragmentation of the bourgeois world is effectively seen as an intellectual regression to a vision that remains frozen in the mode of separateness, a vision that denies the reality of relation and relatedness, a vision that places the part before the whole, a vision that denudes the immediate "fact" of its constituting contexts. Though Emerson talks of nature as the "web of God," he *also* identifies nature with the expanse of the human self; hence, his vision of unity is based less on the idea of the divine than on a particular notion of human subjectivity influenced directly or indirectly by Kant and Hegel, one that sees the apparatus of subjectivity and objectivity as intrinsically commensurate; in other words, our minds and the objects we perceive are mutually adapted to (and constrained by) each other. Kant had said, for example, that we see objects "in" space because spatiality is part of our subjective apparatus for perceiving the world.

The major influences on the scholar include not only nature but also "the mind of the Past," which is transmitted most clearly by books. For Emerson, a book represents the attempt of a previous scholar to receive raw data from the world, to reflect on this, and to give it the "new arrangement of his own mind . . . It came into him, life; it went out from him, truth. It came to him, short-lived actions; it went out from him, immortal thoughts. It came to him, business; it went from him, poetry." Hence, scholarship (which Emerson is using in a broad sense, to encompass, among other things, poetry) is a process of "transmuting life into truth" (61). However, since no scholar or artist can entirely exclude "the conventional, the local, the perishable" from his book, each age must renew the task of interpreting the world: "Each age . . . must write its own books," and cannot simply stand on the authority of books written for an earlier generation or era (61). If books are overprized, as they are by the "sluggish and perverted mind of the multitude" (the similarities to Marx having somewhat receded in Emerson's text), the influence of books becomes tyrannical: they encourage the reliance by scholars on "accepted dogmas" rather than "their own sight of principles." And instead of Man thinking, "we have the bookworm," the book-learned class who would rank books as a third estate along with the world of nature and the soul. Unfortunately, says Emerson, colleges and institutions are built on the book, on the authority of the "past utterance of genius." But the active soul, the true genius, who sees "absolute truth," will not be constrained by the insights of the past, and looks forward. The scholar should rely on books only in times when he cannot "read God directly" (62). In a sense, Emerson's argument here presents an inverted form of what Eliot will later claim in his influential essay "Tradition and the Individual Talent." Eliot urged the individual writer to subordinate himself to tradition, to the "mind of Europe," which itself enabled and set the archetypal patterns of the individual poet's insight into his own present. For Emerson, the "mind of the past," being restrictive, is precisely what the contemporary writer must transcend in expressing the reality of his own era.

The final educative influence on the scholar, according to Emerson, is "action" (as opposed to a life composed exclusively of speculation). Emerson concedes that action is "subordinate" with the scholar but essential: "Without it, he is not yet man. Without it, thought can never ripen into truth." He insists that we possess knowledge only to the extent that we have lived; "we know," he says, "whose words are loaded with life, and whose not" (64). The point here, of course, is that made by all empiricist philosophies: that knowledge arises from experience and cannot indeed go beyond the limits of our actual experience. In other words, we cannot know about the world or about life through abstract reasoning, through the mere testimony of others, or through obeisance to religious or political authority. To this extent, the scholar must seek out varieties of experience, and must be "covetous of action. Life is our dictionary . . . This is the way to learn grammar. Colleges and books only copy the language which the field and the work-yard made" (65). The implication is that the meanings of words are first found in experience; dictionaries merely formalize and artificially stabilize those meanings, while academic institutions provide frameworks of interpretation of experiences after the fact, after they have occurred.

Emerson concludes his essay by outlining the duties and virtues of the scholar: all of these, he says, are comprised in "self-trust," a notion that has several dimensions. To begin with, the scholar is "self-relying and self-directed," being constrained neither by tradition or religion, nor by fashion and the opinion of popular judgment. Indeed, he seems to stand in a relation of "virtual hostility" to society (67). Emerson anticipates Nietzsche in his view that the mass of contemporary humanity are bugs, a mass which acts like a herd; in a thousand years, only one or two men will approximate "to the right state of every man." The remainder are content to bask in the light and dignity of a great man or hero (70). Yet the task of Emerson's heroic scholar, unlike that of Nietzsche's overman who rises above common morality, is to reaffirm and reestablish man's lost connections with his universal, unified self. By having the courage and wisdom to descend into the secrets of his own mind, he fathoms the secrets of all minds and reveals what is "universally true" (68). He is the one who sees "facts amidst appearances," who "raises himself from private considerations" and momentary opinions that cloud the enduring judgment of "Reason from her inviolable seat." It is the scholar alone who knows the world: "He is the world's eye. He is the world's heart" (67). It is he who wakes people from their sleep-walking dream in search of money and power, leading them to this fundamental lesson: "The world is nothing, the man is all; in yourself is the law of all nature . . . in yourself slumbers the whole of Reason." In somewhat Hegelian fashion, Emerson even sees successive scholars as embodying the points of view taken by "the universal mind" (70–71).

Notwithstanding these universalizing functions of the scholar, Emerson welcomes recent literature that explores, not the sublime and the beautiful, but the low and the common, the local and the contemporary (71). Ironically, Emerson's notion of universality is sustained precisely by its refusal to be constrained by past wisdom, by the need to confront what is true and enduring in the present era. And it is here that the duties of the scholar devolve into the *particular* duties of the American scholar: "this confidence in the unsearched might of man belongs, by all motives, by all prophecy, by all preparation, to the American scholar. We have listened too long to the courtly muses of Europe" (73). He appeals to the young man of America to "plant himself indomitably on his instincts," and to attain the perspective of his "own infinite life." He ends with an eloquent call for an independence that is based on relation, on integration within a totality: "We will walk on our own feet; we will work with our own hands; we will speak our own minds . . . A nation of men will for the first time exist, because each believes himself inspired by the Divine Soul which also inspires all men" (74). Emerson's is a powerful voice attempting to situate American ideals such as self-reliance and independence (at both national and individual levels) within a pre-capitalist harmony of self and world, a harmony equated with attunement to the workings of the divine and thereby precariously balanced between secular and religious vision.

In his "Address Delivered before the Senior Class in Divinity College" at Harvard (1838), Emerson undertakes a critique of institutional Christianity in America. Emerson's central criticism is that religion has lost contact with its original impetus, which was exploratory, creative, and intuitive; it is now based on mere precedent, tradition, and expediency. The current decaying state of the Church and the condition of "wasting unbelief" mark the greatest calamity that can befall a nation – loss of worship: "then all things go to decay. Genius leaves the temple to haunt the senate or the market. Literature becomes frivolous. Science . . . Society lives to trifles" (89). Emerson also spurns modern attempts to found a new system of religion, such as the worship of the "goddess of Reason," which ends in "madness and murder" (92).

Emerson's proposed solution to this dismal state of affairs is partly founded on the Stoic doctrine "Obey thyself" (84). He admonishes the future preachers at the Divinity School "to go alone; to refuse the good models . . . and dare to love God without mediator or veil," to cast away "all conformity, and acquaint men at first hand with Deity" (90–91). As he has said in other essays, he reaffirms here that it is in the soul that "redemption must be sought," and it is through such redemption that the world can be transformed, since the world is the mirror of the soul (89, 93). Only such redemption can counter the "loss of the universal" in modern secular democracy, along with the latter's "exaggeration of the finite and selfish" (91). Emerson's essay is an articulate expression of a Romantic view of religion, and indeed of the rootedness of a Romantic view of letters in a transformed conception of religion, one that stresses individuality, creativity, and exploration even in the realm of morality.

In fact, in his essay "The Transcendentalist" (1842), Emerson derides the supposedly "sturdy capitalist" whose apparently solid enterprise actually rests on "quaking foundations" (141). Interestingly, Emerson's very definitions of transcendentalism are forged in the heat of his opposition to the bourgeois obsession with materialism (both as a philosophy and as a way of life, according prominence to economic interests above all else). The term "transcendental," says Emerson, derives from Kant's philosophy, which laid stress on certain forms of perception that belonged to the subjective apparatus (145). Emerson points out that transcendentalism is a form of idealism, and that the transcendentalist's experience "inclines him to behold the procession of facts you call the world, as flowing perpetually outward from an invisible, unsounded center in himself . . . necessitating him to regard all things as having a subjective or relative existence . . . He believes in miracle, in the perpetual openness of the human mind to new influx of light and power; he believes in inspiration, and in ecstasy" (142). Transcendentalists, says Emerson, are characterized by their withdrawal from society, their disinclination even to vote, and their passion for "what is great and extraordinary" (146, 148). They stand aloof from contemporary society, which is marked by "a spirit of cowardly compromise and seeming which intimates a frightful skepticism, a life without love, and an activity without an aim" (149). Their attachment is to "what is permanent," and they speak for "thoughts and principles not marketable or perishable" (153–154). It is clear that the term "transcendental" has acquired a meaning here very different from that which it sustains in Kant's work: it signifies not merely an idealism which rises above the immediacy of the senses, a localized emphasis on materialism, and a mutual isolation or disconnectedness of the phenomena of the world, toward a more unified and longer-term perspective that sees the various elements of the world as the cumulative product of the human mind or spirit; but also a transcendence that refuses to take the bourgeois world as real, that seeks to locate reality itself in another, higher, realm insulated from space, time, and history.

Emerson's essay "Politics" (1844) expresses his skepticism regarding the functioning of government and political parties. He observes that governments exist to protect two types of rights, personal rights and property rights (156). Emerson cautions against the dangers of the "turbulent freedom" of modern times and warns that "in the despotism of public opinion, we have no anchor" (161). Hence he believes in less government and advocates instead, like Socrates, the "influence of private character." The state exists, he says, to "educate the wise man . . . and with the appearance of the wise man, the State expires" (163). The cultivation of character, attuned to nature and higher, spiritual interests, "promises a recognition of higher rights than those of personal freedom, or the security of property" (165).

Many of the foregoing themes, concerning nature, the religious sentiment, and the transcendentalist attitude of withdrawal from the currently degraded state of politics, are brought together in Emerson's essay "The Poet" (1844). In Emerson's eyes, the poet is of course a transcendentalist. The universe, he says, has three children, "the Knower, the Doer and the Sayer. These stand respectively for the love of truth, for the love of good, and for the love of beauty." These three are equal, and the poet "is the sayer, the namer, and represents beauty" (189).

It is the poet whose province is language; nature offers its vast variety to him as a "picture-language." He uses the things in nature as types, as symbols; hence, objects in nature acquire a second value, and nature "is a symbol, in the whole, and in every part" (192). Emerson helps us to make sense of this by reminding us that the "Universe is the externization of the soul," and that its symbolic value lies in its pointing beyond itself, toward the supernatural (193). In this way, the world is a "temple" whose walls are covered with emblems and symbols. The poet, in articulating these symbols, provides a remedy for the "dislocation and detachment from the life of God that makes things ugly." The poet "re-attaches things to nature and the Whole," seeing things "within the great Order" (195). In other words, whereas ordinary perception is filled with images of discrete and unrelated objects, the poet, by "ulterior intellectual perception," is able to see the connectedness of things, especially the symbolic connection between material and spiritual elements (196). Hence the poet's very language, as well as the nature of his perception, is attuned to the workings, the perpetual flux, of nature. By this token, the poet is "the Namer or Language-maker," naming things by their appearance or essence, but always intuitively aware of the connection between these, of the broader, perhaps teleological, picture in which each object exists. Such insight, which Emerson describes as "a very high sort of seeing," is effected by the faculty of imagination (198), which is effectively "the intellect released from all service and suffered to take its direction from its celestial life" (199). In other words, the intellect is freed from its bondage to the restrictive bodily sphere of practical interests and survival.

Emerson refers to poets as "liberating gods . . . They are free, and they make free" (201). They liberate us from the tyranny and fragmentation of conventional perception, from "the jail-yard of individual relations," and enable us to see ourselves and the world in a more comprehensive and far-reaching light (199, 201). Every thought is a prison, says Emerson, and the poet liberates by yielding a new thought. We prize this liberation because "we are miserably dying" (202). As with his essay "The American Scholar," Emerson concludes by calling for poetic universality to comprehend what is peculiarly American. There exists, as yet, no poet of genius in America: "our fisheries, our Negroes and Indians . . . the northern trade, the southern planting . . . are yet unsung. Yet America is a poem in our eyes; its ample geography dazzles the imagination, and it will not wait long for meters" (204). Emerson's words proved prophetic in Whitman's "I sing America." As with the transcendentalist, Emerson calls on the poet to "leave the world, and know the muse only," to "abdicate a manifold and duplex life," and to "lie close hid with nature," away from "the Capitol or the Exchange." The poet is he for whom "the ideal shall be real" (206). Emerson is true to the Romantic inversion of the categories of the bourgeois world: that world is insular, incomplete, and denuded of all relation, all context in which it would find its true meaning. To redeem such relation is the poet's task.

Edgar Allan Poe (1809–1849)

Poe was the first major American writer explicitly to advocate the autonomy of poetry, the freeing of poetry from moral or educational or intellectual imperatives. His fundamental strategy for perceiving such autonomy was to view poetry not as an object but as a series of effects. Hence, while his views are broadly Romantic like Emerson's, they differ deeply from Emerson's in that they present an affective and expressionist view of poetry. While he is usually considered a Romantic, Poe's concern with technique and construction exhibit a formalist disposition and anticipate some of the more modern formalistic theories.

Poe's genius has often been seen as pathological: he lost both his parents at an early age, was informally adopted and later broke with his adoptive parents; he abandoned his studies at the University of Virginia, which he had entered in 1826; he was expelled from West Point Military Academy in 1831; he led a controversial life as a contributor to, and editor of, journals; he indulged in bouts of drinking, suffered from depression and paranoia. Yet his image as an outcast, his emphasis on beauty rather than morality or truth, his view of poetry as affording us a glimpse of an ideal world, as well as his insistence on the close union of poetry and music, exerted a considerable fascination and impact on writers such as Baudelaire, who translated a number of his tales, and Mallarmé, who translated his poems, as well as Lacan, who published in 1966 his seminar on Poe's story "The Purloined Letter."

Poe's most famous tales include "The Black Cat," "The Fall of the House of Usher" (1839), and "The Cask of Amontillado" (1846), and among his notable poems are "To Helen," "Israfel," "The City in the Sea," and "The Haunted Palace." His poem "The Raven" (1842) was widely popular. Some of Poe's radical insights into poetry and criticism are expressed in his essay "The Philosophy of Composition" (1846), which purports to explain the origins of his own poem "The Raven." Other critical essays include "The Poetic Principle" and "The Rationale of Verse." In "The Philosophy of Composition," Poe urges that a poet should begin with the "consideration of an effect," i.e., the response that will be produced in the reader or listener.[13] He also urges that the poet should keep "originality *always* in view" ("PC," 178). This effect, he insists, must be produced as a "unity of impression." Poe does not believe that such a unified impression can be achieved by a long poem; since poetry "intensely excites, by elevating, the soul," and since intense excitement must by nature be brief, a long poem "is, in fact, merely a succession of brief ones – that is to say, of brief poetical effects" ("PC," 180). A poem such as *Paradise Lost*, Poe argues, is at least one half composed of prose, with which the poetic passages are interspersed. Hence the first poetic requirement, unity of impression, cannot be satisfied in a long poem.

Poe's second major claim for the nature of poetry is that it must be "*universally appreciable*," and it is beauty that has the power universally to please. Hence, "Beauty is the sole legitimate province of the poem . . . That pleasure which is at once the most intense, the most elevating, and the most pure, is, I believe, found in the contemplation of the beautiful" ("PC," 181). Poe points out that beauty is not, as is commonly supposed, "a quality, . . . but an effect," an "intense and pure elevation of *soul – not* of intellect, or of heart." Truth, which is the aim of the intellect, or passion, which represents an excitement of the heart, says Poe, are both more easily attainable in prose than poetry. In fact, both of these are antagonistic to beauty, "which is the atmosphere and the essence of the poem" ("PC," 182). Hence beauty – not truth, or emotion, or goodness – is the peculiar province of poetry. Moreover, beauty is reconceived by Poe not as a quality belonging to an object but as an effect in the subject; his views, perhaps influenced by Kant via Coleridge, stop short of Kant's sophistication. Whereas, for Kant, beauty was a mode of apprehension on the part of the subject, for Poe it is a response caused in the reader or listener by the literary object or poem. These are the general points made in Poe's essay, the remainder of which attempts to explain the stages of the composition of "The Raven."

Poe's subsequent essay, "The Poetic Principle" (1850), offers a fuller account of his aesthetics. Here also, he urges that a long poem is a contradiction in terms since it cannot sustain the unity, the "totality of effect or impression," that is the "vital requisite" in all works of art.[14] Poe warns also that a poem may be "improperly brief" such that it degenerates into epigrammatism. A poem that is *very* short cannot produce "a profound or enduring effect" ("PP," 890).

One of Poe's chief endeavors in this essay is to identify and undermine what he calls "the heresy of *The Didactic*," which refers to the view that "the ultimate object of all Poetry is Truth" and that every poem "should inculcate a moral." As against this, Poe insists that the most dignified and noble work is the "poem *per se* – this poem which is a poem and nothing more – this poem written solely for the poem's sake" ("PP," 892–893). This is perhaps the first insistence on artistic or poetic autonomy by an American writer; it may be significant, as emerges later in his text, that Poe somewhat aligned himself with Southern values and resented the domination of American letters by Northern liberalism, as instanced by the influence of the *North American Review* ("PP," 899). Poe himself wrote for the *Southern Literary Messenger*, eventually rising to the editorship of this journal. In this context, Poe's insistence on artistic autonomy may have been a call to consider the beauty of a poem regardless of its political, as well as its moral, content; given that his notion of beauty was somewhat Platonic, it may also have been an attempt to lift art out of and above the sphere of everyday life and its entanglement in bitter political and social struggles.

At any rate, Poe makes a sharp distinction between "the truthful and the poetical modes" of apprehension and inculcation. Truth, he says, demands a severity of language: "We must be simple, precise, terse. We must be cool, calm, unimpassioned." Such a mood, says Poe, "is the exact converse of the poetical" ("PP," 893). Such a seemingly Platonic distinction between the language and mode of philosophy as against those of poetry has of course been challenged by many modern writers. Poe locates his views in a broader model of the mind which somewhat recalls Kant's location of aesthetic judgment as situated between the realm of understanding (which addresses the realm of phenomena) and the realm of practical reason (comprehending the realm of morality). Poe likewise divides the mind into three aspects: "Pure Intellect, Taste, and the Moral Sense." He places taste in the middle, acknowledging that it has "intimate relations" with the other two aspects; but he observes a distinction between these three offices: the intellect is concerned with truth; taste apprehends the beautiful; and moral sense disposes us toward duty ("PP," 893). By situating his view of poetic autonomy within such a scheme, Poe is following a Kantian procedure of both identifying a subjective faculty specifically as aesthetic, and establishing boundaries between distinct human endeavors or attributes, boundaries which cannot be violated. Poe admits that the precepts of duty or even the lessons of truth can be introduced into a poem; but they must subserve the ultimate purpose of art, and must be placed "in proper subjection to that *Beauty* which is the atmosphere and the real essence of the poem" ("PP," 895).

Hence poetry should not be realistic, merely copying or imitating the beauties that lie before us. Rather, poetry is "a wild effort to reach the Beauty above . . . to attain a portion of that Loveliness whose very elements, perhaps, appertain to eternity alone"; it is a "struggle to apprehend the supernal Loveliness" ("PP," 894). Platonic passages such as these, urging the poet to rise above the transient world and to focus his gaze upon the eternal form of Beauty, must have attracted Baudelaire and some of the French Symbolists such as Mallarmé. Poe uses the term poetry in a broad sense, to cover all of the arts; but he sees a very close connection between poetry and music; in fact he defines poetry as "*The Rhythmical Creation of Beauty*. Its sole arbiter is Taste . . . In the contemplation of Beauty we alone find it possible to attain that pleasurable elevation, or excitement, *of the soul*, which we recognize as the Poetic Sentiment, and which is so easily distinguished from Truth, which is the satisfaction of the Reason, or from Passion, which is the excitement of the Heart" ("PP," 895). What is not Platonic, however, is the isolated exaltation of Beauty over truth and goodness; the harmony that was possible, even in theory, in Plato's system, between these forms or essences, between these multifold dimensions of human endeavor, has disintegrated into a desperate craving for a beauty that is not found in the actual world, and a retreat from the increasingly troubled realms of truth and morality.

Poe defines the "poetic principle" as "the Human Aspiration for Supernal Beauty," a quest for an excitement of the soul that is distinct from the intoxication of the heart or the satisfaction of reason. Truth may be instrumental in this quest inasmuch as it leads us to "perceive a harmony where none was apparent before." The experience of such a harmony is "the true poetical effect" ("PP," 906). Once again, we glimpse here reflections of Kantian ideas, refracted perhaps through Coleridge. The poet, according to Poe, recognizes in many phenomena the ambrosia that nourishes his soul, especially in "all unworldly motives – in all holy impulses – in all chivalrous, generous, and self-sacrificing deeds" ("PP," 906). What is interesting here is that all of these phenomena appear to pertain to morality: the very morality that is expelled from the poet's quest for beauty returns as the very ground of this quest, resurrected in aesthetic form on the ground of its own beauty. In other words, morality becomes an integral part of the aesthetic endeavor, and becomes justified on aesthetic grounds. Once again, art is seen as salvific, displacing the function of religion in serving as our guide to the world beyond.

Notes

1 *The Letters of John Keats: Volume I*, ed. Hyder Edward Rollins (Cambridge, MA: Harvard University Press, 1958), p. 184. Hereafter cited as *Letters*.

2 The text cited here is the 1850 version, contained in *The Prose Works of William Wordsworth: Volume I*, ed. W. J. B. Owen and Jane Worthington Smyser (Oxford: Clarendon Press, 1974). The editors have included the 1800 version on facing pages, as well as a useful commentary on variants from the 1850 version. Hereafter cited as *PLB*.

3 *Coleridge: Poetical Works*, ed. Ernest Hartley Coleridge (New York and Oxford: Oxford University Press, 1973), p. 11. Hereafter cited as *CPW*.

4 *The Collected Works of Samuel Taylor Coleridge. VII: Biographia Literaria*, ed. James Engell and W. Jackson Bate (Princeton: Princeton University Press, 1983), p. 187. Hereafter cited as *BL*.

5 *The Collected Works of Samuel Taylor Coleridge: Lay Sermons*, ed. R. J. White (Princeton and London: Princeton University Press/Routledge and Kegan Paul), p. 169. Hereafter cited as *LS*.

6 On this point I differ somewhat from the otherwise splendid account offered by James Engell and W. Jackson Bate in their introduction to the *Biographia*. What they attribute to Coleridge as "philosophic imagination" I would prefer to call "reason." Having said that, I acknowledge that this may simply be a difference in nomenclature; I should also acknowledge my general indebtedness to their learned and insightful commentary.

7 For a detailed and lucid explanation of Coleridge's sources, see Introduction, *BL*, pp. lxxxv–lxxxviii.

8 See ibid., pp. xcvii–civ.

9 *The Education of Henry Adams*, ed. Ernest Samuels (1918; rpt. Boston, 1974), p. 33.

10 Ibid., p. 500.

11 Walt Whitman, "Introduction," in *Leaves of Grass: The First (1855) Edition*, ed. Malcolm Cowley (Harmondsworth: Penguin, 1986), pp. 5, 8, 23.

12 *Ralph Waldo Emerson and Margaret Fuller: Selected Works*, ed. John Carlos Rowe (Boston and New York: Houghton Mifflin, 2003), p. 24. Hereafter page citations are given in the text.

13 "The Philosophy of Composition," in *The Complete Poetry and Selected Criticism of Edgar Allan Poe*, ed. Allen Tate (New York and London: New American Library, 1981), p. 178. Hereafter cited as "PC."

14 "The Poetic Principle," in *Complete Tales and Poems of Edgar Allan Poe* (New York: Vintage Books, 1975), p. 889. Hereafter cited as "PP."

PART VII

THE LATER NINETEENTH CENTURY

CHAPTER 18

REALISM AND NATURALISM

Historical Background

The later nineteenth century saw an intensification of developments that had begun several decades earlier with the French Revolution of 1789. The middle classes continued to struggle against absolutist regimes and to establish their own hegemony in the economic, political, and cultural spheres. In 1848 Europe was shaken by revolutions in France, Vienna, Berlin, Venice, Milan, and Prague. Nationalism achieved a sharpened focus, with several countries, notably Germany and Italy, achieving political unity in the 1870s. By the end of the century, imperialism had spread to an unprecedented extent over large portions of the globe. The forces of the Industrial Revolution accelerated, with ever increasing migration to the towns, a vast surge of population, and the development of communication and transportation. It was in this period that there developed in Europe an industrial workforce which began to challenge bourgeois ideology and institutions. Working conditions and industrial unrest were described in the novels of Elizabeth Gaskell (1810–1865), Charles Dickens (1812–1870), and Émile Zola. But it was the middle classes who now controlled the fate of much of Europe, and it was the middle classes who now formed the primary readership.

In the later nineteenth century, the vast unifying systems of thinkers such as Hegel, as well as the unifying visions of the Romantics, collapsed into a series of one-sided systems, such as utilitarianism, positivism, and social Darwinism. To be sure, there were a number of movements that continued the oppositional stance of Romanticism to mainstream bourgeois and Enlightenment ideals: Matthew Arnold criticized the philistinism of bourgeois society, while Thomas Carlyle promoted his own version of German idealism, and John Ruskin perpetuated a Romantic idealization of the Middle Ages. A tradition of alternative philosophy, often pessimistic, was inaugurated by Schopenhauer and ran through thinkers such as Nietzsche, Kierkegaard, and Bergson. More politically forceful were the various movements of socialism inspired by Marx, Engels, and others.

But the values and ideals of the mainstream bourgeois Enlightenment prevailed. In the later nineteenth century, these values were increasingly attuned to the rapid progress of science and technology. As the culmination of a historical pattern beginning in the Renaissance, science effectively displaced religion and theology as the supreme arbiter of knowledge. The economic and social forces mentioned above had led to the institutional demise of religion. Scientific development and broadly scientific attitudes intensified this process. Charles Darwin's *Origin of Species* (1859) was held by some to undermine the biblical accounts of creation; the rise of the German Higher criticism subjected the gospels to a searching "scientific" scrutiny, exposing many inconsistencies and contradictions. David Strauss' *The Life of Jesus* saw Christ in terms of myth rather than fact; Ernest Renan's book of the same title effectively denied the originality of Christ, viewing him as emerging from a religious context already prepared. Life on the agricultural estate or village, once centered around the church or parish, was now supplanted by life in the cities where people's existence – crowded but more anonymous – revolved around the factory or office.

Against the backcloth of these broad transformations, the natural sciences became the model and the measure of other disciplines. The broadest name for this emulation of science is positivism, which derives its name from those self-proclaimed "positive" philosophies of thinkers such as Auguste Comte and Émile Durkheim in France, and Herbert Spencer in England. These thinkers wished to exclude from investigation all hypotheses that were not empirically verifiable, and they rejected as "metaphysical" all inquiries that were not ultimately reducible to supposedly scientific terms of analysis, such as "matter," "motion," and "force." In political terms, the Marxist philosopher and sociologist Herbert Marcuse has shown how positivism, or "positive philosophy," was essentially a conservative reaction against the "negative philosophy" of Hegel.[1] Hegel's entire dialectic had been premised on a rejection of the world as given and an imperative to refashion the world in the image of our own rationality. When the bourgeoisie had been a revolutionary class, attempting to undermine and eventually shatter the irrational system of feudalism, Hegel's philosophy had articulated the bourgeois vision of reason and historical progress. His system had attempted to reconcile the various contradictions and impasses of bourgeois thought (such as the alienation between subject and object, self and world, individual and community) by articulating a vast historical system in which bourgeois values were situated as a predominating but one-sided component in a larger scheme that included the virtues of Romanticism and religion. In Hegel's philosophy, bourgeois thought achieved a momentary and precarious harmony with the history of theology and metaphysics against which it had reacted, and on whose underlying principles it had emerged into self-formation.

With the collapse of Hegel's philosophy into various emphases, as represented by right-wing Hegelianism and left-wing Hegelianism, came also a positivistic reaction against the very principles of Hegelian unity and totality as achieved by some spiritual agency or absolute. The "positive" philosophers and sociologists rejected all divine or spiritual agency and, in their insistence on "nature," on experience, observation, and empirical verifiability, sought what they considered to be a more scientific and piecemeal approach to the acquisition of knowledge. There was no room in their visions for talk of God or a priori laws of perception or laws of history or any other metaphysical entities that transcended the realm of observational certitude. Ideologically, positivism, in its manifold guises, was an attempt to confirm the reality and propriety of the world as given; in other words, these were essentially conservative modes of thought, sanctioning the status quo. Positivism pervaded many domains, in sociology (as exemplified by Durkheim, who attempted to isolate a distinctly "social" fact), psychology (as shown in Freud's obsession with the scientific status of his work), and in social thought (expressed in the evolutionism of Herbert Spencer). Realism and naturalism are the literary expressions of this general tendency, which did not inform the theory and practice of literary criticism until the formalism, structuralism, and New Criticism of the twentieth century. Nonetheless, a scientific approach to literature and literary history had been anticipated by the scientific biography advocated by Charles Augustin Sainte-Beuve and the deterministic theories of Hippolyte Taine.

Realism and Naturalism in Europe and America

Realism was by no means a uniform or coherent movement; a tendency toward realism arose in many parts of Europe and in America, beginning in the 1840s. The major figures included Flaubert and Balzac in France, Dostoevsky and Tolstoy in Russia, George Eliot and Charles Dickens in England, as well as William Dean Howells and Henry James in America. The most general aim of realism was to offer a truthful, accurate, and objective representation of the real world, both the external world and the human self. To achieve this aim, realists resorted to a number of strategies: the use of descriptive and evocative detail; avoidance of what was fantastical, imaginary, and mythical; adhering to the requirements of probability, and excluding events which were impossible or improbable; inclusion of characters and incidents from all social strata, dealing not merely with rulers and nobility; focusing on the present and choosing topics from contemporary life rather than longing for some idealized past; emphasizing the social rather than the individual (or seeing the individual as a social being); refraining from the use of elevated language, in favor of more colloquial idioms and everyday speech, as well as directness and simplicity of expression. All of these aims and strategies were underlain by an emphasis on direct observation, factuality, experience, and induction (arriving at general truths only on the basis of repeated experience). In adopting the strategies listed above, realism was a broad and multipronged reaction against the idealization, historical retrospection, and the imaginary worlds seen as characterizing Romanticism.

Naturalism was the ancient term for the physical sciences or the study of nature. Naturalism explicitly endeavors to emulate the methods of the physical sciences, drawing heavily on the principles of causality, determinism, explanation, and experimentation. Some naturalists also drew on the Darwinian conception of nature and attempted to express the struggle for survival, as embodied in the connections between individuals and their environments, often portraying the physiologically and psychically determined dimensions of their characters as overwhelmed by accidental circumstances rather than acting rationally, freely, and heroically upon the world. Hence naturalism can be viewed as a more extreme form of realism, extending the latter's scientific basis still further to encompass extremely detailed methods of description, a deterministic emphasis upon the contexts of actions and events (which are seen as arising from specific causes), upon the hereditary psychological components of their characters, experimenting with

471

the connections between human psychology and external environment, and refusing to accommodate any kind of metaphysical or spiritual perspective. The theoretical foundations of naturalism were laid by the literary historian Hippolyte Taine (1828–1893), in works such as his *Histoire de la littérature anglaise* (1863–1864), and by Émile Zola, as will be seen, who first formulated its manifesto.

The term "realism" had been used in the 1820s but did not acquire any significant valency in literary strategy and criticism until the 1830s when a reaction started setting in against the predominating ideals of Romanticism. In Germany, a radical group called the Young Germans, whose prominent members included Heinrich Heine (1797–1856) and Carl Gutzkow (1811–1878), voiced their opposition to the perceived reactionary Romanticism of Goethe and Schlegel. This group also rejected the ideal of aesthetic autonomy in favor of a realism that was politically interventional. The atmosphere in Germany, however, was not favorable toward liberalism. Liberal movements had already been curbed by the Carlsbad Decrees of 1819, subjecting the universities to state control and authors to censorship. In 1835 the Young Germans were banned, as was the later Marxist criticism of figures such as Franz Mehring (1846–1919). The repressive political situation, climaxing in the defeat of the 1848 revolution, led to an isolation of literature from political discourse, reflected even in the literary historicism of figures such as Georg Gottfried Gervinus, influenced by Hegel's aesthetics. Hegelian idealism and historicism increasingly gave way before positivism, reflected in various brands of realism and naturalism. Proponents of realism included Julian Schmidt (1818–1886), the novelist Gottfried Keller (1819–1890), the dramatist Friedrich Hebbel (1813–1863), and Friedrich Theodor von Vischer (1807–1887), who endeavored to express a theoretical basis for realism. The naturalist movement, arising in the 1880s through the influence of Zola, was advanced by Arno Holz (1863–1929), Heinrich (1855–1906) and Julius Hart (1859–1930), Wilhelm Bolsche (1861–1939), the social novelist Theodor Fontane (1819–1898), and Wilhelm Scherer (1841–1886), who attempted to base literature on scientific principles. In general, this entire period was marked by a conflict between politically valent criticism and various forms of aestheticism, impressionism, and relativism, as well as by the collision of historicism with positivism.

In France, realism became a force in the 1850s. A controversy was sparked by the painter Gustave Courbet, who exhibited his art under the rubric of realism after his paintings had been rejected by the Paris World Fair in 1855. Courbet aimed to present a "slice of life," cut free of any moral or emotional or even aesthetic investment. Edmond Duranty began a journal called *Réalisme* in 1856, in which realism was equated with truthfulness, sincerity, and the modern. Duranty believed that novels should reflect the lives of ordinary middle-class or working-class people. In 1857 Jules-François-Felix Husson (known as Champfleury) published a collection of essays entitled *Le Réalisme*. Anticipating Zola, he urged the need for scrupulous documentation and freedom from moral constraints. Positivism in France took on a more overt aspect in the work of Taine. Influenced by the Enlightenment rationalist philosophers on the one hand, and by Hegel and Spinoza on the other, Taine sought a totalizing explanation of the causal operations governing both human beings and the world. In a somewhat paradoxical endeavor, he sought to situate positivism within a broader historical scheme. In the famous Introduction to his *History of English Literature*, he advocated, following Sainte-Beuve, an ideal of scientific exactness in literary criticism, urging that the task of the critic was to discover the master characteristic of a writer's work, by using the literary text as an expression of the facts of the author's psychology and biography. This predominating characteristic, he held, was determined by three broad factors: race, milieu, and moment. The broader assumption behind this endeavor was that art expresses not only the psychology of its immediate creator but also the spirit of its age. Taine was a major influence on Zola and writers such as Ferdinand Brunetière (1849–1906), who reaffirmed the ideals of an objective criticism. In 1880, Zola, Guy de Maupassant, Joris-Karl Huysmans, and others jointly published a volume of naturalistic fiction entitled *Les Soirées de Meda*. As in Germany, these "scientific" and positivistic tendencies were countered toward the end of the century by advocates of impressionism (as in Edmond and Jules de Goncourt) and the subjectivism of writers such as Anatole France, which renewed the Romantic emphasis on subjectivity and individuality.

In England, realism had in varying degrees informed the numerous types of novel – political, historical, religious – which had been written by major figures such as Thackeray and Dickens during the nineteenth century. But it was with the novels of George Eliot, Anthony Trollope, George Meredith, and Thomas Hardy that realist fiction flowered. George Eliot's views were influenced by Ludwig Feuerbach and Auguste Comte, and her exposition of realism will be discussed below. Eliot's friend and domestic partner George Henry Lewes was a philosopher, critic, and scientist, who was also influenced by Comte. His impact on realistic thinking lay in his examination of human psychology as intimately related to social conditions. Two other notable realists of this period were George Gissing (1857–1903) and George Moore (1852–1933), who, both influenced by Zola, introduced a strain of naturalism into English letters. Gissing was an admirer of Balzac and wrote novels that offered minutely documented accounts of lower-middle-class life in London. The Irish novelist Moore also adopted and modified the realist strategies of Flaubert and Balzac. Another figure associated with English realism was the artist and critic F. G. Stephens, a member of the group of painters known as the "Pre-Raphaelite Brotherhood," formed in 1848; this group had aimed to revive in art qualities such as moral seriousness, directness, and minute representation of detail. Indeed, as Lilian Furst has pointed out, the subsequent development of photography and the ideal of photographic accuracy had considerable significance for realism in both art and literature.

While realism in America reacted against the fundamental tendencies of Romanticism, it perpetuated the latter's concern with national identity and defining a native tradition. The foremost theorist of realism in America was William Dean Howells, whose views will be considered below. Influenced by De Sanctis and Tolstoy, and drawing on the determinism of Taine and the evolutionary philosophy of Herbert Spencer, Howells was a powerful advocate of verisimilitude in fiction. In his manifesto *Crumbling Idols* (1894), Hamlin Garland advanced a notion of "veritism," a version of naturalism, which would express social concerns while respecting local traditions and individual qualities. The novels of both Theodore Dreiser and Stephen Crane bear the impact of Zola's naturalism and social Darwinism. Frank Norris' influential essay "A Plea for Romantic Fiction" (1901) was effectively a defense of naturalism which accommodated some Romantic qualities. An important figure in realist theory was Henry James, whose emphasis on freedom in fiction will be examined shortly.

Nearly all of these writers in the traditions mentioned, however, recognized that realism was problematic and even impossible to achieve. Many of their own creative works contradicted and counter-exemplified their critical views, often deploying sophisticated techniques of symbolism and authorial perspective. They often gave voice to scathing critiques of oppressive social conditions and were often guilty (inevitably) of manipulating so-called facts. Writers such as Flaubert were well aware that the raw material of life or experience needed to be worked on by art; and George Eliot was profoundly cognizant of the difficulty of expressing truth and reality.

In the light of the broad historical background outlined above, it needs to be stressed that realism – a way of thinking that continues to this day – has been not just a literary technique but a vast historical phenomenon with economic, ideological, philosophic, and religious ramifications. This is neatly indicated in Fredric Jameson's statement that "the realistic mode . . . is one of the most complex and vital realizations of Western culture, to which it is . . . well-nigh unique."[2] Lilian Furst describes realism as a product of "a pervasive rationalist epistemology that turned its back on the fantasies of Romanticism."[3]

Realism is not a new phenomenon, and its history can be traced all the way back through writers such as Defoe, Shakespeare, Chaucer, and Aquinas to many of the classical thinkers such as Aristotle. Some insight into the connections between modern realism, classical realism, and Romanticism might be enabled by looking at their philosophical underpinnings. "Modern realism," Ian Watt has suggested, "begins from the position that truth can be discovered by the individual through his senses: it has its origins in Descartes and Locke."[4] Watt remarks that the scholastic realism of the Middle Ages, deriving from Aristotle, viewed as the true realities universals, classes, and abstractions rather than the particular, concrete objects of sense-perception. Modern realism inverted these priorities, and it is the belief, affirmed in 1713 by Berkeley's Philonous, that *"everything which exists is particular,"* which "gives modern thought since Descartes a certain unity of outlook and method."[5]

Auerbach too distinguishes medieval from modern realism: in the former, "an occurrence on earth signifies not only itself but at the same time another, which it predicts or confirms . . . The connection between occurrences is not regarded as primarily a chronological or causal development but as a oneness within the divine plan, of which all occurrences are parts and reflections."[6] What Auerbach describes is a duality inscribed in each event, a simultaneous significance in two worlds, this world and the "other" world. Such duality confers universal significance upon the smallest particular occurrence. The potential for an event to have isolated meaning in this world only emerged into realization with a rising bourgeois class whose economic interests were expressed in the philosophical domain by an increasing emphasis on the world here and now, on an emancipation of the particular event from its imprisoning exemplification of moral truths or its stunting participation in preemptive categories. Yet, in virtue of their very assaults on universality, the bourgeois thinkers deprived themselves of the ability to relocate the particular within alternative schemes. Realism's reification of the particular implied a world of mutually disconnected objects. Lilian Furst has pointed out that the evolution of realism was affected by the Daguerre–Niépce method of photography, presented in 1839, "which facilitated a more exact reproduction of reality."[7] The self-casting of realism into the mold of photography completed the rebellion of modern literary technique against the universal: the reality thus encaptured was expressed in great detail, in all its immediate particularity, but at the expense of being randomly isolated, literally cut out from its surroundings. The philosophical situation inherited by Kant had been articulated largely by Locke and Hume. It was a situation characterized above all by a separation between the worlds of subject and object; the difficulty of articulating the connection between these indicated that certain profound philosophical problems had been sidestepped by realism in its reductive claim to represent "the" real world.

Watt states that the problem of realism "is essentially an epistemological problem." Fredric Jameson has suggested that "realism is the most complex epistemological instrument yet devised for recording the truth of social reality."[8] The rise of literary realism had been supported by the rise of philosophical realism, of thinkers such as Meinong, G. E. Moore, and Russell, whose assumptions might be traced back to Locke, and which were reaffirmed in the controversial collection of essays in *The New Realism* (1912).

Much literary modernism has reacted against realism's reduction of experience to a single dimension, ascertainable in terms of causality, chronology, definable motive, and development of individual characters. Fredric Jameson has suggested that, as the bourgeoisie begins to decay as a class, not only is realism no longer appropriate as a mode of representing reality but also "the very object of realism itself – secular reality, objective reality – no longer exists either . . . that 'real world' is itself a thing of the past."[9] Other thinkers such as the Hungarian Marxist George Lukács have advocated a realism grounded not on the detailed depiction of particular events and characters but on an expression of these as typical of, or embodying, the broader historical movements of their time. These historical forces are the real subject of the realist novel, which Lukács sees as the epic of the modern world.

Both Marxist and non-Marxist writers – formalists, structuralists, and deconstructionists – have associated realism with deficiency of artistic form, and with a commonplace vision which accepts reality as something given. According to these writers, the political connotations of merely expressing given reality are equally imposing: it is not the function of art simply to mirror and resign itself to the mundane bourgeois reality which surrounds it. This reality is not eternal, as it claims to be, but ephemeral; to express a more substantial reality, the artist must abstract from what lies immediately to hand. It is integral to the artist's function to demystify this falsifying scheme, to lay bare the artifice of eternity. Structuralists such as Tzvetan Todorov have viewed realism as overtly and misleadingly transparent, and have rejected its referential basis: narrative and language, they have argued, refer not to any external reality; rather, they embody a self-contained and internally coherent system of concepts through which we see reality. Reader-response theorists such as Wolfgang Iser regard reality as produced by the interaction of author, text, and reader, rather than somehow existing prior to these linguistic operations. Deconstructive critics such as J. Hillis Miller have also rejected the correspondence theory of meaning and truth underlying realism: even the name of a city such as London is not a pregiven reality but a set of signs for writers such as Dickens.

As seen above, realism, in both literature and philosophy, was one expression of the "scientific" tendency to analyze and divide up the various constituents of the world.

Influenced by psychoanalytic and sociological developments, much twentieth-century thought has tended to view mental states in terms of a complex admixture of previously separated "faculties" such as reason and imagination. It has also rejected the "scientific" assumption behind realism that total objectivity is attainable: the line between mental states and external objects is no longer so clear. This enables a different kind of realism, one which attempts not so much accurately to reflect the world as to express mental states in all their incoherent flux. Proust, Joyce, Woolf, and Bergson were crucial components of this modernist reaction against the rigidity of some nineteenth-century realism. But there is a sense in which these writers, like T. S. Eliot, do not reject realism outright but refine it. In confronting experience in all its complex temporal actuality rather than predefining its elements, modernism could be described as "realistic." Such a reconceived realism is more consonant with twentieth-century modes of thought. As mentioned earlier, however, many of the nineteenth-century realists were well aware of the practical problems that confronted their theoretical claims. What follows is an analysis of central statements of realism and naturalism made in England, France, and America.

George Eliot (1819–1880)

One of the most succinct yet poignant statements of realism was made by the major Victorian novelist George Eliot, the latter being the pseudonym of Mary Ann Evans. Her novels include *Adam Bede* (1859), *The Mill on the Floss* (1860), *Silas Marner* (1861), *Middlemarch* (1871–1872), and *Daniel Deronda* (1874–1876). Her early life was spent in Warwickshire where she fell under the spell of a narrow religious evangelicalism inspired by John Wesley's Methodist movement. Her intellectual and religious horizons were later expanded through various influences. She contributed to, and eventually became assistant editor of, the *Westminster Review*, a position that gave her access to much liberal thought. She was exposed to the ideas of Carlyle, Emerson, Mill, and Huxley, and more intimately acquainted with figures such as Herbert Spencer, as well as George Henry Lewes, with whom she entered in 1865 into a lifelong partnership outside of marriage. A writer and advocate of realism, Lewes was the first person to bring the positivism of Auguste Comte to the attention of English thinkers. George Eliot's translation of David Strauss' controversial work *The Life of Jesus* appeared in 1846; Strauss had argued that we must reject the literal truth of the gospels and accept them as "myths," as archetypal constructs of the social imagination. In 1854 she also produced a translation of Ludwig Feuerbach's *The Essence of Christianity*. Nearly all of these thinkers promoted a humanistic and tolerant, as opposed to a rigidly religious, conception of human nature.

This newer conception is expressed in both the form and content of *Adam Bede*. One of the features of this novel is that its narrative is self-conscious, with the omniscient narrator often pausing to reflect on the story and to mediate between the story and the reader. The most striking example of this occurs in chapter 17, entitled "In Which the Story Pauses a Little." Eliot uses this chapter to outline and justify her narrative technique of realism. She imagines the reader exclaiming that her portrayal of a certain character called Mr. Irwine, rector of Broxton, presents him as "little better than a pagan!"[10] She retorts that as a novelist she wishes to avoid refashioning "life and character" after her "own liking"; rather, she says, "my strongest effort is to avoid any such arbitrary picture, and to give a faithful account of men and things as they have mirrored themselves in my mind. The mirror is doubtless defective; the outlines will sometimes be disturbed, the reflection faint or confused; but I feel as much bound to tell you as precisely as I can what that reflection is, as if I were in the witness-box narrating my experience on oath" (150). Hence, the first principle of her realism is the artistic pursuit of truth, a truth based on direct experience of the world. She is aware, however, of the difficulty of such an enterprise: "Falsehood is so easy, truth so difficult . . . Examine your words well, and you will find that even when you have no motive to be false, it is a very hard thing to say the exact truth, even about your own immediate feelings" (151–152). There is an implicit recognition here of the gulf between language and experience, of the inadequacy of words to express our actual psychological states. Indeed, she imagines the reader asking for the "facts" to be improved and idealized, for characters to be portrayed as unproblematically good or bad, so that they can be admired or condemned "at a glance," and without the "slightest disturbance" of their prepossessions or assumptions (150–151). Eliot's point is that to indulge in such falsehoods and fictions, to paint life in a neatly categorized manner, is far more easy than expressing life in its actual, untidy, complexity. This, then, is a second principle of her realism, which follows from the pursuit of truth: experience is complex and must not be reduced to expression in preconceived categories; the representation of experience must be authentic, refusing to pander to current prejudices and popular taste.

A third principle of the realism advocated by Eliot is its moral basis: we should accept people in their actual, imperfect, state, rather than holding them up to impossible ideals: "These fellow-mortals, every one, must be accepted as they are: you can neither straighten their noses, nor brighten their wit, nor rectify their dispositions; and it is these people – amongst whom your life is passed – that it is needful you should tolerate, pity, and love" (151). Hence Eliot's realism is not the stark realism of a Flaubert or the naturalism of a Zola, which are inspired primarily by a "scientific" zeal for accuracy. Rather, the artistic focus on ordinary people and events has both an epistemological basis – the reliance on one's own experience – and a moral basis of sympathy or "fellow-feeling" with other human beings. Eliot is reacting of course, in part, against the long tradition of "high" style literature which has treated of "tragic suffering or of world-stirring actions." She regards this tradition as essentially idealistic, a tradition which has ignored the reality of "cheap common things" and "vulgar details" (152).

A fourth principle of realism, for Eliot, is given in her view of beauty. She effectively redefines, or at least vastly extends, the medieval conception of beauty as pertaining to the form and proportion of an object. Let us, she says, "love that other beauty too, which lies in no secret of proportion, but in the secret of deep human sympathy." While she does not reject the high style that paints an angel or a Madonna, she states: "but do not impose on us any aesthetic rules which shall banish from the region of Art those old women scraping carrots with their work-worn hands . . . those rounded backs and stupid weather-beaten faces that have bent over the spade and done the rough work of the world . . . It is so needful we should remember their existence, else we may happen to leave them quite out of our religion and philosophy, and frame lofty theories which only fit a world of extremes. Therefore let Art always remind us of them," helping us to "see beauty in these commonplace things" (153). Hence, the obligation of the artist to truth also becomes an obligation to beauty in this revised sense, an obligation to sympathize with, and perceive the beauty in, "ordinary" things and events. Eliot's comments contain the recognition that literature has often been ideologically motivated, intrinsically connected to philosophies and theologies that have expressed the world views and the experience of the upper classes.

Eliot artfully takes this opportunity to connect the principles of her realism with a certain type of religious attitude. She contrasts her character Mr. Irwine, rector of Broxton, with his successor, the "zealous" Mr. Ryde, who "insisted strongly on the doctrines of the Reformation" (154). While Mr. Irwine may not have been the perfect pastor, people warmed to him, they loved and respected him, and his worldly know-ledge enabled him to play a useful role in the lives of his parishioners both inside and outside the church. His preaching was based not on bookish doctrine and "notions" but on feelings, and it is this which actually influenced people to act morally (154). Mr. Ryde, on the other hand, "was severe in rebuking the aberrations of the flesh," and he is presented by George Eliot and her characters as one of those narrow and petty people who ever "pant after the ideal" (154, 157).

Hence, Eliot cleverly presents her realism not merely as pertaining to literary technique but as encompassing an entire way of looking at the world: the pursuit of truth, the reliance on one's own experience, the acceptance of people as they are, the perception of beauty in ordinary things were all aspects of this vision; and they were all underlain by a religious disposition which itself was humane and based on human sympathy rather than endless doctrine and the imposition of unrealistic ideals.

Émile Zola (1840–1902)

The novels of the French writer Émile Zola move toward a more extreme form of realism known as naturalism, taking its name from its allegedly scientific impulse to base its characters, events, and explanations on natural rather than supernatural or divine causes. Perhaps more than any other major literary figure, Émile Zola registered in his fiction and his critical theory the rising tide of scientific advance in the later nineteenth century. Zola was deeply conscious of these movements toward naturalism, toward the restriction of one's inquiries to the realm of nature (the realm of science, as opposed to the realm of supernature or the supernatural), and he saw naturalistic literature as merely a natural extension and completion of a far broader positivistic movement in recent history.

As such, Zola was the leading figure of French naturalism. He wrote a cycle of twenty novels under the rubric of *Les Rougon-Macquart*, concerning the two branches of a family, the Rougons and the Macquarts. Zola traced the "natural and social history" of this family through a number of generations, laying emphasis upon their behavior as influenced by heredity and environment. Some of the best known of these novels are *L'Assommoir* (1877), *Nana* (1880), and *Germinal* (1885). Zola's essay *The Experimental*

Novel (1880) attempted a justification of his own novelistic practice, and became the seminal manifesto of naturalism.

Zola makes it clear at the outset of his essay that the inspiration and foundation of his arguments was Claude Bernard's essay "Introduction à l'Étude de la Médecine Expérimentale," which had endeavored to show that medicine had a scientific basis, namely, the "experimental method."[11] Bernard had argued that this method, already used in the study of inanimate bodies in physics and chemistry, should also be used in the study of living bodies in the fields of physiology and medicine (2). Essentially, Zola sees Bernard's attempt as a symptom of a larger pattern of intellectual development: the nineteenth century, he remarks, is marked by a "return to nature," to natural and scientific explanation of all phenomena. Zola wishes to argue for "a literature governed by science." He wishes to extend Bernard's arguments specifically to the realm of the novel, thereby situating fiction and literature within this overall direction of scientific advance. Where Bernard aims to extend scientific study into the realm of physiology and medicine, Zola desires to extend it even further, into the realm of "the passionate and intellectual life" (2).

What are the premises of the so-called experimental method? According to Bernard, as reported by Zola, the experimentalist is distinguished from the mere observer in that the latter "relates purely and simply the phenomena which he has under his eyes . . . He should be the photographer of phenomena, his observation should be an exact representation of nature" (7). The experimentalist, on the other hand, directly intervenes in, and modifies, these phenomena for specific heuristic purposes, to confirm or disprove an experimental idea or hypothesis (6–7). The experimental method or experimental reasoning is "based on doubt, for the experimentalist should have no preconceived idea, in the face of nature, and should always retain his liberty of thought" (3). Bernard, as quoted by Zola, distinguishes experimental reasoning from scholastic inquiry: "it is precisely the scholastic, who believes he has absolute certitude, who attains to no results . . . by his belief in an absolute principle he puts himself outside of nature . . . It is . . . the experimenter, who is always in doubt . . . who succeeds in mastering the phenomena which surround him, and in increasing his power over nature" (26). Hence this scientific method overturns and rejects all previous authority: "it recognizes no authority but that of facts . . . The experimental method is the scientific method which proclaims the liberty of thought. It not only throws off the philosophical and theological yoke, but it no longer admits scientific personal authority" (44). Zola accepts Bernard's characterization of the stages of progress of the human mind, through "feeling, reason, and experiment": at first, feeling, which dominated reason, created theology; then reason or philosophy, assuming the dominant role, engendered scholasticism; finally, experiment, or the study of natural phenomena, brought us to "the objective reality of things." Hence the experimental method of science is the culmination of a historical development which is progressively rational and naturalistic (33–34).

The second and related major principle of science, according to Bernard, and Zola after him, is the belief in an "absolute determinism" in natural phenomena; in other words, there is no phenomenon, no occurrence in nature, which does not have a determining cause or complex of causes (3). An important aspect of this principle is that science shows us "the limit of our actual knowledge." But such a recognition of what we can and cannot know is empowering: "as science humbles our pride, it strengthens our power" (22). A passage from Zola neatly sums up this part of his argument, whereby he situates literature within the general context of scientific advance:

> the experimental novel is a consequence of the scientific evolution of the century; it continues and completes physiology, which itself leans for support on chemistry and medicine; it substitutes for the study of the abstract and the metaphysical man the study of the natural man, governed by physical or chemical laws, and modified by the influences of his surroundings; it is in one word the literature of our scientific age, as the classical and romantic literature corresponded to a scholastic and theological age. (23)

What does all of this mean in practice for the naturalistic novel? To begin with, Zola's attitude represents an extreme reaction against Romanticism and all forms of mysticism and supernaturalism. Zola sees his own literary era as placing an exaggerated emphasis on form and as "rotten with lyricism" (48). He insists that the subject matter of the experimental novelist is rooted in actuality, in observation of human beings and their passions; he conducts a "real experiment" by altering the conditions and circumstances of the characters he creates, positing certain causes of their actions (10–11). Such an attitude is directly opposed to attitudes such as vitalism, which "consider life as a mysterious and supernatural agent, which acts arbitrarily, free from all determinism" (15). Anticipating Freud, Zola extends the principle of determinism from its application throughout natural phenomena to encompass human behavior. He extends the principle to literature, to the novel, which is a "general inquiry on nature and on man" (38), saying that "there is an absolute determinism for all human phenomena" (18). Zola sees this determinism, then, as both external and internal, as governing the external world and the psychology of man (17). Novelists should, he urges, "operate on the characters, the passions, on the human and social data, in the same way that the chemist and the physicist operate on inanimate beings, and as the physiologist operates on living beings. Determinism dominates everything." As such, "purely imaginary novels" should be replaced by "novels of observation and experiment" (18).

If determinism dominates in both worlds, in nature and in the mind of man, the experimental novel must consider man in both social and psychological aspects. He suggests that "heredity has a great influence in the intellectual and passionate manifestations of man." Considerable importance must also be attached to the "surroundings" (19). Hence, while he acknowledges that the novelist should continue the physiologist's study of the "thoughts and passions," he reminds us that these are not produced in a vacuum: "Man is not alone; he lives in society, in a social condition; and consequently, for us novelists, this social condition unceasingly modifies the phenomena. Indeed our great study is just there, in the reciprocal effect of society on the individual and the individual on society" (20). Zola sees the experimental novel as freeing this literary genre from "the atmosphere of lies and errors in which it is plunged" (42). The following is perhaps Zola's most comprehensive definition of the program of the experimental novel:

> this is what constitutes the experimental novel: to possess a knowledge of the mechanism of the phenomena inherent in man, to show the machinery of his intellectual and sensory manifestations, under the influences of heredity and environment, such as physiology

shall give them to us, and then finally to exhibit man living in social conditions produced by himself, which he modifies daily, and in the heart of which he himself experiences a continual transformation. (21)

Hence, Zola views literature as not merely the expression of an author's mentality; the artist's personality, he says, "is always subject to the higher law of truth and nature." In fact, this personality is manifested only in the formal aspects of the novel rather than in its truth-value, which is independent of any such subjective basis (51). Zola explains that in the experimental novel all existing rhetorical elements are still allowed, since they do not impinge at all on the method of the novel (48).

One of the most interesting aspects of Zola's essay is his attempt, notwithstanding his scientism, to redeem the moral function of literature. Zola sees science as progressing toward a state where humanity will be in control of life and able to direct nature. Ultimately, for Zola, this capacity is directed toward a moral purpose: "We shall enter upon a century in which man, grown more powerful, will make use of nature and will utilize its laws to produce upon the earth the greatest possible amount of justice and freedom. There is no nobler, higher, nor grander end" (25). Sadly, the passage of another century has proved Zola's vision to be inordinately optimistic. His position might well be seen as an attempt to reincarnate the classical idea of the highest good as the end to which all science and art is ultimately directed. He sees this noble dream as directing also the efforts of the experimental novelist who has, fundamentally, the same goal as the scientist: "we also desire to master certain phenomena of an intellectual and personal order, to be able to direct them. We are, in a word, experimental moralists, showing by experiment in what way a passion acts in a certain social condition." The novelist, as moralist, can help analyze and control the mechanism of the passion, and in this, says Zola, "consists the practical utility and high morality of our naturalistic works" (25). This function of the novel, then, coheres with the paths of science and also is integrated with the efforts of legislators and politicians "toward that great object, the conquest of nature and the increase of man's power" (31). Zola effectively sees idealistic novels as morally harmful, operating under the pernicious desire to "remain in the unknown, through all sorts of religious and philosophical prejudices, under the astounding pretense that the unknown is nobler and more beautiful than the known" (27). This of course is a full-frontal attack on all forms of Romanticism and Symbolism, which Platonically project reality into another realm beyond that of experience. The upward flight of such writers, insists Zola, "is followed by a deeper fall into metaphysical chaos" (31). It is only the experimental novelists that "work for the strength and happiness of man." Zola effectively equates the epistemological status of literature with its moral function: "The only great and moral works are those of truth" (37). The foremost writers in this vein, according to Zola, are Balzac and Stendhal. Balzac, for example, shows in his *Cousin Bette* how an entire family is destroyed under the action of Hulot's "amorous temperament" (28–29). Answering some common objections, Zola denies that the naturalistic novel is somehow fatalistic on the grounds that the genius of the novelist is required to arrange and rearrange the natural order of phenomena, in accordance with the hypothesis, concerning human behavior, that he is aiming to test (11, 29). Finally, Zola concedes that philosophical idealism may ennoble and provide stimulus to the scientific enterprise, but on its own account it

481

cannot discover truth (47). Hence, Zola's theory fits squarely into the tradition of positivism.

William Dean Howells (1837–1920)

Regarded by many as the major American novelist and critic of his age, William Dean Howells began his career as a printer and journalist. He became sub-editor and then chief editor of the most prestigious journal on the East coast, the *Atlantic Monthly*, and associate editor of *Harper's Monthly* in New York. His chief fictional work was *The Rise of Silas Lapham* (1885), and his subsequent novels, such as *A Hazard of New Fortunes* (1890) and *The World of Chance* (1893), reflect his move toward both socialism and social realism, whereby he conducted a critique of American capitalism and imperialism. His status as the major American theorist of realism was established by his book *Criticism and Fiction* (1891), which effectively compiled articles he had written for his "Editor's Study" section of *Harper's Monthly*. As influential editor, novelist, and theorist, he occupied a central position in American literature. Influenced by Lowell and Hawthorne, as well as by European and Russian realists such as Dostoevsky, Tolstoy, Flaubert, Zola, and Ibsen, he transmitted the aesthetic of these writers in a refined and revitalized form to his native soil and his own era. He was acquainted with most of the leading writers of his time, including Lowell, Hawthorne, Emerson, Thoreau, and Whitman; he influenced the careers of Henry James, Mark Twain, Charles W. Chesnutt, and Paul Laurence Dunbar. By the time of his death he had exerted a powerful and pervasive influence on American letters, though subsequent generations of critics and writers tended somewhat to devalue his critical and literary reputation.

Howells' *Criticism and Fiction* is a closely argued manifesto for realism. He begins by declaring his common ground with John Addington Symons, who had expressed a hope that future literature might abandon "sentimental or academical seekings after the ideal," that it shall harness "the scientific spirit," and shall "comprehend with more instinctive certitude what is simple, natural, and honest."[12] Howells further suggests that "what is true is always beautiful and good, and nothing else is so," finding sanction for this partly in Keats' poetic line, "Beauty is Truth, Truth Beauty." From Edmund Burke's essay on the sublime and the beautiful, Howells reaffirms the insight that the "true standard of the arts is in every man's power; and an easy observation of the most common, sometimes of the meanest things, in nature will give the truest lights" (298–299). Integrating these various insights, Howells expresses his own hope that "each new author, each new artist, will be considered, not in his proportion to any other author or artist, but in his relation to the human nature, known to us all, which it is his privilege, his high duty, to interpret" (300). The important issue at stake here, as raised by Burke, is the individuality and authenticity of an artist's perception. Howells laments the custom of encouraging young artists to form their observations not upon life but upon the perceptions of previous masters. Instead of being encouraged to describe, for example, an actual grasshopper, the young artist is urged to describe an artificial one, which represents "the grasshopper in general . . . a type." Such a grasshopper, formulated by generations of previous artists, represents a cultivation of the ideal, the ideal grasshopper through the lens of which the real one must be viewed. Howells voices the hope that the artist, as well as the "common, average man," will reject "the ideal grasshopper, the heroic grasshopper, the impassioned grasshopper, the self-devoted, adventureful, good old romantic card-board grasshopper," in favor of the "simple, honest, and natural grasshopper" (301). Howells is of course attempting to extricate the novel from the characteristics of the conventional heroic and adventurous romance. In the passage above, Howells appropriates from Symonds a new criterion for art: it must be judged not by conformity with the so-called classics or with the authority of tradition but by "the standard of the arts which we all have in our power, the simple, the natural, and the honest" (302). In historical terms, Howells sees realism as continuing a rebellion initiated by Romanticism at the beginning of the nineteenth century: "Romanticism then sought, as realism seeks now, to widen the bounds of sympathy, to level every barrier against aesthetic freedom, to escape from the paralysis of tradition. It exhausted itself in this impulse; and it remained for realism to assert that fidelity to experience and probability of motive are essential conditions of a great imaginative literature" (302).

As he himself later acknowledges, Howells' theory of realism is "democratic" in several senses. As seen above, he takes from Burke (ironically, given the anti-democratic strain of Burke's conservative politics) the democratic notion that all people have the potential for aesthetic judgment. Howells adds that the true realist establishes no hierarchy in the material he considers to be at the disposal of art. The true realist "finds nothing insignificant," and "feels in every nerve the equality of things and the unity of men; his soul is exalted, not by ... ideals, but by realities, in which alone the truth lives." For such a person, "no living man is a type, but a character" (302–303). Howells rejects the "tendency to allegorization" in recent fiction, as well as "the exaggerated passions and motives of the stage" (304–305).

In a manner that somewhat anticipates Northrop Frye and some of the New Critics of the earlier twentieth century, Howells drew attention to the deficiencies of literary criticism as conceived and practiced in his era. He suggests that the critic currently has no principles and indeed is amateurish (306–307). He tends to base his assessments of literary works on personal feelings and impressions; and, in general, his practice has been based on a perpetual resistance of whatever is new, and a blind adherence to past models (311). Interestingly, his position might be viewed as a critique of the "touchstone" theory advanced by Matthew Arnold, with whom Howells otherwise has much in common. Arnold erected this very dearth of critical principles itself into a theory, suggesting that we cannot judge literature by means of fixed and teachable concepts but that we must be exposed to past models of literary greatness, which will serve as touchstones for the assessment of any works we read.

Howells also anticipates the New Critics in his insistence that criticism can have only a subsidiary function: it always exists in a relation of dependence to art; it cannot create literature, and it cannot make or unmake the reputation of authors (308–310). To this sorry state of affairs, Howells brings, as Frye was to do later, a message of admonition that criticism must "reconceive its office." What we need is a "dispassionate, scientific" study of current literature (311, 314). The critic must with humility acknowledge that he can learn from the creative author who, like Wordsworth, expresses a "revolution, a new order of things, to which the critical perceptions and habitudes had painfully to adjust themselves" (312). Hence criticism must reduce its office, its function, "to the business of observing, recording, and comparing; to analyzing the material before it, and then synthesizing its impressions. Even then, it is not too much to say that literature as an art could get on perfectly well without it" (311). This sounds much like T. S. Eliot in his essay "The Function of Criticism," where he claimed to be diverging from Arnold and suggested that the critic's function was disinterested "comparison and analysis." Each of these writers in his own way was attempting to reaffirm the genuine creativity of art, a creativity that could neither be anticipated nor entirely formulated by criticism. Such a posture reinvests art with an indefinable aura of authority, as expressed in the Romantic notion of "genius," which soared above any attempts at rational analysis. Yet Howells, true to his democratic aesthetics, rejects the concept of genius outright, as "a mischievous superstition" aimed at mystifying the artistic process.

The democratic strain of Howells' theory of realism is taken in part from the Spanish writer Palacio Valdés, and appears to be inspired also by insights from Emerson and George Eliot. Like George Eliot, Howells recognizes that truthful simplicity is "very difficult," and that "nothing is so hard as to be honest" (315). From Valdés, Howells repeats a number of crucial elements of realism. He quotes with approval Valdés' statement that "in nature there is neither great nor small; all is equal" (316). Following Valdés, Howells urges that artists need to learn how to interest the reader "with the ordinary events of life, and with the portrayal of characters truly human" (317). The novelist must not endeavor to "add anything to reality, to turn it and twist it, to restrict it," but must paint images "as they appear" (319). And he must engage in a "direct, frank, and conscientious study of character" (318). Howells adds that "Realism is nothing more and nothing less than the truthful treatment of material" (319). He cites Emerson's statement: "I embrace the common; I sit at the feet of the familiar and the low" (321).

Where Howells integrates these insights from various writers and makes them speak through his own voice is in his insistence on the political significance of their democratic sentiment. Since the creation and depiction of beauty rest upon truth, the finest effect of the beautiful, says Howells, "will be ethical and not aesthetic merely. Morality penetrates all things, it is the soul of all things" (322). The novelist "must be true to what life has taught me is the truth." His work will be pernicious if it constructs a "metaphysical lie against righteousness and common-sense." Howells looks forward to a day when "the poor honest herd of mankind shall give universal utterance to the universal instinct, and shall hold selfish power in politics, in art, in religion, for the devil that it is" (323). Fiction is harmful if it tells "idle lies about human nature and the social fabric." Howells reacts against the literary "diet" on which readers have been "pampered to imbecility" (333). The truth alone, says Howells, can "exalt and purify men" (326). Hence this is the supreme test of any work of the imagination: "Is it true? – true to the motives, the impulses, the principles that shape the life of actual men and women? This truth . . . necessarily includes the highest morality and the highest artistry" (327). Beauty in literature "comes from truth alone" and the realistic novel has a moral, as well as an aesthetic, mission (331, 334). In the spirit of this mission, Howells admonishes: "let fiction cease to lie about life; let it portray men and women as they are, actuated by the motives and the passions in the measure we all know . . . let it speak the dialect, the language, that most Americans know – and there can be no doubt of an unlimited future, not only of delightfulness but of usefulness, for it" (328). Such is the circuitous historical route by which literary aesthetics returns to the principles of Horace, that the work of art must delight and teach.

On the question of dialect and language, Howells is reluctant to ask writers to be consciously "American." But he does encourage them to speak their own dialect, rather than indulge in a "priggish and artificial" endeavor to be "English" (328). He directly equates the democratic political beliefs of the country with a democratic aesthetic: the political state, he says, was built "on the affirmation of the essential equality of men in their rights and duties . . . these conditions invite the artist to the study and appreciation of the common . . . The arts must become democratic, and then we shall have the expression of America in art" (339).

Howells issues a ringing judgment against the classics: at "least three-fifths of the literature called classic . . . is not alive; it is as dead as the people who wrote it and read it . . . A superstitious piety preserves it" (341). Howells sees literature as one of the last refuges of the aristocratic spirit which is disappearing from the political and social fabric and "is now seeking to shelter itself in aesthetics . . . Democracy in literature is the reverse of all this. It wishes to know and tell the truth, confident that consolation and delight are there; it does not care to paint the marvellous and impossible" (353). Neither arts nor sciences can be viewed as serious pursuits unless they "tend to make the race better and kinder . . . and they cannot do this except from and through the truth" (354).

Henry James (1843–1916)

Though Henry James was an American novelist, he saw the word "American" as embracing a certain cultural openness, or in his words, a "fusion and synthesis of the various National tendencies of the world."[13] The experience underlying James' creative and critical work was international in scope. During his childhood he had spent some years in Europe; in later life he moved to London, often visiting Italy and France. Some of his best-known novels explore intercultural connections; these include *The American* (1877), *The Europeans* (1878), *Daisy Miller* (1879), *The Portrait of a Lady* (1881), *The Ambassadors* (1903), and *The Golden Bowl* (1904). He was influenced by the European as well as American Romantics, and was acquainted with the so-called realist and naturalist writers such as William Dean Howells, Gustave Flaubert, and Émile Zola. His literary-critical views were influenced by Goethe, Matthew Arnold, and Sainte-Beuve. From these writers he acquired the idea of critical "disinterestedness," which he saw as effecting a mediation between history and philosophy (his brother was the pragmatist philosopher William James), since criticism deals with both ideas and facts. James' own influence spanned both sides of the Atlantic, extending to figures such as Ezra Pound and T. S. Eliot.

It is in his essay "The Art of Fiction" (1884) that James most succinctly expressed his critical principles as well as a justification of his novelistic endeavor. The motivation of his essay is threefold. Firstly, he is combating what he takes to be a general reluctance to view the novel as a genuine art form. His text was written in part as a direct response to a lecture and pamphlet of the same title by the novelist and critic Walter Besant. James is concerned to establish the novel as a serious art form rather than as merely an amusing or escapist pastime. Secondly, while he applauds Besant's attempt to foster this serious treatment of fiction, he disputes Besant's assumptions that rules can be somehow prescribed for fiction. James' central claim is that the novelist and the novel must be free. Finally, James is highly conscious of a puritanical environment which views art as having an injurious effect, and as opposed to morality, amusement, or instruction. Hence, for James, novelistic freedom entails also a liberation from moral and educational requirements and constraints.

While James' central thesis is that the novel must be free, its freedom is first worked out in relation to the kind of novelistic realism on which James insists: "The only reason for the existence of a novel is that it does attempt to represent life . . . as the picture is reality, so the novel is history" (166–167). In attempting to represent life, the novelist's task is analogous with that of the painter; and in searching for truth, the novelistic art is analogous with philosophy as well as history. This "double analogy," says James, "is a magnificent heritage" (167).

James suggests as a broad definition of the genre that the novel is "a personal, a direct impression of life," and it is successful inasmuch as it reveals a particular and unique mind (170). Hence, the procedure of artistic realism cannot be prescribed. He is effectively disputing Besant's claim that the "laws of fiction may be laid down and taught with . . . precision and exactness" (170). Moreover, the enterprise of realism is vastly complex. The writer should indeed possess "a sense of reality" but "reality has a myriad forms" and cannot be encompassed within some formula (171). The realism advocated by James seems to consist not, then, in passive imitation but in producing "the illusion of life" (173).

It is equally inconclusive and inexact, says James, to ask the novelist to write from experience. Like reality, experience is a complex concept. Experience "is never limited, and it is never complete; it is an immense sensibility, a kind of huge spiderweb of the finest silken threads suspended in the chamber of consciousness . . . It is the very atmosphere of the mind" (172). A mere glimpse of a situation can afford a perspicacious novelist an entire perspective based on deep insight. Interestingly, James' definition of "experience" reads like a reformulation of the definition of "imagination" by Romantics such as Coleridge. James states that the "power to guess the unseen from the seen, to trace the implication of things, to judge the whole piece by the pattern, the condition of feeling life in general so completely that you are well on your way to knowing any particular corner of it – this cluster of gifts may almost be said to constitute experience" (172). Whereas, for Coleridge, imagination was a power rooted in symbolism, a power to unite general and particular, James' notion of experience as a "gift" is rooted in metonymy, a power essentially of judging the whole from the part. No longer is there some vast symbolic correspondence implied between word and reality; but the world is still considered to be ordered enough to be read in a coherent manner, for the entirety to be able to manifest itself in any particular partial expression. Modernist writers will be deprived of even this metonymic satisfaction. Indeed, James identifies the very freedom of the novel with its potential for realistic – which for him might well read "metonymic" – correspondence: the novel has a "large, free character of an immense and exquisite correspondence with life" (179). Notwithstanding the complex nature of both reality and experience, James, reminding us of his earlier affirmation, states that "the air of reality (solidity of specification) seems to me to be the supreme virtue of a novel – the merit on which all its other merits (including that conscious moral purpose of which Mr. Besant speaks) helplessly and submissively depends. If it be not there they are all as nothing" (173). The choice of words here is telling: all other factors, including any moral purpose, are erected on the enabling foundation of realism.

Owing to the deeply personal nature of experience, as well as its potential breadth and complexity, a novelist cannot be taught how to express reality. An important part of the freedom James seeks for the novelist consists in the liberty to experiment. Form is not achieved in any a priori fashion; it is something that undergoes continual modification through experience of reality (169, 171). The novel must also be free in its choice of theme and subject matter: the province of art, says James, is all life, not only those elements which are beautiful or noble (178). In all art, says James, one becomes "conscious of an immense increase – a kind of revelation – of freedom . . . the province of art is all life, all feeling, all observation, all vision . . . it is all experience." As such, nothing can be forbidden for the novelist, nothing can be out of bounds (177–178). James suggests that the foremost capacity of the novelist must be that of "receiving straight impressions" (178). Fiction must catch "the strange irregular rhythm of life . . . *without* rearrangement" so that "we feel that we are touching the truth" (177). The implication here seems to be that the novelist accurately records "straight" impressions, without somehow distorting them; yet James also concedes that "Art is essentially selection, but it is a selection whose main care is to be typical, to be inclusive" (177). There seems to be a discrepancy between saying, on the one hand, that the novel records life without distortion, and, on the other hand, acknowledging that this record is inevitably subjective, penned from merely one of "innumerable points of view," from a perspective which is in fact unique. James' position might be seen as expressing a precarious balance in the historical transition between classical and modern realism. A vestige of Aristotelian realism persists in James' view that it is still possible to speak of the "typically" human; and a foreshadowing of modernistic subjectivism is pronounced in his equal acceptance that the novelistic vision must be individual and unique. The two factors appear to be unreconciled in James' text.

Finally, James argues against Besant's claim that the novel must have a "conscious moral purpose"; the novel, says James, should be free of moral and other obligations. His reasoning is apparently simple: "questions of art are questions . . . of execution; questions of morality are quite another affair." If art has a purpose, that purpose is artistic: it must aim at perfection (181). James acknowledges that the moral sense and the artistic sense are in one point very closely allied, namely in their conviction that "the deepest quality of a work of art will always be the quality of the mind of the producer. In proportion as that intelligence is fine will the novel, the picture, the statue partake of the substance of beauty and truth. To be constituted of such elements is, to my vision, to have purpose enough" (181). Again, for all of his insistence on realism, the emphasis is here once more deflected toward subjectivity, to the mind and ability of the novelist: it is this subjectivity that the novel most profoundly expresses. Ironically, just at this point where James' conception of the novel points toward modernism, in terms of both its subjective grounding and its subordination of morality to aesthetic purpose, he has recourse to the ancient Aristotelian category of substance, and to the Platonic identification of beauty and truth, together with the Platonic notion of "partaking" as the means whereby earthly beauty is realized through invocation of a transcendent realm.

Notes

1 Herbert Marcuse, *Reason and Revolution: Hegel and the Rise of Social Theory* (London: Routledge and Kegan Paul, 1977), pp. 232–388.
2 It is worth consulting Jameson's entire discussion, *The Ideologies of Theory: Essays 1971– 1986. Volume II: The Syntax of History* (London: Routledge, 1989), pp. 118–122.
3 Lilian Furst, ed., *Realism* (New York and London: Longman, 1992), p. 1.
4 Ian Watt, *The Rise of the Novel* (Harmondsworth: Penguin, 1985), p. 12.
5 Ibid., pp. 16–17.
6 Eric Auerbach, *Mimesis: The Representation of Reality in Western Literature*, trans. Willard R. Trask (Princeton: Princeton University Press, 1974), p. 555.
7 Furst, *Realism*, p. 2.
8 Jameson, *Ideologies of Theory*, pp. 122–124.
9 Ibid., pp. 121–123.
10 George Eliot, *Adam Bede*, ed. John Paterson (Boston and New York: Houghton Mifflin, 1968), p. 150. Hereafter page citations are given in the text.
11 Émile Zola, *The Experimental Novel and Other Essays*, trans. Belle M. Sherman (New York: Haskell House, 1964), p. 1. Hereafter page citations are given in the text.
12 *Criticism and Fiction*, reprinted in *W. D. Howells: Selected Literary Criticism. Volume II: 1886–1869*, ed. Donald Pizer and Christoph K. Lohmann (Bloomington and Indianapolis: Indiana University Press, 1993), p. 298. Hereafter page citations are given in the text.
13 Letter to T. S. Perry, September 20, 1867, quoted in the introduction to Henry James, *The Art of Criticism*, ed. William Veeder and Susan M. Griffin (Chicago and London: University of Chicago Press, 1986), p. 1. Hereafter page citations from this volume are given in the text.

CHAPTER 19

SYMBOLISM AND AESTHETICISM

Even as the currents of realism and then naturalism held sway in European literature, there was also fermenting in the works of poets such as Charles Baudelaire an alternative set of concerns: with language, with poetic form, with evocation of mental states and ideal worlds, and the most intimate recesses of human subjectivity. To some extent, these concerns were inherited from the Romantics, as was the antagonism toward an urban life regulated by the cycles of modern industry and commerce. The followers of Baudelaire eventually became associated with a literary and cultural disposition which stubbornly resisted the main streams of thought stemming from the Enlightenment, and which crystallized toward the end of the nineteenth century as a series of reactions against the realism and naturalism then in vogue. These reactions included symbolism, aestheticism, and impressionism, which have sometimes, and in varying combinations, fallen under the label of "decadence."

This broad anti-realist and anti-bourgeois disposition had already surfaced in many writers and movements: in the Pre-Raphaelite Brotherhood of artists formed in 1848 in England which looked back to the direct and morally serious art of the Middle Ages prior to the advent of the Renaissance artist Raphael; in the Parnassian poets of France, inspired by Théophile Gautier and Leconte de Lisle (1818–1894), who adopted an ethic of "art for art's sake"; and in the theorics of poetic composition elaborated by Edgar Allan Poe. Baudelaire and his successors, such as Paul Verlaine (1844–1896), Arthur Rimbaud (1854–1891), and Stéphane Mallarmé (1842–1898), were the heirs of these aesthetic tendencies; and they have all been associated with French symbolism. This affiliation is retrospective since the symbolist movement as such arose somewhat later, its manifesto being penned by Jean Moréas in 1886. The other symbolists included the poets Jules Laforgue, Henri de Regnier, Gustave Kahn, the novelist Joris-Karl Huysmans, the dramatist Maurice Maeterlinck, and the critic Remy de Gourmont. This movement reached its zenith in the 1890s and thereafter declined, being often derisively viewed as a form of decadence and affectation. It was the precursors of the symbolists – Baudelaire, Verlaine, Rimbaud, and Mallarmé – rather than the symbolists themselves who have had a vast and enduring influence, extending from major poets such as W. B. Yeats and T. S. Eliot, through writers of fiction such as Marcel Proust,

James Joyce, and Virginia Woolf, and dramatists such as August Strindberg, to philosophers of language and modern literary theorists such as Roland Barthes, Jacques Derrida, and Julia Kristeva.

As expressed in Jean Moréas' manifesto, symbolism was a reaction not only against realism and naturalism, which were based on description, but also against Parnassian poetry, which aimed to cultivate a precise and definitive language. Mallarmé's *Divagations* (1897) was another important statement of symbolist aesthetics. Most fundamentally, Mallarmé rejected the idea – on which realism was premised – that language was referential, that words were somehow the signs of a pregiven reality. Reality is an interpretation from a particular perspective, and for Mallarmé, a poem is part of reality and indeed helps to create reality. Mallarmé also rejected the Romantic idea of a poem as expression of an author's subjectivity; rather, the poet enters the world of language which determines both his consciousness and the world. He drew attention to the material dimensions of words, their sounds, their combinations on the page, the spacing between them, and their ability to create and formulate new shades of meaning and perception. Mallarmé voiced a reaction against the French alexandrine, and urged experimentation with freer verse forms. He also attempted to dissolve the distinction between poetry and prose, as well as between critical and creative writing. The major critic of the symbolist movement was Remy de Gourmont, who urged the ideals of subjectivity and artistic purity. He asserted that "only mediocre works are impersonal"[1] and advocated a "pure art" which was "concerned exclusively with self-realization"[2] This affirmation of personality in literature was based upon Gourmont's philosophical dispositions: a staunch subjective idealist, he insisted that idealism found its best formulation in Schopenhauer's statement that "the world is my representation," a formula that Gourmont held to be "irrefutable."[3] These statements embody the central philosophical and aesthetic stance of symbolism.

In general, the symbolists refused to take the material world they had inherited as the real world. Drawing on Platonic philosophy, they saw the present world as an imperfect reflection or expression of a higher, infinite, and eternal realm which could be evoked by symbols. Hence they rejected the descriptive language of the realists and naturalists in favor of a more suggestive, symbolic, and allusive language, a language that could evoke states of consciousness and experience. They spurned all forms of discursive language – argument, debate, and narration – and the ideals of logical coherence or accuracy of reference. They also drew on Baudelaire's notion of "correspondences" between the senses to elaborate an aesthetic of synaesthesia, and their predominant analogy for poetry was with music.

French symbolism was introduced into England through Arthur Symons' book *The Symbolist Movement in Literature* (1899). Symons characterized the later nineteenth century as "the age of science, the age of material things." He viewed the symbolist movement as a "revolt against exteriority, against rhetoric, against a materialistic tradition."[4] With symbolist poetry, he explained, "comes the turn of the soul . . . a literature in which the visible world is no longer a reality, and the unseen world no longer a dream" (4). Symbolist literature, then, offered a redefinition of reality, which saw the contemporary bourgeois world as but a one-sided material dimension pointing to its own self-transcendence in a higher, spiritual reality. Symons characterized the preceding reign of realism under Flaubert, Taine, and Zola as an age where "words, with that facile elasticity which there is in them, did miracles in the exact representation of everything that visibly existed, exactly as it existed" (4).

Hence symbolism was reacting against not only the reduction of the world to a material dimension but also the correlative reduction of language to a literalness which enshrines the possibility of absolute clarity. Symons quotes Carlyle's definition of the symbol as possessing a "double significance," as a locus where "the Infinite is made to blend itself with the Finite" (2–3). Seen in this light, symbolism was an attempt to reinvest language with its powers of ambivalence and mystery, to relieve it of the stultifying burden of representing factitious identity and clear-cut categories. As Symons put it, symbolism "is all an attempt to . . . evade the old bondage of rhetoric, the old bondage of exteriority" (8).

Long before modern literary theory drew upon the insight, Symons stated that language itself is "arbitrary": words and symbols are "mere sounds of the voice to which we have agreed to give certain significations." Such arbitrariness is only legitimized when "it has obtained the force of a convention" (1). In a sense, French symbolism is a return to the arbitrariness beneath the layers of convention, a flight to a deeper subjectivity which negates or situates the literal subjectivity of the bourgeois self. Far from returning to a medieval religious regimentation of the signifying powers of language, French symbolism must erect subjectivity itself – and the literature which uniquely expresses it – into a religion. As Symons says, such literature attains its "authentic speech" only by accepting a heavier burden: "it becomes itself a kind of religion" (9). As so often at the end of the nineteenth century, the totalizing impulses of philosophy and theology were displaced into the realm of poetry.

Modern symbolism's philosophical negation of the world of contingent particulars was unavoidably subjective and idealistic. Trapped as the symbolist poet was between a dream of unity and an "objective" uncontrollable plurality, the only recourse toward unity lay in subjectivity itself, a unity between differing subjective constructions of the external world. The strategy of symbolism was effectively to reject the literalization of language toward which bourgeois thought had been moving since John Locke. The ideals of clarity and precision were rejected as naive and artificial, premised on a narrow conception of reality as material and as composed of particular objects. Lost in this maze of plurality and irredeemable fragmentation, the symbolist sought unity and totality through recourse to a more comprehensive definition of reality, one which did not reject the bourgeois reality of the here and now but accommodated it as part of a vaster scheme, as merely one dimension of a more stratified vision. In this way, the symbolist endeavored to harmonize the mutually disrupted world of intellect and sensation, spirit and body. The struggle for unity is sublimated to the level of form, displaced to a subjective realm where it becomes a conflict of viewpoints, the historically bequeathed bourgeois world being stripped of its objective status and reduced to one possible perspective within a larger scheme of perspectives.

A further and perhaps more extreme development of this attitude of negation was in aestheticism, the doctrine that art exists for its own sake, or for the sake of beauty, in utter indifference to moral or political considerations, and in entire freedom from didactic or educational purposes. Like symbolism, aestheticism arose in opposition to what was viewed as the sordid industrial world of bourgeois utility and calculation. The phrase "l'art pour l'art" (art for art's sake) had been coined by the philosopher

Victor Cousin in 1818; this doctrine reverberated through the aesthetics of Kant, many of the Romantics, the Pre-Raphaelites, the Parnassians, the symbolists, the decadents, and the critical programs of the twentieth-century formalists. As seen in the case of Gourmont, some of the symbolists and so-called decadents were influenced by the pessimism of thinkers such as Schopenhauer and Nietzsche, whose views will be considered in the next chapter. The work of some of the seminal figures of symbolism and aestheticism – Baudelaire, Pater, and Wilde – can now be examined in detail.

Charles Baudelaire (1821–1867)

Known as the founder of French symbolism (though not himself part of the movement), and often associated with the artistic decadence and aestheticism of the later nineteenth century, Baudelaire was born in Paris where he lived a bohemian life, adopting the artistic posture of a dandy, devoted to beauty and disdainfully aloof from the vulgar bourgeois world of materialism and commerce, as well as the pose of the *flâneur*, frequenter and consumer of the city streets. Baudelaire is often credited with expressing one of the first modernistic visions, a vision of the sordidness, sensuality, and corruption of city life, a disposition that profoundly influenced modernist writers such as T. S. Eliot and Ezra Pound. Baudelaire's famous or infamous collection of poems, *Les Fleurs du mal* (*The Flowers of Evil*), was published in 1857 and became the subject of a trial for obscenity in the same year for including some lesbian poems. Baudelaire contracted syphilis and was paralyzed by a stroke before his death.

Notwithstanding his lifestyle and his artistic views, Baudelaire was a believer in original sin, and was deeply repelled by the commercialism of the modern world, which he regarded as a fallen world. In his *Journaux intimes* Baudelaire stated that man is "*naturally* depraved," and ridiculed the idea of progress.[5] He saw progress as possible only within the individual; he affirmed the importance of ultimate questions concerning the purpose of human existence, and was profoundly antipathetic to bourgeois values, describing commerce as "in its very essence, *satanic*" and as "the vilest form of egotism." He did not welcome developments toward democracy and held that there "is no form of rational and assured government save an aristocracy" (*IJ*, 69).

In general, the French symbolists, including Baudelaire and Mallarmé, reacted against the explicit rationalism, materialism, and positivism of the bourgeois world and, like the Romantics, exalted the role of poet and artist. Baudelaire's ideas about beauty may have been inspired by the German philosopher Schelling, and from 1852 he was also deeply influenced by Poe (though he arrived independently at many of his analogous insights), and shared his views on poetic autonomy and the poetic imagination. His famous sonnet "Correspondences" is a succinct expression of his symbolist aesthetic, seeing the material world as a "forest of symbols" pointing to an ideal world. This alleged system of correspondences was a common idea in the eighteenth and nineteenth centuries; it could be seen as a gesturing of the factual toward the ideal (and truly real) or as a synaesthetic correspondence between the data of the various senses such as sight, sound, and touch. Hence, in this influential notion, Baudelaire adapts toward his own ends an idea that had already informed many aesthetic theories (such as those of

Swedenborg, Schelling, Mme. de Staël, and Sainte-Beuve). In his sonnet, Baudelaire sees the earth and its phenomena as a "revelation" of heavenly correspondences, and it is the poet who must decipher these.

Much of Baudelaire's important criticism is contained in his *Salons*, which were reviews of yearly exhibitions at the Louvre museum. In general, Baudelaire's criticism moves toward an aesthetic of modernity, which might also be called a symbolist aesthetic that both distinguishes itself somewhat from Romanticism (in its views of imagination and nature) and anticipates certain dispositions of modernism. Baudelaire had little sympathy with any endeavor toward an objective criticism. In his "Salon" of 1846 he insisted that "the best criticism is that which is amusing and poetic; not a cold, mathematical criticism which . . . deliberately divests itself of every kind of temperament." In fact, he urges, criticism "should be biased, impassioned, partisan" though it should be written from a point of view "that opens up the widest horizons."[6] Baudelaire at this time sees Romanticism as "a manner of feeling," and equates Romanticism with modernity: "To speak of Romanticism is to speak of modern art – that is, of intimacy, spirituality, color, aspiration toward the infinite" (*BLC*, 40). However, Baudelaire initially rejected what he saw as some of the excesses of Romanticism: in an 1851 article on Pierre Dupont (1821–1870), an author of light verse and patriotic songs, Baudelaire exhibits his transitory allegiance to the socialist and democratic ideals of Proudhon, ideals that underlay the 1848 revolution in France. In this article, Baudelaire says of the "Romantic School" that by "excluding morality . . . the puerile Utopia of the school of *art for art's sake* was inevitably sterile. It was flagrantly contrary to the spirit of humanity" (*BLC*, 52). He adds that after the poet Barbier "proclaimed in impassioned language the sacredness of the Revolution of 1830 . . . the question was settled, and art was thereafter inseparable from morality and utility" (*BLC*, 53). Likewise, the poetry of Pierre Dupont, says Baudelaire, echoed the misfortunes and hopes of the later revolution of 1848. He speaks of the reign of King Louis-Philippe as one of "debauchery" (*BLC*, 53, 57). Baudelaire denounced in this essay the Romantic "creations of idleness and solitude," which violate the "spirit of action," and defined poetry as "the negation of iniquity" (*BLC*, 60). Significantly, the period of the 1848 revolution coincided with the early days of literary realism, which spanned roughly the years 1844–1850, and Baudelaire had displayed some sympathy for this movement, sustaining cordial relations with the figureheads of realism such as Courbet and Champfleury. However, partly inspired by his continued study of figures such as Poe and Joseph de Maistre, which deepened his revulsion for the bourgeois world, Baudelaire developed more aristocratic sympathies in both politics and art. In his notes for a planned article on realism, he described realism as "rustic, coarse, dishonest and even boorish," and in fact questioned whether realism had any meaning at all. "Every good poet," he wrote, "was always *realistic*." Prefiguring his more mature views, he states that "Poetry is what is most real, what is completely true only in *another world*." The present world, he maintained, is merely a "dictionary of hieroglyphics" pointing to the world beyond (*BLC*, 87–88).

Baudelaire wrote three major essays on Poe, the first published in 1852 and used in a revised version as an introduction to his first translations of Poe. In this highly influential account of Poe's life and works, Baudelaire expresses his own and Poe's antipathy to utilitarian literature, though his own view is not as strident as Poe's; he accepts that poetry may have a usefulness that is ancillary to its main purpose, which is aesthetic. He points to the discrepancy between Poe's sensibility and that of his country; the latter he sees as steeped in material values "disproportionately emphasized to the point of being a national mania." Poe was alienated by his country's "lack of an aristocracy," a circumstance in which the "cult of the Beautiful" could only degenerate and disappear (*BLC*, 94). Baudelaire points out that, as a "true poet," Poe believed that "poetry . . . should have no object in view other than itself" (*BLC*, 100). Baudelaire even "explains" Poe's drunkenness as arising from this basic incongruity between the poet and his environment.

It was in his third essay on Poe, which formed the preface to his second volume of translations of Poe (1857), that Baudelaire engaged in detail with Poe's critical outlook, citing many of the views expressed in Poe's essay "The Poetic Principle." Once again, Baudelaire stresses how Poe was at odds with, and sought escape from, the values of his bourgeois world: "From the midst of a greedy world, hungry for material things, Poe took flight in dreams." For Poe, however, these dreams were "the only realities." Stifled by this oppressive atmosphere, says Baudelaire, Poe "pours out his scorn and disgust for democracy, progress and *civilization*" (*BLC*, 119). Baudelaire saw Poe not only as an aristocrat, but also as the "Virginian, the Southerner, the Byron gone astray in a bad world" (*BLC*, 120). Poe's "Southern" temperament reacted against both North American puritanism and commercialism: Poe reacted against "a country where the idea of utility, the most hostile in the world to the idea of beauty, dominates and takes precedence over everything" (*BLC*, 126). Baudelaire establishes a special kinship with Poe in regard to the latter's affirmation of "the natural wickedness of man." Poe saw a mysterious force in man which is ignored, according to Baudelaire, by modern thought: "This primitive, irresistible force is natural Perversity," which Baudelaire himself sees as original sin (*BLC*, 121). Clearly, in much of this essay, Poe's views become the mouthpiece for Baudelaire's own sympathies, and Baudelaire reiterates Poe's antipathy to progress and civilization as his own: progress is the "great heresy of decay," on which Poe vented his spleen. The concept of progress merely compensates for man's fallenness: "Civilized man invents the philosophy of progress to console himself for his abdication and for his downfall" (*BLC*, 124).

Baudelaire is in accord with Poe on a number of issues: the mediocrity of the entire bourgeois system of values and their political incarnation in the form of democracy, the natural fallenness of humankind, the autonomy of poetry, and the aim of poetry as beauty. Baudelaire sanctions the fundamental views expressed in Poe's "The Poetic Principle": that an essential function of art is to produce a totality and unity of impression or effect, that a poem is a poem only insofar as it "uplifts the soul," that poetry "has no other goal than itself," and as such must not be subjected to the "heresy of *teaching a lesson*" which includes as inevitable corollaries the heresy of *passion, of truth, and of morality*." Baudelaire acknowledges, however, that poetry can "ennoble manners" and raises "man above the level of vulgar interests" (*BLC*, 130–131). Having said this, Baudelaire insists just as much as Poe on a separation, even a polarization, between the endeavors of poetry on the one hand and of science and philosophy on the other: "Poetry cannot . . . be assimilated to science or morality; it does not have Truth as its object, it has only itself . . . Cold, calm, impassive, the demonstrative mood rejects the diamonds and the flowers of the Muse; it is then absolutely the inverse of the poetic mood" (*BLC*, 132). Finally, Baudelaire accepts completely Poe's formulation of the "poetic principle" as "human aspiration toward a superior beauty." This notion may lie behind the system of correspondences between visible and spiritual worlds that Baudelaire himself was to formulate. He develops Poe's notion into the statement that the "immortal instinct for the beautiful . . . makes us consider the earth and its spectacles as a revelation, as something in correspondence with Heaven" (*BLC*, 132).

Baudelaire's adaptation of Poe's idea that poetry gestures toward a supernal beauty beyond this world is reflected in his definitions of the imagination. Baudelaire notes that for Poe, "Imagination is the queen of faculties." What is interesting, however, is that the definition of imagination offered by Baudelaire is not Poe's but his own, implying a system of correspondences that is not formulated in Poe's work: "Imagination is an almost divine faculty which perceives immediately and without philosophical methods the inner and secret relations of things, the correspondences and the analogies" (*BLC*, 127). In his "Salon" of 1859 Baudelaire further developed his ideas of the imagination, saying that this "queen of faculties . . . affects all the other faculties; it rouses them, it sends them into combat . . . It is analysis, it is synthesis . . . It is imagination that has taught man the moral meaning of color, of outline, of sound, and of perfume. In the beginning of the world it created analogy and metaphor. It decomposes all creation, and from the materials, accumulated and arranged according to rules whose origin is found only in the depths of the soul, it creates a new world, it produces the sensation of the new" (*BLC*, 181). Like Coleridge, Baudelaire sees the imagination as destroying conventional associations and recreating according to primordial imperatives found within human subjectivity, within the soul itself. Such a function falls within an aesthetic domain. Interestingly, however, the spheres of truth and morality, which Baudelaire had been at such pains to demarcate and distinguish from the aesthetic sphere, are now allowed to reenter the very depth of the aesthetic realm inasmuch as they inform the workings of imagination. Baudelaire states that "Imagination is the queen of truth," and that "it plays a powerful role even in morality . . . the strongest weapon in our battles with the ideal is a fine imagination with a vast store of observations at its disposal" (*BLC*, 182). Hence, even though truth and morality are rigidly expelled by Poe and Baudelaire from the province of the aesthetic, they are effectively subsumed under the control of the very power which creates the aesthetic, the power of imagination. They are once again brought into relation with the aesthetic, not as objective forces imposing on it from the outside but as forces subject to redefinition, subject to the control of the aesthetic, and distilled from the essence itself of subjectivity.

Significantly, Baudelaire's notion of imagination is articulated in reaction against the classical precept that one should "copy only nature." Baudelaire's rejoinder to this precept is: "Nature is ugly, and I prefer the monsters of my imagination to the triteness of actuality" (*BLC*, 180). Baudelaire later issues a challenge: "Who would dare to assign to art the sterile function of imitating nature?" (*BLC*, 300). This classical function of art is, in his eyes, as demoded as the "phantoms of reason," which should not be confused with "the phantoms of imagination; the former are equations, the latter living beings and memories" (*BLC*, 312). The true poet, says Baudelaire, should be "*really* true to his own nature" and avoid "borrowing the eyes and emotions of another man." In short, he should rely on his imagination (*BLC*, 181). What we call "nature" is merely the starting point of true reality, which is far more comprehensive: "The whole visible universe is but a storehouse of images and signs to which imagination will give a relative place and value; it is a sort of food which the imagination must digest and transform. All the powers of the human soul must be subordinated to the imagination, which commandeers them all at one and the same time" (*BLC*, 186). What arranges the world, then, is not divine providence or the canons of truth or morality; all of these are now subjected to the aesthetic power of imagination, which is now newly invested with the functions of truth and morality in their subjectively reconstituted and re-authorized form.

Walter Pater (1839–1894)

Walter Pater is best known for his phrase "art for art's sake." In his insistence on artistic autonomy, on aesthetic experience as opposed to aesthetic object, and on experience in general as an ever vanishing flux, he is a precursor of modern views of both life and art. His subjectivist and "impressionistic" criticism, once attacked by the likes of Eliot and Pound, who called for a return to a depersonalized classical objectivity, is now regarded with renewed interest; not only did it influence figures such as Oscar Wilde but it is now also seen as anticipating several strains of modern theory, including those which derive from Nietzsche and Derrida, as well as certain elements of reader-response theory.

Educated at Oxford, Pater visited Italy in 1865 and was deeply affected by the Renaissance paintings he saw in Florence and elsewhere. His experience eventually inspired his *The Renaissance: Studies in Art and Poetry* (1873). His other works included *Marius the Epicurean* (1885), *Imaginary Portraits* (1887), and *Plato and Platonism* (1893). Pater's work belongs to an era of what is called "decadence," marked by a resigned withdrawal from social and political concerns, disillusionment with the consolations available in religion, and a rejection of the philistine and mechanical world which was the legacy of mainstream bourgeois thought and practice, in favor of an exaltation of art and of experience. Needless to say, the views of Pater, Wilde, and other aesthetes and impressionists brought them into conflict not only with the builders of systems and the defenders of religion or morality, but also with those Victorian writers who saw art and literature as having a high moral purpose and civilizing function.

In the preface to his *The Renaissance: Studies in Art and Poetry*, Pater rejects as useless any attempt to define "beauty in the abstract."[7] While on the surface Pater claims to accept Matthew Arnold's imperative that the function of true criticism is to "see the object as in itself it really is," he redefines this formula in a subjective way: to see the object as it really is, he says, "is to know one's own impression as it really is, to discriminate it, to realize it distinctly" (viii). The kinds of questions we should ask are: "What is this song or picture . . . to *me*? What effect does it really produce on me?" The answers to these questions are the "original facts" which must be confronted by the critic (viii).

Pater's views of aesthetic experience are rooted in his account of experience in general. In the conclusion to *Studies* he observes that modern thought tends to view all things as in constant flux. Our physical life is a "perpetual motion" of ever changing combinations of elements and forces. This is even more true of our mental life, of the world of thought and feeling. At first sight, he says, "experience seems to bury us under a flood of external objects . . . But when reflexion begins to play on those objects they are dissipated under its influence . . . the whole scope of observation is dwarfed into the narrow chamber of the individual mind" (234–235). Hence the world which seemed overwhelming, which seemed solid and external and of boundless scope, is actually encompassed within the circle of our impressions, our experience (235). Not only does the whole world reduce itself to our impressions, but these impressions themselves are ever vanishing and in "perpetual flight" (236). Given the brevity of our life, we must "be for ever curiously testing new opinions and courting new impressions, never acquiescing in a facile orthodoxy, of Comte, or of Hegel, or of our own." For Pater, experience must be undertaken for its own sake: "Not the fruit of experience, but experience itself, is the end . . . To burn always with this hard, gem-like flame, to maintain this ecstasy, is success in life" (236–237). Such intense experience is furnished foremost by "the poetic passion, the desire of beauty, the love of art for its own sake" (239).

We have here reached a point in Western culture where experience is dirempted and abstracted from any kind of constraint whatsoever, even from its consensual overlap with that of other individuals. Hegel would have regarded such experience as an abstract category, not even possible; but Pater expresses a desperate attempt to redeem experience from the weight of centuries of oppression and coercion and molding into various socially acceptable forms. He effectively aestheticizes experience, equating the fullness of experience with beauty, in an attempt to extricate the category of experience from the burdens invested in it by bourgeois thought. Experience is no longer a reliable source of knowledge or a basis of scientific inquiry; it is not a realm which constrains the operations of reason; nor is it a realm under the strict surveillance of morality or of religious institutions. It is raised from the mereness of means to the exaltation of end, a celebration of purposelessness, a celebration of indirection, of relativism and randomness.

Oscar Wilde (1854–1900)

Another figure in the aestheticist vein, one who struck an even more decadent and dandyish posture, was Oscar Wilde. A dazzling wit and brilliant conversationalist, he was the author of several plays which took the London stage by storm, as well as of poetry, novels, and criticism. His most notable dramas were *Lady Windermere's Fan* (1892), *An Ideal Husband* (1895), and, most successful of all, *The Importance of Being Earnest* (1895). These plays powerfully satirized the morals and mores of the English middle classes; Wilde's own homosexual practices brought him into conflict with these moral standards. Publicly called a sodomite by the marquis of Queensbury, the father of Wilde's lover Lord Alfred Douglas, Wilde was involved in a lawsuit and eventually imprisoned for "indecency," and given a sentence of two years with hard labor. Wilde also produced historical tragedies such as *Salome* (1893), relating the story of the beheading of John the Baptist; and his novel *The Picture of Dorian Gray*, published in 1890–1891, provoked a storm of critical protest. Notwithstanding his homosexual inclinations, Wilde married Constance Lloyd and wrote "children's" stories for his two children. His main critical work was a collection of essays called *Intentions* (1891), which includes "The Critic as Artist." On his release from prison he spent his remaining days self-exiled in Europe and wrote *The Ballad of Reading Gaol* (1898), as well as a lengthy moving letter entitled *De Profundis* (1905) to Alfred Douglas.

Wilde was educated at Trinity College, Dublin and Magdalen College, Oxford. The major influences on his thought and style were John Ruskin, Walter Pater, and Algernon Swinburne, all of whom had effectively continued in the aesthetic path paved by Théophile Gautier, Edgar Allan Poe, and Charles Baudelaire. No account of Wilde can be complete without mention of the numerous incisive and witty epigrams he wrote and uttered, epigrams which often subverted the moral principles and prejudices of his bourgeois audience. When he came to America on a lecture tour, he said at customs: "I have nothing to declare except my genius." On being questioned over his fastidious dress, he remarked: "I make up for being over-dressed by being over-educated." Other comments that sometimes go to the heart of the bourgeois ethic include: "Punctuality is the thief of time"; "There is no sin except stupidity"; and "the public is wonderfully tolerant. It forgives everything except genius." Wilde's subversiveness has been a source of inspiration for gay and lesbian studies, and his refusal of absolutes aligns him not only with figures such as Pater but also with Nietzsche and indeed the entire heterological tradition.

In the famous preface to *The Picture of Dorian Gray*, Wilde offers a brief and provocative manifesto of his aesthetic outlook. He states that the "artist is the creator of beautiful things."[8] Already, we are worlds away from the notion of art as imitation, art as expressing either reality or ideality, as well as from any purported connection of art with truth or morality. Indeed, Wilde continues, there "is no such thing as a moral or an immoral book" and "No artist has ethical sympathies." Moreover, no "artist desires to prove anything . . . Books are well written, or badly written. That is all." For Wilde, as for Pater, the prime object of pursuit is beauty, beauty absolutely divorced from all other considerations, moral or practical. Kantian aesthetics lurk in the remote background of such sentiments. Wilde emphasizes that "beautiful things mean only Beauty," and that "All art is quite useless." Not only does Wilde withdraw from art the duty of imitating life, but he effectively redefines its imitative function: "It is the spectator, and not life, that art really mirrors" (17). This statement and in fact Wilde's entire account of criticism anticipates reader-response and even some historicist theories: ultimately, what the work of art tells us about is not the world or the author but *ourselves*, our manner of reading, our expectations, cultural assumptions, and psychological constitution.

It is in "The Critic as Artist" that Wilde sets forth his most important views on art and criticism. This text is framed as a dialogue between two characters: Ernest, who tends to value art over criticism, and Gilbert, who voices Wilde's own conception of the nature and superiority of criticism. Wilde even reinterprets Plato and Aristotle in the image of his own aestheticism: Plato, who attempted to display the connection between beauty, truth, and morality, will be remembered, he suggests, as a "critic of Beauty." And Aristotle's notion of *katharsis* or the purification of emotions undertaken by art is essentially an aesthetic, rather than moral, notion (1018). In general, Wilde suggests that whatever "is modern in our life we owe to the Greeks. Whatever is an anachronism is due to medievalism." It is the Greeks, he avers, who have given us "the whole system of art-criticism" (1019).

As for the connection between art and criticism, any proposed antithesis between these, says Wilde, is "entirely arbitrary. Without the critical faculty, there is no artistic creation at all worthy of the name." The reason for this is that art is not merely an outpouring of emotion; on the contrary, it must be directed by the critical faculty, and must be "self-conscious and deliberate" (1020). In response to this, Ernest argues that "it is the function of Literature to create, from the rough material of actual existence, a new world that will be more marvellous, more enduring, and more true than the world that common eyes look upon" (1026). Gilbert's (or Wilde's) rejoinder expresses a much more modern viewpoint: "Criticism is itself an art." And, just as the creative act is critical, so criticism is creative. It is also independent: "criticism is no more to be judged by any low standards of imitation or resemblance than is the work of poet or sculptor. The critic occupies the same relation to the work of art that he criticizes as the artist does to the visible world of form and colour, or the unseen world of passion and of thought" (1027). Wilde now reaches his most comprehensive definition of criticism:

> the highest Criticism, being the purest form of personal impression, is in its way more creative than creation, as it has least reference to any standard external to itself, and is, in fact, its own reason for existing, and, as the Greeks would put it, in itself, and to itself, an end. Certainly it is never trammelled by any shackles of verisimilitude. No ignoble considerations of probability, that cowardly concession to the tedious repetitions of domestic or public life, affect it ever . . . That is what the highest criticism really is, the record of one's own soul. (1027)

What this paragraph makes us realize is the length of the journey undertaken by literary criticism since Plato and Aristotle. We have now moved beyond the call for artistic autonomy, the demand that art itself be extricated from moral, religious, and ideological constraints. The demand for autonomy, having traversed the sphere of art, has now emerged in the realm of criticism, a demand that carries in its wake a subversion of not only previous conceptions of criticism but also the basic tenets of Western philosophy. Just as art should be free of any obligatory relation to reality – such as the relation of imitation or reflection – so criticism should be free of any constraining relationship to art: it should not be bound by imperatives of fidelity or supposed objectivity, and does not even need art to justify the existence of criticism. Far from being merely adjectival of art, a mere means toward the understanding or illumination of art, criticism becomes an end in itself, an end for which art is merely an occasioning, and not a constituting, factor. In this autonomy, criticism is even more free than art of any constrictive relation to reality. For centuries, art and literature had felt bound by the Aristotelian dictum of probability, that they should express what has a realistic or probable chance of happening in the real world. But, like Nietzsche (and Hume in another context), Wilde derides such a notion of probability as expressing merely the tedium of public conventions: probability is here seen as a shallow and philistine predictability characteristic of mediocrity.

What, then, is the self-contained aim of criticism? It is to express personal impressions, to delve into one's soul, to express subjectivity. Wilde rejects Arnold's definition of criticism's task as attempting "to see the object as in itself it really is." On the contrary, criticism "is in its essence purely subjective" (1028). By way of example, Wilde states that we do not care whether or not Ruskin's views on Turner are "sound." What is important is that Ruskin's "mighty and majestic prose . . . is at least as great a work of art as any of those wonderful sunsets" (1028). Indeed, through such criticism, a picture of Turner's "becomes more wonderful to us than it really is, and reveals to us a secret of which, in truth, it knows nothing" (1029). Wilde here anticipates modern critical rejections of the authority of an author's intention, as well as the intrinsically polysemous nature of works of art: such criticism, he insists, "criticises not merely the individual work of art, but Beauty itself," and "Beauty has as many meanings as man has moods" (1030). Wilde's point is that once a work of art is finished, it has "an independent life of its own" which goes far beyond what its author may have intended to say. Part of the inexhaustibility of art is its capacity to evoke endless impressions and moods in the reader or listener or spectator. And to the critic, the work of art "is simply a suggestion for a new work of his own, that need not necessarily bear any obvious resemblance to the thing it criticises." The premise behind these statements is that a beautiful form is the province not so much of artistic expression as of critical discernment: it is the critic, rather than the artist, who can see beauty in an endless multiplicity of things; in this sense, criticism transcends art (1030).

Wilde acknowledges that the critic can be an interpreter: he can pass from his impression of a work of art to an analysis of it; but this is the "lower sphere" of criticism, and the critic does not always attempt to explain a work of art: "He may seek rather to deepen its mystery" and to raise around it "a mist of wonder" (1032). Moreover, the critic does not merely interpret passively, simply repeating a message already formed by the artist; rather, he intensifies his own personality so as to interpret the personality and work of the artist (1033). It is through the critic that the performative potential of the art is realized; it is the critic who gives voice to the work of art. Moreover, it is the critic who is "always showing us the work of art in some new relation to our age. He will always be reminding us that great works of art are living things" (1034). Again, in this very modern statement, Wilde anticipates many theories of art which emphasize the role of the audience, in its historically specific circumstances, in giving shape to the ever renewed meaning of art. Indeed, it is criticism that "takes the cumbersome mass of creative work, and distils it into a finer essence" (1056).

Wilde insists that there is no art that is impersonal and objective: all artistic creation is "absolutely subjective"; anticipating Derrida, he suggests that the "difference between objective and subjective work is one of external form merely. It is accidental, not essential" (1045). The aim of art is "simply to create a mood" and to create "emotion for the sake of emotion" (1042, 1039). The point here is that art stands above and beyond considerations of practicality, utility, morality, and education. The very value of art, of art as distilled into its essence as beauty, is its detachment from the world, from life, from convention, from action. And criticism, cloaked in the same mantle of autonomy, takes this detachment further; it has its life in contemplation, the "life that has for its aim not *doing* but *being*, and not *being* merely, but *becoming* – that is what the critical spirit can give us . . . From the high tower of Thought we can look out at the world." Criticism is needed more than ever in bourgeois society where "Thought is degraded by its constant association with practice" (1041, 1042). Wilde reiterates the concerns of Shelley and many Romantics that modern life has become locked in mechanism, utility, and pragmatism; the artistic worship of beauty represents a rebellion for Wilde against the strictures of reason: as Plato knew, art "creates in listener and spectator a form of divine madness." And both artist and critic require a temperament that is attuned to beauty, that will transcend the "organised ignorance" that is called public opinion (1048–1049, 1056).

Beyond these functions, criticism has a broader and more basic import. Wilde accepts Arnold's claim that criticism is responsible for creating the "intellectual atmosphere" and culture of an age; like Arnold, Babbitt, and other humanists, he laments the bourgeois education that burdens the memory "with a load of unconnected facts" (1055). It is criticism that gives us a sense of unity, that enables us to reconstruct the past, that enables us to rise above provincialism and prejudice into true cosmopolitanism (1053), so criticism insists upon "the unity of the human mind in the variety of its forms" (1056–1057). Again, anticipating some important modern insights, Wilde states that it "is Criticism that, recognizing no position as final, and refusing to bind itself by the shallow shibboleths of any sect or school, creates that serene philosophic temper which loves truth for its own sake . . . Anything approaching to the free play of the mind is practically unknown amongst us . . . The artistic critic, like the mystic, is an antinomian always" (1057).

Notes

1   Remy de Gourmont, *Selected Writings*, trans. and ed. Glenn S. Burne (New York: University of Michigan Press, 1966), p. 124.
2   Remy de Gourmont, *Decadence and Other Essays on the Culture of Ideas*, trans. William Bradley (1922; rpt. London: George Allen and Unwin, 1930), p. 31.
3   Gourmont, "The Roots of Idealism," in ibid., pp. 209–210.
4   Arthur Symons, *The Symbolist Movement in Literature* (1908; rpt. New York: Haskell House, 1971), pp. 4, 9. Hereafter page citations are given in the text.
5   *Intimate Journals*, trans. C. Isherwood, introd. T. S. Eliot (New York and London: Blackamore Press, 1930), pp. 48, 51. Hereafter cited as *IJ*.
6   *Baudelaire as a Literary Critic: Selected Essays*, trans. Lois Boe Hyslop and Francis E. Hyslop, Jr. (Pennsylvania: Pennsylvania State University Press, 1964), p. 38. Hereafter cited as *BLC*. My account of Baudelaire is indebted in part to the insightful prefaces written by the translators.
7   Walter Pater, *The Renaissance: Studies in Art and Poetry* (London: Macmillan, 1913), p. vii. Hereafter page citations are given in the text.
8   *The Complete Works of Oscar Wilde: Stories, Plays, Poems, Essays*, introd. Vyvyan Holland (London and Glasgow: Collins, 1984), p. 17. Hereafter page citations from this volume are given in the text.

CHAPTER 20

THE HETEROLOGICAL THINKERS

T he main streams of modern European and American thought, such as rationalism, empiricism, utilitarianism, and pragmatism, stemmed from the Enlightenment and the colossal series of changes following the American and French
Revolutions, as well as the ongoing Industrial Revolution. Historians such as Eric
Hobsbawm have remarked that nineteenth-century debates in economics, politics,
theology, philosophy, and science were ultimately indissociable from an implicit stance
toward the bourgeois revolutionary ideals of 1789. Hence, the thinkers of nineteenth-
century Europe could be seen as divided along the broad line of opposition or allegiance
to the interests of the bourgeois class. Major advocates of economic liberalism, such as
Smith, Ricardo, Say, and Malthus, and of utilitarianism, such as James Mill, John
Stuart Mill, and Jeremy Bentham, built on the philosophical and political foundations
of Rousseau, Locke, Hume, and other thinkers of the bourgeois Enlightenment. The
range of "oppositional" theorists was vast, including almost the entire constellation
of Romantic writers, anarchists such as William Godwin, Baudelaire and the French
symbolists, Christian and utopian socialists, and eventually the Victorian writers Carlyle,
Ruskin, William Morris, and Arnold.

The relationship of the two major modern European philosophers – Kant and Hegel
– to Enlightenment ideals was complex. The philosophy of Kant occupied an ambivalent relation to those ideals, demarcating a phenomenal realm in which the fruits of
pure reason and scientific advance could reign and a sharply isolated noumenal realm
in which the feudal Christian emphasis on the human will and its relation to the divine
could be preserved in its freedom from the encroachments of mechanistic causality.
Kant also laid the theoretical foundations of many Romantic aesthetics and the notion
of artistic autonomy. Hegel's philosophy, which effected a precarious synthesis of
Enlightenment and Romantic notions, was central to modern European thought in the
dual process of its construction and disintegration. His vast system had amalgamated
and summed up the entire thrust of modern bourgeois thought from Descartes and
Hobbes through the Enlightenment to Kant: the central currents of bourgeois thought
– rationalism, empiricism, and utilitarianism – achieved concurrence in the dialectic.
But his system had also encompassed Romanticism's insistence on the unity of subject

502

and object, as well as the notion of an all-encompassing totality, a unity and totality fragmented by the forces of an increasingly industrialized and commercialized world. Equally constitutive of Hegel's historical centrality is the vast array of systems into which his dialectic collapsed, signifying the merely precarious ability of bourgeois thought to achieve a unified vision of humanity and the world.

There was, however, an important strand of thought which reacted profoundly against Hegel's philosophy as the embodiment of bourgeois principles. This was the "heterological" or alternative tradition initiated by Schopenhauer who, in explicit opposition to Hegel, launched a radical critique of Enlightenment notions such as the scientific progress of civilization and the perfectibility of individual and state through refinement of the faculty of reason. The heterological tradition opened up by Schopenhauer was continued by figures such as Nietzsche, Kierkegaard, Bergson, Freud, Husserl, Heidegger, Derrida, and modern feminists, thinkers who challenged the very discipline of philosophy and its claims to arrive at truth through reason. They emphasized instead the role of emotion, the body, sexuality, the unconscious, as well as of pragmatic interests. This tradition exhibits some historical continuity with the Romantics, the symbolists, and decadents, as well as several affiliations with humanists such as Irving Babbitt in America and Matthew Arnold in England, both of whom deplored the effects of the French Revolution. The literary and aesthetic views of four figures from this heterodox line of thinking will be analyzed below in the important context of their world views: Schopenhauer, Bergson, Nietzsche, and Arnold. The issues raised by these thinkers continue to influence literary debate in our own day at the profoundest levels.

Arthur Schopenhauer (1788–1860)

Schopenhauer – who is the most widely read philosopher in Germany today – offered an incisive critique of the bourgeois world: its vision of the present as alone real, its exaltation of a rationality answering merely to pragmatic needs, and, underlying these, its self-abasement before the "crass materialism" of science.[1] Schopenhauer was especially contemptuous of attempts to historicize and rationalize the evils of the bourgeois world as part of an ordered teleological plan; he dismissed Hegel's "philosophy of absolute nonsense" as comprised of "three-quarters cash and one-quarter crazy notions" (PW, 79, 81). He himself utterly rejected the notion that history exhibited any unity beyond eternal recurrence of the same miserable patterns of events (PW, 108, 290). Schopenhauer argued that the intellect or reason so hypostatized by much Enlightenment thought was actually in bondage to the practical motives of the will to live, a will concentrated in the sexual act, in the unconscious and irrational desire to perpetuate life. Schopenhauer viewed will as the unique noumenal reality in a Kantian sense, a force which operated (1) largely unconsciously, (2) often repressively, and (3) in intimate conjunction with memory and sexuality.

Schopenhauer expressed an intense disillusionment with the concerns and methods of philosophy. He was impatient of what he saw as the intellectual and verbal games, the logical manipulations and groundless speculations of philosophers. He insisted, moreover, on speculation being confined to experience, observation, and testing. Above all, the human subject as described by Schopenhauer was a far cry from the ideal Hegelian subject whose intellectual and ethical behavior rationally complied with the requirements of a rational state. The Schopenhauerian subject was driven by motives scarcely accessible and harbored a perpetual tension and struggle between its constituting elements.

Anticipating Freud, Schopenhauer viewed consciousness as the mere surface of the mind. Human reason is but one faculty, and it is hardly dominant: its knowledge is restricted to the incomplete conscious mind and its operation occurs as a continuous struggle to mediate the claims of the social world and the deepest instinctive drives and desires. In fact, Schopenhauer's concept of the will to live overlaps broadly with Freud's notion of the unconscious as an arena which can harbor contradictions, where events are not temporally organized and where the claims of external reality are replaced by those of psychical reality. Schopenhauer had taken Kant's distinction of phenomena and noumena as his starting point. On the basis of this distinction he regarded the world which appears to us as phenomenal, a representation whose form was governed by the subjective apparatus of time, space, and causality. In this scheme, the self-conscious human subject has a dual position. On the one hand, it takes its place within the scheme of objects in the world: as a subject I am conscious of myself as an object. On the other hand, I experience my self as a subject, as a willing, active, moving agent, whose body and actions objectify my will. This inner consciousness reveals itself to me immediately and irreducibly as my will, the "in-itself" of my phenomenal being. Schopenhauer is at pains to point out repeatedly that the will is not an instrument of the intellect. Nor is the intellect some privileged faculty engaged in a disinterested manner in understanding the world. Rather, the intellect itself is a slave to the will; in its very basis, it is already infected by practical motives and interests. Schopenhauer characterizes the intellect as operating in a temporal medium, of past, present, and future; whereas the will moves in an endless present. The will, then, is our profoundest source of motivation and the primordial means of our engagement with the world. Schopenhauer sees this will to live as a blind, irrational, and purposeless force, which ceaselessly drives the subject like an internal clockwork. This model of the mind is deterministic and the determining factors lie well beneath the reach of reason.

Common to both Freud's and Schopenhauer's models of the mind are the phenomenon of repression and the location of motives in the unconscious. Schopenhauer asserts that we often impose illusory rationalizations on behavior which arises from hidden drives. The will itself prevents potentially embarrassing thoughts and desires rising to consciousness. The will can inspire failure of memory and a complete suppression of events and experiences, together with the replacement of these by delusions and fantasies. In Schopenhauer's words, the will refuses to allow "what is contrary to it to come under the examination of the intellect."[2] The will, says Schopenhauer, periodically withdraws itself from the guidance of the intellect and of the motives. "In this way it then appears as a blind, impetuous, destructive force of nature, and accordingly manifests itself as the mania to annihilate everything that comes in its way" (*WWII*, 402).

Also anticipating Freud, Schopenhauer accords sexuality a central place in the economy of human motives. He described sexuality as the focus of the will. In his chapter on "The Metaphysics of Sexual Love" he described the sexual impulse as "the strongest and most active of all motives . . . It is the ultimate goal of almost all human effort" (*WWII*, 533). He even goes so far as to define the sexual impulse as the will to live (*WWII*, 535). He looked askance at this state of affairs, affirming that sexuality "appears on the whole as a malevolent demon, striving to pervert, to confuse, and to overthrow everything" (*WWII*, 534). What explains the important role of sexuality is that, whatever its proximate aim might be, its ultimate aim is reproduction, to procure the only kind of immortality available, the immortality of the species. Schopenhauer states that the growing attachment of two lovers is in reality the will to live of the new, unborn individual (*WWII*, 536). The indestructibility of man's true being in itself lies in the species rather than in the individual. Schopenhauer himself reflected sardonically on the fact that the entire maintenance of a species depends on an irrational, emotional, instinctual act.

Further anticipating Freud's account of the life and death instincts, Schopenhauer held that death is the "true result and to that extent the purpose of life," while the sexual instinct is the "embodiment of the will to live" (*WWII*, 618). Schopenhauer regards death as the return to a blissful state. In his essay "On Death and its Relation to the Indestructibility of our Inner Nature," he states that "the entire cessation of the life-process must be a wonderful relief for its driving force." Those who have engaged in the terrible struggles for existence, he says, have "the return into the womb of nature as the last resource . . . Like everything else, they emerged from this womb for a short time, enticed by the hope of more favourable conditions of existence than those which have fallen to their lot" (*WWII*, 469). Moreover, for Schopenhauer, the true being of anything survives its own individual death; employing Platonic ideas, he suggests that the eternity of the idea of a given species is distinctly marked in the finiteness of an individual (*WWII*, 482). In fact, "Death and birth are the constant renewal and revival of the will's consciousness. In itself this will is endless and beginningless" (*WWII*, 500). At the end of this chapter, Schopenhauer presents us with the starkness of his pessimism:

> Death is the great reprimand that the will-to-live, and more particularly the egoism essential thereto, receive through the course of nature . . . it is the violent destruction . . . of the fundamental error of our true nature, the great disillusionment. At bottom, we are something that ought not to be; therefore we cease to be. Egoism really consists in man's restricting all reality to his own person, in that he imagines he lives in this alone, and not in others. Death teaches him something better, since it abolishes this person, so that man's true nature, that is his will, will henceforth live only in other individuals. (*WWII*, 507)

Essentially, Schopenhauer's is a pessimistic philosophy which turns away from the world. Before the French symbolists had articulated the need for poetry to aspire toward a Platonic ideal realm, Schopenhauer had affirmed that genuine knowledge, as given exclusively by poetry, the arts, and philosophy, must have as its object not the particulars of the material world but the underlying unity of the Platonic universal (*PW*, 21, 83). Schopenhauer urged that the only avenue of escape from bondage to the utilitarian and rational will lies in the shared endeavor of philosophy and poetry. The "high calling" of the poet and philosopher, claims Schopenhauer, has its root in their common ability to free the intellect from the utilitarian and rational constraints of the subjective will (*PW*, 90). These disciplines have as their object not the world of becoming but the world of being, the permanent unity underlying the ever changing flux of phenomena, the One behind the Many. Such freeing of the intellect was, for Schopenhauer, a stage on the Buddhistic and Hinduistic path to total renunciation of both world and will, a path summarized in his phrase the "turning of the Will" (*PW*, 106–109).

Following Plato, Schopenhauer sees reality or the true content of the phenomena in the world as embodied in ideas; these alone are timeless, existing "outside and independently of all relations." And the kind of knowledge that apprehends ideas is "*art, the work of genius*," whose perspective toward ideas is one of "pure contemplation" and detachment. Schopenhauer equates this "gift of genius" with the achievement of an impersonal and completely objective perspective: "Accordingly, genius is the capacity to remain in a state of pure perception, to remove from the service of the will the knowledge which originally existed only for this service." Genius is an ability to look at the object independently of one's own aims and interest, and one's own will (*WWI*, 184–186). Schopenhauer subsequently elaborates that genius is the capacity to know not individual things but their *ideas*, the essential form of their entire species. In art, philosophy, and ascetic mysticism, the intellect's bondage to the will is suspended, and the intellect is free to view the world more objectively, free of the practical subjective constraints of the will. Only these activities can perceive the Platonic universal underlying the multiplicity of appearances. Schopenhauer defines the aesthetic perspective, then, as comprising, firstly, knowledge of an object not as an individual thing but as an idea; and, secondly, a condition in which the self-consciousness of the knowing subject operates not as an individual "but as *pure, will-less subject*" (*WWI*, 194–195). A universal subject confronts the object in its universal aspect.

Aesthetic pleasure, then, results from a detached contemplation of beauty, which Schopenhauer defines as the propensity of nature to accommodate itself to such a disinterested perspective (*WWI*, 210). Like Aristotle and Sidney before him, Schopenhauer places poetry above history, since history renders individual and contingent truths, whereas the poet "apprehends the Idea, the inner being of mankind outside all relation and all time, the adequate objectivity of the thing-in-itself at its highest grade" (*WWI*, 244–245). Schopenhauer acknowledges, however, that though the poet conveys abstract and general concepts, he must use concrete terms that represent these, and he achieves this through imagination (*WWI*, 243). The other devices enlisted by poetry, such as rhythm and rhyme, give poetry "a certain emphatic power of conviction, independent of all reason or argument" (*WWI*, 243–244). The feeling of sublimity is excited in the observer when the objects of nature appear to have a hostile or threatening relation to the human will, as in spectacles of immeasurable greatness or might. The difference between beauty and sublimity is that in the former case, nature facilitates a detached contemplation of itself, free of all relation to the human will; in the latter case, this detachment is achieved through a process of struggle, a violent tearing away of the object from relations to the will, through overcoming and transcending feelings such as terror and danger. In sublimity we feel the twofold nature of our consciousness, both as individual, enslaved to the will and the mercy of the vast forces of nature, and as "the eternal, serene subject of knowing, who as the condition of every object is the supporter of this whole world . . . free from, and foreign to, all willing and all needs, in the quiet comprehension of the Ideas" (*WWI*, 200–205).

At the heart of Schopenhauer's philosophy and aesthetics, then, is an attitude which continues through Nietzsche, Arnold, Bergson, and others: that rational knowledge can never be adequate to ideas of perception; and that poetry is the paradigm of disinterested and objective knowledge. As in so many nineteenth-century theories, epistemology – the science of knowing – here becomes aestheticized, and the aesthetic becomes a privileged category of human perception, elevated from being just one more discipline to a final resource for seeking harmony, unity, and order in the world. The harmony which was objectively fragmented in the late industrial world is now internalized as a subjective capacity: it is left to the aesthetic to attempt what religion, philosophy, and science can no longer accomplish. The aesthetic is *defined* as a form of perception of reality: poetry could no longer take for granted the reality it was to express. Schopenhauer's insights were influential in the deployment of humor and irony by the French symbolists and Anglo-American modernists.

Friedrich Nietzsche (1844–1900)

Friedrich Nietzsche is most often associated with the announcement of "the death of God" (which in fact is first found in Hegel's *Phenomenology*); he is also remembered by phrases such as the "will to power," as well as the idea of the "overman" or "superman" (*übermensch*) who gloriously rises above the common herd mentality and morality promoted by modern liberal states. His ideas have sometimes been aligned with anti-Semitism and Nazism, and with both extreme individualism and self-annihilating mysticism. Nietzsche himself saw the apparatus of both Church and state as coercing people into a mediocre conformity and uniformity; he called for a new conception of humanity, based on self-creation, passion, power, and subjugation of one's circumstances.

Nietzsche occupies a prominent place in the spectrum of resistance to mainstream Western thought as embodied in Platonic philosophy, Christianity, and the bourgeois Enlightenment. Influenced by Schopenhauer, who reacted archetypally against the systematizing and historicizing philosophy of Hegel, Nietzsche's own thought refuses to present itself in the mold of any system; it challenges the authority of reason and conventional morality, both Christian and utilitarian; it stresses the Dionysian side of human nature, fueled by unconscious impulses and excess, as a counter to the Apollonian side which is conscious, rational, and individuated; it subverts conventional notions of truth; it unashamedly displays scorn for women; and it undermines modern liberal political visions of democracy. Effectively, it challenges the fundamental assumptions of Western philosophy at epistemological, moral, political, and spiritual levels; for these reasons, as well as for his style – poetic, ironic, discontinuous, intimate – it has exerted an enormous influence on modernism, existentialism, the Frankfurt School of Marxism, the philosophy of science, and various branches of poststructuralism, such as those associated with Derrida and Foucault. Nietzsche was also influenced by the German composer Richard Wagner, to whom his first book, *The Birth of Tragedy*

(1870–1871), is dedicated, though he later recoiled in part from the ideas of both Wagner and Schopenhauer.

Born in Prussia in 1844, Nietzsche was a brilliant student, completing his doctorate at the University of Leipzig, and becoming professor of philology at the University of Basel in Switzerland when he was just 24. His final years, however, were given to insanity; he was cared for by his sister Elisabeth, whose edition of his works was stamped with her own views on racial purity. Nietzsche's works include *The Birth of Tragedy*, *Ecce Homo* (1888), *The Antichrist* (1895), and his notebooks published posthumously as *The Will to Power* (1901).

Nietzsche's historical position in Western thought is complex. The Enlightenment had been broadly secular in its outlook, stressing the need for man to use his own reason and to base his observations upon experience, rather than taking his beliefs on external authority, whether religious or political, as exerted through tradition, custom, and popular belief. Much Enlightenment philosophy had been influenced by scientific trends, particularly the emphasis placed on the universal operation of the law of causality throughout the world of phenomena. Theologies subsequent to the Enlightenment, such as those of Hegel, Strauss, and Renan, were obliged to take account of that emphasis, as were the philosophies of major thinkers such as Kant. Nietzsche's call for a new vision of humanity was profoundly atheistic. In *Thus Spoke Zarathustra* (1883–1892), he urges (through the mouthpiece of Zoroaster, founder of the ancient Persian religion that views the universe as a conflict between the forces of good and evil, and, in Nietzsche's eyes, the creator of morality): "Once you said 'God' when you gazed upon distant seas; but now I have taught you to say 'Superman.'"[3] He goes on:

> Could you *conceive* a god? – But may the will to truth mean this to you: that everything shall be transformed into the humanly-conceivable, the humanly evident, the humanly-palpable! You should follow your senses to the end!
> And you yourselves should create what you have hitherto called the World: the World should be formed in your image by your reason, your will, and your love! And truly, it will be to your happiness, you enlightened men! (*TSZ*, 110)

In a profound sense Nietzsche is humanistic: reality, truth, the world, are constructions, projections of human needs and interests, through the medium of human senses, human faculties, and human language. The superman represents perhaps the archetypal instance of such self-awareness: awareness that one is fashioning the world in the image of one's own will. On the other hand, Nietzsche's thought is *not* humanistic in the sense of envisioning a fundamental substratum of human identity and subjectivity; humans, according to Nietzsche, must create not only the world but also themselves: there is no primal archetype or pattern or essence on which they can model their subjectivity. In this sense, Nietzsche stands firmly opposed to the traditions of humanism that have persisted from the Renaissance through the Enlightenment, and in fact has more in common with anti-humanist theories such as structuralism and deconstruction.

Nietzsche anticipates many branches of thought, including various forms of positivism, poststructuralism, and the thinking of the American pragmatists C. S. Peirce, William James, and John Dewey. Nietzsche's definition of reality is much more pragmatic than the definitions found in previous philosophers, released from participation in any larger interpretative scheme. He affirms that "Appearance is an arranged and simplified world, at which our practical instincts have been at work." And he states that the world of appearance "is essentially a world of relationships . . . its being is essentially different from every point." Reality, in fact, is no more than the similarity between various subjective projections: "the world of 'phenomena' is the adapted world which we feel to be real. The 'reality' lies in the continual recurrence of identical, familiar, related things in their logicized character."[4] In other words, Nietzsche denies that there is any independent objectivity, that there can be objects or even things in the world without the workings and activity of our subjective apparatus. He defines an object as "only a kind of effect produced by a subject upon a subject – a *modus of the subject*" (*WP*, 307). These statements anticipate much modern theory which sees reality and truth as intersubjective constructions. It also anticipates much literary theory, such as reader-response theory, which views "meaning" not as somehow embedded in a text or assigned by any individual but rather as generated by a consensus of informed readers.

Like Schopenhauer, Nietzsche is skeptical about our motivations for acquiring knowledge; our pursuit of knowledge is not inspired by any disinterested love of truth. Rather, it is one manifestation of our "will to power," our fundamental motive of self-assertion, subjugation, and conquest, as well as of our need for security. In the following passage (which anticipates several such passages in Derrida), Nietzsche neatly undermines the fundamental categories that have dominated Western thought:

> The inventive force that invented categories labored in the service of our needs, namely of our need for security, for quick understanding on the basis of signs and sounds, for means of abbreviation: – "substance," "subject," "object," "being," "becoming" have nothing to do with metaphysical truths . . .
>
> In the formation of reason, logic, the categories, it was *need* that was authoritative: the need, not to "know," but to subsume, to schematize, for the purpose of intelligibility and calculation. (*WP*, 277–278)

Evident here is the importance that Nietzsche attributes to language in the construction of truth, a theme that will be revisited shortly. Nietzsche states also that the axioms of logic do not correspond to reality but are "a means and measure for us to *create* reality, the concept 'reality,' for ourselves" (*WP*, 306). Interestingly, in this statement, which will be more or less repeated by the Marxist writer Fredric Jameson in his discussion of realism, Nietzsche suggests that even "reality" is not something "out there" but is merely an expedient concept that serves a purpose for us, that answers to a primal need to classify the world, to divide it up for the purpose of various forms of subjugation, to assert the power of one will over another. In fact, what is important about a statement is not that it is true but that it is "life-affirming," that it promotes strength and freedom.

The foregoing account is an overview of the positions at which Nietzsche's thought eventually arrived, the positions with which he is customarily associated. In what follows, two of Nietzsche's texts will be considered. The first is the renowned text of Nietzsche's that has the most direct bearing on literature and criticism: *The Birth of*

Tragedy. This work anticipates many of Nietzsche's later positions, but it contains important differences. For example, at this early stage, Nietzsche is still enamored of the works of Kant and Schopenhauer. He is still talking in a Schopenhauerian fashion about patterns of eternal recurrence, and still using the Kantian terminology of a world of phenomena as contrasted with things in themselves.

Notwithstanding its title, *The Birth of Tragedy* offers two major theses, one purporting to explain the origins of tragedy and the other the death of tragedy at the hands of what Nietzsche calls "Socratism," a rational and scientific outlook toward the world taught first by Socrates and then by his disciple Plato. Hence in a treatise ostensibly about tragedy, Nietzsche effectively attempts to undermine the entire tradition of Western philosophy deriving from Plato. Nietzsche begins by asserting his first thesis: that the evolution of art is based upon a duality, a broad conflict, between two dispositions, represented respectively by the Greek gods Apollo and Dionysus. As a moral deity, Apollo demands self-control, self-knowledge, moderation; in short, he demands due respect and observance of the limits and status – social, psychological, physical – of the individual.[5] In this sense, Apollo is the expression of the *principium individuationis* (the beginning, or principle, of individuation) (*BT*, 22). Dionysus, on the other hand, represents a condition in which this principle is shattered, a state where the "individual forgets himself completely," and all previous social and religious barriers are annulled, in a universal harmony: "Not only does the bond between man and man come to be forged once more by the magic of the Dionysiac rite, but nature itself, long alienated or subjugated, rises again to celebrate the reconciliation with her prodigal son, man . . . Now the slave emerges as a freeman; all the rigid, hostile walls which either necessity or despotism has erected between man are shattered" (*BT*, 23). These two forces, the Apollonian and the Dionysian, are creative tendencies which developed side by side, "usually in fierce opposition . . . until . . . the pair accepted the yoke of marriage and, in this condition, begot Attic tragedy, which exhibits the salient features of both parents" (*BT*, 19).

Nietzsche points out that Apollo was not just one among many Greek gods: the "same drive that found its most complete representation in Apollo generated the whole Olympian world, and in this sense we may consider Apollo the father of that world" (*BT*, 28). What was this drive that created the Greek pantheon, that luxuriant spectrum of gods and goddesses with Zeus enthroned at its center? Nietzsche explains that the Greeks were profoundly aware of the "terrors and horrors of existence; in order to be able to live at all they had to place before them the shining fantasy of the Olympians." Fate or *Moira* was "mercilessly enthroned beyond the knowable world." Hence, the Greek deities answered to the Apollonian need for a beautiful and comforting illusion. It was essentially an artistic drive, an aesthetic drive, says Nietzsche, which generated "that Olympian realm which acted as a transfiguring mirror to the Hellenic will. The gods justified human life by living it themselves" (*BT*, 30). It seems, then, that the realm of the Olympian Greek gods was a projection of an idealized humanity which acted as a mediating or insulating barrier between human vulnerability and the terrible and unhumanizable forces that loomed beyond even the divine realm. Nietzsche's point is that the creation of this pantheon was essentially an aesthetic vindication or justification of human life, of human will (as expressed here in Schopenhauerian terms), to exist; such a vision, which overcomes the "somber contemplation of actuality . . . by means of illusions," Nietzsche calls "naive." And the naiveté of Homer, he says, "must be viewed as a complete victory of Apollonian illusion" (*BT*, 31). A victory, that is, of our oneiric or dreaming capacity over our drive to truth. It was through this "aesthetic mirror" that the "Greek will opposed suffering" (*BT*, 32).

Somewhat ahistorically, Nietzsche locates this "intense longing for illusion" within "the original Oneness" of nature, within "the ground of Being" that "has need of rapt vision and delightful illusion to redeem itself" (*BT*, 32). We ourselves, says Nietzsche, are the very stuff of such illusions and must view ourselves "as the truly non-existent, that is to say, as a perpetual unfolding in time, space, and causality" (*BT*, 33). In such sentiments, Nietzsche anticipates much existentialist and poststructuralist thought: not only do we have no predetermined essence, not only is there no providence directing the course of human history, but it is in the very dimension of unreality, of illusion, of mechanisms of distancing ourselves from reality, that human development unfolds. It is precisely an original *lack* of content which unfolds through our controlling and essence-endowing categories such as "substance," "idea," and the very notion of "reality" itself. Apollo appears "as the apotheosis of the *principium individuationis*, in whom the eternal goal of the original Oneness, namely its redemption through illusion, accomplishes itself" (*BT*, 33). Notwithstanding Nietzsche's overt anti-essentialism and anti-nominalism, his recourse to suprahistorical terms such as "the original Oneness" and "the eternal goal" effectively restabilizes elements previously de-essentialized and dissolved into relational status, allowing these an avenue of reconfiguration as elements of a totalizing primordial cyclical pattern. This pattern is in fact expressed by the "eternal" conflict between Apollonian and Dionysiac forces: Nietzsche notes that though the Dionysiac spirit was viewed as titanic and barbaric by the Apollonian Greeks, they were essentially akin to the barbaric Titans deposed by the Olympian gods. Only Dionysus could reinstate their awareness that their existence was based on suffering and knowledge. Hence, the "elements of titanism and barbarism turned out to be quite as fundamental as the Apollonian element" (*BT*, 34). In the Dionysiac vortex, "extravagance revealed itself as truth, and contradiction, a delight born of pain, spoke out of the bosom of nature. Whenever the Dionysiac voice was heard, the Apollonian norm seemed suspended or destroyed" (*BT*, 35). In a statement that anticipates certain insights of Lacan, Nietzsche suggests that Dionysus "breaks the spell of individuation and opens a path to the maternal womb of being" (*BT*, 97). It might be argued that this dualism or opposition (as also containing the potential for its own abrogation) has resurfaced in many discourses: as Plato's superordination of idea over sense and emotion; as the general philosophical differentiation of reason and emotion; as the dominance of the male principle over the female; as an imperialistic subjugation by civilization of barbarism; as the Romantic contrast of reason and imagination; as Schiller's distinction between naive and sentimental; as Freud's conscious and unconscious; as Lacan's symbolic and imaginary; as Kristeva's symbolic and semiotic; as the Foucauldian exclusion by normality of madness; as the institutional antagonism between science or philosophy and poetry; and, more generally, as the undermining of theory by experience.

The next phase of Nietzsche's argument yields some general implications of his overall thesis. He states that there have been two broad currents in Greek poetry, corresponding respectively to Apollonian and Dionysiac strains (*BT*, 44). The first of these is epic verse, as archetypally embodied in Homer's works. The second is lyric poetry, whose origin is conventionally traced to its archetype Archilochus (*BT*, 36). Nietzsche emphatically rejects the views of recent critics that these two types represent an opposition between the "objective" and the "subjective" artist. The subjective artist, he exclaims, is simply a bad artist, and "we demand above all, in every genre and range of art, a triumph over subjectivity, deliverance from the self, the silencing of every personal will and desire . . . we cannot imagine the smallest genuine art work lacking objectivity and disinterested contemplation" (*BT*, 37). These comments seem to show that Nietzsche cannot be classified as a Romantic: a disinterested or objective approach is integral to the very notion of art. What, then, of the lyric poet, who never tires of saying "I"? Such a poet, says Nietzsche, is "a Dionysiac artist, become wholly identified with the original Oneness, its pain and contradiction, and producing a replica of that Oneness as music . . . The 'I' thus sounds out of the depth of being" (*BT*, 38). In other words, the lyric poet is not expressing his own passion; whereas the epic poet is "committed to the pure contemplation of images," the lyric poet's work is analogous to music; he undergoes a "mystical process of un-selving," which generates a world of images, but these images are "objectified versions of himself. Being the active center of that world he may boldly speak in the first person, only his 'I' is not that of the actual waking man, but the 'I' dwelling, truly and eternally, in the ground of being" (*BT*, 39).

All tragedy, says Nietzsche, provides us with a "metaphysical solace," with the sense that, despite its transience and pain, "life is at bottom indestructibly joyful and powerful." This solace was expressed "most concretely in the chorus of satyrs, nature beings who dwell behind all civilization and preserve their identity through every change of generations and historical movement." Hence the ancient Greek, though open to the deepest suffering, was "saved by art" (*BT*, 50–51). One of the "realities" from which art saves us is the Dionysiac realization, embodied in Hamlet, that no action of ours can alter the "eternal condition of things . . . Understanding kills action, for in order to act we require the veil of illusion" (*BT*, 51). Once we pierce to the truth of existence, we see its "ghastly absurdity" and are invaded by "nausea." This is the "supreme jeopardy of the will," the endangerment of our drive to existence, that is healed by art, by means of the "sublime," which subjugates terror, and by means of the "comic spirit," which releases us from the tedium of absurdity. Hence we can grasp why the "satyr chorus of the dithyramb was the salvation of Greek art" (*BT*, 52). Once again, we can see at the depth of Nietzsche's argument certain insights that anticipate the views and terminology – absurdity, nausea – of existentialism. Nietzsche sees such absurdity as a perennial human condition, which we must always peripheralize to the boundaries of our consciousness if we are to think and act with any conviction. Art is the supreme mechanism at our disposal in achieving this illusion, in navigating the vast expanses of nothingness by means of purpose and meaning: our justification of life is ultimately neither religious nor moral but aesthetic. In short, then, Nietzsche views Greek tragedy "as a Dionysiac chorus which again and again discharges itself in Apollonian images . . . Tragedy is an Apollonian embodiment of Dionysiac insights and powers, and for that reason separated by a tremendous gulf from the epic" (*BT*, 56–57).

Nietzsche's second thesis in this book is of overarching importance, and has wide-ranging implications for many areas of literary and cultural theory. Greek tragedy, he suggests, "died by suicide," in the hands of Euripides who, viewing tragedy as a rational matter of conscious perceptions, attempted to eliminate altogether the Dionysiac strain, battling against the works of Aeschylus and Sophocles (*BT*, 75–76, 80). In so doing, he killed both myth and music (*BT*, 69). What spoke through Euripides in his endeavor to rebuild the drama on the basis of a non-Dionysiac art was a new and powerful daimon. His name was Socrates (*BT*, 77). Nietzsche sees the aims of Euripides and Socrates as closely allied:

> Euripides set out, as Plato was to do, to show the world the opposite of the "irrational" poet; his esthetic axiom, "whatever is to be beautiful must be conscious" is strictly parallel to the Socratic "whatever is to be good must be conscious." We can hardly go wrong then in calling Euripides the poet of esthetic Socratism. (*BT*, 81)

From this point on, says Nietzsche, the real antagonism was between the Dionysiac spirit and the Socratic spirit, and "tragedy was to perish in the conflict" (*BT*, 77). Euripides and Socrates both were unable to understand tragedy; both viewed it as chaotic and irrational; and both condemned it along with its underlying ethics (*BT*, 82–83). Instead of allowing tragedy to present myths expressing the sufferings of Dionysus, Euripides was concerned with "rendering his conscious perceptions" and must have seen himself "as the first rational maker of tragedy" (*BT*, 81).

As for Socrates: who, asks Nietzsche, was this man who dared single-handedly to "challenge the entire world of Hellenism"? The world of Homer, Pindar, and Aeschylus which commands such reverence? With what became the "gigantic driving wheel of logical Socratism"? Socrates was "the perfect pattern of the *non-mystic*, in whom the logical component had become overdeveloped through superfetation" (*BT*, 84–85). As such, he saw in tragedy and in poetry generally something "abstruse and irrational, full of causes without effects," removed from truth and dangerous in its effects (*BT*, 86). His power, exerted primarily through his disciple Plato, was such that it forced poetry into new channels, as in the dialogue developed by Plato himself, a synthesis of available styles and forms which "hovered between narrative, lyric, drama, between prose and poetry" (*BT*, 87). The new status of poetry was one of subordination to dialectical philosophy and, in fact, art is thenceforth obliged to explore its own connections with philosophy. The Apollonian tendency, says Nietzsche, "now appears as logical schematism," with "Socrates, the dialectical hero of the Platonic drama," showing a close affinity to the Euripidean hero. The Socratic maxims "virtue is knowledge," "all sins arise from ignorance," and "only the virtuous are happy" are optimistic formulations which "spell the death of tragedy" (*BT*, 88). In this new view of drama, the chorus is seen as an accidental feature of tragedy, merely a quaint reminder of its origins; indeed, Sophocles no longer gives the chorus a major role, and eventually the chorus disintegrates in a movement that embraces Euripides, Agathon, and the New Comedy (*BT*, 89). Nietzsche raises the question, as indeed Plato had himself, whether "art and Socratism are diametrically opposed to one another" (*BT*, 90).

Socrates is the "despotic logician," the prototype "of an entirely new mode of existence," the "great exemplar" of *theoretical man* who delights in the very process of unveiling truth, thereby assuring himself of his own power (*BT*, 92). In Socrates is the first manifestation of a deep-seated "grand metaphysical illusion," that has become integral to the very nature of scientific endeavor: the illusion that thought can "plumb the farthest abysses of being," to make "existence appear intelligible and thereby justified" (*BT*, 93). Since Socrates, the apparatus of the intellect has been viewed as man's highest power, a "common net of knowledge" has spread over the entire globe, and man's greatest desire is "to complete the conquest, to weave the net absolutely tight." In this sense, Socrates is "the vortex and turning point of Western civilization" (*BT*, 94–95).

Nietzsche warns, however, that the scientific endeavor will confront its own limits: when it recognizes such limits, this itself is a tragic perception, which requires, "to make it tolerable, the remedy of art" (*BT*, 95). The Socratic zest for knowledge, says Nietzsche, is being somewhat dissipated into a "tragic resignation and the need for art" (*BT*, 95). In fact, the present era is marked precisely by this struggle between the quest for knowledge and man's "tragic dependency" on art (*BT*, 96). Tragedy might be reborn, urges Nietzsche, when science, having reached its limits, has been "forced to renounce its claim to universal validity." He suggests that there may be an eternal conflict between the theoretical and the tragic world view (*BT*, 104). One might object that Nietzsche arbitrarily and erringly equates a scientific outlook with the examination of particulars rather than universals. Surely, what he is characterizing is not science but positivism and the most naive empiricism: that which takes so-called immediately given sense-data as reality. It is true, nonetheless, that much modern art and literature, not to mention modern literary theory, effects a dramatic elevation of the particular, beginning with modern realism. Our whole modern world, says Nietzsche, is "caught in the net of Alexandrian culture and recognizes as its ideal the man of theory, equipped with the highest cognitive powers, working in the service of science, and whose archetype and progenitor is Socrates. All our pedagogic devices are oriented toward this ideal." In a statement anticipating Foucault, Derrida, and many other thinkers, Nietzsche points out that any kind of existence that deviates from this model "lives, at best, on sufferance." For example, through most of history, the scholar was the only type of educated man, and even our literary arts "have been forced to develop out of learned imitations" (*BT*, 109). In short, myth "has been paralyzed everywhere" (*BT*, 110).

And yet there is hope. Modern man has begun to realize the limits of Socratic curiosity. And there are, thinks Nietzsche, certain forces that promise a rebirth of tragedy: tragedy, as Nietzsche has argued, was not rational but based on myth, on a "deeper wisdom" ineffable in words and concepts but expressed in the structure of tragedy and its images (*BT*, 103). Accepting Schopenhauer's view that music is the most universal language, that it is the "immediate language of the will," the universal "lust for life," Nietzsche points to a gradual reawakening of the Dionysiac spirit in the "German soul," as expressed in music from Bach through Beethoven to Wagner (*BT*, 98, 101, 119). This awakening, he claims, has also rudely overtaken the dogmatic slumbers of intellectual Socratism in the sphere of German philosophy: Kant and Schopenhauer have both employed the arsenal of science to demonstrate its limitations, and those of the cognitive faculty. They have "authoritatively rejected science's claim to universal validity" and thereby initiated a culture of the tragic (*BT*, 111). Ironically, in Nietzsche's later writings, Kant's subversiveness as alleged here seems to be forgotten and what is stressed is his attempt to elevate "fictions" such as the worlds of noumena and phenomena to the status of unquestioned reality. Headed by this twin

514

onslaught of music and philosophy against Socratism, the latter has begun to "doubt its own infallibility" and "runs eagerly to embrace one new shape after another, only to let go of it in horror" (*BT*, 112). Some critics say much the same about modern literary theory, based as much of this is on a rejection of absolutes, of fixed meaning and identity. The scientific endeavor confronted with its limits, says Nietzsche, "remains eternally hungry" (*BT*, 112). In our present age, man is stripped of myth, and "stands famished among all his pasts," in the grip of a hunger that signifies "the loss of myth, of a mythic home, the mythic womb" (*BT*, 137).

The second text to be considered here is an essay of Nietzsche's that has proved seminal to much poststructuralist theory. "On Truth and Lying in a Non-Moral Sense" was written in 1873 but not published during Nietzsche's life. Nietzsche here scathingly attacks conventional Western conceptions of truth, knowledge, and language. To begin with, he points out the utter insignificance of humanity when taken within the compass of nature as a whole. In such a context, we can see "how pitiful, how insubstantial and transitory, how purposeless and arbitrary the human intellect looks."[6] As against the pride of the philosopher, who exalts the human intellect to a self-motivated and disinterested faculty in pursuit of truth, Nietzsche's own view of the human intellect is much more practical and lowly: it is merely "a means for the preservation of the individual" ("TL," 142). And as such, far from seeking truth, the intellect "shows its greatest strengths in dissimulation." Indeed, the art of dissimulation, in the service of self-preservation, reaches its peak in humankind, where "deception, flattery, lying and cheating . . . keeping up appearances . . . wearing masks, the drapery of convention, play-acting for the benefit of others and oneself . . . is so much the rule." As a whole, human beings are "deeply immersed in illusions and dream-images" ("TL," 142).

Given such circumstances, where, asks Nietzsche, could the drive to truth have come from? He locates the origins of this drive in a human endeavor to avoid a natural state described by the philosopher Hobbes as a "war of all against all." In order to be able to live in peace with one another according to certain laws and commonly accepted perspectives, the notion of truth arises. Truth "is a way of designating things . . . which has the same validity and force everywhere, and the legislation of language also produces the first laws of truth" ("TL," 143). In other words, not only are certain ways of looking at the world privileged and fixed as correct or truthful, but also language itself is regulated to enable this. Nonetheless, truth is desired by human beings, says Nietzsche, only in this limited sense, as engendering "pleasant, life-preserving consequences . . . they are indifferent to pure knowledge if it has no consequences, but they are actually hostile towards truths which may be harmful and destructive." Similarly, the conventions of language are arbitrarily fixed: there is no intrinsic or "perfect match between things and their designations" ("TL," 143). Nietzsche here challenges the entire philosophical tradition, which has theorized so extensively about reality and truth. He utterly rejects the idea that the pursuit of knowledge or truth can be somehow disinterested or free of a broad range of motives: motives of self-preservation or promotion; motives rooted in ideology, economics, and the desire for power. In short, truth is a practical convenience, an efflorescence, no matter how refined, of our ultimately animal nature. In these sentiments, Nietzsche anticipates a great deal of modern thought ranging from Bergson to Derrida and beyond. It is worth noting also that Nietzsche himself was anticipated by Marx in the latter's recognition both of language as a practical activity arising from the material needs of human beings and of truth as necessarily connected with prevailing ideological and political structures.

Nietzsche proceeds to undertake an acute analysis of language. He defines a "word" as the "copy of a nervous stimulation in sounds." In other words, the designations embodied in language are entirely subjective; they tell us not about the world but merely about our own perceptual apparatus. When we say "The stone is hard," the hardness is "an entirely subjective stimulus" ("TL," 144). We categorize things arbitrarily by gender and by stressing the properties of things that we wish to emphasize. Nietzsche now makes some pronouncements which might be said to have enabled Derrida's most fundamental insights into language and its connections with truth or reality:

> The "thing-in-itself" (which would be, precisely, pure truth, truth without consequences) is impossible for even the creator of language to grasp . . . He designates only the relations of things to human beings, and in order to express them he avails himself of the boldest metaphors. The stimulation of a nerve is first translated into an image: first metaphor! The image is then imitated by a sound: second metaphor!
>
> . . . We believe that when we speak of trees, colours, snow, and flowers, we have knowledge of the things themselves, and yet we possess only metaphors of things which in no way correspond to the original entities . . . the mysterious "X" of the thing-in-itself appears first as a nervous stimulus, then as an image, and finally as an articulated sound. ("TL," 145)

Nietzsche concludes that the material with which the philosopher works does not stem from the essence of things. In fact, language itself falsifies the nature of our experience. We have a "unique, utterly individualized, primary experience" of a given entity, and we represent this experience by a word. But we immediately make this word, this sound, a concept by broadening its application to "countless other, more or less similar cases, i.e. cases which, strictly speaking, are never equivalent, and thus nothing more than non-equivalent cases" ("TL," 145). In other words, we are falsifying in at least two ways: we are forcing two unique experiences under the same category, thereby denuding them of what was unique. Secondly, we are arbitrarily focusing on a given point of similarity and highlighting this at the expense of the points of difference. Nietzsche offers an exquisite example: no two leaves are the same, and we form the concept of "leaf" by dropping these individual differences. We then use this concept to *define* all other leaves. In other words, we are regarding the concept "leaf" as a "primal form . . . from which all leaves are woven." We may then argue (like Plato, whose theory of forms is not mentioned but perhaps implied by Nietzsche in this context) that "the leaf is the cause of the leaves" ("TL," 145). In this way, we build up a vast edifice of collective conceptual self-delusion; later generations will inherit these earlier definitions as though they were "natural" and inevitable and the only true representations of experience. We effectively end up interpreting our experiences, even new experiences, *through* the categories we have arbitrarily constructed. The ideological coerciveness of this procedure can be seen if we extrapolate Nietzsche's argument to encompass concepts such as "blackness" or "Jewishness" or "femininity" or "Islam." We can conclude that a person acted in a certain way because she was "black," or "Jewish," or "Muslim": the arbitrary category itself becomes elevated into the primal cause and primal explanation. Nietzsche insists that nature itself contains "neither forms nor concepts and hence no species, but only an 'X' which is inaccessible to us and indefinable by us." Our categories do "not stem from the essence of things" ("TL," 145).

Nietzsche now makes one of his most famous statements, a statement which has cast its long shadow over much modern thought in many disciplines:

> What, then, is truth? A mobile army of metaphors, metonymies, anthropomorphisms, in short a sum of human relations which have been subjected to poetic and rhetorical intensification, translation, and decoration, and which, after they have been in use for a long time, strike a people as firmly established, canonical, and binding; truths are illusions of which we have forgotten that they are illusions. ("TL," 146)

Far from being some kind of correspondence between words and things, truth is here seen as a function of intersubjective human relations, available not through literal language (implying an exact correspondence between language and reality) but only through the vehicle of metaphor: the word's reference to the "real" object is tenuous: through the word we can never arrive at the true nature of the object; we can only use metaphor, substituting or displacing a given word with other words. We never arrive at a point beyond language, beyond a collective subjective designation of meanings. But what is truly radical in Nietzsche's passage is his view that the concept of "truth" is intrinsically distortive and falsifying: truth represents a very partial freezing and fixing of certain privileged elements of experience at the expense of others; through habit, we come to forget about those repressed elements, and indeed forget about this very operation of selection and ossification, an operation that originally served not the end of pure knowledge but, rather, purposes that are practical, political, and ideological.

Nietzsche notes that, in order for a society to exist as a stable and secure entity, it imposes upon people "the obligation to lie in accordance with firmly established convention, to lie *en masse* and in a style that is binding for all" ("TL," 146). This ability to generalize sense-impressions, to sublimate metaphors into a schema, to dissolve images into concepts, is what truly distinguishes human beings from animals. This "great edifice of concepts" ultimately enables the "construction of a pyramidal order based on castes and degrees, the creation of a new world of laws, privileges, subordinations, definitions of borders . . . as something regulatory and imperative" ("TL," 146). A concept is merely the "left-over *residue of a metaphor*," which in turn is produced by "the artistic translation of a nervous stimulus into images" ("TL," 147). Philosophers and scientists measure all things against man, in the "erroneous belief" that these things are directly before them, as "pure objects," taking the "original metaphors of perception" as things in themselves ("TL," 148).

Nietzsche has an interesting way of formulating this human pretense to objectivity: "only because man forgets himself as a subject, and indeed as *an artistically creative* subject, does he live with some degree of peace, security, and consistency" ("TL," 148). The spheres of sense and conceptuality are related, at best, only in an aesthetic manner, and yet we arrive through this process at a world which "finally acquires the same significance for all human beings." We arrive at a conviction of the "eternal consistency, ubiquitousness and infallibility of the laws of nature" ("TL," 149). And yet, says Nietzsche, these laws of nature are known to us not in themselves but only in their effects, only in their relations to one another and, in fact, only as relations, not as essential or substantial entities. Even the representations of time and space we produce "within ourselves." Many of these statements sound Kantian, but they lack Kant's framework of stabilization and his apparatus of establishing certitude, as provided by his phenomena–noumena distinction. Nietzsche goes on to make some Hegelian statements which, again, lack Hegel's historical and idealistic framework: the conformity to laws that we are so keen to find in the universe, says Nietzsche, is identical with the qualities that we ourselves impose on things, so that "what we find imposing is our own activity" ("TL," 150). Both Kant and Hegel, in their own ways, had also seen the world as a construction of human activity, but this activity was sanctioned and situated within an overall system of infallible knowledge; like Derrida after him, Nietzsche takes the insights of these earlier philosophical builders of systems and removes them from their protective, constraining contexts. He states that science continues to build upon the "edifice of concepts" erected by language; "a great *columbarium* of concepts is thereby structured so that the whole of the empirical world can be fit into it in an orderly way" ("TL," 150). Eventually, this structure becomes a "fortress," imprisoning the fundamental human drive to create and form new metaphors; this frustrated creative urge finds new channels for its activity in myth and art ("TL," 151).

In this text, Nietzsche offers a somewhat Schopenhauerian view of art. In myth, art, in festivals and carnival, the intellect, "that master of pretence, is free and absolved of its usual slavery . . . it jumbles metaphors and shifts the boundary stones of abstraction" ("TL," 152). This liberated intellect uses the conventional scheme of concepts as a "mere climbing frame and plaything . . . it smashes this framework, jumbles it up and ironically re-assembles it, pairing the most unlike things . . . it is now guided, not by concepts but by intuitions" ("TL," 152). Hence for Nietzsche the artist is a figure who liberates us from the prison of tradition and conventional perception.

Henri Bergson (1859–1941)

Schopenhauer's thought impinges considerably not only on the thought of Nietzsche but also on Bergson's philosophy and his theories of art and humor. Notwithstanding his self-dissociation from Schopenhauer,[7] Bergson's philosophy stands in direct line of descent. In fact, his student and translator T. E. Hulme saw the commensurability more clearly than his former master. In his essay "Bergson's Theory of Art" (ca. 1913), Hulme comments that Bergson's aesthetic theory "is exactly the same as Schopenhauer's" but devoid of the latter's "cumbrous" metaphysical machinery. Yet Hulme sees Bergson's theory of art as an integral extension of his philosophy, the great advantage of this theory being that "it removes your account of art from the merely literary level," being rather "part of a definite conception of reality."[8] This insight of Hulme's may help us understand why so many later nineteenth-century thinkers, including Eliot, the French symbolists, humanists such as Arnold, and philosophers such as Schopenhauer and Bergson, called for a unity of philosophy and poetry. Behind this was a desire to *define* the aesthetic as a form of perception of reality: poetry could not take for granted the reality it was to express.

Bergson's philosophy was expressed in his *Creative Evolution* (1907), where he had argued that what is most real is precisely what philosophers since Plato have condemned as unreal: time. Both Plato and Plotinus considered the temporal world as a degradation of the eternal. The main streams of Christian theology retained this hierarchy in broadened theological contexts. Bergson's controversial ideas took root in an early twentieth-century intellectual climate exhausted by the tyranny of technology, science, industrial growth, and reason. Bergson attempted to situate reason within a larger context of evolutionary balance between instinct and intellect. For Bergson what is most real is the continuity of immediate experience. The intellect narrowly equates understanding this continuity with immobilizing it, breaking it up into timeless discrete sections. In affirming the reality of time rather than of eternity, Bergson was challenging both the classical Christian legacy and the various strands of Enlightenment thought which had attempted to overturn this. He was returning to the immediacy and authenticity of experience as against the conceptual and linguistic reduction of such experience to conventional categories, whether in the name of feudal Christianity, Enlightenment reason, or conservative humanism. Bergson's notion of *durée* placed emphasis on the human personality, as the locus of the primary reality, duration: "There is at least one reality which we all seize from within, by intuition and not by simple analysis. It is our own person in its flowing through time, the self which endures" (*CM*, 162).

Like Schopenhauer, Bergson ascribes unique powers to art, whose essence he also sees as irony (*CM*, 27–28). Bergson's theory of art also emerges as a reaction against, and transcendence of, bourgeois practical and utilitarian ways of thinking. He suggests that, in everyday life, a veil is interposed between ourselves and nature: our understanding and our senses, conditioned by our needs, furnishes a merely utilitarian, "practical simplication" of reality. We classify things only with a view to their use and it is this classification we ordinarily perceive. We see not actual things but their labels; their individuality escapes us. For example, we do not perceive *this* table but *a* table. These utilitarian habits of perception are mediated through language; words denote genera, not individual things (*Laughter*, 158–160).[9]

The veil is transparent only to the artist and poet. The poet exercises a "virginal" manner of perception, being more detached from life and, as in Schopenhauer's account, more objective since his perceptions are not riveted to practical need. Hence the poet, brushing aside the conventional generalities, has a more direct vision of reality: it is precisely a withdrawal from utilitarian existence, a retreat into ideality, that enables a resumption of contact with the fluid reality lying beneath its own practically simplified and categorized molds. Again, this applies to the inner as well as the outer reality: the artist and poet aim to dissolve this outer crust of the social self, bringing us back to the inner temporal core of ourselves. Hence the poet and artist aim at what is truly individual (*Laughter*, 160–166). It is clear that there are profound affiliations between Bergson, Baudelaire, and the French symbolists. Enid Starkie cites their common reaction against positivism and materialism, their conceptions of nature and intuition, their view of ultimate reality as ineffable, and their exaltation of the role of poet and artist.[10] Yet there is a contrast between Bergson's critique of bourgeois society and those advanced by the French symbolists and Eliot. Bergson's critique, like Schopenhauer's, is debilitated by its ahistorical foundation: what are actually tendencies of a specific era of bourgeois predominance – such as mechanization, exhaustion of individual by group identity, transformation of human into thing – are ascribed by Bergson indiscriminately to "society." In his essay on Baudelaire, Walter Benjamin observes that, while for Bergson memory structures the pattern of experience, he yet rejects any historical determination of memory.[11] Benjamin argues that it is Baudelaire rather than Bergson, the poet rather than the philosopher, who has grasped the historical significance of "bourgeois" experience.[12]

Integral to the views of art formulated by thinkers and poets in the heterological tradition are their views of language. Schopenhauer, Nietzsche, the French symbolists, and Bergson, as well as the modernists who were influenced by this tradition, opposed the bourgeois positivism, scientism, and mechanism embodied in literal language. For all of these writers, a subversion of literal language was the vehicle of access into a deeper reality. This subversion hinges on two broad strategies: first, a dislocation of the syntactical structure of language, the effect of which is to emphasize language as a temporal process rather than viewing it as a spatialized system of conventional concepts. Secondly, literal language is situated as merely one among several registers which undermine it. Such a radical treatment of language is much more than "literary" experimentation; it is a symptom of transformed metaphysical and political premises, embodying a rejection of the world as given, as composed of discrete objects and appearances, and an idealistic attempt to reach a higher reality through art, especially through poetry.

According to Bergson, language is inescapably general; it can never express the true individuality of an object or situation. The most basic premise of Bergson's aesthetics is that art creates novelty. Whereas language is spatial, art is temporal, expressing duration, expressing the authentic flow of experience which is encrusted over by language. The poet's business, then, is to rebel against the generality and conventionality of language. The poet individuates by deploying the materiality of language, treating words as sharing the same individual material status as other objects in the world rather than as universal meanings or atemporal signs of objects. The reality suggested by a poem is partly that envisaged by Bergson: a perpetual flux which always exceeds the linguistic categories of its attempted imprisonment. It is a world where, as urged by Schopenhauer, the "knowledge" offered by the intellect clashes with the deliverances of sense; where bourgeois rationality emerges in its impoverishment and limitation, unable to counter or exceed the authority of immediate experience. For these thinkers, poetry is effectively the conclusion and resting place of philosophy.

Matthew Arnold (1822–1888)

Although Matthew Arnold has been regarded by some as one of the founding figures of modern English criticism, it will be readily apparent that many of the questions he raises were addressed by numerous writers from earlier centuries. Nonetheless, Arnold re-poses these questions in the context of a modern industrial society, and they remain with us today in forms more intense and pervasive than even Arnold might have imagined. Arnold attended Rugby, one of the most prestigious public schools in England.

His father Dr. Thomas Arnold was one of the leaders of the liberal broad Church in England, opposed to the doctrines of Cardinal Henry Newman; he was also headmaster at Rugby and pioneered a number of educational reforms centered on the need to relate liberal studies to the modern world.

Matthew Arnold was not only a cultural critic but also a poet and an educator. After Rugby, he obtained his degree from Oxford. In 1851 he became an inspector of schools and was deeply concerned with the kind of education suitable for subsequent generations of middle-class and working-class students. In 1857 he was appointed Professor of Poetry at Oxford. Arnold's poetry was written mostly during the 1850s; he himself saw his verse as representing the "main mental movement" of the recent past. His poetry, of which "Dover Beach" is perhaps the most famous example, expresses isolation and near despair in a world seemingly abandoned by divine providence, a world on the brink of disastrous wars, a world in which the only faith is in other human beings. He described himself as "wandering between two worlds, one dead, / The other powerless to be born." Arnold's literary and social criticism was produced largely in the 1860s, comprising *Essays in Criticism*, first series (1865) and *Culture and Anarchy* (1869). A second series of *Essays in Criticism* was published in 1888. In the 1870s Arnold wrote on religious and educational matters; he considered his most important prose work to be *Literature and Dogma* (1873).

Central to Arnold's literary criticism is the problem of living adequately in late industrial society. Arnold's world view is deeply humanist, and he writes in the tradition of a humanism that will run through figures such as F. R. Leavis and survives to this day. Arnold's central terms and phrases – "sweetness and light," "perfection," "inwardness," "the best that has been thought and said" – all derive ultimately from his analysis of the malaise of modern culture. He sees the human being in industrial society as mechanized, as wholly given to "external" pursuits, as stunted in his spiritual and moral sensibility. Arnold was somewhat obsessed with the narrow moralism and mercantilism of the bourgeoisie, whom he termed philistines. In his essay "My Countrymen" Arnold affirms: "Philistinism is . . . characteristic of . . . the middle class . . . which has . . . risen into such preponderating importance of late years, and . . . governs the country."[13] His essay "The Function of Criticism" is concerned to counteract the philistinism of the world as defined by the English bourgeoisie, enshrined in the restrictive obsession of this class with practicality, utility, and reason: in a phrase, with the imperatives of the immediate present.

In one sense, Arnold's essay "The Function of Criticism" is original and controversial inasmuch as it seeks to redefine the central responsibilities of criticism. While he acknowledges that the "critical faculty is lower than the inventive," and that the exercise of the "creative power . . . is the highest function of man," he suggests that it is an atmosphere of appropriate criticism that creates the conditions in which creative genius can be realized (*SP*, 132–133). The work of the literary genius, says Arnold, is not, like the philosopher, to discover new ideas; the literary work is not one of analysis and discovery but of "synthesis and exposition." It needs to be inspired by certain conditions: by "a certain intellectual and spiritual atmosphere, by a certain order of ideas." The aim of the literary work is to present these ideas "in the most effective and attractive combinations," in beautiful form. It is precisely the task of criticism to "establish an order of ideas" and "to make the best ideas prevail." It is the business of the critical power "in all branches of knowledge, theology, philosophy, history, art, science, to see the object as in itself it really is" (*SP*, 134). This statement, which Arnold quotes from his own earlier lecture (Lecture II of *On Translating Homer*, 1861), summarizes a positivistic historical trend wherein many branches of knowledge were seeking to gain scientific status by rejecting metaphysics and by focusing their endeavors on what could be empirically verified. Paradoxically, Arnold wishes to extend this scientific status to literary criticism, even though this trend of positivism was one symptom of the mechanization and "externalization" that he so lamented.

Notwithstanding this paradox, Arnold arrives at an insight, formulated previously in other terms by writers such as Pope, that was to influence the practice and critical theory of many modernists, such as Eliot and Pound: he suggests that "the creation of a modern poet . . . implies a great critical effort behind it" (*SP*, 134). If the poet is to express elements of modern life which is so complex, he needs to be nourished by a climate of ideas prepared through a critical endeavor. Arnold holds that the work of Pindar, Sophocles, Shakespeare, and Goethe was sustained and enabled by a "current of ideas" and "fresh thought"; the work of the English Romantics, in contrast, lacked this intellectual framework, and they "did not know enough" (*SP*, 134–135). Interestingly, Arnold traces the causes of this deficiency to the French Revolution. Unlike previous major movements such as the Renaissance and the Reformation, which were "disinterestedly intellectual and spiritual movements," the French Revolution, says Arnold, "took a political, practical character" (*SP*, 136). While Arnold concedes that this Revolution was "the greatest, the most animating event in history," it was characterized by a "fatal" exaltation of reason, by a "fatal" mania for giving "an immediate political and practical application" to the ideas of reason (*SP*, 137). That Revolution appealed, through reason, to "an order of ideas which are universal, certain, permanent." Arnold's argument is that while we must value ideas "in and for themselves," we cannot "transport them abruptly into the world of politics and practice, violently to revolutionise this world to their bidding" (*SP*, 138). This, says Arnold, "was the grand error of the French Revolution; and its movement of ideas, by quitting the intellectual sphere and rushing furiously into the political sphere . . . produced no such intellectual fruit as the movement of ideas of the Renascence" (*SP*, 138). The "fatal" result, as Arnold states in *Culture and Anarchy*, is an inordinate and spiritually stunting "[f]aith in machinery," a utilitarian reduction of the world to a practical mechanism (*SP*, 209). Indeed, by doing this, the Revolution created an epoch of reaction or opposition against itself, an epoch whose most articulate voice was Burke. Arnold's logic here, like Burke's, is that abstract ideas cannot simply be imposed upon a people's constitution or way of life. He commends the "profound, permanent, fruitful, philosophical truth" of Burke's writings (*SP*, 139). Burke was rare among Englishmen in that he inhabited the world of ideas, rather than the world of politics and practice. Most existing criticism, says Arnold, is an organ of some political perspective. And this is where Arnold comes to the heart of his proposals as to the nature of true criticism.

The time is ripe, says Arnold, for true criticism to "avail itself of the field now opening to it . . . The rule may be summed up in one word – *disinterestedness*." How is criticism to be disinterested? By "keeping aloof," says Arnold, from "the practical view of things," by "following the law of its own nature, which is to be a free play of the mind on all subjects which it touches. By steadily refusing to lend itself to any of those ulterior, political, practical considerations about ideas." Criticism must attempt to know "the best that is known and thought in the world, and by in turn making this known, to create a current of true and fresh ideas . . . but its business is to do no more" (*SP*, 142). Criticism must be entirely independent of all interests. And its purpose? To lead man "towards perfection, by making his mind dwell upon what is excellent in itself, and the absolute beauty and fitness of things" (*SP*, 144). Criticism should embrace "the Indian virtue of detachment," the Hindu ideal of ascetic renunciation of all worldly concerns (*SP*, 146).

The mass of people, Arnold acknowledges, will never possess this zeal for "seeing things as they are"; they are satisfied by inadequate ideas, and on such ideas rests the practice of the world (*SP*, 147). But the critic must resist the temptation to be drawn into the vortex, "the rush and roar of practical life"; he must keep out of the region of immediate practice in the political, social, humanitarian sphere, and betake himself "to the serener life of the mind and spirit" (*SP*, 154). Only in this way, by continually enlarging the stock of "true and fresh ideas," can the critic be of true service to the practical world: "Our ideas will, in the end, shape the world all the better for maturing a little" (*SP*, 154). Arnold gives two examples of how such a "free speculative treatment of things" will differ from a practical treatment. From a practical perspective, he says, the British constitution appears to be a "magnificent organ of progress and virtue." A disinterested speculative viewpoint, however, might reveal that this "august" constitution, "with its compromises, its love of facts, its horror of theory, its studied avoidance of clear thoughts," is a "colossal machine for the manufacture of Philistines" (*SP*, 147). Likewise, the English divorce court may have "practical conveniences," but appears "hideous" to an ideal speculative gaze. Without such a disinterested perspective, claims Arnold, "truth and the highest culture" will not be possible. He is particularly concerned with the intrusion into criticism of politics or religion because these are particularly liable to lead it astray (*SP*, 154).

Finally, Arnold cautions that if the critic is truly devoted to expanding the stock of true ideas, he will move beyond insularity, recognizing that much of the "best that is known and thought" will come from outside England. Every critic, in fact, should try to master at least one literature in a language other than his own. Criticism must regard "Europe as being, for intellectual and spiritual purposes, one great confederation, bound to a joint action and working to a common result; and whose members have, for their proper outfit, a knowledge of Greek, Roman, and Eastern antiquity, and of one other" (*SP*, 156). This statement, in the view of tradition it implies, echoes Burke and anticipates T. S. Eliot.

In *Culture and Anarchy* Arnold both redefines "culture" and affirms the need for it in a modern industrial society devoted to mechanism and profit. He calls culture "*a study of perfection. It moves by the force, not merely or primarily of the scientific passion for pure knowledge, but also of the moral and social passion for doing good*" (*SP*, 205). Culture, then, has an intellectual and an ethical component, and just as Arnold sees the time as ripe for true criticism, so he sees a historical opportunity opening for "culture to be of service, culture which believes in making reason and the will of God prevail," terms which Arnold takes from Bishop Thomas Wilson (*SP*, 206). The aims of culture, according to Arnold, are identical with those of religion, which Arnold calls "the greatest and most important of the efforts by which the human race has manifested its impulse to perfect itself, – religion, that voice of the deepest human experience." What they have in common also is the cultivation of inwardness: religion preaches that "The Kingdom of God is within you," and culture "places human perfection in an *internal* condition, in the growth and predominance of our humanity proper, as distinguished from our animality" (*SP*, 208). Culture expands our gifts of thought and feeling, and fosters growth in wisdom and beauty. In famous lines, Arnold states: "Not a having and a resting, but a growing and a becoming, is the character of perfection as culture conceives it; and here, too, it coincides with religion" (*SP*, 208). The final feature shared by culture and religion is that they both require the individual to be part of a general movement toward perfection: "Perfection, as culture conceives it, is not possible while the individual remains isolated." But culture advances beyond religion, according to Arnold, because, through a "disinterested study of human nature," it fosters a "harmonious expansion of *all* the powers which make the beauty and worth of human nature." The implication is, of course, that religion calls for the development of some faculties at the expense of the rest, for example stressing the moral over the aesthetic, whereas culture promotes their harmony. Because culture represents for Arnold an inward condition of the mind and not outward circumstances, he regards its function as especially crucial in our modern civilization which is "mechanical and external" as well as strongly individualistic, specialized, and inflexible (*SP*, 209).

The "besetting danger" of modern civilization is "faith in machinery," whereby we equate greatness and success with industrial output of coal or iron, with the accumulation of wealth, viewing these as ends in themselves (*SP*, 209). The function of culture is to purge our minds of the effects of such material and narrow preoccupations, and to stem "the common tide of men's thoughts in a wealthy and industrial community" (*SP*, 211). Without this purging, Arnold warns, the future as well as the present "would inevitably belong to the Philistines," those who are devoted to the pursuit of wealth. In uniting beauty and intelligence, culture effects a harmony of "sweetness and light," terms taken from Jonathan Swift's *Battle of the Books* (1704). Interestingly, given that culture fosters these twin ideals, Arnold sees it as sharing the same spirit as poetry, whose dominant idea is of "beauty and a human nature perfect on all its sides." This idea, suggests Arnold, is destined to "transform and govern" the dominant idea of religion, that of a "human nature perfect on the moral side" (*SP*, 213). Arnold is here moving toward his later notion that poetry will replace the function of religion.

The task of both criticism and culture, then, is to place the pragmatic bourgeois vision of life in a broader historical and international context. But the notion of "disinterestedness" implies the possibility of a somehow timeless and universal perspective. Arnold's attempt to historicize the bourgeois world view by situating it paradoxically within a timeless context has something in common with T. S. Eliot's later notion of "tradition" which also blanks out history. Arnold's "tradition," if it may be called that, sees the purpose of criticism as explicitly political, as an instrument which might lift us beyond an immediate present governed by the narrow principles of utility, material progress, and the dictation of all theory by the exigencies of practice.

In this endeavor, Arnold is taking to task the very definition of reality by bourgeois interests. Bourgeois thought concentrates on the "outward," practical, mechanical, and commercial capacities of the human subject. This is perhaps why so much of Arnold's writing is obsessed with a human being's "inward" capacities: he defines "perfection" and "culture" as "an *inward* condition of the mind and spirit" and describes the modern world not only as "mechanical" but as "external" (*SP*, 209). Hence Arnold's key notions of criticism, culture, and poetry are all modes of "inwardness," aimed to counteract the "externality" of the bourgeois world.

In Arnold's "The Study of Poetry" (1880) we find an even greater insistence on the notion of seriousness. Where James advanced claims for the serious treatment of fiction as an art form, Arnold is even more hyperbolic in the claims he makes for poetry and literature. Arnold's text is one of the most influential texts of literary humanism; it insists on the social and cultural functions of literature, its ability to civilize and to cultivate morality, as well as its providing a bulwark against the mechanistic excesses of modern civilization. According to Arnold, the status of religion has been increasingly threatened by science, by the ideology of the "fact." Philosophy he regards as powerless since it is hopelessly entrenched in unresolved questions and problems. It is, he claims, to poetry that we must turn, not merely for spiritual and emotional support and consolation but to interpret life for us. He defines poetry as a criticism of life. Poetry's high function is actually to replace religion and philosophy (*SP*, 340).

If poetry is adequately to serve this exalted office, we must be even more certain, says Arnold, of our capacity to distinguish good from bad poetry. His essay contains also the notions of the classic and tradition, which will be further developed by writers such as T. S. Eliot and F. R. Leavis. Arnold suggests that, in the first place, we need to be sure that our estimate of poetry is "real" rather than historical or personal (*SP*, 341). Many critics and scholars fall into the trap of making historical rather than critical estimations of an author. It may be that an author was important for the development of language or certain literary traditions without having himself composed a classic. Arnold's classic example of this is Chaucer. Again, we need to transcend our personal likes and biases so as not simply to place a high value on authors with whom we have an accidental affinity (*SP*, 342).

How do we arrive at this real estimate of what constitutes a classic? Arnold's answer is to offer a "theory," or the practice, of using touchstones. We cannot ever articulate abstractly what comprises great poetry but we know we are in the presence of great poetry when we experience and feel its power. Arnold cites a number of lines of "great" poets in various languages to illustrate his point. His definition of great literature is ostensive: it is simply to point and say, *this* is great literature. And how do we know that it is great literature? Arnold's definition is partly moral, partly cultural: we know when we are in the presence of a great work because it exhibits truth and seriousness (*SP*, 348–349). What is interesting here is Arnold's lack of engagement with formal qualities. He implies that if the content is sufficiently true and serious, it will automatically be expressed in an appropriate form. Also lacking is any sense of engagement in historical context. Arnold effectively dismisses the claims of the French critic he cites regarding the canonization of certain works as classics, a process which forecloses further investigation into the origins, influences, the immediate circumstances and possible motivations of the work. His reliance on some ineffable literary sensibility which somehow knows how to judge could be considered a form of obscurantism, since it is an appeal to experience and to make judgments on the basis of a sensibility which resists articulation.

Notes

1   Arthur Schopenhauer, *Philosophical Writings*, ed. Wolfgang Schirmacher (New York: Continuum, 1994), pp. 20–22, 69, 86. Hereafter cited as *PW*.
2   Arthur Schopenhauer, *The World as Will and Representation*, 2 vols., trans. E. F. J. Payne (New York: Dover, 1958), Vol. II, p. 400. Hereafter cited as *WWI* and *WWII*.
3   Friedrich Nietzsche, *Thus Spoke Zarathustra*, trans. R. J. Hollingdale (Harmondsworth: Penguin, 1978), p. 109. Hereafter cited as *TSZ*.
4   Friedrich Nietzsche, *The Will to Power*, trans. W. Kaufmann and R. J. Hollingdale (London: Weidenfeld and Nicolson, 1968), pp. 306–307. Hereafter cited as *WP*.
5   Friedrich Nietzsche, *The Birth of Tragedy and The Genealogy of Morals*, trans. Francis Golffing (New York: Doubleday, 1956), p. 34. Hereafter cited as *BT*.
6   "On Truth and Lying in a Non-Moral Sense," in Friedrich Nietzsche, *The Birth of Tragedy and Other Writings*, trans. Ronald Speirs (Cambridge: Cambridge University Press, 1999), p. 141. Hereafter cited as "TL."
7   Henri Bergson, *The Creative Mind: An Introduction to Metaphysics* (New York: Philosophical Library, 1946), p. 30. Hereafter cited as *CM*.
8   *The Collected Writings of T. E. Hulme*, ed. Karen Csengeri (Oxford: Oxford University Press, 1994), pp. 193–194, 204.
9   Henri Bergson, *Le Rire: Essai sur la Signification du Comique* (Paris: Alcan, 1900). All references are to the following, easily accessible, translation: *An Essay on Comedy: George Meredith; Laughter: Henri Bergson*, introd. W. Sypher (New York: Doubleday, 1956). Hereafter cited as *Laughter*.
10 See, for example, Enid Starkie, "Bergson and Literature," in *The Bergsonian Heritage*, ed. T. Hanna (New York and London: Columbia University Press, 1962), pp. 78–79, 84–85, 88, 95.
11 Walter Benjamin, *Illuminations*, trans. H. Zohn (1955; rpt. Glasgow: Fontana/Collins, 1977), p. 159.
12 Ibid., p. 187.
13 Matthew Arnold, *Selected Prose* (Harmondsworth: Penguin, 1970), pp. 177, 179. Hereafter cited as *SP*.

CHAPTER 21

MARXISM

The tradition of Marxist thought has provided the most powerful critique of capitalist institutions and ethics ever conducted. Its founder, Karl Heinrich Marx (1818–1883), was a German political, economic, and philosophical theorist and revolutionist. The influence of Marx's ideas on modern world history has been vast. Until the collapse in 1991 of the communist systems of the USSR and Eastern Europe, one-third of the world's population had been living under political administrations claiming descent from Marx's ideas. His impact on the world of thought has been equally extensive, embracing sociology, philosophy, economics, and cultural theory. Marxism has also generated a rich tradition of literary and cultural criticism. Many branches of modern criticism – including historicism, feminism, deconstruction, postcolonial and cultural criticism – are indebted to the insights of Marxism, which often originated in the philosophy of Hegel. What distinguishes Marxism is that it is not only a political, economic, and social theory but also a form of practice in all of these domains.

Marx's thought can be approached in terms of philosophical, economic, and political strata. As a philosopher, Marx's development has its roots in his early life. Born into a Jewish family where his father had imbibed Enlightenment rationalist principles, Marx was exposed to the ideas of Voltaire, Lessing, and Racine. He studied law at the University of Bonn and then Berlin. But much of his time was spent in literary composition and for a while he was enamored of the Romanticism then in vogue. While these influences were never fully to recede, they were superseded by Marx's seminal encounter with the work of G. W. F. Hegel, whose dialectic shaped the form of Marx's earlier, and arguably his later, thought. Also vital was Marx's encounter with Friedrich Engels (1820–1895), whose importance lies in his collaboration with Marx to produce a critique of capitalist society based on a materialistic conception of history. Engels attempted to formulate a "scientific" basis for socialism, to explore the connections between dialectics and natural science, to analyze working-class conditions as well as the development of the family and state. In *The Conditions of the Working Class in England* (1845), Engels argued that the degraded conditions of the English proletariat, generated by their industrial exploitation, would eventually mold it into a revolutionary political force. It was largely Engels who was responsible for the initial dissemination, clarification, and popularization of Marxist ideas.

Fundamental Principles of Marx's Thought

(1) Critique of Capitalist Society

Marx attempted systematically to seek the structural causes behind what he saw as a system of capitalist exploitation and degradation, and to offer solutions in the spheres of economics and politics. As with all socialists, Marx's main objection to capitalism was that one particular class owned the means of economic production: "The bourgeoisie . . . has centralized means of production, and has concentrated property in a few hands." The correlative of this is the oppression and exploitation of the working classes: "In proportion as the bourgeoisie, i.e., capital, is developed, in the same proportion is the proletariat, the modern working class, developed; a class of laborers, who live only so long as they find work, and who find work only so long as their labor increases capital. These laborers, who must sell themselves piecemeal, are a commodity." Marx's third objection is the imperialistic nature of the bourgeois enterprise: in order to perpetuate itself, capitalism must spread its tentacles all over the world: "The bourgeoisie cannot exist without constantly revolutionizing the instruments of production . . . The need of a constantly expanding market . . . chases the bourgeoisie over the whole surface of the globe." Marx tells us in the next few paragraphs that the bourgeoisie must necessarily give a cosmopolitan character to production and consumption in every country; that raw material is drawn from the remotest zones; that demand for new products ever increases; that the bourgeoisie "compels all nations, on pain of extinction, to adopt the bourgeois mode of production." In short, the bourgeoisie "creates a world after its own image." Finally, capitalism reduces all human relationships to a "cash" nexus, self-interest, and egotistical calculation.[1]

(2) Adaptation of the Hegelian Dialectic

The dialectic is often characterized as a triad of thesis, antithesis, and synthesis. It would be more accurate to say that, in Hegel's hands, the dialectic had both logical and historical dimensions. Logically, it was a way of thinking about any object or circumstance in a series of increasingly complex and comprehensive stages. Each stage supersedes the previous stage but retains what was essential in that previous stage. In the first stage an object was apprehended as a simple datum, as simply a given fact about the world; the second stage adopted a broadened perspective which saw the object as "externalized," as having no independent identity but constituted by its relations with other objects. The third stage, from a still wider standpoint, viewed the object as a "mediated" unity, its true identity now perceived as a principle of unity between universal and particular, between essence and appearance. In this way, for example, "plant" could be viewed as the unifying principle of its own developing stages, bud, blossom, and fruit. Previous philosophers had offered one-sided accounts of the world, according to their particular biases. Descartes emphasized reason; Locke and Hume emphasized experience; Hobbes emphasized matter. Hegel saw all of these various systems in historical perspective, as one continuous system of philosophy which was always progressing through new visions while retaining what was important in previous ways of understanding the world.

Hegel also sees the dialectic as operating through history. He regards societies, from the Oriental world through the Greek and Roman to the modern German world, developing through successive stages of the dialectic: the underlying principles of one society eventually give way to a new society based on different principles but which incorporate whatever was valuable in the previous principles. On a political plane, society's laws become more and more rational while the individual's correlative rational growth enables him to see in the law an expression of his own free will. Hegel thus calls history a movement toward freedom, which is also a movement of absolute spirit toward self-realization. Perhaps the most important feature of dialectical thought is its insistence that whatever we examine, we place in a historical context, viewing it as a product of certain historical relations and tendencies.

The importance of the dialectic for Marx stems from his awareness that the "freedom" Hegel speaks of is the freedom of the bourgeois class to bring down the economic and political edifice of feudalism and absolutism whose social hierarchy rested on irrational theology and superstition: society could now be organized on rational principles, a freer market economy, and a human subject who saw his individual interests enshrined in the general law. Hence the dialectic provided a powerful political tool, one which could negate a given state of affairs. It also furnished Marx with a model of history not only as driven by political and ideological conflict but also where earlier phases were "sublated," both preserved and transcended, in their negation by subsequent phases. For a while Marx associated with the "Young Hegelians" who attempted to exploit the negative power of the dialectic in political analysis. But Marx's reading of French socialists such as Proudhon, his concern with immediate political issues, his exposure to Ludwig Feuerbach's materialism, and his encounter with Friedrich Engels' analyses of capitalism impelled him to insist that the dialectic of history was motivated by material forces.

In the *Economic and Philosophical Manuscripts* (1844), Marx praises Hegel's dialectic inasmuch as it grasps the importance of labor, through which man creates himself, but he views the dialectic in Hegel's hands as abstract because it is a "divine process," first negating religion and then restoring it. Marx cites Hegel's standpoint as "that of modern political economy," by which he means the bourgeois economists Smith, Say, and Ricardo. In religious and economic spheres Marx advocates two kinds of humanism: "atheism, being the supersession of God, is the advent of theoretical humanism, and communism, as the supersession of private property, is . . . the advent of practical humanism. Hence for Marx the third stage of the dialectic is practical, not something which can be resolved in theory.[2] Marx's striking equation of religion and private property as expressions of alienation had been hinted at in an earlier article on Hegel. Here, Marx regarded religion as having an ideologically apologetic function, whereby it situated present miseries as part of a larger, justifying and consolatory, providential pattern: "Religion is the sigh of the oppressed creature, the heart of a heartless world . . . It is the *opium* of the people."[3]

(3) The Materialistic Conception of History

The Dialectical Movement of History

In *The German Ideology* (1846), Marx develops his critique of Hegel's dialectic into what he calls the materialistic conception of history. Hegel's dialectic furnished Marx with a model of history which he of course adapted. Like Hegel, he viewed the world, human beings, and history as a product of human labor. But whereas Hegel saw the dialectical movement of history as driven by an absolute spirit or God, Marx insisted that the dialectic of history was motivated by material forces, by upheavals in the forces and relations of economic production. In particular, he viewed history as driven by class struggle. As he declaims in *The Communist Manifesto* (1848): "The history of all hitherto existing society is the history of class struggles" (*MCP*, 40). Marx alludes to the history of class conflict from the ancient world to his own times: between slaves and freemen, patricians and plebeians, lords and serfs. The major class conflict in modern times is between the bourgeoisie and the proletariat or industrial working class. And, just as the capitalist mode of production superseded the feudal mode, so the capitalist mode will give way to socialism. It is the bourgeoisie itself which creates the instrument of its own destruction: the proletariat, on the one hand, who will unite against it; and, on the other hand, increasingly destructive economic crises which are internal to the operations of capitalism.

Finally, Marx opposed previous philosophical systems inasmuch as they were idealistic; he insisted that the dialectic in history involved a necessary combination of theory and practice, that a given economic and political system cannot be abolished by mere thought but by a revolution. His most famous statement in this respect was: "The philosophers have only *interpreted* the world, in various ways; the point, however, is to *change* it" (*MCP*, 95). As will be seen below, Marx thought that the system of bourgeois dominance and capitalist exploitation would end when conditions for the great mass of people had sufficiently deteriorated.

Economic Base and Superstructure

The main premise of the materialist conception of history is that man's first historical act is the production of means to satisfy his material needs. The production of life, through both labor and procreation, is both natural and social: a given mode of production is combined with a given stage of social cooperation. Only after passing through these historical moments, says Marx, can we speak of men possessing "consciousness," which is itself a "social product." Hence the realms of ideology, politics, law, morality, religion, and art are not independent but are an efflux of a people's material behavior: "Life is not determined by consciousness, but consciousness by life" (*GI*, 47–51).

(4) The Division of Labor

This model of superstructure and economic base furnishes the form of Marx's analyses of state, class, and ideology in terms of the history of the division of labor. Marx traces various stages of this history, affirming that they are effectively different forms of ownership. In general terms, Marx argues that division of labor is an index of the extent to which production has been developed. It leads to separation of industrial and commercial from agricultural labor, hence a conflict of interests between town and country. It then effects a separation of individual and community interests (*GI*, 43–46). Moreover, the division of labor which first manifested itself in the sexual act appears eventually in its true shape as a division of material and mental labor; this is the point at which "pure" theory becomes possible.

Marx cites three crucial consequences of the social division of labor: firstly, the unequal distribution of labor and its products, and hence private property. The second consequence is the state. The division of labor implying a contradiction between individual or family and communal interest, the latter assumes an independent form as the state, as an "illusory communal life" divorced from the real interests of both individual and community. It is based especially on classes, one of which dominates the others. It follows, says Marx, that all struggles within the state are disguised versions of the struggle between classes. The third consequence of division of labor is what Marx calls "estrangement" or "alienation" of social activity. Not only does division of labor force upon each person a particular sphere of activity whereby his "own deed becomes an alien power opposed to him," but the social power or "multiplied productive force" as determined by the division of labor appears to individuals, because their mutual cooperation is forced, as "an alien force existing outside them" which develops independently of their will. "How otherwise," asks Marx, "does it happen that trade . . . rules the whole world through the relation of supply and demand?" (*GI*, 54–55).

(5) Marx's Conception of Ideology

Marx observes that the class which is struggling for mastery must gain political power in order to represent its interest as the general interest (*GI*, 52–53). This is the germ of Marx's concept of ideology. He states that the class which is the ruling material force in society is also the ruling intellectual force. Having at its disposal the means of production, it is empowered to disseminate its ideas in the realms of law, morality, religion, and art, as possessing universal verity. Thus, dominant ideas of the aristocracy such as honor and loyalty were replaced after bourgeois ascendancy by ideas of freedom and equality, whose infrastructure is class economic imperatives (*GI*, 64–65). Marx's notion of ideology is this: the ruling class represents its own interests as the interests of the people as a whole. The modern state, as Marx says, "is but a committee for managing the common affairs of the whole bourgeoisie" (*MCP*, 45–47).

(6) Marx's Economic Views

Marx's economic views, which can receive only cursory treatment here, were worked out largely in the *Grundrisse*, a huge manuscript unpublished in his lifetime, and expressed in Volume I of *Capital* (1867). They derive in one sense from his inversion of Hegel's dialectic, expressed by Marx in his famous statement that with Hegel the dialectic "is standing on its head. It must be turned right side up again, if you would discover the rational kernel within the mystical shell."[4] Implied in this inversion is the insistence that labor was the foundation of economic life. The bourgeois economists Smith and Ricardo had expressed the labor theory of value, whereby an object's value was measured by the amount of labor it incarnated. Developing their distinction between use-value and exchange-value, Marx arrived at his notion of surplus value, whereby labor power as embodied in production is incompletely compensated: the worker might be paid for value of the products generated by only four hours' work, whereas he was actually working for eight hours.

Marx saw this form of economic exploitation as underlying the ultimate downfall of capitalism: the first volume of *Capital* describes the "greed" on the part of the capital-ists for surplus labor, and their attempts to intensify labor and profit through both technology and control of resources through imperial expansion, as well as increas-ingly to centralize capital in the hands of fewer and fewer owners. In an apocalyptic passage, he states: "along with the constantly diminishing number of the magnates of capital . . . grows the mass of misery, oppression, slavery, degradation, exploitation; but with this too grows the revolt of the working-class, a class always increasing in numbers, and disciplined, united, organized by the very mechanism of the process of capitalist production itself . . . The knell of capitalist private property sounds. The expropriators are expropriated." Significantly, Marx sees this as part of a dialectical process moving from feudalism through capitalism to communism, whose essential feature is common ownership of land and the means of production: "capitalist produc-tion begets, with the inexorability of a law of Nature, its own negation. It is the negation of negation" (*Capital*, 715). Hence the capitalist world represents the second phase of the dialectic, negating feudalism. Communism is the "negation of the negation" whereby the contradiction between private property and socialized production is resolved by the establishment of socialized property. Equally, the contradictions within the self, hith-erto alienated from its own labor, as well as those between individual and communal interests, are abolished.

In his preface to *A Contribution to the Critique of Political Economy,* Marx had expressed this economic dialectic by saying that it was when "the material productive forces of society" came into conflict with "the existing relations of production" that historical upheavals resulted.[5] In *The German Ideology* Marx suggests that the estrange-ment which governs the second phase of the dialectic, the phase of bourgeois domina-tion, can be abolished by revolution given two practical premises: it must have rendered most men propertyless and also have produced, in contrast, an existing world of wealth and culture (*GI*, 56). But he also emphasizes the universality or world-historical nature of this conflict: such revolution presupposes not only highly developed productive capacities but that individuals have become enslaved under a power alien to them: the world market. Marx accepted that the struggle between classes might begin in specific nations but must inevitably be conducted as an international struggle given that the bourgeois mode of production dictated constant expansion of markets and the coercion of all nations, "on pain of extinction," into the bourgeois economic mold (*MCP*, 47).

In the year after Marx's death in 1883 Engels wrote *The Origin of the Family, Private Property and the State,* a text widely regarded as the pivotal Marxist document for feminist theory since it alone, among the works of Marx and Engels, offers a comprehensive attempt to explain the origins of patriarchy. Drawing on Lewis H. Morgan's book *Ancient Society* (1877), Engels traced the rise of patriarchy through increasingly sophisticated economic and social configurations, from primitive communal systems to a class society based on private property. Following Morgan's schematization, Engels cited three main forms of marriage: "for the period of savagery, group marriage; for barbarism, pairing marriage; for civilization, monogamy supplemented by adultery and prostitution."[6] With the tribe, descent and inheritance were through the female line. But as wealth increased, the man acquired a more important status in the family than the woman and this "mother right" was eventually overthrown in what Engels sees as a momentous revolution in prehistory: "The overthrow of mother right was the *world historical defeat of the female sex*" (*OF*, 87). Engels says that, with the predominance of private property over common property, father right and monogamy thereby gaining ascendancy, marriage becomes increasingly dependent on economic considerations. Because of the economic dependence of the woman on the man in bourgeois society, in the modern family the husband "is the bourgeois, and the wife represents the proletariat" (*OF*, 105). Engels suggests that the first premise for the emancipation of women is the reintroduction of the entire female sex into public industry and that when the means of production become common property, the individual family will cease to be the economic unit of society. Hence the economic foundations of monogamy as it presently exists will vanish, along with the institutions of the state which preserved them.

Summary

The materialistic conception of history is characterized by a number of features: (1) it is the activity and conditions of material production, not mere ideas, which determine the structure of society and the nature of individuals; law, art, religion, and morality are an efflux of these material relations; (2) the evolution of division of labor issues in the concentration of private property, a conflict between individual and communal interests (the latter assuming the status of an independent power as the state), and estrangement or alienation of social activity; (3) all struggles within the state are euphemisms for the real struggle between classes; it is this struggle which generates social change; (4) once technologically assisted capitalist accumulation, concentration, and world expansion have led to a world of sharply contrasting wealth and poverty, and working classes become conscious of their historical role, capitalism itself will yield to a communism which will do away with private property and base itself on human need rather than the greed of a minority for increasing profit; (5) the exploitation of women, an intrinsic feature of capitalist economics, will also be abolished along with private property and the family as an economic unit.

Is Marxism dead? Can we, finally, consign it to historical and political obsolescence? In addressing these questions, we need to recognize that the connection between Marx's canon and Marxism has always been dialectical: the latter has always striven to modify, extend, and adapt the former to changing circumstances rather than treating it as definitive and complete. Marxism is not somehow a finished and static system but has been continually modified according to changing historical circumstances. We should also perhaps bear in mind that most of what has passed for "communism" has had but remote connections with the doctrines of Marx, Engels, or their followers.

Marx's critique of capitalism, it should be recalled, was dialectical. He regarded capitalist society as an unprecedented historical advance from centuries of benighted and superstitious feudalism. The bourgeois emphasis on reason, practicality, its technological enterprise in mastering the world, its ideals of rational law and justice, individual freedom and democracy were all hailed by Marx as historical progress. His point was not that communism would somehow displace capitalism in its entirety but that it would grow out of capitalism and retain its ideals of freedom and democracy. The essential difference is that a communist society would *realize* these ideals. For example, Marx shrewdly points out that the "individual" in capitalist society is effectively the bourgeois owner of property; individual freedom is merely economic freedom, the freedom to buy and sell. The constitution and the laws are entirely weighted in favor of large business interests and owners of property. Private property, Marx points out, is already abolished for the nine-tenths of the population in capitalist society who do not possess it. The labor of this vast majority, being commodified, is as subject to the vicissitudes of the market as any other commodity.

One of the main sins of capitalism, according to Marx, was that it reduced all human relations to commercial relations. Even the family cannot escape such commodification: Marx states that, to the bourgeois man, the wife is reduced to a mere instrument of production. Moreover, once the exploitation of the laborer by the manufacturer has finished, then he is set upon, says Marx, by the other segments of the bourgeoisie: the landlord, the shopkeeper, the pawnbroker. In bourgeois society "capital is independent and has individuality, while the living person is dependent and has no individuality" (*MCP*, 51, 53, 65–70). The aim of a communist society is to procure genuine freedom, genuine individuality and humanity, genuine democracy.

As an internal critique of the tendencies of capitalism and its crises, Marxism is uniquely coherent and incisive. The influence of Marxism has been fundamental in challenging the claims of the law to be eternal, of the bourgeoisie to represent the interests of the entire nation, of individuality and freedom to be universal. It has also been important in the analysis of women's oppression as an economic factor structurally integral to capitalism. And its insights into language as a social practice with a material dimension, its awareness that truth is an interpretation based on certain kinds of consensus, its view of the world as created through human physical, intellectual, and ideological labor, its acknowledgment of the dialectical nature of all thinking, and its insistence that analysis of all phenomena must be informed by historical context were articulated long before such ideas made their way into modern literary theory.

Marxist Literary Criticism: An Overview

Marx and Engels produced no systematic theory of literature or art. Equally, the subsequent history of Marxist aesthetics has hardly comprised the cumulative unfolding of

a coherent perspective. Rather, it has emerged, aptly, as a series of responses to concrete political exigencies. While these responses have sometimes collided at various
theoretical planes, they achieve a dynamic and expansive coherence (rather than the
static coherence of a closed, finished system) through both a general overlap of political
motivation and the persistent reworking of a core of predispositions about literature
and art deriving from Marx and Engels themselves. These predispositions include:

(1) The rejection, following Hegel, of the notion of "identity" and a consequent
    denial of the view that any object, including literature, can somehow exist inde-
    pendently. The aesthetic corollary of this is that literature can only be understood
    in the fullness of its *relations* with ideology, class, and economic substructure.
(2) The view that the so-called "objective" world is actually a progressive construction
    out of collective human subjectivity. What passes as "truth," then, is not eternal but
    institutionally created. "Private property," for example, is a bourgeois reification
    of an abstract category; it does not necessarily possess eternal validity. Language
    itself, as Marx said in *The German Ideology: Part One*, must be understood not as
    a self-sufficient system but as social practice (*GI*, 51, 118).
(3) The understanding of art itself as a commodity, sharing with other commodities
    an entry into material aspects of production. If, as Marx said, human beings
    produce themselves through labor, artistic production can be viewed as a branch
    of production in general.
(4) A focus on the connections between class struggle as the inner dynamic of history
    and literature as the ideologically refracted site of such struggle. This has some-
    times gone hand in hand with prescriptions for literature as an ideological ancillary
    to the aims and results of political revolution.
(5) An insistence that language is not a self-enclosed system of relations but must be
    understood as social practice, as deeply rooted in material conditions as any
    other practice (*GI*, 51).

To these predispositions could be added, for example, Engels' comments on "typicality," recommending that art should express what is typical about a class or a peculiar
intersection of ideological circumstances. One might also include the problem raised
by Engels' granting a "relative autonomy" to art, his comments that art can transcend
its ideological genesis and that superstructural elements are determined only in the
"last instance" by economic relations: what exactly is the connection between art and
the material base into which its constituting relations extend? Given the inconclusive
and sometimes ambiguous nature of Marx's and Engels' scattered comments on art,
the proposed solutions to such dilemmas have been as various as the political soils on
which they were sown.

   After Marx's death in 1883, Engels' attempt to shed light on his colleague's aesthetic
views was less assiduous than his clarifications of other aspects of Marx's work. As
Europe witnessed a widespread nascence of socialist political parties, together with the
impact of Marxism in sociology, anthropology, history, and political science, the first
generation of Marxist intellectuals included the Italian Antonio Labriola (1843–1904),
who attempted the first effective synthesis of Marx's thought and popularized the

premises of Marxism. His works, translated into all the major European languages, exerted enormous influence and made a particularly striking impression on George Plekhanov, who introduced his work to Russia, as well as on Lenin and Trotsky. In his *Essays on the Materialistic Conception of History* (1895–1896) Labriola reaffirms Marx's premise that (material) being determines consciousness rather than vice versa but takes some pains to emphasize that while legal and political systems are "a true and proper projection of economic conditions . . . in artistic or religious production the mediation from the conditions to the products is very complicated." Hence, although art and ideas can have no independent history, they are themselves a part of history in the sense that they too are a causal agency in subsequent economic and superstructural developments.

Another star in the firmament of early Marxist theory was the Prussian-born Franz Mehring (1846–1919). A one-time follower of Ferdinand Lassalle, Mehring became an outstanding Marxist historian and aesthetician who, along with Rosa Luxemburg and others, founded the German Communist Party in 1918. His writings included the first authoritative biography of Marx, *Karl Marx: The Story of His Life* (1918), and *The Lessing-Legend* (1892–1893), which both applied Marxist categories to the analysis of major German literary figures and brought these within the reach of working-class readers. Mehring attempted to situate Marxist aesthetics, and Marxist thought in general, in necessary relation to the German classical philosophy and aesthetics which had preceded it. This elicited censure from such figures as Paul Reimann and F. P. Schiller, and later from György Lukács, who saw Mehring as a reactionary ideologue. There is much in Mehring which might justify such a response. One of the central questions he confronts is: how are objective aesthetic judgments possible, given the subjectivity of taste? Mehring urges that a "scientific aesthetics" must demonstrate, as Kant did, that art is "a peculiar and aboriginal capacity of mankind." But Lukács somewhat overlooks Mehring's account of Kant's weaknesses: Kant's inability, for example, to recognize that his aesthetic laws were historically conditioned and that a "pure" aesthetic judgment, dirempted from logical and moral considerations, was impossible. Moreover, Mehring's analyses of specific literary texts bear out his view that, like all ideology, literary criticism must ultimately be determined by economic infrastructure.

German Marxist theory found a further advocate in Karl Kautsky (1854–1938), whose preeminence endured till around 1915. A propagandist for the Social Democratic Party, he founded in 1883 a prestigious Marxist journal, *Die Neue Zeit*, which offered a forum for the elaboration of Marx's economic and political thought. His works included *Karl Marx's Economic Teachings* (1887) and *The Foundations of Christianity* (1908). In the 1880s he produced a number of reflections on art such as "Development in Art," "Art and Society," and "Artist and Worker." In *The Foundations of Christianity* Kautsky, typifying his method, showed how religious ideas are tied to the levels of artistic and industrial maturity allowed by a particular economic substructure. He developed the thesis that the major monotheistic religions arose in nations bound by a nomadic way of life; they had not developed the industry or art necessary to construct the localized human images of deities which facilitated polytheism. Ironically, these more backward cultures could make a leap beyond polytheism to a higher form of religion whose progress was retarded in more advanced societies.

George Plekhanov (1856–1918), the "father of Russian Marxism," was a founder of the Russian Social Democratic Party. His writings include *Socialism and the Political Struggle* (1883) and *Fundamental Problems of Marxism* (1908), as well as his highly influential *Art and Social Life* (1912) and some shorter pieces such as *The Role of the Individual in History* (1898). In the last of these he argues that the role of gifted individuals, such as Napoleon, in history has been exaggerated. Plekhanov's own position is that such persons appear "wherever and whenever" social conditions facilitate their development: "every talent which becomes a social force, is the fruit of social relations." Moreover, individuals can change only the individual character, not the general direction, of events. Hence particular trends in art or literature do not depend exclusively on certain individuals for their expression; if the trend is sufficiently profound, it will compensate the premature death of one individual by giving rise to other talents who might embody it. The depth of a literary trend is determined by its significance for the class whose tastes it expresses, and by the social role of that class. In *Art and Social Life* Plekhanov raises the crucial question of the relative values of "art for art's sake" and a "utilitarian" view of art which sees it as instrumental in promoting the improvement of the social order. Plekhanov refuses to approach this question by abstractly asserting the priority of one or the other. Rather, he inquires into the principal social conditions in which each of these attitudes arises and arrives at the thesis that the "art for art's sake" tendency arises when an artist is "in hopeless disaccord with the social environment." The utilitarian attitude, which grants art a function in social struggles as well as the power of judgment concerning the real world, "arises and becomes stronger wherever a mutual sympathy exists between the individuals . . . interested in artistic creation and some considerable part of society."[7]

Another area in which Plekhanov pioneered a Marxist standpoint was the significance of "play," whereby human beings pursue an activity not for its usefulness but simply for pleasure. Plekhanov believed that Karl Bucher's theory that in primitive cultures play and art preceded labor and the production of useful objects was a test case for the materialist explanation of history. If Bucher were right, the Marxist explanation would be turned upside down. As against Bucher, Plekhanov, following Herbert Spencer, maintains that play is a dramatization and imitation of labor or useful activity. Hence utilitarian activity precedes play and is what determines its content. The implications of Plekhanov's comments on play were not taken up systematically by a Marxist until Herbert Marcuse's *Eros and Civilization* appeared in 1955.

One of the most striking figures in the Marxist canon was Rosa Luxemburg (1870–1919). Born into a Jewish business background in Poland, she migrated to Germany where she joined the Social Democratic Party, rising to a lofty prominence until her assassination in 1919. Her most renowned contribution was *The Accumulation of Capital* (1913). Centrally concerned with the reasons behind the stagnation and lack of development of Marxist theory, she was also anxious to preserve an aesthetic dimension for art, a recalcitrance to what she saw as reductive analysis. While acknowledging that both Dostoyevsky's and Tolstoy's doctrines were reactionary and mystical, she nevertheless praised their liberating effects on the reader and their profound response to social injustice. Luxemburg justified this by urging that the "social formula" recommended by an artist was secondary to the source or animating spirit of the art. The starting points of Dostoyevsky and Tolstoy, she affirmed, were not reactionary. She urged that a working-class culture could not be produced within a bourgeois economic framework, and that the workers could only advance if they created for themselves the necessary intellectual weapons in their struggle for liberation. Luxemburg believed that Marx provided much more than was directly essential for practically conducting the class war and that the theoretical fruits of his system could only be realized more gradually. Evident here is the implication that, in Luxemburg's eyes, the superstructural world of art, law, and ethics cannot be appropriated by the revolutionary class in a manner consonant with the general displacement of the bourgeois political apparatus but must evolve, lagging slowly behind those more prosaic shifts in economic substructure.

Vladimir Ilyich Lenin (1870–1924) occupied a central role not only in the revolution of 1917 but also in the unfolding of Marxist aesthetics toward a more politically interventionist stance. In the latter respect, Lenin's most celebrated and controversial piece is his "Party Organization and Party Literature" (1905), which, along with certain comments of Marx and Engels, was later misleadingly claimed to authorize "socialist realism," adopted in 1934 as the official party aesthetic. But hostile, non-Marxist critics have also misinterpreted Lenin's essay, viewing it as an attempt to repress free creativity in literature. Such a view overlooks both the context in which the essay was conceived and its actual arguments. Written shortly after the general strike of October 1905, it belongs to a politically volatile period in which the work of revolution was far from complete, as Lenin emphasizes: "While tsarism is *no longer* strong enough to defeat the revolution, the revolution is *not yet* strong enough to defeat tsarism."[8] Moreover, free speech and a free press, as Lenin points out, did not in any case exist. It can come as no surprise, then, that Lenin insists that literature "must become *part* of the common cause of the proletariat, 'a cog and screw' of one single great Social-Democratic mechanism." Lenin is well aware that art cannot be "subject to mechanical adjustment or levelling, to the rule of the majority over the minority." But he is not prescribing partisanship (*partinost*) for all literature, only literature which claims to be party literature. He grants that freedom "of speech and the press must be complete." What he is suggesting is that "freedom of association" must also be complete: the party reserves the right to circumscribe the ideological boundaries of writing conducted under its banner. Lenin also points out that in bourgeois society the writer cherishes but an illusory freedom: "The freedom of the bourgeois writer . . . is simply masked . . . dependence on the money-bag, on corruption, on prostitution." The writers imagine themselves to be free but are actually dependent upon an entire prescriptive network of commercial relations and interests, "prisoners of bourgeois-shopkeeper literary relations." In contrast, the free literature that Lenin desires "will be *openly* linked to the proletariat." Also underscoring Lenin's arguments is his recognition that literature "cannot . . . be an individual undertaking," as liberal-bourgeois individualism would have us believe (149–152).

Lenin's *Articles on Tolstoy*, produced between 1908 and 1911, exemplify through their detailed analyses both the political urgency informing Lenin's aesthetic approach and his ability to explain the circumstances limiting the potential partisanship of great writers. According to Lenin, the contradictions in Tolstoy's works – for example, his "ruthless criticism of capitalist exploitation," his denunciation of "poverty, degradation and misery among the toiling masses" as against his "crazy preaching of 'resist not evil' with violence" and his preaching of a reformed religion – mirror the contradictory conditions of the revolutionary peasantry (9). Tolstoy's misguided renunciation of politics reflected the "seething hatred, a mature striving for a better lot, a desire to get rid of the past – and also immature dreaming, political ignorance and revolutionary flabbiness" characterizing the peasantry (14). But while Tolstoy's doctrines are "certainly utopian," Lenin is able to call them "socialistic" and to hail Tolstoy's portrayal of the epoch of revolution as "a step forward in the artistic development of the whole of mankind" (16). Lenin's methodological insights are equally interesting: the contradictions in Tolstoy can *only* be apprehended from the standpoint of the class which led the struggle for freedom during the revolution (20). This helps to put into perspective some of Lenin's earlier comments on "Party literature": not only is it impossible to write as an individual, but equally, "individual" acts of reading and interpreting are conducted within parameters dictated by class interests. At a deeper level, Lenin's approach to aesthetic value, embracing as it does the totality of historical circumstances including class, preceding literary traditions, and relation to political exigency, can be seen to derive from his acknowledgment of the dialectical character of Marxism. In his *Philosophical Notebooks* he cites "Dialectics" as the theory of knowledge of both Hegel and Marxism, a theory which focuses on the necessary connection between the individual and the universal, the infinite expansibility through various levels of an individual's constituting relations, as well as the connections between necessity and contingency.

It can be seen from the foregoing that the early debates on art during and after the revolutionary period in Russia focused on questions such as the degree of party control over the arts, the stance toward the bourgeois cultural legacy, and the imperative to clarify the connections between the political and the aesthetic. A related question was the possibility of creating a proletarian culture. The other major protagonist in the Russian Revolution, Leon Trotsky (1879–1940), played a crucial role in these debates. His works include *Lenin* (1924), *History of the Russian Revolution* (1932), and *The Revolution Betrayed* (1937), as well as his renowned *Literature and Revolution* (1923). Trotsky, already exiled in 1900 and 1905 for his revolutionary activities, was finally ousted by Joseph Stalin in the struggle for leadership following Lenin's death in 1904. He continued, in exile, to oppose Stalin's regime until his murder in 1940. The literary debates were far from academic: they are indices of bitter political alignments. In *Literature and Revolution* Trotsky stressed that only in some domains can the party offer direct leadership; the "domain of art is not one in which the Party is called upon to command. It can and must protect and help it, but can only lead it indirectly."[9] But, just as Lenin's views on this topic have been misread, so Trotsky's claims for freedom of art have been subject to misprision. He states quite clearly that what is needed is "a watchful revolutionary censorship, and a broad and flexible policy in the field of art." What is important for Trotsky is that the limits of such censorship be defined very clearly: he is against "the liberal principle of *laissez faire* and *laissez passer*, even in the field of art" (221).

Hence Trotsky cannot be accused of blatant tolerance of reactionary literature and ideas, although in a 1938 manifesto, *Towards a Free Revolutionary Art*, drawn up in collaboration with André Breton, Trotsky urges a "*complete freedom for art*" while acknowledging that all true art is revolutionary in nature. The latter position was adopted in reaction to what Trotsky calls Stalin's "police patrol spirit."[10] In *Literature and Revolution* Trotsky also urges that the party should give "its confidence" to what he calls "literary fellow-travelers," those non-party writers sympathetic to the revolution. What lies behind this is Trotsky's insistence that the proletariat cannot begin the construction of a new culture without absorbing and assimilating the elements of the old cultures (226). Given the proletariat's need for a continuity of creative tradition, it currently "realizes this continuity . . . indirectly, through the creative bourgeois intelligentsia which gravitates towards the proletariat" (227). In the same work, Trotsky addresses the question of whether proletarian culture is possible. The question, to Trotsky, is "formless" because not only will the energy of the proletariat be directed primarily toward the acquisition of power but, as it succeeds, it "will be more and more dissolved into a Socialist community and will free itself from its class characteristics and thus cease to be a proletariat . . . The proletariat acquires power for the purpose of doing away forever with class culture and to make way for human culture" (185–186).

Other aspects of Tolstoy's approach to aesthetics are exemplified in his speech of 1924, "Class and Art." Here, Trotsky suggests that art has "its own laws of development" and that there is no guarantee of an organic link between artistic creativity and class interests. Moreover, such creativity "lags behind" the spirit of a class and is not subject to conscious influence. Trotsky maintains that certain great writers, such as Dante, Shakespeare, and Goethe, appeal to us precisely because they transcend the limitations of their class outlook. Throughout his comments on aesthetics, Trotsky seems to travel a fine line between granting art a certain autonomy while viewing it as serving, in a highly mediated fashion, an important social function.

The call to create a proletarian culture was the originating theme of *Proletkult*, a left-wing group of artists and writers whose foremost ideologist was A. A. Bogdanov. This group, opposed by the Bolshevik leadership, insisted on art as a weapon in class struggle and rejected all bourgeois art. Also active in the debates of this period were the Formalists and the Futurists, notably the critic Osip Brik, whose term "social command" embodied the idea of interventionist art, and the poet Mayakovsky, who wrote an influential pamphlet, "How Are Verses Made?" The Formalists and Futurists found a common platform in the journal *LEF* (Left Front of Art). The Formalists, focusing on artistic forms and techniques on the basis of linguistic studies, had arisen in pre-revolutionary Russia but now saw their opposition to traditional art as a political gesture, allying them somewhat with the revolution. All of these groups were attacked by the most prominent Soviet theoreticians, such as Trotsky, Nikolai Bukharin (1888–1937), Anatoly Lunacharsky (1875–1933), and Voronsky, who decried the attempt to break completely with the past and what they saw as a reductive denial of the social and cognitive aspects of art. V. N. Volosinov (Bakhtin) later attempted to harmonize the two sides of the debate, viz., formal linguistic analysis and sociological emphasis, by treating language itself as the supreme ideological phenomenon. A further group was the Association of Proletarian Writers (VAPP; later RAPP), which insisted on communist literary hegemony.

The Communist Party's attitude toward art in this period was, in general, epiphenomenal of its economic policy. A resolution of 1925 voiced the party's refusal to sanction any one literary faction. This reflected the New Economic Policy (NEP) of a limited free market economy. The period of the first Five-Year Plan (1928–1932) saw a more or less voluntary return to a more committed artistic posture, and during the second Five-Year Plan (1932–1936) this commitment was crystallized in the formation of a Writers' Union. The first congress of this union in 1934, featuring speeches by Maxim Gorky and Bukharin, officially adopted socialist realism, as defined primarily by A. A. Zhdanov (1896–1948). Aptly dubbed by Terry Eagleton as "Stalin's cultural thug," it was Zhdanov whose proscriptive shadow thenceforward fell over Soviet cultural affairs. Although Bukharin's speech at the congress had attempted a synthesis of Formalist and sociological attitudes, premised on his assertion that within "the microcosm of the word is embedded the macrocosm of history," Bukharin was eventually to fall from his position as leading theoretician of the party: his trial and execution, stemming from his political and economic differences with Stalin, were also symptomatic of the fact that Formalism soon became a sin once more. Bukharin had called for socialist realism to portray not reality "as it is" but rather as it exists in socialist imagination. Zhdanov defined socialist realism as the depiction of "reality in its revolutionary development. The truthfulness . . . of the artistic image must be linked with the task of ideological transformation."[11] But, as several commentators have pointed out, despite the calls for socialist realism to express social values as embodied in the movement of history (rather than embracing a static naturalism), the actual aesthetic adopted was largely a return to nineteenth-century realist techniques infused with a socialist content.

Socialist realism received its most articulate theoretical expression in the work of the Hungarian philosopher György Lukács, the foremost Marxist aesthetician of the twentieth century. Lukács' ideas are examined in some detail below; here, it is necessary merely to mention that his notion of realism collided with that of Bertolt Brecht (1898–1956). In some ways this debate can be regarded as a collision between two personalities, or between writer (Brecht) and critic (Lukács), since their "definitions" of socialist realism overlap in crucial aspects, a fact which is often ignored. According to Lukács, modern capitalist society is riven by contradictions, by chasms between universal and particular, intelligible and sensible, part and whole. The realist artist expresses a vision of the possible totality embracing these contradictions, a totality achieved by embodying what is "typical" about various historical stages. For example, an individual character might enshrine an entire complex of historical forces. Brecht, in his notebooks, also equates realism with the ability to capture the "typical" or "historically significant." Realists also identify the contradictions in human relationships, as well as their enabling conditions. Socialist realists, moreover, view reality from the viewpoint of the proletariat. Brecht adds that realist art battles false views of reality, thereby facilitating correct views.[12] Perhaps the conflict between the two thinkers is rooted in Lukács' (arguably Stalinist-inspired) aversion to modernist and experimental art on the grounds that the ontological image of humanity it portrayed was fragmented, decadent, and politically impotent. In the 1930s Brecht's work was viewed as tainted, though later he was received into the ranks of Marxist aestheticians. In contrast, Brecht's experimentalism was crucial to his attempts to combine theory and practice in a Marxist aesthetic. Contrasting dramatic theater (which follows Aristotle's guidelines) with his own "epic" theater, Brecht avers that the audience's capacity for action must be roused and, far from undergoing *katharsis*, it must be forced to take decisions, partly by its standard expectations being disappointed (a procedure Brecht called "the alienation effect"). The action on stage must also implicitly point to other, alternative versions of itself. Far from being sterile, the disputes between Lukács and Brecht display the multi-dimensional potential of any concept approached from Marxist viewpoints as well as the inevitable grounding of those viewpoints in political circumstances.

Mention should also be made of the Italian Marxist theorist and political activist Antonio Gramsci (1891–1937), whose main contribution to Marxism is widely thought to lie in his elaboration of the notion of hegemony. Autonomous revolutionary potential on the part of the proletariat could only be realized, argued Gramsci, through political *and* intellectual autonomy. A mass movement alone was insufficient: also, initiated through a vanguard with working-class roots and sympathies, this class "must train and educate itself in the management of society," acquiring both the culture and psychology of a dominant class through its own channels: "meetings, congresses, discussions, mutual education."[13] The transformation to a socialist state cannot be successful without the proletariat's own organic intellectuals forging an alternative hegemony. The notion of hegemony is effectively a metonymic affirmation of the dialectical connection between economic and superstructural spheres, stressing the transformative role of human agency rather than relying on the "inevitability" of economic determinism. Gramsci wrote some thirty-four notebooks while in prison, ranging from literary topics such as Dante and Pirandello to philosophical and political themes. These were not published until after Mussolini's downfall. Gramsci's literary criticism insisted on understanding literary production within its historical and political context (as against Croce's ahistorical view of art as autonomous) and, following De Sanctis, viewed the critic's task as one of harmonizing with the general cultural and political struggle toward a socialist order.

Later critics have continued to reinterpret and develop the insights of Marx and Engels. The Frankfurt School of Critical Theory, whose leading exponents were Max Horkheimer, Theodor Adorno, and Herbert Marcuse, produced a number of philosophical and cultural analyses informed primarily by Hegel's work and also by Freud. In general, these theorists saw modern mass culture as regimented and reduced to a commercial dimension; and they saw art as embodying a unique critical distance from this social and political world. Walter Benjamin argued in his "The Work of Art in the Age of Mechanical Reproduction" that modern technology has transformed the work of art, stripping it of the "aura" of uniqueness it possessed in earlier eras. Modern works are reproduced for mass consumption, and are effectively copies which relate to no original form. However, this new status of art, thought Benjamin, also gave it a revived political and subversive potential.

Subsequent Marxist cultural and literary theory, such as that of Louis Althusser, Lucien Goldmann, and Pierre Macherey, turned away from Hegel and was heavily influenced by the structuralist movements of the earlier twentieth century, which stressed the role of larger signifying systems and institutional structures over individual agency and intention. Louis Althusser emphasized the later Marx's "epistemological break" from his own earlier humanism, and Marx's scientificity and his departure from, rather than his debt to, Hegel. Althusser's structuralist Marxism – as stated in his *Pour Marx*

(*For Marx*, 1965) and his often cited "Ideology and Ideological State Apparatuses," rejected earlier humanist and historicist readings of Marx, as well as literary-critical emphases on authorial intention and subjective agency. Goldmann rejected the Romantic–humanist notion of individual creativity and held that texts are productions of larger mental structures representing the mentality of particular social classes. He stressed the operation of larger forces and doctrines in literary texts, and developed the notion of "homology" to register the parallels between artistic and social forms. Pierre Macherey's *A Theory of Literary Production* (1966) saw the literary text as the product of the artist's reworking of linguistic and ideological raw material, unwittingly exposing, through its lacunae and contradictions, ideological elements which the author had attempted to suppress into a false coherence. In this way, a critique of ideology could emerge through the literary text.

In the Anglo-American world a "cultural materialist" criticism was first revived by Raymond Williams' work, notably *Culture and Society 1780–1950*, which analyzes the cultural critique of capitalism in English literary tradition. Williams rejected a simplistic explanation of culture as the efflux of material conditions, but stressed the contribution of cultural forms to economic and political development. *The Long Revolution* (1961) continued and refined this project using categories such as dominant, residual, and emergent cultures mediated by what Williams called "structures of feeling." Williams' work became overtly Marxist with the publication in 1977 of *Marxism and Literature*. In this work Williams undertook a critical review of earlier Marxist theories and offered his own analyses of fundamental Marxist notions such as ideology, hegemony, base and superstructure. His own cultural materialism as set forth here attempts to integrate Marxist conceptions of language and literature. *Keywords* (1976) examines the history of fundamental concepts and categories. In general, Williams' work analyzed the history of language, the role of the media, mass communications, and the cultural connections between the country and the city.

The major American Marxist critic Fredric Jameson outlined a dialectical theory of literary criticism in his *Marxism and Form* (1971), drawing on Hegelian categories such as the notion of totality and the connection of abstract and concrete. Such criticism recognizes the need to see its objects of analysis within a broad historical context, acknowledges its own history and perspective, and seeks the profound inner form of a literary text. Jameson's *The Political Unconscious* (1981) attempts to integrate this dialectical thinking with insights from structuralism and Freud, using the Freudian notion of repression to analyze the function of ideology, the status of literary texts, and the epistemological function of literary form. In subsequent work such as *Postmodernism, or the Cultural Logic of Late Capitalism* (1991), Jameson performed the valuable task of extending Marx's insights into the central role of postmodernism in determining the very form of our artistic and intellectual experience.

In Britain, Terry Eagleton has outlined the categories of a Marxist analysis of literature, and has persistently rearticulated the terms of communication, as well as the differences, between Marxism and much of modern literary theory. We can now undertake a closer examination of two Marxist critics whose ideas have been highly influential: the Hungarian philosopher György Lukács and the aforementioned critic Terry Eagleton, as his work relates to modern literary theory.

György Lukács (1885–1971)

Born into a wealthy Jewish family in Budapest, the Hungarian philosopher György Lukács was to launch on an intellectual and political journey which, though fraught with antagonism, compromise, and reversals, left him the highest star in the constellation of twentieth-century Marxist aestheticians. His doctorate, conducted under Georg Simmel's supervision in Berlin, was in sociology and his initial interest in Marx was as a sociologist. He subsequently moved in an interdisciplinary circle of acquaintances which included Ernst Bloch and Max Weber. As well as falling under the influence of these figures, he was indebted to Kierkegaard, Heidegger, Georges Sorel, Rosa Luxemburg, Kant, and especially Hegel. The general orientation of his work toward philosophical idealism was expressed in the major works of this period: *Soul and Form* (1911), *History of the Development of Modern Drama* (1911), and *The Theory of the Novel* (1916).

Returning to Budapest in 1917, Lukács joined the Hungarian Communist Party in 1918, his decision inspired largely by the Russian Revolution but also representing the culmination of his lifelong hatred of capitalism. Thereafter, his aesthetic concerns were eclipsed by political imperatives. He became Commissar of Education in the short-lived communist government under Béla Kun of 1919, after whose overthrow he escaped to Austria, traveling thereafter to Germany and Russia. His *History and Class Consciousness* (1923) suffered a hostile reception from the communist movement, on a number of accounts: it overlooked the centrality of labor to Marxist analysis, it offered an idealistic concept of revolutionary praxis, and above all, it attempted to reinstate the Hegelian category of totality at the center of the Marxist system, drawing a direct line of descent from the Hegelian dialectic to historical materialism, relegating the intermediary role of Feuerbach to the background. It also defined orthodoxy in Marxism as exclusively a question of methodology rather than content and conducted an unwelcome polemic against Engels. Lukács was later to admit that in some ways his book had effectively attempted to "out-Hegel Hegel." The book was denounced with particular vehemence by Béla Kun, whose political sectarianism Lukács had strategically and bitterly opposed. But its analysis of class consciousness, and particularly of alienation as central to the critique of capitalist society, exerted a profound influence through not only Marxist theory but also other areas such as French existentialism. It stands in a sense at the center of Lukács' canon, as he himself pointed out. It is the final synthesis of his development since 1918 and marks the point of divergence toward his subsequent intellectual path along an economically grounded vision of Hegel's dialectic. Lukács' strategic publication of a self-criticism and his monograph, *Lenin: A Study on the Unity of His Thought* (1924), a relatively orthodox study, went some way toward reconciling him with the party. He regarded such reconciliation as his "entry-ticket" into history, since communism appeared to furnish the only viable forum for meaningful resistance to the emerging fascism.

In 1928, as the Hungarian Communist Party prepared for its Second Congress, Lukács was asked to draft its political theses. The resulting "Blum Theses," urging the party to work toward an independent rather than soviet republic, were regarded as regressive since Hungary had already been allied as a soviet republic in 1919.

Notwithstanding Lukács' publication of a self-criticism, the climate of fierce antagonism to his proposals obliged him to withdraw from politics in 1929. This initiated his more or less exclusive devotion to Marxist theory and aesthetics. In 1930–1931 he took up a research post at the Marx–Engels Institute in Moscow where his reading of the recently discovered *Economic and Philosophical Manuscripts of 1844* struck him with the force of a revelation. He regarded this text of Marx both as confirming his insistence, in *History and Class Consciousness*, on the importance of alienation in Marxist theory and as underlining that book's essential failure to view alienation as only one specific instance of what Hegel had called objectification or externalization. In an earlier review, Lukács had insisted, as against Bukharin (at the time second only to Stalin in the leadership of the Russian Communist Party), that economic forces are the determinants, not the products, of technological development. His work on Lassalle and Moses Hess also impelled him to define more closely the connection between economics and dialectics, culminating in a massive and brilliantly intricate work, *The Young Hegel* (1938). An imposing feature of this work is its articulate attempt to distinguish between Marxist integrations of Hegel and distorted bourgeois versions which assimilate Hegel to Romantic and irrational thought, which Lukács viewed as a slippery incline plummeting to fascism.

After a two-year stay in Berlin, Lukács was forced to flee in 1933 to the Soviet Union, where he stayed until 1944. Lukács' study of the connections between dialectics and economics and the ontology of social being generated an attempt to construct a Marxist aesthetics. His literary studies during this period also assumed a coded anti-Stalinist role while exhibiting a surface continuity with the official "socialist realism" as prescribed officially by Stalin's cultural right arm, Zhdanov. These studies included *The Historical Novel* (1937) and essays later collected under the titles *Goethe and his Age* (1947), *Studies in European Realism* (1948), and *Essays on Thomas Mann* (1949). In these works Lukács correlates the rise of genres such as the historical novel with a bourgeois growth of historical consciousness, itself grounded in economic transformations. Sir Walter Scott, Balzac, and Tolstoy are viewed as the great exemplars of "realism" in the sense advocated by Lukács.

At the center of Lukács' concept of realism is precisely the category of totality expressed in *History and Class Consciousness*. This category is based on Hegel's notion of the concrete universal whereby the universal is not separate from but immanent in its particular expressions. Hence Lukács advocates a theory of reflection whereby art reflects a totality of historical forces rather than merely documenting mechanically surface details of the world which are accidentally related. Thus, talking of Balzac, whom Lukács regarded as the greatest realist, he points out that his characters in the very texture of their individuality embody certain historically typical traits. As regards realism in drama, Lukács saw Shakespeare as concentrating typical human relations around historical collisions "with a force unparalleled before and after him." Lukács views the mere photographic reproduction of reality by art as naturalism, a category whose derogated status applies to much literature written under the banner of Zhdanovism as well as many of Balzac's realist successors (among whom Lukács somewhat surprisingly includes Flaubert).

Lukács also arrays his notions of realism against the ideology and literary forms of modernism, which he views as a descendent of naturalism. In his view, the ontological image of the human being as offered by modernists such as Joyce, Beckett, and Kafka was asocial, alienated, fragmented, and pathologically inept as a political agent. Lukács rejects the power of this image to act as a critique of capitalism not only because it is ahistorical, but also because it elevates alienation to a seemingly eternal *condition humaine*. He had in fact been embroiled in the 1930s in a controversy with Bertolt Brecht whose own "alienation effect" was, in Lukács' eyes, part of a formalist procedure. But their notions of realism actually overlapped in crucial imperatives, such as that to capture the "typical" or "historically significant," a fact overridden in the perhaps politically motivated mutual opposition of these writers.

After World War II, Lukács was appointed Professor of Aesthetics and Philosophy at the University of Budapest. His works of philosophical and aesthetic synthesis in this period included *The Destruction of Reason* (1954) and *The Meaning of Contemporary Realism*, written in 1956, in which year, after the popular uprising against communism, Lukács became Minister of Culture in Imre Nagy's coalition, whose government was terminated abruptly by Soviet tanks. The first of these works displays Lukács' continuing preoccupation, in the context of German thought and literature, with the struggle between rationalistic humanism and barbaric irrationalism. In *The Specific Nature of the Aesthetic* (1962) Lukács confronts the enormous task of constructing a Marxist aesthetic, a task which involves: viewing the aesthetic contextually as one mode of reflecting reality among others and elaborating the specific traits of the aesthetic mode, which expresses objectivity as conjoined with peculiarity of subjective conditions and genesis; understanding art as another form of man making himself through his work; the articulation of a genuinely dialectical and historical method as well as of the historical nature of objective reality itself; stressing the connections between Marxism and other traditions of thought (Lukács draws upon Aristotelian mimesis as well as ideas from Goethe, Lessing, and others); clarifying the opposition between idealist and materialist aesthetics as well as the historical and ideological relations between immanence and transcendence.

In 1971 Lukács produced *Towards an Ontology of Social Being* and his projected study of ethics, which was still in its initial stages at the time of his death. Whatever unity can be claimed by Lukács' work as a whole rests on his persistent return to Hegel and his sustained endeavor to understand and clarify Marx and the Marxist tradition through the logical and historical schematic avenues opened up by the Hegelian dialectic. His ideas, in particular his articulation of alienation, class consciousness, and the dialectical character of Marxism, have had far-reaching reverberations for those who have opposed the Hegelian orientation of his work as well as those who have developed this. He is arguably the profoundest philosopher that Marxism has yet produced.

A Marxist View of Literary Theory: Terry Eagleton

Terry Eagleton's contribution to Marxist cultural theory is broad in its range. While his earlier writing examined in some depth certain Marxist categories of literary-cultural analysis, his later, more popularizing, work has argued persuasively the need for theory. Eagleton has revaluated the English literary-critical tradition, redefined the critic's function, and reappraised specific authors from his historical materialistic perspective. These are substantive aspects of the general task of a Marxist critic. But what stands out more saliently in Eagleton's recent texts is his resolute critical engagement with, and historical contextualization of, other modern critical trends. It is this engagement that will be considered here.

Eagleton's position, it will be argued here, entails not compromise but a strategism which is compatible with his Marxism. From one point of view, virtually all modern literary theories, each with its own inflections and motives, can be regarded as an implicit if not direct reaction against the New Critical claims as to the autonomy, independence, and objectivity of a literary text. Eagleton, as we shall see, has an ambivalent stance toward what he calls the "radical anti-objectivism" of recent theory.[14] What this reaction against objectivity entails, at a deeper level, is an assault on the notion of identity. It is perhaps at this level that one can see most clearly the nature of overlap and divergence between Eagleton's Marxism and non-Marxist theory.

In traditional logic, as deriving from its comprehensive formulation by Aristotle, the law of identity serves among other things as a basis of categorization and exclusive definition: an entity is what it is precisely because it is not anything else. Its identity is thus born in the process of dirempting its relations with other similarly "identified" things in the world, a process which thereby denies ontical status to those relations, treating them as somehow external to the entities related. This suppression of relations and relegation of them to a contingent status, a procedure closely tied to Aristotle's various definitions of "substance" and "essence," can serve a political and ideological function. For example, the identity of an object (which could be simply a physical entity or something as complex as a system of law or religion) which is in fact historically specific could be passed off as an eternal or natural identity. As Eagleton remarks in his essay on Adorno in *The Function of Criticism*, the notion of identity is "coercive": it is the "ideological element of pure thought" and was "installed at the heart of Enlightenment reason." It is installed also, one can infer, in all philosophies which positivistically accept the apparent given-ness of an object at face value, failing to see the object as essentially the result of a process whether philosophical or political.

The form of thought which most comprehensively impugns the notion of identity is dialectical thought. Hegel's *Logic* is explicitly an attack on the one-sidedness of traditional logic, which fails to see identity as an intrinsic function of difference. It should be said that Eagleton has not sympathized with Hegelian Marxism, an antipathy partly taken over from Althusser. In *Criticism and Ideology* Eagleton was influenced (though by no means uncritically) by Althusser, particularly with regard to the epistemological break between the earlier "humanistic" and later "scientific" attitudes which Althusser claimed to have found in Marx's work: it had been Althusser's intention to divest Marxism of Hegelian notions. But, quite apart from the facts that Eagleton has moved beyond Althusser's influence and has more recently acknowledged the lasting value of Lukács (whom he calls the greatest Marxist aesthetician[15]), it should equally be observed that Eagleton has never denied the dialectical character of Marxism.

Marx, in both his earlier and later work, takes over some central features of the *form* of Hegel's dialectic: firstly, an imperative to abolish or negate the given object (or state of affairs) by articulating the full rationality of that object's relations with a particular social and historical context, showing how these relations constitute the object. That is why, when the bourgeoisie was the revolutionary class, the Hegelian system was called a "negative" philosophy; it could be interpreted as revolutionary. In his 1844 manuscripts, Marx saw the "outstanding achievement" of Hegel's *Phenomenology* as the recognition of the "dialectic of negativity" as the moving principle of history. And of course, as late as the famous preface to *Capital*, Marx still claimed adherence to the form, though not the idealist content, of Hegel's dialectic. Writing in 1859, Engels was at great pains to stress that the superiority of Hegel's thought to previous philosophy lay in "the tremendous historical sense" of the dialectic, though Marx "divested it of its idealistic wrappings" (*CPE*, 55).

The second dialectical feature is a tendency to view an entity as unstable and intrinsically in a state of transition, being part of a more comprehensive process leading beyond it. This was an aspect of Hegel's ontological vision whereby, for example, "existence" itself was viewed as contradictory. For Marx the notion of "contradiction" acquires a social content, characterizing not only the historical relations between classes but also the central bourgeois concepts. The bourgeois notion of the individual, for instance, entails a contradiction between the individual's "human" needs as a member of civil society and that individual's abstract identity as a "citizen" of the state.

The third aspect of the dialectic is the notion of "sublation," which refers to the dual process of negating and transcending a given opposition or state of affairs while retaining certain features of what is negated. The extent to which this informs, for example, Marx's view of communist society as arising out of bourgeois relations of production is problematic, not least in the realm of superstructure. According to Marx, a change in the "economic foundation" is followed by more or less prolonged struggle in the ideological sphere (*CPE*, 4). The point is that one ideology or social structure does not simply replace another in linear fashion; whatever predominance is achieved is preceded by struggle and conflict. But even here it is a question of emphasis. Eagleton has little sympathy with Lukács' view of a Marxist society which Eagleton characterizes as "the triumphant sublation of the bourgeois humanist heritage" (*WB*, 83). But Eagleton acknowledges that "Socialists . . . wish to draw the full, concrete, practical applications of the abstract notions of freedom and democracy to which liberal humanism subscribes."[16]

All three features of Hegel's dialectic, utilized by Marx and Engels, constitute an attack on the notion of simple identity. Eagleton affirms that the "power of the negative . . . constitutes an essential moment of Marxism" (*WB*, 142). This perhaps gives us the clearest perspective from which we can understand how, in Eagleton's eyes, non-Marxist literary theory can be useful to Marxism. For there is a sense in which modern literary theories can be viewed as embodying "negative" philosophies, attacking received notions of identity, subjectivity, objectivity, and language. Non-Marxist theories effectively arrest the Hegelian dialectic at its second phase (of externalization and relationality) and their political valencies depend on the direction of their reintegration of that externality. For example, structuralism uses "structure" and "language" as a basis of reintegration. Psychoanalysis posits the "unconscious," while deconstruction effectively posits "difference." Feminism and socialism use political goals as a basis. Eagleton brings out this "negative" aspect of literary theory in some detail. Among the "gains" of structuralism he ranks its demystification of literature, which it views not as unique or essential discourse but as a construct. The codes of structuralism are indifferent to traditional compartmentalizations. Again, structuralism regards "meaning" not as substantively self-identical but as relational, the product of a shared system of signification. Eagleton acknowledges that these views harbor an implicit "ideological threat" to bourgeois representational and empiricist views of language and literature inasmuch as structuralism shows reality and experience to be discontinuous rather than comprising a simple correspondence (*LT*, 107–109).

Eagleton also sees psychoanalysis as a form of inquiry of some value to Marxism. Eagleton refuses to regard Freud as an individualist. Rather, Freud sees the development of the individual in social and historical terms: "What Freud produces . . . is nothing less than a materialist theory of the making of the human subject" (*LT*, 163). Eagleton skillfully shows how Lacan rewrites Freud on the question of the human subject, its place in society and its relationship to language. Eagleton also demonstrates how, writing under the influence of Lacan, Althusser describes the working of ideology in society. What Eagleton effectively shows here is how the relation between Marxist and non-Marxist theory cannot be reduced to direct commensurability or opposition, and is rather one of extrapolation and varying degrees of mediation.

The most controversial "philosophy" of the negative is deconstruction. Eagleton accepts that there are political possibilities in deconstruction. According to Eagleton, deconstruction's denial of a unity between signifier and signified, as well as its rejection of "meaning" as self-identical and immediately present, can help us to see that certain meanings – such as those of "freedom," "democracy," and "family" – are elevated by social ideologies to a privileged position as the origin or goal of other meanings. Deconstruction shows that so-called first principles are the products, rather than the foundations, of systems of meaning. Moreover, deconstruction's view of all language as metaphorical, as harboring a surfeit over exact meaning, undermines classical structuralism's typically ideological oppositions which draw a rigid line between what is and is not acceptable, for example between truth and falsehood, sense and nonsense, reason and madness. Eagleton also points out that Derrida himself, though not all of his followers, sees deconstruction as a political practice: he sees meaning, identity, intention, and truth as effects of a wider history, of language, the unconscious as well as social institutions and practices.

So far, all are in accord: Hegel, Marx, non-Marxist theory, and Eagleton's Marxism. All view "identity" as somehow coercive, meaning as relational, the objective world as a subjective construction, and truth as institutional. One is tempted to think of the Homeric gods feasting at this banquet of pure difference. But just as Marx's thought, whatever its similarities in form, has a content entirely different from Hegel's thought, so Eagleton's Marxism is marked by a specificity alien to non-Marxist theory.

It is true that some of Marx's insights, such as those listed above, are superficially compatible with those of non-Marxist theory. But Marx's attacks on the various expressions of identity, such as subject, object, and stable meaning, are without exception *necessarily* and internally related to the economic infrastructure. It is not just that the identification "private property" represents the bourgeois reification of an abstract category: such reification hides the nature of private property as a product of alienated labor. It is not just that man is abstractly perceived to have no essence: man is a result of specific productive forces and specific social relations. Again, man as subject is not created in an abstractly perceived interaction with objects: he produces himself through labor. And Marx views language not as a self-enclosed or independent system but as a social practice (*GI*, 18, 21, 51, 118). In each case, the "negative" aspect of Marx's thought is necessarily, not contingently, related to his affirmative material basis.

There are at least two fundamental premises in Marx from which any Marxist criticism must begin. In the first place all forms of consciousness – religious, moral, philosophical, legal, as well as language itself – have no independent history and arise from the material activity of men. Eagleton identifies a twofold specificity of Marxist criticism: material production is regarded as the ultimate determining factor of social existence, and class struggle is viewed as the central dynamic of historical development. Eagleton adds a third, Marxist-Leninist, imperative, namely a commitment to the theory and practice of political revolution.[17] Eagleton is aware of the highly mediated and complex relation between base and superstructure,[18] but his aptly Marxist insistence on the primacy of material production can be seen, as we shall see, to be the basis of virtually all his attacks on non-Marxist literary theory.

The second premise is Marx's view that the class which is the ruling material force is also the ruling intellectual force: it owns the means of production both materially and mentally. In the light of this we can better understand Eagleton's statement of the tasks of a "revolutionary literary criticism." Such a criticism

> would dismantle the ruling concepts of "literature," reinserting "literary" texts into the whole field of cultural practices. It would strive to relate such "cultural" practices to other forms of social activity, and to transform the cultural apparatuses themselves. It would articulate its "cultural" analyses with a consistent political intervention. It would deconstruct the received hierarchies of "literature" and transvaluate received judgments and assumptions; engage with the language and "unconscious" of literary texts, to reveal their role in the ideological construction of the subject; and mobilize such texts ... in a struggle to transform those subjects within a wider political context. (*WB*, 98)

But all of this subserves the "primary task" of Marxist criticism, which is "to actively participate in and help direct the cultural emancipation of the masses" (*WB*, 97). Eagleton repeatedly stresses that the starting point of theory must be a practical, political purpose and that any theory which will contribute to human emancipation through the socialist transformation of society is acceptable (*LT*, 211). He effectively develops Marx's premise above when he emphasizes that the "means of production" includes the means of production of human subjectivity, which embraces a range of institutions such as "literature." Eagleton regards the most difficult emancipation as that of the "space of subjectivity," colonized as it is by the dominant political order. The humanities as a whole serve an ideological function that helps to perpetuate certain forms of subjectivity. Eagleton's views here imply that for Marxist criticism, "ideology" is a crucial focus of the link between material and mental means of production.

Eagleton affirms that the "negation" entailed by Marxist criticism must have an affirmative material basis. There is an internal, not merely epiphenomenal, connection between practical goal and theoretical method. Hence the similarities between Marxism and "negative" non-Marxist theories are purely superstructural: which is itself an impossible contradiction since no Marxist insight can be "purely" superstructural. Whatever "threat" structuralism may pose to received ideology is thwarted by its complicity. As Eagleton shrewdly observes, the reactionary nature of structuralism lies in the very concept of "structure" (*LT*, 141), in the very positing of this received ideological notion as a basis of enquiry. It is only at this expense that structuralism dismantles the ruling ideologies of subjectivity. The general point here is that whatever non-Marxist theory postulates as a base or infrastructure of investigation is in fact an aspect of superstructure. Inasmuch as these theories fail to articulate their connections with the material infrastructure, they lapse into an effective, if sometimes undesired, complicity with ruling ideologies.

This is why Eagleton views non-Marxist theories as both subversive and complicit with capitalism, a contradiction inherent in their superstructural status. He arraigns, for example, structuralism's static ahistorical view of society, as well as its reduction of labor, sexuality, and politics to "language." Structuralism, moreover, ignores both literature and language as forms of social practice and production. Its anti-humanism brackets the human subject, thereby abolishing the subject's potential as a political agent. These factors, Eagleton observes, contributed to a certain integration of structuralism into the orthodox academy (*LT*, 110–115). Similarly, in Eagleton's eyes, the insights of psychoanalysis are not necessarily politically radical. For example, he asserts that the political correlative of Julia Kristeva's theories, which disrupt all fixed structures, is anarchism. And her dismantling of the unified subject is not in itself revolutionary (*LT*, 189–193).

Eagleton's sustained critique of deconstruction hinges on a specifically Marxist notion of "ideology," which he defines as a "set . . . of values, representations and beliefs which, realized in certain material apparatuses . . . guarantee those misperceptions of the 'real' which contribute to the reproduction of the dominant social relations."[19] A historical conception of the "real" underlies any Marxist view of ideology. And we can infer from Eagleton's statement that, for Marxism, the impugnment of ideology entails an attack on identity, on all the "identities" which comprise distorted reality and which are passed off as eternal or natural truths. These identities must be dissolved into their constitutive economic and social relations. Eagleton acknowledges the complex, internal relation between history and ideology (*CI*, 80–99), but the point here is that for Marxism some notion of identity and reality (such as economic relations) must underlie this attack. For both Hegel and Marx, identity presupposes difference. But difference, in turn, presupposes identity, each being an intrinsic function of the other. But deconstruction effects a one-sided hypostatization of "difference" alone, effectively raising it to transcendent status. Derrida states that "the movement of différance, as that which produces different things . . . is the common root of all . . . oppositional concepts."[20] All of Derrida's heuristic concepts – trace, dissemination, spacing, alterity, and supplement – are without exception metaphors for "différance," which Derrida admits is based on the Hegelian notion of sublation (*POS*, 40), the basis of whose movement is identity-in-difference. But what does it mean to say that différance is the "common root" of all oppositions regardless of their content? For Hegel and Marx, the content of "difference" (which, taken historically, embrace both aspects of Derrida's differing/deferring) is not generalizable, being always historically specific. The constitutive causes (ideological, social, and economic) behind various oppositions are quite different. But Derrida abstracts this historical complexity and variety into one indifferent and near-mystical cause: "the movement of différance." Hence Eagleton says in his essay on Adorno: "Pure difference . . . is as blank . . . as pure identity."

Again, there is a recognition in Derrida's work that the manifestations of identity and presence in history are coercive. But this recognition is abstract: he views *every* philosophical opposition, regardless of its content, as a "violent hierarchy." For Derrida, the base–superstructure model is one such deconstructible "opposition." He views the "violence" of "writing" as "originary."[21] Derrida characteristically coerces historically specific texts and institutions into an abstractly uniform assailability in the name of "writing": he defines "grammatology" as "the science of arbitrariness." Hence Eagleton views deconstruction as outflanking every type of knowledge "to absolutely no effect." Eagleton continues to say: "In the deep night of metaphysics, all cats look black. Marx is a metaphysician, and so is Schopenhauer, and so is Ronald Reagan. Has anything been gained by this manoeuvre?" (*WB*, 140).

Eagleton points out in his essay on Adorno that not all identity or unity is equally terroristic and that poststructuralism effects an "indiscriminate conflation" of different orders of power, oppression, and law. He stresses that any effective opposition to a given political order presupposes unity, solidarity, and at least a sense of provisional identity. The point is that Marxist attacks on identity and ideology derive their force from their inclusion within a more comprehensive vision governed by the necessity of their relation to an economic infrastructure.

It is clear that in Eagleton's view, Derrida's insights, whatever their superficial opposition to prevailing orthodoxies, have merely a contingently subversive capacity since they dispense with "identity" altogether and do not claim internal coherence except a coherence of the negative: they can affirm nothing to replace the order they "subvert." Eagleton points out that deconstruction's "dispersal" of the subject, itself a politically disabling gesture, is "purely textual": "the infrastructure . . . for deconstruction is not de(con)structible" (*WB*, 139). As Derrida admits, his thought effectively arrests the Hegelian dialectic at its second phase, of "difference": he abstracts this phase, divests it of all historical content, and employs it as a transcendental principle. As Eagleton has it, deconstruction "fails to comprehend class dialectics and turns instead to *difference*, that familiar ideological motif of the petty bourgeoisie" (*WB*, 134).

Hence Eagleton regards deconstruction as itself ideological. Like much poststructuralism, it effectively "colludes with the liberal humanism it seeks to embarrass." Eagleton insists that deconstruction reproduces common bourgeois liberal themes (the notions of "identity" and "substance" were, after all, attacked by Locke and Hume). Again, Eagleton observes that many of the ideas of deconstruction are already prefigured and developed in Marxist writers such as Benjamin, Macherey, and Adorno, where the empty shell of deconstructive "difference" is imbued with political content. And because deconstruction's insights are divorced from any infrastructure, it is unaware of the historical determinants of its own *aporiai* (*WB*, 133).

Eagleton acknowledges the potential of deconstruction. But he is also aware that this potential is already contained in the dialectical character of Marxism. What is original to Derrida and his followers is their remorseless insistence on "difference" as a basis of impugnment of literary and philosophical texts. Eagleton says of the "negative": "only a powerless petty-bourgeois intelligentsia would raise it to the solemn dignity of a philosophy" (*WB*, 142). The bases of Derrida's insights are already contained, according to Eagleton, in the context of a far vaster historically self-conscious vision, in the writings of Hegel and Marx. In fact, Eagleton's latest work, *After Theory*, suggests that we need to return in some respects to a "plain realism." He cautions that "If cultural theory is to engage with an ambitious global history, it must have answerable resources of its own, equal in depth and scope to the situation it confronts. It cannot afford simply to keep on recounting the same narratives of class, race and gender, indispensable as these topics are."[22]

Notes

1 Karl Marx and Friedrich Engels, *Manifesto of the Communist Party* (1952; rpt. Moscow: Progress Publishers, 1973), pp. 11–16. Hereafter cited as *MCP*.

2 Marx, *Economic and Philosophical Manuscripts of 1844* (1959; rpt. Moscow and London: Progress Publishers/Lawrence and Wishart, 1981), pp. 127–143.

3 Marx and Engels, *On Religion* (1957; rpt. Moscow: Progress Publishers, 1975), p. 39.

4 Marx, *Capital: Volume I* (1954; rpt. London: Lawrence and Wishart, 1977), p. 29. Hereafter cited as *Capital*.

5 "Preface and Introduction," in *A Contribution to the Critique of Political Economy* (Peking: Foreign Languages Press, 1976), p. 3. Hereafter cited as *CPE*.

6 Engels, *The Origin of the Family, Private Property and the State*, introd. Michèle Barrett (Harmondsworth: Penguin, 1985), p. 105. Hereafter cited as *OF*.

7 George V. Plekhanov, *Art and Social Life* (New York: Oriole Editions, 1974), pp. 177–178.

8 V. I. Lenin, *On Literature and Art* (Moscow: Progress Publishers, 1967), p. 148. Hereafter citations from this volume are given in the text.

9 Leon Trotsky, *Literature and Revolution* (New York: Russell and Russell, 1924), p. 218. Hereafter citations are given in the text.

10 Leon Trotsky, *Culture and Socialism and a Manifesto: Art and Revolution* (London: New Park Publications, 1975), pp. 31–34.

11 A. A. Zhdanov, *On Literature, Music and Philosophy* (New York and London: Lawrence and Wishart, 1950), p. 15.

12 Berel Lang and Forrest Williams, eds., *Marxism and Art: Writings in Aesthetics and Criticism* (New York: McKay, 1972), pp. 226–227.

13 Antonio Gramsci, *Selections from Political Writings*, trans. J. Mathews, ed. Q. Hoare (New York: International Publishers, 1977), p. 171.

14 Terry Eagleton, *The Function of Criticism* (London: New Left Books, 1984), p. 93.

15 Terry Eagleton, *Walter Benjamin or Towards a Revolutionary Criticism* (London: New Left Books, 1981), p. 84. Hereafter cited as *WB*.

16 Terry Eagleton, *Literary Theory: An Introduction* (Oxford and Minnesota: Blackwell/University of Minnesota Press, 1983), p. 208. Hereafter cited as *LT*.

17 Terry Eagleton, *Against the Grain: Essays 1975–1985* (London: New Left Books, 1986), pp. 81–82.

18 See *Marxism and Literary Criticism* (London: New Left Books, 1976), pp. 8–10.

19 Terry Eagleton, *Criticism and Ideology* (London: New Left Books, 1976), p. 54. Hereafter cited as *CI*.

20 Jacques Derrida, *Positions*, trans. Alan Bass (Chicago and London: University of Chicago Press, 1981), p. 9. Hereafter cited as *POS*.

21 Jacques Derrida, *Of Grammatology*, trans. Gayatri Chakravorty Spivak (Baltimore and London: Johns Hopkins University Press, 1976), p. 106.

22 Terry Eagleton, *After Theory* (Harmondsworth: Allen Lane and Penguin, 2003), pp. 221–222.

PART VIII

THE TWENTIETH CENTURY

THE TWENTIETH
CENTURY:
BACKGROUNDS
AND PERSPECTIVES

The vastly complex history of the twentieth century could be viewed from many perspectives of profound relevance to literature, criticism, and theory: the history of the women's movement and the struggle for women's rights; the growth, since the later nineteenth century, of various labor parties throughout Europe, and their struggle on behalf of the working classes; the continuation of imperialism and the subsequent world-scale phenomenon of decolonization; the rise to world power of fascism; the growth of the Soviet empire and the Cold War between the Western world and the communist bloc; and, more recently, the changing composition of the so-called Islamic world and its relation to the West. Each one of these complex phenomena has inspired a great deal of literature and criticism, much of which has not merely passively recorded events but often participated in and shaped the ideological atmosphere in which they occurred.

Most of these phenomena were, in important ways, specific to the twentieth century. Other trends of the twentieth century were more obviously continuations or intensifications of tendencies that had long been in movement: rationalization, urbanization, secularization, the increasingly practical deployment of science and technology, the growth of the middle classes, and the increasing refinements of the techniques of capitalism. In many ways, these broad movements came to a head in certain colossal events and phenomena of the twentieth century, whose impact overrode distinctions and interests of class, gender, race, nation, and religion. These events included the Bolshevik Revolution of 1917 in Russia, World War I (1914–1918), the great economic depression of the 1930s, World War II (1939–1945), the Cold War and the arms race, the predominance of America as a world power, the emergence of the so-called "third world," the social and political unrest of the 1960s, and a general swing in the West toward right-wing politics in the 1980s. Many of these developments culminated in the collapse of much of the communist bloc by 1989 and of the Soviet Union by 1991.

Here is how the historian Eric Hobsbawm summarizes the major movements of the twentieth century:

An Age of Catastrophe from 1914 to the aftermath of the Second World War was followed by some twenty-five or thirty years of extraordinary economic growth and social transformation, which probably changed human society more profoundly than any other period of comparable brevity. In retrospect it can be seen as a sort of Golden Age, and was so seen almost immediately it had come to an end in the early 1970s. The last part of the century was a new era of decomposition, uncertainty and crisis – and indeed, for large parts of the world such as Africa, the former USSR and the formerly socialist parts of Europe, of catastrophe. As the 1980s gave way to the 1990s, the mood of those who reflected on the century's past and future was a growing *fin-de-siècle* gloom.[1]

It is worth looking briefly at some of the phenomena cited by Hobsbawm. The devastating impact of World War I, fought between the major powers Germany and Austria on the one side (joined by Turkey and Bulgaria), and France, Russia, and Britain on the other (allied with Japan, Italy, and America), was unprecedented in history. Hobsbawm states that this war "marked the breakdown of the (western) civilization of the nineteenth century." "This civilization," he continues:

> was capitalist in its economy; liberal in its legal and constitutional structure; bourgeois in the image of its characteristic hegemonic class; glorying in the advance of science, knowledge and education, material and moral progress; and profoundly convinced of the centrality of Europe, birthplace of the revolutions of the sciences, arts, politics and industry, whose economy had penetrated, and whose soldiers had conquered and subjugated most of the world. (*AE*, 6)

It is clear from this succinct formulation that the ideals of the Enlightenment, embodied in the various institutions of the capitalist world, had culminated in a catastrophe on many levels, economic, political, and moral. The psychological impact of this catastrophe on the world of thought and letters was equally profound. Arguably, it was World War I, more than any other phenomenon of the twentieth century, which led thinkers in all domains to question not only the heritage of the Enlightenment but also the very foundations of Western civilization. The sheer scale of devastation and carnage produced by the war accelerated the process whereby long-held assumptions – the power of reason, the progress of history, providence, the moral dignity of human beings, the ability of people and nations to live in harmony, as well as our capacity to know ourselves and the world – were plunged into a mode of moral, spiritual, and intellectual crisis.

Subsequently, the Great Depression of the 1930s represented "a world economic crisis of unprecedented depth," bringing "even the strongest capitalist economies to their knees." Hobsbawm remarks that liberal democratic institutions declined between 1917 and 1942, as fascism and various authoritarian regimes rose to power. World War II, waged by the allies (Britain, America, and France) to contain the expansionist ambitions of Nazi Germany (aided by the totalitarian regimes of Italy and Japan), wrought not only a second wave of wide-scale destruction but also, in its aftermath, the disintegration of the huge colonial empires of Britain, France, Belgium, and the Netherlands, which had subjugated one-third of the world's population. It was the "bizarre" alliance of capitalism and communism which, ironically, saved the former, with the Red Army playing an essential role in the defeat of Nazi Germany. This alliance, says Hobsbawm, "forms the hinge of twentieth-century history and its decisive moment" (*AE*, 7). Notwithstanding such measures as the formation of the United Nations (UN) in 1945, and the North Atlantic Treaty Organization (NATO) in 1949, the twentieth century, as Hobsbawm states, "was without doubt the most murderous century of which we have record," both by the scale and frequency of warfare and also "by the unparalleled scale of the human catastrophes it produced, from the greatest famines in history to systematic genocide" (*AE*, 11). All of these phenomena – the two world wars, the rise of fascism, the depression, and decolonization – had a profound impact on literature and criticism.

The subsequent era, from 1947 to 1973, was one of considerable growth and prosperity, which harbored, according to Hobsbawm, the greatest and most rapid economic and cultural transformations in recorded history (*AE*, 11). Apart from the unprecedented technological advances, whereby most of the world's population ceased to live in agricultural economies, this era witnessed numerous political and social revolutions, whose principles were variously expressed by Che Guevara in Latin America, Frantz Fanon in Algeria, and the philosopher Herbert Marcuse, who inspired radical intellectuals in America and Europe. Political revolutions and movements against colonialism erupted in many parts of Africa; the earlier black militancy in America, inspired by figures such as Marcus Garvey and later Malcolm X, broadened into the civil rights movement of the 1950s and 1960s, whose leaders included Martin Luther King, assassinated in 1968. Many of the sentiments behind these movements were powerfully expressed in African-American literature. The African-American heritage has been increasingly explored and theorized in recent decades by critics such as Henry Louis Gates, Jr. In the Middle East, things were no less turbulent. The termination of the British mandate in Palestine and the creation of the state of Israel in 1948 led to persistent conflict between Israel and the Arab nations, fought out in bitter wars in 1948, 1956, 1967, and 1973. This conflict has profoundly shaped the literature and the literary-critical principles of the entire region; it was analyzed in several works of the Palestinian-American scholar Edward Said.

Throughout this period, Western capitalism pursued the path of increasing monopoly and consolidation, often employing the principles advocated by economists such as John Maynard Keynes who thought that the inequities of capitalism could be remedied, and prosperity brought to all, using monetary control rather than the nineteenth-century principles of laissez-faire. A generation of students in America and Europe, however, reacted against what they saw as the repressive, unjust, sexist, racist, and imperialist nature of the late capitalist world, epitomized for many by American involvement in the Vietnam War. In May 1968, left-wing uprisings of students and workers shook the University of Paris, as well as Berkeley, San Francisco State, Kent State, and elsewhere. Much literary theory in France and America, including feminism, took its impetus from this atmosphere of unrest and agitation. The twentieth century saw an acceleration of trends begun much earlier, such as urbanization, an explosion of population, and the spread of capitalism over most of the world. The later twentieth century brought a new awareness of ecology and the extent to which modern industrial life and production had damaged the environment. Modern criticism and theory has broadened to encompass all of these developments.

The collapse of the communist bloc and the Soviet Union led many to proclaim that Marx was dead. As we enter a new century, it is clear that the Cold War has been replaced by a new dynamic, which itself has served as the foundation for much recent criticism and theory. The relatively stable international system of communism was succeeded by local ethnic, tribal, and religious conflicts in Yugoslavia and areas of the former Soviet Union. Since the early 1990s, the core of this new dynamic has been underlain by America's unopposed predominance as *the* major world power, fueled by formulations of a "New World Order." The relative impotence of the political left has left its mark on the nature of theory, and what is viewed as radical or conservative. What has occupied center stage since the attacks of September 11, 2001 on the World Trade centers has been the "war on terror," stereotypically seen as aligning the Western world against what is known as radical Islamism. The more knowledgeable proponents on both sides urge that the war between Islam and the West is an ideological concoction with no basis in either the true nature of American democracy or the true nature of Islam. Islamic scholars such as Leila Ahmed, Fatima Mernissi, Akbar Ahmed, and Aziz al-Azmeh are currently debating questions such as the compatibility of Islam with democracy, the status of women in Islam, and the connections between Islam, Christianity, and Judaism. In doing this, they are revisiting Islamic history, literature, and the Qur'an in the light of modern literary and cultural theories.

To return to a general characterization. Hobsbawm states three ways in which the world has changed from the beginning to the end of the twentieth century: it is no longer Eurocentric, though America, Europe, and Japan are still the most prosperous; the world has in certain important ways become a "single operational unit," primarily in economic terms, but also increasingly in terms of mass culture; and, finally, there has been a massive disintegration of previous patterns of human relationships, with an unprecedented rupture between past and present. Capitalism has become a permanent and continuous revolutionary force that perpetuates itself in time and extends its empire increasingly in space.

Literary Criticism and Theory in the Twentieth Century

Twentieth-century literary criticism and theory has comprised a broad range of tendencies and movements: a humanistic tradition, descended from nineteenth-century writers such as Matthew Arnold and continued into the twentieth century through figures such as Irving Babbitt and F. R. Leavis, surviving in our own day in scholars such as Frank Kermode and John Carey; a neo-Romantic tendency, expressed in the work of D. H. Lawrence, G. Wilson Knight, and others; the New Criticism, arising initially in the 1920s and subsequently formalized and popularized in the 1940s; the tradition of Marxist criticism, traceable to the writings of Marx and Engels themselves; psychoanalytic criticism, whose foundations were laid by Freud and Jung; Russian Formalism, arising in the aftermath of the Russian Revolution; structuralism, which emerged fully in the 1950s, building on the foundations established in the early twentieth century by Saussure and Lévi-Strauss; and the various forms of criticism which are sometimes subsumed under the label of "poststructuralism": Lacanian psychoanalytic theory, which rewrote Freudian concepts; deconstruction, which emerged in the 1960s, as did feminism; reader-response theory, whose roots went back to Husserl and Heidegger; and the New Historicism, which arose in the 1980s.

At the end of the nineteenth century, criticism in Europe and America had been predominantly biographical, historical, psychological, impressionistic, and empirical. With the establishment of English as a separate discipline in England, many influential critics, such as George Saintsbury, A. C. Bradley, and Arthur Quiller-Couch, assumed academic posts. In America, influential theories of realism and naturalism had been propounded by William Dean Howells, Hamlin Garland, and Frank Norris. An important concern of American critics such as John Macy, Randolph Bourne, and Van Wyck Brooks was to establish a sense of national identity through tracing a specifically American literary tradition. In France, the most pervasive critical mode was the *explication de texte*, based on close readings which drew upon biographical sources and historical context. In the humanist tradition of Matthew Arnold, much of this *fin-de-siècle* criticism saw in literature a refuge from, or remedy for, the ills of modern civilization. In both America and Europe, the defenders and proponents of literature sought to preserve the humanities in the educational curriculum against the onslaughts of reformists such as Harvard University President Charles Eliot and John Dewey, who urged that the college education system should be brought into line with prevailing bourgeois scientific and economic interests.

The vast political and economic developments discussed above provided the broad context in which the literature and criticism of the twentieth century arose. The humanist tradition of the late nineteenth century, reacting against the commercialism and philistinism of bourgeois society, was continued and intensified in the polemic of the "New Humanists." Led by Harvard professor Irving Babbitt and including figures such as Paul Elmer More, Norman Foerster, and Stuart Sherman, the New Humanists were conservative in their cultural and political outlook, reacting against what they saw as a relativistic disorder of styles and approaches characterizing early twentieth-century America. They rejected the predominant tendencies stemming from the liberal-bourgeois tradition: a narrow focus on the present at the expense of the past and of tradition; unrestrained freedom in political, moral, and aesthetic domains; a riot of pluralism, a mechanical exaltation of facts, and an uninformed worship of science.

Also reacting against the industrialism and rationalism of the bourgeois world were the neo-Romantic critics in England, including D. H. Lawrence, G. Wilson Knight, John Middleton Murry, Herbert Read, and C. S. Lewis. Lawrence (1885–1930) was an avowed irrationalist, who saw the modern industrial world as sexually repressive and as having stunted human potential. In his own highly idiosyncratic way, Lawrence anticipates the stress on the unconscious, the body, and irrational motives in various areas of contemporary criticism. In general, these critics attempted to reinstate a Romantic belief in pantheism and the organic unity of the world (Murry), and an organicist aesthetic which saw poetry as an organic totality transcending reason and the possibility of paraphrase in prose (Murry, Read). Their literary analyses subordinated intention and biography to artistic concerns (Wilson Knight). Before the debates about authorial intention and the affective dimensions of literature arose in the New Criticism, the scholar E. M. Tillyard (1889–1962) engaged in a debate with C. S. Lewis in *The Personal Heresy* (1939). New Critical trends were also anticipated in America where W. C. Brownell attempted to establish literary criticism as a serious and independent activity, and where James Gibbons Huneker and H. L. Mencken insisted on addressing the aesthetic elements in art as divorced from moral considerations.

Hence, the critical movements of the early twentieth century were already moving in certain directions: the isolation of the aesthetic from moral, religious concerns, and indeed an exaltation of the aesthetic (as transcending reason and the paradigms of bourgeois thought such as utility and pragmatic value) as a last line of defense against a commercialized and dehumanizing world; and a correlative attempt to establish criticism as a serious and "scientific" activity. This broadly humanist trend is far from dead; it not only has persisted through figures such as F. R. Leavis but also has often structured the very forms of critical endeavors which reject it.

Most of the critical movements associated with "literary theory" – ranging from formalism and the New Criticism to poststructuralism – arose in the shadow of the calamitous historical events discussed earlier. It should be remembered that such historical developments bear a complex and often contradictory relation to literary practice and theory. For example, the Russian Revolution of 1917 eventually adopted an official aesthetic of "socialist realism," whereby literature was seen as politically interventional and as expressing class struggle. But the atmosphere of the revolution also spawned other aesthetics such as symbolism and formalism; the latter exerted a considerable influence on structuralism which usually bracketed the human "subject," whether the latter was conceived politically or otherwise. In other words, some movements retreated from political involvement into a preoccupation with form, and this retreat itself had political resonance.

World War I generated verse written by poets such as Wilfred Owen and Siegfried Sassoon who depicted their direct experience of its horrors and devastation. But the so-called "modernists" of this time, such as Pound, Eliot, Woolf, and Lawrence, re-ferred to the war only tangentially in their writings: it is arguable that their work registered the impact of the war on the profounder level of literary form rather than overt content (though such aesthetic distancing and mediation has been viewed also as evasive). T. S. Eliot's *The Waste Land* (1922) might be said to enact both the disintegration of Western culture and a search into previous mythology and tradition for forms of reintegration and spiritual regeneration. Virginia Woolf's *To the Lighthouse* (1927) registers the impact of the war in the sense of loss and destitution that pervades the last third of this novel. It is significant that much modernism draws upon an aesthetic of symbolism, which itself was a reaction against nineteenth-century scientism and materialism, and which sought a pure poetic language divested of any pretensions to express the real world. Twentieth-century modernism embodied an acute self-consciousness with regard to language and its limitations in expressing human experience. It was marked by a crisis of belief, by a questioning and exploring of the categories of subjectivity, objectivity, and time, as well as by a withdrawal into preoccupation with literary form, into the past, into tradition and myth.

The Bloomsbury Group, composed of a circle of writers and art critics centered around Virginia Woolf, fell under many of the influences that had shaped modernism, such as the notion of time advanced in the philosophy of Bergson. In its own way, this group also, under the influence of the philosopher G. E. Moore, exalted what it saw as an "aesthetic" approach to life. It was during this period that the foundations of the

New Criticism were laid by figures such as William Empson and I. A. Richards; the latter's *Principles of Literary Criticism* (1924) and *Practical Criticism* (1929) were widely and enduringly influential. Here, too, the literary artifact was treated as an autonomous and self-contained verbal structure, insulated from the world of prose, as in Richards' distinction between emotive and referential language. In France also, the somewhat positivistic earlier mode of criticism, the *explication de texte*, was opposed by influential figures such as Bergson, whose novel conceptions of time and memory, and whose view of art as uniquely transcending the mechanistic concepts of bourgeois society, profoundly influenced Proust and other modernists. Paul Valéry (1871–1945) formulated a criticism drawing on the earlier French symbolists, one which prioritized the aesthetic verbal structure over historical and contextual elements.

With the Great Depression of the 1930s and the rise of fascism, literature and criticism in both Europe and America took a turn away from formalism and humanism toward a more socially conscious mode, as in socialist and Marxist criticism, and in the work of many poets. The humanists were challenged by more liberal-minded critics such as Edmund Wilson, Allen Tate, and R. P. Blackmur, by philosophers such as George Santayana who pointed to their inconsistencies, as well as by the left-wing and Marxist critics discussed below. Other schools of criticism also rejected the New Humanism: the Chicago School, the New York intellectuals, and the New Critics reacted against the New Humanists' subordination of aesthetic value to moral criteria and their condemnation of modern and innovative literature.

During this decade of economic collapse, Marxism became a significant political force. Socially and politically conscious criticism had a long heritage in America, going back to figures such as Whitman, Howells, and Emerson and running through the work of writers such as John Macy, Van Wyck Brooks, and Vernon L. Parrington. Notable Marxist critics of the 1920s and 1930s included Floyd Dell, Max Eastman, V. F. Calverton, Philip Rahv, and Granville Hicks. Eastman and Dell edited the important radical journal the *Masses* and then the *Liberator* (1918–1924). Calverton interpreted the tradition of American literature in terms of Marxist categories such as class and economic infrastructure. This period saw the growth of a number of other radical journals as well as the voicing of revolutionary views by non-Marxist critics such as Kenneth Burke and Edmund Wilson. The latter's most influential work, *Axel's Castle* (1931), traced the development of modern symbolist literature, identifying in this broad movement a "revolution of the word," which might open up new possibilities of thought and literature. The tradition of socialist criticism in Britain went back to William Morris, who first applied Marxist perspectives on the theory of labor and alienation to artistic production. In 1884 the Fabian Society was formed with the aim of substituting for Marxist revolutionary action a Fabian policy of gradually introducing socialism through influencing government policy and disseminating pamphlets to raise awareness of economic and class inequalities. The dramatist and critic George Bernard Shaw (1856–1950) was a leader of this society and produced one of its first pamphlets, *A Manifesto* (1884). Shaw edited *Fabian Essays in Socialism* (1899) and advocated women's rights, economic equality, and the abolition of private property. George Orwell (1903–1950) in his later career saw himself as a political writer and a democratic socialist, who, however, became disillusioned with communism, as shown in his political satire *Animal Farm* (1945).

With the menace of fascism and the threat of war, several writers began to engage in Marxist criticism. In Germany, a critique of modern capitalist culture was formulated by the Frankfurt School, whose major figures included Theodor Adorno (1903–1969), Max Horkheimer (1895–1973), Herbert Marcuse (1898–1979), and Walter Benjamin (1892–1940). Some of these thinkers drew on Hegel, Marx, and Freud in attempting to revive the "negative dialectics" or negative, revolutionary potential of Hegelian Marxist thought. They sharply opposed the bourgeois positivism which had risen to predominance in reaction against Hegel's philosophy, and insisted, following Hegel, that consciousness in all of its cultural modes is active in creating the world. These thinkers had a large impact on the New Left and the radical movements of the 1960s.

In Britain, Marxist writers included the art historian Anthony Blunt and the economist John Strachey. A group of Marxist thinkers was centered around *The Left Review* (1934–1938). The poets W. H. Auden, Stephen Spender, and C. Day Lewis at various times espoused and propagated left-wing views. The most significant Marxist theorist of this generation was Christopher Caudwell (1907–1937), who died in Spain fighting in the International Brigade. Caudwell's best-known work is his *Illusion and Reality: A Study of the Sources of Poetry* (1937). Here, Caudwell offered a Marxist analysis of the development of English poetry, somewhat crudely correlating the stages of this development with economic phases such as primitive accumulation, the Industrial Revolution, and the decline of capitalism.

Liberal critics such as F. O. Matthiessen employed a historical approach to literature, but insisted on addressing its aesthetic dimensions. This formalist disposition became intensified in both the New Criticism and the Chicago School. The American New Critics such as John Crowe Ransom and Allen Tate aligned themselves with the values of the South, and, despite their insistence on isolating the literary artifact, were in this very gesture retreating into the aesthetic from what they saw as the vulgar commercialism of the North, viewing in literary form models of unity and a harmony between conflicting forces that was allegedly absent in the world. In this respect, the major English critic F. R. Leavis (1895–1978) stood on common ground with the New Critics: like them, he believed that literary criticism should be a serious and separate discipline. And, as expressed during his editorship of the journal *Scrutiny* from 1932 to 1953, he repeatedly insisted that literature should be approached *as* literature and not as a social, historical, or political document. Moreover, like the New Critics, Leavis attempted to foster an elite which might safeguard culture against the technological and populist vulgarities of an industrial society. What separated him from the New Critics, however, was his equally forceful counter-insistence – in the moralistic and humanistic tradition of Matthew Arnold – that literary study cannot be confined to isolated works of art nor to a realm of purely literary values. Leavis invoked Eliot's notion of tradition as representing "a new emphasis on the social nature of artistic achievement." This social nature, for Leavis, is grounded in what he calls an "inherent human nature." Hence, the study of literature is a study of "the complexities, potentialities and essential conditions of human nature." The apparent contradiction in Leavis' approach between viewing literature as literature and literature as inseparable from all aspects of life seems to be "resolved" by an appeal to the assimilating capacity of intuition and a maturing *experience* of literature, for which no conceptual or theoretical subtlety can substitute.

The Chicago School of critics, drawing on Aristotle, also propounded a formalist conception of criticism, and shared the New Critics' emphasis on the aesthetic and on the organic unity of a literary text. These critics included R. S. Crane, Richard McKeon, and Elder Olson. The New York intellectuals included Irving Howe, Lionel Trilling, and Susan Sontag. Drawing on the work of Edmund Wilson, these writers considered themselves aloof from bourgeois society, commercialism, Stalinism, and mass culture; they viewed themselves as liberals or democratic socialists and wrote criticism with a social and political emphasis. They promoted literary modernism, and valued complexity, irony, and cosmopolitanism in literature.

The conclusion of World War II formalized the opposition between the Western powers and the Soviet bloc of nations. While some literature participated in the ideological implications of this conflict, much writing retreated into a longer-term contextualization of the confrontation as futile and resting on debased values. This retreat from an "objective" reality reached a climax in philosophies such as phenomenology, which parenthesized the objective world, viewing it as a function of perception, and existentialism, which called into question all forms of authority and belief, as well as literary developments such as the Theater of the Absurd, whose proponents such as Samuel Beckett and Eugene Ionesco dramatized the existential absurdity, anguish, and ultimate isolation of human existence. The Italian thinker Benedetto Croce formulated an aesthetic which revived Hegelian idealist principles as against the tradition of bourgeois positivism and scientism. The German existentialist philosopher Martin Heidegger (1889–1976) increasingly saw poetry as transcending the discursive and rational limitations of philosophy. In France, the philosopher Gaston Bachelard (1884–1962) formulated a phenomenological and surrealist account of poetry, while the existentialist Jean-Paul Sartre (1905–1980) advocated a literature of political engagement. The phenomenological emphasis was further elaborated by Georges Poulet (1902–1991), Jean-Pierre Richard (b. 1922), and Georges Bataille (1897–1962), and given a linguistic orientation in the work of Maurice Blanchot (1907–2003).

It was in the 1950s that structuralism – another tendency which parenthesized or diminished the agency of the human subject by situating it within a broad linguistic and semiological structure – began to thrive through figures such as the anthropologist Claude Lévi-Strauss and the narratologist A. J. Greimas, who drew upon Saussure and the earlier Russian Formalism. Roland Barthes analyzed the new myths of Western culture and proposed a revolutionary oppositional discourse which was aware of its own mythical status. Barthes proclaimed the "death of the author," and his later works moved in poststructuralist directions. Notable among the formalist thinkers of this period were Roman Jakobson (1896–1982), Émile Benveniste, Tzvetan Todorov, and Gerard Genette.

It was, ironically, the period of relative economic prosperity after World War II that eventually gave impetus to the civil rights movements and the women's movement. The revolutionary fervor of the 1960s gave Marxist criticism a revived impetus. A group of Marxist critics was centered around the *New Left Review*, founded in 1960 and edited first by Stuart Hall and then by Perry Anderson. Its contributors included E. P. Thompson, Raymond Williams, and Terry Eagleton. This was also the period in which the radical journal *Tel Quel*, established in 1960 in France, fostered an intellectual milieu in which the writings of Derrida, the founder of deconstruction, Lacan, who reinterpreted Freudian concepts in linguistic terms, and several major feminist thinkers such as Julia Kristeva were fomented, eventually displacing the prominence of French existentialism. Drawing on the insights of Bachelard, Barthes, and others, *Tel Quel* moved from an initial aesthetic emphasis toward activism. Its general aim was to draw on literary texts and new critical approaches to redeem the revolutionary power of language. Significantly, many of the thinkers associated with the journal challenged the categories and binary oppositions which had acted as the foundation of much Western thought since Plato and Aristotle, oppositions which represented political and social hierarchies. Lacan's understanding of the unconscious as linguistic was seen by some as having revolutionary implications, though some feminists, notably Luce Irigaray and Hélène Cixous, indicted both Freud and Lacan's own discourse, which they saw as privileging the male and even misogynistic. Feminists such as Monique Wittig and Julia Kristeva reflected on the possibility of an *écriture féminine*.

In the next era, the political mood in both Europe and America swung to the right. The increasingly unchallenged predominance of capitalism in the 1980s and 1990s oversaw the emergence or intensified popularity of New Historicism, which called for the literary text to be situated not, as in Marxist criticism, within the context of an economic infrastructure, but within a superstructural fabric of political and cultural discourses, with the economic dimension itself given no priority and indeed treated as another superstructural discourse. One of the prime influences on New Historicism was Michel Foucault, who saw knowledge as a form of power and analyzed power as highly diffused and as not distinctly assignable to a given set of political or ideological agencies. Reader-response theory, whose roots went back to the reception theories of the German writers Hans Robert Jauss and Wolfgang Iser, engaged in a recognition of the dialogical nature of textual production, redefining the meaning of the text as the product of an interaction between text and an appropriately qualified community of readers.

These movements drew on the previous challenges to binary oppositions and on the "textual" nature of all phenomena, viewing even history and economics as interpretative narratives. Marxist critics in this era, notably Terry Eagleton and Fredric Jameson, have been obliged to define the connections and divergences between their own stances and the various other branches of criticism; they have drawn on the analyses of Althusser as well as Adorno, Horkheimer, and Benjamin in attempting to account for various phenomena of a mass consumer society and the spectrum of ideas falling under the labels of poststructuralism and postmodernism. Writers such as Gilles Deleuze and Félix Guattari and Jean Baudrillard have variously offered powerful analyses of capitalist society in terms of psychological categories and drives, as well as of the symbolic processes that structure consciousness, and the lack of foundations for arriving at intellectual or moral judgment. More recent thinkers such as Clement Rosset, Jacques Bouveresse, and Richard Rorty have turned away from the tenets of poststructuralism, such as its reductive view of reality as ultimately linguistic. Vincent Descombes has returned to the principles of early twentieth-century analytical philosophers such as Wittgenstein, and whereas many poststructuralists drew heavily on Hegelian notions, thinkers such as Jean-François Lyotard have turned instead to Kant. Lyotard has theorized influentially about the "postmodern condition," seeing it as marked by an absence of totalizing schemes of explanation, and the dissolution of human subjectivity.

Most of the literary-critical movements cited above saw themselves as "oppositional," as undermining and challenging the prevailing power structures and ideologies of late capitalism and, in some cases, of communism. In philosophy, this tradition of "heterological" thought can be traced back to Schopenhauer's critique of Enlightenment philosophy and of a totalizing Hegelian vision, a critique that has continued through Nietzsche, Freud, Bergson, Wittgenstein, Saussure, Heidegger, and Sartre to modern literary and cultural theory. This entire tradition has tended to view art and literature as a kind of bulwark against the crude consumerist values of an industrial society. It should be remembered, however, that these movements do not represent the mainstream impetus of liberal-humanist Western thought, which does derive from the Enlightenment and which continues through the utilitarianism of J. S. Mill, the pragmatism of John Dewey and Henry James, the positivism of Auguste Comte, Émile Durkheim, and Herbert Spencer, as well as through the new realism, analytic philosophy, and logical positivism of the early twentieth century, not to mention the modes of literary and cinematic realism which have persisted into our own day, alongside the postmodernist descendents of symbolism. Indeed, it could be argued that even the oppositional tendencies of modern literary theory are internally structured in their very form by the prevailing liberal-bourgeois notions descended from the Enlightenment. For example, the impulse to make literary criticism a scientific discipline – as in Northrop Frye, much structuralism, and New Criticism – is part of a widespread positivistic trend in bourgeois society: science achieved an exaltation whereby other disciplines, including psychology, sociology, philosophy, and literary criticism, sought to found themselves on scientific principles. The desire of New Criticism to treat not only literature but also the discipline of literary criticism as autonomous is part of a larger impetus toward specialization and separation of disciplines. Marxists have argued that deconstruction, notwithstanding its genuinely and profoundly radical gestures, effectively reproduces a liberal-humanist ethic of non-commitment. Hence, as feminists are well aware when they are obliged to utilize a language inherited from patriarchal theory, institutions, and practice, the oppositional nature of much twentieth-century criticism and theory is marked by a deeply structured complicity with prevailing power structures.

Notwithstanding their extraordinary richness and diversity, many of these modern critical tendencies tend to converge in one aspect, namely, their recognition of the importance of language in structuring our world. Derrida has expressed this exquisitely in his statement that our epoch "*must* finally determine as language the totality of its problematic horizon."[2] We can read this statement as an indication that language has been instituted at the heart of every philosophical problem or inquiry. For example, where neo-Hegelian philosophers in the later nineteenth century were exploring the connections between thought and reality, what is now investigated is the connection between thought, language, and reality: language is viewed as integral to both the process of thought and the construction of reality. Language has been similarly instituted within the connections between "man" and "woman," between social classes, between conflicting moral and political systems, between various ideological perspectives, between present and past, and between differing readings of "history." Since the beginning of the twentieth century (and even before this, in the work of Locke, Hume, Hegel, and others), there has been an increasing recognition that, for example, "man" and "woman" are not fixed categories but represent our ways of conceiving the world: gender is at least in part a social and historical construct that is embodied in the concepts expressed by language. "Woman," then, does not somehow designate a reality; it is, rather, a sign existing in complex and multifold interaction with other signs, as part of a system of perception. The increasing primacy attached to the role of language is effectively an acknowledgment not only of the constructed nature of all of the above terms, but also of the need to examine our own perceptual apparatus and the constitution of our own perspectives. In this, we are as much the heirs of Kant as we are of Saussure.

Hence, the twentieth century witnessed an unprecedented preoccupation with, and self-consciousness concerning, language, in a vast range of disciplines, as expressed in a wide range of ideological perspectives. This preoccupation and obsession is the most comprehensive manner in which literature, criticism, and theory have been molded by the economic and political transformations discussed earlier. The work of modernists such as Proust, Pound, Eliot, Faulkner, and Woolf was marked by an intense awareness, derived from the French symbolists, of the limitations of language and its inadequacy for expressing the highest truths and the most profound strata of experience. The work of Marx, Freud, Bergson, Nietzsche, and Wittgenstein was informed by an understanding of language as a system of concepts and signs whose referential value, whose capacity to refer to or represent the real world or the human self, is merely conventional and practical. Many of Saussure's insights into language had long been anticipated and were hardly new; what was new was perhaps the fact that Saussure based an entire theory of language on its relational and conventional nature, as a system of signs. Such a view of language was not only applied by anthropologists such as Lévi-Strauss to the analysis of cultures, but also acted as a model for his study of the language of myth.

Much modern theory was founded on this recognition of the internally constitutive role of language. Russian Formalism and New Criticism held that poetic language was unique and untranslatable into prose. The New Critics tended to view poetic language as non-referential, not somehow expressing or describing any real world but erecting a self-contained verbal structure which had emotive impact. Bakhtin, who combined insights of formalism and Marxism, regarded language as the site of ideological struggle. Structuralism examined literary texts and broader cultural phenomena as patterned after language, as a structure of sign systems. In other words, the very form of those phenomena was linguistic. The analysis of language has been central to the work of feminists, who have seen it as embodying male modes of thought and oppression, and as potentially transformable to express feminine experience. The psychoanalyst Jacques Lacan effectively rewrote much Freudian theory in linguistic terms, and held that the unconscious was linguistic in its structure and operation. For Jacques Derrida, the founder of deconstruction, there was no possible externality to language, nothing beyond the textual nature of all phenomena. For much reader-response theory, the language and meaning of a text were dialogic in their very nature, arising from an interaction of authorial and readerly registers. The New Historicism not only sees literature as one discourse among others, but also, following Foucault, Derrida, and others, views the social and historical context of literature as itself composed of a network of discourses, of ways of signifying and understanding the world.

If, as Derrida says, our era has instituted language at the foundation of its inquiries, it is evident that much of the literature, criticism, and theory of our era enacts a retreat from referentiality, recognizing "reality" as an intellectual and even ideological construct. But once again, we might remind ourselves that the perspectives of the academy, rich and astute as they are, do not always coincide with the mainstream traditions of thought or with popular practice. The tradition of liberal-humanist philosophy has often displayed an equal, if not quite as obsessive, concern with language. Following Descartes' insistence on employing only "clear and distinct" ideas, John Locke held that language should be made more precise, more denotative, and less figurative in order to achieve clarity of understanding. Comte, Durkheim, Spencer, and the entire positivistic tradition well into the twentieth century insisted on expunging what they saw as vague metaphysical terminology from the vocabulary of philosophy and science. Bertrand Russell and G. E. Moore also saw clarity of language as indispensable to the formulation and solution of philosophical problems. Hence, the main streams of liberal-humanist thought in both philosophy and literature have been more inclined toward various kinds of realism, insisting on clarity and accuracy of reference.

Many of the traditions of twentieth-century criticism and theory, in retreating from referentiality, might be said to perpetuate in their own ways the Romantic and late nineteenth-century reaction against bourgeois ideals and practice by exalting the category of the aesthetic, elevating the aesthetic itself into a vehicle of perception both higher than the mechanical plane of reason, and able to incorporate the sensuous and bodily aspects of human existence which were traditionally scorned by reason as institutionalized within philosophy and theology. Even the insistence of much modern theory on the artificiality of the distinction between the literal and the metaphorical, the philosophical and the aesthetic, and indeed on the metaphorical nature of all language (even that of science), might be seen as a return to a Romantic exaltation of the aesthetic to a mode of perception (rather than merely an object of study), a mode that is more comprehensive than reason, accommodating both intellectual and sensuous dimensions, both conscious and unconscious impulses, a particular disposition of subjectivity *through* which the world can be viewed and analyzed. The aesthetic, in this new elevation, is distinguished by an overarching self-consciousness whose irreducible medium is language. It is aware of itself as a historical and social product and of the world as its creation; language is integral to the creation of both. Alternatively, we might say that the aesthetic embodies a consciousness that the worlds of both subjectivity and objectivity are internally structured by language.

Nearly all of these critical movements see human subjectivity as a function of language, as a position within a network of signs which spreads ultimately across numerous registers – of culture, politics, aesthetics, ethnicity, class, and gender – in both time and space. Recent discourses, however, have reacted somewhat against this institution of language at the heart of our inquiries, returning to notions of social subjectivity, empirical analysis, and a resignation to the possibility of theorizing on the basis of exclusively localized concerns and interests, whether these be grounded in ethnicity, race, or region.

Notes

1   Eric Hobsbawm, *The Age of Extremes: A History of the World, 1914–1991* (New York: Pantheon, 1994), p. 6. Hereafter cited as *AE*.
2   Jacques Derrida, *Of Grammatology*, trans. Gayatri Chakravorty Spivak (Baltimore and London: Johns Hopkins University Press, 1974), p. 6.

CHAPTER 22

PSYCHOANALYTIC
CRITICISM

C ritics, rhetoricians, and philosophers since Aristotle have examined the psychological dimensions of literature, ranging from an author's motivation and
intentions to the effect of texts and performances on an audience. The application of psychoanalytic principles to the study of literature, however, is a relatively
recent phenomenon, initiated primarily by Freud and, in other directions, by Alfred
Adler and Carl Jung. The notion of the "unconscious" was not in itself new, and it can
be found in many thinkers prior to Freud, notably in some of the Romantics such as
Schlegel, in Schopenhauer, and in Nietzsche. Freud's fundamental contribution was to
open up the entire realm of the unconscious to systematic study, and to provide a language and terminology in which the operations of the unconscious could be expressed.

The positing of an unconscious as the ultimate source and explanation of human
thought and behavior represented a radical disruption of the main streams of Western
thought which, since Aristotle, had held that man was essentially a rational being,
capable of making free choices in the spheres of intellection and morality. To say that
the unconscious governs our behavior is to problematize all of the notions on which
philosophy, theology, and even literary criticism have conventionally rested: the ideal
of self-knowledge, the ability to know others, the capacity to make moral judgments,
the belief that we can act according to reason, that we can overcome our passions and
instincts, the ideas of moral and political agency, intentionality, and the notion – held
for centuries – that literary creation can be a rational process. In a sense, Freud postulated
that we bear a form of "otherness" within ourselves: we cannot claim fully to comprehend even ourselves, why we act as we do, why we make certain moral and political
decisions, why we harbor given religious dispositions and intellectual orientations.
Even when we think we are acting from a given motive, we may be deluding ourselves;
and much of our thought and action is not freely determined by us but driven by
unconscious forces which we can barely fathom. Moreover, far from being based on
reason, our thinking is intimately dependent upon the body, upon its instincts of
survival and aggression, as well as obstinate features that cannot be dismissed (as in the
Cartesian tradition where the mind is treated as a disembodied phenomenon) such as
its size, color, gender, and social situation. The fact that I am a black working-class

female will determine my world view just as much, and perhaps far more, than anything I consciously learn in the realm of ideas.

Clearly, this general problematization of conventional notions extends to literature: if the unconscious is a founding factor of our psyche, we can no longer talk unequivocally of an author's intention, or take for granted, as Aristotle did, that a drama structured according to certain rules will produce a precise effect upon its audience. We cannot assume that we are fully in control of what we say or that readers are fully in control of their responses. We cannot presume that our intended meanings will be conveyed, or that our conscious purposes represent our true aims. Neither can we presume that language is a transparent medium of communication, of either thought or emotion.

Freud was aware of the problematic nature of language itself, its opaqueness and materiality, its resistance to clarity and its refusal to be reduced to any one-dimensional "literal" meaning. His own writings contain many literary allusions, and some of his major concepts, such as the Oedipus complex, were founded on literary models such as *Oedipus Rex* and *Hamlet*. Freud's own literary analyses tend to apply his models of dream interpretation to literary texts, viewing the latter as expressions of wish fulfillment and gratifying projections of the ego of an author. Subsequent psychologists and literary critics, developing Freud's ideas, have extended the field of psychoanalytic criticism to encompass: analysis of the motives of an author, of readers and fictional characters, relating a text to features of the author's biography such as childhood memories, relationship to parents; the nature of the creative process; the psychology of reader's responses to literary texts; interpretation of symbols in a text, to unearth latent meanings; analysis of the connections between various authors in a literary tradition; examination of gender roles and stereotypes; and the functioning of language in the constitution of the conscious and unconscious. What underlies nearly all of these endeavors is the perception of a broad analogy, fostered by Freud himself, between the psychoanalytic process and the production of a narrative. In a sense, the psychoanalyst himself creates a fiction: triggered by a patient's neurosis and recollection of traumatic events, the psychoanalyst creates a coherent narrative about the patient within which the traumatic event can take its place and be understood.

After Freud, psychoanalytic criticism was continued by his biographer Ernest Jones (1879–1958), whose book *Hamlet and Oedipus* (1948) interpreted Hamlet's indecisive behavior in killing his uncle in terms of his ambivalent feelings toward his mother. Another of Freud's disciples, Otto Rank (1884–1939), produced *The Myth of the Birth of the Hero* (1909), which reaffirmed Freud's notions of the artist producing fantasies of wish fulfillment, and which compiled numerous myths on subjects such as incest, and on the notion of the hero. Ella Freeman Sharpe (1875–1947) treated language and metaphor from a psychoanalytic perspective. Marie Bonaparte (1882–1962) wrote a large study of Edgar Allan Poe, attributing much of his creative disposition to the loss of his mother when he was a child. Melanie Klein (1882–1960) modified Freudian theory of sexuality, rejecting the primacy of the Oedipus complex and elaborating a theory of the drive.

Another generation of literary critics – not necessarily Freudians – drew upon psychoanalysis in their interpretations of literary texts. These included I. A. Richards, William Empson, Lionel Trilling, Kenneth Burke, and Edmund Wilson, who in various ways searched texts for latent content. Harold Bloom's theory of literary influence as mediated through "anxiety" drew upon Freud's account of the Oedipus complex. Poets and critics such as Robert Graves and W. H. Auden (who wrote a poem in memory of Freud) also had recourse to Freudian concepts in their prose writings. Indeed, the influence of Freud's ideas was so pervasive that it can be seen in the very conception of character in many modern novelists, such as William Faulkner and James Joyce. Interestingly, D. H. Lawrence appears to have arrived independently at ideas very similar to Freud's, as for example in his novel *Sons and Lovers*, where Oedipal feelings figure powerfully.

The influence of psychoanalysis has extended into nearly all dimensions of modern literary theory. Simon O. Lesser (1909–1979) furnished a psychoanalytic account of the reading process. Influenced by Lesser, Norman Holland (b. 1927) used ego psychology and the notion of the literary text as fantasy to elaborate his version of reader-response criticism, studying the manner in which texts appeal to the repressed fantasies of readers. Feminist critics such as Juliet Mitchell have used Freud's ideas in their explanations of the operations of patriarchy; others, such as Kristeva, have modified his notions in undertaking their analyses of language and gender. Members of the Frankfurt School of Marxist thinkers, such as Herbert Marcuse, have enlisted Freudian concepts in their analyses of mass culture and ideology. Other significant theorists include Norman O. Brown (b. 1913), D. W. Winnicott, and Gilles Deleuze and Félix Guattari, who have explored the ideological bases of psychoanalysis; and Jacques Lacan, whose ideas will be examined later in this chapter. The following account of Freud's own literary analyses places them in the context of his theories as a whole.

Sigmund Freud (1856–1939)

Sigmund Freud was born in 1856 to Jewish parents in Moravia, a small town in what is now the Czech Republic.[1] His father was somewhat aloof and authoritarian while his mother was a warmer and more accessible figure. When Freud was 4 years old his family moved to Vienna where he received all of his education. Freud recounts how his engrossment in the Bible profoundly affected the direction of his interests. He was, however, also attracted to Darwin's theories, which had recently generated controversy, on account of their attempt to increase our understanding of the world. It was not until he heard a "beautiful essay on Nature" (misattributed, according to some, by Freud to Goethe) that he decided to become a medical student.

When Freud first began his medical studies at the University of Vienna in 1873 he found himself somewhat excluded from the academic community and looked down upon, on account of his Jewish origins. He saw this period, where he was forced into the role of outsider, as furnishing the foundation for his independence of thought. Eventually, however, in the physiological laboratory of Ernst Brucke he found congenial colleagues and an atmosphere of mutual respect. His acquaintance here with the physician Josef Breuer was to have an enormous impact on his thinking. He worked here from 1876 to 1882 and was drawn to only one branch of medicine, psychiatry. He took his medical degree in 1881.

Within a few years Freud had turned his attention to the study of nervous diseases. Initially influenced by Jean-Martin Charcot's investigations of hysteria, Freud developed the idea that neuroses might have a psychological rather than physiological origin. Freud settled in Vienna in 1886 as a specialist in nervous diseases, and in the same year married Martha Bernays, a girl from a high-ranking Jewish family who bore him six children, including Anna Freud, who was herself to become a psychoanalyst. In treating patients with nervous illnesses, Freud relied initially on electrotherapy and hypnosis. Freud seems to have had no shortage of work. He talks of the "crowds of neurotics" whose numbers multiplied as they moved frantically from one doctor to another. Intent on improving his hypnotic technique, he visited the school in Nancy, and it was here that he was struck by the "possibility that there could be powerful mental processes which nevertheless remained hidden from the consciousness of men" (*Freud*, 10).

In 1895 Freud and Breuer jointly published their findings as *Studies on Hysteria*, a text which stressed the emotional life of the patient, distinguished conscious and unconscious mental acts, and introduced the idea of "conversion," whereby a symptom was viewed as arising from the damming-up of an emotional affect or impulse (*Freud*, 13). Freud eventually arrived at a number of conclusions. Firstly, in considering the aetiology (the causes and origins) of neuroses, he reasoned that it was not just any kind of emotional excitement behind these but specifically excitement of a sexual nature. Thus, all neuroses, he claimed, derived from disturbances of the sexual function. Freud eventually abandoned hypnosis in favor of what he would call psychoanalysis, though he retained his practice of asking the patient to lie upon a sofa with the analyst seated unseen behind him. Freud's major theories concerning repression, sexuality, the interpretation of dreams, and instincts can now be outlined.

Repression and the Unconscious

Reasoning that everything forgotten by a patient must have been somehow distressing (alarming, painful, shameful), Freud concluded that this was precisely why it had been expunged from the conscious memory. Freud hypothesized that, in the neurotic, any powerful impulse or instinct which was embarrassing continued to operate in the realm of the unconscious where it retained its full "cathexis" or investment of energy. This instinct began to seek substitutive satisfaction by circuitous routes and would produce neurotic symptoms. This is the process that Freud called repression, which he regarded as a primary mechanism of defense whereby the ego was obliged to protect itself against any renewed threat of the repressed impulse by a permanent investment of energy. Freud saw repression as the foundation of our understanding of neuroses. His new conclusions changed the nature of the physician's task: he was no longer simply redirecting an impulse which had found an abnormal outlet, but rather attempting to uncover repressions and to replace them with conscious acts of judgment. From this time on, Freud called his investigative method not catharsis but psychoanalysis.

Infantile Sexuality

As if Freud had not sufficiently violated conventional thinking, his subsequent claims regarding infantile sexuality aroused even more hostility and indignation. As Freud was investigating the conflicts between subjects' sexual impulses and their resistance to sexuality, he was led further and further back into patients' lives into the period of childhood. It was in this period, he found, that the dispositions of subsequent nervous disorders were established. Freud's assertion that the sexual function began in childhood profoundly contradicted conventional beliefs and prejudices, expressed in theology, poetry, and popular opinion, about the "innocence" of childhood.

Again challenging conventional notions, Freud not only saw sexuality as operative from the beginning of a person's life, but also viewed normal adult sexual life as the result of a long and complicated development of the sexual function in an individual. At first this function is attached to other vital functions of the body and only later achieves independence from them and concentration in the reproductive function. The sexual function initially expresses itself in component instincts classified according to various erotogenic zones in the body. Hence at first the sexual function is auto-erotic, finding its objects of pleasure in the subject's own body. The first stage of organization is dominated by the oral components; there follows an anal-sadistic stage; and only then does sexuality concentrate its expression through the genitals as serving the end of reproduction. Freud used the term "libido" to designate the energy of the sexual instincts (*Freud*, 22).

The Oedipus Complex

The organization of the libido occurs side by side with an important element in mental life, the seeking after an object. After the first stage of auto-eroticism, the first love-object for both sexes is the mother, who is not yet perceived as distinct from the child's own body. As infancy progresses, sexual development undergoes the Oedipus complex: the boy focuses his sexual wishes upon his mother and develops hostile impulses toward his father. At this stage, Freud thought that girls underwent an analogous development but his views on this changed drastically. Again in the face of established beliefs, Freud saw the constitution of the human being as "innately bisexual." Only later was sexuality differentiated in terms of gender, children being initially unclear as to the differences between the sexes. Under the threat of castration, the male child represses its desire for the mother and accepts the rules laid down by the father. Freud saw as unique in human sexuality the fact that it was *diphasic*: the first climax, as described above, occurs in the fourth or fifth year of a child's life. This is followed by a long period of latency which lasts until puberty, which is the second climactic phase; during this interim period certain repressions have taken effect and reaction-formations impelled by morality, such as shame and disgust, are built up. The onset of puberty reanimates the sexual impulses and there occurs a conflict between the urges of the early years and the inhibitions of the period of latency.

Freud saw himself as having extended the concept of sexuality in two important ways. Firstly, sexuality was now divorced from its exclusive connection with the geni-tals and occupied a broader bodily function, having pleasure as its goal and only subsequently serving a reproductive function. Secondly, sexuality now encompassed all of the emotions of affection and friendliness traditionally subsumed under the word "love" (*Freud*, 23). These affectionate impulses were originally sexual in nature but became inhibited or sublimated; such diversion of the sexual instincts has produced, according to Freud, some of the most important cultural contributions. This extension of the realm of sexuality, Freud thought, would allow for a greater understanding, rather than merely dismissal or moral condemnation, of the sexuality of children and perverts, which had hitherto been neglected. Homosexuality, in particular, was hardly a perversion; rather, it could be traced back to the constitutional bisexuality of *all* human beings. Freud adds that psychoanalysis has no concern whatsoever with judgments of moral value.

As was seen earlier, Freud's initial analytic method for uncovering a patient's resistance relied on hypnosis; this gave way to a method of insistence and encouragement; this in turn gave place to another method, that of free association. Instead of directing the patient's thoughts, Freud would allow the patient to abandon himself to a process of free association, on the condition that the patient report literally everything that had occurred to him, no matter how irrelevant or meaningless it seemed. The advantages of free association were that the patient was subjected to the least compulsion, that no element related to the neurosis would be overlooked, and that the course of the analysis would be guided by the patient rather than the expectations of the analyst (*Freud*, 24–25). Nonetheless, the patient's resistance still finds a way to express itself: the repressed material itself will never occur directly to the patient but will be expressed allusively, in the form a substitutive association. Hence the analyst must master the art of interpretation, since he must infer the unconscious or repressed material from the patient's allusions or recognize its character from the associations the patient makes.

The most important feature of the technique of analysis, according to Freud, was the phenomenon of *transference*, which took the form of an intense emotional relationship between patient and analyst. The emotion could range between passionate love and embittered defiance and hatred. In the patient's mind, transference replaces the desire to be cured; if it comprises positive feelings for the analyst, the latter can use it to influence the patient. If it is negative, it becomes the main tool of the patient's resistance. What the analyst must do is make the patient conscious of the transference and convince him that in his transference attitude he is reexperiencing emotional relations originating in his earliest object attachments during the repressed period of his childhood. Thus transference is changed from a weapon of resistance to an instrument for the patient's cure. Analysis without transference, said Freud, was an impossibility. This phenomenon, however, he saw as universal and not merely created by analysis (*Freud*, 26).

The Interpretation of Dreams

Free association and skilled interpretation allowed psychoanalysis to make another breakthrough, in Freud's eyes, which contravened conventional scientific wisdom: to discover the meaning of dreams. Ancient cultures attached various kinds of significance to dreams, such as foretelling the future or expressing a means of communication between divine and human; modern science, however, regarded the reading of dreams as belonging to the realm of superstition. Yet psychoanalysis insisted that dreams could be scientifically interpreted. From the associations produced by the dreamer, the analyst could infer a thought structure, composed of *latent dream thoughts*. These were expressed not directly but only as translated and distorted into the *manifest* dream, which was composed largely of visual images. In his study *The Interpretation of Dreams*

(1900), Freud argued that among the latent dream thoughts, one in particular stands out from the others (which are residues of waking life) and governs the construction of the dream, using the day's residues as its material. This prominent, isolated thought is a wishful impulse and the dream represents the satisfaction of this impulse. During sleep, Freud argued, the ego is focused on withdrawing energy from all the interests of life, and relaxes its expenditure of energy upon repression. The unconscious impulse uses this opportunity to make its way into consciousness via the dream. But the ego maintains some of its repressive resistance as a kind of censorship of the dream: the latent dream thoughts are obliged to undergo alteration, a process Freud called *dream distortion*, so that the forbidden meaning of the dream is unrecognizable. Hence Freud defined a dream as the disguised fulfillment of a repressed wish (*Freud*, 28). The *dream-work*, or process by which the latent thoughts are converted into the manifest or explicit content of the dream, occurs through a number of functions: *condensation* of the component parts of the preconscious material of the dream; *displacement* of the psychical emphasis of the dream; and *dramatization* of the entire dream by translation into visual images. While a dream expresses fulfillment of a repressed wish, it can also continue the preconscious activity of the previous waking day, expressing an intention, a warning, or a reflection. Psychoanalysis can exploit this dual feature of the dream to obtain knowledge of the patient's conscious and unconscious processes.

The Theory of the Instincts

Freud's continuing observations led him to believe that the Oedipus complex was the nucleus of the neuroses. It was both the climax of infantile sexual life and the foundation for all of the later developments of sexuality. This in turn brought Freud to believe that neurotics failed to overcome difficulties that were resolved by normal people. In other words, psychoanalysis expressed the psychology of the normal human mind. Before the Oedipal phase in which the libido is attached to images of the parents, there is a period of *narcissism* or self-love in which the subject's libido has his own ego for an object. This state, Freud surmised, never completely ceases, and for all of his life his libido moves back and forth from the self to objects in the world. In other words, narcissistic libido is continually being transformed into object-libido and vice versa, as well exemplified in the state of being in love, where the subject can range between self-sacrifice and self-indulgence. These considerations led Freud to reformulate the mechanism of repression. The main agency of repression, urged Freud, was the instincts of self-preservation, or the "ego-instincts." It is precisely these instincts which constitute the narcissistic libido. In the process of repression, narcissistic libido is opposed to the object-libido; the self-preservative instincts defend themselves against the demands of object-love (*Freud*, 36).

In some of his later works, such as *Beyond the Pleasure Principle* (1920), *Group Psychology and the Analysis of the Ego* (1921), and *The Ego and the Id* (1923), Freud considered a new account of the operation of the instincts. He used the word *eros* (Greek for "love") to designate the instincts of self-preservation as pertaining to both the individual and the species. He opposed this instinct to another instinct of death or destruction, which he called *thanatos* (Greek for "death"). He viewed these two forces as engaged in a constant struggle, which is the broader context of our mental experience.

Psychoanalysis as an Institution

Freud recounts that after his separation from Breuer, there was an "official anathema" against psychoanalysis. For over ten years he had no followers and was shunned. His *Interpretation of Dreams* was largely ignored. The result of this ostracization was to bring members of the psychoanalytic movement into a cohesive body. A small group of disciples joined Freud in Vienna, and psychiatrists in Switzerland such as E. Bleuler and Carl Jung began to take an active interest in psychoanalysis. Freud was given a different reception in America, where he was invited to give his *Five Lectures on Psycho-Analysis* (1910) by the psychologist G. Stanley Hall. Psychoanalysis had also obtained a following among the public in America.

During 1911–1913 two movements broke away from psychoanalysis, led respectively by Alfred Adler and Carl Jung. Jung, attempting to circumvent the issues of infantile sexuality and the Oedipus complex, attempted to give to the findings of psychoanalysis an impersonal and non-historical interpretation. Adler went even further in repudiating the importance of sexuality, tracing neurosis and character development to men's desire for power. Significantly, Freud refers to these two figures as "heretics," while he uses the word "loyal" to describe the individuals, such as Otto Rank, Ernest Jones, and Hanns Sachs, who continued to collaborate with him (*Freud*, 33).

Freud and Culture

Around 1907 Freud's interests in the implications of psychoanalysis began to extend over the entire domain of culture. He sought to apply psychoanalytic principles to the study of art, religion, and primitive cultures. In his studies of religion, Freud viewed obsessional neurosis as a distorted private religion and religion itself as a universal obsessional neurosis. In studies such as *Totem and Taboo* (1912–1913) Freud explored taboos or prohibitions in primitive cultures, and analogized the various postulates of primitive beliefs with neurosis. In works such as *Civilization and its Discontents* (1930) Freud suggested the extension of the analysis of neurosis in individuals to the examination of the imaginative and cultural creations of social groups and peoples. Some of Freud's disciples, such as Ernest Jones and Otto Rank, followed through the implications of psychoanalytic theory in the realms of literary analysis, mythology, and symbolism. All in all, Freud hoped that psychoanalysis, while yet underdeveloped, might offer valuable contributions in the most varied regions of knowledge.

Freud's Literary Analyses

Even in his earlier work, Freud had appealed to literary texts – notably *Oedipus Rex* and *Hamlet* – not only to exemplify and illuminate, but even to ground some of his theoretical notions. He saw Sophocles' play *Oedipus Rex* as expressing a "universal law of mental life," and interpreted fate in that play as the materialization of an "internal necessity." He also saw the Oedipus complex as governing the tragedy of *Hamlet*, though he later altered his views on this play. As for poetic and artistic creation in general, Freud wrote a paper, "Creative Writers and Day-Dreaming" (1907), which viewed works of art as the imaginary satisfactions of unconscious wishes, just as dreams were. What the psychoanalyst can do is to piece together the various elements of an artist's life and his works, and to construct from these the artist's mental constitution and his instinctual impulses. Freud conducted such an analysis of Leonardo da Vinci's picture of *The Madonna and Child with St. Anne* (1910). His lengthy examination of Leonardo da Vinci's character generated a prototype for psychoanalytic biography. He wrote a psychoanalytic account of the novella *Gradiva* by the German author Wilhelm Jensen, as well as psychological readings of other works. In 1914 he published (anonymously) an acute reading of the "meaning" of Michelangelo's statue of Moses in Rome. Notwithstanding his own readings of literary and artistic texts, Freud never claimed that psychoanalysis could adequately explain the process of artistic creation. In his paper "Dostoevsky and Parricide" (1928), he stated: "Before the problem of the creative artist analysis must, alas, lay down its arms."[2]

We can obtain a sense of Freud's psychoanalytic "literary-critical" procedure by looking at his paper "Creative Writers and Day-Dreaming." This was initially delivered as a lecture before an audience of laymen, which perhaps accounts for some of its views on literature. Freud admits at the outset that the creative writer is a "strange being" who himself cannot explain his power to arouse new and intense emotions in us. He suggests that, in seeking an explanation, we might think of an analogy between creative activity and some activity of "normal" people (*Freud*, 436). He suggests that the "first traces of imaginative activity" can be discerned in childhood: "every child at play behaves like a creative writer, in that he creates a world of his own, or, rather, re-arranges the things of this world in a new way which pleases him." The child takes this "play" very seriously, investing (or "cathecting") it with much emotion. Yet the opposite of "play," says Freud, is "not what is serious but what is real." In fact, the child distinguishes his world of play "quite well from reality; and he likes to link his imagined objects and situations to the tangible and visible things of the real world." This ability to link the two worlds differentiates the child's playing from phantasying (*Freud*, 437).

As people grow up, says Freud, they cease to play, but they do not give up the pleasure they once derived from playing. As always in mental life, "we can never give anything up; we only exchange one thing for another. What appears to be a renunciation is really the substitute or surrogate" (*Freud*, 438). What the growing child does instead of playing is to phantasize, indulging in day dreams. There is one difference, however: whereas the child takes no pains to hide his play, the adult is "ashamed of his phantasies and hides them from other people. He cherishes his phantasies as his most intimate possessions" (*Freud*, 438). The difference in behavior between those who play and those who phantasize, says Freud, can be attributed to a difference in motives: the child's play is motivated by a wish, the wish to imitate adults. The adult's phantasies are also motivated by a wish, but in many cases this is of a nature that he would prefer to conceal.

How, then, do we have any knowledge of phantasies, if people are so reluctant to reveal them? Freud remarks that there is one class of people upon whom falls the task of "telling what they suffer and what things give them happiness." These are "victims of nervous illness, who are obliged to tell their phantasies . . . to the doctor by whom they expect to be cured" (*Freud*, 438). Taking a characteristic leap, Freud stretches this insight to claim that such neurotics "tell us nothing that we might not also hear from healthy people" (*Freud*, 439). He proceeds to enumerate some of the characteristics of phantasying. To begin with, he claims, "a happy person never phantasies, only an unsatisfied one [*sic*]"; and the motive forces of phantasies are "unsatisfied wishes, and every single phantasy is the fulfilment of a wish, a correction of unsatisfying reality" (*Freud*, 439).

Freud divides the motivating wishes that give rise to phantasy into two main types: they are either erotic wishes or ambitious wishes. In "young women," says Freud, "the erotic wishes predominate almost exclusively, for their ambition is as a rule absorbed by erotic trends. In young men egoistic and ambitious wishes come to the fore clearly enough alongside of erotic ones" (*Freud*, 439). The predictable sexism of Freud's account here, as elsewhere in his work, indicates inevitably that his model of the mind, far from being somehow universal, is grounded indissolubly in his own social era. Freud does temper his own position in this case by suggesting that the two kinds of wishes "are often united." In either case, however, there are sound motives for concealment of these wishes and their resultant phantasies: young women are typically "only allowed a minimum of erotic desire," while the young man must suppress his excessive self-regard, so that he can adjust to a society "full of other individuals making equally strong demands" (*Freud*, 439).

The content and form of a phantasy, explains Freud, are unique to a given individual. A phantasy is intimately related to the three dimensions of time: it is linked, firstly, to "some provoking occasion in the present" which arouses one of the major wishes of a person; this triggers the memory of an earlier experience, usually in childhood, in which this wish was fulfilled; the mind then imagines a situation in the future where the wish is fulfilled. What is thus created, says Freud, is a daydream or phantasy, which carries in it traces of the present, past, and future: "Thus past, present and future are strung together . . . on the thread of the wish that runs through them" (*Freud*, 439). In phantasy, the dreamer regains "what he possessed in his happy childhood." However, if phantasies become "over-luxuriant and over-powerful," they can express the onset of neurosis or psychosis. Freud reminds us that our dreams at night are nothing more than phantasies expressing, in distorted form, wishes that our own minds have repressed (*Freud*, 440).

Freud proceeds to analyze creative writing in terms of the foregoing concepts: the creative writer also engages in a kind of play: "He creates a world of phantasy which he takes very seriously – that is, which he invests with large amounts of emotion – while separating it sharply from reality" (*Freud*, 437). (Someone cynical of Freud's account might observe the neat circularity of his argument: the child's play is analogous to creative writing; therefore, we can begin to understand creative writing if we recognize that this too is a form of play.) Freud divides creative writers into two broad groups: those who, "like the ancient authors of epics and tragedies, take over their material ready-made," and those who "seem to originate their own material" (*Freud*, 440). Oddly, Freud states that he will choose for analysis "not the writers most highly esteemed by the critics, but the less pretentious authors of novels, romances and short stories," who have the "widest and most eager circle of readers of both sexes" (*Freud*, 440). Behind this preference may lie the fact that Freud's immediate audience consists of laymen, and also a desire to examine creative writing as a phenomenon in popular culture rather than a professional or academic elite. It is clear, also, that Freud often offended the academic establishment; he sometimes observed that the popular reception of his works was more telling than its assessments by experts. Whatever the reason behind Freud's focus on popular fiction, it is surely questionable whether his claims can be unproblematically extended to higher forms of literature.

Nonetheless, within the terms of his own inquiry, Freud does open up certain pathways of literary-critical analysis. He observes that popular stories typically have "a hero who is the centre of interest," a hero whom the writer appears to "place under the protection of a special Providence." No matter what dangers and adventures he undergoes, he is invulnerable: knowing that he will eventually survive allows the reader to follow his journey with a feeling of security, which Freud describes as "the true heroic feeling." Through "this revealing characteristic of invulnerability," says Freud, "we can immediately recognize His Majesty the Ego, the hero alike of every day-dream and of every story" (*Freud*, 441). Freud's point here is that the fiction is not a "portrayal of reality" but has all the constituents of a phantasy or daydream: the hero is invulnerable, women invariably fall in love with him, and the other characters in the story are "sharply divided into good and bad" in a manner that contravenes the more subtle variations found in real life (*Freud*, 441). Hence the story expresses a phantasy on the part of the creative writer, who can indulge in this parading and projection of his ego.

We might readily agree that such features characterize a romance novel intended for popular consumption, and written according to an explicit formula. But how can such features belong to great literature, which surely is somehow original and exceeds such formulaic constraints? Freud acknowledges that many "imaginative writings are far removed from the model of the naive day-dream." But he suspects that "even the most extreme deviations from that model could be linked with it through an uninterrupted series of transitional cases" (*Freud*, 441). Freud offers the example of "psychological" novels, in which the author inhabits the mind of the hero and views the other characters from the outside; such novels denote the tendency of "the modern writer to split up his ego, by self-observation, into many part-egos, and, in consequence, to personify the conflicting currents of his own mental life in several heroes." In other words, even where the author does not exert a godlike authorial omnipotence that can delve into the mentality of every character, even in cases of "limited" omniscience, the author's phantasies are nonetheless being played out.

Freud acknowledges that certain other kinds of novels, such as the naturalistic novels of Émile Zola, seem to "stand in quite special contrast to the type of the day-dream." Here, he concedes, the hero plays only a small active role and "sees the actions and sufferings of other people pass before him like a spectator" (*Freud*, 441). How can such novels accord with the model of the daydream? Freud's answer (again characteristic) is to say that *some* daydreams are precisely like naturalistic novels: in these dreams "the ego contents itself with the role of spectator" (*Freud*, 442). A cynical observer might remark that it would be difficult for a novel *not* to conform with Freud's model, since that model itself can be modified to accord with the nature of the novel in question.

Freud's inquiry moves to the connection between the life of a writer and his works. He applies to the creative artist his earlier formula for phantasies: "A strong experience in the present awakens in the creative writer a memory of an earlier experience (usually belonging to his childhood) from which there now proceeds a wish which finds its fulfilment in the creative work." Freud points out that his emphasis on a writer's childhood memories derives from his assumption that a creative work is "a continuation of, and a substitute for, what was once the play of childhood" (*Freud*, 442). It might be remarked that while Freud's notion of "play" is not quite the same as the concept of "play" or "free play" in the work of Barthes, Lacan, Derrida, Kristeva, and others, there are perhaps continuities between all of these uses, which might usefully be pursued. For example, Freud's understanding of play implies a self-created world of language, a language that reconfigures the conventional idioms that are held to express reality; it also lays stress on the writer's highly subjective entry into the system of language, an entry marked by psychological make-up as well as by social and political circumstances; it implies, like much of Bakhtin's thought, that language is appropriated by the artist for her own ends; it implies a kind of "return" to a Lacanian imaginary realm of infantile security and satisfying wholeness, a realm where everything is ordered just as we might *wish* it; and that, whatever the author's explicit aims or intentions, there is an underlying subtext, working unconsciously, whose motivations may be different. The kind of psychoanalytic literary criticism enabled by Freud's account here would be one that analyzed both the form and content of art in relation to the author's psychology and biography. For example, despite T. S. Eliot's disclaiming insistence on writing "impersonal" poetry, his poem "The Love Song of J. Alfred Prufrock" might be analyzed in terms of the history of Eliot's own attitudes toward women and the derivation of these attitudes from his childhood relationship with his mother and father, as well as from figures such as Baudelaire and Laforgue who sustained tortuous relationships with the "feminine."

As for the other main category of imaginative works, such as epics, which entail a "re-fashioning of ready-made and familiar material," Freud acknowledges that the writer has some independence in her choice and presentation of material. The material itself, however, is derived from "the popular treasure-house of myths, legends and fairy tales." Freud surmises that further investigation into folk-psychology might reveal myths to be "distorted vestiges of the wishful phantasies of whole nations, the *secular dreams* of youthful humanity" (*Freud*, 442). Unfortunately, Freud himself does not pursue this fascinating hypothesis; it is clear that certain myths become associated with the identity of particular nations or cultures. A striking example might be the Germany of the Third Reich, or the self-conception of "Britishness" as articulated by Thomas Babington Macaulay and other "cultural ambassadors" during the nineteenth and early twentieth centuries.

Freud ends his paper by confronting the question: how does a creative work afford us pleasure? It is not usually pleasurable, he argues, to listen to the self-aggrandizing phantasies of others. Why, then, do we enjoy the narratives of creative artists? Freud suggests that the writer "softens the character of his egoistic day-dreams by altering and disguising it," perhaps in the same way that our own minds disguise the content of our dreams during sleep (*Freud*, 443). A second method is the writer's providing us with aesthetic pleasure through purely formal techniques. Freud refers to such pleasure as "fore-pleasure": our enjoyment of an imaginative work issues from "a liberation of tension in our minds," perhaps because the writer enables us to "enjoy our own day-dreams without self-reproach or shame" (*Freud*, 443).

One of the interesting features of Freud's account is that it (typically) ignores the entire history of its subject, in this case, aesthetics and literary criticism, almost blundering onto the scene with its radically new insights, infusing yet another perspective, drawn from psychoanalysis, into the repertoire of literary criticism. In this brief paper, Freud opens up a number of literary-critical avenues: the linking of a creative work to an in-depth study of an author's psychology, using a vastly altered conception of human subjectivity; the tracing in art of primal psychological tendencies and conflicts; and the understanding of art and literature as integrally related to more general patterns of human activity.

It is not difficult to be skeptical of Freud's trains of reasoning, riddled as these are with leaps of imagination, logical inconsistencies, contradictions, and the molding of the available matter to the desired form of his interpretation. Yet his procedure in this paper demonstrates that the context of literary interpretation can be deepened into dimensions of individual and collective human subjectivity little explored hitherto. Beyond the immediately discernible themes and issues raised by a literary text, beyond its formal attributes, beyond its apparent entry into certain literary traditions, a text can be approached in terms of its probings of deeper, unconscious, impulses that lie hidden in recurring human obsessions, fears, and anxieties. Such paths will be further explored by Carl Jung, Northrop Frye, Lacan, and others.

Freud on History and Civilization

In later works such as *Civilization and its Discontents* Freud did indeed deal with social and religious phenomena as expressed in collective, as well as individual, psychology. He situates the human psyche within the fabric of social institutions: what we call civilization is to some extent the cumulative product of our psychology, its intrinsic character, and the ways in which it reacts upon its environments; civilization is also in some ways analogous with the human psyche, exhibiting a collective psychology that develops according to similar rules. It is in this text that Freud situates the production and enjoyment of creative art and other forms of sublimation within the contexts of broader questions such as the purpose of human life, the pursuit of happiness, and the functions of culture and religion.

Freud initially raises the question: what is the purpose of human life? This indeed is the fundamental question that religion tries to answer, and the very idea of purpose, says Freud, stands or falls with religion (*Freud*, 729). In contrast with religious accounts, Freud argues that the basic purpose of human life, as revealed by the actual behavior of people, is the pursuit of happiness. He defines "happiness" narrowly, as correlative with the gratification of our desires according to the "pleasure principle," which has both positive and negative aspects: the experience of intense pleasures, and the elimination or avoidance of pain and discomfort (*Freud*, 729). There are in fact three sources of suffering: our own bodies, the external world, and our relationships with others. The inevitability of suffering increasingly moderates our demands for happiness in accordance with the "reality principle": we transfer, defer, and deflect our instinctual aims into directions that cannot be so easily frustrated by the external world. Our alternative pleasures, then, are more tempered and diffused, as expressed in the realms of art, science, and religion (*Freud*, 731). An artist's joy in creating exemplifies this kind of satisfaction; yet it is marked by at least two weaknesses: it is accessible to only a few people, and such "substitutive satisfactions, as offered by art, are illusions in contrast with reality" (*Freud*, 728, 731). The region from which these illusions arise, says Freud, is "the life of the imagination; at the time when the development of the sense of reality took place, this region was expressly exempted from the demands of reality-testing and was set apart for the purpose of fulfilling wishes which were difficult to carry out. At the head of these satisfactions through phantasy stands the enjoyment of works of art" (*Freud*, 732). Here, as in his earlier essay about creative writers, Freud sees the entire realm of art as arising from a psychical constitution on the part of human beings that allows them a channel of escape or release from the harsh demands of reality; in this view, art is of the same order as phantasy, issuing from the demands of wish fulfillment, and by its very nature opposed to reality. Freud's brief comments on beauty are in the same vein: when we adopt an "aesthetic attitude to the goal of life," we seek happiness predominantly in the enjoyment of beauty, even though beauty "has no obvious uses" and even though there is no "clear cultural necessity" for it. Beauty, like art, can offer no protection against suffering. Nonetheless, the enjoyment of beauty, entailing a "mildly intoxicating quality of feeling . . . can compensate for a great deal" and "civilization could not do without it" (*Freud*, 733).

Freud's argument concerning art is fundamental: the human psyche, frustrated in its attempts to mold the world in a self-comforting image, resorts to art to create its world in phantasy. Art – in a broad sense that includes science, philosophy, and religion – is the highest form of such an impulse, and is the embodiment of civilization itself, whose foundations are erected on the graveyard of repressed instincts. Indeed, Freud views religion as one of the schemes of human thought that regard "reality as the sole enemy," and encourage a turning away from the world, as is embodied in the delusive behavior of hermits or madmen. The "religions of mankind," exclaims Freud, "must be classed among the mass-delusions of this kind" (*Freud*, 732). By arresting people in a state of "psychical infantilism . . . religion succeeds in sparing many people an individual neurosis. But hardly anything more" (*Freud*, 734–735).

Freud notes that one of the sources of our suffering – our relations with other people, on the levels of family, community, and state – is self-created (*Freud*, 735). It is apparently the function of culture to regulate such relations. Yet why, Freud asks, does such regulation fail to procure happiness? He cites two causes, the one being our own mental constitution: we can experience happiness only as a contrast with suffering, and it is by nature transitory (*Freud*, 729). The second factor is that culture regulates social relations precisely by restricting our possibilities of instinctual gratification, in two broad spheres: sexuality and aggression. Sexual life must be restricted in the interests of binding together the members of a community by libidinal ties, as well as by the bonds of common work and common interests (*Freud*, 747). Freud speaks of the kind of love that is used for this purpose as "aim-inhibited love": such love was originally sensual but is now modified so that it no longer attaches to a specific object (person) but to all people equally, creating new bonds (*Freud*, 744–745). Sexuality is also restricted in other ways in Western civilization, where object-choice is narrowed to allow only the opposite sex and where there is basically one standard of sexual life for all. Such constraints, says Freud, ignore the actual sexual constitution of individuals, which was originally bisexual. The only non-censured sexual outlet is heterosexual genital love, constrained even further by the stipulations of legitimacy and monogamy (*Freud*, 746). Interestingly, Freud makes an analogy similar to that made in Plato's *Republic* between the constitution of a state or civilization and the constitution of the human psyche. Civilization, says Freud, "behaves toward sexuality as a people or a stratum of its population does which has subjected another one to its exploitation. Fear of a revolt by the suppressed elements drives it to stricter precautionary measures" (*Freud*, 746). Freud acknowledges, however, that in practice civilization has been obliged to "pass over in silence" many sexual transgressions (*Freud*, 746). Acknowledging this line of thought, Foucault was later to propound a theory whereby sexual repression occurred through more subtle means of categorization and control.

Our other primal urge, toward aggression, must be restricted because it threatens to disintegrate society. It is well known that thinkers such as Thomas Hobbes had a dismal view of human beings in a state of "nature," as being embroiled in a "war of all against all." In a sense, Freud's view of human nature is even more dismal since it sees a cruel aggressiveness as an intrinsic instinctual disposition, regardless of external threats. Humans see in their neighbor "not only a potential helper or sexual object, but also someone who tempts them to satisfy their aggressiveness on him, to exploit his capacity for work without compensation, to use him sexually without his consent, to seize his possessions, to humiliate him, to cause him pain, to torture and to kill him" (*Freud*, 749). Needless to say, Freud rejects the view advanced by "the communists" that "man is wholly good" and that abolition of private property would remove ill-will and hostility among men. Private property, says Freud, is only one of the instruments of aggression; aggressiveness "was not created by property . . . it already shows itself in the nursery . . . it forms the basis of every relationship of affection and love among people (with the single exception, perhaps, of the mother's relation to her male child)" (*Freud*, 750–751). Having said all this, Freud expresses some good will toward the struggle against "the inequality of wealth among men and all that it leads to" (*Freud*, 751n.). He also acknowledges the potential value of "a real change in the relations of human beings to possessions" (*Freud*, 770).

This "primary mutual hostility of human beings" threatens civilization with disintegration. Civilization must use its utmost efforts to deflect these aggressive instincts into "identifications and aim-inhibited relationships of love" (*Freud*, 750). Civilization checks aggression by fostering its internalization into the superego. The resulting tension between the superego and the ego is characterized by Freud as the sense of guilt. We can see, then, that this sense of guilt answers to two factors: the dread of authority, and dread of the superego. The first of these compels us to renounce instinctual gratification, and the second urges the need for punishment, both factors generating unhappiness (*Freud*, 759). The place of the father or of both parents, says Freud, is taken by the larger human community. The sense of guilt that began in relation to the father ends as a relation to the community (*Freud*, 756–757). Even whole peoples, remarks Freud, have behaved in this way, bowing to a higher power or Fate which is "regarded as a substitute for the parental agency" (*Freud*, 758).

Hence the price of progress in civilization is the forfeiting of happiness through an increase in the sense of guilt. This sense of guilt, says Freud, is "the most important problem in the development of civilization" (*Freud*, 763). In fact, when the external demands of the community or higher power are internalized within the superego, we have effectively exchanged a "threatened external unhappiness . . . for a permanent internal unhappiness, for the tension of the sense of guilt" (*Freud*, 759). On a broader, "phylogenetic" level, Freud traces man's sense of guilt ultimately to the Oedipus complex, arguing that it was established at the killing of the primitive father by the band of brothers who challenged his harsh authority: this sense of guilt, acquired on actually having committed a crime, Freud calls *remorse*, which resulted from the sons' ambivalent feelings of love and hatred toward their father. After their act of aggression had satisfied their hatred, their love "set up the super-ego by identification with the father; it gave that agency the father's power . . . as a punishment for the deed of aggression" (*Freud*, 762). This scenario, says Freud, makes clear "the part played by love in the origin of conscience and the fatal inevitability of the sense of guilt" (*Freud*, 762–763). Freud also characterizes this conflict by viewing sexuality as the representative of the life instinct *eros* and aggression as the representative of the death instinct *thanatos*. He states that aggressiveness "is an original, self-subsisting instinctual disposition in man," which "constitutes the greatest impediment to civilization . . . civilization is a process in the service of Eros, whose purpose is to combine single human individuals, and after that families, then races, peoples and nations, into one great unity, the unity of mankind." Since civilization develops by restricting sexuality and aggression, the evolution of culture is a struggle between *eros* and *thanatos* (*Freud*, 755–756). The sense of guilt, he says, arises from precisely this primordial ambivalence, and is the expression of this "eternal struggle" (*Freud*, 763).

This struggle between the two primal urges, in fact, characterizes not only the development of human civilization but also that of the individual. Freud insists on the analogy: the same process is being "applied to different kinds of object" (*Freud*, 767). There is, however, one important distinction: in the development of the individual, "the programme of the pleasure principle, which consists in finding the satisfaction of happiness, is retained as the main aim . . . But in the process of civilization things are different. Here by far the most important thing is the aim of creating a unity out of the individual human beings . . . the aim of happiness is still there, but it is pushed into the background" (*Freud*, 768). Freud extends further the analogy between individual and social development: the community itself "evolves a super-ego under whose influence cultural development proceeds" (*Freud*, 769). Freud attributes the origins of communal superegos to the influence of great personalities such as Jesus; what is interesting is his acknowledgment that the demands of an individual's superego will "coincide with the precepts of the prevailing cultural super-ego" (*Freud*, 769). This is an implicit acknowledgment that the content of the superego is not somehow patterned on some primal or timeless myth but that it is profoundly and locally rooted in an individual's ethical environment. Freud even states that entire communities and civilizations might be regarded as "neurotic": the difficulty of diagnosing such "communal neuroses" would be that, if all members of a group were afflicted with the neurosis, the standards of normality would be difficult to define. Nonetheless, Freud ventures the hope that the "pathology of cultural communities" will someday be studied. Like Schopenhauer and Nietzsche, Freud has no illusions about where our ideas ultimately derive from: "man's judgments of value follow directly his wishes for happiness – that, accordingly, they are an attempt to support his illusions with arguments" (*Freud*, 771). Once again, Freud stands opposed to Enlightenment notions of man's rational potential: his very capacity to "reason" is premolded to conform to his deepest-rooted instinctual demands.

But what exactly is "civilization" according to Freud? He sees it as characterized by a number of traits: the exploitation and protection of nature's resources; a facility for order and cleanliness; and the reverence of practically useless things such as beauty (*Freud*, 737–739). What most seems to epitomize civilization, in Freud's eyes, is its esteeming of ideas and higher mental activities, as expressed in religious and philosophical systems, as well as in human ideals for the individual, society, and humanity (*Freud*, 739–740). A final and essential element of civilization, insists Freud, is the regulation of social regulations. He states that the decisive step toward civilization was the substitution of the power of a united number of men for the power of a single man. The essence of this substitution was the restriction of possibilities of gratification by the members of a community, whereas the individual recognized no such restrictions. The final outcome, says Freud, "should be a rule of law to which all . . . have contributed by a sacrifice of their instincts" (*Freud*, 740–741). Hence, "sublimation of instinct" is a conspicuous feature of cultural development, and is what makes possible for "higher psychical activities, scientific, artistic or ideological, to play such an important part in civilized life." Effectively, then, "civilization is built up upon a renunciation of instinct." This cultural privation, Freud says, dominates all social relations between human beings and, unless it is compensated, serious disorders will result (*Freud*, 742).

Finally, it is worth stressing that Freud's entire view of civilization – in particular, its construction of art as well as religious and scientific systems – rests ultimately on his account of the infantile ego, an account that has profoundly influenced thinkers such as Lacan and which finds important parallels in the work of Derrida and some feminist writers such as Julia Kristeva. Freud sees religious feeling as a kind of unbounded "oceanic feeling," which he characterizes as the "feeling of an indissoluble bond, of being one with the external world as a whole" (*Freud*, 723). What interests Freud is the question: what is the source of such a feeling? Normally, says Freud, "there is nothing of which we are more certain than the feeling of our own self, of our own ego. This ego appears to us as something autonomous and unitary, marked off distinctly from everything else" (*Freud*, 724). Yet this feeling of certainty, says Freud, has been shown by psychoanalysis to be "deceptive" and that in fact "the ego is continued inwards, without any sharp delimitation, into an unconscious mental entity which we designate as the id." Freud acknowledges, however, that "towards the outside . . . the ego seems to maintain clear and sharp lines of demarcation." In other words, the conscious ego is continuous with the unconscious mind; but it is still fairly clearly distinguished from the external world (*Freud*, 724). But even this feeling of separation has not always existed, and has undergone a process of development. An infant at the breast, says Freud, "does not as yet distinguish his ego from the external world," and only gradually detaches itself from the external causes of its sensations. Originally, says Freud, "the ego includes everything, later it separates off an external world from itself. Our present ego-feeling is, therefore, only a shrunken residue of a much more inclusive – indeed, an all-embracing – feeling which corresponded to a more intimate bond between the ego and the world about it." It is this that accounts for the "oceanic feeling" characteristic of religious experience: this "primary ego-feeling" persists in many people *alongside* the more mature perception of the ego's separation from the world (*Freud*, 725). Hence Freud traces religious feeling to an early phase of ego-feeling: "The origin of the religious attitude can be traced back in clear outlines as far as the feeling of infantile helplessness" (*Freud*, 727).

Clearly, Freud challenges many of the central impulses of Enlightenment thought: the (Cartesian) view of the human self as an independent unit; the view – extending through many Enlightenment thinkers into the work of Kant – of the ego as autonomous and rational agent; the idea (culminating in the philosophy of Hegel) of human progress in history; the notion that the external world and nature can be subjugated both intellectually and materially; and, perhaps above all, the view deriving from Plato and Aristotle and reaching into the later nineteenth century, that human beings can understand themselves. But neither is Freud part of the Romantic reaction against Enlightenment thought. He is indeed a rationalist, and wishes to extend the domain of science over the terrain of the human mind itself. But, like Schopenhauer, Nietzsche, and Bergson, he sees human reason as intrinsically practical and self-preservative in its orientation, and ultimately involved in an intense struggle with our sexual and aggressive instincts. What Freud gives to, and shares with, much cultural and literary theory is a view of the human self as constructed to a large extent by its environment, as a product of familial and larger social forces; a profound sense of the limitations of reason and of language itself; an intense awareness of the closure effected by conventional systems of thought and behavior, of the severe constraints imposed upon human sexuality; a view of art and religion as issuing from broader patterns of human need; and an acknowledgment that truth-value and moral value are not somehow absolute or universal but are motivated by the economic and ideological demands of civilization.

Jacques Lacan (1901–1981)

The work of the French psychoanalyst Jacques Lacan centers around his extensive re-reading of Freud in the light of insights furnished by linguistics and structuralism. Lacan's project was not merely to apply these discourses to psychoanalysis, but rather to enable the mutual reinterpretation of all of these areas of inquiry. He effectively employed these disciplines, as well as mathematics and logic, to reformulate Freud's account of the unconscious and his own account of human subjectivity in a (somewhat altered) Saussurean terminology of the connections between signifier and signified. Lacan's highly esoteric personality and views involved him in unusual and often stormy relationships with family, friends, spouses, and the psychoanalytic establishment. He was born in Paris to Roman Catholic parents who gave him the name "Jacques-Marie." It is arguable that his (anti-nominalist) views of language and subjectivity found their initial inspiration here, in reaction against this moment of primordial naming. He later de-nominated himself, removing the appellation "Marie," and went on to study medicine, after which he undertook training in psychiatry. In 1939 he joined the Psychoanalytic Society of Paris and became president of this organization in 1953. He was criticized, however, for his irregular and unorthodox techniques and was eventually made something of an outcast. He responded by establishing his own Freudian School, which he himself dissolved in 1980, just before his death.

Apart from Freud, the main influences on Lacan's work were Saussure, Roman Jakobson, and Hegel (Alexandre Kojève's famous lectures on whom Lacan had attended). Lacan's reputation was established by his publication of *Écrits* (1966), a large collection of essays and papers, which were translated into English in a much abbreviated format in 1977. Like Derrida, Julia Kristeva, Louis Althusser, and other notable French thinkers, Lacan participated in a landmark conference in 1966 at Johns Hopkins University. Lacan's influence not only has extended over the field of psychoanalysis but also reaches into the work of Marxists such as Louis Althusser (whose theories were influenced by Lacan and who, ironically, became Lacan's patient, after which, even more ironically, he killed his wife) and feminists such as Julia Kristeva and Jane Gallop, as well as deconstructive thinkers such as Barbara Johnson. Other feminists have reacted strongly against the phallocentric thrust (a not altogether inapt expression) of Lacan's own work.

Before examining some of Lacan's most influential texts, it may be useful to outline some of his pivotal views. As stated earlier, Lacan rewrites Freud's account of the unconscious using linguistic terminology and concepts. Lacan posits three orders or states of human mental disposition: the *imaginary* order, the *symbolic* order, and the *real*. The imaginary order is a pre-Oedipal phase where an infant is as yet unable to distinguish itself from its mother's body or to recognize the lines of demarcation between itself and objects in the world; indeed, it does not as yet know itself as a coherent entity or self. Hence, the imaginary phase is one of unity (between the child and its surroundings), as well as of immediate possession (of the mother and objects), a condition of reassuring plenitude, a world consisting wholly of images (hence "imaginary") that is not fragmented or mediated by difference, by categories, in a word, by language and signs. The mirror phase – the point at which the child can recognize itself and its environment in the mirror – marks the point at which this comforting imaginary condition breaks down, pushing the child into the symbolic order, which is the world of predefined social roles and gender differences, the world of subjects and objects, the world of language.

In this way, Lacan effectively reformulates in linguistic terms Freud's account of the Oedipus complex. Freud had posited that the infant's desire for its mother is prohibited by the father, who threatens the infant with castration. Faced with this threat, the infant represses his desire, thereby opening up the dimension of the unconscious, which is for Lacan (and Freud as seen through Lacan) not a "place" but a relation to the social world of law, morality, religion, and conscience. According to Freud, the child internalizes through the father's commands (what Lacan calls the Law of the Father) the appropriate standards of socially acceptable thought and behavior. Freud calls these standards internalized as conscience the child's "superego." The child now identifies with the father, sliding into his own gendered role, in the knowledge that he too is destined for fatherhood. Of course, the repressed desire(s) continue to exert their influence on conscious life. As Lacan rewrites this process, the child, in passing from the imaginary to the symbolic order, continues to long for the security and wholeness it previously felt: it is now no longer in full possession of its mother and of entities in the world; rather, it is distinguished from them in and through a network of signification. The child's desire, as Lacan explains it, passes in an unceasing movement along an infinite chain of signifiers, in search of unity, security, of ultimate meaning, in an ever elusive signified, and immaturely clinging to the fictive notion of unitary selfhood that began in the imaginary phase. The child exists in an alienated condition, its relationships with objects always highly mediated and controlled by social structures at the heart of whose operations is language. For Lacan, the phallus is a privileged signifier, signifying both sexual distinction and its arbitrariness. Lacan never accurately describes the "real": he seems to think of it as what lies beyond the world of signification, perhaps a primordial immediacy of experience prior to language or a chaotic condition of mere thinghood prior to objectivity. For Lacan, the real is the impossible. Lacan rejects any notion that the mind of either child or adult has any intrinsic psychical unity; it is merely a "subject" rather than a self or ego, merely the occupant of an always moving position in the networks of signification; hence, for Lacan, as he indicates in a famous statement, even "the Unconscious is structured like a language." The unconscious is as much a product of signifying systems, and indeed is itself as much a signifying system, as the conscious mind: both are like language in their openness, their constant deferral of meaning, their susceptibility to changing definition, and their constitution as a system of relations (rather than existing as entities in their own right). In Lacan's view, the subject is empty, fluid, and without an axis or center, and is always recreated in his encounter with the other, with what exceeds his own nature and grasp. Influenced by Hegel's master–slave dialectic, as well as by his account of objectivity, Lacan sees the individual's relation to objects as mediated by desire and by struggle.

Lacan elaborates his most renowned concept, that of the "mirror stage," in a 1949 paper of that title.[3] He suggests that this concept can shed light on "the formation of the *I* as we experience it in psychoanalysis" (*Écrits*, 1). This experience, he says, will result in a rejection of any philosophy resulting from Descartes' proposition *cogito ergo sum*, a proposition that grounds existence in thought, that sees man's thinking as the essence of his being. As Lacan states later in his paper, one such philosophy, based on the presumption that thought or consciousness forms a coherent unity, is existentialism, which erringly grants the ego "the illusion of autonomy" (*Écrits*, 6).

When does the mirror stage occur? Lacan locates it in the development of a child between the ages of 6 and 18 months. Such a child can "recognize as such his own image in a mirror." In the case of intelligent animals such as monkeys, this act of recognition is self-exhausting and its implications extend no further. In the case of the child, however, this recognition has a profound and enduring impact: in his mirrored gestures and his reflected play, the child experiences "the relation between the movements assumed in the image and the reflected environment, and between this virtual complex and the reality it reduplicates – the child's own body, and the persons and things, around him" (*Écrits*, 1). In other words, whereas the monkey sees in the mirror simply another monkey, the child sees reflected *himself* and his relationship with his environment.

Lacan stresses, then, that we must "understand the mirror stage *as an identification*," which results in a "transformation" in the subject: though the child is somewhat helpless, unable to walk or even stand up, he exhibits a "jubilant assumption of his specular image" [*speculum* meaning "mirror"], an image which "would seem to exhibit in an exemplary situation the symbolic matrix in which the *I* is precipitated in a primordial form, before it is objectified in the dialectic of identification with the other, and before language restores to it, in the universal, its function as subject" (*Écrits*, 2). The child is "jubilant" because the image reflected in the mirror is what Lacan calls "the Ideal-I," an idealized, coherent, and unified version of itself. The child's ego is precipitated into the symbolic matrix of language, the symbolic order: the word "primordial" indicates that the experience of the child is somewhat premature, anticipating its entry into language, and into the entire relation of subject and object which will govern its engagement in the world. In other words, the mirror stage occurs prior to the child's actual acquisition of a sense of self, a sense of itself as subject in distinction from objects in the world: the child experiences, as projected in its mirror image, itself and its surroundings as an integrated unity. It has not consciously entered the symbolic order, even though it is already surrounded by the effects of that order and even though that order indeed governs its present experience.

What is also important, however, is that this present experience of illusory unity is not entirely left behind even when the child grows beyond the mirror stage. Lacan states that the form of the ideal "I" "situates the agency of the ego, before its social determination, in a fictional direction, which will always remain irreducible for the individual" (*Écrits*, 2). The "fiction" is the unity of the ego, a fiction which is entrenched in the child's psyche prior to its direction or constitution by social factors, and which will continue (since it is "irreducible") even as the child's mind is influenced and formed by social determinants. The child "anticipates in a mirage the maturation of his power," in a mirror image which exhibits a symmetry that contrasts with the child's actual feelings of turbulence. This power the child sees only as a gestalt or pattern of totality which "symbolizes the mental permanence of the *I*, at the same time as it prefigures its alienating destination" (*Écrits*, 2). Hence, the illusion of unity and enduring identity that occurs in the mirror phase also anticipates the life-long alienation of the ego, not only from the objects that surround it, objects of its desire, but also from itself.

Lacan is led to view the "function of the mirror-stage as a particular case of the function of the *imago*, which is to establish a relation between the organism and its reality," between the inner world and the outer world (*Écrits*, 4). *Imago* is an ancient Latin term that can refer to an image, likeness, copy, picture, statue, mask, or apparition. The Romans sometimes used it to refer to statues of distinguished ancestors which were placed in the atria or central courts of their houses. Freud had used the term to indicate the impression made by parental strictures on the child's mind. Lacan appears to use the term to mean something like the assuming of an image: it is this assumption of an image of itself that establishes the child's relation to reality. But Lacan suggests that in the case of the human child, this "relation to nature is altered by a certain dehiscence at the heart of the organism, a primordial Discord" betrayed by the infant's lack of motor coordination (*Écrits*, 2). The word "dehiscence," referring in botany to the gaping or bursting open of vessels containing the seeds of plants, could refer both to the fragmenting or breaking up of the child's sense of unity and to the persistence of this false sense through its later life. This process, as well as the child's assuming an image, is elaborated in an important passage:

> This development is experienced as a temporal dialectic that decisively projects the formation of the individual into history. The *mirror stage* is a drama whose internal thrust is

591

precipitated from insufficiency to anticipation – and which manufactures for the subject, caught up in the lure of spatial identification, the succession of phantasies that extends from a fragmented body-image to a form of its totality that I shall call orthopaedic – and, lastly, to the assumption of the armour of an alienating identity, which will mark with its rigid structure the subject's entire mental development. (*Écrits*, 4)

Lacan also speaks of the "spatial captation manifested in the mirror-stage." What he seems to be suggesting in the passage above is that the mirror stage is a phase where the temporally discrete experiences of the child in reality are projected, in their mirrored idealization, into the form of space, a form in which totality and permanence can obtain. Space, as the dimension in which images subsist, is thereby also the medium in which fantasies of imaginary unity can be constructed. Lacan suggests that the movement of the mirror phase is from the child's actual "insufficiency" through its "anticipation" of its entry into the symbolic order to the child's "assumption" of the protection of a unified identity; this identity, however, is alienating: it is fictive, a spatialized projection into unity of the child's actually temporally discrete "self." Lacan's point seems also to be that the recourse to this "rigid" fiction, to this brittle and breakable identity, will haunt the remainder of the child's mental development.

Lacan continues the metaphor of armor and protection, explaining that "the formation of the *I* is symbolized in dreams by a fortress, or a stadium – its inner arena and enclosure, surrounded by marshes and rubbish-tips, dividing it into two opposed fields of contest where the subject flounders in quest of the lofty, remote inner castle whose form . . . symbolizes the id in a quite startling way." Lacan adds that likewise, on the mental plane, fortified structures are metaphors designating the "mechanisms of obsessional neurosis – inversion, isolation, reduplication, cancellation and displacement" (*Écrits*, 5). According to Lacan's metaphors, the id – the locus of unconstrained instincts and desires, and perhaps the projection of remembered, imagined unity and totality – is the lofty inner castle, to whose protection the floundering "subject" – the "I" that has entered the constraints and self-alienation of the symbolic order – wishes to return. And yet it seems that the metaphor of fortification expresses not only the formation of the "I" but also the operations of neurosis: it expresses both the "defences of the ego" and the alienating, neurosis-generating nature of these defenses, dating from the end of the mirror stage, from the "deflection of the specular *I* into the social *I*" (*Écrits*, 5).

In other words, the passing of the mirror stage marks the transition from the child's jubilant and comforting assumption of his satisfying total image or "I" in the mirror to his entry into the social world. As Lacan puts it, the ending of the mirror stage "inaugurates . . . the dialectic that will henceforth link the *I* to socially elaborated situations" (*Écrits*, 5). Lacan adds that this moment corresponds to a "natural maturation," which itself is normalized by "cultural mediation" as in the case of the Oedipus complex (*Écrits*, 5–6). The child has effectively passed from the imaginary order to the symbolic order. What Lacan seems to be suggesting is that from this point onward, the child's knowledge or awareness will never be immediate, will never be based on a somehow pure experience which precedes identity formation and the categories of subject and object; rather it will enter a "socially elaborated" system where all knowledge will be relational and highly mediated (through social, educational, and ideological structures), and where the child as "subject" will confront elements of the world as "objects," as forms of otherness or foreignness to his identity; his relation to these objects will assume the form of desire, which is, according to Hegel, the form of consciousness itself (since it is desire of a subject for an object that defines their mutual relation as one of mutual demarcation, separation, and definition). Moreover, these objects are constituted in "an abstract equivalence by the co-operation of others," in other words by a socially based consensus that determines the criteria of sameness and difference between objects, that determines – abstractly, rather than by any natural or essential connections between them – how objects will be categorized.

Opposing the philosophy of existentialism which, according to Lacan, takes consciousness as a primary datum in the fashion of Descartes, Lacan does not regard "the ego as centred on the *perception-consciousness system*," or as organized by the "reality principle." He insists that "we should start instead from the *function of méconnaissance* that characterizes the ego in all its structures" (*Écrits*, 6). The word *méconnaissance* refers to a failure to recognize or appreciate, a misreading, a misprizing, or even a disavowal or repudiation of an action. Lacan's point seems to be that the ego, far from being the coherent, unified, and rational agency that has been bequeathed by Descartes and by Enlightenment philosophy, is characterized by its very failure to achieve unity, by its very failure to achieve self-understanding, by its perpetual propensity to misprision. At the end of his article, Lacan seems to imply that the very process of the formation of the "I," of which the mirror stage is a founding moment, itself harbors "the most extensive definition of neurosis" (*Écrits*, 7). Is Lacan, like Freud, redefining the human being as the "neurotic animal"? If so, he hints at certain historical conditions underlying our general neurosis: his opposition to existentialism is based in part on its failure to explain the "subjective impasses" arising from a society based primarily on utilitarian functions and a lack of true freedom, and the recognition of another consciousness only by what Lacan calls "Hegelian murder," by a stagnant immersion in (rather than progression through) Hegel's master–slave dialectic (*Écrits*, 6). Lacan also seems to see neurosis and psychosis as a function of the "deadening of the passions in society." Whereas anthropology has long examined the connections of nature and culture, says Lacan, it is psychoanalysis alone that recognizes the "knot of imaginary servitude that love must always undo again, or sever" (*Écrits*, 7). Is this an appeal, like Kristeva's, to return to the fullness of the imaginary as a resource for subversive thinking, as a locus that preexists the bondage of the symbolic, weighed down as this is in convention and tradition? The general tenor of Lacan's thought is more conservative, though he does at times invoke Dali and the concept of "paranoiac knowledge," an obsession with order and unity and terror of fragmentation, an obsession that has worked its way through Western thought for many centuries.

Lacan's theories of language and the unconscious are formulated in a widely known paper called "The Agency/Insistence of the Letter in the Unconscious since Freud." This paper was delivered initially as a lecture in 1957 to a philosophy group at the Sorbonne, and subsequently reprinted in *Écrits*. In the first part of his paper, entitled "The Meaning of the Letter," Lacan urges that psychoanalysis "discovers in the unconscious ... the whole structure of language" (*Écrits*, 147). Lacan is reacting implicitly against a psychological view of the unconscious as a locus of desire and instinct. He observes, in a cryptically tautological gesture, that "letter" is to be taken "literally" here: it is the "material support that concrete discourse borrows from language" (*Écrits*, 147). Lacan attempts to clarify this definition: language does *not* consist of "the various psychical and somatic functions that serve it in the speaking subject." Language and its structure exist prior to the moment at which the speaking subject makes his entry into it (*Écrits*, 148). Lacan seems to imply here that the various elements which are immediately involved in an individual subject's making of utterances – sound-image, visual image, and the impressions of these upon sensation, together with psychic associations of sounds and meanings – do not constitute language, whose structure is itself their enabling foundation. Another way of putting this is to say that language is not innate (the individual is not born possessing it), nor is it merely a form of behavior.

Lacan proceeds to talk of the subject as "the slave of language," whose place is already "inscribed at birth" (*Écrits*, 148). Hence, it is not the subject who gives rise to language or who controls it; rather, it is language which governs and constitutes the subject. Language is not generated by a communal experience comprising the aggregate or even accumulation of individual speech acts. It is language, then, which determines and authorizes the range of cultural structures and possible experience. The point is that language does not *arise* from these, for there cannot be meaningful experiences which are somehow prelinguistic (*Écrits*, 148).

The only assumptions allowed by Lacan are those through which language has become an object of scientific investigation. He observes that linguistics itself has attained the status of an object of scientific investigation, and currently this science occupies a key position: the reclassification of the sciences around linguistics is tantamount to "a revolution in knowledge" (*Écrits*, 149). He observes that the constitutive moment of the emergence of linguistics, the founding moment of this science, is contained in an algorithm:

$$
\begin{array}{ll}
S & \text{(Signifier)} \\
s & \text{(Signified)}
\end{array}
$$

This algorithm is essentially Saussure's formulation. But the position of Saussurean linguistics, says Lacan, is suspended at this precise distinction between two orders "separated initially by a barrier resisting signification" (*Écrits*, 149). We need to understand this limitation in order to grasp the connections proper to the signifier and their function in the genesis of the signified. What Lacan seems to be pointing out is that the bar or barrier, in Saussure's scheme, is itself outside of the structure of language, imposed, as it were, from without. This primordial distinction or barrier, says Lacan, transcends the discussion of arbitrariness of the sign, which is constrained to the relation of word and thing. In other words, the extra-linguistic nature of the barrier cannot be accounted for or explained simply as signifying arbitrariness (in the connection between signifier and signified).

In sum, no signification can be sustained other than by reference to another signification. There is no language (*langue*) which cannot cover the whole field of the signified. If we grasp in language the constitution of an object, this constitution is found at the level of a concept (which is very different from simple naming). To grasp an object in language, we find the object constituted only at the level of the concept, not as a thing.

594

In other words, it is an illusion that "the signifier answers to the function of representing the signified" (*Écrits*, 150). This illusion or heresy – that the signifier represents the signified – leads logical positivism to search for the "meaning of meaning," or to search for the final signified (treating this as the actual thing or entity) to which the signifier points, excluding the apparatus of interpretation (*Écrits*, 150). The relation between signifier and signified is not one of parallelism.

Saussure's diagram of TREE/Picture of tree (as an illustration of the connection between signifier and signified) could be replaced, to better illustrate this connection, with two identical doors over which, respectively, are inscribed "Ladies" and "Gentlemen." This, says Lacan, should silence the "nominalist debate" by showing how "the signifier enters the signified" (*Écrits*, 151). In other words, the signifier or soundimage "Ladies" does not merely *point* to a signified or concept that somehow is already there, outside of it: it *enters* the signified, it alters or creates the meaning or concept. The bathroom doors are identical but they do not have the same meaning; this meaning is structured or "entered" by the signifier. As Lacan says later, the signifier "always anticipates meaning by unfolding its dimension before it." When we say "I shall never ..." or "And yet there may be ... ," these interrupted remarks are not without meaning, and are all the more oppressive inasmuch as they make us wait for this meaning (*Écrits*, 153).

But no contrived example, warns Lacan, can be as telling as the actual experience of truth. If a train arrives at a station and a little brother and sister are sitting face to face in a compartment, one of them will see the sign "Ladies," and the other, "Gentlemen." They will disagree on what they are seeing. This signifier (seen differently) will become subject to "the unbridled power of ideological warfare." For these children, "ladies" and "gentlemen" will henceforth be "two countries towards which each of their souls will strive on divergent wings" (*Écrits*, 152). Another way of putting this might be to say that each signified is the "same" country, traversed from different points of view; the difference in point of view, however, creates a difference in the signified.

In the algorithm signifier/signified, access from one to the other cannot have a signification. The algorithm can reveal only the structure of the signifier in this transfer. In other words, the algorithm cannot reveal the connection between signifier and signified but only the connections between the signifier in this algorithm and the signifiers in other algorithms. These units (signifiers) are subjected to a double condition: (1) being "reducible to ultimate differential elements" in a synchronic system; these elements are phonemes, the smallest units of sound that can indicate differences in meaning; the differential connection of phonemes present the "letter," which Lacan calls "the essentially localized structure of the signifier"; and (2) "combining them according to laws of a closed order"; this second property of the signifier reflects the "topological substratum of ... the signifying chain." Lacan sees this chain as "rings of a necklace that is a ring in another necklace made of rings" (*Écrits*, 152–153). The connections between the various rings is differential: meaning is not contained in any one of these rings but is a movement through them; and even these connections between rings on one level or circle ultimately depend on the entire necklace, which is itself but one ring on an even larger necklace. As Lacan has it, "it is in the chain of the signifier that the meaning 'insists' but that none of its elements 'consists' in the signification of which it is at the moment capable" (*Écrits*, 153). The Latin *sistere* means "to stand"; hence *insistere* means "to stand upon" but can also mean to stop or pause, to dwell upon, and to doubt or withhold one's assent. The word *consistere* means to place oneself somewhere, to stand still, stop, to settle or take up an abode, to stand or remain, to endure or subsist. The point seems to be, then, that meaning does not settle or halt at any one element in the signification chain: none of these elements in itself consists of meaning. Rather, meaning pauses, or stands upon, elements in the chain, always moving from one to another, none of the elements, therefore, being stable.

We are forced then, says Lacan, in a statement that was to become widely cited, "to accept the notion of an incessant sliding of the signified under the signifier" (*Écrits*, 154). What he appears to mean by this is that (1) we can never reach the pure signified; (2) that the realm of the signifier is far more extensive, both structuring and controlling the realm of the signified; the latter realm can never somehow extend or protrude beyond the domains of the signifier since that would imply that concepts (and ultimately things, entities) can exist prior to, and independently of, the process of signification; (3) the relation between the two realms, contrary to Saussure's formulation of it, is not linear. In fact, says Lacan, all "our experience runs counter to this linearity"; at most, one can speak of "anchoring points" when considering the subject's constitution and transformation by language (*Écrits*, 154). Saussure's view of the "chain of discourse" as linear can only apply in a temporal dimension. Otherwise, one has only to listen to poetry "for a polyphony to be heard." And Lacan sees all discourse as marked by such polyphony: "all discourse is aligned along the several staves of a score" (*Écrits*, 154). Lacan appears to be following Jakobson here. Indeed, as an example of this polyphonic process, of the sliding of the signified under the signifier, of the crossing of the bar (*barre*) of Saussure's algorithm, he looks again at the word "tree" (pointing out that *arbre* is an anagram of *barre*). The signifier "tree" can bring to mind a range of significations, from the strength and majesty of nature, through biblical connotations (the shadow of the cross), to various pagan symbolisms: what these multiple significations show is that an element in the signifying chain can be used "to signify *something quite other* than what it says" (as "tree" was used to refer to the cross, etc.). And this function of speech is also the "function of indicating the place of this subject in the search for the true" (*Écrits*, 155). Hence, in the very process of using signification, the subject or speaker is herself inserted at a specific point into the signifying chain. This "properly signifying function . . . in language," this process whereby one word is used to mean something else, has a name (that Lacan purports vaguely to recall from Quintilian): this name is metonymy (*Écrits*, 156). Lacan cites an example of metonymy: when "thirty sails" is used to refer to "ship"; in other words, when the part is taken for the whole. Lacan's immediate point here is that "the connexion between ship and sail is nowhere but in the signifier, and that it is in the *word-to-word* connexion that metonymy is based" (*Écrits*, 156). Metonymy, then, the core of the signifying process, is a connection between signifiers, between words, and not between signifiers and signifieds.

Lacan states: "I shall designate as metonymy, then, the one side (*versant*) of the effective field constituted by the signifier, so that meaning can emerge there . . . The other side is *metaphor*" (*Écrits*, 156). Lacan acknowledges his debt to Roman Jakobson in viewing metonymy and metaphor as lying at the heart of the signifying process. Lacan urges that metaphor does not spring from the presentation of two images, i.e., of "two signifiers equally actualized." Rather, the creative spark of metaphor "flashes between two signifiers one of which has taken the place of the other in the signifying chain, the occulted signifier remaining present through its (metonymic) connexion with the rest of the chain . . . *One word for another*: that is the formula for metaphor" (*Écrits*, 157). Hence, in Lacan's eyes, the "occulted" or displaced word remains, though reduced to the same level of metonymic presence as other signifiers (*Écrits*, 158). If metonymy yields a certain power to "circumvent the obstacles of social censure," metaphor reminds us that the spirit could not "live without the letter" (*Écrits*, 158). It was "none other than Freud who had this revelation, and he called his discovery the unconscious" (*Écrits*, 159). By the end of this section, Lacan has, with several forms of wordplay, discussed the "meaning of the letter," laying down his basic positions regarding language and the signifying process, viewing the notions of truth, subjectivity, and objectivity as immanent in this process (created within it rather than assuming any externality or independence from it). His final sentence, concerning Freud's revelation, anticipates his forthcoming examination of structuring of the unconscious by the operations of the linguistic process.

In the second part of his paper, entitled "The Letter in the Unconscious," Lacan points out Freud's increasing attention to language as he examined the unconscious. In fact, Freud's "royal road to the unconscious," his "Interpretation of Dreams," is concerned throughout with "the letter of the discourse, in its texture, its usage" (*Écrits*, 159). Freud was aware of the linguistic grounding of mental processes, and just as the linguistic structure enables discourse, so it "enables us to read dreams" (*Écrits*, 159–160).

Lacan has spoken of the "sliding of the signified under the signifier." He sees this process designated as "distortion" or "transposition" in Freud's account of the dream. According to Freud, dream distortion, referring to the repressive transformation or disguising of embarrassing elements by the conscious ego, was accomplished by at least two strategies, condensation and displacement. Lacan equates these two strategies with what he has described as the two "sides" of the effect of the signifier on the signified: metaphor and metonymy. Condensation corresponds to metaphor, whose field is "the structure of the superimposition of the signifiers" (*Écrits*, 160). Lacan, we may remember, had defined metaphor as the substitution of one signifier for another, with the displaced one remaining in metonymic form. The second strategy, that of "displacement," Lacan sees as corresponding to metonymy, a "veering off" on the part of the signifying process, so as to foil the censoring ego. In short, Lacan sees the mechanisms that are fundamental to the signifying process in language – metaphor and metonymy – as equally fundamental to the dream. The dream is "a form of writing," and the "dream-work follows the laws of the signifier" (*Écrits*, 161).

Lacan now turns to the function and place of the subject in the signifying process. Descartes' *cogito ergo sum*, he suggests, avers a "link between the transparency of the transcendental subject and his existential affirmation" (*Écrits*, 164). Descartes' statement "I think, therefore I am" assumes that the human self is "transcendental": it exists as a unity prior to its empirical experience. It is transparent because, in principle, everything is knowable about it, and it provides a clear, detached, perspective onto the world, being uncolored or smeared by the opacity of a specific historically conditioned subjectivity. This transparent self affirms its own existence, locating this in its very ability to think. In other words, its "being" is equated or identified with its "thought"

597

in an unmediated relationship. Lacan cites a more modern, and perhaps less impugn-able, version of Descartes' formula: "'*cogito ergo sum*,' *ubi cogito, ibi sum*" (I think, therefore I am, where I think, there I am) (*Écrits*, 165).

It was Freud's "Copernican Revolution" (which we might see as a second such revolution, Kant having claimed the first) that created "the Freudian universe," in which was questioned for a second time "the place man assigns to himself at the centre of a universe." According to Lacan, the place that I occupy as signifier will be a place in language, a grammatical function; the place that I occupy as a signified will be a concept that is also situated within the networks of language. The "I" which speaks (known to linguists as the "subject of enunciating," the actual person pronouncing a sentence about herself) is not definable as a coherent unity and cannot be adequately represented or signified by the "I" which is the subject of the sentence (the "subject of enunciation"). The question, says Lacan, is one of "knowing whether I am the same as that of which I speak" (*Écrits*, 165). In other words, is my *being* the same as that being which is *signified* in the language that expresses my *thought*? Lacan's answer is negative: the very process of signification, of conceptualization in thought and language, is a substitution for actual existence (Hegel – whose views on the connection between existence and signification anticipate Lacan's – would say a "mediation" of existence). Language, as a network of signifiers, displaces and redistributes the world of immediate existence, a world that can be known only as it is mediated by language. We might recall that the self that emerged from the imaginary stage was a split subject, with its repressed desire opening up the field of its unconscious; hence the child is split between unconscious desire (for the mother, for wholeness, for unity, for absolute meaning, all vestiges of the imaginary stage) and its conscious obligations in the sym-bolic order. In the passage above, Lacan describes this split as a desire split between "a refusal of the signifier and a lack of being." The choice, for my desire, is between signifying and existing: to refuse the signifier is to opt for an imaginary fullness and unity of being; if I choose to subsist as a signifier, I take my place in a vast network of signification but I have distanced myself from the world of existence: I cannot "situate myself," my real being, in the signifying chain. Hence, "my" thought, far from being under my control or identifiable as the basis of my identity, is actually part of a vaster signifying process in which I find myself and which largely controls me; and when I am caught up in this vast chain of signification, the situation of myself as signified is not the situation of myself as existing. The second part of the formula seems to suggest that my immediate self-consciousness involves a (perhaps temporary or provisional) repression of my knowledge that these larger structures of thought and signification constitute me. It might be said that certain of Lacan's insights here, such as the distinc-tion between the ontological and semiotic dimensions of any entity, were already formulated by Hegel and a number of neo-Hegelian philosophers on a somewhat higher intellectual plane.

Indeed, the desire that comprises the unconscious, a desire that mocks philosophy and the infinite, a desire that associates knowing and dominating with *jouissance*, is an endless journey through an infinite chain of signifiers. The subject is "caught in the rails – eternally stretching forth towards the *desire for something else* – of metonymy" (*Écrits*, 167). After the mirror phase, the subject is on an endless quest for unity, for wholeness, for security, a quest that must take place metonymically along a chain of signifiers, one being displaced for another (*Écrits*, 167). Lacan draws attention to the rhetorical nature of the "talking cure" in psychoanalysis, whereby the unconscious mechanisms correspond with the figures of style and the tropes enumerated by rhetoricians such as Quintilian (*Écrits*, 169). He ends this section by issuing a caution against psychoanalysts who are "busy remodelling psychoanalysis into a right-thinking movement whose crowning expression is the sociological poem of the *autonomous ego*" (*Écrits*, 171).

The third section of Lacan's paper is called "The Letter, Being and the Other." His concern here is to show how psychoanalysis has been bypassing the "truth discovered by Freud," which affirms, in Lacan's words, "the self's radical ex-centricity to itself with which man is confronted" (*Écrits*, 171). The notion of the unconscious indicates that the self bears an otherness within itself; or, rather, the self's otherness can be seen as external, as alien, to itself. Psychoanalysis has "compromised" this insight, which is contained in both the letter and spirit of Freud's works. The psychoanalytic institution has fallen prey to a humanism long prevalent in Western thought, one of its tenets being the idea of a unified personality, an idea that has persisted through Descartes' *cogito* and Enlightenment philosophy into the present: the idea of the human being as a rational, autonomous, free agent. Psychoanalysis has fallen under this general disposition, engaging in "moralistic tartufferies" and talking endlessly about the "total personality" (*Écrits*, 172). The underlying idea being that neurosis can be cured once placed in the totalizing narrative of the coherent conscious life of the patient.

But this, insists Lacan, is to compromise and domesticate Freud's radical discovery: the unconscious cannot be treated as simply an aberration that must somehow be reintegrated into the total, normal personality, into the customary bourgeois-Enlightenment conception of the ego. The unconscious, as constituted by desire, is not only structured like a language in its operations through mechanisms such as metaphor and metonymy, but also thereby extends the nature of its operations, fueled by desire – including the endless search for unity along an infinite chain of signifiers, the deferment and displacement of meaning, the inability to accede to reality other than through language – into the realm of the conscious, there in fact being no sharp demarcation between these. Freud taught us that we witness our nature "as much and more in our whims, our aberrations, our phobias and fetishes, as in our more or less civilized personalities" (*Écrits*, 174). We cannot simply place the unconscious alongside our rational selves as inherited from the Renaissance and the Enlightenment: our conception of the operations of reason itself must be transformed; madness has been used by the philosopher to adorn the "impregnable burrow of his fear . . . the supreme agent forever at work digging its tunnels is none other than reason, the very Logos that he serves" (*Écrits*, 174). Reason has been used to hide and define madness, an operation inspired by fear rather than love of knowledge. Since Freud's discovery, however, of a "radical heteronomy . . . gaping within man," this gap can never be hidden over again. Repeating his famous statement, Lacan reminds us that the "unconscious is the discourse of the Other (with a capital O)" (*Écrits*, 172). It is with the appearance of language that "the dimension of truth emerges" and the existence of subjects can be recognized in "the manifested presence of intersubjectivity" (*Écrits*, 172). The slightest alteration "in the relation between man and the signifier . . . changes the whole course of history by modifying the moorings that anchor his being" (*Écrits*, 174). It is precisely in this, says Lacan, that Freudianism has "founded an intangible but radical revolution . . . everything has been affected" (*Écrits*, 174). What Lacan is calling for, then, is a return to Freud, a return to the letter (and spirit) of the Freudian text, a return to the truly radical nature of his discovery of the unconscious, as well as an endeavor to formulate this discovery – and to realize its radical potential – in linguistic terms. Lacan reminds us that the patient's symptom is indeed a metaphor, and that man's desire is a metonymy: it is the concept of humanistic man, man as a total, integrated being, that has stood in the way, through "many centuries of religious hypocrisy and philosophical bravado," of our being able to articulate the connection between metaphor and the question of being, and between metonymy and a lack of being (*Écrits*, 175).

In insisting on the self's "radical ex-centricity" to itself, this phrase refers not to simple externality (as in the self being outside of itself) but perhaps also to the idea that the self is not centered on itself, it does not move on the same axis as itself. What does it mean to say that the self in these ways is external to itself? To say that the unconscious is not so much within us, centered on the same axis as the conscious mind of which it is a kind of controlled depth or projection, but that the unconscious is "radically" exterior to the conscious mind; it is not "beneath" it, not somehow secondary to it, not adjectival upon it. Rather, the unconscious is engaged in a dialectically uneven series of connections with the conscious mind whereby *it* structures the conscious mind somewhat and the conscious mind thus structured in turn exerts its influence on the unconscious. In answering the questions just posed, we need to be careful not to think of the conscious mind itself as some sort of unity – this is precisely what Lacan is rejecting – any more than the unconscious is a unity. The two notions do not stand in binary opposition. The point is that by viewing the unconscious as radically exterior and "other," Lacan forces into visibility the notion that the unconscious is not somehow tucked away, hidden and protected from the social structures which govern the world, a world they construct and define through language. Rather, the unconscious is *part of* that world; it is subject to, and constituted by, the same fundamental linguistic processes as is the conscious mind; as such, like the conscious mind, it is without a center, without an essence, without a psychological substratum; it is nothing more than the series of positions it occupies in language, a series of positions that can only artificially and for convenience be coerced into identity as a "subject," and, with even more coercion, molded into the coherence of an ego or self.

In this way, Lacan, through "insisting" on the agency of the "letter" in the unconscious, brings out the truly radical and subversive nature of the otherness discovered by Freud: the unconscious. In Freud's work (in spite of its actually radical implications), the unconscious – often treated as one controllable and aberrational element in a broader overall and normalizable structure of the mind – is in danger of being tamed and domesticated, of subserving the very notion of a coherent ego or self, descended through centuries of theology, humanism, and Enlightenment, that it set out to subvert. By dethroning the unconscious from this unwitting disposition toward transcendence in Freud's work, by immanentalizing it within the vast networks of signification into which the child is born and which in effect constitute the child's psychology as a network of significations, by resituating the unconscious within language, by redefining it *as* and *through* language, Lacan returns us to the startling and revolutionary nature of the Freudian discovery. This extension of the genuine implications of Freud's theories was furthered by the structuralist Marxist Louis Althusser, who adapted Lacan's insights in his account of the workings of the ideological apparatus of the political state, thereby exploring the connections – which are merely latent in Freud – between the unconscious and social structures.

Notes

1   This treatment of Freud's life and work is based on his own account as offered in "An Autobiographical Study" (1925). It is included in *The Freud Reader*, ed. Peter Gay (New York and London: W. W. Norton, 1989). The following accounts of Freud's various works draw upon some of Peter Gay's insights, and all further citations of Freud's works refer to this excellent and easily accessible collection. Hereafter cited as *Freud*.
2   Quoted by Peter Gay in *Freud*, p. 444.
3   Reprinted in Jacques Lacan, *Écrits: A Selection*, trans. Alan Sheridan (London: Tavistock, 1977). Hereafter citations from this volume are given in the text.

CHAPTER 23

FORMALISMS

Introduction

Literary critics and thinkers of various historical periods have placed emphasis on the formal aspects of art and literature. Aristotle, ancient and medieval rhetoricians, Kant, many of the Romantics, and writers in the nineteenth-century movements of symbolism and aestheticism all placed a high priority on literary form. This emphasis reached a new intensity and self-consciousness in the literatures and critical theories of the early twentieth century, beginning with the Formalist movement in Russia and with European modernism, extending subsequently to the New Criticism in England and America and later schools such as the neo-Aristotelians. In general, an emphasis on form parenthesizes concern for the representational, imitative, and cognitive aspects of literature. Literature is no longer viewed as aiming to represent reality or character or to impart moral or intellectual lessons, but is considered to be an object in its own right, autonomous (possessing its own laws) and autotelic (having its aims internal to itself). Moreover, in this formalist view, literature does not convey any clear or paraphrasable message; rather it communicates what is otherwise ineffable. Literature is regarded as a unique mode of expression, not an extension of rhetoric or philosophy or history or social or psychological documentary. Critics have variously theorized that preoccupation with form betokens social alienation, a withdrawal from the world, an acknowledgment of political helplessness, and a retreat into the aesthetic as a refuge of sensibility and humanistic values. Such an insular disposition also betokens a retreat from history and biography, effectively isolating the literary artifact from both broad social forces and the more localized and personal circumstances of its author.

Russian Formalism

Along with movements in futurism and symbolism, the Russian Formalists were a group of writers who flourished during the period of the Russian Revolution of 1917.

The Formalists and the futurists were active in the fierce debates of this era concerning art and its connections with ideology. The Formalists and futurists found a common platform in the journal *LEF* (Left Front of Art). The Formalists, focusing on artistic forms and techniques on the basis of linguistic studies, had arisen in pre-revolutionary Russia but now saw their opposition to traditional art as a political gesture, allying them somewhat with the revolution. However, all of these groups were attacked by the most prominent Soviet theoreticians, such as Trotsky, Nikolai Bukharin (1888–1937), Anatoly Lunacharsky (1875–1933), and Voronsky, who decried the attempt to break completely with the past and what they saw as a reductive denial of the social and cognitive aspects of art. V. N. Volosinov and Bakhtin later attempted to harmonize the two sides of the debate, viz., formal linguistic analysis and sociological emphasis, by treating language itself as the supreme ideological phenomenon, as the very site of ideological struggle. Other groups, called "Bakhtin Circles," formed around this enterprise.

There were two schools of Russian Formalism. The Moscow Linguistic Circle, led by Roman Jakobson, was formed in 1915; this group also included Osip Brik and Boris Tomashevsky. The second group, the Society for the Study of Poetic Language (*Opoyaz*), was founded in 1916, and its leading figures included Victor Shklovsky, Boris Eichenbaum, and Yuri Tynyanov. Other important critics associated with these movements included Leo Jakubinsky and the folklorist Vladimir Propp.

It should be said that the Russian Formalists' emphasis on form and technique was different in nature from that of the later New Critics. The Formalists' analyses were far more theoretical, seeking to understand the general nature of literature and literary devices, as well as the historical evolution of literary techniques; the New Critics were more concerned with the practice (rather than the theory) of close reading of individual texts. Though Russian Formalism as a school was eclipsed with the rise of Stalin and the official Soviet aesthetic of socialist realism, its influence was transmitted through figures such as Jakobson and Tzvetan Todorov to their own structuralist analyses and those of writers such as Roland Barthes and Gerard Genette. Even reception theorists such as Hans Robert Jauss have drawn upon Shklovsky's notion of defamiliarization.

Victor Shklovsky (1893–1984)

Having studied at the University of St. Petersburg in Russia, Shklovsky became a founding member of one of the two schools of Russian Formalism, the Society for the Study of Poetic Language, formed in 1916. His essay "Art as Technique" (1917) was one of the central statements of formalist theory. Like others in his group, he was denounced by Leon Trotsky for his formalist views.

It is in "Art as Technique"[1] that Shklovsky introduces one of the central concepts of Russian Formalism: that of defamiliarization. As our normal perceptions become habitual, they become automatic and unconscious: in everyday speech, for example, we leave phrases unfinished and words half-expressed. Shklovsky sees this as symptomatic of a process of "algebraization" which infects our ordinary perceptions: "things are replaced by symbols"; we fail to apprehend the object, which "fades and does not leave even a first impression; ultimately even the essence of what it was is forgotten." It is this process of algebraization or over-automatization of an object which permits the greatest economy of perceptive effort, whereby objects are reduced to one salient feature or function as though by formula (11).

Shklovsky quotes Tolstoy as saying that "the whole complex of lives of many people go on unconsciously . . . such lives are as if they had never been." Hence habituation can devour work, clothes, furniture, one's wife, and the fear of war. It is against this background of ordinary perception in general that art assumes its significance: "art exists that one may recover the sensation of life; it exists to make one feel things, to make the stone *stony* . . . The technique of art is to make objects 'unfamiliar,' to make forms difficult, to increase the difficulty and length of perception because the process of perception is an aesthetic end in itself and must be prolonged. *Art is a way of experiencing the artfulness of an object; the object is not important*" (12).

Shklovsky even goes on to say that the meaning of a work of art broadens to the extent that artfulness diminishes. Using Tolstoy as an example, he illustrates the ways in which art removes objects from the automatism of perception. One of these is a refusal to *name* the familiar object; another is to describe situations from an unusual point of view, such as that of a horse; Shklovsky claims that defamiliarization "is found almost everywhere form is found." Art's purpose is not to make us perceive meaning but to create a specific perception of the object: "*it creates a 'vision' of the object instead of serving as a means for knowing it*" (13–18). Shklovsky views the language of poetry as a "roughened" language, which impedes and slows down perception. The object is perceived not in its extension in space but in its continuity (22). However, Shklovsky acknowledges that ordinary speech and poetic language can often change places and metamorphose into each other. Should disordering of rhythm become a convention, it would be ineffective as a device for the roughening of language (24).

Hence Shklovsky's formalism can possibly accommodate cultural change and the relative status of radical innovation. But it is unclear to what extent his view of art as transforming the perception of an object may have epistemological implications. For example, if art *represents* the stone as stony, this surely implies that the quality of stoniness is somehow an objective attribute which has faded from recognition owing to automatism. But, to rediscover an attribute which convention has ignored is not necessarily to offer a new perception; nor, for that matter, could such a recovery be formalistically divorced from the meaning of the object.

Boris Eichenbaum (1886–1959)

Like Shklovsky, Eichenbaum was one of the leaders of the Russian Formalist group known as the Society for the Study of Poetic Language, founded in 1916. Like others of his school, Eichenbaum was denounced by Trotsky, and wrote an important essay, "The Theory of the 'Formal Method'" (1926, 1927), expounding the evolution of the central principles of the formalist method.

Origins of Formalism and the Science of Literature

Eichenbaum begins by stating that formalism is "characterized only by the attempt to create an independent science of literature which studies specifically literary material." And it is formalism's insistence on "empirical study" which comprised its most significant "quarrel with the old traditions."[2] The chief characteristic of the Formalists, says Eichenbaum, was their rejection of all "ready-made aesthetics and general theories" (103–104).

Eichenbaum observes that, before the appearance of formalism, literary analysis had been the province of academic research, marked by antiquated and unscientific aesthetic and psychological attitudes. However, there was almost no struggle between formalism and this theoretical heritage of conventional Russian scholars such as Alexander Potebnya (1835–1891) and Alexander Veselovsky (1838–1906). Instead, another avant-garde group of theorists and writers, the symbolists, had appropriated literary-critical discourse, transposing it from the academy to the journals. The symbolists, drawing inspiration from their French precursors, had tried to revitalize Russian literature by emphasizing aestheticism, the value of art for its own sake, and adopted an impressionistic and highly subjective mode of criticism. It was at this juncture that the Formalists entered the debate: they opposed the symbolists "in order to wrest poetics from their hands – to free it from its ties with their subjective philosophical and aesthetic theories and to direct it toward the scientific investigation of facts" (106).

According to Eichenbaum, the Formalists were aware that "history demanded . . . a really revolutionary attitude . . . Hence our Formalist movement was characterized by a new passion for scientific positivism – a rejection of philosophical assumptions, of psychological and aesthetic interpretations, etc. Art, considered apart from philosophical aesthetics and ideological theories, dictated its own position on things. We had to turn to facts and, abandoning general systems and problems, to begin 'in the middle,' with the facts which art forced upon us. Art demanded that we approach it closely; science, that we deal with the specific" (106). It is clear from these lines that the ideology behind formalism was positivism, an attempt to emulate the models and methods of what is perceived as "science," an attempt to focus on immediately given empirical data rather than on general schemes or theories for uniting and understanding such isolated information. It is hardly surprising that the spokesmen of the official Russian aesthetic saw such a posture as reductive, tearing art from its historical and political contexts, denying its ideological function, and attempting to view it as an independent, autonomous domain. In the context of early twentieth-century Russia, Eichenbaum evidently sees this strategy as revolutionary, as attempting to free art from serving ideological and political ends.

The Independent Value of Poetic Sound

In impugning previous approaches to literature, says Eichenbaum, the Formalists sought to isolate the study of literature from "secondary, incidental features" that might belong to philosophy, psychology, or history (107). And it is this isolation that makes the study of literature scientific. Eichenbaum quotes Roman Jakobson's affirmation that the "object of the science of literature is not literature, but literariness – that is, that which makes a given work a work of literature" (107). Hence, says Eichenbaum, instead of looking to these other disciplines, the Formalists focused on linguistics, a science which borders on poetics and shares material with it.

This focus on linguistics was inspired in part by the studies of the Russian linguist Leo Jakubinsky, who devised a basic principle of the formalist approach to poetics: the contrast between poetic and practical language (108). In his essay "On the Sounds of Poetic Language" (1916), Jakubinsky had argued that practical language contains a linguistic pattern of sounds and morphological features that "have no independent value and are merely a *means* of communication." But in other linguistic systems, such as those employed in poetry, the linguistic patterns of these elements "acquire *independent value*" (108). A brief example might illustrate Jakubinsky's claim: if I say to a friend "There is a strong wind blowing," my purpose is primarily to communicate information, perhaps about weather conditions or my reaction to them. And the various parts of my statement depend on one another for their meaning; they are not independent. But when the poet Shelley states: "O Wild West Wind, thou breath of Autumn's being," the purpose here is not merely or primarily to communicate a message: as such, the various elements of this line (such as a consecutive stress on four syllables, the alliteration of the "w" and "b" sounds) achieve an independence (a kind of excess) over their merely communicative content. We value the sounds for their own sake, not merely as they contribute to meaning. As Eichenbaum observes, Shklovsky had even argued, in his essay "On Poetry and Nonsense" (1916), that "meaningless-ness" was "a phenomenon characteristic of poetry." According to Shklovsky, "a great part of the delight of poetry consists in pronunciation, in the independent dance of the organs of speech" (109). Eichenbaum also cites Osip Brik's essay "Sound Repetitions" (1917), which had argued that sounds "are not only euphonious accessories to meaning; they are also the result of an independent poetic purpose" (111).

The Formalists' Redefinition of Form

Eichenbaum points out that the fundamental formalist distinction between poetic and practical language led to the formulation of a whole group of basic questions. Potebnya and others had presupposed the conventional notion of the harmony of form and content; the Formalists rejected this notion, whereby form was viewed as an "envelope" or vessel into which a liquid (the content) is poured. The new, formalist notion of form required no correlative content; instead of being an envelope, form is viewed as "a complete thing, something concrete, dynamic, self-contained" (112). Eichenbaum cites Shklovsky's definition of artistic or poetic perception as "that perception in which we experience form" (112). This view represented a break from both symbolism, which saw content as somehow shining through the form, and aestheticism, which isolated certain elements of form from content (113). In the formalist view, form is *itself* understood as content. The principle of perceptible form, the heightened perception of form, results from "special artistic techniques which force the reader to experience the form" (113). Eichenbaum notes that Shklovsky repudiated the principle of artistic economy, opposing it with the principle of defamiliarization: instead of art abbreviating and concentrating the process of perception, it should increase "the difficulty and span of perception" (114). Eichenbaum points out that the major earlier achievements of the Formalists included examining the differing uses of poetic and practical language, as well as replacing the notion of form (as bound to content) with the notion of technique, the latter being more closely tied to the features that distinguish poetic and practical speech (115).

Plot and Literary Evolution

The next phase of formalist studies, as Eichenbaum explains, attempted to move toward a general theory of verse and the study of narrative plot and specific techniques (115). He cites Shklovsky's theory of plot and fiction which identified special devices of plot construction. Most importantly, Shklovsky rejected the traditional notion of plot as a combination of *motifs* (the smallest units of narrative); plot was no longer viewed as synonymous with "story"; rather, it was viewed as a compositional device rather than a thematic concept. In other words, plot comprised the distinguishing feature of narrative art, and as such became an important focus of formalist inquiry (116). The idea of "motivation" (the rationale behind the use and function of a given device) enabled Shklovsky to distinguish between "story," which was merely a "description of events," and "plot," which was a structure. Techniques of plot construction, according to the Formalists, included parallelism, framing, and the weaving of motifs. The story, on the other hand, was merely "material for plot formulation," material which also included choice of motifs, characters, and themes (119, 122).

The Formalists – again, notably, Shklovsky – also rejected conventional accounts of the evolution of literary form, such as Veselovsky's view that "the purpose of new form is to express new content" (118). Veselovsky's critical enterprise was ethnographic, aiming to explain literary devices in terms of their social and cultural backgrounds. Instead, Shklovsky had argued that the purpose of a new form is "*to change an old form which has lost its aesthetic quality.*" This new formula was based on the view propounded by the German aesthetician Broder Christiansen that art is characterized by dynamism, by "repeated violations of established rules." It was also based on an insight offered by the French writer Ferdinand Brunetière, namely, that the most significant influence in the history of literature "is the influence of *work on work*" (118). What is being argued here is that literature has its own, relatively independent, history, and it is this history – comprised by the interaction and influence between literary works themselves, rather than "external" influences of society, morals, or manners – that is the appropriate object of formalist analysis. Clearly, such a model of literary history anticipates later theories such as those of Pound and T. S. Eliot; the latter saw works of literature as forming an "ideal order" among themselves, an order that both influenced new works and was in turn slightly modified by these new additions. As Eichenbaum sees it, the Formalists realized that their study of theoretical poetics had to broaden to include a study of literary history: "We found that we could not see the literary work in isolation, that we had to see its form against a background of other works rather than by itself. Thus the Formalists definitely went beyond 'Formalism'" (119). Hence, while formalist analysis in principle rejects the isolation of the literary artifact, an isolation practiced later by the New Critics, their invocation of history is confined to the history of literary form, to an autonomous historical development of literature abstracted from all other influences and circumstances.

Formalist Conceptions of Poetry

Eichenbaum observes that the Formalists insisted upon a clear demarcation between poetry and prose, as opposed to the symbolists, who were attempting to erase this boundary. The formalist position was first stated in Osip Brik's "On Rhythmic-Syntactic Figures" (1920), which argued that rhythm was not merely a "superficial appendage" but rather the "structural basis" of verse; rhythmic patterns were indissolubly connected with syntactical and grammatical patterns (124). In his own book *Verse Melody* (1922), Eichenbaum had maintained that stylistic features were mainly lexical; he also formulated the idea of the *dominant*, the chief element in a hierarchy of compositional factors. On the basis of certain dominant elements, he distinguished three styles of lyric poetry: declamatory (oratorical), melodic, and conversational (125). The most fundamental point here is that poetic form was not understood as an outer expression of a given content; rather, form itself was viewed as the "genuine content of poetic speech" (127). Eichenbaum puts this another way: form is not dependent upon content; it is self-sufficient and must be considered "in relation to its purpose" (130).

Eichenbaum himself had argued in his book on the Russian poet of that name, *Anna Akhmatova* (1923), that words used in verse are "taken out of ordinary speech. They are surrounded by a new aura of meaning and perceived not against the background of speech in general but against the background of poetic speech." He had added that "the formation of collateral meanings, which disrupts ordinary verbal associations, is the chief peculiarity of the semantics of poetry" (129). The suggestion here is that poetry, or more specifically poetic form, comprises a kind of speech of its own, which is cumulatively developed by a tradition of poets. Rhythms are developed that are peculiar to poetry, and so are shades of meaning and syntactical structures. In this view of poetic form, the notion of content or material, as explained in Yuri Tynyanov's *The Problem of Poetic Language* (1924), does not lie opposed to or outside of or beyond form; rather, content is itself a formal element (130). Again, Eichenbaum stresses that formalist advances in the study of poetry were enabled not by some rigid "formal method" but by close attention to an appropriately isolated object of inquiry, by a "study of the specific peculiarities of verbal art" (130). He reiterates his position that the "ability to see facts" is "far more important than the construction of a system. Theories are necessary to clarify facts; in reality, theories are made of facts. Theories perish and change, but the facts they help discover and support remain" (125). Such statements, one imagines, might tempt Hegel to rise from the grave.

Historical Criticism and Literary Evolution

As against the broad histories of the Russian academics and the effective rejection of history by the symbolists, the Formalists adopted a new understanding of literary history which rejected the idea of some overall unity, coherence, and purpose, as well as the idea of historical "progress" and "peaceful" linear succession in some directly continuing line. Rather, the Formalists saw literary tradition as involving struggle, a destruction of old values, competition between various schools in a given epoch, and persistence of vanquished movements alongside the newly dominant groups (134–135). The Formalists insisted that literary evolution had a distinctive character and that it "stood alone, quite independent of other aspects of culture." This evolution, moreover, they held to be independent of biography and psychology: "For us, the central problem of the history of literature is the problem of evolution without personality – the study of literature as a *self-formed social phenomenon*." This study focused rather on topics such as the formation and evolution of genres (136). Such methods clearly anticipate certain tenets of structuralism, such as the location of an author's subjectivity within linguistic and social structures. As a result of formalist inquiry, "many forgotten names and facts came to light, current estimates were shown to be inaccurate, traditional ideas changed" (137).

At the end of his essay, Eichenbaum provides a useful and provocative summary of the evolution of the Formalists' method. Their initial distinction between poetic and practical language led them to differentiate these in terms of their various functions. Their new conception of "form" as dynamic, self-contained, and as not dependent upon some external content led them to stress first the notion of technique, and then the notion of function. Taking rhythm as an integral element in the construction of a poem – as an element not extraneous to but intrinsically connected with syntax – the Formalists viewed poetry as a special form of speech having its own linguistic (syntactical, lexical, semantic) features (138).

Formalist analyses of prose fiction led in the same general direction. Eichenbaum insists yet again that formalism is not "a fixed, ready-made system," and that the Formalists "are too well trained by history itself to think that it can be avoided" (139). Yet a critic of this method might well argue that the "history" to which formalism appeals is an abstraction, comprised by a series of literary forms embroiled in complex mutual connections but dirempted, cut off entirely, from their broader contexts, in the interests of isolating a specifically literary object of study. The method might be seen as a kind of historical positivism or perhaps as a positivistic conception of history which reduces the latter in two ways: firstly, by rejection of any data not perceived to be immediate and of any purported schemes of historical unity; and secondly, by severing all temporal and lateral connections surrounding the literary object so that the "history" being addressed is effectively a series of static constructs laid out in mutual relations frozen in the inertness of spatiality.

Mikhail M. Bakhtin (1895–1975)

Mikhail Bakhtin is increasingly being recognized as one of the major literary theorists of the twentieth century. He is perhaps best known for his radical philosophy of language, as well as his theory of the novel, underpinned by concepts such as "dialogism," "polyphony," and "carnival," themselves resting on the more fundamental concept of "heteroglossia." Bakhtin's writings were produced at a time of momentous upheavals in Russia: the Revolution of 1917 was followed by a civil war (1918–1921), famine, and the dark years of repressive dictatorship under Joseph Stalin. While Bakhtin himself was not a member of the Communist Party, his work has been regarded by some as Marxist in orientation, seeking to provide a corrective to the abstractness of extreme formalism. Despite his critique of formalism, he has also been claimed as a member of the Jakobsonian formalist school, as a poststructuralist, and even as a religious thinker. Bakhtin's fraught career as an author reflects the turbulence of his times: of the numerous books he wrote in the post-revolutionary decade and in the 1930s, only one was published under his own name. The others, such as the influential *Rabelais and his World* (1965), were not published until much later. After decades of obscurity, he witnessed in the 1950s a renewed interest in his works and he became a cult figure in the Soviet Union. In the 1970s his reputation extended to France and in the 1980s to England and America.

Born in the town of Orel in Russia, Bakhtin subsequently obtained a degree in classics and philology from the University of St. Petersburg (Petrograd) in 1918. St. Petersburg at this time was the locus of heated literary-critical debate involving the symbolists, futurists, and Formalists. Bakhtin was influenced by figures such F. F. Zelinski, a classicist, and the Kantian thinker Vvedenski.[3] Fleeing the ensuing civil war, Bakhtin moved to Nevel, where he worked as a schoolteacher. It was here that the first "Bakhtin Circle" convened, including such figures as the musicologist (and later linguist) Valentin Volosinov, the philologist Lev Pumpianskij, and the philosopher Matvej Isaic Kagan. In 1920 Bakhtin moved to Vitebsk, a haven for many artists, where Pavel Medvedev joined the Circle. He married and returned with his wife to St. Petersburg in 1924. His "Circle" now included the poet N. J. Kljuev, the biologist I. I. Kanaev, and the Indologist M. I. Tubianskij. In 1929 Bakhtin's first major publication appeared, entitled *Problems of Dostoevsky's Art*, which formulated the concept of "polyphony" or "dialogism." In the same year, however, Bakhtin was sentenced to ten years' imprisonment for alleged affiliation with the underground Russian Orthodox Church; mercifully, the sentence was commuted to six years' exile in Kazakhstan. In 1936 he obtained a teaching position at the Mordovia State Teachers' College in Saransk; but the threat of more purges prompted him to resign and to move to a more obscure town. Afflicted by a bone disease, on which account his leg was amputated in 1938, he did not subsequently procure a professional appointment. After World War II, in 1946 and 1949 he defended his dissertation on Rabelais, creating an uproar in the scholarly world; the professors who opposed acceptance of the thesis won the day, and Bakhtin was denied his doctorate. His friends, however, procured him a teaching position in Saransk, as Chair of the Department of Literature. These colleagues – comprising a third "Bakhtin Circle" – included scholars at the University of Moscow and the Gorkij Institute, such as V. Kozinov, S. Bocarov, and the linguist V. V. Ivanov. The final years of Bakhtin's life brought him a long-elusive recognition. His book on Dostoevsky, republished in 1963, was a success, as was the volume on Rabelais, appearing two years later.

Bakhtin's major works as translated into English include *Art and Answerability: Early Philosophical Essays* (1990), *Rabelais and his World* (1965; trans. 1968), *Problems of Dostoevsky's Poetics* (1929; trans. 1973), *The Dialogic Imagination: Four Essays* (1930s; trans. 1981), and *Speech Genres and Other Late Essays* (1986). His important early essay "Towards a Philosophy of the Act" (1919) was not published until 1986. This and other early writings, such as "Art and Responsibility" and "Author and Hero," are Kantian in orientation, offering a phenomenological account of the intersubjective connection of human selves in language. Bakhtin's interest in the nature of language was formed in part by members of his Circle. Indeed, the authorship of some of the Bakhtin Circle's publications is still in dispute: two books, *Freudianism* (1927) and *Marxism and the Philosophy of Language* (1929, 1930), were published under the name of V. N. Volosinov. A further title, *The Formal Method in Literary Scholarship* (1928), was published under the name of P. N. Medvedev. The dispute was provoked by the linguist V. V. Ivanov, who claimed that these texts were in fact written by Bakhtin. Bakhtin himself refrained from resolving the matter, and the debate continues. It may well be, in any case, that these texts were collaboratively authored or that they express to some extent the shared ideas of members of the Circle.

Bakhtin's major achievements include the formulation of an innovative and radical philosophy of language as well as a comprehensive "theory" of the novel (though Bakhtin's work eschews systematic theory that attempts to explain particular phenomena through generalizing and static schemes). The essay to be examined here, "Discourse in the Novel," furnishes an integrated statement of both endeavors. Indeed, what purports to be a theory of the novel entails not only a radical account of the nature of language but also a radical critique of the history of philosophy and an innovative explanation of the nature of subjectivity, objectivity, and the very process of understanding.

At the outset, Bakhtin states that his principal object in this essay is to overcome the divorce between an abstract "formal" approach and an equally abstract "ideological" approach to the study of "verbal art" (here referring to the language of poetry and the novel). He insists that form and content in discourse "are one," and that "verbal discourse is a social phenomenon" (*DI*, 259). Bakhtin's point is that traditional stylistics have ignored the social dimensions of artistic discourse, which has been treated as a self-subsistent phenomenon, cut off from broader historical movements and immersion in broad ideological struggles. Moreover, traditional stylistics have not found a place for the novel, which, like other "prosaic" discourse, has been viewed as an "extra-artistic medium," an artistically "neutral" means of communication on the same level as practical speech (*DI*, 260). He acknowledges that in the 1920s some attempts were made (he appears to be thinking of the Russian Formalists) to recognize "the stylistic uniqueness of artistic prose as distinct from poetry." However, Bakhtin suggests that such endeavors merely revealed that traditional stylistic categories were not applicable to novelistic discourse (*DI*, 261).

Bakhtin lists the stylistic features into which the "unity" of the novel is usually divided: (1) direct authorial narration, (2) stylization of everyday speech, (3) stylization of semiliterary discourse such as letters and diaries, (4) various types of extra-artistic speech, such as moral, philosophical, and scientific statements, and (5) the individualized speech of characters. His point is that each of these "heterogeneous stylistic unities" combines in the novel to "form a structured artistic system" and that the "stylistic uniqueness of the novel as a genre consists precisely in the combination of these subordinated, yet still relatively autonomous, unities . . . into the higher unity of the work as a whole." Hence the novel can be "defined as a diversity of social speech types (sometimes even diversity of languages) and a diversity of individual voices, artistically organized" (*DI*, 262).

It quickly becomes apparent that Bakhtin's view of the novel is dependent upon his broader view of the nature of language as "dialogic" and as comprised of "heteroglossia." In order to explain the concept of dialogism, we first need to understand the latter term: "heteroglossia" refers to the circumstance that what we usually think of as a single, unitary language is actually comprised of a multiplicity of languages interacting with, and often ideologically competing with, one another. In Bakhtin's terms, any given "language" is actually stratified into several "other languages" ("heteroglossia" might be translated as "other-languageness"). For example, we can break down "any single national language into social dialects, characteristic group behavior, professional jargons, generic languages, languages of generations and age groups, . . . languages of the authorities, of various circles and of passing fashions . . . each day has its own slogan, its own vocabulary, its own emphases." It is this heteroglossia, says Bakhtin, which is "the indispensable prerequisite for the novel as a genre" (*DI*, 263).

"Dialogism" is a little more difficult to explain. On the most basic level, it refers to the fact that the various languages that stratify any "single" language are in dialogue with one another; Bakhtin calls this "the primordial dialogism of discourse," whereby all discourse has a dialogic orientation (*DI*, 275). We might illustrate this using the following example: the language of religious discourse does not exist in a state of ideological and linguistic "neutrality." On the contrary, such discourse might act as a "rejoinder" or "reply" to elements of political discourse. The political discourse might encourage loyalty to the state and adherence to material ambitions, whereas the religious discourse might attempt to displace those loyalties with the pursuit of spiritual goals. Even a work of art does not come, Minerva-like, fully formed from the brain of its author, speaking a single monologic language: it is a response, a rejoinder, to other works, to certain traditions, and it situates itself within a current of intersecting dialogues (*DI*, 274). Its relation to other works of art and to other languages (literary and non-literary) is dialogic.

Bakhtin has a further, profounder, explanation of the concept of dialogism. He explains that there is no direct, unmediated relation between a word and its object: "no living word relates to its object in a *singular* way." In its path toward the object, the word encounters "the fundamental and richly varied opposition of . . . other, alien words about the same object." Any concrete discourse, says Bakhtin,

> finds the object at which it was directed already as it were overlain with qualifications, open to dispute, charged with value, already enveloped in an obscuring mist – or, on the contrary, by the "light" of alien words that have already been spoken about it. It is entangled, shot through with shared thoughts, points of view, alien value judgments and accents. The word, directed toward its object, enters a dialogically agitated and tension-filled environment . . . it cannot fail to become an active participant in social dialogue . . . The way in which the word conceives its object is complicated by a dialogic interaction within the object between various aspects of its socio-verbal intelligibility. (*DI*, 276–277)

Offering a summary of his view, Bakhtin states that the "word is born in a dialogue as a living rejoinder within it; the word is shaped in dialogic interaction with an alien word that is already in the object. A word forms a concept of its own object in a dialogic way" (*DI*, 279). The underlying premise here is that language is not somehow a neutral medium, transparently related to the world of objects. Any utterance, whereby we assign a given meaning to a word, or use a word in a given way, is composed not in a vacuum in which the word as we initially encounter it is empty of significance. Rather, even before we utter the word in our own manner and with our own signification, it is already invested with many layers of meaning, and our use of the word must accommodate those other meanings and in some cases compete with them. Our utterance will in its very nature be dialogic: it is born as one voice in a dialogue that is already constituted; it cannot speak monologically, as the only voice, in some register isolated from all social, historical, and ideological contexts.

We might illustrate this notion of dialogism with an example taken from the stage of modern international politics. Those of us living in Europe or America tend to think of the word (and concept of) "democracy" as invested with a broad range of positive associations: we might relate it generally with the idea of political progress, with a history of emancipation from feudal economic and political constraints, with what we think of as "civilization," with a secular and scientific worldview, and perhaps above all with the notion of individual freedom. But when we attempt to export this word, this concept, to another culture such as that of Iraq, we find that *our* use of this word encounters a great deal of resistance in the linguistic and ideological registers of that nation. For one thing, the word "democracy" may be overlain in that culture with associations of a foreign power, and with some of the ills attendant upon democracy (as noted by thinkers from Plato to Alexis de Tocqueville): high crime rates, unrestrained individualism, the breakdown of family structure, a lack of reverence for the past, a disrespect for authority, and a threat to religious doctrine and values.

What occurs here, then, is precisely what Bakhtin speaks of: an ideological battle *within* the word itself, a battle for meaning, for the signification of the word, an endeavor to make one's own use of the word predominate. The battle need not occur between cultures; it can rage within a given nation. For example, a similar battle could exist between conservative religious groups and progressive groups in either America or Iraq. Similar struggles occur over words such as "terrorism," welded by the Western media to a certain image of Islam, and qualified in the Arab media with prefixes such as "state-sponsored." In such struggles, the word itself becomes the site of intense ideological conflict. We can see, then, that according to Bakhtin's view of language, language is not some neutral and transparent expression of conflict; it is the very medium and locus of conflict.

In formulating this radical notion of language, Bakhtin is also effecting a profound critique not only of linguistics and conventional stylistics but also of the history of philosophy. He sees traditional stylistics as inadequate for analyzing the novel precisely because it bypasses the heteroglossia that enables the style of the novel. Stylistics views style as a phenomenon of language itself, as an "individualization of the general language." In other words, the source of style is "the individuality of the speaking subject" (*DI*, 263–264). In this view, the work of art is treated as a "self-sufficient whole" and an "authorial monologue," whose "elements constitute a closed system," isolated from all social contexts (*DI*, 273–274). Bakhtin sees such a view of style as founded on Saussure's concept of language, itself premised on a polarity between general and particular, between *langue* (the system of language) and *parole* (the individual speech act). This notion of style presupposes both a "unity of language" and "the unity of an individual person realizing himself in this language" (*DI*, 264). Such a notion leads to a distorted treatment of the novel, selecting "only those elements that can be fitted within the frame of a single language system and that express, directly and without mediation, an authorial individuality in language" (*DI*, 265). Stylistics, linguistics, and the philosophy of language all postulate a unitary language and a unitary relation of the speaker to language, a speaker who engages in a "monologic utterance." All these disciplines enlist the Saussurean model of language, based on the polarity of general (language system) and particular (individualized utterance) (*DI*, 269).

Bakhtin's essential point is that such a unitary language is not real but merely *posited* by linguistics: "A unitary language is not something given . . . but is always in essence posited . . . and at every moment of its linguistic life it is opposed to the realities of heteroglossia. But at the same time it makes its real presence felt as a force for overcoming this heteroglossia, imposing specific limits to it, guaranteeing a certain maximum of mutual understanding and crystallizing into a real, although still relative, unity – the unity of the reigning conversational (everyday) and literary language, 'correct language'" (*DI*, 270). Hence, when we speak of "a language" or "the language," we are employing an ideal construct whose purpose is to freeze into a monologic intelligibility the constantly changing dialogic exchange of languages that actually constitute "language." In this respect, the historical project of literary stylistics, philosophy, and linguistics has been one:

> Aristotelian poetics, the poetics of Augustine, the poetics of the medieval church, of "the one language of truth," the Cartesian poetics of neoclassicism, the abstract grammatical universalism of Leibniz (the idea of a "universal grammar"), Humboldt's insistence on the concrete – all these, whatever their differences in nuance, give expression to the same centripetal forces in socio-linguistic and ideological life; they serve one and the same project of centralizing and unifying the European languages. (*DI*, 271)

Bakhtin sees this project as deeply ideological and political: it was a project that entailed exalting certain languages over others, incorporating "barbarians and lower social strata into a unitary language of culture," canonizing ideological systems and directing attention away "from language plurality to a single proto-language." Nonetheless, insists Bakhtin, these centripetal forces are obliged to "operate in the midst of heteroglossia" (*DI*, 271). Even as various attempts are being made to undertake the project of centralization and unification, the processes of decentralization and disunification continue. As Bakhtin puts it, alongside "the centripetal forces, the centrifugal forces of language carry on their uninterrupted work" (*DI*, 272).

This dialectic between the centripetal forces of unity and the centrifugal forces of dispersion is, for Bakhtin, a constituting characteristic of language. Every utterance, he says, is a point where these two forces intersect: every utterance participates in the "unitary language" and at the same time "partakes of social and historical heteroglossia." The environment of an utterance is "dialogized heteroglossia." Hence the utterance itself – any utterance – consists of "a contradiction-ridden, tension-filled unity of two embattled tendencies in the life of language" (*DI*, 272). What is fundamental to Bakhtin's view of language, then, is that no utterance simply floats in an ideally posited atmosphere of ahistorical neutrality; every utterance *belongs* to someone or some class or group and carries its ideological appurtenance within it. As Bakhtin states: "We are taking language not as a system of abstract grammatical categories, but rather language conceived as ideologically saturated, language as a world view" (*DI*, 271). In contrast, the disciplines of linguistics, stylistics, and the philosophy of language have all been motivated by an "orientation toward unity." Given that their project must occur amid the actual diversity, plurality, and stratification of language, i.e., amid heteroglossia, their project has effectively been that of seeking "*unity* in diversity," and they have ignored real "ideologically saturated" language consciousness (*DI*, 274). They have been oriented toward an "artificial, preconditioned status of the word, a word excised from dialogue" (*DI*, 279).

Bakhtin's own view recognizes that the actual word in living conversation is "directed toward an *answer* . . . it provokes an answer, anticipates it and structures itself in the answer's direction. Forming itself in the atmosphere of the already spoken, the word is at the same time determined by that which has not yet been said" (*DI*, 280). Bakhtin here draws attention to the temporal nature of language, to the fact that the word exists in real time, that it has a real history, a real past, and a real future (as opposed to the static time constructs posited by linguistics), all of which condition its presence. His views bear comparison to Bergson's views of language as a medium that is essentially spatialized and that has contributed to our conceptual spatializing of time, rather than dealing with real time or *durée*. What Bakhtin, like Bergson, is doing is reconceiving not merely the nature of language but the act of understanding itself: this, too, is a dialogic process. Every concrete act of understanding, says Bakhtin, is active; it is "indissolubly merged with the response, with a motivated agreement or disagreement . . . Understanding comes to fruition only in the response. Understanding and response are dialectically merged and mutually condition each other; one is impossible without the other" (*DI*, 282). This "internal dialogism" of the word involves an encounter not with "an alien word within the object itself" (as in the previously explained level of dialogism) but rather with "the subjective belief system of the listener" (*DI*, 282).

What Bakhtin appears to be saying is that the clash of different significations within a word is part of a broader conflict, between subjective frameworks, which is the very essence of understanding. Using this model, Bakhtin emphasizes that the dialogic nature of language entails "a struggle among socio-linguistic points of view" (*DI*, 273). Every verbal act, he explains, can "infect" language with its own intention; each social group has its own language, and, at any given moment, "languages of various epochs and periods of socio-ideological life cohabit with one another . . . every day represents another socio-ideological semantic 'state of affairs,' another vocabulary, another accentual system, with its own slogans, its own ways of assigning blame and praise" (*DI*, 291). The point, again, is not just that language is "heteroglot" and stratified; it is also that "there are no 'neutral' words and forms – words and forms that can belong to 'no one'; language has been completely taken over, shot through with intentions and accents" (*DI*, 293). Moreover, it is not merely that language is always socially and ideologically charged and is the locus of constant tension and struggle between groups and perspectives: in its role of providing this locus, it also furnishes the very medium for the interaction of human subjects, an interaction that creates the very ground of human subjectivity. For the individual consciousness, says Bakhtin, language "lies on the borderline between oneself and the other. The word in language is half someone else's. It becomes 'one's own' only when the speaker populates it with his own intention, his own accent, when he appropriates the word" (*DI*, 293). Prior to this moment of appropriation, the "word does not exist in a neutral and impersonal language"; rather, it is serving other people's intentions; moreover, not all words are equally open to this "seizure and transformation into private property . . . Language is not a neutral medium that passes freely and easily into the private property of the speaker's intentions; it is populated – overpopulated – with the intentions of others" (*DI*, 294).

Bakhtin's account of language as constitutively underlying the interactions of human subjects bears a certain resemblance to Hegel's account of the formation of the human subject in interaction with others; whereas Hegel sees subjectivity as a reciprocal effect, arising from the mutual acknowledgment between the consciousnesses of two people, Bakhtin's exposition explicitly posits language as the medium of such interaction, and hence sees subjectivity as a linguistic effect, though no less reciprocal and dialogic. As Bakhtin puts it, consciousness is faced with "the necessity of *having to choose a language*. With each literary-verbal performance, consciousness must actively orient itself amidst heteroglossia" (*DI*, 295).

Given these political and metaphysical implications of Bakhtin's views of language, it is clear that for him, the study of works of literature cannot be reduced to the examination of a localized and self-enclosed verbal construct. Even literary language, as Bakhtin points out, is stratified in its own ways, according to genre and profession (*DI*, 288–289). The various dialects and perspectives entering literature form "a dialogue of languages" (*DI*, 294). It is precisely this fact which, for Bakhtin, marks the characteristic difference between poetry and the novel. According to Bakhtin, most poetry is premised on the idea of a single unitary language; poetry effectively destroys heteroglossia; it strips the word of the intentions of others (*DI*, 297–298). Everything that enters the poetic work "*must immerse itself in Lethe, and forget its previous life in any other contexts: language may remember only its life in poetic contexts*" (*DI*, 297). In other words, the language of poetry is artificial; the meanings and connotations of words are accumulated through a specifically literary tradition insulated from the life of language beyond this self-enclosed system (T. S. Eliot's notion of literary tradition as an "ideal order" might fit very neatly into Bakhtin's conception). The language thereby built up is a language that, according to Bakhtin, has largely bypassed the heteroglossia and dialogism of language as used in other registers. Everywhere in poetry, says Bakhtin, "there is only one face – the linguistic face of the author, answering for every word as if it were his own." Such a treatment of language "presumes precisely this unity of language, an unmediated correspondence with its object" (*DI*, 297–298). Another way of characterizing this "project" of poetry is to say, as Bakhtin does, that the poetic image carves a direct path to the object, ignoring the numerous other paths laid down to that object, and the meanings previously attached to it, by "social consciousness" (*DI*, 278).

In the novel, on the contrary, this dialogization of language "penetrates from within the very way in which the word conceives its object" (*DI*, 284). In the novel, the actual dialogism and heteroglossia of language are fundamental to style; they comprise the enabling conditions of novelistic style, which thrives on giving expression to them. Poetic style extinguishes this dialogism or, at least, does not exploit it for artistic purposes (*DI*, 284). For the poet, language is an obedient organ, fully adequate to the author's intention; the poet is completely "within" his language and sees everything through it (*DI*, 286). Heteroglossia can be present in poetry only as a "depicted thing," seen through the eyes of the poet's own language. The novel, on the contrary, integrates heteroglossia as part of its own perspective; it will deliberately deploy alien languages, and the heteroglot languages of various social registers (*DI*, 287). Words for the novelist are regarded as "his" only as "things that are being transmitted ironically" (*DI*, 299n). Indeed, the "stratification of language . . . upon entering the novel establishes its own special order within it, and becomes a unique artistic system . . . This constitutes the distinguishing feature of the novel as a genre" (*DI*, 299–300). Hence, any stylistics capable of dealing with the novel must be a "*sociological stylistics*" that does not treat the work of literature as a self-enclosed artifact but exposes "the concrete social context of discourse" as the force that determines *from within* "the entire stylistic structure of the novel" (*DI*, 300).

Bakhtin acknowledges that in actual poetic works, it is possible to find "features fundamental to prose," especially in "periods of shift in literary poetic languages" (*DI*, 287n). Heteroglossia can exist also in some of the "low" poetic genres. In general, however, the language of poetic genres often becomes "authoritarian, dogmatic and conservative, sealing itself off from the influence of extraliterary social dialects," and fostering the idea of a special "poetic language" (*DI*, 287). He also acknowledges that "even the poetic word is social" but poetic forms reflect lengthier social processes, requiring "centuries to unfold" (*DI*, 300). Bakhtin sees the novel's history as far lengthier than conventional accounts, deriving from a variety of prose forms, some of which reflect his notion of "carnival" as elaborated in earlier works such as *Rabelais and his World*. His account is worth quoting at length:

> At the time when major divisions of the poetic genres were developing under the influence of the unifying, centralizing, centripetal forces of verbal-ideological life, the novel – and those artistic prose genres that gravitate toward it – was being historically shaped by the current of decentralizing, centrifugal forces. At the time when poetry was accomplishing the task of cultural, national and political centralization of the verbal-ideological world in the higher official socio-ideological levels, on the lower levels, on the stages of local fairs and at buffoon spectacles, the heteroglossia of the clown sounded forth, ridiculing all "languages" and dialects; there developed the literature of the *fabliaux* and *Schwänke* of street songs, folksayings, anecdotes, where there was no language-center at all, where there was to be found a lively play with the "languages" of poets, scholars, monks, knights and others, where all "languages" were masks and where no language could claim to be an authentic, incontestable face.
>
> Heteroglossia, as organized in these low genres, was . . . consciously opposed to this literary language. It was parodic, and aimed sharply and polemically against the official languages of its given time. It was heteroglossia that had been dialogized. (*DI*, 273)

It might be objected that Bakhtin's conception of poetry is narrow; that some species of poetry do indeed enlist heteroglossia and are politically subversive; it might also be urged that the novelistic form per se may not be subversive, that some novelists express deeply conservative visions. But clearly, in the passage above, Bakhtin sees the genres of poetry and the novel as emblematic of two broad ideological tendencies, the one centralizing and conservative, the other dispersive and radical.

It may even be that "poetry" and "novel" are used by Bakhtin as metaphors for these respective tendencies: thus poetry can indeed be radical, but inasmuch as it challenges official discourses, it enlists attributes of language that are typically deployed by prose. What is interesting is that for Bakhtin, the ideological valency of any position is intrinsically tied to the particular characteristics of language deployed. The "novel" embodies certain metaphysical, ideological, and aesthetic attitudes: it rejects, intrinsically, any concept of a unified self or a unified world; it acknowledges that "the" world is actually formed as a conversation, an endless dialogue, through a series of competing and coexisting languages; it even proposes that "truth" is dialogic. "The development of the novel," says Bakhtin, "is a function of the deepening of dialogic essence . . . Fewer and fewer neutral, hard elements ('rock bottom truths') remain that are not drawn into dialogue" (*DI*, 300). Hence, truth is redefined not merely as a consensus (which by now is common in cultural theory) but as the product of verbal-ideological struggles, struggles which mark the very nature of language itself.

Roman Jakobson (1896–1982)

The work of Roman Jakobson occupies a central and seminal place in the development of formalism and structuralism. Essentially a linguist, Jakobson was born in Moscow, where he co-founded the Moscow Linguistic Circle in 1915, which also included Osip Brik and Boris Tomashevsky. Along with Victor Shklovsky and Boris Eichenbaum, he was also involved in a second Russian Formalist group, the Society for the Study of Poetic Language, formed in 1916. The Formalists were in some ways precursors of structuralism: in 1926 Jakobson founded the Prague Linguistic Circle, which engaged critically with the work of Saussure. And, fleeing from Nazi occupation, he moved to America in 1941 where he became acquainted with Claude Lévi-Strauss; in 1943 he co-founded the Linguistic Circle of New York. His ideas proved to be of greatest impact first in France and then in America.

In his paper "Linguistics and Poetics" (1958) Jakobson argues that, since poetics concerns the artistic features of a "verbal message," and linguistics is the "global science of verbal structure," poetics is an integral part of linguistics. His point here is that poetic elements belong to the science of language as a whole; indeed, they belong to the yet broader field of semiotics or theory of signs since they are not confined to verbal art.[4] Jakobson insists that "literary criticism," which often evaluates literature in subjective terms, must be distinguished from "literary studies" proper, which engage in "objective scholarly analysis of verbal art" (*LL*, 64). Like linguistics, literary studies, whose focal point is poetics, are concerned with problems of synchrony and diachrony. Synchronic description views the various elements of a literary tradition as they occur at a given point in time; these elements will include, however, literary values and figures whose influence has persisted. A diachronic study would analyze the various changes in a given tradition or system over a period of time (*LL*, 64–65).

Jakobson urges that the poetic function of language must be situated among the other functions of language, which he schematizes as follows:

	CONTEXT	
ADDRESSER	MESSAGE	ADDRESSEE
	CONTACT	
	CODE	

In any act of verbal communication, the "addresser" sends a message to the "addressee"; the message requires a "context" that is verbal or at least capable of being verbalized; a "contact" which is a physical channel or psychological connection between them; and a "code" that is shared by them (*LL*, 66). Jakobson explains that each of these factors determines a different function of language, and that the verbal structure of any given message depends on the predominant function. For example, many messages are oriented primarily toward the "context" and the predominant function here will be referential or cognitive or denotative. However, while Jakobson accepts that language is primarily concerned with the transmission of ideas, he cautions that the "emotive" elements of language cannot be excluded from linguistic study. Verbal messages usually do not fulfill merely one function, and other, accessory functions will contribute to the message. For example, the emotive or expressive function is focused on the "addresser," and will convey the speaker's attitude, which itself may convey some information (*LL*, 66). A message that is oriented toward the "addressee" will have a "conative" function, which finds its purest expression in the vocative and imperative uses of language, which address people or things directly or issue commands (*LL*, 67–68). Such sentences differ from normal "declarative" sentences in that they have no relation to truth-value.

The three functions of language so far mentioned by Jakobson – referential, emotive, and conative – belong, as he notes, to the traditional model of language as formulated by the German psychologist Karl Buhler. Jakobson suggests that this model can be augmented to include additional verbal functions. One of these might be a "magic, incantatory" function, where the person addressed in a conative message would be an absent or inanimate third person, as in prayers or supplications to various forces considered to be divine (*LL*, 68). There are also messages whose main function is to establish or prolong communication ("Hello, do you hear me?"); this is the "phatic" function, which might involve an exchange of "ritualized formulas." This, says Jakobson, is the first verbal function acquired by infants (*LL*, 68–69). The third additional function is metalinguistic. Jakobson notes the distinction made by modern logicians between two levels of language: "object language," which speaks of objects and events, and "metalanguage," which speaks about language itself (*LL*, 69).

What distinguishes the poetic function from the others mentioned above is that it focuses on the "message" for its own sake (*LL*, 69); this function is by no means the sole function of "verbal art" but it is its dominant function, whereas in most verbal activities it is merely an accessory function. Hence the poetic function, by "promoting the palpability of signs, deepens the fundamental dichotomy of signs and objects." And the poetic function extends beyond poetry itself into many uses of language, as in the American election campaign slogan "I like Ike," which presents a "paronomastic image of the loving subject enveloped by the beloved object. The secondary, poetic function of this campaign slogan reinforces its impressiveness and efficacy" (*LL*, 70).

In poetry itself, diverse genres employ the other verbal functions along with the poetic function. For example, epic poetry involves the referential function; lyric, the emotive. Here is how Jakobson schematizes the various functions:

	REFERENTIAL	
EMOTIVE	POETIC	CONATIVE
	PHATIC	
	METALINGUAL	

What is the distinguishing feature of poetry? To answer this, Jakobson reminds us that the two basic modes of verbal arrangement are *selection*, which is based on verbal relations of equivalence, similarity, or synonymy; and *combination*, whereby a sequence of words is built up on the basis of contiguity. The poetic function, he says, "*projects the principle of equivalence from the axis of selection into the axis of combination*" (*LL*, 71). This difficult sentence might be interpreted as follows. In a non-poetic use of language, where we simply intend to communicate information, we might choose between a number of different words for "child": we might use "tot," "toddler," or "infant," words which are *equivalent* to one another. In other words, we are using the principle of *equivalence* to make our selection. Our next step will be to *combine* this word with another word which we also select on the basis of equivalence. For example, we might use one of the following words which are equivalent to one another: "sleep," "doze," "nap." Hence our *combination* will be something like: "The child sleeps." What Jakobson appears to be saying is that we use the principle of equivalence at the level of combination: we make one combination equivalent to another. In other words, regardless of the different meanings of various combinations, we make them formally equivalent, in terms of features such as their metrical stress and pattern. Another way of reading Jakobson's statement might be to say that poetry will not merely select from a number of possible equivalent terms but will combine them, maximizing focus on the message for its own sake. Poetry, however, is not a form of metalanguage: in poetry the equivalence is used to build a sequence whereas metalanguage uses the sequence to build an equation (*LL*, 71).

Jakobson's essay "Two Aspects of Language and Two Types of Aphasic Disturbances" (1956) suggests that language has a bipolar structure, oscillating between the poles of metaphor and metonymy. This dichotomy, he urges, "appears to be of primal significance and consequence for all verbal behavior and for human behavior in general" (*LL*, 112). The development of any discourse takes place along two different semantic lines: one is metaphoric, where one topic leads to another through similarity or substitution. The other is metonymic, where one topic suggests another via contiguity (closeness in space, time, or psychological association). In normal behavior, says Jakobson, both processes operate, but one is usually preferred, according to cultural and personal conditions (*LL*, 110–111). In verbal art, also, while the two processes richly interact, one is often given predominance. Jakobson notes that the primacy of metaphor in literary Romanticism and symbolism has been widely acknowledged. What has been neglected, he thinks, is the predominance of metonymy in realism: the realist author often "metonymically digresses from the plot to the atmosphere and from the characters to the setting in space and time" (*LL*, 111). He is also fond of synecdochic details such as "hair on the upper lip" and "bare shoulders" that are used to express character.

Jakobson notes that a competition between metaphoric and metonymic devices occurs in any symbolic process. In analyzing the structure of dreams, for example, the decisive question, he says, is "whether the symbols and the temporal sequences are based on contiguity (Freud's metonymic 'displacement' and synecdochic 'condensation') or on similarity (Freud's 'identification and symbolism')" (*LL*, 113). Here Jakobson anticipates Lacan's analysis of Freud's contrast between condensation and displacement in terms of metaphor and metonymy. In general, Jakobson holds that poetry is focused upon the sign and is based on the principle of similarity; thus poetry in general leans toward metaphor. Prose, on the other hand, is focused primarily upon the referent, and is based on contiguity; hence its underlying strategy is metonymy. Yet this bipolarity of language has actually been reduced, thinks Jakobson, to a unipolar scheme since the study of poetical tropes has been directed primarily toward metaphor while metonymy has suffered an undue neglect (*LL*, 113–114). What Jakobson effectively does here is to introduce an opposition between two terms which had been thought to cohere in traditional rhetoric.

The New Criticism

Around the beginning of the twentieth century, the predominant critical modes were biographical, historical, psychological, romantic, and impressionistic. Liberal critics such as Parrington and F. O. Matthiessen employed a historical approach to literature but Matthiessen insisted on addressing its aesthetic dimensions. This formalist disposition became intensified in both the New Criticism and the Chicago School. The term "The New Criticism" was coined as early as 1910 in a lecture of that title by Joel Spingarn who, influenced by Croce's expressionist theory of art, advocated a creative and imaginative criticism which gave primacy to the aesthetic qualities of literature over historical, psychological, and moral considerations. Spingarn, however, was not directly related to the New Criticism that developed in subsequent decades. Some of the important features of the New Criticism originated in England during the 1920s in the work of T. S. Eliot and Ezra Pound, as well as in seminal studies by I. A. Richards and William Empson. Richards' *Principles of Literary Criticism* (1924) advanced literary-critical notions such as irony, tension, and balance, as well as distinguishing between poetic and other uses of language. His *Practical Criticism* (1929), based on student analyses of poetry, emphasized the importance of "objective" and balanced close reading which was sensitive to the figurative language of literature. Richards' student William Empson produced an influential work, *Seven Types of Ambiguity* (1930), which was held up as a model of New Critical close reading.

Across the Atlantic, New Critical practices were also being pioneered by American critics, known as the Fugitives and the Southern Agrarians, who promoted the values of the Old South in reaction against the alleged dehumanization of science and echnology in the industrial North. Notable among these pioneers were John Crowe Ransom and Allen Tate, who developed some of the ideas of Eliot and Richards. Ransom edited the poetry magazine the *Fugitive* from 1922 to 1925 with a group of writers including Tate, Robert Penn Warren, and Donald Davidson. Other journals associated with the New Criticism included the *Southern Review*, edited by Penn Warren and Cleanth Brooks (1935–1942), the *Kenyon Review*, run by Ransom (1938–59), and the still extant *Sewanee Review*, edited by Tate and others. During the 1940s the New Criticism became institutionalized as the mainstream approach in academia, and its influence, while pervasively undermined since the 1950s, still persists. Some of the central documents of New

Criticism were written by relatively late adherents: W. K. Wimsatt and Monroe Beardsley's essays "The Intentional Fallacy" (1946) and "The Affective Fallacy" (1949) (it is worth noting, in this context, the enormous influence of E. D. Hirsch's book *Validity in Interpretation*, published in 1967, which equated a text's meaning with its author's intention); Austin Warren's *The Theory of Literature* (1949); W. K. Wimsatt's *The Verbal Icon* (1954); and Murray Krieger's *The New Apologists for Poetry* (1956). Some of these documents can now be examined.

John Crowe Ransom (1888–1974)

The seminal manifestos of the New Criticism, however, had been proclaimed earlier by Ransom, who published a series of essays entitled *The New Criticism* (1941) and an influential essay, "Criticism, Inc.," published in *The World's Body* (1938). This essay succinctly expresses a core of New Critical principles underlying the practice of most "New Critics," whose views often differed in other respects. As Ransom acknowledges, his essay is motivated by the desire to make literary criticism "more scientific, or precise and systematic"; it must, says Ransom, become a "serious business."[5] He urges that the emphasis of criticism must move from historical scholarship to aesthetic appreciation and understanding. Ransom characterizes both the conservative New Humanism and left-wing criticism as focusing on morality rather than aesthetics. While he accepts the value of historical and biographical information, Ransom insists that these are not ends in themselves but instrumental to the real aim of criticism, which is "to define and enjoy the aesthetic or characteristic values of literature." In short, Ransom's position is that the critic must study literature, not *about* literature. Hence criticism should exclude: (1) personal impressions, because the critical activity should "cite the nature of the object rather than its effects upon the subject" (*WB*, 342); (2) synopsis and paraphrase, since the plot or story is an abstraction from the real content of the text; (3) historical studies, which might include literary backgrounds, biography, literary sources, and analogues; (4) linguistic studies, which include identifying allusions and meanings of words; (5) moral content, since this is not the whole content of the text; (6) "Any other special studies which deal with some abstract or prose content taken out of the work" (*WB*, 343–345). Ransom demands that criticism, whose proper province includes technical studies of poetry, metrics, tropes, and fictiveness, should "receive its own charter of rights and function independently" (*WB*, 346). Finally, in this essay and other works, Ransom insists on the ontological uniqueness of poetry, as distinct from prose and other uses of language, as in prose. "The critic should," he urges, "regard the poem as nothing short of a desperate ontological or metaphysical manoeuvre," which cannot be reduced to prose (*WB*, 347–349). All in all, he argues that literature and literary criticism should enjoy autonomy both ontologically and institutionally. His arguments have often been abbreviated into a characterization of New Criticism as focusing on "the text itself" or "the words on the page."

William K. Wimsatt, Jr. (1907–1975) and Monroe C. Beardsley (1915–1985)

In addition to their other works, the critic Wimsatt and the philosopher Beardsley produced two influential and controversial papers that propounded central positions of New Criticism, "The Intentional Fallacy" (1946) and "The Affective Fallacy" (1949). In the first of these, they lay down certain propositions that they take to be axiomatic: while acknowledging that the cause of a poem is a "designing intellect," they refuse to accept the notion of design or intention as a standard of literary-critical interpretation.[6] In stating their second "axiom," they raise the question of how a critic might find out what a poet's intention was and state what is effectively their central claim: "If the poet succeeded in doing it, then the poem itself shows what he was trying to do. And if the poet did not succeed, then the poem is not adequate evidence, and the critic must go outside the poem – for evidence of an intention that did not become effective in the poem." The third axiom is the American poet Archibald's MacLeish's statement that a "poem should not mean but be." Wimsatt and Beardsley explain this statement as follows: "A poem can *be* only through its *meaning* – since its medium is words – yet it *is*, simply *is*, in the sense that we have no excuse for inquiring what part is intended or meant . . . In this respect poetry differs from practical messages, which are successful if and only if we correctly infer the intention" (*VI*, 4–5). This is an effective restatement of a New Critical position that the poem is an autonomous verbal structure which has its end in itself, which has no purpose beyond its own existence as an aesthetic object. It is not answerable to criteria of truth, accuracy of representation or imitation, or morality. Finally, Wimsatt and Beardsley insist that the thoughts and attitudes of a poem can be imputed only to the dramatic speaker or persona of the poem, not directly to the author (*VI*, 5).

The foregoing "axioms" are merely stated rather than argued. The first argument of the essay is Horatian: a poem, once published, no longer belongs to the author but to the public: "It is embodied in language, the peculiar possession of the public, and it is about the human being, an object of public knowledge" (*VI*, 5). The implication here is that, as an object in public language, the poem is available to the public for interpretation; the author has no privileged claim over language and his word outside of the poem cannot be taken as somehow authoritative. They acknowledge that an author can offer useful practical advice for a would-be poet, but such advice falls under the "psychology of composition rather than criticism" (*VI*, 9).

What Wimsatt and Beardsley are opposing is what they take to be a Romantic intentional fallacy: the Romantic idea, expressed in ancient times by Longinus and more recently by figures such as the great German writer Goethe and the Italian philosopher Benedetto Croce, that a poem echoes the soul of its author, that it embodies his intentions or psychological circumstances (*VI*, 6). The most influential recent statement of intentionalism, according to the authors of this essay, is I. A. Richards' fourfold characterization of meaning as "sense," "feeling," "tone," and "intention." The passwords of the intentional school are Romantic words such as "spontaneity," "sincerity," "authenticity," and "originality." These need to be replaced, say the authors, with terms of analysis such as "integrity," "relevance," "unity," and "function," terms which they claim to be more precise (*VI*, 9).

Like Ransom, Wimsatt and Beardsley are concerned to exclude from criticism certain related studies such as author psychology, biography, and history. They in fact make a distinction between "internal" and "external" evidence for the meaning of a poem. Internal evidence is actually public: it is evidence that is internal to the poem itself, evidence discovered through the poem's semantics and syntax and the knowledge of how these operate within the larger context of language and culture. External evidence is private or idiosyncratic: it is evidence gleaned from outside the poem, and may include diaries, journals, letters, and reported conversations. Wimsatt and Beardsley acknowledge that there may be a third kind of evidence which is "intermediate": evidence about an author's character, or semi-private meanings attached to words and concepts by the author and his circle (*VI*, 10).

Strictly speaking, it is only internal evidence that the authors allow. They give examples of how resort to evidence of the other types can distort a poem's meaning: if we approach John Donne's poem "A Valediction Forbidding Mourning" through our prior knowledge of his interest in astronomy, we might interpret the following stanza in the poem as centered on a metaphor involving geocentric and heliocentric views of the world:

> Moving of th'earth brings harmes and feares,
>   Men reckon what it did and meant,
> But trepidation of the spheares,
>   Though greater farre, is innocent.

But to advance such an interpretation, the authors warn, is "to disregard the English language, to prefer private evidence to public, external to internal" (*VI*, 14). In other words, we are reading the poem through our knowledge of Donne's "private" interests, rather than attending to what the words themselves might signify.

One of the major problems arising in literary scholarship from the intentional fallacy, according to the authors, concerns the poetic use of allusion by writers such as T. S. Eliot and Ezra Pound, whose verse extensively alludes or refers to lines and phrases of earlier poets. Taking as an example Eliot's inclusion of a lengthy series of notes explaining the various allusions found in his long poem *The Waste Land*, the authors suggest that Eliot's use of these notes attempts to justify his poetic practice through recourse to his own intention. Yet the notes, they say, should be held up to the same scrutiny as the lines of the poem itself; if the force of the allusions is not felt by the reader through the poem itself, then recourse to the notes is superfluous (*VI*, 15–16). As far as allusions are concerned, we must be able to justify their use in terms of their objectively discerned function in the poem, not by consulting the author as an oracle for his intention (*VI*, 18).

There are many possible objections to Wimsatt and Beardsley's argument. To begin with, it presupposes that we can treat the poem as an isolated artifact, torn from all of its contexts, including the circumstances of its reading or reception. Clearly, the distinction between internal and external evidence cannot be absolute and will vary according to the reader's knowledge and literary education. Moreover, many interpretative disputes arise not from questions of content but rather from questions of form and tone: we may agree on the most basic meaning of a poem but disagree on the significance we attach to this meaning. For example, Horace's famous "Ode to Pyrrha" could be translated in a tone of polite urbanity or one of crude sarcasm. Broad considerations of the intention behind the poem may legitimately help us clarify such issues. Many poems, such as satires or mock-heroic poems, presuppose a reader's prior acquaintance with certain literary traditions and conventions: it is important to acknowledge, for example, that Pope's *The Rape of the Lock* is intended to employ epic conventions for the purpose of satire. Recourse to intention can yield necessary insight into the relations between form and content, as well as relations between an artist and his audience. Moreover, given that the same statement made by different speakers in differing contexts could have vastly divergent meanings, it seems implausible to attribute autonomy to any statement or group of words, whether embodied in poetic language or not. As Frank Cioffi has remarked, to refute the intentionalist, Wimsatt and Beardsley should have shown that our response to a poem is not altered by reference to intentional information; but all they have shown is that this does not always or need not happen.

Wimsatt and Beardsley's later essay "The Affective Fallacy" is motivated by the same presupposition, namely, that literature or poetry is an autonomous object, independent not only of author psychology, biography, and history but also of the reader or audience that consumes it. The word "affection" is used by philosophers to refer to emotion, mental state, or disposition. Hence, the "affective fallacy" occurs, according to Wimsatt and Beardsley, when we attempt to explicate or interpret a poem through recourse to the emotions or mental state produced in the reader or hearer. As these authors put it, just as the intentional fallacy "is a confusion between the poem and its origins," so the affective fallacy "is a confusion between the poem and its *results* (what it *is* and what it *does*)."[7] Again, part of their problem with using the reader's response as a criterion of interpretation is that it makes criticism a subjective rather than objective activity, a discourse about the subject (the reader) rather than the object (the text). An affective reading of a poem "begins by trying to derive the standard of criticism from the psychological effects of the poem and ends in impressionism and relativism. The outcome of either Fallacy, the Intentional or the Affective, is that the poem itself, as an object of specifically critical judgment, tends to disappear" (*VI*, 21).

Wimsatt and Beardsley reject the attempts of critics such as I. A. Richards and philosophers such as Charles L. Stevenson to separate emotive from referential meaning, to distinguish what a word *suggests* and what it *means*. There is no evidence, they argue, that what a word *does* to a person is to be ascribed to anything except what it *means*, or what it *suggests* (*VI*, 22, 26). In other words, describing the effect of a poem is tantamount to describing its meaning. Wimsatt and Beardsley fear that the doctrine of emotive meaning, as separated from cognitive meaning, results in affective relativism and potentially endless license: on reading a given line of poetry, a reader could feel a certain emotion regardless of the cognitive quality of the line's context; there is no linguistic rule to stabilize or systematize emotional responses, and therefore there can be no parallel between cognitive meaning and emotional suggestion (*VI*, 27–28).

625

Certain schools of anthropology, the authors observe, have promoted affective relativism of a historical or cultural kind by using as the criterion of poetic value "the degree of feeling felt by the readers of a given era" (*VI*, 27).

Wimsatt and Beardsley trace various manifestations of affective theory back to Plato's view of poetry as inciting the passions, Aristotle's conception of *katharsis* whereby certain emotions were purged by tragedy, through Longinus' notion of sublimity as a state of the reader's soul, through Romantic conceptions of the imagination to modern impressionist critics (*VI*, 28–31). They even see the affective fallacy operating in the neoclassical unities of place and time: the idea that a drama should span one day and occur only in one location is designed to have a hallucinatory effect on the audience, convincing it that the action is realistic or probable (*VI*, 30). The most impressive recent champion of psychologistic or affective theory, in their eyes, is I. A. Richards, whose own critical practice, however, somewhat undermines his theories, given his demonstration that the suggestive aspects of poetic rhythm and form are actually connected with "other and more precise parts of poetic meaning" (*VI*, 32).

In general, Wimsatt and Beardsley argue that when readers report that a poem or story induces in them "vivid images, intense feelings, or heightened consciousness," such statements are too vague to be refuted or to be used by the objective critic. Indeed, an accurate account of what a poem does to the reader will ipso facto be a description of the poem itself, of its meaning (*VI*, 32–33). The critic, they insist, is not a reporter of his own affective and subjective states, not even a creator or facilitator of intersubjective consensus: he is "not a contributor to statistically countable reports about the poem, but a teacher or explicator of meanings." His report will only speak of emotions as stable and as "dependent upon a precise object" (*VI*, 34). The authors deny that there is a poetry of "pure emotion." Poetry, they say, "is characteristically a discourse about both emotions and objects, or about the emotive quality of objects, and this through its preoccupation with symbol and metaphor." The point is that even emotions are treated objectively, as part of the poetic subject matter (*VI*, 38). Indeed, for Wimsatt and Beardsley, "Poetry is a way of fixing emotions or making them more permanently perceptible when objects have undergone a functional change from culture to culture" (*VI*, 38). Rejecting, then, all models of reader-response or affective theory, whether these be highly subjective or intersubjective historical models, the authors affirm that criticism should not lose sight of its specifically literary objects of inquiry, that it should not become dependent on social history or of anthropology: "though cultures have changed and will change, poems remain and explain" (*VI*, 39).

The arguments of this essay are subject to many of the same criticisms that have been leveled against their positions in "The Intentional Fallacy." Perhaps the most fundamental objection is the impossibility and artificiality of treating literature as a self-contained object, an object which is not somehow realized in its performance, in interaction with readers who legitimately bring to the texts their own cultural backgrounds, interests, and assumptions. Moreover, the insistence on the text as an isolated object in itself effectively represents a philosophical regression to a world atomistically conceived as composed of separate and independent objects; despite its persistence on many levels of ideology and politics, it is a view that has been discredited by many thinkers, from Hegel and Marx, through Bergson, Sartre, and Derrida.

The Chicago School

Another group of critics, known as the Chicago School or the Neo-Aristotelians, began formulating their central ideas around the same time as the New Critics were voicing their manifestos. In the 1930s, departments of humanities at the University of Chicago were undergoing a radical transformation in an attempt to revive them and make them institutionally more competitive with the sciences. Six of the figures later known as the Chicago critics were involved in these changes: R. S. Crane, Richard McKeon, Elder Olson, W. R. Keast, Norman Maclean, and Bernard Weinberg. These critics later produced the central manifesto of the Chicago School, *Critics and Criticism: Ancient and Modern* (1952), which both attacked some of the important tenets of the New Criticism and elaborated an alternative formalistic method of criticism derived in part from Aristotle's *Poetics*.

In an earlier essay of 1934, Crane had anticipated (and influenced) Ransom's call that professional criticism should move from a primarily historical toward an aesthetic focus. However, Crane and the Chicago School generally diverged from the New Criticism in their insistence that literary study should integrate both systematic theory of literature (being informed by the history of literary theory) and the practice of close reading and explication of literary texts. Moreover, the Chicago School drew from Aristotle's *Poetics* a number of characteristic critical concerns, such as the emphasis on literary texts as "artistic wholes," the analytical importance of locating individual texts within given genres, and the need to identify textual and generic (as opposed to authorial) intention. Whereas the New Critics had focused attention on specifically poetic uses of language, irony, metaphor, tension, and balance, the Chicago School followed Aristotle in emphasizing plot, character, and thought. In general, the Neo-Aristotelians offered an alternative formalist poetics which acknowledged the mimetic, didactic, and affective functions of literature. The influence of this school, however, was overshadowed by the widespread adoption of New Critical dispositions throughout the American education system.

The Poetics of Modernism: Ezra Pound and T. S. Eliot

Modernism comprised a broad series of movements in Europe and America that came to fruition roughly between 1910 and 1930. Its major exponents and practitioners included Marcel Proust, James Joyce, Ezra Pound, T. S. Eliot, William Faulkner, Virginia Woolf, Luigi Pirandello, and Franz Kafka. These various modernisms were the results of many complex economic, political, scientific, and religious developments over the nineteenth century, which culminated in World War I (1914–1918). The vast devastation, psychological demoralization, and economic depression left by the war intensified the already existing reactions against bourgeois modes of thought and economic practice. Rationalism underwent renewed assaults from many directions: from philosophers such as Bergson, from the sphere of psychoanalysis, from neoclassicists such as T. E. Hulme, the New Humanists in America, and neo-Thomists such as

627

Jacques Maritain. These reactions were often underlain by a new understanding of language, as a conventional and historical construct. The modernist writer occupied a world that was often perceived as fragmented, where the old bourgeois ideologies of rationality, science, progress, civilization, and imperialism had been somewhat discredited; where the artist was alienated from the social and political world, and where art and literature were marginalized; where populations had been subjected to processes of mass standardization; where philosophy could no longer offer visions of unity, and where language itself was perceived to be an inadequate instrument for expression and understanding.

Hence, over the last fifty years or so, we have come to appreciate more fully the complexity and heterogeneity of literary modernism, in its nature and genesis. It is no longer regarded as simply a symbolist and imagistic reaction against nineteenth-century realism or naturalism or later versions of Romanticism. It is not so much that modernism, notwithstanding the political conservatism of many of its practitioners, turns away from the project of depicting reality; what more profoundly underlies modernistic literary forms is an awareness that the definitions of reality become increasingly complex and problematic. Modernists came to this common awareness by different paths: Yeats drew on the occult, on Irish myth and legend, as well as the Romantics and French symbolists. Proust drew on the insights of Bergson; Virginia Woolf, on Bergson, G. E. Moore, and others; Pound drew on various non-European literatures as well as French writers; T. S. Eliot, whose poetic vision was profoundly eclectic, drew on Dante, the Metaphysical poets, Laforgue, Baudelaire, and a number of philosophers.

In general, literary modernism was marked by a number of features: (1) the affirmation of a continuity, rather than a separation, between the worlds of subject and object, the self and the world. The human self is not viewed as a stable entity which simply engages with an already present external world of objects and other selves; (2) a perception of the complex roles of time, memory, and history in the mutual construction of self and world. Time is not conceived in a static model which separates past, present, and future as discrete elements in linear relation; rather, it is viewed as dynamic, with these elements influencing and changing one another. Human history is thus not already written; even the past can be altered in accordance with present human interests, motives, and viewpoints; (3) a breakdown of any linear narrative structure following the conventional Aristotelian model which prescribes beginning, middle, and end. Modernist poetry tends to be fragmented, creating its own internal "logic" of emotion, image, sound, symbol, and mood; (4) an acknowledgment of the complexity of experience: any given experience is vastly more complex than can be rendered in literal language. For example, the experience of "love" could be quite different from one person to another, yet language coercively subsumes these differing experiences under the same word and concept. Modernist poetry tends to veer away from any purported literal use of language which might presume a one-to-one correspondence between words and things; it relies far more on suggestion and allusion rather than overt statement; (5) a self-consciousness regarding the process of literary composition. This embraces both an awareness of how one's own work relates to the literary tradition as a whole, and also an ironic stance toward the content of one's own work; (6) finally, and most importantly, an awareness of the problematic nature of language.

This indeed underlies the other elements cited above. If there is no simple correspondence between language and reality, and if these realms are mutually constituted through patterns of coherence, then a large part of the poet's task lies in a more precise use of language which offers alternative definitions of reality. Eliot once said that the poet must "distort" language in order to create his meaning.

Of all the Western modernists, T. S. Eliot (1888–1965) has been the most pervasively influential through both his poetry and his literary criticism. He was initially influenced by the American New Humanists such as Irving Babbitt and Paul Elmer, and his early ideas owed a great deal to their emphasis on tradition, classicism, and impersonality. Eliot was also indebted to later nineteenth-century French poets and particularly to Ezra Pound and the imagist movement. Pound assumed a broad range of critical roles: as poet-critic, he promoted his own work and the works of figures such as Frost, Joyce, and Eliot; he translated numerous texts from Anglo-Saxon, Latin, Greek, and Chinese; and, associating with various schools such as imagism and vorticism, he advocated a poetry which was concise, concrete, precise in expression of emotion, and appropriately informed by a sense of tradition. As a result of his suggestions, Eliot's major poem *The Waste Land* was radically condensed and transformed.

Eliot took his so-called theory of "tradition" from both Babbitt and Pound, though it had political precedents in conservative theories of tradition such as that of Edmund Burke. Eliot's theory claimed that the major works of art, both past and present, formed an "ideal order" which is continually modified by subsequent works of art. The central implication here was that contemporary writers should find common ground with that tradition even as they extended it. Eliot effectively succeeded in redefining the European literary tradition, continuing the humanists' onslaught against the Romantics, and bringing into prominence Dante, the Metaphysical poets, and the French symbolists. Eliot also advanced an "impersonal" notion of poetry, whereby the poet expresses not a personality but a precise formulation of thought and feeling such as is lacking in "ordinary" experience. The poet, according to Eliot, employs an "objective correlative," whereby objects and events in the external world are used to express complexes of thought and emotion.

In terms of literary history, Eliot held that a "dissociation of sensibility" had set in after the seventeenth century that entailed a disjunction of various human faculties such as reason and emotion which had previously been integrated within a unified sensibility. Eliot's ideas bore an ambivalent relationship with the claims of the New Criticism. On the one hand, he believed that the aesthetic dimension of works of art is irreducible; on the other, he believed, with increasing insistence throughout his career, that art is irreducibly bound to its social, religious, and literary context. The ideas of Pound and Eliot have had a lasting influence but their most forceful impact occurred between the 1920s and the 1940s.

Notes

1   Victor Shklovsky, "Art as Technique," in *Russian Formalist Criticism: Four Essays*, trans. Lee T. Lemon and Marion J. Reis (Lincoln: University of Nebraska Press, 1965), p. 5. Hereafter page citations are given in the text.

2   Boris Eichenbaum, "The Theory of the 'Formal Method,'" in *Russian Formalist Criticism*, trans. Lemon and Reis, p. 103. Hereafter page citations are given in the text.

3   Part of this account is indebted to the valuable introduction to M. M. Bakhtin, *The Dialogic Imagination: Four Essays*, ed. Michael Holquist, trans. Caryl Emerson and Michael Holquist (Austin: University of Texas Press, 1981). Bakhtin's essay "The Dialogic Imagination" is contained in this volume, which is hereafter cited as *DI*.

4   "Linguistics and Poetics," in Roman Jakobson, *Language in Literature*, ed. Krystyna Pomorska and Stephen Rudy (Cambridge, MA and London: Harvard University Press, 1987), p. 63. Hereafter cited as *LL*.

5   John Crowe Ransom, *The World's Body* (Baton Rouge: Louisiana State University Press, 1968), p. 329. Hereafter cited as *WB*.

6   W. K. Wimsatt, Jr. and Monroe C. Beardsley, "The Intentional Fallacy," in W. K. Wimsatt, Jr., *The Verbal Icon* (Lexington: University of Kentucky Press, 1967), p. 4. Hereafter cited as *VI*.

7   W. K. Wimsatt, Jr. and Monroe C. Beardsley, "The Affective Fallacy," in *VI*, p. 21.

CHAPTER 24

STRUCTURALISM

M uch criticism since the 1950s can be regarded as an implicit impugnment of widely institutionalized New Critical practices. A sustained challenge came from structuralism and some of its descendents such as deconstruction. In the West, the influx of structuralism was to some extent anticipated in the work of the Canadian Northrop Frye, who was the most influential theorist in America of what is called Myth Criticism, which was in vogue from the 1940s to the mid-1960s and whose practitioners included Richard Chase, Leslie Fiedler, Daniel Hoffman, and Philip Wheelwright. Drawing on the findings of anthropology and psychology regarding universal myths, rituals, and folktales, these critics were intent on restoring spiritual content to a world they saw as alienated, fragmented, and ruled by scientism, empiricism, positivism, and technology. They wished to redeem the role of myth, which might comprehend magic, imagination, dreams, intuition, and the unconscious. They viewed the creation of myth as integral to human thought, and believed that literature emerges out of a core of myth, where "myth" is understood as a collective attempt on the part of various cultures and groups to establish a meaningful context for human existence. Frye's *Anatomy of Criticism* (1957) continued the formalist emphasis of the New Criticism but insisted even more strongly that criticism should be a scientific, objective, and systematic discipline. Moreover, Frye held that such literary criticism views literature itself as a system. For example, the mythoi of Spring, Summer, Autumn, and Winter gave rise to fundamental literary modes such as comedy, tragedy, irony, and romance. Given the recurrence of basic symbolic motifs, literary history is a repetitive and self-contained cycle. Hence the historical element ostensibly informing Frye's formalism is effectively abrogated, literature being viewed as a timeless, static, and autonomous construct.

Frye's static model, exhibiting recurrent patterns, is a feature shared by structuralist views of language and literature. The foundations of structuralism were laid in the work of the Swiss linguist Ferdinand de Saussure, whose insights were developed by the French anthropologist Claude Lévi-Strauss (b. 1908), Roland Barthes, and others. In his *Course in General Linguistics* (1916), Saussure distinguished *langue*, the system and rules of language, from *parole* or speech. It was the former, according to Saussure, which lent itself to synchronic structural analysis: the system of language could be analyzed at a given point in time as a set of interdependent elements (as opposed to a diachronic study which looked at developments over time). Moreover, Saussure attacked the conventional correspondence theory of meaning whereby language was viewed as a naming process, each word corresponding to the thing it names. Saussure urged that the sign unites not a thing and a name but a concept (signified) and sound-image (signifier). He argued that the bond between signifier and signified is arbitrary (and not natural) in that a concept is not intrinsically linked to a particular signifier. The meaning is determined by collective behavior or convention and is fixed by rules. Hence language is a system of signs and meaning itself is relational, produced by interaction of various signifiers and signifieds within that system. In addition to these insights, what Claude Lévi-Strauss and others took from Saussure was an emphasis on linguistic features described as structures; they also stressed the deep structures underlying various phenomena and sometimes referred these structures to basic characteristics of the human mind.

Lévi-Strauss arrived at some influential insights into the nature of myth. He observed that, despite their contingent character, myths throughout the world exhibited an astounding similarity. Drawing on Saussure's ideas, he suggested that myth was a specific form and use of language. What is specific to myth, according to Lévi-Strauss, is that in addition to *langue* and *parole*, it uses a third referent which combines the properties of the first two. On the one hand, a myth refers to events having taken place long ago; but what gives the myth an enduring value is that the specific pattern described is timeless: it explains the present and past as well as the future. He considered that in modern societies myth has been largely replaced by politics: for example, the French Revolution is viewed as both a sequence of events in the past and as a timeless pattern detectable in contemporary French social structure. Hence the myth had a double structure, historical and ahistorical. Lévi-Strauss held that the structure of mythical thought addresses our inability to connect two kinds of relationship by asserting that contradictory relationships are identical inasmuch as they are both self-contradictory in a similar way. Hence the Oedipus myth is a kind of logical tool. He saw the purpose of myth as providing a logical model capable of overcoming a contradiction.

An important claim of Lévi-Strauss was that his method eliminates the problematic quest for a true or earlier version of a myth. He defined the myth as consisting of all of its versions. Even Freud's account of the Oedipus myth is part of the myth. Even when variants exhibit differences, the latter can themselves be correlated. Hence there is no single true version of which all the others are but copies or distortions. Every version belongs to the myth. A myth displays a "slated" structure, which comes to the surface through repetition. Myth grows spiral-wise until the intellectual impulse behind it is exhausted. Its growth is a continuous process whereas its structure remains discontinuous. Lévi-Strauss saw his theory as generating a novel view of the progress of thought: the logic in mythical thought is as rigorous as that of modern science; the difference, or apparent improvement, lies not in the progress of man's mind but in the discovery of new areas to which it may apply.

Also entailed in structuralist analyses was the anti-humanist view that, since language is an institution, individual human agency is unprivileged, neither human beings nor social phenomena having essences. Hence, structuralism diverged sharply from the

Romantic notion of the author as the source of meaning, and shifts emphasis away from authorial intention toward the broader and impersonal linguistic structure in which the author's text participates, and which indeed enables that text.

Many of these principles underlay the methods of American structuralists. Structuralism was imported into America from France during the 1960s and its leading exponents included Roman Jakobson, Jonathan Culler, Michael Riffaterre, Claudio Guillen, Gerald Prince, and Robert Scholes. Other American thinkers working in the field of semiotics have included C. S. Peirce, Charles Morris, and Noam Chomsky. In his renowned study *Structuralist Poetics* (1975), Jonathan Culler explained that structuralist investigations of literature would seek to identify the systems of conventions underlying literature. Robert Scholes, in *Structuralism in Literature: An Introduction* (1974), sought a scientific basis for the study of literature as an interconnected system of various texts. Other key texts of structuralism in America included a special issue of *Yale French Studies* (1966), and volumes entitled *Structuralism* (1970) edited by Jacques Ehrmann and *The Structuralist Controversy* (1970) edited by Richard Macksey and Eugenio Donato. Also influential in America was the work of Roman Jakobson, who taught for many years at various American universities, and who worked out an influential model of communication as well as a distinction between metaphor and metonymy in the analysis of narratives. The major principles of structuralism can now be examined in detail in the work of Saussure and Roland Barthes.

Ferdinand de Saussure (1857–1913)

Ferdinand de Saussure was effectively the founder of modern linguistics, as well as of structuralism; and, while much poststructuralism arose in partial reaction against his thought, it nonetheless presupposed his theoretical advances in linguistics. Born into a Swiss family, Saussure studied at the universities of Berlin and Leipzig; he taught, in Paris and later at the University of Geneva, a wide range of subjects including Gothic, Old German, Latin, and Persian, as well as courses in historical and comparative linguistics. It was, however, his lectures in general linguistics, posthumously compiled by his colleagues as *Course in General Linguistics* (1916), that proved to be of seminal influence in a broad range of fields, including anthropology, as in the work of Lévi-Strauss; the semiological work of Roland Barthes; the literary-philosophical notions of Derrida; the analyses of ideology by structuralist Marxists such as Louis Althusser; the psychoanalytic theories of Jacques Lacan; and the analyses of language conducted by feminists such as Julia Kristeva.

Prior to Saussure, the predominant modes of analyzing language were historical and philological. As opposed to a diachronic approach which studies changes in language over a period of time, Saussure undertook a synchronic approach which saw language as a structure that could be studied in its entirety at a given point in time. Saussure pioneered a number of further influential and radical insights. Firstly, he denied that there is somehow a natural connection between words and things, urging that this connection is conventional. This view of language also challenges the view of reality as somehow independent and existing outside of language, reducing language to merely a "name-giving system." Saussure's view implies that we build up an understanding of our world by means of language and view the world *through* language. Secondly, Saussure argued that language is a system of signs in relation: no sign has meaning in isolation; rather, its signification depends on its difference from other signs and generally on its situation within the entire network of signs. Finally, Saussure made a distinction between two dimensions of language: *langue*, which refers to language as a structured system, grounded on certain rules; and *parole*, the specific acts of speech or utterance which are based on those rules.

In his *Course in General Linguistics* Saussure explains that it is *langue*, not the acts of speech, which must be the object of scientific investigation. Indeed, the "science of language" is possible only if many elements of speech are excluded.[1] Understood in this sense, language (as opposed to speech) is "outside of the individual who can never create nor modify it by himself." It exists through an implicit contract between the members of a community, and it must be learned in order for a person to communicate through speech (*CGL*, 14). Saussure goes so far as to say that the "distinguishing character of the sign . . . is that in some way it always eludes the individual or social will" (*CGL*, 17). He points out other differences between language and speech. Whereas speech is homogeneous, language is heterogeneous: "It is a system of signs in which the only essential thing is the union of meanings and sound-images, and in which both parts of the sign are psychological." Moreover, language is no less concrete than speech: language is constituted by linguistic signs which are collectively approved, and these signs "are realities that have their seat in the brain." Finally, unlike speech, language can be classified among human phenomena: it is a social institution, with unique features that distinguish it from other, political and legal, institutions (*CGL*, 15).

Saussure suggests that the study of language should be situated within a larger investigative province, which he names semiology, from the Greek word *semeion* meaning "sign." Semiology, he explains, "would show what constitutes signs, what laws govern them . . . Linguistics is only a part of the general science of semiology; the laws discovered by semiology will be applicable to linguistics" (*CGL*, 16). Saussure proposes that semiology be "recognized as an independent science with its own object like all the other sciences." Language needs to be studied "in itself," rather than, as in the past, in its connection with other things. The task of linguistics is to discover what makes language a "special system," but to do this, the linguist must learn what language has in common with other semiological systems (*CGL*, 17).

Saussure's exposition in his *Course* of the "Nature of the Linguistic Sign" is worth considering in some detail since it provides a reference point for much subsequent literary and cultural theory. Especially important is his use of the terms "sign," "signifier," and "signified." He attacks the conventional correspondence theory of meaning whereby language is viewed as a naming process, each word corresponding to the thing it names. Saussure offers three objections to this view: it assumes that ready-made ideas exist before words; it fails to tell us whether a name is vocal or psychological in nature; finally, it assumes that the linking of a name and thing is a simple operation (*CGL*, 65).

As against this conventional view, Saussure urges that *both* terms of the linguistic sign are psychological in nature; the sign unites not a thing and a name but a *concept* and *sound-image*. The latter is not the material sound but the "psychological imprint of the sound," the impression it makes on our senses; hence it too is psychological (*CGL*, 66). To avoid ambiguity, Saussure suggests a new terminology: *sign* designates the whole construct; *signified* designates the *concept*; and *signifier* designates the *sound-image*. As Saussure states, the linguistic sign in its totality is "a two-sided psychological entity," consisting of both signifier and signified. The sign as a whole refers to the actual object in the world, as displayed in the following diagram:

Signifier (the word or sound-image "table")

Sign > Actual object: table

Signified (the concept of "table")

The sign has two primordial characteristics: firstly, the bond between signifier and signified is *arbitrary*: by this, Saussure means that the concept (e.g., "sister") is not linked by any inner relationship to the succession of sounds which serves as its signifier (in French, s-o-r). Saussure offers another clarification: the bond is not *natural* but unmotivated, based on collective behavior or convention, fixed by rules. Signifiers and gestures don't have any intrinsic value. Saussure is careful to suggest that "arbitrary" does not imply that the choice of the signifier is left entirely to the speaker: the individual has no power to change a sign in any way once it has become established in the linguistic community (*CGL*, 69).

The second characteristic of the signifier is its linear nature. Being auditory, it is unfolded in time and thus represents a span which is measurable in a single dimension. In contrast, visual signifiers can offer groupings in several dimensions. Auditory signifiers, having only the dimension of time, are presented in succession, forming a chain; this is apparent when they are represented in writing, where a spatial line of graphic marks is substituted for succession in time (*CGL*, 70).

In part II of his *Course*, Saussure addresses the important connection between thought and language. Prior to language, he suggests, our thought is "a shapeless and indistinct mass," and we "would be unable to make a clear-cut, consistent distinction between two ideas." There are no ideas, he insists, before the appearance of language (*CGL*, 111–112). Equally, however, sounds by themselves are not delimited or clear prior to their expression of thought and ideas. Saussure pictures what he calls the total "linguistic fact," i.e., the two elements involved in the functioning of language, as comprising two series: a series of "jumbled ideas" on one plane, and "the equally vague plane of sounds" (*CGL*, 112). The role of language is to "serve as a link between thought and sound" under conditions that bring about a "reciprocal delimitation" of the units of both thought and sound. It is not a question of thoughts being given material form or of sounds being transformed into mental entities. The reciprocal nature of the process means that we must think of a combination "thought-sound": language takes shape "between two shapeless masses," with ideas and sounds achieving definition at the same time (*CGL*, 112). To illustrate this process, Saussure imagines language as a piece of paper: thought is the front and sound is the back; one cannot cut the front without also cutting the back. Likewise, says Saussure, in language, "one can neither divide sound from thought nor thought from sound." If we were to make this division, it would be artificial, and the result would be the domain of pure psychology (ideas) or pure phonology (sounds). The domain of linguistics is precisely this area where sound and thought combine, and *"their combination produces a form, not a substance,"* a statement that Saussure will elaborate later (*CGL*, 113).

The combination of thought and sound helps explain the arbitrary nature of the sign: the choice of a given piece of sound to name a certain idea is, says Saussure, "completely arbitrary." Hence a linguistic system can be created only by a community since the meanings and values of words "owe their existence solely to usage and general acceptance" (*CGL*, 113). What the union of thought and sound also shows us is that one cannot start with isolated correlations of given sounds and thoughts and build up a linguistic system by adding them together. Conversely, one must begin with the entire "interdependent whole" and obtain the particular elements of the linguistic system by analysis (*CGL*, 113).

Saussure makes a crucial distinction between linguistic *value* and *signification*. While he concedes that value is one element in signification, he insists that the two terms are not identical. The value of a term in language, he states, arises from the simultaneous presence of other, dissimilar, terms that can be exchanged for it or other similar terms that can be compared with it. A word may have a certain signification or meaning but this will not be the same as its value since the latter is determined by "the concurrence of everything that exists outside it." For example, the French word *mouton* may have the same signification as the English word "sheep"; but these words do not have the same value since the English language has a further word, "mutton," to designate a piece of meat ready to be eaten, whereas the French language does not (*CGL*, 115–116). Another example might be the word "love" in the English language, which will have a different value from the various words for love in the Greek language, such as *agape*, *eros*, and *charitas*. All such values, says Saussure, emanate from the linguistic system. When these values "are said to correspond to concepts, it is understood that the concepts are purely differential and defined not by their positive content but negatively by their relations with the other terms of the system. Their most precise characteristic is in being what the others are not" (*CGL*, 117). An example may clarify Saussure's point: when we talk of the color "green," we are not identifying some self-subsistent essence of green-ness; in other words, our definition is not "positive." Rather, if we say that something is green, we are also implicitly stating that it is not blue or red or any other color. In this sense, our statement is "negative" since we are identifying the color in relation to what it is *not*, and our designation presupposes an entire network or system of preexisting linguistic values in order to be possible at all. If we had no conception of other colors, it would be impossible in isolation to attribute the adjective "green" to any object.

Just as linguistic value, when approached from the standpoint of concepts, "is made up solely of relations and differences with respect to the other terms of language," so the same can be said of the "material" dimension of value, i.e., sound. The important element in a word, says Saussure, is not the sound alone but "the phonic differences that make it possible to distinguish this word from all others, for differences carry signification" (*CGL*, 118). This is an important statement: just as concepts have values that are differential, i.e., determined by their differences from other concepts, so the sounds themselves of words exist in a large network of sounds; each sound acquires value not in itself in isolation but through its difference from other sounds. Moreover, sound in itself does not even belong to language: it is only sounds that have acquired signification and value through interaction and difference from other sounds that belong to language. And even here, it is not the sounds themselves that pertain to language; it is the *differences* between sounds that form part of language. This helps to explain Saussure's earlier statement that the signifier is *psychological*, not material. As he now elaborates, "the linguistic signifier . . . is not phonic but incorporeal – constituted not by its material substance but by the differences that separate its sound-image from all others" (*CGL*, 118–119). Saussure sees an identical state of affairs in writing, where signs are arbitrary, the value of letters is purely negative and differential, and linguistic value functions through reciprocal opposition (*CGL*, 120).

Summarizing, Saussure states that "in language there are only differences." He observes that "a difference generally implies positive terms between which the difference is set up; but in language there are only differences *without positive terms* . . . language has neither ideas nor sounds that existed before the linguistic system" (*CGL*, 120). As mentioned earlier, if language is a system of relations between terms, it is these very relations that constitute the terms themselves; in other words, it is not a question of having a set of terms and then relating these to one another; the terms are *created* by the process of relation-forming. However, this negative and differential status, says Saussure, obtains only if the signifier and signified are considered separately; in other words, if the system of concepts and the system of sounds are considered independently of one another. If we consider the sign in its totality, i.e., if we consider the system of concepts and the system of sounds together as a system of signs, "their combination," says Saussure, "is a positive fact: it is even the sole type of fact that language has, for maintaining the parallelism between the two classes of differences is the distinctive function of the linguistic institution" (*CGL*, 120–121). Saussure explains this as follows: when we compare two total signs (two sets of signifiers with their signifieds) we can no longer speak of difference, since difference can apply only to the comparison of two ideas or two sound-images. Between signs there is not difference but distinctness and opposition: this kind of opposition is the basis for the "entire mechanism of language." A sign is constituted by whatever distinguishes it from other signs (*CGL*, 121). In language, says Saussure, there are no simple terms, only complex ones: "everywhere and always there is the same complex equilibrium of terms that mutually condition each other. Putting it another way, *language is a form and not a substance*" (*CGL*, 122). In this renowned statement, Saussure appears to claim that language is not constituted by terms that have any independent essence or substance but by varying sets of relations which comprise the terms themselves.

Saussure points out that the relations and differences between linguistic terms fall into two distinct groups, corresponding to two forms of our mental activity, both "indispensable to the life of language." In discourse, the relations acquired by words are based on the linear nature of language "because they are chained together." These linear relations are "syntagmatic" (*CGL*, 123). Outside of discourse, however, words can acquire many additional kinds of relationships, which are not linear: they can be based on associations of meaning, or similarity of form (such as having the same prefix or suffix or ending). Such relationships are "associative" and in these a given word is "like the center of a constellation" (*CGL*, 126); whereas a syntagm comprises a fixed order of succession and a fixed number of elements, associative relations are characterized by an indeterminate order and indefinite number.

Roland Barthes (1915–1980)

Roland Barthes' theoretical development is often seen as embodying a transition from structuralist to poststructuralist perspectives, though certain of his works are characterized by a Marxian perspective. Barthes effectively extended structural analysis and semiology (the study of signs) to broad cultural phenomena, and it was he also who confronted the limits of structuralism, pointing the way to freer and more relativistic assessments of texts and their role in culture. It was Barthes who made famous the notion of the "death of the author," the idea of the text as a site of free play or pleasure, and differences such as those between "work" and "text," and "writerly" and "readerly" works of art. As such, he anticipates many facets of poststructuralism, including certain elements of deconstruction, cultural studies, and queer studies.

Barthes was born in Cherbourg in France, and later moved with his mother (having lost his father when he was only a year old) to Paris. Notwithstanding his suffering from tuberculosis, his homosexuality, and his esoteric and eclectic worldview, he was at times affiliated with certain mainstream French institutions, such as the National Center for Scientific Research (CNRS), the École des Hautes Études, and the Collège de France. His first works derived inspiration from Saussure, Sartre, and Marxist writers such as Brecht: *Writing Degree Zero* (1953) and *Mythologies* (1957). Then came a number of influential works in the structuralist vein, such as *Elements of Semiology* (1964) and his seminal essay "Introduction to the Structural Analysis of Narrative" (1966). His renowned essay "The Death of the Author" appeared in 1968. Barthes' multivalent analysis of Balzac's novella *Sarrasine* in his *S/Z* (1970) marks the point of transition between Barthes' earlier structuralism and his later poststructuralist dispositions. These dispositions were elaborated in his essay "From Work to Text" (1971) and books such as *The Pleasure of the Text* (1973).

In *Writing Degree Zero* Barthes examines the development of literary forms. Viewing language as inescapably bound to social institutions and norms, he sees the literary movements represented by Flaubert and Mallarmé as aiming toward a "zero degree of writing," an attempt to extricate language from its sociality, to promote the creation of form as an end in itself, or, in Barthes' terms, as "the end-product of craftsmanship," and to create "neutral" modes of writing.[2] Barthes sees this phase of literary history as coinciding with and expressing a "disintegration of bourgeois consciousness" (*WDZ*, 5). Since the period of bourgeois triumph, he notes, one mode of writing was exalted, a writing drilled toward the task of definition. By 1660, he says, clarity had become a predominant value of language, expressing a bourgeois "essentialist mythology" of man. It was when such bourgeois universality became questionable that modes of writing began to multiply and form itself became a kind of ethics (*WDZ*, 58). At this stage, says Barthes, writing absorbs the whole identity of a literary work: writing is a blind alley because society itself is a blind alley. Literature becomes the "Utopia of language" (*WDZ*, 56–60, 85–88).

Barthes said that the motivation for his subsequent book, *Mythologies*, was resentment at the bourgeois confusion of nature and history, as in the attempts of the bourgeois class to pass off their values and agenda – which were historically produced and historically specific – as somehow natural and universal.[3] In this book, Barthes undertook an ideological critique of various products of mass bourgeois culture (rang-ing from soap to advertising to images of Rome), attempting to account for this mys-tification of culture or history into a "universal nature" (*Myth.*, 9). He argued that such mystification is explained by the notion of "myth," and he devotes the second part of his book to a theoretical analysis of myth.

Barthes' most fundamental suggestion is that myth is not an object, a concept, or an idea but a language, a type of speech. It is a mode of signification and is defined by the way in which it utters its message (*Myth.*, 109). He cautions that there are no eternal myths; it is human history that "converts reality into speech" (*Myth.*, 110). Mythical speech, says Barthes, is composed of material that has already been worked on to make it suitable for communication. In explaining the nature of myth, Barthes reiterates Saussure's view that semiology is comprised of three (rather than two) terms: the *signifier*, which is an acoustic (mental) image, the *signified*, which is a concept, and the *sign*, which is a word and which consists of the combination of signifier and signified. In other words, the sign is a *relation* (*Myth.*, 113). The structure of myth repeats this tridimensional pattern: myth is a second-order semiological system. An entire sign in the first system becomes a mere signifier (only one component of the sign) in the second system:

```
Language:  Signifier————————Signified
                    Sign
Myth:           SIGNIFIER——————————SIGNIFIED
                        SIGN
```

Hence in myth there are two semiological systems, one being staggered; the object of the first is language, and the object of the second is myth, or metalanguage. In other words, myth is a second language *in which* one speaks about the first language (*Myth.*, 115). We can use an example offered by Barthes himself to illustrate this process: on the cover of a Parisian magazine, "a young Negro in a French uniform is saluting, with his eyes uplifted," probably gazing at the French flag (*Myth.*, 116). We can break down the semiological structure of this as follows:

```
Language: Signifier: Negro saluting————Signified: Frenchness/militariness
                    Sign = Meaning
Myth:                   Signifier = Form——  —Signified: French imperiality
                        Signification
```

In the first semiological system, that of language, the signifier is the black soldier giving the French salute, and this signifies perhaps a "mixture of Frenchness and militariness." Barthes reminds us that the entire sign of the first system provides the signifier for the second, mythical, system. As the final term of the first system, the signifier is equivalent to *meaning*; but as the first term of the second system, the signifier is *form*. And what this form signifies is something different from the original meaning of the picture: indeed, this original meaning and its entire history are left behind. In other words, we are no longer concerned with the black soldier, his peculiar biography or location. All of this history, as attached to the original meaning, is left behind, is emptied out of the form. We are now confronted with a new signification: "that France is a great Empire, that all her sons, without any colour discrimination, faithfully serve under her flag, and that there is no better answer to the detractors of an alleged colonialism than the zeal shown by this Negro in serving his so-called oppressors" (*Myth.*, 116). The new signifier, the new form, then, signifies nothing personal about the black soldier but the ideal of French imperiality in general. Barthes calls the final term of the mythical system "signification" so as to distinguish it from "sign," which is the final term of the linguistic system (*Myth.*, 117). Indeed, he identifies "signification" with myth itself (*Myth.*, 121).

What myth does, then, is to free certain concepts or meanings from their original history and context, and to implant a "whole new history." Hence, "the fundamental character of the mythical concept is to be *appropriated.*" Such appropriation shows that the concept has an open character: it is "not at all an abstract, purified essence." Rather, its unity and coherence derive from the function into which it is coerced (*Myth.*, 119). Mythical concepts are historical, which is why history can suppress them; and they have at their disposal the entirety of language, "an unlimited mass of signifiers" (*Myth.*, 120). Other examples of mythical concepts might be democracy, freedom, and American imperiality, signifiers which are often wrenched from their actual history and made to signify concepts such as peace, world order, and security. Barthes elaborates certain further important features of myth. Myth is a type of speech defined more by its intention than its literal sense. Furthermore, it is a type of speech that is "turned towards me, I am subjected to its intentional force . . . I feel as if I were personally receiving an imperious injunction." And yet, notwithstanding this character of "adhomination" whereby I personally am made to feel called or answerable, myth also has the character of making "itself look neutral and innocent" (*Myth.*, 125). Barthes explains that myth "essentially aims at causing an immediate impression," promoting the reading of myth as a factual system when in fact it is merely a semiological system (*Myth.*, 130–131). Hence myth naturalizes the concept, and this in fact is "the very principle of myth: it transforms history into nature" (*Myth.*, 129). In other words, it deforms and dehistoricizes the original connection between signifier and signified: it removes the recognition that such connections were historically produced in specific circumstances; and it presents those connections as natural and universal. Myth, in transforming meaning into form, "is always a language-robbery" (*Myth.*, 131). As Barthes explains, "myth has the task of giving an historical intention a natural justification, and making contingency appear eternal . . . What the world supplies to myth is an historical reality . . . and what myth gives in return is a *natural* image of this reality . . . myth is constituted by the loss of the historical quality of things: in it, things lose the memory that they once were made. The world enters language as a dialectical relation between activities, between human actions; it comes out of myth as a harmonious display of essences" (*Myth.*, 142). Barthes adds that the function of myth is to "empty reality" and that "*myth is depoliticized speech.*" Barthes uses the term "political" to designate real human relations in their power of making the world; myth makes opaque this process of human labor. For example, in the case of the black French soldier, what myth removes is the contingent, historical, fabricated character of colonialism, presenting it, conversely, as essential, universal, and natural (*Myth.*, 143). In this way, myth establishes a world "without depth," a world of "blissful clarity" where things "appear to mean something by themselves" (*Myth.*, 143). Or, a world where the meaning of things lies no deeper than their isolated existence.

What has been most influential in Barthes' account of myth is his equation of the process of myth-making with the process of bourgeois ideology. After the French Revolution of 1789 which marked the rise to power of the bourgeoisie, this class underwent what Barthes calls an ex-nominating operation: "the bourgeoisie is defined as *the class which does not want to be named*" (*Myth.*, 138). This ex-nominating phenomenon, says Barthes, was effected through the idea of the "nation": the bourgeoisie as a class merges into the concept of "nation," thereby presenting bourgeois values and interests as in the national interest, through such preemptive identification. Through this depoliticizing and "universalistic effort" of its vocabulary, the bourgeoisie was able to postulate its own definitions of justice, truth, and law as universal; it was able to postulate its own definition of humanity as comprising "human nature"; and "bourgeois norms are experienced as the evident laws of a natural order" (*Myth.*, 138–140). Barthes asserts that "our Justice, our diplomacy, our conversations . . . everything, in everyday life, is dependent on the representation which the *bourgeoisie has and makes us have* of the relations between man and the world" (*Myth.*, 140). In fact, this flight from the name "bourgeois" is "the bourgeois ideology itself, the process through which the bourgeoisie transforms the reality of the world into an image of the world, History into Nature" (*Myth.*, 141). The first bourgeois philosophers, observes Barthes, pervaded the world with myths, and subjected all things to rationality. Bourgeois ideology is scientistic (inordinately obsessed with its own scientific status): it records facts but refuses explanations, so that the order of the world is seen as sufficient or ineffable but never significant. It promotes an "image of unchanging humanity, characterized by an indefinite repetition of its identity" (*Myth.*, 142).

According to Barthes, there are two basic ways in which myth can be opposed or undermined. The first is to mythify it in its turn so as to produce an artificial myth. The original myth could be used as a point of departure for a third semiological chain, the signification of the original myth being taken as the first term of a second myth. This has been the practice of writers such as Flaubert who effectively present elements of bourgeois myth and ideology as objects of demythifying analysis (*Myth.*, 135–136). Nonetheless, Barthes denies that a writer can somehow present reality (as opposed to myth) via language: "Language is a form, it cannot possibly be either realistic or unrealistic" (*Myth.*, 136). Barthes sees Flaubert's great merit in the fact that he "gave to the problem of realism a frankly semiological solution." In other words, while Barthes acknowledges that literary form does have a responsibility toward reality, he praises Flaubert for recognizing that this responsibility must be measured in semiological terms. In other words, as Barthes puts it, the "writer's language is not expected to *represent* reality, but to signify it." We must, warns Barthes, deal with the writer's realism either in ideological or in semiological terms, without confusing them (*Myth.*, 137). For Barthes, as for Hegel and Marx, the notion of objectivity is deeply tied to the metaphysics of labor. As seen earlier, Barthes describes the ability to counter myth in terms of the language of the human being as a producer, the speech which has the power to transform reality.

A second manner in which myth might be countered is through the very opposite of myth: if myth is depoliticized speech, it can be opposed through speech which "*remains* political." The language of man as a producer is a language spoken to transform reality rather than to preserve it as an image. In other words, language is linked to the making of things. Barthes' insight may derive from Marx's view, in *The German Ideology*, of language as one material mode of production among others (*GI*, 18, 21, 51, 118). Hence, says Barthes, revolutionary language cannot be mythical: it "announces itself openly as revolution and thereby abolishes myth" (*Myth.*, 145–146). The speech of the oppressed, says Barthes, is monotonous and immediate, expressing their actions (*Myth.*, 148). Barthes ends his book by drawing up a list of the rhetorical forms of bourgeois myth: inoculation, whereby certain evils are acknowledged so as to conceal greater evils; denuding objects of their history; identification, whereby all experiences, even those of confrontation, are reduced to sameness, in a profound inability to imagine the Other; refuge in tautological explanations; neither-norism, or the reduction of the world to balancing and mutually canceling opposites; a quantification of quality, whereby all things are reduced to an economy of commodification; and statement of fact, such as to refuse explanation and to imply an unalterable hierarchy in the world (*Myth.*, 150–154). What we must ultimately seek, says Barthes, is a "reconciliation between reality and men, between description and explanation, between object and knowledge" (*Myth.*, 159).

Barthes' *Elements of Semiology* is in many ways a classic statement of structuralism. In the introduction to this text, Barthes states that "we are . . . a civilization of the written word," suggesting that there is no extensive system of signs outside of language.[4] He admits that objects, images, and behavior could signify but only in virtue of possessing a "linguistic admixture" (*ES*, 9–10). If such insights now seem commonplace to us, that is partly because structuralism has defined the contours of much twentieth-century thought. Barthes suggests that the "elements" of semiology are contained in four sets of terms: (1) language and speech; (2) signifier and signified; (3) syntagm and system; and (4) denotation and connotation (*ES*, 12).

Talking of Saussure's connection between language (as a structure) and speech (as a series of individual acts), Barthes agrees with many other theorists in defining language as "a collective contract which one must accept in its entirety if one wishes to communicate." Arguing that language resists modifications from a single individual, he quotes Jakobson's statement that "private property in the sphere of language does not exist." Hence language is always socialized, even at the individual level (*ES*, 14, 21). Barthes suggests that there is an affinity between Saussure's view of language and Durkheim's concept of a collective conscience which is independent of its particular manifestations (*ES*, 23). Durkheim himself had stressed the transcendent nature of "society": it had been his aim to show that "social facts" existed on a level of causality independent of "individual facts."[5]

On the connection of signifier and signified, Barthes rejects Saussure's renowned claim that this connection is arbitrary: on the contrary, it is a necessary connection, the result of a collective contract and training. Barthes inclines toward Benveniste's view that what is arbitrary is the connection between the signifier and the *thing* (*ES*, 50). The connection, the act of signification, is a process, the result of a collective contract and, over a period of time, the connection becomes naturalized (*ES*, 48, 51). Barthes cites the phenomenon of the inevitable "semanticization" of language: "as soon as there is a society, every usage is converted into a sign of itself." The use of a raincoat, for example, is inseparable from signs of the atmospheric situation. For Barthes, this "universal semanticization expresses the fact that there is no reality except when it is intelligible" (*ES*, 41–42). This statement is seen as one of the central tenets of structuralism. In *Mythologies* Barthes had put the same idea in other terms: "it is human history which converts reality into speech" (*Myth.*, 110).

Barthes' statements above effectively equate reality with intelligibility and the latter with value in a sign system. Moreover, language as a historical and social contract has an infinite potential to subsume anything at all under its system of signification. Barthes cites a Saussurean metaphor: the production of meaning is not merely a correlation of signifier and signified. Rather, it is like cutting a piece of paper, which yields recto and verso at the same time: it is "*an act of simultaneously cutting out* two amorphous masses, two 'floating kingdoms'" (*ES*, 56). Elaborating on this, Barthes suggests that meaning arises from an articulation, a simultaneous division of the signifying layer and the signified mass. Language is "that which *divides* reality" (*ES*, 64). This had been stated in a different formulation much earlier by Hegel and some of the neo-Hegelian philosophers who affirmed that language artificially divides the continuity of our immediate experience into subject and predicate. Notwithstanding his acknowledgment that language is a historically evolved contract, Barthes expresses a further classic statement of structuralist methodology when he affirms that we must give a structural interpretation to heterogeneous elements of reality and must eliminate diachronic elements to the utmost (*ES*, 98).

Saussure had seen the operation of language as an interaction between two axes. Speech, on the horizontal plane, is made possible, in the Saussurean model, by drawing on the codes of langue on the vertical axis. Barthes calls these axes syntagm and system (conventionally called syntagm and paradigm in linguistics). Syntagm refers to the relation between various elements of a sentence at a given level; paradigm refers to the relation between a given element in the sentence and other elements that are interchangeable with it. For example, in the sentences:

He   is   reading.
She was writing.

the connection between "He," "is," and "reading" is syntagmatic, while the connections between "He" and "She" (or between "is" and "was") are paradigmatic. Barthes refers to the syntagmatic axis as a "combination of signs." He views the systematic (paradigmatic) axis as related to Saussure's *langue*, as a plane of associations. Barthes draws attention to Jakobson's development of this distinction as that between metaphor (the associative and systematic order) and metonymy (the syntagmatic order): every discourse emphasizes one or the other of these axes (*ES*, 58–60). The nature of speech is syntagmatic since it expresses a varied combination of recurrent signs (*ES*, 62). Many creative works, says Barthes, result partly from a defiance of the usual distribution of syntagm and system, as exemplified in the use of rhyme in poetry (*ES*, 86–87).

While Barthes accepts Saussure's position that language is possible because signs recur, he does not concede that language is *entirely* differential or relational in its nature; it does, he says, contain some positive elements. For example, Barthes speaks of a "zero degree of opposition" which "testifies to the power held by any system of signs, of creating meaning 'out of nothing'": Barthes quotes Saussure's statement that "the language can be content with an opposition of something and nothing" (*ES*, 77). Structuralism has often been upbraided for its reliance on binary oppositions. It is interesting that Barthes himself questions the universality of binarism and affirms that "binarism is the great unknown in semiology, whose types of opposition have not yet been outlined." He speculates that perhaps binarism is "a metalanguage, a particular taxonomy meant to be swept away by history, after having been true to it for a moment" (*ES*, 81–82). Behind this speculation lies his earlier claim that bourgeois consciousness is disintegrating: the clear-cut language of definition and opposition which it originally used to express its political causes is now losing its authority, its power to name, just as much as the essentialist views of the human being on which it is based. Talking of metalanguages, Barthes suggests that each science contains "the seeds of its own death, in the shape of the language destined to speak it" (*ES*, 93).

In his section on "Denotation and Connotation," Barthes explains that any system of signification has three components: the plane of expression E (the signifier), the plane of content C (the signified), and the relation R between the two planes. This entire complex ERC can become a mere element of a second system of signification which is staggered in relation to the first:

Plane of Denotation:	ERC		
Plane of Connotation:	E	R	C

In literature, says Barthes, language forms the first system, and suggests, following Hjelmslev, that the second plane could be the basis of a connotative semiotics. In the case of a metalanguage, the first system becomes the signified of the second system (*ES*, 90–93). Clearly, this is a variation of the scheme that Barthes had laid out for the structure of myth in *Mythologies*.

In his classic essay "Introduction to the Structuralist Analysis of Narratives" (1966), Barthes had talked of the "problem of the subject, insisting on viewing an author or persona as a grammatical rather than a psychological subject. Barthes' most well-known formulation of this problem occurs in his essay "The Death of the Author" (1968), a phrase which has come to be associated with both Barthes and structuralism, just as the phrase "God is dead" had been attributed to Nietzsche (though in fact it had first occurred in Hegel's *Phenomenology*). Barthes begins this essay by quoting a sentence from Balzac's novella *Sarrasine*: "This was woman herself, with her sudden fears, her irrational whims, her instinctive worries."[6] Barthes asks, who is the speaker of these words? Is it the hero of the story, or Balzac himself drawing on his experience of women? Or Balzac the author professing literary notions of femininity? Or is it universal wisdom? Barthes' answer is that we can never know, because "writing is the destruction of every voice, of every point of origin. Writing is that neutral, composite, oblique space where our subject slips away, the negative where all identity is lost, starting with the very identity of the body writing" (*IMT*, 142).

Barthes' argument is that as soon as narration occurs without the practical purpose of acting on reality, as soon as narrative occurs as an end in itself, "this disconnection occurs, the voice loses its origin, the author enters into his own death, writing begins"

(*IMT*, 142). One is reminded here of Horace's statement that the voice once sent forth can never return, can never be reclaimed by the author as his own. Barthes also points out that the idea of an individual author is a modern one: in many previous societies, the author or poet was regarded as a mediator between higher powers and humanity. Often, authorship was collective, progressing through oral traditions of storytelling, as was the case with the *Iliad* and the *Odyssey*, conventionally attributed to Homer. The modern, individual author, says Barthes, was "a product of our society insofar as, emerging from the Middle Ages with English empiricism, French rationalism and the personal faith of the Reformation, it discovered the prestige of the individual . . . It is thus logical that in literature it should be this positivism, the epitome and culmination of capitalist ideology, which has greatest importance to the 'person' of the author." Even in the present, says Barthes, our studies of literature and literary history are "tyrannically centred on the author." The newer modes of criticism (by which he presumably means phenomenological and psychoanalytical criticism), he claims, have often consolidated this obsession (*IMT*, 143).

Recently, as Barthes observes, many writers have challenged this centrality of the author. Mallarmé recognized that it is "language which speaks, not the author." Valéry stressed the "essentially verbal condition" of literature, a condition that renders super-fluous any recourse to a writer's interiority. Proust blurred the relation between the writer and his characters. And surrealism, though not preoccupied with language, "contributed to the desacralization of the image of the Author" by stressing the disappointment of expectations of meaning. Linguistics, moreover, has shown that enunciation "is an empty process . . . the author is never more than the instance writing . . . language knows a 'subject', not a 'person', and this subject [is] empty out-side of the very enunciation which defines it" (*IMT*, 145).

This removal of the author, explains Barthes, transforms the modern text. For example, the temporality is changed. Previously, the author was conceived as the past of his own book, the preexisting cause and explanation. In contrast, "the modern scriptor is born simultaneously with the text . . . there is no other time than that of the enunciation and every text is eternally written *here* and *now*" (*IMT*, 145). Hence we can no longer think of writing in the classical ways, as recording, representing, or depicting. Rather, writing is a "performative" act in which "the enunciation has no other content (contains no other proposition) than the act by which it is uttered – something like the *I declare* of kings or the *I sing* of very ancient poets" (*IMT*, 146). In writing, the modern scriptor traces a field with no origin, or at least one which has "no other origin than language itself, language which ceaselessly calls into question all origins" (*IMT*, 146).

What is more, a text can no longer be viewed as releasing in a linear fashion a single "theological" meaning, as the message of the "Author-God." Rather, it is "a multi-dimensional space in which a variety of writings, none of them original, blend and clash. The text is a tissue of quotations drawn from the innumerable centres of culture" (*IMT*, 146). The writer has only the power to mix writings. As for expressing himself, the interiority that he wishes to express is itself "only a ready-formed dictionary . . . the scriptor no longer bears within him passions, humours, feelings, impressions, but rather this immense dictionary from which he draws . . . life never does more than imitate the book, and the book itself is only a tissue of signs, an imitation that is lost, infinitely deferred" (*IMT*, 146–147). The demise of the author spells the demise of criticism: deciphering a text becomes a futile endeavor: "To give a text an Author is to impose a limit on that text, to furnish it with a final signified, to close the writing" (*IMT*, 147). In the multiplicity of writing, says Barthes, "everything is to be *disentangled*, nothing *deciphered.*" We can follow the text's structure but we will find nothing beneath. Hence Literature, by refusing to assign an "ultimate meaning . . . to the text (and to the world as text)," facilitates an "anti-theological" activity which is revolutionary since "to refuse to fix meaning is, in the end, to refuse God and his hypostases – reason, science, law" (*IMT*, 147).

Barthes concludes by pointing out that the multiplicity of writing – its drawing from various cultures and styles – is focused and unified in one place: the reader (not the author). A text's unity, says Barthes, "lies not in its origin but in its destination" (*IMT*, 148). Yet Barthes cautions that the humanism we have rejected via removal of the author should not be reintroduced through any conception of the reader as a personal and complete entity. The reader of which Barthes speaks is a reader "without history, biography, psychology; he is simply that *someone* who holds together in a single field all the traces by which the written text is constituted." In other words, the reader, like the author, is a function of the text. In this sense "the birth of the reader must be at the cost of the death of the Author" (*IMT*, 148).

In a subsequent essay, "From Work to Text" (1971), Barthes provides a succinct statement of a poststructuralist perspective. Barthes notes that in recent decades conceptions of language and literature, influenced by developments in linguistics, anthropology, Marxism, and psychoanalysis, have been marked by an increasing tendency toward interdisciplinarity. The object of linguistic and literary studies accordingly has been changed: it is no longer the stable, fixed object enclosed within one discipline but an object that is fluid, has many levels of meaning, and ranges across disciplinary boundaries. The former is the "work" and the latter is the "text." In recent history, Barthes sees Marxism and Freudianism as the major forces of change in our conceptions of knowledge: subsequent changes have merely reiterated the fundamental insights furnished by these forces. Our history, says Barthes, "allows us today . . . merely to slide, to vary, to exceed, to repudiate" (*IMT*, 155). The cumulative forces of Marxism, Freudianism, and structuralism have led to the demand for an altered conception of the literary object; they amount to a demand for "the relativization of the relations of writer, reader and observer (critic)," a demand for a replacement of the "work" by the "text."

It is worth reminding ourselves that in distinguishing between work and text as differing "objects," Barthes is not describing a difference between two material entities but, rather, a difference between two perspectives. "Work" and "text" are two ways in which the literary object might be viewed. Barthes acknowledges that, traditionally, a work is associated with certain material qualities, occupying a place on a bookshelf, having certain dimensions, and tangibility. A text, on the other hand, is a "methodological field," a "process of demonstration," that is held in language, that only "exists in the movement of a discourse" and is experienced only in an activity of production (*IMT*, 157). Moreover, a text cannot be identified with a given work: it may span several works. Nor can it be contained within hierarchies of good literature or of genres; indeed, the text is marked by a "subversive force in respect of the old classifications," and poses a problem of classification since it can span a range of disciplines as well as of genres.

Whereas a work offers up to analysis a closed signified or definite meaning, a text "practises the infinite deferment of the signified . . . its field is that of the signifier." The "infinite" nature of the signifier perpetuates itself not in an organic and orderly process of deepening investigation but in "disconnections, overlappings, variations" (*IMT*, 158). In other words, the text can never allow investigation to halt at some signified, some concept which represents the ultimate meaning of a work; rather, it forces investigation along a path of signifiers, one replacing another but none offering itself as the final meaning, none pointing to a signified. The logic regulating the text is not comprehensive but metonymic, an activity of associations and displacements. In this way, says Barthes, the text is "restored to language," or restored to a position of relatedness within the network of signs rather than wallowing in some privileged and protected meaning. Like language, the text "is structured but off-centred, without closure" (*IMT*, 159).

Barthes states an important feature of poststructuralist analysis when he says that the text "is plural." This plurality, he claims, is irreducible; in other words, it is not the plurality of mere coexistence of meanings that can answer to interpretation. Rather, it is a plurality issuing from "a disconnected, heterogenous variety of substances and perspectives," a plurality that marks the text as comprised by difference, by a "weave of signifiers" that brings together a variety of citations, echoes, and cultural codes. Every text is held in "intertextuality," in a network of signifiers of which no part can be arbitrarily separated as possessing unity. Barthes seems to suggest that such a conception of plurality is not conceived as the opposite of unity but as outside of the entire opposition of unity and plurality, as external to the opposition of identity and difference. He suggests that such plurality is disturbing for monistic philosophy, the kind of thinking which would see all things as part of a vast and ordered unity. He cites theological monism – which coerces Holy Scripture into a unitary and coherent structure and meaning – and Marxism as examples of two monistic discourses. The plurality of the text, he says, will bring "fundamental changes in reading," especially of the scriptures and the Marxist "institution" (*IMT*, 160–161).

Another difference between work and text is that the former "is caught up in a process of filiation." It is seen as determined by race, by history, and by its "father," the author. The text, on the contrary, "reads without the inscription of the Father." Whereas the work is seen as an organism that develops, the text expresses a network. Hence, "no vital 'respect' is due to the Text . . . the restitution of the inter-text paradoxically abolishing any legacy." The author may indeed come back in the text, but only as a "guest." The novelist is inscribed in his novel like one of his characters, and he becomes a "paper-author: his life is no longer the origin of his fictions but a fiction contributing to his work." In this way, authors allow "their lives to be read as a text." Barthes also points out that a work is the object of consumption. In contrast, the text "decants the work . . . from its consumption and gathers it up as play, activity, production, practice." In other words, the work is consumed more or less passively, such reading being reduced to an "inner mimesis." The text, however, makes the process of reading active, productive, and constitutive. The text "requires that one try to abolish . . . the distance between reading and writing . . . by joining them in a single signifying practice." It asks of the reader a "practical collaboration" in the production of the work (*IMT*, 162–163).

Indeed, the pleasure we derive from the work, says Barthes, is nonetheless the pleasure of consumption: we do not participate in the production, we do not rewrite. The text, on the other hand, "is bound to *jouissance*," to bliss or ecstasy, to "a pleasure without separation." The implication here is that the text invites participation in its own play, in its subversion of hierarchies, its endless deferment of the definite. Finally, Barthes points out that there cannot be a theory of the text, since such a theory would involve the "destruction of meta-language," the abolition of generality and system. Any discourse on the text, says Barthes, "should itself be nothing other than text." He ends with a sentence that anticipates or echoes Derrida: "The theory of the Text can coincide only with a practice of writing" (*IMT*, 164).

The tide of structuralism has somewhat receded before the advance of more recent theoretical movements which have impugned, among other things, its lack of historicity, its use of binary oppositions, its centralizing of the notion of structure as well as its reduction of "real" referents to elements in a self-enclosed linguistic system. It may be, however, that certain concepts of structuralism, such as binarism, need to be revisited, if only to situate our rejection of them alongside their positive potential, a potential which may well have political dimensions, as in Barthes' earlier work.

Notes

1 Ferdinand de Saussure, *Course in General Linguistics*, ed. Charles Bally, Albert Sechehaye, and Albert Reidlinger, trans. Wade Baskin (New York: Philosophical Library, 1959), p. 15. Hereafter cited as *CGL*.

2 Roland Barthes, *Writing Degree Zero*, trans. Annette Lavers and Colin Smith, preface by Susan Sontag (New York: Farrar, Straus, and Giroux, 1968), pp. 4–5. Hereafter cited as *WDZ*.

3 Roland Barthes, *Mythologies*, trans. Annette Lavers (London: Collins, 1973), p. 11. Hereafter cited as *Myth*.

4 Roland Barthes, *Elements of Semiology*, trans. Annette Lavers and Colin Smith (New York: Farrar, Straus, and Giroux, 1967), p. 10. Hereafter cited as *ES*.

5 Émile Durkheim, *The Rules of Sociological Method*, trans. Sarah A. Solovay and John H. Mueller (London and New York: Collier Macmillan/ Free Press, 1964), pp. 62–65.

6 Roland Barthes, *Image: Music: Text*, trans. Stephen Heath (Glasgow: Fontana, 1982), p. 142. Hereafter cited as *IMT*.

CHAPTER 25

DECONSTRUCTION

Jacques Derrida (1930–2004) is responsible for the pervasive phenomenon in modern literary and cultural theory known as "deconstruction." While Derrida himself has insisted that deconstruction is not a theory unified by any set of consistent rules or procedures, it has been variously regarded as a way of reading, a mode of writing, and, above all, a way of challenging interpretations of texts based upon conventional notions of the stability of the human self, the external world, and of language and meaning.

Derrida was born in Algeria to a Jewish family and suffered intensely the experience of being an outsider. While in Algeria he undertook a study of several major philosophers, including Søren Kierkegaard and Martin Heidegger. He then studied at various prestigious institutions in Paris, eventually becoming a teacher of philosophy. He also worked at Harvard and, in 1975, began teaching at Yale University. More recently, he has taught at various American institutions, in particular at the University of California at Irvine. He established a reputation in France during the 1960s, a reputation which crossed to the United States in the 1970s. Derrida's transatlantic influence can be traced to an important seminar held at Johns Hopkins University in 1966. A number of leading French theorists, such as Roland Barthes, Jacques Lacan, and Lucien Goldmann, spoke at this conference. Derrida himself presented what was quickly recognized as a pioneering paper entitled "Structure, Sign, and Play in the Discourse of the Human Sciences," a text which shows both what Derrida owes to structuralism and his paths of divergence from it.

The following year, 1967, marked Derrida's explosive entry onto the international stage of literary and cultural theory, with the publication of his first three books: *La Voix et le phenomène* (*Speech and Phenomena*), concerning Edmund Husserl's theory of signs; *De la grammatologie* (*Of Grammatology*), whose subject was the "science" of writing; and *L'Écriture et la différence* (*Writing and Difference*), which contained important essays on Hegel, Freud, and Michel Foucault. Later works included *La Dissemination* (*Dissemination*) (1972), which included a lengthy engagement with Plato's views of writing and sophistry; *Marges de la philosophie* (*Margins of Philosophy*) (1982), which included essays on Hegel's semiology and the use of metaphor in philosophy; *Positions* (1972), containing three illuminating interviews with Derrida, touching on his attitude to Marxism, Hegel, and other issues; *Circumfessions* (1991), an autobiographical work that engages with the text of Augustine's *Confessions*; and *Spectres de Marx* (*Specters of Marx*) (1994), which looks at the various legacies of Marx.

Proponents of deconstruction often point out that it is not amenable to any static definition or systematization because the meaning of the terms it employs is always shifting and fluid, taking its color from the localized contexts and texts with which it engages. Indeed, deconstruction is often regarded as undermining all·tendency toward systematization. However, there are a number of concerns, and certain heuristic terms, that can be said to characterize deconstruction. The most fundamental project of deconstruction is to display the operations of "logocentrism" in any "text" (where the meaning of "text" is broadened to include not merely written treatises in a variety of disciplines but the entire range of their political, theological, social, and intellectual contexts, as manifested primarily in their use of language).

What is logocentrism? Etymologically and historically, this term refers to any system of thought which is founded on the stability and authority of the *Logos*, the divine Word. The various meanings accumulated by this word in the Hebrew, ancient pagan, and early Christian worlds are complex. The scholar C. H. Dodd explains that *logos* is both a thought and a word, and the two are inseparable: the *logos* is the word as determined by and conveying a meaning. He also observes that the root of the Hebrew equivalent for *logos* means "to speak," and that this expression is used of God's self-revelation. Moreover, in Hebrew culture, the word once spoken was held to have a substantive existence. The word and concept *logos* may have derived in part from the Greek thinker Heraclitus and the Jewish philosopher Philo of Alexandria; in its simplest meaning it can signify "statement," "saying," "discourse," or science.[1] In the gospel of John, the plural *logoi* refers to the words spoken by Jesus or others; but the singular *logos* signifies the whole of what Jesus said, his message as both revelation and command. The life of Jesus is the *Logos* incarnate, and events in this life are signs of eternal realities. And the gospel in general is the record of a life that expresses the eternal thought of God, the meaning of the universe (Dodd, 284–285). Dodd states that all of these senses accord with the fundamental Greek connotation of *logos* as the spoken word *together* with its meaning or rational content. A further sense of *Logos* in the fourth gospel is the "Word of God," his self-revelation to man; it denotes the eternal truth revealed to men by God. Hence the *Logos* is not simply an uttered word; it *is* truth itself, it has a rational content of thought corresponding to the ultimate reality of the universe. And this reality is revealed *as spoken and heard* (Dodd, 266–267). As such, the *Logos* is the thought of God which is the "transcendent design of the universe and its immanent meaning" (Dodd, 285). In its ancient Greek philosophical and Judeo-Christian meaning, then, the *Logos* referred both to the Word of God which created the universe and to the rational order of creation itself. In other words, it is in the spoken *Logos* that language and reality ultimately coincide, in an identity that is invested with absolute authority, absolute origin, and absolute purpose or teleology. If we think of the orders of language and reality as follows, it is clear that one of the functions of the *Logos* is to preserve the stability and closure of the entire system:

LOGOS

Language		Reality
Signifier 1 -*a*- Signified 1	————*b*————	Object 1
Signifier 2 – Signified 2	———————————	Object 2
Signifier 3 – Signified 3	———— ————	Object 3
Signifier 4 – Signified 4	———————————	Object 4

Ad Infinitum

It is because the *Logos* holds together the orders of language and reality that the relation between signifier (word) and signified (concept), i.e., relation *a*, is stable and fixed; so too is relation *b*, the connection between the sign as a whole and the object to which it refers in the world. For example, in a Christian scheme, the signifier "love" might refer to the concept of "self-sacrifice" in relation to God. And this sign as a whole, the word "love" as meaning "self-sacrifice," would refer to object 1, which might be a system of social or ecclesiastical relationships institutionally embodied in a given society, enshrining the ideal of self-sacrifice. In other words, the meaning of "love" is sanctioned by a hierarchy of authority, stretching back through institutional Church practice, theology, philosophy, as well as political and economic theory, to the authority of the scriptures and the Word of God himself. In the same way, all of the other signifiers and signifieds in language would be constrained in their significance, making for a stable and closed system in terms of which the world and the human self could be interpreted in terms of their origins, their meaning and purpose in life, what counts as good and evil, what kind of government is legitimate, and so forth. The *Logos* thereby authorizes an entire world view, sanctioned by a theological and philosophical system and by an entire political, religious, and social order.

If, now, the *Logos* is *removed* from this picture, what happens? The entire order will become destabilized; historically, of course, this disintegration does not happen all at once but takes centuries, as indeed does the undermining of the *Logos*. Once the *Logos* vanishes from the picture, there is nothing to hold together the orders of language and reality, which now threaten to fly apart from each other. The relations *a* and *b* both become destabilized: if we are not constrained by a Christian perspective, we might attribute *other* meanings to the word "love," meanings which may even conflict with the previously given Christian signification. Moreover, various groups might give different meanings to the word so that a general consensus is lost. In this way, signifier 1 may be defined by a meaning attributed to signified 1. But since there is no authoritative closure to this process, it could go on ad infinitum: signified 1 will itself need to be defined, and so this signified will itself become a signifier of something else; this process might regress indefinitely so that we never arrive at a conclusive signified but are always moving along an endless chain of signifiers. Derrida attributes the name of "metaphor" to this endless substitution of one signifier for another: in describing or attempting to understand our world, we can no longer use "literal" language, i.e., language that actually describes the object or reality. We can only use metaphor, hence language in its very nature is metaphorical. Hence there cannot be a sharp distinction between, say, the spheres of philosophy and science, on the one hand, which are often presumed to use a "literal" language based on reason, and literature and the arts, on the other hand, which are characterized as using metaphorical and figurative language in a manner inaccessible to reason. Even the languages of mathematics, science, and philosophy are ultimately metaphorical, and cannot claim any natural and referential connection with the world they purport to describe.

Logocentrism, however, is not uniform but takes a variety of guises: for example, the stabilizing function of the *Logos* might be replaced by other notions. For Plato, this notion might be *eidos* or the Form; what holds Aristotle's metaphysics together, as its foundation, is the concept of substance; similarly, we could cite Hegel's "absolute idea" or Kant's categories of the understanding. Modern equivalents in Western society might be concepts such as freedom or democracy. All of these terms function as what Derrida calls "transcendental signifieds," or concepts invested with absolute authority, which places them beyond questioning or examination. An important endeavor of deconstruction, then, is to show the operation of logocentrism in all of its forms, and to bring back these various transcendental signifieds within the province of language and textuality, within the province of their relatability to other concepts.

Hence, in one sense, the most fundamental project of deconstruction is to reinstate *language* within the connections of the various terms that have conventionally dominated Western thought: the connections between thought and reality, self and world, subject and object. In deconstructive thought, these connections are not viewed as already existing prior to language, with language merely being the instrument of their expression or representation. Rather, all of these terms are linguistic to begin with: they are enabled by language. We don't simply have thought which is then expressed by language; thought takes place in, and is made possible by, language. The notion of language that is thereby reinstituted by deconstruction is partly influenced by Saussure: it is a notion of language as a system of relations; the terms which are related have no semantic value outside of the network of relations in which they subsist; they *depend* on those relations for their meaning and significance. Also implicit in this view of language is the arbitrary and conventional nature of the sign: there is no natural connection between the sign "table" and an actual table in the world. Equally arbitrary and conventional is the connection between the signifier "table" and the concept of a "table" to which it points.

Moreover, there is no "truth" or "reality" which somehow stands outside or behind language: truth is a relation of linguistic terms, and reality is a construct, ultimately religious, social, political, and economic, but always of language, of various linguistic registers. Even the human self, in this view, has no pregiven essence but is a linguistic construct or narrative. Derrida's much-quoted statement that "il n'y a pas de hors-texte," often translated as "there is nothing outside the text," means precisely this: that the aforementioned features of language, which together comprise "textuality," are all-embracing; textuality governs all interpretative operations. For example, there is no history outside of language or textuality: history itself is a linguistic and textual construct. At its deepest level, the insistence on viewing language (as a system of relations and differences) as lying at the core of any world view issues a challenge to the notion of *identity*, a notion installed at the heart of Western metaphysics since Aristotle. Identity, whether of the human self or of objects in the world, is no longer viewed as having a stable, fixed, or pregiven essence, but is seen as fluid and dependent, like linguistic terms, on a variety of contexts. Hence a deconstructive analysis tends to prioritize language and linguistic operations in analyzing texts and contexts.

While this prioritization of language is the fundamental form of deconstruction's exhibition and undermining of logocentrism, deconstructive analysis enlists other strategies and terms toward the same general endeavor. One of these strategies is the unraveling and undermining of certain oppositions which have enjoyed a privileged place in Western metaphysics. Derrida points out that oppositions, such as those between intellect and sense, soul and body, master and slave, male and female, inside and outside, center and margin, do not represent a state of equivalence between two terms. Rather, each of these oppositions is a "violent hierarchy" in which one term has been conventionally subordinated, in gestures that embody a host of religious, social, and political valencies. Intellect, for example, has usually been superordinated over sense; soul has been exalted above body; male has been defined as superior in numerous respects to female. Derrida's project is not simply to reverse these hierarchies, for such a procedure would remain imprisoned within the framework of binary oppositional thinking represented by those hierarchies. Rather, he attempts to show that these hierarchies represent privileged relationships, relationships that have been lifted above any possible engagement with, and answerability to, the network of concepts in general.

Perhaps the most significant opposition treated by Derrida, an opposition which comprehends many of the other hierarchies, is that between speech and writing. According to Derrida, Western philosophy has privileged speech over writing, viewing speech as embodying an immediate presence of meaning, and writing as a mere substitute or secondary representation of the spoken word. Speech implies, as will be seen shortly, an immediate connection with the *Logos*, a direct relation to that which sanctions and constrains it; while writing threatens to depart from the *Logos*, the living source of speech and authority, and to assert its independence. The very centrality of this opposition generates the importance of certain deconstructive strategies: Derrida imputes a meaning to "writing" that far exceeds the notion of "graphic signifier" or "inscription" of letters and words. For him, "writing" designates the totality of what makes inscription possible: all of the differences by which language is constituted. Writing refers to the diffusion of identity (of self, object, signifier, signified) through a vast network of relations and differences. Writing expresses the movement of difference itself. Indeed, it is in an attempt to subvert the conventional priority of speech over writing that Derrida both extends the meaning of "writing" and coins a term that many regard as central to his thought: différance. The significance of this term derives partly from Saussure's concept of "difference" as the constituting principle of language: a term is defined by what it is *not*, by its differences from other terms. Also, however, Derrida incorporates into his term an ambivalence in the French word *différer*, which can mean both "to differ" and "to defer" in time. Hence Derrida adds a temporal dimension to the notion of difference. Moreover, the substitution of *a* for *e* in the word différance cannot be *heard* in French: it is a silent displacement that can only be discerned in writing, as if to counter the superior value previously accorded to speech. The terms that recur in Derrida's texts – their meanings often changing according to contexts – are usually related to the extended significance that Derrida accords to "writing." Such terms include "trace," "supplement," "text," "presence," "absence," and "play."

Logocentrism, then, is sanctioned and structured in a multitude of ways, all of which are called into question by deconstruction. The privileging of speech over writing, for example, has perpetuated what Derrida calls a "metaphysics of presence," a systematization of thought and interpretation that relies on the stability and self-presence of meaning, effecting a closure and disabling any "free play" of thought which might threaten or question the overall structure. Another way of explaining the term "metaphysics of presence" might be as follows: conventionally, philosophers have made a distinction between the "thisness" or haecceity of an entity and its "whatness" or quiddity. The term "whatness" refers to the *content* of something, while "thisness" refers to the *fact* that it exists in a particular place and time. A metaphysics of "presence" would be a metaphysics of complete self-identity: an entity's content is viewed as coinciding completely with its existence.

For example, an isolated entity such as a piece of chalk would be regarded as having its meaning completely within itself, completely in its immediate "presence." Even if the rest of the world did not exist, we could say what the piece of chalk was, what its function and constitution were. Such absolute self-containment of meaning must be sanctioned by a higher authority, a *Logos* or transcendental signified, which ensured that all things in the world had specific and designated meanings. If, however, we were to challenge such a "metaphysics of presence," we might argue that in fact the meaning of the chalk does *not* coincide with, and is not confinable within, its immediate existence; that its meaning and purpose actually lie in relations that extend far beyond its immediate existence; its meaning would depend, for example, upon the concept of a "blackboard" on which it was designed to write; in turn, the relationship of chalk and blackboard derives its meaning from increasingly broader contexts, such as a classroom, an institution of learning, associated industries and technologies, as well as political and educational programs. Hence the meaning of "chalk" would extend through a vast network of relations far beyond the actual isolated existence of that item; moreover, its meaning would be viewed as relative to a given social and cultural framework, rather than sanctioned by the presence of a *Logos*. In this sense, the chalk is *not* self-identical since its identity is *dispersed* through its relations with numerous other objects and concepts. Viewed in this light, "chalk" is not a name for a self-subsistent, self-enclosed entity; rather, it names the provisional focal point of a complex set of relations. It can be seen, then, that a metaphysics of "presence" refers to the *self-presence*, the immediate presence, of meaning, as resting on a complete self-identity that is sanctioned and preserved by the "presence" of a *Logos*.

A deconstructive reading of a text, then, as practiced by Derrida, will be a multifaceted project: in general, it will attempt to display logocentric operations in the text, by focusing on a close reading of the text's language, its use of presuppositions or transcendental signifieds, its reliance on binary oppositions, its self-contradictions, its *aporiai* or points of conceptual impasse, and the ways in which it effects closure and resists free play. Hence deconstruction, true to its name (which derives from Heidegger's term *Destruktion*), will examine all of the features that went into the *construction* of text, down to its very foundations. Derrida has been criticized for his lack of clarity, his oblique and refractive style: his adherents have argued that his engagement with the history of Western thought is not one of mere confrontation but necessarily one of inevitable complicity (where he is obliged to use the very terms he impugns) as well as of critique. This dual gesture must necessarily entail play on words, convolution of language that accommodates its fluid nature, and divergence from conventional norms of essayistic writing. It might also be argued that the very form of his texts, not merely their content, is integral to his overall project.

Derrida has conducted deconstructive readings of numerous major thinkers, including Plato, Rousseau, Hegel, Freud, Husserl, Lévi-Strauss, and Saussure. His style and approach might be illustrated by examining two of his important essays: his seminal work, "Structure, Sign, and Play," which exhibits some of the persistent concerns of deconstruction and reveals both what he owes to structuralism and his divergence from it; and "Plato's Pharmacy," which engages with issues central to the very definition of philosophy by Plato, a definition which laid the foundations of the subsequent history of philosophy.

In "Structure, Sign, and Play," Derrida's endeavor might be seen as threefold: (1) to characterize certain features of the history of Western metaphysics, as issuing from the fundamental concepts of "structure" and "center"; (2) to announce an "event" – in effect, a complex series of historical movements – whereby these central notions were challenged, using the work of the structuralist anthropologist Lévi-Strauss as an example; and (3) to suggest the ways in which current and future modes of thought and language might deploy and adapt Lévi-Strauss' insights in articulating their own relation to metaphysics.

According to Derrida, the concept of structure that has dominated Western science and philosophy has always been referred to as a "center or . . . a point of presence, a fixed origin."[2] The function of such a center has been both to organize the structure and to limit the *free play* of terms and concepts within it, in other words, to foreclose such play. The center, says Derrida, is the point at which any substitution or permutation of elements or terms is no longer possible. Although the structure thereby depends on the center, the center itself is fixed and "escapes structurality," since it is beyond the transformative reach of other elements in the structure. Hence the center is, paradoxically, *outside* the structure, and the very concept of a centered structure is only "contradictorily coherent" (*WD*, 279). What it expresses is a desire for a "reassuring certitude" which stands beyond the subversive or threatening reach of any play which might disrupt the structure. The center, that which gives stability, unity, and closure to the structure, can be conceived as an "origin" or a "purpose," terms which invoke the notion of a "full presence" (such as the *Logos*) that can guarantee such stability and closure (*WD*, 279).

Derrida suggests that the history of Western metaphysics can be viewed as the history of this concept of structure, with various philosophies substituting one center for another. These successive centers have received different metaphorical names, all of which are grounded on "the determination of Being as *presence*." The names of this presence have included *eidos* (the Platonic Form), *arche* (the concept of an absolute beginning), *telos* (the, often providential, purpose and direction attributed to human existence), *ousia* (the Aristotelian concept of "substance" or "essence" as the underlying reality of things), as well as the concepts of truth, God, and man. Each of these concepts has served as a center, as a transcendental signified, stabilizing a given system of thought or world view.

Derrida announces an "event" which has begun to disrupt this system of Western metaphysics. The "event" metaphorically refers to a complex network of historical processes. Most fundamentally, the "event" signifies the "moment when language invaded the universal problematic, the moment when, in the absence of a center or origin, everything became discourse" (*WD*, 280). Here, Derrida refers to a phase in modern intellectual history when central problems in a variety of fields – such as the connection between thought and reality, self and world – were reposited or newly posed as problems of language, where "language" was understood as a system of differences. For example, where previously the term "God" was held to refer to an actual entity independent of language, this term was now seen as one signifier among many others, a signifier which took its meaning and function from its *relation* to a vast system of signifiers; the term was no longer exalted above such relational status in a posture of absolute privilege and authority. Hence, the term "God," which once acted as a "center" (or origin or purpose) of many systems of thought, was brought back within the province of relatability to other elements of language, being dethroned from its status as a transcendental signified to one more signifier on the same level as other signifiers. In this sense, the concept of God moves from being a reality beyond language to a concept *within* language: it becomes discourse. And the systems of thought that depended on the understanding of God as a reality become "decentered," losing their former stability and authority.

When did such a process of decentering occur in Western thought? Derrida suggests that certain names can be associated with this process: Nietzsche, for example, undertook a radical critique of metaphysics, especially of the concepts of being and truth (and, we might add to Derrida's list, of space and time), regarding these as convenient fictions; Freud engaged in a critique of consciousness and the self-identity of the human subject; again, Heidegger reexamined the conventional metaphysics of being and time. The discourses of each of these thinkers put into question some of the central concepts and categories that have dominated Western thought since Plato and Aristotle. Yet Derrida is careful to point out that each of these newer, radical discourses, while attempting to break free of the traditional metaphysical enclosure, is nonetheless trapped in a circle of its own. The critique of metaphysics is inevitably a dual gesture, one which involves not only confrontation and destruction of traditional concepts but also a necessary complicity with them: we must employ the very language of metaphysics to criticize it, a duality that extends even to our discussion of the sign itself (*WD*, 280– 281). We might cite as a further example the dilemma of some modern feminists who wish to break free of "male" language: we cannot simply create from nothing a "female" language, and are obliged to use in our critique terms and concepts from the very language that we wish to undermine. However, as Derrida acknowledges, there are "several ways of being caught in this circle," and it is these differences between the radical discourses that often lead them into mutual confrontation and destruction (*WD*, 281).

The examples of "radical" discourses given by Derrida suggest that the "event" or process of "decentering" was initiated in the nineteenth century. Apart from the critiques advanced by thinkers such as Nietzsche, Freud, and Heidegger (Derrida might equally have mentioned Schopenhauer, Hegel, Marx, and Bergson), there was, according to Derrida, a profounder, structural shift in the orientation of Western thinking, as pertaining to the "human sciences" in general. In the nineteenth century, a decentering occurred in European culture, and consequently in European metaphysics and science: for a complex of political, economic, and philosophical reasons, European culture was "forced to stop considering itself as the culture of reference" (*WD*, 282). In other words, Europe was obliged to retreat from its conception of itself as the political and cultural "center" of the world stage. It was at this moment, says Derrida, this moment of retreat from ethnocentrism, that the "science" of ethnology emerged; while this science undertook a critique of ethnocentrism and the conventional categories of thought underlying it, it was obliged to borrow the very terms and concepts of that heritage itself (*WD*, 282).

In order to illustrate this dual posture of ethnology, Derrida chooses the work of the French structural anthropologist Claude Lévi-Strauss. He begins with Lévi-Strauss' treatment of an opposition – between nature and culture – that is "congenital to philosophy," an opposition that predates Plato and goes back at least at far as the Sophists of the fifth century BC. In fact, this opposition encompasses "a whole historical chain which opposes 'nature' to law, to education, to art, to technics – but also to liberty, to the arbitrary, to history, to the mind, and so on" (*WD*, 283). Derrida points out that Lévi-Strauss' research has entailed both the need to use this opposition and the "impossibility of accepting it." In his first book, *The Elementary Structures of Kinship*, Lévi-Strauss defines "nature" as encompassing that which is universal and spontaneous, whereas "culture" comprehends what is relative, variable, and dependent on a system of social norms (*WD*, 282). However, as Derrida recounts, Lévi-Strauss encounters a "scandalous" threat to this opposition in the notion of "incest-prohibition." This notion, says Lévi-Strauss, refuses to conform to either side of the opposition, since it is both a norm *and* universal, thereby combining characteristics of both culture and nature. Derrida extends the significance of this recalcitrance to conventional categories to the entire conceptual system of philosophy, in which the nature–culture opposition operates systematically. He cites this as an example of the fact that "language bears within itself the necessity of its own critique" (*WD*, 284).

In general, this critique, suggests Derrida, can follow two broad paths. The first would be systematically to question the "founding concepts of the entire history of philosophy, to deconstitute them." This would indeed be the most daring way to take "a step outside of philosophy," but it would be an enormously difficult, if not impossible, task. The second path would be that effectively taken by Lévi-Strauss: to conserve all the old concepts while recognizing their limits, to refrain from attributing any truth-value to them while using them as tools or instruments. In this way, they can be used to "destroy the old machinery to which they belong." In this way, Lévi-Strauss, according to Derrida, effectively attempts to separate *method* from *truth*, and he uses, for example, the opposition between nature and culture not as a historical truth but as a methodological truth. Lévi-Strauss' "double intention" is to "preserve as an instrument something whose truth value he criticizes." And this, says Derrida, is "how the language of the social sciences criticizes *itself*" (*WD*, 284).

Hence, in his later book *The Savage Mind*, Lévi-Strauss both continues to contest the value of the nature–culture opposition and articulates a discourse based on *bricolage*. *Bricolage* means that we use whatever instruments we find at our disposal, instruments that are not designed for our specific purposes and which we may have to adapt or abandon on the basis of trial and error. Derrida sees the procedure of *bricolage* as a critique of language, even a critical language itself. Yet again, however, he extends the implications of this strategy: if *bricolage* involves the need to borrow one's concepts from the very heritage one is challenging, *every* discourse is *bricoleur* (*WD*, 285). The opposite of the *bricoleur*, who works piecemeal and in a tentative manner, would be the *engineer*, someone who envisages and designs his entire project beforehand, constructing "the totality of his language, syntax, and lexicon" (*WD*, 285). But as far as discourse is concerned, such an engineer is a myth: a subject who would be the "absolute origin of his own discourse," constructing it out of nothing. Hence the notion of the engineer is "a theological idea" (*WD*, 285). But if this idea is mythical, and if all discourse, including the language of science and philosophy, is *bricoleur*, then the entire opposition of engineer and *bricoleur* threatens to collapse, erasing the difference that gave *bricolage* its meaning in the first place (*WD*, 285).

Derrida observes that for Lévi-Strauss *bricolage* is not only an intellectual activity but also *mythopoetic*: it makes myths. What does this mean? Derrida explains that Lévi-Strauss' discourse on myths "reflects on itself and criticizes itself." Based on *bricolage*, it attempts to abandon "all reference to a *center*, to a *subject*, to a privileged *reference*, to an origin, or to an absolute *archia*" (*WD*, 286). His discourse is decentered. It attains this status not only in virtue of employing *bricolage* but also by refusing to treat any myth as the privileged ground or source of other myths; by insisting that there is no unity or source of a myth; that such unity is merely a projection of our interpretative endeavors; that myths cannot be studied in a linear fashion according to the Cartesian principle of breaking down a problem into its component parts; in other words, by exhibiting myth to be an "acentric structure." But in order to express this decentered notion of myth, Lévi-Strauss' own discourse on myth can itself have no absolute subject or center; it must in its own strategies reflect "the form and movement of myth"; in short, the discourse about myth must *itself* be a myth (*WD*, 286–287). Derrida quotes Lévi-Strauss' statement in his book *The Raw and the Cooked*, to the effect that this book is itself "a kind of myth"; and this is how ethnographic *bricolage* has a mythopoetic function, a function which makes the conventional philosophical requirement of a center appear as mythological, as a "historical illusion" (*WD*, 287).

In this way, Lévi-Strauss points toward a direction beyond conventional philosophical discourse. Yet Derrida cautions that "the passage beyond philosophy does not consist in turning the page of philosophy . . . but in continuing to read philosophers *in a certain way*" (*WD*, 288). We cannot, that is, simply dispense with previous philosophy and start anew: that would be a project of engineering, whereas we are obliged to engage in *bricolage*, to use the materials already at our disposal to read philosophy in a more radical manner. To illustrate such a radical approach, Derrida elaborates the divergent relationships that conventional philosophy and Lévi-Strauss' more radical structuralism have with empiricism. Empiricism, the notion that knowledge derives primarily from experience, has acted as the foundation of much modern philosophy and science since the Enlightenment. Derrida states that any discourse that considers itself "scientific" encounters problems and impasses that rest ultimately on empiricism: for example, if we amass a great deal of data from experience, how do we make generalizations on the basis of these data, how do we establish unity and totality among observed phenomena? Derrida accepts that "structuralism justifiably claims to be the critique of empiricism": he may be thinking, for example, of structuralism's central claim that language and other social institutions are not somehow created cumulatively by aggregated experiences, but rather, that it is the *structure* of these institutions that enables individual experiences (such as individual acts of language) in the first place.

Equally, however, Derrida seems to think that Lévi-Strauss' research is in one sense empirical in character, since it always awaits completion or invalidation by new information (WD, 288). To illustrate this, Derrida quotes a passage from Lévi-Strauss asserting that the grammar of both myths and language can be worked out on the basis of a relatively small amount of empirical detail, since it is in fact this grammar or body of rules that enables the production of the empirical instances of myth or language and not vice versa. Lévi-Strauss adds that fresh data can certainly be used to modify such grammatical laws (WD, 288–289). Derrida sees these comments as implying that a *totalized*, finished, system of grammar is useless and perhaps impossible. He points out that there are two ways in which the limitations of totalization can be viewed: one is the conventional or classical understanding that no totalizing system can hope to comprehend the infinite richness of empirical detail. The other perspective has recourse to the notion of free play: language in its very nature is a field of free play, with no center (or origin) which could arrest and freeze the play of substitution between various terms.

Derrida calls this movement of play a "movement of *supplementarity*" (WD, 289). Whatever sign takes on the function of the center in the latter's absence, whatever sign replaces the center, occurs as a surplus or supplement. In other words, if there is no center, there is no transcendental signified; this signified is replaced by a signifier whose function, as elaborated by Lévi-Strauss, is not to signify anything in particular but simply to oppose the absence of signification that threatens the system without its center (WD, 290). Given the kind of decentered discourse that Lévi-Strauss aims at, states Derrida, the concept of play is important in his work, where it exists in tension with two concepts, that of history and that of presence.

Lévi-Strauss' treatment of history is appropriately reductive, says Derrida, since history has always been the accomplice of a metaphysics of presence, a metaphysics that is teleological and eschatological. "History," he says, "has always been conceived as the movement of a resumption of history, as a detour between two presences" (WD, 291). In other words, what has actually been a *becoming*, something in process, has always been reduced to *being* in order to unify it. In a slightly different fashion, Lévi-Strauss' structuralism also "compels a neutralization of time and history," effectively placing history between brackets: it studies structures as finished products, as dirempted from their origins and causes, as ruptured from their past. For example, Lévi-Strauss sees language as having been born "in one fell swoop," rather than in a progressive fashion (WD, 291).

There is also a tension between "play" and presence. Play, says Derrida, "is the disruption of presence" (WD, 292). It is a play of absence and presence, but it preexists both. Despite Lévi-Strauss' insights into the notion of play, Derrida discerns in his work "a sort of ethic of presence, an ethic of nostalgia for origins, ... of a purity of presence and self-presence in speech" (WD, 292). Derrida calls this the "Rousseauistic" manner of thinking about play, an attitude that is "*negative*, nostalgic, guilty." The other side, for Derrida, is the joyous "Nietzschean *affirmation* ... of the play of the world ... of a world of signs without fault, without truth, and without origin." This type of affirmation, unlike Lévi-Strauss', "plays without security" (WD, 292).

In conclusion, Derrida states that there are "two interpretations of interpretation, of structure, of sign, of play." The one dreams of arriving at a truth or origin which "escapes play and the order of the sign . . . The other, which is no longer turned toward the origin, affirms play and tries to pass beyond man and humanism," man being he who has "dreamed of full presence, the reassuring foundation, the origin and the end of play." These two interpretations, he thinks, are "absolutely irreconcilable," and our current task is to chart both the common ground and the différance of their irreducible difference, in the interests of the "as yet unnameable which is proclaiming itself" (*WD*, 293).

Derrida's attempt to illustrate the subordination of writing to speech in Western metaphysics is perhaps most articulately expressed in his essay "Plato's Pharmacy," which primarily concerns Plato's dialogue *Phaedrus*. Opposing a tradition, deriving from the third-century historian Diogenes Laertius, that held this text to be badly composed, Derrida suggests that Plato's use of a myth to denigrate writing in this text is not somehow extraneous but forms an integral part of the text as a whole.[3] There are, as he reminds his reader, two myths in the text, one being a fable concerning cicadas and the other the story of Theuth. While, at the textual surface of Plato's dialogue, Socrates proposes that myths should be left behind since they do not constitute knowledge, these two myths, both concerned with the status of writing, will actually be invoked later in the Platonic text ("PP," 68).

Derrida points out that Socrates' "learned explanation" of the myth of the cicadas cites Boreas, the North Wind, playing with a nymph named Pharmacia, and wonders whether this evocation of Pharmacia is merely an accident. Derrida's suspicion is that it is not: *pharmakeia*, he points out, is related to *pharmakon*, which can mean both "drug" or "medicine" and "poison." This term is thereby introduced into Plato's text in its ambivalence ("PP," 70). Indeed, the polysemy of this word has permitted its translation variously as "remedy," "recipe," "poison," "drug," and "philter" ("PP," 71). The very problem of translation, Derrida suggests, is inextricably linked to the foundation of philosophy; it is the "problem of the very passage into philosophy" ("PP," 72). In other words, Derrida sees translation as having played a crucial role in the way Plato's philosophy has been received and constructed, especially in its attempt to distinguish philosophy as pursuit of the truth from rhetoric and sophistry, which merely teach the art of persuasion.

Even before writing is explicitly condemned in the myth later invoked by Plato, there is a connection established between books and *pharmakon*, between "mere bookish knowledge, and the blind usage of drugs": Socrates compares the written speeches Phaedrus has brought with him to a drug (*pharmakon*) ("PP," 72). Books represent "dead and rigid" knowledge, which is alien to "living knowledge and dialectics," just as myth is foreign to true knowledge. In the last phase of Plato's dialogue, where the myth of Theuth is narrated, writing is explicitly, says Derrida, "proposed, presented, and asserted as a *pharmakon*" ("PP," 73). Moreover, the question of writing is approached as a *moral* question, since the propagation of writing is intimately concerned with political developments in Plato's city and with the "activity of the sophists and speechwriters" ("PP," 74). What Plato's text declares, according to Derrida, is a kinship of writing and myth, "both of them distinguished from *logos* and dialectics" ("PP," 75). Yet, ironically, this truth about writing is itself not the object of a science but accessible only by means of a myth, a fable that is handed down by tradition and repeated ("PP," 74).

Briefly, the myth runs as follows: Theuth was an ancient divinity of Egypt who invented numbers, calculation, geometry, astronomy, and writing. He visited Thamus, the king of all Egypt, exhibited his arts, and suggested that they should be imparted to the other Egyptians. When he came to writing, Theuth claimed that this art would make the Egyptians wiser and improve their memories ("PP," 75). Thamus, says Derrida, represents Ammon, the king of the gods, who is thus the "origin of value" ("PP," 76). This king rejects the claim of Theuth, suggesting rather that writing will degrade people's powers of memory since they will come to rely on it. This myth, suggests Derrida, points to a "Platonic schema that assigns the origin and power of speech, precisely of *logos*, to the paternal position" ("PP," 76). The origin, or "speaking subject," of *logos* is its father; writing would thus be "intimately bound to the absence of the father." Indeed, writing claims to achieve "emancipation" from the father with "complacent self-sufficiency" ("PP," 77). Derrida sees the opposition between the "living" discourse of speech (which is backed by the presence of the father) and the inanimate discourse of writing as correlative with the contrast Socrates insists on between mere persuasion (as advocated by the Sophists and rhetors) and pursuit of the truth ("PP," 78). Plato describes *logos* as a *zoon*, a living being, in contrast with the "cadaverous rigidity of writing"; yet, in doing this, says Derrida, he is actually following certain rhetors and Sophists who had "held up the living spoken word, which infallibly conforms to the necessities of the situation at hand, to the expectations and demands of the interlocutors present" ("PP," 79). And the father (for which the Greek word *pater* means also the "chief," the "capital," the "good") is the "blinding source" of *logos*: he cannot be looked in the eye, cannot be questioned, cannot be subjected to the operations of reason ("PP," 82–83).

Despite Plato's overt intentions, says Derrida, the play of the chain of significations in which the word *pharmakon* is caught goes on working of its own accord ("PP," 96). The king's reply to Theuth suggests that writing is both an occult and therefore suspect power; but also that the effectiveness of the *pharmakon* can be reversed, since it can actually make the memory worse ("PP," 97). And, for Plato, writing is no more effective as a remedy than as a poison ("PP," 99). The *pharmakon* goes against "natural life": in Plato's eyes, a drug interferes with the natural course of life, hence it is the "enemy of the living in general." King Thamus, as Plato recounts the myth, tells Theuth that writing will equip people not with true wisdom but merely a semblance of wisdom: students will read for themselves "without the benefit of a teacher's instruction." They will have access not to reality and truth but to appearances, and will suffer from the delusion that they possess knowledge. Thus, says Derrida, "The king, the father of speech, has thus asserted his authority over the father of writing" ("PP," 102).

Derrida's point here is that Plato himself (like his translators) attempts to reduce the ambiguity inherent in the word *pharmakon* to a series of "clear-cut oppositions" between good and evil, inside and outside, true and false, essence and appearance. Thus, through his invocation of the myth, Plato condemns writing as "bad, external to memory, productive not of science but of belief, not of truth but of appearances" ("PP," 103). The danger, in Derrida's eyes, is that writing or *pharmakon*, which is reduced by Plato to one term of an opposition, a term which correlates with other oppositional terms (bad, external, false, appearance), returns to haunt these opposi-tions, as the very condition of their possibility. In other words, the very ambiguity at the heart of *pharmakon* or writing is what precedes and enables this entire system of oppositions ("PP," 103).

There is an ulterior motive, according to Derrida, behind Plato's diatribe against writing: it is directed above all against Sophists and sophistry, since writing is associ-ated, like sophistry, with the mere semblance of truth and wisdom. The man who relies on writing, says Derrida, the man "who brags about the knowledge and powers it assures him," is a "simulator" who has "all the features of a sophist" ("PP," 106). The Sophist merely "sells the signs and insignia of science . . . He thus answers the demands of wealthy young men, and that is where he is most warmly applauded." The Sophist merely pretends to know everything and writing is the emblem and medium of such pretense since it is foreign to the notion of living truth, truth which lives in the process of its presentation in the form of dialectics ("PP," 107).

And yet, as Derrida initially hints, the notion of writing and *pharmakon* threatens to undermine the entire opposition of sophistry and philosophy: instead of these terms subsisting as mutually "other," writing will insinuate itself as the "entirely-other of *both* sophistics and Platonism," exhuming all of the "signposts marking out the battle lines between sophistics and philosophy" ("PP," 107–108). To begin with, the diatribe against writing actually derives *from* the Sophists. The Attic school of rhetoricians (Gorgias, Isocrates, Alcidamas) had already "extolled the force of the living *logos*," though for reasons different from Plato's: they viewed speech as adaptable to present circumstances, while writing merely engages in mechanical repetition ("PP," 114–115). Hence "Plato imitates the imitators in order to restore the truth of what they imitate: namely, truth itself" ("PP," 112).

Secondly, living memory and speech, for Plato, repeat the presence of the *eidos*, the unchanging Platonic Form; for Plato, all knowledge derives from the (imperfect) recol-lection and imitation of the eternal Forms. Hence truth is the signifier of the signified *eidos*. The *eidos* or Form is thus repeated in its identity. The phonic signifier, as ex-pressed by speech, would remain in living proximity to the *eidos*. In writing, however, the graphic or written signifier is effectively an imitation of the phonic signifier, an imitation of an imitation, which is inanimate and mechanical, falling "outside of life" ("PP," 110–111). As Derrida puts it, writing "would indeed be the signifier's capacity to repeat itself by itself, mechanically, without a living soul to sustain or attend it in its repetition" ("PP," 111). Writing would thus be a signifier pointing to a signified, the phonic signifier of the *eidos*. Using Saussure's metaphor, Derrida points out that writing would be therefore "separated" from speech only as a signifier is separated from its signified: writing (and sophistics) would be the recto, and speech (philosophy, Platonism) the verso of a leaf of paper. It is this difference between signified and signifier that provides "the governing pattern within which Platonism institutes itself and determines its opposition to sophistics" ("PP," 112). Yet this alleged "difference" also marks an inseparability (as Saussure said, one can't cut one side of the leaf without cutting the other): "philosophy and dialectics are determined in the act of determining their other" ("PP," 112). In other words, Plato attempts to *define* philosophy by its opposition to sophistry, yet overlooks the fact that this opposition itself bespeaks their necessary connection. Plato cannot "explain what dialectics is without recourse to writing" ("PP," 112). Writing is a necessary element, then, in the very definition of philosophy and dialectics.

Thirdly, apart from the "banal" fact that Plato himself was a writer, there are passages in Plato's texts where he himself judges writing to be indispensable. The example Derrida gives is Plato's perception of the need for the law to be in writing: "the immutable, petrified identity of writing is not simply added to the signified law . . . it assures the law's permanence and identity with the vigilance of a guardian" ("PP," 113). Writing ensures that the law will always be "on record" and accessible to scrutiny. Hence, writing is not an addition to the law, imitating and repeating it. The "law can be *posited* only in writing . . . The legislator is a writer. And the judge is a reader" ("PP," 113).

Finally, the earlier Sophists such as Gorgias who extolled the power of speech or *logos* over writing, on the grounds that the *logos* was a more effective drug or *pharmakon*, recognized that initially the *logos* as a *pharmakon* could be used for both good and bad purposes. Gorgias prefigured Plato's later more systematic gesture in attempting to associate the *logos* with truth and an ordered structure of the world. This initial indeterminate status of the *logos*, in which the ambivalence of *pharmakon* was embodied, was suppressed by Plato ("PP," 115). And Socrates himself, as Derrida points out, is often charged by interlocutors in Plato's dialogues as being a master of the *pharmakon*, who can cast his spell over others. Derrida observes that, for all Plato's endeavors, Socrates himself is the "spitting image of a sophist," and that there is a ceaseless dialectic between the "socratic *pharmakon*" and the "sophistic *pharmakon*" ("PP," 119).

In all these ways, then, writing, in all of its associations (with sophistry, relativism, independence of thought), returns to haunt and undermine Plato's systematic endeavor to suppress and exclude it, a gesture central not only to his thought but also to the reception of his philosophy as whole by subsequent generations, and thus to the demarcation of philosophy as a discipline.

Deconstruction: An Assessment

Derrida's influence in America and Europe was unparalleled in the latter twentieth century. His American disciples included the Yale critics Paul de Man, J. Hillis Miller, and Geoffrey Hartman, as well as Barbara Johnson and, arguably, Harold Bloom. These critics applied and richly extended Derridean techniques such as searching for impasses or *aporiai* in various texts, displaying the hidden presuppositions and contradictions of literary and philosophical works, and demonstrating how their central claims and oppositions undermined themselves. In *Blindness and Insight* (1971), for example, de Man argues that the insights produced by critics are intrinsically linked to certain blindnesses, the critics invariably affirming something other than what they intended. De Man's *Allegories of Reading* (1979) explores the theory of tropes or figurative language, affirming that language is intrinsically metaphorical and that literary texts above all are highly self-conscious of their status as such and are self-deconstructing. Hence criticism inevitably misreads a text, given that figurative language mediates between literary and critical text. Harold Bloom, also centrally concerned with the function of tropes in literature, is best known for his assessment of poetic tradition on the basis of the "anxiety of influence." Each writer, asserts Bloom, attempts to carve out an imaginative space free from overt domination by his or her predecessors; to this end, as Bloom argues in *A Map of Misreading* (1975), the writer assumes an Oedipal disposition, creatively misreading those predecessors or "fathers" by way of certain tropes such as irony, synecdoche, and metonymy.

A number of critics have explored the implications of deconstruction for other fields of study and other literary and cultural perspectives. Barbara Johnson's *A World of Difference* (1987) furnished powerful examples of deconstructive criticism in the context of broader issues of gender, race, and the institution of literary criticism. Gayatri Spivak has brought deconstructive insights to bear on her feminist and postcolonial concerns. Michael Ryan's *Marxism and Deconstruction* (1982) explores the commensurability and sharp contrasts between Marxist and deconstructive perspectives. Shoshana Felman and Stephen W. Melville have related Derrida's work to psychoanalysis.

It is clear that deconstruction has had a profound influence in a wide range of disciplines. Its remorseless insistence on exposing the foundations of and assumptions behind important concepts is a strategy that can be valuably enlisted by many forms of thought which endeavor to scrutinize conventional ways of thinking. It is also true, however, that deconstruction has met with substantial criticism on a number of accounts. One of the sharpest objections, voiced by Marxist critics such as Terry Eagleton, is that deconstruction exhibits a merely destructive or "negative" capability, whereby it criticizes various systems and institutions without offering any alternatives. Hence, its critique is abstract, leaving everything as it was. As scholars such as Jean-Michel Rabaté have pointed out, in his more recent writings Derrida resists this characterization of his endeavor as "negative." Rather, he sees even his earlier work as harboring an "affirmative" dimension, asking pertinent questions about essentiality, presence, and the usual philosophical oppositions such as sense and intellect, appearance and reality. Moreover, Derrida's later work ventured into areas such as politics, law, and the academy. A case in point is his *Specters of Marx* (1994), written in response to the concerns of various scholars over the fate of Marxism after the collapse of communism.[4] Derrida aligns the deconstructive spirit with certain legacies of Marx; even in his earlier work, he had acknowledged his debt to the same Hegelian dialectic that shaped Marx's thought.

Notwithstanding these qualifications, Derrida's thought is nonetheless open to further substantive criticisms. The notions of "difference" and "différance" on which so much of Derrida's thought rests are abstract. What Derrida calls "the movement of différance" extends through everything except itself. Difference, as Derrida conceives it, is itself self-identical. It is nothing other than pure identity. The notion of difference is an abstraction from the logical movement of the Hegelian dialectic. The notion of différance is a dual abstraction from the logical and historical movement of the dialectic, and involves a third abstraction from the progressive unity of logic and history. It suspends the entry into itself of all relations, logical or historical; it freezes the second phase of the dialectic into a self-bounded immunity from movement. Thus the movement of difference is nothing other than pure stasis. It coerces the movement from logic to ontology, as well as the ontological differences between past, present, and future, into one uniform ideal plane, of textuality. Having no past or future nor acknowledging *itself* as a result or product of previous thought, it usurps the place of movement, situating itself as an absolute beginning, a beginning defined not by its subsequent extension or emergence as such through various relations but by the very suppression of relations between itself and all else: by an act of willful self-positing, willful return to itself as the undiluted principle of beginning. It does not endure process but rather imprisons itself within an eternal circle of beginning which, for that very reason, is no beginning at all because nothing develops from it except its own uniform priority. Whatever might genuinely develop and differ from it is coerced into the shadow of its indiscriminate determination. Not only does it abolish historical specificity but also all possibility of logical precedence leading up to it. It is simply inserted into logic from the outside; it is not shown to be an inner development of any logic whatsoever or of any history. It is simply textuality abstracting into its own self-identical structure all the endless variety of true historical relation; it dissolves actual relations into a principle of abstract relationality. For Derrida, différance is effectively elevated to the status of a transcendental signified. Given that this notion underlies Derrida's critiques of philosophical systems that vary widely from one another, it is evident that he coerces all of these systems into a uniform assailability: they all suffer from the same defects, the same kinds of *aporiai* or impasses.

Furthermore, Derrida's concepts derive their possibility and force of articulation from metaphysical targets premolded into their most positivistic shape. It is only against a positivistic understanding of truth, meaning, presence, and subjectivity that his notions of trace, difference, and writing can articulate themselves. For example, his critique and alleged destabilization of subjectivity imposes a liberal atomistic view of the self indiscriminately on every philosophy. He says, for example, that seventeenth-century Cartesian rationalism determined absolute presence as self-presence, as subjectivity.[5] And that eighteenth-century thought began to question logocentrism by restoring the rights of sensibility and affirming the sensible origin of ideas (*OG*, 75, 98, 282). But the very terms of Derrida's impugnment of the ego presuppose as its target the isolated, atomistic Cartesian ego. Derrida says that "writing" both constitutes and dislocates the subject (*OG*, 68). But *which* subject does he mean? Does writing equally constitute and dislocate the Aristotelian and Cartesian subjects? When confronted with notions of truth and subjectivity which already bear the mark of difference and constitutive relations – such as those of Hegel – Derrida's notions vanish completely into that which they criticize. There is no notion or entity in Hegel's philosophy which is free of difference or relation.

Finally, there has been a tendency to overestimate Derrida's originality (though he himself was well aware of his debt to other thinkers). The relational and arbitrary nature of language has been perceived by many thinkers, ranging from Hellenistic philosophers and rhetoricians through Locke and Hume to Hegel, Marx, the French symbolists and Saussure. The notions that "reality" is a construction, that "truth" is an interpretation, that human subjectivity is not essentially fixed, and that there are no ultimate transcendent foundations of our thought and practice are as old as the Sophists of Athens in the fifth century BC. Many of the *aporiai* "revealed" by Derrida were encountered as such long ago by the neo-Hegelian philosophers in connecting phenomena to their various absolutes. Derrida's contribution is to have transferred the appurtenance of those *aporiai* within from the relation between thought and reality to the institution of language within that relation. And whether he has added anything to our understanding of time or of logic – both important in his thought – is uncertain.

What is certain is that we can benefit from a detailed reading of Derrida's texts, one which situates them in a balanced manner within the history of thought rather than merely using them as a privileged lens to view that history.

Notes

1   C. H. Dodd, *The Interpretation of the Fourth Gospel* (Cambridge: Cambridge University Press, 1953), pp. 263–265. Hereafter cited as Dodd.
2   "Structure, Sign, and Play in the Discourse of the Human Sciences," in *Writing and Difference*, trans. Alan Bass (Chicago: University of Chicago Press, 1978), p. 278. Hereafter cited as *WD*.
3   Jacques Derrida, "Plato's Pharmacy," in *Dissemination*, trans. Barbara Johnson (Chicago: University of Chicago Press, 1981), p. 67. Hereafter cited as "PP."
4   Jacques Derrida, *Specters of Marx: The State of the Debt, the Work of Mourning, and the New International*, trans. Peggy Kamuf (New York and London: Routledge, 1994).
5   Jacques Derrida, *Of Grammatology*, trans. Gayatri Chakravorty Spivak (Baltimore and London: Johns Hopkins University Press, 1976), p. 26. Hereafter cited as *OG*.

CHAPTER 26

FEMINIST CRITICISM

eminist criticism is not a uniquely twentieth-century phenomenon. It has antecedents going all the way back to ancient Greece, in the work of Sappho and arguably in Aristophanes' play *Lysistrata*, which depicts women as taking over the treasury in the Acropolis, a female chorus as physically and intellectually superior to the male chorus, and the use of sexuality as a weapon in an endeavor to put an end to the distinctly masculine project of the Peloponnesian War. Feminism also surfaces in Chaucer's Wife of Bath, who blatantly values "experience" over authority and was more than a match for each of her five husbands. In the Middle Ages, Christine de Pisan had the courage to enter into a debate with the predominant male critics of her day. During the Renaissance a number of women poets such as Catherine Des Roches emerged in France and England. In the seventeenth century, writers such as Aphra Behn and Anne Bradstreet were pioneers in gaining access to the literary profession. After the French Revolution, Mary Wollstonecraft argued that the ideals of the Revolution and Enlightenment should be extended to women, primarily through access to education. And the nineteenth century witnessed the flowering of numerous major female literary figures in both Europe and America, ranging from Mme. de Staël, the Brontës, Jane Austen, George Eliot, and Elizabeth Barrett Browning to Margaret Fuller and Emily Dickinson. Modernist female writers included Hilda Doolittle (H. D.), Gertrude Stein, Katherine Mansfield, and Virginia Woolf.

For most of this long history women were not only deprived of education and financial independence, they also had to struggle against a male ideology condemning them to virtual silence and obedience, as well as a male literary establishment that poured scorn on their literary endeavors. Indeed, the depiction of women in male literature – as angels, goddesses, whores, obedient wives, and mother figures – was an integral means of perpetuating these ideologies of gender. It was only with women's struggles in the twentieth century for political rights that feminist criticism arose in any systematic way. Since the early twentieth century feminist criticism has grown to encompass a vast series of concerns: a rewriting of literary history so as to include the contributions of women; the tracing of a female literary tradition; theories of sexuality and sexual difference, drawing on psychoanalysis, Marxism, and the social sciences; the representation of women in male literature; the role of gender in both literary creation and literary criticism (as studied in so-called "gynocriticism"); the connection between gender and various aspects of literary form, such as genre and meter (it is clear, for example, that certain genres such as epic embody masculine values of heroism, war, and adventure, while the lyric has sometimes been seen as feminine, expressing private emotion); above all, feminist critics have displayed a persistent concern with both experience and language: is there a specifically female experience that has been communicated by women writers? And how do women confront the task of being historically coerced into using a language dominated by male concepts and values? Some feminists have urged the need for a female language, while others have advocated appropriating and modifying the inherited language of the male oppressor.

The significance of language rests ultimately on its expression of male ways of thinking that go all the way back to Aristotle: the laws of logic, beginning with the law of identity, as well as the Aristotelian categories divide up the world into strictly demarcated entities. These binary oppositions, as many modern theorists have argued, are coercive: for example, according to Aristotle's laws, *either* one is a man *or* one is a woman; a person is *either* black *or* white, *either* master *or* slave. Feminists have often rejected these divisive ways of viewing the world, stressing instead the various shades between female and male, between black and white, and indeed urging a vision of unity rather than opposition. In this process, such categories are recognized to be founded on no essence or natural distinctions, but are viewed as cultural and ideological constructions. Hence, another fundamental feminist concern has been the rejection of "theory" as such, since in its very nature it houses these masculine presuppositions. Feminism thus advocates a principled recalcitrance to definition, a conceptual fluidity and openness which laughs in the face of tyrannizing attempts to fix it as just one more category to be subsumed by the vast historical catalogue of male-generated concepts.

Indeed, one of the invaluable accomplishments of feminism has been utterly to reject the notions of objectivity and neutrality; feminists have pioneered a new honesty in acknowledging that they write from subjective positions informed by specific circumstances. This position rests largely on feminists' acknowledgment that thought is not somehow a disembodied and abstract process, but is intimately governed by the nature and situation of the body in place and time. The "body" has become a powerful metaphor of such specificity and concreteness, which rejects the male Cartesian tradition that thinking can somehow occur on a plane of disembodied universality. The body that I inhabit will shape my thinking at the profoundest levels: if my body happened to be born into a rich family with political ties, my political, religious, and social affiliations will inevitably reflect this. Whether my body is male or female will initially determine my thought and experience at a far deeper level than which books I read. Notwithstanding these insights of feminism, the days are still not past in which high school students are forbidden to use the word "I" in their compositions, effectively perpetuating the pretense and self-delusion of objectivity.

It is clear, also, that feminism has potential areas of overlap with certain theories such as deconstruction and Marxism, as well as with certain philosophers such as Hegel, who opposed traditional logic, and Schopenhauer and Bergson, who recognized the subjection of reason to bodily needs, and with poetic visions such as those enshrined in French symbolism and modernism (notwithstanding the often misogynistic leanings of male figures in these movements). Having said all of this, it should be remembered that feminism is not comprised of any one movement or set of values; it has been broadly international in scope and its disposition is dictated by many local as well as general factors. For example, writers from Arab traditions such as Fatima Mernissi and Leila Ahmed have attempted to articulate a feminist vision distinctly marked by their specific cultural concerns; the same is true of African-American feminists such as Alice Walker and feminists of Asian heritage such as Gayatri Spivak. What follows is a brief account of feminism in French, American, and British traditions. Two of the landmark works of feminism in the early twentieth century, whose influence was disseminated through all three of these traditions, were Virginia Woolf's *A Room of One's Own* (1929) and Simone de Beauvoir's *The Second Sex* (1949), which will receive detailed treatment below.

French Feminism

The impetus for much modern French feminism was drawn from the revolutionary atmosphere of May 1968 which saw massive unrest on the part of students and workers. In that atmosphere, an integral component of political revolution was seen as the transformation of signifying practices and conceptions of subjectivity, based on a radical understanding of the power of language. Drawing heavily on the ideas of Jacques Lacan and Jacques Derrida (which they often modified against the grain of these thinkers), feminists such as Annie Leclerc, Marguerite Duras, Julia Kristeva, Luce Irigaray, and Hélène Cixous variously participated in advancing a notion of *l'écriture féminine*, a feminine writing that would issue from the unconscious, the body, from a radically reconceived subjectivity, in an endeavor to circumvent what they held to be phallocentric discourse.

For Kristeva, such language came from a pre-Oedipal state, from the realm of the "semiotic," prior to the process of cultural gender formation. She was aware, however, that reliance solely on this "maternal" language would entail the risk of political marginalization. Indeed, Luce Irigaray advocates undermining patriarchal discourse from within, a strategy she pursues in her readings of several discourses from Plato through Freud and Marx to Lacan. She does, however, indicate that a feminine language would be more diffuse, like her sexuality, and less rigidly categorizing than male discourse. Hélène Cixous also sees a "solidarity" between logocentrism and phallocentrism (where the phallus is a signifier, a metaphor of male power and dominance), an alliance that must be questioned and undermined. Women, she urged, must write their bodies, to unfold the resources of the unconscious. All of these writers revaluate the significance of the maternal, viewing this as empowering rather than as oppressed. Other feminists, however, such as Christine Fauré, Catherine Clément, and Monique Wittig, have challenged this emphasis on the body as biologically reductive, fetishistic, and politically impotent. Monique Wittig wishes to do away with the linguistic categories of sex and gender.

American Feminism

Feminist criticism in America received a major stimulus from the civil rights movement of the 1960s, and has differed somewhat in its concerns from its counterparts
in France and Britain, notwithstanding the undoubted impact of earlier figures such
as Virginia Woolf and Simone de Beauvoir. A seminal work, *The Feminine Mystique*
(1963), was authored by Betty Friedan, who subsequently founded the National
Organization of Women in 1966. This widely received book expressed the fundamental
grievance of middle-class American women, their entrapment within private, domestic
life, and their inability to pursue public careers. A number of other important feminist
texts were produced around this time: Mary Ellman's *Thinking About Women* (1968),
Kate Millett's *Sexual Politics* (1969), Germaine Greer's *The Female Eunuch* (1970), and
Shulamith Firestone's *The Dialectic of Sex* (1970), which used gender rather than class
as the prime category of historical analysis. Millett's influential book concerned female
sexuality and the representation of women in literature. It argued that patriarchy was a
political institution which relied on subordinated roles for women. It also distinguished
between the concept of "sex," which was rooted in biology, and that of "gender,"
which was culturally acquired. Other critics in this tradition of examining masculine
portrayals of women included Carolyn Heilbrun and Judith Fetterly.

A number of feminist texts have attempted to identify alternative and neglected
traditions of female writing. These have included Patricia Meyer Spacks' *The Female
Imagination* (1975), Ellen Moers' *Literary Women* (1976), and Sandra Gilbert and
Susan Gubar's *The Madwoman in the Attic* (1979). The most influential work of
this kind was Elaine Showalter's *A Literature of their Own* (1977), which traced three
phases of women's writing, a "feminine" phase (1840–1880) where women writers
imitated male models, a "feminist" phase (1880–1920) during which women challenged those models and their values, and a "female" phase (from 1920) which saw
women advocating their own perspectives. Recent debates within American feminism,
conducted by figures such as Showalter, Lillian Robinson, Annette Kolodny, and
Jane Marcus, have concerned the relationship of female writers to male theories, the
need for feminist theory and a female language, the relation of feminism to poststructuralist perspectives, as well as continuing problems of political and educational
activism.

Also hotly debated has been the possible connection of feminism and Marxism.
Michèle Barrett's *Women's Oppression Today: Problems in Marxist Feminist Analysis*
(1980) attempts to reconcile Marxist and feminist principles in analyzing the representation of gender. Other works in this vein include Judith Newton and Deborah
Rosenfelt's *Feminist Criticism and Social Change* (1985), which also argues for feminist
analysis that takes account of social and economic contexts. A notable recent development has been the attempt to think through feminism from black and minority perspectives, as in Alice Walker's *In Search of Our Mothers' Gardens* (1983) and Barbara
Smith's *Toward a Black Feminist Criticism* (1977). Finally, significant contributions by
lesbian critics include Mary Daly's *Gyn/Ecology* (1978) and Adrienne Rich's "Compulsory
Heterosexuality and Lesbian Existence" (1980). Judith Butler's groundbreaking *Gender
Trouble* (1990) was a powerful critique of heterosexual assumptions in feminist theory,

of the dualism of masculinity and femininity, in the contexts of Western metaphysics, psychoanalysis, and power structures.

British Feminism

Twentieth-century British feminist criticism might be said to begin with Virginia Woolf, whose work is considered in detail below. Much British feminist criticism has had a political orientation, insisting on situating both feminist concerns and literary texts within a material and ideological context. In her landmark work "Women: The Longest Revolution," later expanded and produced as *Women's Estate* (1971), Juliet Mitchell examined patriarchy in terms of Marxist categories of production and private property as well as psychoanalytic theories of gender. Her later works such as *Psychoanalysis and Feminism* (1974) continue to refine her attempt to integrate the insights of Marxism and psychoanalysis. Another seminal text was Michèle Barrett's *Women's Oppression Today* (1980), which attempted to formulate a materialist aesthetics and insisted on integrating Marxist class analysis with feminism in analyzing and influencing gender representation. Other important critics have included Jacqueline Rose and Rosalind Coward, who have integrated certain insights of Jacques Lacan into a materialist feminism, Catherine Belsey, who also has drawn upon Lacan in assessing Renaissance drama from a materialist feminist perspective, and the Norwegian-born Toril Moi, who has developed insights from Woolf and engaged in a critique of the humanism and implicit essentialism of some American feminists. Also critical of the tendency of American feminists to combat male stereotypes and to recover female traditions are Judith Newton and Deborah Rosenfelt. Finally, a number of critics such as Cora Kaplan, Mary Jacobus, and Penny Boumelha have comprised the UK Marxist-Feminist Collective, formed in 1976.

Virginia Woolf (1882–1941)

Though her views have been criticized by some feminists, Virginia Woolf was in many ways a pioneer of feminist literary criticism, raising issues – such as the social and economic context of women's writing, the gendered nature of language, the need to go back through literary history and establish a female literary tradition, and the societal construction of gender – that remain of central importance to feminist studies. Woolf's most significant statements impinging on feminism are contained in two lectures presented at women's colleges at Cambridge University in 1928, subsequently published as *A Room of One's Own* (1929), and in *Three Guineas* (1938), an important statement concerning women's alienation from the related ethics of war and patriarchy. Woolf is also known as one of the foremost modernist writers of the English-speaking world. The most famous of her many novels include *Mrs. Dalloway* (1925), *To the Lighthouse* (1927), and *Orlando* (1928). She also produced several collections of essays on a broad range of literary topics and writers.

671

As the daughter of the Victorian agnostic philosopher Leslie Stephen, Woolf had access to his substantial library, and it was here that she received her education. After her parents' deaths, she settled, with her brothers and sisters, in Bloomsbury, a fashionable area of London which later gave its name to the intellectual circle in which Virginia and her sister Vanessa moved. The "Bloomsbury Group" included the economist John Maynard Keynes, the historian and biographer Lytton Strachey, the art critic Clive Bell, and the writer Leonard Woolf, whom Virginia was to marry in 1912. The group was associated with certain other intellectuals from Cambridge, notably the analytic philosopher G. E. Moore, who may have had some impact on Woolf's thinking (an impact integrated into the influences of figures such as the French philosopher Henri Bergson and the novelist Marcel Proust). This group was unconventional in its outlooks and often in its sexuality. Woolf's own views of femininity and gender relations must have been rooted partly in her own sexuality; she was engaged in a relationship with the writer Vita Sackville-West, on whom Woolf's novel *Orlando* was based.

In 1917 Virginia and Leonard Woolf established the Hogarth Press. Though this printing press was small, it became an important outlet for the work of many modernist writers, including T. S. Eliot, E. M. Forster, and Katherine Mansfield; Woolf's own work was published there, as well as the translated works of Sigmund Freud. Woolf suffered from nervous breakdowns and was acutely and sometimes debilitatingly conscious of her status as a female writer in an intellectual milieu dominated by males and masculine values. In 1941 she walked into a river, her pockets loaded with stones, and drowned herself, suffering the same fate as her imaginative character Shakespeare's sister, who was driven to suicide on account of the overwhelming forces and institutions thwarting her female genius.

Woolf's literary criticism is closely tied to the modernist nature of her fiction, and expresses the broad philosophical and feminist dispositions underlying her novels. Her work is modernist in its complexity of characterization, its use of multiple and shifting narrative perspectives, its manipulation of time, its intricate conception of experience, its accumulation of esoteric symbolism, its treatment of the connections between human identity and its surroundings, and, above all, in its implicit acknowledgment that language does not intrinsically refer to some "external" reality, but itself shapes the realities that we experience. Indeed, the "reality" explored in Woolf's novels is largely that of the "internal" psychology of given characters as this interacts with the "external" world (the distinction between "internal" and "external" being blurred), as well as the reality of their relationships with one another. In some ways, these modernist features are made to overlap with Woolf's feminist concerns: the well-known portrait of Mr. Ramsay in *To the Lighthouse*, for example, has been held to represent Woolf's father, Leslie Stephen, or even the philosopher G. E. Moore; at the very least, this character has been thought to embody a conventionally "male" academic perspective, marked by dry rationality, self-indulgence, and emotional debility.

Hence, Woolf's literary criticism, like her fiction, can be approached from at least two series of perspectives, those of modernism and feminism. The extent to which the concerns and interests of modernism (which was often overarchingly conservative in political terms) overlap with those of feminism is a complex issue that is still being explored. Perhaps the most fundamental point on which feminism and modernism overlap is their common rejection of the mainstream legacy of the bourgeois

Enlightenment and what is often characterized as the Enlightenment view of the human being as a free, rational agent, enabled through progressive knowledge to subjugate the world of nature on many levels, intellectual, material, and economic. Like many Romantics, modernists, and feminists, Woolf reacted against the primacy accorded by the Enlightenment to the faculty of human reason, as well as the presumption that reason could master the world and reduce it to total intelligibility.

At various points in her fiction and essays, Woolf expresses what has come to be seen as a characteristically feminist distrust of theorizing, which is seen as imbued with centuries of male values and strategies. Talking of Mary Wollstonecraft, for example, Woolf remarks that this pioneer was "no cold-blooded theorist – something was born in her that thrust aside her theories and forced her to model them afresh . . . Mary's life had been an experiment from the start."[1] In another essay, she asserts that to "know the reason of things is a poor substitute for being able to feel them" (CR, 192). She notes a tendency in modern writers that they "cannot generalize. They depend on their senses and emotions, whose testimony is trustworthy, rather than on their intellects whose message is obscure" (CR, 329–330). Indeed, in contrast with Enlightenment views of the ultimate intelligibility of the world, and of the human self, Woolf states that human nature is "infinitely mysterious" (CR, 95). Like most modernists, Woolf questioned the idea of an external reality that somehow existed independently of our minds. In an autobiographical sketch, Woolf voiced her sentiment that "reality" is something deeper than the appearances that confront our senses, and that ultimately, it is we ourselves who construct this reality:

> the shock-receiving capacity is what makes me a writer . . . a shock is a token of some real thing behind appearances; and I make it real by putting it into words . . . From this I reach what I might call a philosophy; at any rate it is a constant idea of mine; that behind the cotton wool is hidden a pattern; that we – I mean all human beings – are connected with this; that the whole world is a work of art; that we are parts of the work of art. *Hamlet* or a Beethoven quartet is the truth about this vast mass that we call the world. But there is no Shakespeare, there is no Beethoven; certainly and emphatically there is no God; we are the words; we are the music; we are the thing itself. And I see this when I have a shock.[2]

Hence, for Woolf the world is a construction out of a primordial and undifferentiated "vast mass," and the deeper reality that we might discern beneath appearances is not some unknowable thing in itself but our own operations, especially the operations of art, which can see a pattern and a unity in phenomena such as are inaccessible to reason or discursive thought. In her diary Woolf observes how "the creative power at once brings the whole universe to order."[3] Other diary entries confirm her view of reality as a construct. After noting another writer's charge that her characters fail, she writes: "I haven't that 'reality' gift. I insubstantise, wilfully to some extent, distrusting reality – its cheapness" (WD, 57). In a later entry she muses over the thought that she is "haunted by some semi-mystic very profound life of a woman, which shall all be told on one occasion; and time shall be utterly obliterated; future shall somehow blossom out of the past. One incident – say the fall of a flower – might contain it. My theory being that the actual event practically does not exist – nor time either" (WD, 102).

Hence for Woolf, as for many modernists and feminists, "reality" is not somehow already there but is the result of a complex interaction between human subjects and the "external" world. Moreover, this reality is viewed not as stable but as inherently changing and dynamic. Woolf says in an essay on Montaigne: "Movement and change are the essence of our being; rigidity is death; conformity is death" (*CR*, 94). These attitudes which Woolf attributes to Montaigne also characterize much of her own work. The emphasis on change, in particular, is profoundly symptomatic of a modernist perspective, and in Woolf's case it may well have been inspired by Bergson and Proust. Bergson's emphasis on the primary reality of time challenged the "spatial" disposition of mainstream Western philosophy from Plato through the Enlightenment. This mainstream tradition had effectively ignored the reality of time in its viewing of the world as laid out according to categories in space: the world had been classified and divided up into enduring entities with stable identities.

The mainstream Enlightenment view of the external world as a categorizable inventory of stable objects and events persisted into Woolf's time in the form of various philosophies of realism and logical positivism. It is well known that Woolf studied and admired the realist-analytic philosophy of G. E. Moore, as attested to by her close friends and biographers. Quentin Bell, for example, records that Woolf read Moore's *Principia Ethica* "with some difficulty and great admiration."[4] In his seminal essay of 1903, "The Refutation of Idealism," Moore had characterized the central claim of idealism as the assertion that "the object of experience is inconceivable apart from the subject." According to him, an idealist views the universe as spiritual, which he interprets to mean that the universe is intelligent, purposive, and that it has many properties which it doesn't seem to possess on the surface. What bothers Moore is the "vast difference" between these idealist positions and the "ordinary view of the world," as given by common sense.[5] Moore's pursuit of "common sense" led him, in his lecture series published as *Some Main Problems of Philosophy*, to describe the purpose of philosophy as an attempt to provide an inventory of the things we know and do not know in the universe as well as to clarify our ways of knowing. Common sense suggests that there are two different kinds of things in the universe, material objects and mental acts or acts of consciousness.[6] It also suggests that these two series of things are very different in nature, that material objects are situated in space and time, and that their existence is independent of acts of consciousness. Moore defines the views of "common sense" as those which are "universally held." While acknowledging that some components of common sense may change over time, he suggests that others, such as the belief in a plurality of material objects, have remained the same (*MPP*, 2–3).

These commonsense beliefs not only project a view of the world as something stable and categorizable but are embodied in equally atomistic attitudes toward language and the process of thought: thought can be refined and corrected by polishing its instrument of expression, language. Hence a belief in analytical rigor, clear definition, and precise use of language. In other words, these common sense beliefs are enshrined in a certain conception of *style*.

It is important to understand that the "common sense" wisdom advocated by figures such as G. E. Moore embodies certain central presuppositions of the Western philosophical tradition – the distinction between mind and reality, the independent existence of all entities, the equation of knowledge with various modes of classification of these entities – that were challenged by modernism, which insisted on reality as a productive interaction between subject and object and which stressed the reality of change and the profoundly temporal nature of all phenomena. Those same main-stream presuppositions have also been characterized as "male": the "wisdom" that figures such as G. E. Moore or Edmund Burke have equated with consensually achieved common sense has been characterized by feminists as a distinctly "male" wisdom, based on male-generated categories through which the world has been seen. And while some critics, notably Eric Auerbach and S. P. Rosenbaum, have seen Woolf as a realist, perhaps influenced by Moore, it might be well to remember that Woolf's attitude toward Moore and the entire "masculine" milieu of Cambridge was at best ambivalent. It is true that, reminiscing over her Bloomsbury activities, Woolf herself describes with some excitement how "Moore's book had set us all discussing philosophy, art, religion" (*MB*, 168). And yet she goes on to remark how she became "intolerably bored." Why, she asks, "were the most gifted of people also the most barren? . . . Why was it all so negative?" (*MB*, 172). In the essay on Montaigne, she had lashed out against the "virtues" of common sense and non-contradiction: "let us say what comes into our heads, repeat ourselves, contradict ourselves, fling out the wildest nonsense . . . without caring what the world thinks or says" (*CR*, 94). At one level, it may well be "nonsense" that Woolf wishes to fling in the face of Moore's "common sense," and that of the entire male philosophical tradition. Whether this attitude makes her a realist or an idealist is open to debate.

What is not in question is Woolf's defiant refusal to accept "reality" as anything more than a convention, or set of conventions, which do not grasp what is most private and authentic about our experience. In an autobiographical sketch she talks of her "sensation that we are sealed vessels afloat on what it is convenient to call reality" (*MB*, 122). And in a diary entry of 1933 she states: "I will go on adventuring, opening my mind and my eyes, refusing to be stamped and stereotyped. The thing is to free one's self: to let it find its dimensions, not be impeded" (*WD*, 213). In her essay on Montaigne she observed that this deeper self or soul corresponds very "little to the version which does duty for her in public." She in fact warns that the "laws are mere conventions, utterly unable to keep touch with the vast variety and turmoil of human impulses; habits and customs are a convenience devised for the support of timid natures who dare not allow their souls free play. But we, who have a private life . . . hold it infinitely the dearest of our possessions" (*CR*, 90–93).

Hence Woolf seems to reject both terms of the realist vision of the world, a vision with its roots in Enlightenment thought: a stable subject perceiving a world of inde-pendent and stable objects. If reality is actually a complex and ever-changing interac-tion between subject and object, then the project of conventional realism is misguided – not necessarily in its attempt to provide an accurate reflection or impression of reality but in its very definition of reality as piecemeal and static. Modernism in general did not react against the attempt to express reality but against the conception of reality that underlay that endeavor. In her famous essay "Modern Fiction," Woolf takes issue with the novelistic realism of writers such as Wells, Bennett, and Galsworthy. She labels these writers "materialists" because they imitate only surface phenomena, "making the trivial and the transitory appear the true and the enduring." These writers are in thrall to the methods of conventional realism: "to provide a plot, to provide comedy, tragedy, love, interest, and an air of probability." But, Woolf asks: "Is life like this?" (*CR*, 210–212). What she questions is the assumption that we somehow experience reality in a neatly ordered manner; actual experience is much less tidy and more complex:

> The mind receives a myriad impressions – trivial, fantastic, evanescent, or engraved with the sharpness of steel. From all sides they come, an incessant shower of innumerable atoms; and as they fall, as they shape themselves into the life of Monday or Tuesday, the accent falls differently from of old . . . if a writer were a free man and not a slave, if he could write what he chose, not what he must, if he could base his work upon his own feeling and not upon convention, there would be no plot, no comedy, no tragedy, no love interest or catastrophe in the accepted style . . . Life is not a series of gig lamps symmetrically arranged; but a luminous halo, a semi-transparent envelope surrounding us from the beginning of consciousness to the end.
>
> Let us record the atoms as they fall upon the mind in the order in which they fall, let us trace the pattern, however disconnected and incoherent in appearance, which each sight or incident scores upon the consciousness. (*CR*, 212–213)

Woolf's language, urging the novelist to "record the atoms as they fall upon the mind," implies a call for a refined realism, one that is not constrained by frigid imperatives pertaining to plot, character, and probability. When Woolf rejects these imperatives, she does so on the grounds that they *cannot* generate a "likeness to life" (*CR*, 211–212). In reacting against the realism of her literary predecessors, Woolf seeks a more complex and deeper vision of reality and experience as the basis of fiction. Reviewing Dorothy Richardson's *The Tunnel*, Woolf insists that: "We want to be rid of realism, to penetrate without its help into the regions beneath it, and further require that Miss Richardson shall fashion this new material into something which has the shapeliness of the old accepted forms."[7]

But, although Woolf clearly wishes to shift novelistic attention away from the "actual event" and time-frame of conventional realism, she seems to advocate a more refined realism. It seems that Woolf does wish the novelist to engage with "reality," but this reality itself is reconceived: it is no longer an atomistic reality of independent objects but something beneath these surface appearances, something which binds them in a farther-reaching totality. On a philosophical plane, it will be recalled that this attempt to characterize the world as "other than what it seems," to penetrate beyond appearances to an underlying reality, was regarded by Moore as the supreme claim of idealism. If Virginia Woolf is a realist, her realism seems to comprise a call for viewing things in their relatedness rather than in isolation, a fact which places her in the deepest opposition to philosophical realism. Whatever label we place on her philosophical disposition, that disposition was shared by both modernism and feminism, though it sprang from differing motivations: in the case of modernism, reality was seen as a complex and dynamic construction; in the case of feminism, the tradition of realism embodied a static and hierarchical vision of the world according to male categories founded on the notion – on the philosophy and logic – of stable identity.

In *A Room of One's Own* Woolf raised a number of issues that would remain of central concern to feminists. This book comprises two lectures, delivered by Woolf in 1928 at two women's colleges in Cambridge, on the topic of women and fiction. The "room" of the book's title is a skillfully used metaphor around which the entire text is woven: Woolf's central claim is that "a woman must have money and a room of her own if she is to write fiction."[8] The most obvious meaning of this claim is that women need financial and psychological independence in order to exercise their creative potential. But the claim itself is complex and the rest of Woolf's text effectively elaborates the metaphorical significance of "room."

At the most fundamental level, Woolf's claim situates literature within a material (economic, social, political) context. She compares fiction, for example, to a spider's web: this web is not spun in midair (literature does not arise in a vacuum) but is "attached to life at all four corners." Indeed, it is "attached to grossly material things" (*Room*, 43–44). Hence, literature cannot be produced without economic independence or backing: our "mothers," Woolf notes (talking to a female audience), were never given the chance to learn the art of making money, and it is this economic poverty that has underlain the intellectual impoverishment of women (*Room*, 21). Woolf notes of her own circumstances that when she began to receive a fixed income through inheritance, this initiated a change of temper in her entire outlook toward men, moving from fear and bitterness to pity and toleration, and finally to a calmer state of mind in which she felt the "freedom to think of things in themselves" (*Room*, 38–39). Hence, intellectual freedom, the "power to think for oneself," rests on financial freedom (*Room*, 106).

Historically, this "freedom of the mind" for women was pioneered by Aphra Behn, the first female writer to earn her living by writing. It was she who earned for women "the right to speak their minds" (*Room*, 64, 66). It was the "solid fact" of this economic basis that enabled the relative profusion of middle-class female writers in the later eighteenth century (*Room*, 65). It is also this fact which explains women's apparent silence through most of history. Even up until the beginning of the nineteenth century, Woolf notes, it would have been out of the question for a woman "to have a room of her own, let alone a quiet room or a sound-proof room . . . unless her parents were exceptionally rich or very noble." Women were debarred from any "separate lodging" which might shelter them "from the claims and tyrannies of their families" (*Room*, 52).

But beyond the material circumstances forestalling her independence, the immaterial difficulties were much worse. Woolf relates her famous anecdote of "Shakespeare's sister" Judith, who, being "wonderfully gifted," attempts to seek her fortune in the theater like her brother. The opposition to her endeavors ranges from her father's violent anger to the laughter and exploitation of men in the theater company; such is her frustration and fragility that she kills herself (*Room*, 46–48). Woolf's point is that "genius like Shakespeare's is not born among labouring, uneducated, servile people." And if a woman had been born with potential for genius, she "would certainly have gone crazed, shot herself, or ended her days in some lonely cottage" (*Room*, 48–49). While Shakespeare's sister is fictional, her parable is extrapolated from actual circumstances: Woolf cites the examples of women such as Lady Winchilsea who were mocked for their attempts to write; many women – including Currer Bell, George Eliot, and George Sand – sought the refuge of anonymous authorship (*Room*, 50).

The metaphor of one's own "room," as embodying the ability to think independently, takes another level of significance from its resistance to the appropriation of language, history, and tradition by men. Woolf notes that most of the books on women have been written by men, defining women so as to protect men's image of their own superiority (*Room*, 27, 34). She observes a deep ambivalence and irony in male attitudes toward women: "women have burnt like beacons in all the works of all the poets." In literature, woman has been treated as full of character and importance; in reality, "she was locked up, beaten and flung about the room." Hence, in poetry, in the imagination of man, woman has occupied a position "of the highest importance." In practical life, however, she "is completely insignificant" and "is all but absent from history" (*Room*, 43). Conventionally, woman "never writes her own life and scarcely keeps a diary." What is needed, according to Woolf, is a rewriting of history by women so as to present a more accurate account of the conditions in which women have lived (*Room*, 45).

A related task for women, as they look back through history, is to seek out the hitherto neglected and blurred outlines of a female literary tradition. "Poetry," affirms Woolf, "ought to have a mother as well as a father" (*Room*, 103). The work of the great female writers in the English tradition – including Jane Austen, the Brontës, George Eliot – was made possible by predecessors such as Aphra Behn, Fanny Burney, and others. For literary masterpieces are not, says Woolf, "single and solitary births; they are the outcome of many years of thinking in common" (*Room*, 65). Woolf points out that "books continue each other," and we must read newer women authors as descendents of previous female writers (*Room*, 80). However, when we think back through the great female writers, we find that, in addition to the material and psychological impediments to their creativity, they were faced with an even greater obstacle: "they had no tradition behind them, or one so short and partial that it was of little help. For we think back through our mothers if we are women. It is useless to go to the great men writers for help" (*Room*, 76). Implied in these statements is the need to establish a tradition of women's writing which, however closely it might be related to the male tradition, has its own emblems of distinctness in terms of both content and style. In this broader sense, the "room" might encompass a female tradition and female perspectives toward history.

A room of one's own might also represent the possibility, or ideal, of writing in a female language or at least appropriating language for female use. Woolf holds that women should not write in the same way as men do, notwithstanding the fact that many female authors have felt under enormous pressure to think and write like men. This pressure has stemmed partly from the unsuitability of language as hitherto developed to express the experience of women. Some writers, such as Jane Austen and Emily Brontë, succeeded in ignoring the persistent domineering male voice invading their consciousness, and managed to write as women, as able to reflect upon things in themselves rather than answering (perhaps unconsciously) to the voice of external authority (*Room*, 75). But most women writers, including George Eliot and Charlotte Brontë, failed to transcend or ignore the imposing conventions of external authority; debilitated by the lack of a female tradition, they found in the language no "common sentence" ready for their use; the "weight, the pace, the stride of a man's mind" was too unlike their own to be of use; these female writers succumbed to anger, irritation, the need to prove themselves and other such obstacles to their clarity of vision, a clarity that would allow them to view things in themselves rather than things as they ought to be seen from male perspectives (*Room*, 74). The "male" language they inherited could not express their female experience; this language, habituated to showing women exclusively in their relationship to men, could not express, for example, the liking of one woman for another (*Room*, 82). Encountering the sentence "Chloe liked Olivia" in a novel by Mary Carmichael, Woolf observes that such a sentiment – the liking of one woman for another – is expressed here perhaps for the first time in literature, and, were it to find adequate expression, it might "light a torch in that vast chamber where nobody has yet been" (*Room*, 82, 84). This novel experience requires a specifically female creativity and female appropriation of language in order to be articulated. Woolf notes how woman has been at the "centre of some different order and system of life," contrasting sharply with the world inhabited by men (*Room*, 86).

Indeed, so much of the literary tradition was a repository of male values – for example, the form of the epic – that, when women did begin to write in relative profusion, they expressed themselves largely in the form of the novel, which "alone was young enough to be soft" in their hands (*Room*, 77). Moreover, the domestic situation of middle-class women, obliging them to write in the common sitting room, was more conducive to novel writing than poetry; and the only literary training that such women had "was training in the observation of character, in the analysis of emotion" (*Room*, 67). Not only must women craft a sentence, a language that will grasp the rhythms of their own experience, but also a literary form that is "adapted to the body . . . women's books should be shorter, more concentrated, than those of men, and framed so that they do not need long hours of steady and uninterrupted work" (*Room*, 78). Broad shifts in economic conditions since Woolf's day may undermine her particular formula here for women's writing; but her general point – that language and thought are ultimately and irreversibly grounded in the rhythms of the body, of one's particular situation in place and time – is one that has been richly pursued by a variety of feminisms. What Woolf might have meant by a "female" use of language can perhaps be clarified by her characterization of male language: a man's writing, she said, appeared "so direct, so straightforward . . . It indicated such freedom of mind, such liberty of person, such confidence in himself." But all of these virtues – if such self-certainty and pretense to objectivity can be deemed virtues – fall, according to Woolf, under the shadow of a mighty male egotism, the shadow of the "I" that aridly dominates the male text, permeating it with an emotion incomprehensible to a woman, an emotion which lacks "suggestive power" and which Woolf associates with certain transcendental signifieds of the male world, such as "Work" and the "Flag" as found in authors such as Galsworthy and Kipling (*Room*, 99–102).

Ultimately, however, Woolf is calling on women to write *as* women but without consciousness of their sex occluding their creative vision. She states that Mary Carmichael "mastered the first great lesson; she wrote as a woman, but as a woman who has forgotten that she is a woman, so that her pages were full of that curious sexual quality which comes only when sex is unconscious of itself" (*Room*, 93). Indeed, the mental state that Woolf sees as most creative is what she calls "unity of the mind," a unity in which the sexes are not viewed as distinct (*Room*, 97). Her advocacy of this notion of "androgyny" is also impelled by her instinct that the greatest human happiness results from the natural cooperation of the sexes. She characterizes this "theory" of androgyny (a Greek term fusing the words for "man" and "woman"; the term is taken over from Coleridge, and ultimately from Plato) as follows: "in each of us two powers preside, one male, one female; and in the man's brain, the man predominates over the woman, and in the woman's brain, the woman predominates over the man. The normal and comfortable state of being is that when the two live in harmony together, spiritually co-operating . . . Coleridge perhaps meant this when he said that a great mind is androgynous" (*Room*, 98). Without this mixture, suggests Woolf, "the intellect seems to predominate and the other faculties of the mind harden and become barren." If we are to be creative, our minds must engage in this collaboration between male and female elements, and some "marriage of opposites has to be consummated. The whole of the mind must lie wide open if we are to get the sense that the writer is communicating his experience with perfect fullness" (*Room*, 104).

It is significant that Woolf alludes to Romantic notions of unity, as in Coleridge's view of androgyny and Blake's marriage of opposites. What her allusion brings out clearly is that the primacy of reason, advocated by the mainstream Enlightenment, against which the Romantics reacted on account of the abstractness and one-sidedness of such reason, was also a profound index and culmination of a long tradition of *male* thought and male categorization of the world. What the Romantics saw as an indeterminate deficiency of reason becomes in much feminism precisely a deficiency of male perspectives. In other words, the Romantics' perception of reason's deficiency or incompleteness was itself somewhat abstract; feminism, like Marxism, sees it as a political deficiency, ingrained in the social and economic fabric of gender relations.

A room of one's own is imbued with a further intensity of metaphorical significance: Woolf equates having such a room with living "in the presence of reality." The writer, she says, lives more than others in the presence of reality and attempts to convey it to the rest of us. What this means for women is that, when they have a room of their own (a tradition, a language, economic and intellectual independence), they will be free to be themselves, to see reality as it is, without their relation to the male sex weighing down their judgment; they will be able to "[t]hink of things in themselves" (*Room*, 110–111). And "reality," according to Woolf, comprises the "common life" we lead, not "the little separate lives which we live as individuals." She stresses that our essential relation is not to the world of men and women but to the "world of reality." Women need to see "human beings not always in their relation to each other but in relation to reality" (*Room*, 113–114). Ultimately, then, Woolf's call is for women to redefine their relationship to reality independently of prior definitions by men; their relation to men is but one element in this newly broadened vision of reality.

Woolf's other major "feminist" text, *Three Guineas* (1938), is written as a response to three requests for money (for an English guinea) for certain causes: the rebuilding of a woman's college, the promotion of women's entry into the professions, and the prevention of war together with the protection of culture and intellectual liberty. Woolf's response to these requests takes the form of a public meditation on issues at the heart of a modern liberal-democratic bourgeois state: the nature of education, the ethics underlying the professions, and the attributes of both spheres – grounded on an unequal distribution of property and wealth – that foster a mentality leading to war and imperialism. Woolf is in no doubt that the ruling values of such a state are male values: the entire ethos of war, she points out, is exclusively male. The splendid military uniforms, the distinctions of rank, the rosettes and medals which are invested by men with so much significance, appear "ridiculous" to women.[9] And the truth about war would reveal its horror, beneath its long-vaunted glory (*TG*, 97). Interestingly, Woolf sees the impulse to war and the conquest of other peoples as inhering in the very machinery of the liberal-democratic state. Traditional education, she urges, has not fostered freedom or peace; on the contrary, it has taught the arts of competition, domination, killing, and the acquiring of land and capital (*TG*, 29, 33–34). The professions, too, are infested with these same tendencies: founded on the acquisition of property and wealth, they foster – in the name of God, Nature, Law, and Empire – possessiveness, jealousy, and combativeness, qualities that cannot but lead to war (*TG*, 63, 66).

What of the position of women in such a political state founded on a male-oriented matrix of economic and cultural values? Should women be educated? Should they be encouraged to enter the professions? Can they exert any influence in the direction of peace? Woolf calls for "new words" and "new methods" (*TG*, 143). Women are in a historical position – having been excluded for so long – to take a more disinterested view of culture than men, and to initiate new schemes of education that will not breed fruitless individualism and competition, and new methods of participating in public life based on common interests rather than self-interest (*TG*, 100). An example of such disinterestedness lies in woman's justified indifference to patriotism. The notion of the "nation," enshrined at the heart of bourgeois culture and economy, engenders a patriotism that is all too often harmful and divisive. What meaning, asks Woolf, does patriotism have for a woman? Does she have the same reasons for loving, and being proud of, her country? Woolf points out – as World War II looms over the horizon – that dictatorship is not limited to the Nazis and fascists: as far as the oppression of women is concerned, dictatorship is universal. And how can we "trumpet our ideals of freedom and justice to other countries" when these ideals are far from being realized at home (*TG*, 53)? A woman, Woolf points out, will be justified in exclaiming to her patriotic brothers:

> Our country . . . throughout the greater part of its history has treated me as a slave; it has denied me education or any share in its possessions . . . Therefore if you insist upon fighting to protect me, or "our" country, let be understood, soberly and rationally between us, that you are fighting to gratify a sex instinct which I cannot share; to procure benefits which I have not shared and probably will not share . . . in fact, as a woman, I have no country. As a woman I want no country. As a woman my country is the whole world. (*TG*, 108–109)

Though Woolf has sometimes been criticized for the insufficient stridency of her feminism, few feminist statements could be more far-reachingly subversive than this effective rejection of the entire apparatus and logic of patriotism. This rejection, for reasons given above, is equally a rejection of the entire infrastructure of the modern nation, an infrastructure which disposes the nation toward a perpetual posture of war. Women, says Woolf, should have no share in the displays and trimmings of patriotism and all ceremonies that "encourage the desire to impose 'our' civilization or 'our' dominion upon other people" (*TG*, 109). Woolf calls upon women to reject the unbridled pursuit of wealth and profit, the prostituting of professions (whatever these might be) for money, and the external emblems of rank and status. She also urges them to dissociate themselves from "unreal" loyalties: "you must rid yourself of pride of nationality in the first place; also of religious pride, college pride, school pride, family pride, sex pride and those unreal loyalties that spring from them" (*TG*, 80).

Woolf's feminism has sometimes been viewed as problematic. Feminists have criticized her support of androgyny and her advice to the woman writer. Some feminists have been shocked by Woolf's apparently premature claim that the word "feminist" could be expunged from the language. The definition of "feminist" that Woolf had in mind in *Three Guineas* is "one who champions the rights of women," and since "the only right, the right to earn a living, has been won, the word no longer has a meaning. And a word without meaning is a dead word . . . Let us therefore celebrate this occasion by cremating the corpse" (*TG*, 80). Feminists would argue, with much justification, that the struggle for women's rights on a worldwide basis is far from over. Nonetheless, *Three Guineas* is a powerful statement of the fact that women's rights cannot simply be included as an additive element in bourgeois society, and that for women's rights to be realized, the very infrastructure of that society, as well as its fundamental values, need to be transformed. The importance of Woolf's work for feminism cannot be overestimated: the issues she raises, such as female tradition and language, the need for a broad critique of education and the professions, the core values of the modern nation, and the reflection of gendered dispositions in the very definition of reality and history, are still very much alive and still mark the sites of fierce political, economic, and intellectual debate.

Simone de Beauvoir (1908–1986)

Another classic feminist statement, *Le Deuxième Sexe* (1949; translated as *The Second Sex*, 1952), was produced by Simone de Beauvoir, a leading intellectual of her time, whose existentialist vision was forged partly in her relationship, as companion and colleague, with the existentialist philosopher Jean-Paul Sartre. De Beauvoir's text laid the foundations for much of the feminist theory and political activism that emerged during the 1960s in western Europe and America. Since then, its impact, if anything, has broadened and deepened: its basic thesis and premises continue to underlie the broad spectrum of feminist concerns. The book's central argument is that, throughout history, woman has always occupied a secondary role in relation to man, being relegated to the position of the "other," i.e., that which is adjectival upon the substantial subjectivity and existential activity of man. Whereas man has been enabled to transcend and control his environment, always furthering the domain of his physical and intellectual conquests, woman has remained imprisoned within "immanence," remaining a slave within the circle of duties imposed by her maternal and reproductive functions. In highlighting this subordination, the book explains in characteristic existentialist fashion how the so-called "essence" of woman was in fact created – at many levels, economic, political, religious – by historical developments representing the interests of men.

De Beauvoir was born in Paris; while studying at the Sorbonne, she made the acquaintance of Jean-Paul Sartre and Maurice Merleau-Ponty; with these two philosophers, she founded a literary and political journal. She belonged to a feminist collective and was politically active in feminist causes. She wrote several novels and a number of philosophical works, the most notable of which was *The Ethics of Ambiguity* (1947), articulating an existentialist ethics. Her existentialism, while influenced by Sartre, was also influenced by Marxism, psychoanalysis, and Hegel. Her view of freedom is distinguished from Sartre's view by its Hegelian emphasis on mutual recognition: it is through acknowledging another person's humanity that I confirm my own humanity and freedom. Another moment in Hegel's philosophy that underlies de Beauvoir's analyses of male–female relations through history and ideology is the master–slave relationship. According to Hegel, human consciousness strives for recognition and mastery, placing itself initially in a posture of hostility toward every other consciousness; a crucial phase in this endeavor for mastery is the willingness of one consciousness to risk everything in a life and death struggle. The consciousness that takes this risk becomes the "master," reducing its opponent to the status of a slave. Because of the nature of his duties, however, the slave is actually more attuned to the world than the master and it is the slave who gains mastery of his environment. Ultimately, the master is forced to recognize his own dependence on the slave, to see that his own human worth is gained in a relationship of reciprocity, of mutual recognition between himself and the slave: if he is to be recognized as human, he must acknowledge the slave's own humanity, else the latter's recognition of the master will be meaningless. In other words, humanity cannot arise in one person or in one group of people unilaterally: it is something born only of mutual recognition. This master–slave dialectic represents an important stage in Hegel's account of the development of human consciousness, and de Beauvoir skillfully bases the entire argument of her book on this intersubjective model of human consciousness and humanity. She views Hegel's master–slave dialectic as peculiarly applicable to the evolution of the male–female relationship.[10]

In her renowned introduction to *The Second Sex*, de Beauvoir points out the fundamental asymmetry of the terms "masculine" and "feminine." Masculinity is considered to be the "absolute human type," the norm or standard of humanity. A man does not typically preface his opinions with the statement "I am a man," whereas a woman's views are often held to be grounded in her femininity rather than in any objective perception of things. A man "thinks of his body as a direct and normal connection with the world, which he believes he apprehends objectively, whereas he regards the body of woman as a hindrance, a prison . . . Woman has ovaries, a uterus; these peculiarities imprison her in her subjectivity, circumscribe her within the limits of her own nature" (*SS*, xv). De Beauvoir quotes Aristotle as saying that the "female is a female by virtue of a certain *lack* of qualities," and St. Thomas as stating that the female nature is "afflicted with a natural defectiveness" (*SS*, xvi). Summarizing these long traditions of thought, de Beauvoir states: "Thus humanity is male and man defines woman not in herself but as relative to him; she is not regarded as an autonomous being . . . she is the incidental, the inessential as opposed to the essential. He is the Subject, he is the Absolute – she is the Other" (*SS*, xvi). De Beauvoir's Hegelian terminology highlights the fact that man's relegation of woman to the status of "other" violates the principle of mutual recognition, thereby threatening the very status that man has for so long jealously accorded to himself, to his own subjectivity. And yet, as de Beauvoir points out (drawing on both Hegel and Lévi-Strauss), "otherness" is a "fundamental category of human thought," as primordial as consciousness itself. Consciousness always entails positing a duality of Self and Other: indeed, no group "ever sets itself up as the One without at once setting up the Other over against itself" (*SS*, xvi–xvii). Our very conception of our identity entails consciousness of what we are not, of what stands beyond us and perhaps opposed to us.

The problem with demoting another consciousness or group to the status of "other" is that this other consciousness or ego "sets up a reciprocal claim": from *its* perspective, we are the stranger, the other. Interaction with other individuals, peoples, nations, and classes forces us to acknowledge the relativity of the notion of otherness. But this relativity and reciprocity, in the case of women, has not been recognized (*SS*, xvii). Woman's otherness seems to be absolute because, unlike the subordination of other oppressed groups such as Jews and black Americans, her subordination was not the result of a historical event or social change but is partly rooted in her anatomy and physiology. Also in contrast with these other groups, women have never formed a minority and they have never achieved cohesion as a group, since they have always lived dispersed among males: if they belong to the middle class, they identify with the males of that class rather than with working-class women; white women feel allegiance to white men rather than to black women (*SS*, xviii–xix). The "division of the sexes," de Beauvoir points out, "is a biological fact, not an event in human history . . . she is the Other in a totality of which the two components are necessary to one another." Indeed, woman has no autonomous history (*SS*, xix). Another contributing factor to women's subordination is her own reluctance to forego the traditional advantages conferred on them by their protective male superiors: if man supports woman financially and assumes responsibility for defining her existence and purpose, then she can evade both economic risk and the metaphysical "risk" of a freedom in which she must work out her own purposes (*SS*, xxi).

Men, of course, have had their own reasons for perpetuating such a duality of Self and Other: "Legislators, priests, philosophers, writers, and scientists have striven to show that the subordinate position of woman is willed in heaven and advantageous on earth" (*SS*, xxii). A long line of thinkers, stretching from Plato and Aristotle through Augustine and Aquinas into modern bourgeois philosophers, has insisted on stabilizing woman as an object, on dooming her to immanence, to a life of subjection to given conditions, on barring her from property rights, education, and the professions (*SS*, xviii). As well as procuring the obvious economic and political benefits of such subordination, men have reaped enormous psychological reassurance: their hostility toward women conceals a fundamental desire for self-justification, as well as a fundamental insecurity (*SS*, xxii). While de Beauvoir acknowledges that by the eighteenth century certain male thinkers such as Diderot and John Stuart Mill began to champion the cause of women, she also notes that, in contradiction of its ostensible disposition toward democracy, the bourgeois class "clung to the old morality that found the guarantee of private property in the solidity of the family." Woman's liberation was thwarted all the more harshly as her entry into the industrial workforce furnished an economic basis for her claims to equality (*SS*, xxii–xxiii).

From her own perspective of "existentialist ethics," as informed by Heidegger, Sartre, and Merleau-Ponty, de Beauvoir rejects all attempts to stabilize the condition of women under the pretext that happiness consists in stagnation and stasis. Every human subject, she insists, must engage in exploits or projects that serve as a mode of transcendence, as a means of rising above and controlling the conditions into which one is born (*SS*, xxvii). In the first part of her book, de Beauvoir examines the views of women advanced by biology, psychology, and historical materialism, in an endeavor to show how the concept of the feminine has been fashioned and to consider why woman has been defined as the other. Regarding the data afforded by biology, she acknowledges that a physiological burden is imposed on woman by her reproductive function. She points out, however – anticipating the manifold importance subsequently placed on the concept of the "body" by feminists – that the body is not a *thing* but a *situation* (*SS*, 30–31). Human beings achieve self-definition only as part of a larger, social framework, and the so-called facts of biology must be viewed in the light of economic, social, and moral circumstances: the benefits or disadvantages attaching to these facts are dependent upon the arbitration of social norms. For example, if violence is morally or legally forbidden, man's superior physical strength is not an intrinsic asset (*SS*, 32–33).

In her account of psychoanalytic views of woman, de Beauvoir objects that Freud, Adler, and other psychoanalysts "allot the same destiny to woman," namely, an internal conflict between her "viriloid" and "feminine" tendencies, arising from her inferiority complex. De Beauvoir's critique of psychoanalysis spans a number of points. Firstly, male sexual and emotional development is taken as the norm, and Freud assumes that the woman feels herself to be a "mutilated man," suffering from penis envy; Adler sees her envy as based on her "total situation" of disadvantage (*SS*, 36–39). This asymmetry is expressed in the significance attached to the phallus, which is the "incarnation of transcendence" for the male, on account of its being at the same time a part of the male *and* a foreign object, at once self and other (*SS*, 43). Hence the phallus comes to symbolize a dominance that is exercised in all domains, not just that of sexuality. In viewing the phallus as a symbol of male transcendence of his environment, de Beauvoir here anticipates much that has been written about phallocentrism by Lacan and other psychoanalysts.

A further problem with psychoanalysis, in de Beauvoir's eyes, is its exclusive focus on sexuality, taken as an irreducible and primordial datum. But from an existential perspective, there is a more original and more fundamental "quest of being," of which sexuality is only one aspect: man interacts not only with other bodies but also with the entire world of nature, finding important modes of being in work, war, play, and art. These modes of existing cannot be reduced to sexuality, and indeed, the significance of sexuality must be brought into relation with these other human endeavors (*SS*, 41, 45). A related problem is that psychoanalysis assumes that "the drama of the individual unfolds within him," overlooking the fact that the truths of psychoanalysis must be situated in a social and historical context (*SS*, 44). Finally, and perhaps most importantly, psychoanalysis reduces human behavior to determinism, to determined patterns and fixed causal connections, thereby rejecting the concept of choice (*SS*, 42). Psychoanalysis ignores the possibility that human behavior might be "motivated by purposes freely envisaged." De Beauvoir defines the situation of woman in contradistinction from the views of psychoanalysis: "I shall place woman in a world of values and give her behavior a dimension of liberty. I believe that she has the power to choose between the assertion of her transcendence and her alienation as object; she is not the plaything of contradictory drives" (*SS*, 45–46).

De Beauvoir next considers the perspective of historical materialism, as expressed by Friedrich Engels in his book *The Origin of the Family, Private Property and the State*.

685

She acknowledges that Engels offers some important truths: humanity is not an animal species but a historical reality; and woman's self-awareness far exceeds her sexuality, reflecting the economic organization of society (*SS*, 47). Engels' central argument was that the history of woman depended essentially on the history of technological progress: before the discovery of bronze and iron, women played a significant role in economic life, complementing the hunting and fishing of men with their own domestic productive labor, making pottery, weaving, and gardening. With the invention of new tools, however, the scope of agriculture was enlarged and intensive labor was called for; as a result, women's domestic work sank into relative insignificance. This was the point at which private property appeared, in turn giving rise to the patriarchal family. Engels argued that, just as women's economic and social oppression was brought about by technology, so her emancipation would arise in virtue of technological progress, when she could "take part on a large social scale in production" (*SS*, 49).

While de Beauvoir sees this socialist perspective as an advance over the previously considered viewpoints, she regards it as deficient. To begin with, Engels nowhere explains how the "turning point of history," the passage from communal to private ownership, could have come about. Nor does he show how the oppression of women is a necessary outcome of private property (*SS*, 50–51). Again, mere technological changes alone cannot explain the economic fortunes of women: it was not simply the discovery of bronze that transformed gender roles but rather the innate "imperialism of the human consciousness," the very nature of consciousness which, forever seeking to exercise its sovereignty, includes the original category of the other and a desire to dominate this other (*SS*, 52). Finally, Engels reduces the antagonism of the sexes to class conflict; but the analogy, thinks de Beauvoir, is unjustified since there is no biological basis for the separation of classes (*SS*, 52). While de Beauvoir accepts that the contributions of biology, psychoanalysis, and historical materialism are valuable, they must be situated within a broader context of social life and values that only an existentialist outlook can furnish. The "body, the sexual life, and the resources of technology exist concretely for man" only within the "total perspective" of his existence (*SS*, 55).

De Beauvoir proceeds to offer her own existentialist overview of women's history, an account that challenges certain male-generated myths about women. From earliest nomadic times, women have suffered the "bondage of reproduction," a function which must be viewed as natural and not as comprising a deliberate project through which she might affirm her existence (*SS*, 57). Man, on the other hand, was able to transcend his animal nature through invention, risk-taking, and refashioning the earth. While woman's activity was "immanent," remaining closely bound to her body, man's activity created values, and "prevailed over the confused forces of life," subduing both nature and woman (*SS*, 59–60). In the earliest agricultural communities, woman's status was enlarged: it was recognized that the life of the clan was propagated through her, and maternity was held to be a "sacred function." The children often belonged to the mother's clan and communal property was handed down through women. This matrilineal regime was characterized by an assimilation of woman to the earth: to man, all nature seemed "like a mother." Man felt himself to be at the mercy of natural forces, and in "woman was summed up the whole of alien Nature." Woman's otherness, her alien power, was projected into powerful female deities associated with life and fertility, as well as death: she was the Great Goddess, the Great Mother, the queen of heaven, the empress of hell, variously called Ishtar in Babylonia, Astarte among the Semitic peoples, Gaea, Rhea, or Cybele by the Greeks, and Isis in Egypt. These goddesses were elevated above male divinities (*SS*, 61–64).

And yet de Beauvoir disputes the view of Engels and others that there was ever a matriarchy in history, a reign of women. Such a golden age of woman, she insists, is a myth. Even in the era just described, woman's power was viewed as alien, as other, as always beyond the human realm. The female goddesses were projections of the male mind, and actual political power "has always been in the hands of men" (*SS*, 65). Indeed, as agriculture was refined and expanded through technological invention based on the discovery of bronze and iron, man was able to master the soil: instead of passively relying on the produce of mother earth, he could now apply rational techniques to agriculture. Hence man's mastery of the soil was concomitant with his mastery of himself: the religion of woman, based on magic and mystery, was overthrown by the male principle of rationality, intellect, and self-creation (*SS*, 69–71). The Great Mother was dethroned in favor of Ra, Zeus, and Jupiter; woman lost the economic role she had enjoyed in the tribe and patrilineal descent replaced inheritance through the mother. Hence, de Beauvoir agrees with Engels that woman was dethroned by the advent of private property; she herself was property, first of her father and then of her husband (*SS*, 72–75). Woman came to embody otherness: "she is passivity confronting activity, diversity that destroys unity, matter as opposed to form, disorder against order." Hence woman becomes chaos, darkness, and evil (*SS*, 74).

Tracing the history of women through patriarchal times and classical antiquity, de Beauvoir observes woman's subservience among the Hebrews: Ecclesiastes speaks of her as "more bitter than death" (*SS*, 78). Throughout the Oriental world, women had little prestige and few rights, notable exceptions being Babylon, where the laws of Hammurabi gave her rights to part of the paternal estate, and Egypt, where goddess mothers retained their prestige and women had similar rights to men (*SS*, 78–79). In classical Greece, woman was reduced to a state of semi-slavery, being "firmly shut away in the gynecaeum," the women's apartments in a house, and expected to be a prudent and watchful mistress of the home (*SS*, 84). In Rome, after the death of Tarquin, patriarchal authority was established, and agricultural property in the form of the private estate – and, therefore, the family – became the basis of society. Woman "lived a life of legal incapacity and servitude," being excluded from public affairs and treated as a minor in civil life. The father's authority was unlimited and he was "absolute ruler of wife and children." Though women's situation improved during the later years of the empire, their relative emancipation (in such matters as inheritance and divorce) did not bring them any increase in political power. De Beauvoir calls this a "negative" emancipation (*SS*, 84–88).

During the Middle Ages, Christian ideology "contributed no little to the oppression of woman" (*SS*, 89). De Beauvoir remarks that the anti-feminist Hebrew tradition was affirmed through St. Paul, who based the wife's subordination to husband on both Old and New Testaments. Christianity's holding of the body in low esteem lowered the rank of woman further, imposing on her the status of a temptress. The Church Fathers were almost unanimous in viewing woman as an agent of the devil's temptation. De Beauvoir's quotations are worth reproducing: "Woman, you are the devil's doorway," scolded Tertullian. St. Ambrose pronounced that "it is just and right that woman accept as lord and master him whom she led to sin." And St. John Chrysostom averred that "Among all savage beasts none is found so harmful as woman." St. Jerome saw marriage as a "fruitless tree," and from the time of Gregory VI celibacy was imposed on the priesthood, thereby highlighting further the dangerous nature of woman. St. Thomas declared that woman was a kind of incomplete man and that man "is above woman, as Christ is above man" (SS, 90). Woman was treated as legally incompetent and powerless by canon law; the masculine occupations were closed to her and she was forbidden to make depositions in court. The state laws throughout the Holy Roman Empire also held woman subservient to her functions of wife and mother. These laws came into contact with Germanic traditions, in which woman was in a state of absolute dependence on father and husband (SS, 91). Like Engels, De Beauvoir sees courtly love as a "compensation for the barbarism of the official mores": the wife sought an extramarital lover to compensate for the tyranny and guardianship of her feudal husband (SS, 93).

All the European legal codes were based on canon law, Roman law, and Germanic law, all of which were unfavorable to women. In fact, women's legal status remained almost unchanged from the beginning of the fifteenth century until the nineteenth (SS, 97). The essential institutions that demanded such subordination were private property and the family (SS, 94). As the bourgeois class rose to power, it continued the basic patterns of subordination, allowing rights to widows and unmarried girls but not to married women. The rigorous monogamy required of the bourgeois family, and woman's continued enslavement to the family, gave rise to prostitution throughout Europe (SS, 94–95). While the rising middle class imposed a strict morality on wives, women of leisure since the sixteenth century had been enjoying greater freedom and license. During the Renaissance, a few women were powerful sovereigns, artists, and writers. Their role in culture expanded in the seventeenth century and they played an important part in the salons. Women's advocates since the Renaissance included Erasmus, Marguerite de Navarre, Molière, and Poulain de la Barre, whose De l'égalité des deux sexes was published in 1673. In the eighteenth century, women's champions included Voltaire, Diderot, Montesquieu, Helvetius, Mercier, and Condorcet (SS, 98–100).

Notwithstanding these endeavors of prominent individuals, the French Revolution did very little to change the lot of women; there was a certain amount of feminist agitation which proposed, for example, a "Declaration of the Rights of Woman" in 1789, to match the "Declaration of the Rights of Man" actually adopted by the French National Assembly. The Revolution was essentially a middle-class revolution, respectful of middle-class values and institutions, and was accomplished almost exclusively by men (SS, 100). Though some rights were granted to women, the post-revolutionary Napoleonic Code greatly retarded women's emancipation, perpetuating their dependency in marriage; and various middle-class spokesmen, including Auguste Comte and Balzac, reaffirmed the vision of the anti-feminist bourgeoisie, which wished to exclude women from labor and public life (SS, 100–102).

Paradoxically, however, some of the historical forces through which the bourgeoisie drove to power themselves furthered the emancipation of women. The liberal-democratic ideas of the Enlightenment and the Revolution initiated at least a theoretical basis for women's claims; even more importantly, the technological and industrial revolutions destroyed landed property and concretely furthered the emancipation of woman. She regained an economic importance through her productive role in the factory: it is this that de Beauvoir calls "the grand revolution of the nineteenth century, which transformed the lot of woman and opened for her a new era" (SS, 104). A number of regulations over the late nineteenth and early twentieth centuries improved women's working conditions throughout Europe. Women achieved a degree of political organization in the nineteenth century; the Socialist Congress of 1879 proclaimed the equality of the sexes; and the first feminist congress – which gave its name to the movement – was held in 1892. As a result of various suffragette movements, women received the vote in England and Germany in 1918, and in America in 1920 (SS, 113–116).

Two essential factors paved the way for women's prospective equality: one was her ability (conferred by technology, which abrogated any innate male advantages of strength) to share in productive labor; and the second was her recently acquired freedom from the slavery of reproduction through contraception, adopted by many of the middle and then the working classes from the eighteenth century onward (SS, 109). Woman could now make her reproductive function, her pregnancies and child-rearing duties, a rationally integral part of her life, instead of being enslaved by her generative function (SS, 108, 111). Woman was now almost in a position to assume a role of economic independence (SS, 112). And yet, a major factor retarding her freedom was the continued existence of the family, sanctioned by the various ideologies – political and religious – which aimed to detain her in her traditional roles. De Beauvoir's formulation of the central problem of woman is as pertinent today as in her own era: woman's obstinate dilemma is the reconciliation of her productive and reproductive roles. De Beauvoir regards the present as a period of transition, in which woman's desire for transcendence is still constrained by her perpetuated subjugation and the defining of her choices by men (SS, 123–124, 128).

Not least among the factors inhibiting woman's social and economic freedom is the perpetuation of certain obstinate myths of woman, in the realms of art and literature as well as in daily life. De Beauvoir examines the literary presentation of the feminine by writers such as Montherlant, D. H. Lawrence, Claudel, Breton, and Stendhal, authors whose attitudes toward women she takes to be "typical" (SS, 188). Montherlant, like Aristotle and St. Thomas, believes in "that vague and basic essence, femininity," defining it negatively (SS, 188). These writers, says de Beauvoir, reflect the "great collective myths" of woman: woman as *flesh*, as first womb then lover to the male; woman as the incarnation of *nature* and the door to the supernatural; woman as poetry, as the mediatrix between this world and the beyond. She appears as the "*privileged Other*, through whom the subject fulfills himself: one of the measures of man, his counterbalance, his salvation, his adventure, his happiness" (SS, 233). But these myths are orchestrated very differently by each author: the Other is defined according to the terms in which the One sets himself up. And for each of them the ideal woman is "she who incarnates most exactly the *Other* capable of revealing him to himself."

De Beauvoir notes that all of these writers – notwithstanding the affection and sympathy for women displayed by some of them – require woman to "forget self and to love." Montherlant seeks "pure animality" in her; Lawrence sees her as summing up the feminine sex in general; Claudel, as a soul-sister, Breton, as a woman-child, and Stendhal, as an "equal." With varying degrees of insistence, they express a need for feminine devotion and altruism (*SS*, 236). De Beauvoir's point is that, no matter how exalted or debased woman is in the works of these writers, she fulfills the role of otherness, being always an integral aspect of man's self-definition, of the fulfillment of his being, rather than enjoying true autonomy. Another way of saying this is that her "existence" is always attenuated, always adjectival, ever mired in the mode of objectivity, never blossoming into true subjectivity, true humanity. De Beauvoir notes, however, that Stendhal views woman not merely as object but as a subject in her own right. As de Beauvoir puts it: he rejects "the mystifications of the serious, as he rejects the false poetry of the myths. Human reality suffices him. Woman according to him is simply a human being" (*SS*, 233).

In an important chapter entitled "Myth and Reality," de Beauvoir observes that the myth of woman exerts an important influence not only in the world of literature but equally in everyday life. She points out that the myth of woman is a static myth: it "projects into the realm of Platonic ideas a reality that is directly experienced." In other words, the myth *substitutes* for actual experience a transcendent idea which is timeless and unchangeable; because this idea is beyond or above the realm of actual experience, it is endowed with absolute truth. Hence mythical thought opposes this fixed, universal, and unitary idea of the "Eternal Feminine" to the "dispersed, contingent, and multiple existences of actual women." If we say, for example, that "woman is flesh" or that she is "Night" or "Death" or "Nature," we are effectively abandoning terrestrial and empirical truth and soaring "into an empty sky" (*SS*, 239). And the myth is unassailable: if the behavior of a real woman contradicts the mythical idea, she is told that she is not feminine; the "contrary facts of experience are impotent against the myth" (*SS*, 237). In short, what the mythical treatment of woman does is to pose woman as "the absolute Other, without reciprocity, denying against all experience that she is a subject, a fellow human being" (*SS*, 238).

Of all these myths, the one most deeply "anchored in masculine hearts" is that of the feminine "mystery." This myth allows man the luxury of "legitimately" not understanding woman, and, above all, it enables man to remain alone by living in the company of an enigma: such an experience is more attractive for many than "an authentic relation with a human being" (*SS*, 240). De Beauvoir argues that such feminine mystery is an illusion: in truth, there is mystery on both sides, male and female. But the male perspective is elevated into an absolute and normal perspective, and from that vantage point, woman appears essentially mysterious. What underlies the feminine mystery is an "economic substructure" of subordination: mystery always belongs to the vassal, the colonized, the slave (*SS*, 242–243).

In the conclusion to her book, de Beauvoir argues that the age-old conflict between the sexes no longer takes the form of woman attempting to hold back man in her own prison of immanence, but rather in her own effort to emerge into the light of transcendence. Woman's situation will be transformed primarily by a change in her economic condition; but this change must also generate moral, social, cultural, and psychological transformations. If girls were brought up to expect the same free and assured future as boys, even the meanings of the Oedipus and castration complexes would be modified, and the "child would perceive around her an androgynous world and not a masculine world" (*SS*, 683). Moreover, if she were brought up to *understand*, rather than inhibit, her own sexuality, eroticism and love would take on the nature of free transcendence rather than resignation: the notions of dominance and submission, victory and defeat, in sexual relations might give way before the idea of exchange (*SS*, 685). De Beauvoir is confident that women will arrive at "complete economic and social equality, which will bring about an inner metamorphosis" (*SS*, 686). And both man and woman will exist *both* for self and for the other: "mutually recognizing each other as subject, each will yet remain for the other an *other*." In this recognition, in this reciprocity, will "the slavery of half of humanity" be abolished (*SS*, 688).

Elaine Showalter (b. 1941)

An influential American feminist critic has been Elaine Showalter, who developed "gynocriticism," a criticism concerned with the specificity of women's experience and women's writing. Showalter's most influential book has been *A Literature of their Own* (1977), whose title reflects Woolf's *A Room of One's Own*. Indeed, Showalter here takes up the issue initially posed by Woolf, that of a female literary tradition. Her book's title, however, derives not from Woolf but from the philosopher John Stuart Mill, one of the few males to have championed the rights of women. In his polemical text *The Subjection of Women* (1869), Mill had observed how difficult it would be for women to free themselves from the constraints and influences of the male literary tradition; had they been able to live apart from men, they "would have a literature of their own."[11] Ironically, then, Showalter's book sets out to contradict Mill's well-intended statement, to show that, if we re-read literary history carefully, we can in fact discern a female literary heritage.

The most fundamental undertaking and achievement of Showalter's book is her formulation of the female literary tradition as an evolution through three phases. She observes that literary subcultures (such as black, Jewish, Anglo-Indian) tend to pass through three stages. First, there is a phase of *imitation* of the modes of the dominant tradition; the artistic standards of that tradition, as well as the social roles it implies, are internalized. The second is a stage of *protest* against these standards and values, and a call for autonomy. The final stage is one of *self-discovery*, a "turning inward freed from some of the dependency of opposition, a search for identity" (*LTO*, 13). Viewing the women's literary tradition in terms of these phases, Showalter suggests that the first phase might be called the *feminine* phase, spanning the period from the appearance of the male pseudonym in the 1840s to the death of George Eliot in 1880. The *feminist* period extends from 1880 until the year 1920 when women won the vote. And the third, or *female*, phase runs from 1920 until around 1960, at which point women's writing enters "a new stage of self-awareness" (*LTO*, 13).

While Showalter acknowledges that the female subculture was "uniquely divided against itself by ties to the dominant culture," she points out that women writers "were united by their roles as daughters, wives, and mothers; by the internalized doctrines of evangelicalism, with its suspicion of the imagination and its emphasis on duty; and by legal and economic constraints on their mobility." And from the beginning, she says, the woman novelist shared a "covert solidarity" with other women writers and with her female audience, which would "read the messages between her lines" (*LTO*, 14–15).

Moreover, from about 1750, women made steady inroads into the literary profession. Notwithstanding these rudiments of solidarity, women writers exhibit almost no sense of "communality and self-awareness" before the 1840s, the decade in which the novel, according to some critics, became the dominant form. In this first phase of *feminine* writing, women did not see their writing as an expression of their female experience. That their vocation to write stood in conflict with their status as women was indicated by the use of the male pseudonym.

Yet the repressive circumstances imposed on it forced the feminine novel to find "innovative and covert ways to dramatize the inner life, and led to a fiction that was intense, compact, symbolic, and profound." We are presented with figures such as the mad wife locked in the attic, the crippled artist, and the murderous wife. And many female novels offer fantasies of money and power, often projecting the ideology of success, and the elements of success in the author's own experience, onto male characters. Another set of strategies was embodied in protest fiction, which championed the rights not only of women but also of workers, child laborers, and prostitutes. Despite its restrictions, the woman's novel from Jane Austen to George Eliot had moved "in the direction of an all-inclusive female realism, a broad, socially informed exploration of the daily lives and values of women within the family and the community" (*LTO*, 29).

Indeed, with the death of George Eliot, the woman's novel moved into a "feminist" phase that confronted male society and sexual stereotypes. The feminists challenged the restrictions of women's language, denounced the ethic of self-sacrifice, and used their fictional dramatization of oppression to urge changes in the social and political system. While the writers of the feminist period were not important as artists, they embodied a crucial stage, "a declaration of independence," in the female tradition. They explored and defined womanhood, they rejected the ideal of self-sacrifice and stood up to the male establishment in an outspoken manner. They insisted on the right to use male sexual vocabulary, and most importantly, challenged the monopoly of the male press; feminist journals challenged the judgments of men of letters and some, like Virginia Woolf, controlled their own presses (*LTO*, 31). Feminists such as Mona Caird, Elizabeth Robins, and Olive Schreiner were producing theories of women's relationship to labor, to the class structure, and to the family. The vote was won in 1918. Showalter points out that the death of many male writers during World War I "left English women writers with a poignant sense of carrying on a national literary tradition" (*LTO*, 32).

The last generation of women Victorian writers moved beyond feminism to a "female" phase "of courageous self-exploration, but it carried with it the double legacy of feminine self-hatred and feminist withdrawal" (*LTO*, 33). The withdrawal by feminist writers from male society and culture had been symbolized by the "enclosed and secret room," which was identified with the womb and female conflict. As Showalter puts it, "the secret room, the attic hideaway, the suffragette cell came to stand for a separate world, a flight from men and from adult sexuality" (*LTO*, 33). As for the "feminine self-hatred," this was projected into narrative form. The fiction of writers such as Virginia Woolf and Katherine Mansfield "created a deliberate female aesthetic, which transformed the feminine code of self-sacrifice into an annihilation of the narrative self, and applied the cultural analysis of the feminists to words, sentences, and structures of language in the novel. Their version of modernism was a determined response to the material culture of male Edwardian novelists like Arnold Bennett and H. G. Wells, but, like D. H. Lawrence, the female aestheticists saw the world as mystically and totally polarized by sex" (*LTO*, 33). This female aesthetic, however, paradoxically repressed sexuality and treatment of the female body to the periphery of its concerns, taking flight in androgyny, the sexual ethic of the Bloomsbury group. A favorite image, as in the title of Woolf's book, was that of "a room of one's own," implying both artistic autonomy and, according to Showalter, "disengagement from social and sexual involvement" (*LTO*, 34). Showalter insists that this aesthetic was a "form of self-annihilation," marked by retreat: "retreat from the ego, retreat from the physical experience of women, retreat from the material world, retreat into separate rooms and separate cities" (*LTO*, 240). The stream of consciousness technique, she claims, was in part an attempt to transcend the dilemma of expressing female transcendence of the given world in language and in categories of thought that had been developed by men (*LTO*, 260).

Later women writers reacted against female aestheticism and the strategy of disengagement, returning to more realistic modes of expression untouched by modernism. But it was not until the 1960s that the female novel entered a "new and dynamic" phase, fueled by the international women's movement. Writers such as Iris Murdoch, Muriel Spark, Doris Lessing, and Margaret Drabble undertook an authentic expression of female experience, using a new range of language, accepting anger and sexuality as sources of creative power, while reasserting their continuity with women of the past (*LTO*, 302). There is "a new frankness about the body" (*LTO*, 299). Showalter's book examines the developments outlined above in detail, concluding with a discussion of the dilemmas faced by contemporary women novelists, such as being torn between commitment to feminist revolution and individual exploration, expression of female experience and sexuality and addressing the dominant culture's definition of what constitute the most important issues (*LTO*, 318).

Michèle Barrett: The Marxist/Feminist Encounter

In her seminal text *Women's Oppression Today* (1980), Michèle Barrett outlines some of the central problems facing any attempt to forge a coalition of Marxist and feminist perspectives. How can a Marxist analysis, conceived on the basis of "a primary contradiction between labour and capital," be reconciled with a feminist approach, which must begin with the relations of gender?[12] In general terms, suggests Barrett, the object of Marxist feminism must be to "identify the operation of gender relations" as they relate to the "processes of production and reproduction understood by historical materialism." Marxist feminism must "explore the relations between the organization of sexuality, domestic production . . . and historical changes in the mode of production and systems of appropriation and exploitation." Such an approach will stress the "relations between capitalism and the oppression of women" (*WT*, 9).

Barrett focuses on three concepts that have been central to the Marxist feminist dialogue: patriarchy, reproduction, and ideology. She begins by noting the enormous problems inhering in the concept of patriarchy: radical feminists such as Kate Millett

693

have used this concept as "an over-arching category of male dominance." Millett sees patriarchy as a system of domination that is analytically independent of the capitalist or any other mode of production; its apparent mediation by class is merely tangential. Shulamith Firestone goes even further and aims to ground the analysis of class in the "biological division of the sexes," her aim being "to substitute sex for class as the prime motor in a materialist account of history" (*WT*, 11). Barrett objects to these uses of patriarchy as a "universal and trans-historical category of male dominance," grounded in biological determinants (*WT*, 12). Such uses are reactionary (treating social arrangements as somehow naturally given) and regressive since they overlook "one of the early triumphs" of feminist analysis, namely, a "distinction between sex as a biological category and gender as a social one" (*WT*, 13).

Other feminists such as Christine Delphy, however, have formulated a materialist analysis of patriarchy, stressing social rather than biological relations. Delphy argues that the material basis of women's oppression "lies not in capitalist but in patriarchal relations of production" (*WT*, 14). But most recent theorists, says Barrett, attempt to represent contemporary capitalism as patriarchy. Such an endeavor not only poses patriarchy as a universal and transhistorical mode, but also reveals a confusion between two meanings of patriarchy, between "patriarchy as the rule of the father and patriarchy as the domination of women by men" (*WT*, 17). This is the case, according to Barrett, with Annette Kuhn's theory that the crucial site of women's oppression is the family, which has a relative autonomy from capitalist relations. Kuhn argues that patriarchy unites psychic and property relations (*WT*, 18–19).

Another concept used by recent theorists to relate women's oppression to the organization of production in society is "reproduction." Interest in this concept derives from Engels' formulation that the "determining factor in history is . . . the production and reproduction of immediate life." Engels is referring here both to "the production of the means of subsistence" and "the production of human beings themselves, the propagation of the species" (*WT*, 20). Also important is Louis Althusser's treatment of social production in his essay "Ideology and Ideological State Apparatuses." Again, part of the problem with this concept is its range of definition: women's role in biological reproduction can have only a highly refracted relationship with their role in economic and social production. In fact, the "fundamental problem" faced by Marxist feminism is "to combine an analysis of social reproduction with an analysis of patriarchal human reproduction" (*WT*, 29).

The third important but problematic notion in Marxist feminism is that of ideology. As Barrett points out, feminists have insisted that Marxism take account of the sexual division of labor and the familial ideology that sustain women's oppression; this insistence has coincided with a "revolution" in the Marxist theory of ideology. This shift in Marxist theory was largely occasioned by Louis Althusser's rejection of ideology "as a distortion or manipulation of reality by the ruling class," as well as of the vulgar Marxist view that "ideology is simply a mechanical reflection (in ideas) of a determining economic base." While Althusser accepts the basic Marxist premise that the economic substructure determines the ideological superstructure "in the last instance," he nonetheless sees ideology as having a "relative autonomy," and stresses its experiential character as "the imaginary relationship of individuals to their real conditions of existence" (*WT*, 29–30).

694

Althusser's attempt to rethink the Marxist notion of ideology is part of a widespread challenge to the economism – the insistence on the determining power of the economic base – that has prevailed within Marxism. Feminists have participated in this challenge, prioritizing ideology such that questions of gender division can be accommodated. Feminists have emphasized the ideological construction of gendered subjects and familial relations, seeking to rethink psychoanalytic theory from a Marxist feminist perspective (*WT*, 31). In short, some feminists, such as Rosalind Coward, have rejected traditional Marxism's implicit location of women's oppression as merely an ideological effect, secondary to the primary economic contradiction of labor and capital. Coward sees the primacy of the economic level over the ideological as no longer necessary, and based on an outdated model of scientific realism (*WT*, 33–34). Barrett points out that this rejection of the "real" represents a radical break not only with the Marxism of Althusser but also with Marxism per se since it abandons any materialist analysis of history (*WT*, 36). While such feminists have rightly affirmed the importance of gender in the construction of individual subjects, they are misguided in rejecting "all determinate relations," a position that is not at all Marxist (*WT*, 38).

Barrett's own general position is that the oppression of women in capitalist society must be situated within the oppression of women throughout the world, and that male domination stretches far beyond this context, hence socialist revolution will not of itself achieve women's liberation. Barrett stresses also the intimate connections between economic oppression and the "role of familial and domestic ideology," as well as the changing form of the family organization during and since the transition from feudalism to capitalism. The most significant elements, then, of the oppression of women under capitalism are "the economic organization of households and its accompanying familial ideology, the division of labor and relations of production, the educational system and the operations of the state," as well as the processes of creation and recreation of gendered subjects (*WT*, 40–41).

Indeed, this last element is taken up in an important chapter called "Ideology and the Cultural Production of Gender," where Barrett addresses the function of literature and of culture generally in the social construction of gender and female subjectivity. She begins by noting that recent feminist theorists have challenged the classical Marxist theory of representation, which views ideology and discourse in general as a reflection of given historical conditions: for example, a work of literature in the twentieth century might be seen as an ideological reflection or representation of economic conditions in late capitalism. Such a view is based on a classical Marxist model of economic base and ideological superstructure, the latter somehow "reflecting" the former. As Barrett points out, the attempt by recent feminists to undermine this model is rooted in a more general challenge to classical models of representation or discourse generally, models which held that language or discourse (or representation) somehow corresponds with a reality which is already there. Much modern theory in several fields has of course impugned this assumption, saying that there is no reality prior to language and discourse, and that language is in fact instrumental in creating what we call reality. Such feminists, says Barrett, deny, for example, that there is any such phenomenon as "sexual difference" that precedes discourse: the difference itself, they claim, is *created* by discourse; in other words, the difference is located in the realm of ideology, the realm of conflicting discourses, rather than as a reflection of economic conditions. Such feminists reject the distinction between ideology and material conditions; they see ideology itself as material and as largely autonomous in respect of those material conditions (*WT*, 89–90). A literary text, for example, would not necessarily represent social and economic relations.

In Marxist fashion, Barrett rejects these views: she rejects the claim that ideology itself is either material or autonomous. She also rejects the view that reality is merely constructed by language or discourse. To insist on a "non-correspondence" of language and reality, she affirms, is to slide into the very dogmatism one is purporting to condemn; and language or representation is linked to actual and specific historical conditions that cannot be reduced to discourse (*WT*, 91–94). Nor can the connection between women's oppression and the conditions of economic production be reduced to discourse (*WT*, 97). Recent feminists see discourse itself as the site of political struggle; but such struggle, says Barrett, is merely ideological, and will not of itself produce any type of social revolution (*WT*, 95). Barrett's own view is that we need not accept a mechanical model of reflection or representation; but this does not mean that we abandon the model altogether; we can specify the limits to the autonomous operation of ideology. She also insists that there is an integral connection between ideology and the relations of production, a connection all the more important in the case of gender: the ideology of gender plays an important role in the capitalist division of labor as well as in the reproduction of labor power (*WT*, 98). The term "relations of production," she insists, comprehends differences not only of class but also of race and forms of labor. We can make a useful distinction, she says, between these *relations* of production, in which ideology plays a crucial role, and the means and forces of production which lie beyond (and beneath) the sphere of ideology (*WT*, 99).

Hence, Barrett accepts the claim of Marxists such as Terry Eagleton that literature might be a "paradigm case" for the examination of ideology; but she warns that such an analysis will give us insight into the production of meaning and discourse, not into the social formation itself (*WT*, 97). She suggests that if we are to analyze the production of gender ideology, for example, in literature, we cannot merely focus on literary texts; as Eagleton points out, these texts have internalized their material conditions of production and express these albeit in highly refracted ways (*WT*, 100–101). Our analysis must take account of the material conditions in which men and women produce literary works; it must be informed by a theory of reading which acknowledges that aesthetic judgment is grounded in social contexts, that meaning is not intrinsic to any text but is a social construction, and the representation of women in literature is often a complex and oblique process (*WT*, 104–107). She stresses that literature has a fictional status which makes it facile, for example, to condemn male authors (as Kate Millett does) for presenting images of women in negative terms. Such images may be motivated by ambivalence and are necessarily constrained and dictated by historical conditions (*WT*, 107). In short, Barrett argues that while cultural practice is an essential site of revolutionary struggle, and that literature can play an important role in the transformation of subjectivity, culture alone cannot liberate women: a more fundamental revolution in means and forces of production is required (*WT*, 112–113).

In the conclusion to her book, Barrett revisits the three essential components of Marxist feminist analysis with which she began. She urges that arguments concerning the "reproduction" thesis – that capital supports the reproduction of labor power through domestic labor – should be historicized (*WT*, 249). And, while the concept of patriarchy should not be jettisoned, its use might be restricted to contexts where male domination is "expressed through the power of the father over women" (*WT*, 250). As for ideology, our recognition of its role in gender construction must move to deeper analysis of subjectivity and identity, effectively continuing the work of earlier feminists such as Simone de Beauvoir (*WT*, 251). In general, Barrett stresses that there is no "programmatic answer" to the question of whether women's liberation can be achieved under capitalism. She does affirm, however, that such liberation would require: first, a redivision of labor and the responsibilities of childcare; second, the extrication of women from dependence on a male wage or capital; lastly, the ideology of gender would need to be transformed. None of these changes, she observes, is compatible with capitalism as it exists at present. Hence, although the women's movement needs to be autonomously organized, it can profitably collude with socialism on the basis of over-lapping political objectives. These might include the need to improve women's wages and working conditions, and to abolish the use of female labor as a means of keeping general wages down (*WT*, 257–258). Since women's oppression is "entrenched in the structure of capitalism," the struggle for women's liberation and the struggle for socialism cannot be disengaged (*WT*, 258–259).

Julia Kristeva (b. 1941)

Aptly characterizing herself as a "female intellectual," Julia Kristeva has been a powerful influence on literary theory. She integrates insights from linguistics, psychoanalysis, and philosophy into her theories, the most important of which concern the development of subjectivity in relation to both language and the play of drives and impulses anterior to language. Born in Bulgaria, Kristeva studied in France from 1965; her teachers in Paris included Roland Barthes, Lucien Goldmann, and Claude Lévi-Strauss. In the late 1960s, she was appointed to the editorial board of *Tel Quel*, an outlet for structuralist and poststructuralist perspectives. Her work exhibits the profound impact of Hegel and Freud, as well as the influences of Mikhail Bakhtin, Jacques Lacan, and the psychologist Melanie Klein. Kristeva's first book, *Semeiotike: Recherches pour une Semanalyse* (1969), advances a theory of the sign. Her later publications are psycho-analytic in their approach and emphasis. Her best-known and most influential work is *Revolution in Poetic Language* (1974), some of the central ideas of which will be examined here.

Kristeva starts out by observing that modern linguistic theories treat language as a formal object which is marked by arbitrary relations between signifiers and signifieds, the substitution of the sign for the extra-linguistic (or reality outside of language), the discreteness of its elements, and finitude.[13] However, language considered as such a formal object lacks a *subject* of enunciation; and it merely passes over the question of "externality" or the possible existence of the subject beyond language. Two recent trends have addressed this issue of externality. The first attempts to examine signifying systems in which the arbitrary connection of signifier and signified is seen as "motivated" by unconscious processes: the externality to which linguistic relations are here connected is the psychosomatic realm, the "body divided into erogenous zones." These theories rehabilitate the notion of the pre-Oedipal fragmented body, but fail to explain this body's link to the post-Oedipal subject and his symbolic language (*RPL*, 22). The other trend begins from the subject of enunciation or transcendental ego and, purveying the necessary connections that linguistics bears with semantics and logic, views signification as an ideological and historical process (*RPL*, 23). Kristeva calls the first trend "the semiotic," and the second "the symbolic." These two modes, she says, "are inseparable within the *signifying process* that constitutes language, and the dialectic between them determines the type of discourse (narrative, metalanguage, theory, poetry, etc.) involved." And this necessary dialectic between the two modes of the signifying process, she says, is also "constitutive of the subject," a subject which is thus both semiotic and symbolic (*RPL*, 24).

Kristeva adopts from Plato's *Timaeus* the term *chora*, which refers to the space that is occupied by a thing; it can also refer to place or position or station, and, in Kristeva's extension, receptacle or womb. Adapting this term, she suggests that the *chora* is "a nonexpressive totality" formed by the bodily drives and what Freud calls the primary processes of the unconscious (such as displacement and condensation); it stresses the mobile and provisional nature of the way these drives are articulated, as characterizing the semiotic process (*RPL*, 25). The *chora* has no fixed unity or identity; it precedes "evidence, verisimilitude, spatiality and temporality." Indeed, the *chora* is not yet a signifier: it precedes the linguistic sign, which articulates (as Lacan claims) both the absence of the object itself and the distinction between real and symbolic (*RPL*, 26). This *chora* which regulates the drives is to be distinguished from the realm of the symbolic, which is the realm of spatial intuition and of language. Following some comments of Plato, as well as insights of Freud, Lacan, and Melanie Klein, Kristeva associates the prelinguistic semiotic process with the mother: the mother's body, as the site around which the oral and anal drives are structured, is the "ordering principle" of the semiotic *chora* and is also "what mediates the symbolic law organizing social relations" (*RPL*, 27). Following Freud's observation that the most instinctual drive is the death drive, she suggests that the semiotic *chora* is "no more than the place where the subject is both generated and negated" by a process of "charges and stases." Kristeva assigns the term *negativity* to this dual process of generation and negation (*RPL*, 28). The semiotic is organized not only by the primary processes such as condensation and displacement but also by the connections among bodily zones and between these and what will later be formed as external subjects and objects. Hence the semiotic is "a psychosomatic modality of the signifying process" (*RPL*, 28). The realm of the symbolic is a "social effect" of the natural or sociohistorical constraints (such as biological difference or family structure) which ultimately organize the *chora* (*RPL*, 27, 29). The French poet Mallarmé, according to Kristeva, speaks of the semiotic as a rhythm or space which is feminine, enigmatic and indifferent to language; it underlies what is written and is irreducible to verbal translation; it is, however, constrained by one factor: syntax (*RPL*, 29). Kristeva sees her notion of the semiotic as positing a post-Freudian subject which decenters the transcendental ego of conventional Western thought (*RPL*, 30).

While Kristeva diverges from a Cartesian notion of language and consciousness which sees thought as preconditioned by "natural" facts, she builds on a central insight of Husserlian phenomenology, namely, the positing of "an ego as the single, unique constraint which is constitutive of all linguistic acts as well as all trans-linguistic prac-tice" (*RPL*, 31–32). She distinguishes the semiotic realm from the Husserlian notion of meaning as intentionality, as constituted by a bracketing of the real object so as to highlight the "intentional experience" and "intentional object" (*RPL*, 33). She states that the semiotic is "pre-thetic," i.e., prior to the positing of the subject (understood as possessing thetic or positing or naming or propositional functions). Hence no meaning as such exists within the semiotic, but there do exist "articulations heterogeneous to signification and to the sign: the semiotic *chora*" (*RPL*, 36). For Kristeva, the ego is a "speaking subject," which she differentiates not only from the Cartesian ego but also ultimately from the phenomenological transcendental ego: it is a subject in process/on trial [*sujet en procès*], as in the "practice of the *text*" (*RPL*, 37).

Hence, Kristeva sees the semiotic as part of a larger signifying process, which in-cludes the symbolic realm, and which is ultimately "the process of the subject. The semiotic is thus a modality of the signifying process with an eye to the subject posited (but posited as absent) by the symbolic" (*RPL*, 41). If the semiotic is the realm of drives and their articulations, the symbolic is the realm of signification, the realm of proposition or judgment, a realm of *positions*. And this positionality, says Kristeva, is "structured as a break in the signifying process, establishing the *identification* of the subject and its object as preconditions of propositionality." This break, which produces the positing of signification, she calls a "*thetic* phase." Even a child's first enunciations, including gesture and noises, are "thetic" insofar as they separate an object from the subject and attribute to the object (either metaphorically or metonymically) a signifying function (*RPL*, 43). Given that this thetic phase is the "deepest structure" of signification and the proposition, Kristeva is concerned to move beyond the mere phenomenological tracing of this phase to the ego, to showing, with the help of Freud and Lacan, the process whereby this phase is produced (*RPL*, 44).

Kristeva points out that we can view the semiotic *chora* as preceding the symbolic order only for purposes of theoretical analysis. In practice, the semiotic functions *within* the symbolic, as a transgression of it. Though semiotic functioning is discernible before the mirror stage, it is the semiotic that functions within the signifying practices of the symbolic realm, i.e., *after* the symbolic break, that can be analyzed in both psychoanalytic discourse and artistic practice (*RPL*, 68). Hence, the semiotic is pro-duced "recursively" on the basis of the thetic break, and represents a second "return of instinctual functioning within the symbolic, as a negativity introduced into the symbolic order, and as the transgression of that order" (*RPL*, 69). However, this "return" is not analogous with the movement of the Hegelian dialectic whereby one phase sublates (transcends and preserves in a higher synthesis) another: the eruption of the semiotic within the symbolic does not lead to the restoration, on a higher plane, of some primordial presymbolic unity or synthesis; rather, this negativity tends to "de-syn-thesize" and disrupt the thetic phase. Hence textual practice, as in art and literature, embodies a risk for the subject, threatening to sweep away entirely the symbolic: negativity is checked, and the semiotic regulated, by the operation of lan-guage (*RPL*, 69–70).

Kristeva suggests that in all known ancient societies, this founding break of the symbolic order, as theorized by Freud in his account of the death drive, was repre-sented by sacrifice, a thetic event that has long been central to the discourses of religion

(*RPL*, 70). Kristeva explains that the act of sacrifice focuses violence on a victim, thereby displacing this violence "onto the symbolic order *at the very moment* this order is being founded. Sacrifice sets up the symbol and the symbolic order at the same time, and this 'first' symbol, the victim of a murder, merely represents the structural violence of language's irruption as the murder of soma, the transformation of the body, the captation of drives" (*RPL*, 75). In other words, sacrifice represents the point at which the social order and the symbolic order of language are simultaneously created, both orders being based on representation (as in the body being withheld and made to signify).

If sacrifice represents one aspect of the thetic function – the prohibition of *jouissance* or play by language – art, having its roots in the representative ritual accompanying sacrifice, expresses a different aspect, the "introduction of jouissance into and through language" (*RPL*, 80). Religion controls the first aspect in instituting the symbolic order, an institution justified first by myth and then by science. On the other hand, poetry, music, dance, and theater enact trans-symbolic *jouissance* which threatens "the unity of the social realm and the subject" (*RPL*, 80). Poetry becomes, in fact, "an explicit confrontation between jouissance and the thetic . . . a permanent struggle to show the facilitation of drives within the linguistic order itself." It is the "eternal function" of poetry to introduce through the symbolic that which threatens it (*RPL*, 81).

Hence the subject herself is marked by this irreconcilable contradiction. Kristeva sees literature as the "most explicit realization of the signifying subject's condition," and this "dialectical condition" of the subject in language was expressed especially by Lautréamont and Mallarmé (*RPL*, 82). Kristeva views this as a revolution in poetic language at the end of the nineteenth century, and continuing into the practice of writers such as Bataille and Joyce. In her view, poetry since the Renaissance through the French Revolution and Romanticism has become "mere rhetoric, linguistic formalism, a fetishization, a surrogate for the thetic," reduced to "a decorative uselessness" with no subversive power (*RPL*, 83). The nineteenth-century "revolution" moved beyond both madness and realism, in a leap that maintained both delirium and logic (*RPL*, 82). In confronting the world of discourse, poetry, which represents a "semiotization of the symbolic," splits open the socio-symbolic order, "changing vocabulary, syntax, the word itself, and releasing from beneath them the drives borne by vocalic or kinetic differences" (*RPL*, 79–80). It was, however, only with Freud's designation of sexuality as "the nexus between language and society, drives and the socio-symbolic order" that the radical practice of Mallarmé, Lautréamont, and Joyce could be adequately assessed (*RPL*, 84–85).

In summary, the semiotic process includes "drives, their disposition, and their division of the body, plus the ecological and social system surrounding the body, such as objects and pre-Oedipal relations with parents." The realm of the symbolic encompasses the emergence of subject and object as well as the constitution of meaning structured according to categories tied to the social order (*RPL*, 86). Kristeva makes a distinction between two aspects of a text: *genotext* refers to the "underlying foundation" of language, the underlying play of energies and drives which give rise to a text and which can be discerned through various linguistic devices (such as rhyme, melody, intonation, and rhythm) but which is itself not linguistic. The term *phenotext*, on the other hand, denotes communicative language; it is a structure which obeys the rules of communication and "presupposes a subject of enunciation and an addressee." The *genotext* is not a structure but a *process* that is not restricted to "the two poles of univocal information between two full-fledged subjects" (*RPL*, 86–87). This process is potentially infinite, encompassing "the flow of drives, material discontinuity, political struggle, and the pulverization of language." The *phenotext* represents the constraints on this infinite, plural, and heterogeneous signifying process; these constraints are ultimately "sociopolitical" (*RPL*, 88).

Hence, the revolutionary poetic language of which Kristeva speaks has a subversive potential inasmuch as it threatens to reach back into the semiotic *chora*, to release energies and drives that have been thwarted by the conventional structure of the symbolic, disrupting the symbolic from within and reconceiving its notions of subject, object, and their connections. In the signifying practices of late capitalism, according to Kristeva, only certain avant-garde literary texts, such as those of Mallarmé and Joyce, have the ability to transgress the boundaries between semiotic and symbolic, genotext and phenotext; such texts can open up new possibilities of meaning, new modes of signification. The text, therefore, is instrumental in social and political change: it is the site where the explosive force of the semiotic *chora* expresses itself (*RPL*, 103). Reading such a text is to subject one's subjectivity to "impossible dangers" and risks, such as leaving behind one's identity, family, state, and religion, as well as the very notions of continuity and constancy (*RPL*, 104). This "infinite" process can occur through various modalities, through art or revolutionary processes of labor and political practice. The radical transformation of linguistic and signifying practices is "logically (if not chronologically) contemporaneous" with transformations in the social, political, and economic order (*RPL*, 104). Quoting Marx's comment that freedom can arise only when the notion of labor is transformed, Kristeva urges that the signifying process as practiced by "free" texts "transforms the opaque and impenetrable subject of social relations and struggles into a subject in process/on trial." She thus draws attention to the "social function of texts: the production of a different kind of subject, one capable of bringing about new social relations, and thus joining in the process of capitalism's subversion" (*RPL*, 105).

Hélène Cixous (b. 1937)

The radical nature and impact of Hélène Cixous' work is rooted in the political and social protests and upheavals of the 1960s, a period when leading French intellectuals such as Roland Barthes, Jacques Derrida, Jacques Lacan, and Julia Kristeva were reexamining some of the basic categories and assumptions of Western thought, especially as these were embodied in the structure of language. All of these thinkers challenged conventional representational or idealist views of language; they variously explored the implications of Saussure's observation of the discrepancy and distance between signifier and signified; and they variously promoted conceptions of writing or *écriture* which emphasized the relational, sensuous, material, and cultural-historical dimensions of language, and the "textuality" of discourse. Cixous' peculiar contribution to this radical project was to promote *écriture féminine* or feminine writing, as expressed in her powerful and outspoken manifesto "Le Rire de la Méduse" (1975), translated as "The Laugh of the Medusa" (1976).

Like Derrida, Cixous was born to an Algerian Jewish family and suffered the experience of imperialism. During the Algerian uprising against the French she went to study in Paris; her doctoral dissertation, translated as *The Exile of James Joyce*, was published in 1976. Assuming both teaching and administrative responsibilities at the University of Paris, she made the acquaintance of Derrida, Lacan, Foucault, and Luce Irigaray. She was, along with Tzvetan Todorov and Gerard Genette, one of the founders of the journal *Poétique*, as well as the originator of France's first PhD program in women's studies. Her subsequent literary theoretical writings have been collected in two volumes.

"The Laugh of the Medusa" might be seen as structured like a poem in its implicit refusal to engage with the conventional rhetorical formats of argumentation and expository prose. While its themes – the need for a female writing, the nature of such writing, and its momentous implications at both personal and societal levels – are clear, these themes surface into prominence in Cixous' text through an almost poetic refrain, through patterns of recurrence and reiteration in altering contexts. What is more, the "argument" of this text relies heavily on the materiality of language, the texture of words, the effect of word combinations and wordplay, as well as on an overtness of metaphor that peripheralizes the possibility of attributing literal meaning – grounded as this spurious notion is on centuries-old traditions of masculine categorizations of concepts – to any portion of the text. The text attempts to move beyond even poetic stratagems inasmuch as its "parts" resist assimilation into unity or into any preceding literary-critical tradition or into any reductive hierarchy that might assign a status of centrality to any of its claims.

Given its deliberated fluidity, it would be difficult to claim that Cixous' text revolves around any central metaphor: the very notion of centrality is treated as tentative and transitory, one set of concerns sliding into centrality, then receding as they are continually displaced by other notions. It may be worth beginning, however, by looking at the metaphor that issues from the text's title: the laugh of the Medusa. This metaphor is not taken up until the middle of Cixous' text, where, addressing women (as she does throughout the text), she charges that men have "riveted us between two horrifying myths: between the Medusa and the abyss."[14] The "abyss" refers to the connotations and implications of Freud's designation of woman as a "dark continent," pregnant with a mystery recalcitrant to analysis and understanding, and signifying lack, castration, negativity, and dependence (on the positive identity of the male). Cixous of course resists this view, this myth, of woman as unexplorable. And, countering the other myth, that of woman as Medusa, she affirms: "You only have to look at the Medusa straight on to see her. And she's not deadly. She's beautiful and she's laughing" ("LM," 289). Why beautiful? And why laughing? For Cixous, as for symbolist poets like Laforgue and heterological thinkers such as Schopenhauer and Bergson, laughter is a symbolic mode of refusing the history of (male) conceptuality, of truth as defined by masculine traditions of thought. It is not that laughter *opposes* truth with some other truth in the same conceptual mold. Rather, laughter is a way of *exceeding* the very notion of truth, of refusing to engage in the thought processes and categorizations of the world that have generated this notion. Another way of putting this would be to say that laughter exceeds or transcends "theory," which, by its very (historically determined) nature, is "male." Cixous states that a "feminine text" is "more than subversive," designed to "smash everything, to shatter the framework of institutions, to blow up the law, to break up the 'truth' with laughter" ("LM," 292). And it is the Medusa, in her newly envisaged beauty, who wears this laughing countenance, beyond the assaulting reach of her own reflectedness in the male shield of self-protective truth. In her demythified and remythified status, she cannot be destroyed like the Medusa of myth.

The myth of Medusa: in classical mythology, the Medusa was one of three sisters known as Gorgons, daughters of Phorcys and Ceto. The first two sisters, Stheno and Euryale, were immortal, but Medusa was mortal. Serpents were entwined in their hair, their bodies were covered with armor-like scales, and their hands were made of brass. Their gaze turned any onlooker to stone. Perseus, the son of Zeus and Danae, was sent to bring back the head of the Medusa. Armed by Pluto with a helmet that made him invisible, by Athena with a shield of brilliant bronze that would serve as a mirror, and by Hermes with winged feet, he was able to avoid the gaze of the Gorgons by viewing their reflection in his shield, and he cut off the Medusa's head, which nonetheless retained its power. Eventually, Perseus placed the Medusa's head on the shield of Athena, where (or on her breastplate) it was conventionally represented. In his *Metamorphoses*, Ovid has Perseus explain to his in-laws why the Medusa had snakes twining in her hair. The Medusa, he says, "was once renowned for her loveliness, and roused jealous hopes in the hearts of many suitors. Of all the beauties she possessed, none was more striking than her lovely hair." But Poseidon, he continues, "robbed her of her virginity" in the temple of Athena, who punished her "immodesty" by changing her hair into revolting snakes: "To this day, in order to terrify her enemies and numb them with fear, the goddess wears as a breastplate the snakes that were her own creation."[15]

If the Medusa represents one of the archetypal myths into which men have molded the image of woman, this myth expresses the repression of female sexuality and beauty: the very symbol of this sexuality, the Medusa's hair, becomes a symbol of terror in its draconian transformation. And although the agent of this repression and punishment was a female goddess, Athena, this happens to be a goddess with very "masculine" attributes, as expressed in her conventionally represented fierce countenance, and her powerful frame, robed in the attire of war. What Cixous effectively does is to redeem that part of the Medusa myth which has been repressed: the Medusa as she was prior to the repression of her sexuality, prior to the disfigurement of her beauty, and prior to her metamorphosis into a monster. To focus on the "laugh" of the Medusa, then, is to redeem woman, to liberate her from her degraded status in the history of male mythology. It is also to undermine the entire conceptual apparatus that has perpetuated the myths of woman. The Medusa's laugh returns woman to a premythical state, to the state of actuality behind the myth, to the reality that has been repressed: it does not oppose theory but laughs in its face, creating through its laughter a mode of engagement with theory that cannot be reduced to simple opposition but gestures toward a reformulation of the very grounds of communication between the system of language on which conventional notions of truth are grounded, and an alternative, female language. This new language will subsist in the relation of laughter (not opposition) to conventional male language.

Indeed, what recurs throughout this text is a poetic exhortation to women to bring into being a female language: "Woman must write her self . . . Woman must put herself into the text – as into the world and into history – by her own movement" ("LM," 279). These broad categories – text, world, history – underlie the movement of Cixous' account of the significance and implications of female writing. First and foremost, feminine writing acknowledges its rootedness in the body: "Write your self. Your body must be heard" ("LM," 284). The significance of "body" in this context, as in many of the texts of feminism, is complex and far-reaching, since it is the body, the female body, that has been repressed historically by the apparatus of male theology and philosophy, social systems, and even psychoanalysis. Male visions of the world have achieved the status of "theory" precisely by abstracting from the data of actual experience, by withdrawing from the world of the senses and the unconscious into an ideal world, whether of pure forms, substance, the absolute idea, the transcendental ego, or the soul. The most blatant cases of such repression of the body occur in theologies which advocate negation or denial of one's body and its drives and desires, and in particular the female body, which is regarded as a source of temptation and often as unclean; the most explicit examples in philosophy occur in Plato, who denies the status of reality to the world of the body, the physical world of sensation, and also in Descartes' dualism between mind and matter, between the human self identified as a disembodied thinking substance and its body which occupies the world of matter and extension, and is external to the human self as such.

Historically, then, to write *without* the body, to refuse to accommodate the claims of the body in a given view of the world, has been the norm, from Plato to the movements in modern philosophy commencing with Descartes. To write *with* the body implies facilitating a return of the repressed, a resurrection of that which has been subordinated and treated as secondary, as dirty, as weighing us down and preventing us from rising to the perception of higher truths. It is to reinstate the claims of the body as legitimate in the overall constitution of humanity, a restitution that is initially most visible in the constitution of femininity and its expression in feminine writing. Cixous suggests that, more "than men who are coaxed toward social success, toward sublimation, women are body" ("LM," 290). Whereas Simone de Beauvoir had viewed the rootedness of woman's experience in bodily functions as a kind of imprisonment within immanence, Cixous regards woman's greater attunement to bodily needs and drives as potentially liberating.

For it is indeed, in a sense, the body that resists pure theory: the latter, if not constrained, can ascend through infinite orbits of speculation and can envelop us, as Kant showed, in a spiraling regression of contradiction. We can use pure theory to prove almost anything: that God exists and that he doesn't exist: in either case, our conclusion is not rooted in the world of actual experience. The body is a name, a metaphor for many things: the uniqueness of experience which refuses to be subsumed under a general category or to be reduced to exemplificatory status; and, as Cixous reminds us, it can express the individuality of the self, inhabiting a determinate position in place, time, class, color, race, and religion. To write with the body is to refuse to annul these differences. If I am a black woman, born into a certain economic class and raised in a specific ideological and cultural climate, all of these factors will of course influence my reading of any given situation. I cannot, as the male tradition would have me do, simply dismiss these factors to arrive at some neutral perspective, which is somehow based on "pure" reason or pure thought and which thereby pretends to objectivity.

704

One of the great achievements of feminism as a whole has been to remind us on many levels that we *all* – not just women – speak from a perspective that is over-determined, that is highly conditioned by numerous factors beyond our control. For me to be aware of my body when I write, then, is to recognize the profundity of its contribution to, and determination of, my thought processes; we do not think in some Cartesian vacuum, in some pure mind abstracted from all of the concrete circumstances in which it is embodied. It has become conventional for us, in the process of understanding anything, to see how a number of particular entities or events can be brought under universals or general concepts: this attempt to see patterns of unity or similarity in the vast diversity of phenomena is one of the fundamental ways in which we have tried to make sense of the world. But feminism has shown that individuality cannot be wholly abrogated, its richness and uniqueness cannot be wholly left behind, in the process of thinking through general concepts. As Cixous insists, "there is . . . no general woman." One can talk of what women have in common, but the "infinite richness of their individual constitutions" prevents us from talking about "*a* female sexuality" that might be "uniform, homogeneous, classifiable into codes" ("LM," 280).

If the body represents resistant particularity, particularity that is recalcitrant to the generalization of its nature, this is because it harbors an irreducible and unique richness. Indeed, it is a "unique empire" which "knows unheard-of songs," an empire built on acknowledgment of the "fantastic tumult of her drives," and on a "precise interrogation of her erotogeneity" ("LM," 280). Each body is unique inasmuch as it distributes desires in its own special way ("LM," 295). And when this body is "heard," when it is expressed through writing, then "will the immense resources of the unconscious spring forth," the unconscious being the place where the repressed survives ("LM," 284). This new writing, expressing the "new woman," and based on the "empire" of the body, will resist the "analytic empire" built up in the language and categories of men ("LM," 296): "Women must write through their bodies, they must invent the impregnable language that will wreck partitions, classes, and rhetorics, regulations and codes . . . A woman's body, with its thousand and one thresholds of ardor – once, by smashing yokes and censors, she lets it articulate the profusion of meanings that run through it in every direction – will make the old single-grooved mother tongue reverberate with more than one language" ("LM," 289–290).

Noting that writing has so far has been run by a masculine economy, as "a locus where the repression of women has been perpetuated," Cixous equates the history of writing with the history of reason; and this history "has been one with the phallocentric tradition," an "enormous machine that has been operating and turning out its 'truth' for centuries" ("LM," 283). Hence the implications of a "new," feminine, writing will be momentous: "writing is precisely *the very possibility of change*, the space that can serve as a springboard for subversive thought, the precursory movement of a transformation of social and cultural structures" ("LM," 283). This new, "insurgent writing" will cause a "rupture" in the history of women, at two levels: it will effect a "return" of woman to her body, whereby she can realize a "decensored" relation to her sexuality; and it will tear her away from the "superegoized structure in which she has always occupied the place reserved for the guilty." Writing will emancipate "the marvelous text of her self that she must urgently learn to speak." Secondly, when woman thus seizes the occasion to speak, this will mark her "shattering entry into history," her use of writing as "the antilogos weapon" ("LM," 284). Woman's writing will confirm a place for her other than that reserved by the symbolic order, the order established by male institutions and history. In contrast with the writing that structures the symbolic order, woman's writing is closest to the drives; woman "dares and wishes to know from within . . . She lets the other language speak . . . which knows neither enclosure nor death . . . Her language does not contain, it carries" ("LM," 293). A woman's language is never abstract, never loses touch with the presymbolic and with the resources of the unconscious: "it's with her body that she vitally supports the 'logic' of her speech . . . Her speech, even when 'theoretical' or political, is never simple or linear or 'objectified,' generalized: she draws her story into history." Since no woman "stockpiles" defenses for countering the drives, "a woman is never far from 'mother' . . . There is always within her at least a little of that good mother's milk. She writes in white ink" ("LM," 285).

It is time, says Cixous, to "liberate the New Woman from the Old," to break with male-written history, and to write a new history ("LM," 279, 282). As subject for history, woman "un-thinks [spends] the unifying, regulating history that homogenizes and channels forces, herding contradictions into a single battlefield. In woman, personal history blends together with the history of all women, as well as national and world history" ("LM," 286). Cixous insists that one cannot "*define* a feminine practice of writing . . . this practice can never be theorized, enclosed, coded . . . it will always surpass the discourse that regulates the phallocentric system" ("LM," 287). The "New Women" will "dare to create outside the theoretical," even at the risk of being "called in by the cops of the signifier" who will try to reassign them their "precise place in the chain that's always formed for the benefit of a privileged signifier," who would use a privileged signifier to take them back to the "authority of a signified" ("LM," 296).

The body, then, is an emblem of drives, the resistant particularity of experience, the uniqueness of individuals that cannot be subsumed under coercive classifications, the impossibility of abstracting the historical and the national from the personal. And the writing that writes the body refuses codification and closure, resists obeisance to the throne of reason, and insists on its living connections with the materiality of the body, its drives, the unconscious, the libido. For a brief period in her text, Cixous even addresses the "defenders of 'theory,' the sacrosanct yes-men of Concept, enthroners of the phallus," denying their potential charges of idealism and mysticism ("LM," 295). In fact, she stresses that to escape her imprisonment within the discourse of man, she cannot merely appropriate male concepts and instruments: she must, rather, "fly" and "steal" ("LM," 291). She must, that is, "take pleasure in jumbling the order of space, in disorienting it, in changing around the furniture, dislocating things and values, breaking them all up, emptying structures, and turning propriety upside down" ("LM," 291). She must, with her body, puncture the "system of couples and opposition . . . successiveness, connection, the wall of circumfusion" ("LM," 291–292). She treads outside of the history governed by the phallocentric values of "[o]pposition, hierarchizing exchange, the struggle for mastery which can end only in at least one death (one master – one slave . . .)" ("LM," 297).

In terms somewhat reminiscent of de Beauvoir's, Cixous suggests that the new woman will embody "risk," the danger of being a self-creating woman; woman's oppressed history gives her a better knowledge "about the relation between the economy of the drives and the management of the ego than any man." Moreover, unlike man, "who holds so dearly to his title and his titles," woman is a "giver," who seeks not herself but the other in the other, who attempts to "unhoard," who thrills in endless change and becoming ("LM," 297), and who "stands up against separation" ("LM," 286). She is "an integral part of all liberations," carrying on the class struggle into "a much vaster movement" ("LM," 286). She will bring about "a mutation in human relations," embodying a new, *other bisexuality*," that designates "each one's location is self . . . of the presence . . . of both sexes," a bisexuality that will supersede man's "glorious phallic monosexuality" ("LM," 288). If there is a "propriety of woman," urges Cixous, it is her "capacity to depropriate unselfishly: body without end . . . If she is a whole, it's a whole composed of parts that are wholes," as distinguished from masculine sexuality comprised of a phallic centrality "under the dictatorship of its parts" ("LM," 293). When we write, "everything we will be calls us to the unlagging, intoxicating, unappeasable search for love. In one another we will never be lacking" ("LM," 297).

Notes

1 Virginia Woolf, *The Common Reader: First and Second Series* (New York: Harcourt Brace, 1948), p. 172. Hereafter cited as *CR*.
2 Virginia Woolf, *Moments of Being: Unpublished Autobiographical Writings*, ed. J. Schulkind (New York and London: Harcourt Brace, 1976), p. 72. Hereafter cited as *MB*.
3 *A Writer's Diary: Being Extracts from the Diary of Virginia Woolf*, ed. Leonard Woolf (London: Hogarth Press, 1953), p. 220. Hereafter cited as *WD*.
4 Quentin Bell, *Virginia Woolf: A Biography* (New York, 1972), p. 145.
5 Moore, "The Refutation of Idealism" (1903), in *Philosophical Studies* (London, 1922), pp. 1–2. Hereafter cited as "RI."
6 *Some Main Problems of Philosophy* (London and New York, 1953), p. 4. Hereafter cited as *MPP*.
7 Virginia Woolf, *Contemporary Writers* (New York and London: Harcourt Brace Jovanovich, 1965), p. 122. Hereafter cited as *CW*.
8 Virginia Woolf, *A Room of One's Own* (1929; rpt. San Diego, New York, London: Harvest/ Harcourt Brace Jovanovich, 1989), p. 4. Hereafter cited as *Room*.
9 Virginia Woolf, *Three Guineas* (1938; rpt. New York and London: Harcourt Brace, 1966), pp. 19–21. Hereafter cited as *TG*.
10 Simone de Beauvoir, *The Second Sex*, trans. H. M. Parshley (New York: Bantam/Alfred A. Knopf, 1961), p. 59. Hereafter cited as *SS*.
11 Elaine Showalter, *A Literature of their Own: British Women Novelists from Brontë to Lessing* (Princeton: Princeton University Press, 1977), p. 3. Hereafter cited as *LTO*.
12 Michèle Barrett, *Women's Oppression Today: Problems in Marxist Feminist Analysis* (New York and London: Verso, 1980), p. 8. Hereafter cited as *WT*.
13 Julia Kristeva, *Revolution in Poetic Language*, trans. Margaret Waller (New York: Columbia University Press, 1984), p. 21. Hereafter cited as *RPL*.
14 Hélène Cixous, "The Laugh of the Medusa," trans. Keith Cohen and Paula Cohen, in *The Signs Reader: Women, Gender, and Scholarship*, ed. Elizabeth Abel and Emily K. Abel (Chicago and London: University of Chicago Press, 1983), p. 289. Hereafter cited as "LM."
15 Ovid, *Metamorphoses*, trans. Mary Innes (Harmondsworth: Penguin, 1977), IV.774–803.

CHAPTER 27

READER-RESPONSE AND RECEPTION THEORY

The role of the reader or audience of a literary work or performance has been recognized since classical times. Plato was acutely aware of the disturbing power of poetry to affect people at the level of their passions and morality, as well as their basic conceptions of the gods and indeed of reality itself. He saw poetry as appealing to our lower natures, disposing us toward irrational behavior, and distracting us from the rational pursuit of truth. Aristotle, who had a more tolerant conception of poetry, made the response of the audience an integral component of his famous definition of a properly structured tragedy: such a tragedy must inspire the purgative emotions of fear and pity in the audience. Many classical and medieval writers viewed literature as a branch of rhetoric, the art of persuasive speaking or writing. As such, literature had to be highly aware of the composition and expectations of its audience. Subsequently, several Romantic theories stressed the powerful emotional impact of poetry on the reader, and various later nineteenth-century theories such as symbolism and impressionism stressed the reader's subjective response to literature and art. Several other kinds of theories, such as feminism and Marxism, have long acknowledged that literature, necessarily operating within certain social structures of class and gender, is always oriented toward certain kinds of audiences, in both aesthetic and economic terms. The hermeneutic theories developed by Friedrich Schleiermacher, Martin Heidegger, and Hans Georg Gadamer, as well as the phenomenological theories inspired by Edmund Husserl, such as that of Roman Ingarden, examined the ways in which readers engaged cognitively and historically with literary texts.

It was partly in reaction to both the subjectivist theories of the nineteenth century and theories that situated literature within larger historical contexts that various kinds of formalism, including the New Criticism, emerged. The formalists wanted to carve out the domain of literature as a scientific, autonomous realm, where the emphasis lay not on mere subjective reactions of the reader nor on the connections of the text to its broader social circumstances but on the literary work itself: they saw the study of literature as an objective activity, and they saw the literary object itself as the repository of meaning. What needed to be studied, they argued, was the "objective" verbal structure of the literary artifact, and what needed to be identified were its specifically literary qualities, as opposed to any moral, religious, or other significance it might contain.

At one level, reader-response theory was a reaction against such formalism and objectivism; it was also, however, a renewal of a long and diversified tradition that had acknowledged the important role of the reader or audience in the overall structure of any given literary or rhetorical situation. There are elements of a reader-response outlook in the theoretical writings of Virginia Woolf, Louise Rosenblatt, and Wayne Booth. All of these figures recognized that the author of a literary text uses certain strategies to produce given effects in their readers or to guide their responses. A number of poststructuralist movements such as deconstruction had challenged the formalist and New Critical assertion of the objectivity of the text. But it was not until the 1970s that a number of critics at the University of Constance in Germany (the "Constance School") began to formulate a systematic reader-response or "reception" theory. The leading members of this school were Wolfgang Iser and Hans Robert Jauss. The aesthetics of this school had its roots not only in the hermeneutic and phenomenological traditions mentioned above but also in the earlier thought of Alexander Baumgarten, Immanuel Kant, and Friedrich von Schiller.

Edmund Husserl (1859–1938)

Much reader-response theory had its philosophical origins in the doctrine known as phenomenology, whose foundations were laid by the German philosopher Edmund Husserl. The Greek word *phainomenon* means "appearance." Hence, as a philosophical attitude, phenomenology shifts our emphasis of study away from the "external" world of objects toward examining the ways in which these objects *appear* to the human subject, and the subjective contribution to this process of appearing. This "bracketing" of the external world is referred to by Husserl as the "phenomenological reduction," and it underlies his attempt to achieve certainty in philosophy. Husserl argues that we cannot be sure of the nature of the outside world; but we can have certainty about the nature of our own perception and about the ways in which we construct the world, the ways in which that world appears to our subjective apparatus. This emphasis on subjectivity proved to be enormously influential; it provided the foundations of the Geneva School of phenomenological criticism (including figures such as Georges Poulet and Jean Starobinski), which read literature as embodying the consciousness of its author; it exerted a considerable impact on the reception theories of Wolfgang Iser and Hans Robert Jauss; and it provided a starting point against which Martin Heidegger's thought reacted.

Husserl wished to establish philosophy on a rational and scientific basis. In his early essay "Philosophy as a Rigorous Science" (1911), he maintains that at no stage in its development has philosophy ever lived up to its claim of being rigorously scientific. He sees the various philosophies since the Renaissance as following "an essentially unitary line of development."[1] Husserl acknowledges that a "conscious will for rigorous science dominated the Socratic–Platonic revolution of philosophy and also, at the beginning of the modern era, the scientific reactions against Scholasticism, especially the Cartesian

709

revolution." This scientific impulse, says Husserl, renews itself in Kant's critique of reason and in the philosophy of Fichte. After that, however, the scientific endeavor of philosophy is weakened by Romantic philosophy, of which Husserl sees the archetypal exemplar as the philosophy of Hegel. It was in reaction against Hegel, partly due to the progress of the exact sciences, that naturalism gained an "overwhelming impetus." Indeed, the skeptical attitude of naturalism, says Husserl, has decisively shaped philosophy over the last few decades (*PCP*, 76–77). Such naturalism has been warring against a "sceptical historicism" adapted from Hegel's "metaphysical philosophy of history" (*PCP*, 77).

Husserl engages in a critique of both these tendencies, naturalism and historicism, the one professing to attain scientific objectivity and the other denying the possibility of such objectivity and affirming a historical relativism. In contrast with the "metaphysical irresolution and scepticism" of the previous age, Husserl calls for a philosophical science based on "sure foundations," one that will answer to the urgent spiritual need of our time, one that will satisfy "both intellect and feeling" (*PCP*, 140, 142). Like Descartes, Husserl insists that, in the spirit of genuine philosophical science, we "accept nothing given in advance" (*PCP*, 145). Philosophy is "essentially a science of true beginnings, or origins, of *rizomata panton* [the roots of all things]." We must begin not from previous philosophies, previous biases, misconceptions, and prejudices; rather, we must begin from "things and from the problems connected with them." Ideas, Husserl insists, are largely given in "immediate intuition," and it is through philosophical intuition that we will achieve a "phenomenological grasp of essences" (*PCP*, 147).

Husserl gives a fairly succinct account of his own philosophical position in a lecture of 1917 entitled "Pure Phenomenology, its Method and its Field of Investigation."[2] Here, Husserl announces that, in response to an urgent need, a "new fundamental science, pure phenomenology" has developed, and he defines this as "the science of pure phenomena" ("PP," 4–5). One of Husserl's accomplishments in this lecture is to define and refine the concept of "phenomenon," which in its simplest meaning refers to "something which appears" (to the subject or observer). Husserl's most general claim is that "objects would be nothing at all for the cognizing subject if they did not 'appear' to him, if he had of them no 'phenomenon.' Here, therefore, 'phenomenon' signifies a certain content that intrinsically inhabits the intuitive consciousness" ("PP," 7). Husserl is not only claiming, as Kant did, that we can know the object only as it appears to us, regardless of what it might be in itself; he is also urging that the object is *nothing* in itself, and its very constitution as an object, as a phenomenon or object which appears, is grounded on the subjective apparatus which intuits it as an object. In a sense, what Husserl is doing is removing the Kantian notion of noumenon which acts as a constraint or limitation upon the constitution of phenomena by the mind: for Husserl, there is nothing beyond the sphere and status of phenomena. The phenomenal world is not merely the only reality we can know; it *is* the only reality.

Husserl points out the complexity of the term "phenomenon" as it is used in his thought. When we perceive an object (i.e., when an object "appears" to us), this is not a single or simple operation: the object might be given to us, or appear to us, in differing ways. We might look at it from above, below, near, far, past, and present. So we in fact have several single intuitions of the "same" object. And these single intuitions are combined and integrated into "the unity of one continuous consciousness of one and the same object." Hence, "one unitary 'phenomenon' permeates all the manifolds of phenomenal presentation." In other words, what we call a phenomenon, or object as it appears to us, is in fact an intuited unity of a *series of perceptions* of an object" ("PP," 8). On the other side, consciousness itself is a unity of a variety of processes that are performed upon phenomena, such as remembering, referring, combining, contrasting, and ultimately, theorizing. So we have a situation where the "unity of one consciousness . . . constitutes intrinsically a single synthetic objectivity" ("PP," 9). Again, this situation seems similar to that outlined in Kant's description of the transcendental ego, which unifies the individual perceptions of the empirical ego; but again, Husserl's emphasis is different: the entire world of phenomena, ranging from the simplest designations of objectivity to complex groupings and sub-groupings of objects, is constituted by acts of consciousness, by a variety and hierarchy of such acts which themselves must form part of a pattern of ordered unity.

The point here is that it is consciousness that determines objectivity, that classifies and arranges the world of objects and phenomena: without this activity, there simply would be no objects as such. Hence, Husserl has extended the notion of "phenomenon" to "include the whole realm of consciousness with all the ways of being conscious of something . . . all values, all goods, all works, can be experienced, understood, and made objective as such only through the participation of emotional and volitional consciousness." By way of example, Husserl suggests that no object in the category "work of art" could occur in the world of someone who was "devoid of all aesthetic sensibility" ("PP," 13–14). The implication, clearly, is that a work of art (like any other phenomenon) cannot somehow exist prior to its reception; it is *constituted* by the sensibility which receives it as such, *as* a work of art.

The task of phenomenology, then, is to examine not the world of objects "in itself" but how this world is constituted by a vast range of acts of consciousness. For example, if something is remembered, we will examine not the object that is remembered but the object *as it is remembered*. In other words, we will consider how the process of remembering constitutes the object. As Husserl says, a phenomenological investigation will address "the intrinsic nature . . . of the perceiving itself, of remembering (or any other way of representing) itself, and of thinking, valuing, willing, and doing themselves . . . In Cartesian terms, the investigation will be concerned with the cogito in its own right," i.e., the thinking itself, as well as the object that is thought about ("PP," 15). As such, phenomenology will be a "science of consciousness" ("PP," 16).

Husserl insists on making a distinction between "phenomena" and "objects." Objects, such as all natural objects, are "foreign to consciousness," whereas phenomena comprise the processes and constituents of consciousness itself. This distinction indicates a sharp contrast, says Husserl, between phenomenology and the so-called "objective" sciences ("PP," 17–18). These contrasted fields deal with fundamentally different kinds of experience and intuition: phenomenology deals with "immanent" experience, which is a reflection through which we grasp both consciousness and whatever consciousness is aware of. The objective sciences deal with "external" or "transcendent" experience, i.e., experience of something external that is presented to our senses. Husserl claims that what is given to "immanent" reflection is given "absolutely," and is always certain, always indubitable; whereas, the object of external experience may be proven (through further experiences) to be illusory. For example, the mental process of "desiring" or "liking" is given absolutely: it is intrinsic (not foreign) to our consciousness, and we do not "view" it, as an object, from various perspectives. Another way of putting this is to say that desiring or liking *is* one of the ways of being conscious; as Husserl says, "to like is intrinsically to be conscious" ("PP," 19–20). Desiring or liking, then, is one of the forms in which an object is given to us; and we intuit the unity of desire and the object of desire as a phenomenon.

Husserl urges that we can pass from transcendent to immanent experience (since it is the latter alone that yields certainty). When we are in the "natural" (or transcendent) attitude, we execute certain acts of consciousness such as referring and combining; but our focus is not on these acts but on the objects which our consciousness intends. But we can convert this "natural attentional focus into the phenomenologically reflective one," by fixing our attention on our own "currently flowing consciousness and, thus, the infinitely multiform world of phenomena" ("PP," 22–23). In other words, our focus is now on not the objects as objects, but the objects as phenomena: the objects as they appear to consciousness, together with the structures of consciousness that condition these modes of appearing. As stated earlier, Husserl distinguishes phenomenology as the science of consciousness from mere psychology; the latter, he considers, is inadequate to the task of examining consciousness since it misapplies natural laws to the mind and in fact treats the mind as just another event in the spatiotemporal world of nature and matter ("PP," 25–26).

In contrast with "psychological experiencing," phenomenology engages in an intuiting which remains within "pure reflection" and which excludes nature ("PP," 27). In phenomenology, consciousness "is taken purely as it intrinsically is with its own intrinsic constituents, and no being that transcends consciousness is coposited" ("PP," 28). Husserl sees his "phenomenological reduction" as a development of Descartes' *cogito ergo sum* toward non-Cartesian aims: "phenomenological reduction is the method for effecting radical purification of the phenomenological field of consciousness from all obtrusions from Objective actualities" ("PP," 30). What does such a reduction involve? First of all, it entails suspending or bracketing or "putting out of action" the whole of "material Nature," and the entire corporeal world, including my own body, the "body of the cognizing subject" ("PP," 32). Secondly, we must exclude "all psychological experience," all consideration of conscious processes being grounded in the body or nature. Hence, "the Objective world," as comprehending both nature and the psyche, "is as if it were placed in brackets" ("PP," 33–34).

Once we have done this, what is left over? What is left for phenomenological analysis? Husserl's answer is "the totality of the phenomena of the world . . . Consciousness and what it is conscious of . . . is what is left over as field for pure reflection" ("PP," 34–35). He elaborates, saying that we can investigate "every kind of theoretical, valuational, practical consciousness," and all the objects constituted in it. The difference is that, in our phenomenological investigation, we will treat objects not as independent entities but as "correlates of consciousness." We can still examine everything that we would have done prior to the advent of this wondrous phenomenological science: "Things in Nature, persons and personal communities, social forms and formations, poetic and plastic formations, every kind of cultural work." Only, now, we will regard these not as "actualities" but in relation to the consciousness that constitutes them through its "wealth of structures" ("PP," 35). Hence, in examining pure consciousness, we are examining not only the structures of thought and perception that are immanent in consciousness but also the entire range of "external" phenomena as they *appear* to, and are structured by, consciousness.

But if our (hypothetical) starting point is a Cartesian one, of an individual consciousness, doesn't Husserl's procedure entrap us in solipsism, the narrow belief that the world and its contents are merely the product or projection of a single mind? Husserl explains that pure phenomenology is not an empirical science, viewing each consciousness as imprisoned within an individual body: rather, it is an a priori science, concerned "with the ideally possible and the pure laws thereof" ("PP," 38–41). Pure phenomenology, then, is concerned with the "essential laws" to which consciousness and its phenomena are subject ("PP," 41–42). The philosophical problems involved in a critique of reason must be reformulated in terms of "essential coherences" between various spheres of objectivity "and the consciousness in which it is immanently constituted." Following Brentano, Husserl sees acts of consciousness as *intentional*: consciousness is always conscious *of* something, and it posits or intends the objects toward which it is directed. Such objects are therefore "immanent" in the thinking process of the subject; and, since such immanent objectivity is ideal (certain qualities being abstracted from an object and recognized as its essence), it is an objectivity that is valid for all subjects.

According to Husserl, what phenomenology grasps is the ideal essences of objects; and, since these essences are immanent in (rather than external to) consciousness, they are grasped intuitively. Husserl sees his method as characterized not only by a "phenomenological reduction" but also by an "eidetic reduction," a reduction or abstraction to the ideal form (the Greek *eidos* meaning type or form). As Husserl states, the critique of reason must be regrounded by "a kind of research that draws intuitively upon what is given phenomenologically" ("PP," 43). In short, Husserl replaces the notion of objectivity with a model of intersubjectivity: coherences are found no longer in nature itself or in objects themselves but in the patterns of our perceptions of objects.

Husserl ends his paper with a confident prediction that phenomenology will "overcome all resistance and stupidity and will enjoy enormous development" ("PP," 44). While it may not have overcome all stupidity, phenomenology has certainly inaugurated, and has been symptomatic of, an enormous shift, discernible in many fields, including modernist literature, existentialism, deconstruction, and many branches of psychoanalytic and feminist theory, toward examining the world as integrally related to the apparatus of human subjectivity. Where the modern world has left Husserl behind, however, is his Cartesian insistence on isolating the mind from the body and conceiving the mind in an individualistic and atomistic way; subsequent thinkers have indeed built on Husserl's insights but have tended to ground human subjectivity in a social and historical framework, after the model of Hegel rather than that of Descartes.

Husserl himself, however, saw his "scientific" method of philosophy as answering to a much-needed exigency of the modern world. His inaugural lecture, just examined, was delivered in 1917, while Europe was still being devastated by World War I. In a subsequent lecture, "Philosophy and the Crisis of European Man" (1935), Husserl examined the connection between philosophy and history, and, more specifically, between his phenomenological method and the current malaise of Europe. Husserl effectively begins with the truism, in the wake of world war and economic depression, that the "European nations are sick." Husserl attributes this condition in part to the failure of the "humanistic sciences" to perform their function of guiding humanity in the spheres of culture, spirituality, and creativity (*PCP*, 150–151, 153). Blinded by naturalism, says Husserl, the practitioners of humanistic science have neglected to seek a "pure science of the spirit" (*PCP*, 155).

Husserl sees Europe as a unity transcending national conflicts and localized differences; this unity is "a special inner affinity of spirit," the "unity of one spiritual image." Husserl traces this spiritual unity back to the development of philosophy and science in the ancient Greek world; it is the emergence of the spirit of such science and philosophy, claims Husserl, that makes European culture unique (*PCP*, 156–157). This spirit consisted essentially in a new kind of attitude of people toward their environment: instead of being concerned solely with survival and practical needs, the Greeks acquired interest in systematic and universal knowledge that transcended any immediate application to their own, localized situation. They became interested in knowledge for its own sake, in the concept of a universal truth, and universal standards of morality (*PCP*, 160). Such an attitude transformed the lives of the Greeks, who began to live according to "ideal norms." Husserl designates this attitude, interested as it is in the universal, the "theoretical" attitude, carried out by philosophers and scientists "bound together in a common interpersonal endeavor" and devoted to *theoria* (*PCP*, 164–165). Such an attitude is unique to European culture (though it has been exported and imitated), and contrasts sharply with the "natural attitude," with the "naively direct living immersed in the world" that has characterized other cultures (*PCP*, 166). The theoretical attitude can, however, be integrated into a higher-level practical attitude. In this way, *theoria* is "called upon . . . to serve humanity in a new way," by offering "a universal critique of all life and of its goals . . . it is a practical outlook whose aim is to elevate mankind through universal scientific reason in accord with norms of truth in every form, and thus to transform it into a radically new humanity" (*PCP*, 169).

Indeed, Husserl suggests that the "European crisis" has its roots in the "mistaken rationalism" that has descended from the Enlightenment (*PCP*, 179). He views Enlightenment notions of reason as "one-sided," and warns that no one line of "truth must be absolutized. Only in such a supreme consciousness of self, which itself becomes a branch of the infinite task, can philosophy fulfill its function of putting itself, and therewith a genuine humanity, on the right track" (*PCP*, 181). Husserl once again denounces the objectivism that has descended from the Renaissance and was especially pronounced over the last two centuries, an objectivism that has taken the form of naturalism and psychologism. Husserl sees the crisis of Europe not as due to the collapse of rationalism but as the diversion or exteriorization of reason into forms such as naturalism and objectivism. He ends with a prescient warning: Europe can move from its present ruins into further alienation from its "rational sense of life, fallen into a barbarian hatred of spirit." Or it can find rebirth "from the spirit of philosophy, through a heroism of reason that will definitively overcome naturalism." Husserl urges Europeans to rise like the phoenix from "the annihilating conflagration of disbelief" and to engage once again in "the West's mission to humanity" (*PCP*, 192). His words have echoed loudly through the mouths of politicians speaking into the twenty-first century.

Martin Heidegger (1889–1976)

Husserl's student Martin Heidegger proved to be one of the most influential philosophers of the twentieth century, and the major modern exponent of existentialism. His impact extends not only to existentialist philosophers such as Merleau-Ponty, Sartre, and Simone de Beauvoir but also to psychiatrists such as Ludwig Binswanger and to theologians such as Rudolph Bultmann, Paul Tillich, Martin Buber, and Karl Barth, as well as to poststructuralist thinkers such as Jacques Derrida. Influenced by the phenomenological method of his mentor as well as by writers in the hermeneutic tradition of Friedrich Schleiermacher and Wilhelm Dilthey, Heidegger's central project consisted in a radical reexamination of the notion of "being," in its intrinsic relationship with time. His major work, *Sein und Zeit* (*Being and Time*), was published in 1927, making an immediate impact in both the halls of professional philosophy and the educated reading public. Heidegger argued that we had inadequately addressed the question of what Being is, and that the answer to this question would determine the future of humankind. Heidegger, moreover, developed his own hermeneutic or method of interpretation of texts; his later work focuses increasingly on the analysis of poetry and language.

Born into a Roman Catholic family, Heidegger was originally trained in theology, writing a thesis on Duns Scotus (1915); his philosophical studies at Freiberg University, where Husserl was Professor of Philosophy, brought him into contact with the work of Husserl and Brentano, as well as thinkers in the neo-Kantian tradition of Windelband and Rickert. Heidegger was appointed Professor of Philosophy at the University of Marburg in 1923; he was subsequently, in 1929, elected Husserl's successor to the Chair of Philosophy at Freiberg and then elected rector in 1933 under Hitler's recently inaugurated regime. It was in this year that Heidegger joined the National Socialist Party; in fact, in his inaugural address at the university, "The Role of the University in the New Reich," he decried freedom of speech in the interests of national unity, and lauded the advent of a glorious new Germany. He resigned his position as rector in early 1934. Did these events represent merely a brief flirtation on Heidegger's part with Nazism or an enduring collaboration and commitment? The controversy remains, yet it is undoubted that his work is marked by a vehement nationalism (he thought, for example, that philosophizing was possible only in German and Greek). Other significant works by Heidegger include "Kant and the Problem of Metaphysics," which offers a new interpretation of Kant's *Critique of Pure Reason*; and his inaugural lecture, "What is Metaphysics?"

In his *Being and Time* (1927) Heidegger insisted that philosophers to date had still failed to answer the question raised by Plato and Aristotle: what is being?[3] In this work, Heidegger analyzes what he terms *dasein* or *human* being. What characterizes human being is its "thrownness" into the world or "facticity": a human being is already cast into a series of relationships and surroundings that constitute his or her "world" (*BT*, 82–83). A second feature is "existentiality" or "transcendence," whereby a human being appropriates her world, impressing on it the unique image of her own existence and potential. In other words, she uses the various elements of her world as given to realize herself (*BT*, 235–236). Yet this positive feature is accompanied by a third characteristic, that of "fallenness": in attempting to create herself, the human being falls from true Being, becoming immersed instead in the distractions of day-to-day living, becoming entangled in particular beings (*BT*, 220). The authentic being, the authentic self, is thus buried beneath the cares and distractions of life (*BT*, 166–168).

How does a human being overcome such inauthentic existence, such loss of true being? Heidegger's answers to this question comprise one of the classic statements of existentialism. Inauthenticity consists in losing sight of the unity of human being, of human existence, caused by attention to the practical interests and cares of daily existence; human being is thereby prescinded and experienced as a series of desultory phenomena. Heidegger suggests that there is one particular state of mind which is unique: "dread" or angst (*BT*, 227–235). This refers to a sense of nothingness, of loss, of the emptiness, when we look at life or existence in its totality, as essentially oriented toward death. In such a mood, the human self attains knowledge of itself as a whole, as "being-to-death." In other words, death is the fundamental fact that shapes our existence and the course of our life. And the mental state of "dread" enables us to rise above our immanence, our dispersion in the immediate and transitory affairs of the world, to reflect upon our life as a whole, in the fullest glare of its finitude and its potential to lack meaning (*BT*, 293–299). The vehicle through which we acknowledge this responsibility to ourselves is "conscience," which acknowledges both our facticity, our being placed within a world and our obligation actively to fashion our selves in relation to this very world. Conscience makes us aware of this guilt or obligation (*BT*, 313, 317–319).

Like Bergson, Heidegger views time as integral to the constitution of the self or human being. As in Bergson's concept of *durée* or "internal" time (as opposed to mechanical "clock" time which merely spatializes time), time for Heidegger is integral to being; it is the profoundest substratum of human existence (*BT*, 466–472). What Heidegger calls existential time is time that is unique to a particular person's consciousness; a person's life, her traversing of the journey between birth and death, is most fundamentally constituted by time (*BT*, 376). Hence, her sense of existential responsibility is a temporal notion, lying in the ability to view her life from beginning to end (to a projected end) (*BT*, 395–396). This ability to situate my present (immersed inauthentically in temporary distractions) within a broader context of past and future, this attempt actively to engage in the world into which I have been cast, this assertion of my freedom in the midst of determination, is seen by Heidegger as living out one's "destiny" (*BT*, 416–417, 436–437).

In his later works, such as *Introduction to Metaphysics* (1953), Heidegger warns that we have fallen away from Being and have lost ourselves in the distractions of worldly and proximate aims, as well as in technology and gadgetry. In tones which are reminiscent of Husserl, Heidegger wishes to save Western man from this dire fate. Ironically, like humanists such as Arnold, he attaches overwhelming importance to poetry in this salvific enterprise. The works of Heidegger which directly concern literary theory and criticism include "The Origin of the Work of Art" (1935), "Hölderlin and the Essence of Poetry" (1936), and "Language" (1950). In these later works, Heidegger appeals increasingly to the power of poetry to express the truths of authentic being.

Indeed, in his essay "The Origin of the Work of Art," Heidegger states that the origin of a work of art is art itself: "art is by nature an origin: a distinctive way in which truth comes into being, that is, becomes historical."[4] We can attempt to follow Heidegger's elaboration of these general statements. He defines art as "the setting-into-work of truth." This process has two aspects: art fixes truth in place within a particular figure, and it also preserves truth. Heidegger broadens his definition of art to "the creative preserving of truth in the work. *Art then is the becoming and happening of truth*" (*PLT*, 71). What Heidegger seems to be indicating here is that art does not simply express prior or ready-made truths: rather, it both *creates* truths and *preserves* them, the latter being a historical function, for, as Heidegger says, art grounds history (*PLT*, 77). Heidegger proceeds to say that, in the midst of ordinary objects, art "breaks open an open place, in whose openness everything is other than usual . . . everything ordinary and hitherto existing becomes an unbeing" (*PLT*, 72). Hence, art has the power to transform our earlier and "ordinary" conceptions of truth, exposing the unreality of the arrangements of our ordinary life, releasing us from the closure and rigidity of conventional perception. Heidegger states that the "truth that discloses itself in the work [of art] can never be proved or derived from what went before" (*PLT*, 75).

Like many twentieth-century theorists, Heidegger insists that language has an important role beyond its merely communicative function: "language alone brings what is . . . into the Open for the first time . . . Language, by naming beings for the first time, first brings beings to word and to appearance" (*PLT*, 73). The emphasis here is characteristic of Heidegger's later, somewhat mystically oriented, writing: language not only creates but also reveals the true being that is already there, bringing this being to the light of expression. In this sense, language "itself is poetry." Poetry "takes place in language because language preserves the original nature of poetry" (*PLT*, 74). Heidegger calls this type of revelation of being through language and poetry "projective" statement. Such projection renounces the "dim confusion" which conceals things, and brings to light what was previously "unsayable." Such revelations, such bringing of realities to light and exposing the narrowness of previous conceptions, is projective also in a historical sense: it lays the groundwork for a people's understanding of itself, its self-image and its entrance into world history (*PLT*, 74).

Given this historical function and nature of art, Heidegger insists that, just as poetic as the actual creation of a work of art is the process of its preservation. He proceeds to affirm that the "nature of poetry, in turn, is the founding of truth." He sees "founding" as consisting of "bestowing," "grounding," and as "beginning" (*PLT*, 75). A genuine beginning, he says, is always a leap, and "always contains the undisclosed abundance of the unfamiliar and the extraordinary, which means that it also contains strife with the familiar and ordinary. Art as poetry is founding . . . of the strife of truth" (*PLT*, 76). Hence, whenever "art happens," Heidegger explains, "history either begins or starts over again" (*PLT*, 77). In other words, art's relation to history is one of founding but also of strife, since it transforms the fundamental concepts and truths by which individuals and nations live.

In his epilogue, Heidegger quotes Hegel's statement that in the modern era, art is no longer the highest expression of truth, this function having been assumed by philosophy. Heidegger points to the fact that in the work of art, the truth of being appears as beauty: "the beautiful belongs to the advent of truth . . . It does not exist merely relative to pleasure" (*PLT*, 81). In other words, in contrast with some modern affective theories which view beauty as a function of the taste or pleasure of the reader or listener, Heidegger views beauty as intrinsic to the expression of truth in art. In Western

717

thought, he says, there is "concealed a peculiar confluence of beauty with truth" (*PLT*, 81). Ironically, perhaps, Heidegger's position here hints at a return to Platonic and even medieval conceptions of the connection between being, truth, and beauty.

In "Hölderlin and the Essence of Poetry" (1936), Heidegger develops certain insights of the poet Hölderlin. The first of these is that poetry is the "most innocent of all occupations."[5] Heidegger takes this to refer to poetry's unfettered invention of a world of images, in the guise of "play" (*EB*, 272). He attempts to reconcile this insight with Hölderlin's further comment that language is the "most dangerous of possessions," given to man so that "he may affirm what he is" (*EB*, 273). It is language that creates the danger of confusion and loss of existence, of falsehood: "only where there is language, is there world, i.e. the perpetual circuit of decision and production, of action and responsibility" (*EB*, 274–276).

Hölderlin's line "We have been a conversation" is analyzed by Heidegger as indicating that only in conversation is language realized, and that the single, unitary "conversation" of man grounds his historical existence: "it is precisely in the naming of the gods, and in the transmutation of the world into word, that the real conversation, which we ourselves are, consists" (*EB*, 279). Language is indeed "the supreme event of human existence," and poetry is "the establishing of being by means of the word" (*EB*, 280–281). Through Hölderlin, we can understand poetry, says Heidegger, as "the inaugural naming of the gods and of the essence of things":

> poetry is the inaugural naming of being and of the essence of all things – not just any speech, but that particular kind which for the first time brings into the open all that which we then discuss and deal with in everyday language. Hence poetry never takes language as a raw material ready to hand, rather it is poetry which first makes language possible. (*EB*, 283)

In poetry, "man is re-united on the foundation of his existence. There he comes to rest." As in his earlier essay on the origin of art, Heidegger sees poetry as "an act of firm foundation" (*EB*, 286). In the language of Hölderlin, the poet stands between the gods and men, interpreting the signs of the gods and making them available to humanity. On the other hand, he is also the voice of the people, and it is these two tendencies in himself that mark his position of "betweenness" (*EB*, 288–289).

This notion of "betweenness" is developed and imbued with further associations in Heidegger's subsequent essay "Language" (1950). Here, Heidegger analyzes a poem entitled *Ein Winterabend* ("A Winter Evening") by Georg Trakl in order to arrive at certain insights into the nature of language. Heidegger's "analysis," like much of his later work, is itself written poetically and presents the kind of difficulties that we might encounter in a complex and obscure poem. The style and the insights of this piece anticipate Derrida's prose, as well as Derrida's rejection of a distinction between philosophy and literature, between prose and poetry, and between literal and figurative language. Heidegger begins by reaffirming his view that "only speech enables man to be the living being he is as man" (*PLT*, 189). Given this primordial status of language, Heidegger makes it clear that he does not wish to ground language "in something else that is not language itself" (*PLT*, 191). He notes that certain broad views of language have persisted for two and a half millennia. These are: language as expression (whereby something internal is externalized); language as an activity of man; and, finally, language as the presentation or representation of reality or unreality. But these views, says Heidegger, fail to confront language *as* language. By this, he appears to indicate that language cannot be treated merely as an appendage or adjective of the "human," an instrument of human communication and self-definition. It is not man, says Heidegger, but language, which speaks: "It is language that first brings man about, brings him into existence." In this sense, man is "bespoken by language" (*PLT*, 192–193).

Heidegger's "explication" of Trakl's poem anticipates some of the central positions of much reception and reader-response theory. The language of Trakl's poem, says Heidegger, does not merely name familiar objects such as "snow," "bell," "window," "falling," and "ringing." Rather, it "calls into the word . . . The calling calls into itself," into a "presence sheltered in absence" (*PLT*, 199). Inasmuch as we can "explain" this statement, we might take it to indicate that language does not name things which are somehow already there, waiting to be named. They achieve their very status as "things" only by being called into the word, only by being given a status, a position, a situation, in language. The status they occupy in the uniqueness of their current combination in language is different from that which they occupied prior to this combination, this current "calling" of language. Moreover, they are called into the act of calling itself: they achieve their very thinghood only in the process of this calling, of which they are an integral element. As things they are called into "presence"; but this is not a literal or immediate presence. The "falling snow" of which the poem speaks is not actually present in the immediate world of the listener or reader: it is called into presence in her mind, hence it is a "presence sheltered in absence."

The various images of the poem, according to Heidegger, such as snowfall, the vesper bell, house, and table set with bread and wine, evoke respectively the sky, the divine, mortals, and earth. Heidegger refers to this combination as the "unitary fourfold" which makes up the "world" (*PLT*, 199). It is this "world" that is called into being by the things that are named in the poem: "In the naming, the things named are called into their thinging. Thinging, they unfold world, in which things abide . . . The world grants to things their presence. Things bear world." Language speaks by "bidding things come to world, and world to things . . . For world and things do not subsist alongside one another. They penetrate each other" (*PLT*, 199–200, 202). If "world" expresses the core elements of a vision of unity or totality (sky, earth, mortals, divinities), and "things" express isolated features within that world (such as snowfall, or the ringing of a bell), the language that names these things does not merely name them in their isolation previous to the poem; rather, it names them *as* things in their current mutual combination, and as such, it is language which brings into visibility – into being – the bearing by each thing of its participation in a larger scheme, the self-gesturing of each thing toward its own essential relatedness, its implication of its own environment. In other words, language allows things to achieve their thinghood by bringing to light the "world" borne by them or implicitly contained within them. A thing becomes a thing only by release, through the power of language, from its bare immediate particular existence (a condition that can be only hypothetical) and access into its own mediation by more general categories, access into the fullness of its thinghood as part of a relational complex through the naming of it in language.

719

Heidegger's further explication of this situation appears to anticipate certain features of Derrida's notion of difference. He states that the "intimacy of world and thing is not a fusion." There is a persistent separation between the two. Between world and thing prevails a condition of "betweenness," or what Heidegger calls *dif-ference* where the latter part of this noun may refer to the "bearing" or "carrying" of world by thing. The intimacy of world and thing, says Heidegger, "is present in the separation of the between; it is present in the dif-ference. The word dif-ference is now removed from its usual and customary usage. What it now names is not a generic concept for various kinds of differences. It exists only as this single difference" (*PLT*, 202). This formulation anticipates Derrida's hypostatization of difference – his treating of it as a primordial essence, a linguistic primum mobile, an aseitic first cause prescinded from the very relationality into which it plunges all else. But what can Heidegger possibly intend? He has told us that it is language which speaks, language which brings together world and things *in their intimacy which is a relation of absolute difference*. He proceeds to tell us that the "dif-ference carries out world in its worlding, carries out things in their thinging. Thus carrying them out, it carries them toward one another" (*PLT*, 202). The neologisms "thinging" and "worlding" represent an extension of the gerund verbal form to the nouns "thing" and "world." In everyday language, the gerund form (which has the form of the present participle, such as "singing"), could be used as the subject of a sentence ("singing is healthy") or as an object ("she likes singing"). What is thereby emphasized, by the ending "ing," is not a noun (such as "song") but the *act* of singing. Hence, Heidegger's extension of this *verbal* form to a noun such as "world," transforming this into "worlding," draws attention to the world not as a thing but as an act; to be more accurate, it stresses the nature of the world or thing *as* an act. Hence, it is language, language that speaks, which brings the processes of world-composition and thing-composition into the mutuality in which alone either can be realized.

Heidegger proceeds to explain that the "dif-ference does not mediate after the fact by connecting world and things through a middle added on to them. Being in the middle, it first determines world and things in their presence, i.e. in their being toward one another, whose unity it carries out" (*PLT*, 202). In other words, dif-ference is not an external relation that connects two entities (world and thing) that are already there: rather, dif-ference is internal to their relation, shaping the very entities themselves. Heidegger insists, then, that the word is not merely our way of representing a distinction between objects; nor is it merely a relation between world and thing. If language speaks by bidding, by calling "thing and world, what is really called is: the dif-ference" (*PLT*, 203). Language speaks by bidding "thing-world and world-thing, to come to the between of the dif-ference. What is so bidden is commanded to arrive from out of the dif-ference into the dif-ference" (*PLT*, 206). If dif-ference primordially preexists identity, if dif-ference is prior to the constitution of world and thing, then language is the vehicle by which world and thing are called into being, through mutual relation, from this primordial dif-ference into the dif-ference which is language itself: "Language goes on as the taking place or occurring of the dif-ference for world and things" (*PLT*, 207). What ultimately takes place in the speaking of language is the creation of what is human: "What has thus taken place, human being, has been brought into its own by language" (*PLT*, 208). Man speaks, says Heidegger, "in that he responds to language," and "mortals live in the speaking of language" (*PLT*, 210).

While much of what Heidegger says in these later works leans toward mysticism, his insights into language overlap with those of many modern theorists such as Barthes and even Lacan. Heidegger indicates not only that the human being is "thrown" into the world (his or her particular world), but also that the human is characterized by a thrownness into language. It is the language that we are born into (not this or that particular language but language in general) that speaks through us and that speaks to us. At the core of language is dif-ference, the irreducible relation between world and thing, the irreducible self-transcendence of all of the elements of our world in a larger unity toward which they point; it is language that constitutes the human; all of our attempts to understand and act upon the world and thereby to create ourselves are mediated by the speaking of language, a speaking in which we must enter to find our own voice. In other words, it is when we arrive at a dialogue with language that we truly speak.

Hans Robert Jauss (b. 1921)

The phenomenological method of Husserl and the hermeneutics of Heidegger paved the way for what became known as reception theory. One of the foremost figures of reception theory, Hans Robert Jauss, studied at the University of Heidelberg with the hermeneutic philosopher Hans Georg Gadamer. In 1966 he became a professor at the University of Constance where, along with other leading proponents of reception theory such as Wolfgang Iser, he established the "Constance School." One of his most important texts was "Literary History as a Challenge to Literary Theory" (1969, 1970), a refined version of a lecture he had given at the University of Constance as his inaugural address. In this text, Jauss challenged objectivist views of both literary texts and literary history, urging that the history of a work's reception by readers played an integral role in the work's aesthetic status and significance.

Part of Jauss' purpose, as he states, is to bridge the gap between historical and aesthetic approaches to literature, the former exemplified by Marxism and the latter by formalism. The factor of the audience or listener or reader, he urges, is largely neglected in these approaches.[6] He insists that the audience of literature does not merely play a passive or formal role; indeed, the "historical life of a literary work is unthinkable without the active participation of its addressees." Literary studies have largely been confined to a "closed circle" of inquiry which has highlighted the processes of literary production and representation. This circle must be opened up to "an aesthetics of reception and influence" if we are to gain a coherent understanding of literary history (*TAR*, 19).

To begin with, we must overcome objectivist prejudices: instead of grounding the history of literature on so-called "literary facts," we must ground it on the history of a work's reception, on the succession of readers' experiences of that work. A literary work, Jauss insists, "is not an object that stands by itself and that offers the same view to each reader in each period. It is not a monument that monologically reveals its timeless essence" (*TAR*, 21). Rather, literature is "dialogic": it exists only in the form of a dialogue between text and reader, a dialogue whose terms and assumptions are ever being modified as we pass from one generation of readers to the next. As such, litera-ture is not an object or a thing but an *event* and it can exert a continued effect only if readers continue to respond to it. Jauss uses the hermeneutic philosophical term "horizon of expectations" to designate the framework of expectations and assump-tions that bring the worlds of reader and author together in the constitution and interpretation of texts. The "coherence of literature as an event is primarily mediated in the horizon of expectations of the literary experience of contemporary and later readers, critics, and authors" (*TAR*, 22).

Jauss counters the "widespread scepticism," as exemplified in the objectivism of critics such as René Wellek, which assumes that any study of readers' responses will inevitably be reduced to "an arbitrary series of merely subjective impressions" (*TAR*, 23). The responses of individual readers, he argues, do not occur in a vacuum but are situated within a horizon of expectations (a framework of assumptions) that can be objectified. The "continuous establishing and altering of horizons," he urges,

> determines the relationship of the individual text to the succession of texts that forms the genre. The new text evokes for the reader (listener) the horizon of expectations and rules familiar from earlier texts, which are then varied, corrected, altered, or even just reproduced . . . the question of the subjectivity of the interpretation and of the taste of different readers or levels of readers can be asked meaningfully only when one has first clarified which transsubjective horizon of understanding conditions the influence of the text. (*TAR*, 23)

Hence the concept of "horizon of expectations" is both historical and transsubjective, furnishing a common framework against which the differing responses of individual readers might be assessed. This "objective" status of the horizon of expectations is most clearly visible in cases where a literary work evokes "the reader's horizon of expectations, formed by a convention of genre, style, or form, only to destroy it step by step." For example, Cervantes in *Don Quixote* allows the horizon of expectations of old tales of knighthood and adventure to arise before parodying it (*TAR*, 24). Another integral part of this objectifying of the horizon of expectations lies in the fact that the reception of a text consists of "the carrying out of specific instructions in a process of directed perception" (*TAR*, 23). The author's anticipation of an audience's disposition toward a given work is effected by means of three "generally presupposed" factors: the familiar norms of the genre to which the work belongs; the implicit relationship between this work and others in its literary-historical surroundings; and through the contrast between fiction and reality, between the poetic and practical function of language (*TAR*, 24). By this last point, Jauss means that a reader can view the literary work within both the "narrower horizon" of literary expectations and through the "wider horizon" of her actual experience of life.

If the "horizon of expectations" of a work is formulated in this way, says Jauss, we can determine the artistic character of the work by the nature and extent of its influ-ence on a presupposed audience. He uses the term "aesthetic distance" to characterize the discrepancy between a given or already established horizon of expectations and the appearance of a new work, which might simply conform to, or subvert in varying degrees, this horizon. In the latter case, the reception of a "subversive" work might result in a change of horizons or a "horizonal change," a concept taken over from Husserl (*TAR*, 25). Jauss suggests that this concept of aesthetic distance can provide a criterion of the artistic value of a work: to the extent that no change in aesthetic values is demanded of a work, which merely relies on familiar conceptions and experiences, the work might be seen as belonging to the sphere of mere "culinary" or entertainment art. Such a work demands no horizonal change, but fulfills previous established norms and expectations, satisfies the prevalent norms of taste, and confirms familiar sentiments (*TAR*, 25). A work which does demand a horizonal change will create an aesthetic distance between the audience's expectations and its own new and alienating perspective.

However, this distance can disappear for later readers, as the work initiates an alternative horizon, and as it becomes increasingly understood and its value recognized. So-called literary masterpieces belong in this category, of a second horizonal change: the "self-evidence" of their beauty and their "eternal meaning" – in other words, the very pervasiveness of their acceptance – bring them "dangerously close" to being a mere "culinary" art, so that it requires a special effort of reading "against the grain" to bring out their truly artistic character once again (*TAR*, 26). Some new works only gradually develop an audience for themselves. For example, Flaubert's *Madame Bovary* appeared in 1857, the same year as his friend Ernest Aimé Feydeau's novel *Fanny*. At the time, Feydeau's novel was far more popular. However, as *Madame Bovary* formed an increasingly wider audience attuned to a newer horizon of expectations (such as Flaubert's principle of "impersonal narration"), these newer expectations saw clearly the weaknesses of Feydeau's novel, which is now forgotten (*TAR*, 27–28).

Deriving certain insights from Hans Georg Gadamer's *Truth and Method*, Jauss urges that the reconstruction of the horizon of expectations also highlights the differences between past and present understandings of a particular work, calling into question the objectivist dogma that "literature . . . is eternally present, and that its objective meaning, determined once and for all, is at all times immediately accessible to the interpreter" (*TAR*, 28). Following Gadamer's critique of historical objectivism, Jauss states that such a focusing on the history of a work's reception precludes the dangers of historical objectivism where the interpreter, "supposedly bracketing himself, nonetheless raises his own aesthetic preconceptions to an unacknowledged norm and unreflectively modernizes the meaning of the past text." Such an interpreter pretends that "he had a standpoint outside history," beyond all error, and denies the presuppositions that "govern his own understanding" (*TAR*, 29). On the contrary, as Gadamer points out, understanding can never occur outside of history: we do not have access to the original horizon of a work because this horizon is already enveloped within the present horizon. Jauss cites Gadamer's statement that "Understanding is always the process of fusion of these horizons that we suppose to exist by themselves" (*TAR*, 30). In the light of the intrinsically historical nature of understanding, the claim of critics such as Wellek, that we must "isolate the object," is a "relapse into objectivism." The significance of a literary work over time "is the successive unfolding of the potential for meaning that is embedded in a work and actualized in the stages of its historical reception," via the understanding achieved through the process of fusion of horizons (*TAR*, 30).

This theory of the aesthetics of reception insists not only on the development of the work's form and meaning through historical understanding, but also on the insertion of the individual work into a "literary series": we must undertake not only a diachronic analysis of the responses to the text over time but also a series of synchronic perspectives that reveal the text's relationship with other texts, genres, and overarching norms at a given time (TAR, 36). In this way, we can view literary history – represented both synchronically and diachronically – as a "special history" with its own unique relationship to "general history" (TAR, 39). The social function of literature, says Jauss, occurs when the literary experience of the reader enters into the horizon of expectations of his lived experience and "preforms his understanding of the world" as well as shaping his social behavior. Jauss resists the notion of literature as a representational art: the specific achievement of literature is that it does not simply reflect, at another remove, the processes of general history; rather, literary history as a special kind of history shows that literature has a *socially formative* function, and it "competes with other arts and social forces in the emancipation of mankind from its natural, religious, and social bonds" (TAR, 45).

Wolfgang Iser (b. 1926)

Iser's theories of reader response were initially presented in a lecture of 1970 entitled "The Affective Structure of the Text," and then in two major works, *The Implied Reader* (1972) and *The Act of Reading* (1976). After examining a number of English novels in *The Implied Reader*, Iser outlines his approach in a section of this book entitled "The Reading Process: A Phenomenological Approach."[7] Iser begins by pointing out that, in considering a literary work, one must take into account not only the actual text but also "the actions involved in responding to that text." He suggests that we might think of the literary work as having two poles: the "artistic" pole is the text created by the author, and the "aesthetic" pole refers to "the realization accomplished by the reader" (IR, 274). We cannot identify the literary work with either the text or the realization of the text; it must lie "half-way between the two," and in fact it comes into being only through the convergence of text and reader (IR, 275). His point here is that reading is an active and creative process. It is reading which brings the text to life, which unfolds "its inherently dynamic character" (IR, 275). If the author were somehow to present a story completely, the reader's imagination would have nothing to do; it is because the text has unwritten implications or "gaps" that the reader can be active and creative, working things out for himself. This does not mean that *any* reading will be appropriate. The text uses various strategies and devices to limit its own unwritten implications, but the latter are nonetheless worked out by the reader's own imagination (IR, 276).

To explain this process, Iser draws on Roman Ingarden's concept of "intentional sentence correlatives," according to which a series of sentences in a work of literature does not refer to any objective reality outside itself. Rather, the complex of these sentences gives rise to a "particular world," the world presented in the literary work (IR, 277). Iser's point is that the *connections* between various sentences or complexes of sentences are not established by the work itself, but are determined by the reader. A sentence in any literary work, claims Iser, characteristically "aims at something beyond what it actually says." Iser reminds us of Husserl's observation that a group of sentences creates an expectation in the reader; but what tends to happen, says Iser, is that in truly literary works these expectations are continually modified as we go on reading; indeed, a good literary work will usually frustrate our expectations. When we read expository texts (of science or philosophy, for example), we look for our expectations to be confirmed. But we regard such confirmation in literary works as a defect, since we are likely to be bored if a text merely rehearses what we already know and if our imagination is not called upon to work (*IR*, 278). The text produced by our response when reading is called by Iser its "virtual dimension," which represents the "coming together of text and imagination" (*IR*, 279).

Iser draws attention to two important features of the reading process. The first is that reading is a temporal activity, and one that is not linear. As readers, we cannot absorb even a short text in a single moment, nor does the fictional world of the text pass in linear fashion before our eyes (*IR*, 277, 280). Whatever we read sinks into our memory and is "foreshortened"; it may be evoked again later against a different background, enabling us to develop connections we had not anticipated: "the reader, in establishing these interrelations between past, present and future, actually causes the text to reveal its potential multiplicity of connections. These connections are the product of the reader's mind working on the raw material of the text, though they are not the text itself – for this consists just of sentences, statements, information, etc." (*IR*, 278). As readers, we occupy a perspective that is continually moving and changing according to the way we make sense of the accumulating fictional material. Moreover, our second reading of the same text will proceed along a different time sequence: we already know the ending, for example, and we will make connections that we had earlier missed. The text thus created by our reading is a product of our processes of anticipation and retrospection (*IR*, 281).

The second important feature of the reading process is that, when we are confronted with "gaps" or unwritten implications or frustrated expectations in the text, we attempt to search for consistency. Though our expectations are continually shifting, and images are continually being modified in their significance, we will "strive, even if unconsciously, to fit everything together in a consistent pattern" (*IR*, 283). According to Iser, this consistency of images or sentences and coherence of meaning is not given by the text itself; rather, we, as readers, project onto the text the consistency that *we* require. Hence, such textual consistency is the product of the "meeting between the written text and the individual mind of the reader with its own particular history of experience, its own consciousness, its own outlook" (*IR*, 284). We attempt to understand the material of the text within a consistent and coherent framework because it is this which allows us to make sense of whatever is unfamiliar to us in the text (*IR*, 285).

This search for consistency has a number of implications. Firstly, it makes us aware of our own capacity for providing links, our own interpretative power: we thereby learn not only about the text but also about ourselves. The non-linear nature of the reading process, says Iser, is akin to the way we have experiences in real life. Hence the "reading experience can illuminate basic patterns of real experience" (*IR*, 281). As

Iser states, the manner "in which the reader experiences the text will reflect his own disposition, and in this respect the literary text acts as a kind of mirror" (*IR*, 280–281). On the other hand, by making certain semantic decisions and ruling out others, for the sake of a consistent reading, we acknowledge the inexhaustibility of the text, its potential to have other meanings that may not quite fit into our own scheme. Indeed, our desire for consistency involves us to some extent in a world of illusion: as we leave behind our own reality somewhat to enter the reality of the text, we build up a textual world whose illusory consistency helps us make sense of unfamiliar elements. The consistency is illusory because we "reduce the polysemantic possibilities to a single interpretation in keeping with the expectations aroused, thus extracting an individual, configurative meaning" (*IR*, 285).

Iser sees the polysemantic nature of the text and the illusion-making of the reader as "opposed factors," but both are necessary in the process of reading: if the illusion were destroyed completely, the text would be alien to us; and if the illusion were all-embracing, then the polysemantic nature of the text would be reduced to one level of meaning. Hence we try to find a balance between these two conflicting tendencies. According to Iser, however, the "dynamism" of the text, its sense of life-likeness, presupposes that we do *not* actually achieve this balance. Even as we seek a consistent pattern in the text, we are also uncovering other textual elements and connections that resist integration into our pattern (*IR*, 285). In other words, even "in forming our illusions, we also produce at the same time a latent disturbance of these illusions." It is the reader's attempt to conduct this balancing operation, oscillating between consistency and alien associations, between "involvement in and observation of the illusion . . . that forms the esthetic experience offered by the literary text" (*IR*, 286). In seeking a balance, we start out with certain expectations, and it is the shattering of these expectations that lies at the core of our aesthetic experience. The very indeterminacy of the text, the very fact that parts of it are unformulated or unwritten, is the driving force behind our attempt to work out a "configurative" meaning, a meaning that is consistent and coherent (*IR*, 287). It is the very shifting of our perspective that makes us feel that a novel is true to life, and we ourselves impart to the text this dynamic life-likeness which allows us to absorb unfamiliar experiences into our personal world (*IR*, 288).

Following an insight in John Dewey's *Art as Experience* (1958), Iser believes that in reading a text, we undergo a process of organization similar to that undertaken by the creator of the text. In other words, we must *recreate* the text in order to view it as a work of art. And this act of aesthetic recreation, says Iser, is not a smooth or linear process and it actually relies on continual interruption of the flow of reading: "We look forward, we look back, we decide, we change our decisions, we form expectations, we are shocked by their nonfulfillment, we question, we muse, we accept, we reject; this is the dynamic process of recreation" (*IR*, 288). Two factors govern this process of re-creation: firstly, a familiar repertoire of literary patterns, themes, and social contexts; secondly, strategies that are used to "set the familiar against the unfamiliar." It is the "defamiliarization" of what the reader thought she knew which creates the tension between her intensified expectations and her distrust of those very expectations (*IR*, 288). Hence it is the interplay between "illusion-forming and illusion-breaking that makes reading essentially a recreative process" (*IR*, 289).

726

The bases of the connection between reader and text, then, are: anticipation and retrospection, hence the unfolding of the text as a living event and consequently an impression of life-likeness (*IR*, 290). During the reading process, the work's efficacy is caused by its evocation and subsequent negation of the familiar; in other words, the reader thinks her assumptions are affirmed by the text; she is then led to see that these assumptions are overturned and she enters the assumptions of the textual world itself, her reorientation marking an expansion of her experience, which learns to incorporate unfamiliar perspectives (*IR*, 290–291). Reading, for Iser, reflects the way in which we gain experience: once our preconceptions are held in abeyance, the text becomes our "present" while our own ideas fade into the past. We suspend the ideas and attitudes governing our own personality so that we can experience the "unfamiliar world of the literary text" (*IR*, 291).

But how does this happen? Many critics have suggested that the reader "identifies" with certain attitudes or characters in the fictional world. Iser's explanation of such identification derives in part from Georges Poulet's essay "Phenomenology of Reading" (1969). Following Poulet, Iser insists that in reading, it is the reader, not the author, who becomes the subject that does the thinking. Even though the text consists of ideas thought out by the author, in reading we must think the thoughts of the author, and we place our consciousness at the disposal of the text. According to Poulet, consciousness is the point at which author and reader converge, and the work itself can be thought of as a consciousness which takes over the mentality of the reader, who is obliged to shut out his individual disposition and character (*IR*, 292–293).

Iser modifies Poulet's insights to urge that reading abrogates the dualism of subject and object that constitutes ordinary perception, and this division now takes place within the reader's consciousness. Though we may be thinking the thoughts of the author, our own personality and disposition will not disappear completely but remain as "a more or less powerful virtual force," and in reading there will be "an artificial division of our personality." We, as readers, "assume" the individuality of the author as a division within our personality, thereby establishing the alien "me" and the real, virtual "me." Indeed, it is this relationship between the alien themes of the text and the virtual background of familiar assumptions that allows "the unfamiliar to be understood" (*IR*, 293–294). Someone else's thoughts can only take shape in our consciousness if our own unformulated faculty for deciphering those thoughts is brought into play and achieves formulation. In this way, reading is a genuinely dialectical process with myself being infused by the author's subjectivity and perpetually negotiating between the illusionary world of the fiction and the real world of which my own subjectivity is a part (*IR*, 293–294).

The production of meaning in literary texts not only entails our discovering unformulated or unwritten elements of the text; it also gives us the chance to formulate our own deciphering capacity, to formulate ourselves and to expand our experience by incorporating the unfamiliar (*IR*, 294). Hence, for Iser, the reading process mimes the process of experience in general: the aesthetic dimension of a literary work is located in the act of its *recreation* by the reader, a process that is temporal and also dialectical insofar as it allows the assumptions of the reader to interact with those of the text, yielding knowledge not only of the text but also of the reader herself.

But if the text at one level "mirrors" the reader, and if it is the reader who makes the connections between a text's various elements, what is to stop the reading process from being entirely subjective and even impressionistic? While Iser acknowledges and even insists that "the potential text is infinitely richer than any of its individual realizations," and that the reading process will vary from individual to individual, he also urges that such variation can occur only "within the limits imposed by the written as opposed to the unwritten text." He compares the variety of possible readings with the way two people might gaze on the same constellation of stars: one might "see" a plough and the other a dipper. The "stars" in a literary text, says Iser, "are fixed; the lines that join them are variable" (IR, 280, 282). One might also argue in Iser's defense that his concept of the reader as split between two personalities, the author's and her own, also disables complete arbitrariness of interpretation since it is a prerequisite of the reading process that the reader's preconceptions are held in suspension or, at the very least, compelled into dialogue with the assumptions and attitudes in the text.

In fact, this possible charge of uncontrolled subjectivism is confronted in Iser's *The Act of Reading*.[8] In this book, Iser enlists two basic arguments against such a charge. The first argument is based on the nature of meaning, and the second hinges on the question of whether a truly objective interpretation is possible. The meaning of a literary text, says Iser, is not a fixed and "definable entity" but a "dynamic happening" (AR, 22). It is, in other words, an event in time. Every fictional structure, according to Iser, is two-sided: it is both "verbal" and "affective." The verbal structure of effects embodied in the text "guides the [reader's] reaction and prevents it from being arbitrary"; the affective aspect is the realization in the reader's response of a meaning that has been "prestructured by the language of the text" (AR, 21).

However, though the textual structures guide the reader's response, they do not completely control it: some elements of the text are indeterminate and their meaning must be worked out by the reader. It is this mixture of determinacy and indeterminacy that "conditions the interaction between text and reader, and such a two-way process cannot be called arbitrary" (AR, 24). In this way, literary texts initiate "performances" of meaning "rather than actually formulating meanings themselves." Indeed, the very aesthetic quality of a text, says Iser, lies in this "performing" structure, which could not occur without the reader (AR, 27). Hence, not only is "meaning" an event in time, but also it is located in the interaction between text and reader. Iser effectively extricates the notion of meaning from its status as a spatial concept, as an entity somehow hidden in the textual object, and sees it as a temporal concept, as a *relation* that is produced in the reader's consciousness.

Again, we might object: even if we grant that the text somehow guides the reader's reaction, could not the meaning thereby generated in the mind of a given reader be entirely subjective and private? Iser acknowledges that what *is* private is the reader's eventual incorporation of the text "into his own treasure-house of experience" (AR, 24). However, such arbitrariness is limited by the fact that the act of understanding a text is "intersubjective": though readers may draw very different conclusions from what they read, they will often respond to the same things: "a literary text contains intersubjectively verifiable instructions for meaning-production, but the meaning produced may then lead to a whole variety of different experiences and hence subjective judgments" (AR, 25). The point is that the process of "meaning-production" itself will occur within a range limited by the textual structures; different readers may then draw widely diverging conclusions from this range of meanings. Iser sees this intersubjective model of reading as an advance over objectivist theories which presume that a text itself contains a single hidden meaning or set of meanings that can be discovered by the critic.

Iser points out that such objectivism is based on an "ideal standard" to which literary works should conform: and, far from being objective, this ideal standard is open to dispute. Who, moreover, defines this standard? The critic? But the critic, says Iser, is hardly infallible; he is another reader who will bring his own background and dispositions into play when judging the meaning or value of a literary work. Such "objective" judgments, then, may rest on intensely private foundations (AR, 24).

In *The Act of Reading*, Iser further elaborates his important concept of the "implied reader." He points out that when critics talk about literature in terms of its effects, they invoke two broad categories of reader: the "real" reader and the "hypothetical" reader. The former refers to an actual reader whose response is documented, whereas the hypothetical reader is a projection of all possible realizations of the text (AR, 27). Iser sees both of these concepts as deficient. The documented response of real readers has often been thought to mirror the cultural norms or codes of a given era. The main problem Iser sees with this approach is that any reconstruction of real readers depends on the survival of documents from their era; and the further back we go in history, such documentation becomes increasingly sparse, and we must reconstruct the real readership of a text from the text itself (AR, 28). On the other hand, Iser points out that the "hypothetical" or what is sometimes called the "ideal" reader is often nothing more than a creation of the critic's mind. Moreover, the code of an ideal reader would be identical to that of the author, thereby making reading superfluous (AR, 28–29). Since the "ideal reader" must encompass all the potential meanings of a text, Iser acknowledges that such a concept might be useful in order to "close the gaps that constantly appear in any analysis of literary effects and responses" (AR, 29).

Iser evaluates newer models of the reader that have arisen in more recent years, models that have sought to break free of the traditional restrictive models cited above: the "superreader" of Michael Riffaterre, the "informed reader" of Stanley Fish, the "intended reader" of Erwin Wolff, and the "psychological reader" of Norman Holland and Simon Lesser. Iser has criticisms of all of these models. Riffaterre's concept of the "superreader" refers to a "group of informants" who converge at "nodal points in the text," and their common reactions establish the existence of a "stylistic fact" (AR, 30). Iser acknowledges the value of Riffaterre's concept in showing that stylistic qualities cannot be constrained within the province of linguistics but must be discerned by readers. But he points out that Riffaterre hopes to guard against inordinate variation of response among readers by appealing to the "sheer weight of numbers." Also, his concept depends on the historical position of a group of readers in relation to the literary work (AR, 30–31). Iser sees this weakness also in Fish's concept of the "in-formed" reader, characterized by Fish as a competent speaker of the language, having "mature" semantic knowledge and possessing "literary competence." What he views as positive in Fish's model is its demand that the reader engage in a process of self-observation while reading, and its stressing, like Riffaterre's model, the insufficiency of a merely linguistic model (AR, 31). Iser insists that the reader's role is larger than that of the fictitious reader, who is only one aspect of the former. His critique of the psychological models of reading is centered on his objection that they do not adequately describe our reading of literature as an aesthetic experience: the text tends to lose its aesthetic quality and is merely regarded as material to demonstrate the functioning of our psychological dispositions (*AR*, 40).

According to Iser, all of the models cited above are restricted in their general applicability. His concept of the "implied reader" is intended to overcome these restrictions. In analyzing responses to a literary work, he says, "we must allow for the reader's presence without in any way predetermining his character or his historical situation." It is this reader, who is somehow lifted above any particular context, whom Iser designates the implied reader (*AR*, 34). The implied reader is a function not of "an empirical outside reality" but of the text itself. Iser points out that the concept of the implied reader has "his roots firmly planted in the structure of the text; he is a construct and in no way to be identified with any real reader." He defines the implied reader as "a textual structure anticipating the presence of a recipient without necessarily defining him." The implied reader, then, designates "a network of response-inviting structures," which prestructure the role of the reader in the latter's attempt to grasp the text (*AR*, 34).

Iser explains that there are two aspects of the concept of the implied reader: "the reader's role as a textual structure, and the reader's role as a structured act." By the first of these, Iser refers to those elements in a text that help a reader to "actualize" unfamiliar or new textual material. The text must be able to bring about a standpoint or perspective from which the reader will be able to do this. For example, in a novel, there are four main perspectives: those of the narrator, characters, plot, and the fictitious reader. The meaning of the text is generated by the convergence of these perspectives, a convergence that is not itself set out in words but occurs during the reading process. During this process, the reader's role is to occupy shifting perspectives that are to some extent prestructured, and then to fit these various viewpoints "into a gradually evolving pattern" (*AR*, 35). The components that prestructure the reader's role are: the different perspectives represented in the text, the perspective from which the reader holds these together, and their point of convergence (*AR*, 36). Indeed, the second aspect of the concept of the "implied reader" is the "reader's role as a structured act." By this, Iser means the reader's active role in bringing together the various perspectives offered in the text; the text itself does not bring about this convergence. Iser sees "textual structure" and "structured act" – the two aspects of the "implied reader" – as related in the manner of intention and fulfillment (*AR*, 36).

Iser also sees the notion of the "implied reader" as explaining the tension that occurs within the reader during the reading process, a tension between the reader's own subjectivity and the author's subjectivity which overtakes the reader's mentality, a tension between two selves that directs the reader's ability to make sense of the text. The reader's own subjective disposition, says Iser, will not be totally left behind: "it will tend instead to form the background to and a frame of reference for the act of grasping and comprehending." Every text, says Iser, constructs its work, in varying degrees unfamiliar to possible readers; these readers, therefore, must be placed in a position to actualize the new perspectives. It is part of the reader's role to be a fictitious reader, and her existing stock of experience will provide a referential background against which the unfamiliar can be conceived and processed (*AR*, 36–37). Given that the text's structure allows for different realizations and interpretations, any one actualization, says Iser, "represents a selective realization of the implied reader" and it can be judged against the background of the other realizations "potentially present in the textual structure of the reader's role." As such, the notion of the "implied reader" performs the vital function of providing "a link between all the historical and individual actualizations of the text." In short, the "implied reader" is a "transcendental model" which allows us to describe and analyze the structured effects of literary texts (*AR*, 37–38).

Iser's concept of "negativity" is important in his analysis of the reading process. All of the text's formulations, he says, are punctuated by "blanks" and "negations." The former refer to omissions of various elements between the formulated "positions" of a text; "negations" refer to cancelations or modifications or contradictions of positions in the repertoire of the text. These blanks and negations, says Iser, refer to an unformulated background: this fact he calls "negativity." It is negativity that enables words to transcend their literal meaning and to assume multiple layers of reference (*AR*, 225–227). Negativity, urges Iser, is the basic force in literary communication, making possible: (1) an understanding based on the reader's linkage of individual positions in a text, directed in part by blanks and negations; (2) deformations of organized structures of familiar knowledge and their remedy or the reader's search for the underlying cause of those deformations; here, negativity is a mediator between representation and reception, enabling the reader to construct the text's meaning on a question–answer basis. In this sense, negativity is the "infrastructure" of the literary text; (3) since literature presents something (knowledge or perspectives) that is not already in the world, it can reveal itself only through negativity, through the dislocation of external norms from their real context. In other words, everything that has been incorporated into a literary text has been deprived of its reality, and is subjected to new and unfamiliar connections. Negativity is the structure underlying this invalidation or questioning of the manifested reality (*AR*, 229). The reader must formulate the cause underlying this questioning of the world, and to do this, she must transcend that world, observing it, as it were, from the outside.

Hence negativity provides a "basic link between the reader and the text." Iser sees it as characteristic of a work of art that it enables us to transcend our own lives, entangled as they are in the real world. Negativity, then, as a basic element of communication, is an "enabling structure" that gives rise to a fecundity or richness of meaning that is aesthetic in character. Each decision we make as readers must stabilize itself against the alternatives that we have rejected, alternatives which arise from an interaction between the text and the reader's dispositions. The richness of meaning derives partly from the fact that there are no rigid criteria of right and wrong, but this, according to Iser, does not mean that meaning is purely subjective: the "very existence of alternatives makes it necessary for a meaning to be defensible and so intersubjectively accessible." Moreover, as we gain insights from a literary work, we do not merely use these mechanically to complement our previous insights, or our previous understanding of earlier parts of the text; rather, an interaction occurs that leads to a *new* meaning. Hence the production of meaning of literary works does not take place according to "regulative or constitutive rules" but is "conditioned by a structure which allows for contingencies." Iser acknowledges that it is the reader's own competence that will enable the various possibilities of meaning and interpretation to be narrowed down: it is the reader who provides the "code" that will govern her communicative relation with the text, rather than there being a preexisting code between text and reader already in place. In the latter case, literature would have nothing, or at least nothing valuable, to communicate (*AR*, 230).

What Iser is reacting against in his account of the reading process is what he considers to be the "classical norm" of interpretation, and the implications of this norm. According to Iser, the aim of conventional, classical interpretation was to uncover "a single hidden meaning" within the text. Meaning was considered as "representative," having a direct reference to the outside world; and hence the literary work was considered to be a vehicle for the expression of truth (*AR*, 10–12). Beyond this, interpretation aimed to instruct the reader as to the text's meaning, value, and significance (*AR*, 22). Such a model of interpretation promoted the treatment of a literary work as a document, testifying to characteristics of its era and the disposition of its author. What this model ignored, according to Iser, was the status of the text as an event as well as the experience of the reader (*AR*, 22). Iser sees his own project as emerging from a more modern constellation of approaches which rejected the idea that art somehow expresses or represents truth and which focused more on the connections between the text and either its historical context or its audience (*AR*, 14).

And yet, Iser points out, various elements of the classical norm have persisted, even within approaches that aim to reject it. The New Criticism, for example, "called off the search for meaning," rejecting the idea that the literary work contains "the hidden meaning of a prevailing truth," and focusing on the interaction of elements within the text. Nonetheless, elements of the classical norm have crept into this new approach: the New Critical values of harmony, order, completeness, and removal of ambiguity differ from the classical norm only inasmuch as these values are freed from their subservience to the expression of truth. In the New Critical approach, qualities such as harmony are considered valuable in their own right. In many modern conceptions of art Iser sees the classical values of symmetry, balance, order, and totality as occupying a central role. Why this obstinate persistence of the age-old classical norm, even within the texture of theories that claim to subvert or transcend it?

The main reason, according to Iser, is that consistency is essential to the very act of comprehension. And the very fact, acknowledged in modern theories, that a reader cannot grasp a text all at once obliges her to engage in the process of "consistency-building" to make sense of the text (*AR*, 15–16). The meaning of the text is not formulated by the text itself but is a projection of the reader. Hence as readers we have recourse to the classical values of symmetry, harmony, and totality, values that enable us to construct a frame of reference against which we can make unfamiliar elements accessible. The fragmented or disjointed nature of the literary work – leaving many blanks, gaps, and connections for the reader to work out – conditions "consistency-building throughout both the writing and the reading process" (*AR*, 17). So, in historical terms, the task of the critic has altered: instead of explaining how a text, with all its qualities of harmony, order, and totality, contains a hidden meaning, she must now acknowledge that consistency-building, as a "structure of comprehension," depends on the reader rather than the work. The critic must explain, then, not the work itself (which is an abstraction from the entire situation of reader interacting with text) but "the conditions that bring about its various possible effects." In other words, what is needed is not instruction passing from critic to reader in the meaning of the text but an analysis of the reading process (*AR*, 18–19). It is here that Iser's own work is designed to intervene.

Stanley Fish (b. 1938)

In historical terms, then, Iser aims to shift critical focus away from the text toward the reader, and while he stresses the experience of the reader during the reading process, his analyses are concerned primarily with individual acts of reading. It may be useful to consider here the work of another reader-response theorist, Stanley Fish, who attempts to situate the reading process in a broader, institutional context. Fish's earlier work, focusing on the reader's experience of literary texts, included an important study of Milton, *Surprised by Sin: The Reader in "Paradise Lost"* (1967), and *Self-Consuming Artifacts: The Experience of Seventeenth-Century Literature* (1972). His essay "Interpreting the *Variorum*" (1976) introduced his concept of "interpretive communities," a concept explored more fully in his book *Is There a Text in this Class? The Authority of Interpretive Communities* (1980),[9] where he addresses the important question of the role of institutions, and in particular the literary institution, in the construction of meaning.

Fish's essay "Interpreting the *Variorum*" takes its title and point of departure from the then recently published "Variorum" edition (containing variant textual versions) of the poems of John Milton.[10] Fish suggests that the controversies over meaning in Milton's sonnets are not "*meant* to be solved but to be experienced" and that "any procedure that attempts to determine which of a number of readings is correct will necessarily fail." For example, noting that certain commentators draw opposing conclusions from exactly the same evidence, Fish warns that any analyses generated by the assumption that meaning is embedded in the text itself "will always point in as many directions as there are interpreters." He urges that we need a "new set of questions based on new assumptions." In each of the disputes analyzed by Fish, he points out that the responsibility for judgment and interpretation is transferred from the text to its readers: the meaning of the lines at stake coincides with the experience of the readers. Meaning is not somehow contained in the text but is created within the reader's experience.

A formalist analysis, which locates meaning within the forms and verbal structure of the text itself, will ignore the reader's experience of the text, which is temporal and contains modifications and shifts of viewpoint. The central assumption of formalist analysis to which Fish stands opposed is that "there *is* a sense, that it is embedded or encoded in the text, and that it can be taken in at a single glance." Fish calls these assumptions "positivist, holistic, and spatial." The goal of such analysis is "to settle on a meaning," to step back from the text, and then to put together or calculate "the discrete units of significance it contains." Fish's objection to such an approach is that it takes the text as a self-sufficient entity, and ignores or devalues the reader's activities.

What we should be describing, he believes, is "the structure of the reader's experience rather than any structures available on the page." The reader's activities should be "the center of attention, where they are regarded not as leading to meaning but as *having* meaning." These activities, which include the making and revising of many kinds of decisions, are already interpretative; hence a description of them will be an interpretation. Fish points out that his approach differs from the formalist methods primarily through its emphasis on the temporal dimension of the reading process and the creation of meanings.

Fish acknowledges that the intended reader he has in mind is the "reader whose education, opinions, concerns, linguistic competences . . . make him capable of having the experience the author wished to provide." Notwithstanding Fish's insistence that it is the reader's experience of the text that creates meaning (or, in his terminology, *has* meaning), he views this meaning as always constrained by the central goal of readers: "the efforts of readers are always efforts to discern and therefore to realize (in the sense of becoming) an author's intention." The difference between Fish's model of reading and traditional intentional models is that whereas those earlier models saw the grasping of an author's purpose as a "single act," Fish sees this as "the succession of acts readers perform in the continuing assumption that they are dealing with intentional beings." Fish equates this understanding of an author's intention with "all the activities which make up . . . the structure of the reader's experience." Hence, according to Fish, if we describe these activities of the reader, or the structure of the reader's experience, we will also be describing the structure of the author's intention. So Fish's overall thesis, in his own words, is: "that the form of the reader's experience, formal units, and the structure of intention are one, that they come into view simultaneously."

Fish recognizes a potential problem here: if interpretative acts are the source of forms and of the intentions we ascribe to an author, what is to prevent an endless relativism, where there are as many interpretations as there are readers? In response to this problem, Fish argues that readers, or at least competent readers, belong to "interpretive communities" which are "made up of those who share interpretive strategies not for reading (in the conventional sense) but for writing texts, for constituting their properties and assigning their intentions." These strategies, he points out, exist prior to the act of reading and therefore "determine the shape of what is read."

In his book *Is There a Text in this Class?* (containing Fish's widely anthologized essay of the same title), Fish argues that what constrains interpretation is not fixed meanings in a linguistic system but the practices and assumptions of an institution. It is not the linguistic system that gives determinacy to the meaning of an utterance but rather the context of the utterance. Fish offers an anecdote about a student who asked a professor, one of his colleagues, before taking his course: "Is there a text in this class?" The professor heard this utterance in one context, assuming the question to be an inquiry about the textbook that might be required for his class. The student's question, however, referred to the concept of textuality as advanced in some modern literary theory. Fish uses this example to show that his colleague, having initially heard the question in one context (which includes whatever is associated with "the first day of class"), was obliged to modify this context (to embrace the concerns of modern literary theory) in order to understand the utterance (*ITC*, 309–311). His point is that "it is impossible even to think of a sentence independently of its context," and that our making sense of an utterance and our identifying of its context occur simultaneously: we do not, as M. H. Abrams and E. D. Hirsch imply, first scrutinize an utterance and then give it meaning (*ITC*, 313). We hear an utterance as already embedded within, not prior to determining, a knowledge of its purposes and interests (*ITC*, 310).

Fish's overall account is a sensible and balanced counter to the formalists who claim that the text is an object in its own right and that it somehow possesses stable meaning independently of any reader. The notion of intersubjectivity on which Fish's idea of "interpretive communities" rests goes back of course at least as far as Hegel; it is developed by neo-Hegelian philosophers, hermeneutic scholars, and sociologists, as well as thinkers such as Nietzsche and Bergson. Fish is effectively applying a well-known and previously extensively articulated insight to the act of reading. The same applies to his claim that facts do not exist independently of, or prior to, the interpretations and viewpoints that construct them as such. There are some problems with Fish's account: in his model of the reading process, Fish insists that this process of constructing or "writing" the text is equivalent to grasping, in a temporal fashion, the author's intention, which is itself a product of interpretation. The problem here, as Fish effectively acknowledges, is that the text disappears. Whereas for the formalists the text was a stable object, for Fish there is *nothing* beyond intersubjective agreement, and the text is reduced to merely the area of overlap of subjective responses. The problem here is that the process of *interaction* between text and reader is elided: where Iser saw reading as a dialectical interaction between a "virtual" text and an implied reader, Fish removes even that virtual status, reducing textuality to an effect of intersubjectivity.

Fish employs a naive notion of objectivity as somehow entirely independent of subjectivity. But philosophers for more than a century have been arguing that objectivity and subjectivity arise in the same, mutually constructive, process. Fish fails, moreover, to distinguish *degrees* of objectivity, whereby we might agree that certain "factual" elements of the text are less open to interpretation, or open to a far smaller range of interpretation, than, say, lines or phrases or themes in a poem which are overtly controversial. In this way we could talk about an objectivity which we understood to be constructed but which offered certain markers or foundations for such construction, rather than blandly saying that all objects are of equal status regarding the degree of intersubjective construction that constitutes them. The difficulty with Fish's procedure is that it freezes our analytical power within the abstract insight that all objectivity is the product of collective subjectivity: once we acknowledge this, we still have to make distinctions and evaluations of the vast variety of "objects."

Fish's procedure sensibly states what is undeniably true: we bring our assumptions (learned from our community) to bear on what we see "in" a literary text: but if this is true for all literary texts, it remains frozen as a general insight and does not furnish a basis from which to analyze the ways in which a particular work might actively direct our response as readers. Different texts obviously constrain and direct readers' responses in different ways, and simply to say that all of the strategies of the text are products of interpretation does not help us in describing the process of such constrainment and direction. Indeed, Fish does not explain how our mere "experience" of a work can *have* meaning (his phrase); how does this experience enter a structure of signification? It might also be objected that Fish invokes a naive, pre-Kantian, empiricism whereby the notion of "experience" is blandly opposed to thought and conceptuality: each element in a reader's experience is somehow "legitimate" simply because it is experience (*ITC*, 207–209). Fish claims that a formalist analysis is incapable of analyzing an experiential, temporal process. But his own description of this temporal process is couched in terms that are (as Bergson might observe) inescapably spatial: he talks of a "sequence" where the reader "structures" the "field" he "inhabits" and is then asked to "restructure" it (*ITC*, 207–209). Each of the enquoted words is spatial, and Fish's analyses follow the reader's response in a linear, sequential manner. Notwithstanding Fish's claim that "[e]verything depends on the temporal dimension," he offers almost no analysis of this dimension of the reader's response; his model in some ways rehearses the old intentional model of reading within an abstractly conceived temporality.

Notes

1 Edmund Husserl, *Phenomenology and the Crisis of Philosophy*, trans. Quentin Lauer (New York: Harper and Row, 1965), p. 71. Hereafter cited as *PCP*.

2 In *Husserl: Shorter Works*, ed. Peter McCormick and Frederick A. Elliston (Notre Dame, IN: University of Notre Dame Press, 1981). Hereafter cited as "PP." Numbers refer to paragraphs.

3 Martin Heidegger, *Being and Time*, trans. John Macquarrie and Edward Robinson (New York: Harper and Row, 1962), pp. 19, 21–23. Hereafter cited as *BT*. Given the necessarily brief nature of my account, I have referred the reader to passages that provide useful summaries or definitions of important terms.

4 "The Origin of the Work of Art," in Martin Heidegger, *Poetry, Language, Thought*, trans. Albert Hofstadter (New York and London: Harper and Row, 1975), p. 78. Hereafter cited as *PLT*.

5 "Hölderlin and the Essence of Poetry," trans. Douglass Scott, in Martin Heidegger, *Existence and Being*, ed. Werner Brock (Indiana: Gateway, 1949), p. 270. Hereafter cited as *EB*.

6 Hans Robert Jauss, "Literary History as a Challenge to Literary Theory," in *Toward an Aesthetic of Reception*, trans. Timothy Bahti (Minneapolis: University of Minnesota Press, 1982), pp. 18–19. Hereafter cited as *TAR*.

7 Wolfgang Iser, *The Implied Reader: Patterns of Communication in Prose from Bunyan to Beckett* (Baltimore and London: Johns Hopkins University Press, 1974). Hereafter cited as *IR*.

8 Wolfgang Iser, *The Act of Reading: A Theory of Aesthetic Response* (Baltimore and London: Johns Hopkins University Press, 1978). Hereafter cited as *AR*.

9 Stanley Fish, *Is There a Text in this Class? The Authority of Interpretive Communities* (Cambridge, MA and London: Harvard University Press, 1980). This book contains the revised version of "Interpreting the *Variorum*" which is cited in the current chapter. Hereafter cited as *ITC*.

10 *A Variorum Commentary on the Poems of John Milton*, gen. ed. Merritt Y. Hughes, 4 vols. (New York: Columbia University Press, 1970–1975).

CHAPTER 28

POSTCOLONIAL CRITICISM

Since the complex phenomenon of "postcolonialism" is rooted in the history of imperialism, it is worth briefly looking at this history. The word imperialism derives from the Latin *imperium*, which has numerous meanings including *power*, *authority*, *command*, *dominion*, *realm*, and *empire*. Though imperialism is usually understood as a strategy whereby a state aims to extend its control forcibly beyond its own borders over other states and peoples, it should be remembered that such control is usually not just military but economic and cultural. A ruling state will often impose not only its own terms of trade, but also its own political ideals, its own cultural values, and often its own language, upon a subject state.

The term imperialism as we know it dates back to the last half of the nineteenth century. But the concept and practice is as old as civilization itself. Both the Western world and the Eastern world have seen a series of vast empires which have extended over vast territories, often in the name of bringing the blessings of their civilization to the subject peoples who were regarded as barbarians. These include the Chinese empires extending from the eleventh century BC to the tenth century after Christ; the Sumerian, Babylonian, Egyptian, Assyrian, and Persian empires; the empires of the Greeks, which reached a climax with the conquests of Alexander the Great; the Roman Empire, the Byzantine Empire, and the various empires of Islam which lasted until the early twentieth century.

In modern times, there have been at least three major phases of imperialism. Between 1492 and the mid-eighteenth century, Spain and Portugal, England, France, and the Netherlands established colonies and empires in the Americas, the East Indies, and India. Then, between the mid-nineteenth century and World War I, there was an immense scramble for imperialistic power between Britain, France, Germany, Italy, and other nations. By the end of the nineteenth century, more than one fifth of the land area of the world and a quarter of its population had been brought under the British Empire: India, Canada, Australia, New Zealand, South Africa, Burma, and the Sudan. The next largest colonial power was France, whose possessions included Algeria, French West Africa, Equatorial Africa, and Indochina. Germany, Italy, and Japan also entered the race for colonies. In 1855 Belgium established the Belgian Congo in the heart of

Africa, a colonization whose horrors were expressed in Conrad's *Heart of Darkness* (1899). Finally, the periods during and after World War II saw a struggle involving the countries just mentioned as well as a conflict between America and the communist Soviet Union for extended control, power, and influence. Needless to say, these imperialistic endeavors have survived into the present day in altered forms and with new antagonists.

What concerns us is not only the history of imperialism itself but also the various narratives of imperialism. The motives behind imperialism have usually been economic (though liberal economists such as Adam Smith and David Ricardo were skeptical of imperialism's economic benefits, arguing that it only benefited a small group but never the nation as a whole). Marxists, especially Lenin and Bukharin, saw imperialism as a late stage of capitalism, in which monopolistic home markets were forced to subjugate foreign markets to accommodate their overproduction and surplus capital. A second and related motive has been (and still is) the security of the home state. A third motive is related to various versions of social Darwinism. Figures such as Machiavelli, Bacon, Hitler, and Mussolini saw imperialism as part of the natural struggle for survival. Like individuals, nations are in competition, and those endowed with superior strength and gifts are able and fit to subjugate the weaker nations. Karl Pearson's "arguments" belong to this category. The final motive, propounded by figures such as Rudyard Kipling (in poems such as "The White Man's Burden") and questioned by writers such as Conrad, rests on moral grounds: imperialism is a means of bringing to a subject people the blessings of a superior civilization, and liberating them from their benighted ignorance. Clearly, much of this rationale rests on Western Enlightenment notions of civilization and progress.

After the end of World War II in 1945 there occurred a large-scale process of decolonization of the territories subjugated by most of the imperial powers (Britain, France, the Netherlands, Belgium), with the significant exception of the Soviet Union and the United States, beginning with the independence of India in 1947. The collapse of the communist regimes in 1991 left America as the only major remaining colonial power (though America itself had of course held the status of a colony). Indeed, colonial struggle is hardly dead: it has continued until very recently in East Timor, and still persists bitterly in Tibet, Taiwan, Kashmir, and the Middle East.[1]

Postcolonial literature and criticism arose both during and after the struggles of many nations in Africa, Asia, Latin America (now referred to as the "tricontinent" rather than the "third world"), and elsewhere for independence from colonial rule. The year 1950 saw the publication of seminal texts of postcolonialism: Aimé Césaire's *Discours sur le colonialisme*, and Frantz Fanon's *Black Skin, White Masks*. And in 1958 Chinua Achebe published his novel *Things Fall Apart*. George Lamming's *The Pleasures of Exile* appeared in 1960 and Fanon's *The Wretched of the Earth* followed in 1961. According to Robert Young, the "founding moment" of postcolonial theory was the journal the *Tricontinental*, launched by the Havan Tricontinental of 1966, which "initiated the first global alliance of the peoples of the three continents against imperialism" (Young, 5). Edward Said's landmark work *Orientalism* appeared in 1978. More recent work includes *The Empire Writes Back* (1989) by Bill Ashcroft, Gareth Griffiths, and Helen Tiffin and Gayatri Spivak's *The Post-Colonial Critic* (1990), as well as important work by Abdul JanMohamed, Homi Bhabha, Benita Parry, and Kwame

Anthony Appiah. Robert Young sees postcolonialism as continuing to derive its inspiration from the anti-colonial struggles of the colonial era. Anti-colonialism had many of the characteristics commonly associated with postcolonialism such as "diaspora, transnational migration and internationalism" (Young, 2). Ashcroft, Griffiths, and Tiffin also use the term postcolonial in a comprehensive sense, "to cover all the culture affected by the imperial process from the moment of colonization to the present day," on account of the "continuity of preoccupations" between the colonial and postcolonial periods.[2]

Postcolonial criticism has embraced a number of aims: most fundamentally, to reexamine the history of colonialism from the perspective of the colonized; to determine the economic, political, and cultural impact of colonialism on both the colonized peoples and the colonizing powers; to analyze the process of decolonization; and above all, to participate in the goals of political liberation, which includes equal access to material resources, the contestation of forms of domination, and the articulation of political and cultural identities (Young, 11). Early voices of anti-imperialism stressed the need to develop or return to indigenous literary traditions so as to exorcize their cultural heritage of the specters of imperial domination. Other voices advocated an adaptation of Western ideals toward their own political and cultural ends. The fundamental framework of postcolonial thought has been furnished by the Marxist critique of colonialism and imperialism, which has been adapted to their localized contexts by thinkers from Frantz Fanon to Gayatri Spivak.

This struggle of postcolonial discourse extends over the domains of gender, race, ethnicity, and class. Indeed, we should avoid the danger of treating either the "West" or the "tricontinent" as homogeneous entities which can somehow be mutually opposed. Such a rigid opposition overlooks the fact that class divisions and gender oppression operate in both the West and in colonized nations. Many commentators have observed that exploitation of workers occurred as much in Western countries as in the areas that they subjugated. Equally, colonization benefited primarily a tiny portion of the population of imperial nations. In this sense, colonialism is a phenomenon internal to imperial nations as well as extending beyond their frontiers (Young, 8–9). Hence, postcolonial discourse potentially embraces, and is intimately linked with, a broad range of dialogues within the colonizing powers, addressing various forms of "internal colonization" as treated by minority studies of various kinds such as African-American, Native American, Latin American, and women's studies. All of these discourses have challenged the main streams of Western philosophy, literature, and ideology. In this sense, the work of African-American critics such as Henry Louis Gates, Jr., of African-American female novelists and poets, of commentators on Islam, and even of theorists such as Fredric Jameson, is vitally linked to the multifarious projects of postcolonialism.

One of these projects, or rather, one point of convergence of various postcolonial projects has been the questioning and revaluation of the literary and cultural canon in Western institutions, through what is loosely called "multiculturalism." In explaining the rise of multiculturalism, Paul Berman suggests that a new "postmodern" generation of activists from the 1960s came into power in American universities. The year 1968 saw left-wing uprisings against the elements of liberal humanism: Western democracy, rationalism, objectivity, individual autonomy. These were all considered to be slogans which concealed the society's actual oppression of blacks, working-class people, gays, women, as well as the imperialistic exploitation of third world countries. These oppressive ideas, according to radicals, were embodied and reproduced in the conventional canons of literature and philosophy which we offer to our students: the literary tradition from Homer to T. S. Eliot and the philosophical spectrum from Plato to logical positivism. Berman suggests that this reaction against the Western mainstream tradition was fostered largely by the rise of French literary theory, which insisted that the text was an indirect expression and often a justification of the prevailing power structure. This structure was inevitably a hierarchy in which the voices of minorities, women, and the working classes were suppressed. These voices now had to be heard.

The central conservative argument against multiculturalism was advanced by Allan Bloom, Arthur Schlesinger, and others. It assumed, firstly, that in the past there existed a period of consensus with regard to the aims of education, political ideals, and moral values; secondly, that this consensus, which underlies the national identity of America, is threatened by the cacophonic irreconcilable voices of multiculturalism. Multiculturalists respond that this past consensus is imaginary: the educational curricula adopted at various stages both in the United States and elsewhere have been the products of conflicting political attitudes. In late nineteenth-century America, conservatives, who desired a curriculum that would foster religious conformism and discipline, were opposed by those, like the pragmatist John Dewey, who wished to stress liberal arts, utility, and advanced research. In 1869, President Charles W. Eliot of Harvard initiated a program of curricular reform, amid much controversy. Disciplines such as history, sociology, and English itself struggled to gain admission into various liberal arts curricula. In 1890 the Modern Language Association (MLA) witnessed a heated debate over the relative merits of the classics and the moderns. And the 1920s and 1930s saw a struggle to make American literature part of the English program.

A third assumption of conservatives is that great literature somehow conveys "timeless truths"; Schlesinger states that history should be conducted as "disinterested intellectual inquiry," not as therapy; William Bennett, Lynne V. Cheney, and the National Academies have all appealed to the notion of timeless truths. But, to speak in such language is to dismiss the traditions of Hegelianism, Marxism, existentialism, historicism, hermeneutic theory, and psychoanalysis, which have attempted to situate the notion of truth in historical, economic, and political contexts. Various theorists have responded that, in fact, the appeal to "timeless truths" has always subserved a political function. The growth of English literature was from the beginning imbued with ideological motives. Arnold and subsequent professors at Oxford saw poetry as the sole salvation for a mechanical civilization. The timeless truths of literature were intended as a bulwark against rationalist and ideological dogma. Literature was to "promote sympathy and fellow feeling among all classes," to educate citizens as to their duties, to inculcate national pride and moral values. And English was a pivotal part of the imperialist effort. In 1834 Macaulay argued the merits of English as the medium of instruction in India, stating: "I have never found one . . . who could deny that a single shelf of a good European library was worth the whole native literature of India and Arabia." We can refrain from commenting on this except to add Macaulay's own subsequent statement that "I have no knowledge of either Sanskrit or Arabic." Such statements reveal the depth to which constructions of Europe's self-image, resting on the Enlightenment project of rationality, progress, civilization, and moral agency, were premised on the positing of various forms of alterity or "otherness," founded on polarized images such as superstitiousness, backwardness, barbarism, moral incapacity, and intellectual impoverishment.

In many areas of the globe – including the United States, where the study of English literature often overbalances that of American writers – the English literary tradition continues to act as a foundation and norm of value, with texts from other traditions often being "incorporated" and viewed through analytical perspectives intrinsic to the English heritage. In India, where English replaced Persian (the language of the former rulers, the Mughals) as the official state language in 1835, English continues to exert a pervasive influence on language, literature, and legal and political thought. It is in profound recognition of this integral relationship between the literary canon and cultural values that writers such as the Kenyan Ngugi Wa Thiong'o have written essays with such titles as "On the Abolition of the English Department" (1968), and important texts such as *Decolonizing the Mind* (1986). Many writers, notably Chinua Achebe, have struggled with the dilemma of expressing themselves in their own dialect, to achieve an authentic rendering of their cultural situation and experience, or in English, to reach a far wider audience. It should be noted also that what conventionally passes as "English" is Southern Standard English, spoken by the middle classes in London and the south of England. This model of English has effectively peripheralized the English spoken not only in other parts of England but also in other areas of the world. Today, there are innumerable varieties of English spoken in many countries, and only recently has their expression in literature been institutionally acknowledged. These various debates can now be examined in some of the major figures who have made contributions to postcolonial criticism and theory.

Frantz Fanon (1925–1961)

A leading theorist and activist of third world struggle against colonial oppression, Frantz Fanon was one of the most powerful voices of revolutionary thought in the twentieth century. Born on the French island colony of Martinique, Fanon fought against Nazism in France where he subsequently trained as a psychiatrist. His origins and his experience in both Martinique and France exposed him to the issues of racism and colonialism. An important influence on him was his teacher Aimé Césaire, a leader of the so-called negritude movement which called for cultural separation rather than assimilation of blacks. Fanon's books included *Peau noire, masques blancs* (1952), translated as *Black Skin, White Masks* (1967), which explored the psychological effects of racism and colonialism.

In 1954, while Fanon was working as a psychiatrist in Algeria, the Algerians rebelled against French rule. The violent struggle for Algerian independence was led by the National Liberation Front. Fanon edited the Front's newspaper and remained involved in the revolution until his death in 1961. Independence was not achieved until 1962. Fanon produced a number of writings connected with Algerian and African revolution; his most comprehensive and influential work was *Les Damnés de la terre* (1961), translated as *The Wretched of the Earth* (1963). This now classic text analyzed the conditions and requirements for effective anti-colonial revolution from a Marxist perspective, modified somewhat to accommodate conditions specific to colonized nations. It also articulated the connections between class and race. Indeed, Fanon points out the utter difference in historical situation between the European bourgeois class, a once revolutionary class which overturned feudalism, and the African bourgeoisie emerging as successor to colonial rule. In an important chapter called "The Pitfalls of National Consciousness," Fanon points out the limitations of nationalist sentiment: while such sentiment is an integral stage in the struggle for independence from colonial rule, it proves to be an "empty shell." The idea of the unified nation crumbles into pre-colonial antagonisms based on race and tribe.

Fanon attributes this failure of national consciousness and truly national unity to the deficiencies of what he calls the national middle class, the bourgeois class in the subject nation that takes over power at the end of colonial rule.[3] This class is underdeveloped: it has little economic power or knowledge, it is not engaged in production or invention or labor. Such is the narrow vision of this class that it equates "nationalization" with "transfer into native hands of those unfair advantages which are a legacy of the colonial period" (*WE*, 149–152). In other words, the national bourgeoisie appropriates for itself the privileges formerly held by the colonial power. Indeed, according to Fanon, this is precisely the "historic mission" of the new bourgeoisie: that of intermediary between its own nation and imperial capitalism (*WE*, 152). This bourgeoisie is historically stagnant, its entire existence absorbed in its identification with, and pandering to, the Western bourgeoisie, "from whom it has learnt its lessons" (*WE*, 153). And because the national bourgeoisie can provide no intellectual, political, or economic leadership or enlightenment, national consciousness, and the loudly hailed promise of African unity, dissolve into the regional, racial, and tribal conflict which existed before colonial rule (*WE*, 158–159). Colonial powers, of course, exploit these divisions to the fullest, and encourage, for example, the division of Africa into "White" and "Black" Africa (north and south of the Sahara, respectively). White Africa is held to have a long cultural tradition, and is seen as sharing in Greco-Roman civilization, whereas Black Africa is looked on as "inert, brutal, uncivilized" (*WE*, 161). The national bourgeoisie of each of these regions assimilates racist colonial philosophy long propagated by the Western bourgeoisie; but unlike their Western counterparts, whose chauvinism wore the mask of democratic and humanist ideals, the African bourgeoisie is devoid of any humanist ideology (*WE*, 163).

Fanon's overall point and conclusion is twofold: firstly, "the bourgeois phase in the history of underdeveloped countries is a completely useless phase" (*WE*, 176). In Marxist thought, the rise of the bourgeoisie is of course an integral and decisive stage in the ultimate historical progress toward socialism and a classless society. Communism does not merely sweep away the capitalist world: rather, it acknowledges the vast progress made by the bourgeoisie over feudalism in economic, legal, political, and social terms. The aim of communism, according to Marx, was to *realize* the promise of freedom, democracy, and equality which was articulated but not fulfilled by the bourgeois class. In stark contrast with the rich and revolutionary contributions of the Western bourgeoisie, the national bourgeoisie of colonized countries has none of the virtues of its counterparts in the West; it came to power in the name of a narrow nationalism which scarcely masked its pursuit of its own interests. As such, it must be opposed and neutralized, with the aid of the "honest intellectuals" who truly desire revolutionary change for the mass of people (*WE*, 177). The second point is that "a rapid step must be taken from national consciousness to political and social consciousness." By this, Fanon means that nationalist sentiment must be enriched by a consciousness of social and political needs, as framed by a humanistic outlook (*WE*, 203–204).

In another chapter entitled "On National Culture" (originally delivered as a talk in 1959), Fanon addresses the important connections between the struggle for freedom and the various elements of culture, including literature and the arts. Colonialism, says Fanon, entirely disrupts the cultural life of a conquered people. Moreover, every "effort is made to bring the colonized person to admit the inferiority of his culture . . . to recognize the unreality of his 'nation,' and, in the last extreme, the confused and imperfect character of his own biological structure" (*WE*, 236). A culture under colonial domination is a "contested culture," whose destruction is systematically sought. The native culture freezes into a defensive posture: there are no new developments or initiatives, only a rigid adherence to "a hard core of culture" which is identified with resistance to the colonial oppressor (*WE*, 238).

The various tensions caused by colonial exploitation – poverty, famine, cultural and psychological emaciation – have their repercussions on the cultural plane. Gradually, the progress of "national consciousness" among the people gives rise to substantial changes in literary styles and themes: tragic and poetic styles give way to novels, short stories, and essays; themes of hopelessness and resignation, once couched in florid traditional expression, give way before stinging denunciation of the occupying power and hard realistic exposure of the conditions of life. Eventually, even the audience for literature changes: the intellectuals, who formerly wrote for the oppressor, now address their own people. It is only when national consciousness reaches a certain stage of maturity that we can speak of a national literature, a literature which takes up and explores themes that are nationalist. This literature, says Fanon, is a "literature of combat" because "it calls on the whole people to fight for their existence as a nation," and "molds the national consciousness" (*WE*, 240). Hence literature is not merely a superstructural effect of economic struggle: it is instrumental in shaping the nation's conscious articulation of its own identity and the values at stake in that struggle.

A number of broad changes result in literature: in the oral tradition, for example, stories, epics, and songs which followed traditional and now inert formulae are imbued with new episodes, modernized struggles, and conflict. In Algeria, the epic reappeared, as "an authentic form of entertainment which took on once more a cultural value." And traditional methods of storytelling were overturned: instead of treating time-worn themes, the storyteller "once more gives free reign to his imagination," relating fresh and topical episodes, interpreting the vast panorama of present political and psychological phenomena, and presenting a new type of man – man free from the shackles of colonialism. Significantly, as in Algeria, such literary developments often led to the systematic arrest of the storytellers by the colonial power (*WE*, 241).

Fanon's essential point is that, in the circumstance of colonial domination, the "nation" is a necessary condition of culture. The "nation gathers together the various indispensable elements necessary for the creation of a culture." The struggle of a colonized people to reestablish the sovereignty of their nation "constitutes the most complete and obvious cultural manifestation that exists" (*WE*, 245). It is this struggle that leaves behind a fundamentally different set of relations between men, marked not only by the disappearance of colonialism but also by the disappearance of the colonized man (*WE*, 246). What Fanon is stressing here is that, given that culture is the expression of "national consciousness," the stage of national identity cannot be somehow bypassed, as we progress to a view of our general participation in humanity (*WE*, 247). Fanon insists that "it is at the heart of national consciousness that international consciousness lives and grows" (*WE*, 247–248).

At the end of his book, Fanon stresses that the way forward for the colonized nations of Africa and other parts of the globe lies not in the imitation of Europe but in the working out of new schemes on the basis of the unity of humankind: "For Europe, for ourselves, and for humanity, comrades, we must turn over a new leaf, we must work out new concepts, and try to set afoot a new man" (*WE*, 316). Much of what Fanon says of African nations applies equally well to other colonized areas, including the Indian subcontinent and much of the Middle East. His account of culture and national consciousness, which implicates political struggle in the very fabric of literary production, provides a revealing counterbalance to certain Western aesthetic attitudes which have insisted on isolating literature from its social and political contexts, or at least, in staking out an autonomous domain of purely literary analysis which might be complemented by considerations of context as long as its borders remain uninfringed. In a sense, this type of theory presupposes the luxury of political stability or stagnation, as well as the luxury of the marginalization of literature: in a culture where literature has no direct impact in the political sphere, there may well be justification for viewing the literary sphere as a relatively autonomous and self-enclosed domain. This domain can accommodate the most "radical" perspectives precisely because of its overall insulation from the political and economic realms. In short, we can be as subversive as we wish in poetry, because, unfortunately, it makes no difference. Such is the marginalization of poetry in our culture that its lines of intersection with the mainstream political process are delicate to the point of indiscernibility. Fanon's account reminds us, however, that there are cultures around the world – which in recent times have included much of the Middle East, the Indian subcontinent, parts of Russia and Yugoslavia – where literature is often directly and deeply involved in the political process, not merely as effect but as cause, in a profoundly reciprocal relationship.

Edward Said (1935–2004)

Known as a literary and cultural theorist, Edward Said was born in Jerusalem, Palestine. Having attended schools in Jerusalem, Cairo, and Massachusetts, he received his BA from Princeton in 1960 and his PhD from Harvard in 1964. From 1963 until his death he was Parr Professor of English and Comparative Literature at Columbia University. He was also visiting professor at Harvard, Stanford, Johns Hopkins, and Yale.

Said's thinking has embraced three broad imperatives: firstly, to articulate the cultural position and task of the intellectual and literary critic. Said's formulations in this area, influenced by Foucault, provided a crucial impetus to the so-called New

Historicism in the 1980s which was in part a reaction against the tendency of American adherents of structuralism, poststructuralism, and deconstruction either to isolate literature from its various contexts or to reduce those contexts to an indiscriminate "textuality." Said's second concern has been to examine the historical production and motivations of Western discourses about the Orient in general, and about Islam in particular. Said's own origin (or "beginning" as he would prefer) has defined a third, more immediately political commitment: an attempt to bring to light and clarify the Palestinian struggle to regain a homeland. Some regarded him as a model of the politically engaged scholar while others viewed his enterprise as incoherent. This account of Said's work will pursue the three lines indicated above.

Beginnings (1975) was Said's first influential book. Focusing on the question "What is a beginning?," Said traces the ramifications and diverse understandings of this concept in history. Adapting insights from the Italian philosopher Giambattista Vico's *New Science* (1744), Said distinguishes between "origin," which is divine, mythical, and privileged, and "beginning," which is secular and humanly produced. An "origin," as in classical and neoclassical thought, is endowed with linear, dynastic, and chronological eminence, centrally dominating what derives from it, whereas a beginning, especially as embodied in much modern thought, encourages orders of dispersion, adjacency, and complementarity.[4] Said defines beginning as its own method, as a first step in the intentional production of meaning, and as the production of difference from pre-existing traditions. If beginning comprises such an activity of subversion, it must be informed by an inaugural logic which authorizes subsequent texts; it both enables them and limits what is acceptable (*Beginnings*, 32–34). Drawing on insights of Vico, Valéry, Nietzsche, Saussure, Lévi-Strauss, Husserl, and Foucault, Said argues that the novel represents the major attempt in Western literary culture to give beginnings an authorizing function in experience, art, and knowledge. In postmodernist literature, beginning embodies an effort to achieve knowledge and art through a "violently transgressive" language.

The problematics of language lie at the heart of "beginnings." Given their exposure of the hierarchical and often oppressive system of language, Said places Foucault and Deleuze within the "adversary epistemological current" running through Vico, Marx, Engels, Lukács, and Fanon. Following Foucault, he redefines writing as the act of "taking hold" of language, which means beginning again rather than taking up language at the point ordained by tradition. To do so is an act of discovery and is indeed the "method" of "beginning," which intends difference and engages in an "other" production of meaning (*Beginnings*, 13, 378–379). The task for the intellectual or critic is to combat institutional specialization, ideological professionalism, and a hierarchical system of values which rewards traditional literary and cultural explanations and discourages "beginning" critiques. Criticism should be a constant reexperiencing of beginning, promoting not authority but non-coercive and communal activity (*Beginnings*, 379–380).

But in *The World, the Text, and the Critic* (1983),[5] Said argues that critical theory has retreated into a "labyrinth of textuality" whereby it betrays its "insurrectionary" beginnings in the 1960s. Said sees even the "radical" factions of the intellectual establishment, along with the traditional humanists, as having sold out to the "principle of non-interference" and the triumph of the ethic of professionalism, a self-domestication he sees as concurrent with the rise of Reaganism (*WTC*, 3–4). He sees contemporary criticism as an institution for publicly affirming the values of culture as understood in a Eurocentric, dominative, and elitist sense. Having thereby lost touch with the "resistance and heterogeneity of civil society," criticism has effectively presided over its own (paradoxically) cultural marginality and political irrelevance (*WTC*, 25–26). The notion of the "text" thus dirempted from the "world" is what Said is at pains to combat. He effectively redefines the text as "worldly," as implication in real social and political conditions in a number of ways: the most important feature of a text is the fact of its production (*WTC*, 50). The specific conditions of a text's production are constitutive of its capacity to produce meaning; they constrain their own interpretation by placing themselves, intervening in given ideological and aesthetic conjunctures. Texts are marked by an interplay between their speech and the contours of its projected reception (*WTC*, 39–40). Moreover, as texts dislodge and displace other texts, they are essentially facts of power, not of democratic exchange (*WTC*, 45). Following Foucault, Said rejects formulations of the discursive situation as one of democratic equality or political neutrality but likens it to the relation between colonizer and colonized, or oppressor and oppressed (*WTC*, 48–49). In short, "Texts are a system of forces institutionalized by the reigning culture at some human cost to its various components" (*WTC*, 53).

Following Foucault, Said sees culture as that which fixes the range of meanings of "home," "belonging," and "community"; beyond this is anarchy and homelessness. It is within this outright opposition that Said, as he had already hinted in *Beginnings*, wishes to carve out a space within civil society for the intellectual and critic, a space of "in-betweenness." Echoing Arnold, whose ultimate identification of culture with state authority he rejects, Said suggests that the "function of criticism at the present time" is to stand between the dominant culture and the totalizing forms of critical systems (*WTC*, 5). Said articulates this in terms of the notions of filiation (which embodies given ties of family, home, class, and country) and affiliation (an acquired allegiance, part voluntary and part historically determined, of critical consciousness to a system of values). Much modernist literature, Said argues, having experienced the failure of filiative ties, turned to compensatory affiliation with something broader than the parameters of their original situation in the world. Examples are Joyce and Eliot who both shed their original ties of family, race, and religion to affiliate themselves, from an exilic position, with broader visions of the world. The kind of criticism Said advocates lies precisely in its difference from other cultural activities and from totalizing systems of thought and method. This "secular" criticism focuses on local and worldly situations and opposes itself to the production of massive hermetic systems (*WTC*, 26, 291). It must combat every form of tyranny, domination, and abuse; to promote non-coercive knowledge in the interests of human freedom and to articulate possible alternatives to the prevailing orthodoxies of culture and system (*WTC*, 29–30). Said regards Vico and Swift as important prototypes of the oppositional stance. His characterization of Swift as "anarchic in his sense of the range of alternatives to the status quo" (*WTC*, 27) might well be applied to himself.

Interestingly, Said traces the emergence of Eurocentrism itself to Renan's transference of authority from sacred, divinely authorized texts to an ethnocentric philology which diminished the status of both Semitic languages and the "Orient," a theme which is developed in *Orientalism* (1978).[6] Here, Said examines the vast tradition of Western "constructions" of the Orient. This tradition of Orientalism has been a "corporate institution" for coming to terms with the Orient, for authorizing views about it and ruling over it. Central to Said's analysis is that the Orient is actually a production of Western discourse, a means of self-definition of Western culture as well as of justifying imperial domination of Oriental peoples (*Orientalism*, 3). Said concentrates on the modern history of British, French, and American engagement with primarily the Islamic world. Given his crucial treatment of Orientalism as a discourse, his aim is not to show that this politically motivated edifice of language somehow distorts a "real" Orient, but rather to show that it is indeed a language, with an internal consistency, motivation, and capacity for representation resting on a relationship of power and hegemony over the Orient.

The book is also an attempt to display Orientalism as but one complex example of the politically and ideologically rooted nature of all discourse, even those forms which have been veiled under the mantle of innocence. Thus, "liberal cultural heroes" such as Mill, Arnold, and Carlyle all had views, usually overlooked, on race and imperialism (*Orientalism*, 14). Using a vast range of examples, from Aeschylus' play *The Persians* through Macaulay, Renan, and Marx to Gustave von Grunbaum and the *Cambridge History of Islam*, Said attempts to examine the stereotypes and distortions through which Islam and the East have been consumed. These stereotypes include: Islam as a heretical imitation of Christianity (*Orientalism*, 65–66); the exotic sexuality of the Oriental woman (*Orientalism*, 187); Islam as a uniquely unitary phenomenon and as a culture incapable of innovation (*Orientalism*, 296–298). Also considering America's twentieth-century relations with the Arab world, Said suggests that the electronic postmodern world reinforces dehumanized portrayals of the Arabs, a tendency both aggravated by the Arab–Israeli conflict and intensely felt by Said himself as a Palestinian.

In *The Question of Palestine* (1979) Said, himself a member of the Palestine National Council, attempts to place before the American reader a historical account of the Palestinian experience and plight. *Covering Islam* (1981) aims to reveal how media representations "produce" Islam, and, in reducing its adherents to anti-American fanatics and threatening fundamentalists, continue the centuries-old function of Western self-definition. Said's subsequent book *Culture and Imperialism* (1993) is effectively a continuation of the themes raised in *Orientalism* in that it examines in a more focused manner the power relations between Occident and Orient hinted at in the earlier work. Said's uniqueness as a cultural critic lay in the range of his interests, which allowed him to explore the nexus of connections between literature, politics, and religion in a global rather than national or Eurocentric context.

Gayatri Chakravorty Spivak (b. 1942)

Born in Calcutta, India, Gayatri Spivak was educated at both Indian and American universities; one of her teachers at Cornell was Paul de Man. She is known for her translation of, and lengthy preface to, Derrida's *Of Grammatology*, and her central concern with the structures of colonialism, the postcolonial subject, and the possibility of postcolonial discourse draws on deconstructive practices, the feminist movement, Marxism, and Freud. In her influential and controversial essay "Can the Subaltern Speak?" (1983), later expanded in her book *Critique of Postcolonial Reason* (1999), she addresses precisely this issue of whether peoples in subordinate, colonized positions are able to achieve a voice. A "subaltern" refers to an officer in a subordinate position; the term was used by the Italian Marxist Antonio Gramsci to refer to the working masses that needed to be organized by left-wing intellectuals into a politically self-conscious force. The term as Spivak uses it also insinuates the "Subaltern Studies Group" in India, a radical group which attempted to articulate and give voice to the struggles of the oppressed peasants of the Indian subcontinent.

In broad terms, Spivak sees the project of colonialism as characterized by what Foucault had called "epistemic violence," the imposition of a given set of beliefs over another. Such violence, she says, marked the "remotely orchestrated, far-flung, and heterogeneous project to constitute the colonial subject as Other."[7] Spivak suggests that this epistemic violence, perpetrated in colonized nations, was a corollary of the epistemic overhaul in Europe at the end of the eighteenth century, of which Foucault speaks: she is both extending Foucault's own argument and situating it within a larger, global, context, suggesting that the narrative of political and economic development in Europe was part of a broader narrative that included imperialism and the definition of Europe in relation to the colonial other. Certain knowledges in both Europe and colonized countries were subjugated or "disqualified as inadequate" (*CPCR*, 267). Spivak gives as an example the British reformulations of the Hindu legal system. Spivak in fact cites a statement from the English historian and statesman Thomas Babington Macaulay's notorious "Minute on Indian Education" (1835), a statement which is worth requoting in full:

> We must at present do our best to form a class who may be interpreters between us and the millions whom we govern; a class of persons, Indian in blood and colour, but English in taste, in opinions, in morals, and in intellect. To that class we may leave it to refine the vernacular dialects of the country, to enrich those dialects with terms of science borrowed from the Western nomenclature, and to render them by degrees fit vehicles for conveying knowledge to the great mass of the population. (*CPCR*, 268)

These words are all the more chilling in the light of their continued application in the transformed imperialist economy of the modern world. Nothing has changed in strategy, merely the name of the new rulers. Spivak's point is the epistemic violence enshrined in the imperialist legal project was equally enshrined in the project of cultural imposition. Her underlying point is that such violence perpetuated – and was perhaps underlain by – the project of establishing "*one* explanation and narrative of reality . . . as the normative one" (*CPCR*, 267–268).

However, as Spivak has already said, this uniform project was in fact itself heterogeneous, as Foucault had pointed out concerning its operations in Europe. She also points out that "the colonized subaltern *subject* is irretrievably heterogenous" (*CPCR*, 270). Hence she rejects any possibility of an outright opposition between colonizer and colonized, oppressor and victim. Even radical intellectuals, she explains, who would speak on behalf of the oppressed, effectively romanticize and essentialize the other:

possibly, she says, "the intellectual is complicit in the persistent constitution of the Other as the Self's shadow" (*CPCR*, 266). The temptation is great simply to view the other as a projection or shadow of oneself: an example might be a Western feminist imposing her schema for liberation onto women in colonized areas, a procedure that might overlook the culturally specific character of both oppression and liberation. Such a binary opposition overlooks and perpetuates the complicity between radical discourses and the colonial discourses they seek to undermine. Spivak even sees the Subaltern Studies Group in India as tainted by an essentialist agenda in some ways, as, for example, in this group's endeavor to characterize "subaltern consciousness" (*CPCR*, 271–272). Spivak astutely remarks that, although many radical discourses, such as those of feminism, are opposed to essentialism and positivism, a "stringent binary opposition between positivism/essentialism . . . may be spurious" since it represses "the ambiguous complicity between essentialism and critiques of positivism." Her statement here is supported by the insight that the notion of essence pervades the work of Hegel, the modern inaugurator of "the work of the negative," and is recognized by Marx as persisting within the dialectic (*CPCR*, 282).

In this chapter, Spivak recounts a powerful story of a young woman in India, Bhubaneswari Bhaduri, who committed suicide in 1926 on account of her inability to perform a political assassination that had been assigned to her. Spivak notes that she timed this suicide to occur when she was menstruating so as to deter what would be the usual diagnosis of her act: that she had become pregnant. This suicide, says Spivak, was "an unemphatic, ad hoc, subaltern rewriting of the social text of *sati*-suicide." And yet, when Spivak herself questioned the girl's nieces about the incident, they "recalled" it as a "case of illicit love" (*CPCR*, 306–307). Spivak was so unnerved by this "failure of communication" that she emphatically stated (in her first version of this essay) that "the subaltern cannot speak." While she calls her own remark "inadvisable," she proceeds to point out how Bhubaneswari's own "emancipated" granddaughters actually continued the process of her silencing: one of them became a US immigrant and attained an executive position in a transnational company. Hence, "Bhubaneswari had fought for national liberation. Her great grandniece works for the New Empire. This too is a historical silencing of the subaltern" (*CPCR*, 311). Spivak's point is that the new empire, the new imperialism, had become global, and that complicity within its circuits and its operations is inevitable. While she recognizes that the speech of the subaltern girl was made to speak in her own (Spivak's) text, even radical intellectuals are complicit in the muting of subaltern voices (*CPCR*, 309–310).

Yet Spivak's stance is not entirely negative. To some extent, we must undertake an "unlearning" project, acknowledging our participation, even complicity, in the objects of our own investigation and impugnment (*CPCR*, 284). Elsewhere, Spivak talks usefully of a "strategic" essentialism whereby we can use essentialist language in a self-conscious way for practical, political purposes. In this essay she makes a number of suggestions that might prevent one's own position being indeterminate and merely a negative critique. She suggests that intellectuals recognize the importance of the economic sphere but without investing it with any kind of absolute or ultimate explanatory power (*CPCR*, 267). She adds that participation in the political process – access to citizenship, becoming a voter – will help to mobilize the subaltern on "the long road to hegemony" (*CPCR*, 310).

Homi K. Bhabha (b. 1949)

Like Gayatri Spivak, Homi Bhabha extends certain tenets of poststructuralism into discourses about colonialism, nationality, and culture. These tenets include a challenging of the notion of fixed identity, the undermining of binary oppositions, and an emphasis on language and discourse – together with the power relations in which these are imbricated – as underlying our understanding of cultural phenomena. But, as in the case of Spivak, this "extension" is not a simple extrapolation of poststructuralist principles in their purity to colonial subject matter; the process of extension itself is used to display the limits of these principles and the altered nature of their applicability. Bhabha takes some of the foregoing ideas from Derrida; from Mikhail Bakhtin he draws the notion of the "dialogic" (indicating the mutuality of a relationship) in order to characterize the connection between colonizer and colonized; he draws also on Frantz Fanon's revolutionary work on colonialism, as well as on the concept of "nation" as defined in Benedict Anderson's book *Imagined Communities* (1983).

The notion of "hybridity" is central to Bhabha's work in challenging notions of identity, culture, and nation as coherent and unified entities that exhibit a linear historical development. Hybridity expresses a state of "in betweenness," as in a person who stands between two cultures. The concept is embodied in Bhabha's own life (as in the lives of many intellectuals from colonial nations who have been raised in Western institutions): born into a Pharsi community in Bombay, India, he was educated both in his native country and at Oxford University; he subsequently taught at universities in England and America, and now teaches at Harvard.

In his important essay "The Commitment to Theory" (1989), Bhabha attempts to respond to recent charges that literary and cultural theory (including deconstruction, Lacanianism, and the various tendencies of poststructuralism) suffers from at least two crippling defects: it is inscribed within, and complicit with, a Eurocentric and imperialist discourse; and, as such, it is insulated from the real concerns, the "historical exigencies and tragedies" of third world peoples.[8] Bhabha sees this "binarism of theory vs. politics" as reproducing, in mirror image, the "ahistorical nineteenth century polarity of Orient and Occident which, in the name of progress, unleashed the exclusionary imperialist ideologies of self and other." It is a "mirror image" because, in the modern situation, it is depoliticized Western theory itself (rather than the Orient) which is the "Other." Bhabha questions this binarism: "must we always polarize in order to polemicize?" Must we, he asks, simply invert the relation of oppressor and oppressed (*LC*, 19)?

Bhabha himself is in no doubt about the continued aspirations of imperialism, as it presses into a "neo-imperialist" phase: "there is a sharp growth in a new Anglo-American nationalism which increasingly articulates its economic and military power in political acts that express a neo-imperialist disregard for the independence and autonomy of peoples and places in the Third World." Bhabha cites, as recent examples, Britain's war against Argentina over the Falklands in 1982 and the first Gulf War of 1991. Such economic and political domination, he adds, "has a profound hegemonic influence on the information orders of the Western world, its popular media and its specialized institutions and academics" (*LC*, 20). There is a tacit admission here that Western academic institutions will fall to some extent under the sway of the Western ideology of political dominance. Nonetheless, he raises the question as it concerns the "new" languages of theoretical critique in the West: "Are the interests of 'Western' theory necessarily collusive with the hegemonic role of the West as a power bloc? Is the language of theory merely another power ploy of the culturally privileged Western elite to produce a discourse of the Other that reinforces its own power–knowledge equation?" (*LC*, 20–21).

Bhabha reposes these questions within the specific perspective of postcolonial discourse: he asks what the function of "a committed theoretical perspective might be, once the cultural and historical hybridity of the postcolonial world is taken as the paradigmatic place of departure" (*LC*, 21). In addressing this, Bhabha begins by rejecting the opposition between "theory" and "activism" since, he argues, they are both "forms of discourse" which "produce rather than reflect their objects of reference" (*LC*, 21). In other words, as Bhabha explains using insights from the British cultural critic Stuart Hall, political positions cannot be charted out in advance as true or false, progressive or reactionary, bourgeois or radical, prior to the specific conditions in which they emerge. In this sense, they are marked by the hybridity and ambivalence of "the process of emergence itself" (*LC*, 22). This is a way of acknowledging "the force of writing, its metaphoricity and its rhetorical discourse, as a productive matrix which defines the 'social' and makes it available as an objective of and for, action" (*LC*, 23). Bhabha is here using "writing" in a Derridean sense, signifying the intrinsically metaphorical nature of language and discourse, their inability to make statements which are absolutely clear and unequivocal since they are constituted by a vast network of signifiers in which any given position is structured by what is outside of it, this externality infecting with its diversity and ambivalence any presumed internal coherence of the position itself. Bhabha cites J. S. Mill's essay "On Liberty," which describes knowledge and a given political stance as arising only through continual self-questioning and confronting at each stage of its articulation other stances that are opposed to it. As Bhabha interprets it, Mill sees "the political as a form of debate and dialogue"; the political is dialogic not by abstractly acknowledging other perspectives and then circumventing them but by recognizing that its *own* perspective, recognizing its own limitations in their light, is at every point riven by ambivalence. It is this discursive ambivalence in the subject of enunciation itself that marks the truly public and political (*LC*, 24). This type of political "negotiation," says Bhabha, "goes beyond the unsettling of the essentialism or logocentrism of a received political tradition, in the name of an abstract free play of the signifier" (*LC*, 25).

Hence, the language of political critique is effective not because it maintains rigid oppositions between terms such as master and slave but because it "overcomes the given grounds of opposition and opens up a space of translation: a place of hybridity" which engages in the construction of a *new* (rather than preconceived) political object and endeavor. Such a language will be dialectical without recourse to "a teleological or transcendent History . . . the event of theory becomes the *negotiation* of contradictory and antagonistic instances that open up hybrid sites and objectives of struggle, and destroy those negative polarities between knowledge and its objects, and between theory and practical-political reason." Bhabha notes that there can be "no simplistic, essentialist opposition between ideological miscognition and revolutionary truth." Between these is a "historical and discursive *différance*" (*LC*, 25). Hence our political priorities and referents – such as the people, class struggle, gender difference – "are not there in some primordial, naturalistic sense. Nor do they reflect a unitary or homogeneous political object" (LC, 26). All of this makes us recognize, claims Bhabha, that the "question of commitment" is "complex and difficult." This should not lead, however, to quietism or inertia, but to a demand that "questions of organization are theorized and socialist theory is 'organized'" (LC, 26).

As an example of this refusal of outright opposition, Bhabha cites the miners' strike in Thatcher's Britain of 1984–1985. Originally this conflict might have been seen in the received terminology of a class struggle. But when miners' wives were interviewed, they began to question their roles within the community and family, and challenged elements of the very culture they were ostensibly defending. This circumstance, says Bhabha, displays the "importance of the hybrid moment of political change," whereby there was a rearticulation of the terms of the struggle that was "*neither the One* (unitary working class) *nor the Other* (the politics of gender) *but something else besides,* which contests the terms and territories of both. There is a negotiation between gender and class." Bhabha sees in Stuart Hall's suggestion that "the British Labour Party should seek to produce a socialist alliance among progressive forces that are widely dispersed and distributed across a range of class, culture and occupational forces" as an acknowledgment of the "historical necessity" of his own notion of "hybridity" (LC, 28).

Returning to his original question of whether critical theory is "Western," Bhabha sees this as "a designation of institutional power and ideological Eurocentricity." He acknowledges that much European theory, having "opened up the chasm of cultural difference," uses the metaphor of Otherness to "contain the effects of difference . . . the Other text is forever the exegetical horizon of difference, never the active agent of articulation." Being analyzed and showcased, "the Other loses its power to signify, to negate . . . to establish its own institutional and oppositional discourse." In these ways, critical theory has reproduced "a relation of domination" (LC, 31). But Bhabha chooses to distinguish between the institutional history of critical theory and "its conceptual potential for change and innovation." He cites Althusser, Lacan, and Foucault as opening up other possibilities of understanding history, the relations of production, and the ambivalent structure of subjectivity (LC, 31–32). Many poststructuralist ideas, he notes, are "themselves opposed to Enlightenment humanism and aesthetics. They constitute no less than a deconstruction of the moment of the modern" (LC, 32).

According to Bhabha, such a revision of the history of critical theory is informed by a notion of "cultural difference" (rather than cultural "diversity," which embodies a received and static recognition), which foregrounds the ambivalence of even Western cultural authority in its own moment of enunciation or articulation. This notion of difference "problematizes the binary division of past and present, tradition and modernity" (LC, 35). It harbors the recognition that cultures "are never unitary in themselves, nor simply dualistic in the relation of Self to Other. It embodies an acknowledgment that the "act of cultural enunciation . . . is crossed by the *différance* of writing." The pact of interpretation, says Bhabha, is never just an act of communication between two interlocutors; these two "places" must pass through a "Third Space, which represents both the general conditions of language and the specific implication of the utterance" (LC, 36). This Third Space, "though unrepresentable in itself," makes meaning and reference "an ambivalent process," which challenges "our sense of the historical identity of culture as a homogenizing, unifying force, authenticated by the originary Past, kept alive in the national tradition of the People." We must recognize, then, the "hybridity" of all cultural statements. Fanon recognized, says Bhabha, that those who initiate revolutionary change "are themselves the bearers of a hybrid identity" (*LC*, 38). By way of example, Bhabha cites the Algerian struggle for independence, which "in the moment of liberatory struggle" destroyed many elements of the very nationalist tradition that had opposed colonial cultural imposition.

In closing, Bhabha claims that theoretical recognition of "the split-space of enunciation" may open the way to thinking of "*inter*national culture, based . . . on the inscription and articulation of culture's *hybridity*." It is the "*in-between* space . . . that carries the burden of meaning of culture . . . And by exploring this Third Space, we may elude the politics of polarity and emerge as the others of our selves" (*LC*, 38–39). Bhabha curiously understands the notion of différance as the embodiment of ambivalence rather than of endless relationality. In asserting the need to recognize the ambivalence of enunciation, he effectively perpetuates the very binarism he seeks to avoid.

One of the problems with Bhabha's argument is that it is uncritically founded on Derrida's notion of différance, which is itself abstract. Bhabha even admits that his own "Third Space" is "unrepresentable in itself," denying any possibility of its articulation and allowing it to wallow in transcendence. The central valuable insight in Bhabha's essay is that political endeavors cannot be fully theorized in advance because they must always be adapted to local conditions and possibilities. But this insight is somewhat marred by its coercion into more generalized and somewhat vague assertions about the way language functions. The notion of hybridity bears within itself the origins of whatever polarization it was intended to transcend; as such, it is inadequate for comprehending the diverse constitution of political commitment, which is often not marked by a mere blending of two factors such as class and gender. Finally, Bhabha sets up many straw targets: who *does* claim that "culture" or "subjectivity" or "truth" is somehow an unproblematic unity? The so-called opposition between ideological error and truth that Bhabha's notions of ambivalence and hybridity are intended to overcome has already been abrogated – in a dialectic deriving from Hegel – in the long tradition of Marxist thought, which has seen truth as institutionally grounded and as itself the formalized projection of various ideologies.

Henry Louis Gates, Jr. (b. 1950)

The most prominent contemporary scholar of African-American literature, Henry Louis Gates, Jr. has sought to map out an African-American heritage of both literature and criticism, as well as to promote and establish this heritage in academic institutions, the popular press, and the media. Central to this project has been his endeavor to integrate approaches from modern literary theory, such as deconstructive and structuralist notions of signification, with modes of interpretation derived from African literary traditions. Born in West Virginia, Gates was educated at the universities of Yale and Cambridge; he has taught at Yale, Cornell, Duke, and Harvard, where he is Chair of African-American Studies and directs the W. E. B. Du Bois Institute for African-American Research. He has edited a number of pioneering anthologies such as *Black Literature and Literary Theory* (1984), *"Race," Writing, and Difference* (1986), and *The Norton Anthology of African American Literature* (1997), as well as helping to found African-American journals. The important works authored by Gates include *Figures in Black: Words, Signs, and the "Racial" Self* (1987) and *The Signifying Monkey: A Theory of African-American Literary Criticism* (1988). One of his goals in these texts is to redefine the notions of race and blackness in the terms of poststructuralist theory, as effects of networks of signification and cultural difference rather than as essences. Gates has been criticized for the integrative and assimilative nature of his work: radicals have seen him as overtly compromising toward the white, elitist, mainstream Anglo-American and European traditions. Yet his work has influenced, and displays analogies with, the output of critics such as Houston A. Baker, Jr. and Wahneema Lubiano.

In essays such as "Writing, 'Race,' and the Difference it Makes" (1985), he conducts an acute analysis of the concept of race, and draws attention to the explicit or implicit assumptions about race that inform the Western literary and philosophical traditions. Gates acknowledges that in twentieth-century literature and theory, race has been an "invisible quality," at best only implicitly present. But this, he explains, was not always the case. By the mid-nineteenth century, metaphors such as "national spirit" and "historical period" were widely used in the study and creation of literature. It was the French literary historian Hippolyte Taine who posited "race, moment, and *milieu*" as the foundational criteria for analyzing of any work of art. This notion, says Gates, was the "great foundation" upon which subsequent notions of "national literatures" were erected.[9] In race Taine had located the peculiar character of the "intellect and . . . heart," and race was "the first and richest source of these master faculties from which historical events take their rise" (*LCNCW*, 46). Gates acknowledges that Taine's originality lay not in expressing such ideas about race – which were derived "from the Enlightenment, if not from the Renaissance" – but in their "scientific" application to literary history. The growth of "national" literatures, says Gates, "was coterminous with the shared assumption among intellectuals that 'race' was a 'thing,' an ineffaceable quantity, which irresistibly determined the shape and contour of thought and feeling" (*LCNCW*, 46–47). Moreover, discourses about race often have their sources in the "dubious pseudo-science" of the eighteenth and nineteenth centuries. Race in these usages "pretends to be an objective term of classification, when it is in fact a trope." Though it is a fiction, it has been accorded the "sanction of God, biology, or the natural order." Indeed, race has become "a trope of ultimate, irreducible difference between cultures, linguistic groups, or practitioners of specific belief systems . . . Race is the ultimate trope of difference because it is so very arbitrary in its application" (*LCNCW*, 48–49). Writers in many European traditions have sought to make the metaphors of race "literal" by making them "natural, absolute, essential . . . they have *inscribed* these differences as fixed and finite categories . . . But it takes little reflection to recognize that these pseudoscientific categories are themselves figures of thought. Who has seen a black or red person, a white, yellow, or brown? These terms are arbitrary constructs, not reports of reality" (*LCNCW*, 50).

The metaphors of race lay at the heart of a widespread European debate, since the Renaissance and through the Enlightenment, over "the nature of the African." This debate prompts Gates into an "alternative" reading of Enlightenment philosophy, one

754

which reveals its "nether side" (*LCNCW*, 57). He notes that after Descartes, "reason" was privileged among human characteristics; and writing, especially after the advent and proliferation of the printing press, was taken as the "visible sign of reason." The Enlightenment, says Gates,

> used the absence and presence of "reason" to delimit and circumscribe the very humanity of the cultures and people of color which Europeans had been "discovering" since the Renaissance. The urge toward the systematization of all human knowledge, by which we characterize the Enlightenment, led directly to the relegation of black people to a lower rung on the Great Chain of Being. (*LCNCW*, 54–55)

Gates traces this "extraordinary *subdiscourse*" of European philosophy and aesthetics through a number of major writers. The "subdiscourse" consisted largely in the privileging of writing, the visible sign of reason, as the "principal measure" of the humanity of blacks and of their capacity for progress (*LCNCW*, 56). Sir Francis Bacon, in his *The New Organon* (1620), turned to the arts as the "ultimate measure of a race's place in nature." Bacon averred that the difference between the life of civilized and savage races sprang "not from soil, not from climate, not from race, but from the arts" (*LCNCW*, 57–58). A few years later, Peter Heylyn published his *Little Description of the Great World*, affirming that Black Africans "lacked completely" the use of reason, and were possessed of "little Wit" (*LCNCW*, 58). Literacy – the *mastery* of reading and writing – was directly correlated with political rights, and writing was transformed into a commodity: learning to read and write was reserved for the master and was a violation of the law for a slave. There was a "direct relation between freedom and discourse" (*LCNCW*, 58–59). By 1705, says Gates, the Dutch explorer William Bosman had "encased Peter Heylyn's bias into a myth," the myth that, given a choice by God, blacks had chosen gold whereas whites had chosen the alternative, the knowledge of letters. As punishment for their avarice, God decreed that blacks should always be slaves to whites. It was David Hume, Gates suggests, who "gave to Bosman's myth the sanction of Enlightenment philosophical reasoning" (*LCNCW*, 59). In his essay "Of National Characteristics" (1748), Hume had stated that the negroes were "naturally inferior to the whites," and that one index of this difference of "nature" was that negroes had "*no arts, no sciences*" (*LCNCW*, 60).

Predictably, says Gates, Hume's opinion became "prescriptive." In an essay of 1764 entitled "Observations on the Feelings of the Beautiful and the Sublime," Kant had extrapolated Hume's comments into an affirmation of a fundamental difference of "mental capacities" between the black and white races, squarely correlating "blackness" and "stupidity." Kant based his "observations" on the absence of published writing among blacks (*LCNCW*, 60–61). Thomas Jefferson's opinion was hardly more salutary: "Never yet could I find that a black had uttered a thought above the level of plain narration." He vehemently denied that the blacks were capable of poetry (*LCNCW*, 61). Gates also recounts – all too briefly – Hegel's strictures concerning the lack of history and of writing among black people. Gates points out that Hegel was echoing Hume and Kant, and that all of these writers shared the assumption about the "absence of memory," a collective, cultural memory. Gates adroitly summarizes the connections made or implied by these thinkers between reason, writing, history, and humanity:

"Without writing, there could exist no *repeatable* sign of the workings of reason, of mind. Without memory or mind, there could exist no history. Without history, there could exist no 'humanity,' as defined consistently from Vico to Hegel" (*LCNCW*, 62).

Gates observes a change in the visibility of the concept of race in twentieth-century literature and theory, a movement away from Taine's "race, moment, and *milieu*" toward the New Critical focus on the "language of the text." Like other allegedly "extrinsic" features, race was bracketed or suspended. Yet it remained implicit in ideas of "canonical *cultural* texts that comprise the Western tradition in Eliot's simultaneous order." The Anglo-American, Gates notes, "was the castle in which Taine's criteria took refuge . . . a canon of texts whose authors purportedly shared a 'common culture' inherited from *both* the Greco-Roman and the Judeo-Christian traditions" (*LCNCW*, 47). Hence even this reductive formalism, which purported to exclude material not readable in the text "itself," was premised upon a canon, a "republic of literature," whose citizens "were all white, and mostly male." Gates detects a racism in the works of Southern Agrarians/New Critics such as I. A. Richards and Allen Tate (*LCNCW*, 47–48).

Gates suggests that Anglo-African writing "arose as a response to allegations of its absence" (from the Renaissance onward). The need to record an authentic black voice as proof of the blacks' humanity was so "central . . . to the birth of the black literary tradition" that the earliest slave narratives drew upon the same tropes correlating blackness with silence, such as the trope of the "talking book" (whereby a book is seen as "talking" only to whites, and as being urged to speak to blacks). Such narratives, suggests Gates, formed the "very first black chain of signifiers," which implicitly signified upon another chain, the "metaphorical Great Chain of Being . . . these writers implicitly were Signifyin(g) upon the figure of the chain itself, simply by publishing autobiographies that were indictments of the received order of Western culture" (*LCNCW*, 64). Gates questions, "how can the black subject posit a full and sufficient self in a language in which blackness is a sign of absence? Can writing, the very 'difference' it makes and marks, mask the blackness of the black face that addresses the text of Western letters, in a voice that 'speaks English'?" (*LCNCW*, 65). Similar questions confront the use of theory by black critics, a topic addressed only summarily in this essay. Gates states that it is imperative to "'deconstruct' . . . the ideas of difference inscribed in the trope of race, to take discourse itself as our common subject . . . to reveal the latent relations of power and knowledge inherent in popular and academic usages of 'race'" (*LCNCW*, 50). He urges that "to use contemporary theories of criticism to explicate these modes of inscription [of racial difference] is to demystify large and obscure ideological relations and indeed theory itself" (*LCNCW*, 51).

In the Introduction to his *Figures in Black*, which is perhaps the most succinct statement of his overall endeavor as a black critic, Gates offers a more detailed account of his own engagement with contemporary European and American literary theories and his use of these in analyzing black literary traditions, situating his endeavor within the broader historical development of African-American literary criticism. Gates openly declares, adopting a term from Lévi-Strauss and Derrida, that he practices "a sort of critical bricolage," a making do with the materials already at hand, materials which may have been constructed originally for other purposes, rather than somehow starting anew. Yet this very necessity (for it is of course impossible to start anew) poses a problem for Gates: can black critics "escape a mockingbird relation to theory, one

756

destined to be derivative," and mechanically imitative?[10] His point here is that a core of racism runs through much of the Western intellectual tradition. Can black critics "escape the supposed racism of so many theorists of criticism, from David Hume and Immanuel Kant through the Southern Agrarians [later known as the New Critics] . . . Aren't we justified in being suspicious of a discourse in which blacks are signs of absence?" (*FB*, xviii). The dilemma is somewhat analogous to that formulated by many feminists and other oppressed groups: can the oppressed escape speaking the language of the oppressor, thereby perpetuating the basic concepts and the broad world view contained in that language? In Derridean terms, can the language of marginal groups even be spoken without drawing on the syntax and vocabulary of the centers of domination and power? Gates uses Derridean terminology in explaining that some black critics (like many feminist critics) resist the very notion of theory, in "healthy reactions against the marriage of logocentrism and ethnocentrism in much of Western aesthetic discourse" (*FB*, xix). Gates notes, however, that in the eyes of other black critics, "the racism of the Western critical tradition was not a sufficient reason for us to fail to theorize about our own endeavor." He also observes a renewed interest in theory inspired by a recognition that close textual reading has been "repressed" in African-American literary criticism; hence much theory is driven by a need to address "the very language of the black text" (*FB*, xix).

Gates characterizes his own use of theory as a practice of transformation rather than mere application: "I have tried to work through contemporary theories of literature not to apply them to black texts, but to transform these by translating them into a new rhetorical realm" (*FB*, xx). One assumes that the antecedent of "these" is left deliberately ambiguous: what will be "transformed," then, are both the theories and the texts. Only by such critical activity, thinks Gates, can the "profession" – which, presumably, is the profession of black criticism – "redefine itself away from a Eurocentric notion of a hierarchical canon of texts – mostly white, Western, and male – and encourage and sustain a truly comparative and pluralistic notion of the institution of literature" (*FB*, xx). Gates emphasizes that using theory to analyze the language of a black text is an endeavor to "respect the integrity, the tradition, of the black work of art," and to "produce richer structures of meaning than are possible otherwise" (*FB*, xx–xxi). Summarizing this general endeavor, Gates suggests that this "is the challenge of the critic of Afro-American literature: not to shy away from literary theory, but rather to translate it into the black idiom, renaming principles of criticism where appropriate, but especially naming indigenous black principles of criticism and applying these to explicate our own texts" (*FB*, xxi).

Gates recounts that he has drawn upon variants of formalism, structuralism, and poststructuralism in order to "defamiliarize the black text" (*FB*, xxii, xxiv). He wished to see the text as "a structure of literature" rather than as a simple reflection of black experience (*FB*, xxiv). Gates suggests that the connection between the development of African-American criticism and contemporary literary theory can be charted in four stages, corresponding broadly to his own development: the first was the phase of the "Black Aesthetic"; the second was a phase of "Repetition and Imitation"; the third, "Repetition and Difference"; and, finally, "Synthesis" (*FB*, xxv).

The Black Aesthetic theorists of the first stage attempted both to resurrect "lost" black texts and to formulate a "genuinely black" aesthetic, and were persistently concerned with the "nature and function of black literature vis-à-vis the larger political struggle for Black Power" (*FB*, xxvi). Gates identifies his own radical innovation as lying in the emphasis he accorded to the "language of the text," a hitherto repressed concern in African-American criticism. His engagement with formalism and structuralism led to the second phase of his development, that of "Repetition and Imitation." Realizing that a more critical approach to theory was called for, Gates' work moved into the stage of "Repetition and Difference," using theory to read black texts but thereby also implicitly offering a critique of the theory itself. The final stage of Gates' work, that of "Synthesis," involved a "sustained interest in the black vernacular tradition as a source field in which to ground a theory of Afro-American criticism, a theory at once self-contained and related by analogy to other contemporary theories" (*FB*, xxix).

Gates urges that an analysis of the connection between a black text and its "critical field" constitutes implicitly "a theory of the origins and nature of Afro-American literature" (*FB*, xxxi). This theory, argued in the current book and elsewhere, is basically that, since its origins in the seventeenth century at least through the New Negro Renaissance of the 1920s, black literature has been produced in defiant response to, and counter-exemplification of, assertions that the dearth of a black literary tradition signifies the black's "innate mental inequality with the European" (*FB*, xxxi). Charged with such lack of intellectual capacity and correlative lack of humanity, black authors have literally attempted to write themselves into existence, to achieve an identity through the narratives of their own lives, an identity that subsists primarily in language: the very language in which they had been designated as absences was itself appropriated as the sign of presence.

Yet it could be argued that such gestures – effectively creating a literary tradition in response to allegations of its absence – implicitly accept the racist terms and operate within the racist outlook that is ostensibly in question. Such unwitting complicity, as Gates has already intimated, leads to a "dead end." In an essay of 1988 entitled "Talking Black: Critical Signs of the Times," Gates recounts the intellectual journey of the nineteenth-century pan-Africanist Alexander Crummell. Falling prey to the "tragic lure of white power," Crummell "never stopped believing that mastering the master's tongue was the sole path to civilization, intellectual freedom, and social equality for the black person" (*LCNCW*, 73). Nonetheless, while Gates cautions against Crummell's "mistake of accepting the empowering language of white critical theory as 'universal,'" he is equally insistent that "We [black critics] must redefine theory itself from within our own black cultures, refusing to grant the racist premise that theory is something that white people do ... We are all heirs to critical theory, but critics are also heir to the black vernacular critical tradition as well" (*LCNCW*, 83). Black critics must, says Gates, "turn to our own peculiarly black structures of thought and feeling to develop our own languages of criticism," using the black "vernacular to ground our theories." Those critics must "don the empowering mask of blackness and talk *that* talk, the language of black difference"; only by doing this can they escape the possibility that using theory might be "merely another form of intellectual indenture, a mental servitude" (*LCNCW*, 77).

While Gates addresses in these texts the genuinely problematic issue of what kind of language is available to black critics, it could be argued that the terms of his inquiry tend somewhat to perpetuate the subordination of black criticism to the languages of modern critical theory. For example, to talk of "the language of black difference" is merely to transpose into black studies a hypostatization of the very concept of difference: why ground an "alternative" language on a trope that is often abstract even on its native soil? Gates speaks of "theory" as if somehow engagement with "it" will automatically replenish black studies. Yet modern theories do not all speak the same language, and indeed often conflict profoundly with one another's claims and insights. The lately privileged concept of "difference" is merely one of the latest reifications propagated by the aesthetics of late capitalism; as used by many modern theorists, it is torn from its history in philosophy and the history of its connection with the notion of identity. Why accept these categories – dating all the way back to Aristotle (himself an owner of slaves and theorist of slavery) – as overseeing the project of black criticism? Why even refer to them as a starting point? It may be that there is no choice but to use the "master's" language for one's own ends, but surely our starting point could be more substantial than the contentless and clichéd abstraction of pure "difference." Surely the use of this effectively rehearses – at the level of theoretical reflection – Crummell's strategy in the face of the grand Enlightenment claims concerning blacks, that of accepting the master's tropes and the master's critical idiom. In fairness to Gates, he valuably articulates the problems surrounding any black critical use of so-called "theory." And his own project is indeed informed by recourse to native African idioms and traditions.

Notes

1 Several points in this account are taken from the excellent chapter "Colonialism and the Politics of Postcolonial Critique," in Robert Young's *Postcolonialism: An Historical Introduction* (Oxford: Blackwell, 2001). Hereafter cited as Young.

2 Bill Ashcroft, Gareth Griffiths, and Helen Tiffin, *The Empire Writes Back: Theory and Practice in Post-Colonial Literatures* (New York and London: Routledge, 1989), p. 2. Hereafter cited as EWB.

3 Frantz Fanon, *The Wretched of the Earth*, trans. Constance Farrington (New York: Grove Press, 1963), pp. 148–149. Hereafter cited as WE.

4 Edward Said, *Beginnings: Intention and Method* (New York: Columbia University Press, 1985), pp. xii, 373. Hereafter cited as *Beginnings*.

5 Edward Said, *The World, the Text, and the Critic* (Cambridge, MA: Harvard University Press, 1983). Hereafter cited as WTC.

6 Edward Said, *Orientalism* (New York: Vintage, 1978). Hereafter cited as *Orientalism*.

7 Gayatri Chakravorty Spivak, *A Critique of Postcolonial Reason* (Cambridge, MA and London: Harvard University Press, 1999), p. 266. Hereafter cited as CPCR.

8 Homi K. Bhabha, *The Location of Culture* (New York and London: Routledge, 1994), p. 19. Hereafter cited as LC.

9 "Writing, 'Race,' and the Difference it Makes," in Henry Louis Gates, Jr., *Loose Canons: Notes on the Culture Wars* (New York and Oxford: Oxford University Press, 1992), p. 45. Hereafter cited as LCNCW.

10 Henry Louis Gates, Jr., *Figures in Black: Words, Signs, and the "Racial" Self* (New York and Oxford: Oxford University Press, 1987), p. xviii. Hereafter cited as FB.

CHAPTER 29

NEW HISTORICISM

Historicism began toward the end of the eighteenth century with German writers such as Herder, and continued through the nineteenth-century historians Von Ranke and Meinecke to twentieth-century thinkers such as Wilhelm Dilthey, R. G. Collingwood, Hans Georg Gadamer, Ernst Cassirer, and Karl Mannheim. Powerful historical modes of analysis were formulated by Hegel and Marx, who themselves had a profound impact on historicist thinking; and literary historians such as Sainte-Beuve and Hippolyte Taine also insisted on viewing literary texts as integrally informed by their historical milieux. Much of what passes under the rubric of the "New" Historicism is not radically new, but represents a return to certain foci of analysis as developed by previous traditions of historicism.

Historicism has been characterized by a number of concerns and features. Most fundamentally, there is an insistence that all systems of thought, all phenomena, all institutions, all works of art, and all literary texts must be situated within a historical perspective. In other words, texts or phenomena cannot be somehow torn from history and analyzed in isolation, outside of the historical process. They are determined in both their form and content by their specific historical circumstances, their specific situation in time and place. Hence, we cannot bring to our analyses of Shakespeare the same assumptions and methods that we bring to Plato; the fact that they belong to different historical periods and different social, political, and economic circumstances will profoundly shape their notions of truth, of art and polity, and hence whatever meanings we might attribute to their texts. In other words, literature must be read within the broader context of its culture, in the context of other discourses ranging over politics, religion, and aesthetics, as well as its economic context.

A second feature of historicism is that the history of a given phenomenon is sometimes held to operate according to certain identifiable laws, yielding a certain predictability and explanatory power; this feature is pronounced in the writings of Hegel and Marx. A third concern arises from the recognition that societies and cultures separated in time have differing values and beliefs: how can the historian "know" the past? The historian operates within the horizon of her own world view, a certain broad set of assumptions and beliefs; how can she overcome these to achieve an empathetic understanding of a distant culture? How, for example, can students fed on the epistemological fat of a New Critical diet begin to appreciate the world of the Homeric epics, the language of which we are not even sure how to pronounce, and the actions of whose characters are, by our moral standards, often bizarre? How can we avoid imposing our own cultural prejudices, not to mention our own interests and motives, on texts historically removed from us?

Thinkers such as Dilthey, Gadamer, and E. D. Hirsch have offered various answers to this dilemma. Hirsch's position aspires to be "objectivist," effectively denying the historical and context-bound nature of knowledge and proposing a distinction between "meaning," which embraces what the author meant or intended by his particular use of language, and "significance," which comprehends the subjective evaluation of the text according to the values and beliefs of the critic. Gadamer proposed a notion of "horizonfusion" whereby we both acknowledge that what we call the "text" is in fact a product of a tradition of interpretation (with no "original" meaning) and that our own perspective is informed by the very past we are seeking to analyze. Recognizing both of these limitations, we can begin to effect an empathetic fusion of our own cultural horizon with that of the text.

Hence, the dilemma of historical interpretation can easily lead to a kind of aesthetic formalism on the one hand, which denies history any constitutive role in the formation of texts, and, on the other hand, to a historical view of texts as culturally and socially determined, a view that reduces emphasis on authorial intention and agency. The fundamental principles of historicism, then, are opposed to those of many twentieth-century movements such as Russian Formalism and New Criticism. In general, structuralism also has been ahistorical, focusing on synchronic analyses of language and literature. Yet structuralism differs from rigid formalism in that it does not isolate the literary text but situates it within the broader codes, sign systems, and registers of other discourses. In this sense, its endeavors are compatible with those of historicism. Also, certain adaptations of structuralism, as for example in the work of Mikhail Bakhtin, have a strongly historical dimension in which language itself is seen as an ideological phenomenon. Elements of historicism also inform hermeneutics and reader-response theory, which is obliged to take into account the different meanings that a text might have for readers of various historical periods. Indeed, the influence of Schleiermacher, usually viewed as the founder of hermeneutics, has extended not only to historicists such as Dilthey and Gadamer but also to reception theorists such as Hans Robert Jauss.

The "New" Historicism which arose in the 1980s reacted against both the formalist view of the literary text as somehow autonomous and Marxist views which ultimately related texts to the economic infrastructure. It saw the literary text not as somehow unique but as a kind of discourse situated within a complex of cultural discourses – religious, political, economic, aesthetic – which both shaped it and, in their turn, were shaped by it. If there was anything new about this procedure, it was its insistence, drawn from Foucault and poststructuralism, that "history" itself is a text, an interpretation, and that there is no single history. It also rejected any notion of historical progress or teleology, and broke away from any literary historiography based on the study of genres and figures. In the same way, the "culture" in which New Historicism situated literary texts was itself regarded as a textual construct. Hence, New Historicism refused to accord any kind of unity or homogeneity to history or culture, viewing both as harboring networks of contradictory, competing, and unreconciled forces and interests.

Perhaps the most general direction in which Foucault influenced the New Historicism was that his contextualizations were "superstructural" (rather than referring literary and cultural phenomena to an economic base): even the realm of economics, like history itself, was seen as a discourse, as textual. Indeed, the language of economics gave way before Foucault's terminology of power, viewed as operating in diffuse and heterogeneous ways without clear appurtenance to any given agency. The New Historicists tended, then, to view literature as one discourse among many cultural discourses, insisting on engaging with this entire complex in a localized manner, refusing to engage in categorical generalizations or to commit to any definite political stance. Indeed, New Historicists have been criticized for a political quietism that accompanies their alleged principled indefiniteness, as well as for accepting uncritically Foucault's somewhat disembodied and abstract notion of power which floats free of political and economic agency. They are also accused of arbitrariness in the ways in which they relate literary texts to other cultural discourses. Notwithstanding such reservations, New Historicism – perhaps precisely because it appears to open the possibility of accommodating social context from a non-committed perspective – has enjoyed considerable influence since the 1980s and has arguably contributed to a more pervasive concern among formerly liberal-humanist and New Critical academics with the larger cultural patterns and forces within which literature operates. Having said all of this, it should be noted that many New Historicists and cultural materialists have been profoundly concerned not only with situating literary texts within power structures, but also with seeing them as crucially participating in conflicts of power between various forms of social and political authority.

The "New" Historicism dates back to Stephen Greenblatt's use of the term in 1982 in an introduction to an issue of the journal *Genre* devoted to the Renaissance. His statements concerning the new movement will be considered below. In general, both Greenblatt and subsequent critics identified with New Historicism rejected the notion that it was a theory or a specific doctrine. Rather, they identified some persistent concerns and approaches, some of which have been indicated above, such as the rejection of the formalist notion of aesthetic autonomy and the situating of literature within a broader cultural network. Louis Montrose stressed that this contextualization of literature involved a reexamination of an author's position within a linguistic system. Montrose also points out that New Historicists variously recognize the ability of literature to challenge social and political authority.

It is significant that this subversive potential of literature has been brought out by many New Historicist critics – who in Britain have identified themselves in Raymond Williams' terminology as "cultural materialists" – in relation to Renaissance thought and literature. Greenblatt's own work has focused on this period, and critics such as Jonathan Dollimore have produced groundbreaking studies such as *Radical Tragedy* (1984), which have reassessed the work of Shakespeare and his contemporaries, rejecting critical orthodoxies such as art ordering the chaos of reality, essentialist and providentialist readings of texts, the Bradleyan notion of tragedy as Hegelian reconciliation, the criterion of coherence whereby discontinuity is viewed as artistic failure, and recognizing the increasingly historical and ideological functions of drama.[1] The book

Political Shakespeare, edited by Jonathan Dollimore and Alan Sinfield, also challenged the liberal-humanist notion of Shakespeare as a timeless and universal genius. Instead, the political dimension of Shakespeare's work is emphasized, embracing a broad range of issues such as the subversion of authority, sexuality, and colonialism, as well as modern receptions and appropriations of Shakespeare in education, film, and theater.[2] Another powerful reinterpretation was formulated in *Alternative Shakespeares* (1985), in which a range of writers, including Catherine Belsey, Terence Hawkes, Jacqueline Rose, John Drakakis, and Francis Barker, challenged the liberal-humanist language of character analysis, artistic coherence, and harmony. Drawing on a vast range of theories, ranging from psychoanalysis and structuralism to Marxism and feminism, they drew attention to the manner in which Shakespeare's texts produce meaning, construct the human subject, and engage in larger structural and ideological issues.[3]

These studies have not only questioned prevailing images of the Renaissance but have also shown how issues raised in the Renaissance context have implications for theory itself. For example, the complexity of the cultural processes of the Renaissance were seen as undermining any attempt to treat the culture of any period as a homogeneous or coherent entity. Other critics such as Jerome McGann have extended New Historical concerns into other historical periods such as Romanticism. Some of the major principles of New Historicism can now be examined as they are formulated in two important statements by Stephen Greenblatt, and as they are practiced by the figure who is perhaps the primary influence on this critical tendency, Michel Foucault.

Stephen Greenblatt (b. 1943)

While he was teaching at the University of California, Berkeley, Greenblatt helped to found a journal called *Representations*, in which some of the earlier important New Historicist criticism appeared. As mentioned earlier, however, it was his introduction to *The Power of Forms in the English Renaissance* (1982) that spurred the growth of the New Historicism. In this introduction, Greenblatt differentiated what he called the "New Historicism" from both the New Criticism, which views the text as a self-contained structure, and the earlier historicism which was monological and attempted to discover a unitary political vision. Both of these earlier modes of analysis, according to Greenblatt, engaged in a project of uniting disparate and contradictory elements into an organic whole, whether in the text itself or in its historical background. The earlier historicism, moreover, viewed the resulting totality or unity as a historical fact rather than the product of interpretation or of the ideological leanings of certain groups. Such a homogenizing procedure allows the unified vision of historical context to serve as a fixed point of reference which could form the background of literary interpretation.

In contrast with this earlier formalism and historicism, the New Historicism questions its own methodological assumptions, and is less concerned with treating literary works as models of organic unity than as "fields of force, places of dissension and shifting interests, occasions for the jostling of orthodox and subversive impulses." New Historicism also challenges the hierarchical distinction between "literary foreground" and "political background," as well as between artistic and other kinds of production.

It acknowledges that when we speak of "culture," we are speaking of a "complex network of institutions, practices, and beliefs."

Greenblatt elaborated his statements about New Historicism in a subsequent influential essay, "Towards a Poetics of Culture" (1987). He begins by noting that he will not attempt to "define" the New Historicism but rather to "situate it as a practice." What distinguishes it from the "positivist historical scholarship" of the early twentieth century is its openness to recent theory; Greenblatt remarks that his own critical practice has been informed by Foucault, as well as anthropological and social theory. He proposes to situate this practice in relation to Marxism, on the one hand, and poststructuralism, on the other. Citing passages from the Marxist Fredric Jameson and the poststructuralist Jean-François Lyotard, Greenblatt questions the generalizations made about "capitalism" in each passage. Both writers are addressing the question of the connection between art and society:

> Jameson, seeking to expose the fallaciousness of a separate artistic sphere and to celebrate the materialist integration of all discourses, finds capitalism at the root of the false differentiation; Lyotard, seeking to celebrate the differentiation of all discourses and to expose the fallaciousness of monological unity, finds capitalism at the root of the false integration. History functions in both cases as a convenient anecdotal ornament upon a theoretical structure, and capitalism appears not as a complex social and economic development in the West but as a malign philosophical principle.[4]

Greenblatt further charges that both Jameson and Lyotard are trying to provide a "single, theoretically satisfactory" answer to the question of the relation between art and society. Neither of these theorists can "come to terms with the apparently contradictory historical effects of capitalism." Jameson treats capitalism as the agent of "repressive differentiation," and Lyotard treats it as the agent of "monological totalization" ("TPC," 5).

In contrast to these reductive theories, Greenblatt espouses a critical practice that would recognize capitalism's production of "a powerful and effective oscillation between the establishment of distinct discursive domains and the collapse of those domains into one another. It is this restless oscillation . . . that constitutes the distinct power of capitalism" ("TPC," 6). Greenblatt wishes to move beyond literary criticism's familiar terminology for treating the relationship between art and society: allusion, symbolism, allegory, representation, and mimesis. We need to develop, he urges, terms to describe the ways in which material "is transferred from one discursive sphere to another and becomes aesthetic property," a process which is not unidirectional because the "social discourse is already charged with aesthetic energies" ("TPC," 11). The New Historicism is marked by a "methodological self-consciousness," rather than the old historicist "faith in the transparency of signs and interpretative procedures." The New Historicism will view the work of art itself as "the product of a set of manipulations . . . the product of a negotiation between a creator or class of creators, equipped with a complex, communally shared repertoire of conventions, and the institutions and practices of society" ("TPC," 12). The general movement here is away from a mimetic theory of art to an interpretative model that will "more adequately account for the unsettling circulation of materials and discourses that is . . . the heart of modern aesthetic practice" ("TPC," 12).

There are some problems with Greenblatt's arguments as stated above. To some extent, the allegedly unifying models from which New Historicism would distinguish itself are straw targets. The best New Critics engage in intricate analyses which acknowledge the contradictions and tensions in a given literary text. And the best Marxist critics do not engage in naive reflectionist theories of the connection between literary or philosophical texts and their historical contexts. Lukács' *The Young Hegel*, for example, does precisely the opposite, situating Hegel's work within a complex network of economic and political discourses in a manner that exposes reductive liberal-humanist accounts, treating complex notions such as "contradiction" and "totality" on a high intellectual level. Greenblatt's characterization of what he takes to be "the" Marxist perspective violates his own New Historicist principles by treating it in isolation: clearly, the statements of a critic such as Fredric Jameson should be taken within the context of a vast tradition of Marxist thinking which has indeed recognized the complex and contradictory nature of capitalism. Jameson's own formulation of a "dialectical criticism" at the conclusion of his *Marxism and Form* is a highly articulate testimony to the non-reductive and genuinely complex character of his Marxist thought, informed as it is (or was at that time) by Hegelian concepts. In fact, Greenblatt's own characterization of the "distinctive feature" of capitalism as the "oscillation" between totalizing and fragmenting tendencies is as reductive as the positions he impugns; moreover, this insight is already contained in the work of previous Marxist thinkers. Finally, there appears to be absent in Greenblatt's formulation of the New Historicism any assessment of its connections with the earlier forms of historicism discussed at the beginning of this chapter. The historicism of figures such as Dilthey and Gadamer demonstrated anything but a "faith in the transparency of signs and interpretative procedures." It should be noted that, in both of the articles discussed above, when Greenblatt refers to the "earlier historicism," he is thinking not of the historicism descending from Hegel or of figures such as Gadamer and Dilthey, but of the historical literary scholarship which preceded the New Criticism and which was continued in the work of figures such as Dover Wilson. In the second article, as we have seen, Greenblatt refers to this as "the positivist historical scholarship of the early twentieth century" ("TPC," 1). The connections between the earlier lines of historicism (as opposed to positivist historical scholarship – which is anything but positivistic) and Greenblatt's version of historicism remain unformulated.

Notwithstanding such objections, Greenblatt's own books, such as *Renaissance Self-Fashioning* (1980) and *Shakespearean Negotiations* (1988), are illustrious examples of the critical practice he advocates. The former book, for example, explores the complex ways in which identity was created in the sixteenth century in an atmosphere of competition between various institutions, authorities, and ideologies, political, religious, domestic, and colonial. And, as mentioned earlier, New Historicists have profoundly reassessed the entire image of the Renaissance and other periods, questioning conventional categories of analysis and infusing a new energy, revitalized by recent theories, into the study of literature within its cultural contexts. New Historicism has been of further value inasmuch as it has refused to align itself with a definite series of positions, and as such, it has drawn upon insights from Marxism, feminism, structuralism, and poststructuralism; in turn, its insights have been enlisted by critics from a broad range of perspectives. Some of the fundamental principles of New Historicism can now be examined in the practice of Michel Foucault.

Michel Foucault (1926–1984)

Along with figures such as Jacques Derrida, Foucault has exerted an enormous influence on many branches of thought in the latter twentieth century, including what is broadly known as "cultural studies." He had a seminal impact on the New Historicism that was initiated by Stephen Greenblatt, as well as on queer theory. Born in France the son of a physician, Foucault criticized the institutions of medical practice in his first two publications, *Madness and Civilization* (1961) and *The Birth of the Clinic* (1963). Indeed, the central theme of most of Foucault's works was the methods with which modern civilization creates and controls human subjects, through institutions such as hospitals, prisons, education, and knowledge; corollary to these investigations was Foucault's examination of power, its execution and distribution. Foucault's next works, *The Order of Things* (1966) and *The Archaeology of Knowledge* (1969), offered a characterization of the growth of knowledge in the modern Western world, as manifested in the emergence of disciplines such as linguistics, economics, and biology. He elaborated a historical scheme of three "epistemes" (outlooks underlying the institutional organization of knowledge) that characterized the Middle Ages, the Enlightenment (called the "Classical" period in this text), and the modern world. Foucault's essay "What is an Author?" (1969) questions and examines the concept of authorship and, in insights that were taken up by the New Historicism, argued that analysis of literary texts could not be restricted to these texts themselves or to their author's psychology and background; rather, the larger contexts and cultural conventions in which texts were produced needed to be considered. Subsequently, Foucault offered extended critiques respectively of the institutions of the prison and of sexuality in *Discipline and Punish: The Birth of the Prison* (1975) and *The History of Sexuality* (1976).

In his essay "What is an Author?," Foucault observes the fundamental role that the notion of the author occupies in the institution and practice of literary criticism. In fact, the "man and his work" is a "fundamental critical category."[5] Foucault notes two tendencies in recent writing which militate against this exaltation of the author. The first, exemplified by writers such as Brecht, is a view of writing as free from the necessity of expression, from the need to express the thoughts and emotions of an individual. This "reversal," he says, "transforms writing into an interplay of signs, regulated less by the content it signifies than by the very nature of the signifier" (*LCP*, 116). Foucault is now beginning to sound like a poststructuralist. The second theme is the "kinship between writing and death." Traditionally, writing (as in epic narratives) has been viewed as a means of overcoming death, of achieving immortality by recording heroic and noble actions. But, says Foucault, our culture has transformed this conception of writing as "a protection against death." Writing is now a "voluntary obliteration of the self" and effects a "total effacement of the individual characteristics of the writer," canceling out the "signs of his particular individuality." Writing creates "an opening where the writing subject endlessly disappears" (*LCP*, 116–117).

According to Foucault, the consequences of Barthes' proclamation of the "death of the author" have not been fully explored, largely due to two developments. The first of these might be attributed to formalistic, New Critical, and certain structuralist approaches: a position that effectively replaces the privileged position of the author with an equally privileged status of the work. This perspective sees criticism as concerned with "the structures of a work, its architectonic forms, which are studied for their intrinsic and internal relationships" (*LCP*, 118). But, Foucault argues, if we are rejecting the term "author" as designating some coherent entity systematically grounding the text, we must equally reject any simple definition of the "work" as a unitary entity. Does, for example, everything that an author wrote count as his "work"? Where do we draw the line between those portions of an author's writings that contribute to his "work" and those that do not (*LCP*, 118–119)?

The second notion that has impeded a proper examination of the author's "disappearance" is that of *écriture*, or writing, where this term implies a signifying system constituted by relation and difference, embodying a rejection of the notion of simple, self-contained identity. While Foucault acknowledges that this notion "stands for a remarkably profound attempt to elaborate the conditions of any text," he charges it with subtly perpetuating the "existence of the author." This (poststructuralist) notion of writing, says Foucault, has "merely transposed the empirical characteristics of an author to a transcendental anonymity" (*LCP*, 120). Implicit in Foucault's accusation is the idea that difference, so integral to this concept of writing, is itself elevated to transcendent status. As a result, a "primordial status" is granted to the notion of writing: the "play of representations" which were previously gathered up into an image of the author is now "extended within a gray neutrality." Hence the "privileges of the author" are effectively sustained by attributing a "transcendental" causality to "writing" itself, and there is effectively reintroduced into criticism "the religious principle of hidden meanings" requiring interpretation (*LCP*, 120–121).

Hence, acknowledging that "god and man died a common death," we should examine the "empty space left by the author's disappearance" (*LCP*, 121). The name of an author, says Foucault, does not merely function as a proper name among others; it oscillates, rather, "between the poles of description and designation." For example, when we say "Aristotle," we are not simply designating a person but are invoking a series of descriptions such as "the author of the *Analytics*" or "the founder of ontology" (*LCP*, 121). If we were to establish that Shakespeare had not written the sonnets attributed to him, his name would function in a different manner (*LCP*, 122). The author's name, then, is not just an element of speech that functions as a subject in a sentence, replaceable by a pronoun. The name is functional: it serves as a means of classification, of establishing relationships among texts. In short, the function of an author "is to characterize the existence, circulation, and operation of certain discourses within a society" (*LCP*, 124).

Foucault suggests four crucial features of the "author-function." The first feature is its imbrication in the systems of law and property that controlled the realm of discourses: speeches and books "were assigned real authors . . . to the extent that . . . discourse was considered transgressive." It was when a system of strict ownership and copyright rules was established in the late eighteenth and early nineteenth centuries that "the transgressive properties always intrinsic to the act of writing became the forceful imperative of literature" (*LCP*, 125). The second feature is that the author-function does not operate in a universal manner in all discourse. For example, earlier texts in Western culture – stories, folk tales, epics – were accepted without any consideration of the identity of their authors. In the Middle Ages, texts purporting to be scientific were considered truthful only if the name of the author was cited as an authority. In the seventeenth and eighteenth centuries, however, a "totally new conception" was developed: scientific texts were accepted on the basis of their merits and their position "within an anonymous and coherent system of established truths . . . the role of the author disappeared as an index of truthfulness" (*LCP*, 126). On the other hand, *literary* discourse was acceptable only if it bore an author's name, as well as the date, place, and circumstance of its composition; in our day, "literary works are totally dominated by the sovereignty of the author," apart from a few areas of study such as genre or recurring textual motifs.

The third characteristic of the author-function is that it is not somehow formed spontaneously but is a "complex operation whose purpose is to construct the rational entity we call an author." The aspects of an individual that we select as significant to comprising him as an author are "projections, in terms always more or less psychological, of our way of handling texts" (*LCP*, 127). In a fascinating paragraph, Foucault suggests that the traditional methods used by literary criticism for defining an author (for "determining the configuration of the author from existing texts") derives largely from the methods of Christian exegesis. Foucault cites the work of St. Jerome, the fourth-century Church Father who produced the first translation of the Bible into Latin (the Vulgate translation). Jerome had suggested four criteria for determining the authorship of several texts by the same person: uniformity of quality among the works; coherence of doctrine and absence of contradiction between works; uniformity of style; and historical congruity (a text, for example, referring to events after the author's death could not be included among his works). The strategies used by modern criticism for defining the author, says Foucault, are strikingly similar: the author constitutes "a principle of unity in writing," such that any unevenness of quality must be explained; further, the author "serves to neutralize the contradictions that are found in a series of texts"; finally, the author is "a particular source of expression who . . . is manifested equally well . . . in a text, in letters, fragments, drafts" (*LCP*, 128).

The fourth and final characteristic of the author-function is that it does not bear a simple reference to an actual individual who speaks in a given text: clearly, in a novel narrated in the first person, the "I" need not refer directly to the writer but to a "second self." The author-function arises out of the scission, the "division and distance" between these two selves. Moreover, this phenomenon does not merely apply to novels or poetry: all discourse that supports this author-function, says Foucault, "is characterized by this plurality of egos" (*LCP*, 130).

Foucault suggests that certain authors – such as Homer, Aristotle, and the Church Fathers – occupy a "transdiscursive position": they authored not merely books but theories or traditions in which new works could proliferate. But Foucault sees the nineteenth century as having given rise to yet another kind of author, distinct from the founders of science or the authors of canonical religious texts: the initiator of a discursive practice. Marx and Freud, he says, are the prime example of such initiating authors: they "both established the endless possibility of discourse." Not only did they enable a certain number of concepts and analogies that could be adopted by future texts, but they also opened up a space for divergences from their own hypotheses (*LCP*, 132). Foucault argues that there is a fundamental difference between the founders of science (who date from the present all the way back to antiquity) and the exclusively modern initiators of discourse. The founding of a science is on an "equal footing with its future transformations . . . the founding act may appear as little more than a single instance of a more general phenomenon that has been discovered." In contrast, "the initiation of a discursive practice . . . overshadows and is necessarily detached from its later developments" (*LCP*, 134). Practitioners of such discourses, says Foucault, inevitably "return to the origin," seeking a refined understanding of the founding texts: "A study of Galileo's works could alter our knowledge of the history, but not the science, of mechanics; whereas, a re-examination of the books of Freud or Marx can transform our understanding of psychoanalysis or Marxism" (*LCP*, 135–136). Such returns, says Foucault, tend to reinforce the "enigmatic" connection between an author and his works; these returns are an important aspect of discursive practice and establish a relationship between "fundamental" and "mediate" authors (*LCP*, 136).

Foucault suggests that the work he has undertaken in this brief essay could point in a number of directions. It could provide the basis for a "typology of discourse," which would venture into the "larger categories" of discourse beyond merely grammatical and logical features. Also, it might foster a historical analysis of discourse since the author-function could show how discourse "is articulated on the basis of social relationships." Finally, the notion of the "subject" should not be abandoned entirely but reexamined in terms of its function and its position in discourse. Indeed, the subject "must be stripped of its creative role and analyzed as a complex and variable function of discourse" (*LCP*, 138). Foucault stresses that the author-function is "only one of the possible specifications of the subject." He insists that we "can easily imagine a culture where discourse would circulate without any need for an author. Discourses . . . would unfold in a pervasive anonymity." Instead of the "tiresome" questions "Who is the real author?" and "Have we proof of his authenticity and originality?," we will ask (the no doubt tireless) questions such as "What are the modes of existence of this discourse?" as well as asking where it comes from, who controls it, and what placements within it are possible for the subject (*LCP*, 138). Foucault seems dangerously poised on the very precipice at whose edge he envisaged Derrida's notion of writing: the notion of "discourse" is happily invoked in his own text as the new throne of the transcendental.

In the first part of *The History of Sexuality*, entitled "We 'Other Victorians,'" Foucault examines the conventional "repressive hypothesis": that, at the beginning of the seventeenth century, a certain frankness was still common in sexual discourse and practice. But this "bright day" was followed by the "monotonous nights of the Victorian bourgeoisie." Sexuality was confined to the home, silence became the rule, and sex was repressed into the heterosexual bedroom for procreative purposes.[6] Modern puritanism, the argument goes, "imposed its triple edict of taboo, nonexistence, and silence" (*HS*, 5). This theory of modern sexual repression, says Foucault, appears on the surface to hold up well: repression is made "to coincide with the development of capitalism: it becomes an integral part of the bourgeois order" (*HS*, 5). The principle of explanation behind this is that sex, the dissipation of oneself in pleasure, is "incompatible with a general and intensive work imperative" (*HS*, 6). But this definition of the connection between sex and power in terms of repression, rejoins Foucault, is sustained by the opportunity it gives us to speak out against the prevailing powers, and to enter into a (professional) discourse about sex (*HS*, 7). Hence, this alleged repression has been "coupled with the grandiloquence of a discourse purporting to reveal the truth about sex, modify its economy within reality, subvert the law that governs it, and change its future." Foucault's point is that the two phenomena, the repression and the discourse, are "mutually reinforcing" (*HS*, 8).

Foucault raises doubts about this repressive hypothesis, questioning its historical veracity, its equation of power with repression, and pointing out the complicity of the discourse on sexuality with the process of repression itself (*HS*, 10). He states that his aim is not to show that the repressive hypothesis is mistaken but to situate it within "a general economy of discourses on sex in modern societies." He intends to "define the regime of power–knowledge–pleasure that sustains the discourse on human sexuality" (*HS*, 11). His own thesis is that since the end of the sixteenth century, the discourse on sexuality, "far from undergoing a process of restriction, on the contrary has been subjected to a mechanism of increasing incitement; that the techniques of power exercised over sex have not obeyed a principle of rigorous selection, but rather one of dissemination and implantation of polymorphous sexualities; and that the will to knowledge . . . has persisted in constituting . . . a science of sexuality" (*HS*, 12–13). It is clear that Foucault's investigation of the discourse on sexuality is equally an investigation into the workings of power, which will be seen as far more complex and subtle than a procedure of mere repression.

Foucault's general hypothesis, then, is that bourgeois society did not refuse to recognize sex but rather "put into operation an entire machinery for producing true discourses concerning it . . . it also set out to formulate the uniform truth of sex" (*HS*, 69). The aim was to inscribe sex within an economy of pleasure and an "ordered system of knowledge." In speaking the truth about itself, sex also tells us the deeply buried truth about ourselves, its part in the constitution of the subject. Indeed, the science of the subject has "gravitated . . . around the question of sex" (*HS*, 70). The proliferation of discourses about sex has been "carefully tailored to the requirements of power" (*HS*, 72). Within a few centuries, says Foucault, the inquiry into what we are has led us to sex, to "sex as history, as signification and discourse." After being immersed in binary oppositions (body/soul, flesh/spirit, instinct/reason) that relegated sex to irrationality, the West has effectively annexed "sex to a field of rationality" and brought us "almost entirely – our bodies, our minds, our individuality, our history – under the sway of a logic of concupiscence and desire." This logic provides the "master key" to what we are: sex, as grounding our psychology and reproduction, the very mechanisms of life, is seen as "the explanation for everything" (*HS*, 78).

Foucault offers an explicit statement of his conception of power, a conception that has underlain his arguments on sexuality. He rejects the conventional notion of power that is based on a "juridico-discursive" model. This conception of power is essentially juridical, based on the statement of the law and taboo, and is seen as straightforwardly restrictive and repressive. Such a conception of power, deriving from the development of monarchic power and the concept of right, says Foucault, overlooks precisely what makes power so effective and accepted (*HS*, 85–86). New methods of power, he maintains, operate not "by right but by technique, not by law but by normalization, not by punishment but by control." And, in order to operate effectively, power must mask at least a part of itself (*HS*, 87, 89). Foucault states that power is not " a group of institutions and mechanisms that ensure the subservience of the citizens of a given state." Nor is it a "mode of subjugation" or a "general system of domination exerted by one group over another ... these are only the terminal forms that power takes" (*HS*, 92). Nor must power be sought "in the primary existence of a central point, in a unique source of sovereignty from which secondary and descendent forms would emanate" (*HS*, 93). Nor is power something that is "acquired, seized, or shared." Moreover, "there is no binary and all-encompassing opposition between rulers and ruled at the root of power relations" (*HS*, 94).

What *is* it, then? According to Foucault, power "must be understood in the first instance as the multiplicity of force relations immanent in the sphere in which they operate and which constitute their own organisation ... as the support which these force relations find in one another, thus forming a chain or system ... and lastly, as the strategies in which they take effect" (*HS*, 92). Foucault insists that power "is everywhere; not because it embraces everything, but because it comes from everywhere." It is "simply the over-all effect that emerges from all these mobilities" (*HS*, 93). A conventional Marxist critique of Foucault would impugn his apparent removal of political agency from the operations of power. Yet he characterizes power relations as "both intentional and nonsubjective." He acknowledges that "there is no power that is exercised without a series of aims and objectives. But this does not mean that it results from the choice or decision of an individual subject" (*HS*, 94–95). He also concedes that where "there is power, there is resistance, and yet ... this resistance is never in a position of exteriority in relation to power." Foucault stresses that there is "no single locus of great Refusal, no soul of revolt, source of all rebellions, or pure law of the revolutionary. Instead there is a plurality of resistances, each of them a special case" (*HS*, 95–96). These resistances can exist only "in the strategic field of power relations." But this does not mean, says Foucault, that they are "doomed to perpetual defeat" (*HS*, 96). Foucault admits that there are occasionally "great radical ruptures," but for the most part there are "mobile and transitory points of resistance" which have the effect of producing cleavages in a society, breaking up unities and effecting regroupings. Just as power relations form a "dense web" through apparatuses and institutions, so the points of resistance "traverse social stratifications and individual unities." What makes revolution possible is a "strategic codification of these points of resistance" (*HS*, 96).

Notes

1   Jonathan Dollimore, *Radical Tragedy: Religion, Ideology and Power in the Drama of Shakespeare and his Contemporaries* (New York and London: Harvester Wheatsheaf, 1984), pp. 8, 18, 54, 59, 63, 78.

2   Jonathan Dollimore and Alan Sinfield, *Political Shakespeare: New Essays in Cultural Materialism* (New York and London: Cornell University Press, 1985).

3   John Drakakis, ed., *Alternative Shakespeares* (New York and London: Routledge, 1985).

4   Stephen Greenblatt, "Towards a Poetics of Culture," in *The New Historicism*, ed. H. Aram Veeser (New York and London: Routledge, 1989), p. 5. Hereafter cited as "TPC."

5   Michel Foucault, "What is an Author?," in *Language, Counter-Memory, Practice: Selected Essays and Interviews*, ed. and trans. Donald F. Bouchard (New York and Ithaca: Cornell University Press, 1977), p. 115. Hereafter cited as *LCP*.

6   Michel Foucault, *The History of Sexuality: An Introduction*, trans. Robert Hurley (Harmondsworth: Penguin, 1978), p. 3. Hereafter cited as *HS*.

EPILOGUE

In the past decade or so, there has been a spate of claims that "theory" is dead and that we inhabit a "post-theoretical" environment. But, as we have seen, literary theory did not arise in the twentieth century; it is at least two and a half thousand years old, and it cannot be reductively aligned with a group of theories that happened to emerge in our recent history. Moreover, the claim that theory is dead presupposes that practice – the practice of literary criticism – can somehow proceed without theory, without some kind of systematic reflection on its underlying principles. Such a practice, even if it were possible, would be a profoundly impoverished and superficial enterprise. It would involve an intellectual regression to certain literary-critical attitudes that refuse to articulate themselves, that insist on first-order direct impressions, on philosophically discredited notions such as "immediate experience," and vague notions of "sensibility."

It is perhaps true, however, that "theory" in the sense of a grand narrative of historical development, or a series of archetypes with claims to universal explanatory power, has become increasingly problematic. By the standards of the early twenty-first century, even deconstruction, structuralism, and New Historicism are viewed as excessively comprehensive in their heuristic scope and explanatory ambition. There is somewhat less tolerance for grand schemes as well as for difficult language. Critiques of "metaphysics" or generalizations about "history" or indeed of "theory" itself are now seen in many quarters as impossibly general. What has displaced these larger visions is a series of more empirical inquiries, based on more narrowly defined fields and interests. Cases in point are ecocriticism, which examines the manifold significance of nature (treated as a reality rather than as a construct) and the environment in literature, returning to writers such as Emerson, Thoreau, and the English Romantics for inspiration; gay and lesbian criticism, which makes sexual orientation a fundamental category of analysis; narratology, or the study of narrative, which has assumed a considerable degree of independence from its sources in structuralist theory; and the detailed, empirical, and factual study of specific historical periods, localities, and authors. Even the concept of "reality" – for more than two millennia the central pursuit of philosophy – is now viewed as not only an intellectual but also an ideological construct, serving to privilege certain ways of viewing the world. In a strange historical development, we have come full circle, returning to a rhetorical and skeptical vision, whereby we recognize not only the constitution of our perceptual and conceptual capacity by language but also the constitutive role of the linguistic situation itself, fraught with the multifold dimensions of performance, all of the historically specific circumstances which internally shape the process of communication, whether philosophical, political, or literary.

Looking back over the history of literary criticism (or at least one version of that history), it is evident that, since the time of Plato, there has been a series of complex tendencies moving first in the direction of universality, reaching a climax in the intellectual hierarchies of the Middle Ages in which theology stood at the apex and where all dimensions of humanity – bodily, emotional, intellectual, and spiritual – had their appointed place, and where humanity itself had a defined location both within the universe and within the historical scheme of providence. Since the Renaissance or early modern period, there has been a dissolution of these coherent and totalizing visions, spurred by economic and political development, the Protestant Reformation, the Enlightenment, the French Revolution, and the rise to hegemony throughout Europe of the middle classes. This movement from general to particular has been underlain by the location of the source of the intellect in sense-perception, of rationality within our physical and emotional apparatus of survival, and of an increasing awareness that the world is not an objective datum but a human historical and social construct. Certain totalizing philosophies such as that of Hegel attempted to construct a unified vision of the fragmented modern world, situating it as the latest phase of historical development. But Hegel's system itself was shattered, leaving in its aftermath various more localized approaches (many of which reacted against it), including Marxism, positivism, Anglo-American idealism, and existentialism. Hence, the preoccupation with the particular and the local which we now witness, in literary theory and criticism as well as in mass culture, is not in itself new (though it has reached new intensities), but the product of a long historical development.

It could be argued that all of these denials of totalizing schemes, all of these forms of elevation of the local and particular, are ideologies into which the mainstream modes of bourgeois thought have been dissipated, and that they are taking us deeper and deeper into the core of late bourgeois ideology, reaching back into and unearthing its deepest foundation: a positivistic exaltation of the particular, a refusal of so-called "theory," a refusal to discern connections and patterns beyond those that comprise any local situation, beyond what can be comprehended in one view, concentrated into the diminished time and diminished space of a consumerist mode of apprehension. There is a danger that even well-intentioned radicalism at this level of diminished and localized context, radicalism whose very language insulates itself from the political process, is smoothly integrated into the untouched and unchallenged totality of the political and ideological status quo. Recently, a number of writers and thinkers have called for a redemption of concepts such as reality, truth, morality, and practicable notions of political agency.

Such a redemption might itself prove radical and necessary in a world that increasingly presents endless surfaces with no depth, in proliferating images with no connection. This is the case even with the best-intentioned media. For example, we have C-Span providing detailed coverage of anti-war demonstrations followed by, say, coverage of a day in the life of the defense secretary and his subalterns. If the viewer herself does not bring a larger context in which both perspectives can be connected and situated, there is otherwise no broader context offered; in fact, each smaller, localized perspective threatens to occupy temporarily the entire perspective of a viewer, either sequentially by displacement or by outright rejection of the other perspective. The point is that each "text" – even in a television channel that makes concrete gestures in the direction of fairness – is offered up in isolation, divorced from any dialogue with its own background or with other texts. In attempting to link these texts, in attempting to arrive at a broader vision – provided that this attempt itself is not already stifled and castigated as excessive – an uninformed viewer will naturally fall back on the very same assumptions with which he began, assumptions that are themselves articulated only with reference to the broadest and vaguest generalities, as rote-learned from the major TV networks and official press briefings in which only certain types of questions – those motivated by the same assumptions as the answers provided – can be asked.

Nowadays, Marxism ironically appears old-fashioned in its belief that there is an objective world (though as a construction, a product of historical development), that there is a sphere of civic society, moral action, and political agency. As mentioned earlier, even deconstruction and feminism have suffered similar dismissive assessments. And postcolonial theory, which feels the need to take account of the insights of poststructuralist thinkers, is facing many dilemmas which are both institutional and theoretical. Will these discourses continue to be accommodated within our educational institutions, insulated from their potential connections with political practice? The history of literary criticism suggests that this need not be the case. If one point emerges saliently from this history, it is surely that literary criticism has been related at the profoundest levels not only to other fields of inquiry such as philosophy and theology, but also to fundamental economic and political developments. Its inquiries have ranged over vast areas: in philosophy, it has examined the notions of subjectivity, objectivity, the nature of experience, the categories of unity and identity, and the connection between universal and particular; its psychological inquiries have embraced the connection between various human faculties such as understanding, imagination and reason, emotion, instinct and the unconscious; its formal and rhetorical concerns have extended over the concepts of imitation, structure, free play, pleasure, symbol, allegory, and other figures of speech, as well as the nature and composition of audiences; educationally, it has addressed the moral, intellectual, and ideological functions of literature; politically, it has delved into questions of class, gender, and race; theologically, it has reflected on the status of literature within a scheme of discourses or sciences, as well as the ability of literature to express the highest spiritual truths. And of course, it has been embroiled for over two thousand years in ideological, political, and religious debates, entangled in the conflicts of various power structures.

What has underlain nearly all of these inquiries of literary criticism has been an attention – both theoretical and practical – to language, to the process of composition, and to the processes of reading and interpretation. In this sense, the activities and issues involved in literary criticism and theory underlie all kinds of inquiries; it is increasingly recognized in schools, for example, that sound language skills are needed to comprehend mathematical and scientific problems. Hence the fundamentality of literary criticism to the projects of human understanding, of molding human subjectivity and of informing the political process, cannot be overstressed.

Our sometimes narrow conception of the "purely" aesthetic or literary dimension of a text would have been regarded as strange and puzzling by virtually any writer, thinker, or critic before the end of the eighteenth century. Since the inception of literary criticism over two thousand years ago, the aesthetic has been viewed as necessarily imbricated in political, moral, and educational issues. Neither Plato nor the ancient Greek poets such as Homer and Hesiod, neither Vergil nor Dante nor Shakespeare nor contemporary Russian, Israeli, or Palestinian poets, would understand the notion of "art for art's sake" or the idea that we should read literature *as* literature. This narrow aestheticism is primarily a creature of luxury, arising in a highly secluded and depoliticized academic environment where the study of literature can afford to be a mere exercise, a study of mere verbal virtuosity. Such an attitude – along with the so-called "theory" that it has attempted to reject – has sometimes helped foster the self-isolation of academia from the political, economic, and cultural process. In spite of our best intentions, we lovers of literature and proponents of radical theory have unwittingly conspired – through the very sophistication of our language – to deprive ourselves of any voice, to seal off our studies from their potential application to the important issues that engulf our lives.

There have been times, however, when the sheer urgency of what is at stake in literary criticism threatens to batter down the academic walls insulating it from the political process and the concerns of the mass media. One example is the debate concerning "multiculturalism" in the 1980s and 1990s. Institutional and theoretical developments in ethnic studies, gender studies, feminism, and education, and above all, worldwide economic and political developments, brought the issues contained under the rubric of "literary criticism" – modes of reading, interpretation, rhetorical strategies, canon formation, curriculum construction, audience – under the glare of ferocious public debate and interest. The modes and direction of literary criticism were suddenly seen once more in the light of their implications for democracy, national identity, national interest, and cultural-political diversity. Such a debate was hardly new in either European or American history: it had raged during the nineteenth century in Europe, with profound implications for national identity, the nature of imperialism, and the nature of the colonized peoples. It had marked the intense debates for educational reform in American institutions in the late nineteenth and early twentieth centuries, involving figures such as Charles Eliot, Irving Babbitt, and John Dewey. Resurfacing in the final decades of the twentieth century, this complex of debates was played out in newspapers and leading magazines, television, and the halls of political power, and indeed is currently reaching a new intensity with talk of an "advisory committee" that might oversee the curricula of institutions of higher education in an attempt to control what is taught – in the interests of national security. In the Indian subcontinent and much of the Middle East, the debate in the nineteenth century took the form of a conflict between Western and Eastern, modern and traditional, modes of learning and has erupted more recently as an ideological struggle between sacred and secular modes of education.

The overall point here is that education in general, and the theory and practice of literary criticism in particular, can no longer be artificially marooned from the political, social, and economic framework. Conservatives and liberals in America seem to be agreed at least upon this, though their motives lie far apart. There is an increasingly pervasive acknowledgment, then, that the acts of reading, writing, and interpretation are not somehow value-free and do not subsist in some atemporal, academic vacuum; these once purportedly "neutral" acts are informed by the points of our entry into a much broader cultural and political fabric: reading a work of literature involves strategies that are similar to, and continuous with, the strategies we use to "read" television, advertisements, political speeches, domestic and foreign policy. These developments are welcomed by those who see their classroom activities as helping students understand their world, their own identities, and the history and future possibilities of both. The political implications of reading may not be immediately obvious to a student reading poetry in a climate of New Criticism; but they are inescapably and vividly transparent to Middle Eastern readers of Palestinian or Israeli poetry, to the readers of Indian and Pakistani novels, to the audiences of drama in various regions of the former Soviet Union, and to scholars and politicians in countries such as Iran and Malaysia who are re-reading the texts and traditions of Islamic law. Having said that, the propulsion in recent times of America's foreign policy into an overtness of worldwide concern and stark visibility has, ironically, brought into sharp relief the connections between literature and other realms of public discourse, connections that had hitherto been suppressed by certain schools of literary criticism; it is far more difficult for the American and European student today to escape the awareness that the texts she reads deal with issues whose ramifications explode far beyond the classroom, and that the rhetorical strategies she is called upon to enlist are those that command a widespread currency in the broader languages of politics and culture.

We need to draw on the richness of our literary, philosophical, and literary-critical heritage in order to realize the potential of the humanities to foster increased understanding of our world. Literary criticism furnishes the tools for analyzing not only Shakespeare and Milton, Toni Morrison and Naguib Mahfouz, but also the "texts" of a soccer game, advertisements, political speeches, press conferences, rock concerts, and news presentations. We can draw on the insights furnished by a host of thinkers – ranging from Plato and Aristotle through Emerson and Whitman to Alexis de Tocqueville and contemporary politicians – to analyze the nature of democracy in an array of uniquely modern contexts. We can probe the various findings of the connection between "literal" and figurative language – from Augustine through Aquinas and Ibn Rushd to Locke, Schleiermacher, and Derrida – to facilitate analyses of the Qur'an and the various texts of Islam. Both of these tasks face us with a dire urgency. The "war on terror" has become the latest grand narrative, one which stands in sore need of analysis. In more general terms, we need to ensure that the skills fostered by our diverse and rich critical heritage are not insulated within academia: not by adopting the languages of the public sphere but by forging at least a continuity between it and the critical languages we construct, by articulating the political implications of our work, by extending our inquiries over the fields of popular culture, by refashioning our departments in the humanities to accommodate prevailing cultural concerns, and by supporting the participation of our institutions in the larger community. We may then draw on our philosophical and literary-critical heritage in actively shaping the political, educational, and economic discourses that will determine our future.

SELECTIVE
BIBLIOGRAPHY

This bibliography cites some of the major texts of each period, followed by suggestions for further reading and useful anthologies.

(1) Classical

Aristophanes. *Frogs*. In *Aristophanes, Volume II: The Peace, The Birds, The Frogs*. Trans. Benjamin Bickley Rogers. Loeb Classical Library. Cambridge, MA and London: Harvard University Press/Heinemann, 1968.

Aristotle. *The Art of Rhetoric*. Trans. H. C. Lawson-Tancred. Harmondsworth: Penguin, 1991.

——. *The Categories; On Interpretation; Prior Analytics*. Trans. Harold P. Cooke and Hugh Tredennick. Loeb Classical Library. Cambridge, MA and London: Harvard University Press/ Heinemann, 1973.

——. *The Metaphysics I–IX*. Trans. Hugh Tredennick. Loeb Classical Library. Cambridge, MA and London: Harvard University Press/Heinemann, 1947.

——. *Nicomachean Ethics*. Trans. H. Rackham. Loeb Classical Library. London and New York: Heinemann/Harvard University Press, 1934.

——. *Poetics*. In *Aristotle: Poetics; Longinus: On the Sublime; Demetrius: On Style*. Trans. W. Hamilton Fyfe. Cambridge, MA and London: Harvard University Press/Heinemann, 1965.

——. *Poetics*. In *Aristotle: Poetics; Longinus: On the Sublime; Demetrius: On Style*. Trans. Stephen Halliwell, W. Hamilton Fyfe, Doreen C. Innes, and W. Rhys Roberts. Cambridge, MA and London: Harvard University Press/Heinemann, 1996.

——. *Politics*. Trans. T. A. Sinclair. Harmondsworth: Penguin, 1986.

——. *Posterior Analytics; Topica*. Trans. Hugh Tredennick and E. S. Forster. Loeb Classical Library. Cambridge, MA and London: Harvard University Press/Heinemann, 1976.

Cicero, Marcus Tullius. *De inventione; De optimo genere oratorum; Topica*. Trans. H. M. Hubbell. Loeb Classical Library. Cambridge, MA and London: Harvard University Press/Heinemann, 1968.

——. *De oratore*. Cambridge, MA: Harvard University Press, 1967–1968.

——. *De re publica; De legibus*. Trans. Clinton Walker Keyes. Cambridge, MA and London: Harvard University Press/Heinemann, 1966.

[Cicero]. *Ad C. Herennium: De ratione dicendi (Rhetorica ad Herennium)*. Trans. Harry Caplan. Cambridge, MA and London: Harvard University Press/Heinemann, 1968.

Horace. *The Art of Poetry*. Trans. Burton Raffel. New York, 1974.

——. *The Odes of Horace*. Trans. James Michie. Harmondsworth: Penguin, 1976.

Juvenal. *The Sixteen Satires*. London: Penguin, 1974.

Plato. *Collected Dialogues of Plato*. Ed. Edith Hamilton and Huntington Cairns. Princeton: Princeton University Press, 1969.

——. *Gorgias*. Trans. Robin Waterfield. New York and Oxford: Oxford University Press, 1994.

Plutarch. *Fall of the Roman Republic*. Harmondsworth: Penguin, 1968.

Quintilian. *Quintilian: On the Teaching of Speaking and Writing: Translations from Books One, Two, and Ten of the Institutio oratoria*. Ed. James J. Murphy. Carbondale: Southern Illinois University Press, 1987.

Suetonius. *The Twelve Caesars*. Trans. Robert Graves. Harmondsworth: Penguin, 1989.

Tacitus. *The Complete Works of Tacitus*. Ed. M. Hadas. Trans. A. J. Church and W. J. Brodribb. New York: Random House, 1942.

Further Reading and Anthologies

Commager, Steele. *The Odes of Horace: A Critical Study*. Bloomington and London: Indiana University Press, 1967.

Daiches, David, and Anthony Thorlby, eds. *Literature and Western Civilization: The Classical World*. London: Aldus Books, 1972.

Ford, Andrew. *The Origins of Criticism: Literary Culture and Poetic Theory in Classical Greece*. Princeton: Princeton University Press, 2002.

Kennedy, George A. *A New History of Classical Rhetoric*. Princeton: Princeton University Press, 1994.

——, ed. *The Cambridge History of Literary Criticism. Volume I: Classical Criticism*. Cambridge: Cambridge University Press, 1997.

Kraut, Richard, ed. *The Cambridge Companion to Plato*. Cambridge: Cambridge University Press, 1992.

Ledbetter, Grace M. *Poetics Before Plato: Interpretation and Authority in Early Greek Theories of Poetry*. Princeton: Princeton University Press, 2003.

Levin, Susan. *The Ancient Quarrel between Philosophy and Poetry Revisited: Plato and the Greek Literary Tradition*. Oxford: Oxford University Press, 2001.

Murphy, James J., and Richard A. Katula. *A Synoptic History of Classical Rhetoric*. Davis, CA: Hermagoras Press, 1994.

Roberts, Jennifer Tolbert. *Athens on Trial: The Antidemocratic Tradition in Western Thought*. Princeton: Princeton University Press, 1994.

Russell, Bertrand. *History of Western Philosophy*. London: George Allen and Unwin, 1974.

Russell, D. A., and M. Winterbottom, eds. *Ancient Literary Criticism: The Principal Texts in New Translations*. Oxford: Clarendon Press, 1972.

Ste. Croix, G. E. M. de. *The Class Struggle in the Ancient Greek World*. Ithaca and New York: Cornell University Press, 1981.

Too, Yun Lee. *The Idea of Ancient Literary Criticism*. Oxford: Oxford University Press, 1998.

Zeitlin, Irving M. *Plato's Vision: The Classical Origins of Social and Political Thought*. Englewood Cliffs, NJ: Prentice-Hall, 1993.

(2) Medieval

Boccaccio, Giovanni. *Boccaccio on Poetry: Being the Preface and the Fourteenth and Fifteenth Books of Boccaccio's Genealogia Deorum Gentilium*. Introd. Charles Osgood. Indianapolis and New York: Bobbs-Merrill, 1956.

Boethius. *The Consolation of Philosophy*. Trans. Richard H. Green. New York: Dover, 2002.

Christine de Pisan. *The Book of the City of Ladies.* Trans. Earl Jeffrey Richards. New York: Persea, 1982.

Dante. *Il Convivio: The Banquet.* Trans. Richard H. Lansing. New York and London: Garland, 1990.

——. *De Vulgari Eloquentia.* In *The Latin Works of Dante: De Vulgari Eloquentia, De Monarchica, Epistles, Eclogues, and Quaestio de Aqua et Terra.* Trans. A. G. Ferrers Howell. New York: Greenwood Press, 1904.

——. *Literary Criticism of Dante Alighieri.* Trans. Robert S. Haller. Nebraska: University of Nebraska Press, 1973.

Geoffrey of Vinsauf. *Poetria Nova.* Trans. Margaret F. Nims. Toronto and Wetteren, Belgium: Pontifical Institute of Medieval Studies/Universa Press, 1967.

Hugh of St. Victor. *The Didascalicon of Hugh of St. Victor.* Trans. Jerome Taylor. New York: Columbia University Press, 1991.

John of Salisbury. *The Metalogicon of John of Salisbury: A Twelfth-Century Defense of the Verbal and Logical Arts of the Trivium.* Trans. Daniel D. McGarry. Gloucester, MA: Peter Smith, 1971.

Macrobius. *Commentary on the Dream of Scipio.* Trans. William Harris Stahl. New York: Columbia University Press, 1990.

Plotinus. *The Essence of Plotinus: Extracts from the Six Enneads and Porphyry's Life of Plotinus.* Trans. Stephen Mackenna. Ed. Grace H. Turnbull. New York and Oxford: Oxford University Press, 1948.

St. Augustine. *City of God.* Trans. Henry Bettenson. Harmondsworth: Penguin, 1984.

——. *The Confessions of St. Augustine.* Trans. Rex Warner. New York: Mentor, 1963.

——. *De Doctrina Christiana.* Calvin College: Christian Classics Ethereal Library, 2003. This translation can be found at: www.ccel.org/ccel/augustine/doctrine.iii.html.

St. Thomas Aquinas. *An Introduction to the Metaphysics of St. Thomas Aquinas: Texts Selected and Translated.* Ed. James F. Anderson. Indiana: Regnery/Gateway, 1953.

Further Reading and Anthologies

Anderson, Perry. *Passages From Antiquity to Feudalism.* London: Verso, 1985.

Curtius, Ernst Robert. *European Literature and the Latin Middle Ages.* Trans. Willard R. Trask. London: Routledge and Kegan Paul, 1979.

Eco, Umberto. *The Aesthetics of Thomas Aquinas.* Trans. Hugh Bredin. Cambridge, MA: Harvard University Press, 1988.

Hardison, Jr., O. B., ed. *Medieval Literary Criticism: Translations and Interpretations.* New York: Frederick Ungar, 1974.

Irvine, Martin. *The Making of Textual Culture: "Grammatica" and Literary Theory, 350–1100.* Cambridge and New York: Cambridge University Press, 1994.

Kretzmann, Norman, and Eleonore Stump, eds. *Cambridge Companion to Aquinas.* Cambridge: Cambridge University Press, 1993.

Minnis, A. J., A. B. Scott, and David Wallace, eds. *Medieval Literary Theory and Criticism, c.1100–c.1375: The Commentary Tradition.* Oxford: Clarendon Press, 1988.

Montgomery Watt, W. *Islamic Philosophy and Theology.* Edinburgh: Edinburgh University Press, 1985.

Ouyang, Wen-chin. *Literary Criticism in Medieval Arabic-Islamic Culture: The Making of a Tradition.* Edinburgh: Edinburgh University Press, 1997.

(3) Early Modern

Castelvetro, Lodovico. *On the Art of Poetry: An Abridged Translation of Lodovico Castelvetro's Poetica d'Aristotele vulgarizzata e sposta.* Trans. Andrew Bongiorno. Binghamton, NY: Medieval and Renaissance Texts and Studies, 1984.

Corneille, Pierre. "Of the Three Unities of Action, Time, and Place." Trans. Donald Schier. In *The Continental Model: Selected French Critical Essays of the Seventeenth Century, in English Translation*. Ed. Scott Elledge and Donald Schier. Ithaca and London: Cornell University Press, 1970.

Du Bellay, Joachim. *La Deffence et Illustration de la Langue Francoyse*. Paris: Société des Textes Français Modernes, 1997.

Gascoigne, George. "Certayne Notes of Instruction." Reprinted in *English Renaissance Literary Criticism*. Ed. Brian Vickers. Oxford: Clarendon Press, 1999.

Giraldi, Giambattista. *Giraldi Cinthio on Romances: Being a Translation of the Discorso intorno al comporre dei romanzi*. Trans. Henry L. Snuggs. Lexington: University of Kentucky Press, 1968.

Mazzoni, Giacopo. *On the Defense of the Comedy of Dante: Introduction and Summary*. Trans. Robert L. Montgomery. Tallahassee: University Presses of Florida, 1983.

Puttenham, George. *The Arte of English Poesie*. Ed. Gladys Doidge Willcock and Alice Walker. Cambridge: Cambridge University Press, 1970.

Ronsard, Pierre de. "A Brief on the Art of French Poetry." Trans. J. H. Smith. In *The Great Critics*. Ed. James Harry Smith and Edd Winfield Parks. New York: W. W. Norton, 1951.

Sidney, Sir Philip. *A Defence of Poetry*. Ed. J. A. Van Dorsten. Oxford: Oxford University Press, 1966.

——. *The Selected Poetry and Prose of Sir Philip Sidney*. Ed. David Kalstone. New York and Toronto: New American Library, 1970.

Tasso, Torquato. *Discourses on the Heroic Poem*. Trans. Mariella Cavalchini and Irene Samuel. Oxford: Clarendon Press, 1973.

Further Reading

Matz, Robert. *Defending Literature in Early Modern England: Renaissance Literary Theory in Social Context*. Cambridge: Cambridge University Press, 2000.

Norbrook, David. "Introduction." In *The Penguin Book of Renaissance Verse 1509–1659*. Ed. H. R. Woudhuysen. Harmondsworth: Penguin, 1993.

——. *Poetry and Politics in the English Renaissance*. Revised edition. Oxford: Oxford University Press, 2002.

——. *Writing the English Republic: Poetry, Rhetoric and Politics 1627–1660*. Cambridge: Cambridge University Press, 2000.

Norton, Glyn P., ed. *The Cambridge History of Literary Criticism. Volume III: The Renaissance*. Cambridge: Cambridge University Press, 1999.

(4) Neoclassical

Behn, Aphra. *The Works of Aphra Behn: Volume I*. Ed. Montague Summers. New York: Benjamin Blom, 1967.

——. *The Works of Aphra Behn: Volume III*. Ed. Montague Summers. New York: Benjamin Blom, 1967.

Boileau, Nicolas. *The Art of Poetry: The Poetical Treatises of Horace, Vida, and Boileau*. Trans. Francis Howes, Christopher Pitt, and Sir William Soames. Ed. Albert S. Cook. Boston: Ginn, 1892.

Dryden, John. *Essays of John Dryden*, 2 vols. Ed. W. P. Ker. New York: Russell and Russell, 1961.

Johnson, Samuel. *Essays from the Rambler, Adventurer, and Idler*. Ed. W. J. Bate. New Haven and London: Yale University Press, 1968.

——. *The History of Rasselas, Prince of Abyssinia.* Harmondsworth: Penguin, 1986.

——. *Lives of the English Poets.* Introd. John Wain. London and New York: Dent/Dutton, 1975.

——. *The Yale Edition of the Works of Samuel Johnson. Volume VII: Johnson on Shakespeare.* Ed. Arthur Sherbo. Introd. Bertrand H. Bronson. New Haven and London: Yale University Press, 1968.

Further Reading

Nisbet, H. B., and Claude Rawson, eds. *The Cambridge History of Literary Criticism. Volume IV: The Eighteenth Century.* Cambridge: Cambridge University Press, 1997.

Smallwood, Philip. *Reconstructing Criticism: Pope's Essay on Criticism and the Logic of Definition.* Cranbury, NJ: Associated University Presses, 2003.

(5) Enlightenment

Addison, Joseph, and Richard Steele. *Selections from the Tatler and the Spectator.* Ed. Robert J. Allen. New York: Holt, Rinehart, and Winston, 1961.

Bacon, Francis. *The New Organon.* Ed. Fulton H. Anderson. Indianapolis: Bobbs-Merrill, 1960.

Burke, Edmund. *A Philosophical Enquiry into the Origins of Our Ideas of the Sublime and Beautiful.* New York and Oxford: Oxford University Press, 1990.

Descartes, René. *The Philosophical Works of Descartes: Volume I.* Trans. E. S. Haldane and G. R. T. Ross. NP: Dover, 1955.

Hume, David. *Four Dissertations.* New York: Garland, 1970.

——. *A Treatise of Human Nature: Book One.* Ed. D. G. C. Macnabb. Glasgow: Fontana/Collins, 1978.

Locke, John. *An Essay Concerning Human Understanding.* Ed. A. D. Woozley. Glasgow: Fontana/Collins, 1975.

Vico, Giambattista. *The New Science of Giambattista Vico.* Revised translation of third edition. Thomas Goddard Bergin and Max Harold Fisch. Ithaca and New York: Cornell University Press, 1968.

Wollstonecraft, Mary. *Vindication of the Rights of Woman.* Ed. Miriam Brody Kramnick. Harmondsworth: Penguin, 1985.

Further Reading

Hobsbawm, E. J. *The Age of Revolution: Europe, 1789–1848.* London: Abacus, 1977.

Muthu, Sankar. *Enlightenment Against Empire.* Princeton: Princeton University Press, 2003.

(6) The Modern Period

Brewer, John, and Eckhart Hellmuth. *Rethinking Leviathan: The Eighteenth-Century State in Britain and Germany.* London and Oxford: German Historical Institute/Oxford University Press, 1999.

Briggs, Asa. *A Social History of England.* London: Weidenfeld and Nicolson, 1983.

——. *The Age of Improvement, 1783–1867.* Harlow, England, and New York: Longman, 2000.

——, and Patricia Clavin. *Modern Europe: 1789–1989.* London and New York: Longman, 1997.

Burns, Edward McNall. *Western Civilizations: Volume 2*. New York: W. W. Norton, 1973.

Cook, Chris. *The Longman Handbook of Modern European History, 1763–1997*. New York: Addison Wesley Longman, 1997.

Darnton, Robert. *What was Revolutionary about the French Revolution?* Waco, TX: Baylor University Press, Markham Press, 1990.

Doty, Charles Stewart, ed. *The Industrial Revolution*. New York: Holt, Rinehart, and Winston, 1969.

Forrest, Alan I. *The French Revolution*. Cambridge, MA and Oxford: Blackwell, 1995.

Hanlon, Gregory. *Early Modern Italy, 1550–1800: Three Seasons in European History*. New York: Macmillan, 2000.

Hibbert, Christopher. *The French Revolution*. London: Allen Lane, 1980.

Hunt, Lynn Avery. *Politics, Culture, and Class in the French Revolution*. Berkeley: University of California Press, 1984.

——. *Revolution and Urban Politics in Provincial France: Troyes and Reims, 1786–1790*. Stanford: Stanford University Press, 1978.

Lefebvre, Georges. *The French Revolution: From its Origins to 1793*. Trans. Elizabeth Moss Evanson. London and New York: Routledge and Kegan Paul/Columbia University Press, 1965.

McCraw, Thomas K., ed. *Creating Modern Capitalism: How Entrepreneurs, Companies, and Countries Triumphed in Three Industrial Revolutions*. Cambridge, MA: Harvard University Press, 1997.

Roche, Daniel. *France in the Enlightenment*. Trans. Arthur Goldhammer. Cambridge, MA: Harvard University Press, 1998.

Royle, Edward. *Modern Britain: A Social History, 1750–1997*. London: Edward Arnold, 1997.

Rürup, Reinhard, ed. *The Problem of Revolution in Germany, 1789–1989*. Oxford and New York: Berg/New York University Press, 2000.

Simpson, William, and Martin Jones. *Europe, 1783–1914*. London and New York: Routledge, 2000.

Stearns, Peter N. *The Industrial Revolution in World History*. Boulder, CO: Westview Press, 1993.

Taine, Hippolyte Adolphe. *The French Revolution*. New York: Henry Holt, 1878–1885.

Welch, David. *Modern European History, 1871–2000: A Documentary Reader*. London and New York: Routledge, 1999.

(7) Kant and Hegel

Hegel, G. W. F. *Hegel's Introduction to Aesthetics: Being the Introduction to the Berlin Aesthetic Lectures of the 1820s*. Trans. T. M. Knox. Oxford: Oxford University Press, 1979.

——. *Hegel's Lectures on the History of Philosophy, III*. Trans. E. S. Haldane and Frances H. Simson. London and New York: Routledge and Kegan Paul/Humanities Press, 1963.

——. *Hegel's Logic: Being Part One of the Encyclopaedia of the Philosophical Sciences (1830)*. Trans. William Wallace. Oxford: Oxford University Press, 1982.

——. *Hegel's Science of Logic*. Trans. A. V. Miller. London and New York: George Allen and Unwin/Humanities Press, 1976.

——. *Phenomenology of Spirit*. Trans. A. V. Miller. Oxford: Oxford University Press, 1977.

Kant, Immanuel. *Critique of Judgment*. Trans. Werner S. Pluhar. Indianapolis and Cambridge: Hackett, 1987.

——. *Critique of Practical Reason*. Trans. L. W. Beck. Indianapolis: Bobbs-Merrill, 1978.

——. *Critique of Pure Reason*. Trans. Norman Kemp Smith. London: Macmillan, 1978.

——. *Political Writings*. Trans. H. B. Nisbet. Ed. Hans Reiss. Cambridge: Cambridge University Press, 1991.

(8) Romanticism

Coleridge, Samuel Taylor. *Coleridge: Poetical Works*. Ed. Ernest Hartley Coleridge. New York and Oxford: Oxford University Press, 1973.

——. *The Collected Works of Samuel Taylor Coleridge. VII: Biographia Literaria*. Ed. James Engell and W. Jackson Bate. Princeton: Princeton University Press, 1983.

——. *The Collected Works of Samuel Taylor Coleridge: Lay Sermons*. Ed. R. J. White. Princeton and London: Princeton University Press/Routledge and Kegan Paul.

Ralph Waldo Emerson and Margaret Fuller: Selected Works. Ed. John Carlos Rowe. Boston and New York: Houghton Mifflin, 2003.

Gautier, Théophile. "Preface." In *Mademoiselle de Maupin*, 1835; rpt. Paris: Garnier, 1955.

Keats, John. *The Letters of John Keats: Volume I*. Ed. Hyder Edward Rollins. Cambridge, MA: Harvard University Press, 1958.

Poe, Edgar Allan. "The Philosophy of Composition." In *The Complete Poetry and Selected Criticism of Edgar Allan Poe*. Ed. Allen Tate. New York and London: New American Library, 1981.

——. "The Poetic Principle." In *Complete Tales and Poems of Edgar Allan Poe*. New York: Vintage Books, 1975.

Schiller, Friedrich. "On the Aesthetic Education of Man." In *Friedrich Schiller: Poet of Freedom*. Trans. William F. Wertz, Jr. New York: New Benjamin Franklin House, 1985.

Schlegel, Friedrich von. "On Incomprehensibility." In *German Aesthetic and Literary Criticism: The Romantic Ironists and Goethe*. Ed. Kathleen M. Wheeler. Cambridge and New York: Cambridge University Press, 1984.

——. *Philosophical Fragments*. Trans. Peter Firchow. Minneapolis and Oxford: University of Minnesota Press, 1991.

Schleiermacher, Friedrich. *Hermeneutics and Criticism and Other Writings*. Trans. and ed. Andrew Bowie. Cambridge: Cambridge University Press, 1998.

Shelley, Percy Bysshe. "A Defence of Poetry." In *The Complete Works of Percy Bysshe Shelley: Volume VII*. Ed. Roger Ingpen and Walter E. Peck. London and New York: Ernest Benn/Gordian Press, 1965.

Staël, Germaine de, "Essay on Fiction." In *Madame de Staël on Politics, Literature and National Character*. Trans. Morroe Berger. London: Sidgwick and Jackson, 1964.

——. *On Literature Considered in its Relationship to Social Institutions*. In *An Extraordinary Woman: Selected Writings of Germaine de Staël*. Trans. Vivian Folkenflik. New York: Columbia University Press, 1987.

Whitman, Walt. "Introduction." In *Leaves of Grass: The First (1855) Edition*. Ed. Malcolm Cowley. Harmondsworth: Penguin, 1986.

Wordsworth, William. *The Prose Works of William Wordsworth: Volume I*. Ed. W. J. B. Owen and Jane Worthington Smyser. Oxford: Clarendon Press, 1974.

Further Reading

Armstrong, Charles I. *Romantic Organicism: From Idealist Origins to Ambivalent Afterlife*. New York: Palgrave Macmillan, 2003.

Brown, Marshall, ed. *The Cambridge History of Literary Criticism. Volume V: Romanticism*. Cambridge: Cambridge University Press, 2000.

Hamilton, Paul. *Metaromanticism: Aesthetics, Literature, Theory*. Chicago: University of Chicago Press, 2003.

Plekhanov, George V. *Art and Social Life*. New York: Oriole Editions, 1974.

(9) Realism, Naturalism, Symbolism

Baudelaire, Charles. *Intimate Journals*. Trans C. Isherwood. Introd. T. S. Eliot. New York and London: Blackamore Press, 1930.

——. *Baudelaire as a Literary Critic: Selected Essays*. Trans. Lois Boe Hyslop and Francis E. Hyslop, Jr. Pennsylvania: Pennsylvania State University Press, 1964.

Eliot, George. *Adam Bede*. Ed. John Paterson. Boston and New York: Houghton Mifflin, 1968.

Gourmont, Remy de. *Selected Writings*. Trans. and ed. Glenn S. Burne. New York: University of Michigan Press, 1966.

——. *Decadence and Other Essays on the Culture of Ideas*. Trans. William Bradley. London: George Allen and Unwin, 1930.

Howells, William Dean. *W. D. Howells: Selected Literary Criticism. Volume II: 1886–1869*. Ed. Donald Pizer and Christoph K. Lohmann. Bloomington and Indianapolis: Indiana University Press, 1993.

James, Henry. *The Art of Criticism*. Ed. William Veeder and Susan M. Griffin. Chicago and London: University of Chicago Press, 1986.

Pater, Walter. *The Renaissance: Studies in Art and Poetry*. London: Macmillan, 1913.

Wilde, Oscar. *The Complete Works of Oscar Wilde: Stories, Plays, Poems, Essays*. Introd. Vyvyan Holland. London and Glasgow: Collins, 1984.

Zola, Émile. *The Experimental Novel and Other Essays*. Trans. Belle M. Sherman. New York: Haskell House, 1964.

Further Reading

Auerbach, Eric. *Mimesis: The Representation of Reality in Western Literature*. Trans. Willard R. Trask. Princeton: Princeton University Press, 1974.

Furst, Lilian, ed. *Realism*. New York and London: Longman, 1992.

McGuinness, Patrick, ed. *Symbolism, Decadence and the Fin de Siècle: French and European Perspectives*. Exeter: University of Exeter Press, 2000.

Marcuse, Herbert. *Reason and Revolution: Hegel and the Rise of Social Theory*. London: Routledge and Kegan Paul, 1977.

Symons, Arthur. *The Symbolist Movement in Literature*, 1908; rpt. New York: Haskell House, 1971.

Watt, Ian. *The Rise of the Novel*. Harmondsworth: Penguin, 1985.

(10) The Heterological Thinkers

Arnold, Matthew. *Selected Prose*. Harmondsworth: Penguin, 1970.

Benjamin, Walter. *Illuminations*. Trans. H. Zohn. Glasgow: Fontana/Collins, 1977.

Bergson, Henri. *The Creative Mind: An Introduction to Metaphysics*. New York: Philosophical Library, 1946.

Nietzsche, Friedrich. *The Birth of Tragedy and The Genealogy of Morals*. Trans. Francis Golffing. New York: Doubleday, 1956.

——. "On Truth and Lying in a Non-Moral Sense." In Friedrich Nietzsche, *The Birth of Tragedy and Other Writings*. Trans. Ronald Speirs. Cambridge: Cambridge University Press, 1999.

——. *Thus Spoke Zarathustra*. Trans. R. J. Hollingdale. Harmondsworth: Penguin, 1978.

——. *The Will to Power*. Trans. W. Kaufmann and R. J. Hollingdale. London: Weidenfeld and Nicolson, 1968.

Schopenhauer, Arthur. *Philosophical Writings*. Ed. Wolfgang Schirmacher. New York: Continuum, 1994.

——. *The World as Will and Representation*, 2 vols. Trans. E. F. J. Payne. New York: Dover, 1958.

(11) Marx and Marxism

Aczel, Richard. "Eagleton and English," *New Left Review*, CLIV (November/December, 1985): 113–123.

Bellamy, R., and Schecter, D. *Gramsci and the Italian State*. Manchester and New York: Manchester University Press/St. Martin's Press, 1993.

Eagleton, Terry. *After Theory*. Harmondsworth: Allen Lane and Penguin, 2003.

——. *Against the Grain: Essays 1975–1985*. London: New Left Books, 1986.

——. *Criticism and Ideology*. London: New Left Books, 1976.

——. *The Function of Criticism*. London: New Left Books, 1984.

——. *Literary Theory: An Introduction*. Oxford and Minnesota: Blackwell/University of Minnesota Press, 1983.

——. *Marxism and Literary Criticism*. London: New Left Books, 1976.

——. *Walter Benjamin or Towards a Revolutionary Criticism*. London: New Left Books, 1981.

Engels, Friedrich. *The Origin of the Family, Private Property and the State*. Introd. Michèle Barrett. 1972; rpt. Harmondsworth: Penguin, 1985.

——. *Socialism: Utopian and Scientific*. Trans. Edward Aveling. New York: International Publishers, 1975.

Fontana, B. *Hegemony and Power*. Minneapolis: University of Minneapolis Press, 1993.

Gill, S., ed. *Gramsci, Historical Materialism and International Relations*. New York and Cambridge: Cambridge University Press, 1993.

Gramsci, A. *The Modern Prince and Other Writings*. Trans. L. Marks. New York: International Publishers, 1968.

——. *Selections from Political Writings*. Trans. J. Mathews, ed. Q. Hoare. New York: International Publishers, 1977.

——. *Selections from Prison Notebooks*. Trans. Q. Hoare and G. N. Smith. London: Lawrence and Wishart, 1971.

Jay, Martin. "The Two Holisms of Antonio Gramsci." In *Marxism and Totality*. Berkeley: University of California Press, 1984.

Lang, Berel, and Forrest Williams, eds. *Marxism and Art: Writings in Aesthetics and Criticism*. New York: McKay, 1972.

McLellan, David. *Karl Marx*. New York: Viking Press, 1975.

Marx, Karl. *Capital: Volume I*, 1954; rpt. London: Lawrence and Wishart, 1977.

——. *Early Writings*. Trans. and ed. T. B. Bottomore. 1963; rpt. New York and London: McGraw-Hill, 1964.

——. *Economic and Philosophical Manuscripts of 1844*. 1959; rpt. Moscow and London: Progress Publishers/Lawrence and Wishart, 1981.

——. "Preface and Introduction." In *A Contribution to the Critique of Political Economy*. Peking: Foreign Languages Press, 1976.

Marx, Karl, and Friedrich Engels. *Feuerbach: Opposition of the Materialist and Idealist Outlooks: The First Part of "The German Ideology."* London: Lawrence and Wishart, 1973.

785

——. *The German Ideology: Part One.* Ed. C. J. Arthur. 1970; rpt. London: Lawrence and Wishart, 1982.

——. *The Holy Family, or Critique of Critical Criticism: Against Bruno Bauer and Company.* 1956; rpt. Moscow: Progress Publishers, 1975.

——. *Manifesto of the Communist Party.* 1952; rpt. Moscow: Progress Publishers, 1973.

——. *On Religion.* 1957; rpt. Moscow: Progress Publishers, 1975.

——. *Selected Works.* 1968; rpt. London: Lawrence and Wishart, 1977.

Further Reading and Anthologies

Bennett, Tony. *Formalism and Marxism.* London: Routledge, 2003.

Eagleton, Terry, and Drew Milne, eds. *Marxist Literary Theory: A Reader.* Cambridge, MA and Oxford: Blackwell, 1996.

Mulhern, Francis. *Contemporary Marxist Literary Criticism.* New York and London: Longman, 1992.

(12) Psychoanalysis

Freud, Sigmund. *The Freud Reader.* Ed. Peter Gay. New York and London W. W. Norton, 1989.

Lacan, Jacques. *Écrits: A Selection.* Trans. Alan Sheridan. London: Tavistock, 1977.

Further Reading and Anthologies

De Berg, Frank. *Freud's Theory and its Use in Literary and Cultural Studies.* Rochester, NY: Camden House, 2003.

Ellman, Maud, ed. *Psychoanalytic Literary Criticism.* New York and London: Longman, 1994.

Wright, Elizabeth. *Psychoanalytic Criticism: Theory in Practice.* New York and London: Routledge, 1984.

(13) Formalisms

Bakhtin, M. M. *The Dialogic Imagination: Four Essays.* Ed. Michael Holquist. Trans. Caryl Emerson and Michael Holquist. Austin: University of Texas Press, 1981.

Eichenbaum, Boris. "The Theory of the 'Formal Method.'" In *Russian Formalist Criticism: Four Essays.* Trans. Lee T. Lemon and Marion J. Reis. Lincoln: University of Nebraska Press, 1965.

Jakobson, Roman. *Language in Literature.* Ed. Krystyna Pomorska and Stephen Rudy. Cambridge, MA and London: Harvard University Press, 1987.

Ransom, John Crowe. *The World's Body.* Baton Rouge: Louisiana State University Press, 1968.

Shklovsky, Victor. "Art as Technique." In *Russian Formalist Criticism: Four Essays.* Trans. Lee T. Lemon and Marion J. Reis. Lincoln: University of Nebraska Press, 1965.

Wimsatt, Jr., W. K., and Monroe C. Beardsley. "The Affective Fallacy." In W. K. Wimsatt, Jr., *The Verbal Icon.* Lexington: University of Kentucky Press, 1967.

——. "The Intentional Fallacy." In W. K. Wimsatt, Jr., *The Verbal Icon.* Lexington: University of Kentucky Press, 1967.

Further Reading and Anthologies

Bann, Stephen, ed. *Russian Formalism: A Collection of Articles and Texts in Translation*. New York: Barnes and Noble, 1973.

Davis, Todd F., and Womack, Kenneth. *Formalist Criticism and Reader-Response Theory*. New York: Palgrave, 2002.

Erlich, Victor. *Russian Formalism: History, Doctrine*. New Haven: Yale University Press, 1981.

Jameson, Fredric. *The Prison-House of Language: A Critical Account of Structuralism and Russian Formalism*. Princeton: Princeton University Press, 1972.

Jancovich, Mark. *The Cultural Politics of the New Criticism*. Cambridge and New York: Cambridge University Press, 1993.

Lemon, Lee T., and Marion J. Reis, eds. *Russian Formalist Criticism: Four Essays*. Lincoln: University of Nebraska Press, 1965.

Litz, A. Walton, Louis Menand, and Lawrence Rainey, eds. *The Cambridge History of Literary Criticism. Volume VII: Modernism and the New Criticism*. Cambridge: Cambridge University Press, 2000.

Royden, Mark. *Cleanth Brooks and the Rise of Modern Criticism*. Charlottesville: University Press of Virginia, 1996.

Selden, Raman, ed. *The Cambridge History of Literary Criticism. Volume VIII: From Formalism to Poststructuralism*. Cambridge: Cambridge University Press, 1995.

(14) Structuralism and Deconstruction

Barthes, Roland. *Elements of Semiology*. Trans. Annette Lavers and Colin Smith. New York: Farrar, Straus, and Giroux, 1967.

——. *Mythologies*. Trans. Annette Lavers. London: Collins, 1973.

——. *Writing Degree Zero*. Trans. Annette Lavers and Colin Smith. Preface by Susan Sontag. New York: Farrar, Straus, and Giroux, 1968.

Derrida, Jacques. *Dissemination*. Trans. Barbara Johnson. Chicago: University of Chicago Press, 1981.

——. *Of Grammatology*. Trans. Gayatri Chakravorty Spivak. Baltimore and London: Johns Hopkins University Press, 1976.

——. *Positions*. Trans. Alan Bass. Chicago and London: University of Chicago Press, 1981.

——. *Specters of Marx: The State of the Debt, the Work of Mourning, and the New International*. Trans. Peggy Kamuf. New York and London: Routledge, 1994.

——. *Writing and Difference*. Trans. Alan Bass. Chicago: University of Chicago Press, 1978.

Saussure, Ferdinand de. *Course in General Linguistics*. Ed. Charles Bally, Albert Sechehaye, and Albert Reidlinger. Trans. Wade Baskin. New York: Philosophical Library, 1959.

Further Reading and Anthologies

Berman, Art. *From the New Criticism to Deconstruction: The Reception of Structuralism and Post-Structuralism*. Urbana: University of Illinois Press, 1988.

Kamuf, Peggy, ed. *A Derrida Reader: Between the Blinds*. New York: Columbia University Press, 1991.

Lane, Michael, ed. *Structuralism: A Reader*. London: Cape, 1970.

McQuillan, Martin, ed. *Deconstruction: A Reader*. New York: Routledge, 2001.

Rajan, Tilottama. *Deconstruction and the Remainders of Phenomenology: Sartre, Derrida, Foucault, Baudrillard*. Stanford: Stanford University Press, 2002.

Sturrock, John. *Structuralism*. With a new introduction by Jean-Michel Rabaté. Oxford: Blackwell, 2003.

Zima, Peter. *Deconstruction and Critical Theory*. Trans. Rainer Emig. New York: Continuum, 2002.

(15) Feminism

Barrett, Michèle. *Women's Oppression Today: Problems in Marxist Feminist Analysis*. New York and London: Verso, 1980.

Beauvoir, Simone de. *The Second Sex*. Trans. H. M. Parshley. New York: Bantam/Alfred A. Knopf, 1961.

Cixous, Hélène. "The Laugh of the Medusa." Trans. Keith Cohen and Paula Cohen. In *The Signs Reader: Women, Gender, and Scholarship*. Ed. Elizabeth Abel and Emily K. Abel. Chicago and London: University of Chicago Press, 1983.

Kristeva, Julia. *Revolution in Poetic Language*. Trans. Margaret Waller. New York: Columbia University Press, 1984.

Showalter, Elaine. *A Literature of their Own: British Women Novelists from Brontë to Lessing*. Princeton: Princeton University Press, 1977.

Woolf, Virginia. *The Common Reader: First and Second Series*. New York: Harcourt Brace, 1948.

——. *Contemporary Writers*. New York and London: Harcourt Brace Jovanovich, 1965.

——. *A Room of One's Own*. San Diego, New York, London: Harvest/Harcourt Brace Jovanovich, 1989.

——. *Three Guineas*. New York and London: Harcourt Brace, 1966.

Further Reading and Anthologies

Bordo, Susan. *Unbearable Weight: Feminism, Western Culture, and the Body*. Berkeley: University of California Press, 1993.

Gamble, Sarah. *The Routledge Companion to Feminism and Postfeminism*. New York and London: Routledge, 2002.

McCann, Carole R., and Seung-Kyung Kim, eds. *Feminist Theory Reader: Local and Global Perspectives*. New York: Routledge, 2002.

Mohanty, Chandra Talpade. *Feminism Without Borders: Decolonizing Theory, Practicing Solidarity*. Durham, NC and London: Duke University Press, 2003.

Warhol, Robyn, and Diane Price Herndl, eds. *Feminisms: An Anthology of Literary Theory and Criticism*. New Brunswick: Rutgers University Press, 1991.

(16) Hermeneutics and Reader-Response Theory

Fish, Stanley. *Is There a Text in this Class? The Authority of Interpretive Communities*. Cambridge, MA and London: Harvard University Press, 1980.

Heidegger, Martin. *Being and Time*. Trans. John Macquarrie and Edward Robinson. New York: Harper and Row, 1962.

——. *Existence and Being*. Trans. Douglass Scott. Ed. Werner Brock. Indiana: Gateway, 1949.

——. *Poetry, Language, Thought*. Trans. Albert Hofstadter. New York and London: Harper and Row, 1975.

Husserl, Edmund. *Phenomenology and the Crisis of Philosophy*. Trans. Quentin Lauer. New York: Harper and Row, 1965.

——. *Husserl: Shorter Works*. Ed. Peter McCormick and Frederick A. Elliston. Notre Dame, IN: University of Notre Dame Press, 1981.

Iser, Wolfgang. *The Act of Reading: A Theory of Aesthetic Response*. Baltimore and London: Johns Hopkins University Press, 1978.

——. *The Implied Reader: Patterns of Communication in Prose from Bunyan to Beckett*. Baltimore and London: Johns Hopkins University Press, 1974.

Jauss, Hans Robert. "Literary History as a Challenge to Literary Theory." In *Toward an Aesthetic of Reception*. Trans. Timothy Bahti. Minneapolis: University of Minnesota Press, 1982.

Further Reading and Anthologies

Beach, Richard. *A Teacher's Introduction to Reader-Response Theories*. Urbana, IL: National Council of Teachers of English, 1993.

Tompkins, Jane P., ed. *Reader-Response Criticism: From Formalism to Post-Structuralism*. Baltimore: Johns Hopkins University Press, 1980.

(17) Postcolonialism

Bhabha, Homi K. *The Location of Culture*. New York and London: Routledge, 1994.

Fanon, Frantz. *The Wretched of the Earth*. Trans. Constance Farrington. New York: Grove Press, 1963.

Gates, Jr., Henry Louis, *Figures in Black: Words, Signs, and the "Racial" Self*. New York and Oxford: Oxford University Press, 1987.

——. *Loose Canons: Notes on the Culture Wars*. New York and Oxford: Oxford University Press, 1992.

Said, Edward. *Beginnings: Intention and Method*. New York: Columbia University Press, 1985.

——. *Orientalism*. New York: Vintage, 1978.

——. *The World, the Text, and the Critic*. Cambridge, MA: Harvard University Press, 1983.

Spivak, Gayatri Chakravorty. *A Critique of Postcolonial Reason*. Cambridge, MA and London: Harvard University Press, 1999.

Further Reading and Anthologies

Ashcroft, Bill, Gareth Griffiths, and Helen Tiffin. *The Empire Writes Back: Theory and Practice in Post-Colonial Literatures*. New York and London: Routledge, 1989.

——, eds. *The Post-Colonial Studies Reader*. New York and London: Routledge, 1995.

Booth, Howard, ed. *Modernism and Empire*. New York: St. Martin's Press, 2000.

Young, Robert. *Postcolonialism: An Historical Introduction*. Oxford: Blackwell, 2001.

(18) New Historicism

Dollimore, Jonathan. *Radical Tragedy: Religion, Ideology and Power in the Drama of Shakespeare and his Contemporaries*. New York and London: Harvester Wheatsheaf, 1984.

Foucault, Michel. *Discipline and Punish: The Birth of the Prison*. Trans. Alan Sheridan. New York: Vintage Books, 1995.

——. *The History of Sexuality: An Introduction*. Trans. Robert Hurley. Harmondsworth: Penguin, 1978.

——. *Language, Counter-Memory, Practice: Selected Essays and Interviews*. Ed. and trans. Donald F. Bouchard. New York and Ithaca: Cornell University Press, 1977.

——. *The Order of Things: An Archaeology of the Human Sciences*. New York: Vintage Books, 1994.

Greenblatt, Stephen. *Renaissance Self-Fashioning: From More to Shakespeare*. Chicago: University of Chicago Press, 1984.

——. *Shakespearean Negotiations: The Circulation of Social Energy in Renaissance England*. Berkeley: University of California Press, 1988.

——. "Towards a Poetics of Culture." In *The New Historicism*. Ed. H. Aram Veeser. New York and London: Routledge, 1989.

Further Reading and Anthologies

Brannigan, John. *New Historicism and Cultural Materialism*. New York: St. Martin's Press, 1998.

During, Simon, ed. *The Cultural Studies Reader*. New York and London: Routledge, 1993.

Gallagher, Catherine, and Stephen Greenblatt. *Practicing New Historicism*. Chicago: University of Chicago Press, 2000.

Veeser, H. Aram, ed. *The New Historicism Reader*. New York: Routledge, 1994.

(19) Epilogue

Bissell, Elizabeth Beaumont. *The Question of Literature: The Place of the Literary in Contemporary Theory*. Manchester and New York: Manchester University Press, 2002.

Hutcheon, Linda, and Mario J. Valdés, eds. *Rethinking Literary History: A Dialogue on Theory*. Oxford: Oxford University Press, 2002.

McQuillan, Martin, ed. *Post-Theory: New Directions in Criticism*. Edinburgh: Edinburgh University Press, 1999.

(20) Anthologies of Modern Theory and Criticism

Newton, K. M., ed. *Twentieth-Century Literary Theory: A Reader*. New York: St. Martin's Press, 1997.

Rivkin, Julie, and Michael Ryan, eds. *Literary Theory: An Anthology*. Oxford: Blackwell, 2004.

INDEX

INDEX

imagination (*cont'd*)
  de Staël on   425
  Dryden on   290
  Enlightenment   319, 326–327, 337–338
  fancy and   290, 326, 396, 445–446, 447–448
  Hegel on   396
  Johnson on   303–304
  Kant on   379–380, 410, 446, 447
  Longinus on   122–123
  neoclassical views   303–304
  perceptual function   447
  phantasia   81
  poetic imagination   446–447, 492
  reproductive imagination   446
  Romantic theory   122, 327, 408, 410, 417, 432–433, 436, 443–444, 626
  Schelling and   447
  Shelley on   410
  Wordsworth on   432–433, 436
imagist movement   629
imago   591
imitation   107, 239, 240
  and action   50–51
  Aristotelian view   49–50, 51–54, 55, 59, 244
  Castelvetro on   244
  Ibn Rushd on   198, 201
  John of Salisbury on   187, 188
  Johnson on   307
  Mazzoni on   246
  medieval practice   173, 187–188
  moral function   53–54
  neoclassical theory   274, 307
  Plato on   36–37, 38, 39, 50, 121–122, 135
  Plotinus on   135
  poetic imitation   36–37, 38, 39
  Sidney on   263
  Tasso on   250, 251, 252
  see also mimesis
immanence   546, 704
  De Beauvoir on   682, 684, 686, 704
  Heidegger on   716
  Husserl on   711, 712, 713
imperialism   255, 350–351, 469, 737
  anti-imperialism   739
  and the bourgeoisie   528
  and capitalism   738
  economic and cultural   737, 738

linguistic subjugation   255
Marxist critique   528, 532, 738, 739
neo-imperialism   750
phases   737–738
impressionism   472, 473, 489, 496, 708
inauthenticity   716
Incarnation theology   152, 202
individualism   237, 296, 507
  economic individualism   356
  liberal-bourgeois individualism   538
  Nietzsche and   507
  Pope on   296, 297
  Renaissance   273, 274
  Romanticism and   409
induction, Bacon and   312–313
Industrial Revolution   349, 354–355, 469
Ingarden, Roman   708, 724
Inkhorn term controversy   270
Innes, Doreen C.   106
instincts, Freudian theory of   505, 577, 586, 698
intellect
  Nietzsche on   514
  Schopenhauer on   504, 506
intentional fallacy   623, 624, 625, 626
intentional sentence correlatives   724–725
intentionalism   623–624, 625, 699
interdisciplinarity   646
interpretation
  allegorical   420
  grammatical   421, 422
  hermeneutic circle   420
  psychological   422
  Schleiermacher on   418–423
  see also exegesis; hermeneutics
interpretive communities   733, 734, 735
intersubjectivity   735
intertextuality   178, 647
invention   273
  Boccaccio on   218, 219
  Castelvetro on   243
  early modern theory   266
  Gascoigne on   267–268
  neoclassical theory   274
  Ronsard on   259
Ionesco, Eugene   565
Irigaray, Luce   566, 669
irony   99, 332
  classical irony   410–411
  Hegel on   400

812